LEARNING
CANADIAN
CRIMINAL LAW

Twelfth Edition

LEARNING CANADIAN CRIMINAL LAW

Twelfth Edition

by

DON STUART
B.A., LL.B., Dip. Crim., D. Phil.
Faculty of Law
Queen's University

and

STEVE COUGHLAN
B.A., M.A., LL.B., Ph.D.
Faculty of Law
Dalhousie University

and

RONALD JOSEPH DELISLE
B.Sc., LL.B., LL.M.
Faculty of Law
Queen's University

CARSWELL®

ISBN 978-0-7798-4925-3

Composition: Computer Composition of Canada Inc.

A cataloguing record for this publication is available from Library and Archives Canada.

Printed in the United States by Thomson Reuters.

 **THOMSON REUTERS**

CARSWELL, A DIVISION OF THOMSON REUTERS CANADA LIMITED

One Corporate Plaza	Customer Relations
2075 Kennedy Road	Toronto 1-416-609-3800
Toronto, Ontario	Elsewhere in Canada/U.S. 1-800-387-5164
M1T 3V4	Fax: 1-416-298-5082
	www.carswell.com
	E-mail www.carswell.com/email

PREFACE TO THE TWELFTH EDITION

In our view the major focus for studying criminal law in first-year law school should be on the tools that lawyers and judges must know and use in the daily business of the conduct of a criminal trial. It is obvious that law students, teachers and lawyers can better understand criminal law if they seek help from the many disciplines that now offer insights into the criminal justice system. However, time and energy are limited and choices have to be made. It is also quite impossible to properly address all the basic legal principles of the substantive, procedural, evidentiary and sentencing aspects of the criminal justice system in one first-year course. Such a survey would belittle the worth of each. Our choice is to concentrate on substantive principles and the trial context: the adversary system, how the elements of crime are proved, defences, and sentencing issues. We promote a full inquiry into the methods of determining legal guilt and the major legal justifications and excuses.

With the arrival of an entrenched *Charter of Rights and Freedoms* in 1982, the subject of teaching the criminal justice system became even more demanding and complex. We have integrated throughout consideration of the impact of the *Charter* on substantive principles and also on the presumption of innocence and matters of proof. In order to leave the task manageable, we leave the detailed study of police powers under the *Charter,* concerning such important matters as search and seizure, arrest, right to counsel, right to silence and racial profiling, to more specialist upper-year courses. We have not considered the controversial issue of exclusion of evidence obtained in violation of the *Charter* as this topic turns on assessing the seriousness of the violation, which would require a full understanding of procedural rights. Likewise, we do not address the complex laws of evidence respecting proof through witnesses and real evidence. Although we end with a chapter on sentencing we leave more technical aspects of sentencing and release from prison to other courses.

Although the development of a critical perspective is key to any university environment, we believe it essential to ensure that we first provide a full and complete analysis of the existing laws before we turn to critical analysis. Our students need to be informed before they can be truly critical. Criminal law teachers should encourage a learning process rather than just lecture. Our approach throughout has been to concentrate on the major sources: the *Criminal Code* itself, key judicial decisions and critical review. Increasingly, major decisions, especially those from the Supreme Court of Canada, tend to be long. Although we have, of course, had to resort to editing, we have tried not to be too intrusive, especially as to the most key rulings. We try to pose questions rather than provide answers. We have also used the device of problems, sometimes based on actual decisions, sometimes to provoke thought on current social problems. We have also included general review questions.

Although the focus in these materials is on substantive law, our first "Introductory Chapter" is intended to introduce readers to sources of criminal law: judge-made law, statutes and statutory interpretation, and the *Charter*. We have also grouped together the now well-established s. 7 *Charter* challenges of vagueness, overbreadth and arbitrariness, with special consideration of the unsuccessful challenges to marihuana laws in *Malmo-Levine* and the child spanking case of *Foundation for Youth, Children and the Law*. Under "Role of the Criminal Justice System" we have put together the Supreme Court's inconsistent consideration of a principle of objective harm in *Malmo-Levine* (marihuana) and *Labaye* (swinger clubs not indecent). We address the controversial issues of balancing victims' rights. "Truths of Criminology" includes extracts from an important study by criminologists Tony Doob and Cheryl Webster accepting the null hypothesis that there is no evidence that stiff sentences deter. We consider the adversary system and some major criticisms of it. Included are the controversial and complex cases where bias was alleged against a black judge in *R.D.S.* and the Ontario Court of Appeal's decision in *Hamilton* that a trial judge had gone too far in initiating an inquiry into the impact of race in sentencing drug traffickers.

Chapter 2 on the "Act Requirement" considers general principles respecting acts of commission, responsibility for omissions, voluntariness not associated with mental disorder, acting through an innocent agent, and tests for factual and legal cause for offences which require that a particular consequence be caused.

We have always stressed the importance of a logical order that builds on understanding. In early editions we began the subject of fault by a chapter entitled "The Aware State of Mind Requirement *(Mens Rea)*" and followed it by a chapter on "Departures from the Subjective *Mens Rea* Principle", where we addressed public welfare offences and negligence offences. Here we continue to reflect the major structural change first made in the 5th edition to reflect the Supreme Court's major decision on fault in *Creighton*. Chapter 3 now amalgamates these chapters into one entitled "The Fault Requirement *(Mens Rea* or Negligence)". This starts with an introductory analysis of the distinction between subjective and objective standards as outlined by Supreme Court judgments. We then move to public welfare offences, reviewing the due diligence compromise of *Sault Ste. Marie* and how this became a *Charter* standard for any offence which threatens the liberty interest—a constitutional standard unique to Canada. We then turn to *Criminal Code* offences and first examine how the Supreme Court decided that subjective awareness would only be constitutionally mandated for a few crimes, such as murder. Then, following the dictates of *Creighton,* we analyze in detail the three types of crimes the Court envisages: those of subjective *mens rea,* objective crimes requiring a marked departure from the norm and, finally, those based on predicate offences, which have a much-reduced fault requirement. This allows us to postpone to the end consideration of the difficult decisions in *DeSousa, Creighton* (respecting unlawful act manslaughter) and *Godin* (aggravated assault).

Our separate Chapter 4 on Rape and Sexual Assault continues to allow for consideration of this controversial subject in a wider context: gender bias in rape laws, the 1982 change from rape to sexual assault, striking down of the statutory rape shield in *Seaboyer* and the 1992 Bill C-49 changes respecting the mistaken belief in consent defence and consent. We focus on the blockbuster ruling of the Supreme Court in *Ewanchuk* on the issue of consent and imposing new limits on the defence of mistaken belief in consent. We have constructed problems so that the decision can be better assessed in less emotive contexts. We deal with the latest law respecting the duty to take reasonable steps to ascertain consent and consider possible outstanding *Charter* issues especially concerning Parliament's denial of any intoxication defence. We have included the Supreme Court's controversial decision in *J.(A.)*, which holds that a person is legally incapable of giving advance consent to sexual activity if that person will not be in a position to retract the consent at the relevant time. The Supreme Court's controversial and complex rulings in *O'Connor* and *Mills,* respecting discovery of medical and counselling records of complainants in sexual assault cases, are mentioned but full treatment is left to Criminal Procedure and Evidence courses. We assess enforceable equality rights under s. 15 of the *Charter.* We note that in *Shearing,* respecting cross-examination on a complainant's diary, the majority of the Supreme Court later speaks of equality "interests" rather than equality rights.

After the special treatment given to sexual assault we return to general principles with chapters on Mistake of Fact and Law. For the officially induced error defence, we examine the Supreme Court's definitive pronouncement in *City of Levis v. Tetreault.* The chapter on Incapacity considers issues of age, mental disorder, the defence of sane automatism (much limited by *Stone, Luedecke* and *Bouchard-Lebrun*) and intoxication, which is still wedded to the distinction between specific and general intent offences.

For ease of teaching, Chapter 7 now starts with the statutory defence of self-defence and the defence of property. We then turn to the common law defence of necessity where we consider the Supreme Court's acceptance of the philosophical distinction between justification and excuse and its rejection of a defence of necessity to murder in the tragic case of *Latimer.* We then consider the defence of duress and the partial striking down of the limits of that defence in *Ruzic* (asserting a new *Charter* standard of moral involuntariness).

Chapter 8 on Parties to a Crime now includes separate treatment of principals before proceeding to liability for lesser involvement, such as aiding and abetting. Chapter 9 considers incomplete crimes such as Attempts and Conspiracy.

Chapter 10 addresses Parliament's recent embracing of various forms of group responsibility—guilt by association some would say. This starts with new *Criminal Code* provisions declaring a wide form of criminal responsibility, not just for corporations but also for broadly defined "organizations". This was Parliament's response to the failure of the courts to find criminal responsibility for the deaths of 26 miners in the Westray mine explosion. We also consider anti-gang laws Parliament passed in 1997 in response to violent biker wars in Quebec and its stiffening of those provisions in 2001. Finally, we consider the controversial anti-terrorist provisions Parliament rushed into place to address issues of terrorism following the 9/11 attacks on the World Trade Center in New York and note that *Charter* challenges to the wide provisions have largely failed.

Section 11 on sentencing addresses general principles and sentencing reforms, and provides an outline of different forms of sentences

This 12th edition has been thoroughly updated and re-edited. Major additions are:

- Supreme Court decisions in: *PHS Community Services* (Minister's refusal to grant exemption to supervised injection site contrary to *Charter*); *Morelli* (possessing child pornography on computer); *Briscoe* (definition of willful blindness as deliberate ignorance and liability as aider); *A.(J.)* (majority holding that person cannot validly consent to sexual activity in advance); and *Tran* (estranged wife having sexual conduct with another not allowing for partial provocation defence to murder)

- Court of Appeal rulings in *Moquin* (Man. C.A.: meaning of bodily harm); *Mabior* (Man. C.A.: failure to disclose HIV status not resulting in significant risk of bodily harm to vitiate consent); *Maybin* (B.C. C.A.: test for intervening cause); *Shand* (Ont. C.A.: restricting s. 229(c) murder); *Khawaja* (Ont. C.A.: requiring proof of motive in terrorist offence not violating *Charter*); *Ball* (B.C. C.A.: co-principals); *S.R.B.* (Alta. C.A.: abandonment) and *Arcand* (Alta. C.A.: criticizing disparities in trial sentencing)

- Updated material on context of sexual assault (for which we are indebted to Pam Hrick, a third-year law student at Queen's).

We thank Ken Murphy and Graham Peddie of Carswell for their continuing support. Many thanks to our Content Editor, Claire Cheverie, for hours of meticulous work at the production stage.

Don Stuart
Steve Coughlan
March 1, 2012

ACKNOWLEDGMENTS

We gratefully thank the following authors, publishers or organizations for permission to reproduce excerpts from the material listed below.

Aboriginal Peoples and Criminal Justice
Law Reform Commission of Canada

Acts of Will and Responsibility
H.L.A. Hart
Oxford University Press

Adversary System Excuse
Rowman and Allanheld

Case for the Defence
E. Greenspan and Macmillan of Canada

The Charter, the Supreme Court and the Invisible Politics of Fault
Rosemary Cairns Way

Code of Professional Conduct
Canadian Bar Association

Comment
Cambridge Law Journal
Cambridge University Press
Glanville L. Williams

Criminal Law. The General Part
Glanville L. Williams
Stevens and Sons Ltd.
Sweet and Maxwell Ltd.

Criminal Responsibility for Omissions
H.R.S. Ryan

Culpable Mistakes and Rape: Harsh Words on Pappajohn
T. Pickard
University of Toronto Law Journal
University of Toronto Press

Dancing with a Ghost
Rupert Ross

Diagnostic and Statistical Manual of Mental Disorders
American Psychiatric Association

Dimensions of Criminal Law
Toni Pickard and Phil Goldman

False Memory Syndrome
Nicholas Bala
Queen's Law Journal

The Intoxicated Offender — A Problem of Responsibility
S.M. Beck
Canadian Bar Review
G.E. Parker

The Jury in Criminal Trials
Law Reform Commission of Canada

Our Criminal Law
Law Reform Commission of Canada

Portia in a Different Voice
Berkeley Women's Law Journal

Principles of Criminal Liability
Canadian Bar Association

Psychiatry, Ethics and the Criminal Law
Columbia Law Review
T. Szasz

Punishment and Responsibility
H.L.A. Hart
Oxford University Press

Recodifying Criminal Law
Law Reform Commission of Canada

Re-Thinking Criminal Law
G.P. Fletcher

Report of the Committee on Mentally Abnormal Offenders
Her Majesty's Stationery Office

Sentencing Reform: A Canadian Approach
Minister of Supply and Services, Canada

Sentence Severity and Crime: Accepting the Null Hypothesis
Anthony N. Doob and Cheryl Marie Webster
Crime and Justice: A Review of Research

Teaching Rape Law
Susan Estrich
Yale Law Journal

Textbook of Criminal Law
Glanville L. Williams
Stevens and Sons Ltd.
Sweet and Maxwell Ltd.

TABLE OF CONTENTS

Chapter 3.   THE FAULT REQUIREMENT (*MENS REA* OR NEGLIGENCE)

Chapter 6.   INCAPACITY

Chapter 11.   SENTENCING

APPENDIX A

APPENDIX B

TABLE OF CASES

The bold entries reflect those cases where the text of the judgment is given.

Chapter 1

INTRODUCTION

1. SOURCES

(a) Common Law (Judge-made Law)

(i) Offence definition

R. v. SEDLEY

(1663) as described in Curll, *Cobbett's Complete Collection of State Trials*,
Vol. 17 (1727), 155

Sir Charles Sedley was indicted at common law for several misdemeanors against the King's peace, and which were to the great scandal of Christianity; and the cause was, for that he shewed his naked body in a balcony in Covent Garden to a great multitude of people, and there did such things, and spoke such words, & c. mentioning some particulars of his misbehaviour, as throwing down bottles (pissed in) *vi et armis* among the people. Fortescue's Reports, 99, 100. And this indictment was openly read to him in court; and the justices told him, that notwithstanding there was not then any Star-chamber, yet they would have him know, that the Court of King's bench was the *custos morum* of all the king's subjects; and that it was then high time to punish such profane actions, committed against all modesty, which were as frequent, as if not only Christianity, but morality also had been neglected. After he had been kept in court by recognizance from Trinity term to the end of Michaelmas term, the court required him to take his trial at bar: but being advised, he submitted himself to the court, and confessed the indictment. The Michaelmas term following, the court considered what judgment to give; and inasmuch as he was a gentleman of a very ancient family (in Kent) and his estate incumbered, (not intending his ruin, but his reformation) they fined him only 2,000 marks, and to be imprisoned a week without bail, and to be of good behaviour for three years.

In 1892 Parliament enacted Canada's first *Criminal Code*. It was modelled on the English Draft Code of 1879 which in turn was primarily the work of Sir James Stephen, a remarkable English jurist. The English Draft Code was rejected in England and there is still no *Criminal Code* there. Most U.S. states have a

Criminal Code. Criminal law there differs from state to state. Our *Criminal Code* is federal and applies across Canada, including Quebec. It declares offences and defences and also procedure. There are also a number of other federal offences declared in other federal statutes and regulations and also provincial offences such as driving and liquor offences declared in provincial statutes and regulations.

Can you guess how many offences exist in law in Canada?

FREY v. FEDORUK

[1950] S.C.R. 517, 10 C.R. 26, 97 C.C.C. 1, 1950 CarswellBC 1

Frey had been seen on Fedoruk's property looking into a lighted side window of the house where Fedoruk's mother was preparing for bed. Fedoruk chased him brandishing a butcher's knife. He caught and detained him. A policeman, Stone, was called and, after some investigation, arrested Frey without warrant. Frey sued for damages for malicious prosecution and for false imprisonment. The suit was dismissed by the trial judge and this was affirmed by a majority in the British Columbia Court of Appeal on the ground that Frey had been guilty of a criminal offence at common law and therefore that there had been legal justification for the arrest without warrant. The appeal to the Supreme Court was concerned only with the claim for false imprisonment. The court decided that criminal offences were to be found in the *Criminal Code* and established common law. Since being a "peeping tom" was not an offence known to the law, there was no justification in law for Fedoruk and Stone to have imprisoned Frey, and Frey was entitled to succeed against both of them.

CARTWRIGHT J.: —

. . . .

I do not think that it is safe to hold as a matter of law, that conduct, not otherwise criminal and not falling within any category of offences defined by the criminal law, becomes criminal because a natural and probable result thereof will be to provoke others to violent retributive action. If such a principle were admitted, it seems to me that many courses of conduct which it is well settled are not criminal could be made the subject of indictment by setting out the facts and concluding with the words that such conduct was likely to cause a breach of the peace. Two examples may be mentioned. The speaking of insulting words unaccompanied by any threat of violence undoubtedly may and sometimes does produce violent retributive action, but is not criminal. The commission of adultery has, in many recorded cases, when unexpectedly discovered, resulted in homicide; but, except where expressly made so by statute, adultery is not a crime.

If it should be admitted as a principle that conduct may be treated as criminal because, although not otherwise criminal, it has a natural tendency to provoke violence by way of retribution, it seems to me that great uncertainty would result.

. . . .

I do not understand O'Halloran J.A. to suggest in his elaborate reasons that there is precedent for the view that the plaintiff's conduct in this case was criminal. Rather he appears to support the finding of the trial judge to that effect on the grounds stated in the following paragraph:

> Criminal responsibility at common law is primarily not a matter of precedent, but of application of generic principle to the differing facts of each case. It is for the jury to apply to the facts of the case as they find them, the generic principle the judge gives them. Thus by their general verdict the jury in practical effect decide both the law and the facts in the particular case, and have consistently done so over the centuries, and *cf.* Coke on Littleton (1832 ed.) vol. 1, note 5, para. 155(*b*). The fact-finding judge in this case, as the record shows, had not the slightest doubt on the evidence before him that what the appellant had been accused of was a criminal offence at common law.

In my opinion when it is read against the background of the rest of the reasons of O'Halloran J.A., it appears that, in relation to the facts of this case, the "generic principle" which the learned judge has in mind is too wide to have any value as a definition. The genus appears to be a "breach of the King's Peace" in the wider signification which is attached to that expression elsewhere in the reasons.

It appears to me that so understood, the genus is wide enough to include the whole field of the criminal law. As it is put in Pollock and Maitland, History of English Law (1895), vol. 1, p. 22: "all criminal offences have long been said to be committed against the King's peace." And in vol. 2 of the same work at p. 452, it is stated: "to us a breach of the King's peace may seem to cover every possible crime."

Once the expression "a breach of the King's peace" is interpreted, as O'Halloran J.A. undoubtedly does interpret it, not to require as an essential ingredient anything in the nature of "riots, tumults, or actual physical violence" on the part of the offender, it would appear to become wide enough to include any conduct which in the view of the fact-finding tribunal is so injurious to the public as to merit punishment. If, on the other hand, O'Halloran J.A. intended to give to the expression a more limited meaning so that it would include only conduct of a nature likely to lead to a breach of the peace in the narrower sense of which he speaks, the authorities referred to elsewhere in this judgment seem to me to show that this is not an offence known to the law.

I am of opinion that the proposition implicit in the paragraph quoted above ought not to be accepted. I think that if adopted, it would introduce great uncertainty into the administration of the criminal law, leaving it to the judicial officer trying any particular charge to decide that the acts proved constituted a crime or otherwise, not by reference to any defined standard to be found in the *Code* or in reported decisions, but according to his individual view as to whether such acts were a disturbance of the tranquillity of people tending to provoke physical reprisal.

To so hold would, it seems to me, be to assert the existence of what is referred to in Stephen's *History of the Criminal Law of England*, vol. 2, p. 190, as:

> the power which has in some instances been claimed for the judges of declaring anything to be an offence which is injurious to the public although it may not have been previously regarded as such.

The writer continues: "this power, if it exists at all, exists at common law."

In my opinion, this power has not been held and should not be held to exist in Canada. I think it safer to hold that no one shall be convicted of a crime unless the offence with which he is charged is recognized as such in the provisions of the *Criminal Code*, or can be established by the authority of some reported case as an offence known to the law. I think that if any course of conduct is now to be declared criminal, which has not up to the present time been so regarded, such declaration should be made by Parliament and not by the courts.

———————————

In its 1955 revision of the *Criminal Code*, Parliament went further than the Supreme Court and, in s. 9, largely abolished common law offences. The possibility of common law defences was, however, preserved in s. 8(3). These will be discussed in later chapters.

THE CRIMINAL CODE

R.S.C. 1985, c. C-46

8. (1) The provisions of this Act apply throughout Canada except

    (*a*) in the Northwest Territories, in so far as they are inconsistent with the *Northwest Territories Act*, and

    (*b*) in the Yukon Territory, in so far as they are inconsistent with the *Yukon Act*.

(2) The criminal law of England that was in force in a province immediately before the 1st day of April 1955 continues in force in the province except as altered, varied, modified or affected by this Act or any other Act of the Parliament of Canada.

(3) Every rule and principle of the common law that renders any circumstance a justification or excuse for an act or a defence to a charge

continues in force and applies in respect of proceedings for an offence under this Act or any other Act of the Parliament of Canada, except in so far as they are altered by or are inconsistent with this Act or any other Act of the Parliament of Canada.

9. Notwithstanding anything in this Act or any other Act no person shall be convicted or discharged under section 736

> (*a*) of an offence at common law,
>
> (*b*) of an offence under an Act of the Parliament of England, or of Great Britain, or of the United Kingdom of Great Britain and Ireland, or
>
> (*c*) of an offence under an Act or ordinance in force in any province, territory or place before that province, territory or place became a province of Canada,

but nothing in this section affects the power, jurisdiction or authority that a court, judge, justice or magistrate had, immediately before the 1st day of April 1955, to impose punishment for contempt of court.

Shortly after *Frey v. Fedoruk* was decided, in S.C. 1953-54, c. 51, Parliament added the following offence to the *Criminal Code*:

Trespassing at night

177. Every one who, without lawful excuse, the proof of which lies on him, loiters or prowls at night on the property of another person near a dwelling-house situated on that property is guilty of an offence punishable on summary conviction.

On July 20, 2005, Royal Assent was given to the following amendment to the *Criminal Code*, which came into effect on November 1, 2005:

Voyeurism

162. (1) Every one commits an offence who, surreptitiously, observes — including by mechanical or electronic means — or makes a visual recording of a person who is in circumstances that give rise to a reasonable expectation of privacy, if

(a) the person is in a place in which a person can reasonably be expected to be nude, to expose his or her genital organs or anal region or her breasts, or to be engaged in explicit sexual activity;

(b) the person is nude, is exposing his or her genital organs or anal region or her breasts, or is engaged in explicit sexual activity, and the observation or recording is done for the purpose of observing or recording a person in such a state or engaged in such an activity; or

(c) the observation or recording is done for a sexual purpose.

Do you have any concerns as to the breadth of the new voyeurism offence?

Is someone who watches a couple skinny dipping at a nearby but secluded cottage guilty of voyeurism? What if he or she makes a video recording?

(ii) Doctrine of precedent

As there are no common law offences in Canada, legislation is the pre-eminent source of criminal law in Canada. A charge must always allege a breach of a statutory provision. However the common law (judge-made law) remains essential to the criminal justice system. Many mental elements of crimes and defences are defined by the common law rather than being specified in the *Criminal Code* or other statute. Some important procedural rules (such as the presumption of innocence) began as, or continue to be, common law rules.

The common law also helps guide judicial reasoning through a practice of relying on earlier decisions as "precedents". The long established tradition is for decisions of higher courts to be *binding* on lower courts, with courts of co-ordinate jurisdiction merely *persuasive* — meaning that they can but need not be followed. In Canada each province has a hierarchy of courts which we will examine later under "Procedural Overview". Every province has two levels of criminal trial court, a Court of Appeal, with a final appeal going to the Supreme Court in Ottawa. The Supreme Court's decisions are binding on all lower courts. In *R. v. Henry* (see below) the Supreme Court recently confirmed that its practice is not to depart from its own precedents unless there are compelling reasons to do so (as there were held to be in *Henry* itself).

In relying on previous decisions, a distinction is sometimes drawn between the "*ratio decidendi*" of a case — the point or points it actually decides — and "*obiter dicta*", which are other statements made in the course of the decision which are not strictly essential to a resolution of that particular dispute. In *R. v. Henry* the Supreme Court considered this distinction, and the extent to which it should affect the way in which Supreme Court decisions are used as precedents.

R. v. HENRY

33 C.R. (6th) 215, 202 C.C.C. (3d) 449, 2005 SCC 76,
2005 CarswellBC 2972, 2005 CarswellBC 2973

BINNIE J.: —

52 ... I believe the submissions of the attorneys general presuppose a strict and tidy demarcation between the narrow *ratio decidendi* of a case, which is binding, and *obiter*, which they say may safely be ignored. I believe that this supposed dichotomy is an oversimplification of how the common law develops.

53 The traditional view expressed by the Earl of Halsbury L.C. was that "a case is only an authority for what it actually decides", and that

> every judgment must be read as applicable to the particular facts proved, or assumed to be proved since the generality of the expressions which may be found there are not intended to be expositions of the whole law, but governed and qualified by the particular facts of the case in which such expressions are to be found. (*Quinn v. Leathem*, [1901] A.C. 495 (H.L.), at p. 506)

The caution was important at the time, of course, because the House of Lords did not then claim the authority to review and overrule its own precedents. This is no longer the case. Even in the time of the Earl of Halsbury L.C., however, the challenge was to know how broadly or how narrowly to draw "what it actually decides". In Canada in the 1970s, the challenge became more acute when this court's mandate became oriented less to error correction and more to development of the jurisprudence (or, as it is put in s. 40(1) of the *Supreme Court Act*, R.S.C. 1985, c. S-26, to deal with questions of "public importance"). The amendments to the Supreme Court Act had two effects relevant to this question. Firstly, the court took fewer appeals, thus accepting fewer opportunities to discuss a particular area of the law, and some judges felt that "we should make the most of the opportunity by adopting a more expansive approach to our decision-making role": Bertha Wilson, "Decision-making in the Supreme Court" (1986), 36 U.T.L.J. 227, at p. 234. Secondly, and more importantly, much of the court's work (particularly under the *Charter*) required the development of a general analytical framework which necessarily went beyond what was essential for the disposition of the particular case. In those circumstances, the court nevertheless intended that effect be given to the broader analysis. In *R. v. Oakes*, [1986] 1 S.C.R. 103, for example, Dickson C.J. laid out a broad purposive analysis of s. 1 of the *Charter*, but the dispositive point was his conclusion that there was no rational connection between the basic fact of possession of narcotics and the legislated presumption that the possession was for the purpose of trafficking. Yet the entire approach to s. 1 was intended to be, and has been regarded as, binding on other Canadian courts. It would be a foolhardy advocate who dismissed Dickson C.J.'s classic formulation of proportionality in *Oakes* as mere *obiter*. Thus if we were to ask "what *Oakes* actually decides", we would likely offer a more expansive definition in the post-*Charter* period than the Earl of Halsbury L.C. would have recognized a century ago.

54 From time to time there have been statements of some members of this court that have been taken to suggest that other courts are bound by this court's considered ruling on a point of law, even a point not strictly necessary to the conclusion. Most famously, in *Sellars v. The Queen*, [1980] 1 S.C.R. 527, at p. 529, Chouinard J. resolved an issue respecting jury instructions by reference to an earlier decision of this court and said:

> ... this is the interpretation that must prevail.

As it does from time to time, the court has thus ruled on the point, although it was not absolutely necessary to do so in order to dispose of the appeal.

55 This statement was perfectly understandable in context. So far as Chouinard J. was concerned, the court of which he was a member had ruled on the point, and he proposed to be consistent and follow it. However, the "*Sellars* principle", as it came to be known, was thought by some observers to stand for the proposition that whatever was said in a majority judgment of the Supreme Court of Canada was binding, no matter how incidental to the main point of the case or how far it was removed from the dispositive facts and principles of law; for varying views, see e.g., *Re Haldimand-Norfolk Regional Health Unit and Ontario Nurses' Association* (1981), 120 D.L.R. (3d) 101 (Ont. C.A.); *R. v. Sansregret*, [1984] 1 W.W.R. 720 (Man. C.A.); *R. v. Barrow* (1984), 65 N.S.R. (2d) 1 (S.C.); *Clark v. Canadian National Railway Co.* (1985), 17 D.L.R. (4th) 58 (N.B.C.A.); *Scarff v. Wilson* (1988), 33 B.C.L.R. (2d) 290 (C.A.); *Moses v. Shore Board Builders Ltd.* (1993), 106 D.L.R. (4th) 654 (B.C.C.A.); *Friedmann Equity Developments Inc. v. Final Note Ltd.* (1998), 41 O.R. (3d) 712 (C.A.); *Cardella v. Minister of National Revenue* (2001), 268 N.R. 168, 2001 FCA 39. Other cases are more critical: *R. v. Chartrand* (1992), 74 C.C.C. (3d) 409 (Man. C.A.); *R. v. Hynes* (1999), 26 C.R. (5th) 1 (Nfld. C.A.); *R. v. Vu* (2004), 184 C.C.C. (3d) 545, 2004 BCCA 230; *McDiarmid Lumber Ltd. v. God's Lake First Nation* (2005), 251 D.L.R. (4th) 93, 2005 MBCA 22.

56 Some of these comments simply reflect the practical consideration that disregarding the majority view of this court on a point of law, even if it was not strictly necessary for the disposition of the case in which it was expressed, may just precipitate a successful appeal. Other comments suggested that the "*Sellars* principle" had ripened into a new doctrine of law. This extension was challenged in "*Ratio Decidendi* and *Obiter Dicta*" (1993), 51 Advocate (B.C.) 689, by the Honourable Douglas Lambert, writing extra-judicially, who canvassed the case law and concluded that at least some of the confusion was due to an error translating Chouinard J.'s opinion from French to English as well as by an overstatement by the writer of the English headnote in *Sellars* itself. More recently, Professor M. Devinat, in "L'Autorité des *obiter dicta* de la Cour suprême" (1998), 77 Can. Bar Rev. 1, suggested that some courts were only too willing to broaden the scope of the "*Sellars* principle" to lighten their own workload by minimizing what remained for them to decide. If Professor Devinat is correct, the effect would be to deprive the legal system of much creative thought on the part of counsel and judges in other courts in continuing to examine the operation of legal principles in different and perhaps novel contexts, and to inhibit or skew the growth of the common law. This would be a consequence totally unforeseen and unintended by the court that decided *Sellars*. Thus the notion of "binding effect" as a matter of law was disavowed by this court in *Reference re Remuneration of Judges of the Provincial Court of Prince*

Edward Island, [1997] 3 S.C.R. 3, at para. 168, for example, where Lamer C.J., writing for six members of the seven-judge panel said that "the remarks of Le Dain J. [writing for the court in *Valente v. The Queen*, [1985] 2 S.C.R. 673] were strictly *obiter dicta*, and do not bind the courts below".

57 The issue in each case, to return to the Halsbury question, is what did the case decide? Beyond the *ratio decidendi* which, as the Earl of Halsbury L.C. pointed out, is generally rooted in the facts, the legal point decided by this court may be as narrow as the jury instruction at issue in *Sellars* or as broad as the *Oakes* test. All *obiter* do not have, and are not intended to have, the same weight. The weight decreases as one moves from the dispositive *ratio decidendi* to a wider circle of analysis which is obviously intended for guidance and which should be accepted as authoritative. Beyond that, there will be commentary, examples or exposition that are intended to be helpful and may be found to be persuasive, but are certainly not "binding" in the sense the *Sellars* principle in its most exaggerated form would have it. The objective of the exercise is to promote certainty in the law, not to stifle its growth and creativity. The notion that each phrase in a judgment of this court should be treated as if enacted in a statute is not supported by the cases and is inconsistent with the basic fundamental principle that the common law develops by experience.

The pronouncement in *Henry* that not all *obiter dicta* of the Supreme Court are binding is expressly intended to foster creativity by lower courts. However the court does still insist (see para. 57 above) that some *obiter dicta* obviously intended to give guidance should be accepted as authoritative. In contrast *obiter* that are "commentary, examples or exposition that are intended to be helpful and may be found to be persuasive" are not binding. This may well be a difficult distinction to make! It seems clear that lower courts have been given the green light to try.

Swift, in *Gulliver's Travels* (1977 ed., O.U.P.) p. 249 has Gulliver say:

> It is a maxim among these lawyers, that whatever hath been done before, may legally be done again: and therefore they take special care to record all the decisions formerly made against common justice and the general reason of mankind. These under the name of precedents, they produce as authorities, to justify the most iniquitous opinions; and the judges never fail of decreeing accordingly.

Jerome Frank, *Law and the Modern Mind* (1949) p. 48 is even more sceptical:

> Lawyers and judges purport to make large use of precedents; that is, they purport to rely on the conduct of judges in past cases as a means of procuring analogies for action in new cases. But since what was actually decided in the earlier cases is seldom revealed, it is impossible, in a real sense, to rely on these precedents. What the courts in fact do is to manipulate the language of former decisions. They could approximate a system of real precedents only if the judges, in rendering those former decisions, had reported with fidelity the precise steps by which they arrived at their decisions. The paradox of the situation is that, granting there is a value in a system of

precedents, our present use of illusory precedents makes the employment of real precedents impossible.

The decision of a judge after trying a case is the product of a unique experience . . . [The] "*decision is reached after an emotive experience in which principles and logic play a secondary part*".

While Gulliver's view that precedent is a slavish adherence to bad rules and Frank's view that no credence can be put on what judges say they are doing are both overstatements, they point to the ideal. It is widely accepted that the doctrine of precedent is a working ingredient of the judicial function and achieves a compromise between a goal of certainty and predictability and one of flexibility. It is recognized that there are indeed several powerful devices with which to manipulate rules. An unwelcome precedent can be distinguished on its facts and the proposition or propositions of law involved can be restated at a different level of generality, consigned to mere *obiter dicta* (*i.e.*, not logically necessary for the decision) or qualified by reference to other precedent. Few would be content to see the judicial function as a mere exercise of these linguistic skills. Surely our judges should do more than search for and then assert rules espoused by other judges. Each rule or principle, if not absolutely binding (and few are) should be independently evaluated for its soundness in respect of the particular case and for other cases as well. Although this is a much more intellectually demanding mandate upon judges, it is only by a frank discussion of these factors of justification that a sound approach to the law can be developed.

(b)   Statute

(i)   *General principles of statutory interpretation*

While at the time of *Sedley's* trial it fell to the judges to punish those activities which they believed violated contemporary community morals, we see that in Canada today the pre-eminent source of criminal law is legislation. The judges are given the task of interpreting the legislation and applying it to the activities in their particular case. **In interpreting the law, is there room for creativity? To what extent are they restricted by the words of statutes and the doctrine of precedent?**

APPLICATION UNDER S. 83.28 OF THE CRIMINAL CODE, RE

[2004] 2 S.C.R. 248, 21 C.R. (6th) 82, 184 C.C.C. (3d) 449,
2004 SCC 42, 2004 CarswellBC 1378, 2004 CarswellBC 1379

In the course of a decision concerning the constitutionality of an aspect of anti-terrorist provisions in the *Criminal Code*, one of the majority judgments summarised the modern approach to statutory interpretation as follows.

IACOBUCCI and ARBOUR JJ.:

34 The modern principle of statutory interpretation requires that the words of the legislation be read "in their entire context and in their grammatical and ordinary sense harmoniously with the scheme of the Act, the object of the Act, and the intention of Parliament": E. A. Driedger, *Construction of Statutes* (2nd ed. 1983), at p. 87. This is the prevailing and preferred approach to statutory interpretation: see, e.g., *Rizzo & Rizzo Shoes Ltd. (Re)*, [1998] 1 S.C.R. 27, at para. 21; *R. v. Sharpe*, [2001] 1 S.C.R. 45, 2001 SCC 2, at para. 33; *Bell ExpressVu Limited Partnership v. Rex*, [2002] 2 S.C.R. 559, 2002 SCC 42, at para. 26. The modern approach recognizes the multi-faceted nature of statutory interpretation. Textual considerations must be read in concert with legislative intent and established legal norms.

35 Underlying this approach is the presumption that legislation is enacted to comply with constitutional norms, including the rights and freedoms enshrined in the *Charter*: R. Sullivan, *Sullivan and Driedger on the Construction of Statutes* (4th ed. 2002), at p. 367. This presumption acknowledges the centrality of constitutional values in the legislative process, and more broadly, in the political and legal culture of Canada. Accordingly, where two readings of a provision are equally plausible, the interpretation which accords with *Charter* values should be adopted: see *Slaight Communications Inc. v. Davidson*, [1989] 1 S.C.R. 1038, at p. 1078; *R. v. Nova Scotia Pharmaceutical Society*, [1992] 2 S.C.R. 606, at p. 660; *R. v. Lucas*, [1998] 1 S.C.R. 439, at para. 66; and *Sharpe, supra*, at para. 33.

R. v. CLARK

[2005] 1 S.C.R. 6, 2005 SCC 2, 25 C.R. (6th) 197, 193 C.C.C. (3d) 289, 2005 CarswellBC 137, 2005 CarswellBC 138

The judgment of the court was delivered by

Fish J. : —

1 The appellant stands convicted for having masturbated near the uncovered window of his illuminated living room.

2 He was first noticed by Mrs. S., a neighbour who was watching television with her two young daughters in their partially lit family room. Mrs. S. moved to another room for a better view and then alerted her husband. Together, they observed the appellant for 10 to 15 minutes from the privacy of their darkened bedroom, across contiguous backyards, from a distance of 90 to 150 feet.

3 The police were summoned and the appellant was charged under both s. 173(1)(a) and s. 173(1)(b) of the *Criminal Code*, R.S.C. 1985, c. C-46.

4 Section 173(1)(a) makes it an offence to wilfully perform an indecent act "in a public place in the presence of one or more persons"; s. 173(1)(b), on the other hand, makes it an offence to wilfully commit an indecent act "in any place, with intent thereby to insult or offend any person"...

16 The appellant was first noticed by Mrs. S. while she was watching television with her two young daughters in their family room, which was lit up only by the television screen and by light from the adjoining kitchen. Mrs. S. agreed with counsel's suggestion that, from there, she "didn't really see anything untoward other than some movement". But for reasons that she explained at trial, Mrs. S. was troubled and, to get "a better angle to view", she "ran" to her bedroom and then summoned her husband.

17 From that vantage point, Mr. and Mrs. S. observed the appellant for 10 or 15 minutes. Taking care to escape his notice, they looked out through the uncovered part of their bedroom window, below their partially lowered blinds. And, to ensure that the appellant was in fact doing what he appeared to them to be doing, Mr. S. fetched a pair of binoculars and a telescope. He also tried, unsuccessfully, to videotape the appellant in action.

18 Mr. and Mrs. S. were understandably concerned. In the words of Mr. S., they feared that the appellant was "masturbating to our children". They therefore called the police.

19 The first officer arrived within five minutes. From the bedroom of Mr. and Mrs. S., the officer could see the appellant from "just below the navel up". The appellant had his hand in front of him "and there was a hand motion consistent with somebody masturbating". At the back of the house, looking up to the appellant's living room from street level, the officer could only see the appellant "from about maybe the neck or the shoulders up because of the angle".

20 It did not appear to the trial judge "that [the appellant] actually knew he was being watched". There was nothing to suggest, the trial judge said, "that [the appellant] was aware that [Mrs. S.] was watching from the darkened bedroom window". He found that the evidence in fact indicated the contrary. The appellant was, however, seen by Mrs. S. and "could easily have been seen by the children, but apparently was not".

21 On these facts, the trial judge concluded that the appellant had wilfully committed "an indecent act . . . in a public place in the presence of one or more persons", thereby committing the offence set out in s. 173(1)(a) of the *Criminal Code*.

22 The trial judge was not satisfied, however, that the appellant had committed this indecent act "with intent thereby to insult or offend any person", as required

by s. 173(1)(b) of the *Code*. He therefore acquitted the appellant of the charge laid against him under that section.

23 The appellant's conviction under s. 173(1)(a) was affirmed by the Court of Appeal for British Columbia. He now appeals to this court, with leave, from the decision of the Court of Appeal...

33 The appellant does not contest the trial judge's finding that he committed an "indecent act" within the meaning of s. 173(1)(a) of the *Criminal Code*. He concedes, at least implicitly, that masturbating in an illuminated room near an uncovered window visible to neighbours can be "indecent" within the meaning of that section.

34 The appellant contends, however, that he did not wilfully commit this indecent act "in a public place in the presence of one or more persons", as required by s. 173(1)(a). He raises three grounds: first, that his living room was not a "public place" within the meaning of s. 173(1)(a); second, that the complainants were "surreptitiously watching him from beneath the blinds of a window in their own private bedroom some distance away" — and, therefore, not "in his presence", as likewise required by s. 173(1)(a); third, that he cannot be said to have wilfully committed an indecent act in the presence of anyone, since the trial judge found there was no evidence that he knew he was being observed...

37 It is common ground that the appeal must succeed if the appellant did not commit an indecent act in a public place within the meaning of ss. 150 and 173(1)(a) of the *Criminal Code*.

38 These provisions read:

> 150. In this Part, . . .
>
> "public place" includes any place to which the public have access as of right or by invitation, express or implied; ...
>
> 173. (1) Every one who wilfully does an indecent act
>
> > (a) in a public place in the presence of one or more persons, or
> >
> > (b) in any place, with intent thereby to insult or offend any person, is guilty of an offence punishable on summary conviction.

· · · ·

41 There is thus no need to choose in this case between the English and French versions of s. 150. The parties agree that both versions require public access by right or invitation: their disagreement is limited to the meaning of "access" in this context.

42 On that issue, which is decisive in this case, the appellant submits that ss. 150 and 173(1)(a) contemplate physical access to the place in which the impugned act was committed; the respondent, that visual access is sufficient. In my view, the appellant's position is supported by the prevailing rules of statutory construction. The respondent's position is not.

43 It is now well established that "the words of an Act are to be read in their entire context and in their grammatical and ordinary sense harmoniously with the scheme of the Act, the object of the Act, and the intention of Parliament": *Bell ExpressVu Limited Partnership v. Rex*, [2002] 2 S.C.R. 559, 2002 SCC 42, at para. 26, quoting E. A. Driedger, *Construction of Statutes* (2nd ed. 1983), at p. 87; *Rizzo & Rizzo Shoes Ltd. (Re)*, [1998] 1 S.C.R. 27, at para. 21.

44 As a matter of semantics, the "ordinary" meaning of a disputed term will, of course, often vary with the context in which it is being used. Thus, for example, "access" has one "ordinary meaning" in relation to the rights of non-custodial parents, another as regards on-line computing, and yet another with respect to a place.

45 Section 150 of the *Criminal Code* uses the word "access" in reference to a "place" — in this case, a private home. And our concern is with access to that place "as of right or by invitation". In common usage, "access" to a place to which one is invited or where one has a right to be refers to entering, visiting or using that place — and not, as I said earlier, to looking or listening in from the outside. When we are told that someone has access, as of right or by invitation, to an apartment, a workshop, an office, or a garage, this does not signify to us a mere opportunity or ability to look through a window or doorway and to see what is happening inside.

46 This "grammatical and ordinary sense" of "access" in relation to a place must, of course, be read harmoniously with the legislative context that concerns us here and the intention of Parliament as it appears from the *Criminal Code*: *Bell ExpressVu and Rizzo & Rizzo Shoes*.

47 I begin with the immediate legislative context.

48 First, interpreting "public place" in a manner consistent with physical as opposed to visual access, renders the whole of s. 173(1) more coherent. The offences under ss. 173(1)(a) and 173(1)(b) are circumscribed in distinct ways. Section 173(1)(a) prohibits indecent acts in public places, while s. 173(1)(b) prohibits indecent acts in any place — public or private — when they are committed with intent to insult or offend.

49 Moreover, as I mentioned earlier, Parliament has distinguished in the *Code* between conduct that is criminal because it occurs in a public place and conduct

that is criminal because it is exposed to public view. Section 173(1)(a), as we have seen, grounds liability in the fact that the prohibited act is committed in a public place. The offence of nudity is set out in the very next section of the *Code*:

174. (1) Every one who, without lawful excuse,

   (a) is nude in a public place, or

   (b) is nude and exposed to public view while on private property, whether or not the property is his own,

is guilty of an offence punishable on summary conviction.

50 Section 174(1) makes it perfectly clear that the definition of "public place" in s. 150 of the *Criminal Code* was not meant to cover private places exposed to public view. Were it otherwise, s. 174(1)(b) would be entirely superfluous.

51 Section 150 applies equally to s. 174(1) and s. 173(1)(a). If "public place" does not, for the purposes of s. 174(1), include private places exposed to public view, this must surely be the case as well for s. 173(1)(a). And I hasten to emphasize that ss. 173(1) and 174 of the *Criminal Code* were enacted in their present form simultaneously, as ss. 158 and 159, when the present *Code* was revised and enacted as S.C. 1953-54, c. 51. Parliament could not have intended that identical words should have different meanings in two consecutive and related provisions of the very same enactment.

52 Section 213(1) of the *Code* provides further support, if any were needed, for the proposition that the grammatical and ordinary meaning I have ascribed to "access" is consistent with its legislative context and with Parliament's intention in enacting s. 150. Section 213(1) makes it an offence for anyone "in a public place or in any place open to public view" to commit certain specified acts for the purposes of prostitution.

53 The underlined, alternative route to liability in s. 213 was added by R.S.C. 1985, c. 51 (1st Supp.), s. 1. Parliament shortly thereafter directed its attention to s. 173, adding subs. (2): see R.S.C. 1985, c. 19 (3rd Supp.), s. 7. The respondent notes, correctly, that s. 213, unlike s. 173, is not in Part V of the *Criminal Code* and suggests that it was amended in response to comments by this court in *Hutt v. The Queen*, [1978] 2 S.C.R. 476. This may well be so, but Parliament is deemed to act deliberately. It is therefore not unreasonable to suppose that Parliament, when it expanded s. 213 to include places open to public view, did not add similar language to s. 173(1)(a) because it did not intend acts committed in such places to be caught under the latter section.

54 I think it inappropriate for this court to do now what Parliament declined to do then and remains free in its wisdom to do still.

55 For all of these reasons, as indicated at the outset, I would allow the appeal, vacate the appellant's conviction and enter an acquittal.

[The court also noted a separate issue around appeals, and the deference which must be paid to findings such as that of the trial judge here that the accused was not aware that he was being watched.]

8 In affirming the appellant's conviction, the Court of Appeal nonetheless concluded that the appellant "intentionally conducted himself in an indecent way, seeking to draw the attention of others (members of the public) to himself on the evening in question" ((2003), 185 B.C.A.C. 87, 2003 BCCA 408, at para. 10). It was "an inescapable inference from the facts", said the Court of Appeal, "that what the appellant was doing here was acting in an exhibitionist manner and seeking to draw attention to himself in a residential neighbourhood while he was in view of other residents" (para. 5).

9 The appellant submits that the Court of Appeal, in this regard and in other respects as well, departed impermissibly from the trial judge's appreciation of the evidence. With respect, I agree. But since I would in any event allow the appeal on other grounds, I find it sufficient for present purposes simply to reaffirm the governing principles. Appellate courts may not interfere with the findings of fact made and the factual inferences drawn by the trial judge, unless they are clearly wrong, unsupported by the evidence or otherwise unreasonable. The imputed error must, moreover, be plainly identified. And it must be shown to have affected the result. "Palpable and overriding error" is a resonant and compendious expression of this well-established norm: see *Stein v. The Ship "Kathy K"*, [1976] 2 S.C.R. 802; *Lensen v. Lensen*, [1987] 2 S.C.R. 672; *Geffen v. Goodman Estate*, [1991] 2 S.C.R. 353; *Hodgkinson v. Simms*, [1994] 3 S.C.R. 377; *Toneguzzo-Norvell (Guardian ad litem of) v. Burnaby Hospital*, [1994] 1 S.C.R. 114; *Schwartz v. Canada*, [1996] 1 S.C.R. 254; *Housen v. Nikolaisen*, [2002] 2 S.C.R. 235, 2002 SCC 33.

10 It has not been suggested that the trial judge in this case committed a palpable and overriding error in his appreciation of the evidence. This appeal therefore falls to be decided by applying the law as set out by Parliament to the facts as found by the trial judge.

Appeal allowed; conviction quashed and acquittal substituted.

. . . .

In *Clark*, the neighbour Mr. S. goes to his bedroom in order to have a better view of the accused, and attempts to videotape him. **If the new s. 162(1) of the Code (p. 5) had been in force at the relevant time, should he be found guilty of committing that offence?**

(ii)   Bilingual interpretation

An issue which sometimes arises in Canada is understanding the meaning of a statute which has been written in two languages, since both the English and French versions are considered equally authoritative. In most cases no issue arises, since the two versions will express the same meaning. There can sometimes be discrepancies between the two versions, however. In such cases, the Supreme Court held in *Schreiber v. Canada (Attorney General)*, [2002] 3 S.C.R. 269, 167 C.C.C. (3d) 51 that:

> 56 A principle of bilingual statutory interpretation holds that where one version is ambiguous and the other is clear and unequivocal, the common meaning of the two versions would *a priori* be preferred; see: *Côté, supra*, at p. 327; and *Tupper v. The Queen*, [1967] S.C.R. 589. Furthermore, where one of the two versions is broader than the other, the common meaning would favour the more restricted or limited meaning...

So, for example, the English version of section 24(2) of the *Charter* provides for the possible exclusion of evidence where its admission "would bring the administration of justice into disrepute". The court noted in *R. v. Collins*, [1987] 1 S.C.R. 265, 56 C.R. (3d) 193, 33 C.C.C. (3d) 1 that:

> 43 . . . The French text of s. 24(2) provides "est susceptible de déconsidérer l'administration de la justice", which I would translate as "could bring the administration of justice into disrepute". This is supportive of a somewhat lower threshold than the English text. As Dickson J. (as he then was) wrote in *Hunter v. Southam Inc., supra*, at p. 157:
>
> Since the proper approach to the interpretation of the *Charter of Rights and Freedoms* is a purposive one, before it is possible to assess the reasonableness or unreasonableness of the impact of a search or of a statute authorizing a search, it is first necessary to specify the purpose underlying s. 8: in other words, to delineate the nature of the interests it is meant to protect.
>
> As one of the purposes of s. 24(2) is to protect the right to a fair trial, I would favour the interpretation of s. 24(2) which better protects that right, the less onerous French text. Most courts which have considered the issue have also come to this conclusion (see Gibson, *supra*, at pp. 63 and 234-35). Section 24(2) should thus be read as "the evidence shall be excluded if it is established that, having regard to all the circumstances, the admission of it in the proceedings could bring the administration of justice into disrepute".

(iii)   Strict construction

Do Canadian courts construe penal statutes "strictly"? Should they?

Interpretation Act, R.S.C. 1985, c. I-21, s. 12:

> Every enactment shall be deemed remedial, and shall be given such fair, large and liberal construction and interpretation as best ensures the attainment of its objects.

Interpretation Act, R.S.O. 1990, c. I.11, s. 10:

Every Act shall be deemed to be remedial, whether its immediate purport is to direct the doing of anything that the Legislature deems to be for the public good or to prevent or punish the doing of anything that it deems to be contrary to the public good, and shall accordingly receive such fair, large and liberal construction and interpretation as will best ensure the attainment of the object of the Act according to its true intent, meaning and spirit.

R. v. GOULIS

(1981), 20 C.R. (3d) 360 at 365, 60 C.C.C. (2d) 347,
1981 CarswellOnt 164 (Ont. C.A.)

MARTIN J.A.: —

. . . .

This court has on many occasions applied the well-known rule of statutory construction that if a penal provision is reasonably capable of two interpretations that interpretation which is the more favourable to the accused must be adopted: see, for example, *Cheetham v. R.* (1980), 17 C.R. (3d) 1, 53 C.C.C. (2d) 109; *Negridge v. R.* (1980), 17 C.R. (3d) 14. I do not think, however, that this principle always requires a word which has two accepted meanings to be given the more restrictive meaning. Where a word used in a statute has two accepted meanings, then either or both meanings may apply. The court is first required to endeavour to determine the sense in which Parliament used the word from the context in which it appears. It is only in the case of an ambiguity which still exists after the full context is considered, where it is uncertain in which sense Parliament used the word, that the above rule of statutory construction requires the interpretation which is the more favourable to the defendant to be adopted. This is merely another way of stating the principle that the conduct alleged against the accused must be clearly brought within the proscription.

For an extreme example of strict construction, see *R. v. Steer* (1982), 30 C.R. (3d) 269 (B.C. Prov. Ct.). On a charge of leaving the scene of an accident, the accused was acquitted since the trial judge found that the accused had deliberately rammed the other vehicle in a fit of temper and thus was not leaving an accident.

R. v. PARÉ

[1987] 2 S.C.R. 618, 60 C.R. (3d) 346, 38 C.C.C. (3d) 97,
1987 CarswellQue 19, 1987 CarswellQue 97

The accused, aged 17, lured a seven-year-old boy to a place under a bridge, where he indecently assaulted him. When the boy told the accused that he would tell his mother, the accused threatened to kill him if he did. When the accused became certain that the boy would nevertheless tell, he held the boy down on his back for two minutes and then killed him through strangulation and hitting him with an oil filter. The accused was charged with and convicted of first degree murder on the basis of s. 214(5) [now s. 231(5)] of the *Criminal Code*, in that "murder is first degree murder ... when the death is caused ... *while committing*" an indecent assault (now sexual assault).

WILSON J.: —

. . . .

(iii)   Strict Construction

Counsel for the respondent argue that the doctrine of strict construction of criminal statutes requires that this court adopt the interpretation most favourable to the accused. According to this argument the words "while committing" must be narrowly construed so as to elevate murder to first degree only when the death and the underlying offence occur simultaneously. In order to assess the validity of this position we must examine the doctrine of strict construction.

The doctrine is one of ancient lineage. It reached its pinnacle of importance in a former age when the death penalty attached to a vast array of offences. As Stephen Kloepfer points out in his article "The Status of Strict Construction in Canadian Criminal Law" (1983), 15 Ottawa L. Rev. 553, at pp. 556-60, the doctrine was one of many tools employed by the judiciary to soften the impact of the Draconian penal provisions of the time. Over the past two centuries criminal law penalties have become far less severe. Criminal law remains, however, the most dramatic and important incursion that the state makes into individual liberty. Thus, while the original justification for the doctrine has been substantially eroded, the seriousness of imposing criminal penalties of any sort demands that reasonable doubts be resolved in favour of the accused.

This point was underlined by Dickson J. (as he then was) in *Marcotte v. Deputy Attorney General for Canada*, [1976] 1 S.C.R. 108, at p. 115:

> It is unnecessary to emphasize the importance of clarity and certainty when freedom is at stake. No authority is needed for the proposition that if real ambiguities are found, or doubts of substance arise, in the construction and application of a statute affecting the liberty of a subject, then that statute should be applied in such a manner as to favour the person against whom it is sought to be enforced. If one is to be incarcerated, one should at least know that some Act of Parliament requires it in express terms, and not, at most, by implication.

The continued vitality of the doctrine is further evidenced by the decisions in *R. v. Goulis* (1981), 60 C.C.C. (2d) 347 (Ont. C.A.), and *Paul v. The Queen*, [1982] 1 S.C.R. 621. The question, therefore, is not whether the doctrine of strict construction exists but what its implications are for this case.

(iv)   Applying the Doctrine

As we have noted above, it is clearly grammatically possible to construe the words "while committing" in s. 214(5) as requiring murder to be classified as first degree only if it is exactly coincidental with the underlying offence. This, however, does not end the question. We still have to determine whether the narrow interpretation of "while committing" is a reasonable one, given the scheme and purpose of the legislation.

In my view, the construction that counsel for the respondent would have us place on these words is not one that could reasonably be attributed to Parliament. The first problem with the exactly simultaneous approach flows from the difficulty in defining the beginning and end of an indecent assault. In this case, for example, after ejaculation the respondent sat up and put his pants back on. But for the next two minutes he kept his hand on his victim's chest. Was this continued contact part of the assault? It does not seem to me that important issues of criminal law should be allowed to hinge upon this kind of distinction. An approach that depends on this kind of distinction should be avoided if possible.

A second difficulty with the exactly simultaneous approach is that it leads to distinctions that are arbitrary and irrational. In the present case, had the respondent strangled his victim two minutes earlier than he did, his guilt of first degree murder would be beyond dispute. The exactly simultaneous approach would have us conclude that the two minutes he spent contemplating his next move had the effect of reducing his offence to one of second degree murder. This would be a strange result. The crime is no less serious in the latter case than in the former; indeed, if anything, the latter crime is more serious since it involves some element of deliberation. An interpretation of s. 214(5) that runs contrary to common sense is not to be adopted if a reasonable alternative is available.

In my view, such an interpretation has been provided by Martin J.A. in *Stevens, supra*. As noted above, Martin J.A. suggested that "where the act causing death and the acts constituting the rape, attempted rape, indecent assault or an attempt to commit indecent assault, as the case may be, all form part of one continuous sequence of events forming a single transaction" the death was caused "while committing" an offence for the purposes of s. 214(5). This interpretation eliminates the need to draw artificial lines to separate the commission and the aftermath of an indecent assault. Further, it eliminates the arbitrariness inherent in the exactly simultaneous approach. I would, therefore, respectfully adopt Martin J.A.'s single transaction analysis as the proper construction of s. 214(5).

This approach, it seems to me, best expresses the policy considerations that underlie the provision. Section 214, as we have seen, classifies murder as either first or second degree. All murders are serious crimes. Some murders, however, are so threatening to the public that Parliament has chosen to impose exceptional penalties on the perpetrators. One such class of murders is that found in s. 214(5), murders done while committing a hijacking, a kidnapping and forcible confinement, a rape, or an indecent assault. An understanding of why this class of murder is elevated to murder in the first degree is a helpful guide to the interpretation of the language.

The Law Reform Commission of Canada addressed this issue in its paper on Homicide (Working Paper 33, 1984). At page 79, the paper states:

> . . . there is a lack of rationale in the law. Subsection 214(5) provides that, whether planned and deliberate or not, murder is first degree murder when committed in the course of certain listed offences. It is curious that the list there given is considerably shorter than that given in section 213 which makes killing murder if done in the commission of certain specified offences. Inspection and comparision of the two lists, however, reveal no organizing principle in either of them and no rationale for the difference between them.

With respect, I disagree. The offences listed in s. 214(5) are all offences involving the unlawful domination of people by other people. Thus an organizing principle for s. 214(5) can be found. This principle is that where a murder is committed by someone already abusing his power by illegally dominating another, the murder should be treated as an exceptionally serious crime. Parliament has chosen to treat these murders as murders in the first degree.

Refining then on the concept of the "single transaction" referred to by Martin J.A. in *Stevens, supra*, it is the continuing illegal domination of the victim which gives continuity to the sequence of events culminating in the murder. The murder represents an exploitation of the position of power created by the underlying crime and makes the entire course of conduct a "single transaction". This approach, in my view, best gives effect to the philosophy underlying s. 214(5).

. . . .

4.   Conclusion

The respondent murdered Steve Duranleau minutes after indecently assaulting him. The killing was motivated by fear that the boy would tell his mother about the indecent assault. The jury found the respondent guilty of first degree murder. They were entitled to do so. The murder was temporally and causally connected to the underlying offence. It formed part of one continuous sequence of events. It was part of the same transaction.

I would allow the appeal and restore the conviction of first degree murder.

R. v. MAC

(2001), 40 C.R. (5th) 138, 152 C.C.C. (3d) 1, 2001 CarswellOnt 328
(Ont. C.A.)

The accused was tried on charges related to the large scale manufacture and sale of forged credit cards. The charges were laid under s. 369(*b*) of the *Criminal Code* alleging that the accused was in possession of various machines and materials adapted for and intended to be used to create forged credit cards. On appeal the accused argued that the trial judge erred in instructing the jury that the word "adapted" in s. 369(*b*) meant "suitable for". The accused argued that it means "altered so as to be suitable for". The material and machines relied on for some of the charges were suitable for use in the making of forged credit cards but had not been altered in any way.

DOHERTY J.A. (CHARRON and MACPHERSON JJ.A. concurring): —

. . . .

The principle identified in these cases (*Paré* and *McIntosh*) and countless others is justified on at least two grounds. Persons who are subject to the coercive and stigmatizing power of the criminal law are entitled to fair notice of the conduct which will subject them to that power. Where a crime is defined in ambiguous terms, fair notice is only given with respect to the conduct which is captured by each of the meanings which are reasonably available upon a reading of the statute: A. Ashworth, *Principles of Criminal Law, supra*, at 76-78.

The second justification underlying the principle arises out of our commitment to individual liberty, particularly where the criminal law power is engaged. Canadian society operates on the basis that individuals are free to do as they choose, subject to constitutionally permissible limits on that liberty imposed by Parliament (and not the courts). Where it is unclear whether Parliament has chosen to prohibit conduct by making it criminal, the commitment to individual liberty commands that the doubt be resolved in favour of the maintenance of individual liberty: D. Stuart, *Canadian Criminal Law, supra*, at 37-40.

The principle that ambiguous penal provisions must be interpreted in favour of an accused does not mean that the most restrictive possible meaning of any word used in the penal statute must always be the preferred meaning. The principle applies only where there is true ambiguity as to the meaning of a word in a penal statute: *R. v. Hasselwander* (1993), 81 C.C.C. (3d) 471 at 476-77 (S.C.C.). The meaning of words cannot be determined by examining those words in isolation. Meaning is discerned by examining words in their context. True ambiguities in a statute exist only where the meaning remains unclear after a full contextual analysis of the statute.

The court held that, given real ambiguity, the offence of possession of machines "adapted" for creating credit cards had to be given the strict construction of "altered so as to be suitable for" rather than just "suitable for".

On further appeal the Supreme Court reversed in a brief oral judgment by Bastarache J. (see [2002] 1 S.C.R. 856, 50 C.R.(5th) 50, 163 C.C.C.(3d) 1). The court accepted that "courts may resort to strict construction of penal statutes where ordinary principles of interpretation do not resolve an ambiguity" but held that there was no ambiguity given the wording of the French version of the *Code*.

The majority judgments of the B.C. Court of Appeal in *Scott* (2000), 34 C.R. (5th) 322, 145 C.C.C. (3d) 52 (B.C. C.A.), are far less sympathetic to strict construction. The majority there decided that the offence of using a firearm in the commission of offences under s. 85(2), which requires consecutive sentencing on conviction, did not require the Crown to establish whether the weapon was real or an imitation.

(c)   Division of Powers under the *Constitution Act 1867*

THE CONSTITUTION ACT, 1867

(formerly the British North America Act)

1867, 30 and 31 Vic., c. 3

VI.—DISTRIBUTION OF LEGISLATIVE POWERS.

Powers of the Parliament.

91. It shall be lawful for the Queen, by and with the Advice and Consent of the Senate and House of Commons, to make Laws for the Peace, Order, and good Government of Canada, in relation to all Matters not coming within the Classes of Subjects by this Act assigned exclusively to the Legislatures of the Provinces; and for greater Certainty, but not so as to restrict the Generality of the foregoing Terms of this Section, it is hereby declared that (notwithstanding anything in this Act) the exclusive Legislative Authority of the Parliament of Canada extends to all Matters coming within the Classes of Subjects next hereinafter enumerated; that is to say,—

. . . .

27. The Criminal Law, except the Constitution of Courts of Criminal Jurisdiction, but including the Procedure in Criminal Matters.
28. The Establishment, Maintenance, and Management of Penitentiaries.

. . . .

Exclusive Powers of Provincial Legislatures.

92. In each Province the Legislature may exclusively make Laws in relation to Matters coming within the Classes of Subject next hereinafter enumerated; that is to say,—

. . . .

6. The Establishment, Maintenance, and Management of Public and Reformatory Prisons in and for the Province.

. . . .

13. Property and Civil Rights in the Province.
14. The Administration of Justice in the Province, including the Constitution, Maintenance, and Organization of Provincial Courts, both of Civil and of Criminal Jurisdiction, and including Procedure in Civil Matters in those courts.
15. The Imposition of Punishment by Fine, Penalty, or Imprisonment for enforcing any Law of the Province made in relation to any Matter coming within any of the Classes of Subjects enumerated in this Section.

REFERENCE RE FIREARMS ACT (CANADA)

[2000] 1 S.C.R. 783, 144 C.C.C. (3d) 385, 34 C.R. (5th) 1,
2000 SCC 31, 2000 CarswellAlta 517, 2000 CarswellAlta 518

The following is the judgment delivered by THE COURT —

I. Introduction

1 In 1995, Parliament amended the *Criminal Code*, R.S.C., 1985, c. C-46, by enacting the *Firearms Act*, S.C. 1995, c. 39, commonly referred to as the gun control law, to require the holders of all firearms to obtain licences and register their guns. In 1996, the Province of Alberta challenged Parliament's power to pass the gun control law by a reference to the Alberta Court of Appeal. The Court of Appeal by a 3:2 majority upheld Parliament's power to pass the law. The Province of Alberta now appeals that decision to this court.

2 The issue before this court is not whether gun control is good or bad, whether the law is fair or unfair to gun owners, or whether it will be effective or ineffective in reducing the harm caused by the misuse of firearms. The only issue is whether or not Parliament has the constitutional authority to enact the law.

3 The answer to this question lies in the Canadian Constitution. The Constitution assigns some matters to Parliament and others to the provincial legislatures: *Constitution Act, 1867*. The federal government asserts that the gun control law falls under its criminal law power, s. 91(27), and under its general power to legislate for the "Peace, Order and Good Government" of Canada. Alberta, on the other hand, says the law falls under its power over property and civil rights, s. 92(13). All agree that to resolve this dispute, the court must first determine what the gun control law is really about—its "pith and substance"—and then ask which head or heads of power it most naturally falls within.

4 We conclude that the gun control law comes within Parliament's jurisdiction over criminal law. The law in "pith and substance" is directed to enhancing public safety by controlling access to firearms through prohibitions and penalties. This brings it under the federal criminal law power. While the law has regulatory aspects, they are secondary to its primary criminal law purpose. The intrusion of the law into the provincial jurisdiction over property and civil rights is not so excessive as to upset the balance of federalism.

II. Reference Questions

5 ... Simply put, the issue before us is whether or not the licensing and registration provisions in the *Firearms Act*, as they relate to ordinary firearms, were validly enacted by Parliament. . .

III. Legislation

6 For many years, the *Criminal Code* has restricted access to firearms, mainly automatic weapons and handguns, by classifying some as prohibited and some as restricted. The *Firearms Act* amendments extended this regulation to all firearms, including rifles and shotguns. As a result, s. 84 of the *Criminal Code* now controls three classes of firearms: (1) prohibited firearms (generally automatic weapons); (2) restricted firearms (generally handguns); and (3) all other firearms (generally rifles and shotguns). The third class of guns is variously referred to as "ordinary firearms", "long guns", and "unrestricted firearms". We will refer to this class as "ordinary firearms".

7 The reference questions focus on the validity of the licensing and registration provisions for ordinary firearms introduced by the *Firearms Act*. The licensing sections of the Act provide that a person must be licensed in order to possess a firearm. Eligibility for a licence reflects safety interests. An applicant with a criminal record involving drug offences or violence, or a history of mental illness, may be denied a licence. An applicant who seeks to acquire a firearm must pass a safety course which requires a basic understanding of firearm safety and the legal responsibilities of firearm ownership. The chief firearms officer, who issues licences, may conduct a background check on the applicant in order

to determine eligibility, and may attach conditions to a licence. Once issued, a licence is valid for five years, but it may be revoked for contravention of its conditions or for certain criminal convictions. A licence refusal or revocation may be appealed to a court.

8 The registration provisions of the Act are more limited. A firearm cannot be registered unless the applicant is licensed to possess that type of firearm. Registration is generally done by reference to the serial number on the firearm. A registration certificate is valid as long as its holder owns the weapon. If ownership of a registered weapon is transferred, the new owner must register the weapon. In order to give gun owners time to register their weapons, people who owned ordinary firearms as of January 1, 1998 are deemed to hold registration certificates that are valid until January 1, 2003. Possession of an unregistered firearm of any type is an offence. All licences and registration certificates, along with imported, exported, lost and stolen guns, are recorded in the Canadian Firearms Registry, which is operated by a federal appointee.

. . . .

V. Analysis

15 The issue before us is whether the licensing and registration provisions of the *Firearms Act* constitute a valid federal enactment pursuant to Parliament's jurisdiction over criminal law or its peace, order and good government power. In order to answer this question, we must engage in the division of powers analysis used so often by this court, and most recently summarized in *Global Securities Corp. v. British Columbia (Securities Commission)*, [2000] 1 S.C.R. 494, 2000 SCC 21; see also *Whitbread v. Walley*, [1990] 3 S.C.R. 1273, *R. v. Big M Drug Mart Ltd.*, [1985] 1 S.C.R. 295, and *R. v. Morgentaler*, [1993] 3 S.C.R. 463. There are two stages to this analysis. The first step is to determine the "pith and substance" or essential character of the law. The second step is to classify that essential character by reference to the heads of power under the *Constitution Act, 1867* in order to determine whether the law comes within the jurisdiction of the enacting government. If it does, then the law is valid.

A. Characterization: What Is the Pith and Substance of the Law?

16 The first task is to determine the "pith and substance" of the legislation. To use the wording of ss. 91 and 92, what is the "matter" of the law? What is its true meaning or essential character, its core? To determine the pith and substance, two aspects of the law must be examined: the purpose of the enacting body, and the legal effect of the law.

17 A law's purpose is often stated in the legislation, but it may also be ascertained by reference to extrinsic material such as Hansard and government

publications: see *Morgentaler, supra,* at pp. 483-84. While such extrinsic material was at one time inadmissible to facilitate the determination of Parliament's purpose, it is now well accepted that the legislative history, Parliamentary debates, and similar material may be quite properly considered as long as it is relevant and reliable and is not assigned undue weight: see *Global Securities, supra,* at para. 25; *Rizzo & Rizzo Shoes Ltd. (Re),* [1998] 1 S.C.R. 27, at para. 35; and *Doré v. Verdun (City),* [1997] 2 S.C.R. 862, at para. 14. Purpose may also be ascertained by considering the "mischief" of the legislation—the problem which Parliament sought to remedy: see *Morgentaler, supra,* at pp. 483-84.

18 Determining the legal effects of a law involves considering how the law will operate and how it will affect Canadians. The Attorney General of Alberta states that the law will not actually achieve its purpose. Where the legislative scheme is relevant to a criminal law purpose, he says, it will be ineffective (e.g., criminals will not register their guns); where it is effective it will not advance the fight against crime (e.g., burdening rural farmers with pointless red tape). These are concerns that were properly directed to and considered by Parliament. Within its constitutional sphere, Parliament is the judge of whether a measure is likely to achieve its intended purposes; efficaciousness is not relevant to the court's division of powers analysis: *Morgentaler, supra,* at pp. 487-88, and *Reference re Anti-Inflation Act,* [1976] 2 S.C.R. 373. Rather, the inquiry is directed to how the law sets out to achieve its purpose in order to better understand its "total meaning": W. R. Lederman, Continuing Canadian Constitutional Dilemmas (1981), at pp. 239-40. In some cases, the effects of the law may suggest a purpose other than that which is stated in the law: see *Morgentaler, supra,* at pp. 482-83; *Attorney-General for Alberta v. Attorney-General for Canada,* [1939] A.C. 117 (P.C.) (Alberta Bank Taxation Reference); and *Texada Mines Ltd. v. Attorney-General of British Columbia,* [1960] S.C.R. 713; see generally P. W. Hogg, *Constitutional Law of Canada* (loose-leaf ed.), at pp. 15-14 to 15-16. In other words, a law may say that it intends to do one thing and actually do something else. Where the effects of the law diverge substantially from the stated aim, it is sometimes said to be "colourable".

19 Against this background, we turn to the purpose of the *Firearms Act.* Section 4 states that the purpose of the Act is "to provide . . . for the issuance of licences, registration certificates and authorizations under which persons may possess firearms" and "to authorize . . . the manufacture of" and "transfer of" ordinary firearms. This is the language of property regulation. However, this regulatory language is directly tied to a purpose cast in the language of the criminal law. The licensing, registration and authorization provisions delineate the means by which people can own and transfer ordinary firearms "in circumstances that would otherwise constitute [a criminal] offence". Those who challenge the legislation point to the first part of the section and its regulatory focus. Those

who seek to uphold the law point to the second part of the section and its criminal focus.

20 The statements of the Honourable Allan Rock, Minister of Justice at the time, in his second-reading speech in the House of Commons, reveal that the federal government's purpose in proposing the law was to promote public safety. He stated: "The government suggests that the object of the regulation of firearms should be *the preservation of the safe, civilized and peaceful nature of Canada*" (House of Commons Debates, vol. 133, No. 154, 1st Sess., 35th Parl., February 16, 1995, at p. 9706 (emphasis added)). Mr. Rock went on to describe the contents of the bill in more detail (at p. 9707):

> First, tough measures to deal with the *criminal misuse of firearms*; second, specific *penalties to punish those who would smuggle illegal firearms*; and third, measures overall to provide a context in which the legitimate use of firearms can be carried on in a manner consistent with *public safety*. [Emphasis added.]

> (See also the judgment of Fraser C.J.A., at paras. 169-72.)

Later, the Minister referred to the problems of suicide, accidental shootings, and the use of guns in domestic violence, and detailed some of the shooting tragedies that had spurred public calls for gun control. Russell MacLellan, the Parliamentary Secretary of Justice at the time, underscored the government's concerns, noting that the Act pursues "three fundamental policies: the deterrence of the misuse of firearms, general controls on persons given access to firearms, and controls placed on specific types of firearms" ("Canada's firearms proposals" (1995), 37 Can. J. Crim. 163, at p. 163).

21 Another way to determine the purpose of legislation is to look at the problems it is intended to address—the so-called "mischief" approach. The *Firearms Act* is aimed at a number of evils or "mischiefs". One is the illegal trade in guns, both within Canada and across the border with the United States: see The Government's Action Plan on Firearms Control, tabled in the House of Commons in 1994. Another is the link between guns and violent crime, suicide, and accidental deaths. In a paper commissioned by the Department of Justice in 1994, *The Impact of the Availability of Firearms on Violent Crime, Suicide, and Accidental Death: A Review of the Literature with Special Reference to the Canadian Situation*, Thomas Gabor found that all three causes of death may increase in jurisdictions where there are the fewest restrictions on guns. Whether or not one accepts Gabor's conclusions, his study indicates the problem which Parliament sought to address by enacting the legislation: the problem of the misuse of firearms and the threat it poses to public safety.

22 Finally, there is a strong argument that the purpose of this legislation conforms with the historical public safety focus of all gun control laws. This reference challenges the licensing and registration provisions of the Act only as

they relate to ordinary firearms. Alberta does not question the licensing and registration of restricted and prohibited weapons. It freely admits that the restrictions on those categories of weapons are constitutional. Indeed, Alberta would have difficulty alleging otherwise, as numerous courts have upheld the validity of different aspects of the federal gun control legislation that existed prior to the enactment of this Act: see *R. v. Schwartz*, [1988] 2 S.C.R. 443; *McGuigan v. The Queen*, [1982] 1 S.C.R. 284; and *Attorney General of Canada v. Pattison* (1981), 30 A.R. 83 (C.A.).

23 More specifically, before the introduction of the *Firearms Act*, the registration of all restricted weapons was upheld by the British Columbia Court of Appeal in *Martinoff v. Dawson* (1990), 57 C.C.C. (3d) 482. Furthermore, the *Criminal Code* required anyone seeking to obtain any kind of firearm to apply for a firearms acquisition certificate. This requirement was upheld in *R. v. Northcott*, [1980] 5 W.W.R. 38 (B.C. Prov. Ct.). These cases upheld the previous gun control legislation on the basis that Parliament's purpose was to promote public safety. The *Firearms Act* extends that legislation in two respects: (1) it requires all guns to be registered, not just restricted and prohibited firearms; and (2) eventually all gun owners will be required to be licensed, not just those who wish to acquire a firearm. These changes represent a continuation of Parliament's focus on safety concerns, and constitute a limited expansion of the pre-existing legislation. Given the general acceptance of the gun control legislation that has existed for the past hundred years, the constitutional validity of which has always been predicated on Parliament's concern for public safety, it is difficult to now impute a different purpose to Parliament. This supports the view that the law in pith and substance is about public safety.

24 The effects of the scheme—how it impacts on the legal rights of Canadians—also support the conclusion that the 1995 gun control law is in pith and substance a public safety measure. The criteria for acquiring a licence are concerned with safety rather than the regulation of property. Criminal record checks and background investigations are designed to keep guns out of the hands of those incapable of using them safely. Safety courses ensure that gun owners are qualified. What the law does not require also shows that the operation of the scheme is limited to ensuring safety. For instance, the Act does not regulate the legitimate commercial market for guns. It makes no attempt to set labour standards or the price of weapons. There is no attempt to protect or regulate industries or businesses associated with guns (see *Pattison, supra*, at para. 22). Unlike provincial property registries, the registry established under the Act is not concerned with prior interests, and unlike some provincial motor vehicle schemes, the Act does not address insurance. In short, the effects of the law suggest that its essence is the promotion of public safety through the reduction of the misuse of firearms, and negate the proposition that Parliament was in fact attempting to achieve a different goal such as the total regulation of firearms

production, trade, and ownership. We therefore conclude that, viewed from its purpose and effects, the *Firearms Act* is in "pith and substance" directed to public safety.

B. Classification: Does Parliament Have Jurisdiction to Enact the Law?

25 Having assessed the pith and substance or matter of the law, the second step is to determine whether that matter comes within the jurisdiction of the enacting legislature. We must examine the heads of power under ss. 91 and 92 of the *Constitution Act, 1867* and determine what the matter is "in relation to". In this case, the question is whether the law falls under federal jurisdiction over criminal law or its peace, order and good government power; or under provincial jurisdiction over property and civil rights. The presumption of constitutionality means that Alberta, as the party challenging the legislation, is required to show that the Act does not fall within the jurisdiction of Parliament: see *Nova Scotia Board of Censors v. McNeil*, [1978] 2 S.C.R. 662.

26 The determination of which head of power a particular law falls under is not an exact science. In a federal system, each level of government can expect to have its jurisdiction affected by the other to a certain degree. As Dickson C.J. stated in *General Motors of Canada Ltd. v. City National Leasing*, [1989] 1 S.C.R. 641, at p. 669, "overlap of legislation is to be expected and accommodated in a federal state". Laws mainly in relation to the jurisdiction of one level of government may overflow into, or have "incidental effects" upon, the jurisdiction of the other level of government. It is a matter of balance and of federalism: no one level of government is isolated from the other, nor can it usurp the functions of the other.

27 As a general rule, legislation may be classified as criminal law if it possesses three prerequisites: a valid criminal law purpose backed by a prohibition and a penalty: *RJR-MacDonald, supra*; *Hydro-Québec, supra*; and *Reference re Validity of Section 5(a) of the Dairy Industry Act*, [1949] S.C.R. 1 (the "*Margarine Reference*"). The Attorney General of Canada argues that the 1995 gun control law meets these three requirements, and points to commentary on this legislation which supports its position: D. Gibson, "The Firearms Reference in the Alberta Court of Appeal" (1999), 37 Alta. L. Rev. 1071; D. M. Beatty, "Gun Control and Judicial Anarchy" (1999), 10 Constitutional Forum 45; A. C. Hutchinson and D. Schneiderman, "Smoking Guns: The Federal Government Confronts The Tobacco and Gun Lobbies" (1995), 7 Constitutional Forum 16; and Peter W. Hogg's testimony before the Standing Senate Committee on Legal and Constitutional Affairs, October 26, 1995.

28 Before determining whether the three criminal law criteria are met by this legislation, some general observations on the criminal law power may be apposite. Criminal law, as this court has stated in numerous cases, constitutes a

broad area of federal jurisdiction: *RJR-MacDonald, supra; Hydro-Québec, supra;* and *Margarine Reference, supra.* The criminal law stands on its own as federal jurisdiction. Although it often overlaps with provincial jurisdiction over property and civil rights, it is not "carved out" from provincial jurisdiction, contrary to the view of Conrad J.A. It also includes the law of criminal procedure, which regulates many aspects of criminal law enforcement, such as arrest, search and seizure of evidence, the regulation of electronic surveillance and the forfeiture of stolen property.

29 Not only is the criminal law a "stand-alone" jurisdiction, it also finds its expression in a broad range of legislation. The *Criminal Code* is the quintessential federal enactment under its criminal jurisdiction, but it is not the only one. The *Food and Drugs Act*, the *Hazardous Products Act*, the *Lord's Day Act*, and the *Tobacco Products Control Act* have all been held to be valid exercises of the criminal law power: see *Standard Sausage Co. v. Lee*, [1933] 4 D.L.R. 501 (B.C.C.A.); *R. v. Cosman's Furniture* (1972) Ltd. (1976), 73 D.L.R. (3d) 312 (Man. C.A.); *Big M Drug Mart, supra* (legislation struck down on other grounds); and *RJR-MacDonald, supra* (legislation struck down on other grounds), respectively. Thus the fact that some of the provisions of the *Firearms Act* are not contained within the *Criminal Code* has no significance for the purposes of constitutional classification.

30 Although the criminal law power is broad, it is not unlimited. Some of the parties before us expressed the fear that the criminal law power might be illegitimately used to invade the provincial domain and usurp provincial power. A properly restrained understanding of the criminal law power guards against this possibility.

31 Within this context, we return to the three criteria that a law must satisfy in order to be classified as criminal. The first step is to consider whether the law has a valid criminal law purpose. Rand J. listed some examples of valid purposes in the *Margarine Reference* at p. 50: "Public peace, order, security, health, morality: these are the ordinary though not exclusive ends served by [criminal] law". Earlier, we concluded that the gun control law in pith and substance is directed at public safety. This brings it clearly within the criminal law purposes of protecting public peace, order, security and health.

32 In determining whether the purpose of a law constitutes a valid criminal law purpose, courts look at whether laws of this type have traditionally been held to be criminal law: see *Morgentaler, supra,* at p. 491, and *RJR-MacDonald, supra,* at para. 204; see also *Scowby v. Glendinning*, [1986] 2 S.C.R. 226, *Westendorp v. The Queen*, [1983] 1 S.C.R. 43, and *R. v. Zelensky*, [1978] 2 S.C.R. 940. Courts have repeatedly held that gun control comes within the criminal law sphere. As Fraser C.J.A. demonstrated in her judgment, gun control has been a matter of criminal law since before the enactment of the *Criminal Code* in 1892,

and has continued since that date (see also E. M. Davies, "The 1995 *Firearms Act*: Canada's Public Relations Response to the Myth of Violence" (2000), 6 Appeal 44, and M. L. Friedland, A Century of Criminal Justice (1984), at pp. 125 ff.).

33 Gun control has traditionally been considered valid criminal law because guns are dangerous and pose a risk to public safety. Section 2 of the *Criminal Code* (as amended by s. 138(2) of the *Firearms Act*) defines a "firearm" as "a barrelled weapon from which any shot, bullet or other projectile can be discharged and that is capable of causing serious bodily injury or death to a person" (emphasis added). This demonstrates that Parliament views firearms as dangerous and regulates their possession and use on that ground. The law is limited to restrictions which are directed at safety purposes. As such, the regulation of guns as dangerous products is a valid purpose within the criminal law power: see *R. v. Felawka*, [1993] 4 S.C.R. 199; *RJR-MacDonald, supra; R. v. Wetmore*, [1983] 2 S.C.R. 284; and *Cosman's Furniture, supra*.

34 The finding of a valid criminal law purpose does not end the inquiry, however. In order to be classified as a valid criminal law, that purpose must be connected to a prohibition backed by a penalty. The 1995 gun control law satisfies these requirements. Section 112 of the *Firearms Act* prohibits the possession of a firearm without a registration certificate. Section 91 of the *Criminal Code* (as amended by s. 139 of the *Firearms Act*) prohibits the possession of a firearm without a licence and a registration certificate. These prohibitions are backed by penalties: see s. 115 of the *Firearms Act* and s. 91 of the *Code*.

35 It thus appears that the 1995 gun control law possesses all three criteria required for a criminal law. However, Alberta and the provinces raised a number of objections to this classification which must be considered.

. . . .

(4) Is Moral Content Required?

54 Yet another argument is that the ownership of guns is not criminal law because it is not immoral to own an ordinary firearm. There are two difficulties with this argument. The first is that while the ownership of ordinary firearms is not in itself regarded by most Canadians as immoral, the problems associated with the misuse of firearms are firmly grounded in morality. Firearms may be misused to take human life and to assist in other immoral acts, like theft and terrorism. Preventing such misuse can be seen as an attempt to curb immoral acts. Viewed thus, gun control is directed at a moral evil.

55 The second difficulty with the argument is that the criminal law is not confined to prohibiting immoral acts: see *Proprietary Articles Trade Association*

v. Attorney-General for Canada, [1931] A.C. 310 (P.C.). While most criminal conduct is also regarded as immoral, Parliament can use the criminal law to prohibit activities which have little relation to public morality. For instance, the criminal law has been used to prohibit certain restrictions on market competition: see *Attorney-General for British Columbia v. Attorney-General for Canada*, *supra*. Therefore, even if gun control did not involve morality, it could still fall under the federal criminal law power.

(5) Other Concerns

56 We recognize the concerns of northern, rural and aboriginal Canadians who fear that this law does not address their particular needs. They argue that it discriminates against them and violates treaty rights, and express concerns about their ability to access the scheme, which may be administered from a great distance. These apprehensions are genuine, but they do not go to the question before us—Parliament's jurisdiction to enact this law. Whether a law could have been designed better or whether the federal government should have engaged in more consultation before enacting the law has no bearing on the division of powers analysis applied by this court. If the law violates a treaty or a provision of the *Charter*, those affected can bring their claims to Parliament or the courts in a separate case. The reference questions, and hence this judgment, are restricted to the issue of the division of powers.

57 We also appreciate the concern of those who oppose this Act on the basis that it may not be effective or it may be too expensive. Criminals will not register their guns, Alberta argued. The only real effect of the law, it is suggested, is to burden law-abiding farmers and hunters with red tape. These concerns were properly directed to and considered by Parliament; they cannot affect the court's decision. The efficacy of a law, or lack thereof, is not relevant to Parliament's ability to enact it under the division of powers analysis. Furthermore, the federal government points out that it is not only career criminals who are capable of misusing guns. Domestic violence often involves people who have no prior criminal record. Crimes are committed by first-time offenders. Finally, accidents and suicides occur in the homes of law-abiding people, and guns are stolen from their homes. By requiring everyone to register their guns, Parliament seeks to reduce misuse by everyone and curtail the ability of criminals to acquire firearms. Where criminals have acquired guns and used them in the commission of offences, the registration system seeks to make those guns more traceable. The cost of the program, another criticism of the law, is equally irrelevant to our constitutional analysis.

VI. Conclusion

58 We conclude that the impugned sections of the *Firearms Act* contain prohibitions and penalties in support of a valid criminal law purpose. The

legislation is in relation to criminal law pursuant to s. 91(27) of the *Constitution Act, 1867* and hence *intra vires* Parliament. It is not regulatory legislation and it does not take the federal government so far into provincial territory that the balance of federalism is threatened or the jurisdictional powers of the provinces are unduly impaired.

In 2011 the Conservative Government abolished the long gun registry.

(d) *Charter of Rights and Freedoms*

Another potential source of substantive criminal law is the *Canadian Charter of Rights and Freedoms,* entrenched by the *Constitution Act, 1982,* of December 8, 1981 [en. by the *Canada Act, 1982* (U.K.), c. 11, Sched. B], Pt. 1. Unlike its predecessor, the *Canadian Bill of Rights,* R.S.C. 1970, App. III, it applies to provincial as well as federal laws by virtue of s. 32. Furthermore s. 52(1) reads:

> The Constitution of Canada is the supreme law of Canada, and any law that is inconsistent with the provisions of the Constitution is, to the extent of the inconsistency, of no force or effect.

This provision is a significant inroad on the principle of parliamentary supremacy and grants to the courts the power to measure legislation against a now entrenched yardstick of human rights and freedoms. Arguments against such a judicial function (for example, that it constitutes an unjustifiable transfer of legislative power to the courts, that the courts are not democratically elected and should not therefore be ruling on such value questions, and that judges, particularly at the lower levels are not sufficiently equipped to handle these large questions) should now be at an end. The courts have the power and arguments such as these can only be made in seeking to persuade judges to exercise their power with restraint.

The *Charter* has had a considerable impact on the criminal courts. In thousands of cases, judges at all levels have grappled with the meaning of various aspects of the *Charter.* The impact of the *Charter* has been most marked on procedural law. It enshrines several procedural rights quite specific to the criminal trial. Most are to be found under the heading of "Legal Rights" — the protection against unreasonable search or seizure (s. 8), the right not to be arbitrarily detained (s. 9), the right on arrest or detention to be informed promptly of the reasons (s. 10(*a*)), the right to retain and instruct counsel without delay and to be informed of that right (s. 10(*b*)), the right of an accused not to be compelled to be a witness (s. 11(*c*)) and the protection against self-incrimination (s. 13). Such purely procedural topics will not be considered here. This book is primarily concerned with substantive criminal law and not procedure. This material is concerned with examining the elements of a crime (what has to be proved) and not with how the crime will be investigated or prosecuted. However we will consider the broadly interpreted s. 7, which reads:

> Everyone has the right to life, liberty and security of the person and the right not to be deprived thereof except in accordance with the principles of fundamental justice.

We shall also deal with the presumption of innocence under s. 11(*d*), different types of burdens of proof and with what constitutes a demonstrably justified reasonable limit under s. 1.

By s.1 the rights set out in the *Charter* are subject to

such reasonable limits prescribed by law as can be demonstrably justified in a free and democratic society.

When it is found that there has been a *Charter* violation and that that violation cannot be saved under s. 1, the question of remedy arises. These include personal remedies under s. 24 (including possible exclusion of evidence) or remedies which strike down or in some way rewrite the offending statutory provision under s. 52.

For a review of the impact of the *Charter* on all aspects of the criminal justice system, see Stuart, *Charter Justice in Canadian Criminal Law* (5th ed., 2010, Carswell).

(i) Purposive approach

In its second ruling under the *Charter,* the Supreme Court in *Hunter v. Southam* was called upon to interpret s. 8 which guarantees protection against unreasonable search and seizure. Before doing so, the Court announced a purposive approach to the interpretation of any provision of the *Charter*, which has been followed ever since.

HUNTER v. SOUTHAM INC.

(1984), 41 C.R. (3d) 97, [1984] 2 S.C.R. 145, 14 C.C.C. (3d) 97,
1984 CarswellAlta 121, 1984 CarswellAlta 415

DICKSON J.: — . . . The task of expounding a constitution is crucially different from that of construing a statute. A statute defines present rights and obligations. It is easily enacted and as easily repealed. A constitution, by contrast, is drafted with an eye to the future. Its function is to provide a continuing framework for the legitimate exercise of governmental power and, when joined by a bill or a charter of rights, for the unremitting protection of individual rights and liberties. Once enacted, its provisions cannot easily be repealed or amended. It must therefore be capable of growth and development over time to meet new social, political and historical realities often unimagined by its framers. The judiciary is the guardian of the constitution and must, in interpreting its provisions, bear these considerations in mind. Professor Paul Freund expressed this idea aptly when he admonished the American courts "not to read the provisions of the Constitution like a last will and testament lest it become one".

The need for a broad perspective in approaching constitutional documents is a familiar theme in Canadian constitutional jurisprudence. It is contained in Viscount Sankey L.C.'s classic formulation in *Edwards v. A.G. Can.*, [1930] A.C. 124 at 136-37, (P.C.), cited and applied in countless Canadian cases:

> The British North America Act planted in Canada a living tree capable of growth and expansion within its natural limits. The object of the Act was to grant a Constitution to Canada
> . . .

> Their Lordships do not conceive it to be the duty of this Board — it is certainly not their desire — to cut down the provisions of the Act by a narrow and technical construction, but rather to give it a large and liberal interpretation.

More recently, in *Min. of Home Affairs v. Fisher*, [1980] A.C. 319 (P.C.), dealing with the Bermudian constitution, Lord Wilberforce reiterated at p. 329 that a constitution is a document "sui generis, calling for principles of interpretation of its own, suitable to its character", and that as such a constitution incorporating a bill of rights calls for [p. 328]:

> . . . a generous interpretation avoiding what has been called 'the austerity of tabulated legalism', suitable to give individuals the full measure of the fundamental rights and freedoms referred to.

Such a broad, purposive analysis, which interprets specific provisions of a constitutional document in the light of its larger objects, is also consonant with the classical principles of American constitutional construction enunciated by Marshall C.J. in *McCulloch v. Maryland*, 17 U.S. (4 Wheat.) 316, 4 L. Ed. 870 (1819). It is, as well, the approach I intend to take in the present case.

I begin with the obvious. The Canadian *Charter of Rights and Freedoms* is a purposive document. Its purpose is to guarantee and to protect, within the limits of reason, the enjoyment of the rights and freedoms it enshrines. It is intended to constrain governmental action inconsistent with those rights and freedoms; it is not in itself an authorization for governmental action.

The court determined that under this purposive approach the interest to be protected under s. 8 was privacy, and the purposive way to protect that interest was to require a police officer to obtain a search warrant to search unless that was not feasible. There is a mountain of jurisprudence on s. 8 and exceptions to the *Hunter v. Southam* warrant requirement which is beyond the scope of this book.

There are two types of *Charter* challenge: challenges to conduct and challenges to the law. Challenges to conduct typically concern a challenge that a police officer infringed a *Charter* standard such as s. 8 and s. 9: where, for example, racial profiling is alleged. Whether there was a breach turns on the evidence in the case. If a breach is found, the judge typically decides whether evidence should be excluded under s. 24(2).

Where the challenge is to the law, it is important to remember that, as Chief Justice Lamer once put it, the law is on trial so the court is not concerned with the evidence in the particular case. Where a statutory provision is found to be a violation of the *Charter,* the usual remedy is a declaration of invalidity under s. 52. It is here that the Crown will argue that the violation can be saved under s. 1.

As we analyse substantive criminal law in subsequent chapters, we shall discover that the *Charter*, and s. 7 in particular, has been used by the courts to establish major new standards, such as those relating to requirements of act, fault and fair defences.

(ii) Vagueness, overbreadth, arbitrariness and gross disproportionality

We turn now to a consideration of grounds the courts have developed under s. 7 of the *Charter* upon which criminal charges can be challenged and declared unconstitutional: vagueness, overbreadth and arbitrariness. We shall discover that, although those standards are in place, the courts have been resistant to accepting such challenges in particular cases.

Before the advent of the *Charter*, void for uncertainty was a well-recognized ground of challenge to by-law offences (see, *e.g., Harrison v. Toronto* (1982), 31 C.R. (3d) 244, (H.C.)), but our courts had recoiled from its availability in the case of other types of criminal sanction. In *R. v. Pink Triangle Press* (1979), 45 C.C.C. (2d) 385 (Ont. Prov. Ct.), Harris Prov. J. held that the undefined term "immoral" in s. 164 of the *Criminal Code* was so "ambiguous and indefinite" (p. 407) that it had "no legally enforceable meaning" (p. 408). This decision was, however, soon reversed (51 C.C.C. (2d) 485 (Co. Ct.)) and on further appeal the Ontario Court of Appeal (19 C.R. (3d) 393 (sub nom. *Popert v. R.*), 58 C.C.C. (2d) 505) confirmed that the trial judge had erred. On behalf of the court, Zuber J.A. agreed that the meaning of "immoral" was imprecise but, observing that the courts often had to interpret imprecise terms such as "reasonable", "undue" and "dangerous", held at p. 398 that the courts had "to work as best they can with the tools in hand".

Since the *Charter*, the Supreme Court of Canada has determined, in a series of decisions, that any penal law should be declared unconstitutional if it is too vague. According to *Canada v. Pharmaceutical Society (Nova Scotia)*, [1992] 2 S.C.R. 606, 15 C.R. (4th) 1, 74 C.C.C. (3d) 289 the test is whether there "is sufficient room for legal debate". A challenge should normally be brought under s. 7 on the basis that it is a principle of fundamental justice that laws may not be too vague. Sometimes the issue will arise where there has been a breach of a *Charter* right such as freedom of expression; then the issue is whether that violation is a demonstrably justified reasonable limit prescribed by law under s. 1. The court has confirmed that a law that is too vague cannot be "prescribed by law". Although the court has thus recognized a constitutional doctrine of void for vagueness, the Supreme Court has been most reluctant to strike down penal law. It has, for example, dismissed vagueness challenges against the *Criminal Code* offences of keeping a common bawdy house (s. 193) and communicating for the purposes of prostitution (s. 195.1(1)(*c*)) (*Prostitution Reference* (1990), 77 C.R.

(3d) 1 (S.C.C.), and against the obscenity definition in s. 163(8) of an undue exploitation of sex or of sex and violence (*Butler* (1992), 11 C.R. (4th) 137 (S.C.C.)).

R. v. HEYWOOD

[1994] 3 S.C.R. 761, 34 C.R. (4th) 133, 94 C.C.C. (3d) 481,
1994 CarswellBC 592, 1994 CarswellBC 1247

The accused was convicted in 1987 of two counts of sexual assault. In 1989 he was charged with two offences of committing vagrancy by being a person who had been convicted of a sexual offence, and "found loitering at or near a school ground, playground, public park or bathing area" contrary to s. 179(1)(*b*) of the *Criminal Code*. He had been observed carrying a camera with a telephoto lens near children's playground areas in parks and, in one case, had been seen taking photographs. One of the pictures and several found in his residence showed the crotch areas of young girls.

The accused was convicted. The trial judge ruled that although s. 179(1)(*b*) of the *Criminal Code* was contrary to ss. 7 and 11(*d*) of the *Charter* it was demonstrably justified as a reasonable limit under s. 1. The British Columbia Court of Appeal declared s. 179(1)(*b*) unconstitutional and allowed the appeal.

The majority of the Supreme Court dismissed the Crown's further appeal, confirming that s. 179(1)(*b*) was unconstitutional. By the time of the appeal Parliament had already replaced the provision with a more narrowly worded s. 161.

Section 179(1)(*b*) provided that:

179. (1) Every one commits vagrancy who

(*b*) having at any time been convicted of an offence under section 151, 152 or 153, subsection 160(3) or 173(2) or section 271, 272 or 273, or of an offence under a provision referred to in paragraph (*b*) of the definition "serious personal injury offence" in section 687 of the *Criminal Code*, chapter C-34 of the Revised Statutes of Canada, 1970, as it read before January 4, 1983, is found loitering in or near a school ground, playground, public park or bathing area.

"serious personal injury offence" in s. 687 of the *Criminal Code*, as it read before January 4, 1983, was rape, attempted rape, sexual intercourse with a female under fourteen or between fourteen and sixteen, indecent assault or gross indecency.

CORY J. (LAMER C.J. and SOPINKA, IACOBUCCI and MAJOR JJ. concurring):

— Section 179(1)(*b*) of the *Criminal Code*, R.S.C., 1985, c. C-46, as amended, makes it a crime for persons convicted of specified offences to be "found loitering in or near a school ground, playground, public park or bathing area". It must be determined whether the section infringes ss. 7 or 11(*d*) of the *Canadian Charter of Rights and Freedoms*.

· · · ·

What then is the ordinary meaning of the word "loiter"? The *Oxford English Dictionary* (2nd ed. 1989), defines "loiter" in this manner:

> 1. In early use: To idle, waste one's time in idleness. Now only with more specific meaning: To linger indolently on the way when sent on an errand or when making a journey; to linger idly about a place; to waste time when engaged in some particular task, to dawdle. Freq. in legal phr. to loiter with intent (to commit a felony).

Similarly, *Black's Law Dictionary* (5th ed. 1979), defines "loiter" as follows:

> To be dilatory; to be slow in movement; to stand around or move slowly about; to stand idly around; to spend time idly; to saunter; to delay; to idle; to linger; to lag behind.

None of these definitions requires a malevolent intent or makes any reference to such a requirement. Cases which have considered the meaning of "loiter" in other sections of the *Code* support the use of the ordinary meaning of "loiter" in s. 179(1)(*b*). ...The ordinary definition of "loiter" is also consistent with the purpose of s. 179(1)(*b*). The section is aimed at protecting children from becoming victims of sexual offences. This is apparent from the places to which the prohibition of loitering applies. School grounds, playgrounds, public parks and public bathing areas are typically places where children are likely to congregate. The purpose of the prohibition on loitering is to keep people who are likely to pose a risk to children away from places where they are likely to be found. Prohibiting any prolonged attendance in these areas, which is what the ordinary definition of "loiter" does, achieves this goal.

There can be no question that s. 179(1)(*b*) restricts the liberty of those to whom it applies. Indeed, the appellant made no argument to the contrary. The section prohibits convicted sex offenders from attending (except perhaps to quickly walk through on their way to another location) at school grounds, playgrounds, public parks or bathing areas — places where the rest of the public is free to roam. The breach of this prohibition is punishable on summary conviction and, as this case demonstrates, imprisonment is the consequence.

The question this court must decide is whether this restriction on liberty is in accordance with the principles of fundamental justice. The respondent conceded in oral argument that a prohibition for the purpose of protecting the public does not per se infringe the principles of fundamental justice. *R. v. Lyons*, [1987] 2 S.C.R. 309, at pp. 327-34, held that the indeterminate detention of a dangerous offender, the purpose of which was the protection of the public, did not per se violate s. 7. ...The question, then, is whether some other aspect of the prohibition contained in s. 179(1)(*b*) violates the principles of fundamental justice. In my opinion it does. It applies without prior notice to the accused, to too many places, to too many people, for an indefinite period with no possibility of review. It restricts liberty far more than is necessary to accomplish its goal.

A. Overbreadth

This court considered the issue of overbreadth as a principle of fundamental justice in *R. v. Nova Scotia Pharmaceutical Society*, [1992] 2 S.C.R. 606. Writing for the court, Gonthier J. discussed the relationship between overbreadth and vagueness at pp. 627-31.

Overbreadth and vagueness are different concepts, but are sometimes related in particular cases. As the Ontario Court of Appeal observed in *R. v. Zundel* (1987), 58 O.R. (2d) 129, at pp. 157-58, cited with approval by Gonthier J. in *R. v. Nova Scotia Pharmaceutical Society*, *supra*, the meaning of a law may be unambiguous and thus the law will not be vague; however, it may still be overly broad. Where a law is vague, it may also be overly broad, to the extent that the ambit of its application is difficult to define. Overbreadth and vagueness are related in that both are the result of a lack of sufficient precision by a legislature in the means used to accomplish an objective. In the case of vagueness, the means are not clearly defined. In the case of overbreadth the means are too sweeping in relation to the objective.

Overbreadth analysis looks at the means chosen by the state in relation to its purpose. In considering whether a legislative provision is overbroad, a court must ask the question: are those means necessary to achieve the State objective? If the State, in pursuing a legitimate objective, uses means which are broader than is necessary to accomplish that objective, the principles of fundamental justice will be violated because the individual's rights will have been limited for no reason. The effect of overbreadth is that in some applications the law is arbitrary or disproportionate.

Reviewing legislation for overbreadth as a principle of fundamental justice is simply an example of the balancing of the State interest against that of the individual. ... However, where an independent principle of fundamental justice is violated, such as the requirement of *mens rea* for penal liability, or of the right to natural justice, any balancing of the public interest must take place under s. 1 of the *Charter*: *Re B.C. Motor Vehicle Act*, *supra*, at p. 517; *R. v. Swain*, [1991] 1 S.C.R. 933, at p. 977.

In analyzing a statutory provision to determine if it is overbroad, a measure of deference must be paid to the means selected by the legislature. While the courts have a constitutional duty to ensure that legislation conforms with the *Charter*, legislatures must have the power to make policy choices. A court should not interfere with legislation merely because a judge might have chosen a different means of accomplishing the objective if he or she had been the legislator. ...However, before it can be found that an enactment is so broad that it infringes s. 7 of the *Charter*, it must be clear that the legislation infringes life, liberty or security of the person in a manner that is unnecessarily broad, going beyond what is needed to accomplish the governmental objective.

The purpose of s. 179(1)(*b*) is to protect children from becoming victims of sexual offences. This is apparent from the prohibition which applies to places where children are very likely to be found. In determining whether s. 179(1)(*b*) is overly broad and not in accordance with the principles of fundamental justice, it must be determined whether the means chosen to accomplish this objective are reasonably tailored to effect this purpose. In those situations where legislation limits the liberty of an individual in order to protect the public, that limitation should not go beyond what is necessary to accomplish that goal. ... In my opinion, s. 179(1)(*b*) suffers from overbreadth and thus the deprivation of liberty it entails is not in accordance with the principles of fundamental justice.

The section is overly broad in its geographical ambit. It applies not only to school grounds and playgrounds, but also to all public parks and bathing areas. Its application to schools and playgrounds is appropriate, as these are the very places children are likely to congregate. But its application to all public parks and bathing areas is overly broad because not all such places are places where children are likely to be found. Public parks include the vast and remote wilderness parks. Bathing areas would include all the lakes in Canada with public beaches. Prohibiting individuals from loitering in all places in all parks is a significant limit on freedom of movement. Parks are places which are specifically designed to foster relaxation, indolent contemplation and strolling; in fact it may be assumed that "hanging around" and "idling" is encouraged in parks. ... Section 179(1)(*b*) is also overly broad in another aspect. It applies for life, with no possibility of review. The absence of review means that a person who has ceased to be a danger to children (or who indeed never was a danger to children), is subject to the prohibition in s. 179(1)(*b*). ...Section 179(1)(*b*) is overly broad in respect to the people to whom it applies. It applies to all persons convicted of the listed offences, without regard to whether they constitute a danger to children. ...A new s. 161 was passed following the decision of the British Columbia Court of Appeal in this case and is set out later in these reasons. It is significant and telling that the new section only applies to persons who have committed the listed offences in respect of a person who is under the age of 14 years. In addition, under the new section, the order is discretionary, so that only those offenders who constitute a danger to children will be subject to a prohibition. I would add that in certain circumstances, legislative provisions for notice and for review of the prohibition may reduce the significance of the factor of overbreadth in the application of one impugned provision. It is noteworthy that the new s. 161 provides for both notice and review of the prohibition. These provisions are absent in s. 179(1)(*b*). In summary, s. 179(1)(*b*) is overly broad to an extent that it violates the right to liberty proclaimed by s. 7 of the *Charter* for a number of reasons. First, it is overly broad in its geographical scope embracing as it does all public parks and beaches no matter how remote and devoid of children they may be. Secondly, it is overly broad in its temporal aspect with the prohibition applying for life without any process for review. Thirdly, it is too broad in the number of persons it encompasses.

The violation of s. 7 of the *Charter* is thus established. It is now necessary to consider whether the section may be saved by the provisions of s. 1 of the *Charter*.

This court has expressed doubt about whether a violation of the right to life, liberty or security of the person which is not in accordance with the principles of fundamental justice can ever be justified, except perhaps in times of war or national emergencies: *Re B.C. Motor Vehicle Act*. In a case where the violation of the principles of fundamental justice is as a result of overbreadth, it is even more difficult to see how the limit can be justified. Overbroad legislation which infringes s. 7 of the *Charter* would appear to be incapable of passing the minimal impairment branch of the s. 1 analysis.

The objective of s. 179(1)(*b*) is certainly pressing and substantial. The protection of children from sexual offences is obviously very important to society. Furthermore, at least in some of their applications, the means employed in s. 179(1)(*b*) are rationally connected to the objective. However, for the same reasons that s. 179(1)(*b*) is overly broad, it fails the minimal impairment branch of the s. 1 analysis. ...Section 179(1)(*b*) cannot be justified under s. 1 of the *Charter*.

Counsel for the appellant argued that even if s. 179(1)(*b*) of the *Criminal Code* is so overbroad as to result in a violation of s. 7 which cannot be saved by s. 1, rather than striking the section down in its entirety, the section should be read down so as to come within constitutional limits. In my opinion reading down is not appropriate in this case. The changes which would be required to make s. 179(1)(*b*) constitutional would not constitute reading down or reading in; rather, they would amount to judicial rewriting of the legislation.

GONTHIER J. (LA FOREST, L'HEUREUX-DUBÉ and MCLACHLIN JJ. concurring) (dissenting): —

. . . .

In my view s. 179(1)(*b*) should be interpreted as prohibiting the persons affected from being in one of the enumerated places for a malevolent or ulterior purpose related to the predicate offences. My reasons for favouring this interpretation are drawn from the purpose and legislative history of s. 179(1)(*b*) as well as precedent and statutory context.

. . . .

My review of the legislative history, purpose and context of s. 179(1)(*b*) thus leads to the conclusion that the offence should be interpreted as lingering or hanging about the enumerated areas for a malevolent or ulterior purpose related to any of the predicate offences. This interpretation is suggested by the terms of the offence and general desire to limit the intrusiveness of the prohibition while still achieving the objectives of public safety and offender treatment. As will be seen in the next section, this interpretation is also consistent with the *Charter*.

C. Section 179(1)(*b*) and Its Conformity with the *Charter*

The two primary *Charter* concerns raised by s. 179(1)(*b*) pertain to vagueness and overbreadth. Cory J.'s broader interpretation of s. 179(1)(*b*) eliminates any vagueness problem, but, in his view, leads to a prohibition which is unjustifiably overbroad. The interpretation I have adopted avoids both these problems.

As discussed in *R. v. Nova Scotia Pharmaceutical Society*, [1992] 2 S.C.R. 606, at p. 643, a provision which is unconstitutionally vague provides an intolerable level of prosecutorial discretion and fails to give those subject to the provision notice of its content. Put in its most simplistic form, what is prohibited will be what those charged with law enforcement decide at any given moment should be prohibited. Interpreting s. 179(1)(*b*) to prohibit lingering with an "untoward or improper motive" would arguably be an example of an unconstitutionally vague restriction on liberty. "Untoward or improper motive" gives little basis for legal debate within the terms of *Nova Scotia Pharmaceutical Society*. It is difficult to identify the factors to be considered or the determinative elements in ascertaining whether a motive is untoward or improper. Qualifying malevolent or ulterior purposes by reference to the predicate offences, however, eliminates any concerns as to vagueness. The enumerated offences provide a clear basis for legal debate and narrow the scope of potential liability. The persons affected would thus have notice of what is prohibited and prosecutorial discretion would be sufficiently restricted.

Cory J., however, suggests that the prohibition created by s. 179(1)(*b*) is overbroad in terms of the persons, places and time period to which it applies. I express no opinion on the soundness of this analysis of liberty because it is not necessary in this case to decide the issue. The interpretation I advocate eliminates Cory J.'s concern that the prohibition is overbroad. A lifetime prohibition of activities with a malevolent or ulterior purpose related to re-offending is in no way objectionable or overbroad. Such a prohibition would impose a restriction on the liberty of the affected individuals to which ordinary citizens are not subject, but that restriction is directly related to preventing re-offending. The affected persons' history of offending, the uncertainties prevalent in treating offenders and a desire to disrupt the cycle of re-offending justify what is in effect a minor intrusion which does not breach the principles of fundamental justice.

That restraint of the affected persons' liberty is minor and easily illustrated. As noted above, use of public parks for the legitimate purposes for which they are intended would not be caught. Furthermore, though trite, it must be remembered that the Crown will bear the burden of proving all elements of the offence beyond a reasonable doubt. This burden guarantees that only loitering which can be proven to be related to one of the predicate offences will be subject to the criminal prohibition. I recognize that this formulation of the offence will likely lead to certain evidentiary presumptions which, absent a satisfactory explanation, may cause a judge to draw an adverse inference. Take for example a person with a history of offences in relation to children who is observed hanging around a playground and offering children candy. Similarly, as discussed above, just lingering about a school yard with no apparent purpose, as distinct from a public park, would give rise to legitimate suspicions. Such presumptions, however, in no way reverse the burden of proof, nor do they violate the accused's right to silence.

Prohibiting lingering or hanging about the enumerated areas for a malevolent or ulterior purpose related to one of the predicate offences thus survives *Charter* scrutiny. The predicate offences provide an ample basis for limiting prosecutorial discretion and giving guidance as to what is prohibited to those affected. Furthermore, prohibiting only conduct which can be demonstrated to be part of the cycle of re-offending carefully balances the objectives of public safety and offender treatment with a desire to limit the intrusiveness of the prohibition.

From the point of view of defence counsel is an overbreadth argument easier to win on the current law than one of vagueness? Was it wise for the Supreme Court to establish constitutional doctrines of vagueness and overbreadth?

In *R. v. Sharpe* (2000), [2001] 1 S.C.R. 45, 39 C.R. (5th) 72, 150 C.C.C. (3d) 321, the Supreme Court upheld the validity of the prohibition against child pornography in s. 163.1(4) of the *Criminal Code*. McLachlin C.J., writing for six justices, concluded that the prohibition was a demonstrably justified reasonable limit on freedom of expression guaranteed in s. 2(*b*) of the *Charter*. However, the court identified a problem of overbreadth and, apart from making careful clarification of many of the provisions, found it necessary to read in two exclusions dealing with self-authored works of imagination and visual representation of sexual activity by teenagers for private use. The court makes no mention of the doctrines of vagueness under *Nova Scotia Pharmaceutical Society* or overbreadth under *Heywood*.

On December 23, 2003, in *Malmo-Levine, Caine* and *Clay*, three appeals heard together and resulting in the release of two separate judgments, a 6-3 majority of the Supreme Court rejected a number of constitutional challenges to marihuana laws then under the *Narcotic Control Act*. In so doing it signaled a much less active role for the courts in s. 7 review: (2003) 16 C.R. (6th) 1 and 117 (S.C.C.).

The court unanimously quickly rejected the division of powers challenge. Ample constitutional power is found under the federal criminal law power under s. 91(27) of the *Constitution Act, 1867*. This power, the court held, extends to those laws that are designed to promote public peace, safety, order, health or some other legitimate public purpose. The purpose of the *Narcotic Control Act* fits within the criminal law power, which includes the protection of vulnerable groups. It was unnecessary to consider whether marihuana laws also fall under the peace, order and good government power.

The division in the court occurs respecting the *Charter* challenges. The lengthy majority judgment of Gonthier and Binnie JJ. (McLachlin C.J., and Iacobucci, Major, Bastarache JJ. concurring) in *Malmo-Levine*, *Caine*, rejected various challenges under s. 7, and those under ss. 12 and 15.

The majority justices started by reviewing the trial judge's findings that the effects of marihuana use are neither insignificant nor trivial. They then looked to the Senate and House of Commons and concluded that it seems clear that the use of marihuana has less serious and permanent effects than was once claimed, but its psychoactive and health effects can be harmful, and in the case of members of vulnerable groups the harm may be serious and substantial.

Turning to the s. 7 challenges, the majority ruled that the availability of imprisonment for the offence of simple possession engages the liberty interest sufficiently to trigger scrutiny under s. 7 of the *Charter*. However, Justices Gonthier and Binnie bluntly decided that a desire to build a lifestyle around the recreational use of marihuana does not attract *Charter* protection. There is no free-standing constitutional right to smoke "pot" for recreational use.

The majority further held that the criminalization of marihuana possession does not violate principles of fundamental justice under s. 7. The principle that criminal law cannot be resorted to where there is no reasonable risk of harm, accepted by the B.C. Court of Appeal in the court below, was determined by the majority, over the sole dissent of Arbour J., not to be a principle of fundamental justice (see later in Chapter 1, under Scope). Marihuana prohibition is also held not to offend fundamental principles of justice under s. 7 of the *Charter* that a law not be arbitrary or irrational, and that effects on the accused of enforcement not be grossly disproportionate.

According to the majority, for a rule or principle to constitute a principle of fundamental justice for the purposes of s. 7, it must be a legal principle, there must be significant societal consensus that it is fundamental to the way in which the legal system ought fairly to operate, and it must be identified with sufficient precision to yield a manageable standard against which to measure deprivations of life, liberty or security of the person. The "harm principle" did not meet these criteria.

Two of the trio of dissenting judges, LeBel and Deschamps JJ., also dismissed the argument that the harm principle was a principle of fundamental justice under s. 7. Both justices however were of the view, in short separate opinions, that marihuana possession should be struck down because the criminal law in question was an arbitrary and disproportionate response to the social problem.

In her lengthy dissenting judgment Justice Arbour was the sole justice to hold the view that a law that has the potential to convict a person whose conduct causes little or no reasoned risk of harm to others offends s. 7 of the *Charter* where there is a risk of imprisonment. Here the evidence of the risk of harm as found by the trial judge did not outweigh the harm resulting from enforcement.

In the companion case of *Clay* the same 6-3 majority rejected arguments that marihuana laws offended s. 7 of the *Charter* on privacy considerations or because the prohibition was too broad. The court also rejected as an unreasonable interpretation that the prohibition should be interpreted not to apply to cannabis sativa without tetrahydrocannabinol — an argument designed to de-criminalize possession of hemp. The court found that position had a disputed scientific basis and that it would be impractical.

It is crystal clear that six justices of the Supreme Court of Canada have decided that criminal sanctions for marihuana possession do not offend division of powers or *Charter* principles and raise policy issues that should be left to Parliament. The court left just one issue open: that of a medical exemption which was said to raise different considerations. The Ontario Court of Appeal in *Parker* (2000), 37 C.R. (5th) 97 (Ont. C.A.) and *Hitzig* (2003), 14 C.R. (6th) 1 (Ont. C.A.), held that the *Charter* requires such an exemption but the issue has not been pursued before the Supreme Court of Canada.

The marihuana judgments have important implications for *Charter* challenges in other contexts, especially those based on s. 7. The majority confirms that a *Charter* challenge under s. 7 may be based on arbitrariness or irrationality or, alternatively, on a test of "gross disproportionality". In both cases the majority's application of these principles to marihuana laws shows that that threshold test will be very hard to meet. On the issue of arbitrariness, for example, the majority sees no validity in the argument that it is arbitrary to criminalize and even jail for simple possession of marihuana but to have no such criminal laws against use of cancer-producing tobacco. **Do you agree with this ruling?**

The principle of gross disproportionality is derived by the majority from *United States v. Burns*, [2001] 1 S.C.R. 283 (grossly disproportional to extradite suspected murderers to a country likely to impose the death sentence) and *Suresh v. Canada* (*Minister of Citizenship & Immigration*), [2002] 1 S.C.R. 3 (not grossly disproportional to permit the extradition of a suspected terrorist to face torture in another country).

It is clear from the companion case of *Clay* that the majority saw gross disproportionality as the organizing principle not only for s. 12 of the *Charter* respecting cruel and unusual punishment but also for several s. 7 issues. The assertion of a gross disproportionality test is clearly designed to lessen the power of judicial review under s. 7. A criminal law can be disproportional but will only offend the *Charter* when it is grossly disproportional and shocks the conscience of Canadians. The only recent acceptance by the court of such a challenge was the unanimous ruling in *Burns*. Section 7 challenges based on vagueness, overbreadth, arbitrariness and now gross disproportionality are still possible but the standards have few teeth such that most such challenges will fail.

Do you see this as a fortunate or unfortunate development?

In another controversial ruling a slightly differently composed majority of the court rejected a number of *Charter* challenges to s. 43 of the *Criminal Code* (often referred to as the "spanking law"):

> Every schoolteacher, parent or person standing in the place of a parent is justified in using force by way of correction toward a pupil or child, as the case may be, who is under his care, if the force does not exceed what is reasonable under the circumstances.

Do you agree with the majority's ruling below that s. 43 is not too vague and not too broad?

CANADIAN FOUNDATION FOR CHILDREN, YOUTH & THE LAW v. CANADA (ATTORNEY GENERAL)

[2004] 1 S.C.R. 76, 16 C.R. (6th) 203, 180 C.C.C. (3d) 353,
2004 CarswellOnt 252, 2004 CarswellOnt 253 (S.C.C.)

McLACHLIN C.J.C. (GONTHIER, IACOBUCCI, MAJOR, BASTARACHE and LeBEL JJ. concurring): —

. . . .

(1) *Vagueness*

. . . .

a. *The Standard for "Vagueness"*

A law is unconstitutionally vague if it "does not provide an adequate basis for legal debate" and "analysis"; "does not sufficiently delineate any area of risk"; or "is not intelligible". The law must offer a "grasp to the judiciary": *R. v. Nova Scotia Pharmaceutical Society*, [1992] 2 S.C.R. 606, at pp. 639-40. Certainty is not required. . . .

A law must set an intelligible standard both for the citizens it governs and the officials who must enforce it. The two are interconnected. A vague law prevents the citizen from realizing when he or she is entering an area of risk for criminal sanction. It similarly makes it difficult for law enforcement officers and judges to determine whether a crime has been committed. This invokes the further concern of putting too much discretion in the hands of law enforcement officials, and violates the precept that individuals should be governed by the rule of law, not the rule of persons. The doctrine of vagueness is directed generally at the evil of leaving "basic policy matters to policemen, judges, and juries for resolution on an *ad hoc* and subjective basis, with the attendant dangers of arbitrary and discriminatory application": *Grayned v. City of Rockford*, 408 U.S. 104 (1972), at p. 109.

Ad hoc discretionary decision making must be distinguished from appropriate judicial interpretation. Judicial decisions may properly add precision to a statute. Legislators can never foresee all the situations that may arise, and if they did, could not practically set them all out. It is thus in the nature of our legal system that areas of uncertainty exist and that judges clarify and augment the law on a case-by-case basis.

It follows that s. 43 of the *Criminal Code* will satisfy the constitutional requirement for precision if it delineates a risk zone for criminal sanction. This achieves the essential task of providing general guidance for citizens and law enforcement officers.

b.   Does Section 43 Delineate a Risk Zone for Criminal Sanction?

The purpose of s. 43 is to delineate a sphere of non-criminal conduct within the larger realm of common assault. It must, as we have seen, do this in a way that permits people to know when they are entering a zone of risk of criminal sanction and that avoids *ad hoc* discretionary decision making by law enforcement officials. People must be able to assess when conduct approaches the boundaries of the sphere that s. 43 provides.

To ascertain whether s. 43 meets these requirements, we must consider its words and court decisions interpreting those words. The words of the statute must be considered in context, in their grammatical and ordinary sense, and with a view to the legislative scheme's purpose and the intention of Parliament: *Rizzo & Rizzo Shoes Ltd., (Re)*, [1998] 1 S.C.R. 27, at paras. 21; *Bell ExpressVu Limited Partnership v. Rex*, [2002] 2 S.C.R. 559, 2002 SCC 42, at paras. 26. Since s. 43 withdraws the protection of the criminal law in certain circumstances, it should be strictly construed: see *Ogg-Moss v. The Queen*, [1984] 2 S.C.R. 173, at p. 183.

Section 43 delineates who may access its sphere with considerable precision. The terms "schoolteacher" and "parent" are clear. The phrase "person standing in the place of a parent" has been held by the courts to indicate an individual who has assumed "all the obligations of parenthood": *Ogg-Moss, supra*, at p. 190. These terms present no difficulty.

Section 43 identifies less precisely what conduct falls within its sphere. It defines this conduct in two ways. The first is by the requirement that the force be "by way of correction". The second is by the requirement that the force be "reasonable under the circumstances". The question is whether, taken together and construed in accordance with governing principles, these phrases provide sufficient precision to delineate the zone of risk and avoid discretionary law enforcement.

I turn first to the requirement that the force be "by way of correction". These words, considered in conjunction with the cases, yield two limitations on the content of the protected sphere of conduct.

First, the person applying the force must have intended it to be for educative or corrective purposes: *Ogg-Moss, supra*, p. 193. Accordingly, s. 43 cannot exculpate outbursts of violence against a child motivated by anger or animated by frustration. It admits into its sphere of immunity only sober, reasoned uses of force that address the actual behaviour of the child and are designed to restrain, control or express some symbolic disapproval of his or her behaviour. The purpose of the force must always be the education or discipline of the child: *Ogg-Moss, supra*, p. 193.

Second, the child must be capable of benefiting from the correction. This requires the capacity to learn and the possibility of successful correction. Force against children under two cannot be corrective, since on the evidence they are incapable of understanding why they are hit (trial decision, (2000), 49 O.R. (3d) 662, at paras. 17). A child may also be incapable of learning from the application of force because of disability or some other contextual factor. In these cases, force will not be "corrective" and will not fall within the sphere of immunity provided by s. 43.

The second requirement of s. 43 is that the force be "reasonable under the circumstances". The Foundation argues that this term fails to sufficiently delineate the area of risk and constitutes an invitation to discretionary *ad hoc* law enforcement. It argues that police officers, prosecutors and judges too often assess the reasonableness of corrective force by reference to their personal experiences and beliefs, rendering enforcement of s. 43 arbitrary and subjective. In support, it points to the decision of the Manitoba Court of Appeal in *R. v. K. (M.)* (1992), 74 C.C.C. (3d) 108, in which, at p. 109, O'Sullivan J.A. stated that "[t]he discipline administered to the boy in question in these proceedings [a kick to the rear] was mild indeed compared to the discipline I received in my home".

Against this argument, the law has long used reasonableness to delineate areas of risk, without incurring the dangers of vagueness. The law of negligence, which has blossomed in recent decades to govern private actions in nearly all spheres of human activity, is founded upon the presumption that individuals are capable of governing their conduct in accordance with the standard of what is "reasonable". But reasonableness as a guide to conduct is not confined to the law of negligence. The criminal law also relies on it. The *Criminal Code* expects that police officers will know what constitutes "reasonable grounds" for believing that an offence has been committed, such that an arrest can be made (s. 495); that an individual will know what constitutes "reasonable steps" to obtain consent to sexual contact (s. 273.2(b)); and that surgeons, in order to be exempted from criminal liability, will judge whether performing an operation is "reasonable" in "all the circumstances of the case" (s. 45). These are merely a few examples; the criminal law is thick with the notion of "reasonableness".

The reality is that the term "reasonable" gives varying degrees of guidance, depending upon the statutory and factual context. It does not insulate a law against a charge of vagueness. Nor, however, does it automatically mean that a law is void for vagueness. In each case, the question is whether the term, considered in light of principles of statutory interpretation and decided cases, delineates an area of risk and avoids the danger of arbitrary *ad hoc* law enforcement.

Is s. 43's reliance on reasonableness, considered in this way, unconstitutionally vague? Does it indicate what conduct risks criminal sanction and provide a principled basis for enforcement? While the words on their face are broad, a number of implicit limitations add precision.

The first limitation arises from the behaviour for which s. 43 provides an exemption, simple non-consensual application of force. Section 43 does not exempt from criminal sanction conduct that causes harm or raises a reasonable prospect of harm. It can be invoked only in cases of non-consensual application of force that results neither in harm nor in the prospect of bodily harm. This limits its operation to the mildest forms of assault. People must know that if their conduct raises an apprehension of bodily harm they cannot rely on s. 43. Similarly, police officers and judges must know that the defence cannot be raised in such circumstances.

Within this limited area of application, further precision on what is reasonable under the circumstances may be derived from international treaty obligations. Statutes should be construed to comply with Canada's international obligations: *Ordon Estate v. Grail*, [1998] 3 S.C.R. 437, at paras. 137. Canada's international commitments confirm that physical correction that either harms or degrades a child is unreasonable.

Canada is a party to the United Nations *Convention on the Rights of the Child*. Article 5 of the Convention requires state parties to

> respect the responsibilities, rights and duties of parents or . . . other persons legally responsible for the child, to provide, in a manner consistent with the evolving capacities of the child, appropriate direction and guidance in the exercise by the child of the rights recognized in the present Convention.

Article 19(1) requires the state party to

> *protect the child from all forms of physical or mental violence, injury or abuse, neglect or negligent treatment, maltreatment or exploitation*, including sexual abuse, while in the care of parent(s), legal guardian(s) or any other person who has the care of the child. [Emphasis added.]

Finally, Art. 37(a) requires state parties to ensure that "[n]*o child shall be subjected to torture or other cruel, inhuman or degrading treatment or punishment*" (emphasis added). This language is also found in the *International Covenant on Civil and Political Rights*, Can. T.S. 1976 No. 47, to which Canada is a party. Article 7 of the Covenant states that "[no] one shall be subjected to torture or to cruel, inhuman or degrading treatment or punishment". The preamble to the *International Covenant on Civil and Political Rights* makes it clear that its provisions apply to "all members of the human family". From these international obligations, it follows that what is "reasonable under the circumstances" will seek to avoid harm to the child and will never include cruel, inhuman or degrading treatment.

Neither the *Convention on the Rights of the Child* nor the *International Covenant on Civil and Political Rights* explicitly require state parties to ban all corporal punishment of children. In the process of monitoring compliance with the *International Covenant on Civil and Political Rights*, however, the Human Rights Committee of the United Nations has expressed the view that corporal punishment of children in schools engages Art. 7's prohibition of degrading treatment or punishment: see for example, *Report of the Human Rights Committee*, Vol. I, UN GAOR, Fiftieth Session, Supp. No. 40 (A/50/40) (1995), at paras. 426 and 434; *Report of the Human Rights Committee*, Vol. I, UN GAOR, Fifty-fourth Session, Supp. No. 40 (A/54/40) (1999), at paras. 358; *Report of the Human Rights Committee*, Vol. I, UN GAOR, Fifty-fifth Session, Supp. No. 40 (A/55/40) (2000), at paras. 306 and 429. The Committee has not expressed a similar opinion regarding parental use of mild corporal punishment.

Section 43's ambit is further defined by the direction to consider the circumstances under which corrective force is used. National and international precedents have set out factors to be considered. Article 3 of the *European Convention on Human Rights*, 213 U.N.T.S. 221, forbids inhuman and degrading treatment. The European Court of Human Rights, in determining whether parental treatment of a child was severe enough to fall within the scope of Article 3, held that assessment must take account of "all the circumstances of the case, such as the nature and context of the treatment, its duration, its physical and mental effects and, in some instances, the sex, age and state of health of the victim": Eur. Court H.R., *A. v. the United Kingdom*, judgment of 25 September 1998, Reports of Judgments and Decisions 1998-VI, 2692, pp. 2699-2700. These factors properly focus on the prospective effect of the corrective force upon the child, as required by s. 43.

By contrast, it is improper to retrospectively focus on the gravity of a child's wrongdoing, which invites a punitive rather than corrective focus. "[T]he nature of the offence calling for correction", an additional factor suggested in *R. v. Dupperon* (1984), 16 C.C.C. (3d) 453 (Sask. C.A.), at p. 460, is thus not a relevant contextual consideration. The focus under s. 43 is on the correction of the child, not on the gravity of the precipitating event. Obviously, force employed in the absence of any behaviour requiring correction by definition cannot be corrective.

Determining what is "reasonable under the circumstances" in the case of child discipline is also assisted by social consensus and expert evidence on what constitutes reasonable corrective discipline. The criminal law often uses the concept of reasonableness to accommodate evolving mores and avoid successive "fine-tuning" amendments. It is implicit in this technique that current social consensus on what is reasonable may be considered. It is wrong for caregivers or judges to apply their own subjective notions of what is reasonable; s. 43 demands an objective appraisal based on current learning and consensus. Substantial consensus, particularly when supported by expert evidence, can provide guidance and reduce the danger of arbitrary, subjective decision making.

Based on the evidence currently before the court, there are significant areas of agreement among the experts on both sides of the issue (trial decision, paras. 17). Corporal punishment of children under two years is harmful to them, and has no corrective value given the cognitive limitations of children under two years of age. Corporal punishment of teenagers is harmful, because it can induce aggressive or antisocial behaviour. Corporal punishment using objects, such as rulers or belts, is physically and emotionally harmful. Corporal punishment which involves slaps or blows to the head is harmful. These types of punishment, we may conclude, will not be reasonable.

Contemporary social consensus is that, while teachers may sometimes use corrective force to remove children from classrooms or secure compliance with instructions, the use of corporal punishment by teachers is not acceptable. Many school boards forbid the use of corporal punishment, and some provinces and territories have legislatively prohibited its use by teachers: see, e.g., *Schools Act*, 1997, S.N.L. 1997, c. S-12.2, s. 42; *School Act*, R.S.B.C. 1996, c. 412, s. 76(3); *Education Act*, S.N.B. 1997, c. E-1.12, s. 23; *School Act*, R.S.P.E.I. 1988, c. S-2.1, s. 73; *Education Act*, S.N.W.T. 1995, c. 28, s. 34(3); *Education Act*, S.Y. 1989-90, c. 25, s. 36. This consensus is consistent with Canada's international obligations, given the findings of the Human Rights Committee of the United Nations noted above. Section 43 will protect a teacher who uses reasonable, corrective force to restrain or remove a child in appropriate circumstances. Substantial societal consensus, supported by expert evidence and Canada's treaty obligations, indicates that corporal punishment by teachers is unreasonable.

Finally, judicial interpretation may assist in defining "reasonable under the circumstances" under s. 43. It must be conceded at the outset that judicial decisions on s. 43 in the past have sometimes been unclear and inconsistent, sending a muddled message as to what is and is not permitted. In many cases discussed by Arbour J., judges failed to acknowledge the evolutive nature of the standard of reasonableness, and gave undue authority to outdated conceptions of reasonable correction. On occasion, judges erroneously applied their own subjective views on what constitutes reasonable discipline — views as varied as different judges' backgrounds. In addition, charges of assaultive discipline were seldom viewed as sufficiently serious to merit in-depth research and expert evidence or the appeals which might have permitted a unified national standard to emerge. However, "[t]he fact that a particular legislative term is open to varying interpretations by the courts is not fatal": *Reference re ss. 193 and 195.1(1)(c) of the Criminal Code (Man.)*, [1990] 1 S.C.R. 1123, at p. 1157. This case, and those that build on it, may permit a more uniform approach to "reasonable under the circumstances" than has prevailed in the past. Again, the issue is not whether s. 43 has provided enough guidance in the past, but whether it expresses a standard that can be given a core meaning in tune with contemporary consensus.

When these considerations are taken together, a solid core of meaning emerges for "reasonable under the circumstances", sufficient to establish a zone in which discipline risks criminal sanction. Generally, s. 43 exempts from criminal sanction only minor corrective force of a transitory and trifling nature. On the basis of current expert consensus, it does not apply to corporal punishment of children under two or teenagers. Degrading, inhuman or harmful conduct is not protected. Discipline by the use of objects or blows or slaps to the head is unreasonable. Teachers may reasonably apply force to remove a child from a classroom or secure compliance with instructions, but not merely as corporal punishment. Coupled with the requirement that the conduct be corrective, which rules out conduct stemming from the caregiver's frustration, loss of temper or abusive personality, a consistent picture emerges of the area covered by s. 43. It is wrong for law enforcement officers or judges to apply their own subjective views of what is "reasonable under the circumstances"; the test is objective. The question must be considered in context and in light of all the circumstances of the case. The gravity of the precipitating event is not relevant.

The fact that borderline cases may be anticipated is not fatal. As Gonthier J. stated in *Nova Scotia Pharmaceutical*, at p. 639, ". . . it is inherent to our legal system that some conduct will fall along the boundaries of the area of risk; no definite prediction can then be made. Guidance, not direction, of conduct is a more realistic objective".

Section 43 achieves this objective. It sets real boundaries and delineates a risk zone for criminal sanction. The prudent parent or teacher will refrain from conduct that approaches those boundaries, while law enforcement officers and judges will proceed with them in mind. It does not violate the principle of fundamental justice that laws must not be vague or arbitrary.

My colleague, Arbour J., by contrast, takes the view that s. 43 is unconstitutionally vague, a point of view also expressed by Deschamps J. Arbour J. argues first that the foregoing analysis amounts to an impermissible reading down of s. 43. This contention is answered by the evidence in this case, which established a solid core of meaning for s. 43; to construe terms like "reasonable under the circumstances" by reference to evidence and argument is a common and accepted function of courts interpreting the criminal law. To interpret "reasonable" in light of the evidence is not judicial amendment, but judicial interpretation. It is a common practice, given the number of criminal offences conditioned by the term "reasonable". If "it is the function of the appellate courts to rein in overly elastic interpretations" (Binnie J., at paras. 122), it is equally their function to define the scope of criminal defences.

Arbour J. also argues that unconstitutional vagueness is established by the fact that courts in the past have applied s. 43 inconsistently. Again, the inference does not follow. Vagueness is not argued on the basis of whether a provision has been interpreted consistently in the past, but whether it is capable of providing guidance for the future. Inconsistent and erroneous applications are not uncommon in criminal law, where many provisions admit of difficulty; we do not say that this makes them unconstitutional. Rather, we rely on appellate courts to clarify the meaning so that future application may be more consistent. I agree with Arbour J. that Canadians would find the decisions in many of the past cases on s. 43 to be seriously objectionable. However, the discomfort of Canadians in the face of such unwarranted acts of violence toward children merely demonstrates that it is possible to define what corrective force is reasonable in the circumstances. Finally, Arbour J. argues that parents who face criminal charges as a result of corrective force will be able to rely on the defences of necessity and "*de minimis*". The defence of necessity, I agree, is available, but only in situations where corrective force is not in issue, like saving a child from imminent danger. As for the defence of *de minimis*, it is equally or more vague and difficult in application than the reasonableness defence offered by s. 43.

(2) *Overbreadth*

Section 43 of the *Criminal Code* refers to corrective force against children generally. The Foundation argues that this is overbroad because children under the age of two are not capable of correction and children over the age of 12 will only be harmed by corrective force. These classes of children, it is argued, should have been excluded.

This concern is addressed by Parliament's decision to confine the exemption to reasonable correction, discussed above. Experts consistently indicate that force applied to a child too young to be capable of learning from physical correction is not corrective force. Similarly, current expert consensus indicates that corporal punishment of teenagers creates a serious risk of psychological harm: employing it would thus be unreasonable. There may however be instances in which a parent or school teacher reasonably uses corrective force to restrain or remove an adolescent from a particular situation, falling short of corporal punishment. Section 43 does not permit force that cannot correct or is unreasonable. It follows that it is not overbroad.

ARBOUR J. (dissenting): —

[After a comprehensive review of existing s. 43, emphasizing the number of acquittals, she decided that the phrase "reasonable under the circumstances" in s. 43 violated children's security of the person interest in s. 7 and that the principle was too vague to be in accordance with fundamental justice.]

The doctrine of vagueness does not "require that a law be absolutely certain; no law can meet that standard" (*Prostitution Reference, supra*, at p. 1156). However, while discretion is inevitable, a law will be too vague if "the legislature has given a plenary discretion to do whatever seems best in a wide set of circumstances" (*Irwin Toy Ltd. v. Quebec (Attorney General)*, [1989] 1 S.C.R. 927, *per* Dickson C.J., Lamer and Wilson JJ., at p. 983, albeit within s. 1).

. . . .

In my view, the case law speaks for itself with respect to whether s. 43 delineates the appropriate boundaries of legal debate. It is wholly unpersuasive for this court to declare today what the law is *de novo* and to assert that this now frames the legal debate: i.e., anything outside the framework was simply wrongly decided! This approach robs the test in *Nova Scotia Pharmaceutical, supra*, of any usefulness. There is no need to speculate about whether s. 43 is capable, in theory, of circumscribing an acceptable level of debate about the scope of its application. It demonstrably has not succeeded in doing so. Canadian courts have been unable to articulate a legal framework for s. 43 despite attempts to establish guidelines. . . .

Judges themselves have often referred to the lack of consensus in this area of the law, with Weagant Prov. J. in *James, supra*, at paras. 8, for instance, noting:

> Exactly what is needed to establish, or what legal test demonstrates that the force exceeds what is reasonable, is a matter of some variance across this nation. For some trial courts, the act speaks for itself, especially if there is bodily harm or an injury which may endanger life, limbs or health (*R. v. Dupperon* (1985), 16 C.C.C. (3d) 453 (Sask. C.A.)). Other courts pay lip service to the necessity of having a view to community standards, although just how that is established through evidence remains unclear (*R. v. Halcrow* (1993), 80 C.C.C. (3d) 320 ([B.C.] C.A.): the Appeal Court noted that the defendant had called no evidence suggesting the treatment of the foster children was in accordance with community standards, a burden our Court of Appeal has decided falls upon the Crown). Other trial courts have rejected the notion that a judge can take notice of community standards (*R. v. Myers*, [1995] P.E.I.J. No. 180, P.E.I. Prov. Ct., November 27, 1995, per Thompson, P.C.J.). Yet another trial court says it is the trier of fact's responsibility to reflect community standards, as a jury would (*R. v. R.S.D.*, [1995] O.J. No. 3341, Ontario Prov. Ct., October 30, 1995, per Megginson, P.J.O.). And still another court was of the view that section 43 does not deal with the concept of a community standard of tolerance at all (*R. v. Peterson*, [1995] O.J. No. 1366, Ontario Prov. Ct., April 26, 1995, per Menzies, P.J.O.).

That judges have been at a loss to appreciate the "reasonableness" referred to by Parliament is not surprising and yet is not endemic to the notion of reasonableness.

"Reasonableness" with respect to s. 43 is linked to public policy issues and one's own sense of parental authority. "Reasonableness" will always entail an element of subjectivity. As McCombs J. recognized in the case at bar, "[b]ecause the notion of reasonableness varies with the beholder, it is perhaps not surprising that some of the judicial decisions applying s. 43 to excuse otherwise criminal assault appear to some to be inconsistent and unreasonable" ((2000), 49 O.R. (3d) 662, at paras. 4). It is clear, however, that the concept of reasonableness, so widely used in the law generally, and in the criminal law in particular, is not in and of itself unconstitutionally vague. "Reasonableness" functions as an intelligible standard in many other criminal law contexts. . . .

Other instances of the words "reasonable under the circumstances" may not be overly vague because they occur in contexts in which the factors for assessing reasonableness are clear and commensurable. Some general agreement as to the standard against which to measure the "reasonableness" of conduct will assist in providing sufficient clarity to a standard of "reasonableness". For example, reasonable force in self-defence can be measured for proportionality against the assault for which one is defending oneself. Similarly, it is possible to frame a legal debate about the proper boundaries of the use of reasonable force in performing an arrest (see *Asante-Mensah, supra*, per Binnie J., at paras. 51-59). This is not so in the case of corporal punishment of children, where there is no built-in commensurability between physical punishment and bad behaviour that can be used to assess proportionality. Indeed the Chief Justice concludes, at paras. 35, that the gravity of the child's conduct is not a "relevant contextual consideration" as it invites a punitive, rather than a corrective focus.

Corporal punishment is a controversial social issue. Conceptions of what is "reasonable" in terms of the discipline of children, whether physical or otherwise, vary widely, and often engage cultural and religious beliefs as well as political and ethical ones. Such conceptions are intertwined with how other controversial issues are understood, including the relationship between the state and the family and the relationship between the rights of the parent and the rights of the child. Whether a person considers an instance of child corporal punishment "reasonable" may depend in large part on his or her own parenting style and experiences. While it may work well in other contexts, in this one the term "reasonable force" has proven not to be a workable standard. Lack of clarity is particularly problematic here because the rights of children are engaged. This court has confirmed that children are a particularly vulnerable group in society (*Sharpe, supra*, at paras. 169, and *Winnipeg Child and Family Services v. K.L.W.*, [2000] 2 S.C.R. 519, 2000 SCC 48, at paras. 73). Vagueness in defining the terms of a defence which affects the physical integrity of children may be even more invidious than is vagueness in defining an offence or a defence in another context, and may therefore call for a stricter standard.

Canada's international obligations with respect to the rights of the child must also inform the degree of protection that children are entitled to under s. 7 of the *Charter*. As the Chief Justice notes (at paras. 32), Canada is a party to both the *United Nations Convention on the Rights of the Child*, Can. T.S. 1992 No. 3 and the *International Covenant on Civil and Political Rights*, Can. T.S. 1976 No. 47. The Chief Justice has referred, at paras. 33, to the *Report of the Human Rights Committee*, Vol. I, UN GAOR, Fiftieth Session, Supp. No. 40 (A/50/40) (1995) with respect to corporal punishment of children in schools. I would also make reference to the *Concluding Observations of the Committee on the Rights of the Child*. Article 43(1) of the *Convention on the Rights of the Child* establishes a Committee on the Rights of the Child "[f]or the purpose of examining the progress made by State Parties in achieving the realization of the obligations undertaken" in the Convention. *The Concluding Observations of the Committee on the Rights of the Child: United Kingdom of Great Britain and Northern Ireland*, which has a legal provision similar to s. 43 dealing with reasonable chastisement within the family, state:

> The imprecise nature of the expression of reasonable chastisement as contained in these legal provisions may pave the way for it to be interpreted in a subjective and arbitrary manner. Thus, the . . . legislative and other measures relating to the physical integrity of children do

not appear to be compatible with the provisions and principles of the Convention. [Emphasis added.]

Committee on the Rights of the Child, Report adopted by the Committee at its 209th meeting on 27 January 1995, Eighth Session, CRC/C/38, at paras. 218.

The Committee has identified the vagueness inherent in provisions such as s. 43 in this and other Concluding Observations.

It is notable that the Committee has not recommended clarifying these laws so much as abolishing them entirely. The Chief Justice notes, at paras. 33, that neither the *Convention on the Rights of the Child* nor the *International Covenant on Civil and Political Rights* "require state parties to ban all corporal punishment of children". However, the *Committee's Concluding Observations on Canada's First Report* are illustrative:

[P]enal legislation allowing corporal punishment of children by parents, in schools and in institutions where children may be placed [, should be considered for review]. *In this regard . . . physical punishment of children in families [should] be prohibited.* In connection with the child's right to physical integrity . . . and in the light of the best interests of the child, . . . the possibility of introducing new legislation and follow-up mechanisms to prevent violence within the family [should be considered], and . . . educational campaigns [should] be launched with a view to changing attitudes in society on the use of physical punishment in the family *and fostering the acceptance of its legal prohibition.* [Emphasis added.]

Committee on the Rights of the Child, Report adopted by the Committee at its 233rd meeting on 9 June 1995, Ninth Session, CRC/C/43, at paras. 93.

In its most recent Concluding Observations, the Committee expressed "deep concern" that Canada had taken "no action to remove section 43 of the *Criminal Code*" and recommended the adoption of

legislation to remove the existing authorization of the use of "reasonable force" in disciplining children and explicitly prohibit all forms of violence against children, however light, within the family, in schools and in other institutions where children may be placed.

Committee on the Rights of the Child, Consideration of Reports submitted by State Parties Under Article 40 of the Convention, Thirty-fourth session, CRC/C/15/Add. 215 (2003), at paras. 32-33.

I doubt that it can be said, on the basis of the existing record, that the justification of corporal punishment of children when the force used is "reasonable under the circumstances" gives adequate notice to parents and teachers as to what is and is not permissible in a criminal context. Furthermore, it neither adequately guides the decision making power of law enforcers nor delineates, in an acceptable fashion, the boundaries of legal debate. The Chief Justice rearticulates the s. 43 defence as the delineation of a "risk zone for criminal sanction" (paras. 18). I do not disagree with such a formulation of the vagueness doctrine in this context. Still, on this record, the "risk zone" for victims and offenders alike has been a moving target.

The other dissenters, Justices Binnie and Deschamps, found that s. 43 violated equality protections under s. 15. Binnie J. was of the view that the violation could be saved under s. 1 for parents and those standing in the place of parents but not for teachers. Deschamps J. found that the violation could not be demonstrably justified.

Which judgment is more activist? That of Chief Justice McLachlin or that of Justice Arbour?

Are there problems with the regime for s. 43 declared by the majority? See critical comments by Tim Quigley, "Correction of Children: The Supreme Court Divided" (2004) 16 C.R. (6th) 286 and Sanjeev Anand, "Reasonable Chastisement: A Critique of the Supreme Court's Decision in the Spanking Case" (2003) 42 Alberta. L.Rev. 871.

The tougher criteria read in by the majority have since not always been faithfully applied so judicial subjectivity and acquittals are still a major problem. See for example *R. v. Kaur* (2004), 27 C.R. (6th) 224 (Ont. C.J.) (mother lightly tapped cheek of 12 year old daughter because of her silent treatment), criticised by Drew Mitchell, "Child Assault and Children's Rights after Foundation for Children", ((2005) 27 C.R. (6th) 230), *Plummer*, Ont. C.J., June 6, 2006 (use of belt to correct causing no pain) and *Swan*, Ont. S.C. March 13, 2008 (throwing teenage daughter into truck to rescue her from party and her boyfriend).

Should s. 43 be repealed? Corinne Robertshaw, Co-ordinator of the Repeal 43 Committee has long campaigned for this result, supported by groups who work with children across the country: see www.repeal43.org.

In *Swan* the trial judge convicted on the basis of s. 43 based on the synopsis in Martin's *Criminal Code* that s. 43 "does not apply to force to children under two or teenagers". On appeal Justice Robertson acquitted, deciding this was a misreading as the SCC was referring at that point only to corporal punishment. This is certainly true and it seems clear that the Supreme Court envisaged s. 43 as capable of authorising physical restraint by parents as well as teachers. However, Robertson J. overlooks other general limits required by the Supreme Court, in particular against the use of force where there is a risk of bodily harm and the quite clear pronouncement that the gravity of the precipitating event is not to be considered.

It is fundamentally problematic as pointed out by Arbour J. that, unlike normal defences to assault such as self-defence, the Supreme Court allows no consideration of proportionality given that the gravity of the precipitating event is stated to be irrelevant. It doesn't matter whether the child spat or burnt down the barn. The assaulter also cannot be acting out of frustration or anger. So we are left with justifying coolly premeditated minor physical correction without reference to context. Trial judges will surely have difficulty, as did Robertson J., in not considering the precipitating event.

Would the better approach be to repeal s. 43 and catch Canada up to the worldwide trend to abolish the right to physically discipline children? By 2008, 26 countries including New Zealand and almost all those in Europe have enacted laws prohibiting corporal punishment of children. If Canada followed this trend defences available to parents, caregivers and teachers would be those available to anyone charged with assault, include the defences of self-defence, duress and necessity, and possibly the emerging doctrine of *de minimis non curat lex* (see later). The power of physical restraint would be limited to that presently authorised in s. 27, which allows physical force where reasonably necessary to prevent crime or harm to others and which involves an assessment of what the child actually did. Section 27 would indeed have been the better basis for the acquittal of *Swan*.

CANADA (ATTORNEY GENERAL) v. PHS COMMUNITY SERVICES SOCIETY

2011 SCC 44, (2011) 86 C.R. (6th) 223 (S.C.C.)

Sections 4(1) and 5(1) of the *Controlled Drugs and Substances Act* prohibit possession and trafficking of illegal drugs subject to exemption from the federal Minister of Health. In 2003 authorities in Vancouver's downtown Eastside set up a supervised injection site (Insite) pursuant to a federal ministerial exemption granted under s. 56 of the Act. Insite does not provide drugs but supervises safe injections. The current Minister subsequently failed to renew the exemption.

Chief Justice McLachlin, writing for a unanimous nine-justice bench of the Supreme Court of Canada, held that the criminal prohibitions on possession in the CDSA are constitutionally valid and applicable to Insite as an exercise of the federal criminal power under s. 92(27) of the *Constitution Act 1867*. The health services offered by Insite were acting within the provincial health power but Insite could not operate without a federal exemption.

The Court further held that the prohibition of drug possession engages the rights to life and security of the person under s. 7 of the *Charter* of the clients and staff of Insite. The prohibition itself did not violate the principles of fundamental justice: it was not overbroad because the Minister's power under s. 56 to grant an exemption meant that it could be limited to appropriate circumstances. However, the Minister's refusal to grant such an exemption in this case was not in accordance with principles of fundamental justice as it was arbitrary and grossly disproportionate in its effects.

McLACHLIN C.J.: —

. . . .

> (3) Does the Minister's Refusal to Grant an Exemption to Insite Accord with the Principles of Fundamental Justice?

[127] The next question is whether the Minister's decision that the CDSA applies to Insite is in accordance with the principles of fundamental justice. On the basis of the facts established at trial, which are consistent with the evidence available to the Minister at the relevant time, I conclude that the Minister's refusal to grant Insite a s. 56 exemption was arbitrary and grossly

disproportionate in its effects, and hence not in accordance with the principles of fundamental justice.

[128] As noted above, the Minister, when exercising his discretion under s. 56, must respect the rights guaranteed by the *Charter*. This means that, where s. 7 rights are at stake, any limitations imposed by ministerial decision must be in accordance with the principles of fundamental justice. The Minister cannot simply deny an application for a s. 56 exemption on the basis of policy *simpliciter*; insofar as it affects *Charter* rights, his decision must accord with the principles of fundamental justice.

(a) *Arbitrariness*

[129] When considering whether a law's application is arbitrary, the first step is to identify the law's objectives. Decisions of the Minister under s. 56 of the CDSA must target the purpose of the Act. The legitimate state objectives of the CDSA (then the *Narcotic Control Act*, R.S.C. 1986, c. N-1) were identified by this Court in *Malmo-Levine* as the protection of health and public safety.

[130] The second step is to identify the relationship between the state interest and the impugned law, or, in this case, the impugned decision of the Minister. The relationship between the general prohibition on possession in the CDSA and the state objective was recognized in *Malmo-Levine* with respect to marihuana:

> The criminalization of possession is a statement of society's collective disapproval of the use of a psychoactive drug such as marihuana . . ., and, through Parliament, the continuing view that its use should be deterred. The prohibition is not arbitrary but is rationally connected to a reasonable apprehension of harm. In particular, criminalization seeks to take marihuana out of the hands of users and potential users, so as to prevent the associated harm and to eliminate the market for traffickers. [para. 136]

The question is whether the decision that the CDSA apply to the activities at Insite bears the same relationship to the state objective. As noted above, the burden is on the claimants to establish that the limit imposed by the law is not in accordance with the principles of fundamental justice.

[131] The trial judge's key findings in this regard are consistent with the information available to the Minister, and are those on which successive federal Ministers have relied in granting exemption orders over almost five years, including the facts that: (1) traditional criminal law prohibitions have done little to reduce drug use in the DTES; (2) the risk to injection drug users of death and disease is reduced when they inject under the supervision of a health professional; and (3) the presence of Insite did not contribute to increased crime rates, increased incidents of public injection, or relapse rates in injection drug users. On the contrary, Insite was perceived favourably or neutrally by the

public; a local business association reported a reduction in crime during the period Insite was operating; the facility encouraged clients to seek counselling, detoxification and treatment. Most importantly, the staff of Insite had intervened in 336 overdoses since 2006, and no overdose deaths had occurred at the facility. (See trial judgment, at paras. 85 and 87-88.) These findings suggest not only that exempting Insite from the application of the possession prohibition does not undermine the objectives of public health and safety, but furthers them.

[132] The jurisprudence on arbitrariness is not entirely settled. In *Chaoulli*, three justices (per McLachlin C.J. and Major J.) preferred an approach that asked whether a limit was "necessary" to further the state objective: paras. 131-32. Conversely, three other justices (per Binnie and LeBel JJ.), preferred to avoid the language of necessity and instead approved of the prior articulation of arbitrariness as where "[a] deprivation of a right . . . bears no relation to, or is inconsistent with, the state interest that lies behind the legislation": para. 232. It is unnecessary to determine which approach should prevail, because the government action at issue in this case qualifies as arbitrary under both definitions.

(b) *Gross Disproportionality*

[133] The application of the possession prohibition to Insite is also grossly disproportionate in its effects. Gross disproportionality describes state actions or legislative responses to a problem that are so extreme as to be disproportionate to any legitimate government interest: *Malmo-Levine*, at para. 143. Insite saves lives. Its benefits have been proven. There has been no discernable negative impact on the public safety and health objectives of Canada during its eight years of operation. The effect of denying the services of Insite to the population it serves is grossly disproportionate to any benefit that Canada might derive from presenting a uniform stance on the possession of narcotics.

(c) *Overbreadth*

[134] Having found the Minister's decision arbitrary and its effects grossly disproportionate, I need not consider this aspect of the argument.

[135] I conclude that, on the basis of the factual findings of the trial judge, the claimants have met the evidentiary burden of showing that the failure of the Minister to grant a s. 56 exemption to Insite is not in accordance with the principles of fundamental justice.

(4) *Conclusion on the Challenge to Minister's Decision*

[136] The Minister made a decision not to extend the exemption from the application of the federal drug laws to Insite. The effect of that decision, but for the trial judge's interim order, would have been to prevent injection drug users

from accessing the health services offered by Insite, threatening the health and indeed the lives of the potential clients. The Minister's decision thus engages the claimants' s. 7 interests and constitutes a limit on their s. 7 rights. Based on the information available to the Minister, this limit is not in accordance with the principles of fundamental justice. It is arbitrary, undermining the very purposes of the CDSA, which include public health and safety. It is also grossly disproportionate: the potential denial of health services and the correlative increase in the risk of death and disease to injection drug users outweigh any benefit that might be derived from maintaining an absolute prohibition on possession of illegal drugs on Insite's premises.

VII.   Remedy

[145] Section 24(1) confers a broad discretion on the Court to craft an appropriate remedy that is responsive to the violation of the respondents' *Charter* rights...

[150] In the special circumstances of this case, an order in the nature of *mandamus* is warranted. I would therefore order the Minister to grant an exemption to Insite under s. 56 of the CDSA forthwith. (This of course would not affect the Minister's power to withdraw the exemption should the operation of Insite change such that the exemption would no longer be appropriate.) On the trial judge's findings of fact, the only constitutional response to the application for a s. 56 exemption was to grant it. The Minister is bound to exercise his discretion under s. 56 in accordance with the *Charter*. On the facts as found here, there can be only one response: to grant the exemption. There is therefore nothing to be gained (and much to be risked) in sending the matter back to the Minister for reconsideration.

[151] This does not fetter the Minister's discretion with respect to future applications for exemptions, whether for other premises, or for Insite. As always, the Minister must exercise that discretion within the constraints imposed by the law and the *Charter*.

[152] The dual purposes of the CDSA — public health and public safety — provide some guidance for the Minister. Where the Minister is considering an application for an exemption for a supervised injection facility, he or she will aim to strike the appropriate balance between achieving the public health and public safety goals. Where, as here, the evidence indicates that a supervised injection site will decrease the risk of death and disease, and there is little or no evidence that it will have a negative impact on public safety, the Minister should generally grant an exemption.

[153] The CDSA grants the Minister discretion in determining whether to grant exemptions. That discretion must be exercised in accordance with the *Charter*.

This requires the Minister to consider whether denying an exemption would cause deprivations of life and security of the person that are not in accordance with the principles of fundamental justice. The factors considered in making the decision on an exemption must include evidence, if any, on the impact of such a facility on crime rates, the local conditions indicating a need for such a supervised injection site, the regulatory structure in place to support the facility, the resources available to support its maintenance, and expressions of community support or opposition.

IX.   Disposition

[156] The CDSA is constitutionally valid and applies to the activities at Insite. However, the Minister of Health's actions in refusing to exempt Insite from the operation of the CDSA are in violation of the respondents' s. 7 *Charter* rights. The Minister is ordered to grant an exemption for Insite under s. 56 of the CDSA.

The Court here identifies three separate *Charter* challenges: arbitrariness, gross disproportionality and overbreadth. In *Malmo-Levine* the majority required a test of gross disproportionality for each head. Not so here.

Note that the Court has not settled the meaning of arbitrariness.

(iii)   Oakes test for section 1

R. v. OAKES

[1986] 1 S.C.R. 103, 50 C.R. (3d) 1, 24 C.C.C.(3d) 321,
1986 CarswellOnt 95, 1986 CarswellOnt 1001

DICKSON C.J.C. (CHOUINARD, LAMER, WILSON and LE DAIN JJ. concurring):

It is important to observe at the outset that s. 1 has two functions: first, it constitutionally guarantees the rights and freedoms set out in the provisions which follow; and, second, it states explicitly the exclusive justificatory criteria (outside of s. 33 of the *Constitution Act, 1982*) against which limitations on those rights and freedoms must be measured. Accordingly, any s. 1 inquiry must be premised on an understanding that the impugned limit violates constitutional rights and freedoms — rights and freedoms which are part of the supreme law of Canada. As Madam Justice Wilson stated in *Singh et al. v. Ministry of Employment and Immigration, supra*, at pp. 218-19: "... it is important to remember that the courts are conducting this inquiry in light of a commitment to uphold the rights and freedoms set out in the other sections of the *Charter*."

A second contextual element of interpretation of s. 1 is provided by the words "free and democratic society". Inclusion of these words as the final standard of justification for limits on rights and freedoms refers the court to the very purpose for which the *Charter* was originally entrenched in the Constitution: Canadian society is to be free and democratic. The court must be guided by the values and principles essential to a free and democratic society which I believe embody, to name but a few, respect for the inherent dignity of the human person, commitment to social justice and equality, accommodation of a wide variety of beliefs, respect for cultural and group identity, and faith in social and political institutions which enhance the participation of individuals and groups in society. The underlying values and principles of a free and democratic society are the genesis of the rights and freedoms guaranteed by the *Charter* and the ultimate standard against which a limit on a right or freedom must be shown, despite its effect, to be reasonable and demonstrably justified.

The rights and freedoms guaranteed by the *Charter* are not, however, absolute. It may become necessary to limit rights and freedoms in circumstances where their exercise would be inimical to the realization of collective goals of fundamental importance. For this reason, s. 1 provides criteria of justification for limits on the rights and freedoms guaranteed by the *Charter*. These criteria impose a stringent standard of justification, especially when understood in terms of the two contextual considerations discussed above, namely, the violation of a constitutionally guaranteed right or freedom and the fundamental principles of a free and democratic society.

The onus of proving that a limit on a right or freedom guaranteed by the *Charter* is reasonable and demonstrably justified in a free and democratic society rests upon the party seeking to uphold the limitation. It is clear from the text of s. 1 that limits on the rights and freedoms enumerated in the *Charter* are exceptions to their general guarantee. The presumption is that the rights and freedoms are guaranteed unless the party invoking s. 1 can bring itself within the exceptional criteria which justify their being limited. This is further substantiated by the use of the word "demonstrably" which clearly indicates that the onus of justification is on the party seeking to limit: *Hunter v. Southam Inc.*, *supra*.

The standard of proof under s. 1 is the civil standard, namely, proof by a preponderance of probability. The alternative criminal standard, proof beyond a reasonable doubt, would, in my view, be unduly onerous on the party seeking to limit. Concepts such as "reasonableness", "justifiability" and "free and democratic society" are simply not amenable to such a standard. Nevertheless, the preponderance of probability test must be applied rigorously. Indeed, the phrase "demonstrably justified" in s. 1 of the *Charter* supports this conclusion. Within the broad category of the civil standard, there exist different degrees of probability depending on the nature of the case: see Sopinka and Lederman, *The*

Law of Evidence in Civil Cases (Toronto: 1974) at p. 385. As Lord Denning explained in *Bater v. Bater*, [1950] 2 All E.R. 458 (C.A.) at p. 459:

> The case may be proved by a preponderance probability, but there may be degrees of probability within that standard. The degree depends on the subject-matter. A civil court, when considering a charge of fraud, will naturally require a higher degree of probability than that which it would require if considering whether negligence were established. It does not adopt so high a standard as a criminal court, even when considering a charge of a criminal nature, but still it does require a degree of probability which is commensurate with the occasion.

This passage was cited with approval in *Hanes v. Wawanesa Mutual Insurance Co.*, [1963] S.C.R. 154 at p. 161. A similar approach was put forward by Cartwright J. in *Smith v. Smith & Smedman*, [1952] 2 S.C.R. 312 at pp. 331-32:

> I wish, however, to emphasize that in every civil action before the tribunal can safely find the affirmative of an issue of fact required to be proved it must be satisfied, and that whether or not it will be so satisfied must depend on the totality of the circumstances on which its judgment is formed including the gravity of the consequences.

Having regard to the fact that s. 1 is being invoked for the purpose of justifying a violation of the constitutional rights and freedoms the *Charter* was designed to protect, a very high degree of probability will be, in the words of Lord Denning, "commensurate with the occasion". Where evidence is required in order to prove the constituent elements of a s. 1 inquiry, and this will generally be the case, it should be cogent and persuasive and make clear to the court the consequences of imposing or not imposing the limit. See: *Law Society of Upper Canada v. Skapinker, supra,* at p. 384; *Singh et al. v. Ministry of Employment and Immigration, supra,* at p. 217. A court will also need to know what alternative measures for implementing the objective were available to the legislators when they made their decisions. I should add, however, that there may be cases where certain elements of the s. 1 analysis are obvious or self-evident.

To establish that a limit is reasonable and demonstrably justified in a free and democratic society, two central criteria must be satisfied. First, the objective, which the measures responsible for a limit on a *Charter* right or freedom are designed to serve, must be "of sufficient importance to warrant overriding a constitutionally protected right or freedom": *R. v. Big M Drug Mart Ltd., supra,* at p. 352. The standard must be high in order to ensure that objectives which are trivial or discordant with the principles integral to a free and democratic society do not gain s. 1 protection. It is necessary, at a minimum, that an objective relate to concerns which are pressing and substantial in a free and democratic society before it can be characterized as sufficiently important.

Second, once a sufficiently significant objective is recognized, then the party invoking s. 1 must show that the means chosen are reasonable and demonstrably justified. This involves "a form of proportionality test": *R. v. Big M Drug Mart*

Ltd., supra, at p. 352. Although the nature of the proportionality test will vary depending on the circumstances, in each case courts will be required to balance the interests of society with those of individuals and groups. There are, in my view, three important components of a proportionality test. First, the measures adopted must be carefully designed to achieve the objective in question. They must not be arbitrary, unfair or based on irrational considerations. In short, they must be rationally connected to the objective. Second, the means, even if rationally connected to the objective in this first sense, should impair "as little as possible" the right or freedom in question: *R. v. Big M Drug Mart Ltd., supra*, at p. 352. Third, there must be a proportionality between the *effects* of the measures which are responsible for limiting the *Charter* right or freedom, and the objective which has been identified as of "sufficient importance".

With respect to the third component, it is clear that the general effect of any measure impugned under s. 1 will be the infringement of a right or freedom guaranteed by the *Charter*; this is the reason why resort to s. 1 is necessary. The inquiry into effects must, however, go further. A wide range of rights and freedoms are guaranteed by the *Charter*, and an almost infinite number of factual situations may arise in respect of these. Some limits on rights and freedoms protected by the *Charter* will be more serious than others in terms of the nature of the right or freedom violated, the extent of the violation, and the degree to which the measures which impose the limit trench upon the integral principles of a free and democratic society. Even if an objective is of sufficient importance, and the first two elements of the proportionality test are satisfied, it is still possible that, because of the severity of the deleterious effects of a measure on individuals or groups, the measure will not be justified by the purposes it is intended to serve. The more severe the deleterious effects of a measure, the more important the objective must be if the measure is to be reasonable and demonstrably justified in a free and democratic society.

In *Oakes* the reverse onus was held to be unconstitutional as it did not meet the rational connection part of the *Oakes* test for s. 1. The court has subsequently changed what is meant by "rational connection": as the test is now understood, the reverse onus would likely pass rational connection but would fail minimal impairment.

A review of many decisions in the Supreme Court applying the *Oakes* blueprint to s. 1 shows that the *Oakes* test is formalistic. Whether a limit can be demonstrably justified under s. 1 almost always turns on what has become known as the "minimal impairment" test of whether the limitation restricts the *Charter* right as little as possible. Even in the context of criminal law, there seems to be a trend towards judicial deference to legislative choices.

In *R. v. Edwards Books & Art Ltd.*, [1986] 2 S.C.R. 713, the issue was whether a Sunday observance law was unconstitutional through a violation of the freedom of religion guaranteed by s. 2(*a*) of the *Charter*. In applying his *Oakes* test, Chief

Justice Dickson stated that the nature of the proportionality test would "vary depending on the circumstances" and that, both in the articulation of the standard of proof and in the applicable criteria, the court had been "careful to avoid rigid and inflexible standards". The Chief Justice saw the question as whether the Act abridged freedom of religion as "little as is reasonably possible". Was there "some reasonable alternative scheme which would allow the province to achieve its objective with fewer detrimental effects on religious freedom?"

In *R. v. Chaulk*, [1990] 3 S.C.R. 1303, it was argued that the presumption of sanity then contained in s. 16(4) of the *Criminal Code*, placing the onus of proving the defence of insanity on the accused, was an unconstitutional violation of the presumption of innocence in s. 11(*d*). Chief Justice Lamer, writing for himself and four other judges, held that there had been a violation but it could be justified under s. 1. The objective of the presumption was to "avoid placing an impossible burden of proof on the Crown". Citing recent judgments of the court, indicating that Parliament was not required to adopt the absolutely least intrusive means, Chief Justice Lamer saw the issue as "whether a less intrusive means would achieve the same objective or would achieve the same objective as effectively". The Chief Justice concluded that the alternative of an evidentiary burden requiring that the accused merely raise a reasonable doubt would not be as effective, accepting arguments by Attorneys General that it would be very easy for accused persons to "fake" such a defence.

The sole dissent on this point in *Chaulk* was Madam Justice Wilson, who held that this was not a case for relaxing the minimal impairment test. This might be done where a legislature, mediating between competing groups of citizens or allocating scarce resources, had to compromise on the basis of conflicting evidence. But in *Chaulk* the state was acting as "singular antagonists" of a very basic legal right of an accused and the strict standard of review in *Oakes* should be applied. The government's objective could be quite readily met by a mere burden on the accused to adduce evidence that made insanity "a live issue fit and proper to be left to the jury".

In the more than two decades of jurisprudence since *Oakes*, s. 1 consideration has invariably started with a recitation of the *Oakes* approach, almost as if it were a legislative replacement of the words of s. 1. In *RJR-MacDonald Inc. v. Canada (Attorney General)*, [1995] 3 S.C.R. 199, a major decision on s. 1, McLachlin J. reasserts for the majority that:

> The factors generally relevant to determining whether a violative law is reasonably and demonstrably justified in a free and democratic society remain those set out in *Oakes*. The first requirement is that the objective of the law limiting the *Charter* right or freedom must be of sufficient importance to warrant overriding it. The second is that the means chosen to achieve the objective must be proportional to the objective and the effect of the law — proportionate, in short, to the good which it may produce. Three matters are considered in determining proportionality: the measures chosen must be rationally connected to the objective; they must impair the guaranteed right or freedom as little as reasonably possible (minimal impairment); and there must be overall proportionality between the deleterious effects of the measures and the salutary effects of the law.

In *R. v. Laba* (1994), 34 C.R. (4th) 360 (S.C.C.) the issue was the constitutionality of a provision under s. 394(1)(*b*) of the *Criminal Code* requiring a person charged with possessing or selling minerals to establish the defence of ownership or lawful authority. Sopinka J., for a court unanimous on this point, held that the Crown could not demonstrably justify this persuasive burden on an accused given a reasonable legislative alternative of an evidentiary burden. In the course of the judgment a reference to *Chaulk* is followed by the remark that:

> it is also important to remember that this is not a case in which the legislature has attempted to strike a balance between the interests of competing individuals or groups. Rather it is a case in which the government (as opposed to other individuals or groups) can be characterised as the singular antagonist of an individual attempting to assert a legal right which is fundamental to our system of criminal justice (at 392).

This appears to endorse the minority Wilson position in *Chaulk*. Since the court has changed its basic premise, previous s. 1 rulings justifying various *Charter* violations in criminal cases, especially but not only those concerning reverse onus clauses, may well have to be revisited and/or properly distinguished on fresh challenges.

The court in *Laba* also noted that the "rational connection" portion of the *Oakes* test did not require any internal logical connection. They stated at p. 1008:

> Before moving on to consider the next step in the *Oakes* test I would like to address the respondents' argument that s. 394(1)(b) fails the rational connection test because it creates an unreasonable presumption that any ore which has been purchased or sold was stolen. This argument is premised upon the notion that in order for a legislatively created presumption to pass this portion of the *Oakes* test it must be internally rational in the sense that there is a logical connection between the presumed fact and the fact substituted by the presumption. This argument was made by the appellant in *R. v. Downey*, [1992] 2 S.C.R. 10. It was contended that a presumption which is not internally rational unduly enmeshes the innocent in the criminal process. This argument was not accepted by the majority. Consequently, I regard it as settled that there is no general requirement that a presumption be internally rational in order to pass the rational connection phase of the proportionality test. The only relevant consideration at this stage of the analysis is whether the presumption is a logical method of accomplishing the legislative objective.

In its very lengthy judgment in *RJR-MacDonald* the Supreme Court held that a federal ban on advertising and promotion of tobacco without health warnings under the *Tobacco Products Act* violated freedom of expression guaranteed by s. 2(*b*) of the *Charter*. The court further held, 5-4, that the violation could not be saved under s. 1. The judgment turns on s. 1 with the degree of deference to be paid to Parliament being the pivotal issue. The majority finds it crucial that the federal government did not tender evidence in support of the need for a total ban. The minority through Mr. Justice La Forest would have allowed Parliament considerable latitude in its decision that a total ban was appropriate. On minimal intrusion the court again seems agreed that the issue is whether the measure restricted as little as reasonably possible.

One of the majority judgments, by Madam Justice McLachlin, Major and Sopinka JJ. concurring, engages in the most wide-ranging and thoughtful consideration of *Oakes* since that decision. Unfortunately the extent to which she is speaking for the court is unclear given a much shorter concurring judgement by Justice Iacobucci, Lamer C.J. concurring, which indicates that he differs "somewhat" with McLachlin J.'s s. 1 analysis. The extent of the disagreement is left unclear.

McLachlin J. calls for a new stress by courts on the words "reasonable" and "demonstrably justified":

> While remaining sensitive to the social and political context of the impugned law and allowing for difficulties of proof inherent in that context, the courts must nevertheless insist that before the state can override constitutional rights, there must be a reasoned demonstration of the good which the law may achieve in relation to the seriousness of the infringement. It is the task of the courts to maintain this bottom line if the rights conferred by our Constitution are to have force and meaning. The task is not easily discharged, and may require the courts to confront the tide of popular public opinion.

McLachlin J. agrees with La Forest J. that the *Oakes* test, being a fact-specific inquiry, must be applied flexibly having regard to the factual and social context of each case. However she warns that this should not undercut the obligation of Parliament to justify limitations on *Charter* rights by reasoned demonstration. Her Ladyship later warns that care must be taken not to overstate the objective of the measure under challenge:

> The objective relevant to the s. 1 analysis is *the objective of the infringing measure*, since it is the infringing measure and nothing else which is sought to be justified. If the objective is stated too broadly, its importance may be exaggerated and the analysis compromised.

On the degree of deference courts should show Parliament McLachlin J. accepts that context is relevant. She gives a qualified answer to the question of whether a tougher approach should always be demanded in criminal law:

> It has been suggested that greater deference to Parliament or the legislature may be appropriate if the law is concerned with competing rights between different sections of society than if it is a contest between the individual and the state.... However, such distinctions may not always be easy to apply. For example, the criminal law is generally seen as involving a contest between the state and the accused, but it also involves an allocation of priorities between the accused and the victim, actual or potential.

McLachlin J. also suggests that care should be taken not to extend the notion of deference to the point of relieving the government of its burden of demonstrating reasonable and justified limits:

> Parliament has its role: to choose the appropriate response to social problems within the limiting framework of the Constitution. But the courts also have a role: to determine, objectively and impartially, whether Parliament's choice falls within the limiting framework of the Constitution.

For McLachlin J. the standard of proof is not to the standard required by science nor proof beyond reasonable doubt. The standard of proof on a balance of probabilities may be established by the application of common sense to what is known. However she determines that this standard must be applied at all stages of the proportionality analysis, including the demonstration of a rational connection.

Her final general point relates to deference by appeal courts to findings by trial judges. There should be more deference to findings based on evidence of a purely factual nature but less where the trial judge has considered social science and other policy oriented evidence.

For further consideration of this controversial jurisprudence on the s. 1 test, see Stuart, *Charter Justice in Canadian Criminal Law* (Toronto: Carswell, 5th ed., 2010) Chapter 1.

2. PROCEDURAL OVERVIEW

(a) Procedural Classification of Offences

At common law a distinction was drawn between indictable offences (treasons, felonies and misdemeanours) triable only by judge and jury, and offences triable only summarily by justices of the peace sitting without a jury. The distinction between felonies and misdemeanours was important in that the former (e.g., murder, burglary and rape) were punishable by death and resulted in forfeiture of the felon's property, while the latter never involved the death penalty and only rarely forfeiture. It is still maintained in the United States, but was abolished in England in 1967 and in Canada by the *Criminal Code* as early as the nineteenth century.

In the Canadian *Criminal Code* there are, broadly speaking, three types of offences: summary conviction, indictable, and dual (or hybrid) offences. (There is also a fourth type of offence, contraventions offences under the *Contraventions Act*, S.C. 1992, c. 47. These latter offences are regulatory offences and will not be discussed here.) The type of offence is always expressly stipulated in the offence definition; however, this categorization is somewhat misleading. The category of dual (hybrid) offences is not actually a third category, it simply means that the Crown has an election as to whether to proceed by indictment or by summary conviction. Further, for purposes of mode of trial at least, there are three types of indictable offences. Adding to the confusion, the trial court is determined by the classification of the offence and the *Code* does not set out the classification in an orderly way. Instead, the provisions are haphazardly strewn across the *Code* and are less than explicit in some instances. The best way to explain them, therefore, is by a process of elimination. But, first, a definition of each of the types of offences:

(i) Offences triable only on indictment

These are more serious offences. Usually the offence section or its penalty section sets out the punishment applicable to the offence. If it does not, s. 743 of the *Code* provides a maximum of five years imprisonment. Indictable offences are of three types and the type involved has a large bearing on the forum for trial. Where an accused is charged with an indictable offence, generally speaking, he must be personally present at all stages of the proceedings, although ss. 650, 650.01, and 650.02 of the *Criminal Code* now permit appearing in other ways in some circumstances.

The most serious offences are given into the exclusive jurisdiction of the superior court of criminal jurisdiction, in Ontario, the Superior Court of Justice.

See ss. 468 and 469. The least serious indictable offences are absolutely within the jurisdiction of a provincial court judge, in Ontario, a judge of the Ontario Court of Justice. See s. 553. For the great bulk of the indictable offences remaining, the accused is entitled to choose the mode of trial. By s. 536(2) the accused will be put to an election and will be asked to choose to be tried by a provincial court judge without a jury, a judge without a jury, or by a court composed of a judge and jury. If the accused does not elect a mode of trial, he will be deemed to have elected trial by judge and jury, s. 565(1)(c). It is important to note the difference between the exclusive jurisdiction of the superior court at one end of the scale and the absolute jurisdiction of the provincial court judge at the other. The superior court has exclusive jurisdiction: no other court can try these offences. The provincial court judge has absolute jurisdiction: the provincial court judge is absolutely entitled to try these offences in the sense that she is not dependent on the accused's electing to be so tried. Other courts of criminal jurisdiction are nevertheless entitled to try the accused for offences within the provincial court judge's absolute jurisdiction should the matter come before them: see *R. v. Holliday* (1973), 12 C.C.C. (2d) 56, 26 C.R.N.S. 279 (Alta. CA).

Notwithstanding that the accused has elected trial by provincial court judge, the provincial court judge may decide that the matter should be proceeded with by a judge or jury, s. 555, and the Attorney General may also override an accused's decision and compel a jury trial where the offence is punishable by more than five years, s. 568.

There are detailed provisions in the *Criminal Code* which allow an accused person to change his or her mind and to re-elect his mode of trial: see ss. 561 to 563.1 and 565. The heart of the re-election provisions is s. 561 which conditions the right to re-elect on the basis of a combination of: (a) the original election; (b) the point in time in the process when the accused wishes to re-elect; and (c) whether the Crown consents to the re-election. The labyrinthine nature of elections is described by Professor Tim Quigley in Procedure in *Canadian Criminal Law*, 2nd ed. (Toronto: Carswell, 2005).

(ii)   Summary conviction offences

Part XXVII of the *Criminal Code* sets out the procedure for the trial of summary conviction offences (i.e., trial before a provincial judge without a jury and without a preliminary inquiry). The maximum penalty for any summary conviction offence, unless otherwise provided, is $5,000 or six months imprisonment or both: s. 787(1).

Summary conviction offences are always tried in Provincial Court (or its equivalent) or by a justice of the peace (although superior court judges also have the jurisdiction to do so, they rarely exercise it in practice). In theory, Parliament could establish a maximum penalty of up to five years less one day imprisonment without violating the right to a jury trial under s. 11 (f) of the *Charter*.

An accused charged with a summary conviction offence normally need not appear personally in court but may instead choose to have a lawyer or some other agent appear for him unless the judge orders that he must appear personally: s. 800(2) of the *Code*.

(iii) Crown election offences (dual, hybrid)

These are offences for which the prosecution may choose whether to proceed by way of summary conviction or by indictment. If the Crown elects summary conviction, such offences are in all respects summary conviction offences. If the Crown proceeds by indictment, the forum for the trial will depend upon the type of indictable offence involved. As with straight indictable offences, the penalty is usually specified in the enactment but, if not, is governed by s. 743.

Various tactical considerations enter into the Crown election. The higher available penalty for indictable offences, a prior criminal record by the accused, or a desire to require the accused's personal presence throughout may be among the reasons. Sometimes it is a matter of judge shopping or wishing to get the matter over more quickly.

In 1994 Parliament increased the maximum penalty for several hybrid offences when proceeded against by way of summary conviction to 18 months: see, e.g., assault causing bodily harm (s. 267) and sexual assault (s. 271). Only when the prosecutor elects to proceed by indictment does the accused have the choice under s. 536. If the Crown chooses summary conviction proceedings, the accused no longer has a choice of a preliminary inquiry, trial in superior court or a jury trial. The prosecutor should indicate the nature of the proceeding prior to trial.

The *Interpretation Act*, R.S.C. 1985, c. 1-21, provides:

> 34. (1) Where an enactment creates an offence,
>
>> (a) the offence is deemed to be an indictable offence if the enactment provides that the offender may be prosecuted for the offence by indictment;

Section 34(1) has been applied to equate Crown election offences with indictable offences in various contexts such as arrest and for the purposes of fingerprinting under the *Identification of Criminals Act*, R.S.C. 1985, c. 11.

PROBLEM 1

How are the following *Criminal Code* offences classified? What options for trial will an accused have in each case? What factors will you as counsel take into account in determining how to exercise your options?

1. frightening the Queen (s. 49)
2. murder (s. 235(1))
3. operating vehicle while impaired (ss. 253, 255)
4. shoplifting (s. 334)
5. robbery (ss. 343, 344)
6. assault (s. 266)
7. assault causing bodily harm (s. 267)
8. sexual assault (s. 271)
9. causing a disturbance in a public place (s. 175)

10. possession of stolen property over $5000 (s. 355(a))
11. attempted murder (s. 239)
12. conspiracy to commit murder (s. 465(1)(a))

PROBLEM 2

You are Crown counsel prosecuting a charge of assault causing bodily harm. The accused is charged with striking his wife with his fist. His blow cut her cheek. This required three sutures at the hospital. A senior Crown asks you to try hard to avoid the matter being bumped up to a court in which the accused could choose trial by jury. In the higher court, there is a huge backlog of cases. She advises you to elect to proceed by way of summary conviction. Consider carefully whether you should follow this advice.

PROBLEM 3

A person has been charged with the following three offences: (1) Possession of cocaine for the purposes of trafficking, contrary to s. 5(2) and (3) of the *Controlled Drugs and Substances Act*; (2) Possession of marijuana, contrary to s. 4(1), (4) and (5) of the *Controlled Drugs and Substances Act*; and (3) Driving while "over 80", contrary to ss. 253(b) and 255(1) of the *Criminal Code*. How will he be tried on each charge? What considerations should be taken into account by the Crown or defence counsel in making any election which may be available?

It has been well documented that the criminal jurisdiction of superior courts is shrinking and that the vast percentage of criminal trials now occur in provincial courts (see Webster and Doob, "The Superior/Provincial Criminal Court Distinction: Historical Anachronism or Empirical Reality?" (2004) 48 Crim. L.O. 77). The major difference is that murder trials and all jury trials are confined to the superior courts.

The general and serious problems of systemic delays, complexity and judge-shopping could be better addressed by returning to the vision of those such as former Attorney General Ian Scott and others (see Martin Friedland, "The Provincial Court and the Criminal Law" (2004) 98 Crim. L.O. 14) who called for just one federal trial court to handle all criminal trials with or without juries. He was pilloried for that view by many members of the superior courts, some members of the profession, and politicians wishing to retain provincial powers to appoint. The *status quo* is currently propped up by claims of special expertise by judges of higher status which increasingly ring hollow given the calibre and workload of current provincial court judges. The single court is already the reality in Nunavut.

LAW REFORM COMMISSION OF CANADA,
THE JURY IN CRIMINAL TRIALS

W.P. No. 27, (1980), 76-77

Questions of law are decided by the judge; questions of fact are decided by the jury. This well-known dichotomy of functions raises the problem of who applies the law to the facts. Because the jury in criminal cases returns a general verdict of guilty or not-guilty, it must discharge this responsibility. Thus, to enable the jury to carry out its duties, the judge instructs the jury on the law which governs the case. In reaching a verdict the jury must then apply those instructions to the facts as it finds them.

Jury instructions must, therefore, satisfy two conflicting requirements: the need to state accurately the relevant law and the need to state the law so that the jury understands it. The need to state the law accurately is, of course, an obvious requirement. If the case is appealed, counsel will scrutinize the charge for all possible errors in the statement of law. The Court of Appeal will hold the instructions to be in error unless the judge has correctly stated the law in all respects. (Of course, not every error causes a substantial wrong or miscarriage of justice.) Because strict legal correctness is the primary concern of the appellate courts, it is naturally the concern of trial judges as well. Indeed, to eliminate the possibility of error from their statements of the law, trial judges will sometimes include long quotations from appellate court judgments in their instructions and in other ways generally attempt to "boiler-plate" them. This often results in instructions which are long, repetitious, and disjointed.

The need to state the law correctly may thus often conflict with the other important requirement of jury instructions: that they be understandable to the jury. The allocation of responsibility between the judge and jury is premised on the jury's ability to understand and apply the law. It is often alleged that one of the most serious deficiencies of trial by jury, and indeed an aspect of it which is sometimes said to place the institution of the jury in jeopardy, is the jury's inability to follow and comprehend the instructions given by the judge. If jurors are confused about the law they are to apply, they cannot perform their function properly, and a just verdict will be reached only by chance.

Our survey of judges also led us to the conclusion that something to improve the quality of jury instructions ought to be attempted. Only 23 percent of the judges were quite certain that juries generally understand the judge's instructions. And while most (82 percent) felt that it was at least probable that juries understood what was being told to them, a significant minority (18 percent) felt that it was probable that juries did not understand what was being told them.

(b) What is Evidence?

The Crown, we have seen, has the obligation of proving the allegations. How do we prove things? By evidence. What is evidence? Evidence may take the form of oral testimony, I saw the accused stab the victim, or real evidence, clothes belonging to the accused with bloodstains matching the victim's bloodtype. Whatever the form of the evidence it must be relevant. To understand the meaning of relevance and the reason for its necessity we should first trace briefly the developments of our fact-finding process.

The methods employed by the Anglo-Saxons at the time of the Conquest involved the invocation of the Deity. One method was known as compurgation or wager of law. The litigants would assemble specified numbers of oath-takers who would swear to their belief in the correctness of "their" litigant's claim or defence or to his trustworthiness; these oath-takers would have no personal knowledge of the facts of the case. The supernatural sanction for a false oath was seen as assuring the correctness of the decision. Another method of fact-finding was known as trial by ordeal. The litigant would grasp a hot iron and God would directly indicate the litigant's righteousness by producing a clean, healed wound after three days. The accused would be bound and thrown into a body of water; if the water accepted him and he sank he was innocent. Trial by ordeal ended in the early 13th century when the Pope forbade participation by the clergy. The early Anglo-Norman technique of fact-finding, trial by combat, was based on the belief that God would assist the innocent and the honest.

By the late 13th century the Norman Inquest had largely supplanted the earlier modes of fact-finding. The Inquest was revolutionary in its emphasis on a rational inquiry and consisted of sworn investigators, or jurors, who undertook to discover the facts and relate the same to the judge who would pass judgment thereon. Gradually these jurors came to rely on sworn witnesses to the facts in question and by the 17th century the functions of jurors and witnesses were formally separated.

The fact-finding process has developed into a system of inquiry which is *considered* to be rational. There must therefore be a rational connection between the evidence tendered and the proposition sought to be established. This connection is labelled relevance.

When evidence about a material proposition is led, the proponent seeks to persuade the trier to draw the inference from the fact led to the proposition. If there is a rational connection between them, if the fact will, according to reason and experience, support the inference, the fact will be adjudged relevant and received. The facts tendered in evidence are normally classified as either testimonial or circumstantial, but in each case inferences are necessary and problems of relevancy therefore occur. With testimonial evidence, sometimes called direct evidence, the trier is asked to infer from the fact that the witness made a statement to the truth of the matter stated. If the witness is seen to be sincere and possessed of an ability to observe and accurately recall, and clearly had the opportunity to see the matter in issue, there will be reason to draw the inference and testimony will be credited. Though a true problem of relevance exists, it is more common, however, to examine and discuss the probative worth of such evidence under the heads of testimonial qualifications and credibility.

Commonly we reserve the concept of relevancy for discussions involving circumstantial evidence. In cases of circumstantial evidence certain facts connected with the material fact are proved and the trier is asked to infer from these facts that the material fact exists. If reason and experience support the connection the evidence led is relevant.

If a witness is willing to testify that she saw the accused shoot the deceased, this is direct evidence of that fact. The trial judge will first ensure the witness's competence to speak, then the evidence may be evaluated according to the trier of fact's assessment of the witness's credibility. If a witness is willing to testify that she heard the deceased scream and moments later saw the accused standing over the body holding a smoking gun this is circumstantial evidence of the accused shooting the deceased. The trial judge will assess the relevance of the evidence led; if received the trier of fact will then assess its sufficiency.

Having said that evidence must be relevant it is important to emphasize the requirement of materiality. The concept of materiality demands a rational connection between the tendered evidence and a fact in issue. Sometimes writers and judges avoid the term "materially" and speak of the need for relevance to a legal issue. The trial of an action or a criminal allegation is not designed to review all that has occurred between the parties or all of the accused's past delinquencies, but rather a particular section of that history. A particular slice of life is to be examined and that slice is dictated by the substantive law and the pleadings of the parties. In the criminal area the "pleadings" of the parties are confined to the information and particulars ordered by the court; sometimes the issues are narrowed by formal admissions made by the accused.

For evidence to be received it must then be relevant to a material issue. We have seen that relevancy and materiality are not dictated by the laws of evidence. The laws of evidence are concerned with canons of exclusion which render inadmissible evidence which is both relevant and material. For a variety of policies the law of evidence excludes material which might aid in the search for truth. Some of these rules are due to a concern regarding the ability of the trier of fact to adequately assess the evidence, some out of concern for values inherent in the adversary system, and some to protect certain relationships in society as we recognize the competition with values other than truth. Evidence, then, is information which clears all three hurdles and is therefore receivable.

(c) Presumption of Innocence

The cornerstone precepts of the presumption of innocence and that the Crown must normally prove to a standard of proof beyond a reasonable doubt were asserted by the House of Lords relatively recently.

(i)   *Common law*

WOOLMINGTON v. D.P.P.

[1935] A.C. 462 (H.L.)

May 23. VISCOUNT SANKEY L.C.: — My Lords, the appellant, Reginald Woolmington, after a trial at the Somerset Assizes at Taunton on January 23, at which, after an absence of one hour and twenty-five minutes, the jury disagreed, was convicted at the Bristol Assizes on February 14 of the wilful murder of his wife on December 10, 1934, and was sentenced to death.

. . . .

The facts are as follows. Reginald Woolmington is 21-1/2 years old. His wife, who was killed, was 17-1/2 years old last December. They had known each other for some time and upon August 25 they were married. Upon October 14 she gave birth to a child. Shortly after that there appears to have been some quarrelling between them and she left him upon November 22 and went to live with her mother. Woolmington apparently was anxious to get her to come back, but she did not come. The prosecution proved that at about 9.15 in the morning of the 10th Mrs. Daisy Brine was hanging out her washing at the back of her house at 25 Newtown, Milborne Port. While she was engaged in that occupation, she heard voices from the next door house, No. 24. She knew that in that house her niece, Reginald Woolmington's wife, was living. She heard and could recognize the voice of Reginald Woolmington saying something to the effect "are you going to come back home?" She could not hear the answer. Then the back door in No. 24 was slammed. She heard a voice in the kitchen but could not tell what it said. Then she heard the sound of a gun. Upon that she looked out of the front window and she saw Reginald Woolmington, whose voice she had heard just before speaking in the kitchen, go out and get upon his bicycle, which had been left or was standing against the wall of her house, No. 25. She called out to him but he gave no reply. He looked at her hard and then he rode away.

According to Reginald Woolmington's own story, having brooded over and deliberated upon the position all through the night of December 9, he went on the morning of the 10th in the usual way to the milking at his employer's farm, and while milking conceived this idea that he would take the old gun which was in the barn and he would take it up that morning to his wife's mother's house where she was living, and that he would show her that gun and tell her that he was going to commit suicide if she did not come back. He would take the gun up for the purpose of frightening her into coming back to him by causing her to think that he was going to commit suicide. He finished his milking, went back to his father's house, had breakfast and then left, taking with him a hack saw.

He returned to the farm, went into the barn, got the gun, which had been used for rook shooting, sawed off the barrels of it, then took the only two cartridges which were there and put them into the gun. He took the two pieces of the barrel which he had sawn off and the hack saw, crossed a field about 60 yards wide and dropped them into the brook. Having done that, he returned on his bicycle, with the gun in his overcoat pocket, to his father's house and changed his clothes. Then he got a piece of wire flex which he attached to the gun so that he could suspend it from his shoulder underneath his coat, and so went off to the house where his wife was living. He knocked at the door, went into the kitchen and asked her: "Are you coming back?" She made no answer. She came into the parlour, and on his asking her whether she would come back she replied she was going into service. He then, so he says, threatened he would shoot himself, and went on to show her the gun and brought it across his waist, when it somehow went off and his wife fell down and he went out of the house. He told the jury that it was an accident, that it was a pure accident; that whilst he was getting the gun from under his shoulder and was drawing it across his breast it accidentally went off and he was doing nothing unlawful, nothing wrong, and this was a pure accident. There was considerable controversy as to whether a letter in which he set out his grievances was written before or after the above events. But when he was arrested at 7.30 on the evening of the 10th and charged with having committed murder he said: "I want to say nothing, except I done it, and they can do what they like with me. It was jealousy I suppose. Her mother enticed her away from me. I done all I could to get her back. That's all."

The learned judge in summing-up the case to the jury said:—

> If you accept his evidence, you will have little doubt that she died in consequence of a gunshot wound which was inflicted by a gun which he had taken to this house, and which was in his hands, or in his possession, at the time that it exploded. If you come to the conclusion that she died in consequence of injuries from the gun which he was carrying, you are put by the law of this country into this position: The killing of a human being is homicide, however he may be killed, and all homicide is presumed to be malicious and murder, unless the contrary appears from circumstances of alleviation, excuse, or justification. "In every charge of murder, the fact of killing being first proved, all the circumstances of accident, necessity, or infirmity are to be satisfactorily proved by the prisoner, unless they arise out of the evidence produced against him: for the law will presume the fact to have been founded in malice until the contrary appeareth." That has been the law of this country for all time since we had law. Once it is shown to a jury that somebody has died through the act of another, that is presumed to be murder, unless the person who has been guilty of the act which causes the death can satisfy a jury that what happened was something less, something which might be alleviated, something which might be reduced to a charge of manslaughter, or was something which was accidental, or was something which could be justified.

At the end of his summing-up he added:

> The Crown has got to satisfy you that this woman, Violet Woolmington, died at the prisoner's hands. They must satisfy you of that beyond any reasonable doubt. If they satisfy you of that, then he has to show that there are circumstances to be found in the evidence which has been given from the witness-box in this case which alleviate the crime so that it is

only manslaughter or which excuse the homicide altogether by showing that it was a pure accident.

In the argument before the Court of Criminal Appeal cases were cited by the learned counsel on either side and textbooks of authority were referred to, but the learned judges contented themselves with saying "there can be no question to start with that the learned judge laid down the law applicable to a case of murder in the way in which it is to be found in the old authorities." They repeated the learned judge's words and said: "No doubt there is ample authority for that statement of the law." They then relied, as I have already mentioned, upon the proviso to s. 4 of the *Criminal Appeal Act, 1907*, and dismissed the appeal.

It is true as stated by the Court of Appeal that there is apparent authority for the law as laid down by the learned judge. But your Lordships' House has had the advantage of a prolonged and exhaustive inquiry dealing with the matter in debate from the earliest times, an advantage which was not shared by either of the courts below. Indeed your Lordships were referred to legal propositions dating as far back as the reign of King Canute (994-1035). But I do not think it is necessary for the purpose of this opinion to go as far back as that. Rather would I invite your Lordships to begin by considering the proposition of law which is contained in Foster's Crown Law, written in 1762, and which appears to be the foundation for the law as laid down by the learned judge in this case. It must be remembered that Sir Michael Foster, although a distinguished judge, is for this purpose to be regarded as a textbook writer, for he did not lay down the doctrine in any case before him, but in an article which is described as the "Introduction to the Discourse of Homicide." In the folio edition, published at Oxford at the Clarendon Press in 1762, at p. 255, he states:

> In every charge of murder, the fact of killing being first proved, all the circumstances of accident, necessity, or infirmity, are to be satisfactorily proved by the prisoner, unless they arise out of the evidence produced against him; for the law presumeth the fact to have been founded in malice, until the contrary appeareth. And very right it is, that the law should so presume. The defendant in this instance standeth upon just the same foot that every other defendant doth: the matters tending to justify, excuse, or alleviate, must appear in evidence before he can avail himself of them.

Now the first part of this passage appears in nearly every textbook or abridgment which has been since written. To come down to modern times, the passage appears in Stephen's Digest of the Criminal Law; also in the well-known treatise of Archbold, Criminal Pleading, Evidence and Practice, which is the companion of lawyers who practise in the criminal courts. It also appears most textually in Russell on Crimes and in the second edition of Halsbury's Laws of England, which purports to state the law as on May 1, 1933, where it is said:

> When it has been proved that one person's death has been caused by another, there is a *prima facie* presumption of law that the act of the person causing the death is murder, unless the

contrary appears from the evidence either for the prosecution or for the defence. The onus is upon such person when accused to show that his act did not amount to murder.

The authority for that proposition is given as Foster, pp. 255, 290, and also the case of *Rex v. Greenacre*.

The question arises, Is that statement correct law? Is it correct to say, and does Sir Michael Foster mean to lay down, that there may arise in the course of a criminal trial a situation at which it is incumbent upon the accused to prove his innocence? To begin with, if that is what Sir Michael Foster meant, there is no previous authority for his proposition, and I am confirmed in this opinion by the fact that in all the textbooks no earlier authority is cited for it. Before, however, one considers the earlier criminal law several facts have to be remembered.

First, it was not till 1907 that the Court of Criminal Appeal was set up. It is perfectly true that from time to time there have been famous occasions on which the Judges and Barons were called together to give their opinion upon the law bearing on murder. Examples of this will be found; in the year 1611, in the case of *Mackalley*, all the Judges and Barons were moved to give their opinion; in 1706, in the case of *Reg. v. Mawgridge*, which case was argued before all the judges and all of them except Lord Chief Justice Trevor were of opinion that Mawgridge was guilty of murder; and in 1843 in the case of *Reg. v. M'Naghten*, where all the Judges gave answers to your Lordships' House upon the test of insanity.

M'Naghten's case stands by itself. It is the famous pronouncement on the law bearing on the question of insanity in cases of murder. It is quite exceptional and has nothing to do with the present circumstances. In *M'Naghten's* case the onus is definitely and exceptionally placed upon the accused to establish such a defence. See *Rex v. Oliver Smith*, where it is stated that the only general rule that can be laid down as to the evidence in such a case is that insanity, if relied upon as a defence, must be established by the defendant. But it was added that all the judges had met and resolved that it was not proper for the Crown to call evidence of insanity, but that any evidence in the possession of the Crown should be placed at the disposal of the prisoner's counsel to be used by him if he thought fit. See also Archbold, 29th Edition. It is not necessary to refer to *M'Naghten's* case again in this judgment, for it has nothing to do with it.

It is true that at a later period certain cases were reserved by the judges for the consideration of the Court of Crown Cases Reserved, but many of the propositions with regard to criminal law are contained either in the summing-up of the judges or in text-books of authority as distinguished from a court sitting in banc.

The learned author of Stephen's Digest of the Criminal Law has an interesting note on the definition of murder and manslaughter. But his remarks are rather directed to the ingredients of the crime than to the proof of it. None the less, the author does not hesitate to tread a path of very robust criticism of the previous authorities. He speaks of the "intricacy, confusion and uncertainty of this branch of the law." He refers to the definition of Coke (1552-1623) and says "these passages, overloaded as Coke's manner is, with a quantity of loose, rambling gossip, form the essence of his account of murder." He describes Coke's chapter on manslaughter as "bewildering" and adds that Hale (1609-1676) treats manslaughter in a manner so meagre and yet so confused that no opinion of it can be obtained except by reading through chapters 38 to 40 and trying to make sense of them, and concludes by saying (p. 466) that Sir Michael Foster "to some extent mitigates the barbarous rule laid down by Coke as to unintentional personal violence."

Next it must be remembered that prisoners were not entitled to be represented by counsel, except in cases of felony, where counsel might argue the law on their behalf.

Thirdly, it must not be forgotten that the prisoner himself was not allowed to give evidence before the Act passed in 1898.

Bearing these considerations in mind, I now turn to some of the cases cited to us.

. . . .

The case of *Rex v. Greenacre* was certainly heard by a very distinguished Judge, Tindal, C.J. But it is to be observed that the dictum relied upon by the prosecution in this case — namely:

> that where it appears that one person's death has been occasioned by the hand of another, it behoves that other to show from evidence, or by inference from the circumstances of the case, that the offence is of a mitigated character, and does not amount to the crime of murder,

was contained in the summing-up of the learned judge to the jury. It is the passage in Sir Michael Foster and this summing-up which are usually relied on as the authority for the proposition that at some particular time of a criminal case the burden of proof lies on the prisoner to prove his innocence. The presumption of innocence in a criminal case is strong: see Taylor On Evidence, and it is doubtful whether either of these passages means any such thing. Rather do I think they simply refer to stages in the trial of a case. All that is meant is that if it is proved that the conscious act of the prisoner killed a man and nothing else appears in the case, there is evidence upon which the jury may, not must, find him guilty of murder. It is difficult to conceive so bare and meagre a case, but that does not mean that the onus is not still on the prosecution.

If at any period of a trial it was permissible for the judge to rule that the prosecution had established its case and that the onus was shifted on the prisoner to prove that he was not guilty, and that unless he discharged that onus the prosecution was entitled to succeed, it would be enabling the judge in such a case to say that the jury must in law find the prisoner guilty and so make the judge decide the case and not the jury, which is not the common law. It would be an entirely different case from those exceptional instances of special verdicts where a judge asks the jury to find certain facts and directs them that on such facts the prosecution is entitled to succeed. Indeed, a consideration of such special verdicts shows that it is not till the end of the evidence that a verdict can properly be found and that at the end of the evidence it is not for the prisoner to establish his innocence, but for the prosecution to establish his guilt. Just as there is evidence on behalf of the prosecution so there may be evidence on behalf of the prisoner which may cause a doubt as to his guilt. In either case, he is entitled to the benefit of the doubt. But while the prosecution must prove the guilt of the prisoner, there is no such burden laid on the prisoner to prove his innocence and it is sufficient for him to raise a doubt as to his guilt; he is not bound to satisfy the jury of his innocence.

This is the real result of the perplexing case of *Rex v. Abramovitch*, which lays down the same proposition, although perhaps in somewhat involved language. Juries are always told that, if conviction there is to be, the prosecution must prove the case beyond reasonable doubt. This statement cannot mean that in order to be acquitted the prisoner must "satisfy" the jury. This is the law as laid down in the Court of Criminal Appeal in *Rex v. Davies*, the headnote of which correctly states that where intent is an ingredient of a crime there is no onus on the defendant to prove that the act alleged was accidental. Throughout the web of the English Criminal Law one golden thread is always to be seen, that it is the duty of the prosecution to prove the prisoner's guilt subject to what I have already said as to the defence of insanity and subject also to any statutory exception. If, at the end of and on the whole of the case, there is a reasonable doubt, created by the evidence given by either the prosecution or the prisoner, as to whether the prisoner killed the deceased with a malicious intention, the prosecution has not made out the case and the prisoner is entitled to an acquittal. No matter what the charge or where the trial, the principle that the prosecution must prove the guilt of the prisoner is part of the common law of England and no attempt to whittle it down can be entertained. When dealing with a murder case the Crown must prove (*a*) death as the result of a voluntary act of the accused and (*b*) malice of the accused. It may prove malice either expressly or by implication. For malice may be implied where death occurs as the result of a voluntary act of the accused which is (i.) intentional and (ii.) unprovoked. When evidence of death and malice has been given (this is a question for the jury) the accused is entitled to show, by evidence or by examination of the circumstances adduced by the Crown that the act on his part which caused death was either unintentional or provoked. If the jury are either satisfied with his explanation or, upon a review of all the evidence, are left in reasonable doubt whether, even if his explanation be not accepted, the act was unintentional or provoked, the prisoner is entitled to be acquitted. It is not the law of England to say, as was said in the summing-up in the present case:

> if the Crown satisfy you that this woman died at the prisoner's hands then he has to show that there are circumstances to be found in the evidence which has been given from the witness-box in this case which alleviate the crime so that it is only manslaughter or which excuse the homicide altogether by showing it was a pure accident.

If the proposition laid down by Sir Michael Foster or in the summing-up in *Rex v. Greenacre* means this, those authorities are wrong.

We were then asked to follow the Court of Criminal Appeal and to apply the proviso of s. 4 of the *Criminal Appeal Act, 1907*, which says:

> the court may, notwithstanding that they are of opinion that the point raised in the appeal might be decided in favour of the appellant, dismiss the appeal if they consider that no substantial miscarriage of justice has actually occurred.

There is no doubt that there is ample jurisdiction to apply that proviso in a case of murder. The Act makes no distinction between a capital case and any other case, but we think it impossible to apply it in the present case. We cannot say that if the jury had been properly directed they would have inevitably come to the same conclusion.

In the result we decline to apply the proviso and, as already stated, we order that the appeal should be allowed and the conviction quashed.

While the prosecution must satisfy the trier of all ingredients of the offence, and thus negative all possible defences, a defence is not properly in the case unless there is evidence capable of supporting it.

Why do we presume innocence in criminal law?

C.K. ALLEN, LEGAL DUTIES AND OTHER ESSAYS IN JURISPRUDENCE

(1931), 286-288

Again, "it is better that ten guilty persons should be acquitted than that one innocent person should be convicted". As Stephen dryly observes, it all depends on what the guilty persons have been doing. It also depends on the general social conditions in which they have been doing it. I have already called attention to the vague fluctuations in the proverbial ratio between the guilty and the innocent; and I have done so in no spirit of levity, for the ratio which it assumes is not without significance. I dare say some sentimentalists would assent to the proposition that it is better that a thousand, or even a million, guilty persons should escape than that one innocent person should suffer; but no sensible and practical person would accept such a view. For it is obvious that if our ratio is extended indefinitely, there comes a point when the whole system of justice has broken down and society is in a state of chaos. In short, it is only when there is a reasonable and uniform probability of guilty persons being detected and convicted that we can allow humane doubt to prevail over security. But we must never forget that ideally the acquittal of ten guilty persons is exactly ten times as great a failure of *justice* as the conviction of one innocent person.

What is a reasonable doubt? Can we define it? Is this standard of proof different from that of proof on a balance of probabilities in civil cases?

(ii) Reasonable doubt

R. v. LIFCHUS

[1997] 3 S.C.R. 320, 9 C.R. (5th) 1, 118 C.C.C. (3d) 1,
1997 CarswellMan 392, 1997 CarswellMan 393

The accused was charged with fraud. The trial judge told the jury in her charge on the burden of proof that she used the words "'proof beyond a reasonable doubt' . . . in their ordinary, natural every day sense", and that the words "doubt" and "reasonable" are "ordinary, every day words that . . . you understand". The accused was convicted of fraud. On appeal, he contended that the trial judge had erred in instructing the jury on the meaning of the expression "proof beyond a reasonable doubt". The Court of Appeal allowed the appeal and ordered a new trial. The Supreme Court dismissed the Crown's appeal.

CORY J. (LAMER C.J., SOPINKA, MCLACHLIN, IACOBUCCI and MAJOR JJ. concurring): —

. . . .

The phrase "beyond a reasonable doubt", is composed of words which are commonly used in everyday speech. Yet, these words have a specific meaning in the legal context. This special meaning of the words "reasonable doubt" may not correspond precisely to the meaning ordinarily attributed to them. In criminal proceedings, where the liberty of the subject is at stake, it is of fundamental importance that jurors fully understand the nature of the burden of proof that the law requires them to apply. An explanation of the meaning of proof beyond a reasonable doubt is an essential element of the instructions that must be given to a jury. That a definition is necessary can be readily deduced from the frequency with which juries ask for guidance with regard to its meaning. It is therefore essential that the trial judge provide the jury with an explanation of the expression.

. . . .

Perhaps a brief summary of what the definition should and should not contain may be helpful. It should be explained that:

- the standard of proof beyond a reasonable doubt is inextricably intertwined with that principle fundamental to all criminal trials, the presumption of innocence;
- the burden of proof rests on the prosecution throughout the trial and never shifts to the accused;
- a reasonable doubt is not a doubt based upon sympathy or prejudice;
- rather, it is based upon reason and common sense;
- it is logically connected to the evidence or absence of evidence;[1]
- it does not involve proof to an absolute certainty; it is not proof beyond *any* doubt nor is it an imaginary or frivolous doubt; and
- more is required than proof that the accused is probably guilty — a jury which concludes only that the accused is probably guilty must acquit.

On the other hand, certain references to the required standard of proof should be avoided. For example:

- describing the term "reasonable doubt" as an ordinary expression which has no special meaning in the criminal law context;
- inviting jurors to apply to the task before them the same standard of proof that they apply to important, or even the most important, decisions in their own lives;
- equating proof "beyond a reasonable doubt" to proof "to a moral certainty";
- qualifying the word "doubt" with adjectives other than "reasonable", such as "serious", "substantial" or "haunting", which may mislead the jury; and
- instructing jurors that they may convict if they are "sure" that the accused is guilty, before providing them with a proper definition as to the meaning of the words "beyond a reasonable doubt".

A charge which is consistent with the principles set out in these reasons will suffice regardless of the particular words used by the trial judge. Nevertheless, it may . . . be useful to set out a "model charge" which could provide the necessary instructions as to the meaning of the phrase beyond a reasonable doubt.

---

1 The court observed elsewhere in the decision that "certain doubts, although reasonable, are simply incapable of articulation. For instance, there may be something about a person's demeanor in the witness box which will lead a juror to conclude that the witness is not credible. It may be that the juror is unable to point to the precise aspect of the witness's demeanor which was found to be suspicious, and as a result cannot articulate either to himself or others exactly why the witness should not be believed. A juror should not be made to feel that the overall, perhaps intangible, effect of a witness's demeanor cannot be taken into consideration is the assessment of credibility." (para 29)

Suggested Charge

Instructions pertaining to the requisite standard of proof in a criminal trial of proof beyond a reasonable doubt might be given along these lines:

The accused enters these proceedings presumed to be innocent. That presumption of innocence remains throughout the case until such time as the Crown has on the evidence put before you satisfied you beyond a reasonable doubt that the accused is guilty.

What does the expression "beyond a reasonable doubt" mean?

The term "beyond a reasonable doubt" has been used for a very long time and is a part of our history and traditions of justice. It is so engrained in our criminal law that some think it needs no explanation, yet something must be said regarding its meaning.

A reasonable doubt is not an imaginary or frivolous doubt. It must not be based upon sympathy or prejudice. Rather, it is based on reason and common sense. It is logically derived from the evidence or absence of evidence.

Even if you believe the accused is probably guilty or likely guilty, that is not sufficient. In those circumstances you must give the benefit of the doubt to the accused and acquit because the Crown has failed to satisfy you of the guilt of the accused beyond a reasonable doubt.

On the other hand you must remember that it is virtually impossible to prove anything to an absolute certainty and the Crown is not required to do so. Such a standard of proof is impossibly high.

In short if, based upon the evidence before the court, you are sure that the accused committed the offence you should convict since this demonstrates that you are satisfied of his guilt beyond a reasonable doubt.

This is not a magic incantation that needs to be repeated word for word. It is nothing more than a suggested form that would not be faulted if it were used

. . . .

Further, it is possible that an error in the instructions as to the standard of proof may not constitute a reversible error. It was observed in *R. v. W. (D.)*, [1991] 1 S.C.R. 742, at p. 758, that the verdict ought not be disturbed "if the charge, when read as a whole, makes it clear that the jury could not have been under any misapprehension as to the correct burden and standard of proof to apply". On the other hand, if the charge as a whole gives rise to the reasonable likelihood that the jury misapprehended the standard of proof, then as a general rule the verdict will have to be set aside and a new trial directed.

R. v. STARR

[2000] 2 S.C.R. 144, 36 C.R. (5th) 1, 147 C.C.C. (3d) 449, 2000 CarswellMan 449, 2000 CarswellMan 450

The accused had been convicted of two counts of first degree murder. The majority of the court decided that the reasonable doubt instruction given in the case fell prey to many of the same difficulties outlined in *Lifchus*, and likely misled the jury as to the content of the criminal standard of proof. In allowing the accused's appeal they gave further advice.

IACOBUCCI J. (MAJOR, BINNIE, ARBOUR and LEBEL JJ. concurring): —

. . . .

In the present case, the trial judge did refer to the Crown's onus and to the presumption of innocence, and he stated that the appellant should receive the benefit of any reasonable doubt. The error in the charge is that the jury was not told *how a reasonable doubt is to be defined.* As was emphasized repeatedly in *Lifchus* and again in *Bisson,* a jury *must* be instructed that the standard of proof in a criminal trial is higher than the probability standard used in making everyday decisions and in civil trials. Indeed, it is this very requirement to go beyond probability that meshes the standard of proof in criminal cases with the presumption of innocence and the Crown's onus. However, as Cory J. explained in these earlier decisions, it is generally inappropriate to define the meaning of the term "reasonable doubt" through examples from daily life, through the use of synonyms, or through analogy to moral choices. The criminal standard of proof has a special significance unique to the legal process. It is an exacting standard of proof rarely encountered in everyday life, and there is no universally intelligible illustration of the concept, such as the scales of justice with respect to the balance of probabilities standard. Unlike absolute certainty or the balance of probabilities, reasonable doubt is not an easily quantifiable standard. It cannot be measured or described by analogy. It must be explained. However, precisely because it is not quantifiable, it is difficult to explain.

In my view, an effective way to define the reasonable doubt standard for a jury is to explain that it falls much closer to absolute certainty than to proof on a balance of probabilities. As stated in *Lifchus,* a trial judge is required to explain that something less than absolute certainty is required, and that something more than probable guilt is required, in order for the jury to convict. Both of these alternative standards are fairly and easily comprehensible. It will be of great assistance for a jury if the trial judge situates the reasonable doubt standard appropriately between these two standards. The additional instructions to the jury set out in *Lifchus* as to the meaning and appropriate manner of determining the existence of a reasonable doubt serve to define the space between absolute certainty and proof beyond a reasonable doubt. In this regard, I am in agreement with Twaddle J.A. in the court below, when he said, at p. 177:

> If standards of proof were marked on a measure, proof "beyond reasonable doubt" would lie much closer to "absolute certainty" than to "a balance of probabilities". Just as a judge has a duty to instruct the jury that absolute certainty is not required, he or she has a duty, in my view, to instruct the jury that the criminal standard is more than a probability. The words he or she uses to convey this idea are of no significance, but the idea itself must be conveyed.

See further Patrick Healy, "Direction and Guidance on Reasonable Doubt in the Charge to the Jury" (2001), 6 Can. Crim. L.R. 161.

In 1991 the Supreme Court handed down a decision, *R. v. W. (D.)*, [1991] 1 S.C.R. 742, 63 C.C.C. (3d) 397, 3 C.R. (4th) 302 that was intended to give guidance to judges on how to explain to a jury the process of considering whether they were left with a reasonable doubt or not. Subsequently that court has recognised various criticisms of the *W. (D.)* approach and held that it should not be applied as a "magical incantation".

R. v. S. (J.H.)

2008 SCC 30, 2008 CarswellNS 270, 2008 CarswellNS 271, 57 C.R. (6th) 79, [2008] 2 S.C.R. 152, 231 C.C.C. (3d) 302

A stepfather was charged with sexual assault after the complainant alleged that he had sexually abused her over a number of years, starting when she was approximately four years old. She twice complained to her mother who did not believe her. When the complainant was 15 she went to the police. The accused denied all the allegations and suggested that they were falsely made after he threatened to send her to a Catholic school because of her uncontrollable behaviour. The issue at trial before judge and jury was whether the alleged events had ever happened. The complainant and the accused were the principal witnesses. The trial judge charged the jury on the credibility of the witnesses, instructing them they had to consider all the evidence and that the trial was not a choice between two competing versions of events. The defence raised no objection to the charge. The jury returned a verdict of guilty.

A majority of the Nova Scotia Court of Appeal set aside the conviction and ordered a new trial. The trial judge had insufficiently explained the principles of reasonable doubt as they applied to credibility. While the *W. (D.)* phrasing was not a magical incantation the charge had failed to express the second *W. (D.)* principle that disbelief in the accused's testimony does not amount to proof of his guilt beyond a reasonable doubt. The dissenting judge found that the charge was sufficient.

BINNIE J. (for seven justices): —

8 A series of decisions over at least the past 20 years has affirmed and reaffirmed the proposition that where credibility is a central issue in a jury trial, the judge must explain the relationship between the assessment of credibility and the Crown's ultimate burden to prove the guilt of the accused to the criminal standard. A general instruction on reasonable doubt without adverting to its relationship to the credibility (or lack of credibility) of the witnesses leaves open too great a possibility of confusion or misunderstanding. The so-called *W. (D.)* instruction has long roots: *R. v. Challice* (1979), 45 C.C.C. (2d) 546 (Ont. C.A.), at p. 556; *R. v. Chan* (1989), 52 C.C.C. (3d) 184, (Alta. C.A.), at p. 186; *R. v. Morin*, [1988] 2 S.C.R. 345, at p. 362; *R. v. H. (C.W.)* (1991), 68 C.C.C. (3d) 146 (B.C.C.A.), at p. 155; *R. v. MacKenzie*, [1993] 1 S.C.R. 212, at pp. 219 and 239; *R. v. Levasseur*, [1994] 3 S.C.R. 518 (upholding Fish J.A.'s dissent reported at (1994), 89 C.C.C. (3d) 508 (Que. C.A.), at p. 534). *W. (D.)* has been cited by Canadian courts at all levels in no fewer than 3,743 subsequent reported cases. It has proven to be a fertile source of appellate review. For a recent application, see *R. v. C.L.Y.*, [2008] 1 S.C.R. 5, 2008 SCC 2.

9 The passage from *W. (D.)* at issue in this case, as in so many others, is found at pp. 757-58, where Cory J. explained:

> Ideally, appropriate instructions on the issue of credibility should be given, not only during the main charge, but on any recharge. A trial judge might well instruct the jury on the question of credibility along these lines:
>
>> First, if you believe the evidence of the accused, obviously you must acquit.
>> Second, if you do not believe the testimony of the accused but you are left in reasonable doubt by it, you must acquit.
>> Third, even if you are not left in doubt by the evidence of the accused, you must ask yourself whether, on the basis of the evidence which you do accept, you are convinced beyond a reasonable doubt by that evidence of the guilt of the accused.
>
> If that formula were followed, the oft repeated error which appears in the recharge in this case would be avoided. The requirement that the Crown prove the guilt of the accused beyond a reasonable doubt is fundamental in our system of criminal law. Every effort should be made to avoid mistakes in charging the jury on this basic principle.
> Nonetheless, the failure to use such language is not fatal if the charge, when read as a whole, makes it clear that the jury could not have been under any misapprehension as to the correct burden and standard of proof to apply...

Essentially, *W. (D.)* simply unpacks for the benefit of the lay jury what reasonable doubt means in the context of evaluating conflicting testimonial accounts. It alerts the jury to the "credibility contest" error. It teaches that trial judges are required to impress on the jury that the burden never shifts from the Crown to prove every element of the offence beyond a reasonable doubt.

10 The precise formulation of the *W. (D.)* questions has been criticized. As to the first question, the jury may believe inculpatory elements of the statements of an accused but reject the exculpatory explanation. In *R. v. Latimer*, [2001] 1 S.C.R. 3, 2001 SCC 1, the accused did not testify, but his description of the killing of his daughter was put into evidence by way of statements to the police. His description of the event itself was obviously believed. The exculpatory explanation did not amount to a defence at law. He was convicted. The principle that a jury may believe some, none, or all of the testimony of any witness, including that of an accused, suggests to some critics that the first *W. (D.)* question is something of an oversimplification.

11 As to the second question, some jurors may wonder how, if they believe none of the evidence of the accused, such rejected evidence may nevertheless of itself raise a reasonable doubt. Of course, some elements of the evidence of an accused may raise a reasonable doubt, even though the bulk of it is rejected. Equally, the jury may simply conclude that they do not know whether to believe the accused's testimony or not. In either circumstance the accused is entitled to an acquittal.

12 The third question, again, is taken by some critics as failing to contemplate a jury's acceptance of inculpatory bits of the evidence of an accused but not the exculpatory elements. In light of these possible sources of difficulty, Wood J.A. in *H. (C.W.)* suggested an additional instruction:

> I would add one more instruction in such cases, which logically ought to be second in the order, namely: "If, after a careful consideration of all the evidence, you are unable to decide whom to believe, you must acquit". [p. 155]

13 In short the *W. (D.)* questions should not have attributed to them a level of sanctity or immutable perfection that their author never claimed for them. *W.(D.)*'s message that it must be made crystal clear to the jury that the burden never shifts from the Crown to prove every element of the offence beyond a reasonable doubt is of fundamental importance but its application should not result in a triumph of form over substance. In *R. v. S. (W.D.)*, [1994] 3 S.C.R. 521, Cory J. reiterated that the *W. (D.)* instructions need not be given "word for word as some magic incantation" (p. 533). In *R. v. Avetysan*, [2000] 2 S.C.R. 745, 2000 SCC 56, Major J. for the majority pointed out that in any case where credibility is important "[t]he question is really whether, in substance, the trial judge's instructions left the jury with the impression that it had to choose between the two versions of events" (para. 19). The main point is that lack of credibility on the part of the accused does not equate to proof of his or her guilt beyond a reasonable doubt.

14 In the present case Oland J.A. agreed that the trial judge did not "call upon the jury to simply decide which of the complainant or [the accused] it believed" (para. 19). Nevertheless, in her view:

> The charge only instructed that probable guilt was not enough to meet the standard of proof beyond a reasonable doubt, that the appellant was to be given the benefit of the doubt, and they did not have to accept or reject all of the testimony of any witness including his, and that they were to consider all of the evidence. Nowhere did it provide any guidance as to how, in the event they were uncertain or unable to resolve the issue of credibility, they were to proceed with their deliberations. *The charge failed to direct that if the jury did not believe the testimony of the accused but were left in a reasonable doubt by that evidence, they must acquit.* [Emphasis added; para. 20.]

In my view, with respect, the reasoning of the majority brushes uncomfortably close to the "magic incantation" error. At the end of the day, reading the charge as a whole, I believe the instruction to this jury satisfied the ultimate test formulated by Cory J. in *W. (D.)* as being whether "the jury could not have been under any misapprehension as to the correct burden and standard of proof to apply" (p. 758).

15 Here the trial judge explained that any reasonable doubt must be resolved in favour of the accused. She also explained that even if they did not accept all of the accused's testimony, they could still accept some of it. She also explained to the jury that they should not see their task as that of deciding between two versions of events. She told them that they could not decide the case simply by choosing between the evidence of the complainant and that of the accused. She reminded them, in that context, that they must consider all of the evidence when determining reasonable doubt. She stated:

> You do not decide whether something happened simply by comparing one version of events with another, or choosing one of them. You have to consider all the evidence and decide whether you have been satisfied beyond a reasonable doubt that the events that form the basis of the crime charged, in fact, took place. [A.R., at p. 54.]
>
> ...
>
> Again, you do not decide whether something happened simply by comparing one version of events with the other, or by choosing one of them. You have to consider all of the evidence and decide whether you have been satisfied beyond a reasonable doubt that the events that form the basis of the crimes charges, in fact, took place. [A.R., at p. 55.]

16 In my view, the trial judge got across the point of the second *W. (D.)* question without leaving any realistic possibility of misunderstanding. As stated, she told the jury:

> It is for the Crown counsel to prove beyond a reasonable doubt that the events alleged in fact occurred. It is not for [the accused] to prove that these events never happened. If you have a reasonable doubt whether the events alleged ever took place, you *must* find him not guilty. [Emphasis added; A.R., at p. 54.]

17 There was much discussion at the hearing about defence counsel's failure to object. In my view, he correctly ascertained that the jury had been adequately instructed on the relationship between the assessment of credibility and the ultimate determination of guilt beyond a reasonable doubt. Before the recharge was given he told the trial judge he would "feel more comfortable if simply the wording that was read previously was re-read to the jury again" (A.R., at p. 77). He discharged his duty to the respondent.

Appeal allowed; conviction restored.

Should the Supreme Court have expressly and clearly abandoned the *W. (D.)* **approach?** It has been responsible for many, many prolix appeals and orders of new trials. The main problem is that the second question is potentially confusing and/or too generous to accused. See especially the late Jack Gibson, "*R. v. W.D.* Revisited: Is Step Two a Misdirection?" (2003) 11 C.R. (6th) 323. Justice Binnie might have mentioned the remark of McLachlin J. dissenting in *R. v. S. (W.D.)*, [1994] 3 S.C.R. 521, 93 C.C.C. (3d) 1, 34 C.R. (4th) 1:

> Certainly if the jury rejected (as opposed to being merely undecided about) all of the evidence of the accused, it is difficult to see how that very evidence, having been rejected, could raise a reasonable doubt.

Trial judges are at least now free to reject the complexity of *W. (D.)* as long as they make sure that the jury is warned of the Crown's burden of proof, that it is not just a choice between competing versions and that they may believe some, none or all of any witness, including the accused. These principles, of course, apply equally to judge alone trials.

R. v. MULLINS-JOHNSON

(2007), 50 C.R. (6th) 265, 228 C.C.C. (3d) 505, 2007 CarswellOnt 6660
(C.A.)

In 1993 parents found their four year old daughter lying dead on her bed. Her uncle, the accused, who had babysat her the night before, was arrested and charged with first degree murder. He was convicted. He had protested his innocence from the very outset but his appeals to the Ontario Court of Appeal and Supreme Court were rejected. He spent twelve years in jail from the time of his arrest until he was released in 2005 on bail. The Minister of Justice referred the matter to the Court of Appeal under s. 696.3(3)(a)(ii) of the *Criminal Code*, R.S.C. 1985, c. C-46, to determine the case as if it were an appeal on the issue of fresh evidence. The court heard a number of experts who re-examined the earlier evidence that had led to conviction.

The Ontario Court of Appeal allowed the appeal, quashed the murder conviction and acquitted.

PER O'CONNOR A.C.J.O. (Rosenberg and Sharpe JJ.A concurring):—

...There is no doubt that the new expert opinions in this case are credible and highly cogent. They go to the very core of whether there was an offence committed in this case. The opinions have been provided by some of the leading Canadian and international experts in forensic pathology and pathology. The opinions not only have a profound impact on the reliability of the jury verdict reached at trial, it is submitted that they are dispositive of the result.

Finally, in their excellent factums the parties have fully reviewed for us the entire body of evidence aside from the expert evidence. In short, without the expert evidence there is no case against the appellant and no evidence of a crime. The non-expert evidence, if anything, is inconsistent with guilt and, again, is not indicative of a crime. Now that the trial expert evidence has been completely discredited, there is no case against the appellant and he is clearly entitled to an acquittal.

THE DECLARATION OF INNOCENCE

The fresh evidence shows that the appellant's conviction was the result of a rush to judgment based on flawed scientific opinion. With the entering of an acquittal, the appellant's legal innocence has been re-established. The fresh evidence is compelling in demonstrating that no crime was committed against Valin Johnson and that the appellant did not commit any crime. For that reason an acquittal is the proper result.

There are not in Canadian law two kinds of acquittals: those based on the Crown having failed to prove its case beyond a reasonable doubt and those where the accused has been shown to be factually innocent. We adopt the comments of the former Chief Justice of Canada in The Lamer Commission of Inquiry Pertaining to the Cases of: Ronald Dalton, Gregory Parsons, Randy Druken, Annex 3, pp. 342:

> [A] criminal trial does not address "factual innocence". The criminal trial is to determine whether the Crown has proven its case beyond a reasonable doubt. If so, the accused is guilty. If not, the accused is found not guilty. There is no finding of factual innocence since it would not fall within the ambit or purpose of criminal law.

Just as the criminal trial is not a vehicle for declarations of factual innocence, so an appeal court, which obtains its jurisdiction from statute, has no jurisdiction to make a formal legal declaration of factual innocence. The fact that we are hearing this case as a Reference under s. 696.3(3)(a)(ii) of the *Criminal Code* does not expand that jurisdiction. The terms of the Reference to this court are clear: we are hearing this case "as if it were an appeal". While we are entitled to express our reasons for the result in clear and strong terms, as we have done, we cannot make a formal legal declaration of the appellant's factual innocence.

In addition to the jurisdictional issue, there are important policy reasons for not, in effect, recognizing a third verdict, other than "guilty" or "not guilty", of "factually innocent". The most compelling, and, in our view, conclusive reason is the impact it would have on other persons found not guilty by criminal courts. As Professor Kent Roach observed in a report he prepared for the Commission of Inquiry into Certain Aspects of the Trial and Conviction of James Driskell, "there is a genuine concern that determinations and declarations of wrongful convictions could degrade the meaning of the not guilty verdict" (p. 39). To recognize a third verdict in the criminal trial process would, in effect, create two classes of people: those found to be factually innocent and those who benefited from the presumption of innocence and the high standard of proof beyond a reasonable doubt.

Nothing we have said in these reasons should be taken as somehow qualifying the impact of the fresh evidence. That evidence, together with the other evidence, shows beyond question that the appellant's conviction was wrong and that he was the subject of a terrible miscarriage of justice. We conclude these reasons by paraphrasing what the president of the panel said to Mr. Mullins-Johnson at the conclusion of the oral argument after entering the verdict of acquittal: it is profoundly regrettable that as a result of what has been shown to be flawed pathological evidence Mr. Mullins-Johnson was wrongly convicted and has spent such a very long time in jail.

(iii) Section 11(d) of the Charter

With the advent of the *Canadian Charter of Rights and Freedoms*, the presumption of innocence has taken on a constitutional dimension. The *Charter* provides in s. 11:

11. Any person charged with an offence has the right

. . . .

(d) to be presumed innocent until proven guilty according to law in a fair and public hearing by an independent and impartial tribunal.

There is an important distinction between persuasive burdens of proof and evidentiary burdens:

Persuasive burdens of proof (sometimes called legal or ultimate burdens) have three main features. They apply at the end of a case, never shift in the sense it is known from the start who bears the burden, and the trier of fact must find against the burdenholder in a borderline case. Normally the burden is on the Crown to prove to a standard of beyond a reasonable doubt. Sometimes the persuasive burden of an issue is placed by Parliament or the courts on the accused to prove on a balance of probabilities. This is called a reverse onus.

There is considerable confusion amongst writers and judges as to the meaning of "evidentiary burdens". This term usually refers to the burden of pointing to evidence to put a legal issue into play (*R. v. Schwartz*, [1988] 2 S.C.R. 443, 45 C.C.C. (3d) 97, 66 C.R. (3d) 251, at 466 [S.C.R.] per Dickson C.J.).

Sometimes this is referred to as giving a matter an "air of reality" (an issue we will return to when we discuss defences), providing an evidentiary foundation or a tactical burden. It can be discharged through cross-examination of opposing witnesses or by calling witnesses. It can shift during the ebb and flow of a trial. Used in this sense it has nothing to do with the burden of proof. However, the term "evidentiary burden" is also sometimes used to describe a reverse onus which merely calls upon the accused to provide some evidence to doubt the fact or conclusion in question (see the discussion in "Doubt Mountain and the Presumption of Innocence", p. 89).

Oakes concerned the constitutionality of a persuasive burden on the accused:

R. v. OAKES

[1986] 1 S.C.R. 103, 50 C.R. (3d) 1, 24 C.C.C.(3d) 321,
1986 CarswellOnt 95, 1986 CarswellOnt 1001

DICKSON C.J.C. (CHOUINARD, LAMER, WILSON and LE DAIN JJ. concurring): —

This appeal concerns the constitutionality of s. 8 of the *Narcotic Control Act*, R.S.C. 1970, c. N-1. The section provides, in brief, that if the court finds the accused in possession of a narcotic, he is presumed to be in possession for the purpose of trafficking. Unless the accused can establish the contrary, he must be convicted of trafficking. The Ontario Court of Appeal held that this provision constitutes a "reverse onus" clause and is unconstitutional because it violates one of the core values of our criminal justice system, the presumption of innocence, now entrenched in s. 11 (*d*) of the *Canadian Charter of Rights and Freedoms*. The Crown has appealed.

. . . .

The respondent, David Edwin Oakes, was charged with unlawful possession of a narcotic for the purpose of trafficking, contrary to s. 4(2) of the *Narcotic Control Act*. He elected trial by magistrate without a jury. At trial, the Crown adduced evidence to establish that Mr. Oakes was found in possession of eight one gram vials of *cannabis* resin in the form of hashish oil. Upon a further search conducted at the police station, $619.45 was located. Mr. Oakes told the police that he had bought ten vials of hashish oil for $150 for his own use, and that the $619.45 was from a workers' compensation cheque. He elected not to call evidence as to possession of the narcotic. Pursuant to the procedural provisions of s. 8 of the *Narcotic Control Act*, the trial judge proceeded to make a finding that it was beyond a reasonable doubt that Mr. Oakes was in possession of the narcotic.

Following this finding, Mr. Oakes brought a motion to challenge the constitutional validity of s. 8 of the *Narcotic Control Act*, which he maintained imposes a burden on an accused to prove that he or she was not in possession for the purpose of trafficking. He argued that s. 8 violates the presumption of innocence contained in s. 11(*d*) of the *Charter*.

[The trial judge found s. 8 to be inoperative as in conflict with s. 11(*d*). He afforded the Crown an opportunity to adduce further evidence and the Crown declined. The trial judge acquitted on the offence charged and found the accused guilty of possession only.]

. . . .

To interpret the meaning of s. 11(*d*), it is important to adopt a purposive approach. As this court stated in *R. v. Big M Drug Mart Ltd.*, [1985] 1 S.C.R. 295 at p. 344:

> The meaning of a right or freedom guaranteed by the *Charter* was to be ascertained by an analysis of the *purpose* of such a guarantee; it was to be understood, in other words, in the light of the interests it was meant to protect.
>
> In my view this analysis is to be undertaken, and the purpose of the right or freedom in question is to be sought by reference to the character and the larger objects of the *Charter* itself, to the language chosen to articulate the specific right or freedom, to the historical origins of the concepts enshrined, and where applicable to the meaning and purpose of the other specific rights and freedoms.

To identify the underlying purpose of the *Charter* right in question, therefore, it is important to begin by understanding the cardinal values it embodies.

The presumption of innocence is a hallowed principle lying at the very heart of criminal law. Although protected expressly in s. 11(*d*) of the *Charter*, the presumption of innocence is referable and integral to the general protection of life, liberty and security of the person contained in s. 7 of the *Charter* (see *Reference re s. 94(2) of the Motor Vehicle Act*, December 17, 1985, unreported, per Lamer J.). The presumption of innocence protects the fundamental liberty and human dignity of any and every person accused by the State of criminal conduct. An individual charged with a criminal offence faces grave social and personal consequences, including potential loss of physical liberty, subjection to social stigma and ostracism from the community, as well as other social, psychological and economic harms. In light of the gravity of these consequences, the presumption of innocence is crucial. It ensures that until the State proves an accused's guilt beyond all reasonable doubt, he or she is innocent. This is essential in a society committed to fairness and social justice. The presumption of innocence confirms our faith in humankind; it reflects our belief that individuals are decent and law-abiding members of the community until proven otherwise.

The presumption of innocence has enjoyed longstanding recognition at common law. In the leading case, *Woolmington v. Director of Public Prosecutions*, [1935] A.C. 462 (H.L.), Viscount Sankey wrote at pp. 481-482:

> Throughout the web of the English Criminal Law one golden thread is always to be seen, that it is the duty of the prosecution to prove the prisoner's guilt subject to what I have already said as to the defence of insanity and subject also to any statutory exception. If, at the end of and on the whole of the case, there is a reasonable doubt, created by the evidence given by either the prosecution or the prisoner, as to whether the prisoner killed the deceased with a malicious intention, the prosecution has not made out the case and the prisoner is entitled to an acquittal. No matter what the charge or where thc trial, the principle that the prosecution must prove the guilt of the prisoner is part of the common law of England and no attempt to whittle it down can be entertained.

Subsequent Canadian cases have cited the *Woolmington* principle with approval (see, for example, *Manchuk v. The King*, [1938] S.C.R. 341, at p. 349; *R. v. City of Sault Ste. Marie*, [1978] 2 S.C.R. 1299, at p. 1316).

Further evidence of the widespread acceptance of the principle of the presumption of innocence is its inclusion in the major international human rights documents. Article 11(1) of the *Universal Declaration of Human Rights*, adopted December 10, 1948 by the General Assembly of the United Nations, provides:

> Art. 11(1) Everyone charged with a penal offence has the right to be presumed innocent until proved guilty according to law in a public trial at which he has had all the guarantees necessary for his defence.

In the *International Covenant on Civil and Political Rights*, 1966, art. 14(2) states:

> Art. 14(2) Everyone charged with a criminal offence shall have the right to be presumed innocent until proved guilty according to law.

Canada acceded to this Covenant, and the Optional Protocol which sets up machinery for implementing the Covenant, on May 19, 1976. Both came into effect on August 19, 1976.

In light of the above, the right to be presumed innocent until proven guilty requires that s. 11(*d*) have, at a minimum, the following content. First, an individual must be proven guilty beyond a reasonable doubt. Second, it is the State which must bear the burden of proof. As Mr. Justice Lamer stated in *Dubois v. The Queen* (November 21, 1985, unreported) at p. 6:

> Section 11 (*d*) imposes upon the Crown the burden of proving the accused's guilt beyond reasonable doubt as well as that of making out the case against the accused before he or she need respond, either by testifying or calling other evidence.

Third, criminal prosecutions must be carried out in accordance with lawful procedures and fairness. The latter part of s. 11(*d*), which requires the proof of guilt "according to law in a fair and public hearing by an independent and impartial tribunal", underlines the importance of this procedural requirement.

. . . .

The *Woolmington* case was decided in the context of a legal system with no constitutionally entrenched human rights document. In Canada, we have tempered parliamentary supremacy by entrenching important rights and freedoms in the Constitution. Viscount Sankey's statutory exception proviso is clearly not applicable in this context and would subvert the very purpose of the entrenchment of the presumption of innocence in the *Charter*. . . . Section 8 of the *Narcotic Control Act* is not rendered constitutionally valid simply by virtue of the fact that it is a statutory provision.

. . . .

In general one must, I think, conclude that a provision which requires an accused to disprove on a balance of probabilities the existence of a presumed fact, which is an important element of the offence in question, violates the presumption of innocence in s. 11(*d*). If an accused bears the burden of disproving on a balance of probabilities an essential element of an offence, it would be possible for a conviction to occur despite the existence of a reasonable doubt. This would arise if the accused adduced sufficient evidence to raise a reasonable doubt as to his or her innocence but did not convince the jury on a balance of probabilities that the presumed fact was untrue.

The fact that the standard is only the civil one does not render a reverse onus clause constitutional. As Sir Rupert Cross commented in the *Rede Lectures*, "The Golden Thread of the English Criminal Law: The Burden of Proof", delivered in 1976 at the University of Toronto, at pp. 11-13:

> It is sometimes said that exceptions to the Woolmington rule are acceptable because, whenever the burden of proof on any issue in a criminal case is borne by the accused, he only has to satisfy the jury on the balance of probabilities, whereas on issues on which the Crown bears the burden of proof the jury must be satisfied beyond a reasonable doubt. . . . The fact that the standard is lower when the accused bears the burden of proof than it is when the burden of proof is borne by the prosecution is no answer to my objection to the existence of exceptions to the Woolmington rule as it does not alter the fact that a jury or bench of Magistrates may have to convict the accused although they are far from sure of his guilt.

As we have seen, the potential for a rational connection between the basic fact and the presumed fact to justify a reverse onus provision has been elaborated in some of the cases discussed above and is now known as the "rational connection test". In the context of s. 11(*d*), however, the following question arises: if we apply the rational connection test to the consideration of whether s. 11(*d*) has been violated, are we adequately protecting the constitutional principle of the presumption of innocence? As Professors MacKay and Cromwell point out in their article "Oakes: A Bold Initiative" (1983), 32 C.R. (3d) 221, at p. 233:

> The rational connection test approves a provision that *forces* the trier to infer a fact that may be simply rationally, connected to the proved fact. Why does it follow that such a provision does not offend the constitutional right to be proved guilty beyond a reasonable doubt?

A basic fact may rationally tend to prove a presumed fact, but not prove its existence beyond a reasonable doubt. An accused person could thereby be convicted despite the presence of a reasonable doubt. This would violate the presumption of innocence.

I should add that this questioning of the constitutionality of the "rational connection test" as a guide to interpreting s. 11(*d*) does not minimize its importance. The appropriate stage for invoking the rational connection test, however, is under s. 1 of the *Charter*. This consideration did not arise under the *Canadian Bill of Rights* because of the absence of an equivalent to s. 1. At the Court of Appeal level in the present case, Martin J.A. sought to combine the analysis of s. 11(*d*) and s. 1 to overcome the limitations of the *Canadian Bill of Rights* jurisprudence. To my mind, it is highly desirable to keep s. 1 and s. 11(*d*) analytically distinct. Separating the analysis into two components is consistent with the approach this court has taken to the *Charter* to date (see *R. v. Big M Drug Mart Ltd., supra; Hunter v. Southam Inc.*, [1984] 2 S.C.R. 145; *Law Society of Upper Canada v. Skapinker*, [1984] 1 S.C.R. 357).

To return to s. 8 of the *Narcotic Control Act*, I am in no doubt whatsoever that it violates s. 11(*d*) of the *Charter* by requiring the accused to prove on a balance of probabilitics that he was not in possession of the narcotic for the purpose of trafficking. Mr. Oakes is compelled by s. 8 to prove he is *not* guilty of the offence of trafficking. He is thus denied his right to be presumed innoccent and subjected to the potential penalty of life imprisonment unless he can rebut the presumption. This is radically and fundamentally inconsistent with the societal values of human dignity and liberty which we espouse, and is directly contrary to the presumption of innocence enshrined in s. 11(*d*). Let us turn now to s. 1 of the *Charter*.

Subsequently, the Supreme Court has determined that any persuasive burden placed on the accused, whether this relates to an element of the offence or a defence, violates s. 11(d) and the only issue is whether it is saved under s. 1.

Sometimes Parliament resorts to the evidentiary device of a rebuttable presumption to assist the burdenholder. This is usually achieved by a provision that "in the absence of evidence to the contrary" something is presumed. In such cases where the accused points to credible evidence to the contrary the presumption no longer exists. This type of burden is sometimes also confusingly referred to as an evidentiary burden. It has a greater significance than the usual meaning of pointing to evidence in the case. With rebuttable presumptions if the accused does nothing to displace the presumption the presumed fact must be considered proved.

The task of the Crown in proving that a particular element is proven is sometimes made easier by the presence of a "deeming" provision in the *Criminal Code*. Consider an accused who finds a partly-completed building on which no door has yet been installed in the doorway, and who steps halfway in before leaving. Has that accused broken and entered for the purposes of the offence of "break and enter" in s. 348? See s. 350(b)(ii) of the *Criminal Code*. For similar provisions, see s. 139(3), s. 198(2), s. 366(3) and (4), or s. 461. Provisions can also establish that certain matters are *not* proven: see, for example, ss. 304-315 or s. 333.

In *Downey*, the court decided that rebuttable presumptions also offend s. 11(d) (and would have to be justified under s.1):

R. v. DOWNEY

[1992] 2 S.C.R. 10, 13 C.R. (4th) 129, 72 C.C.C. (3d) 1,
1992 CarswellAlta 56, 1992 CarswellAlta 467

The accused was charged under s. 195 of the *Criminal Code* (now s. 212) with living off the avails of prostitution. Section 195(2) of the *Code* stated that "[e]vidence that a person lives with or is habitually in the company of prostitutes. . . is, in the absence of evidence to the contrary, proof that the person lives on the avails of prostitution". The accused challenged the constitutionality of that mandatory presumption. The court took the opportunity to articulate the principles governing reverse onus clauses and the presumption of innocence.

. . . .

CORY J.: —

. . . .

Perhaps it may be helpful to summarize the principles to be derived from the authorities.

I - The presumption of innocence is infringed whenever the accused is liable to be convicted despite the existence of a reasonable doubt.

II - If by the provisions of a statutory presumption, an accused is required to establish, that is to say to prove or disprove, on a balance of probabilities either an element of an offence or an excuse, then it contravenes s. 11(d). Such a provision would permit a conviction in spite of a reasonable doubt.

III - Even if a rational connection exists between the established fact and the fact to be presumed, this would be insufficient to make valid a presumption requiring the accused to disprove an element of the offence.

IV - Legislation which substitutes proof of one element for proof of an essential element will not infringe the presumption of innocence if as a result of the proof of the substituted element, it would be unreasonable for the trier of fact not to be satisfied beyond a reasonable doubt of the existence of the other element. To put it another way, the statutory presumption will be valid if the proof of the substituted fact leads inexorably to the proof of the other. However, the statutory presumption will infringe s. 11(d) if it requires the trier of fact to convict in spite of a reasonable doubt.

V - A permissive assumption from which a trier of fact may but not must draw an inference of guilt will not infringe s. 11(d).

VI - A provision that might have been intended to play a minor role in providing relief from conviction will nonetheless contravene the *Charter* if the provision (such as the truth of a statement) must be established by the accused (see *Keegstra, supra*).

VII - It must of course be remembered that statutory presumptions which infringe s. 11(d) may still be justified pursuant to s. 1 of the *Charter*. (As for example in *Keegstra, supra*.)

The court decided that the rebuttable presumption in s. 195(2) violated s. 11(d) but, by a 4-3 majority, it was saved under s. 1.

STEVE COUGHLAN, DOUBT MOUNTAIN AND THE PRESUMPTION OF INNOCENCE

It can be difficult to conceptualize the various burdens on the Crown and the defence. This is particularly true of the interplay between the onus on the Crown to prove the elements of an offence beyond a reasonable doubt, and the occasional reverse onus provisions in the *Code* which sometimes require an accused to prove or raise doubt about a particular element. The thought experiment below can be helpful in understanding these issues.

Imagine a hill - Doubt Mountain - on which a two-person game is played (see figure 1, below). The player at the top of the hill is called the "accused"; the player at the bottom is the "Crown". A number of boxes are placed at the bottom of the hill, next to the Crown. Halfway up the hill the "balance of probabilities" (BOP) line is marked on the ground. Somewhere quite close to the top of the hill, but not actually marked on the ground, is the "beyond a reasonable doubt" (BARD) line.

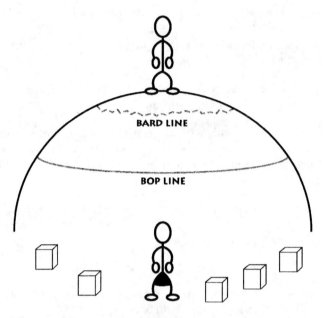

The rules of the game are very simple. The Crown is required to push every box up the hill past the BARD line: if the Crown succeeds in doing this, she wins. If not, the accused wins. Making the game more challenging is the fact that the BARD line does not appear on the hill: until the game is over both players are required to guess, based on their experience with the game, whether a box has been pushed past it or not.

Note that the simplest strategy for the accused is simply to lie down and have a nap. This is not likely to be the *best* strategy, but the rules do not actually require the accused to do anything at all in order to win. At a certain point in the game, though, a lot of the boxes are likely to be a long way up the hill. The accused is likely to think "unless I push some of those boxes below the BARD line, I'm going to lose". A neutral observer (perhaps the neutral observer who will eventually decide the winner) is likely to agree. At that stage it would be true to say that the accused had better do some work or he will lose the game. Note that this does not change the *rule* that the accused is not required to do anything. Tactically, however, it is obvious to everyone that if the accused does nothing he will lose, and so as a practical reality he had better push some boxes down the hill.

Over time it will become obvious to players and observers that some particular routes up the hill are quite easy. In those circumstances an observer will recognize that some boxes are going to be pretty easy to get to the top of the hill, and practically speaking they will almost always end up past the BARD line unless the accused does something about them. Again, though, no change in the rules is implied by this fact.

Now, though, let us consider a possible change in the rules: the addition of a conveyor belt in front of one or more boxes. In those circumstances, we know for certain that the moment the game begins, those boxes shoot up the hill and are past the BARD line. Here we have actually changed the rules: the rules now require the accused to push some boxes down the hill, rather than requiring the Crown to push them up. We could leave the change in the rules at that, and say that the accused is required to push the box below the BARD line. However, we could also make the game even harder than that for the accused. We could say that unless the accused pushes the conveyor belt box down the hill below the BOP line, he loses.

The rules of Doubt Mountain correspond fairly readily to the burdens imposed on the Crown and accused in the criminal justice system. The Crown bears the onus of proof beyond a reasonable doubt, and it is an error to instruct a jury that an accused is required to establish doubt. As a practical matter, however, it is as true in a courtroom as it would be on Doubt Mountain (that is to say, not absolutely clear but reasonably predictable to an informed observer) that sometimes the Crown has done a pretty good job of fulfilling the obligations imposed on it. In those cases, as a tactical decision, the accused ought to choose do some work. It is in one sense accurate in those circumstances to say that unless the accused shows doubt, he will be convicted: the challenge is to distinguish clearly that this is not making it a *rule* that the accused must show doubt. It is simply recognizing that within the rules, which don't insist on the accused doing anything, it has nonetheless become a tactical necessity for the accused to act.

This situation is particularly likely to occur when there is an obvious and reasonable inference to be drawn from facts: or on Doubt Mountain, when the box is on an easy route up the hill. It has often been said, for example, that a person is presumed to intend the natural consequences of his or her actions: if we see an adult pick up a rock, cock her arm, and throw the rock through a pane of glass, we are likely to conclude without any further evidence that she intended to break the window. Unless we hear a reason to think otherwise, we will take the facts to be sufficient to prove the intent. The accused isn't by the rules of the criminal justice system *required* to prove an absence of intent to break the window, just as an easy route up Doubt Mountain isn't a conveyor belt. Still, tactically the accused had better do something or the element will almost certainly be proven. This situation is sometimes described as a "tactical burden".

Sometimes, however, the *Criminal Code* actually imposes a reverse onus on the accused, just as there are sometimes conveyor belts on Doubt Mountain. In those cases it is true *as a matter of law* that an accused who does not show the existence of some doubt will be convicted. If the *Code* provision says that an accused must show "evidence to the contrary",[2] or similar words, that corresponds to pushing the box below the BARD line: the accused is required to show that there is doubt. This type of provision is referred to by the court as an "evidentiary burden." (It is important to note that the phrase "evidentiary burden" is also, and more frequently, used by the court to describe the obligation to present enough evidence to put some legal issue into play, such as, for example, whether an accused acted in self-defence or not). On the other hand if the *Code* provision

---

2 See for example, s. 348(2): "For the purposes of proceedings under this section, evidence that an accused (a) broke and entered a place or attempted to break and enter a place is, in the absence of any evidence to the contrary, proof that he broke and entered the place or attempted to do so, as the case may be, with intent to commit an indictable offence therein."

actually requires the accused to "establish" or "prove" some point,[3] that corresponds to a requirement that the accused push a box far enough down Doubt Mountain that it is below the BOP line. This type of provision is referred to as a "legal burden" on the accused.

Note that a tactical burden and an evidentiary burden (as used in this context) do not differ in the amount of work they call on the accused to do: in each case the accused must show the existence of doubt about whether a particular element has been proven. Those two differ because of the *reason* the accused must do this: because the Crown has done its job well, or because the rules require it. A legal burden, like an evidentiary burden, arises from statute. It differs, though, in that it requires a greater amount of work from the accused: not merely to show that there is doubt whether a point is true, but actually to prove that it is false (that is, push the box halfway down, not just a little way down).

It can be difficult to understand these distinctions in the cases, because judges and the *Code* tend to talk about whether an accused has "proved" a point, but also about whether the Crown has proved its points. As Doubt Mountain attempts to illustrate, it is important to recognize that the Crown and the accused are pushing in different directions. Really it is better to conceptualize the accused as trying to *dis*prove elements, rather than proving anything. The language tends also to talk about an accused "raising" a doubt, which again suggests some positive proof of a point. It is easier to keep the different roles distinct if one thinks of the accused's job as "showing" doubt rather than raising it. This helps keep clear that the accused's task in relation to the "beyond a reasonable doubt" standard is actually easier, not harder, than in relation to the "balance of probabilities" standard.

3.   ROLE OF THE CRIMINAL JUSTICE SYSTEM IN CANADIAN SOCIETY

(a)   Victims' Rights

It is clear that victims have in the past been ignored and sometimes denigrated by the criminal justice system. Abuses have included unwarranted humiliation on cross-examination, especially in sexual assault trials, the trauma of endless court appearances and delays often without proper explanation, and no consideration in sentencing of the impact of the offence on the victim. Clearly victims have a right to be treated with respect. Legislative changes to better protect interests of victims have included rape shield laws, greater restitution provisions, fine surcharge programs to support victim services, and provisions for bans on publicity of the identity of victims, written victim impact statements on sentencing and victim input into parole decisions.

Although there are often now calls to recognize new legal and constitutional rights for victims and complaints that accused have too many rights, there is room

---

3   See for example, s. 57(3): "Everyone who without lawful excuse, the proof of which lies on him, has in his possession a forged passport or a passport in respect of which an offence under subsection (2) has been committed is guilty of an indictable offence and liable to imprisonment for a term not exceeding five years."

for considerable caution and concern. A criminal trial is about determining guilt and just punishment of an accused, not about personal redress for victims. What, for example, if the input of victims were to be determinative on the issue of sentence? Would it be just to have the length of a prison sentence determined by whether the victim wants revenge or compassion? Wouldn't a general right of representation of victims at trial, even on the determination of guilt, hopelessly burden and confuse an already overtaxed and under-resourced criminal justice system?

Constitutional rights for those alleging crimes were directly recognized by the Supreme Court for the first time in its controversial decision in *R. v. O'Connor* (1996) 44 C.R. (4th) 1 (S.C.C.). The court adopted a special balancing procedure respecting discovery of medical records in the possession of third parties. L'Heureux-Dubé, J., with La Forest, Gonthier and McLachlin JJ. concurring, saw the need to balance the accused's right to a fair trial and full answer and defence with the complainant's rights to privacy and to equality without discrimination. The majority, through a joint judgment by Lamer C.J. and Sopinka J., with Cory, Iacobucci and Major JJ. concurring, determined that the accused's right to full answer and defence should be balanced against the complainant's rights to privacy under ss. 7 and 8. However the majority, in not referring to a s. 15 equality right for complainants, although it was fully argued, implicitly reject it.

Section 15 equality rights for complainants in sexual assault cases were later asserted by the Supreme Court in *R. v. Mills* (1999), 28 C.R.(5th) 207 (S.C.C.). In *R. v. Shearing* (2002), 2 C.R.(6th) 213 (S.C.C.), the majority of the court however refers to them as "equality interests". See further below in Chapter 4 on Sexual Assault.

For full discussion of issues of criminal trials and victims' rights, see Paciocco, *Getting Away With Murder*, (1999) pp. 351-382. See also Christine Boyle and Marilyn MacCrimmon, "The Constitutionality of Bill C-49: Analysing Sexual Assault as if Equality Really Mattered" (1998), 41 Crim. L.Q. 198-237.

For strong arguments opposing and supporting *Charter* rights for victims see respectively David Paciocco, "Why the Constitutionalisation of Victims' Rights Should Not Occur" (2005), 49 Crim. L.Q. 393 and Alan Young, "Crime Victims and Constitutional Rights" (2005), 49 Crim. L.Q. 432. See too Kent Roach, "Victims' Rights and the *Charter*" (2005), 49 Crim. L.Q. 474, who concludes that "a workable victims' rights amendment to the *Charter* would not benefit crime victims to a significant extent" (at p. 514).

(b) Scope

"There are acts of wickedness so gross and outrageous that self-protection apart they must be prevented as far as possible at any cost to the offender and punished if they occur with exemplary severity." (J.F. Stephen, *Liberty, Fraternity and Equality*, 2nd ed., (1874), p. 178.)

"The only purpose for which power can rightfully be exercised over any member of a civilized community against his will is to prevent harm to others." (John Stuart Mill, *On Liberty*, (1859), Chapter 1.)

CANADIAN COMMITTEE ON CORRECTIONS, TOWARDS UNITY: CRIMINAL JUSTICE AND CORRECTIONS (OUIMET REPORT)

(1969), 12-13

1. No act should be criminally proscribed unless its incidence, actual or potential, is *substantially damaging to society*.
2. No act should be criminally prohibited where its incidence may adequately be controlled by social forces other than the criminal process. Public opinion may be enough to curtail certain kinds of behaviour. Other kinds of behaviour may be more appropriately dealt with by non-criminal legal processes, *e.g.* by legislation relating to mental health or social and economic condition.
3. No law should give rise to social or personal damage greater than that it was designed to prevent.

To designate certain conduct as criminal in an attempt to control anti-social behaviour should be a last step. Criminal law traditionally, and perhaps inherently, has involved the imposition of a sanction. This sanction, whether in the form of arrest, summons, trial, conviction, punishment or publicity is, in the view of the Committee, to be employed only as an unavoidable necessity. Men and women may have their lives, public and private, destroyed; families may be broken up; the state may be put to considerable expense: all these consequences are to be taken into account when determining whether a particular kind of conduct is so obnoxious to social values that it is to be included in the catalogue of crimes. If there is any other course open to society when threatened, then that course is to be preferred. The deliberate infliction of punishment or any other state interference with human freedom is to be justified only where manifest evil would result from failure to interfere.

LAW REFORM COMMISSION OF CANADA, STUDIES ON STRICT LIABILITY

(1974), 56

Total Numbers: Federal and Provincial

Total number of offences — Federal Statutes 3,582
Federal Regulations 19,460
Provincial Statutes 4,420
Provincial Regulations ... 14,120
Total 41,582
Strict liability offences   — Federal Statutes 1,587 (44%)
Federal Regulations 18,820 (96%)
Provincial Statutes 3,640 (82%)
Provincial Regulations ... 13,920 (98%)
Total 37,967

LAW REFORM COMMISSION OF CANADA, REPORT: OUR CRIMINAL LAW

(1976), 27-28

But criminal law is not the only means of bolstering values. Nor is it necessarily always the best means. The fact is, criminal law is a blunt and costly instrument — blunt because it cannot have the human sensitivity of institutions like the family, the school, the church or the community, and costly since it imposes suffering, loss of liberty and great expense.

So criminal law must be an instrument of last resort. It must be used as little as possible. The message must not be diluted by overkill — too many laws and offences and charges and trials and prison sentences. Society's ultimate weapon must stay sheathed as long as possible. The watchword is restraint — restraint applying to the scope of criminal law, to the meaning of criminal guilt, to the use of the criminal trial and to the criminal sentence.

1.   Scope of Criminal Law

In re-affirming values criminal law denounces acts considered wrong. Accordingly it has to stick to really wrongful acts. It must not overextend itself and make crimes out of things most people reckon not really wrong or, if wrong, merely trivial. Only those acts thought seriously wrong by our society should count as crimes.

Not all such acts, however, should be crimes. Wrongfulness is a necessary, not a sufficient condition of criminality. Before an act should count as a crime, three further conditions must be fulfilled. First, it must cause harm to other people, to society or, in special cases to those needing protection from themselves. Second, it must cause harm that is serious both in nature and degree. And third, it must cause harm that is best dealt with through the mechanism of the criminal law. These conditions would confine the criminal law to crimes of violence, dishonesty and other offences traditionally in the centre of the stage. Any other offences, not really wrong but penally prohibited because this is the most convenient way of dealing with them, must stay outside the *Criminal Code* and qualify merely as quasi-crimes or violations.

1. Are there dangers in the Commission's last recommendation?
2. Are the proposed criteria of crime helpful?

R. v. MALMO-LEVINE

16 C.R. (6th) 1, 179 C.C.C. (3d) 417,
2003 CarswellBC 3133, 2003 CarswellBC 3134 (S.C.C.)

In the course of upholding the constitutionality of Canada's marihuana laws the Supreme Court, over the sole dissent of Justice Arbour, firmly rejected the notion that there is a principle of fundamental justice under s. 7 that a criminal prohibition will offend the *Charter* where it can be established that the conduct involved no risk of harm.

GONTHIER and BINNIE JJ.:—

(i) *History and Definition of the Harm Principle*

What is "the harm principle"? The appellants rely, in particular, on the writings of the liberal theorist, J. S. Mill, who attempted to establish clear boundaries for the permissible intrusion of the state into private life:

> The object of this Essay is to assert one very simple principle, as entitled to govern absolutely the dealings of society with the individual in the way of compulsion and control, whether the means used be physical force in the form of legal penalties, or the moral coercion of public opinion. That principle is, that the sole end for which mankind are warranted, individually or collectively, in interfering with the liberty of action of any of their number, is self-protection. That *the only purpose for which power can be rightfully exercised over any member of a civilised community, against his will, is to prevent harm to others.* His own good, either physical or moral, is not a sufficient warrant. . . . The only part of the conduct of any one, for which he is amenable to society, is that which concerns others. In the part which merely concerns himself, his independence is, of right, absolute. Over himself, over his own body and mind, the individual is sovereign. [Emphasis added.]

> (J. S. Mill, *On Liberty and Considerations on Representative Government*, R. B. McCallum, ed. (1946), at pp. 8-9.)

Thus Mill's principle has two essential features. First, it rejects paternalism — that is, the prohibition of conduct that harms only the actor. Second, it excludes what could be called "moral harm". Mill was of the view that such moral claims are insufficient to justify use of the criminal law. Rather, he required clear and tangible harm to the rights and interests of others.

At the same time, Mill acknowledged an exception to his requirement of harm "to others" for vulnerable groups. He wrote that "this doctrine is meant to apply to human beings in the maturity of their faculties. . . . Those who are still in a state to require being taken care of by others, must be protected against their own actions as well as against external injury" (p. 9).

Mill's statement has the virtues of insight and clarity but he was advocating certain general philosophic principles, not interpreting a constitutional document. Moreover, even his philosophical supporters have tended to agree that justification for state intervention cannot be reduced to a single factor — harm — but is a much more complex matter. One of Mill's most distinguished supporters, Professor H.L.A. Hart, wrote:

> *Mill's formulation of the liberal point of view may well be too simple. The grounds for interfering with human liberty are more various than the single criterion of "harm to others" suggests*: cruelty to animals or organizing prostitution for gain do not, as Mill himself saw, fall easily under the description of harm to others. Conversely, even where there is harm to others in the most literal sense, there may well be other principles limiting the extent to which harmful activities should be repressed by law. So *there are multiple criteria, not a single criterion, determining when human liberty may be restricted.*
>
> (H. L. A. Hart, "Immorality and Treason", originally appearing in *The Listener* (July 30, 1959), at pp. 162-63, reprinted in *Morality and the Law* (1971), 49, at p. 51 (emphasis added).)

To the same effect, see Professor J. Feinberg, *The Moral Limits of the Criminal Law*, (1984), vol. 1: Harm to Others, at p. 12; also vol. 4: Harmless Wrongdoing, at p. 323.

(ii)   *Is the Harm Principle a Principle of Fundamental Justice?*

The appellants submit that the harm principle is a principle of fundamental justice for the purposes of s. 7 that operates to place limits on the type of conduct the state may criminalize. This limitation exists independently of the division of powers under ss. 91 and 92 of the *Constitution Act, 1867*. In other words, the appellants contend that there is a double threshold. Even if the Crown is able to establish that the creation of a particular criminal offence is a valid exercise of the criminal law power, there is a second level of constraint on the type of conduct that can be made criminal by virtue of s. 7 of the *Charter*.

We agree that there is a form of "double threshold", in that the *Charter* imposes requirements that are separate from those imposed by ss. 91 and 92 of the *Constitution Act, 1867*. However, we do not agree with the attempted elevation of the harm principle to a principle of fundamental justice. That is, in our view the harm principle is not the constitutional standard for what conduct may or may not be the subject of the criminal law for the purposes of s. 7.

In *Re B.C. Motor Vehicle Act*, *supra*, Lamer J. (as he then was) explained that the principles of fundamental justice lie in "the basic tenets of our legal system. They do not lie in the realm of general public policy but in the inherent domain of the judiciary as guardian of the justice system" (p. 503). This court provided further guidance as to what constitutes a principle of fundamental justice for the purposes of s. 7, in *Rodriguez, supra, per* Sopinka J. (at pp. 590-91 and 607):

> A mere common law rule does not suffice to constitute a principle of fundamental justice, rather, as the term implies, principles upon which there is *some consensus* that they are vital or fundamental to our societal notion of justice are required. Principles of fundamental justice must not, however, be so broad as to be no more than vague generalizations about what our society considers to be ethical or moral. They must be capable of being *identified with some precision* and *applied* to situations in a manner which yields an understandable result. They must also, in my view, be *legal principles*.
>
> . . . .
>
> While the principles of fundamental justice are concerned with more than process, reference must be made to principles which are "fundamental" in the sense that they would have *general acceptance among reasonable people*. [Emphasis added.]

The requirement of "general acceptance among reasonable people" enhances the legitimacy of judicial review of state action, and ensures that the values against which state action is measured are not just fundamental "in the eye of the beholder *only*": *Rodriguez*, at pp. 607, and 590 (emphasis in original). In short, for a rule or principle to constitute a principle of fundamental justice for the purposes of s. 7, it must be a legal principle about which there is significant societal consensus that it is fundamental to the way in which the legal system ought fairly to operate, and it must be identified with sufficient precision to yield a manageable standard against which to measure deprivations of life, liberty or security of the person.

a.   Is the Harm Principle a Legal Principle?

In our view, the "harm principle" is better characterized as a description of an important state interest rather than a normative "legal" principle. Be that as it may, even if the harm principle could be characterized as a legal principle, we do not think that it meets the other requirements, as explained below.

b.   There is No Sufficient Consensus that the Harm Principle is Vital or Fundamental to Our Societal Notion of Criminal Justice

Contrary to the appellants' assertion, we do not think there is a consensus that the harm principle is the sole justification for criminal prohibition. There is no doubt that our case law and academic commentary are full of statements about the criminal law being aimed at conduct that "affects the public", or that constitutes "a wrong against the public welfare", or is "injurious to the public", or that "affects the community". No doubt, as stated, the presence of harm to others may justify legislative action under the criminal law power. However, we do not think that the absence of proven harm creates the unqualified barrier to legislative action that the appellants suggest. On the contrary, the state may sometimes be justified in criminalizing conduct that is either not harmful (in the sense contemplated by the harm principle), or that causes harm only to the accused.

The appellants cite in aid of their position the observation of Sopinka J., writing for the majority in *Butler, supra,* that "[t]he objective of maintaining conventional standards of propriety, independently of any harm to society, is no longer justified in light of the values of individual liberty which underlie the *Charter*" (p. 498). However, Sopinka J. went on to clarify that it is open to Parliament to legislate "on the basis of some fundamental conception of *morality* for the purposes of safeguarding the values which are integral to a free and democratic society" (p. 493 (emphasis added)).

Several instances of crimes that do not cause harm to others are found in the *Criminal Code*. Cannibalism is an offence (s. 182 of the *Code*) that does not harm another sentient being, but that is nevertheless prohibited on the basis of fundamental social and ethical considerations. Bestiality (s. 160 of the *Code*) and cruelty to animals (s. 446 of the *Code*) are examples of crimes that rest on their offensiveness to deeply held social values rather than on Mill's "harm principle".

A duel fought by consenting adults is an example of a crime where the victim is no less culpable than the perpetrator, and there is no harm that is not consented to, but the prohibition (s. 71 of the *Code*) is nevertheless integral to our ideas of civilized society. See also *R. v. Jobidon*, [1991] 2 S.C.R. 714. Similarly, in *R. v. F. (R.P.)* (1996), 105 C.C.C. (3d) 435, the Nova Scotia Court of Appeal upheld the prohibition of incest under s. 155 of the *Criminal Code* despite a *Charter* challenge by five consenting adults. In none of these instances of consenting adults does the criminal law conform to Mill's expression of the harm principle that "[o]ver himself, over his own body and mind, the individual is sovereign", as referenced earlier at para. 106.

Various jurists and commentators are said by the appellants to have endorsed the idea that harm is required, but we think that these sources, read in context, do not support the "harm principle" as defined by the appellants.

One source relied on by the appellants — the writings of Sir James Fitzjames Stephen — illustrates this point. Reference was made to Stephen's statement that the criminal law

> ... must be confined within narrow limits, and can be applied only to definite overt acts or omissions capable of being proved, which acts or omissions inflict definite evils, either on specific persons or on the community at large.

(J. F. Stephen, A History of the Criminal Law of England (1883), vol. II, at pp. 78-79.)

However, Stephen himself was a prominent critic of Mill's harm principle. He believed that "immoral" behaviour can be a proper subject for the criminal law. Clearly, his reference to "evils" inflicted on the community includes the idea of moral harm, which Mill specifically excluded from the scope of his "harm principle". Stephen thus supported a much larger view of the legitimate purposes of the criminal law than is permitted by the appellants' argument.

The appellants also rely on a 1982 report by the Law Reform Commission of Canada entitled *The Criminal Law in Canadian Society* which concludes, at p. 45, that the criminal law "ought to be reserved for reacting to conduct that is seriously harmful". This seems, on its face, to support the harm principle. However, the report goes on to state, at p. 45, that such harm

> ... may be caused or threatened to the collective safety or integrity of society through the infliction of direct damage or the *undermining of what the Law Reform Commission terms fundamental or essential values — those values or interests necessary for social life to be carried on, or for the maintenance of the kind of society cherished by Canadians.* [Emphasis added.]

Such a definition of "harm" is clearly contrary to Mill's harm principle as endorsed by the appellants.

c. Nor Is There Any Consensus that the Distinction Between Harm to Others and Harm to Self Is of Controlling Importance

Our colleague Arbour J. takes the view that when the state wishes to make imprisonment available as a sanction for criminal conduct, it must be able to show the potential of such conduct to cause harm to others (para. 56). With respect, we do not think there is any such principle anchored in our law. As this court noted in *Rodriguez, supra*, attempted suicide was an offence under Canadian criminal law (found in the original *Code* at s. 238) until its repeal by S.C. 1972, c. 13, s. 16. Sopinka J. emphasized, at p. 597, that

> ... the decriminalization of attempted suicide cannot be said to represent a consensus by Parliament or by Canadians in general that the autonomy interest of those wishing to kill themselves is paramount to the state interest in protecting the life of its citizens.

The offence of attempted suicide was removed from the *Criminal Code* because Parliament came to prefer other ways of addressing the problem of suicide. In that case, as here, there was an important distinction between constitutional competence, which is for the courts to decide, and the wisdom of a particular measure, which, within its constitutional sphere, is up to Parliament.

Putting aside, for the moment, the proper approach to the appropriateness of imprisonment (which, as stated, we think should be addressed under s. 12 rather than s. 7), we do not accept the proposition that there is a general prohibition against the criminalization of harm to self. Canada continues to have paternalistic laws. Requirements that people wear seatbelts and motorcycle helmets are designed to "save people from themselves". There is no consensus that this sort of legislation offends our societal notions of justice. Whether a jail sentence is an appropriate penalty for such an offence is another question. However, the objection in that aspect goes to the validity of an assigned punishment — it does not go to the validity of prohibiting the underlying conduct.

A recent discussion policy paper from the Law Commission of Canada entitled *What is a Crime? Challenges and Alternatives* (2003) highlights the difficulties in distinguishing between harm to others and harm to self. It notes that "in a society that recognizes the interdependency of its citizens, such as universally contributing to health care or educational needs, harm to oneself is often borne collectively" (p. 17).

In short, there is no consensus that tangible harm to others is a necessary precondition to the creation of a criminal law offence.

d.   The Harm Principle Is Not a Manageable Standard Against Which to Measure Deprivation of Life, Liberty or Security of the Person

Even those who agree with the "harm principle" as a regulator of the criminal law frequently disagree about what it means and what offences will meet or offend the harm principle. In the absence of any agreed definition of "harm" for this purpose, allegations and counter-allegations of non-trivial harm can be marshalled on every side of virtually every criminal law issue, as one author explains:

> The harm principle is effectively collapsing under the weight of its own success. Claims of harm have become so pervasive that the harm principle has become meaningless: the harm principle no longer serves the function of a critical principle because non-trivial harm arguments permeate the debate. Today, the issue is no longer whether a moral offence causes harm, but rather what type and what amount of harms the challenged conduct causes, and how the harms compare. On those issues, the harm principle is silent.
>
> (B. E. Harcourt, "The Collapse of the Harm Principle" (1999), 90 J. Crim. L. & Criminology 109, at p. 113)

Professor Harcourt goes on to point out that "[i]t is the hidden normative dimensions . . . [that] do the work in the harm principle, not the abstract, simple notion of harm" (p. 185). In other words, the existence of harm (however defined) does no more than open a gateway to the debate; it does not give any precise guidance about its resolution.

Harm, as interpreted in the jurisprudence, can take a multitude of forms, including economic, physical and social (e.g., injury and/or offence to fundamental societal values). In the present appeal, for example, the respondents put forward a list of "harms" which they attribute to marihuana use. The appellants put forward a list of "harms" which they attribute to marihuana prohibition. Neither side gives much credence to the "harms" listed by the other. Each claims the "net" result to be in its favour.

In the result, we do not believe that the content of the "harm" principle as described by Mill and advocated by the appellants provides a manageable standard under which to review criminal or other laws under s. 7 of the *Charter*. Parliament, we think, is entitled to act under the criminal law power in the protection of legitimate state interests other than the avoidance of harm to others, subject to *Charter* limits such as the rules against arbitrariness, irrationality and gross disproportionality. . . .

R. v. LABAYE

203 C.C.C. (3d) 170, 34 C.R. (6th) 1,
2005 CarswellQue 11495, 2005 CarswellQue 11496, 2005 SCC 80

R. v. KOURI

203 C.C.C. (3d) 217, 34 C.R. (6th) 86,
2005 CarswellQue 11497, 2005 CarswellQue 11498, 2005 SCC 81

The operators of a Montreal "swingers" establishment were charged with keeping a common bawdy-house for the practice of acts of indecency under s. 210(1) of the *Criminal Code*. A 7-2 majority of the Supreme Court abandons the community standard of tolerance test for indecency in favour of an objectively determined harms approach. On that new approach the majority finds that both accused should be acquitted.

In *Labaye* the purpose of the club was to permit couples and single people to meet each other for group sex. Only members and their guests were admitted to the club. Prospective members were interviewed to ensure that they were aware of the nature of the activities of the club and to exclude applicants who did not share the same views on group sex. Members paid an annual membership fee. A doorman manned the main door of the club to ensure that only members and their guests entered. Group sex only took place in an apartment on the third floor. Two doors separated the third floor apartment from the rest of the club. One was marked "Privé" and the other was locked with a numeric key pad. Members of the club were supplied with the appropriate code and permitted to gain access to the third floor apartment. Entry to the club and participation in the activities were voluntary.

At trial, the accused was convicted. The trial judge found that the accused's apartment fell within the meaning of "public place", as defined in s. 197(1) of the *Criminal Code* and that the sexual practices fell below the Canadian community standard of tolerance. She found social harm in the fact that sexual exchanges took place in the presence of other members of the club. This conduct was indecent under the *Criminal Code* because it was degrading and dehumanizing, calculated to induce anti-social behaviour in its disregard for moral values, and raised the risk of sexually transmitted diseases.

A majority of the Quebec Court of Appeal upheld the accused's conviction.

In *Kouri* the accused operated a licensed bar in Montréal. Access to the bar was restricted to couples. A doorman asked prospective clients if they were a "liberated couple", and only couples answering yes were permitted to enter after paying a $6 fee. Every half hour, a translucent curtain closed around the dance floor where people would engage in group sex activities. The trial judge convicted the accused. However the majority of the Quebec Court of Appeal set aside the conviction, concluding that the acts at issue did not constitute criminal indecency.

In the Supreme Court both appeals were heard together.

MCLACHLIN C.J. (MAJOR, BINNIE, DESCHAMPS, FISH, ABELLA and CHARRON JJ. concurring): —

. . . .

2 Defining indecency under the *Criminal Code* is a notoriously difficult enterprise. The *Criminal Code* offers no assistance, leaving the task to judges. The test developed by the cases has evolved from one based largely on subjective considerations, to one emphasizing the need for objective criteria, based on harm. This heightened emphasis on objective criteria rests on the principle that crimes should be defined in a way that affords citizens, police and the courts a clear idea of what acts are prohibited. (See *Reference re ss. 193 and 195.1 (1)(c) of the Criminal Code* (Man.), [1990] 1 S.C.R. 1123, per Lamer J.) We generally convict and imprison people only where it is established beyond a reasonable doubt that they have violated objectively defined norms. Crimes relating to public indecency are no exception.

3 This appeal requires us to apply the norms developed in recent cases to the operation of clubs established to facilitate group sex, a practice colloquially referred to as "swinging". This in turn invites further refinement of the objective criteria for indecency under the *Criminal Code*.

. . . .

4. Analysis

4.1 The Legal Test for Criminal Indecency

4.1.1 The History of Criminal Indecency

13 Section 210(1) of the *Criminal Code* makes it an offence, punishable by two years in prison, to keep a common bawdy-house. A bawdy-house is defined in s. 197(1) of the *Code* as a place kept, occupied, or resorted to "by one or more persons for the purpose of prostitution or the practice of acts of indecency". The

only question in this case is whether what went on at l'Orage constituted "acts of indecency".

14 Indecency has two meanings, one moral and one legal. Our concern is not with the moral aspect of indecency, but with the legal. The moral and legal aspects of the concept are, of course, related. Historically, the legal concepts of indecency and obscenity, as applied to conduct and publications, respectively, have been inspired and informed by the moral views of the community. But over time, courts increasingly came to recognize that morals and taste were subjective, arbitrary and unworkable in the criminal context, and that a diverse society could function only with a generous measure of tolerance for minority mores and practices. This led to a legal norm of objectively ascertainable harm instead of subjective disapproval.

· · · ·

4.1.2 Toward a Theory of Harm

26 Developing a workable theory of harm is not a task for a single case. In the tradition of the common law, its full articulation will come only as judges consider diverse situations and render decisions on them. Moreover, the difficulty of the task should not be underestimated. We must proceed incrementally, step by cautious step.

27 The facts of this case require the further exploration of what types of harm, viewed objectively, suffice to found a conviction for keeping a bawdy-house for the purposes of act of indecency. This exploration must be based on the purposes that the offence serves. More precisely, what harms are sought to be curtailed by targeting indecent conduct?

28 The first step is to generically describe the type of harm targeted by the concept of indecent conduct under the *Criminal Code*. In *Butler* at p. 485 and *Little Sisters* at para. 59 , this was described as "conduct which society formally recognizes as incompatible with its proper functioning".

29 Two general requirements emerge from this description of the harm required for criminal indecency. First, the words "formally recognize" suggest that the harm must be grounded in norms which our society has recognized in its Constitution or similar fundamental laws. This means that the inquiry is not based on individual notions of harm, nor on the teachings of a particular ideology, but on what society, through its laws and institutions, has recognized as essential to its proper functioning. Second, the harm must be serious in degree. It must not only detract from proper societal functioning, but must be incompatible with it.

30 It follows that the analysis to be performed in a particular case involves two steps. The first step is concerned with the nature of the harm. It asks whether the Crown has established a harm or significant risk of harm to others that is grounded in norms which our society has formally recognized in its Constitution or similar fundamental laws. The second step is concerned with the degree of the harm. It asks whether the harm in its degree is incompatible with the proper functioning of society. Both elements must be proved beyond a reasonable doubt before acts can be considered indecent under the *Criminal Code*.

. . . .

4.1.5 Summary of the Test

62 Indecent criminal conduct will be established where the Crown proves beyond a reasonable doubt the following two requirements:

1. That, by its nature, the conduct at issue causes harm or presents a significant risk of harm to individuals or society in a way that undermines or threatens to undermine a value reflected in and thus formally endorsed through the Constitution or similar fundamental laws by, for example:

   (a) confronting members of the public with conduct that significantly interferes with their autonomy and liberty; or

   (b) predisposing others to anti-social behaviour; or

   (c) physically or psychologically harming persons involved in the conduct, and

2. That the harm or risk of harm is of a degree that is incompatible with the proper functioning of society.

As the above makes clear, the categories of harm capable of satisfying the first branch of the inquiry are not closed, nor is any one of the listed categories in itself an integral part of the definition of harm. For example, predisposition to anti-social behaviour, while central to this court's analysis in *Butler*, is but one illustration of the type of harm that undermines or threatens to undermine one of society's formally recognized values.

63 This test, applied objectively and on the basis of evidence in successive cases as they arise, is directed to articulating legal standards that enhance the ability of persons engaged in or facilitating sexual activities to ascertain the boundary between non-criminal conduct and criminal conduct. In this way, the basic requirements of the criminal law of fair notice to potential offenders and clear enforcement standards to police will, it is hoped, be satisfied.

4.2 Application of the Test

64 The first question is whether the conduct at issue harmed, or presented a significant risk of harm to individuals or society.

65 The sexual acts at issue were conducted on the third floor of a private club, behind doors marked "Privé" and accessed only by persons in possession of the proper numerical code. The evidence establishes that a number of steps were taken to ensure that members of the public who might find the conduct inappropriate did not see the activities. Pre-membership interviews were conducted to advise of the nature of the activities and screen out persons not sharing the same interests. Only members and guests were admitted to the premisses. A doorman controlled access to the principal door.

66 On these facts, none of the kinds of harm discussed above was established. The autonomy and liberty of members of the public was not affected by unwanted confrontation with the sexual conduct in question. On the evidence, only those already disposed to this sort of sexual activity were allowed to participate and watch.

67 Nor was there evidence of the second type of harm, the harm of predisposing people to anti-social acts or attitudes. Unlike the material at issue in *Butler*, which perpetuated abusive and humiliating stereotypes of women as objects of sexual gratification, there is no evidence of anti-social attitudes toward women, or for that matter men. No one was pressured to have sex, paid for sex, or treated as a mere sexual object for the gratification of others. The fact that l'Orage is a commercial establishment does not in itself render the sexual activities taking place there commercial in nature. Members do not pay a fee and check consent at the door; the membership fee buys access to a club where members can meet and engage in consensual activities with other individuals who have similar sexual interests. The case proceeded on the uncontested premise that all participation was on a voluntary and equal basis.

68 Finally, there is no evidence of the third type of harm—physical or psychological harm to persons participating. The only possible danger to participants on the evidence was the risk of catching a sexually transmitted disease. However, this must be discounted as a factor because, as discussed above, it is conceptually and causally unrelated to indecency.

69 As stated above, the categories of harm are not closed; in a future case other different harms may be alleged as a basis for criminal indecency. However, no other harms are raised by the evidence in this case. All that is raised, in the final analysis, is the assessment that the conduct amounted to "an orgy" and that Canadian society does not tolerate orgies. (Rochon J.A., at para. 133) This reasoning erroneously harks back to the community standard of tolerance test,

which has been replaced, as discussed, by the harm-based test developed in *Butler*.

70 I conclude that the evidence provides no basis for concluding that the sexual conduct at issue harmed individuals or society. *Butler* is clear that criminal indecency or obscenity must rest on actual harm or a significant risk of harm to individuals or society. The Crown failed to establish this essential element of the offence. The Crown's case must therefore fail. The majority of the court of Appeal erred, with respect, in applying an essentially subjective community standard of tolerance test and failing to apply the harm-based test of *Butler*.

71 It is unnecessary to proceed to the second branch of the test. However, if one did, there appears to be no evidence that the degree of alleged harm rose to the level of incompatibility with the proper functioning of society. Consensual conduct behind code-locked doors can hardly be supposed to jeopardize a society as vigorous and tolerant as Canadian society.

72 I would allow the appeal and set aside the conviction.

LeBel J. (Bastarache J. concurring) (dissenting): —

. . . .

75 The majority is in this way departing from the case law of this court and proposing a new approach to indecency that is, in our view, neither desirable nor workable. It constitutes an unwarranted break with the most important principles of our past decisions regarding indecency. Our colleagues' approach replaces the community standard of tolerance with a test that treats harm as the basis of indecency rather than as a criterion for determining the community's level of tolerance. Whether or not serious social harm is sustained has never been the determinative test for indecency, and it cannot take the place of a contextual analysis of the Canadian community standard of tolerance without completely transforming the concept of indecency and rendering it meaningless.

76 In contrast to our colleagues, we propose to continue applying the original test for indecency, which focusses on a contextual analysis of the impugned acts and incorporates the concept of harm as a significant, but not determinative, factor to consider in establishing the applicable level of tolerance. Whether or not harm is sustained is merely one of several indicators or contextual factors that make it possible to gauge the degree of tolerance of the Canadian community. In our view, all the contextual factors must be considered in every case. The application of this test to the facts of the case at bar leads to the conclusion that the impugned acts were indecent and that the appellant's establishment was a common bawdy-house within the meaning of s. 210(1) Cr. C.

. . . .

98 In principle, we consider the change to the legal order proposed by the majority to be inappropriate, particularly because no valid justification is given for departing from the existing test. We are convinced that this new approach strips of all relevance the social values that the Canadian community as a whole believes should be protected.

99 First, our colleagues' approach changes the role of the judge in establishing the standard of tolerance. It is clear from the case law that the judge's role is, through contextual analysis, to interpret the community's view of sexual practices as expressed in various places at various times. Whether the impugned acts met the Canadian community standard of tolerance is thus a question of law: see *Mara*, at para. 26; *Tremblay*, at p. 946 (per Gonthier J., dissenting, but not on this issue). However, by adopting certain categories of harm that emphasize the mere exposure of the general public to sexual acts or the risk of serious psychological or physical harm, the majority's approach tends to reduce the judge's analysis to a purely fact-based one. The inquiry into the standard of tolerance thus becomes more a question of fact, which is contrary to this court's case law.

100 Second, when the standard of tolerance is established on the basis of the three categories of harm adopted by the majority, it becomes impossible to take into account the multitude of situations that could exceed the threshold for indecency. Granted, the harm-based test for indecency will in most cases yield the same result as a contextual approach. However, it is easy to conceive of situations in which the categories will not reflect the Canadian community standard of tolerance. For example, it is possible that, even in the absence of degrading acts or of harm to the participants, the Canadian community will not tolerate certain acts committed in a given context and place, regardless of whether spectators are present or whether they consent. In other words, sexual acts of any nature performed without an audience would de facto fall outside the ambit of the provisions aimed at prohibiting indecency. In our view, indecency cannot be based solely on the exposure of the general public to sexual acts. This outcome is unacceptable.

101 The Canadian community's tolerance for sexual practices must be assessed independently of the presence of spectators. The nature of the principle that is to be applied must not be forgotten. It consists in establishing not what Canadians think is right for themselves, or what the spectators or participants in question think is right for themselves, but what Canadians would not abide other Canadians seeing: *Towne Cinema*, at pp. 508-9. In a situation in which the Canadian community's tolerance for sexual acts must be established, as opposed to the situation in *Mara*, which concerned indecent performances, the principle will necessarily concern what Canadians would not abide other Canadians doing,

taking into account the place and general context, of course. Another thing to bear in mind is that it is the standards of the community as a whole that must be considered and not the standards of a small segment of the community: *Towne Cinema*, at p. 508. Consequently, indecency cannot be based solely on the presence of participants or on their views. The contextual approach allows us to take into account the private nature of the place where the acts are carried out. But for sexual practices in places to which the public has access not to be subject to the standard of tolerance because of their allegedly private nature - we are referring here to the ambiguous concept of relatively private places - would be incompatible with a proper interpretation of the standard of tolerance. An approach that in many situations, like the situation in the instant case, systematically prevents the standard of tolerance from being established and applied must be rejected.

102 Furthermore, the majority's approach poses serious problems in light of the practical consequences that would result from adopting it. To successfully defend against a charge under s. 210(1) Cr. C. in a context in which there are no degrading acts or in which the participants do not suffer serious harm, it would be enough to ensure that the general public is not a spectator, regardless of the number of participants. It would then be difficult to characterize the acts as indecent, as there would be no evidence of harm.

103 In our opinion, the test adopted by the majority introduces a concept of tolerance that does not seem to be justifiable according to any principle whatsoever. This concept cannot be accepted on the pretext that harm is easier to prove or that it is desirable for this type of offence to have the same rationale as the vast majority of other criminal offences, namely the need to protect the community from harm. Social morality, which is inherent in indecency offences and is expressed through the application of the standard of tolerance, must still be allowed to play a role in all situations where it is relevant. Otherwise, the social values that the Canadian community as a whole considers worth protecting would be stripped of any relevance.

104 Furthermore, the existence of harm is not a prerequisite for exercising the state's power to criminalize certain conduct. The existence of fundamental social and ethical considerations is sufficient: see *R. v. Malmo-Levine*, [2003] 3 S.C.R. 571, 2003 SCC 74, at p. 635. There is no principle that supports the harmonization of offences.

105 The philosophical underpinnings of the majority's harm-based approach are found in the liberal theories of J. S. Mill. This philosopher argued that the only purpose for which state power can be rightfully exercised over a member the community is to prevent harm to others: see J. S. Mill, *On Liberty and Considerations on Representative Government*, at p. 8. This court had occasion to address the principle of harm in *Malmo-Levine*. Although that case concerned

the constitutional limits on the state's power to legislate in criminal matters, the majority's reasons stressed that the justification for state intervention cannot be reduced to a single factor. There are multiple criteria for justifying state intervention in criminal matters, even if it restricts human liberty: see *Malmo-Levine*, at p. 632. Offences under the *Criminal Code* are thus based on principles and values other than harm. In the case at bar, the offence relates to social morality. To place excessive emphasis on the criterion of harm will therefore make it impossible to give effect to the moral principles in respect of which there is a consensus in the community.

4.3 Conclusion Regarding Indecency

153 In the case at bar, the impugned sexual acts were very explicit acts, and they took place in a commercial establishment that was easily accessible to the general public. This situation caused a certain form of social harm resulting from the failure to meet the minimum standards of public morality. In light of these contextual factors, we are of the opinion that the sexual acts performed in the appellant's establishment clearly offended the Canadian community standard of tolerance and were therefore indecent. Our analysis does not permit us to conclude that the Canadian community would tolerate the performance, in a commercial establishment to which the public has easy access, of group sexual activities on the scale of those that took place in this case. The appellant's establishment is therefore a common bawdy-house within the meaning of s. 210(1) Cr. C.

5. Disposition

154 We would have dismissed the appeal and upheld the appellant's conviction.

Clarity is a noble and commendable goal when our courts review the exercise of massive state power against the individual. Whether this shift away from the community standard test of tolerance applied in *R. v. Butler*, [1992] 1 S.C.R. 452, *R. v. Tremblay*, [1993] 2 S.C.R. 932 and *R. v. Mara*, [1997] 2 S.C.R. 630 to objectively defined harm has, or will, achieve greater clarity is however debatable. The dissenters are clearly not convinced. **Are you?**

Under the community standard of tolerance test, the Supreme Court has previously decided that strippers dancing for men while the men masturbate is not indecent (*Tremblay*), whereas lap dancing in strip clubs is indecent (*Mara*). Presumably these decisions should now be re-litigated under the objective harm criteria. One wonders, too, whether, given the new approach, there is not now an argument that a keeping a common bawdy house charge can no longer be sustained based on acts of prostitution in private. See Elaine Craig, "Re-interpreting the Criminal Regulation of Sex Work in Light of *Labaye*" (2008) 1 C.C.L.R. 327. The majority in *Labaye* stress that no-one paid for the group sex. **But what about the membership fee?**

The emphasis on evidence of objective harm appears, as Lebel J. points out, to be at odds with the court's earlier decision in *R. v. Malmo-Levine*. **Should Parliament intervene?**

1. The population is aging. Statistics show that 40 percent of hospital beds are occupied by geriatric patients and that 30 percent of the intensive care space is used for the treatment of geriatric patients, many of whom are on life support systems.

Medical science prides itself on its ability to prolong life. But at what cost? Many members have received mail urging legislation to give patients the right to die with dignity; to give patients and their families the right to determine treatment and the right to decline treatment. The Netherlands now recognizes a limited form of mercy killing conducted under medical supervision. Assume you are a member of a committee advising Parliament. Within this context a private member's bill is before the committee to legalize euthanasia or mercy killing. Under the present law such killing is culpable homicide, likely first or second degree murder resulting in minimum sentences of 25 years and 10 years respectively.

In *Rodriguez v. B.C. (A.G.)*, [1993] 3 S.C.R. 519, 24 C.R. (4th) 281, 85 C.C.C. (3d) 15, the majority of the court held that the *Criminal Code* offence under s. 241(*b*) of the *Criminal Code*, forbidding counselling or aiding and abetting suicide, did not violate *Charter* guarantees of principles of fundamental justice under s. 7, protection against cruel and unusual treatment under s. 12 nor equality before the law under s. 15.

The Law Reform Commission of Canada addressed this issue and concluded:

> The Commission recommends against legalizing or decriminalizing voluntary active euthanasia in any form and is in favour of continuing to treat it as culpable homicide.
>
> The Commission recommends that mercy killing not be made an offence separate from homicide and that there be no formal provision for special modes of sentencing for this type of homicide other than what is already provided for homicide.

Two sub-committees were appointed by the committee to consider the issue: the first advocates the legalization of euthanasia or mercy killing under prescribed conditions, and the second urges the retention of the law as it stands — culpable homicide.

Prepare your arguments for submission before the full committee. The committee may well vote on the proposal at the next meeting. Therefore, your presentation is critical to sway "undecided" members.

(c) Truths of Criminology

Many disciplines other than law have devoted considerable time and energy to a serious study of the causes, nature, punishment or treatment of criminal behaviour. Are there truths of criminological research that should be taken into account in the development of substantive criminal law principles?

Few researchers now attempt to explain "crime". Even assuming that an inquiry into legally-defined criminality is adequate, there is the Barbara Wootton contention[4] that criminal behaviour covers too large a range of human behaviour to be classified and analysed, a miscellaneous aggregate of quite different kinds of action.

> It seems time that we recognised that delinquency or criminality (even with its major motoring component left out) is not a rational field of discourse. . . . The inherent stupidity of treating criminals, delinquents, or prisoners, even of a given sex and age group, as sufficiently homogeneous for rational study had been repeatedly demonstrated.[5]

Even if one could reject this view, a researcher into criminality must look wider than officially recorded crime. It is universally accepted that the figures often represent the "tip of the iceberg" due to such factors as police discretion, the low reporting of some crimes and the vagaries of recording practices. The researcher must also contend with the observation, stemming from the controversial study by Sutherland of "white-collar" criminality,[6] that conduct which is not officially criminal sometimes appears similar. In the Canadian context we could not ignore motoring offenders on the legalistic basis that they were mostly provincial offences,[7] that false advertising by companies which looks like fraud is not a *Criminal Code* offence[8] and that the distinction between tax evasion which is an offence and tax avoidance which is not is sometimes fudgy.[9]

Even if an acceptable typology of conduct is arrived at, most researchers now agree that any attempt to seek a mono-causal theory is doomed to failure and that the best we can do is to suggest that there are a host of interacting predisposing factors — biological, psychological and sociological. The invariable problem with a monolithic theory such as "'poverty causes crime" is that it does not explain the exceptions. David Matza[10] has used the phrase "embarrassment of riches" to describe this deficiency. Why do so many poor people not commit crimes? The modern approach of avoiding extravagant claims characterizes the recent Senate Report, *Child at Risk* (1980).[11] For example, it firmly rejects the concept of a "natural born criminal" in these terms:

> Some individuals may be more likely than others to become criminal or violent as a result of inheritance, but it is never inevitable that they will become so. At most, genetic make-up must be considered as one factor, among many others, that can place a child at risk.[12]

---

4 *Social Science and Social Pathology*, (1959).

5 At 306.

6 "Is 'White Collar Crime' Crime?" (1945), 10 Am. Soc. Rev. 132.

7 T.C. Willett, *Criminal on the Road*, (1964).

8 Cf. C. Goff and C.E. Reasons, "Corporations in Canada: A Study of Crime and Punishment" (1976), 18 Crim. L.Q. 468, who survey prosecution statistics under the *Combines Investigation Act* and conclude that the Federal Government is devoting less effort to proceed against Canada's largest companies. See now their book *Corporate Crime in Canada: A Criticial Analysis of Anti-Combines Legislation*, (1978). See too, L. Snider, "Corporate Crime in Canada: A Preliminary Report" (1978), 20 Can. J. of Crim. 142.

9 See R.S. Rice, "Judicial Techniques in Combating Tax Avoidance" (1953), 51 Mich. L. Rev. 1021.

10 *Delinquency and Drift*, (1964).

11 3, 8-9, 60, 50-2.

12 At 9.

Thus no magic answers exist, or are ever likely to exist, on the question of what causes crime. We should thus retain a healthy scepticism of claims that the explanation is to be found in the "extra Y chromosome,"[13] "brain dysfunction,"[14] or in the rational challenge to inequities in the structure of ownership and the distribution of wealth.[15] Social labelling theorists[16] who assert that it is the quality of societal reaction to deviancy rather than the quality of the act or actor himself that determines criminality have a point — decriminalizing everything would "solve" crime — but it is a limited truth. What initiates the act?

This marshy base leads to the conclusion that human behaviour is so complex that we should be careful about generalizing, let alone talking about an individual case which is what concerns a criminal trial. It is not surprising that the truths from what may be called applied criminology are equally guarded and limited.

Research has been undertaken on the effectiveness of different forms of punishment or treatment, predictions of dangerousness, and the notion of general deterrence.

Research on the effectiveness of punishments and treatments almost inevitably encounters grave methodological problems. Not the least of these is the widely perceived unethical nature of the best research model of experimentation with a controlled group. Yet even the most sophisticated research[17] has produced very pessimistic results, particularly if we are concerned with the acid test: the rate of recidivism. Different forms of punishment or treatment seem equally ineffective, even if we compare such markedly different punishments as long- and short-term prison sentences, probation and institutional punishments, and authoritarian institutions and therapeutic communities. The greatest hope is with the first offenders but it does not seem to matter what the disposition is. The gloom is so pervasive that Dr. Fattah's conclusion[18] appears optimistic:

---

13 N. Wade, "Born Criminals" New Society, December 19, 1968, made the monstrous suggestion that once computer methods made it feasible to culture the blood cells of all new-born babies it may not be "ethically" correct to let XYY babies live. Researchers are now extremely cautious: see especially H.A. Witkin *et al*, "Criminality in XYY and XXY Men" (1976), 193 Science 547.

14 M. Yeudall, "Neuropsychological Assessment of Forensic Disorders" (1977), 25 Canada's Mental Health 7.

15 See L. McDonald, *The Sociology of Law and Order*, (1976) for a description of "conflict theories" stemming from the work of I. Taylor, P. Walton, and J. Young, *The New Criminology*, (1973) and *Critical Criminology*, (1975). See also A.E.C. Antony, "Radical Criminology" in R.A. Silverman and J.J. Teevan Jr., eds., *Crime in Canadian Society*, 2nd ed., (1980), 234.

16 E.M. Lemert, *Social Pathology*, (1951), H.S. Becker *Outsiders*, (1963) and generally E. Rubington and M.S. Weinberg, *Deviance: The Interactionist Perspective*, (1968). In Canada, see R.V. Ericson, *Criminal Reactions: The Labelling Perspective*, (1975).

17 R. Hood, "Research on the Effectiveness of Punishments and Treatments" (1967), 1 Collected Studies in Criminological Research 73; W. Outerbridge, "The Tyranny of Treatment?" (1968), 10 Can. J. of Corr. 378; R. Martinson, "What Works? Questions and Answers About Prison Reform" (1974), 35 The Public Interest 22; N. Morris, *The Future of Imprisonment* (1974); K. Jobson, "Reforming Sentencing Laws: A Canadian Perspective", in B. Grossman, (ed.), *New Directions in Sentencing* (1980), p. 73 at 75-76. Before his death, Martinson however reversed his "nothing works" stance: R. Martinson, "New Findings, New Views: A Note of Caution Regarding Sentencing Reform" (1979), 7 Hofstra L. Rev. 243. See also P. Gendreau and B. Ross, "Effective Correctional Treatment: Bibliography for Cynics" (1979), 25 Crime & Delinquency 463.

18 "Deterrence: A Review of the Literature" in L.R.C., *Fear of Punishment*, (1976).

Recidivism rates appear to vary greatly for different types of crime and for different types of offenders. More research is needed to establish what types of offences or what types of offenders are relatively immune to the influence of intimidation.

On the basis of existing evidence it appears that there are persistent offenders who are very likely to be reconvicted whatever is done to them. On the other hand there are offenders who have relatively good chances of avoiding reconviction no matter what penal measure they were subjected to. Between these two extremes there is a group of offenders, probably the largest group, for whom differential sentencing is needed and for whom the choice of sentence makes a difference. . . .

The development of a typology of crime and of the criminal would, no doubt, be very useful in selecting appropriate deterrent measures.[19]

The difficulty with putting our hope in typologies is that no one has yet been able to develop them. Although accurate figures in respect of recidivism rates of those sent to Canadian prisons and penitentiaries are not available, few would suggest that the rates are not very high.[20]

On the topic of prediction of dangerousness there is now strong evidence denying the expertise of psychiatrists or anybody else to make reasonably accurate predictions. Clinical analysis is as ineffective as an examination of past behaviour. After their exhaustive review of research findings, Ennis and Litwack[21] conclude:

Whatever may be said for the reliability and validity of psychiatric judgments in general, there is literally no evidence that psychiatrists reliably and accurately can predict dangerous behaviour. To the contrary, such predictions are wrong more often than they are right. It is inconceivable that a judgment could be considered an "expert" judgment when it is less accurate than the flip of a coin.[22]

---

19 At 97.

20 See I. Waller, *Men Released from Prison*, (1974) and see, as to parole, P. Macnaughton-Smith, *Permission to be Slightly Free*, L.R.C. (1976). The most optimistic findings are by R.B. Cormier, "Canadian Recidivism Index" (1981), 23 *Can. J. Crim.* 103.

21 "Psychiatry and the Presumption of Expertise: Flipping Coins in the courtroom" (1974), 62 Cal. L. Rev. 693, discussed in the Canadian context by N. Boyd, "Ontario's Treatment of the 'Criminally Insane' and the Potentially Dangerous: The Questionable Wisdom of Procedural Reform" (1980), 22 Can. J. of Crim. 151. See also, for example, R. Price, "Psychiatry, Criminal Law Reform and the Mythophilic Impulse: on Canadian Proposals for the Control of the Dangerous Offender" (1970), 4 Ottawa L. Rev.; J. Klein, "Habitual Offender Legislation and the Bargaining Process" (1973), 15 Crim. L.Q. 417; "The Dangerousness of Dangerous Offender Legislation: Forensic Folklore Revisited" (1976), 18 Can. J. of Crim. and Corr. 109; R. Price and A. Gold, "Legal Controls for the Dangerous Offender" in L.R.C., *Studies on Imprisonment*, (1976), 153; More recent studies in the United States are discussed by Jobson, note 14 above at 78-80; and see T.P. Thornberry and J.E. Jacoby, *The Criminally Insane: A Community Follow-Up of Mentally Ill Offenders*, (1979). See, however, Canadian claims for risk assessment based on a combination of actuarial and clinical assessment: C.D Webster, G.T. Harris, M.E. Rice, C. Cormier and V.L. Quinsey, *The Violence Prediction Scheme: Assessing Dangerousness in High Risk Men* (1994). The authors are themselves cautious: "No one claims that its use will guarantee 'fairness', 'accuracy' and 'absence of bias' in each and every case" (at p. 65). For highly critical reviews of such risk assessment measures see, for example, P. Gendreau, C. Goggin and P. Smith, "Is the PCL-R Really the Unparalleled Measure of Offender Risk? A Lesson in Knowledge Cumulation" (2002) 29 *Criminal Justice and Behaviour* 397-426 and David MacAlister, "Use of Risk Assessment by Canadian Judges in the Determination of Dangerous and Long-Term Offender Status, 1997-2002", in Law Commission of Canada, *Law And Risk* (2005, U.B.C. Press) pp. 20-40. See too David Nussbaum and Melanie MacEacheron, "Legal and Psychological Complexities in Prediction of Severity of Violent Recidivism Necessitate New Research" (2011) 57 *Crim. L. Q.* 242.

22 At 737.

Research on the general deterrent effect of penalties[23] faces tremendous methodological barriers. Again the greatest barrier is that ethical considerations strongly militate against experimentation with real subjects in the criminal justice system. Most researchers now go out of their way to emphasize how complex the issue of general deterrence is and how little we know.

. . . .

There is research indicating that any deterrent effect or penalty depends more on its certainty than its severity. There is evidence that certainty of detection is even more important, while there is research, and indeed common sense would indicate the same, that what will act as a deterrent is likely to differ markedly from crime to crime. Thus traffic offences including drunken driving or parking violations might be responsive to changes in law enforcement or penalty. Although the question is particularly controversial, there would seem to be no evidence that an extreme penalty such as death or a long maximum prison sentence deters murder. The crime is typically committed in volatile and emotional circumstances in which there is little time for reason.

The truths of criminology are limited. There are no clear explanations, definitions or answers. We can no longer develop our substantive law principles without taking this reality into account.

ANTHONY N. DOOB and CHERYL MARIE WEBSTER, SENTENCE SEVERITY AND CRIME: ACCEPTING THE NULL HYPOTHESIS

Michael Tonry (ed.), (2003) 30 *Crime and Justice: A Review of Research* pp. 143-195 (University of Chicago Press)

Abstract

The research literature which examines the impact of sentence severity on crime levels has been reviewed numerous times in the past 25 years. Most of these reviews have concluded that there is little or no consistent evidence that harsher sanctions reduce crime rates in western populations. Nevertheless, most reviewers have been reluctant to come to a firm conclusion that variation in the severity of sentence does not have differential deterrent impacts. We suggest that a reasonable assessment of the research to date – with a particular focus on studies conducted in the past decade – is that sentence severity has no effect on the level of crime in society. It is time to accept the null hypothesis.

[After a detailed analysis of some 50 studies published in the United States, Canada and Europe and elsewhere, the authors conclude as follows:]

---

23 See the careful assessment by Fattah, note 15 above. See also F. Henry, "Imprisonment as a General Deterrent" (1978), 21 Crim L.Q 69 and C.T. Griffiths, J F. Klein, and S.N. Verdun-Jones, *Criminal Justice in Canada*, (1980), 179-82.

IV. CONCLUSION

... Can we conclude that variation in the severity of sentences would have differential (general) deterrent effects? Answered simply, our reply is a resounding no. Indeed, we could find no conclusive evidence that supports the hypothesis that harsher sentences would reduce crime through the mechanism of general deterrence. Particularly given the significant body of literature from which this conclusion is based, the consistency of the findings over time and space and the multiple measures and methods employed in the research conducted, we would suggest that a stronger conclusion is warranted. More specifically, we propose that the null hypothesis that variation in sentence severity does not cause variation in crime rates should be conditionally accepted. The condition that we would impose is a simple one: If a "deterrent effect" of harsh sentences were to be consistently demonstrated under specified conditions at some point in the future, our broad conclusion would require revision.

In coming to this conclusion, we have not attempted to review every paper ever published on the topic of deterrence in this essay. Rather, we began with the published reviews of the deterrence literature and moved from there to the studies that are held out, occasionally, as evidence that harsher sentences would deter crime. We subsequently examined the research which does not find support for a deterrent effect on variation in sentence severity, focusing largely — albeit not exclusively — on those that assessed the general deterrent impacts of the structural changes in sentencing laws that have occurred in the last decade in the U.S. In brief, this essay looks not only at other reviews but also at research which purports to support as well as challenge the view that variation in sentence severity affects the levels of crime in society. The findings of our inquiry can be summarized as follows:

1) With two exceptions - neither of which purports to be comprehensive - the reviews of the deterrence literature are pessimistic about the possibility that harsher sentences handed down in criminal courts would decrease crime. Indeed, our assessment of general deterrence is consistent with the views expressed by most criminologists who have reviewed the current body of literature and concluded that the evidence does not support the hypothesis that variation in sentence severity will differentially affect crime rates. Further, the summaries which challenge this conclusion not only constitute sporadic anomalies but also do not address most of the relevant research literature on the topic.

2) The studies that have found support for the notion that harsher sentences deter are relatively few in number. Additionally, they suffer from one or more methodological, statistical or conceptual problems which render their findings problematic. In some cases, causal inferences between sentence severity and crime cannot be drawn because of the basic nature of the data under analysis (e.g., a simple comparison of crime and punishment in two locations). In other

cases, alternative explanations (e.g., incapacitation) are more plausible than deterrence. In still others, there are data selection, measurement, or methodological questions that raise sufficient doubt about the generality of the findings that inferences are dangerous. Finally, while some findings do, in fact, seem to support a deterrent effect, they appear in unstable and inconsistent ways (e.g., for some offenses but not others, in some locations but not others). In brief, we suggest that the data held out as supportive of the general deterrent impact of sentence severity are not strong enough to allow one to conclude that there is a relationship between the severity of sanctions and crime. A strong finding would be one that appears to be reliable across time, space, and, perhaps, offense. The research examined in this essay which is favorable to the conclusion that there is a deterrent impact of the severity of sentences clearly does not fulfill these criteria.

3) An impressive body of literature has appeared in the past 10 years which has largely taking advantage of dramatic sentencing changes that have occurred in the United States (e.g., three-strikes legislation). The studies that we examined vary in their scope, but not their findings. More precisely, there is no consistent and plausible evidence that harsher sentences deter crime. Moreover, these studies were frequently conducted in almost ideal research conditions in which one would, in fact, expect to find a deterrent effect. In particular, there was generally a substantial amount of publicity surrounding the introduction of these new sentencing laws. Hence, people would be likely to know (or at least believe) that harsh sentences would follow conviction for the offenses covered by these laws. Further, these sentencing changes have been studied in different countries and with different units of analysis (e.g., states, counties, cities, etc.). Finally, some of these studies were able to break down "punishment" into its various components (i.e., apprehension, conviction, sentencing), permitting an assessment of the separate or unique effects of sentence severity. Even under these conditions, sentencing levels do not appear to be important in determining crime. Indeed, the effects are consistent: the severity of sentence does not matter. The hypothesis that harsher sentences would reduce crime through general deterrence – which is to say that there are marginal effects of general deterrence – is not supported by the research literature.

IV.A. Accepting the null hypothesis.

We started this essay by pointing out that we cannot logically "prove" that harsher sentences do not deter. Strictly speaking, one cannot prove the absence of a phenomenon. It may exist somewhere, but research may not have (yet) identified where this is. Having said this, one can still conclude that no consistent body of literature has developed over the last 25-30 years indicating that harsh sanctions deter. While one must always reserve judgment for the possibility that - in the future - someone may discover persons or situations in which the relative severity of sentences does, in fact, have an impact on crime, it would not seem unreasonable to conclude that at the present time in western populations and with the current methods and measures available, variation in sentence severity does not affect the levels of crime in society.

We are conscious that our conclusion – as well as, for that matter, those of the majority of criminologists who have examined the hypothesis that variation in sentence severity has of a deterrent effect – defies an intuitive appeal which is inherent in the logic of deterrence. Indeed, we seem to naturally (want to) accept the notion that any reasonable person – like ourselves – would be deterred by the threat of a more severe sanction. However, we suggest that this continued belief in the deterrent effect of harsh sentences – even in the face of consistent evidence to the contrary – is rooted, at least in part, in a simplistic form of reasoning about deterrence. On the one hand, we may not adequately separate the effects of certainty of apprehension and severity of punishment in our minds and, by extension, think of the latter largely within the context of a high likelihood of the former. As research has shown us (see Ross 1982, for a pertinent example), the assumption that the majority of offenses have a high probability of apprehension is clearly not a safe one.

On the other hand, we may not adequately break down the actual process by which deterrence works. Indeed, many people may not be aware of the complex sequence of conditions which must be met in order that variation in sentence severity can potentially affect levels of crime. As von Hirsch et al. (1999, p.7) have outlined, for a harsher sanction to have an impact, individuals must first believe that there is a reasonable likelihood that they will be apprehended for the offense and receive the punishment that is imposed by a court. Second, they must know that the punishment has changed. It does no good to alter the sanction if potential offenders do not know that it has been modified. Indeed, consequences that are unknown to potential offenders cannot affect their behavior. Third, the individual must be a person who will consider the penal consequences in deciding whether to commit the offense. Finally, the potential offender – who knows about the change in punishment and perceives that there is a reasonable likelihood of apprehension – must calculate that it is "worth" offending for the lower level of punishment but not worth offending for the increased punishment. In other words, in arguing that a 3-year sentence will deter more people than a 2-year sentence, one is, in fact, suggesting that there is a measurable number of people who would commit the offense with a reasonable expectation of serving a 2-year sentence who would not do the same thing if they thought that they would serve a 3-year sentence.

When viewed from this strictly logical perspective, the lack of evidence in favor of a deterrent effect for variation in sentence severity may gain its own intuitive appeal. Clearly, the number of intervening processes that must take place between (a) the change in penalties for a crime and (b) the possible impact of that alteration on the population of potential offenders may be considerably greater than most of us imagine. When one factors in the perceptual element at the root of deterrence, the complexity of the process only increases. In fact, the very logic upon which deterrence rests may break down. As Foglia (1997) found in her study of the perceived likelihood of arrest on the behavior of inner-city teenagers in a large U.S. northeastern city, "the threat of formal sanctions means little to young people from economically depressed urban neighbourhoods. The irrelevance of arrest is understandable considering these young people have less to lose if arrested; also, they perceive less of a connection between behaviour and legal consequences because they see many commit crimes with impunity and view law enforcement as arbitrary" (1997, p. 433).

Simply put, if penalty structures are irrelevant to potential offenders, it does not matter how severe they might be. Or more broadly, the deterrence process – as a perceptual model – is not nearly as simple as that which one might assume or the economist might contemplate when employing utility functions to explain why the chicken crossed the road against the red light.

IV.B. The consequences of accepting the null hypothesis.

As we have pointed out, we would suggest that the time has come to conditionally accept the null hypothesis: severity of sentences does not affect crime levels. Obviously, this analysis is based on variation in sentence severity within fixed limits. We are not suggesting that a one-dollar fine for armed robbery would be the same as a three-year prison sentence. Rather, we are proposing that we can accept the null hypothesis that variation within the limits that are plausible in western countries will not make a difference.

Within this context, potentially the most intriguing ramification of this conclusion is for sentencing objectives. Principled arguments against sentencing according to deterrence principles have been made by others (e.g. von Hirsch, 1985). It is not our purpose to review those arguments here. We would simply suggest that in addition to those more theoretically based discussions, we should add another of a more practical or pragmatic nature. More specifically, deterrence based sentencing makes false promises to the community in dealing with crime. Further, as long as the public believes that crime can be deterred by legislatures or judges through harsh sentences, there is no need to consider other approaches to crime reduction.

Indeed, it may not be a coincidence that sentencing systems which do not subscribe to general deterrence – in part or in whole – already exist in several western nations. For example, Finland currently bases its sentencing provisions on a principle of "general prevention" (i.e., educating the public about the seriousness of offending) rather than general deterrence (Lappi-Seppälä, 2000). In addition, Canada's new youth justice legislation focuses on imposing proportional sentences and avoids the notion that youths will be deterred by harsh sentences imposed on others (Doob and Sprott, 2003). Similarly, the Law Reform Commission of Ireland has suggested that general deterrence has no place in a modern sentencing structure in large part because there is no credible evidence of its effectiveness (Law Reform Commission 1996, p.6). Finally, the Swedish Ministry of the Attorney General notes in a discussion of sanctions that prison is not a deterrent (National Council for Crime Prevention Sweden 1997, p.22). In other words, it no longer appears to constitute a radical suggestion to accept that - like the missing sock - the general deterrent impact of harsher sentences does not exist.

4. ROLES AND RESPONSIBILITIES OF JUDGES AND LAWYERS

(a) The Adversary System

The method of inquiry in our courts is quite distinct from the scientific method; the method of ascertaining the facts at common law is known as adversarial while the scientific might be labelled inquisitorial. The principal distinguishing characteristic between the two methods resides in the relative passivity of the judge in the adversarial method. The judge's function is to make the ultimate finding of facts but not to personally investigate; rather, to judge the merits of two positions. The tradition in the English-speaking world is to regard the "over-speaking 'judge as no well-tuned cymbal'" (Bacon L.C. as quoted by Lord Denning in *Jones v. National Coal Board*, [1957] 2 Q.B. 55 (C.A.) at 64 (Q.B.)) and should a trial judge intervene too frequently during the trial he or she runs the risk of being reversed on appeal and a new trial ordered. A frank description of our method of inquiry by the Ontario Court of Appeal appears in *Phillips v. Ford Motor Co.* (1971), 18 D.L.R. (3d) 641 at 657 (Ont. C.A.) where Evans J.A. wrote:

> Our mode of trial procedure is based upon the adversarial system in which the contestants seek to establish through relevant supporting evidence, before an impartial trier of facts, those events or happenings which form the bases of their allegations. This procedure assumes that the litigants, assisted by their counsel, will fully and diligently present all the material facts which have evidentiary value in support of their respective positions and that these disputed facts will receive from a trial judge a dispassionate and impartial consideration in order to arrive at the truth of the matters in controversy. A trial is not intended to be a scientific exploration with the presiding judge assuming the role of a research director; it is a forum established for the purpose of providing justice for the litigants. Undoubtedly a court must be concerned with truth, in the sense that it accepts as true certain sworn evidence and rejects other testimony as unworthy of belief, but it cannot embark upon a quest for the "scientific" or "technological" truth when such an adventure does violence to the primary function of the court, which has always been to do justice, according to law.

The adversary method, however, has been justified over the years by many lawyers as capable of promoting the finest approximation to the truth. As Jerome Frank said:

> They think that the best way for the court to discover the facts in a suit is to have each side strive as hard as it can, in a keenly partisan spirit, to bring to the court's attention the evidence favourable to that side. Macauley said that we obtain the fairest decision "when two men argue, as unfairly as possible, on opposite sides" for then "it is certain that no important consideration will altogether escape notice". (*Courts on Trial*, (1949), p. 80.)

The diligence of the parties in ferreting out evidence favourable to their side and the vigour with which they attack their opponent's case are seen as finer guarantees of approximating the historical truth than giving the problem for resolution to some government official whose motivation can rarely be of the magnitude of the parties. Also, it is believed that the bias of the decision-maker can be minimized if played to a much less active role than is demanded in the inquisitorial method. The judge who conducts the examination of witnesses is seen as "descend[ing] into the arena and is liable to have his vision clouded by the dust of the conflict. Unconsciously he deprives himself of the advantage of calm and dispassionate observation". (Lord Green M.R. in *Yuill v. Yuill*, [1945] 1 All E.R. 183 (C.A.) at 189.)

Whether the adversary method will more closely approximate truth is certainly open to question. The lawyer is trained to seek success for the client, to win the game. The goal is to present the best picture of the client's position and not the most complete picture. Also, the adversary system presupposes for success some equality between the parties and when this is lacking the "truth" becomes too often simply the view of the more powerful. Most judges will confess to the frequent temptation to reach out and "even the match" but the system cautions against such practice. Perhaps most importantly, while it may be true that in deciding between the validity of two competing theories the decision-maker may be considerably aided by advocates on each side presenting their respective position in the strongest arguments possible, it is certainly questionable whether such a technique is valuable in ensuring that all of the available evidence has been presented by the parties for examination. As Professor Peter Brett has noted:

> observe the practice of scientists and historians in carrying out their investigations. . . . [A] lengthy search will fail to reveal one competent practitioner in either discipline who will willingly and in advance confine himself, in deciding any question involving factual data, to a choice between two sets of existing data proffered to him by rival claimants. In short, the inquisitorial method is the one used by every genuine seeker of the truth in every walk of life (not merely scientific and historical investigations) with only one exception . . . the trial system in the common-law world. (Brett, "Legal Decision-Making Bias: A Critique" (1973), 45 U. Col. L. Rev. 1.)

One large impediment to our search for truth is that the facts to be discovered by our courts are almost always past facts. Our method of discovering them is normally through the oral testimony of witnesses who have personal knowledge about what happened. This personal "knowledge" might perhaps better be described as personal beliefs about what they now remember of facts which they believe they observed. The trier of fact then has regard to what the witness says and, based on observations of what the witness said and of the manner of saying it, comes to an opinion as to whether that is an honest belief. One can do no more. One cannot, as the scientist might, duplicate in the laboratory the actual facts and test the hypothesis proposed. Facts as found by the court are really then only guesses about the actual facts. "Subjectivity piled on subjectivity . . . a trial court's finding of fact is, then, at best, its belief or opinion about someone else's belief or opinion". (Frank, *Courts on Trial*, p. 22). Recently Mr. Justice Haines of the Ontario Supreme Court described it this way:

> A trial is not a faithful reconstruction of the events as if recorded on some giant television screen. It is an historical recall of that part of the events to which witnesses may be found and presented in an intensely adversary system where the object is quantum of proof. Truth may be only incidental. (*R. v. Lalonde* (1972), 15 C.R.N.S. 1, 5 C.C.C (2d) 168 (H.C.), at 4 (C.R.N.S.)

Besides searching for a different truth than the scientist, our methods are circumscribed by other considerations which require our fact-finding to be done in a way which is acceptable to the parties and to society. Our courts provide a forum for the purpose of resolving disputes between parties which they themselves have been unable to resolve in any other way. Our modern form of trial began simply as a substitute for private duels and feuds which had later been dignified by the process of trial by battle. The resolution of the conflict must be done in a way which ensures social tranquillity generally and is also acceptable to the individual parties. The parties should be able to leave the court feeling that they have had their say, that their case has been presented in the best possible light and that they have been judged by an impartial trier. In judging the efficacy of the legal system's method of fact-finding we must remember that:

> A contested law suit is society's last line of defense in the indispensable effort to secure the peaceful settlement of social conflicts — it is a last-ditch process in which something more is at stake than the truth only of the specific matter in contest. There is at stake also that confidence of the public generally in the impartiality and fairness of public settlement and disputes which is essential if the ditch is to be held and the settlements accepted peaceably. . . . While it is important that the court be right . . . a decision must be made now, one way or the other; . . . to require certainty . . . would be impracticable and undesirable. The law thus compromises. (Hart and McNaughton, *Evidence and Inference in the Law*, D. Lerner, ed., (1958), p. 57.)

With these thoughts in mind we might better understand, and even accept, some of the rules and procedures at work in a criminal trial. For additional thoughts along this line see Brooks, "The Judge and the Adversary System," *The Canadian Judiciary*, A. Linden, ed., (1976).

It would be quite misleading to view the criminal justice system as always leading to an adversarial contest at trial. A large percentage of accused plead guilty. Estimates as to the number of accused charged with criminal offences who plead guilty range between 70 and 90 percent. A large number of guilty pleas are reached as a result of a plea bargain where there is an agreement by the accused to plead guilty with a view to some consideration, usually relating to charge or sentence. The agreement may be reached quite formally after protracted discussion or it may involve a hurried hallway discussion. Usually the plea bargain is entered into following a discussion between the Crown Attorney and the defence counsel but sometimes, although less frequently in Canada, the judge is involved. Sometimes the reality is that the plea bargain can be traced to a discussion between the accused and the police without any lawyer being involved. See generally Klein, *Let's Make A Deal* (1976), Ericson and Baranek, *The Ordering of Justice: A Study of Persons as Dependants in the Criminal Process* (1982) and Warner and Renner, "The Bureaucratic and Adversary Models of the Criminal Courts: The Criminal Sentencing Process", (1981) 1 *Windsor Yearbook of Access to Justice* 81.

STEVE COUGHLAN, "THE 'ADVERSARY SYSTEM': RHETORIC OR REALITY"

(1993), 8 C.J.L.S. 139 at 154-158

In virtually every criminal case, one of the parties will be the Crown prosecutor. What is the role of the prosecutor? The Supreme Court of Canada has said:

> It cannot be over-emphasized that the purpose of a criminal prosecution is not to obtain a conviction, it is to lay before a jury what the Crown considers to be credible evidence relevant to what is alleged to be a crime. Counsel have a duty to see that all available legal proof of the facts is presented; it should be done firmly and pressed to its legitimate strength but it must also be done fairly. *The role of prosecutor excludes any notion of winning or losing*: his function is a matter of public duty than which in civil life there can be none charged with greater personal responsibility. It is to be efficiently performed with an ingrained sense of the dignity, the seriousness and the justness of judicial proceedings.[24] [emphasis added]

The court has also referred to the "fundamental difference in the respective roles of the prosecution and the defence," stating that "the tradition of Crown counsel in this country carrying out their role as 'ministers of justice' and not as adversaries has generally been very high."[25]

Similarly, the Canadian Bar Association Code of Professional Conduct says:

> When engaged as a prosecutor, the lawyer's prime duty is not to seek a conviction, but to present before the trial court all available credible evidence relevant to the alleged crime in order that justice may be done through a fair trial upon the merits. The prosecutor exercises a public function involving much discretion and power, and must act fairly and dispassionately.[26]

These authorities do not attach restrictions to the adversarial ways in which a prosecutor may behave: they say that the prosecutor's role is not adversarial. The Crown and defence attorneys in a criminal trial do not occupy equal and opposite positions, as the adversary system would require – Crown counsel is not there as an adversary. How, one must ask, can one have an adversary system with only one adversary?

Most lawyers know prosecutors who clearly do not regard their role in this way: some prosecutors seem to regard themselves as advocates for the police, and are for example unwilling to exercise their own discretion to drop charges.[27] Problems have also been noted owing to Crown prosecutors failing to provide

---

24 G.R. Williams, *Legal Negotiation and Settlement* (St. Paul, Mn: West Publishing, 1983) also notes that it is difficult for even the most competent negotiator to reach a reasonable settlement if she is not also a competent trial lawyer: in judging the strength of her case, she is required to take into account her own weakness in court.

25 *R. v. Stinchcombe* (1991), 8 C.R. (4th) 277 (S.C.C.) at pp. 283-289.

26 Canadian Bar Association, *Code of Professional Conduct*, (Ottawa: Canadian Bar Association, 1987) commentary 9 to rule IX.

27 See, for example, H. Lilles, "Some Problems in the Administration of Justice in Remote and Isolated Communities" (1990) 15 *Queens' L.J.* 327 at 340, suggesting that Crown attorneys in the Yukon and Northwest Territories" appear to be reluctant to exercise any significant prosecutorial discretion."

adequate disclosure to the defence.[28] But to the extent that this is true, these Crown prosecutors are failing to perform their jobs properly. Further, this failure illustrates precisely the difficulty in adopting the rhetoric of adversarialism: if prosecutors believe they are adversaries in a competitive activity, we cannot be surprised if they try to win.

One might suggest that the adversary system functions differently in civil and criminal matters, and so the non-adversarial role of Crown counsel is not sufficient to prove that criminal cases are not adversarial. But consider also the role of defence counsel.

One study found, for example, that in 80% of cases where bail was in issue, no hearing took place: 65% of accused were released without formality, and 15% remained in custody.[29] In the remaining 20% of cases, where a bail hearing was held, the accused was released half the time. This means that in two-thirds of all cases, the accused was released on bail because of an agreement between Crown and defence, while only 10% of the time did the defence get the accused released by adversarial means. That is, defence counsel negotiated the release of six clients for every one released through adversarial means.

Similarly, other studies have found that for every charge that results in an acquittal, approximately four charges are stayed or withdrawn without trial.[30] One cannot simply infer from these figures that defence counsel were four times as successful in having clients released through negotiation;[31] it seems, however, a reasonable inference that this strategy must be at least as successful as going to trial.[32]

Of course, one cannot simply say that these results depended solely on the strategy of defence counsel. In most cases it will be obvious to trained counsel whether a particular accused is likely to be released on bail, for example, and if so on what types of conditions. In those cases, defense counsel and prosecutors who reach an agreement are only making use of their expertise. In fact, it is the metasystem, not the system, that is operating. It is not necessary to invoke the rules of the adversary system, or adversary behavior in the broad sense, to

---

28 See, in particular, *Report of the Commission of Inquiry into the Prosecution of Donald Marshall, Jr.* (Halifax: 1989), finding 1, 4, and *R. v. Stinchcombe, supra* note 25.

29 E. MacKaay, *The Paths of Justice: A Study of the Operation of Criminal Courts in Montreal* (Montreal: Groupe de recherché en jurimétrie, 1976) at 36.

30 See Canada, Policy, Programs and Research Branch, Research and Statistics Section, Department of Justice, *Some Statistics on the Preliminary Inquiry in Canada* (Ottawa: Department of Justice, 1984) at 33, which found that 25% of the charges in the study were stayed or withdrawn, compared to a 6% acquittal rate. See also Canadian Centre for Justice Statistics, "Processing Time in Youth Courts, 1986-87 to 1989-90" 11:4 Juristat 1 at 11, which shows the number of charges stayed or withdrawn in the four years studied ranging from 20.9% to 24.0%, while the number of dismissals or finding of not guilty range from 5.3% to 5.7%.

31 Charges may have been stayed with the intention of relaying them at a later time, for example.

32 A similar example, though one where the benefit to the accused is less obvious, concerns preliminary inquiries. In principle, one would expect lawyers who are trying "to save that client by all means and expedients" (see note 5) routinely to try to use preliminary inquiries as a way of having their client not face trial. In fact, 52% of the time an accused is committed for trial at the preliminary by consent, and a further 40% of the time the defence consents to the admission of some of the Crown's evidence. Only 6% of the time is a preliminary inquiry fully contested. See *Some Statistics on the Preliminary Inquiry in Canada, supra* note 30 at 24-27.

explain how these decisions, the majority, are reached. In a system that expects these types of agreements to be reached, excessive adversarial behavior is out of place.[33]

Consider other things a partisan defence counsel will do for a client. If the client is a young offender, alternative measures may be available, provided that the prosecutor believes it is appropriate to use them. Producing that opinion in a prosecutor requires consensus-building and co-operation: a prosecutor must be persuaded, not forced, to recommend alternative measures. The same is true of plea bargaining: the prosecutor cannot be forced to agree. Only a bargain that both parties can accept will be successful – in effect, the win/win model of commercial negotiations, though the "winning" on the part of the accused is a limitation of loss.[34] Indeed, one empirical study of the plea-bargaining process has argued that the prosecutor and defence lawyer generally reach "an agreement that merely reflects the going rate":[35] once again, the meta-system.

Further, a great percentage of criminal charges concern minor offences – shoplifting and similar small-scale property offences.[36] The great majority of these criminal charges result in a finding of guilty, generally by way of guilty plea.[37] Accordingly, one of the most common tasks for many defence counsel is to speak to sentence on a minor matter.[38] Particularly if Crown counsel's role is limited to noting that the facts are unexceptional and that a penalty in the normal range is called for, it is difficult for any defence counsel, try as she might, to be very adversarial.

That is not to say that defence counsel will not zealously act in the interests of her client. Competent defence counsel will call witnesses on sentencing where appropriate, take steps in advance to have the accused enter a treatment program or pay restitution, and argue strongly for the most lenient sentence appropriate. But doing these things is not what we would describe in any other circumstances as adversarial. Counsel is being partisan, and is taking steps to assist the accused;

---

33 But see the discussion below, under "Some Defences of Adversarialism Rejected," for the ethical implications of this observation.

34 But see the Canadian Bar Association *Code of Professional Conduct*, *supra* note 26, commentary 12 to rule IX, allows plea bargaining only where the client is prepared to admit guilt, and so some sentence is inevitable.

35 R.V. Ericson & P.M. Baranek, *The Ordering of Justice: A Study of Accused Persons as Dependants in the Criminal Process* (Toronto: Toronto University Press, 1982) at 117. This study is discussed at greater length below, under "Some Defences of Adversarialism Rejected."

36 Canadian Centre for Justice Statistics, "Preliminary Crime Statistics – 1989," 10:9 Juristat at 2 indicates that in 1989, approximately 90% of Criminal Code offences reported by the police were property crime (59.5%, the majority of which was theft under $1,000) or other crime – "i.e., mischief, disturbing the peace, bail violations" (30.3%).

37 *Some Statistics on the Preliminary Inquiry in Canada*, *supra* note 30 at 66-67 indicates that, in provincial court, a "not guilty" plea is entered only 18% of the time.

38 One cannot make direct inferences about the tasks counsel perform from the statistics on crime. Some counsel restrict themselves to more serious cases. More importantly, the less serious the offence, the less likely it is that an accused person will have counsel: many guilty pleas to minor offences will be entered by the accused personally. Nonetheless, particularly given the existence of legal aid schemes, it seems reasonable to expect a general correlation between the crime statistics and the role of counsel.

but seeing to it that the accused receives counseling and a psychiatric evaluation is not acting as an adversary.

On the whole, the role of criminal lawyers involves more non-adversarial than adversarial functions. Certainly there are times when counsel will behave adversarially, but non-adversarial roles dominate the criminal lawyer's time.

See further David Paciocco, "Understanding the Accusatorial System" (2010) 14 *Can. Crim. L. Rev.* 307.

Is the adversary system and the criminal-law precept that the State must prove guilt beyond reasonable doubt compatible with values of women and aboriginal people? In arriving at your opinion consider the following views:

CARRIE MENKEL-MEADOW, PORTIA IN A DIFFERENT VOICE: SPECULATION ON A WOMEN'S LAWYERING PROCESS

(1985), 1 Berkeley Women's L.J. 39, at pp. 44-55

In her book, *In a Different Voice: Psychological Theory and Women's Development*, Gilligan observes that much of what has been written about human psychological development has been based on studies of male subjects exclusively. As a consequence, girls and women have either not been described, or they are said to have "failed" to develop on measurement scales based on male norms. Just as Gilligan has observed that studies of human psychological development have been centred on males, feminists have observed the law to be based on male values and behaviours. As Frances Olsen notes:

> Law is supposed to be rational, objective, abstract and principled, like men; it is not supposed to be irrational, subjective, contextualized or personalized like women. The social, political and intellectual practices that constitute "law" were for many years carried out almost exclusively by men. Given that women were long excluded from the practice of law, it should not be surprising that the traits associated with women are not greatly valued by law. Moreover, in a kind of vicious cycle, the "maleness" of law was used as a justification for excluding women from practicing law. While the number of women in law has been rapidly increasing, the field continues to be heavily male dominated.

The male-derived model of moral reasoning and psychological development described by Gilligan values hierarchical thinking based on the logic of reasoning from abstract, universal principles. Gilligan measures her findings against the work of her colleague, Lawrence Kohlberg. His theory of moral development comprised of six "universal" stages is based on a study of 84 *boys* from childhood through adulthood. Gilligan explains that when Kohlberg's model is applied to women, they tend to score at a stage three, a stage characterized by seeing morality as a question of interpersonal relations and caring for and pleasing others. In looking at moral judgments and hearing the "women's voice," Gilligan discovered that:

When one begins with the study of women and derives developmental constructs from their lives, the outline of a moral conception different from that described by Freud, Piaget, or Kohlberg begins to emerge and informs a different description of development. In this conception, the moral problem arises from conflicting responsibilities rather than from competing rights and requires for its resolution a mode of thinking that is contextual and narrative rather than formal and abstract.

An example drawn from Gilligan's work best illustrates the duality of girls' and boys' moral development. In one of the three studies on which her book is based, a group of children are asked to solve Heinz's dilemma, a hypothetical moral reasoning problem used by Kohlberg to rate moral development on his six-stage scale. The dilemma is that Heinz's wife is dying of cancer and requires a drug which the local pharmacist has priced beyond's Heinz's means. The question is posed: should Heinz steal the drug?

To illustrate and explain the differences between the ways boys and girls approached this problem, Gilligan quotes from two members of her sample, Jake and Amy. Jake, an 11-year-old boy, sees the problem as one of "balancing rights," like a judge who must make a decision or a mathematician who must solve an algebraic equation. Life is worth more than property, therefore Heinz should steal the drug. For Amy, an 11-year-old girl, the problem is different. Like a "bad" law student she "fights the hypo"; she wants to know more facts: Have Heinz and the druggist explored other possibilities, like a loan or credit transaction? Why couldn't Heinz and the druggist simply sit down and talk it out so that the druggist would come to see the importance of Heinz's wife's life? In Gilligan's terms, Jake explores the Heinz dilemma with "the logic of justice" while Amy uses the "ethic of care." Amy scores lower on the Kohlberg scale because she sees the problem rooted in the persons involved rather than in the larger universal issues posed by the dilemma.

In conventional terms Jake would make a good lawyer because he spots the legal issues of excuse and justification, balances the rights, and reaches a decision, while considering implicitly, if not explicitly, the precedential effect of his decision. But as Gilligan argues, and as I develop more fully below, Amy's approach is also plausible and legitimate, both as a style of moral reasoning and as a style of lawyering. Amy seeks to keep the people engaged; she holds the needs of the parties and their relationships constant and hopes to satisfy them all (as in a negotiation), rather than selecting a winner (as in a lawsuit). If one must be hurt, she attempts to find a resolution that will hurt least the one who can least bear the hurt. (Is she engaged in a "deep pocket" policy analysis?) She looks beyond the "immediate lawsuit" to see how the "judgment" will affect the parties. If Heinz steals the drug and goes to jail, who will take care of his wife? Furthermore, Amy is concerned with *how* the dilemma is resolved; the process by which the parties communicate may be crucial to the outcome. (Amy cares as much about procedure as about substance.) And she is being a good lawyer when she inquires whether all the facts have been discovered and considered.

The point here is not that Amy's method of moral reasoning is better than Jake's, nor that she is a better lawyer than Jake. (Some have read Gilligan to argue that the women's voice is better. I don't read her that way.) The point is that Amy does some things differently from Jake when she resolves this dilemma, and these things have useful analogies to lawyering and may not have been sufficiently credited as useful lawyering skills. Jake and Amy have something to learn from one another.

Thus, although a "choice of rights" conception (life v. property) of solving human problems may be important, it is not the only or the best way. Responsibilities to self and to others may be equally important in measuring moral, as well as legal decision making, but have thus far been largely ignored. For example, a lawyer who feels responsible for the decisions she makes with her client may be more inclined to think about how those decisions will hurt other people and how the lawyer and client feel about making such decisions. (Amy thinks about Heinz, the druggist, and Heinz's wife at all times in reaching her decision; Jake makes a choice in abstract terms without worrying as much about the people it affects.)

. . . .

III. THE ADVOCACY-ADVERSARIAL MODEL

The basic structure of our legal system is premised on the adversarial model, which involves two advocates who present their cases to a disinterested third party who listens to evidence and argument and declares one party a winner. In this simplified description of the Anglo-American model of litigation, we can identify some of the basic concepts and values which underlie this choice of arrangements: advocacy, persuasion, hierarchy, competition, and binary results (win/lose). The conduct of litigation is relatively similar (not coincidentally, I suspect) to a sporting event — there are rules, a referee, an object to the game, and a winner is declared after the play is over. As I have argued elsewhere, this conception of the dispute resolution process is applied more broadly than just in the conventional courtroom. The adversarial model affects the way in which lawyers advise their clients ("get as much as you can"), negotiate disputes ("we can really get them on that") and plan transactions ("let's be sure to draft this to your advantage"). All of these activities in lawyering assume competition over the same limited and equally valued items (usually money) and assume that success is measured by maximizing individual gain. Would Gilligan's Amy create a different model?

By returning to Heinz's dilemma we see some hints about what Amy might do. Instead of concluding that a choice must be made between life and property, in resolving the conflict between parties as Jake does, Amy sees no need to hierarchically order the claims. Instead, she tries to account for all the parties' needs, and searches for a way to find a solution that satisfies the needs of both. In her view, Heinz should be able to obtain the drug for his wife and the pharmacist should still receive payment. So Amy suggests a loan, credit arrangement, or a discussion of other ways to structure the transaction. In short, she won't play by the adversarial rules. She searches outside the system for a way to solve the problem, trying to keep both parties in mind. Her methods substantiate Gilligan's observations that women will try to change the rules to preserve the relationships.

Furthermore, in addition to looking for more substantive solutions to the problem (i.e., not accepting the binary win/lose conception of the problem), Amy also wants to change the process. Amy sees no reason why she must act as a neutral arbiter of a dispute and make a decision based only on the information she has. She "belie[ves] in communication as the mode of conflict resolution and [is convinced] that the solution to the dilemma will follow from its compelling representation...." If the parties talk directly to each other, they will be more likely to appreciate the importance of each other's needs. Thus, she believes direct communication, rather than third party mediated debate, might solve the problem, recognizing that two apparently conflicting positions can both be simultaneously legitimate, and there need not be a single victor.

The notion that women might have more difficulty with full-commitment-to-one-side model of the adversary system is graphically illustrated by Hilary, one of the women lawyers in Gilligan's study. This lawyer finds herself in one of the classic moral dilemmas of the adversary system: she sees that her opponent has failed to make use of a document that is helpful to his case and harmful to hers. In deciding not to tell him about the document because of what she sees as her "professional vunerability" in the male adversary system, she concludes that "the adversary system of justice impedes not only the supposed search for truth (the conventional criticism), but also *the expression of concern for the person on the other side*." Gilligan describes Hilary's tension between her concept of rights (learned through legal training) and her female ethic of care as a sign of her socialization in the male world of lawyering. Thus, the advocacy model, with its commitment to one-side advocacy, seems somehow contrary to "apprehending the reality of the other" which lawyers like Hilary experience. Even the continental inquisitorial model, frequently offered as an alternative to the adversarial model, includes most of these elements of the male system — hierarchy, advocacy, competition and binary results.

So what kind of legal system would Amy and Hilary create if left to their own devices? They might look for ways to alter the harshness of win/lose results; they might alter the rules of the game (or make it less like a game); and they might alter the very structures and forms themselves. Thus, in a sense Amy and Hilary's approach can already be found in some of the current alternatives to the adversary model such as mediation. Much of the current interest in alternative dispute resolution is an attempt to modify the harshness of the adversarial process and expand the kinds of solutions available, in order to respond the better to the varied needs of the parties. Amy's desire to engage the parties in direct communication with each other is reflected in mediation models where the parties talk directly to each other and forge their own solutions. The work of Gilligan and Noddings, demonstrating an ethic of care and a heightened sense of empathy in women, suggests that women lawyers may be particularly interested in mediation as an alternative to litigation as a method of resolving disputes.

Even within the present adversarial model, Amy and Hilary might, in their concern for others, want to provide for a broader conception of interested parties, permitting participation by those who might be affected by the dispute (an ethic of inclusion). In addition, like judges who increasingly are managing more of the details of their cases, Amy and Hilary might seek a more active role in settlement processes and rely less on court-ordered relief. Amy and Hilary might look for other ways to construct their lawsuits and remedies in much the same ways as courts of equity mitigated the harshness of the law court's very limited array of remedies by expanding the conception of what was possible.

The process and rules of the adversary system itself might look different if there were more female voices in the legal profession. If Amy is less likely than Jake to make assertive, rights-based statements, is she less likely to adapt to the male-created advocacy mode? In my experience as a trial lawyer, I observed that some women had difficulty with the "macho" ethic of the courtroom battle. Even those who did successfully adapt to the male model often confronted a dilemma because women were less likely to be perceived as behaving properly when engaged in strong adversarial conduct. It is important to be "strong" in the courtroom, according to the stereotypic conception of appropriate trial behavior. The woman who conforms to the female stereotype by being "soft" or "weak" is a bad trial lawyer, but if a woman is "tough" or "strong" in the courtroom, she is seen as acting inappropriately for a woman. Note, however, that this stereotyping is contextual: the same woman acting as a "strong" or "tough" mother with difficult children would be praised for that conduct. Women's strength is approved of with the proviso that it be exerted in appropriately female spheres.

Amy and Hilary might create a different form of advocacy, one resembling a "conversation" with the fact finder, relying on the creation of a relationship with the jury for its effectiveness, rather than on persuasive intimidation. There is some anecdotal evidence that this is happening already. Recently, several women prosecutors described their styles of trial advocacy as the creation of a personal relationship with the jury in which they urge jurors to examine their own perceptions and values and encourage them to think for themselves, rather than "buying" the arguments of one of the advocates. This is a conception of the relationship between the lawyer and the fact-finder which is based on trust and mutual respect rather than on dramatics, intimidation and power, the male mode in which these women had been trained and which they found unsatisfactory.

In sum, the growing strength of women's voice in the legal profession may change the adversarial system into a more cooperative, less war-like system of communication between disputants in which solutions are mutually agreed upon rather than dictated by an outsider, won by the victor, and imposed upon the loser. Some seeds of change may already be found in existing alternatives to the litigation model, such as mediation. It remains to be seen what further changes Portia's voice may make.

Compare D.L. Rhode, "The Woman's Point of View" (1988), 38 J. Leg. Ed. 39.

MADAM JUSTICE BERTHA WILSON,* WILL WOMEN JUDGES REALLY MAKE A DIFFERENCE?

(1990), 28 Osgoode Hall L.J. 507

. . . .

In the literature which is required reading for every newly appointed judge, it is repeatedly stated that judges must be both independent and impartial, that these qualities are basic to the proper administration of justice and fundamental to the legitimacy of the judicial role. The judge must not approach his or her task with preconceived notions about law or policy, with personal prejudice against parties or issues, or with bias toward a particular outcome of a case. Socrates defined the essential qualities of a judge in the following manner: "Four things belong to a judge: to hear courteously, to answer wisely, to consider soberly, and to decide impartially."

. . . .

Many have criticized as totally unreal the concept that judges are somehow superhuman, neutral, above politics and unbiased, and are able to completely separate themselves from their personal opinions and predispositions when exercising their judicial function.

. . . .

Judge Rosalie Abella (Chair of the Ontario Law Reform Commission) also doubts that judicial impartiality is a realistic requirement. In her article "The Dynamic Nature of Equality," she emphasizes that "[e]very decisionmaker who walks into a courtroom to hear a case is armed not only with the relevant legal texts, but with a set of values, experiences and assumptions that are thoroughly embedded."

. . . .

But what has all this got to do with the subject: "Will women judges really make a difference?" It has a great deal to do with it, and whether you agree or not will probably depend on your perception of the degree to which the existing law reflects the judicial neutrality or impartiality we have been discussing. If the existing law can be viewed as the product of judicial neutrality or impartiality, even although the judiciary has been very substantially male, then you may conclude that the advent of increased numbers of women judges should make no difference, assuming, that is, that these women judges will bring to bear the same neutrality and impartiality. However, if you conclude that the existing law, in some areas at least, cannot be viewed as the product of judicial neutrality, then your answer may be very different.

. . . .

Taking from my own experience as a judge of 14 years' standing, working closely with my male colleagues on the bench, there are probably whole areas of the law on which there is no uniquely feminine perspective. This is not to say that the development of the law in these areas has not been influenced by the fact that lawyers and judges have all been men. Rather, the principles and the underlying premises are so firmly entrenched and so fundamentally sound that no good would be achieved by attempting to re-invent the wheel, even if the revised version did have a few more spokes in it. I have in mind areas such as the law of contract, the law of real property, and the law applicable to corporations. In some other areas of the law, however, a distinctly male perspective is clearly discernible. It has resulted in legal principles that are not fundamentally sound and that should be revisited when the opportunity presents itself. Canadian feminist scholarship has done an excellent job of identifying those areas and making suggestions for reform. Some aspects of the criminal law in particular cry out for change; they are based on presuppositions about the nature of women and women's sexuality that, in this day and age, are little short of ludicrous.

But how do we handle the problem that women judges, just as much as their male counterparts, are subject to the duty of impartiality? As was said at the outset, judges must not approach their task with preconceived notions about law and policy. They must approach it with detachment and, as Lord MacMillan said, purge their minds "not only of partiality to persons, but of partiality to arguments." Does this then foreclose any kind of "judicial affirmative action" to counteract the influence of the dominant male perspective of the past and establish judicial neutrality through a countervailing female perspective? Is Karen Selick, writing recently in the *Lawyers Weekly*, correct when she argues that offsetting male bias with female bias would only be compounding the injustice? Does the nature of the judicial process itself present an insuperable hurdle so that the legislatures rather than the courts must be looked to for any significant legal change?

In part this may be so. Certainly, the Legislature is the more effective instrument for rapid or radical change. But there is no reason why the judiciary cannot exercise some modest degree of creativity in areas where modern insights and life's experience have indicated that the law has gone awry. However, and this is extremely important, it will be a Pyrrhic victory for women and for the justice system as a whole if changes in the law come only through the efforts of women lawyers and women judges. The Americans were smart to realize that courses and workshops on gender bias for judges, male and female, are an essential follow-up to scholarly research and learned writing. In Canada, we are just beginning to touch the fringes.

. . . .

I return, then, to the question of whether the appointment of more women judges will make a difference. Because the entry of women into the judiciary is so recent, few studies have been done on the subject. Current statistics show that just over 9 percent of federally appointed judges are women; it is reasonable to assume that more women will be appointed to the Bench as more women become licensed to practise law. Will this growing number of women judges by itself make a difference?

The expectation is that it will, that the mere presence of women on the bench will make a difference. In her article "The Gender of Judges," Suzanna Sherry (an Associate Law Professor at the University of Minnesota) suggests that the mere fact that women are judges serves an educative function; it helps to shatter stereotypes about the role of women in society that are held by male judges and lawyers, as well as by litigants, jurors, and witnesses.

Judge Gladys Kessler (former President of the National Association of Women Judges in the United States) defends the search for competent women appointees to the bench. She says: "But the ultimate justification for deliberately seeking judges of both sexes and all colors and backgrounds is to keep the public's trust. The public must perceive its judges as fair, impartial and representative of the diversity of those who are being judged." Justice Wald has expressed similar sentiments. She believes that women judges are indispensable to the public's confidence in the ability of the courts to respond to the legal problems of all classes of citizens.

. . . .

Some feminist writers are persuaded that the appointment of more women judges will have an impact on the process of judicial decision-making itself and on the development of the substantive law. As was mentioned earlier, this flows from the belief that women view the world and what goes on in it from a different perspective from men. Some define the difference in perspective solely in terms that women do not accept male perceptions and interpretations of events as the norm or as objective reality. Carol Gilligan (a Professor of Education at Harvard University) sees the difference as going much deeper than that. In her view, women think differently from men, particularly in responding to moral dilemmas. They have, she says, different ways of thinking about themselves and their relationships to others.

. . . .

Gilligan's work on conceptions of morality among adults suggests that women's ethical sense is significantly different from men's. Men see moral problems as arising from competing rights; the adversarial process comes easily to them. Women see moral problems as arising from competing obligations, the one to the other; the important thing is to preserve relationships, to develop an ethic of caring. The goal, according to women's ethical sense, is not seen in terms of winning or losing but, rather, in terms of achieving an optimum outcome for all individuals involved in the moral dilemma. It is not difficult to see how this contrast in thinking might form the basis of different perceptions of justice.

There is merit in Gilligan's analysis. In part, it may explain the traditional reluctance of courts to get too deeply into the circumstances of a case, their anxiety to reduce the context of the dispute to its bare bones through a complex system of exclusionary evidentiary rules. This is one of the characteristic features of the adversarial process. We are all familiar with the witness on cross-examination who wants to explain his or her answer, who feels that a simple yes or no is not an adequate response, and who is frustrated and angry at being cut off with a half-truth. It is so much easier to come up with a black and white answer if you are unencumbered by a broader context which might prompt you, in Lord MacMillan's words, to temper the cold light of reason with the warmer tints of imagination and sympathy.

. . . .

Professor Patricia Cain, in her article "Good and Bad Bias: A Comment on Feminist Theory and Judging," says:

> What we want, it seems to me, are lawyers who can tell their clients' story, lawyers who can help judges to see the parties as human beings, and who can help remove the separation between judge and litigant. And, then, what we want from our judges is a special ability to listen with connection before engaging in the separation that accompanies judgment.

Obviously, this is not an easy role for the judge — to enter into the skin of the litigant and make his or her experience part of your experience and only when you have done that, to judge. But we have to do it; or at least make an earnest attempt to do it. Whether the criticism of the justice system comes to us through Royal Commissions, through the media, or just through our own personal friends, we cannot escape the conclusion that, in some respects, our existing system of justice has been found wanting. And as Mr. Justice Rothman says, the time to do something about it is *now*.

One of the important conclusions emerging from the Council of Europe's Seminar on Equality between Men and Women held in Strasbourg last November is that the universalist doctrine of human rights must include a realistic concept of masculine and feminine humanity regarded as a whole, that humankind *is* dual and must be represented in its dual form if the trap of an asexual abstraction in which *human being* is always declined in the masculine is to be avoided. If women lawyers and women judges through their differing perspectives on life can bring a new humanity to bear on the decision-making process, perhaps they *will* make a difference. Perhaps they will succeed in infusing the law with an understanding of what it means to be fully human.

ABORIGINAL PEOPLES AND CRIMINAL JUSTICE

Law Reform Commission of Canada, Report No. 34: (1991), 5-7

The Aboriginal Perspective on Criminal Justice

Aboriginal communities number in the several hundreds and each has had a distinctive experience of the Canadian criminal justice system. Given this diversity, there is necessarily some oversimplification in the following general description of Aboriginal perceptions and aspirations. Nevertheless, we have been struck by the remarkably uniform picture of the system that has been drawn by Aboriginal speakers and writers.

I.   Aboriginal Perceptions

From the Aboriginal perspective, the criminal justice system is an alien one, imposed by the dominant white society. Wherever they turn or are shuttled throughout the system, Aboriginal offenders, victims or witnesses encounter a sea of white faces. Not surprisingly, they regard the system as deeply insensitive to their traditions and values: many view it as unremittingly racist.

Abuse of power and the distorted exercise of discretion are identified time and again as principal defects of the system. The police are often seen by Aboriginal people as a foreign, military presence descending on communities to wreak havoc and take people away. Far from being a source of stability and security, the force is feared by them even when its services are necessary to restore a modicum of social peace to the community.

For those living in remote and reserve communities, the entire court apparatus, quite literally, appears to descend from the sky — an impression that serves to magnify their feelings of isolation and erects barriers to their attaining an understanding of the system.

The process is in reality incomprehensible to those who speak only Aboriginal languages, especially where little or no effort is made to provide adequate interpretation services. Even the English- or French-speaking inhabitants of these communities find the language of the courts and lawyers difficult to understand. Understanding is more than a problem of mere language. Aboriginal persons contend that virtually all of the primary actors in the process (police, lawyers, judges, correctional personnel) patronize them and consistently fail to explain adequately what the process requires of them or what is going to happen to them. Even those who are prepared to acknowledge certain well-intentioned aspects of the present system nevertheless conclude that the system has utterly failed.

Such efforts as have been made to involve the community in the administration of justice are seen as puny and insignificant, and there is little optimism about the future. Elders see the community's young people as the primary victims of the system — cut adrift by it and removed from the community's support as well as from its spiritual and cultural traditions. They recount experiences of children taken from their communities at an early age who later emerge, hardened from the court and correctional processes and ultimately beyond the reach of even imaginative initiatives designed to promote rehabilitation.

Evident and understandable weariness and frustration attend any discussion of approaches to fixing the system or setting it right. For Aboriginal persons, the system presents an unending course of barriers and obstacles, with no avenues of effective complaint or redress. Their sense of injustice is bottomless. They have little or no confidence in the legal profession or in the judiciary to bring about justice or to effect a just resolution of any particular dispute in which they are involved. If the truth be told, most have given up on the criminal justice system.

II.   Aboriginal Aspirations

Aboriginal people have a vision of a justice system that is sensitive to their customs, traditions and beliefs. This vision is a natural outgrowth of their aspirations to self-government and sovereignty. They desire a criminal justice system that is Aboriginal-designed, -run and -populated, from top to bottom.

Undoubtedly there are many contrasting visions as to what constitutes an Aboriginal justice system, but fundamental is the belief that the system must be faithful to Aboriginal traditions and cultural values, while adapting them to modern society. Hence, a formal Aboriginal justice system would evince appropriate respect for community Elders and leaders, give heed to the requirements of Aboriginal spirituality and pay homage to the relation of humankind to the land and to nature.

The Aboriginal vision of justice gives pre-eminence to the interests of the collectivity, its overall orientation being holistic and integrative. Thus, it is community-based, stressing mediation and conciliation while seeking an acknowledgment of responsibility from those who transgress the norms of their society. While working toward a reconciliation between the offender and the victim, an Aboriginal justice system would pursue the larger objective of reintegrating the offender into the community as a whole.

The Aboriginal vision challenges both common and civil law concepts. Statute law becomes less important. Within an Aboriginal justice system, laws would not be uniform or homogeneous; they would vary from community to community, depending on customary practices. Customary law would be the binding force promoting harmony within the community.

While possessing common general characteristics, an Aboriginal justice system would of necessity be pluralistic. What such a system would actually look like is unclear. This haziness is a source of frustration. Much essential detail is missing, and Aboriginal people are hesitant to provide that detail, not because they are incapable of providing it — some communities have well-developed and well-articulated models — but because, in their view, they should not have to do so. They aspire to local control. Their contention is essentially: "Give us the keys. Let us control the system. We can hardly do worse than you have."

For accounts of one judge's struggle to deal with cultural diversity in the Yukon Territory, see H. Lilles, "Some Problems in the Administration of Justice in Remote and Isolated Communities" (1990) 15 Queen's L.J. 327 and "A Plea for More Human Values in Our Justice System" (1992) 17 Queen's L.J. 328.

RUPERT ROSS, DANCING WITH A GHOST

Exploring Indian Reality
(Octopus Publishing, 1992), 41-46

[Rupert Ross was an assistant Crown Attorney for the District of Kenora, Ontario, where he worked closely with the Ojibway and Cree peoples to make the court system more responsive to the needs of their communities.]

. . . .

Gradually, though, I began to see and hear things which made me suspect that there might exist a whole range of different explanations where Native people are concerned. One young victim of a rape refused to testify because, as she put it, "It's not right to do this after so much time. He should be finished with it now and getting on with his life." She was 16 years old.

Another woman, the victim of a violent assault by her dangerous nephew, went over her evidence with me in great detail just before court. She insisted (uncharacteristically, I should add) that I do whatever I could to send this uncontrollably violent young man out of the community for as long as possible so that she and her children could live in peace. When she took the witness stand minutes later, however, her refusal to say anything at all about the attack led to his acquittal.

In another case, after a lengthy review of her evidence, the victim, a 15-year-old who had been sexually assaulted by her former boyfriend, told me she thought she could repeat her story in court. As we walked into the courtroom, though, she tugged at my sleeve and asked, "Should I say these things in court? Is it right?"

"Is it right?" That was a dumbfounding question for me. I knew of many significant reasons which made it difficult for people to testify, but it had never occurred to me that in their eyes it might not be the *right* thing to do. I had always assumed that even the most frightened and reluctant witness shared my conviction that testifying was what they should do, even if competing concerns made it impossible for them to go through with it.

What, I asked myself, if we are wrong in that assumption when we deal with Native people? Could they actually believe that coming forward in this fashion was an improper thing to do? If that was the case, then factors such as fear or embarrassment only reinforced the basic disinclination.

It was not until 1986, at a conference in Whitehorse dealing with Native justice issues, that I began to see a little further into the dynamics of such reluctance. It was commonly agreed by the conference participants that Native people, with their belief in consensus decision-making, might find our adversarial system foreign and inappropriate. To explore alternate forms of dealing with social disruption we play-acted a more informal mediation process. In this exercise we devised a scenario in which a youth had broken into the community store and vandalized it. We selected some volunteers from the audience to act as the boy, the store manager and the mediation panel. That panel then asked them both about the break-in, the value of the damage, about how they felt towards each other, and about what could be done to set matters straight between them. It seemed a sensible alternative approach.

One of the mediators, however, was Charlie Fisher, whom I mentioned in Chapter 1. He was asked if such a technique bore any resemblance to what might have been done at Whitedog in more traditional times. His response was a very vehement "no". He then volunteered to make the appropriate changes.

He began by getting rid of the chairs and tables, everyone sat on the floor in a circle, as equals. He then asked for two other people to act as "Representing Elders", one each for the boy and the store manager. As he continued, it became clear that our little experiment in non-adversarial mediation was flawed in virtually every respect. In Charlie's version, the boy and the store manager never spoke in the presence of the panel of Elders. There was no discussion whatever about the break-in, the damage, the feelings of the disputants, or what might be done to set matters straight. There was no *talk* of compensation or restitution, much less the actual imposition of such measures.

Once we understood what was *not* going to take place, we had only one question left: "Why, then, is there a panel at all?"

Charlie Fisher tried to answer us in this way. The duty of each Representing Elder, he explained, was not to speak for the young man or the store manager, but to counsel them in private. That counselling was intended to help each person "rid himself of his bad feelings". Such counselling would continue until the Elder was satisfied that "the person's spirit had been cleansed and made whole again". When the panel convened, an Elder could signify that such cleansing had taken place by touching the ceremonial pipe. The panel would continue to meet until both Elders so signified. At that point, the pipe would be lit and passed to all. As far as the community was concerned, that would be the end of the matter. Whether the two disputants later arranged recompense of some sort was entirely up to them. Passing the pipe signified, as Charlie phrased it, that each had been "restored to the community and to himself".

What was going on here? No fact finding? No allocation of responsibility? No imposition of consequences? Weren't these the very things our courts were created to do? Why didn't the Whitedog people do them in traditional times?

. . . .

I suggest that we must react differently than we have in the past when we find ourselves puzzled by something a Native person has done or, more importantly, when we are about to come to a negative conclusion about it. Rather than assuming that their behaviour stems from principles similar to ours, and then judging that behaviour badly because it does not conform to our own typical behaviour, we must realize that their behaviour is different because it flows from different basic principles. We are not seeing, despite what we *seem* to be seeing, a people who don't care if their friends make dangerous mistakes or if their loved ones fall into self-destructive habits, who don't care about the peace, health and security of their communities. We are instead seeing people whose traditional commandments require that they demonstrate their care in two ways which are fundamentally different from our ways: by conferring virtually absolute freedom on everyone and, when damaging events do occur, by doing whatever is possible to put those events behind them, to let bygones be bygones and to restore essential harmony.

Until we realize that Native people have a highly developed, formal, but radically different set of cultural imperatives, we are likely to continue misinterpreting their acts, misperceiving the real problems they face and imposing, through government policies, potentially harmful "remedies".

We also need to realize that these ethics and attitudes are not necessarily seen as "rules" by Native people themselves, just as we are often unaware that vigorous introspection is an acquired cultural trait with us. These sorts of habits represent, to each group respectively, the way they assume all people are naturally. We are seldom conscious of the fact that at some time we *learned* them, and that we could just as easily have learned different approaches instead.

. . . .

It is also clear that at this stage in history Native people are declaring that they have had enough. After putting up politely with our all-encompassing interference for so long, they are asking us to leave them alone, for in many spheres they have seen only negative results.

The court system is one clear example. The function of traditional Native dispute-resolution systems was the real resolution of disputes. They hoped that at the end of their process the parties would be returned to cooperative co-existence, to real interpersonal harmony. Naturally, they expected that our courts would have the same goal. Little did they know that we do not even pretend to that goal. Our society is a society of strangers. Our judicial processes do not aim at restoring friendship or harmony, if only because between strangers these qualities do not exist in the first place. Instead, we aim at deterring harmful *activity* so that each stranger can continue to follow his private path without interference.

It is little wonder that one Chief recently complained that the court doesn't do what it should do. As he put it, "your court only comes in here to take money in fines and to take our people out to jail, leaving us with the problem." That problem, needless to say, was the unresolved original dispute between people, or the uncorrected dysfunction within an individual accused. Until recently, Native people have been willing to endure many of the traditionally unethical requirements of our legal system in the belief that we too aimed at restoring interpersonal harmony and individual mental health. That belief was mistaken, for our courts focus primarily on the preservation of public peace. They are concerned not with what people are, but with what they do. The Native approach essentially ignores what was done and concentrates instead upon the personal or interpersonal dysfunctions which caused the problem in the first place. Their first priority lies in trying to correct those dysfunctions rather than in trying to keep those continuing dysfunctions from erupting into further harmful or illegal acts.

It is now the judgment of many bands that our system is inappropriate both in its processes and in its goals. If we are not even going to attempt to do what they believe should be done, they don't want us, for our processes themselves are harmful, involving as they do confrontation and the perpetuation of disruptive issues.

R. v. R.D.S.

[1997] 3 S.C.R. 484, 118 C.C.C. (3d) 353, 10 C.R. (5th) 1,
1997 CarswellNS 301, 1997 CarswellNS 302

The accused, a black 15-year-old, was charged with a series of offences arising out of an incident wherein a white police officer had arrested the accused for interfering with the arrest of another youth. The police officer and the accused were the only witnesses at trial. Their accounts of the relevant events differed widely. The trial judge weighed the evidence and determined that the accused should be acquitted. While delivering her oral reasons, the trial judge remarked:

> The Crown says, well, why would the officer say that events occurred the way in which he has relayed them to the court this morning. I am not saying that the Constable has misled the court, although police officers have been known to do that in the past. I am not saying that the officer overreacted, but certainly police officers do overreact, particularly when they are dealing with non-white groups. That to me indicates a state of mind right there that is questionable. I believe that probably the situation in this particular case is the case of a young police officer who overreacted. I do accept the evidence of [R.D.S.] that he was told to shut up or he would be under arrest. It seems to be in keeping with the prevalent attitude of the day. At any rate, based upon my comments and based upon all the evidence before the court I have no other choice but to acquit.

Judge Sparks, the trial judge, was the first black judge appointed in Nova Scotia. **In her decision, was Judge Sparks simply bringing her "different perspective on life" to the bench as Justice Wilson urges in her articles on women judges, or was she acting improperly?** The Crown challenged these comments as raising a reasonable apprehension of bias. The Crown's appeal was allowed and a new trial ordered. This judgment was upheld by a majority of the Nova Scotia Court of Appeal. The accused appealed further.

The Supreme Court allowed the appeal and restored the acquittals. There was a complex division of opinion. **What are the majority rulings on how judges should approach questions of social context at trial and on whether the trial judge's approach in this case created a reasonable apprehension of bias?**

CORY J. (IACOBUCCI J. concurring): —

. . . .

In some circumstances it may be acceptable for a judge to acknowledge that racism in society might be, for example, the motive for the overreaction of a police officer. This may be necessary in order to refute a submission that invites the judge as trier of fact to presume truthfulness or untruthfulness of a category of witnesses, or to adopt some other form of stereotypical thinking. Yet it would not be acceptable for a judge to go further and suggest that all police officers should therefore not be believed or should be viewed with suspicion where they are dealing with accused persons who are members of a different race. Similarly, it is dangerous for a judge to suggest that a particular person overreacted because of racism unless there is evidence adduced to sustain this finding. It would be equally inappropriate to suggest that female complainants, in sexual assault cases, ought to be believed more readily than male accused persons solely because of the history of sexual violence by men against women.

If there is no evidence linking the generalization to the particular witness, these situations might leave the judge open to allegations of bias on the basis that the credibility of the individual witness was prejudged according to stereotypical generalizations. This does not mean that the particular generalization — that police officers have historically discriminated against visible minorities or that women have historically been abused by men — is not true, or is without foundation. The difficulty is that reasonable and informed people may perceive that the judge has used this information as a basis for assessing credibility instead of making a genuine evaluation of the evidence of the particular witness' credibility. As a general rule, judges should avoid placing themselves in this position.

. . . .

The Crown contended that the real problem arising from Judge Sparks' remarks was the inability of the Crown and Constable Stienburg to respond to the remarks. In other words, the Crown attempted to put forward an argument that the trial was rendered unfair for failure to comply with "natural justice". This cannot be accepted. Neither Constable Stienburg nor the Crown was on trial. Rather, it is essential to consider whether the remarks of Judge Sparks gave rise to a reasonable apprehension of bias. This is the only basis on which this trial could be considered unfair.

. . . .

However, there was *no* evidence before Judge Sparks that would suggest that anti-black bias influenced this particular police officer's reactions. Thus, although it may be incontrovertible that there is a history of racial tension between police officers and visible minorities, there was no evidence to link that generalization to the actions of Constable Stienburg. The reference to the fact that police officers may overreact in dealing with non-white groups may therefore be perfectly supportable, but it is nonetheless unfortunate in the circumstances of this case because of its potential to associate Judge Sparks' findings with the generalization, rather than the specific evidence. This effect is reinforced by the statement "[t]hat to me indicates a state of mind right there that is questionable" which immediately follows her observation.

There is a further troubling comment. After accepting R.D.S.'s evidence that he was told to shut up, Judge Sparks added that "[i]t seems to be in keeping with the prevalent attitude of the day". Again, this comment may create a perception that the findings of credibility have been made on the basis of generalizations, rather than the conduct of the particular police officer. Indeed these comments standing alone come very close to indicating that Judge Sparks predetermined the issue of credibility of Constable Stienburg on the basis of her general perception of racist police attitudes, rather than on the basis of his demeanour and the substance of his testimony.

The remarks are worrisome and come very close to the line. Yet, however troubling these comments are when read individually, it is vital to note that the comments were not made in isolation. It is necessary to read all of the comments in the context of the whole proceeding, with an awareness of all the circumstances that a reasonable observer would be deemed to know.

The reasonable and informed observer at the trial would be aware that the Crown had made the submission to Judge Sparks that "there's absolutely no reason to attack the credibility of the officer". She had already made a finding that she preferred the evidence of R.D.S. to that of Constable Stienburg. She gave reasons for these findings that could appropriately be made based on the evidence adduced. A reasonable and informed person hearing her subsequent remarks would conclude that she was exploring the possible reasons why Constable Stienburg had a different perception of events than R.D.S. Specifically, she was rebutting the unfounded suggestion of the Crown that a police officer by virtue of his occupation should be more readily believed than the accused. Although her remarks were inappropriate they did not give rise to a reasonable apprehension of bias.

. . . .

A high standard must be met before a finding of reasonable apprehension of bias can be made. Troubling as Judge Sparks' remarks may be, the Crown has not satisfied its onus to provide the cogent evidence needed to impugn the impartiality of Judge Sparks. Although her comments, viewed in isolation, were unfortunate and unnecessary, a reasonable, informed person, aware of all the circumstances, would not conclude that they gave rise to a reasonable apprehension of bias. Her remarks, viewed in their context, do not give rise to a perception that she prejudged the issue of credibility on the basis of generalizations, and they do not taint her earlier findings of credibility.

. . . .

I must add that since writing these reasons I have had the opportunity of reading those of Major J. It is readily apparent that we are in agreement as to the nature of bias and the test to be applied in order to determine whether the words or actions of a trial judge raise a reasonable apprehension of bias. The differences in our reasons lies in the application of the principles and test we both rely upon to the words of the trial judge in this case. The principles and the test we have both put forward and relied upon are different from and incompatible with those set out by Justices L'Heureux-Dubé and McLachlin.

MAJOR J. (LAMER C.J. and SOPINKA J. concurring) (dissenting): — The trial judge stated that "police officers have been known to [mislead the court] in the past" and that "police officers do overreact, particularly when they are dealing with non-white groups" and went on to say "[t]hat to me indicates a state of mind right there that is questionable." She in effect was saying, "sometimes police lie and overreact in dealing with non-whites, therefore I have a suspicion that this police officer may have lied and overreacted in dealing with this non-white accused." This was stereotyping all police officers as liars and racists, and applied this stereotype to the police officer in the present case. The trial judge might be perceived as assigning less weight to the police officer's evidence because he is testifying in the prosecution of an accused who is of a different race. Whether racism exists in our society is not the issue. The issue is whether there was evidence before the court upon which to base a finding that *this* particular police officer's actions were motivated by racism. There was no evidence of this presented at the trial.

. . . .

Trial judges have to base their findings on the evidence before them. It was open to the appellant to introduce evidence that this police officer was racist and that racism motivated his actions or that he lied. This was not done. For the trial judge to infer that based on her general view of the police or society is an error of law. For this reason there should be a new trial.

. . . .

The life experience of this trial judge, as with all trial judges, is an important ingredient in the ability to understand human behaviour, to weigh the evidence, and to determine credibility. It helps in making a myriad of decisions arising during the course of most trials. It is of no value, however, in reaching conclusions for which there is no evidence. The fact that on some other occasions police officers have lied or overreacted is irrelevant. Life experience is not a substitute for evidence. There was no evidence before the trial judge to support the conclusions she reached.

. . . .

Canadian Courts have, in recent years, criticized the stereotyping of people into what is said to be predictable behaviour patterns. If a judge in a sexual assault case instructed the jury or him- or herself that because the complainant was a prostitute he or she probably consented, or that prostitutes are likely to lie about such things as sexual assault, that decision would be reversed. Such presumptions have no place in a system of justice that treats all witnesses equally. Our jurisprudence prohibits tying credibility to something as irrelevant as gender, occupation or perceived group predisposition.

. . . .

It can hardly be seen as progress to stereotype police officer witnesses as likely to lie when dealing with non-whites. This would return us to a time in the history of the Canadian justice system that many thought had past. This reasoning, with respect to police officers, is no more legitimate than the stereotyping of women, children or minorities.

. . . .

I agree with the approach taken by Cory J. with respect to the nature of bias and the test to be used to determine if the words or actions of a judge give rise to apprehension of bias. However, I come to a different conclusion in the application of the test to the words of the trial judge in this case. It follows that I disagree with the approach to reasonable apprehension of bias put forward by Justices L'Heureux-Dubé and McLachlin.

L'Heureux-Dubé J. (McLachlin J. concurring): —

. . . .

In our view, the test for reasonable apprehension of bias established in the jurisprudence is reflective of the reality that while judges can never be neutral, in the sense of purely objective, they can and must strive for impartiality. It therefore recognizes as inevitable and appropriate that the differing experiences of judges assist them in their decision-making process and will be reflected in their judgments, so long as those experiences are relevant to the cases, are not based on inappropriate stereotypes, and do not prevent a fair and just determination of the cases based on the facts in evidence.

We find that on the basis of these principles, there is no reasonable apprehension of bias in the case at bar. Like Cory J. we would, therefore, overturn the findings by the Nova Scotia Supreme Court (Trial Division) and the majority of the Nova Scotia Court of Appeal that a reasonable apprehension of bias arises in this case, and restore the acquittal of R.D.S. This said, we disagree with Cory J.'s position that the comments of Judge Sparks were unfortunate, unnecessary, or close to the line. Rather, we find them to reflect an entirely appropriate recognition of the facts in evidence in this case and of the context within which this case arose — a context known to Judge Sparks and to any well-informed member of the community.

. . . .

Cardozo recognized that objectivity was an impossibility because judges, like all other humans, operate from their own perspectives. As the Canadian Judicial Council noted in *Commentaries on Judicial Conduct* (1991), at p. 12, "[t]here is no human being who is not the product of every social experience, every process of education, and every human contact". What is possible and desirable, they note, is impartiality:

> . . . [T]he wisdom required of a judge is to recognize, consciously allow for, and perhaps to question, all the baggage of past attitudes and sympathies that fellow citizens are free to carry, untested, to the grave.

True impartiality does not require that the judge have no sympathies or opinions; it requires that the judge nevertheless be free to entertain and act upon different points of view with an open mind.

. . . .

As discussed above, judges in a bilingual, multiracial and multicultural society will undoubtedly approach the task of judging from their varied perspectives. They will certainly have been shaped by, and have gained insight from, their different experiences, and cannot be expected to divorce themselves from these experiences on the occasion of their appointment to the bench. In fact, such a transformation would deny society the benefit of the valuable knowledge gained by the judiciary while they were members of the Bar. As well, it would preclude the achievement of a diversity of backgrounds in the judiciary. The reasonable person does not expect that judges will function as neutral ciphers; however, the reasonable person does demand that judges achieve impartiality in their judging.

. . . .

An understanding of the context or background essential to judging may be gained from testimony from expert witnesses in order to put the case in context: *R. v. Lavallee*, . . . *R. v. Parks*, . . . and *Moge v. Moge*, . . . from academic studies properly placed before the court; and from the judge's personal understanding and experience of the society in which the judge lives and works. This process of enlargement is not only consistent with impartiality; it may also be seen as its essential precondition.

A reasonable person far from being troubled by this process, would see it as an important aid to judicial impartiality.

. . . .

It is important to note that having already found R.D.S. to be credible, and having accepted a sufficient portion of his evidence to leave her with a reasonable doubt as to his guilt, Judge Sparks necessarily disbelieved at least a portion of the conflicting evidence of Constable Stienburg. At that point, Judge Sparks made reference to the submissions of the Crown that "there's absolutely no reason to attack the credibility of the officer", and then addressed herself to why there might, in fact, be a reason to attack the credibility of the officer in this case. It is in this context that Judge Sparks made the statements which have prompted this appeal.

[The trial judge's] remarks do not support the conclusion that Judge Sparks found Constable Stienburg to have lied. In fact, Judge Sparks did quite the opposite. She noted firstly, that she was *not* saying Constable Stienburg had misled the court, although that could be an explanation for his evidence. She then went on to remark that she was *not* saying that Constable Stienburg had overreacted, though she was alive to that possibility given that it had happened with police officers in the past, and in particular, it had happened when police officers were dealing with non-white groups. Finally, Judge Sparks concluded that, though she was not willing to say that Constable Stienburg did overreact, it was her belief that he *probably* overreacted. And, in support of that finding, she noted that she accepted the evidence of R.D.S. that "he was told to shut up or he would be under arrest".

At no time did Judge Sparks rule that the probable overreaction by Constable Stienburg was motivated by racism. Rather, she tied her finding of probable overreaction to the evidence that Constable Stienburg had threatened to arrest the appellant R.D.S. for speaking to his cousin. At the same time, there was evidence capable of supporting a finding of racially motivated overreaction. At an earlier point in the proceedings, she had accepted the evidence that the other youth arrested that day, was handcuffed and thus secured when R.D.S. approached. This constitutes evidence which could lead one to question why it was necessary for both boys to be placed in choke holds by Constable Stienburg, purportedly to secure them. In the face of such evidence, we respectfully disagree with the views of our colleagues Cory and Major JJ. that there was no evidence on which Judge Sparks could have found "racially motivated" overreaction by the police officer.

While it seems clear that Judge Sparks *did not in fact* relate the officer's probable overreaction to the race of the appellant R.D.S., it should be noted that if Judge Sparks *had* chosen to attribute the behaviour of Constable Stienburg to the racial dynamics of the situation, she would not necessarily have erred. As a member of the community, it was open to her to take into account the well-known presence of racism in that community and to evaluate the evidence as to what occurred against that background.

That Judge Sparks recognized that police officers *sometimes* overreact when dealing with non-white groups simply demonstrates that in making her determination in this case, she was alive to the well-known racial dynamics that may exist in interactions between police officers and visible minorities.

. . . .

Judge Sparks' oral reasons show that she approached the case with an open mind, used her experience and knowledge of the community to achieve an understanding of the reality of the case, and applied the fundamental principle of proof beyond a reasonable doubt. Her comments were based entirely on the case before her, were made after a consideration of the conflicting testimony of the two witnesses and in response to the Crown's submissions, and were entirely supported by the evidence. In alerting herself to the racial dynamic in the case, she was simply engaging in the process of contextualized judging which, in our view, was entirely proper and conducive to a fair and just resolution of the case before her.

GONTHIER J. (LA FOREST J. CONCURRING): — . . . I agree with Cory J. and L'Heureux-Dubé and McLachlin JJ. as to the disposition of the appeal and with their exposition of the law on bias and impartiality and the relevance of context. However, I am in agreement with and adopt the joint reasons of L'Heureux-Dubé and McLachlin JJ. in their treatment of social context and the manner in which it may appropriately enter the decision-making process as well as their assessment of the trial judge's reasons and comments in the present case.

For competing views on *R.D.S.*, see Archibald, "The Lessons of the Sphinx: Avoiding Apprehensions of Judicial Bias in a Multi-racial, Multi-cultural Society" (1998), 10 C.R. (5th) 54; Delisle, "An Annotation to R.D.S." (1998), 10 C.R. (5th) 7 and Paciocco, "The Promise of R.D.S.: Integrating the Law of Judicial Notice and Apprehension of Bias"(1998), 3 Can. Crim. L.R. 319.

R. v. HAMILTON

(2004), 22 C.R. (6th) 1, 186 C.C.C. (3d) 129,
2004 CarswellOnt 3214 (Ont. C.A.)

The accused H and M were each charged with importing cocaine. Each had swallowed pellets of cocaine in order to smuggle them into Canada from Jamaica. H imported 349 grams in November 2000 while M imported 489 grams in May 2001. Both accused were black single mothers supported entirely or in part by social assistance. Neither had any prior criminal record, and both had pleaded guilty to the charges laid. Each accused spent four days in custody on arrest, apologized in court for her behaviour, and received a pre-sentence report stating she was a suitable candidate for community supervision. M was not a Canadian citizen and faced the risk of deportation. At the sentencing hearings before Justice Hill, conducted over 13 separate days, extensive social context evidence concerning poverty, gender bias, systemic racism and rates of incarceration in Canada and other countries was filed. The judge himself provided 700 pages of materials. Based, in part, on this evidence, the trial judge concluded that the accused should not receive the usual sentence of imprisonment but should receive conditional sentences. In his opinion, the background factors of race, gender, and poverty were linked to the commission of the offence because they made these accused particularly vulnerable targets to those who sought out individuals to act as cocaine couriers. H was sentenced to a 20-month conditional sentence of imprisonment. M was sentenced to a 24-month-less-a-day conditional sentence of imprisonment. The Crown appealed.

The Ontario Court of Appeal dismissed the sentence appeal given the time that had passed but made it clear that in their view that trial judge had acted inappropriately:

DOHERTY J.A. (O'CONNOR A.C.J.O. and GILLESE J.A. concurring): —

. . . .

Having read and reread the transcripts, I must conclude that the trial judge does appear to have assumed the combined role of advocate, witness, and judge. No doubt, the trial judge's extensive experience in sentencing cocaine couriers had left him with genuine and legitimate concerns about the effectiveness and fairness of sentencing practices as applied to single poor black women who couriered cocaine into Canada for relatively little gain. The trial judge unilaterally decided to use these proceedings to raise, explore, and address various issues which he believed negatively impacted on the effectiveness and fairness of current sentencing practices as they related to some cocaine importers. Through his personal experience and personal research, the trial judge became the prime source of information in respect of those issues. The trial judge also became the driving force pursuing those issues during the proceedings. No one suggests that a trial judge is obliged to remain passive during the sentencing phase of the criminal process. Trial judges can, and sometimes must, assume an active role in the course of a sentencing proceeding. Section 723(3) of the *Criminal Code* provides that a court may, on its own motion, require the production of evidence that "would assist in the determination of the appropriate sentence." Quite apart from that statutory power, the case law has long recognized that where a trial judge is required by law to consider a factor in determining the appropriate sentence and counsel has not provided the information necessary to properly consider that factor, the court can, on its own initiative, make the necessary inquiries and obtain the necessary evidence: *R. v. Wells* (2000), 141 C.C.C. (3d) 368 at 390-91 (S.C.C.); *R. v. Gladue*, [1999] 1 S.C.R. 688 at paras. 84-85.

Recognition that a trial judge can go beyond the issues and evidence produced by the parties on sentencing where necessary to ensure the imposition of a fit sentence does not mean that the trial judge's power is without limits or that it will be routinely exercised. In considering both the limits of the power and the limits of the exercise of the power, it is wise to bear in mind that the criminal process, including the sentencing phase, is basically adversarial. Usually, the parties are the active participants in the process and the judge serves as a neutral, passive arbiter. Generally speaking, it is left to the parties to choose the issues, stake out their positions, and decide what evidence to present in support of those positions. The trial judge role is to listen, clarify where necessary, and ultimately evaluate the merits of the competing cases presented by the parties.

The trial judge's role as the arbiter of the respective merits of competing positions developed and put before the trial judge by the parties best ensures judicial impartiality and the appearance of judicial impartiality. Human nature is such that it is always easier to objectively assess the merits of someone else's argument. The relatively passive role assigned to the trial judge also recognizes that judges, by virtue of their very neutrality, are not in a position to make informed decisions as to which issues should be raised, or the evidence that should be led. Judicial intrusion into counsel's role can cause unwarranted delay and bring unnecessary prolixity to the proceedings.

Judges must be very careful before introducing issues into the sentencing proceeding. Where an issue may or may not be germane to the determination of the appropriate sentence, the trial judge should not inject that issue into the proceedings without first determining from counsel their positions as to the relevance of that issue. If counsel takes the position that the issue is relevant, then it should be left to counsel to produce whatever evidence or material he or she deems appropriate, although the trial judge may certainly make counsel aware of materials known to the trial judge which are germane to the issue. If counsel takes the position that the issue raised by the trial judge is not relevant on sentencing, it will be a rare case where the trial judge will pursue that issue.

It is also important that the trial judge limit the scope of his or her intervention into the role traditionally left to counsel. The trial judge should frame any issue that he or she introduces as precisely as possible and relate it to the case before the court. This will avoid turning the sentencing hearing into a de facto commission of inquiry.

The manner in which the proceedings were conducted created at least four problems. First, by assuming the multi-faceted role of advocate, witness, and judge, the trial judge put the appearance of impartiality at risk, if not actually compromising that appearance. For example, the trial judge introduced the issues of race and gender bias into the proceedings, and then, through the material he produced and the questions he addressed to Crown counsel, the trial judge appeared to drive the inquiry into those matters towards certain results. Those results are reflected in his reasons. Looking at the entirety of the proceedings, there is a risk that a reasonable observer could conclude that the trial judge's findings as to the significance of race and gender bias in fixing the appropriate sentences had been made before he directed an inquiry into those issues. At the very least, the conduct of the proceedings produced a dynamic in which the trial judge became the Crown's adversary on the issues introduced by the trial judge.

Although the appearance of impartiality was put at risk by the conduct of these proceedings, the trial judge did take steps to try and preserve the appearance of fairness. He gave counsel clear indications of his concerns and any tentative opinions he had formed. He also provided the material to counsel to which he planned to refer in considering the issues he had raised. This procedure was much fairer to the parties and much more likely to produce an accurate result than had the trial judge simply referred to the material without giving counsel any notice: *R. v. Paul* (1998), 124 C.C.C. (3d) 1 (N.B.C.A.); *Cronk v. Canadian General Insurance Co.* (1995), 25 O.R. (3d) 505 at 518 (C.A.); Ian Binnie, "Judicial Notice: How Much is Too Much?" in Law Society of Upper Canada, *Special Lectures 2003: The Law of Evidence* (Toronto: Irwin

Law, 2004) 543 at 564-65. Much of the material produced by the trial judge was not suggestive of any particular answer to the questions raised by the trial judge in the course of the proceedings. The scrupulous fairness with which the trial judge conducted the proceedings went some way towards overcoming the potentially adverse effects of the extraordinary role he assumed in the conduct of the proceedings.

The second problem arising from the trial judge's approach is that it produced a fundamental disconnect between the case on sentencing presented by counsel for the respondents and the case of the paradigmatic cocaine courier constructed by the trial judge. From the time he first introduced race and gender into the proceedings, the trial judge spoke in terms of poor black single women who were "targeted" and "conscripted" by drug overseers to act as couriers. The trial judge referred to these couriers as "virtue-tested" by drug overseers and as living "in the despair of poverty". The trial judge also described these couriers as using the small compensation they received from the drug overseers to pay rent, feed children, and support a subsistence level-existence.

Counsel for the respondents chose to provide next to no information about the respondents' involvement in these crimes. Ms. Hamilton indicated she acted out of financial need. Ms. Mason offered no explanation. There was no evidence that these respondents were conscripted, virtue-tested, or paid minimal compensation, nor was there evidence that such compensation was used to pay for the necessaries of life. The reasons for sentence indicate to me that the trial judge based his sentences more on his concept of the typical drug courier than on the evidence pertaining to these two individuals.

A third problem with the trial judge's conduct of the proceedings is that it created a real risk of inaccurate fact-finding. The trial judge introduced a veritable blizzard of raw statistical information. He also produced various forms of opinion on a wide variety of topics. None of this material was analyzed or tested in any way.

. . . .

I do not think the meaning of the statistics introduced by the trial judge or the inferences that could be properly drawn from them is self-evident. There were real risks that these statistics could be misunderstood and misused absent proper expert evidence. Instead of being treated with the caution that all statistics deserve, these statistics - probably because they were introduced by the trial judge - took on a strong aura of reliability and were treated as if they were self-explanatory.

A fourth difficulty with the way the trial judge conducted these proceedings is evident from his introduction of the "certainty of detection" issues. These issues consumed a good deal of time and effort. In the end, quite properly, they played virtually no role in determining the appropriate sentence..... The trial judge made several findings of fact which were specific to the respondents' involvement in their offences. He relied on these findings to support his conclusion that their personal culpability was significantly reduced. He found as a fact that:

* the respondents were "conscripted" by the "drug distribution hierarchy" to participate in their crimes (para. 198);
* the involvement of the respondents was the result of "virtue-testing" by "drug operation overseers" (para. 195);
* the respondents were paid relatively minimal amounts and used those amounts to provide the bare necessities for their families (para. 191); and
* the respondents' children would be "effectively orphaned" if the respondents were incarcerated (para. 198).

Although the rules of evidence are substantially broadened on the sentencing inquiry, factual findings that are germane to the determination of the appropriate sentence and are not properly the subject of judicial notice must be supported by the evidence. There was no evidence to support the findings of fact outlined immediately above.

The respondents chose not to offer any explanation for, or description of, their involvement in the crimes, apart from Ms. Hamilton's indication that she acted out of financial need. The trial judge had no information as to how the respondents came to be involved in this scheme, what their prior association or relationship was with the individuals who may have hired them, when or where the importation plans were formed, what amount of compensation was paid to the respondents, or how the respondents proposed to use that compensation. He also had no information concerning the care of the children if the respondents went to jail. All of this information was uniquely within the knowledge of the respondents. If the respondents were conscripted - that is, compelled to engage in this activity - they could have said so. If they agreed to be involved in the crimes only after repeated requests, they could have said so, just as they could have provided other details concerning their involvement in the scheme and the compensation they received. Similarly, if the effect of the respondents' imprisonment on the children was as drastic as the trial judge held it to be, I would have expected the respondents to have led evidence to that effect.

The Crown's concession that the respondents were couriers did not constitute an admission that they possessed every characteristic that the trial judge ascribed to couriers. Nor do I accept the contention that requiring the respondents to lead the kind of evidence described above works any hardship on them. This kind of evidence has been given in other cases... Safety concerns rising out of implicating others in the scheme can be addressed if and when they arise. In any event, concerns about the potential safety of the offender should he or she provide certain evidence, do not justify assumptions that have no basis in the evidence.

The trial judge did not purport to base the findings of fact outlined above on any material that actually related to these respondents. Instead, he relied on his experiences in sentencing other individuals who couriered cocaine from Jamaica. He applied those generalizations to these respondents. In doing so, he relied on *R. v. S. (R.D.)* (1997), 118 C.C.C. (3d) 353 (S.C.C.). I read that authority as prohibiting the very kind of fact-finding made by the trial judge. ....The majority of the Supreme Court of Canada rejected the bias allegation. In the course of doing so, the court addressed the extent to which trial judges can use personal judicial experience and judicial understanding of the applicable social context in the course of the fact-finding process. Major J., in dissent, speaking for the three members of the court who would have accepted the bias argument, observed at para. 13:

> The life experience of this trial judge, as with all trial judges, is an important ingredient in the ability to understand human behaviour, to weigh evidence, and to determine credibility. It helps in making a myriad of decisions arising during the course of most trials. It is of no value, however, in reaching conclusions for which there is no evidence. The fact that on some other occasions police officers have lied or overreacted is irrelevant. *Life experience is not a substitute for evidence. There was no evidence before the trial judge to support the conclusions she reached* [emphasis added].

Cory J., speaking for himself and Iacobucci J., joined the majority in rejecting the bias argument. However, he approached the use of judicial experience and social context in a manner that was consistent with that applied by Major J. In referring to trial judges' credibility assessments, Cory J. said at para. 129:

> On one hand, the judge is obviously permitted to use common sense and wisdom gained from personal experience in observing and judging the trustworthiness of a particular witness on the basis of factors such as testimony and demeanour. On the other hand, the judge must avoid judging the credibility of the witness on the basis of generalizations or upon matters that were not in evidence [emphasis added].

Cory J. then addressed the trial judge's reasons at para. 150:

> However, there was *no* evidence before Judge Sparks that would suggest that anti-black bias influenced *this particular police officer's reactions*. Thus, although it may be incontrovertible that there is a history of racial tension between police officers and visible minorities, there was no evidence to link that generalization to the actions of Constable Stienburg. The reference to the fact that police officers may overreact in dealing with non-white groups may therefore be perfectly supportable, but it is nonetheless unfortunate in the circumstances of this case because of its potential to associate Judge Sparks' findings with the generalization, rather than the specific evidence [underline added, italics in original].

I think the trial judge fell into the error described by Cory J. While his generalizations concerning the way in which persons like the respondents come to be involved in couriering cocaine from Jamaica, the amounts they are paid for that service, and the use to which they put those amounts may be true as generalizations, there was no evidence that they had any application to the facts of this case.

Justices L'Heureux-Dubé and McLachlin, speaking for four members of the majority on the bias issue, took a somewhat wider view of the use that trial judges could make of information garnered through personal judicial experience and judicial understanding of applicable social context. Their view is the minority view on this issue. However, even on their analysis, fact-finding has to ultimately have some basis in the evidence. They observed at para. 56:

> While it seems clear that Judge Sparks *did not in fact* relate the officer's probable overreaction to the race of the appellant R.D.S., it should be noted that if Judge Sparks *had* chosen to attribute the behaviour of Constable Stienburg to the racial dynamics of the situation, she would not necessarily have erred. <u>As a member of the community, it was open to her to taken into account the well-known presence of racism in that community and to evaluate the evidence as to what occurred against that background</u> [underline added, italics in original].

R. v. S. (R.D.) draws a distinction between findings of fact based exclusively on personal judicial experience and judicial perceptions of applicable social context, and findings of fact based on evidence viewed through the lens of personal judicial experience and social context. The latter is proper; the former is not.

The proper use of personal experience and social context can be demonstrated by reference to Ms. Hamilton's evidence concerning the motive for her crime. She testified that she acted out of dire financial need. The fact that a crime was committed for financial gain can, in some circumstances, mitigate personal responsibility, and, in different circumstances, it can increase personal responsibility. The trial judge was required to determine what weight should be given on sentencing to Ms. Hamilton's admitted financial motive for committing the crime. In making that assessment, he was entitled to put her statement as to her motive in its proper context by recognizing, based on his experiences and the operative social context, that individuals in the circumstances of Ms. Hamilton often find themselves in very real financial need for reasons that include societal factors, like racial and gender bias, over which those individuals have no control. Used in this way, the tools of personal judicial experience and social context help illuminate the evidence. This use can be contrasted with the trial judge's use of his experience in other cases to make the specific finding of fact that these respondents were conscripted - that is, compelled by drug overseers to engage in this criminal activity - when there was no evidence as to how the respondents came to be involved.

The limits on judicial fact-finding based on prior judicial experience and social context are necessary for at least two reasons. First, fact-finding based on a judge's personal experience can interfere with the effective operation of the adversary process. It is difficult, if not impossible, to know, much less explore or challenge, a trial judge's perceptions based on prior judicial experiences or his or her appreciation of the social issues which form part of the context of the proceedings. Second, fact-finding based on generalities developed out of personal past experience can amount to fact-finding based on stereotyping. That risk is evident in this case. The trial judge appears to have viewed all poor black single women who import cocaine into Canada from Jamaica as essentially sharing the same characteristics. These characteristics describe individuals who, because of their difficult circumstances, have virtually no control over their own lives and turn to crime because they are unable to otherwise provide for their children. While this may be an apt description of some of the individuals who turn to cocaine importing, it is stereotyping to assume that all single black women who import cocaine into Canada fit this description.

Do you agree with the Ontario Court of Appeal's interpretation on R.D.S.? Do you agree that the trial judge overstepped his sentencing role? Academic commentary on the Ontario Court of Appeal has been highly critical: see comments by Song and Boyle, Tanovich and Kaiser in (2004), 22 C.R. (6th) 45, 57 and 86.

(b) Ethical Obligations of Crown and Defence Counsel

See generally, Proulx and Layton, *Ethics and Canadian Criminal Law* (Irwin Law, 2001).

CANADIAN BAR ASSOCIATION'S
CODE OF PROFESSIONAL CONDUCT (2004)

CONFIDENTIAL INFORMATION

RULE

Maintaining Information in Confidence

1. The lawyer has a duty to hold in strict confidence all information concerning the business and affairs of the client acquired in the course of the professional relationship, and shall not divulge any such information except as expressly or impliedly authorized by the client, required by law or otherwise required by this Code.

Public Safety Exception

2. Where a lawyer believes upon reasonable grounds that there is an imminent risk to an identifiable person or group of death or serious bodily harm, including serious psychological harm that would substantially interfere with health or well-being, the lawyer shall disclose confidential information where it is necessary to do so in order

to prevent the death or harm, but shall not disclose more information than is required

THE LAWYER AS ADVOCATE

RULE

When acting as an advocate, the lawyer must treat the tribunal with courtesy and respect and must represent the client resolutely, honourably and within the limits of the law.

Commentary

Guiding Principles

1. The advocate's duty to the client "fearlessly to raise every issue, advance every argument, and ask every question, however distasteful, which he thinks will help his client's case" and to endeavour "to obtain for his client the benefit of any and every remedy and defence which is authorized by law" must always be discharged by fair and honourable means, without illegality and in a manner consistent with the lawyer's duty to treat the court with candour, fairness, courtesy and respect.

Prohibited Conduct

2. The lawyer must not, for example:

. . . .

 (b) knowingly assist or permit the client to do anything that the lawyer considers to be dishonest or dishonourable;

. . . .

 (e) knowingly attempt to deceive or participate in the deception of a tribunal or influence the course of justice by offering false evidence, misstating facts or law, presenting or relying upon a false or deceptive affidavit, suppressing what ought to be disclosed or otherwise assisting in any fraud, crime or illegal conduct.

. . . .

Duties of Prosecutor

9. When engaged as a prosecutor, the lawyer's prime duty is not to seek a conviction, but to present before the trial court all available credible evidence relevant to the alleged crime in order that justice may be done through a fair

trial upon the merits. The prosecutor exercises a public function involving much discretion and power and must act fairly and dispassionately. The prosecutor should not do anything that might prevent the accused from being represented by counsel or communicating with counsel and, to the extent required by law and accepted practice, should make timely disclosure to the accused or defence counsel (or to the court if the accused is not represented) of all relevant facts and known witnesses, whether tending to show guilt or innocence, or that would affect the punishment of the accused. There is a clear distinction between prosecutorial discretion and professional conduct. Only the latter can be regulated by a law society. A law society has jurisdiction to investigate any alleged breach of its ethical standards, even those committed by Crown prosecutors in connection with their prosecutorial discretion.

Duties of Defence Counsel

10. When defending an accused person, the lawyer's duty is to protect the client as far as possible from being convicted except by a court of competent jurisdiction and upon legal evidence sufficient to support a conviction for the offence charged. Accordingly, and notwithstanding the lawyer's private opinion as to credibility or merits, the lawyer may properly rely upon all available evidence or defences including so-called technicalities not known to be false or fraudulent.

11. Admissions made by the accused to the lawyer may impose strict limitations on the conduct of the defence and the accused should be made aware of this. For example, if the accused clearly admits to the lawyer the factual and mental elements necessary to constitute the offence, the lawyer, if convinced that the admissions are true and voluntary, may properly take objection to the jurisdiction of the court, or to the form of the indictment, or to the admissibility or sufficiency of the evidence, but must not suggest that some other person committed the offence, or call any evidence that, by reason of the admissions, the lawyer believes to be false. Nor may the lawyer set up an affirmative case inconsistent with such admissions, for example, by calling evidence in support of an alibi intended to show that the accused could not have done, or in fact had not done, the act. Such admissions will also impose a limit upon the extent to which the lawyer may attack the evidence for the prosecution. The lawyer is entitled to test the evidence given by each individual witness for the prosecution and argue that the evidence taken as a whole is insufficient to amount to proof that the accused is guilty of the offence charged, but the lawyer should go no further than that. A lawyer representing an accused or potential accused must not take unfair or improper advantage of an unrepresented complainant by attempting to influence the complainant or potential complainant with respect to the laying, prosecution or withdrawal of a criminal charge.

JUSTICE PETER CORY,
THE INQUIRY REGARDING THOMAS SOPHONOW

2000, Government of Manitoba

The Role of Crown Counsel in the Administration of Justice

Just as it was necessary to express criticism of police officers, I must be critical of some of the actions and omissions of Crown Counsel. The criticism is limited to this case and must not be taken as a general criticism of their work or the work of any particular Crown Attorney.

The role of Crown Counsel is of great importance to the administration of justice and to the welfare of the community. The Crown prosecutor must proceed with the case against the accused fairly and courageously. Prosecutions must proceed even in the face of threats and attempts at intimidation. These insidious threats can on occasion extend to family members. Despite these threats and the danger in which the Crown and at times the family of the Crown are placed, charges must still be vigorously prosecuted. They must be brought to trial and prosecuted with diligence, dispatch and fairness. Crown Counsel are often overworked and paid less than their contemporaries who are in private practice. Nonetheless, they must be industrious to ensure that all the arduous preparation required for each trial or appeal has been completed before the matter comes to court. Crown Counsel must be of absolute integrity and above all suspicion of favouritism or unfair compromise.

Crown Counsel must be a symbol of fairness, prompt to make all reasonable disclosure. As well, they must be scrupulous in the attention given to the welfare and safety of witnesses. They enjoy the respect of all the members of the judiciary. Much is expected of Crown Counsel by society, their community and by the judiciary. The community looks upon the Crown prosecutor as a symbol of fairness, of authority and as a spokesman for the community.

As a rule, Crown Counsel attain and maintain a very high level of professional excellence and fairness. They fulfil all of society's high expectations. It is truly a high office, honoured by the bench, the bar and the community. They should always have, not only the respect of the public and the legal community, but the resources to handle their ever increasing caseloads and the financial compensation that their important office deserves.

The Role of Defence Counsel

There may be some explicit and some implicit criticism of the actions of Defence Counsel, particularly with regard to the disclosure of the alibi evidence. Once again, that criticism arises from the circumstances of this case and it is certainly not a general comment on their work.

The role of Defence Counsel is of great importance to the administration of justice and to our democratic society. Crown Counsel are often regarded by the community as its protector and champion. Frequently, Defence Counsel are associated with their clients. All too often, they are unfairly thought of as those who take advantage of every "loophole" in the law to gain an acquittal. Yet Defence Counsel too must be courageous. They must defend those charged with offences no matter how heinous they may be. It is Defence Counsel who must ensure that no one is found guilty unless the charge is proven beyond a reasonable doubt. They must prepare their case carefully and present it clearly and fearlessly. They are duty bound to ensure that the case proceeds with due attention to the law which binds us all.

It cannot be forgotten that it is often only the Defence Counsel who stands between the lynch mob and the accused. Defence Counsel must be courageous, not only in the face of an outraged and inflamed community, but also, on occasion, the apparent disapproval of the court. Defence Counsel must always act fairly, can never subvert the law and must remember, no matter how trying the circumstances may be, to uphold the dignity of the court.

Our system of justice works best when able and well prepared counsel on both sides make their presentations to an impartial arbiter.

Defence Counsel must ensure that they put forward every reasonable defence on the part of their clients and strive to ensure that only the guilty are convicted.

It cannot be forgotten that there are innocent people who are charged with murder; that there are innocent people charged with sexual assault; that there are innocent people charged with fraud; and, indeed, that innocent people may be charged with any offence set out in the *Criminal Code*. It is the vitally important role of Defence Counsel to ensure that no person is found guilty unless guilt is proven beyond a reasonable doubt. The penalty of imprisonment takes away the most basic liberty of the subject. Indeed, for serious crimes, the deprivation of that liberty may result in a lifetime of imprisonment. The fundamental importance of the role of Defence Counsel in our democratic society is self-evident.

LUBAN, THE ADVERSARY SYSTEM EXCUSE

The Good Lawyer: Lawyers' Rules and Lawyers' Ethics
(Rowman and Allenheld, 1984), 84-88

On February 7, 1973, Richard Helms, the former director of the Central Intelligence Agency, lied to a Senate committee about American involvement in the overthrow of the Allende government in Chile. Santiago proved to be Helms's Waterloo: he was caught out in his perjury and prosecuted. Helms claimed that requirements of national security led him to lie to Congress. We can only speculate, however, on how the court would have viewed this excuse, for in fact the case never came to trial; Helm's lawyer, the redoubtable Edward

Bennett Williams, found an ingenious way to back the government down. He argued that national security information was relevant to Helms's defense and must be turned over to Helms, thereby confronting the government with the unpleasant choice of dropping the action or making public classified and presumably vital information. The government chose the first option and allowed Helms to plead guilty to a misdemeanor charge.

I don't know if anyone ever asked Williams to justify his actions; had anyone attempted to do so, they would presumably have been told that Williams was simply doing his job as a criminal defense attorney. The parallel with Helms's own excuse is clear — he was doing his job, Williams was doing his — but it is hard to miss the irony. Helms tried to conceal national security information; therefore he lied. Williams, acting on Helms's behalf, threatened to reveal national security information as part of a tactic that has come to be called "graymailing." One man's ends are another man's means. Neither lying nor graymailing (to say nothing of destabilizing elected regimes) are morally pretty, but a job is a job and that was the job that was. So, at any rate, runs the excuse.

We may want to reject these "good soldier" excuses or we may find them valid and persuasive. That is the issue I shall address here. A second graymailing example will warm us to our topic:

> In instances [of merger cases involving firms in competition with each other] in which the [Federal Trade] commission's legal case looked particularly good and none of the usual defenses appeared likely to work, the staff was confronted several times with the argument that if they did not refrain from prosecution and allow the merger, one of the proposed merger partners would close down its operations and dismiss its employees.
>
> ... Of course, the mere announcement of the threat to close the plant generates enormous political pressure on the prosecutor not to go forward. Ought lawyers to be engaged in such strategies for the purpose of consummating an otherwise anticompetitive and illegal transaction involving the joinder of two substantial competitors?

On the lawyers' advice, the firms played a nice game of chicken: closing down by stages, they laid off a few workers each day until the FTC cried uncle.

What could justify the conduct of these lawyers? A famous answer is the following statement of Lord Henry Brougham:

> An advocate, in the discharge of his duty, knows but one person in all the world, and that person is his client. To save that client by all means and expedients, and at all hazards and costs to other persons, and, amongst them to himself, is his first and only duty; and in performing this duty he must not regard the alarm, the torments, the destruction which he may bring upon others. Separating the duty of a patriot from that of an advocate, he must go on reckless of consequences, though it should be his unhappy fate to involve his country in confusion.

This speech, made in his 1820 defense of Queen Caroline against King George IV's charge of adultery, was itself an act of graymail. Reminiscing years later, Brougham said that the king would recognize in it a tacit threat to reveal his secret marriage to a Catholic, a marriage that, were it to become public knowledge, would cost him his crown. Knowing this background of Brougham's oft-quoted statement might make us take a dim view of it; it has, nevertheless, frequently been admired as the most eloquent encapsulation of the advocate's job.

Brougham's statement invites philosophical reflection for at first blush it is equally baffling to utilitarianism, and moral rights theory, and Kantianism. The client's utility matters more than that of the rest of the world put together. No one else's moral rights matter. Other people are merely means to the client's ends. Moral theory seems simply to reject Brougham's imperatives.

They are, however, universalizable over lawyers, or so it is claimed. The idea seems to be that the role of lawyer, hence the social institutions that set up this role, reparse the Moral Law, relaxing some moral obligations and imposing new ones. In the words of an Australian appellate court, "Our system of administering justice necessarily imposes upon those who practice advocacy duties which have no analogies, and the system cannot dispense with their strict observance."

The system of which the court speaks is the so-called "adversary system of justice." My main question is this: does the adversary system really justify Brougham's position? I hope that the example of Helms and his lawyers has convinced you that a more general issue is lurking here, the issue of what I shall call *institutional excuses*. We can state the main question in full generality in this way: can a person appeal to a social institution in which he or she occupies a role in order to excuse conduct that would be morally culpable were anyone else to do it? Plausibly, examples exist in which the answer is yes: we do not call it murder when a soldier kills a sleeping enemy, although it is surely immoral for you or me to do it. There are also cases where the answer is no, as in the job "concentration camp commandant" or "professional strikebreaker." Here, we feel, the immorality of the job is so great that it accuses, not excuses, the person who holds it.

This suggests that an important feature of a successful institutional excuse is that the institution is itself justified. I think that is partly right, but I do not think it is the whole story: I shall argue that the *kind* of justification that can be offered of the institution is germane to the success of the excuses it provides.

GEOFFREY HAZARD, ETHICS IN THE PRACTICE OF LAW

(1978), 128

There are several escapes [from moral responsibility]. It is said that no client is guilty until so found by a court; therefore one cannot know what the truth is until then; therefore, one cannot conclude that a client's testimony will constitute perjury. This is pure casuistry. Of course there are doubtful situations, but there are also ones that are not doubtful. A thing is not made true or not by a court's pronouncing on it, and a lawyer can reach conclusions about an issue without having a judge tell him what to think.

See further, Michel Proulx and David Layton, *Ethics and Canadian Criminal Law* (Irwin Law, 2001) and David Tanovich "Law's Ambition: The Reconstruction of Role Morality in Canada" (2005), 28 *Dal. L.J.* 267.

GREENSPAN AND JONAS,
GREENSPAN: THE CASE FOR THE DEFENCE

(1987), 260-265

Whenever a crime is committed (or whenever some people in the community suspect that an act may amount to a crime), a large, impersonal machinery goes into motion. Its initial purpose is to determine if some act or event was, in fact, a crime — and if it concludes that it was, to find the individual (or group of individuals) responsible for it.

Once this appears to be accomplished, the machinery shifts into second gear. It tries to establish the accused individual's *degree* of responsibility. Then, in third gear, his or her appropriate punishment. Sometimes there is a fourth gear: the machinery may turn its attention to some social or legal condition in the hope of making it easier to define, prevent, or detect such crimes in the future.

This process can involve dozens and dozens of people in its various stages. Ideally — and often in actual fact — they are highly trained, intelligent, dedicated, and hard-working human beings: people of great personal integrity. They are police officers, forensic experts, medical doctors, prosecuting attorneys, court officials, judges, jurors, parole officials, prison administrators, and lawmakers. Except for the jurors, they are all professionals. Many of them have the authority to knock on anybody's door and ask for information and assistance. Even when they cannot compel people's co-operation by law, they can expect people to co-operate with them as a civic or moral duty. They also have at their disposal support personnel and sophisticated, expensive equipment, the best society can provide, to help them in their work.

There is nothing wrong with any of this, of course. Crime cannot go undetected, undefined, or unpunished. No community could function without protecting itself from crime.

However, this great, impersonal, awesome machinery has one built-in bias. It is an unconscious, functional bias, somewhat like an aircraft's bias for leaving the ground as soon as it has attained a certain speed. The bias of the justice system is to find guilt. That is, first, to define any human act that comes to its attention as a crime; then, to define any suspect as a person who has probably committed such an act; and finally, to define any human being who has committed such an act as a criminal. That's the way the justice system flies.

Everyone knows that in a given individual case none of this may be true — yet the great machine of the criminal justice system may thunder down the runway and take off regardless.

. . . .

Our justice system has tried to counteract this potential by two remedies.

First, on an abstract level, the remedy is the law's presumption that every person is innocent until proven guilty on relevant evidence beyond a reasonable doubt.

By saying "on an abstract level" I don't mean to imply that this presumption is unimportant. On the contrary, it is vital and fundamental. Everything else flows from the presumption of innocence. However, without a second remedy on a concrete level, it could remain as ineffectual as a sheathed sword. Or, to use a more up-to-date metaphor, as an engine without a driver.

This second, concrete remedy is the lawyer for the defence. He drives the abstract engine of the presumption of innocence. He is the one person in the entire world, apart from the accused person's mother, who *starts* with the assumption that the authorities must be mistaken.

To balance the awe-inspiring machinery of the criminal-justice system, the law permits one individual to be the accused person's friend. He is, as the legal expression goes, to be "of counsel" to him. Simply put, his job is to "believe" the accused — or at least not to disbelieve him. His job is to look at every circumstance surrounding the allegations against a defendant with the assumption that they prove, or are consistent with, his innocence.

The defence lawyer is to balance the dozens of powerful professionals whose task is to investigate and prosecute an accused person. We give the defence lawyer this task in the knowledge that a defendant may *be* innocent. Innocent, not just as an abstract legal idea (because in that sense he is innocent anyway until found guilty), but as a matter of plain, actual fact. What he is accused of may not amount to a crime, or he may not have committed it. If it is a crime and he did commit it, it may not be as serious a crime as his adversary, the prosecutor, suggests. And even if it is as serious, there may be something about the circumstances, or about the defendant as a human being, that makes him something else than a criminal deserving the worst punishment.

Since this may be so, our system has decided that there must be one person in the defendant's community who acts as if it were so. One man or woman who is not the defendant's inquisitor, accuser, or judge. One who doesn't merely keep an open mind about him. One person who is the defendant's advocate.

Society assigns this role to the defence lawyer. He is the one person whose duty is to assume the best about a defendant at every step of the way. The defence lawyer alone, among all the defendant's fellow citizens and neighbours, must act on the assumption that whatever the defendant says is true. He must act on the assumption that the defendant's accusers are mistaken. Mistaken — or possibly malicious. They may have their own axe to grind. The defence lawyer must put everything they say about the defendant to the strictest test of proof. In so far as the law permits, he must put the accusers on trial.

This is the defence lawyer's duty. It's a duty not just to his client, but to his society. It is not something the defence lawyer decides in his own mind: it is an obligation the community places on him. The defence lawyer chooses his occupation voluntarily, but he does not choose his role: his society defines his role for him. The moral essence of this role has been distilled by the common experience of our legal tradition over the centuries. It is that a community can retain justice and freedom only as long as it gives standing to one person to take, within the limits of the law, the defendant's side in court.

. . . .

The defence lawyer, as many people have pointed out, only defends a client (or a client's act) and not a crime. Central to any defence, other than a submission in mitigation of sentence, is the position that the client didn't do something. Or that whatever he did was not wrong in law, or at least not as wrong as the prosecution contends. If a lawyer suggested that yes, my client did shoot this man deliberately and in cold blood, but the victim was a nasty fellow who deserved to be shot, *then* he would be defending a crime — but no lawyer does that. (The only exceptions in our times have been some "activist" lawyers who attempted to gain the acquittal of murderers on the basis of some "higher" political or social motive.)

But these are only aberrations — albeit dangerous ones — and we need not concern ourselves with them here. Like most criminal lawyers, I defend clients, not crimes. Which is why I find questions like: "How can you defend those people?" or "Is there any kind of crime at which you'd draw a line?" meaningless.

I haven't the slightest moral conflict defending people accused of homicide, sexual assault, business fraud, environmental offences, or even crimes against humanity. I don't "draw the line" at anything. If I defended *crimes*, maybe I would — but I don't defend crimes. I only defend innocent people. Until they are found guilty there are no other kinds of people for me to defend, and what difference does it make what an innocent person is accused of?

Would you represent any and all accused?

Helen Conway, a sole practitioner and defence counsel in Windsor, writing in the *Law Times* of September 10, 2001 under the title "The Spirit of the Law", points to statistics of disproportionate rates of depression, addiction and suicide for lawyers, financial strain from low legal aid rates, high overheads and collection difficulties, and a bureaucratic and inefficient criminal justice system. She concludes that the practice of criminal law

> is not for the faint of heart. Lawyers take the heat from all directions and most have even grown accustomed to the overall disrespect and disapproval towards them which exists in the community. Ultimately, however, moral affirmation and professional certainty have to come not from society but from within the knowledge and belief that perhaps lawyers have in some small measure protected the rights of an individual or defended a client who has been wronged or treated unfairly.

> The practice of [criminal] law is, first and finally, a vocation, a call to represent and to advance the ideal of justice. While public in practice, it is also and always personal in spirit (p. 8).

It has been said that there are broadly two models of the practice of criminal law as a defence counsel. Some defence counsel start by advising potential clients that everything told to them will be kept in strictest confidence but that, having heard the full story, the defence counsel may be limited in the ability to present a defence. The client is told that the lawyer cannot participate in perjured testimony. Subject to these limits, the accused is encouraged to tell the defence counsel everything about the case. On the other model, sometimes called "blind person's bluff" the lawyer remains purposefully ignorant about potentially embarrassing facts and discourages the client from telling everything. The accused is never directly asked for his or her version of the facts. Instead, the questions are entirely limited to such questions as whether the accused gave a statement to the police, which witnesses could be of assistance to the defence and what else is known by the police or the Crown Attorney.

What advantages do you see in these models of practice? Which would you follow?

---

1. John Smith has been charged with assault. He asks you to represent him and you agree. He tells you that he beat on the victim during a drunken rage. He imagines that it was because he has never cared for his manner. He knows that he started this particular fracas but also advises you that the victim himself has two previous convictions of common assault, which, he suggests, could be fertile ground for cross-examination. The victim describes the beating in some detail. When the Crown finishes the examination in chief you turn to your client who advises "That's exactly what happened. Now go get him. Destroy his credibility." What do you do?
Your client is convicted. Would you inform the Crown about two other assault convictions registered against your client under another name?

2. Your client is prosecuted for robbery. He committed the crime at 10:45 and has admitted the same to you. The sole prosecution witness identified your client as the robber but mistakenly placed the time at 10:15. Your client has an airtight alibi for 10:00 to 10:30. Will you present the alibi?

3. You have been assigned to prosecute a case of domestic assault. The police laid the charge after they had been called to investigate a

disturbance. The wife told the police that her husband had beaten her and that this was not the first time. The trial is to take place tomorrow, three months after the alleged incident. The woman approaches you and wants to withdraw the charge. She tells you that her husband has returned to Alcoholics Anonymous and is participating with her in a marriage-counselling program. The incidence of domestic violence in your community is very high. Will you withdraw?

4. Mr. Murray is a member of the Ontario Bar and certified as a specialist in criminal litigation by the Law Society of Upper Canada. He was retained by Paul Bernardo initially in February 1993 in regard to the "Scarborough Rapes" and on May 18, 1993, in connection with the murders of L.M. and K.F. and additional related offences.

On May 6, 1993, he went to the Bernardo home after the search warrant for those premises had expired to retrieve personal possessions and evidence that might be helpful to the defence. He had a letter from his client with written instructions that he was only to open it once inside the house. Once inside he opened the sealed envelope, which contained a map and directions to assist in locating six eight-millimetre videotapes from above a pot light. He did so and removed them to his office. Bernardo's written instructions were for his counsel not to view them. The videotapes depicted gross sexual abuse of K.F., L.M., Jane Doe and T.H. by Bernardo and his co-accused Karla Homolka. Without disclosing their existence to the Crown, he retained the tapes for 17 months. He only viewed them at the instruction of Bernardo after he and Bernardo learned of a deal under which Karla Homolka agreed to plead guilty to two counts of manslaughter, with a joint submission to be made for a sentence of 12 years in exchange for her testifying for the Crown in the first degree murder trial of Bernardo. The tapes would be used to aid the defence that Bernardo was guilty of sexual assault but not murder. The Crown was going to portray Homolka as an abused, manipulated victim, while the tapes showed the reverse: that she was not afraid and was an enthusiastic participant in the sexual crimes. He felt obliged to keep the existence of the tapes secret so that the Crown could not prepare Homolka for defence cross-examination.

Trial motions were to begin on September 12, 1994. On September 2, 1994, the accused, through his counsel, applied to the Law Society of Upper Canada for advice. He was advised the tapes should be turned over to the judge and that he should withdraw from the case. Accepting that advice he appeared before the trial judge, who directed that the tapes, their integrity protected by suitable undertakings, go to John Rosen, new counsel for Bernardo, at which time the accused was given leave to withdraw as counsel. Rosen, on September 22, 1994, turned the tapes over to the police and they were used by Crown counsel at the trial. A jury found Bernardo guilty on all charges.

Did Mr. Murray act unethically? If so, what precisely did he do wrong?

See generally Macdonald and Pink, "Murder, Silence and Physical Evidence: The Dilemma of Client Confidentiality" (1997), 2 Can. Crim. L.R. 111, Kent Roach, "Smoking Guns: Beyond the Murray Case" (2000), 43

Crim. L.Q. 409 and Wayne Renke, "Real Evidence, Disclosure and the Plight of Counsel" (2003,) 47 Crim. L.Q. 175.

Murray was later charged with obstruction of justice but was acquitted on the basis of a lack of proof of intent to mislead and because the rules of professional responsibility in such a situation were quite unclear. An attempt by the Law Society of Upper Canada to craft new rules became mired in controversy and was later abandoned: *Law Times*, August 18, 2003.

5. Your client says that he is innocent, but that he wants to plead guilty "to get it over with". He is tired of the court delay and does not want to lose any more time off work. The offence is a minor one. Would you assist him in entering his guilty plea? Would you advise him to indicate remorse to secure a minimal penalty?

6. John is observed slipping a box of mints, value $1.75, into his jacket. He is arrested by store security and, following store policy, a charge is laid. John is in his second year of university and hopes to go to law school. He has no prior record. Your brief indicates that he was co-operative during the investigation. He had told the security officer, "I'm dumbfounded. I don't know why I took them". You are approached by a senior defence counsel, acting for John. He's also a friend of John's family. He tells you that John has been going through some rough times of late. John's older brother was recently killed in a car accident and John has just broken up with his girl friend. He tells you that John is basically a "good kid" but he's under a lot of pressure because exams are just around the corner. Counsel asks if you'll withdraw the charges. Will you?

Suppose that you decide not to withdraw the charge but just as the case is being called by the court clerk you are advised that the store security officer is not present. You can't prove the charge and the trial judge is known not to grant adjournments in such cases. You know that John is about to plead guilty. What do you do?

Chapter 2

THE ACT REQUIREMENT
(ACTUS REUS)

1. INTRODUCTION

C. HOWARD, CRIMINAL LAW

3rd ed. (1977), 9-10

The traditional analysis of a crime at common law is into *actus reus*, or guilty act, and *mens rea*, or guilty mind, but the codes use neither these expressions nor any exact synonyms for them. A writer on the criminal law in Australia therefore has to decide between using different terms according as he is talking about common law or code rules and abandoning the traditional common law terminology altogether. The opinion acted on in this book is that the expressions *actus reus* and *mens rea* are too obscure to be of practical utility in an exposition of the modern law in any context. They therefore do not justify adopting the otherwise disadvantageous course of discussing the principles of the criminal law at common law and under the codes in different language, especially since the principles themselves are the same in all significant respects in both contexts.

The words *actus reus* and *mens rea* are taken from the maxim, *actus non facit reum nisi mens sit rea*, there is no guilty act without a guilty mind. An alternative statement of this principle in English which stresses the implication that the guilty act must be coincidental in time with the guilty mind is, "The intent and the Act must both concur to constitute the crime". The argument in favour of keeping the terms *actus reus* and *mens rea* in common use is that they are the customary language of the courts and that since in themselves they have no special significance, their content being "only one of legal arrangement", there is no point in replacing them with unfamiliar terminology which can be no less arbitrary. Nevertheless there are reasons for thinking that at the present day these particular expressions are responsible for much confusion of thought and should be abandoned in favour of any language which accurately conveys the effect of the law without in itself imposing an unnecessary burden of translation and explanation.

It was noted in Chapter 1 that, as a general rule, the Crown bears the burden of proving all the elements of an offence. In general terms, a distinction is drawn between the external elements of an offence and the fault elements. Chapter 3 will pursue the fault requirement at length, while the focus of this chapter will be on the act requirement. It is important to recognize, however, that the external elements of an offence include more than just the conduct of the accused: other circumstances or consequences will usually also be relevant. It is not an offence to pull a fire alarm if there is actually a fire, for example, and dangerous driving which causes death is a more serious offence than dangerous driving which does not.

Determine what elements need to be established to prove that an accused is guilty of the following *Criminal Code* offences:

- **Defacing current coins - s. 456(b)**
- **Escape from lawful custody - s. 145(1)(a)**
- **Endangering safety of ship - s. 78.1(2)(a)**
- **Carrying weapon while attending public meeting - s. 89**
- **Public mischief - s. 140(1)(c)**
- **Breach of trust by public officer - s. 122**
- **Assault - s. 265(1)(a)**
- **Assaulting a peace officer - s. 270(1)(a)**
- **Assault causing bodily harm - s. 267(b)**
- **Arson - s. 433(a)**
- **Fraud in relation to fares - s. 393(1)(a)**
- **Carrying concealed weapon - s. 90(1)**
- **Communicating for the purpose of prostitution (s. 213)**

The rest of this chapter will focus on issues surrounding proof that the accused has engaged in the conduct which is forbidden by the offence. It is important to remember, though, that unless *all* elements of the offence are proven by the Crown beyond a reasonable doubt, whether conduct, circumstance or consequence, the accused cannot be found guilty.

R. v. THORNE

192 C.C.C. (3d) 424, 27 C.R. (6th) 366,
2004 CarswellNB 634, 2004 CarswellNB 635 (N.B. C.A.)

1 The appellant, an unrepresented litigant, is an inmate at the Federal Maximum Security Institution at Renous, N.B. In July, 2001, he participated in a riot with some 30 prisoners. The warden of the prison read a proclamation commanding the prisoners to disperse, but the appellant failed to do so. Whether that proclamation conformed with s. 67 of the *Criminal Code* of Canada will be

discussed later. The appellant was convicted by a jury of an offence under s. 68(b) of the *Code*, in that he "... did not peaceably disperse and depart from a place where the riot proclamation referred to in Section 67 was made within thirty minutes after it was made ..." He was sentenced to a term of imprisonment of 3 years consecutive to time being served.

2 He appeals his conviction and seeks leave to appeal sentence.

II. Grounds of Appeal

3 Mr. Thorne appeals his conviction upon the following grounds:

. . . .

b) The trial judge failed to introduce all the evidence. (At the hearing before us, it became clear that Mr. Thorne's argument was that there was no evidence before the jury that the proclamation referred to in s. 67 of the *Code* was read to the rioters and thus, no evidence as to one of the essential elements for his conviction under s. 68(b).

. . . .

B. *The Proclamation Issue*

Sections 67 and 68(b) of the *Code* read as follows:

67. Reading proclamation - A person who is

(a) a justice, mayor or sheriff, or the lawful deputy of a mayor or sheriff,

(b) a warden or deputy warden of a prison, or

(c) the institutional head of a penitentiary, as those expressions are defined in subsection 2(1) of the *Corrections and Conditional Release Act*, or that person's deputy,

who receives notice that, at any place within the jurisdiction of the person, twelve or more persons are unlawfully and riotously assembled together shall go to that place and, after approaching as near as is safe, if the person is satisfied that a riot is in progress, shall command silence and thereupon make or cause to be made in a loud voice a proclamation in the following words or to the like effect:

Her Majesty the Queen charges and commands all persons being assembled immediately to disperse and peaceably to depart to their habitations or to their lawful business on the pain of being guilty of an offence for which, on conviction, they may be sentenced to imprisonment for life. GOD SAVE THE QUEEN.

68. Offences related to proclamation - Every one is guilty of an indictable offence and liable to imprisonment for life who

...(b) does not peaceably disperse and depart from a place where the proclamation referred to in section 67 is made within thirty minutes after it is made; or

6 Section 67 provides for what is commonly referred to as "reading the riot act" by the head of a penitentiary. After commanding silence, the official must then read the proclamation in the words provided for in s. 67 or in words "to the like effect".

7 To comply with s. 67, the words of the proclamation must provide that all persons participating in the riot are required to disperse "on pain of being guilty of an offence for which, on conviction, they may be sentenced to imprisonment for life."

8 As mentioned, Mr. Thorne was charged with committing an offence under s. 68(b), namely, failing to peaceably disperse from the place where the proclamation referred to in s. 67 was made within 30 minutes after it was made. Briefly put, "compliance with s. 67 is an essential ingredient of a s. 68 offence." *R. v. Greenhow*, [2004] A.J. No. 38, para. 9 (Alta. C.A.) (QL).

9 The trial judge was concerned from the outset that one of the essential ingredients to the offence under s. 68(b) was that the accused failed to disperse within the required time after the proclamation under s. 67 had been read. He was fully aware that the Crown would have to adduce evidence of what was in fact read to the rioting prisoners. Of course, evidence of the required proclamation involved a reference by the witnesses to the fact that the failure to heed the command to disperse could result in life imprisonment for the offender.

10 The trial judge wanted to comply with the time-honored rule that the matter of the penalty following conviction is not one of the jury's concerns. *R. v. Stevenson*, [1990] O.J. No. 1657 (QL); 41 O.A.C. 1; *58 C.C.C. (3d) 464; R. v. Cracknell (1931), 56 C.C.C. 190 at 192 (Ont. C.A.); McLean v. The King* (1933), 61 C.C.C. at 13-14 (S.C.C.); *Cathro v. The Queen* (1955), 113 C.C.C. 225 at 241 (S.C.C.).

11 Although the evidence before him (given in the absence of the jury) was to the effect that the proclamation actually read to the rioters matched exactly the wording of the proclamation in s. 67, including the reference to imprisonment "for life", the trial judge made two orders. First, he directed the Crown to instruct witnesses to refrain from mentioning the words "for life" when testifying about the proclamation actually read to the rioters. Secondly, he directed Crown counsel to delete the words life" from the text of the proclamation about to be filed as an exhibit for the jury's consideration. Following the trial judge's directives, two witnesses in fact testified that the proclamation read by the warden of the prison was the proclamation required by s. 67. They proceeded to read an amended text of the proclamation as directed by the trial judge. As a result, the witnesses' statements that what was read to the rioters was the proclamation under s. 67 were not accurate. That is so because the proclamation

that the witnesses described to the jury as having been read to the rioters did not make any reference to imprisonment "for life", but only to "imprisonment".

12 Section 67, as mentioned, does not dictate that the proclamation must be exactly as provided in that section; it may employ words "to the like effect". That said, I am of the view that the proclamation actually read must be in the words referred to in s. 67 or in words which have the same meaning and convey the same message as the words employed in s. 67.

13 The question, then, is whether there was evidence before the jury that the proclamation as worded in s. 67 or in words "to the like effect" was read to the rioters. It is not sufficient, as argued by the respondent, for a witness to state that a proclamation as required by s. 67 was read to the rioters. That question is for the jury to decide after evidence is adduced as to what was in fact read by the authorized official.

14 The appellant could only be convicted if the Crown proved beyond a reasonable doubt that he failed to peaceably disperse and depart, within the statutorily provided time frame, from a place where the proclamation referred to in s. 67 was made. There can be no offence under s. 68(b) for failing to disperse until and unless the proclamation under s. 67 is made. The obligation to disperse under s. 68(b) is triggered and a subsequent conviction possible only if the proclamation under s. 67 is made. Was there, in this case, evidence before the jury that a proclamation in the words prescribed by s. 67 or words "to the like effect" was read to the rioters?

15 The proclamation in the words of s. 67 charges and commands, in the name of Her Majesty the Queen, the rioters immediately to disperse "... on the pain of being guilty of an offence, for which, on conviction", an offender "may be sentenced to imprisonment for life." The message conveyed to the rioters is that their failure to heed the command issued by the authorities carries the potential to bring about the most severe sentence that can be imposed in this country. The evidence before the jury was that the rioters, including the appellant, had been read a proclamation which commanded them to disperse "on pain of being guilty of an offence for which, on conviction", an offender "may be sentenced to imprisonment". In my respectful view, that proclamation simply does not convey the same message nor does it have the same meaning as the proclamation referred to in s. 67.

16 Consequently, Mr. Thorne could not be convicted of having failed to peaceably disperse from a place where the proclamation referred to in s. 67 was made because there was no evidence before the jury that such a proclamation was ever made. Briefly put, there was no evidence before the jury with respect to one of the essential elements or ingredients of the offence under s. 68(b). The

appeal against conviction must be allowed on the basis that the verdict cannot be supported by the evidence: section 686(1)(a)(i).

. . . .

21   As in *Ivall*, I would allow the appeal, quash the conviction and order a new trial.

Why require an act?

E.M. BURCHELL, P.M.A. HUNT and J.M. BURCHELL, SOUTH AFRICAN CRIMINAL LAW AND PROCEDURE

2nd ed. (1983), 106

The reason for requiring an *actus reus* is usually said to be the impossibility of proving a purely mental state. "The thought of man is not triable, for the devil himself knoweth not the thought of man", said Brian C.J. But Glanville Williams draws attention to the fallacy of this argument, and suggests two better reasons for the requirement of *actus reus*:

> (1) the difficulty of distinguishing between day-dream and fixed intention in the absence of behaviour tending towards the crime intended, and (2) the undesirability of spreading the criminal law so wide as to cover a mental state that the accused might be too irresolute even to begin to translate into action.

The invariable rule is then that criminal liability is dependent upon proof of an *actus reus* on the part of the accused. Where *mens rea* is required, there must be some act which puts the accused's guilty mind into action or at least goes part of the way towards doing so.

J.F. STEPHEN, A HISTORY OF THE CRIMINAL LAW OF ENGLAND

Vol. 2, (1883), 78-9

No temper of mind, no habit of life, however pernicious, has ever been treated as a crime, unless it displayed itself in some definite overt act. It never entered into the head of any English legislator to enact, or of any English Court, to hold, that a man could be indicted and punished for ingratitude, for hardheartedness, for the absence of natural affection, for habitual idleness, for avarice, sensuality, pride, or, in a word, for any vice whatever as such. Even for purposes of ecclesiastical censure some definite act of immorality was required. Sinful thoughts and dispositions of mind might be the subject of confession and of penance, but they were never punished in this country by ecclesiastical criminal proceedings.

The reasons for imposing this great leading restriction upon the sphere of criminal law are obvious. If it were not so restricted it would be utterly intolerable; all mankind would be criminals, and most of their lives would be passed in trying and punishing each other for offences which could never be proved.

Criminal law, then, must be confined within narrow limits, and can be applied only to definite overt acts or omissions capable of being distinctly proved, which acts or omissions inflict definite evils, either on specific persons or on the community at large.

There are a few provisions in the *Criminal Code* which contemplate potential future behaviour by an accused, rather than responding to a past act. The "peace bond" provisions in s. 810 have long existed, allowing a person who reasonably fears personal injury or property damage at the hands of another person to obtain a "recognizance" in which that other person promises to "keep the peace and be of good behaviour". A person refusing to sign such a recognizance can be jailed for up to 12 months. In recent years, similar provisions dealing with fear of intimidation offences, criminal organization offences, terrorism offences, sexual offences and serious personal injury offences have been brought in: see ss. 810.01, 810.1 and 810.2. These provisions differ from the "personal remedy" offered by a peace bond in that they do not require that the person seeking the order fear that he or she personally will be the victim.

In *R. v. Budreo* (2000), 46 O.R. (3d) 481, 142 C.C.C. (3d) 225, 32 C.R. (5th) 127 (C.A.), s. 810.1 was challenged on the basis that it created a "status offence" and therefore violated s. 7 of the *Charter*. The court upheld the provision, rejecting that argument on the basis that the provision did not create an offence at all.

Budreo was relied on by the Quebec Superior Court in rejecting a challenge brought by Karla Homolka to the constitutionality of s. 810.2. Karla Homolka had pleaded guilty to manslaughter in a notorious murder trial in Ontario in which her husband, Paul Bernardo, was convicted of two counts of first degree murder. Homolka served her full 12 year sentence. On her release in Quebec, prosecutors applied to the Court of Québec Criminal & Penal Division and obtained a section 810.2 recognizance placing stringent conditions on Homolka's movements. On appeal to the Quebec Superior Court that recognizance was quashed on the facts, but the constitutionality of the legislation was upheld.

TEALE v. NOBLE

(2005), [2005] Q.J. No. 17295, 2005 CarswellQue 10567 (Que. S.C.),
leave to appeal refused 2005 QCCA 1174 (Que. C.A.)

BRUNTON J: —

22 If I am in error in refusing to entertain the challenge, I would nonetheless hold that based upon the record before me, s. 810.2 Cr. C. is constitutional. No cogent reason has been advanced why the decision in *Budreo* should not be followed.

23 As pointed out in that case, a section such as s. 810.2 Cr. C. responds to one of two broad objectives of the criminal justice system which has been recognized for centuries - the prevention of future harm.

> The section (810.1) does not create an offence. It is a preventive provision not a punitive provision. (*Budreo*, Ont. C.A. p. 237)

24 The same is true as regards s. 810.2 Cr. C.

25 Many of Ms. Teale's arguments suggest that s. 810.2 Cr. C. is overbroad and too vague. I respectfully disagree. I adopt the same factors identified in *Budreo* in response to this argument.

- unlike the appellant, I do not believe that s. 810.2 Cr. C. provides the hearing judge with an unfettered discretion to impose any type of condition in the order;

- the impossibility of making exact predictions of future dangerousness does not render s. 810.2 Cr. C. overbroad. Both the dangerous offender legislation and the bail system rely on predictions of future dangerousness;

- the procedural safeguards in s. 810.2 are adequate;

- the recourse to hearsay evidence is not objectionable. Ultimately, the order can only issue on evidence that is judged credible and trustworthy;

- the need for the informant to establish a "fear" of future dangerousness does not render s. 810.2 void for vagueness.

26 As pointed out by Then J., the need to establish the fear on reasonable grounds

> "... equates to a belief, objectively established, that the individual will commit an offence." (*Budreo*, Ont. G.D., p. 281)

27 Finally, Ms. Teale's reliance on s. 11(g) and 11(h) of the *Charter* is misplaced. Those sections have no application as they are available only to persons charged with an offence. The recourse to s. 810.2 Cr. C. did not result in Ms. Teale being charged with an offence.

[On the merits Brunton J. held that the s. 810.2 order issued was invalid. The Crown had not demonstrated by preponderance of probability reasonable grounds to believe that the accused would commit another violent crime. The risk had to be imminent and serious. The judge at first instance had overlooked evidence favourable to Homolka, including psychiatric evidence indicating she was at a low risk of re-offending.]

We next turn to consider each of the five legal aspects of the act requirement:

1. Commission of an unlawful act;

2. Omission where there was a legal duty to act;

3. Voluntariness;

4. Acting through an innocent agent; and

5. If consequences are part of the offence charged, that the act or omission caused the consequence.

2.   COMMISSION OF AN UNLAWFUL ACT

In many, if not most crimes, the act requirement is self-evident. Stealing requires taking something belonging to someone else, assault is a positive act of applying force, etc. In some instances, however, the law's description of the necessary external circumstance of the offence requires careful judicial analysis because it is vague or involves what appears to be a most minimal form of an act. What follows in this section is a selection of a number of different offences where the definition of the act requirement is difficult and often controversial.

(a)   Causing Disturbance in Public Place

R. v. LOHNES

[1992] 1 S.C.R. 167, 10 C.R. (4th) 125, 69 C.C.C. (3d) 289,
1992 CarswellNS 11, 1992 CarswellNS 350

McLACHLIN J.: — This case requires this court for the first time to consider what constitutes a public disturbance under s. 175(1)(*a*) of the *Criminal Code*, R.S.C. 1985, c. C-46, which makes it an offence to cause a disturbance in or near a public place by, inter alia, fighting, screaming, shouting, swearing, singing or using insulting or obscene language. Shouting or swearing or singing are not in themselves criminal offences. They become criminal only when they cause a disturbance in or near a public place. What constitutes such a disturbance? For example, does mere annoyance or emotional disturbance of the complainant suffice? Or is something more required?

The Facts

The case began as a disagreement between two neighbours in the town of Milton, Nova Scotia. The appellant, Donald Lohnes, lived across the street from a certain Mr. Porter. Mr. Porter, it seems, was given to collecting equipment on his premises and running motors which made loud noises. This disturbed Mr. Lohnes. It disturbed him so much that on two occasions a year apart he went onto the veranda of his house and shouted obscenities at Mr. Porter. The essence of Mr. Lohnes's remarks was that he did not want Mr. Porter "to run that chain saw or that lawn mower or to leave that or have that God-damned junk heap". This was embellished by a string of epithets revealing an impressive command of the obscene vernacular. On the second occasion Mr. Lohnes concluded his oration with the assertion that he would shoot Mr. Porter if he had a gun.

Mr. Porter filed a complaint. He was the only Crown witness. There was no evidence that anyone else heard Mr. Lohnes's statements or that Mr. Porter's conduct was affected by them.

Mr. Lohnes was convicted on the ground that his conduct in itself constituted a disturbance within s. 175(1)(*a*) of the *Criminal Code*; the trial judge found, as well, that Mr. Porter was "disturbed" by the impugned conduct. The convictions were upheld by the Summary Convictions Appeal Court. The Nova Scotia Supreme Court, Appeal Division refused leave from that decision: (1990), 100 N.S.R. (2d) 268. He now appeals to this court.

Legislation

Section 175 of the *Criminal Code* states:

175. (1) Every one who

(a) not being in a dwelling house, causes a disturbance in or near a public place,

(i) by fighting, screaming, shouting, swearing, singing or using insulting or obscene language,

. . . .

is guilty of an offence punishable on summary conviction.

(2) In the absence of other evidence, or by way of corroboration of other evidence, a summary conviction court may infer from the evidence of a peace officer relating to the conduct of a person or persons, whether ascertained or not, that a disturbance described in paragraph (1)(a) or (d) was caused or occurred.

Analysis

Section 175(1)(a) creates a two-element offence consisting of: (1) commission of one of the enumerated acts; which, (2) causes a disturbance in or near a public place. There is no doubt on the facts of this case that one of the enumerated acts was committed. The only question is whether the evidence establishes that it caused a disturbance in or near a public place.

The word "disturbance" encompasses a broad range of meanings. At one extreme, it may be something as innocuous as a false note or a jarring colour; something which disturbs in the sense of annoyance or disruption. At the other end of the spectrum are incidents of violence, inducing disquiet, fear and apprehension for physical safety. Between these extremes lies a vast variety of disruptive conduct. The question before us is whether all conduct within this broad spectrum elicits criminal liability under s. 175(1), and if not, where the line should be drawn.

The Nova Scotia Supreme Court, Appeal Division, in dismissing Mr. Lohnes's application for leave to appeal, agreed with the finding implicit to the judgments below: all that is required to establish an offence under s. 175(1)(a) is one of the forms of prohibited conduct (fighting, screaming, shouting, swearing, singing or using insulting or obscene language) which one ought to know would disturb others. The appellant contends that this interpretation is too broad; there must be some overtly manifested disturbance of the public's use and enjoyment of the public place where the act takes place. The main issue thus turns on how "disturbance" in s. 175(1)(*a*) is defined; does foreseeable emotional upset suffice, or must there be an externally manifested disturbance of a public nature? The appeal, like the judgments below, focuses upon the requisite *actus reus* of the offence, although the issue of *mens rea*, as recognized by the respondent, flows necessarily from a discussion of "disturbance". A subsidiary issue concerns whether the act itself may constitute the disturbance, or whether a secondary disturbance is required.

The values at stake on this appeal are readily discerned. On the one hand lies the freedom of the individual to shout, sing or otherwise express himself or herself. On the other lies the collective right of every subject to peace and tranquillity. Neither right is absolute. The individual right of expression must at some point give way to the collective interest in peace and tranquillity, and the collective right in peace and tranquillity must be based on recognition that in a society where people live together some degree of disruption must be tolerated. The question is where the line is to be drawn.

I propose to consider these issues from the perspectives of the authorities, the principles of statutory construction, and the underlying policy issues. On my reading, these considerations point to the conclusion that s. 175(1)(*a*) of the *Criminal Code* requires an externally manifested disturbance in or near a public place, consisting either in the act itself or in a secondary disturbance.

The Authorities

The offence created by s. 175(1)(*a*) finds its origins in the common law of vagrancy, an "offence against public convenience", which proscribed certain behaviour in order to preserve peace and order in the community: see, for example, *An Act Respecting Vagrants*, S.C. 1869, c. 28. In 1947, the *Criminal Code* created a new and distinct offence of causing a disturbance; the offence was moved from the section of the *Code* entitled "Vagrancy" to the nuisance offences falling under Part V labelled "Offences Against Religion, Morals and Public Convenience", S.C. 1947, c. 55, s. 3. Upon the *Code's* revision in 1955, S.C. 1953-54, c. 51, the offence was included in Part IV, renamed "Sexual Offenses, Public Morals and Disorderly Conduct", as s. 160 under the section entitled "Disorderly Conduct".

Our jurisprudence has exhibited two different doctrinal approaches to the offence dating to the first federal vagrancy enactments. The first line of authority adopts an expansive approach to "disturbance"; the second a narrower approach which would limit "disturbance" by requiring external manifestations of disturbance.

. . . .

Whatever their theoretical pronouncements, Canadian courts have entered few if any convictions under (what is now) s. 175(1)(*a*) absent an overtly manifested disturbance which affected people's conduct, be it found in the act itself or in its effect. In *Swinimer* the accused's fighting, shouting and obscene language in front of his residence interfered with the usual activities of a neighbour as well as her children, to judge from her testimony that she had to return to the bedroom during the episode to calm the children down. The conviction in *R. v. Allick* (February 20, 1976), Munroe J. (B.C. S.C.) [unreported] (cited in *R. v. Peters*, *supra*, at p. 90 [C.C.C., p. 256 C.R.]), arose from a spirited barroom brawl. In *R. v. Chikoski* (1973), 14 C.C.C. (2d) 38 (Ont. Prov. Ct.), the police officer testified that the obscenities which the accused had shouted at him not only offended and disturbed him, but caused a group of men working in a field some 200 feet away to stop their work and look up towards the place where the police officer and the accused were standing. In *R. v. D. (C.)*, the trial judge found that the accused caused an affray in the street by shouting and ramming his car into the back of another car, reducing the wife of the owner to tears. Yet, the Court of Appeal overturned even this conviction, finding that the interruption of "tranquillity" of mind or the "emotional upset" caused the owner and his wife was insufficient to constitute a "disturbance". Shouting abusive language without more was held not to trigger the section in *R. v. Eyre* (1972), 10 C.C.C. (2d) 236 (B.C. S.C.) and *R. v. Peters*. In *R. v. Wolgram*, *supra*, shouting obscenities at police in a barroom was similarly held not to offend the section because "[i]t was not made to appear that any person or persons were so disturbed by what occurred as to cause some disorder or agitation to ensue or that there was any interference with the ordinary and customary use by the public of a public place" (p. 537 [C.C.C.]).

I conclude that the weight of the authority, whether viewed from the point of view of theory or result, suggests that before an offence can arise under s. 175(1) of the *Criminal Code*, the enumerated conduct must cause an overtly manifested disturbance which constitutes an interference with the ordinary and customary use by the public of the place in question. This may be proved by direct evidence or inferred under s. 175(2). It is not necessary that there be a separate disturbance secondary to the disturbing act; the act itself may in some cases amount to a disturbance and "cause" it in this sense. Finally, the principle of legality, alluded to in the judgment of Wilson J. in *Skoke-Graham* suggests that only conduct which may reasonably be expected to cause such a disturbance in the particular circumstances of the case falls within s. 175(1)(*a*) (see p. 14, below).

Principles of Statutory Construction

The word "disturbance" is capable of many meanings. The task is to choose the meaning which best accords with the intention of Parliament.

The following arguments support the conclusion that "disturbance" in s. 175(1)(*a*) involves more than mere mental or emotional annoyance or disruption.

First, the noun "disturbance" may have a different connotation than the verb "to disturb". Not everything that disturbs people results in a disturbance (*e.g.*, smoking). A definition which posits identity between "disturb" and "disturbance" is contrary to ordinary usage, the most fundamental principle of statutory construction. This is not to say that one cannot speak of a purely emotional disturbance, but rather that "disturbance" has a secondary meaning which "disturb" does not possess; a meaning which suggests interference with an ordinary and customary conduct or use.

Second, the context of "disturbance" in s. 175(1)(*a*) suggests that Parliament did not intend to protect society from mere emotional disturbance. Had Parliament sought to protect society from annoyance and anxiety, the section would not be confined to acts occurring in or near a public place, nor would it single out particular forms of objectionable conduct — many other types of conduct disturb us. Parliament could have expressly protected against emotional disturbance, as was done in the *Public Order Act 1986* (U.K.), 1986, c. 64. But, to borrow the language of MacKeigan C.J.N.S. in *Swinimer, supra,* Parliament chose to speak of a disturbance in or near a public place, not in someone's mind. By addressing "disturbance" in the public context, Parliament signalled that its objective was not the protection of individuals from emotional upset, but the protection of the public from disorder calculated to interfere with the public's normal activities.

Third, interpretative aids suggest that s. 175(1)(*a*) is directed at publicly exhibited disorder. As noted in *Skoke-Graham, supra,* headings and preambles may be used as intrinsic aids in interpreting ambiguous statutes. Section 175(1)(*a*) appears under the section "Disorderly Conduct". Without elevating headings to determinative status, the heading under which s. 175(1)(*a*) appears supports the view that Parliament had in mind, not the emotional upset or annoyance of individuals, but disorder and agitation which interferes with the ordinary use of a place.

Fourth, the word used for disturbance in the French version of s. 175(1), "tapage", connotes an externally manifested disturbance involving violent noise or confusion disrupting the tranquillity of those using the area in question. For example, Le Petit Robert 1 (Paris: Le Robert, 1990) defines the term as: "10 Bruit violent, confus, désordonné produit par un groupe de personnes; ... *Tapage injurieux ou nocturne*: consistant à troubler la tranquillité des habitants en faisant du bruit, sans motif légitime". [Emphasis in original.]

Finally, it can be argued that the reference in s. 175(2) to an inference of disturbance from evidence "relating to the *conduct* of a person *or persons*" is consistent with the finding that Parliament had in mind the effect of the shouting, swearing or singing, for example, on the conduct of persons other than the accused. In short, Parliament was concerned with how members of the public other than the accused may have been affected by the impugned act.

Policy

Considerations pertaining to the practical application of the criminal law suggest that the narrower "public disturbance" interpretation of s. 175(1)(*a*) is preferable to the broader "emotional disturbance" standard.

The first consideration pertains to fundamental justice, and in particular, the principle of legality, which affirms the entitlement of every person to know in advance whether their conduct is illegal. As Wilson J. points out in *Skoke-Graham, supra*, application of the internal test would mean that "anyone in any given situation would act at the risk of causing some unmanifested emotional upset or 'disturbance' to another person" (p. 131 S.C.R.). Read thus, s. 175(1)(*a*) imposes a duty to ascertain whether one's conduct disturbs or can reasonably be expected to disturb the "mental" or "emotional" tranquillity of others. Such a burden, dependent as it is on time, place, circumstance and the sensitivities of others, verges on the capricious. It may well be questioned whether it could ever be discharged with certainty.

The second consideration is that the narrower "public disturbance" test permits a more sensitive balancing between the countervailing interests at stake. As MacKeigan C.J.N.S. points out in *Swinimer*, the test for a disturbance in or near a public place under s. 175(1)(*a*) should permit the court to weigh the degree and intensity of the conduct complained of against the degree and nature of the peace which can be expected to prevail in a given place at a given time. A test which accepts mental or emotional disturbance as sufficient to establish the offence does not permit such balancing; all that is required is that the accused should have known that someone might be internally disturbed. A test, on the other hand, which turns on whether the effect of the conduct was such as to interfere with the ordinary and customary use of the premises at the time and place in question, permits the countervailing factors to be weighed and balanced. As such, it arguably strikes a more sensitive balance between the individual interest in liberty and the public interest in going about its affairs in peace and tranquillity.

The final policy consideration takes us into the more precarious terrain of pondering the proper goals and limits of the criminal law. The *Swinimer* standard, adopted by the courts below, would make it a criminal offence to sing or shout in circumstances where a person has reason to believe that his or her conduct might annoy or upset someone else, even though no one may have heard the sound, much less have been affected by it. In support of this interpretation, it was argued that such a stringent standard is necessary in order to nip disturbances in the bud before they become truly disruptive to the public. But it is far from self-evident that the goal of peace and order in our public places requires the criminal law to step in at the stage of foreseeability of mental annoyance. Indeed, our society has traditionally tolerated a great deal of activity in our streets and byways which can and does disturb and annoy others sharing the public space. Given the intrusion on public liberty and the uncertainty in the criminal law which such a rule would introduce, it is arguable that some external manifestation of disorder in the sense of interference with the normal use of the affected place should be required to transform lawful conduct into an unlawful criminal offence.

Conclusion on the Ambit of s. 175(1)(a)

The weight of the authorities, the principles of statutory construction and policy considerations, taken together, lead me to the conclusion that the disturbance contemplated by s. 175(1)(*a*) is something more than mere emotional upset. There must be an externally manifested disturbance of the public peace, in the sense of interference with the ordinary and customary use of the premises by the public. There may be direct evidence of such an effect or interference, or it may be inferred from the evidence of a police officer as to the conduct of a person or persons under s. 175(2). The disturbance may consist of the impugned act itself, as in the case of a fight interfering with the peaceful use of a barroom, or it may flow as a consequence of the impugned act, as where shouting and swearing produce a scuffle. As the cases illustrate, the interference with the ordinary and customary conduct in or near the public place may consist in something as small as being distracted from one's work. But it must be present and it must be externally manifested. In accordance with the principle of legality, the disturbance must be one which may reasonably have been foreseen in the particular circumstances of time and place.

Disposition of the Appeal

There was no evidence of a disturbance of the use of the premises in question by anyone in the case at bar. The trial judge applied a mental disturbance test, convicting on the basis that an "ordinary reasonable individual would be disturbed by language of that nature being shouted in a public area". The convictions were upheld. In denying leave to appeal, the Court of Appeal agreed that language such as that used by the accused was "inherently disturbing and was of itself a disturbance" (p. 270 [N.S.R.]). There was no finding that the conduct of the complainant or anyone else was affected or disturbed by the language. In the absence of such findings, the convictions cannot stand.

I would allow the appeal, quash the convictions, and substitute acquittals in their place.

(b)   Vicarious Liability

Under a doctrine of vicarious responsibility, one person is automatically responsible for the wrongdoing of another solely on the basis of a relationship between the parties, irrespective of whether that person was at fault or even acted. In the law of torts it has long been clear common-law doctrine that a "master" may be vicariously liable for a tort committed by a "servant" acting in the course and scope of his employment. Given that the purpose of torts is compensation, the doctrine has a pragmatic rationale: a master is likely to be in a better position to compensate the victim and an employer profits through his employee's work. In this way the employer also bears the risk of employing a bad worker. In the criminal law where the purpose is just punishment, the emphasis is usually on an individual's own act and fault. Our courts have accordingly been reluctant to impose vicarious responsibility. They have generally done so in the past only where there is an express statutory provision. One such statutory provision has now been held to be unconstitutional.

R. v. BURT

(1985), 47 C.R. (3d) 49, 21 C.C.C. (3d) 138,
1985 CarswellSask 201 (Sask. Q.B.)

GEREIN J.: — The accused was charged that he did contrary to "s. 141 via s. 253 [of the Vehicles Act] as registered owner allow someone to operate vehicle and cause excessive noise in its operation". After a trial which proceeded on the basis of an agreed statement of facts, the learned trial Judge concluded that s. 253 contravened the *Canadian Charter of Rights and Freedoms* and entered an acquittal. From said decision the Crown has appealed.

The agreed facts giving rise to the charge were as follows:

1. THAT on the 4th day of September, 1983 at approximately 2:45 a.m. a Ford pick-up truck, being a motor vehicle registered in the name of the defendant, was operated within the Town of Kindersley, in the Province of Saskatchewan on a public highway.

2. THAT the vehicle was operated in a manner which created excessive or unusual noise, contrary to Section 141 of *The Vehicle* [sic] *Act* for the Province of Saskatchewan. The vehicle left approximately 25 feet of tire marks while crossing Main Street.

3. THAT the Royal Canadian Mounted Police constable on patrol pursued the vehicle, which was approximately two blocks ahead of the police car when it pulled to the right and stopped. As the police vehicle approached the registered owner was observed standing next to the vehicle. The police car stopped and the officer called to the owner who ignored the officer and continued walking into his residence.

4. THAT the driver of the motor vehicle was not identified and the accused is charged as the registered owner of the motor vehicle under the provisions of Section 253 of *The Vehicles Act* for the Province of Saskatchewan.

Section 253 (now s. 169(1)) of the *Vehicles Act*, R.S.S. 1978, c. V-3 (since replaced by the *Vehicles Act, 1983* (Sask.), c. V-3.1), provided:

253. The owner of a motor vehicle, tractor or trailer, other than a public service vehicle, is liable for violation of any Provision of this Act in connection with the operation of the motor vehicle, tractor or trailer, unless he proves to the satisfaction of the provincial magistrate or justice of the peace trying the case that at the time of the offence the vehicle, tractor or

trailer was not being operated by him, nor by any other person with his consent, express or implied.

The trial Judge held that s. 253 contravened s. 7 of the *Canadian Charter of Rights and Freedoms*, which provides:

> 7. Everyone has the right to life, liberty and security of the person and the right not to be deprived thereof except in accordance with the principles of fundamental justice.

By reason of s. 253 of the *Vehicles Act* an owner of a motor vehicle became vicariously liable for any violation of the Act in which the motor vehicle was involved: see *R. v. Grant* (1957), 29 C.R. 229, 122 C.C.C. 261 (Sask. Police Ct.); *R. v. Davlyn Corp.*, 8 C.R.N.S. 219, [1970] 3 C.C.C. 115 (Alta. C.A.); and *R. v. Budget Car Rentals (Toronto) Ltd.* (1981), 20 C.R. (3d) 66 (C.A.). Thus an owner became liable to be convicted of the substantive violation and not simply of lending or permitting the use of his motor vehicle. On conviction he was subject to punishment, which could be a fine of up to $1,000, imprisonment, suspension of licence or a combination thereof. A person could be asleep at home when events transpire which ultimately result in that person's imprisonment. This could occur even though the person took no part in the violation, even in the sense of aiding or abetting. Thus an owner could be convicted in the absence of *both mens rea* and *actus reus*.

Does this absence of *actus reus* render the legislation invalid? In my opinion it does.

. . . .

Throughout the history of the common law the conduct of the wrongdoer had to compromise the prohibited act. The *actus reus* had to be present. Thus, in *Fowler v. Padget* (1798), 101 E.R. 1103 at 1106, Lord Kenyon C.J. stated:

> . . . it is a principle of natural justice, and of our law, that *actus non facit reum nisi mens sit rea*. The intent and the act must both concur to constitute the crime . . .

In Russell on Crime, 12th ed. (1964), vol. 1, at p. 22, the learned author states:

> The new conception that merely to bring about a prohibited harm should not involve a man in liability to punishment unless in addition he could be regarded as morally blameworthy came to be enshrined in the well-known maxim *actus non facit reum nisi mens sit rea*. This ancient maxim has remained unchallenged as a declaration of principle at common law throughout the centuries up to the present day. So long therefore as it remains unchallenged no man should be convicted of a crime at common law unless the two requirements which it envisages are satisfied, namely, that there must be both a physical element and a mental element in every crime.

Then, at p. 26:

> We may repeat, then, that to constitute a crime at common law there must always be a result brought about by human conduct, a physical event, which the law prohibits, for example

the death of a man who is under the Queen's peace; and that it has for some time past been the custom to employ the term *actus reus* to denote a deed so prohibited.

In the text *Criminal Law*, 4th ed. (1978), by Smith and Hogan, the learned authors state at p. 31:

> Before a man can be convicted of a crime it is usually necessary for the prosecution to prove (a) that a certain event or a certain state of affairs, which is forbidden by the criminal law, has been caused by his conduct and (b) that this conduct was accompanied by a prescribed state of mind. The event, or state of affairs, is usually called the *actus reus* and the state of mind the *mens rea* of the crime. Both these elements must be proved beyond reasonable doubt by the prosecution.

From my reading, I conclude that traditionally a person was not to be convicted of an offence unless he committed the prohibited act.

The legislative tradition has been more mixed. That a person should not be convicted of an offence committed by someone else unless he has assisted, encouraged, counselled or participated in the offence was enunciated as long ago as *R. v. Huggins* (1730), 92 E.R. 518. However, three exceptions were early recognized, namely: (1) public nuisance committed by an employee; (2) criminal libel; and (3) criminal contempt of court: see *Upholsterers Int. Union of N. Amer., Loc. I v. Hankin & Struck Furniture Ltd.*, [1965] 1 C.C.C. 110 (B.C. C.A.), particularly at p. 40. Then, over the years, other instances of vicarious liability have been created by statute and approved by the courts. By way of example see *Barker v. Levinson*, [1950] 2 All E.R. 825 (Div. Ct.); *R. v. Piggly Wiggly Can. Ltd.* (1933), 60 C.C.C. 104 (C.A.); and *R. v. Kiewel Brewing Co.*(1930), 53 C.C.C. 56 (C.A.). Thus for some considerable time our society has lived with vicarious liability in the field of criminal or quasi-criminal law. Put otherwise, there is a certain legislative tradition of vicarious liability in this country.

Yet instances of vicarious liability have remained the exception rather than the rule. Usually such an approach appears to have been adopted to regulate situations where substantial control over the conduct being regulated and an effective means of enforcing same has reposed in one of the parties, *e.g.*, employment situations: again see *Barker v. Levinson* and *R. v. Kiewel Brewing Co.*

In any event the legislative tradition must be looked at in the light of the then prevailing jurisprudence. More particularly, one must remember that prior to the *Charter* the law was that Parliament and Legislatures were supreme and could enact legislation as they saw fit, subject only to the division of powers as set out in the *British North America Act* [now the *Constitution Act, 1867*]. Thus, it was futile to resist legislation even if it did offend principles of fundamental justice. This situation undoubtedly caused the courts to try to temper certain legislation by resorting to the concept of *mens rea* and implying the requirement of same as often as possible. However, this has now changed. Legislation must now conform to the requirements of the *Charter*.

To ascertain community standards as to *actus reus* is exceedingly difficult. Not only have lay members of society failed to discuss the matter, but the same can be said of the legal community. To my mind this dearth of comment is significant. It suggests that it is generally assumed or taken for granted that *actus reus* will be present when a charge is preferred.

In my opinion, fundamental justice encompasses the concept that a person should not be punished in the absence of a wrongful act. I am satisfied that this is the prevailing view in our society. In speaking about *mens rea* in *R. v. Sault Ste. Marie*, *supra*, Dickson J. (now C.J.C.) said at pp. 362-63:

> Public welfare offences obviously lie in a field of conflicting values. It is essential for society to maintain, through effective enforcement, high standards of public health and safety. Potential victims of those who carry on latently pernicious activities have a strong claim to consideration. On the other hand, there is a generally held revulsion against punishment of the morally innocent.

Surely no less revulsion is held when the person has not even committed the act.

I return now to a consideration of s. 253 itself and in doing so I bear in mind the statement of Dickson J., at p. 51 of *R. v. Big M Drug Mart Ltd.*, *supra*:

> In short, I agree with the respondent that the legislation's purpose is the initial test of constitutional validity and its effects are to be considered when the law under review has passed or, at least, has purportedly passed the purpose test. If the legislation fails the purpose test, there is no need to consider further its effects, since it has already been demonstrated to be invalid. Thus, if a law with a valid purpose interferes by its impact with rights or freedoms, a litigant could still argue the effects of the legislation as a means to defeat its applicability and possibly its validity. In short, the effects test will only be necessary to defeat legislation with a valid purpose; effects can never be relied upon to save legislation with an invalid purpose.

The purpose of the *Vehicles Act* as it existed in 1983, and indeed as it presently exists, was to achieve safe and orderly operation of motor vehicles on public highways. To this end various types of conduct are prohibited and sanctions are provided for any breach thereof. No criticism can be made of the Act as a whole.

The purpose of s. 253 is not so clear. It could not have been enacted to ensure that the owner operates his vehicle in a safe manner. The section itself anticipates that he will not be operating the vehicle and in any event the sections which explicitly govern the operation of a vehicle would cover the situation. I do not think the section was intended to regulate the lending of a motor vehicle. The very wording of the section does not suggest this. Were it otherwise the Legislature could have so stated. It seems to me that the real purpose of the section is to provide a means whereby a form of coercion can be brought to bear upon the owner of a vehicle to disclose who was driving his vehicle or had possession of it at the time when a violation occurred but the actual malefactor was not apprehended or ascertained. In short, it is a device to facilitate enforcement of the provisions of the Act.

It is of interest to note that s. 231 (now s. 172) required an owner, upon request, to furnish a police officer "with such information as he requires in the fulfilment of his duties". However, I am unable to say that the purpose of the section contravenes the *Charter*.

The result is different when one looks at the effect of the legislation. The owner would not be convicted of having improperly permitted the use of his vehicle by another or refusing to provide information. Rather, he would be convicted of the substantive offence or actual violation; in this case, causing excessive noise. As stated earlier, the owner plays no part in the violation of the Act which gives rise to the charge which is preferred. The result is that the owner becomes subject to punishment for the misconduct of another. As I have earlier concluded that this is contrary to principles of fundamental justice, it follows that s. 253 of the *Vehicles Act* has contravened s. 7 of the *Charter*. I use the past tense as I am concerned only with the former section.

Further, it is my opinion that s. 1 of the *Charter* cannot be utilized to maintain the impugned section. I accept that the *Vehicles Act* has the public welfare as its object and to that end seeks to achieve safe and orderly operation of motor vehicles. I also recognize that motor vehicles are numerous and, by their very nature, highly mobile. Difficulties in enforcement of the provisions of the *Vehicles Act* may result therefrom. While the object is laudable and the difficulties unfortunate, the provisions of s. 253 go beyond the reasonable limits envisaged by s. 1 of the *Charter*.

Appeal dismissed.

The decision in *Burt* was confirmed on appeal by the Saskatchewan Court of Appeal, the majority on the basis that there was no requirement of fault. For discussion of this ruling and other decisions see Lee Stuesser, "Convicting the Innocent Owner: Vicarious Liability Under Highway Traffic Legislation" (1989), 67 C.R. (3d) 316.

A car rental company disputes its responsibility for a municipal by-law parking offence arising from a parking meter violation by a lessee of one of its cars. The by-law declares that a driver of a vehicle who was not the owner is liable to any penalty exacted for a parking by-law offence, but that the owner of the vehicle is also liable "to such a penalty unless at the time the offence was committed the vehicle was in the possession of a person other than the owner or his chauffeur without the owner's consent". Do you think that a constitutional defence along the lines of Burt should succeed?
Compare *R. v. Budget Car Rentals (Toronto) Ltd.* (1981), 20 C.R. (3d) 66, 57 C.C.C. (2d) 201 (C.A.).

Should such a constitutional defence bar enforcement of speeding laws through means of photo radar equipment? Would it be material that the scheme of automatically charging the owner of the vehicle involved fines but no demerit points?

(c) Possession Offences

Given the definition of "possession" in s. 4(3) of the *Criminal Code* (the older numbering was s. 3(4)) as interpreted in the following decisions, mount defences to charges of possession of marihuana against each of A, B, C and D. The evidence is that at a party in an apartment, A, a guest, passed on a joint to others in a group, without herself smoking, but knowing full well what it was. B did not touch the joint but joined the group in which the joint was being smoked, knowing full well what it was. C joined the group, grabbed the joint and called the police. D, the tenant of the apartment where the party was being held, was not in the group at the time but knew that some of her guests were smoking marihuana. Are there any possible *Charter* arguments? If so, what are they?

MARSHALL v. R.

[1969] 3 C.C.C. 149, 5 C.R.N.S. 348,
1968 CarswellAlta 69 (Alta. C.A.)

McDERMID J.A.: — The appellant was charged jointly with three other persons that:

> Reginald James Smith, Roy Clare Jones, Daniel Joseph Marshall and Frank Nelson Brander stand charged that you on the 5th day of February, A.D. 1968 in the Province of Alberta, near the City of Calgary, in the said Province, were unlawfully in possession of a narcotic, to wit: Cannabis (Marihuana) for the purpose of trafficking, contrary to the provisions of Section 4, sub-section 2 of the *Narcotic Control Act*.

All of the accused were found guilty and the appellant Marshall has appealed against his conviction and sentence.

At the date of the offence the appellant was 16 years of age and was attending school in the city of Calgary. He decided to accompany his friend, one of the accused, Roy Clare Jones, who owned a car, to Vancouver for a short weekend holiday. Also accompanying them were the accused Brander and one, Wes. Cameron. The appellant Marshall did not know Wes. Cameron before the trip to Vancouver. The appellant Marshall only had $15 when he commenced the trip and upon arrival in Vancouver on Friday, February 2, he slept the first night in the car, but subsequently he slept in a suite of a friend of Cameron. Very early Monday morning, February 5, the four who were jointly charged and Wes. Cameron started driving back to Calgary. Shortly after leaving Vancouver the appellant discovered that there was *cannabis* (marijuana) in the car. On the trip marijuana was smoked in the car but not by Marshall.

At Golden, B.C., which is better than halfway on the Trans-Canada Highway to Calgary from Vancouver, while doing 95 m.p.h., the car was stopped by the R.C.M.P. The driver at the time was Cameron. As the highway does not go directly through Golden the police required the car to follow them into Golden. The marijuana was thrown out of the car, but not by the appellant. At Golden as Cameron did not have an identification or a driver's licence he was detained by the police but the other boys were allowed to proceed. Jones, the owner of the car, then drove it. They returned to where they had thrown out the marijuana and it was picked up by one of the boys but not the appellant. They then proceeded on to Calgary, picking up a hitchhiker east of Banff. On the outskirts of Calgary the boys were again stopped by the R.C.M.P. as they only had one light burning. This was in the evening of Monday, February 5. The appellant was sitting in the left rear seat of the car. The R.C.M.P. searched the car and found the marijuana, which was a kilogram or 2.2 lbs. It was on the floor of the rear seat on the right-hand side partially covered by a sweater which belonged to Wes. Cameron. Also in the sleeve of the sweater was found a bag containing additional marijuana.

The police also found a hookah pipe, which is a pipe used for smoking marijuana, the bowl of which was found in the glove compartment and the stem in the pocket of the sweater. With the exception of the hitchhiker all of the boys in the car were arrested and charged as aforesaid. The appellant, Marshall, gave evidence in his defence, and stated that he did not know the marijuana was in the car until they were about 30 miles out of Vancouver on their way home. When asked why he did not leave the car when he found out about the marijuana he said he had no money and he was just getting a ride back to Calgary as he had to get back to classes. He further testified that it was Cameron's marijuana, that he said he did not want to pick up the marijuana after it had been thrown out of the car at Golden, and that when asked by the police about the marijuana he said that whosoever it was would take him off the hook at the trial. When asked why he said that he answered, "Oh I didn't want to, I didn't actually want to tell, say whose it was at the time, what you say squeal on him."

Nowhere does the trial judge throw any doubt on the credibility of the testimony given by Marshall and he did say that he believed that he (Marshall) "did not do anything to exercise control or take control of the marihuana." Such being the case I have accepted the evidence of Marshall even where there is conflict between it and the evidence of others.

Marshall was convicted along with the others by the learned trial judge who stated:

> In the case of Marshall his role at this time was perhaps less of a participant in the sense that he did not drive the car, but certainly at that point he had an opportunity of leaving the car. He may or may not have had an opportunity before reaching Golden. I make no finding on that question but at Golden it is very clear that he had the opportunity of leaving the car, requesting the assistance of the police to get back to Calgary or simply leaving the car and hitch hiking himself if there were no other means.

. . . .

Although I believe the evidence of Marshall that he did not do anything to exercise control or take control of the marihuana, yet having ridden in the car as long as he did ride in the car, not having indicated in his evidence any protest or any act on his part separating himself from the actions of the others or from their company, and considering the length of time that transpired, which I think is quite a material consideration, I find that he acquiesced in what the others did, and I also find that in the meaning of the *Narcotic Control Act* and the *Criminal Code*, he was in possession.

The Crown relies upon s. 3(4)(*b*) of the *Criminal Code*, 1953-54, ch. 51, to support the conviction of the appellant, Marshall, The *Narcotic Control Act*, 1960-61, ch. 35, provides that possession means possession as defined in the *Criminal Code*. Section 3(4)(*b*) of the *Criminal Code* provides:

(4) For the purposes of this Act,

. . . .

(b) where one of two or more persons, with the knowledge and consent of the rest, has anything in his custody, it shall be deemed to be in the custody and possession of each and all of them.

There is no doubt that Marshall had knowledge of the marijuana being in the car so the question is did he consent to it being there.

The *Shorter Oxford Dictionary* defines "consent" as: "1. Voluntary agreement to or acquiescence in what another proposes or desires; compliance, concurrence, permission."

The meaning of s. 5(2) in the previous *Code*, which is in substantially the same terms as s. 3(4)(*b*) in the present *Code*, has been dealt with by the British Columbia and the Ontario Courts of Appeal in several cases.

. . . .

It was much pressed on us by counsel for the defence that there must be an element of control in order for there to be possession, and the statement of Cartwright J. (now C.J.) was quoted in *Beaver v. Reg.*, [1957] S.C.R. 531, at 541, 26 C.R. 193, 118 C.C.C. 129, reversing (1956), 25 C.R. 53, 116 C.C.C. 231:

In my view the law is correctly stated in the following passage in the judgment of O'Halloran J.A., with whom Robertson J.A. concurred, in *Rex. v. Hess* (1949), 8 C.R. 42, 94 C.C.C. 48, at 50-1 (B.C.):
"To constitute 'possession' within the meaning of the criminal law it is my judgment that where, as here, there is manual handling of a thing, it must be co-existent with knowledge of what the thing is, and both these elements must be co-existent with some act of control (outside public duty). When those three elements exist together, I think it must be conceded that under s. 4(1)(*d*) it does not then matter if the thing is retained for an innocent purpose."

However, in that case s. 5(2) was not being considered. The reference was to manual possession.

I find it unnecessary to decide in this case whether there must be some measure of control in order to find the "knowledge and consent" required by s. 3(4)(*b*) of the *Code*. In my opinion, although Marshall certainly had knowledge of the presence of the marijuana he had no control, right to control, nor did he consent to its presence.

The choice facing Marshall was to leave the car at Golden and run the risk of obtaining a ride to Calgary in time to attend his classes, or to stay with the car containing the marijuana. There can be no doubt that he would have been much wiser to have left the car and hitch-hiked to Calgary no matter how long it took him. But to say that a 16-year-old boy faced with this alternative, by choosing to continue his trip to Calgary has consented or agreed or acquiesced to the presence of marijuana in the car is not maintainable. It was certainly an error of judgment on his part to run the risk of being charged with possession of marijuana by being found as an occupant of the car. The trial judge might not have believed his story but once it was believed his decision to continue the journey was consent to riding in the car, but such consent does not mean he consented to the marijuana being in the car. He said he objected to it being picked up again after it was thrown out at Golden. He did nothing to impede the police, although he did not volunteer any assistance to them.

Crown counsel argued that at the time it was stated to the police that Boltwood the hitchhiker had nothing to do with the marijuana that Marshall at that time should also have said he had nothing to do with it. This is, of course, a matter the trial judge could take into consideration in deciding whether to believe Marshall or not. Marshall had no obligation to make a statement. His conduct in the whole matter was not only childish but silly but this does not make him guilty of the offence.

. . . .

In the circumstances of this case the appellant, Marshall, had no power to control the persons possessing the marijuana. He was not the owner of the car. In my opinion, he could not be found guilty of aiding and abetting.

I have been concerned as to the fact that although Marshall stated he did not smoke the marijuana when the pipe was passed to him, he did pass it on. This I think comes very close to a consent, but it could be due almost as a reflex action just as a lighted squib was passed on in the squib case, and in all of the circumstances I do not think constituted consent.

In my opinion, the learned trial judge was in error in drawing the inferences from the facts which he found and he should not have inferred the appellant, Marshall, consented to the others having possession of the drug. Accordingly I would allow the appeal and quash the conviction.

R. v. TERRENCE

33 C.R. (3d) 193, [1983] 1 S.C.R. 357, 4 C.C.C. (3d) 193,
1983 CarswellOnt 67, 1983 CarswellOnt 807

RITCHIE J.: — This is an appeal brought with leave of this court at the instance of the Attorney-General of Ontario, pursuant to s. 621(1)(*b*) of the *Criminal Code*, from a judgment of the Court of Appeal for Ontario whereby that court allowed the appeal and quashed the conviction of the accused entered at trial before Judge P.H. Megginson in the Ontario Provincial Court (Criminal Division) for the County of Frontenac, Ontario, on a charge that he:

> . . . on or about the 30th day of January, 1980 at the Township of Kingston and elsewhere in the County of Frontenac, unlawfully did have in his possession one 1980 Chevrolet automobile, of a value exceeding $200.00, the property of Trudeau Motors, Belleville, Ontario which had been theretofore obtained by a person unknown by an offence committed in Canada punishable on indictment, to wit: theft, the said Kelly Brett Terrence, then knowing the said automobile to have been obtained and did thereby commit an indictable offence, contrary to s. 313(*a*) of the *Criminal Code* of Canada.

The important question raised by this appeal relates to the true meaning to be attached to the word "possession" as the same occurs in the context of s. 3(4)(*b*) of the *Criminal Code* and more particularly whether "possession" as there employed imports control as an essential element. Section 3(4)(*b*) reads as follows:

> 3(4) For the purposes of this Act
>
> . . . .
>
> (*b*) where one of two or more persons, with the knowledge and consent of the rest, has anything in his custody or possession, it shall be deemed to be in the custody and possession of each and all of them.

The only evidence in the record of this appeal which is in any way descriptive of the manner in which the respondent first became aware of the existence of the automobile in question is the evidence of the respondent himself which is, in my view, accurately summarized in the judgment of Mr. Justice MacKinnon at p. 64 of the case on appeal herein as follows [55 C.C.C. (2d) 183 at pp. 184-5, 17 C.R. (3d) 390]:

> The 17-year-old appellant testified at his trial. His evidence was that Bill Rorback, Rorback's brother and one Rick Hayes lives across the street from him in Belleville. He often went across to visit after dinner and he had done so on the evening of January 29, 1980. When he arrived Rick Hayes was not present and the appellant and the two Rorbacks watched television. At about midnight Hayes drove up to the front of the house in a new Camaro automobile and asked if anybody wanted to go for a ride in his "brother-in-law's new car". The appellant said "sure" and went with Hayes.
>
> According to the appellant's evidence, Hayes and the appellant drove around town for three quarters of an hour or so and then started east along Highway 401 towards Kingston. It

was established that the Camaro had in fact been recently stolen and the licence plates it carried had recently been stolen from another Camaro in Belleville. The appellant knew that Hayes did not own his own motor vehicle but Hayes had, on previous occasions, borrowed his brother-in-law's car which the appellant described as old junker". He thought that it was probably time for Hayes' brother-in-law to acquire a new car and as Hayes had the keys to the car, he had no suspicion at the time that the car was stolen.

Hayes turned onto Highway 2 around Napanee and shortly thereafter an O.P.P. cruiser gave chase. Constable Mallock testified that the stolen vehicle, on being pursued, increased its speed to 150 km/h, although the appellant's evidence was that the vehicle did not speed up but rather continued at a constant pace. The car was finally stopped by an O.P.P. roadblock some time shortly after 2:30 a.m. The Camaro pulled over to the shoulder and was apparently slowing down to a stop when the appellant jumped from the moving vehicle, rolled onto the shoulder and ran into the adjoining field. The Camaro collided with a cruiser and then came to a stop . . .

As I have indicated, this was the account given by the respondent and it remains uncontradicted by any direct evidence; it accordingly appears to me that the only basis for doubting the accuracy of this account was the repeated assertion by the trial judge that he "utterly" disbelieved it.

There is no doubt about the fact that the vehicle had been stolen from a garage in Belleville and, indeed, there was evidence to the effect that the theft occurred on the very night when the respondent accepted the invitation from Hayes to go for a ride "in his brother-in-law's car". It was this latter circumstance which permitted the trial judge to say, ". . . this car was as hot as a car could be, having been taken by someone during the same night . . .".

There was, as I have said, no direct evidence to contradict the respondent's version of what occurred, but it is evident from his somewhat acid comments that the judge's finding of "possession" is in great measure based on his disbelief of the respondent and it is apparent that the Judge proceeded on the assumption that the respondent's knowledge of the stolen character of the vehicle was a proven fact.

Based on the assumption that the respondent knew the car to be stolen property, the trial judge went on to find that:

> Even if the accused was not the operator of the vehicle and in that sense had the control of it, if the person who had control of the vehicle had it with his knowledge and consent and he is in the vehicle as well, in my view, that is sufficient to found the necessary conditions to constitute constructive possession under s. 3(4)(b) of the *Criminal Code* as defined.

In the course of his reasons for judgment rendered on behalf of the court of Appeal, Mr. Justice MacKinnon reviewed the relevant cases concerning the ingredients of possession under s. 3(4)(b) of the *Criminal Code* and concluded that in order to establish "possession" under that section it was necessary that there should be evidence of control on the part of the accused. In the course of these reasons he said [p. 399]:

> In my view, on the proven facts the necessary measure of control was not established beyond a reasonable doubt by the Crown, nor do those facts allow for the invocation of s. 21. If, by

way of example only, it were established that the appellant had directed Hayes to drive to Kingston, that, in light of all the other proven facts, would, in my view, satisfy the requirement of some measure of control over the car. If, by way of further example, he had been seen handing the stolen licence plates to Hayes for them to be placed on the motor vehicle, that, once again in my view, would be sufficient to warrant the application of s. 21 and to establish constructive possession of the car by the appellant.

Section 21 of the *Criminal Code* defines the meaning of "parties" to an offence and involves the question of common intention. It will be remembered that in the present case there is no suggestion that the respondent participated in any way in the actual theft of the car by an unknown person, which took place some time before he was invited to drive in it, and there is nothing to support a finding of common intention in relation to the offence of "possession" with which the respondent is here charged.

The Court of Appeal had reference to the case of *R. v. Lou Hay Hung* (1946), 85 C.C.C. 308, which was a decision of its own court concerned with a charge under the *Opium and Narcotic Drug Act*, 1929 (Can.), c. 49, and in which Mr. Justice Roach in the course of his reasons for judgment, referred to and quoted s. 5(2) of the *Criminal Code*, the predecessor of s. 3(4)(*b*), in the following terms at p. 321 C.C.C.:

> Under s. 5(2), both "knowledge" and "consent" are necessary. I have already stated that, in my opinion, there is no doubt that the appellant knew that the accused Watson had opium in the premises. I have been more than a little concerned with the question whether or not, on the evidence, it should be held that he also consented.

In the same set of reasons, Mr. Justice Roach referred to the judgment of O'Halloran J.A. in *R. v. Colvin and Gladue* (1942), 78 C.C.C. 282 at p. 287, where he said: [at p. 322 C.C.C.]:

> " 'Knowledge and consent' which is an integral element of joint possession in s. 5(2) must be related to and read with the definition of 'possession' in the previous s. 5(1)(*b*). It follows that 'knowledgc and consent' cannot exist without the co-existence of some measure of control over the subject-matter. If there is the power to consent there is equally the power to refuse and vice versa. They each signify the existence of some power or authority which is here called control, without which the need for their exercise could not arise or be invoked."

In the course of the reasons for judgment rendered by Mr. Justice MacKinnon on behalf of the Court of Appeal in the present case, he had occasion to say of the above passage from Mr. Justice O'Halloran's judgment [at pp. 188-9]:

> The judgment of O'Halloran J.A. in *R. v. Colvin and Gladue* (1942), 78 C.C.C. 282, the relevant passage of which for our purposes being the one quoted by Roach J.A., *supra*, to the effect that "knowledge and consent cannot exist without the co-existence of some measure of control over the subject-matter", has been followed by British Columbia Courts in subsequent decisions: *R. v. Sherman* (1929), 1 C.R. 153; *R. v. Bunyon* (1954), 110 C.C.C. 119; *R. v. Dick and Malley* (1969), 7 C.R.N.S. 75; *R. v. Baker* — May 21, 1976 (B.C. C.A.) (unreported as yet) [reported [1976] W.W.D. 132].

The courts in Quebec have adopted the same reasoning as will be seen by reference to *R. v. Sigouin et al.* (1964) 43 C.R. 211, and *R. v. Fournier* (1979), 43 C.C.C. (2d) 468.

As I have indicated, I agree with the Court of Appeal that a constituent and essential element of possession under s. 3(4)(*b*) of the *Criminal Code* is a measure of control on the part of the person deemed to be in possession by that provision of the *Criminal Code* and, accordingly, I do not consider that the Court of Appeal for the Province of Ontario erred in this regard.

. . . .

Appeal dismissed.

In the next case, the Supreme Court addressed the issue of what constitutes possession in the context of digital information. The accused was charged with possession of child pornography after a warrant was issued to search his home computer. The real issue in the case was whether the warrant had been properly issued, but to answer that question the Court had to decide what it meant to possess an image in a computer.

R. v. MORELLI

[2010] 1 S.C.R. 253, 2010 CarswellSask 151, 252 C.C.C. (3d) 273, 72 C.R. (6th) 208

PER FISH J. (MCLACHLIN C.J., BINNIE, and ABELLA JJ. concurring): —

14 In my view, merely viewing in a Web browser an image stored in a remote location on the Internet does not establish the level of control necessary to find possession. Possession of illegal images requires possession of the underlying data files in some way. Simply viewing images online constitutes the separate crime of accessing child pornography, created by Parliament in s. 163.1(4.1) of the *Criminal Code*.

15 For the purposes of the *Criminal Code*, "possession" is defined in s. 4(3) to include personal possession, constructive possession, and joint possession. Of these three forms of culpable possession, only the first two are relevant here. It is undisputed that knowledge and control are essential elements common to both.

16 On an allegation of personal possession, the requirement of knowledge comprises two elements: the accused must be aware that he or she has physical custody of the thing in question, and must be aware as well of what that thing is. Both elements must co-exist with an act of control (outside of public duty): *Beaver v. The Queen*, [1957] S.C.R. 531, at pp. 541-42.

17 Constructive possession is established where the accused did not have physical custody of the object in question, but did have it "in the actual possession or custody of another person" or "in any place, whether or not that place belongs to or is occupied by him, for the use or benefit of himself or of another person" (*Criminal Code*, s. 4(3)(a)). Constructive possession is thus complete where the accused: (1) has knowledge of the character of the object, (2) knowingly puts or keeps the object in a particular place, whether or not that place belongs to him, and (3) intends to have the object in the particular place for his "use or benefit" or that of another person.

18 Here, the appellant is alleged to have had possession of digital images in a computer, rather than tangible objects. The law of possession, however, developed in relation to physical, concrete objects. Its extension to virtual objects—in this case, images stored as digital files and displayed on computer monitors—presents conceptual problems. Unlike traditional photographs, the digital information encoding the image—the image file—can be possessed even if no representation of the image is visible. Likewise, even if displayed on a person's computer monitor, the underlying information might remain firmly outside that person's possession, located on a server thousands of kilometres away, over which that person has no control.

19 Essentially, there are thus two potential "objects" of possession of an image in a computer—the image file and its decoded visual representation on-screen. The question is whether one can ever be said to be in culpable possession of the visual depiction alone, or whether one can only culpably possess the underlying file. Canadian cases appear implicitly to accept only the latter proposition: That possession of an image in a computer means possession of the underlying data file, not its mere visual depiction.

. . .

25 This is a sensible interpretation for a number of reasons. First, and most important, because Parliament, in s. 163.1(4.1) of the *Criminal Code*, has made accessing illegal child pornography a separate crime, different from possession. In virtue of s. 163.1(4.2), a person accesses child pornography by "knowingly caus[ing the] child pornography to be viewed by, or transmitted to, himself or herself".

26 Parliament's purpose in creating the offence of accessing child pornography, as explained by the then Minister of Justice, was to "capture those who intentionally view child pornography on the [Inter]net but where the legal notion of possession may be problematic" (Hon. Anne McLellan, House of Commons Debates, vol. 137, 1st Sess., 37th Parl., May 3, 2001, at p. 3581).

27 What made a charge of possession "problematic", of course, is that possessing a digital file and viewing it are discrete operations—one could be criminalized without also criminalizing the other. In the case of child pornography, Parliament has now criminalized both. But viewing and possession should nevertheless be kept conceptually separate, lest the criminal law be left without the analytical tools necessary to distinguish between storing the underlying data file and merely viewing the representation that is produced when that data, residing elsewhere, is decoded. The ITO here is specifically limited to allegations of possession pursuant to s. 163.1(4) of the *Criminal Code* (ITO, preamble and paras. 2, 4 and 16).

28 Interpreting possession to apply only to the underlying data file is also more faithful to a traditional understanding of what it means to "possess" something. The traditional objects of criminal possession—for example, contraband, drugs, and illegal weapons—are all things that could, potentially at least, be transferred to another person.

29 Without storing the underlying data, however, an image on a screen cannot be transferred. The mere possibility of sharing a link to a Web site or enlarging the visual depiction of a Web site, as one could "zoom in" on a TV screen image, is insufficient to constitute control over the content of that site. It is indeed the underlying data file that is the stable "object" that can be transferred, stored, and, indeed, possessed. More broadly, the object possessed must itself have some sort of permanence.

30 Thus, while it does not matter for the purposes of criminal possession how briefly one is in possession of the object, the thing said to be culpably possessed cannot—like a broadcast image flickering across a TV screen or a digital image displayed transiently on-screen—be essentially evanescent.

31 Plainly, the mere fact that an image has been accessed by or displayed in a Web browser does not, without more, constitute possession of that image. An ITO seeking a warrant to search for evidence of possession (rather than accessing) must therefore provide reasonable and probable grounds to believe that the alleged offender possesses (or has possessed) digital files of an illegal image, and that evidence of that possession will be found in the place to be searched. It is not enough to provide reasonable and probable grounds to believe that the alleged offender viewed or accessed illegal images using a computer, without knowingly taking possession—which includes control—of the underlying files in some way.

32 In applying these principles to the facts of this case, I take care not to be understood to have circumscribed or defined constructive possession of virtual objects. I leave open the possibility, for example, that one could constructively

possess a digital file without downloading it to his or her hard drive, using for example a Web-based e-mail account to store illegal material.

33 In short, my purpose here is not to say what constructive possession of virtual objects necessarily is, but rather what it manifestly is not. Plainly, in my view, previous access and the possibility of again accessing a Web site that contains digital images, located on a distant server over which the viewer has no control, do not constitute—either alone or together—constructive possession. However elastic the notion of constructive possession may be, to stretch it that far is to defy the limits of its elasticity.

34 For the sake of greater clarity, I turn now to consider how this understanding of possession applies to files in an Internet cache (that is, copies of files automatically stored on the hard drive by a Web browser).

35 When accessing Web pages, most Internet browsers will store on the computer's own hard drive a temporary copy of all or most of the files that comprise the Web page. This is typically known as a "caching function" and the location of the temporary, automatic copies is known as the "cache". While the configuration of the caching function varies and can be modified by the user, cached files typically include images and are generally discarded automatically after a certain number of days, or after the cache grows to a certain size.

36 On my view of possession, the automatic caching of a file to the hard drive does not, without more, constitute possession. While the cached file might be in a "place" over which the computer user has control, in order to establish possession, it is necessary to satisfy mens rea or fault requirements as well. Thus, it must be shown that the file was knowingly stored and retained through the cache.

37 In the present case, the charge is not based on the appellant using his cache to possess child pornography. It is hardly surprising as most computer users are unaware of the contents of their cache, how it operates, or even its existence. Absent that awareness, they lack the mental or fault element essential to a finding that they culpably possess the images in their cache. Having said that, there may be rare cases where the cache is knowingly used as a location to store copies of image files with the intent to retain possession of them through the cache.

The dissenting judges (Deschamps J. (Charron and Rothstein JJ. concurring) felt that the majority understanding of "possession" was too narrow. They argued that there was little difference between exercising control over the hard drive of a computer while on the premises where the computer is located and exercising control over the online space of a web-based hosted service. The key feature, in their view, was whether the accused had control over the data, and that requiring proof of downloading was a formalistic approach which was tied to the particular state of technology at the time of the decision.

R. v. PHAM

[2005] O.J. No. 5127, 2005 CarswellOnt 6940 (Ont. C.A.)

KOZAK J. (AD HOC) (BLAIR J.A. concurring): —

1 As a result of a police search that took place on March 5, 2003 at unit #4, 28 Overlea Crescent in Kitchener Ontario, the appellant Kim Thi Pham and Lieng Van Nguyen were jointly charged with possession of cocaine for the purpose of trafficking contrary to Section 5(2) of the *Controlled Drugs and Substances Act*. On May 28, 2003, prior to the trial, the charge against Nguyen was withdrawn without explanation. Following a judge alone trial in which the appellant did not testify, she was convicted. There was no evidence of actual possession in that the appellant was not present in the apartment when the search was conducted, so that the Crown's case rested on constructive or joint possession.

2 Ms. Pham appeals her conviction on two grounds:

(i) the verdict was unreasonable and not supported by the evidence; and

(ii) the trial judge misapprehended the evidence.

3 The sentence appeal was abandoned since the appellant has served her sentence. For reasons that follow, I would dismiss the conviction appeal.

Position of the Parties

4 The drugs were found in premises primarily occupied by the appellant and then later shared with Nguyen. The appellant contends that Nguyen was trafficking in crack cocaine during her absence and therefore the drugs and money, all of which were found in a common area of the apartment (i.e. the bathroom) could reasonably belong to Nguyen alone. The appellant also argues that the trial judge misapprehended the evidence in concluding that the drugs found in the residence at the time of the search had been in the apartment prior to the appellant's departure on March 3, 2003, and that Nguyen had not left the apartment between the time of the appellant's departure on March 3, 2003 and the time of the search on March 5, 2003.

5 The Crown takes the position that on the facts of the case, it has proven constructive or joint possession. In this regard the Crown submits that this was a simple trial in which the requisite elements of possession, i.e. knowledge, consent and control were considered by the trial judge in light of all the direct and circumstantial evidence. The Crown contends that in convicting the

appellant the trial judge made no palpable and overriding error in his factual findings, nor did he draw any inferences that were clearly wrong, unreasonable, or unsupported by the evidence.

The Facts

6 The appellant moved into the apartment at unit #4 during the month of October 2002, at which time she was the sole occupant. Some two months later Lieng Nguyen moved into the apartment. Ms. Lee Ann Poulton occupied unit #3 which was located directly across from unit #4, and from the peek hole in her door she had a clear view of the entranceway of unit #4.

7 After the appellant moved into the building, numerous visitors came to her door on a consistent basis. As a result of watching through the peek hole, Ms. Poulton saw:

(i) people approach the door to unit #4;

(ii) money being slipped under the door; and

(iii) a clear plastic bag would come out containing white stuff.

The visitors would not usually go inside the appellant's apartment but, instead would participate in short exchanges with someone behind the door. On occasion Ms. Poulton heard voices and was able to identify the appellant as one of the people speaking. On two occasions she saw the appellant open the door. The first was when a man asked if fifty dollars was enough and she let him in. The second was on March 1, 2003 when she saw the exchange of money for a small plastic bag with white stuff in it.

8 Some time during the latter part of December 2002, Lieng Nguyen became an occupant of unit #4.

9 The police were contacted and a surveillance of the building, which was a sixplex, was set up on January 3, 2003. The surveillance continued on the following days: January 6, 7 and 8; February 25, 27 and 28; and March 3, 4 and 5, 2003. The comings and goings of persons into and out of the building were noted by the surveillance officers. Many of those people were known to the police to have problems with drug addiction.

10 On March 3, 2003 at 4:40 p.m. the appellant was seen (by surveillance) to leave her apartment and did not return prior to the seizure of the drugs on March 5, 2003.

11 On March 4, 2003, during Ms. Pham's absence a person attended at unit #4 briefly and then departed. The police arrested this person and seized from him

two pieces of crack cocaine. The police then obtained a search warrant to enter unit #4, and during the early morning hours of March 5, 2003, a search of the apartment was conducted. Lieng Nguyen was the only person in the apartment. During the course of the search two pouches were discovered in the bathroom adjacent to the sink. One pouch was described as a small black cloth purse sitting in full view. Upon opening the purse the police found individually wrapped crack cocaine. On the other side of the sink and sitting in full view was an open pink make-up bag which contained $165.00 of Canadian currency, mostly in 20-dollar bills. It was conceded that the 9.8 grams of crack cocaine was seized from the appellant's apartment which she shared with Nguyen.

Legal Considerations

12 The issue at trial was whether the appellant had knowledge and control of the cocaine found in the bathroom and therefore had it in her possession.

13 Section 2 of the *Controlled Drugs and Substances Act*, S.C. 1996 C.19 adopts the definition of "possession" in subsection 4(3) of the *Criminal Code*. That section reads:

> 4(3) For the purposes of this Act,
>
> > (a) a person has anything in possession when he has it in his personal possession or knowingly:
> >
> > > (i) has it in the actual possession or custody of another person or
> > >
> > > (ii) has it in any place, whether or not that place belongs to or is occupied by him for the use or benefit of himself or another person; and
> >
> > (b) where one of two or more persons with the knowledge and consent of the rest has anything in his custody or possession, it shall be deemed to be in the custody and possession of each and all of them.

14 Section 4(3) of the *Code* creates three types of possession:

> (i) personal possession as outlined in section 4(3)(a);
>
> (ii) constructive possession as set out in section 4(3)(a)(i) and section 4(3)(a)(ii); and
>
> (iii) joint possession as defined in section 4(3)(b).

15 In order to constitute constructive possession, which is sometimes referred to as attributed possession, there must be knowledge which extends beyond mere quiescent knowledge and discloses some measure of control over the item to be possessed. See *R. v. Caldwell* (1972), 7 C.C.C. (2d) 285 (Alberta Supreme Court, Appellate Division); *R. v. Grey* (1996), 28 O.R. (3d) 417 (C.A.).

16 In order to constitute joint possession pursuant to section 4(3)(b) of the Code there must be knowledge, consent, and a measure of control on the part of the person deemed to be in possession. See *R. v. Terrence*, [1983] 1 S.C.R. 357 (S.C.C.); *R. v. Williams* (1998), 40 O.R. (3d) 301 (C.A.); *R. v. Barreau*, 9 B.C.A.C. 290, 19 W.A.C. 290 (B.C.C.A.) and *Re: Chambers and the Queen* (1985), 20 C.C.C. (3d) 440 (Ont. C.A.).

17 The element of knowledge is dealt with by Watt J. in the case of *R. v. Sparling*, [1988] O.J. No. 107 (Ont. H.C.) at p. 6:

> There is no direct evidence of the applicant's knowledge of the presence of narcotics in the residence. It is not essential that there be such evidence for as with any other issue of fact in a criminal proceeding, it may be established by circumstantial evidence. In combination, the finding of narcotics in plain view in the common areas of the residence, the presence of a scale in a bedroom apparently occupied by the applicant, and; the applicants' apparent occupation of the premises may serve to found an inference of the requisite knowledge.

The court of appeal decision in *R. v. Sparling*, [1988] O.J. No. 1877 upheld the above passage as being sufficient evidence to infer knowledge.

18 The onus is on the Crown to prove beyond a reasonable doubt, all of the essential elements of the offence of possession. This can be accomplished by direct evidence or may be inferred from circumstantial evidence. In *Re: Chambers and the Queen*, *supra* at 448, Martin J.A. noted that the court may draw "appropriate inferences from evidence that a prohibited drug is found in a room under the control of an accused and where there is also evidence from which an inference may properly be drawn that the accused was aware of the presence of the drug."

ANALYSIS

19 The central issue at trial was whether the appellant had knowledge and control of the cocaine found in the black cloth purse in the bathroom, sufficient to constitute constructive or joint possession as defined in paragraphs 4(3)(a) and (b) of the *Code*. In my view the trial judge was entitled to find on the evidence as he did, that she had constructive possession of the cocaine either alone or jointly with Mr. Nguyen.

20 In dealing with the issue of possession the trial judge made it clear that the evidence of Ms. Poulton and the surveillance officers was used only to support a trafficking scheme and not for the purpose of showing propensity. He considered this evidence in the context of the evidence as a whole, as playing a significant role in his assessment of the elements of constructive possession.

21 The trial judge found that the 9.8 grams of cocaine were in the apartment before the appellant left the unit on March 3, 2003. He relied on the evidence of the surveillance officers that Nguyen was in the unit on March 3rd and 4th

as the various persons were seen coming and going, and that he was still there at the time of the police entry. In his words:

> I would have to speculate given the evidence before me to find that he left the unit at a point after the accused did, and later returned. I find he did not personally bring the cocaine in after the accused left.

22 That Mr. Nguyen left the unit and returned with the drugs in question (or that someone else brought them in), and therefore that the cocaine was not in Ms. Pham's possession on March 5th, is an argument raised by defence counsel, not on the basis of any evidence but merely as a speculative consideration. In *R. v. Jenner* (2005), 195 C.C.C. (3d) 364 (Man. C.A.) at paragraph 16, this type of approach was dealt with as follows:

> The accused's argument is found not on attempting to rebut the evidence tendered by the crown, but on raising questions and issues that although valid in a rhetorical sort of way add nothing to the issues that the trial judge had to address, and the manner in which he did so. Such a manner of attack was dealt with by this court in *R. v. Drury (L.W.) et al.* (2000), 150 Man. R. (2d) 64, 2000 MBCA 100. Huband J.A. addressed the issue as follows (at paragraph 92):
>
>> This is a question that only the accused Drury could answer, but he elected not to testify. Raising the question and inviting the court to speculate as to the answer does nothing to overcome the body of evidence which overwhelmingly points to guilt.

23 I am inclined to the view that the Manitoba Court of Appeal's reasoning applies in the circumstances of this case. However in the end it does not matter for the purpose of the disposition of this appeal.

24 In his companion reasons which I have had the opportunity of considering, Chief Justice R.R. McMurtry concludes that there was no evidentiary basis upon which the trial judge could conclude beyond a reasonable doubt that the particular drugs in question were in the apartment prior to Ms. Pham's departure. He would therefore allow the appeal. Respectfully I would dismiss the appeal even assuming that Mr. Nguyen or someone else brought the drugs into the apartment during Ms. Pham's absence. The evidence and the trial judge's findings support the conclusion that she was in constructive and/or joint possession of the cocaine even if that were so.

25 The following findings and evidence regarding both knowledge and control of the 9.8 grams of crack cocaine by the accused support that conclusion:

> (a) the accused elected to use her home as a drug trafficking center, and was a key figure in the trafficking scheme carried on out of that center; she continued to be the occupant of unit #4 and retained control of the apartment while she was away;

(b) both the black cloth purse containing the drugs and the pink make-up bag containing the money were found in full view in the bathroom, a common area of the apartment;

(c) the cloth purse and the make-up bag are consistent with the personal toiletries of the appellant and were found amidst her personal toiletries and make-up;

(d) there was no evidence of any men's toiletries in the bathroom;

(e) the main bedroom was littered with woman's clothing, contained documents (including a passport) in Ms. Pham's name, and was the source of drug-related "dime bags" and cut up newspapers and grocery bags of the type used to wrap a 40 piece of crack cocaine;

(f) the circumstantial evidence supported as the only logical inference a consistent awareness of, and participation in, all that occurred in her home on the part of Ms. Pham, and demonstrated much more than a quiescent or passive knowledge of the drugs, as well as an element of control over them;

(g) the role of the accused in the trafficking scheme strongly suggested power and authority over the disposal of the cocaine found, and an ability to withhold consent to the keeping of any drugs in her home; and

(h) Mr. Nguyen either filled Ms. Pham's shoes as the primary distributor during her absence or she and Mr. Nguyen jointly operated the trafficking scheme.

26 In my view the foregoing provided ample basis to found an inference of the requisite knowledge and supported the trial judge's finding that the appellant had sufficient knowledge and control to constitute constructive possession of the cocaine either personally or jointly with Nguyen. It was agreed that if possession was established, that the possession was for the purpose of trafficking.

27 Whether someone is in possession of something pursuant to section 4(3) of the Code is a question of fact to be determined on the evidence based on the inferences to be drawn in each case. The difficulty in determining the sufficiency of the evidence required to support an inference of possession is aptly demonstrated in the contrasting decisions of *R. v. Sparling* and *R. v. Grey* mentioned earlier.

28 In *Grey*, the accused was convicted of possession of crack cocaine for the purpose of trafficking. The police found the cocaine hidden in the bedroom of his girlfriend's apartment. The case against the accused rested principally on his regular occupancy of his girlfriend's apartment (i.e. 3 or 4 nights a week) and

on the presence of his clothing and other belongings in the bedroom where the crack cocaine was found. The above evidence was found to be insufficient to infer knowledge in that:

(1) there was no direct evidence of the appellant's knowledge. The Crown did not have a witness who could state affirmatively that the appellant knew about the cocaine;

(2) the drugs seized by the police were not in plain view, they were hidden;

(3) the apartment was rented by the co-accused;

(4) other persons frequented the apartment; and

(5) the appellant was not a permanent occupant.

29 In *Sparling* the accused entered into a joint lease and was a full time tenant. The drugs were in full view on the coffee table. This court agreed with Watt J. that direct evidence of knowledge was not essential and that knowledge could be established by circumstantial evidence. *Sparling* is closer to the facts of this case than *Grey*.

CONCLUSION

30 The trial judge instructed himself on reaching a conviction based on inferences from proven facts. At page 4 of the judgment he states as follows:

> If I am to convict on inferences of fact, I must be satisfied beyond a reasonable doubt that guilt is the only reasonable inference to be drawn from all of the proven facts. In assessing inferences for each piece of evidence the reasonable doubt standard is not to be applied each time. I am to consider the inference suggested against any other reasonable inference that can be drawn and attribute weight accordingly. All of the evidence that I determine merits weight is then assessed on the reasonable doubt standard.

This is in keeping with what Lord Wright emphasized *in Caswell v. Powell Duffy Associated Collieries Ltd.*, [1940] A.C. 152, Where at p. 169 he stated:

> ... that inference must be carefully distinguished from conjecture or speculation and there can be no inferences unless there are objective facts from which to infer other facts which it is sought to establish.

In *R. v. Lukianchuk*, [2001] B.C.J. No. 3000, 2001 B.C.S.C 119, Romilly J. had this to say at page 7 paragraph 19:

> In *R. v. To*, [1992] B.C.J. No. 1700, supra the accused was arrested after placing a plastic bag in a vehicle. The bag contained several videotapes and 4.4 lbs of heroin. The trial judge disbelieved the accused's evidence that he did not know what was in the bag. McEachern C.J.B.C. stated at page 230:

> It must be remembered that we are not expected to treat real life cases as a completely intellectual exercise where no conclusion can be reached if there is the slightest competing possibility. The criminal law requires a very high degree of proof especially for inferences consistent with guilt, but it does not demand certainty. I do not think it can properly be said that the inferences of knowledge in this case would be unreasonable or unsupported by the evidence.

31 It has not been shown that the trial judge committed any palpable and overriding error or made findings of fact including inferences of fact that are clearly wrong, unreasonable or unsupported by the evidence. The trial judge did not misapprehend the evidence. I would accordingly dismiss the appeal.

32 Like Chief Justice R.R. McMurtry, I agree that the appellant might well have been convicted as a party to the offence, under s. 21(2) of the *Criminal Code*. However, the case was not put on that basis, either at trial or on appeal.

McMURTRY C.J.O. (dissenting): —

44 The only evidence available to the trial judge on which such an inference of knowledge might be drawn is that the appellant was the principal occupant of the premises and that she was actively engaged in the trafficking of drugs. However, the evidence established that the appellant had been absent from the apartment for at least 32 hours before the drugs were discovered by the police. The evidence advanced at trial was not capable of excluding the reasonable inference that someone else left the 9.8 grams of crack cocaine in the bathroom during Ms. Pham's extended absence.

R. v. CHALK

(2007), 52 C.R. (6th) 371, 2007 CarswellOnt 7625, 227 C.C.C. (3d) 141
(C.A.)

The accused was convicted by a judge sitting without a jury on a charge of possessing child pornography contrary to s. 163.1(4) of the *Criminal Code*. The pornography consisted of several videos found on the hard drive of a computer kept in the home he occupied with his girlfriend and her two children. The defence acknowledged that several videos found on the computer fell within the definition of child pornography set out in s. 163.1 of the *Criminal Code*. The accused admitted in a statement to the police that he had been aware for several months that there was child pornography on the computer but denied he had intentionally downloaded it to the hard drive. He acknowledged downloading and watching child pornography sometimes alone and sometimes with his girlfriend. He admitted telling his girlfriend to delete them after his arrest because he knew the computer would be investigated by the authorities. He did not testify. The trial judge convicted. The accused appealed.

DOHERTY J.A: —

[17] Section 4(3) of the *Criminal Code* contains a definition of possession. Section 4(3)(a)(ii) contains the relevant part of that definition for present purposes:

> a person has anything in possession when he ... knowingly
> (ii) has it in any place ... for the use or benefit of himself or another person;

[18] Possession requires knowledge of the criminal character of the item in issue. In this case, the Crown had to prove that the appellant had knowledge of the contents of the videos in issue. It was, of course, irrelevant whether the appellant knew the contents constituted child pornography: see *Beaver v. The Queen* (1957), 118 C.C.C. 129 at 140 (S.C.C.); *Rex v. Hess (No. 1)* (1948), 94 C.C.C. 48 at 51-52 (B.C.C.A.). The appellant's knowledge of the nature of the videos was established by his statements to the police.

[19] Knowledge alone will not establish possession. The Crown must also prove that an accused with the requisite knowledge had a measure of control over the item in issue. Control refers to power or authority over the item whether exercised or not: *R. v. Mohamad* (2004), 182 C.C.C. (3d) 97 at paras. 60-61 (Ont. C.A.).

[20] In *R. v. Daniels* (2004), 191 C.C.C. (3d) 393 at para. 12 (Nfld. C.A.), a case which also involved a charge of possession of child pornography in the form of material located on a computer hard drive, Welch J.A. explained the concept of control in these terms:

> To be in possession of child pornography, it is not necessary for the individual to have viewed the material. For example, a person may obtain pornographic material in an envelope, but without viewing it, either place it in a drawer or dispose of it in the garbage. *It is the element of control, including deciding what will be done with the material, that is essential to possession.* [Emphasis added.]

[21] In her submissions, Ms. LeRoy argued first that the evidence did not support a finding that the appellant knew that the files contained child pornography. This submission cannot succeed in the face of the appellant's own admission in his statement to the police.

[22] Ms. LeRoy also submitted that the appellant's direction to Ms. Lewis to delete the files containing the child pornography could not constitute an act of control for the purposes of fixing the appellant with possession of the pornography. She submitted that the appellant's instructions demonstrated an intention to destroy rather than possess the material. She analogized the appellant's position to that of a person who possesses drugs strictly for the purpose of destroying them by flushing them down the toilet. Ms. LeRoy stressed that the trial judge did not find that the appellant played any role in downloading

the pornography on to the computer or that he used the computer to view the pornography. She contended that the finding of control was based solely on the instruction to delete and that this instruction was inconsistent with an intention to possess.

[23] There is a line of authority supporting the proposition that exercising control over contraband with the requisite knowledge, but solely with the intent of destroying the contraband or otherwise permanently removing it from one's control does not constitute criminal possession: see *R. v. Glushek* (1978), 41 C.C.C. (2d) 380 (Alta. S.C. App. Div.); *R. v. Christie* (1978), 41 C.C.C. (2d) 282 (N.B. S.C. App. Div.); *R. v. York* (2005), 193 C.C.C. (3d) 331 (B.C.C.A.). In *Christie, supra*, Chief Justice Hughes, in referring to what I would call "innocent possession", said at p. 287:

> In my opinion, there can be circumstances which do not constitute possession even where there is a right of control with knowledge of the presence and character of the thing alleged to be possessed, where guilt should not be inferred, as where it appears there is no intent to exercise control over it. An example of this situation is where a person finds a package on his doorstep and upon opening it discovers it contains narcotics. Assuming he does nothing further to indicate an intention to exercise control over it, he had not, in my opinion, the possession contemplated by the *Criminal Code*. Nor do I think that a person who manually handles it for the sole purpose of destroying or reporting it to the police has committed the offence of possession. ...

[24] The "innocent possession" line of authorities was helpfully examined by Green J. in *R. v. Loukas*, [2006] O.J. No. 2405 (Ont. C.J.). Green J. points out that some of the "innocent possession" cases recognize a public duty defence as for example where an accused takes possession of contraband to deliver it to the authorities. In other cases, "innocent possession" is said to arise from the absence of an intention to exercise control beyond that needed to destroy the contraband or otherwise put it permanently beyond one's control. Green J. observes that in all of these cases there is, despite the existence of possession in the strict sense, an absence of a blameworthy state of mind or blameworthy conduct. Convictions for criminal possession by a technical application of the concepts of knowledge and control in these circumstances would overreach the purpose underlying the criminal prohibition against possession.

[25] I agree with the analysis described above. There are cases where an individual has the requisite control and knowledge, but cannot be said to be in possession for the purpose of imposing criminal liability. These cases will include cases in which a person takes control of contraband exclusively for the purpose of immediately destroying the contraband or otherwise placing it permanently beyond that person's ability to exercise any control over the contraband. In such cases, the intention is solely to divest oneself of control rather than to possess. Like the other appellate courts whose discussions are

referred to above, I do not think that criminal liability should attach to that kind of brief, "innocent possession": see e.g. *R. v. Glushek*, *supra*; *R. v. York*, *supra*.

[26] I am also satisfied, however, that this line of authority has no application to the findings of the trial judge. His findings negate any suggestion of "innocent possession". On the trial judge's findings, the appellant did not have possession of the child pornography strictly for the purposes of destroying that pornography. He knew that the pornography was on the computer's hard drive for several months. During that time, he regularly used the computer and had control over the pornography in the sense that he could have deleted it from the computer at any time had he chosen to do so. On his own admission, he ultimately decided to delete the pornography because he feared that the police would discover it when they examined his computer. In those circumstances, the appellant's instruction to delete the material was a manifestation of his longstanding power or authority over the material. That control had existed for several months and was not merely incidental to an innocent purpose.

[27] I would dismiss the appeal.

(d)   Consent Making Act Lawful

Lack of consent is often referred to as a defence. Where consent of the complainant operates in law to acquit it is better seen as a denial that the Crown has proved an unlawful act. Consent is often the crucial issue in the crime of sexual assault and will be fully considered below in Chapter 4.

Here we deal more generally with a series of controversial court rulings where apparent consent is vitiated (considered to be of no legal effect) because of policy limits or because consent was induced by fraud.

R. v. JOBIDON

[1991] 2 S.C.R. 714, 7 C.R. (4th) 233, 66 C.C.C. (3d) 454,
1991 CarswellOnt 110, 1991 CarswellOnt 1023

The accused was tried by judge alone on a charge of manslaughter. A fight had begun in a bar. It was stopped by the bar's owner and the two men agreed it was not over. Outside, the accused struck the victim with his fist. The victim was knocked backwards onto the hood of a car. The trial judge found that the victim had been rendered unconscious by this punch. In a brief flurry lasting no more than a few seconds, the accused struck the unconscious victim a further four to six times on the head. There was one single continuing exchange until the victim rolled off the hood and lay limp. He later died of contusions to the head. The trial judge found as a fact that the accused and the victim had consented to a fair fist fight, and that physical injury was intended. He also found that there was no intent to kill or cause serious bodily harm. He further found that the accused did not intentionally exceed the consent that was given and that he struck the last blows under a reasonable but mistaken apprehension that the victim was still capable of returning the fight and was trying to do so. The cause of death was one or more of the punches thrown by the accused in the parking lot. The trial judge acquitted. He decided that there was no unlawful act which could form the basis for a manslaughter conviction. The connection between the two offences of assault and manslaughter is found in s. 222 of the *Code*. The section provides that culpable homicide is either murder or manslaughter and that a person commits culpable homicide when he causes the death of a human being by means of an unlawful act. Since there was a consent to a fair fist fight there was no assault within the meaning of s. 265 of the *Criminal Code* and therefore no unlawful act. The Crown's appeal to the Ontario Court of Appeal was allowed and a conviction of manslaughter substituted. That court decided that the word "consent" in s. 265 of the *Criminal Code*, defining the crime of assault, should be construed subject to common law limits under which consent to a fight in private or public is not a defence to a charge of assault if actual bodily harm is intended and/or caused. The accused appealed. The Supreme Court dismissed the appeal.

GONTHIER J. (LA FOREST, L'HEUREUX-DUBÉ, CORY and IACOBUCCI JJ. concurring): —

. . . .

There is one principal issue raised in this appeal. The principal issue is whether absence of consent is a material element which must be proved by the Crown in all cases of assault or whether there are common law limitations which restrict or negate the legal effectiveness of consent in certain types of cases.

. . . .

Section 265(1)(*a*) states that an assault occurs when, "without the consent of another person, he applies force intentionally to that other person, directly or indirectly". ... In the appellant's opinion, the trial Judge's finding of consent meant that all the elements of the offence of assault had not been proved. The appellant should therefore have been acquitted on that basis, since the Legislature intended that consent should serve as a bar to conviction.

According to the appellant, the Legislature could have specified that in certain situations, or in respect of certain forms of conduct, absence of consent would not be an operative element of the offence. It has done so with other offences. Parliament has provided that no person is entitled to consent to have death inflicted on him (s. 14). It restricted the concept in ss. 150.1 and 159 of the *Code* by denying defences to sexual offences based on a child's consent. It also did this in s. 286 by negating the validity of a young person's consent to abduction. But with the assault provisions in s. 265, it chose not to insert policy-based limitations on the role of consent.

. . . .

The appellant further observed that, in England, the crime of assault is not defined in a *Criminal Code* but in the common law, to which common law limitations and exceptions more naturally apply. In Canada, we have a code of general principles by which, it is presumed, ambiguity is to be construed in favour of the liberty of the subject.

. . . .

There is no indication in s. 265 that the jurisprudence of the criminal common law was to be undermined by its enactment. There was no hint that traditional policy limits on consent, described below in greater detail, were to be ousted by s. 258 of the first *Criminal Code* of 1892, nor by enactment of its successor provision in s. 244 (now s. 265). This should not be surprising. As the foregoing sketch of the history of the offence demonstrates, far from intending to curtail the authority of that law, the *Code* was a partial expression of it.

All criminal offences in Canada are now defined in the *Code* (s. 9). But that does not mean the common law no longer illuminates these definitions nor gives content to the various principles of criminal responsibility those definitions draw from. As the Law Reform Commission of Canada has noted in its 31st report on recodification, the basic premises of our criminal law — the necessary conditions for criminal liability — are at present left to the common law (*Recodifying Criminal Law*, op. cit., at pp. 17, 28 and 34. Reference may also be made to Eric Colvin, *Principles of Criminal Law* (Toronto: Carswell, 1986), at pp. 16-17). The *Code* itself, in s. 8, explicitly acknowledges the ongoing common law influence.

. . . .

Section 8 expressly indicates that the common law rules and principles continue to apply, but only to the extent that they are not inconsistent with the *Code* or other Act of Parliament and have not been altered by them. While little judicial analysis of this section of the *Code* has been undertaken, the references made to it have predominantly concerned exceptional circumstances which provide defences or which deny certain features of an offence. (See Colvin, op. cit., at pp. 16-17.) This court's leading interpretation of s. 8(3) is found in *R. v. Kirzner*, [1978] 2 S.C.R. 487, 1 C.R. (3d) 138, 38 C.C.C. (2d) 131. Chief Justice Laskin expressly rejected a static view of the common law under s. 8(3) (formerly s. 7(3)). Though speaking in the context of alleged prosecutorial impropriety, and a claimed defence of entrapment, Laskin C.J.C. offered an expansive, developmental view, at p. 496 [S.C.R.]:

> There are good reasons for leaving the question open [re: application of an entrapment defence]. Indeed, if that position is based on a static view of s. 7(3) of the *Criminal Code* I

find it unacceptable. I do not think that s. 7(3) should be regarded as having frozen the power of the courts to enlarge the content of the common law by way of recognizing new defences.

The approach of the Chief Justice in *Kirzner* was later reinforced in *R. v. Amato*, [1982] 2 S.C.R. 418, 29 C.R. (3d) 1, 69 C.C.C. (2d) 31. Writing in dissent, on behalf of Laskin C.J.C., McIntyre and Lamer JJ., Estey J. applied what he termed the "ordinary rule of construction where statutes and common law meet" to conclude that "s. 7(3) is the authority for the courts of criminal jurisdiction to adopt, if appropriate in the view of the court, defences including the defence of entrapment" (p. 445 [S.C.R.]). The court's majority did not disagree with this determination.

. . . .

In light of this communicated understanding of the antecedents and purpose of s. 8(3), it can hardly be said that the common law's developed approach to the role and scope of consent as a defence to assault has no place in our criminal law. If s. 8(3) and its interaction with the common law can be used to develop entirely new defences not inconsistent with the *Code*, it surely authorizes the courts to look to preexisting common law rules and principles to give meaning to, and explain the outlines and boundaries of, an existing defence or justification, indicating where they will not be recognized as legally effective —provided of course that there is no *clear* language in the *Code* which indicates that the *Code* has displaced the common law. That sort of language cannot be found in the *Code*. As such, the common law legitimately serves in this appeal as an archive in which one may locate situations or forms of conduct to which the law will not allow a person to consent.

. . . .

We have observed from the general analysis of the *Code* and common law that, in the history of our criminal law, codification did not replace common law principles of criminal responsibility, but in fact reflected them. That history also reveals that policy-based limitations of the sort at issue here boast a lineage in the common law equally as long as the factors which vitiate involuntary consent. Since these policy-based limitations also existed before the codification of Canada's criminal law, there is no reason to think they have been ousted by statutory revisions and amendments made to the *Code* along the way.

. . . .

Furthermore, since s. 8(3) of the *Code* expressly confirms the common law's continued authority and provides that exculpatory defences not expressly struck down by the *Code* continue to operate to exclude criminal liability, in this appeal, where the *Code* has not erased the common law limit in fist fights, it must continue to define the scope of legally effective consent. Some may object that

s. 8(3) cannot be used to support this interpretation because consent is not really a defence, but instead forms part of the offence; indeed it is the absence of consent that is relevant as an element of the offence of assault. For example, Mewett and Manning, op. cit., at p. 567, write that "Real consent is therefore an essential element of assault going to the *actus reus* in the sense that if consent is present no offence can have been committed." Yet while that objection may have some relevance from a strictly formalistic perspective, it is of little consequence from a substantive point of view. Moreover it conflicts with the spirit of this court's previously expressed understanding of s. 8(3).

Whether consent is formally categorized as part of the *actus reus* of the offence, or as a defence, its essential function remains unaltered — if consent is proved, or if absence of consent is not proved, an individual accused of assault will *generally* be able to rely on the consent of the complainant to bar a conviction. He will be able to lean on the consent as a defence to liability. This basic reality has been widely recognized. English and Canadian courts widely refer to consent as being in the nature of a defence. Leading treatises on criminal law conceive it this way. See Watt, op. cit., at p. 216; Clarkson and Keating, op. cit., at pp. 283-292; Glanville Williams, *Textbook of Criminal Law*, 2nd ed. (London: Steven & Sons, 1983), at pp. 549 and 576-578; and Law Reform Commission of Canada, *Assault*, op. cit., at p. 24. We have also observed, in the general interpretive section above, that the law confers on s. 8(3) an open and developmental view of the common law's role. Section 8(3) strongly suggests preservation of the common law approach to consent in assault.

Assault has been given a very encompassing definition in s. 265. It arises whenever a person intentionally applies force to a person "directly or indirectly", without the other's consent. The definition says nothing about the degree of harm which must be sustained. Nor does it refer to the motives for the touching. If taken at face value, this formulation would mean that the most trivial intended touching would constitute assault. As just one of many possible examples, a father would assault his daughter if he attempted to place a scarf around her neck to protect her from the cold but she did not consent to that touching, thinking the scarf ugly or undesirable. (Even an argument for implied consent would not seem to apply in a case like this.) That absurd consequence could not have been intended by Parliament. Rather its intention must have been for the courts to explain the content of the offence, incrementally and over the course of time.

Furthermore, whereas the factors specified in s. 265(3) are readily identifiable, and are generally applicable to all sorts of situations, that is inherently not true of limitations based on policy considerations, which are fact-specific by nature. It would have been quite impractical, if not impossible, for Parliament to establish an adequate list of exceptions to apply to all situations, old and new. Policy-based limits are almost always the product of a balancing of individual autonomy (the freedom to choose to have force intentionally applied to oneself) and some larger societal interest. That balancing may be better performed in the light of actual situations, rather than in the abstract, as Parliament would be compelled to do.

With the offence of assault, that kind of balancing is a function the courts are well-suited to perform. They will continue to be faced with real situations in which complicated actions and motivations interact, as they have in the past. I do not accept the argument that by failing to enact a list of *objects or forms of conduct* to which one could not validly consent, Parliament intended to eliminate their role in the offence of assault and to rely only on the four factors specified in s. 265(3). Such a major departure from well-established policy calls for more than mere silence, particularly as such a list would have been unduly difficult and impractical to prescribe, and was unnecessary given their existing entrenchment in the common law. The common law is the register of the balancing function of the courts — a register Parliament has authorized the courts to administer in respect of policy-based limits on the role and scope of consent in s. 265 of the *Code*.

. . . .

Limits on consent to assault have long been recognized by English and Canadian courts. ... In present times as well, the English courts have on the whole been very consistent when confronted by assaults arising from fist fights and brawls. Since the English cases have set the overall direction for the Canadian common law in the assault context, and apparently continues to do so, it is of particular relevance in the circumstances of this case. The Canadian authorities also favour limits on consent. However, in recent years there has evolved a mixed record across provincial courts of appeal. This appeal therefore presents a timely opportunity for clarification.

[The court then reviewed a number of English decisions.]

Finally, in 1980, the English Court of Appeal was asked to state the law in *Attorney General's Reference* (No. 6 of 1980), [1981] 2 All E.R. 1057. It was a reference prompted by a street fight between two young men who, in a relatively calm fashion, had decided to settle differences between them by resorting to their fists. One suffered a bleeding nose and some bruises. The other was charged with assault, but acquitted. The question put to the appellate court was, at p. 1058:

> Where two persons fight (otherwise than in the course of sport) in a public place can it be a defence for one of those persons to a charge of assault arising out of the fight that the other consented to fight?

The court held that because it is not in the public interest that people should cause each other bodily harm for no good reason, consent is no answer to a charge of assault when "actual bodily harm is intended and/or caused" (p. 1059). This meant that most fights would be unlawful regardless of consent. Only minor struggles, or rough but properly conducted sporting events, which may have some positive social value, were combative activities where consent would be an effective bar to a charge of assault. Of course lawful chastisement and reasonable surgical interference were also activities in which the public interest does not require nullification of consent. In such cases the general rule applies: the Crown must prove absence of consent to get a conviction for assault. The English Court of Appeal added that the public nature of the forum in which the fight occurs is not determinative of the effectiveness of consent. Private fights deserved no more protection than public ones.

If determinative of this appeal, the English authorities would undoubtedly support the decision of the court below. Here the assault occurred in circumstances which appear very nearly to have amounted to a disturbance of the peace. And there is no question that the punches thrown by Jobidon were intentional applications of force intended to cause the deceased bodily harm. Rodney Haggart's apparent consent would provide no defence to Jobidon in England.

. . . .

(d)   *Summary of the Common Law*

(i)   The English Position

Attorney General's Reference makes it clear that a conviction of assault will not be barred if "bodily harm is intended *and/or* caused". Since this test is framed in the alternative, consent could be nullified even in situations where the assailant did not intend to cause the injured person bodily harm but did so inadvertently. In Canada, however, this very broad formulation cannot strictly apply, since the definition of assault in s. 265 is explicitly restricted to *intentional* application of force. Any test in our law which incorporated the English perspective would of necessity have to confine itself to bodily harm intended *and* caused.

(ii)   The Canadian Position

The preceding analysis reveals division in the Canadian jurisprudence. Decisions by courts of appeal in Manitoba, Ontario, Nova Scotia and (lately) Saskatchewan would nullify consent to intentionally inflicted bodily harm arising from a fist fight. Their approach is contained, respectively, in *Buchanan* (1898), *Cullen* (1948), *Squire* (1975), *Jobidon* (1988), *Gur* (1986), *McIntosh* (1991), and *Cey* (1989). (There is of course general support for the idea of policy-based nullification in the Alberta Court of Appeal; witness the language of Laycraft C.J.A. in *R. v. Carriere*, *supra*.) On the other side are decisions of appellate courts in New Brunswick (*MacTavish* (1972)), Quebec (*Abraham*

(1974)), Saskatchewan (*Setrum* (1976)), and Alberta (*Bergner* (1987) and *Loonskin* (1990)).

Although there is certainly no crystal-clear position in the modern Canadian common law, still, when one takes into account the combined English and Canadian jurisprudence, when one keeps sight of the common law's centuries-old persistence to limit the legal effectiveness of consent to a fist fight, and when one understands that s. 265 has always incorporated that persistence, the scale tips rather heavily against the validity of a person's consent to the infliction of bodily injury in a fight.

The thrust of the English common law is particularly important in this regard because it has been consistent for many decades, indeed, centuries. It became an integral component of the Canadian common law and has remained so to this day. Many of the seemingly pivotal pro-consent decisions made by courts in the 1970s were either obiter or were pronounced upon insufficient consideration of the important role of the traditional common law. Moreover they were decided prior to the decision in *Attorney General's Reference* (1980), which offered a very authoritative pronouncement of the common law position. The significance of that decision is perhaps best indicated in the instant appeal, for it provided the basis used by the Ontario Court of Appeal to overrule its decision in *R. v. Dix, supra*. The *Attorney General's Reference* case was again observed to be pivotal in the recent decision of the Appeal Court in Saskatchewan, in *R. v. Cey*. In light of these many considerations, I am of the view that the Canadian position is not as opaque or bifurcated as one might initially think.

Notwithstanding this conclusion, given the residual indeterminacy which admittedly lingers in the recent Canadian cases, it is useful to canvass policy considerations which exert a strong influence in this appeal, for they rather decisively support the respondent, bringing down the scales even more surely in support of the decision in the court below.

(e) *Policy considerations*

Foremost among the policy considerations supporting the Crown is the social uselessness of fist fights. As the English Court of Appeal noted in the *Attorney General's Reference*, it is not in the public interest that adults should willingly cause harm to one another without a good reason. There is precious little utility in fist fights or street brawls. These events are motivated by unchecked passion. They so often result in serious injury to the participants. Here it resulted in a tragic death to a young man on his wedding day.

There was a time when pugilism was sheltered by the notion of "chivalry". Duelling was an activity not only condoned, but required by honour. Those days are fortunately long past. Our social norms no longer correlate strength of character with prowess at fisticuffs. Indeed, when we pride ourselves for making positive ethical and social strides, it tends to be on the basis of our developing reason. This is particularly true of the law, where reason is cast in a privileged light. Erasing longstanding limits on consent to assault would be a regressive step, one which would retard the advance of civilized norms of conduct.

Quite apart from the valueless nature of fist fights from the combatants' perspective, it should also be recognized that consensual fights may sometimes lead to larger brawls and to serious breaches of the public peace. In the instant case, this tendency was openly observable. At the prospect of a fight between Jobidon and the deceased, in a truly macabre fashion many patrons of the hotel deliberately moved to the parking lot to witness the gruesome event. That scene easily could have erupted in more widespread aggression between allies of the respective combatants. Indeed it happened that the brothers of Jobidon and Haggart also took to each other with their fists.

Given the spontaneous, often drunken nature of many fist fights, I would not wish to push a deterrence rationale too far. Nonetheless, it seems reasonable to think that, in some cases, common law limitations on consent might serve some degree of deterrence to these sorts of activities.

. . . .

Wholly apart from deterrence, it is most unseemly from a moral point of view that the law would countenance, much less provide a backhanded sanction to the sort of interaction displayed by the facts of this appeal. The sanctity of the human body should militate against the validity of consent to bodily harm inflicted in a fight.

. . . .

Some may see limiting the freedom of an adult to consent to applications of force in a fist fight as unduly paternalistic; a violation of individual self-rule. Yet while that view may commend itself to some, those persons cannot reasonably claim that the law does not know such limitations. All criminal law is "paternalistic" to some degree — top-down guidance is inherent in any prohibitive rule. That the common law has developed a strong resistance to recognizing the validity of consent to intentional applications of force in fist fights and brawls is merely one instance of the criminal law's concern that Canadian citizens treat each other humanely and with respect.

Finally, it must not be thought that by giving the green light to the common law, and a red light to consent to fights, this court is thereby negating the role of consent in all situations or activities in which people willingly expose themselves to intentionally applied force. No such sweeping conclusion is entailed. The determination being made is much narrower in scope.

(f)   *Conclusion*

How, and to what extent is consent limited?

The law's willingness to vitiate consent on policy grounds is significantly limited. Common law cases restrict the extent to which consent may be nullified; as do the relevant policy considerations. The unique situation under examination in this case, a weaponless fist fight between two adults, provides another important boundary.

The limitation demanded by s. 265 as it applies to the circumstances of this appeal is one which *vitiates consent between adults intentionally to apply force causing serious hurt or non-trivial bodily harm to each other in the course of a fist fight or brawl.* (This test entails that a minor's apparent consent to an adult's intentional application of force in a fight would also be negated.) This is the extent of the limit which the common law requires in the factual circumstances of this appeal. It may be that further limitations will be found to apply in other circumstances. But such limits, if any, are better developed on a case-by-case basis, so that the unique features of the situation may exert a rational influence on the extent of the limit and on the justification for it.

Stated in this way, the policy of the common law will not affect the validity or effectiveness of freely given consent to participate in rough sporting activities, so long as the intentional applications of force to which one consents are within the customary norms and rules of the game. Unlike fist fights, sporting activities and games usually have a significant social value; they are worthwhile. In this regard the holding of the Saskatchewan Court of Appeal in *R. v. Cey*, *supra*, is apposite.

The court's majority determined that some forms of intentionally applied force will clearly fall within the scope of the rules of the game, and will therefore readily ground a finding of implied consent, to which effect should be given. On the other hand, very violent forms of force which clearly extend beyond the ordinary norms of conduct will not be recognized as legitimate conduct to which one can validly consent.

There is also nothing in the preceding formulation which would prevent a person from consenting to medical treatment or appropriate surgical interventions. Nor, for example, would it necessarily nullify consent between stuntmen who agree in advance to perform risky sparring or daredevil activities in the creation of a socially valuable cultural product. A charge of assault would be barred if the Crown failed to prove absence of consent in these situations, insofar as the activities have a positive social value and the intent of the actors is to produce a social benefit for the good of the people involved, and often for a wider group of people as well. This is a far cry from the situation presented in this appeal, where Jobidon's sole objective was to strike the deceased as hard as he physically could, until his opponent either gave up or retreated. Fist fights are worlds apart from these other forms of conduct.

Finally, the preceding formulation avoids nullification of consent to intentional applications of force which cause only minor hurt or trivial bodily harm. The bodily harm contemplated by the test is essentially equivalent to that contemplated by the definition found in s. 267(2) of the *Code*, dealing with the offence of assault causing bodily harm. The section defines bodily harm as "any hurt or injury to the complainant that interferes with the health or comfort of the complainant and that is more than merely transient or trifling in nature".

On this definition, combined with the fact that the test is restricted to cases involving adults, the phenomenon of the "ordinary" schoolyard scuffle, where boys or girls immaturely seek to resolve differences with their hands, will not come within the scope of the limitation. That has never been the policy of the law and I do not intend to disrupt the status quo. However, I would leave open the question as to whether boys or girls under the age of 18 who truly intend to harm one another, and ultimately cause more than trivial bodily harm, would be afforded the protection of a defence of consent. (As was the accused in *R. v. Barron* (1985), 48 C.R. (3d) 334, 23 C.C.C. (3d) 544 (Ont. C.A.), in which a boy was charged with manslaughter, via assault, for pushing another boy down a flight of stairs thereby causing the boy's death. The trial judge held that the deceased boy had impliedly consented to rough-housing on the stairs as they descended.) The appropriate result will undoubtedly depend on the peculiar circumstances of each case.

. . . .

I would uphold the decision of the Court of Appeal. The appeal is dismissed.

SOPINKA J. (STEVENSON J. concurring): —

I have had the advantage of reading the reasons of Gonthier J., and while I agree with his disposition of the matter I am unable to agree with his reasons. This appeal involves the role that consent plays in the offence of criminal assault. Unlike my colleague I am of the view that consent cannot be read out of the offence.

. . . .

While the consent of the victim cannot transform a crime into lawful conduct, it is a vital element in determining what conduct constitutes a crime. It is a well-accepted principle of the criminal law that the absence of consent is an essential ingredient of the *actus reus*. Thus it is not theft to steal if the owner consents and consensual intercourse is not sexual assault. In Don Stuart, *Canadian Criminal Law: A Treatise* 2d ed. (Toronto: Carswell, 1987), the author states [at p. 469]:

> The general principle, to which there are exceptions, that the true consent of the victim is always a defence to criminal responsibility is a fundamental principle of the criminal law.

. . . .

In *R. v. Lemieux*, [1967] S.C.R. 492, 2 C.R.N.S. 1, [1968] 1 C.C.C. 187, this court held that the offence of breaking and entering was not made out when it was carried out by pre-arrangement with the agent of the owner. The consent of the owner deprived the activity of an essential feature of the *actus reus*.

. . . .

There is, moreover, no generally accepted exception to this principle with respect to the intentional infliction of physical harm. There are many activities in society which involve the intentional application of force which may result in serious bodily harm but which are not criminal. Surgical operations and sporting events are examples. It was no doubt the absence of an exception to this principle that led Parliament to enact s. 14 of the *Criminal Code*, R.S.C., 1985, c. C-46, which creates an exception for the most serious of assaults, the intentional infliction of death.

In my view, Parliament has chosen to extend this principle to all assaults save murder in the interests of making this aspect of the criminal law certain. I see no evidence in the clear and simple language of s. 265 that it intended to outlaw consensual fighting in the interests of avoiding breaches of the peace or to allow it if a judge thought that it occurred in circumstances that were socially useful. Rather, the policy reflected in s. 265 is to make the absence of consent a requirement in the definition of the offence, but to restrict consent to those intentional applications of force in respect of which there is a clear and effective consent by a victim who is free of coercion or misrepresentation. Instead of reading the words "without the consent of another person" out of s. 265, I am of the opinion that the intention of Parliament is respected by close scrutiny of the scope of consent to an assault. Instead of attempting to evaluate the utility of the activity, the trial judge will scrutinize the consent to determine whether it applied to the very activity which is the subject of the charge. The more serious the assault, the more difficult it should be to establish consent.

2.   Interpretation of Section 265

Section 265 states that "[a] person commits an assault when *without the consent of another person*, he applies force intentionally to that other person...." (emphasis added). My colleague Gonthier J. concludes that on the basis of cases which applied the common law, that section should be interpreted as excluding the absence of consent as an element of the *actus reus* in respect of an assault with intent to commit intentional bodily harm. In coming to his conclusion my colleague relies on a number of English authorities. The issue was not finally resolved in England until the decision of the English Court of Appeal on a reference to it by the Attorney General in 1980. See *Attorney General's Reference (No. 6 of 1980)*, [1981] 2 All E.R. 1057. Unconstrained by the expression of legislative policy, the court moulded the common law to accord with the court's view of what was in the public interest. On this basis the court discarded the absence of consent as an element in assaults in which actual bodily harm was either caused or intended. Exceptions were created for assaults that have some positive social value such as sporting events. In Canada, the criminal law has been codified and the judiciary is constrained by the wording of sections defining criminal offences. The courts' application of public policy is governed by the expression of public policy in the *Criminal Code*. If Parliament intended to adopt the public policy which the English Court of Appeal developed it used singularly inappropriate language. It made the absence of consent a specific requirement and provided that this applied to *all* assaults without exception. The conflict in the Canadian cases which my colleague's review discloses is largely due to the application of these two disparate strains of public policy.

In my opinion the above observations as to the appropriate use of public policy are sufficient to conclude that the absence of consent cannot be swept away by a robust application of judge-made policy. This proposition is strengthened and confirmed by the specific dictates of the *Code* with reference to the essential elements of a criminal offence. Section 9(*a*) of the *Code* provides that "[n]otwithstanding anything in this Act or any other Act, no person shall be convicted ... (a) of an offence at common law." The effect of my colleague's approach is to create an offence where one does not exist under the terms of the *Code* by application of the common law. The offence created is the intentional application of force with the consent of the victim. I appreciate that my colleague's approach is to interpret the section in light of the common law but, in my view, use of the common law to eliminate an element of the offence that is required by statute is more than interpretation and is contrary to not only the spirit but also the letter of s. 9(*a*). One of the basic reasons for s. 9(*a*) is the importance of certainty in determining what conduct constitutes a criminal offence. That is the reason we have codified the offences in the *Criminal Code*. An accused should not have to search the books to discover the common law in order to determine if the offence charged is indeed an offence at law. Where does one search to determine the social utility of a fight during a hockey game to take one example? There are those that would argue that it is an important part of the attraction. Judges may not agree. Is this a matter for judicial notice or does it require evidence? The problem of uncertainty which the social utility test creates is greater than searching out the common law, a problem which lead to the prohibition in s. 9(*a*).

. . . .

It appears clear from the findings of the trial judge that the accused had an honest belief in consent, but that consent extended only until Haggart "gave up or retreated". The extent of the consent given by Haggart did not, therefore, extend to being struck once he had been knocked unconscious. The accused knew that Haggart's consent did not extend beyond consciousness.

In my opinion, based on his own findings, the trial judge misconstrued the evidence with respect to the accused's belief that all the blows were struck prior to Haggart losing consciousness.

. . . .

Having found that the accused committed an assault, and given that Mr. Haggart died as a result of that unlawful act, the accused is therefore guilty of manslaughter via *Criminal Code* ss. 222(5)(*a*) and 234. I would therefore dispose of the appeal as proposed by Gonthier J.

For a criticism of the majority's position see Upsrich (1992), 7 C.R. (4th) 235. *Jobidon* was re-asserted by the Supreme Court in *R. v. Paice*, [2005] 1 S.C.R. 339, 29 C.R. (6th) 1, 195 C.C.C. (3d) 97. See editorial by Kent Roach in (2005), 50 *Crim. L.Q.* 357.

In *Jobidon*, the Court identifies the limits of consent at "bodily harm" while at other times "serious hurt" or "non-trivial bodily harm." Justice Gonthier later states that the "bodily harm contemplated by [his] test" is "essentially equivalent" to what is now defined in s. 2 of the *Criminal Code* as "any hurt or injury to a person that interferes with the health or comfort of the person and is more than merely transient or trifling in nature."

How have the courts applied this definition of bodily harm?

R. v. MOQUIN

(2010), 73 C.R. (6th) 310, 253 C.C.C. (3d) 96, 2010 CarswellMan 51 (Man. C.A.)

BEARD J.A.: —

23 What constitutes bodily harm within the meaning of . . . s. 2 was considered by Esson J.A. in *Dixon*, as follows (at pp. 331-32):

.... The judge clearly found a number of facts. The victim suffered bruises on her arm and head and a laceration two to three inches in length on the back of her head. That wound took "some 10 days to heal". She was "all better within a matter of a month". Having found those facts, the judge had to apply the *Code's* definition of bodily harm. That required him to decide whether the hurt or injury interfered with the victim's health or comfort and whether it was more than merely transient or trifling in nature. I leave aside the question whether there was interference with health because, if there was interference with comfort, that is enough. Transient, trifling and comfort are all words in common usage. The

Shorter Oxford English Dictionary, 3rd ed., vol. II, defines "transient" at p. 2346 as: *"Transient* 1. Passing by or away with time; not durable or permanent; temporary, transitory; *esp.* passing away quickly or soon, brief, momentary, fleeting". At p. 2362, it defines "trifling" as: *"Trifling* ... 3. Of little moment or value; trumpery; insignificant, petty". At pp. 373-4, vol. I, it defines "comfort" as: *"Comfort* ... The condition or quality of being comfortable".

. . .

> 1 The findings that "there is no evidence of any interference with the victim's health or comfort" and that "an injury that lasts no longer than a month would fall within the definition of being transient and trifling" demonstrate, in my view, an absence of any reasonable regard for the ordinary meaning of the words. From the time of the assault at least until the medical treatment was completed, it is clear that the victim must have been deprived of any sense of comfort which she might have had before being assaulted. The element of interference with comfort, which is all that the definition requires, must have continued for some time after that. The interference with comfort resulted from a significant injury—one which cannot be described as trifling. There is no necessary connection at all between the duration of the injury and the question whether it is trifling—a life-threatening injury is often resolved in a short time. Transient does relate to time but, in this context, it is simply insupportable to describe as transient an injury that "lasts no longer than a month".

> 2 .... [emphasis added]

24 This finding in *Dixon* has been applied in a number of appeal cases, including: *R. v. K.(C.)*, 2001 BCCA 379; *R. v. T.G.*, 1999 BCCA 512, 129 B.C.A.C. 148; and *R. v. Van De Wiel (K.W.)* (1997), 158 N.S.R. (2d) 368 (S.C.).

25 Examples of injuries that have been found by courts of appeal to constitute bodily harm within s. 2 of the *Code* are as follows:

— scrapes, lacerations and bruises, especially around the eye and a large amount of hair which had been pulled out by the roots—the court observed that significant bruising will obviously cause discomfort and inconvenience for more than a brief and transitory period—*R. v. Dorscheid*, [1994] A.J. No. 56 (C.A.) (QL);

— superficial injuries, consisting primarily of bruising and abrasions, were found at trial to have interfered with the complainant's health and comfort, which decision was upheld on appeal—*R. v. Rabieifar*, [2003] O.J. No. 3833 (C.A.) (QL);

— a number of bruises to the neck and arms, a number of lacerations to the face, chest, shoulder and wrist which cleared up within a week, difficulty speaking for three or four days as a result of choking and a scar on her forearm from a laceration—the court noted (1) that it was incorrect to find that an injury that would heal within a week could not constitute bodily harm, as life-threatening injuries can be of short duration, and, (2) one must look at the overall effect of a number of injuries, each of which may be trifling, but taken together may be more than trifling and transient—*Garrett*; and

— a sore neck that lasted for approximately one month - the court also noted that medical evidence is not required before making a finding of bodily harm—*R. v. Giroux*, [1995] A.J. No. 900 (C.A.) (QL).

. . .

27   There is a range of harm occasioned by an assault, and the maximum penalty for the related offences increases as the harm increases. The degrees of harm include bodily harm, serious bodily harm and the harm that is required for an aggravated assault. The Supreme Court of Canada dealt with the interpretation of "serious bodily harm" in *McCraw* as follows (at pp. 80-81):

> 3 .... Giving the word "serious" its appropriate dictionary meaning, I would interpret "serious bodily harm" as being any hurt or injury that interferes in a grave or substantial way with the physical integrity or well-being of the complainant. Thus "serious bodily harm" does not require proof of the same degree of harm required for aggravated assault described in s. 268 of the *Code*; that is to say the wounding, disfiguring or endangering of the life of the complainant. Yet it requires greater harm than the mere "bodily harm" described in s. 267; that is hurt or injury that interferes with the health or comfort of the complainant and that is more than merely transient or trifling in nature.

28   It follows from the decision in *McCraw* that, to constitute bodily harm, an injury does not have to meet the standard of "interferes in a grave or substantial way with the physical integrity or well-being of the complainant," that being the standard for serious bodily harm, which is a higher standard than bodily harm. It should be noted that, for the most part, the offences that incorporated serious bodily harm have been amended to require only bodily harm. Within each offence there is a range of harm, and one of the issues on sentencing is the degree or seriousness of the harm within that range.

PROBLEM

John Jones came into your law office yesterday. He's a man aged 52 who has a son Bill, who is 16. Mr. Jones advised you that his son was involved yesterday in an incident at his school. He says that his son was not the instigator but did respond to taunts from a schoolmate, Spike O'Toole. All of Bill's friends were present in the schoolyard when Spike challenged him to a fight. Bill is a karate expert who is schooled that retreat is always to be preferred but the pressure of the situation got to him and he took up the challenge. In the result Spike went to the hospital with a broken jaw. Mr. Jones has asked you for advice as to Bill's position.

Compare *R. v. W. (G.)* (1994), 30 C.R. (4th) 393, 90 C.C.C. (3d) 139 (Ont. C.A.) and *R. v. B. (T.B.)* (1994), 34 C.R. (4th) 241 (P.E.I. C.A.).

Jobidon has been applied to decide that for policy reasons there cannot be consent to sexual practices that cause harm: *R. v. Welch* (1995) 43 C.R. (4th) 225 (Ont. C.A.) and *R. v. McIlwane* (1996) 3 C.R. (5th) 76 (Que. C.A.). **Any concerns about this determination?**

The Criminal Code used to require that consent is vitiated by "fraud as to the nature and quality of the act".

PROBLEM

A doctor conducts a full vaginal examination of a patient. She consented to the presence of a young medical intern watching the procedure. Unbeknownst to her he was in fact not an intern and the doctor had lied about his status so that his friend could watch. Was her consent vitiated by fraud as to the nature and quality of the act such that the doctor should be convicted of the then-existing crime of indecent assault? Compare *R. v. Bolduc and Bird*, [1967] S.C.R. 677.

In 1983, the law relating to coerced consent was changed. Now, under s. 265(3), applying to all forms of assault and sexual assault,

No consent is obtained where the complainant submits or does not resist by reason of

   (a) the application of force to the complainant or to a person other than the complainant;
   (b) threats or fear of the application of force to the complainant or to a person other than the complainant;
   (c) fraud; or
   (d) the exercise of authority.

The meaning of consent vitiated by "fraud" in the new section was the central issue which divided the Court in *Cuerrier*

What is the meaning of fraud?

R. v. CUERRIER

[1998] 2 S.C.R. 371, 18 C.R. (5th) 1, 127 C.C.C. (3d) 1,
1998 CarswellBC 1772, 1998 CarswellBC 1773

The accused was charged with two counts of aggravated assault pursuant to s. 268 of the *Criminal Code*. The accused had tested positive for HIV in August 1992. At that time a public health nurse explicitly instructed him to use condoms every time he engaged in sexual intercourse and to inform all prospective sexual partners that he was HIV-positive. The accused angrily rejected this advice. He complained that he would never be able to have a sex life if he told anyone that he was HIV-positive. The accused had unprotected sexual relations with the two complainants without informing them he was HIV-positive. The complainants had consented to unprotected sexual intercourse with the accused, but they testified at trial that if they had known that he was HIV-positive they would never have engaged in unprotected intercourse with him. Fortunately, the complainants did not become HIV-positive.

The trial judge entered a directed verdict acquitting the accused. The Court of Appeal upheld the acquittals. The Supreme Court was unanimous in allowing the appeal and ordering a new trial. The court was divided in its reasons.

CORY J. (MAJOR, BASTARACHE and BINNIE JJ. concurring): —

. . . .

In 1983, the *Criminal Code* was amended. The rape and indecent assault provisions were replaced by the offence of sexual assault. The s. 265 assault provision was enacted in its present form, and it, by the terms of s. 265(2), applies to all forms of assault, including sexual assault.

Section 265(3)(c) simply states that no consent is obtained where the complainant submits or does not resist by reason of "fraud". There are no limitations or qualifications on the term "fraud". It is no longer necessary when examining whether consent in assault or sexual assault cases was vitiated by fraud to consider whether the fraud related to the "nature and quality of the act".

. . . .

. . . A principled approach consistent with the plain language of the section and an appropriate approach to consent in sexual assault matters is preferable. To that end, there is no reason why, with appropriate modifications, the principles which have historically been applied in relation to fraud in criminal law cannot be used.

In criminal law cases dealing with commercial transactions, it has been held that mere negligent misrepresentation would not amount to a fraudulent act. However, deliberately practised fraudulent acts which, in the knowledge of the accused, actually put the property of others at risk is subject to criminal sanction. Non-disclosure can constitute fraud where it would be viewed by the reasonable person as dishonest. The essential elements of fraud then are dishonesty, which can include non-disclosure of important facts, and deprivation or risk of deprivation.

It is now necessary to consider the nature of fraud and how it should be applied in the context of the wording of the present s. 265.

. . . .

At the outset it can be accepted that fraud pertaining to the nature and quality of the act or the identity of the partner will still constitute fraud which can be found to vitiate consent. What other acts of dishonesty which give rise to the risk of deprivation can have the same effect?

. . . .

The deadly consequences that non-disclosure of the risk of HIV infection can have on an unknowing victim, make it imperative that as a policy a broad view of fraud vitiating consent . . . should be adopted. . . . [I]t should now be taken that for the accused to conceal or fail to disclose that he is HIV-positive can constitute fraud which may vitiate consent to sexual intercourse.

Persons knowing that they are HIV-positive who engage in sexual intercourse without advising their partner of the disease may be found to fulfil the traditional requirements for fraud namely dishonesty and deprivation. That fraud may vitiate a partner's consent to engage in sexual intercourse.

. . . .

Without disclosure of HIV status there cannot be a true consent. The consent cannot simply be to have sexual intercourse. Rather it must be consent to have intercourse with a partner who is HIV-positive. True consent cannot be given if there has not been a disclosure by the accused of his HIV-positive status. A consent that is not based upon knowledge of the significant relevant factors is not a valid consent. The extent of the duty to disclose will increase with the risks attendant upon the act of intercourse. To put it in the context of fraud the greater the risk of deprivation the higher the duty of disclosure. The failure to disclose HIV-positive status can lead to a devastating illness with fatal consequences. In those circumstances, there exists a positive duty to disclose. The nature and extent of the duty to disclose, if any, will always have to be considered in the context of the particular facts presented. . . . [T]he Crown will have to establish that the dishonest act . . . had the effect of exposing the person consenting to a significant risk of serious bodily harm. The risk of contracting AIDS as a result of engaging in unprotected intercourse would clearly meet that test.

A position that any fraud that is designed to induce the complainant to submit to the act will vitiate consent and constitute an assault would trivialize the criminal process by leading to a proliferation of petty prosecutions instituted without judicial guidelines or directions. To say that any fraud which induces consent will vitiate consent would bring within the sexual assault provisions of the *Code* behaviour which lacks the reprehensible character of criminal acts.

. . . [S]ome limitations on the concept of fraud as it applies to s. 265(3)(c) are clearly necessary or the courts would be overwhelmed and convictions under the sections would defy common sense. The existence of fraud should not vitiate consent unless there is a significant risk of serious harm.

. . . .

It was contended that criminalization would further stigmatize all persons with HIV/AIDS. However it cannot be forgotten that the further stigmatization arises as a result of a sexual assault and not because of the disease. Just as an HIV-positive individual convicted of armed robbery will be further stigmatized but it will not be related to the status of his health. To proceed by way of a criminal charge for assault is not to "criminalize" the accused's activities. Rather, it is simply to apply the provisions of the *Code* to conduct which could constitute the crime of assault and thereby infringe s. 265.

L'HEUREUX-DUBÉ J.: — . . . [T]he 1983 amendment to the *Criminal Code*, in which the rape and indecent assault provisions were reconstituted as the offence of sexual assault, and the words "false and fraudulent representations as to the nature and quality of the act" were removed, evidences Parliament's intention to move away from the unreasonably strict common law approach to the vitiation of consent by fraud.

. . . Parliament has recognized with s. 265(3), that in order to maximize the protection of physical integrity and personal autonomy, only consent obtained without negating the voluntary agency of the person being touched, is legally valid. . . . [F]raud is simply about whether the dishonest act in question induced another to consent to the ensuing physical act, whether or not that act was particularly risky and dangerous. The focus of the inquiry into whether fraud vitiated consent so as to make certain physical contact non-consensual should be on whether the nature and execution of the deceit deprived the complainant of the ability to exercise his or her will in relation to his or her physical integrity with respect to the activity in question.

. . . .

An interpretation of fraud that focuses only on the sexual assault context, and which limits it only to those situations where a "significant risk of serious bodily harm" is evident, is unjustifiably restrictive. Such a particularization and limitation is nowhere present in the assault scheme, because Parliament removed any qualifications to the fraud provision as it relates to sexual assault.

. . . .

Finally, my colleagues' examples of the types of trivial conduct that will be caught by this approach are grossly overstated. Cory J. downplays the limiting effect of the fact that a causal connection must be proven, to the imposing criminal standard, between the accused's dishonest act and his intention to induce the submission of the complainant. For instance, a mere misrepresentation as to a man's professional status, without proof that the man was aware that the complainant was submitting to sexual intercourse with him by reason of his lie, would not constitute sexual assault. See Mewett and Manning, *supra*, at pp. 789-90. Whether a complainant actually submitted to sexual intercourse by reason of an accused's fraud will necessarily depend on an examination of all of the factors, and can only be decided on a case-by-case basis.

McLachlin J.'s predictions are even more cataclysmic. Contrary to her assertion in para. 52 of her reasons, it is not "any deception or dishonesty" that will be criminalized by this approach. McLachlin J. argues that based on the approach to fraud that I have explained, henceforward "the implied consent inherent in the social occasion — the handshake or social buss — are transformed by fiat of judicial pen into crimes". But my approach to fraud will in no way catch such innocent conduct. The very notion of implied consent to touching that is inherent in the social occasion, and indeed, inherent in so many aspects of day to day life, is based on an understanding of social realities and a need for tolerance of a reasonable degree of incidental and trivial contact. Whether or not a man is wearing a false moustache or a woman, alluring make-up, it is inconceivable that the Crown, were it foolish enough to prosecute a case of assault by handshake or social buss, would be capable of establishing beyond a reasonable doubt both that a complainant only consented to the physical contact by reason of the deception, and that the deception was employed with the knowledge and intention of inducing the submission of the complainant. In addition, the principle of *de minimis non curat lex*, that "the law does not concern itself with trifles" might apply in such a case: see *R. v. Hinchey*, [1996] 3 S.C.R. 1128 at para. 69, 111 C.C.C. (3d) 353, 142 D.L.R. (4th) 50, per L'Heureux-Dubé J. Furthermore, I cannot accept McLachlin J.'s criticism that the test suffers from imprecision and uncertainty due to the fact that the dishonesty of the act is to be assessed based on an objective standard. A majority of this court has already accepted such an approach to the assessment of the dishonesty of the act in the criminal fraud context: see *Théroux, supra*, at p. 16, per McLachlin J.

Since Parliament has, through the assault provisions, granted broad protection to individual autonomy and physical integrity in order to guard everyone's right to decide under what conditions another may touch them, it is not for this court to narrow this protection because it is afraid that it may reach too far into the private lives of individuals. One of those private lives presumably belongs to a complainant, whose feeling of having been physically violated, and fraudulently deprived of the right to withhold consent, warrants the protection and condemnation provided by the *Criminal Code*.

Subject to these reasons, I agree with my colleagues' disposition to allow the appeal and order a new trial.

McLACHLIN J. (GONTHIER J. concurring): — For more than a century, the law has been settled; fraud does not vitiate consent to assault unless the mistake goes to the nature of the act or the identity of the partner. Fraud as to collateral aspects of a consensual encounter, like the possibility of contracting serious venereal disease, does not vitiate consent. Parliament did not intend to remove the common law limitations on fraud for assault by amending s. 265(3) of the *Criminal Code* in 1983.

. . . [T]he criminalization of conduct is a serious matter. Clear language is required to create crimes . . . When courts approach the definition of elements of old crimes, they must be cautious not to broaden them in a way that in effect creates a new crime. Only Parliament can create new crimes and turn lawful conduct into criminal conduct . . . [T]he *Interpretation Act*, . . . s. 45(2), . . . provides that an amending enactment shall not be deemed to involve a declaration of a change in the existing law . . . As such, the 1983 amendment of the assault provisions, which removed the qualifier "nature and quality of the act" from the type of fraud sufficient to vitiate consent, should not, in the absence of evidence to the contrary, be taken as a change in the law of assault.

This conclusion is also supported by the rule that where a criminal statute is ambiguous, the interpretation that favours the accused is preferred . . .

. . . [T]he 1983 amendments to the *Criminal Code* did not oust the common law governing fraud in relation to assault. The common law continues to inform the concept of fraud in s. 265(3)(c) of the *Criminal Code*.

. . . .

However, it does not follow that all change to the law of assault is barred. It is open to courts to make incremental changes by extending the common law concepts of nature of the act and identity, provided the ramifications of the changes are not overly complex.

. . . .

It is the proper role of the courts to update the common law from time to time to bring it into harmony with the changing needs and mores of society . . . This applies to the common law concept of fraud in relation to assault.

. . . .

The basic precondition of such change is that it is required to bring the law into step with the changing needs of society.

. . . .

In the case at bar . . . the current state of the law does not reflect the values of Canadian society. It is unrealistic, indeed shocking, to think that consent given to sex on the basis that one's partner is HIV-free stands unaffected by blatant deception on that matter . . . [The] common law [earlier] recognized that deception as to sexually transmitted disease carrying a high risk of infection, constituted fraud vitiating consent to sexual intercourse. Returning the law to this position would represent an incremental change to the law.

. . . .

The final and most difficult question is whether the change would introduce complex and unforeseeable changes of the sort better left to Parliament . . . [O]nce the law leaves the certainty of the dual criteria of nature of the act in the sense of whether it was sexual or non-sexual, and the identity of the perpetrator, the argument is made that to go beyond these criteria would be to open the door to convictions for assault in the case, for example, where a man promises a woman a fur coat in return for sexual intercourse . . . This difficulty is a serious one. The courts should not broaden the criminal law to catch conduct that society generally views as non-criminal. If that is to be done, Parliament must do it. Furthermore, the criminal law must be clear. I agree with the fundamental principle . . . that it is imperative that there be a clear line between criminal and non-criminal conduct. Absent this, the criminal law loses its deterrent effect and becomes unjust.

. . . .

The question is whether a narrower increment is feasible that catches only harm of the sort at issue in this appeal and draws the required bright line . . . [A] return to the [earlier] common law would draw a clear line between criminal conduct and non-criminal conduct . . . [T]he [earlier] law permitted fraud to vitiate consent to contact where there was (a) a deception as to the sexual character of the act; (b) deception as to the identity of the perpetrator; or (c) deception as to the presence of a sexually transmitted disease giving rise to serious risk or probability of infecting the complainant. This rule is clear and contained. It would catch the conduct here at issue, without permitting people to be convicted of assault for inducements like false promises of marriage or fur coats. The test for deception would be objective, focussing on whether the accused falsely represented to the complainant that he or she was disease-free when he knew or ought to have known that there was a high risk of infecting his partner. The test for inducement would be subjective, in the sense that the judge or jury must be satisfied beyond a reasonable doubt that the fraud actually induced the consent.

. . . .

. . . [A]n explanation may be suggested for why deceit as to venereal disease may vitiate consent while deceit as to other inducements, like promises of marriage or fur coats, does not. Consent to unprotected sexual intercourse is consent to sexual congress with a certain person and to the transmission of bodily fluids from that person. Where the person represents that he or she is disease-free, and consent is given on that basis, deception on that matter goes to the very act of assault. The complainant does not consent to the transmission of diseased fluid into his or her body. This deception in a very real sense goes to the nature of the sexual act, changing it from an act that has certain natural consequences (whether pleasure, pain or pregnancy), to a potential sentence of disease or death. It differs fundamentally from deception as to the consideration that will be given for consent, like marriage, money or a fur coat, in that it relates to the physical act itself. It differs, moreover, in a profoundly serious way that merits the criminal sanction.

R. v. MABIOR

(2010) 79 C.R. (6th) 1, 2010 CarswellMan 587, 261 C.C.C. (3d) 520 (Man. C.A.)

The accused was convicted of six counts of aggravated sexual assault. He had had sexual intercourse with six women, all of whom had consented; however, the accused had not disclosed to these women that he was HIV-positive. The question was whether the accused's failure to disclose his HIV-positive status constituted fraud and vitiated the consents, based on *R. v. Cuerrier*, [1998] 2 S.C.R. 371. In particular, the question for the Manitoba Court of Appeal was whether the trial judge had applied the "significant risk of serious bodily harm" test correctly on the particular facts of the case. The Court of Appeal held that she had not done so, and as a result overturned some but not all of the convictions.

Background

6 Between February 2004 and December 2005 the accused had sexual relations with the six complainants, one of whom was under 14 years of age at the time. The accused's knowledge of his HIV status, the dates of his medical tests and his treatments are all relevant facts in determining culpability, and therefore the facts are presented in some detail.

7 The accused was medically diagnosed as HIV-positive on January 14, 2004, as a result of a specimen being drawn on December 22, 2003. The evidence showed that he had been fully counselled by doctors and nurses on all relevant aspects of being HIV-positive, including the potential result of unprotected sex. He was advised by public health officials that he was to use latex condoms that had not expired every time he had sexual intercourse and to tell all sexual partners of his HIV-positive status.

8 The trial judge found as a fact that the accused, despite the advice given him, engaged in acts of both protected and unprotected sexual intercourse with the complainants subsequent to learning of his condition without disclosing to any of them that he was HIV-positive. None of the complainants have to date been diagnosed as HIV-positive.

9 The trial judge also found as a fact that five of the complainants would not have engaged in sexual relations with the accused if they had been told by him that he was HIV-positive. The one exception to this was D.C.S., who learned of his medical condition during the course of their sexual relationship.

10 The scientific and medical evidence at trial were provided by Dr. Richard Smith, Ms Katherine McDonald and Ms Jaime Burgoyne, all three of whom were called by the Crown. Dr. Richard Smith testified as an expert in the area of HIV and AIDS on behalf of the Crown. He was qualified as a medical doctor whose primary emphasis of practice was on the diagnosis, treatment and prevention of HIV and AIDS. He provided an expert's report on HIV/AIDS, which was filed and upon which he was examined. As well, although he did not treat the accused, he reviewed and gave his opinion on the accused's medical and public health records, all of which were also filed.

...

12 In April 2004 the accused was placed on antiretroviral therapy, and his viral loads were checked every three to four months. Dr. Smith testified, and the trial judge accepted, that the accused had viral loads that were consistent with "probably low but possible infectivity" until October 21, 2004, and then from October 22, 2004, to December 28, 2005, there was a very high probability that the accused was not infectious and could not have transmitted HIV throughout that period.

...

Did the Trial Judge Err in Applying the Factual Findings to the Legal Standard of "Significant Risk of Serious Bodily Harm"?

...

The Law of Consent in Sexual Assault

38 The accused was convicted of aggravated sexual assault contrary to s. 273(1) of the *Criminal Code*, which states:

> 273. (1) Every one commits an aggravated sexual assault who, in committing a sexual assault, wounds, maims, disfigures or endangers the life of the complainant.

For a conviction, in the context of this case, the Crown was required to prove beyond a reasonable doubt that the accused intentionally applied force to the complainants, that the complainants did not consent to the application of that force and the accused knew it, that the application of force took place in circumstances of a sexual nature and, finally, that the force endangered the life of the complainants.

39 Although the complainants may have consented to have sex with the accused, they testified that they would not have done so had they known he was HIV-positive. Section 273.1(1) of the *Criminal Code* defines consent as "the voluntary agreement of the complainant to engage in the sexual activity in question." According to s. 265(3), a person's "voluntary" consent, whether to assault, sexual assault or aggravated sexual assault, is vitiated if it was obtained by fraud.

40 Is it criminally fraudulent to lie or fail to disclose one's HIV-positive status to a sexual partner? The Crown says that it is fraudulent based on the principles underlying the law's present treatment of consent in relation to sexual assault. In *R. v. Ewanchuk*, 1999 CanLII 711 (S.C.C.), [1999] 1 S.C.R. 330, the Supreme Court of Canada described the role of consent in relation to sexual assault as follows (at para. 28):

> . . .. Society is committed to protecting the personal integrity, both physical and psychological, of every individual. Having control over who touches one's body, and how, lies at the core of human dignity and autonomy. . . .. The common law has recognized for centuries that the individual's right to physical integrity is a fundamental principle, "every man's person being sacred, and no other having a right to meddle with it, in any the slightest manner": . . ..

41 Parliament seems to have reinforced this attitude toward consent in sexual assault by explicitly placing the onus on the accused to take reasonable steps to ensure the consent of the complainant to the activity in question. See s. 273.2 of the *Criminal Code* and *Ewanchuk*, at paras. 46, 51. Thus, an accused can only rely on a complainant's consent to sexual activity if that consent was clear and unequivocal.

42 The Crown submits that sexual intercourse should not be treated any differently than any other physically invasive procedure. Individuals have a right to know the risks they are accepting when they agree to sexual intercourse. An accused should ensure that a prospective complainant is fully informed of the material risks prior to seeking consent to the acts. The obligation imposed on an accused, it is argued, is relatively minor. He or she is free to have sexual intercourse with anyone he or she pleases so long as their HIV status is disclosed. To hold otherwise removes the ability of a complainant to make any kind of informed decision about his or her own body and is inconsistent with the law of consent in relation to sexual assault.

...

49 A broad interpretation of fraud in relation to consent to sexual activity seems most consistent with protection of bodily integrity. Moreover, fraud with respect to HIV status does relate to a matter which most people would regard as going to the fundamental nature and quality of the sexual act as opposed to, for example, false representations as to financial or social status. See, for example, the arguments made in support of this approach in Diana Ginn, "Can Failure to

Disclose HIV Positivity to Sexual Partners Vitiate Consent? *R. v. Cuerrier*" (2000) 12 Can. J. Women & L. 235, and Isabel Grant, "The Boundaries of the Criminal Law: the Criminalization of the Non-disclosure of HIV" (2008) 31 Dalhousie L.J. 123 at 176 (but see n. 193, on p. 177).

50 However, it is not the law in Canada. The majority decision in *Cuerrier*, written by Cory J., widened the definition of fraud which vitiated consent in assault cases beyond that of the common law. However, it still required that the dishonesty result in a deprivation consisting of actual harm or a significant risk of serious bodily harm. Justice Cory, in examining the development of the doctrine of criminal fraud, found that it had two constituent elements, namely, dishonesty, which can include non-disclosure of important facts, and deprivation or risk of deprivation. By deprivation, it is meant "proof of detriment, prejudice, or risk of prejudice to the economic interests of the victim" (at para. 113).

51 Justice Cory felt that the above principles, which were developed to address the problem of fraud in the commercial context, could, with appropriate modifications, "serve as a useful starting point in the search for the type of fraud which will vitiate consent to sexual intercourse in a prosecution for aggravated assault" (at para. 117).

...

53 As one academic put it:

> The majority in *Cuerrier* was particularly concerned that fraud not be defined so broadly that any risk of harm (such as the emotional harm that may result from deceptive sexual practices), could negate consent to sexual activity and give rise to assault charges. They held that the deception must pose a *significant* risk of *serious* bodily harm in order to negate consent. The Court conceptualized the duty to disclose in direct proportion to "the risks attendant upon the act of intercourse": the greater the risk to the complainant, the more likely it is that the accused has a duty to disclose. . . ..

[Isabel Grant, "Rethinking Risk: The Relevance of Condoms and Viral Load in HIV Nondisclosure Prosecutions" (2009) 54 McGill L.J. 389 at 396]

...

Significant Risk of Serious Bodily Harm

...

Serious Bodily Harm

...

64 ...I do not think it can be disputed that being infected with HIV subjects an individual to serious bodily harm. Although no longer necessarily fatal if treated

medically, HIV is an infection that cannot be cured at this time and is a lifelong, chronic infection. For those who become infected, it is a life-altering disease, both physically and emotionally. Individuals must take medications every day, and the condition is potentially lethal if they do not have access to treatment or fail to take the medications. Even with treatment, HIV infection can still lead to devastating illnesses. Moreover, the emotional and psychological impact of dealing with such a disease is, no doubt, overwhelming. In their factums, both the accused and the intervener acknowledged that acquiring HIV constitutes serious bodily harm.

Significant Risk of Harm – Error of Trial Judge

65 The accused and the intervener argue that the trial judge made two errors when assessing the risk of harm. First, given the nature of the harm that might be suffered, she required that there be no risk of transmission at all. Second, she misapprehended the evidence as to the risk of transmission of the virus in the case of protected sexual activity, and that misapprehension "play[ed] an essential part in the reasoning process resulting in a conviction" (*R. v. C.L.Y.*, 2008 SCC 2 (CanLII), 2008 SCC 2, [2008] 1 S.C.R. 5 at para. 19). I agree with both of those submissions.

66 At various points in her reasons, the trial judge seems to have required proof of no risk at all. For example, she states, ". . . [E]ven with an undetectable viral load, there remains a risk . . ." (at para. 105), and again, "However, the research has not proven that such a situation completely eliminates the risk of transmitting the virus. In such circumstances, I find that the risk constituted a significant risk of serious bodily harm" (at para. 134).

67 The elimination of risk is not the legal test. I do not accept the Crown's argument, which seems to have been accepted by the trial judge and was argued again in front of us on appeal, that given the nature of the serious bodily harm that might occur, <u>any</u> risk of harm is significant. This was the same argument that was made and rejected in the case of *R. v. Jones*, 2002 NBQB 340. In that case, the accused was charged with aggravated assault as a result of having unprotected sexual intercourse while being infected with Hepatitis C. Although the medical evidence was that the risk of transmission through sex was very low, the Crown argued that it was not the risk of transmission that mattered, but rather the serious consequences to one's health after it is contracted. The court rejected this argument, stating (at para. 32):

> I interpret this paragraph [in *Cuerrier*] to mean that the risk referred to by the Supreme Court of Canada is both the risk of contracting the disease <u>and</u> the risk to the health of the person after it is contracted. [emphasis added]

68 I agree that the nature of the harm can affect the determination of what is considered to be a significant risk. As the magnitude of the harm goes up, the

threshold of probability that will be considered significant goes down. However, to have required a complete elimination of risk rather than a significant risk was an error in law.

69 So one must determine what constitutes a "significant risk" of transmission in any particular case. I do agree with the British Columbia Court of Appeal when it stated in *R. v. T. (J.)*, 2008 BCCA 463 (CanLII), 2008 BCCA 463, 256 C.C.C. (3d) 246 (at paras. 19-20):

> I do not accept that *Cuerrier* set an evidentiary benchmark. Risk is a matter of fact to be assessed on the evidence in each and every case. The remark at paragraph 129 of *Cuerrier* concerning the careful use of condoms merely provides an illustration of what "might" (the word chosen by Cory J.) take the risk below the "significant" level. I think the language acknowledges that it is a question of evidence whether in any given prosecution the risk is significant.
>
> *Cuerrier* laid down a proposition of law: a significant risk of substantial harm will vitiate consent when combined with deceit. It did not, in my opinion, purport to prescribe for all cases what facts will determine the significance of the risk.

70 Second, at numerous points in her reasons, the trial judge held that since the use of condoms only resulted in an 80 per cent risk reduction (or, alternatively, that they were only 80 per cent reliable or effective), there still remained a significant risk of transmission of the virus....

71 Although the trial judge quoted the medical evidence of an 80 per cent reduction in risk, she did not go on to consider an 80 per cent reduction "from what." A substantial reduction of an already small number may not necessarily result in a significant risk. As a foundational building block to the legal question of whether a significant risk remains where there is condom use or reduced viral loads, one must first have a baseline of the rate of transmission of HIV in unprotected intercourse.

[The Court of Appeal considered a variety of scientific evidence concerning the transmission rate of HIV, concluding that the risk of transmission of the virus in unprotected intercourse is approximately somewhere between 0.05 per cent and 0.26 per cent. The appropriate use of condoms could reduce that rate by a further 80%. They also noted that Mabior's case was the first in which very detailed information about the accused's own viral load at various times was available, and so the decision had to be made based on that evidence, rather than on evidence of average viral loads. They then applied those facts to an analysis of whether there was a "significant risk" with regard to each of the six complainants separately.]

118 This general evidence with respect to condom use and viral load must now be examined in relation to each complainant.

M.P.

119 The first complainant who had sexual intercourse with the accused after his diagnosis was M.P. M.P. engaged in sexual relations with the accused on 10 or 11 occasions between February 2004 and March or April 2004. I have already indicated that I accept the trial judge's finding that although condoms were used on at least two occasions, there was also unprotected sex on a number of occasions.

120 The accused's viral load counts taken on February 11 and 25, 2004, were 6,100 copies per millilitre and 6,300 copies per millilitre, which, according to Dr. Smith, indicated that the accused had "probably low but possible infectivity" when these tests were taken. Moreover, the impact of STDs has already been discussed, and the accused tested positive for gonorrhea for the second time on February 13, 2004. Consequently, I agree with the trial judge that a significant risk of harm existed during the instances of unprotected sex with M.P.

K.R.

121 K.R. had sexual relations with the accused from April 2004 until approximately November 2004. She testified that condoms were always used and that she and the accused practised safe sex. However, she indicated that on three or four occasions, the condom broke during sexual intercourse. As a result, sexual activity was stopped and a new condom was applied. This breakage may have resulted from any number of causes – improper application or utilization, simple condom failure or intoxication of the accused. Nonetheless, once the condom broke, the complainant became exposed to the risk of transmission as if the sex was unprotected. She was entitled, at that point in time, to disclosure of the accused's serostatus so that she could, if she chose to, take prophylactic measures. As mentioned earlier, where a condom breaks, the non-HIV partner can be treated successfully so long as treatment starts within 72 hours.

122 The accused's viral load near the beginning of this relationship was less than 500 copies per millilitre, which again was consistent with low, but possible infectivity. His viral load was undetectable for the latter portions of his relationship with K.R. (50 copies per millilitre on August 4, 2004, and less than 50 copies per millilitre on October 6, 2004). However, given the increased risk factors, including the fact that he had a higher viral load during the first part of his relationship, he was involved with multiple partners (he had sex with K.G. while in a relationship with K.R.) and he was listed as a Chlamydia contact by another woman during this period, I agree with the trial judge that a significant risk of harm existed in relation to this complainant.

K.G.

123 K.G. had sexual relations on one occasion with the accused in June 2004. Although she was intoxicated at the time, she testified that she was "pretty sure" a condom was used. She testified that she normally required the use of a condom during intercourse. The trial judge found the accused guilty, referring to the "only 80% effectiveness rate of condoms" (at para. 129). I have already commented on the error related to the assessment of risk and condom use. Generally, consistent and careful use of good quality condoms reduces risk to below a significant level.

124 In this case, it is true that there was generally much evidence of inconsistent and careless use of condoms by the accused. However, based on the testimony of the complainant herself, with respect to this one sexual encounter, there is no evidence of failed condom use or human error. Even alcohol did not appear to play a factor. The complainant testified that she did not see the accused drinking or using drugs at any time.

125 Given the evidence of the complainant as to the use of a condom in this particular instance and the medical evidence as to the effect of condom use on the risk of transmission, I find that there was no significant risk of serious bodily harm here.

126 When an appeal is allowed with respect to a conviction, an appellate court may direct that a verdict of acquittal be entered or order a new trial. See s. 686(1)(a) and s. 686(2) of the *Criminal Code*. The appeal court should exercise its discretion and enter an acquittal, rather than order a new trial, where it concludes there was no reasonable evidence of an essential element in the crime charged [citations omitted]. Consequently, I would allow the appeal with respect to this count and substitute an acquittal.

127 With respect to the last three complainants, generally from October 22, 2004, to December 28, 2005, according to Dr. Smith, there was a "high probability" that the accused was not infectious during this period. I do not see how that evidence can support a finding with respect to these complainants that the Crown has proven beyond a reasonable doubt the lack of consent arising from the presence of a significant risk of serious bodily harm. "Significant" means something other than an ordinary risk. It means an important, serious, substantial risk. It is the opposite of evidence of a "high probability" of no infectiousness, especially given the statistical percentages referred to earlier. ...

Conclusion

147 In this case, the Crown proved, and the trial judge correctly accepted, that the accused intentionally applied force to all the complainants in circumstances

of a sexual nature. Further, although the accused knew that he was HIV-positive, and despite medical warnings to the contrary, he did not disclose that condition to the complainants, who, with one exception, would not have consented if they had known he was HIV-positive.

148 I can well understand that those complainants feel, in their opinion, that the nature and quality of the sexual act was fundamentally changed by the lack of disclosure of the risk of disease. Certainly this was especially the case with S.H., who was lied to by the accused as to his HIV status after she specifically asked about the presence of disease. From the complainants' points of view, any risk of contracting HIV is too great because any sexual encounter "could be 'the one', whether the odds are 1 in 100 or 1 in 10,000" (*R. v. J.A.T.*, at para. 54). In fact, other judges (L'Heureux-Dubé J. in *Cuerrier* and Roscoe J.A. in *Hutchinson*) and certain academics agree that misrepresentation coupled with reliance should be sufficient to vitiate consent without the necessity of the element of deprivation. In addition, some argue that there are unique issues for women here. "Thus, the reality for women may be that they cannot always take the best precautions available to prevent transmission of HIV/AIDS; rather they must rely on their male partners to cooperate" (Grant, "The Boundaries of the Criminal Law," at p. 159).

149 In *Cuerrier*, a majority of the court expressed concern that to allow a wider definition of fraud when determining when consent to sexual activity was negated might trivialize the issue. Yet, in other areas, courts are well able to determine when a material matter goes to the heart of consent without trivializing the analysis. For example, courts are very familiar with determining whether an informed consent has been obtained from a medical patient. In determining whether disclosure is required in a medical setting, both the degree of probability of risk and its seriousness are relevant factors. The same analysis may be useful in determining whether non-disclosure of a certain risk affected a person's informed consent to sexual activity.

...

153 At present, however, *Cuerrier* is the law in Canada. The trial judge incorrectly interpreted and applied the test arising from *Cuerrier* and erred in her understanding of the relevant evidence at trial. Specifically, she erred in ruling that a combination of both undetectable viral load <u>and</u> the use of a condom would be required to escape criminal liability.

...

156 I am well aware that respect for one's bodily integrity would favour a legal standard that requires disclosure of facts that so closely impact on one's decision to allow physical intimacies. Everyone would want to be told that a potential

partner was HIV-positive. Most people would agree that there was a moral and ethical obligation to disclose that information. In reaching the conclusion that I have, I do not condone the behaviour of the accused in this case.

157 However, there are other criminal charges possible when actual harm occurs. See McLachlin J.'s comments in *Cuerrier*, at para. 74, and *R. v. Mercer*, (1993), 84 C.C.C. (3d) 41 (Nfld. C.A.). With respect to situations where exposure to risk of harm is at issue, the requirement for a significant risk of serious bodily harm is the legal test, as set out by the Supreme Court of Canada.

158 The appeal is allowed in part. The accused should have a fresh sentencing hearing in the Court of Queen's Bench on the charges for which his conviction has been sustained.

John Flaherty, "Clarifying the Duty to Warn in HIV Transference Cases" (2008) 54 *Crim. L.Q.* 60, calls for a new test of objectivity foresight of bodily harm. For a case for de-criminalization see Isabel Grant, "The Boundaries of the Criminal Law: The Criminalization of the Non-disclosure of HIV" (2008) 31 *Dalhousie L.J.* 123.

PROBLEM

The accused is charged with sexual assault. He testified that he met the complainant on a street corner in the early morning hours and had agreed to pay her $100 for sexual intercourse. He conceded that he had driven the complainant to an underground parking lot and that he had sexual relations with her to which she consented. In the course of his testimony he stated that he never had intended to pay her $100 for sexual services and that he had offered to pay $100 only because he wanted to have some sexual activity. Result? Compare *R. v. P.* (1987), 58 C.R. (3d) 320, 35 C.C.C. (3d) 528 (B.C. C.A.).

In *R. v. Williams*, [2003] 2 S.C.R. 134 the accused had unprotected sexual relations with the complainant during their 18-month relationship. Five months into the relationship the accused learned that he had recently tested positive for HIV. He did not inform the complainant, who tested positive shortly thereafter. The Supreme Court held that he was wrongly convicted of aggravated assault on the principle that the *actus reus* and *mens rea* must coincide. There was no proof beyond reasonable doubt that he had infected the complainant at a time that he knew he was HIV positive. The Court substituted a conviction of attempted aggravated assault.

(e)   *De Minimis Non Curat Lex*

The most supportive consideration of the *de minimis* principle is to be found in the dissenting opinion of Justice Arbour in *Canadian Foundation for Children, Youth & the Law v. Canada (Attorney General)*, 16 C.R. (6th) 203, [2004] 1 S.C.R. 76, 180 C.C.C. (3d) 353. We have seen that in that decision a 6-3 majority upheld the constitutionality of the section 43 defence allowing parents and teachers to use reasonable force in correction of children. In response to the concern that striking down s. 43 would criminalise acts of minor discipline Justice Arbour relied upon the *de minimis* doctrine (paras 202-209). Reviewing the case law she noted that the issue was still open in the Supreme Court, and had not been widely used by courts due to charge screening by police and Crown. In her view it existed as a common law defence preserved by section 8(3) of the *Criminal Code*. In her view *de minimis* does not mean that the act is justified; it remains unlawful but on account of it triviality goes unpunished. The doctrine:

(1) ... reserves the application of the criminal law to serious misconduct;
(2) protects an accused from the stigma of a criminal conviction and from the imposition of serious penalties for relatively trivial conduct; and
(3) ... saves courts from being swamped by enormous number of trivial cases (para 204).

In her majority judgment in *Canadian Foundation* Chief Justice McLachlin J. did not deny the existence of the *de minimis* doctrine, simply saying that it was "equally or more vague and difficult in application than the reasonableness defence offered by s. 43".

Lower courts are often resistant, especially Courts of Appeal:

R. v. KUBASSEK

(2004), 25 C.R. (6th) 340, 2004 CarswellOnt 3425, 188 C.C.C. (3d) 307
(C.A.)

CATZMAN J.A. (WEILER and MACPHERSON JJ.A. concurring): —

The Background

1 In *Halpern v. Canada (Attorney General)* (2003), 65 O.R. (3d) 161, this court held that the common law definition of marriage as a union between a man and a woman violated the Canadian *Charter of Rights and Freedoms* and that it should be reformulated as "the voluntary union for life of two persons to the exclusion of all others". The result was that, in Ontario, same-sex couples were entitled to marry.

2 One of the parties to the proceedings in Halpern was the Metropolitan Community Church, whose senior pastor, Rev. Brent Hawkes, had published the banns of marriage for two same-sex couples on three consecutive Sundays

and officiated at their weddings on January 14, 2001. The two couples whose marriage he celebrated were also parties to the proceedings in Halpern.

3 Erica Kubassek holds very strong views about same-sex marriages. She considers such marriages to be a falling away from God's truth. She believes herself to be a Christian servant of the Lord, endowed with the spiritual gifts of revelation and prophesy.

4 The Metropolitan Community Church had announced that the two same-sex marriages referred to above would be celebrated on Sunday afternoon, January 14, 2001. That Sunday morning, Ms. Kubassek, who was not a congregant of the Metropolitan Community Church, believed that she received a message from the Lord to go to the church, there to speak out for truth and to explain the word of the Lord. She drove from her home in Cambridge to Toronto, where she attended the church's 11:00 a.m. Sunday morning service. At a point in the service when Rev. Hawkes asked the congregation to come forward for anointing for healing, she went to the front, turned around and began to address the congregation. She quoted scripture, saying that homosexuality was an abomination and a sin in God's eyes. Rev. Hawkes went around her, faced her with his back to the congregation and asked her to stop. In response, she pushed or shoved him with her right hand. As a result, Rev. Hawkes stumbled backwards, towards the congregation, and almost fell over a pew that was two or three feet behind him. He did not fall and he was not injured in the incident. He turned to the congregation and asked everyone to sing. A security officer escorted Ms. Kubassek, who was screaming and throwing biblical pamphlets in the air, out of the church.

5 Ms. Kubassek was charged with assault. The trial judge found that she had intended to push Rev. Hawkes, but he dismissed the charge against her on the basis of the principle *de minimis non curat lex*: the law does not concern itself with trifles. The Crown appealed her acquittal to the summary conviction appeal court. The summary conviction appeal court judge agreed that the push had been intentional, but concurred with the trial judge that the *de minimis* principle applied. He affirmed Ms. Kubassek's acquittal.

6 The Crown now seeks leave to appeal and, if granted, to appeal from the decision of the summary conviction appeal court. For the reasons that follow, I would grant leave, allow the appeal, enter a finding of guilt and direct an absolute discharge.

De Minimis Non Curat Lex

17 The Crown's position on this appeal reduces itself to two basic submissions. The first is that the principle *de minimis non curat lex* has no application as a defence in criminal law. The second is that, even if can be raised as a defence

in criminal proceedings, the principle was not available in the circumstances of this case.

18   I agree with the Crown's second submission and do not find it necessary to decide the first.

19   The principle *de minimis non curat lex* is of considerable antiquity. The first record of the principle in the law reports is found in *Taverner v. Dominum Cromwell* (1594), 78 E.R. 601. Over two centuries later, the meaning of the expression was amplified in a case involving the seizure of a British ship for breach of British revenue laws by exporting logwood from Jamaica to the United States, which prohibited its importation: *The Reward* (1818), 2 Dods. 265, 165 E.R. 1482. In rejecting an invitation by the owners of the ship to reverse its condemnation because of the relative insignificance of the amount of logwood in issue, Sir Walter Scott (later Lord Stowell) said, at 269-270 Dods., 1484 E.R.:

> The court is not bound to a strictness at once harsh and pedantic in the application of statutes. The law permits the qualification implied in the ancient maxim, *de minimis non curat lex*. Where there are irregularities of very slight consequence, it does not intend that the infliction of penalties should be inflexibly severe. If the deviation were a mere trifle, which, if continued in practice, would weigh little or nothing on the public interest, it might properly be overlooked.

20   Within the last decade, the Supreme Court of Canada has touched upon, but not resolved, the question whether the *de minimis* principle provides a defence to a criminal charge. In *R. v. Hinchey*, [1996] 3 S.C.R. 1128, 111 C.C.C. (3d) 353 (S.C.C.), which involved a charge of corruption of a government employee, L'Heureux-Dubé J., writing for the majority of the court, acknowledged the possibility that the *de minimis* principle might operate as a defence to criminal culpability, but specifically left the question open. She said in obiter, at para. 691:

> [A]ssuming that situations could still arise which do not warrant a criminal sanction, there might be another method to avoid entering a conviction: the principle of *de minimis non curat lex*, that "the law does not concern itself with trifles". This type of solution to cases where an accused has "technically" violated a Code section has been proposed by the Canadian Bar Association, in *Principles of Criminal Liability* (Ottawa: The Association, 1992), and others: see Professor Stuart, *Canadian Criminal Law*, 3rd ed. (Scarborough, Ont.: Carswell, 1995) at pp. 542-46. I am aware, however, that this principle's potential application as a defence to criminal culpability has not yet been decided by this court, and would appear to be the subject of some debate in the courts below. Since a resolution of this issue is not strictly necessary to decide this case, I would prefer to leave this issue for another day.

21   In *Canadian Foundation for Children, Youth and the Law v. Canada (Attorney General)*, [2004] 1 S.C.R. 76, 180 C.C.C. (3d) 353, the Supreme Court upheld the constitutionality of s. 43 of the *Criminal Code*, which provided that schoolteachers, parents or persons standing in the place of a parent were justified in using force by way of correction of a child under their care if the force did

not exceed what was reasonable in the circumstances. The decision of the majority was rendered by McLachlin C.J.C. Binnie, Arbour and Deschamps JJ. each wrote dissenting reasons. In Arbour J.'s dissent, she expressed the view that *de minimis non curat lex* does exist as a common law defence: see paras. 200-208. But all that McLachlin C.J.C., speaking for the majority of the court, said on the subject, at para. 44, was:

> Arbour J. argues that parents who face criminal charges as a result of corrective force will be able to rely on the defences of necessity and "*de minimis*". The defence of necessity, I agree, is available, but only in situations where corrective force is not in issue, like saving a child from imminent danger. As for the defence of *de minimis*, it is equally or more vague and difficult in application than the reasonableness defence offered by s. 43.

22 Like L'Heureux-Dubé J. in Hinchey and McLachlin C.J.C. in *Canadian Foundation*, I do not find it necessary to determine in the present case whether the *de minimis* principle operates as a defence in criminal law. I say that because even assuming, for the purpose of disposition of this appeal, that it does, the application of the label "trifling" to Ms. Kubassek's conduct constituted an error of law that is amenable to correction by this court.

The Present Case

23 In reaching the conclusion that Ms. Kubassek's conduct was not trivial, I have considered both the assault itself and the context in which it took place.

24 Ms. Kubassek's act of pushing or shoving Rev. Hawkes was intentional. Although he suffered no injury, he did fall backwards and almost tripped over a pew that was behind him. It is instructive to recall the circumstances in which the assault took place. The respondent chose to come to Metropolitan Community Church that Sunday morning. She chose to come to the front of the church for a purpose unconnected with the invitation extended to the congregation. She chose to deliver a message that she knew would fall on unreceptive ears. She chose to ignore the request of the senior pastor of the church not to interrupt the service. She chose to push or shove him to the side so that she could finish what she had to say. That he tripped, but did not fall or suffer injury, was purely fortuitous. She could fully have expected (as the trial judge found) that to go up to the front and preach to the congregants in terms she knew would be offensive could cause a disturbance. Against this backdrop, the push or shove that she intentionally applied to Rev. Hawkes cannot appropriately be characterized as an "irregularit[y] of very slight consequence ... a mere trifle, which, if continued in practice, would weigh little or nothing on the public interest" (*The Reward* (1818), 2 Dods. 265, 165 E.R. 1482: see para. 19). To minimize the assault by ascribing to it the designation "trifling" or "trivial" is to ignore the realities of what transpired between Ms. Kubassek and Rev. Hawkes that Sunday morning.

25 In the result, I conclude that the facts in the present case cannot be said to fall within the ambit of the defence (assuming it to be a defence available at law) of *de minimis non curat lex* and that the Crown's appeal must succeed.

Disposition

26 During the course of the argument, the court suggested to counsel that, if the Crown's appeal were to succeed, it might be appropriate at the penalty stage that Ms. Kubassek be given an absolute discharge. Neither counsel resisted that suggestion, and I consider it to be fair and reasonable.

27 Accordingly, I would grant the Crown's application for leave to appeal and would allow the appeal. I would set aside the respondent's acquittal, enter a finding of guilt, and order that she be discharged absolutely.

. . . .

Do you agree with the trial judge or the Ontario Court of Appeal? The Court of Appeal decides on the remedy of an absolute discharge. The suggested advantage of a judicial power to acquit (or stay) on the basis that the matter is too trivial is that it would be a vehicle for using the criminal sanction with restraint. There would be no criminal record. In contrast the legal effect of a discharge under the *Criminal Code* is that the accused is deemed not to have been convicted. Under the *Criminal Records Act*, R.S. C. 1985, s. 6.1(1) records are maintained and may be disclosed to anyone for a year. After the year disclosure to the police is still allowed: s. 6.2.

The suggested disadvantage to a *de minimis* defence is that it is the role of the Crown, not the judge, to decide whether charges should be laid: the judge's job is to decide whether all the elements of the offence have been proven, not whether he or she approves of the prosecution being brought. To allow a judge to refuse to convict a person where the elements of the offence have been proven can be said to undermine the rule of law.

Earlier in *R. v. Carson* (2004), 185 C.C.C. (3d) 541 (Ont. C.A.), leave to appeal refused (2004), 187 C.C.C. (3d) vi (S.C.C.) the court, with very little analysis, held that the *de minimis* principle had no application to cases involving "the use of force or domestic violence" (at 549).

3. OMISSIONS — LEGAL DUTIES TO ACT

(a) Moral and Legal Duties

As observed earlier, the strong tendency of the criminal law is to require an act on the part of the accused before criminal liability can attach. There are explicit exceptions to this rule, however, in which omissions are made criminal. Under s. 21(1)(b), for example, a party to an offence is someone who:

does or omits to do anything for the purpose of aiding any person to commit it.

In other cases the situation is less clear. Section 446.1, for example, makes the owner of an animal guilty of an offence if he or she "wilfully permits [the animal] to be caused unnecessary pain". The general rule is that positive action is required for liability, but the language of "permitting" might imply that an omission is sufficient in this case.

Often, in cases where an omission is explicitly criminalized it is done so on the basis that an accused had a duty to act. See, for example, the definition of criminal negligence in s. 219, which deals in part with the behaviour of a person:

(a) in doing anything, or

(b) in omitting to do anything that it is his duty to do.

The general common-law principle is that criminal responsibility for omissions is limited to cases where there is a legal and not merely a moral duty to act. A failure to fulfil the moral duty to stop a blind man walking over a cliff, or an animal drowning in a pool, or a person from being stabbed is therefore insufficient to attract the criminal sanction. The vital question of whether there is a legal duty to act is, however, a difficult one to answer with any precision.

BUCH v. AMORY MORTGAGE CO.

(1898), 44 A. 809 at 810 (N.H. S.C.)

CARPENTER C.J.: —

. . . .

With purely moral obligations the law does not deal. For example, the priest and Levite who passed by on the other side were not, it is supposed, liable at law for the continued suffering of the man who fell among thieves, which they might, and morally ought to have, prevented or relieved. Suppose A., standing close by a railroad, sees a two year old babe on the track, and a car approaching. He can easily rescue the child, with entire safety to himself, and the instincts of humanity require him to do so. If he does not, he may, perhaps, justly be styled a ruthless savage and a moral monster; but he is not liable in damages for the child's injury, or indictable under the statute for its death.

H.R.S. RYAN, CRIMINAL RESPONSIBILITY FOR OMISSIONS

(1967), Study Note

In the debate between Bentham and Macaulay — at long range, at the distance of two generations — the former would impose on everybody a duty to act to save another from harm when he can do so without prejudicing himself. So, we may note, would Bracton, writing in mid-13th century.

Bentham used the following examples:

(1) A woman's headdress catches fire;
(2) A drunken man falls face down into a puddle of water;
(3) A man with a lighted candle in his hand is about to enter a room in which gunpowder is lying scattered about.

In each case, somebody who is present and aware of the danger can easily prevent harm without the slightest danger to himself but omits to act and harm follows as a consequence.

"Who is there," asks Bentham, "That in these cases would think punishment misapplied?"

Livingstone, the American early 19th-century theorist and code maker, in his draft *Criminal Code* for Louisiana, proposed to constitute an offence of criminal homicide consisting of death following upon an omission to save life if the accused could have saved the life without personal danger or pecuniary loss.

But Macaulay, the draftsman of the *Indian Penal Code*, rejected this theory and the proposals based on it. He based his rejection on the great difficulty, if not impossibility of defining the conditions and limitations of guilt. His reasoning followed these lines:

(a) Suppose I have refused food to a beggar who must die unless I gave it to him and who has died. Am I guilty of criminal homicide? You cannot answer, "Yes", in all circumstances.

What if I myself am a beggar and have barely a crust between me and starvation?

What if my wife and children are hungry and wish to eat the food?

Are these two cases the same as if I am rich and need too much?

It may seem clear that I am not guilty in the first case. What about the second?

You can imagine an infinite number of readily possible cases in which the answer must be in doubt.

(b) Again, suppose I am a physician coming upon the scene of an accident and finding a victim bleeding to death and refuse to look after him. Am I guilty of criminal homicide?

What if I am on my way to treat a family all of whom are in danger of death from poison accidently taken?

What if I have been on duty for 48 hours at the scene of a disaster and am exhausted?

(c) If I am a surgeon and refuse to operate to save a life, will it make a difference whether I would have to walk a block to do it, or go to Barrifield? Or to Napanee? Or Belleville? Or Windsor?

(d) How far should I travel to give warning of an impending flood? 50 yards? Half a mile? Ten miles?

Many of Macaulay's examples clearly fall outside Bentham's limitation "without prejudicing himself" and Livingstone's "without personal danger or pecuniary loss" but he demonstrates the difficulty in practice of defining the limits of an offence based on an omission. It is, however, arguable that the offence could be so defined as to include only situations in which it is clearly demonstrated beyond question that the actor could have acted without in any way prejudicing himself personally or in property.

In Macaulay's draft *Code*, it was provided that an omission should be illegal if it had caused and had been intended to cause harm or was known to be likely to cause harm or was on other grounds illegal, that is, an offence in itself or a breach of some direction of law, or such a wrong as would be a good ground for a civil action.

He said that any further duty to act must be moral and not legal, enforced by public opinion and by teaching precepts of religion and morality.

As Jerome Hall points out, Macaulay and the English courts of the 18th and early 19th century had reached the same position.

Stephen, the draftsman of the *English Draft Code of 1878* on which the departmental draftsmen of the *Canadian Criminal Code of 1892* drew heavily, accepted Macaulay's position, and it appears in our present *Code*.

QUEBEC CHARTER OF HUMAN RIGHTS AND FREEDOMS

R.S.Q. 1980, c. C-12

2. Every human being whose life is in peril has a right to assistance. Every person must come to the aid of anyone whose life is in peril either personally or calling for aid, by giving him the necessary and immediate physical assistance, unless it involves danger to himself or a third person, or he has another valid reason.

For an assertion that this provision in the Quebec *Charter* has had a marked educative effect on the medical profession see S. Rodgers, "The Right to Emergency Medical Assistance in the Province of Quebec" (1980), 40 R. du B. 373.

FRENCH PENAL CODE

Article 63, translated by G. Hughes in "Criminal Omissions"
(1958), 67 Yale L.J. 590 at 632

Whoever is able to prevent by his immediate action, without risk to himself or others, the commission of a serious crime or offence against the person, and voluntarily neglects to do so shall be liable to imprisonment from one month to three years and a fine of 24,000 to 1,000,000 francs, or one of these penalties only.

The same punishments are applicable to one who voluntarily neglects to give to a person in peril assistance which he could render without risk to himself or others whether by his personal action or by procuring aid.

Should there be a criminal offence for failing to assist another whose safety is threatened?

(b)   What is an Omission?

O.W. HOLMES, THE COMMON LAW

Howe, ed., (1963), 218-219

Although a man has a perfect right to stand by and see his neighbor's property destroyed, or, for the matter of that, to watch his neighbor perish for want of his help, yet if he once intermeddles he has no longer the same freedom. He cannot withdraw at will. To give a more specific example, if a surgeon from benevolence cuts the umbilical cord of a newly-born child, he cannot stop there and watch the patient bleed to death. It would be murder wilfully to allow death to come to pass in that way, as much as if the intention had been entertained at the time of cutting the cord. It would not matter whether the wickedness began with the act, or with the subsequent omission.

FAGAN v. COMMISSIONER OF METROPOLITAN POLICE

[1968] 3 All E.R. 442 (C.A.)

July 31. LORD PARKER C.J.: — I will ask James J. to read the judgment which he has prepared, and with which I entirely agree.

JAMES J.: — The appellant, Vincent Martel Fagan, was convicted by the Willesden magistrates of assaulting David Morris, a police constable, in the execution of his duty on August 31, 1967. He appealed to quarter sessions. On October 25, 1967, his appeal was heard by Middlesex Quarter Sessions and was dismissed. This matter now comes before the court on appeal by way of case stated from that decision of quarter sessions.

The sole question is whether the prosecution proved facts which in law amounted to an assault.

On August 31, 1967, the appellant was reversing a motor car in Fortunegate Road, London, N.W.10, when Police Constable Morris directed him to drive the car forwards to the kerbside and standing in front of the car pointed out a suitable place in which to park. At first the appellant stopped the car too far from the kerb for the officer's liking. Morris asked him to park closer and indicated a precise spot. The appellant drove forward towards him and stopped it with the offside wheel on Morris's left foot. "Get off my foot," said the officer. "Fuck you, you can wait," said the appellant. The engine of the car stopped running. Morris repeated several times "Get off my foot." The appellant said reluctantly "Okay man, okay," and then slowly turned on the ignition of the vehicle and reversed it off the officer's foot. The appellant had either turned the ignition off to stop the engine or turned it off after the engine had stopped running.

The justices at quarter sessions on those facts were left in doubt as to whether the mounting of the wheel on the officer's foot was deliberate or accidental. They were satisfied, however, beyond all reasonable doubt that the appellant "knowingly, provocatively and unnecessarily allowed the wheel to remain on the foot after the officer said 'Get off, you are on my foot'." They found that on those facts an assault was proved.

Mr. Abbas for the appellant relied upon the passage in Stone's Justices' Manual (1968), Vol. 1, p. 651, where assault is defined. He contends that on the finding of the justices the initial mounting of the wheel could not be an assault and that the act of the wheel mounting the foot came to an end without there being any *mens rea*. It is argued that thereafter there was no act on the part of the appellant which could constitute an *actus reus* but only the omission or failure to remove the wheel as soon as he was asked. That failure, it is said, could not in law be an assault, nor could it in law provide the necessary *mens rea* to convert the original act of mounting the foot into an assault.

Mr. Rant for the respondent argues that the first mounting of the foot was an *actus reus* which act continued until the moment of time at which the wheel was removed. During that continuing act, it is said, the appellant formed the necessary intention to constitute the element of *mens rea* and once that element was added to the continuing act, an assault took place. In the alternative, Mr. Rant argues that there can be situations in which there is a duty to act and that in such situations an omission to act in breach of duty would in law amount to an assault. It is unnecessary to formulate any concluded views on this alternative.

In our judgment the question arising, which has been argued on general principles, falls to be decided on the facts of the particular case. An assault is any act which intentionally — or possibly recklessly — causes another person to apprehend immediate and unlawful personal violence. An assault may be committed by the laying of a hand upon another, and the action does not cease to be an assault if it is a stick held in the hand and not the hand itself which is laid on the person of the victim. So for our part we see no difference in principle between the action of stepping on to a person's toe and maintaining that position and the action of driving a car on to a person's foot and sitting in the car whilst its position on the foot is maintained.

To constitute the offence of assault some intentional act must have been performed: a mere omission to act cannot amount to an assault. Without going into the question whether words alone can constitute an assault, it is clear that the words spoken by the appellant could not alone amount to an assault: they can only shed a light on the appellant's action. For our part we think the crucial question is whether in this case the act of the appellant can be said to be complete and spent at the moment of time when the car wheel came to rest on the foot or whether his act is to be regarded as a continuing act operating until the wheel was removed. In our judgment a distinction is to be drawn between acts which are complete — though results may continue to flow — and those acts which are continuing. Once the act is complete it cannot thereafter be said to be a threat to inflict unlawful force upon the victim. If the act, as distinct from the results thereof, is a continuing act there is a continuing threat to inflict unlawful force.

For an assault to be committed both the elements of *actus reus* and *mens rea* must be present at the same time. The "*actus reus*" is the action causing the effect on the victim's mind (see the observations of Park B. in *Regina v. St. George*). The "*mens rea*" is the intention to cause that effect. It is not necessary that *mens rea* should be present at the inception of the *actus reus*; it can be superimposed upon an existing act. On the other hand the subsequent inception of *mens rea* cannot convert an act which has been completed without *mens rea* into an assault.

In our judgment the Willesden magistrates and quarter sessions were right in law. On the facts found the action of the appellant may have been initially unintentional, but the time came when knowing that the wheel was on the officer's foot the appellant (1) remained seated in the car so that his body through the medium of the car was in contact with the officer, (2) switched off the ignition of the car, (3) maintained the wheel of the car on the foot and (4) used words indicating the intention of keeping the wheel in that position. For our part we cannot regard such conduct as mere omission or inactivity.

There was an act constituting a battery which at its inception was not criminal because there was no element of intention but which became criminal from the moment the intention was formed to produce the apprehension which was flowing from the continuing act. The fallacy of the appellant's argument is that it seeks to equate the facts of this case with such a case as where a motorist has accidentally run over a person and, that action having been completed, fails to assist the victim with the intent that the victim should suffer.

We would dismiss this appeal.

BRIDGE J.: — I fully agree with my Lords as to the relevant principles to be applied. No mere omission to act can amount to an assault. Both the elements of *actus reus* and *mens rea* must be present at the same time, but the one may be superimposed on the other. It is in the application of these principles to the highly unusual facts of this case that I have, with regret, reached a different conclusion from the majority of the court. I have no sympathy at all for the appellant, who behaved disgracefully. But I have been unable to find any way of regarding the facts which satisfies me that they amounted to the crime of assault. This has not been for want of trying. But at every attempt I have encountered the inescapable question: after the wheel of the appellant's car had accidentally come to rest on the constable's foot, what was it that the appellant did which constituted the act of assault? However the question is approached, the answer I feel obliged to give is: precisely nothing. The car rested on the foot by its own weight and remained stationary by its own inertia. The appellant's fault was that he omitted to manipulate the controls to set it in motion again.

Neither the fact that the appellant remained in the driver's seat nor that he switched off the ignition seem to me to be of any relevance. The constable's plight would have been no better, but might well have been worse, if the appellant had alighted from the car leaving the ignition switched on. Similarly I can get no help from the suggested analogies. If one man accidentally treads on another's toe or touches him with a stick, but deliberately maintains pressure with foot or stick after the victim protests, there is clearly an assault. But there is no true parallel between such cases and the present case. It is not, to my mind, a legitimate use of language to speak of the appellant "holding" or "maintaining" the car wheel on the constable's foot. The expression which corresponds to the reality is that used by the justices in the case stated. They say, quite rightly, that he "allowed" the wheel to remain.

With a reluctantly dissenting voice I would allow this appeal and quash the appellant's conviction.

Appeal dismissed.

We earlier considered a Supreme Court ruling looking at a series of acts as one transaction. What was that decision and what was the context?

(c) How Do Legal Duties Arise?

Sometimes by statute. For example, consider these provisions of the *Criminal Code*:

215. (1) Every one is under a legal duty

    (a) as a parent, foster parent, guardian or head of a family, to provide necessaries of life for a child under the age of 16 years;

    (b) as a married person, to provide necessaries of life to his spouse; and

    (c) to provide necessaries of life to a person under his charge if that person

        (i) is unable, by reason of detention, age, illness, mental disorder or other cause, to withdraw himself from that charge, and

        (ii) is unable to provide himself with necessaries of life.

216. Every one who undertakes to administer surgical or medical treatment to another person or to do any other lawful act that may endanger the life of another person is, except in cases of necessity, under a legal duty to have and to use reasonable knowledge, skill and care in so doing.

217. Every one who undertakes to do an act is under a legal duty to do it if an omission to do the act is or may be dangerous to life.

217.1 Every one who undertakes, or has the authority, to direct how another person does work or performs a task is under a legal duty to take reasonable steps to prevent bodily harm to that person, or any other person, arising from that work or task. [added by S.C.2003, c.21. s.3]

Can the courts create legal duties? Is this desirable? Remember s. 9 of the *Criminal Code*.

R. v. MILLER

[1983] 1 All E.R. 978, [1983] A.C. 161 (H.L.)

LORD DIPLOCK: — My Lords, the facts which give rise to this appeal are sufficiently narrated in the written statement made to the police by the appellant Miller. That statement, subject to two minor orthographical corrections, reads:

> Last night I went out for a few drinks and at closing time I went back to the house where I have been kipping for a couple of weeks. I went upstairs into the back bedroom where I've been sleeping. I lay on my mattress and lit a cigarette. I must have fell to sleep because I woke up to find the mattress on fire. I just got up and went into the next room and went back to sleep. Then the next thing I remember was the police and fire people arriving. I hadn't got anything to put the fire out with so I just left it.

He was charged on indictment with the offence of 'arson contrary to s. 1(1) and (3) of the *Criminal Damage Act, 1971*'; the particulars of offence were that he —

> on a date unknown between the 13th and 16th days of August 1980, without lawful excuse damaged by fire a house known as No. 9 Grantham Road, Sparkbrook, intending to do damage to such property or recklessly as to whether such property would be damaged.

He was tried in the Crown Court at Leicester before a recorder and a jury. He did not give evidence, and the facts as set out in his statement were not disputed. He was found guilty and sentenced to six months' imprisonment.

From his conviction he appealed to the Court of Appeal on the ground, which is one of law alone, that the undisputed facts did not disclose any offence under s. 1 of the *Criminal Damage Act 1971*. The appeal was dismissed (see [1982] 2 All E.R. 386), but leave to appeal to your Lordships' House was granted by the Court of Appeal, which certified that the following question of law of general public importance was involved:

> Whether the *actus reus* of the offence of arson is present when a Defendant accidentally starts a fire and thereafter, intending to destroy or damage property belonging to another or

being reckless as to whether any such property would be destroyed or damaged, fails to take any steps to extinguish the fire or prevent damage to such property by that fire?

The question speaks of '*actus reus*'. This expression is derived from Coke's brocard (3 Co. Inst. ch. 1, fo. 10), '*Actus non facit reum, nisi mens sit rea*,' by converting incorrectly into an adjective the word *reus* which was there used correctly in the accusative case as a noun. As long ago as 1889 in *R. v. Tolson*, [1886-90] All E.R. Rep. 26 at 36-37 Stephen J. when dealing with a statutory offence, as are your Lordships in the instant case, condemned the phrase as likely to mislead, though his criticism in that case was primarily directed to the use of the expression '*mens rea*'. In the instant case, as the argument before this House has in my view demonstrated, it is the use of the expression '*actus reus*' that is liable to mislead, since it suggests that some positive act on the part of the accused is needed to make him guilty of a crime and that a failure or omission to act is insufficient to give rise to criminal liability unless some express provision in the statute that creates the offence so provides.

My Lords, it would I think be conducive to clarity of analysis of the ingredients of a crime that is created by statute, as are the great majority of criminal offences today, if we were to avoid bad Latin and instead to think and speak (as did Stephen J. in those parts of his judgment in *R. v. Tolson* to which I referred at greater length in *Sweet v. Parsley* [1969] 1 All E.R. 347 at 361) about the conduct of the accused and his state of mind at the time of that conduct, instead of speaking of *actus reus* and *mens rea*.

. . . .

The recorder, in his lucid summing up to the jury (they took 22 minutes only to reach their verdict), told them that the accused, having by his own act started a fire in the mattress which, when he became aware of its existence, presented an obvious risk of damaging the house, became under a duty to take some action to put it out. The Court of Appeal upheld the conviction, but its ratio *decidendi* appears to be somewhat different from that of the recorder. As I understand the judgment, in effect it treats the whole course of conduct of the accused, from the moment at which he fell asleep and dropped the cigarette onto the mattress until the time the damage to the house by fire was complete, as a continuous act of the accused, and holds that it is sufficient to constitute the statutory offence of arson if at any stage in that course of conduct the state of mind of the accused, when he fails to try to prevent or minimise the damage which will result from his initial act, although it lies within his power to do so, is that of being reckless whether property belonging to another would be damaged.

My Lords, these alternative ways of analysing the legal theory that justifies a decision which has received nothing but commendation for its accord with common sense and justice have, since the publication of the judgment of the Court of Appeal in the instant case, provoked academic controversy. Each theory has distinguished support. Professor J.C. Smith espouses the 'duty theory' (see [1982] Crim. L.R. 526 at 528); Professor Glanville Williams who, after the decision of the Divisional Court in *Fagan v. Metropolitan Police Comr.*, [1968] 3 All E.R. 442 appears to have been attracted by the duty theory, now prefers that of the continuous act (see: [1982] Crim. L.R. 773). When applied to cases where a person has unknowingly done an act which sets in train events that, when he becomes aware of them, present an obvious risk that property belonging to another will be damaged, both theories lead to an identical result; and, since what your Lordships are concerned with is to give guidance to trial judges in their task of summing up to juries, I would for this purpose adopt the duty theory as being the easier to explain to a jury; though I would commend the use of the word 'responsibility', rather than 'duty' which is more appropriate to civil than to criminal law since it suggests an obligation owed to another person, *i.e.*, the person to whom the endangered property belongs, whereas a criminal statute defines combinations of conduct and state of mind which render a person liable to punishment by the state itself.

While, in the general run of cases of destruction or damage to property belonging to another by fire (or other means) where the prosecution relies on the recklessness of the accused, the direction recommended by this House in *R. v. Caldwell* is appropriate, in the exceptional case (which is most likely to be one of arson and of which the instant appeal affords a striking example), where the accused is initially unaware that he has done an act that in fact sets in train events which, by the time the accused becomes aware of them, would make it obvious to anyone who troubled to give his mind to them that they present a risk that property belonging to another would be damaged, a suitable direction to the jury would be that the accused is guilty of the offence under s. 1(1) of the 1971 Act if, when he does become aware that the events in question have happened as a result of his own act, he does not try to prevent or reduce the risk of damage by his own efforts or if necessary by sending for help from the fire brigade and the reason why he does not is either because he has not given any thought to the possibility of there being any such risk[1] or because having recognized that there was some risk involved he has decided not to try to prevent or reduce it.

So, while deprecating the use of the expression '*actus reus*' in the certified question, I would answer that question Yes and would dismiss the appeal.

---

1 We will see when we discuss the meaning of the word "recklessnees" in Chapter 3 that this statement would not be consistent with the definition of the term as it is used in Canadian jurisprudence.

MOORE v. R.

[1979] 1 S.C.R. 195, 5 C.R. (3d) 289, 43 C.C.C. (2d) 83,
1978 CarswellBC 500, 1978 CarswellBC 559

SPENCE J. (MARTLAND, RITCHIE, PIGEON and BEETZ JJ. concurring): —
This is an appeal from the judgment of the Court of Appeal for British Columbia
pronounced on June 7, 1977.

The appellant had been acquitted after his trial before His Honour Judge
Millward and a jury upon an indictment charging him:

> THAT at the City of Victoria, County of Victoria, Province of British Columbia, on the
> 19th day of April, 1976, he did unlawfully and wilfully obstruct a Peace Officer, to wit,
> Constable Sutherland, in the execution of his duty as such Peace Officer, contrary to the
> *Criminal Code* of Canada.

The appellant was acquitted by a verdict directed by the learned trial judge
at the close of the Crown's case. The facts are outlined in an admission by
counsel for Moore which I quote:

> If it please, your Honour, I have certain admission of facts to make to expedite matters.
> Firstly, I am instructed to admit that on or about the 19th of April 1976, at or about 9:10 a.m.,
> the Accused, Richard Harvey Moore, was southbound on Government Street at Pandora and
> at that intersection proceeded through a light which had not yet turned green and was, in fact
> red when he proceeded through on his ten-speed bicycle. That is the extent of my admission
> of fact.

and are further dealt with by Carrothers J.A., in his reasons for judgment as
follows [36 C.C.C. (2d) 481 at p. 489, 40 C.R.N.S. 93]:

> Constable Sutherland, a peace officer with the Victoria City Police, in uniform and on
> a motorcycle, observed this infraction on the part of Moore and set about to "ticket" Moore.
> The constable and Moore proceeded side by side on their respective cycles, with Moore
> sometime taking elusive action by riding his bicycle on the sidewalk, with the constable
> repeatedly requesting Moore to "pull over and stop" and Moore lewdly rebuffing each such
> request with an obscene demand to leave him alone as he was in a hurry. I attach no importance
> to the particular salacious vulgarity used by Moore in rejecting the policeman's request to
> stop as it has been used by the unimaginative so excessively and indiscriminately as to have
> lost its literal quality, but there is no doubt that it constituted flat refusals on the part of Moore
> to stop as requested by the policeman.

As a result of this occurrence, Moore was charged upon an indictment, as I
have said above, but he was not charged with failing to stop at a stop light only
with obstructing a peace officer in the performance of his duty. The obstruction
which the Crown put forward as constituting the offence was the failure of the
appellant to give his name when requested to do so by the police constable.

The relevant sections of the provincial statutes with which I shall deal
hereafter are as follows: first, the *Motor-vehicle Act*, R.S.B.C. 1960, c. 253.
Section 2 contains definitions of "motor-vehicle" and "vehicle", as follows:

"motor-vehicle" means a vehicle, not run upon rails, that is designed to be self-propelled or propelled by electric power obtained from overhead trolley-wires;

. . . .

"vehicle" means a device in, upon, or by which a person or thing is or may be transported or drawn upon a highway, except a device designed to be moved by human power or used exclusively upon stationary rails or tracks. [enacted 1963, c. 27, s. 2(*c*)]

Section 58 of the said *Motor-vehicle Act* provides:

58. Every person driving or operating or in charge of a motor-vehicle on any highway who refuses or fails

   (*a*) to stop his motor-vehicle when signalled or requested to stop by any police officer or constable who is in uniform or who displays his police badge conspicuously on the outside of his outer coat; or

   (*b*) to state correctly his name and address and the name and address of the owner of the motor-vehicle when requested by any peace officer or constable to state the same is guilty of an offence.

It will be seen plainly that a bicycle is neither a "motor-vehicle" nor a "vehicle" of any kind under the provisions of the aforesaid definition. A bicycle is plainly not self-propelled and, therefore, cannot be a "motor-vehicle" and it is a device designed to be moved by human power and, therefore, it cannot be a "vehicle" at all. Much argument was spent in the Court of Appeal for British Columbia and in this court in an attempt to say that although a bicycle was neither a "motor-vehicle" nor a "vehicle" s. 58 of the *Motor-vehicle Act* applied thereto because of other sections with which I shall deal hereafter. As the courts below, I am quite unable to accept any such submission and I have come to the conclusion, with respect, that the Court of Appeal for British Columbia was quite correct in holding that the respondent was not in breach of s. 58 of the *Motor-vehicle Act* when he refused to give his name to the constable.

. . . .

After detailed consideration of statutory powers, Spence J. continued:

The constable, therefore, in requesting the appellant Moore to identify himself, was carrying out the duty of enforcing the law of the Province in this summary conviction matter by attempting to identify the accused person so that he might proceed to lay an information or take the more modern form permitted under the said *Summary Convictions Act* of British Columbia of issuing a ticket.

I am of the opinion that the Court of Appeal of British Columbia was correct in finding that when the appellant Moore refused to accede to the constable's request for his identification he was obstructing that constable in the performance of his duties. As did the members of the Court of Appeal, I am confining my consideration of this matter to the actual circumstances which occurred, that is, that a constable on duty observed the appellant in the act of committing an infraction of the statute and that that constable had no power to arrest the accused for such offence unless and until he had attempted to identify the accused so that he might be the subject of summary conviction proceedings.

I also agree, with respect, with the learned members of the Court of Appeal that this conclusion in no way opposes or ignores the judgment of the Queen's Bench in *Rice v. Connolly*, [1966] 2 All E.R. 649. In that case, the appellant was seen by police officers behaving suspiciously. On being questioned, he refused to say where he was going or where he had come from. He refused to give his full name and address, although he did give a name and the name of a road which were not untrue. He refused to accompany the police to a police box for identification purposes saying, "if you want me, you will have to arrest me". He was acquitted by the Court of Appeal upon a charge of obstructing the police. It is paramount to note that the appellant there had not committed any offence in the presence or view of a police officer. He had simply been acting in what the constable regarded as a suspicious manner. I view the situation very differently when a person is actually seen by the constable committing an offence.

Therefore, for the reasons which I have outlined above, I am of the opinion that the officer was under a duty to attempt to identify the wrongdoer and the failure to identify himself by the wrongdoer did constitute an obstruction of the police officer in the performance of his duties.

I add that in coming to this conclusion I have not forgotten the provisions of the *Canadian Bill of Rights* nor the topic of individual freedom generally but I am of the opinion that there is not even minimal interference with any freedom of a citizen who is seen committing an infraction by a police constable in the police constable simply requesting his name and address without any attempt to obtain from that person any admission of fault or any comment whatsoever. On the other hand, the refusal of a citizen to identify himself under such circumstances causes a major inconvenience and obstruction to the police in carrying out their proper duties. So that if anyone were engaged in any balancing of interest, there could be no doubt that the conclusion to which I have come would be that supported by the overwhelming public interest.

I would dismiss the appeal.

DICKSON J. (dissenting) (ESTEY J. concurring): — These proceedings originated in a minor traffic infraction in the City of Victoria, British Columbia. The issue raised, however, is an important one having to do with police power of interrogation and the right of citizens to remain silent. That right has always been regarded as absolute and as being firmly anchored to two fundamental common-law principles: the presumption of innocence and the privilege against self-incrimination. Explicit statutory provisions may impose a duty upon a person to identify himself to police officers in certain situations, but in this appeal the court is being asked to impose such a duty in the absence of any statutory underpinning whatever. In more stark terms, the question is whether a person committing a petty traffic offence exposes himself to a criminal charge of "obstructing" and a maximum penalty of two years' imprisonment, if he refuses to give his name and address to a police officer.

. . . .

The general principle

Any duty to identify oneself must be found in either common law or statute, quite apart from the duties of the police. A person is not guilty of the offence of obstructing a police officer merely by doing nothing, unless there is legal duty to act. Omission to act in a particular way will give rise to criminal liability only where a duty to act arises at common law or is imposed by statute: 11 Hals., 4th ed., p. 15, para. 9. This idea was expressed by Mr. Justice Schroeder in *R. v. Patrick*, 128 C.C.C. 263 at p. 267, [1960] O.W.N. 206, 32 C.R. 338 at p. 343 (Ont. C.A.):

> Counsel for the appellant submitted that to sustain a charge of obstructing a peace officer in the execution of his duty, it was necessary for the Crown to prove either a positive act of interference, or a refusal to perform some act required to be done by a statute. . . . It not having been shown that the appellant was under any duty or obligation to communicate to the peace officer the information required of him under the provisions of either s. 221(2) of the *Cr. Code*, or s. 110(1) of the *Highway Traffic Act*, the Crown has failed to bring home to the appellant the commission of a criminal offence. This is sufficient to dispose of the appeal. . . .

The point under discussion is dealt with at some length by Dr. Glanville Williams in an article entitled "Demanding Name and Address" appearing in 66 *L.Q.R.* 465 (1950). The general principle of the common law is stated:

> neither a private person nor a constable has any effective power to demand the name and address of a person on the ground that he has committed an offence or is under a civil liability.

Dr. Williams refers to the case of *Hatton v. Treeby*, [1897] 2 Q.B. 452 as an illustration of this principle. The head note reads:

> A constable who sees a person riding a bicycle at night without a proper light, contrary to the provisions of s. 85 of the *Local Government Act, 1888*, has no power to stop him for the purpose of ascertaining his name and address.

The constable in that case called on the rider to stop, in order to ascertain his name and address. On the rider failing to do so, the constable caught hold of the handlebar of the bicycle, whereby the rider was thrown to the ground. The rider summoned the constable for assault. The Justices found that the constable did not know the name or address of the rider, and could not have ascertained his name or address in any other way than by stopping him, and that in so stopping him he used no more force than was necessary. They were of opinion that, as the rider was committing an offence punishable on summary conviction within view of the constable, the latter was justified in stopping him as he did in order to prevent a continuance of the offence and to ascertain his name and address. They accordingly dismissed the complaint, subject to a case for the opinion of the court. The appellate court held that the constable had no power to stop the bicycle rider at common law and the only question was whether he had statutory authority to do so. It was found that there was no statutory authority for the constable acting as he did. In the result the constable was convicted of assault.

No statutory duty

It appears to me impossible to extract from the statutory provisions of the British Columbia *Motor-vehicle Act*, R.S.B.C. 1960, c. 253, a duty on a cyclist, caught riding through a red light, to identify himself. Section 58 of the Act specifically places a duty on a person driving a "motor-vehicle" to state correctly his name and address when requested to do so by a peace officer. This in itself appears to recognize the absence of any such duty where there is no statutory requirement. Section 58 does not apply to persons operating either "vehicles" (as defined in s. 2) or bicycles, and there is no other provision in the *Motor-vehicle Act*, or any other relevant statute, placing such a duty on a cyclist caught committing a summary conviction offence under the *Motor-vehicle Act*.

I have had the advantage of reading the reasons of Mr. Justice Spence and I am in full agreement, for the reasons stated by him and by the Court of Appeal of British Columbia, that the accused was not in breach of s. 58 of the *Motor-vehicle Act*, when he refused to give his name and address to the constable.

. . . .

Power of arrest

. . . .

Constable Sutherland could have arrested the accused for the offence of proceeding against a red light if it were necessary to establish his identity. However, with great respect, I cannot agree that, as a consequence, the accused was guilty of the further, and much more serious, offence of obstructing the constable in the performance of his duties by refusing to divulge his name and address.

No common law duty

There is no duty at common law to identify oneself to police. As was stated by Lord Parker in *Rice v. Connolly*, [1966] 2 All E.R. 649 at p. 652 (Q.B.D.):

> It seems to me quite clear that though every citizen has a moral duty or, if you like, a social duty to assist the police, there is no legal duty to that effect, and indeed the whole basis of the common law is the right of the individual to refuse to answer questions put to him by persons in authority, and a refusal to accompany those in authority to any particular place, short, of course, of arrest.

The case stands for the proposition that refusal to identify oneself to the police could not constitute obstruction of the police. The court distinguished a refusal to answer, which is legal, from a "cock and bull" story to the police, which might constitute obstruction. No other distinction was made. Lord Parker said:

> In my judgment there is all the difference in the world between deliberately telling a false story, something which on no view a citizen has a right to do, and silence or refusing to answer, something which he has every right to do.

In *Ingleton v. Dibble*, [1972] 1 All E.R. 275 (Q.B.D.), a distinction was drawn between a refusal to act, on the one hand, and the doing of some positive act, on the other. Bridge J. (with whom Lord Widgery C.J. and Ashworth J. concurred), said, at p. 279:

> In a case, as in *Rice v. Connolly*, where the obstruction alleged consists of a refusal by the defendant to do the act which the police constable has asked him to do — to give information, it might be, or to give assistance to the police constable — one can see readily the soundness of the principle, if I may say so with respect, applied in *Rice v. Connolly*, that such a refusal to act cannot amount to a wilful obstruction under s. 51 unless the law imposes on the person concerned some obligation in the circumstances to act in the manner requested by the police officer.

The legal position in England and Wales has been described in these terms in *Police Powers in England and Wales* (1975), by Leigh, at p. 195:

> and in general it still remains the rule that a citizen has a right to be as unco-operative as he pleases, provided that he does not impede the course of justice by knowingly giving false information to the police.

In the Ontario case of *R. v. Carroll* (1959), 126 C.C.C. 19, 31 C.R. 315 (Ont. C.A.), the facts, as disclosed in the headnote, were these. The accused was charged with unlawfully and wilfully obstructing a police constable while engaged in his duties as a peace officer, contrary to s. 110(*a*) of the *Criminal Code*, 1953-54 (Can.), c. 51. The accused, in company with three other men, was proceeding along a highway at an early hour in the morning. The constable heard them whistling and yelling and he advised them to be quiet and go home. Three of the party followed his advice. The accused remained. The constable asked him to produce his identification but the accused refused to do so and proceeded on his way. The constable caught up to him and again asked accused to identify himself. An argument and struggle followed and the accused was arrested. He was later charged with obstructing a police officer and was convicted. He appealed. The conviction was quashed. It was held that under the circumstances, the accused was not under any duty to identify himself as requested.

The Crown conceded in this court that no such obligation was to be found in the common law. From whence then comes such a duty? Where does one find the legal compulsion to answer? A person cannot "obstruct" by refusing to answer a question unless he is under a legal duty to answer.

An "implied" or "reciprocal" duty?

It was strongly urged in argument before us that because a duty rested upon constables to investigate crime and enforce provincial laws, an "implied" or "reciprocal" duty rested upon a person, suspected of an infraction, to give his name and address, and refusal to do so amounted to such frustration as to constitute the offence of obstructing the police in the execution of their duty.

The Crown perforce had to fall back upon the proposition that because there was a duty upon the police officer to enquire before exercising the power to arrest under s. 450 [rep. & sub. R.S.C. 1970, c. 2, (2nd Supp.), s. 5] of the *Code*, there was a reciprocal duty upon the alleged culprit to respond. The alleged duty, as I understand the argument, is to be limited to divulging name and address, when caught in the commission of an offence and prior to arrest.

. . . .

A limited obligation to respond, effective only when the policeman is an eye witness, introduces into the criminal law, which should rest upon "broad, plain, intelligible" principles a qualification unsound in principle and unworkable in practice.

The fact that a police officer has a duty to identify a person suspected of, or seen committing, an offence says nothing about whether the person has the duty to identify himself on being asked. Each duty is entirely independent. Only if the police have a lawful claim to demand that a person identify himself, does the person have a corresponding duty to do so. As McFarlane J.A. said in *R. v. Bonnycastle*, [1969] 4 C.C.C. 198 at p. 201, 7 C.R.N.S. 37 (B.C. C.A.), the duty of a peace officer to make enquiries must not be confused with the right of a person to refuse to answer questions in circumstances where the law does not require him to answer.

The Legislature deliberately imposed a duty to identify upon the drivers of motor vehicles — perhaps because of their more lethal nature — but chose not to impose such duty on the drivers of other vehicles such as bicycles. The

Legislature must be taken to have intended to relieve bicycle riders of the duty. To require the riders of bicycles to give their names and addresses would be tantamount to amending the *Motor-Vehicle Act*. It would also appear that Parliament, in providing in ss. 450(2) and 452(1)(*f*)(i) [rep. & sub. R.S.C. 1970, c. 2 (2nd Supp.), s. 5] of the *Criminal Code* for arrest and detention for the purpose of establishing identity, did not recognize a duty to identify oneself existing apart from statute, breach of which would expose the offender to a charge of "obstructing". Examples from English legislation of statutory obligation to disclose identity to police constables, unnecessary if the obligation existed otherwise, are to be found in the *Protection of Birds Act*, 1954 (U.K.), c. 30, s. 12(i)(*a*); *Dangerous Drugs Act*, 1965 (U.K.), c. 15, s. 15; *Representation of the People Act*, 1949 (U.K.), c. 68, s. 84(3); *Road Traffic Act*, 1960 (U.K.), c. 16, s. 228; *Prevention of Crime Act*, 1953 (U.K.), c. 14, s. 1(3).

The criminal law is no place within which to introduce implied duties, unknown to statute and common law, breach of which subjects a person to arrest and imprisonment.

The "reciprocal duty" argument advanced by the Crown in this case was considered by Dr. Glanville Williams in the article to which I have referred. Dr. Williams effectively disposed of the argument in words which I should like to adopt, pp. 473-4:

> The question may be asked whether the power of the police to demand name and address is in effect generalised by the statutes creating the offence of obstructing the police in the execution of their duty — so that refusal to comply with the demand amounts to an obstruction. At first sight it would seem that a good case could be made out for an affirmative answer. Although it is not the duty of the police to prosecute every crime, it can be said to be their duty to make inquiries into crimes with a view to prosecution. The courts have held that interference with the police when they are collecting evidence of an offence constitutes an obstruction. Moreover, it has been decided that an obstruction may take place merely by a nonfeasance, where there is a refusal to comply with the lawful orders of the police. Notwithstanding these authorities, it is submitted that the refusal by an offender to give his name and address does not constitute an obstruction, for at least two reasons. First, if it were an obstruction, all the statutes making it an offence to refuse to give name and address in specific situations would have been unnecessary. When, for example, Parliament passed the *Public Order Act* in 1936, it must have been thought that the police had no general power to demand name and address. Secondly, it is a fundamental principle of English law that an accused person cannot be interrogated or at least cannot be forced to answer questions under a legal penalty if he refuses; this principle is absolute, and does not admit of exception even for a demand of name and address, unless a statute has expressly created an exception. To say that the police have a duty to gather evidence, and therefore that a criminal's refusal to give his name and address is an obstruction, is far too wide, because the same premise would yield the conclusion that a criminal's refusal to confess to the crime is an obstruction.

The views expressed by Dr. Williams were adopted in the New Zealand case of *Elder v. Evans*, [1951] N.Z.L.R. 801 at p. 806 (N.Z.S.C.).

I would allow the appeal, set aside the judgment of the Court of Appeal and restore the judgment at trial.

Appeal dismissed.

R. v. THORNTON

(1991), 3 C.R. (4th) 381, 1990 CarswellOnt 73 (Ont. C.A.)

The accused donated blood to the Red Cross. At that time the accused knew that he had twice tested positive for HIV antibodies and that he was therefore infectious. The Red Cross screening process detected the contaminated blood and it was put aside. The accused was charged that he did commit a common nuisance contrary to s. 180 of the *Criminal Code*. This section provides that every one commits a common nuisance who does an unlawful act or fails to discharge a legal duty and thereby endangers the lives, safety or health of the public. He was convicted and sentenced to a term of 15 months' imprisonment. At the trial the Crown did not argue an unlawful act but rather a failure to discharge a legal duty. The trial judge expressed concern with the Crown's position because it seemed to the court that the facts in the case might define and constitute an unlawful act. The trial judge said the conduct of the accused was conduct evidencing marked disregard for safety of others. Nevertheless the trial judge proceeded on the basis that there was an omission. The trial judge found a duty within s. 216 of the *Criminal Code* which provides:

> Everyone who undertakes to administer surgical or medical treatment to another person or to do any other lawful act that may endanger the life of another person is, except in cases of necessity, under a legal duty to have and to use reasonable knowledge, skill and care in so doing.

The trial judge decided that by donating blood to the Red Cross and knowing the purpose for which such donations are collected the accused was involved in a medical procedure. The accused appealed conviction and sentence. One of the grounds of appeal was that the accused's conduct, though reprehensible, did not amount to an offence known to the law. The appeals from conviction and sentence were dismissed.

GALLIGAN J.A. (BROOKE and DOHERTY JJ.A. concurring): —

... For the purposes of this appeal, I am prepared to assume the correctness of Mr. Greenspon's cogent argument that the words "unlawful act" must be taken to mean conduct which is specifically proscribed by legislation. The *Code* does not make it an offence to donate contaminated blood. Counsel were unable to refer the court to any other statutory provision, federal or provincial, which does so. On the assumption, therefore, that the appellant's conduct could not constitute an act", I will examine whether it amounted to a failure to discharge a "legal duty".

I am unable to find any provision in the *Code*, or any other statute which I can read, as specifically imposing a legal duty upon a person to refrain from donating contaminated blood. The immediate issue therefore is two-fold. Can a "legal duty" within the meaning of s. 180(2) be one which arises at common-law, or must it be one found in a statute? Is there a "legal duty" arising at common law the breach of which, assuming the other essential elements of the offence were proved, could be the basis of an offence under s. 180?

There are no cases deciding whether the "legal duty" in s. 180(2) must be a duty imposed by statute or whether it can be a duty according to common law. However, the "duty imposed by law" which forms part of the definition of criminal negligence set out in s. 219 of the *Code* has been held to be either a duty imposed by statute or a duty arising at common law.

. . . .

In *R. v. Coyne* (1958), 31 C.R. 335, 124 C.C.C. 176, the New Brunswick Supreme Court, Appeal Division, considered the criminal negligence provisions of the *Code* in relation to a hunting accident. Speaking for that court, Ritchie J.A. held at pp. 179-180 [C.C.C., p. 338 C.R.]:

> The "duty imposed by law" may be a duty arising by virtue of either the common law or by statute. Use of a firearm, in the absence of proper caution, may readily endanger the lives or safety of others. Under the common law anyone carrying such a dangerous weapon as a rifle is under the duty to take such precaution in its use as, in the circumstances, would be observed by a reasonably careful man. If he fails in that duty and his behaviour is of such a character as to show or display a wanton or reckless disregard for the lives or safety of other persons, then, by virtue of s. 191, his conduct amounts to criminal negligence.

In *R. v. Popen* (1981), 60 C.C.C. (2d) 232, this court also had occasion to consider the nature of the "duty imposed by law" contained in the definition of criminal negligence. It was a child abuse case. In giving the judgment of the court, Martin J.A. said at p. 240 [C.C.C.]:

> [A] parent is under a legal duty at common law to take reasonable steps to protect his or her child from illegal violence used by the other parent or by a third person towards the child which the parent foresees or ought to foresee.

The effect of that judgment is to hold that the common law duty, which was there described, was a "duty imposed by law" within the meaning of s. 219 because the court held that its breach could amount to criminal negligence.

These decisions lead me to the opinion that it is well settled that, for the purpose of defining criminal negligence, a "duty imposed by law" includes a duty which arises at common law.

While the words "legal duty" in s. 180(2) are not the same as a "duty imposed by law" used in s. 219, they have exactly the same meaning. It follows therefore that the meaning given to a "duty imposed by law" in s. 219 should also be given to the "legal duty" contained in s. 180(2). Thus, I am of the opinion that the legal duty referred to in s. 180(2) is a duty which is imposed by statute or which arises at common law. It becomes necessary, then, to decide whether at common law there is a duty which would prohibit the donating of blood known to be HIV-contaminated to the Red Cross.

While this is not a civil case and the principles of tort law are not directly applicable to it, the jurisprudence on that subject is replete with discussions about the legal duties of one person to another which arise at common law. The jurisprudence is constant that those duties are legal ones: that is, they are ones which are imposed by law. Throughout this century and indeed since much earlier times, the common law has recognized a very fundamental duty, which while it has many qualifications, can be summed up as being a duty to refrain from conduct which could cause injury to another person.

This is not the place to make a detailed examination of the jurisprudence on the subject of tort law but a few references to authority are in order.

. . . .

In the course of his oft-quoted speech in the famous case of *M'Alister or (Donoghue) v. Stevenson*, [1932] A.C. 562 (H.L.), Lord Atkin said at p. 580 [A.C.]:

> The rule that you are to love your neighbour becomes, in law, you must not injure your neighbour.

. . . .

That brief reference to jurisprudence in civil matters shows that there is deeply embedded in the common law a broad fundamental duty which, although subject to many qualifications, requires everyone to refrain from conduct which could injure another. It is not necessary to decide in this case how far that duty extends. At the very least, however, it requires everyone to refrain from conduct which it is reasonably foreseeable could cause serious harm to other persons. Accepting, as I have said, that a duty" within the meaning of that term in s. 180(2) includes a duty arising at common law, I think that the common law duty to refrain from conduct which it is reasonably foreseeable could cause serious harm to other persons is a "legal duty" within the meaning of that term in s. 180(2).

Donating blood which one knows to be HIV-contaminated to an organization whose purpose is to make the blood available for transfusion to other persons, clearly constitutes a breach of the common law duty to refrain from conduct which one foresees could cause serious harm to another person. It is thus a failure to discharge a "legal duty" within the contemplation of s. 180(2). It is therefore my conclusion that the indictment which alleges the commission of a nuisance by the donation of blood which the appellant knew to be HIV-contaminated does allege an offence known to law. The first argument made by counsel for the appellant cannot be accepted.

. . . .

In the light of the findings of the trial judge on the issue of credibility, and in the light of all of the other evidence, there can be no doubt that this appellant had personal knowledge that he should not donate his blood, that it was possible for it to get through the testing screen, and that it could cause serious damage to the life and health of members of the public. It follows that he knew that, by giving his blood to the Red Cross, he was endangering the lives and health of other members of the public. ... This appellant knew personally the danger to which the public was subjected by his donation of blood. He clearly had *mens rea*. ...

It is my opinion that the appellant was properly convicted of the offence under s. 180. Accordingly, I would dismiss the appeal from conviction.

With respect to sentence, the trial judge did not impose the maximum sentence prescribed by law. The maximum sentence must be reserved for the worst offender committing the worst category of the offence. The sentence imposed took into account that, because of his prior good record, the appellant would not fall into the category of the worst offender. The offence, however, can certainly be categorized as among the worst offences. The appellant's conduct verges on the unspeakable. It cried out for a sentence which would act as a deterrent to others and which would express society's repudiation of what he did. One must have great compassion for this man. He faces a terrible future. Nevertheless, the sentence demonstrates no error in principle and is one that is eminently fit.

The important issue of principle of whether a criminal omission can be based on a common-law duty, in apparent violation of s. 9(*a*) of the *Criminal Code*, was unfortunately avoided when *Thornton* reached the Supreme Court.

THORNTON v. R.

[1993] 2 S.C.R. 445, 21 C.R. (4th) 215, 82 C.C.C. (3d) 530,
1993 CarswellOnt 98, 1983 CarswellOnt 982

LAMER C.J. (for a unanimous nine-person court, orally): — Section 216 imposed upon the [accused] a duty of care in giving his blood to the Red Cross. This duty of care was breached by not disclosing that his blood contained HIV antibodies. This common nuisance obviously endangered the life, safety and health of the public.

The above is the complete judgment of the court. The court appears to read s. 216 literally to impose a duty of care on those doing lawful acts which endanger others' lives. This seems to establish a new wide measure of criminal responsibility for omissions.

Do you prefer the interpretation of the trial judge, the Court of Appeal or the Supreme Court? Justify your preference.

See, more generally, Winnie Holland, "HIV/AIDS and the Criminal Law" (1994), 36 *Crim. L.Q.* 279.

R. v. BROWNE

(1997), 116 C.C.C. (3d) 183, 1997 CarswellOnt 1715 (Ont. C.A.),
leave to appeal refused (1997), 225 N.R. 396 (note) (S.C.C.)

The accused and the deceased were partners in drug dealing. The deceased swallowed a plastic bag of crack cocaine to avoid detection when they were strip-searched by police. She tried unsuccessfully to vomit it up. Later that night the accused found her shaking and sweating. He said he would take her to hospital. He called for a cab which took ten minutes to arrive and a further 15 minutes to get her to hospital. She had no pulse or heartbeat and was pronounced dead shortly after arrival.

ABELLA J.A. (CATZMAN and LABROSSE JJ.A. concurring): —

. . . .

The statement found by the trial judge to constitute an "undertaking" by Browne is underlined.

> He called her name a couple of times and she did not answer at first, but then she said yes. He said, "*I'm going to take you to the hospital.*" He helped her up the stairs. He asked her if she could get up and there was no response. She sat up and she put her arm around him and he put his arm around her waist and they walked up the stairs. She could not walk on her own. He called a taxi. He testified she got heavy and he laid her on the floor by the front door and waited 10 to 15 minutes for the taxi. She was still sweating, shaking, and was mumbling. The taxi arrived and he could not pick her up and asked his brother to help him take her to the taxi.

. . . .

On her arrival at the hospital, Greiner had no pulse and no heartbeat. She was pronounced dead at 3:10 a.m.

The trial judge found that the appellant told Ms. Greiner at about 2:00 a.m. that he would take her to the hospital and "immediately thereafter embarked on that act". She concluded that this statement was an "undertaking" within the meaning of s. 217 of the *Criminal Code*.

The circumstances giving rise to a legal duty were summarized by the trial judge in the following passages:

> By taking charge of Audrey Greiner after he knew that she had ingested crack, Dexter Browne undertook to care for her while the crack was in her body. That undertaking included rendering

assistance to her which required taking her to the hospital immediately. On this basis, the legal duty to Audrey Greiner within the meaning of section 217 arose just after 11:30 when the accused knew that Audrey Greiner had not vomited the crack cocaine.

Although Dexter Browne testified that he did not say to Audrey Greiner that he would take care of her if something bad happened, he did admit that he would take care of her if she sold to someone who tried to rob her or anything like that.

. . . .

Using a taxi instead of calling 911 reflected, according to the trial judge, a "wanton and reckless disregard" for Audrey Greiner's life contrary to s. 219(1) of the *Criminal Code*.

Analysis

The charge of criminal negligence against the appellant was particularized as follows, mirroring the language found in s. 217 of the *Criminal Code*:

. . . that he . . . failed to render assistance to Audrey Greiner by failing to take her immediately to the hospital after undertaking to render such assistance and did thereby cause the death of Audrey Greiner . . .

The particularization of the charge in this way meant that to find a legal duty, there had first to be a finding of an undertaking. This flows from the language of s. 217 which states that everyone "who *undertakes* to do an act is under a legal duty to do it if an omission to do the act is or may be dangerous to life". In other words, the legal duty does not flow from the relationship between the parties, as it does in s. 215, which creates legal duties between spouses, between parents and children, and between dependants and their caregivers. Under s. 217, there is no pre-existing relationship or situation that creates a legal duty; there must be an undertaking before a legal duty is introduced into the relationship. The relationship or context is relevant only to the determination of whether the breach reflected a "wanton or reckless disregard" under s. 219(1), not to whether there was an undertaking under s. 217.

What kind of an undertaking gives rise to a legal duty within the meaning of s. 217, the breach of which can result in criminal culpability? In my view, the ordinary dictionary definition of "undertaking" is of little assistance. There is no doubt that the definition embraces an interpretive continuum ranging from an assertion to a promise. But it seems to me that when we are deciding whether conduct is caught by the web of criminal liability, the threshold definition we apply must justify penal sanctions. A conviction for criminal negligence causing death carries a maximum penalty of life imprisonment. The word "undertaking" in s. 217 must be interpreted in this context. The threshold definition must be sufficiently high to justify such serious penal consequences. The mere expression of words indicating a willingness to do an act cannot trigger the legal duty.

There must be something in the nature of a commitment, generally, though not necessarily, upon which reliance can reasonably be said to have been placed.

Any other interpretation of "undertaking" imports theories of civil negligence, rendering individuals who breach civil standards of care susceptible to imprisonment. The criminal standard must be — and is — different and higher. Before someone is convicted of recklessly breaching a legal duty generated by his or her undertaking, that undertaking must have been clearly made, and with binding intent. Nothing short of such a binding commitment can give rise to the legal duty contemplated by s. 217.

The trial judge found that the relationship between Dexter Browne and Audrey Greiner as partners in drug dealing gave rise to an implicit undertaking by Browne that he would take Audrey Greiner to the hospital whenever she swallowed cocaine. The fundamental error made by the trial judge was in reversing the analytical steps under s. 217 by starting her analysis with whether a duty of care existed, finding that it did, and then basing her finding of an undertaking on the existence of a legal duty. The inquiry should have begun with whether there was an undertaking. Only if there was an undertaking in the nature of a binding commitment could a legal duty have arisen under s. 217, regardless of the nature of the relationship between the appellant and Audrey Greiner.

In my view, the evidence does not disclose any undertaking of a binding nature. These were two drug dealers who were used to swallowing bags of drugs to avoid detection by the police. There was no evidence that the appellant knew that Audrey Greiner was in a life-threatening situation until 2:00 a.m., when he immediately phoned for a taxi. His words to her at that time — "I'll take you to the hospital" — hardly constitute an undertaking creating a legal duty under s. 217. He said he would take her to the hospital when he saw the severity of her symptoms, and he did. There is no evidence either that a 911 call would have resulted in a significantly quicker arrival at the hospital at that hour, or even that had she arrived earlier, Audrey Greiner's life could have been saved.

There being no undertaking within the meaning of s. 217 of the *Criminal Code*, there can be no finding of a legal duty. There being no duty, there can be no breach contrary to s. 219 of the *Code*.

. . . .

Accordingly, I would allow the appeal, set aside the conviction, and enter an acquittal.

R. v. PETERSON

[2005] O.J. No. 4450, 2005 CarswellOnt 5093, 201 C.C.C. (3d) 220 (C.A.),
leave to appeal refused (2006), 2006 CarswellOnt 1198, 2006 CarswellOnt
1199 (S.C.C.)

1 WEILER J.A. (ARMSTRONG J.A. concurring).:— This appeal requires us to consider when a parent is under the charge of a child thereby requiring the child to provide necessaries of life to that parent pursuant to s. 215 of the *Criminal Code*. The relevant portion of s. 215 states:

> (1) Every one is under a legal duty
>
> . . . .
>
> (c) to provide necessaries of life to a person under his charge if that person
>
>> (i) is unable, by reason of detention, age, illness, mental disorder or other cause, to withdraw himself from that charge, and
>>
>> (ii) is unable to provide himself with necessaries of life.
>
> (2) Every one commits an offence who, being under a legal duty within the meaning of subsection (1), fails without lawful excuse, the proof of which lies upon him,[2] to perform that duty, if
>
> . . . .
>
> (b) with respect to a duty imposed by paragraph (1)(c), the failure to perform the duty endangers the life of the person to whom the duty is owed or causes or is likely to cause the health of that person to be injured permanently.
>
> (3) Every one who commits an offence under subsection (2) is guilty of
>
> (a) an indictable offence and is liable to imprisonment for a term not exceeding two years; or
>
> (b) an offence punishable on summary conviction.

2 Because several members of the affected family have the same last name, where it is not possible to use the last name to identify the person, the first name has been used. No disrespect is intended by this practice.

3 On September 20, 2002, Dennis Peterson was convicted of failing to provide the necessaries of life to his father, Arnold Peterson, thereby endangering Arnold's life. Dennis was sentenced to six months imprisonment, two years probation, and one hundred hours community service on November 15, 2002.

---

2 At trial, it was accepted by counsel that the reverse onus is unconstitutional and that the onus is on the Crown to prove the essential elements of the charge beyond a reasonable doubt.

He appeals from his conviction, seeks leave to appeal his sentence, and, if leave is granted, appeals his sentence.

4 Dennis appeals his conviction on two bases. He submits that the reasons of the trial judge fail to satisfy the functional need to know the basis on which the conviction was entered and, accordingly, a new trial is necessary. Alternatively, Dennis submits that the evidence does not support a finding that Arnold was under his charge. Dennis also submits that the sentence was harsh and excessive in the circumstances.

5 For the reasons that follow I would dismiss the appeal from both conviction and sentence.

Factual Background

6 For over forty years, Arnold, who was approximately eight-four years old in 2000, lived in his three-story house in Toronto. For a period of time, Arnold lived with his adult son, Dennis; daughter, Linda Peterson; grandson, Derek Joyce; and the grandson's girlfriend, Laura Scriver. At that time the house was "open" in the sense that it was not divided into apartments. Linda moved out in January 1999. At the time of the events in question, the house was divided into apartments. Arnold occupied the first floor and the basement. Dennis lived on the second floor and occupied a living room on the first floor. Joyce lived on the third floor. An internal staircase linked the apartments. Dennis kept the doors to the upstairs apartments and to the main floor living room locked.

7 Arnold's living quarters were in disrepair to the point that the kitchen did not function. It had no drywall and the floorboards were lifting. It was also filled with dead cockroaches. Dirty dishes were stacked on the counter and in the sink, and the cupboards were bare. Linda confirmed that this kitchen had not been used for a couple of years and she assumed that her father was eating upstairs with Dennis. However, Scriver, the former girlfriend of Arnold's grandson, testified she never saw Arnold on the second floor and that it was always locked. Arnold would sometimes go to the convenience store to buy bread, chips, or cookies, which he ate on the porch. However, he had not been seen buying groceries since before his deterioration in 1999. A neighbour estimated that over the winter and spring of 2000 Arnold lost up to thirty pounds.

8 There was no bathroom on the main floor where Arnold's apartment was located. There was a broken cistern toilet in the basement and a bathroom on the second floor. The broken dirt floor of the basement was covered in dog feces. The neighbours and Scriver did not see Arnold using the upstairs washroom. Arnold's bedroom was messy and there were no sheets on the bed.

9 Arnold would rake leaves and do repair jobs for the neighbours, including Catherine Raven and Ana Michalsky, until the spring of 2000. Raven or Michalsky would give him meals when he came over. He could not dress himself appropriately and often wore winter clothes in the summer and vice versa. Because of his weight loss, his clothes did not fit. He would wear pants without a belt or zipper and would pin the waist to keep them from falling down. He did not wear underwear. He stopped shaving and began to smell. His clothes became dirty.

10 Raven found Arnold locked out of the house at least a dozen times in the eight months before the police first had contact with the family. He would wait on Raven's porch and she would let him stay in her house until Dennis returned home, usually around midnight. Raven would not go to bed without checking to see if Arnold was locked out.

11 Raven and Scriver testified that the appellant would yell at Arnold, tease him about the Germans (Arnold had lost family in WWII), or ignore him and speak as if he was not there.

12 On April 30, 2000, Officer Houston responded to a call claiming that an old man "sat down rather heavily" in front of someone's house. It is Arnold, who was exhausted. The police helped him to his feet and drove him home. Dennis was not home so Michalsky offered to let Arnold stay with her until Dennis came home.

13 One week later, P.C. Cutmore visited the house. Dennis said it was hard to look after Arnold because he would go for long walks and get lost. P.C. Cutmore explained about community agencies that could help. Dennis did not call these agencies.

14 On June 7, 2000, a man flagged Officer Houston down to help Arnold, who had collapsed on the street close to where he had been found on April 30. He found Arnold sitting on a planter, reclining back on an elbow, looking filthy and exhausted. He was weaker than he had been before and required assistance to stand and walk. He smelled very badly and it appeared he had not showered for some time. He was not answering questions promptly and, other than recognising his name, Officer Houston did not think that Arnold knew what was asked of him. He needed to be reminded where he lived although he recognized the house as his home. No one answered the door when P.C. Houston knocked and, because Arnold could not move on his own, P.C. Houston took Arnold to St. Joseph's Hospital where he was admitted and given a place to lie down. P.C. Houston telephoned the address where Arnold lived and advised Dennis that his father was at the hospital. Arnold was released shortly thereafter.

15 On June 9, 2000, Officer Worth received a call from a gas company employee making meter checks who told him he had found a dead dog at the residence of a confused, elderly man. Officer Worth went to the address in question and found Arnold sitting on the front porch. Arnold was very dirty; his clothes were filthy and did not fit. His pants were too large and he had to hold them up with his hands. The fly was down or broken and he was wearing no underwear. The pants were dirty and wet in the crotch area. There was a very strong odour coming from him and it was obvious that he had not bathed in a number of days. He was quite thin, although he was a big man, and his cheeks were sunken in and unshaven. It was obvious to Officer Worth that Arnold had not eaten in a while. Arnold did not complain about Dennis or his grandson. He did say he was hungry. Officer Worth asked him when was the last time he had eaten and was told that it had been a few days and that his son gave him an apple the day before.

16 Officer Worth apprehended Arnold under the *Mental Health Act*, R.S.O. 1990, c. M.7. Officer Worth did not believe that Arnold was able to care for himself and apprehended him for his safety. He took him to St. Joseph's Hospital where he was admitted. Linda signed the forms to transfer him from St. Joseph's Hospital to a nursing home and he was admitted to Fairview Nursing Home on June 10.

17 Linda described her father as fiercely independent and contrary. He was very stubborn and would do the opposite of what Dennis told him to do. She stated that Arnold would not listen to anyone and that it was not uncommon for him to wear dirty clothes. When she and Dennis bought clothes for their father, it was very hard to get him to wear them. Linda testified that Dennis was concerned about their father and said that Dennis had always been good to him. Besides buying Arnold clothes, Dennis did his laundry, and cut his hair. He was never physically abusive towards his father. Arnold was adamant that he would not go into a nursing home. Linda left the family home in January 1999. She and Dennis did not discuss who would take care of Arnold as they all "helped out". Arnold had a key that he wore around his neck but the last time Linda saw it was in June 1999. She had not been in the house for six months prior to June 7, 2000.

18 On February 28, 2000, Linda and Dennis asked a lawyer to draft two powers of attorney with the two of them acting as joint attorneys: one addressed financial affairs, the other, Arnold's personal care. They thought that if anything happened to Arnold, someone should be able to take care of his financial affairs and "everything".

19 After February 28, 2000, she and Dennis did not discuss their father's welfare and who should take care of him. Dennis never called her to say that their father's health was deteriorating.

20 Dr. Lam, a general practitioner who works at the nursing home, examined Arnold. He found him to be a little underweight for his height and build but not emaciated. Although he was pleasant and cooperative, Arnold seemed confused. He did not know where he was and was not able to tell Dr. Lam his home address when asked. Further testing to determine the extent of Arnold's cognitive impairment led Dr. Lam to the conclusion that Arnold was in the early stages of Alzheimer's dementia and that this dementia could have been going on for six months to two years. In Dr. Lam's opinion, given how Arnold was acting in the fall and winter of 1999 and the spring of 2000, he was likely suffering from some dementia process.

21 On admission, Arnold was incontinent in terms of urine. Dr. Lam doubted that Arnold would bathe himself without being reminded to do so. He would also need direction and assistance. Further, he would probably need supervision in terms of dressing and would not know how to dress appropriately for the weather. Arnold was able to feed himself, but he needed supervision, guidance, and direction. At the nursing home, he had to be taken to the dining hall when the meal was served and have it placed in front of him. Dr. Lam stated that Arnold would probably forget to eat if he were not called down to the dining hall.

22 Dr. Lam opined that Arnold's living situation was a totally unsafe environment for him. He was in danger of falling and the environment was very non-hygienic. The state of the rooms meant that Arnold probably could not take care of himself at all and that it was likely that Arnold was not even aware of the environment he was in. Arnold should have had supervision by a person who saw him at least once every half hour so that he could not wander off or fall and break a hip.

. . . .

The Issues

28 The appellant's first submission is that the trial judge failed "to explain the basis upon which he arrived at his conclusion that Arnold was in the Appellant's charge" and therefore the reasons fail to satisfy the basis upon which the conviction was entered in accordance with *R. v. Sheppard*, [2002] 1 S.C.R. 869. His second submission is that "the evidence does not support a finding beyond a reasonable doubt that Mr. Peterson was in the care of the appellant". The appellant further submits that there is at least a reasonable doubt that Arnold was not in Dennis's care having regard to the following factors:

* Arnold was energetic, physically active, and walked the neighbourhood on a regular basis.

* Arnold was fiercely independent, very stubborn, and would never look to anyone for help nor listen to his children.

* Linda Peterson testified that she and Dennis did not consider invoking their power of attorney because their father was well and there was no reason to think he would need care.

29 I propose to deal with the appellant's submissions together...

The Meaning of "Under His Charge"

33 This appears to be the first case to reach an appellate court in which the meaning of the phrase "under his charge" in s. 215(1)(c) as between an adult child and his or parent is in issue. That said, the section must be read and interpreted as a whole.

34 Section 215(1)(c) differs from section s. 215(1)(a), which imposes a duty on a "parent, foster parent, guardian or head of a family" to provide necessaries "for a child under the age of sixteen years", and from s. 215(1)(b), which imposes a duty on spouses and common-law partners to provide necessaries of life to their spouses and partners. Section 215(1)(c) makes it clear that the duty to provide necessaries is not limited to these relationships but can arise in other circumstances. The duty arises when one person is under the other's charge, is unable to withdraw from that charge, and is unable to provide himself or herself with necessaries of life. The phrase "necessaries of life" includes not only food, shelter, care, and medical attention necessary to sustain life but also appears to include protection of the person from harm: *R. v. Popen* (1981), 60 C.C.C. (2d) 232 (Ont. C.A.) at 240. Thus, s. 215(1)(c) obligations are driven by the facts and the context of each case.

35 Subsection 215(2) imposes liability on an objective basis. The offence is made out by conduct showing a marked departure from the conduct of a reasonably prudent person having the charge of another in circumstances where it is objectively foreseeable that failure to provide necessaries of life would risk danger to life or permanent endangerment of the health of the person under the charge of the other. The personal characteristics of the accused, falling short of capacity to appreciate the risk, are not a relevant consideration. The use of the word "duty" is indicative of a societal minimum that has been established and is aimed at establishing a uniform minimum level of care: *R. v. Naglik*, [1993] 3 S.C.R. 122 at paras. 37, 51 and 33 respectively.

36 The objective basis of liability includes an assessment of whether the person in charge could have acted other than as he or she did. For example, in *Naglik* at para. 36, a "crucial consideration" was that the evidence indicated the services

of a public health nurse were made available to *Naglik* to help her in caring for her child, given her age, education, and lack of experience with children. She refused to accept any assistance.

37 The words "without lawful excuse" in s. 215(2) provide a defence and serve to prevent the punishment of the morally innocent. The obligation to provide necessaries is not absolute and may be excused, for example, where there is financial inability: *Naglik, supra*, and *R. v. Yuman* (1910), 17 C.C.C. 474 (Ont. C.A.).

38 On the other hand, I note that contributory negligence by the victim is not a defence for an accused charged with criminal negligence unless the injuries incurred are attributable solely to the victim: see Eugene G. Ewaschuk, *Criminal Pleadings and Practice in Canada,* 2d ed. looseleaf (Aurora: Canada Law Book, 1987) at para. 28:180, citing *R. v. Lesuk*, [2000] 7 W.W.R. 462 (Man. C.A.) at para. 31 and other appellate decisions from Alberta, Saskatchewan, Nova Scotia, and Prince Edward Island.

39 Section 215(2)(b) indicates that the failure to provide necessaries includes not only a failure to do a discrete act but also includes a failure to act in an ongoing relationship over a period of time: see *Naglik, supra*, at para. 36 in relation to section 215(2)(a)(ii), which is similar in wording to s. 215(2)(b).

40 In addition to the foregoing, I would make the following observations. First, the relationship of the parties to each other is among the factors to consider in determining whether a person is in the charge of another. The dependency of the parent under a disability on an independent adult child is justified not only by their past course of dealing in which the parent supported the child but also by their relationship to one another in which an element of trust will usually be present. The history of the section supports the interpretation that the section was intended to require certain minimal standards in relation to dependants such as wives and children and was later broadened: see *R. v. Middleton*, [1997] O.J. No. 2758, at paras. 10-14. The mere breach of a federal or provincial statute, such as s. 32 of *the Family Law Act*, which imposes a duty on a child to support a parent, does not constitute a crime. It is nevertheless proper for the trier of fact to consider legislation governing the accused in order to determine whether the accused's actions or inactions show a "marked departure" from the conduct expected: see by analogy *R. v. Leblanc*, [1977] 1 S.C.R. 339, *R. v. Bergeron* (1999), 132 C.C.C. (3d) 45 (Que. C.A.).

41 Second, the word "charge" is not unknown to the criminal law in other contexts involving adults. In the impaired driving context, the court characterized having "care, charge or control" of a vehicle as requiring "a kind of domination as in the master-servant relationship and as in the parent-child or teacher-beginner relationship": *R. v. Slessor*, [1970] 1 O.R. 664 at 674. The court

did not restrict the meaning of charge too far, however, stating, "'Charge', too, is a word of broad comprehension. One speaks of a person who is fixed with responsibility of supervision as one who is in 'charge'". The Ontario Environmental Appeal Board also considered the meaning of the word charge in *Re Karge* (1996), 21 C.E.L.R. (N.S.) 5 at para. 68-69. It referred to the dictionary meanings of the word and concluded essentially that it means to have the responsibility to take care of someone, something, or somewhere.

42 Used in these contexts the word "charge" connotes, among other things, the duty or responsibility of taking care of a person or thing. Similarly, one of the definitions of charge in *Black's Law Dictionary*, 8th ed. (St. Paul, Minneapolis: West Publishing, 2004) is "to entrust with responsibilities or duties e.g. to charge the guardian with the ward's care". What the definitions have in common is the exercise of an element of control by one person and a dependency on the part of the other.

43 In assessing whether one person is in the charge of another, the relative positions of the parties and their ability to understand and appreciate their circumstances is a factor to consider. A parent who is not in full possession of his or her faculties may not appreciate that he or she cannot provide himself or herself with the necessaries of life and may not have the capacity to understand that he or she is in an unsafe or unhealthy environment that is likely to cause permanent injury. Just as some contributory negligence by the victim is not a defence to a charge of criminal negligence, the inability of the victim to appreciate his or her need for necessaries and the victim's unwillingness to cooperate is not a defence for an accused charged with failure to provide necessaries. If the parent is otherwise in the child's charge and the child cannot care for the parent due to the parent's refusal to accept care, the child is obliged to seek the help of a community agency. See *Regina v. Stone & Dobinsons*, [1977] Q.B. 354 at 361.

44 A further consideration in determining whether a person is in the charge of another is whether one person has explicitly assumed responsibility for the other, for example, by obtaining a power of attorney for personal care or by publicly acknowledging to others in the community by words or conduct an assumption of responsibility.

45 The non-exhaustive criteria below illuminate the trial judge's findings and the path he took to his conclusion that Arnold was in the charge of the appellant:

> 1. Arnold was dependent: The trial judge found that in his state of dementia, Arnold was unable to provide himself with the necessaries of life. As he never cooked, had no food in the apartment, and sometimes went days without food, he was dependent on someone else to provide him with food. The trial judge also accepted Dr. Lam's evidence that Arnold needed

assistance in choosing appropriate clothing to wear as well as assistance with his personal grooming.

2. The appellant had a familial relationship with Arnold and was aware of his father's dependency. The trial judge found that Dennis was fully aware that his father was in need of the necessaries of life. It was manifestly obvious, particularly because Arnold lost up to thirty pounds during the winter and spring of 2000.

3. The appellant controlled Arnold's living conditions and kept him in an unsafe environment. The trial judge found that the appellant had free access to Arnold's rooms but kept all of the rooms he occupied locked when he was not there. The logical inference is that Dennis prevented Arnold from having access to the only working kitchen, bathing facilities, and properly working toilet in the house. The trial judge also found that the toilet in the basement had no seat, was filthy, worked poorly; and the environment in which it was located was unsafe because the stairs to the basement were poorly lit and had no handrail until near the bottom. The trial judge further found that the kitchen was unsafe even for a fit person.

4. The appellant had control over Arnold's personal care. The appellant took steps to obtain the power to make decisions respecting Arnold's personal care and had the ability to make decisions about his personal care. Put another way, at the request of Dennis and his sister, Arnold entrusted them with the ability to make decisions respecting his personal care. Quite apart from the power of attorney, when Dennis came home and Arnold was locked out, as frequently happened, the appellant took Arnold into his charge from the neighbours. Thus, both legally and publicly Dennis assumed responsibility for Arnold.

5. The appellant chose not to make decisions that would result in Arnold receiving the necessaries of life. Dennis was made aware of community services that could assist him with the care of his father. He took no steps pursuant to Const. Cutmore's suggestions. (One suggestion, as revealed in the evidence, was to contact a church across the street that operated an extensive Meals-on-Wheels program.)

6. Arnold was incapable of withdrawing himself from the appellant's "charge" due to age and illness. He was too old, feeble, and senile to withdraw himself from the appellant's charge.

46 When the trial judge's reasons are considered in this manner, they disclose why the trial judge found that Arnold was under the appellant's charge as well as why Arnold was unable to withdraw from his son's charge. Thus, the reasons

disclose why the trial judge convicted Arnold and satisfy the requirements of *Sheppard, supra.*

47 With respect to the third element of the offence, namely, the failure to provide Arnold with the necessaries of life, the appellant relied on Linda's evidence as contradicting the evidence that Dennis failed to provide Arnold with the necessaries of life and was under his charge. The appellant submits that the trial judge was required to resolve the conflict in the evidence. However, as Linda had not entered the house for at least six months prior to Arnold being apprehended, she was not in a position to testify about whether Dennis failed to provide Arnold with the necessaries of life. Her evidence did not raise a conflict that necessitated resolution by the trial judge. Thus the trial judge correctly found that the evidence was not really in dispute.

48 Insofar as the legal test for determining when a person is under the charge of another is concerned, the evidence that Arnold did not wish to bathe or change his clothes does not negate the appellant's having charge of him. The evidence simply supports the conclusion that Arnold had a mental disability that prevented him from exercising sound judgment to provide himself with the necessaries of life. This disability cannot be used by Dennis as a defence for failing to provide Arnold with the necessaries of life. Dennis could have called a community agency for help and did not. Further, there was no evidence that Arnold ever refused food yet, Dennis did not provide him with food regularly.

49 The trial judge's reasons are sufficient to permit his decision to be reviewed and do not disclose any error in law. Accordingly, I would dismiss the conviction appeal.

. . . .

The majority upheld the trial judge's sentence of six months imprisonment followed by two years' probation and a hundred hours of community service. Borins J.A. would have upheld the sentencing portion of the appeal, substituting a conditional sentence, on the basis that failure to provide necessaries cases involving children were not sufficiently analogous. He agreed with the majority's conclusions on guilt, however, making the following comments:

BORINS J.A. (dissenting in part):—

66 In my view, contemporary legislation is required to deal with the issue of parent/child role reversal, which is one of the results of human longevity. An estimated 22.4 million households in the United States - nearly one in four - are providing care to a relative or friend aged fifty or older according to a 1997 survey by the National Alliance for Caregiving and the American Association of Retired Persons. It is likely that adults born between 1946 and 1965 will spend more years caring for a parent than for their children. As Susan Dominus

pointed out in an article in *The New York Times Magazine*: "The philosophical impact [of human longevity] on family dynamics will be profound, as parents continue to lean on children long past retirement themselves, and people in their 80's learn what it means, at that age, to still be somebody's child." ("Life in The Age of Old, Old Age", *The New York Times Magazine*, February 22, 2004.)

67 In an article, "Longer Lives Reveal the Ties That Bind Us" (*The New York Times*, October 2, 2005), David Brooks points out that between now and 2050, the percentage of the population above age eighty-five is expected to quadruple. Brooks quotes Dr. Leon Kass, the former Chairman of the President's Council on Bioethics, as stating: "The defining characteristic of our time seems to be that we are both younger longer and older longer." To which Brooks adds:

> Parents have to spend more time preparing their children for the new economy and children have to spend a lot more time caring for their parents when they are old.

In other words, technology, which was supposed to be liberating, actually creates more dependence. We spend more of our lives while young and old dependent upon others, and we spend more time in between caring for those who depend on us.

68 Although these data and comments apply to the United States, there is little doubt that they also apply to Canada. This is why it is no longer satisfactory to rely on legislation designed for another purpose in another era to define what contemporary society requires of its members who have aging parents in need of care. Children of aging parents no doubt accept that their parents require some form of care, be it in respect to financial affairs or personal care. As the elderly lose their ability to remain self-sufficient, their adult children are gradually required to assume caregiving responsibilities. As a result of rising life expectancy, the child who becomes his or her parent's caregiver, is often well within the "senior citizen" age category. In addition, given that the age at which children are conceived is rising, the expectation is that there will be a sizeable group of children who will face a double "necessaries" duty in respect to both their children and their parents, raising, perhaps, the need to chose between the welfare of their children and their parents. It is, therefore, of critical importance that if the duty to care for an aging population continues to be within the ambit of the criminal law, that care is taken to clearly define what constitutes criminal neglect or penal negligence.

69 Unlike its role in shaping the duty to provide care for very young children, which is easily defined and recognized, and which is governed by s. 215(1)(a) of the *Criminal Code*, the challenge for government is to address the issue of the child caregiver of an aging parent in a way that clearly defines the circumstances in which criminal liability will be imposed. Determining the level of responsibility that an adult child should bear for an elder parent together with

defining the appropriate standard of care are difficult and challenging issues. Indeed, one may ask whether they should continue to be governed by criminal law. Useful contemporary legislative models may be found in several states in the United States that have enacted specific laws related to elder abuse and elder care, entrenching a defined duty of care. I refer, in particular, to legislation in California, Massachusetts and Illinois. The Massachusetts legislation is especially instructive in its comprehensive definition of "caretaker" in defining appropriate boundaries for criminal liability.

This decision is useful for beginning to analyse the question of when an elderly parent should be taken to be in the "charge" of an accused, thereby placing the accused under a duty to provide necessaries of life.* As Borins J.A. notes in his dissent, the demographics of the Canadian population make this an issue likely to arise more frequently in the future than it has in the past. More complete presentation by counsel of social sciences research into the issue of elder abuse and neglect would be helpful in allowing later decisions to flesh out these criteria even more fully.

The Supreme Court has regularly noted that it is important to avoid reliance on unsupported stereotypical thinking in legal reasoning: this has affected their reasoning around equality rights and around sexual assault, for example. There are a number of stereotypes about the elderly in society: that the typical elderly person is frail and dependent, for example. In fact, most elderly persons remain healthy and competent to make decisions for most of their lives: see, for instance, Chappel, N., Gee, E., McDonald, L. & Stones, M., *Aging in Contemporary Canada* (Toronto: Prentice Hall, 2003). Similarly, it is often supposed that the typical victim of "elder abuse" is dependent on the abuser. In fact, research suggests that more typically it is the abuser who is dependent on the victim in some way: see McDonald, L. and Collins, A., *Abuse and Neglect of Older Adults: A Discussion Paper* (Ottawa: National Clearinghouse on Family Violence, Health Canada, 2000). Similarly, the elderly are often presumed typically to refuse services due to incompetence. Again this assumption is false. Competent older people most often refuse services because they see those services as a threat to their independence, their privacy, their ability to remain in their own homes, or even their ability to continue a relationship with the "abuser": see J. Aronson and S. Naismith, "Manufacturing Social Exclusion in the Home Care Market" (2001), 27(2) *Canadian Public Policy* 151-164.

These stereotypes can be seen to have affected some social services legislation in various provinces. Although some provinces avoid relying on these stereotypes by making the wishes of the adult a primary consideration, others do not. The four Atlantic provinces, for instance, have all adopted versions of an "Adult Protection Act". This approach in essence assumes that the elderly are like children, and is modelled quite closely on child protection legislation. Generally

---

* This note originally appeared in the *Criminal Reports* as an annotation to the *Peterson* decision: see Steve Coughlan, *R. v. Peterson*: Annotation, 34 C.R. (6th) 120.

speaking, these statutes give little or no weight to the wishes of the adult, and rather require courts to decide based on what a third party thinks are the adult's "best interests". The fact that an adult in need of protection might not (as the father in this case did not) wish to be placed in a nursing home would be of no consequence.

It is important that a proper understanding of the situation and attitudes of the elderly be incorporated into a full understanding of when an elderly person can be said to be in the "charge" of someone else. Here, the court is content to limit discussion of the father's refusal to enter a nursing home to the issue of whether contributory negligence is a defence to criminal negligence. The majority hold at para. 43:

> If the parent is otherwise in the child's charge and the child cannot care for the parent due to the parent's refusal to accept care, the child is obliged to seek the help of a community agency.

The issue is not pursued at length, but there is the danger here that the parent's wishes are being treated merely as an obstacle, not as a legitimate consideration to be taken into account. Similarly the court notes at para 48:

> Insofar as the legal test for determining when a person is under the charge of another is concerned, the evidence that Arnold did not wish to bathe or change his clothes does not negate the appellant's having charge of him. The evidence simply supports the conclusion that Arnold had a mental disability that prevented him from exercising sound judgment to provide himself with the necessaries of life.

In the adult protection context, particularly in cases of "self-neglect", this same catch-22 situation reduces the likelihood of an adult's wishes being respected: those very wishes are taken as evidence to justify overriding the adult's wishes. We do not generally take this approach with other people, who are assumed to be entitled to make potentially foolish and hazardous decisions, like taking part in extreme skiing, eating live insects on a reality show, or investing in high risk ventures. Similarly, if a 30-year-old ceases to bathe often enough, we try not to sit next to them on the bus: if the person is 70, we try to place them in a nursing home. Treating older adults differently seems like a natural approach if we stereotype them as like children. The ultimately negative impact this approach actually has on the elderly whom the law aims to "protect" has been noted and criticized: see Joan Harbison et al., *Mistreating Elderly People: Questioning the Legal Response to Elder Abuse and Neglect* (Halifax: Dalhousie University Health Law Institute, 1995).

If courts too readily assume that care for the elderly involves a "parent/child role reversal" (para. 66), it is likely that the elderly will, in this context as well, be treated like children rather than like adults. In this criminal context, those stereotypes are likely to work to the detriment of those associated with the elderly, and who might be found to have failed to provide necessaries in circumstances where the accused might have thought he or she was simply recognizing the adult's independence and respecting his or her right to make decisions.

PROBLEM

In a controversial old United States decision in *People v. Beardsley*, 113 N.W. 1128 (Mich. S.C., 1907) the trial judge convicted the accused of manslaughter in the following circumstances:

"He was a married man living at Pontiac, and at the time the facts herein narrated occurred, he was working as a bartender and clerk at the Columbia Hotel. He lived with his wife in Pontiac, occupying two rooms on the ground floor of a house. Other rooms were rented to tenants, as was also one living room in the basement. His wife being temporarily absent from the city, respondent arranged with a woman named Blanche Burns, who at the time was working at another hotel, to go to his apartments with him. He had been acquainted with her for some time. They knew each other's habits and character. . . . On the evening of Saturday, March 18, 1905, he met her at the place where she worked, and they went together to his place of residence. They at once began to drink and continued to drink steadily, and remained together, day and night, from that time until the afternoon of the Monday following, except when respondent went to his work on Sunday afternoon. There was liquor at these rooms, and when it was all used they were served with bottles of whiskey and beer by a young man who worked at the Columbia Hotel, and who also attended respondent's fires at the house. . . . On Monday afternoon, about one o'clock, the young man went to the house to see if anything was wanted. . . . During this visit to the house the woman sent the young man to a drug store to purchase, with money she gave him, camphor and morphine tablets. He procured both articles. There were six grains of morphine in quarter-grain tablets. She concealed the morphine from respondent's notice, and was discovered putting something into her mouth by him and the young man as they were returning from the other room after taking a drink of beer. She in fact was taking morphine. Respondent struck the box from her hand. Some of the tablets fell on the floor, and of these, respondent crushed several with his foot. She picked up and swallowed two of them, and the young man put two of them in the spittoon. Altogether it is probable she took from three to four grains of morphine. The young man went away soon after this. Respondent called him by telephone about an hour later, and after he came to the house requested him to take the woman into the room in the basement which was occupied by a Mr. Skoba. She was in a stupor and did not rouse when spoken to. Respondent was too intoxicated to be of any assistance and the young man proceeded to take her downstairs. While doing this Skoba arrived, and together they put her in his room on the bed. Respondent requested Skoba to look after her and let her out the back way when she waked up. Between nine and ten o'clock in the evening Skoba became alarmed at her condition. He at once called the city marshal and a doctor. An examination by them disclosed that she was dead."

On appeal the accused was acquitted on the basis that there had been no legal duty to act. How would that issue be decided under current Canadian law as reviewed in preceding pages?

4.   VOLUNTARINESS

(a)   Defining Conduct that is Not "Voluntary"

R. v. KING

[1962] S.C.R. 746 at 749, 38 C.R. 52, 133 C.C.C. 1,
1962 CarswellOnt 18 (S.C.R.)

TASCHEREAU J.: — It is my view that there can be no *actus reus* unless it is the result of a willing mind at liberty to make a definite choice or decision, or in other words, there must be a willpower to do an act whether the accused knew or not that it was prohibited by law.

RABEY v. R.

[1980] 2 S.C.R. 513, 54 C.C.C. (2d) 1, 15 C.R. (3d) 225 at 232, 235, 255,
1980 CarswellOnt 35, 1980 CarswellOnt 71

RITCHIE J.: —

. . . .

Automatism is a term used to describe unconscious, involuntary behaviour, the state of a person who, though capable of action, is not conscious of what he is doing. It means an unconscious involuntary act, where the mind does not go with what is being done.

DICKSON J.: —

. . . .

Although the word "automatism" made its way but lately to the legal state, it is basic principle that absence of volition in respect of the act involved is always a defence to a crime. A defence that the act is involuntary entitles the accused to a complete and unqualified acquittal. That the defence of automatism exists as a middle ground between criminal responsibility and legal insanity is beyond question. Although spoken of as a defence, in the sense that it is raised by the accused, the Crown always bears the burden of proving a voluntary act.

. . . [A] . . . principle, fundamental to our criminal law, which governs this appeal is that no act can be a criminal offence unless it is done voluntarily. Consciousness is a *sine qua non* to criminal liability.

R. v. PARKS

[1992] 2 S.C.R. 871, 15 C.R. (4th) 289, 75 C.C.C. (3d) 287,
1992 CarswellOnt 107, 1992 CarswellOnt 996

LA FOREST J.: —
Automatism occupies a unique place in our criminal law system. Although spoken of as a "defence", it is conceptually a subset of the voluntariness requirement, which in turn is part of the *actus reus* component of criminal liability.

R. v. STONE

[1999] 2 S.C.R. 290, 24 C.R. (5th) 1, 134 C.C.C. (3d) 353,
1999 CarswellBC 1064, 1999 CarswellBC 1065

BASTARACHE J.: — I . . . prefer to define automatism as a state of impaired consciousness, rather than unconsciousness, in which an individual, though capable of action, has no voluntary control over that action. . . .

. . . .

[V]oluntariness, rather than consciousness, is the key legal element of automatistic behaviour since a defence of automatism amounts to a denial of the voluntariness component of the *actus reus*.

In *Stone*, Bastarache, for a 5-4 majority, also held that accused had to prove any defence of automatism on a balance of probabilities.

The leading decisions in *Rabey* (disassociated state), *Parks* (sleepwalking) and *Stone* will be considered much later after a consideration of the defence of insanity when voluntariness is re-visited under the heading of automatism.

In *R. v. Ruzic* (2001), 41 C.R. (5th) 1 (S.C.C.) (considered later under duress), the court distinguished the issue of physical voluntariness required for proof of the *actus reus* from the issue of moral involuntariness arising in the case of justifications and excuses. The physical voluntariness requirement applies to any offence, and is distinct from any issue of fault. There is here no reference to a reverse onus, as compared to the onus of proof the majority placed on the accused for the defence of automatism in *Stone*.

COBB, FOUNDATIONS OF NEUROPSYCHIATRY

(1958), 117-18, quoted by S.J. Fox, "Physical Disorder Consciousness and Criminal Liability" (1963), 63 Col. L. Rev. 645 at 651

When the human organism is working well, functioning as a whole, there is probably the highest degree of consciousness, and a feeling of well being and capability. In such a state attention is usually directed to certain objects with neglect of others. Therefore there is never a state that could be called full consciousness. ... When tired, bored, or slightly poisoned by alcohol, we are suffering from a partial loss of consciousness. From the excited state of great efficiency under stress, through normal work-a-day moods, to states of dullness, coma and stupor, there is a continuous series of states where consciousness is less and less active. ... Only in deep sleep is the cortex inactive, as judged by the electroencephalograph. There are different degrees of consciousness in sleep. Persons lightly asleep can differentiate between ordinary noises and sounds that may mean danger. Dreaming is a form of consciousness. A sense of time may be carried through hours of sleep, allowing one to wake at a desired hour.

(b)   Why Have a Voluntary Requirement for the *Actus Reus*?

H.L.A. HART, ACTS OF WILL AND RESPONSIBILITY

Punishment and Responsibility, (1968), 104-106

The General Doctrine Reconstructed.

Most people, lawyers and laymen alike, would I think agree that in our list of examples of involuntary conduct (conscious and unconscious), some radical defect is present, and some vital component of normal action is absent, even if Austin's terminology of "desire" or muscular movement or volitions misdescribes it. For the cases do not seem to be a *mere* list without any unifying feature to justify treating them alike as cases where conduct is not voluntary. If it is the policy of the law to mark these cases off, there seems some good factual basis for this policy. Is it then possible to give a more adequate account than that of the traditional theory? Or must we leave the dark phrases "not governed by the will", "no act of will", "involuntary", "no operation of the will" etc. unexplained?

In fact, I think it would not be difficult to construct an account which would explain and justify the intuitive feeling that, in all these cases, there is some more fundamental defect than lack of knowledge or foresight. By a "more adequate" account I mean one which involves no fictions; which is better fitted to the facts of ordinary experience; and which could be used by the courts in order to identify a range of cases where the minimum mental element required for responsibility is not satisfied. Such an account could cover both the conscious and unconscious examples suggested in the books, but it would necessarily differ from the kind of general explanation given there in two main ways. First it would be disassociated from any claim that the ordinary way of talking about actions was inferior, or less accurate than the definition of acts as muscular contractions. Secondly, omissions would have to be treated separately from positive interventions. Granted these two things, we could then characterise involuntary movements such as those made in epilepsy, or in a stroke, or mere reflex actions to blows or stings, as movements of the body which occurred although they were not appropriate, *i.e.* required for any action (in the ordinary sense of action) which the agent believed himself to be doing. This, I think, reproduces what is in fact meant by ordinary people when they say a man's bodily movements are uncontrolled, as in the case of a reflex or St. Vitus dance. Such movements are "wild" or not "governed by the will" in the sense that they are not subordinated to the agent's conscious plans of action: they do not occur as part of anything the agent takes himself to be doing. This is the feature which the Austinian theory represents in a distorted form by identifying the involuntary movements as those which are not caused by a desire for them.

In the unconscious cases, *e.g.* of epilepsy, automatism, etc. the same test can be used. Here too, the movements which we call involuntary are not part of any action the agent takes himself to be doing, because, being unconscious, he does not take himself to be doing any action. This test, it should be noted, preserves the distinction between involuntary conduct and mere lack of knowledge of circumstances or foresight of consequences, and so reproduces the sense that we have in involuntary movements a different and more fundamental defect. For one who merely fails to foresee that the gun he fires will harm someone still makes voluntary muscular movements, *i.e.* movements appropriate to the action of firing the gun, which he knows he is doing; whereas the involuntary tremors of the palsied man, who breaks a glass, are appropriate to no action which he believes himself to be doing.

Omissions must, I think, be catered for separately, though this can and should be done in a way which reveals that their voluntary or involuntary character depends on the same general principle as positive interventions. When a man fails to do some positive action demanded by the law, his failure to act is involuntary if he is unconscious and so *unable* to do any conscious action, or if, though conscious, he is *unable* to make the particular muscular movements required for the performance of actions demanded by the law.

I.H. PATIENT, SOME REMARKS ABOUT THE ELEMENT OF VOLUNTARINESS IN OFFENCES OF ABSOLUTE LIABILITY

(1968), Crim. L. Rev. 23 at 25-26

It is important at this stage to stress that involuntariness goes beyond lack of *mens rea*. A series of examples may show this.

Case 1: A shoots B meaning to kill him and B is indeed killed. A kills intentionally.

Case 2: A is not sure whether the shape in the distance is a human being or a tree, he nevertheless shoots. It was in fact B, who was killed by the shot. A kills recklessly.

Case 3: A is convinced he is shooting at a tree trunk. In fact it is B. A reasonable man would have realised it was a human being. B is killed by A's shot. A kills negligently.

Case 4: A shoots in a pistol club at a target. Suddenly B falls from the spectator's gallery into A's line of fire. He is killed. Even a reasonable man could not foresee this. A kills with blameless inadvertence, *i.e.*, accidentally.

In all four cases A's shooting was voluntary.

Case 5: A has an epileptic fit. One of his movements causes a gun which is lying beside him on a table to go off and kill B.
or:
A is aiming at a target. The physically stronger X takes hold of A's hand and forces him to point the gun at B and to pull the trigger. B is hit and killed.
or:
A is aiming at a target. He is attacked by a swarm of bees. His defensive reflex movement causes the gun to go off in B's direction and B is killed.

In all these cases there was a lack of voluntariness. There was no act on A's part. A cannot be said to have "shot" B. He caused his death, just as lightning can cause a man's death. Since there was no act neither was there an *actus reus*. To bring out the difference between involuntariness and *mens rea*, cases 4 and 5 have to be compared. In case 4, A kills accidentally, *i.e.*, without *mens rea*. Though there was no *mens rea* with regard to the killing, there was nonetheless a voluntary act. A did shoot. Moreover, he implemented the full *actus reus* of homicide, he killed a human being. If homicide were an offence of strict liability, *i.e.*, an offence which makes you liable even without *mens rea*, then A would be guilty of homicide in case 4. As the law stands he luckily will not be so liable. In case 5, however, there is not even an *actus reus*. An *actus reus* presupposes an act. There was no such act. A's movements were causal in bringing about B's death, but A did not "shoot" B. The defect in case 5 is therefore more fundamental than the defect in case 4. Even if homicide were an offence of strict liability, A would nevertheless not be liable in case 5. For strict [absolute] liability means liability without *mens rea*. In case 5 there is more than lack of *mens rea*. There is not even an *actus reus*.

O.W. HOLMES, THE COMMON LAW

Howe, ed., (1963), 46

The reason for requiring an act is, that an act implies a choice, and that it is felt to be impolitic and unjust to make a man answerable for harm, unless he might have chosen otherwise. But the choice must be made with a chance of contemplating the consequence complained of, or else it has no bearing on responsibility for that consequence. If this were not true, a man might be held answerable for everything which would not have happened but for his choice at some past time. For instance, for having in a fit fallen on a man, which he would not have done had he not chosen to come to the city where he was taken ill.

H.L. PACKER, THE LIMITS OF THE CRIMINAL SANCTION

(1968), 76-77

Conduct must be, as the law's confusing term has it, "voluntary." The term is one that will immediately raise the hackles of the determinist, of whatever persuasion. But, once again, the law's language should not be read as plunging into the deep waters of free will vs. determinism, Cartesian duality, or any of a half-dozen other philosophic controversies that might appear to be invoked by the use of the term "voluntary" in relation to conduct. The law is not affirming that some conduct is the product of the free exercise of conscious volition; it is excluding, in a crude kind of way, conduct that in any view is not. And it does so primarily in response to the simple intuition that nothing would more surely undermine the individual's sense of autonomy and security than to hold him to account for conduct that *he* does not think he can control. He may be deluded, if the determinists are right, in his belief that such conduct differs significantly from any other conduct in which he engages. But that is beside the point. *He* thinks there is a difference, and that is what the law acts upon.

(c)   Examples Not Associated with Mental Disorder

R. v. LUCKI

(1955), 17 W.W.R. 446, 1995 CarswellSask 72 (Sask. Pol. Ct.)

GOLDENBERG Q.C., P.M. — The charge against the accused is as follows:

[O]n the 22nd day of November, A.D., 1955, at the City of Saskatoon in the said Province did operate a motor vehicle, to wit, an automobile bearing Saskatchewan License Number 139-212 on a public highway in the said City of Saskatoon, to wit, Saskatchewan Crescent, and did fail to keep to the right half of the said highway, and did thereby inconvenience other persons using the said highway, contrary to the provisions of Section 125 (9) of *The Vehicles Act* of the Province of Saskatchewan.

The facts are not in dispute. The accused operated a car on 17th Street in the city of Saskatoon at a speed of from 10 to 15 miles per hour. He had proceeded on 17th Street a distance of only about 150 feet, and made a right turn onto Saskatchewan Crescent East. While doing so, his car skidded over onto the left or north side of the road, and as a result he collided with another car which was proceeding in an opposite direction.

It is clear that his car was not on the right half of the road and that another car was inconvenienced thereby. It is clear to me that he got onto the wrong side of the road by an involuntary act, caused by the condition of the road, and I cannot say upon the evidence before me that it was his faulty driving that placed him in the position where he ended up. I think it was an involuntary act, for which he is not to blame.

Do these facts render him guilty of an offence under sec. 125 (9) of *The Vehicles Act*, R.S.S., 1953, ch. 344 [amended by 1955, ch. 82, sec. 27 (3)]? There are many sections under that Act that require no *mens rea*. Is this one of them? I do not think so. Were it otherwise some grave injustices would arise.

I can think of a case where a person drives a car carefully and a drunken driver runs into him and pushes his car over on to the left side of the road. I do not believe that the legislature intended such a person to be convicted under the section in question. And yet, if *mens rea* was not an essential ingredient of this offence, he would be guilty of it, since he did drive on the left side of the road.

No general rule can be formulated beyond stating that a person who by an involuntary act for which he is not to blame gets onto the wrong side of the road is not guilty under the section in question.

I find the accused not guilty.

R. v. WOLFE

(1975), 20 C.C.C. (2d) 382 (Ont. C.A.)

The judgment of the court was delivered orally by GALE C.J.O.: — The appellant was found guilty following a trial on a charge of assault causing bodily harm. After the finding of guilt was registered, the trial judge granted the appellant a conditional discharge. The appellant now appeals from the finding of guilt and this court is unanimously of the opinion that the appeal ought to be allowed, the finding of guilt set aside and a verdict of acquittal entered.

The appellant is a part-owner of a hotel in Kingston. On previous occasions, the complainant had been told, for good reason, that he was not to enter the hotel premises. On the evening in question, despite that prohibition, he entered the hotel. The appellant, using discretion and restraint, ordered him to leave. The complainant would not leave. The appellant then went to the telephone and while he was calling the police for the purpose of having him removed, the complainant punched the appellant who turned quickly and hit the complainant on the head with the telephone receiver. The complainant had a rather serious cut on his forehead, but that was really all that happened.

In giving judgment the learned trial judge said:

> Now, there is evidence that Mr. Brown-Keay hit the accused Mr. Wolfe and then in a reflex action (if you can call it that) Mr. Wolfe, who was calling the police, hit Mr. Brown-Keay on the forehead and caused a four-inch cut on his forehead. . . .

If, as it would seem to us, the trial judge regarded the action by the accused as being the result of a reflex action then no offence was committed because some intent is a necessary ingredient in an assault occasioning bodily harm.

Mr. Campbell argues, not very vigorously, however, that, because of the limitation in brackets in the above quotation, the trial judge did not regard the action of the appellant as resulting from his reflexes. However, that was in fact what the judge said and we see no reason to depart from his conclusion.

In any event, the encounter was a trifling one and we have come to the conclusion that the appeal ought to be allowed and the finding of guilt set aside, as I have already indicated. The appeal will therefore be allowed.

Appeal allowed.

R. v. SWABY

44 C.R. (5th) 1, 155 C.C.C. (3d) 235, 2001 CarswellOnt 2160 (Ont. C.A.)

Acting on a confidential tip, police officers followed a car driven by the accused in which J. was a passenger. The car stopped and J. ran into a nearby backyard. The accused drove off. Both men were arrested shortly thereafter. The police found a loaded, unregistered, restricted handgun in the backyard. J., the main Crown witness at the accused's trial, had pleaded guilty to possession of the handgun and received a sentence of time served (42 days). J. had a significant criminal record and was the subject of immigration proceedings. The accused was tried before a judge and jury on an indictment containing eight counts. He was convicted of being an occupant in a vehicle knowing there was present an unlicensed, restricted weapon contrary to s. 91(3) of the *Criminal Code*, but acquitted on all other counts. According to J.'s testimony the gun was the accused's and he gave it to J. to dispose of. According to the accused the gun was J.'s and he only learned of it after the arrest. The accused appealed his conviction.

The majority of the Ontario Court of Appeal allowed the accused's appeal, set aside the conviction and ordered a new trial.

Per SHARPE J.A. (FELDMAN J.A. concurring): —

. . . .

The charging provision under which the appellant was convicted was s. 91(3) of the *Criminal Code*, R.S.C. 1985, c. C-46:

91(3) Every one who is an occupant of a motor vehicle in which he knows there is a restricted weapon is, unless some occupant of the motor vehicle is the holder of a permit under which he may lawfully have that weapon in his possession in the vehicle, or he establishes that he had reason to believe that some occupant of the motor vehicle was the holder of such permit,

(a) guilty of an indictable offence and liable to imprisonment for a term not exceeding five years; or

(b) guilty of an offence punishable on summary conviction.

. . . .

To establish guilt on this count, the Crown had to prove the coincidence of the two essential elements of the offence as defined by s. 91(3), namely occupancy of the vehicle and the appellant's knowledge of the weapon. In my view, it is implicit as well that the Crown had to prove that the coincidence of occupancy and knowledge was attributable to something amounting to voluntary conduct on the part of the appellant. Although the section under which the appellant was charged contained no explicit defence in the terms of the present s. 94(3), it must be interpreted so as to exclude the possibility of conviction for what would amount to an involuntary act.

Voluntary conduct is a necessary element for criminal liability: see A.W. Mewett & M. Manning, *Mewett & Manning on Criminal Law*, 3rd ed. (Toronto, Butterworths: 1994) at pp. 129-32; Glanville Williams, *Textbook of Criminal Law*, 2nd ed. (London, Stevens & Sons: 1983) at pp. 146-54. The requirement for voluntary conduct applies even if the provision creating the offence does not expressly require one: see D. Stuart, *Canadian Criminal Law: A Treatise*, 3rd ed. (Toronto, Carswell: 1995) at p. 94: "There is no general Code stipulation that the guilty act be voluntary. The requirement exists by virtue of judicial reasoning . . .". As explained by McLachlin J. in *R. v. Théroux*, [1993] 2 S.C.R. 5, 79 C.C.C. (3d) 449 at p. 17 S.C.R., p. 458 C.C.C.: ". . . the act must be the voluntary act of the accused for the *actus reus* to exist."

If one acquires knowledge of an illegal weapon while travelling in a moving vehicle, it surely cannot be the law that criminal liability instantly attaches. There must be some period of time, however short, afforded to the person who has acquired that knowledge to deal with the situation. If a passenger tells the driver that the passenger has a gun, it cannot be the case that the driver is immediately guilty. Should the driver immediately stop the vehicle and tell the passenger to leave, the driver would have known of the gun while he was an occupant of the vehicle, but he would have done all the law could expect. The driver's occupancy of the vehicle would have coincided with his knowledge of the gun, but it could not be said that the coincidence of knowledge and occupancy amounted to voluntary conduct on the part of the driver. It is the conduct of the driver following the coincidence of occupancy and knowledge that counts, and if the driver acts with appropriate dispatch to get either the gun or himself out of the vehicle, there is no voluntary act for the criminal law to punish.

Accordingly, it is my view that if the appellant acquired knowledge of the weapon while the vehicle was in motion, he would have to be given a reasonable opportunity to either remove himself or to see that the weapon was removed from the vehicle. If the appellant only acquired knowledge of the weapon at the point when J. was leaving the vehicle, he would be entitled to an acquittal.

. . . .

It is my view that the appellant was entitled to a fuller explanation from the trial judge of the necessary elements of this offence dealing more thoroughly with the circumstances in which guilt would follow if knowledge of the weapon were acquired after the vehicle was set in motion. For these reasons, I would allow the appeal, set aside the conviction, and order a new trial.

. . . .

Per MACPHERSON J.A. (dissenting): — The appellant testified that at no time until after charges were laid did he know that there was a gun in his car. In spite of this testimony, the appellant now contends that, in response to the jury's questions, the trial judge should have given a broad answer that would have included an instruction on a scenario in which there was no evidence — namely, that the appellant became aware that J. had a gun at some point during their ride together in the car. In such a circumstance, I do not think that the trial judge erred by answering the jury's questions within the context of the evidence they had heard:

He must know of the existence of the weapon. You must be satisfied on the evidence you have heard in total throughout the trial but with respect to this particular question that you have asked, it must be proven by the Crown to have known of the existence of that weapon in that vehicle while both he and Mr. J. were in it.

In my view, this was a precise and, in light of the evidence (especially the appellant's position at trial), appropriate response to the jury's questions.

R. v. RYAN

(1967), 40 A.L.J.R. 488 (Aus. H.C.)

The accused, aged 20, read a novel in which the hero, feeling obliged to his parents, decided to rob a service station to obtain money to "invest" in the Irish sweepstake. In the book, the hero, armed with a gun, tied up the garage attendant's hands behind his back after having obtained his money. He subsequently won the lottery, repaid the owner of the service station handsomely and gave the balance of his winnings to his parents.

The accused, as an act of bravado and for excitement and self-aggrandizement, decided to emulate his hero. On arrival at the service station where he intended the drama to occur he left his companion outside and went in armed with a sawn-off rifle, loaded and cocked. He demanded money from the sole attendant, threatening him with the weapon. The attendant produced some money. The accused then told him to put his hands behind his back, and went to tie them together with a piece of cord he had brought with him for the purpose. At this point, according to the accused, the attendant made a sudden movement and the gun accidentally discharged, killing the attendant. It was clear that slight pressure by the accused's finger had caused the gun to discharge. The jury dismissed the defence of accident and convicted of murder. The accused was sentenced to life imprisonment.

On appeal the accused argued that the jury ought to have been instructed on the issue of involuntariness which, if accepted, would have resulted in an acquittal. The firing of the gun was a reflex response to a sudden movement by the victim and was unwilled action on his part. The police had conducted several re-enactments of this scenario and on each occasion the actor had pulled the trigger. However the Australian High Court unanimously rejected the view that the jury ought to have been so instructed.

WINDEYER J. (one of four judgments delivered): —

The essential that the act be a voluntary act is .... generally spoken of as a necessary quality of a criminal act; but it is perhaps more accurately regarded as a mental quality or attribute of the actor....

That an act is only punishable as a crime when it is the voluntary act of the accused is a statement satisfying in its simplicity. But what does it mean? What is a voluntary act? The answer is far from simple, partly because of ambiguities in the word "voluntary" and its supposed synonyms, partly because of imprecise, but inveterate, distinctions which have long dominated men's ideas concerning the working of the human mind. These distinctions, between will and intellect, between voluntary and involuntary action, may be unscientific and too simple for philosophy and psychology today. However that may be, the difficulty of expressing them in language is obvious and may be illustrated. The word "involuntary" is sometimes used as meaning an act done seemingly without the conscious exercise of the will, an "unwilled" act: sometimes as meaning an act done "unwillingly", that is by the conscious exercise of the will, but reluctantly or under duress so that it was not a "wilful" act. Words and phrases such as involuntary, unintentional, inadvertent, accidental, unmeditated, unthinking, not deliberate, unwilled and so forth are used by different writers. Their connotations often depend upon their context, and they are used in discussions which seem to drift easily off into psychological questions of consciousness, sanity and insanity and philosophical doctrines of free-will and of events uncontrolled by will. There is a discussion of some aspects of this subject in the American work, *Reflex Action, a Study in the History of Physiological Psychology.* I mention it, not because I profess any knowledge in this field, but because of the readiness with which the phrase "reflex action" was used in the course of the argument as a presumably exculpatory description of the act of the applicant when he pressed the trigger of the firearm.

The conduct which caused the death was of course a complex of acts all done by the applicant — loading the rifle, cocking it, presenting it, pressing the trigger. But it was the final act, pressing the trigger of the loaded and levelled rifle, which made the conduct lethal. When this was said to be a reflex action, the word "reflex" was not used strictly in the sense it ordinarily has in neurology as denoting a specific muscular reaction to a particular stimulus of a physical character. The phrase was, as I understood the argument, used to denote rather the probable but unpredictable reaction of a man when startled. He starts. In doing so he may drop something which he is holding, or grasp it more firmly. Doctor Johnson in his Dictionary — and his definition has been in substance repeated by others — said that "to start" means "to feel a sudden and involuntary twitch or motion of the animal frame on the apprehension of danger". The Oxford Dictionary speaks of a start as "a sudden involuntary movement of the body occasioned by surpise, terror, joy or grief ... ". But assume that the applicant's act was involuntary, in the sense in which the lexicographers use the word, would that, as a matter of law, absolve him from criminal responsibility for its consequences? I do not think so. I do not think that, for present purposes, such an act bears any true analogy to one done under duress, which, although done by an exercise of the will, is said to be involuntary because it was compelled. Neither does it, I think, bear any true analogy to an act done in convulsions or an epileptic seizure, which is said to be involuntary because by no exercise of the will could the actor refrain from doing it. Neither does it, I think, bear any true analogy to an act done by a sleepwalker or a person for some other reason rendered unconscious whose action is said to be involuntary because he knew not what he was doing.

Such phrases as "reflex action" and "automatic reaction" can, if used imprecisely and unscientifically, be, like "blackout", mere excuses. They seem to me to have no real application to the case of a fully conscious man who has put himself in a situation in which he has his finger on the trigger of a loaded rifle levelled at another man. If he then presses the trigger in immediate response to a sudden threat or apprehension of danger, as is said to have occurred in this case, his doing so is, it seems to me, a consequence probable and foreseeable of a conscious apprehension of danger, and in that sense a voluntary act. The latent time is no doubt barely appreciable, and what was done might not have been done had the actor had time to think. But is an act to be called involuntary merely because the mind worked quickly and impulsively? I have misgivings in using any language descriptive of psychological processes and phenomena, especially as I doubt whether all those skilled in this field employ their descriptive terms uniformly. Guided however by what has been said in other cases and by writers on criminal law whose works I have read, and especially by the judgments in the House of Lords in *Bratty v. Attorney-General for Northern Ireland*, [1963] A.C. 386, I have come to the conclusion that if the applicant, being conscious of the situation in which he had put himself, pressed the trigger as a result, however spontaneous, of the man whom he was threatening making some sudden movement, it could not be said that his action was involuntary so as to make the homicide guiltless. The act which caused the death was. ... an act of the accused. The question for the jury was whether it was an act done by him in such a way as to make the resulting homicide murder. This was the issue submitted to the jury. The application for special leave to appeal must I consider be refused.

KILBRIDE v. LAKE

[1962] N.Z.L.R. 590 (S.C.)

WOODHOUSE J.: — On Thursday, 15 June 1961, the appellant drove his wife's car into Queen Street in the City of Auckland where he left it parked. He returned to it a short time later to find stuck to the inside of the windscreen a traffic offence notice drawing his attention to the fact that a current warrant of fitness was not displayed in terms of Reg. 52 of the Traffic Regulations 1956 (S.R. 1956/217). It was agreed before me that the warrant had been in its correct position when he left the vehicle, but that it could not be found upon his return. It was further agreed that during the period of his absence from the car the warrant had become detached from the windscreen in some way and been lost, or it had been removed by some person unknown. The fact that it was a current warrant was proved conclusively by records showing that on 13 April it had been issued by the Auckland Municipal Motor Vehicle Testing Station under No. 4513, and in respect of voucher No. 115456. Thus it had been issued for only two months, and four months would elapse before it required to be renewed. Despite a written explanation to this general effect which he had forwarded on the same day, a prosecution followed and he was convicted before Justices on an information alleging that he "did operate a motor vehicle . . . and did fail to display in the prescribed manner a current warrant of fitness". The proceedings were defended, but no note of the evidence was taken and no reasons for the decision were given. In these circumstances the appeal was argued on agreed facts as I have summarised them.

So far as it is applicable the regulation reads:

(1) . . . No person shall operate a motor vehicle . . . unless there is carried on the vehicle a current warrant of fitness as described in subclause (2) of this Regulation.

Subclause (2) provides that in the case of a vehicle fitted with a windscreen the warrant shall be affixed to the inside of the windscreen. The word "operate" is defined in Reg. 3 as meaning

to use or drive or ride, or cause or permit to be driven or ridden, or to permit to be on any road whether the person operating is present in person or not.

The appeal was argued on the basis that the appellant operated the vehicle by permitting it to be on the road, and the facts do not support any wider application of the word "operate". Accordingly the regulation under review may be written, for the present purpose, as follows:

No person shall permit a motor vehicle to be on a road whether the person operating it is present or not unless there is carried on the vehicle a current warrant of fitness.

The case for the appellant was that if he could show an absence of *mens rea*, then he could not be convicted, and he had succeeded in doing this as the warrant had disappeared without his knowledge during his absence from the car. On the other hand it was claimed for the respondent that this statutory offence was one which excluded *mens rea* as an ingredient to be proved. On this basis it was submitted that the offence was one of strict liability, and therefore the knowledge or the intention of the appellant was irrelevant. The issue thus raised on these simple facts directly poses the important question as to whether something done perfectly lawfully by the appellant could become an offence on his part by reason of an intervening cause beyond his influence or control, and which produced an effect entirely outside his means of knowledge.

It has long been established, of course, that if there is an absolute prohibition, and the prohibited act is done by the defendant, then the absence of *mens rea* affords no defence. This principle derives its justification from the general public interest, and any consequential injustice which might seem to follow in individual cases has necessarily been accepted. In the present case the respondent has conceded that the appellant had no opportunity of dealing with the situation which arose. But, it is said, however unfair a conviction might be to him personally, this offence has been made one of absolute liability as it is essential to put strong pressure on drivers of motor vehicles to do their whole duty. He permitted the car to be on the road, it was found there without a warrant, and accordingly he is guilty of the offence. With all respect to the arguments of both counsel, however, I am of the opinion that the emphasis which has been put on the matter of *mens rea* has obscured the real issue in this case.

It is fundamental that quite apart from any need there might be to prove *mens rea*,

> a person cannot be convicted of any crime unless he has committed an overt act prohibited by the law, or has made default in doing some act which there was a legal obligation upon him to do. The act or omission must be voluntary. (*10 Halsbury's Laws of England*, 3rd ed., 272.)

He must be shown to be responsible for the physical ingredient of the crime or offence. This elementary principle obviously involves the proof of something which goes behind any subsequent and additional inquiry that might become necessary as to whether *mens rea* must be proved as well. Until that initial proof exists arguments concerning *mens rea* are premature. If the first decision to be made is that the offence excludes *mens rea*, then that finding is likely to disguise the fact that there is an absence of proof showing that the accused has done all that is charged against him, should this in fact be the case. The missing link in the chain of causation, if it is noticed at all, appears to be provided by notions of absolute liability. But it is impossible, of course, to prove the one ingredient by eliminating the need to prove another. It appears to me that this confusion has arisen in this case. The primary question arising on this appeal, in my opinion, is whether or not the physical element in the offence was produced by the appellant. This physical element may be described by the convenient term *actus reus*, in contrast to the mental element or *mens rea* which is also an ingredient of a crime or offence, unless expressly excluded by its statutory definition.

In considering whether the *actus reus* can be attributed to a defendant, it is important to recognize that this is something which occurs following acts or omissions. It is not the line of conduct which produces the prohibited event, but it is the event itself. It is an occurrence brought about by some activity or inactivity, or by both. The crime therefore (excluding for the moment the possible ingredient of *mens rea*) is constituted by the event, and not by the discrete acts or omissions which preceded it: *Russell on Crime*, 11th ed., pp. 25, *et seq.* Accordingly it is not sufficient to show by some single act or omission that the accused produced the event. It is this fact which produces difficulties of causation when attempting to attribute responsibility for the *actus reus* to a given person. It is easy to do this when the *actus reus* can result from a single act, as, for example, a death by shooting. When it depends, however, upon supervening acts, and particularly when omissions are added to them, then the difficulties tend to multiply. Of course, when *mens rea* is an ingredient to be proved against an accused person, all these difficulties disappear as soon as they arise, because he usually cannot be proved to have intended acts done by others. He is thereupon acquitted on that ground. As *mens rea* is so frequently an ingredient of crimes and offences, this is a problem which rarely arises, and for that reason is not always recognized.

In the present case the definition of the offence takes the form of a prohibition followed by an exception. The prohibited event, however, in the sense of the term *actus reus* is not merely to permit a vehicle to be on a road. It is the doing of that act accompanied by an omission to observe the obligation to carry the current warrant of fitness. The *actus reus* occurs only when the second of these factual ingredients co-exists with the first. There must be the presence of the car combined with the absence of the warrant. Did this appellant produce that prohibited event, or did he merely set the stage?

There can be no doubt that the appellant permitted the vehicle to be on the road, and his conduct in this respect was a continuing act which did not end when he left the vehicle. Nevertheless, at this latter point of time the warrant was on the car, and there was no unlawful situation. Only when some extraneous cause subsequently removed the warrant did the event occur which the regulation is directed to prevent. If he is to be regarded as responsible for that *actus reus*, therefore, the decision must be made on the basis that he omitted immediately to replace the warrant.

It is, of course, difficult to demonstrate that an omission to act was not, in a causal sense, an omission which produced some event. All omissions result from inactivity, and in this matter of the warrant the appellant was necessarily inactive. But, in my opinion, it is a cardinal principle that, altogether apart from the mental element of intention or knowledge of the circumstances, a person cannot be made criminally responsible for an act or omission unless it was done or omitted in circumstances where there was some other course open to him. If this condition is absent, any act or omission must be involuntary, or unconscious, or unrelated to the forbidden event in any causal sense regarded by the law as involving responsibility. See for example *Salmond on Jurisprudence*, 11th ed. 401, *Causation in the Law* by Hart and Honore 292, *et seq.*, and the passage in *10 Halsbury's Laws of England*, 3rd ed., 272 cited above. In my opinion a correct emphasis is now given by this last paragraph to the need for the act or omission making up the *actus reus* to be voluntary, whereas in the corresponding paragraph of the second edition this distinction was blurred in discussion of *mens rea*. Naturally the condition that there must be freedom to take one course or another involves free and conscious exercise of will in the case of an act, or the opportunity to choose to behave differently in the case of omissions. But this mental stimulus required to promote acts or available to promote omissions if the matter is adverted to, and consequently able to produce some forbidden condition, is entirely distinct from the mental element contained in the concept of *mens rea*. The latter is the intention or the knowledge behind or accompanying the exercise of will, while the former is simply the spark without which the *actus reus* cannot be produced at all. In the present case there was no opportunity at all to take a different course, and any inactivity on the part of the appellant after the warrant was removed was involuntary and unrelated to the offence. In these circumstances I do not think it can be said that the *actus reus* was in any sense the result of his conduct, whether intended or accidental. There was an act of the appellant which led up to the prohibited event (the *actus reus*), and that was to permit the car to be on the road. The second factual ingredient was not satisfied until the warrant disappeared during his absence. The resulting omission to carry the warrant was not within his conduct, knowledge, or control: on these facts the chain of causation was broken.

For the foregoing reasons I am of the opinion that the physical ingredient of this charge was not proved against the appellant. Accordingly, I express no opinion on the submission that *mens rea* is excluded as an ingredient of the offence. On the view I have taken of the case the point does not arise.

Before I part with this appeal I think it should be said that the true purpose of the regulation is to ensure that motor vehicles are kept off the highway unless they are shown to be roadworthy by means of a current warrant of fitness. The additional requirement that the current warrant be displayed in a particular manner is, of course, an effective and sensible means of promoting that purpose. It keeps the matter before the notice of the driver, and also it enables traffic officers to check the position regularly, and with a minimum of difficulty. This latter fact, however, should not be elevated to such a level that charges are laid almost automatically against ordinary folk who have shown promptly and conclusively that a missing warrant was in fact current, and that there was an acceptable and proper explanation for its absence from the windscreen. As I have already stated, this appellant provided the Traffic Department of the Corporation concerned with a written explanation of the whole position on the day of the alleged offence, and he included in his letter all the numerical details concerning the issue of the warrant to which I have referred. I was informed by counsel that if he had also enclosed the voucher itself, his explanation would probably have been accepted and no further action would have been taken. If there was any real doubt in the mind of the officer concerned as to the currency of the warrant, it is a pity that he did not check with the Municipal Testing Station, or invite the appellant to produce the voucher. To the extent that this is a mandatory requirement it is a weapon intended to put appropriate pressure on people to do their duty. This general purpose is not likely to be promoted by prosecuting people who cannot reasonably be expected to do more than in fact they have done. It seems a proper case to award costs against the respondent, and accordingly I allow the appellant 10 guineas and disbursements. The appeal is allowed and the conviction quashed.

Appeal allowed.

5. ACTING THROUGH INNOCENT AGENT

R. v. MICHAEL

(1840), 9 C. & P. 356 (C.C.C.R.)

The prisoner was indicted for the wilful murder of George Michael. She was also charged on the coroner's inquisition with the same offence.

The indictment stated, that the prisoner, contriving and intending to kill and murder George Michael on the 31st day of March, in the third year of the reign of her present Majesty, upon the said George Michael feloniously, &c., did make an assault, and that the prisoner, a large quantity, to wit, half an ounce weight, of a certain deadly poison called laudanum, feloniously, &c., did give and administer unto the said George Michael, with intent that he should take and swallow the same down into his body (she then and there well knowing the said laudanum to be a deadly poison), and the said George Michael the said laudanum so given and administered unto him by the said Catherine Michael as aforesaid, did take and swallow down into his body; by reason and by means of which said taking and swallowing down the said laudanum into his body, as aforesaid, the said George Michael became and was mortally sick and distempered in his body, of which said mortal sickness and distemper the said George Michael from &c. till &c. did languish, &c., and died; and concluding in the usual form, as in cases of murder.

It appeared that the deceased was a child between nine and ten months old, and that the prisoner was its mother, and was a single woman living in service as wet nurse at Mrs. Kelly's, in Hunter Street, Brunswick Square. The child was taken care of by a woman named Stevens, living at Paddington, who received five shillings a week from the prisoner for its support. A few days before its death the prisoner told Mrs. Stevens that she had an old frock for the child, and a bottle of medicine, which she gave her, telling her it would do the baby's bowels good. Mrs. Stevens said the baby was very well, and did not want medicine; but the prisoner said it had done her mistress's baby good, and it would do her baby good, and desired Mrs. Stevens to give it one teaspoonful every night. Mrs. Stevens did not open the bottle, or give the child any of its contents, but put the bottle on the mantel-piece, where it remained till Tuesday, the 31st of March, on which day, about half-past four in the afternoon, Mrs. Stevens went out, leaving the prisoner's child playing on the floor with her children, one of whom, about five years of age, during the absence for about ten minutes of his elder sister, gave the prisoner's child about half the contents of the bottle, which made it extremely ill, and in the course of a few hours it died. The bottle was found to contain laudanum. The prisoner said that a young man, an assistant of Dr. Reid's, had given the bottle by mistake. This was proved to be untrue; and Dr. Reid stated, that in the course of a conversation he had with the prisoner, she used these remarkable words, speaking of the death of the child, and the probability of an inquest being held upon the body: — "If I am hanged for it, I could not support the child on my wages." It was also proved that the prisoner purchased the laudanum at the chemist's in Tavistock Place, Russell Square, saying that it was for her mistress, Mrs. Kelly, who was in the habit of taking it, being a bad sleeper. One of the medical men examined at the trial said, that a teaspoonful administered to a child of the age of the deceased would be sure to destroy life.

Alderson, B., in his summing up, told the jury, that if the prisoner delivered the laudanum to Sarah Stevens with the intention that she should administer it to the child, and thereby produce its death, and the quantity so directed to be administered was sufficient to cause death, and while the prisoner's original intention continued, the laudanum was administered by an unconscious agent, the death of the child, under such circumstances, would sustain the charge of murder against the prisoner. His Lordship added, that if the teaspoonful of laudanum was sufficient to produce death, the administration by the little boy of a much larger quantity would make no difference.

The jury found the prisoner guilty. The judgment was respited, that the opinion of the Judges might be taken, whether the facts above stated constituted an administering of the poison by the prisoner to the deceased child.

Ryland, for the prosecution.

Ballantine, for the prisoner.

At a subsequent Session, Mr. Baron Alderson, in passing sentence upon the prisoner, said, that the Judges were of opinion that the administering of the poison by the child of Mrs. Stevens, was, under the circumstances of the case, as much, in point of law, an administering by the prisoner as if the prisoner had actually administered it with her own hand. They therefore held that she was rightly convicted.

Would it have made any difference if the laudanum had been administered by a conscious agent who acted for his own purposes?

For Canadian authority applying the "doctrine of acting through an innocent agent" see *R. v. MacFadden* (1971), 5 C.C.C. (2d) 204, 16 C.R.N.S. 251 at 253 (N.B. C.A.); *R. v. Berryman* (1990), 78 C.R. (3d) 376, 57 C.C.C. (3d) 375, (B.C. C.A.); *R. v. Ali* (1990), 79 C.R. (3d) 382 (Ont. Prov. Ct.) and *R. v. Toma* (2000), 147 C.C.C. (3d) 252 (B.C. C.A.).

In *R. v. Devgan* (2007) 53 C.R. (6th) 104 (Ont. S.C.J.) Justice Ducharme held that a doctor could be guilty of trafficking drugs as the acts of the pharmacist unaware of the illegal scheme could be considered his acts even though he exercised independent judgment. Under the doctrine the instigator is deemed to be the actual perpetrator even though the agent's acts were non-criminal specific to the agent, such as the absence of *mens rea*, a defence, mental disorder or infancy. Requiring that the innocent agent cannot exercise independent judgment would lead to undesirable results.

The doctrine of acting through an agent has been relied on to confer some criminal responsibility as a perpetrator for injuries committed through animals (e.g. getting a dog to attack a person). We shall see much later under Parties to an Offence that there is also wide criminal responsibility in Canadian law beyond the actual perpetrator to those who merely assist or facilitate.

6. CAUSATION

(a) *Criminal Code*

In the case of some but not all offences the *actus reus* requires the causing of certain consequences. These offences include all homicides (s. 222), wilful damage to property (s. 430), arson (s. 433), and causing bodily harm (s. 221) or death (s. 220) by criminal negligence. The latter two offences illustrate that graver consequences may attract a higher maximum penalty — life imprisonment in the case of death and ten years imprisonment in the case of bodily harm. Since 1985 the maximum penalty of five years for the offence of dangerous operation of a vehicle increases to ten years where that conduct causes bodily harm and to 14 years where death results (s. 249 (3) and (4) and see similarly for impaired driving (s. 255 (2) and (3)).

Our *Code* contains no general principles concerning causation but only a number of special rules concerning homicide: see ss. 222 and 224-228.

B.C. ELECTRIC RY. v. LOACH

[1916] 1 A.C. 719 at 727-728 (P.C.)

LORD SUMNER: —

. . . .

It is surprising how many epithets eminent judges have applied to the cause, which has to be ascertained for this judicial purpose of determining liability, and how many more to other acts and incidents, which for this purpose are not the cause at all. or effective cause," "real cause," "proximate cause," "direct cause," "decisive cause," "immediate cause," "causa causans," on the one hand, as against, on the other, "causa sine qua non," "occasional cause," "remote cause," "contributory cause," "inducing cause," "condition," and so on. No doubt in the particular cases in which they occur they were thought to be useful or they would not have been used, but the repetition of terms without examination in other cases has often led to confusion, and it might be better, after pointing out that the inquiry is an investigation into responsibility, to be content with speaking of the cause of the injury simply and without qualification.

(b)   Common Law

SMITHERS v. R.

[1978] 1 S.C.R. 506, 40 C.R.N.S. 79, 34 C.C.C. (2d) 427,
1977 CarswellOnt 25, 1977 CarswellOnt 479F

DICKSON J.: — This is an appeal from a judgment of the Court of Appeal for Ontario dismissing an appeal brought by the appellant from his conviction by judge and jury on a charge of manslaughter. The indictment alleges that the appellant did unlawfully kill Barrie Ross Cobby by kicking him.

On February 18, 1973, a hockey game was played between the Applewood Midget Team and the Cooksville Midget Team at the Cawthra Park Arena in the Town of Mississauga. The leading player on the Applewood team was the deceased, Barrie Cobby, 16 years of age; the leading player on the Cooksville team was the appellant. The game was rough, the players were aggressive and feelings ran high. The appellant, who is black, was subjected to racial insults by Cobby and other members of the Applewood team. Following a heated and abusive exchange of profanities, the appellant and Cobby were both ejected from the game. The appellant made repeated threats that he was going to "get" Cobby. Cobby was very apprehensive and left the arena at the end of the game, some 45 minutes later, accompanied by eight or ten persons including friends, players, his coach and the team's manager. The appellant repeated his threats and challenges to fight as the group departed. Cobby did not take up the challenge. Instead, he hurried toward a waiting car. The appellant caught up with him at the bottom of the outside steps and directed one or two punches to Cobby's head. Several of Cobby's team mates grabbed the appellant and held him. Cobby, who had taken no steps to defend himself, was observed to double up and stand back while the appellant struggled to free himself from those holding him. While Cobby was thus bent over, and approximately two to four feet from the appellant, the appellant delivered what was described as a hard, fast kick to Cobby's stomach area. Only seconds elapsed between the punching and the kick. Following the kick, Cobby groaned, staggered towards his car, fell to the ground on his back, and gasped for air. Within five minutes he appeared to stop breathing. He was dead upon arrival at the Mississauga General Hospital.

Doctor David Brunsdon, who performed an autopsy, testified that in his opinion death was due to the aspiration of foreign materials present from vomiting. He defined aspiration as the breathing, or taking in, of foreign material through the windpipe into the lungs. It appears from the medical evidence that aspiration is generally due to barbiturate overdosage, alcohol intoxication, motor vehicle accidents or epilepsy. One medical witness testified to the possibility of spontaneous aspiration, whereby foreign material may be aspirated without any precipitating cause. This witness had seen three such cases out of the 900 to

1,000 cases of aspiration which he had experienced. In none of the three cases was the aspiration preceded by a blow. The consensus among the doctors was that spontaneous aspiration was a rare and unusual cause of death in the case of a healthy teenager such as Cobby. Normally, when a person vomits the epiglottis folds over to prevent the regurgitated stomach contents from entering the air passage. In the instant case this protective mechanism failed.

. . . .

The ground of dissent in the Ontario Appeal Court forms the first ground of appeal in this court. Counsel for the appellant submits that the trial judge, in emphasizing the act of assault as a constituent element in the crime of manslaughter, did not make it clear to the jury that the act of assault must also cause the death of the deceased and, secondly, that in giving his summation of the Crown and defence theories, the trial judge referred to the issue of causation as defence counsel's argument that the cause of death had not been proven beyond a reasonable doubt. It is contended that the effect of these remarks was to minimize this issue in the minds of the jury. The jury was never instructed, it is said, that as a matter of law one of the issues on which they had to be satisfied beyond a reasonable doubt was that the kick caused the vomiting.

. . . .

I agree with the majority view in the Ontario Court of Appeal that the issue as to the cause of death was properly and sufficiently delineated by the trial judge. It was not an unduly complicated issue. The assault by the appellant upon the deceased boy was undoubtedly an unlawful act. The principal issue was whether the appellant had committed homicide by directly or indirectly, by any means, causing the death of Cobby and whether such homicide was culpable for the reason that it was caused by an unlawful act. The Crown quite properly chose to establish causation principally through medical evidence and the doctors, men of high professional standing, understandably were disinclined to speak in absolute terms.

Doctor Brunsdon testified as to the effect of a sudden blow in the abdominal area. He said:

> I couldn't say always, but it certainly I think, would be predisposed to regurgitation. I am certainly not going to say it would happen in every case, but I think it could be predisposed to.

During cross-examination, Dr. Brunsdon used the expressions "very possible" and "very probable" to describe the cause and effect of the kick and the vomiting. As to the relationship of the kick and aspiration, he said: "I can amplify that a bit. It is a rare condition, but the kick would have made it more likely to aspirate." The following passage appears in the testimony of Dr. Hillsdon Smith, Professor of Forensic Pathology at the University of Toronto:

I have already given in evidence that fear by itself can cause vomiting, a kick by itself can cause vomiting. The two together have simply a greater effect than either of those singly.

The jury was not limited to the evidence of the medical experts. In considering the issue of causation the jury had the benefit of uncontradicted evidence of a number of lay witnesses to the effect that the appellant kicked the deceased boy in the stomach area, that the kick was followed by immediate distress, and that the death occurred within minutes. This was cogent evidence to which the jury could apply common sense in considering the issue of causality. In my opinion, the first ground of appeal cannot be maintained.

The second ground, not unrelated to the first ground, is that the court of Appeal erred in holding that there was evidence on the basis of which the jury was entitled to find that it had been established beyond a reasonable doubt that the kick caused the death. This broad question is unfortunately phrased, in that it leaves doubt whether the issue raised is one of sufficiency of evidence, a question of fact to which the jurisdiction of this court does not extend, or an entire absence of evidence upon which a finding could be made that the kick caused the death, a question of law. The appellant's factum tends to remove the uncertainty by subsuming, within the broad question, three narrower questions. The first of these is whether the jury was restricted to a consideration of the expert medical evidence in making its determination on the issue of causation. It is conceded that the jury was entitled to consider all of the evidence, expert and lay, in its deliberations with respect to the issue of causation but on the precise question of whether or not the kick caused the vomiting or the aspiration, it is contended the jury was restricted to the medical evidence. It seems to me to be a novel proposition, subversive of the usual jury procedure, that on a particular issue the jury should be denied the evidence of certain witnesses. I have difficulty also in reconciling the concession that the jury is entitled to consider all of the evidence on the issue of causation but something less than all the evidence when considering the only causative questions in the case, namely, whether the kick caused the vomiting and whether the kick caused the aspiration. In support of his submission counsel cited *Walker v. Bedard and Snelling*, [1945] 1 D.L.R. 529. That was a civil case tried by LeBel J., without a jury in which damages were claimed against a surgeon and an an anaesthetist for the death of a patient following the injection of nupercaine into the spinal canal. LeBel J. quoted with approval a passage from the American decision in *Ewing v. Goode* (1897), 78 Fed. Rep. 442 at p. 444, in which the following words appear [p. 536 D.L.R.]:

"But when a case concerns the highly specialized art of treating an eye for cataract, or for the mysterious and dread disease of glaucoma, with respect to which a layman can have no knowledge at all, the court and jury must be dependant on expert evidence. There can be no other guide, and, where want of skill or attention is not thus shown by expert evidence applied to the facts, there is no evidence of it proper to be submitted to the jury."

The other case cited was *State v. Minton* (1952), 68 S.E. 2d 844, in which the death of the deceased was caused by a pistol bullet fired by one of the defendants, and a resulting haemorrhage. The judgment contains these words:

> The State did not undertake to show any causal relation between the wound and the death by a medical expert. For this reason, the question arises whether the cause of death may be established in a prosecution for unlawful homicide without the use of expert medical testimony. The law is realistic when it fashions rules of evidence for use in the search for truth. The cause of death may be established in a prosecution for unlawful homicide without the use of expert medical testimony where the facts in evidence are such that every person of average intelligence would know from his own experience or knowledge that the wound was mortal in character.
>
> There is no proper foundation, however, for a finding by the jury as to the cause of death without expert medical testimony where the cause of death is obscure and an average layman could have no well grounded opinion as to the cause.

In my opinion, neither of the cases cited lends any support to the proposition sought to be advanced by the appellant. No useful comparison is possible between an operation for glaucoma and the circumstances in the case at bar. In *Minton's* case the causal relation between the wound and the death was established without medical evidence.

It is important in considering the issue of causation in homicide to distinguish between causation as a question of fact and causation as a question of law. The factual determination is whether A caused B. The answer to the factual question can only come from the evidence of witnesses. It has nothing to do with intention, foresight or risk. In certain types of homicide jurors need little help from medical experts. Thus, if D shoots P or stabs him and death follows within moments, there being no intervening cause, jurors would have little difficulty in resolving the issue of causality from their own experience and knowledge.

Expert evidence is admissible, of course, to establish factual cause. The work of expert witnesses in an issue of this sort, as Glanville Williams has pointed out ("Causation in Homicide", [1957] *Crim. L.R.* 429 at p. 431), is "purely diagnostic and does not involve them in metaphysical subtleties"; it does not require them to distinguish between what is a "cause", *i.e.*, a real and contributing cause of death, and what is merely a "condition", *i.e.*, part of the background of the death. Nor should they be expected to say, where two or more causes combine to produce a result, which of these causes contributes the more.

In the case at bar, the Crown had the burden of showing factual causation, that beyond a reasonable doubt the kick caused the death. In my view, the trial judge did not err in failing to instruct the jury that in determining that issue they could consider only the medical evidence. The issue of causation is for the jury and not the experts. The weight to be given to the evidence of the experts was entirely for the jury. In the search for truth, the jury was entitled to consider all of the evidence, expert and lay, and accept or reject any part of it. Non-medical testimony is available to both the Crown and the accused, and in the instant case, lay evidence was vital to the defence raised by the appellant. That evidence tended to show that all the circumstances preceding the kick were such as to create in the deceased boy a highly emotional state which might well have given rise to spontaneous vomiting, unassociated with the kick.

The second sub-question raised is whether there was evidence on the basis of which the jury was entitled to find that it had been established beyond a reasonable doubt that the kick caused the death. In answer to this question it may shortly be said that there was a very substantial body of evidence, both expert and lay, before the jury indicating that the kick was at least a contributing cause of death, outside the *de minimis* range, and that is all that the Crown was required to establish. It is immaterial that the death was in part caused by a malfunctioning epiglottis to which malfunction the appellant may, or may not, have contributed. No question of remoteness or of incorrect treatment arises in this case.

I should like to adopt two short passages from a case note on *R. v. Larkin* (1942), 29 Cr. App. R. 18, by G.A. Martin, as he then was, which appeared in 21 *Can. Bar Rev.* 503 at pp. 504-5 (1943):

> There are many unlawful acts which are not dangerous in themselves and are not likely to cause injury which, nevertheless if they cause death, render the actor guilty of culpable homicide, *e.g.*, the most trivial assault, if it should, through some unforeseen weakness in the deceased, cause death, will render the actor guilty of culpable homicide.
>
> . . . .
>
> In the case of so-called intentional crimes where death is an unintended consequence the actor is always guilty of manslaughter at least. The act of the accused in *R. v. Larkin* fell within the class of intentional crimes because he was engaged in committing an assault upon Nielsen, and the fact that he caused a different type of harm to that which he intended did not free him from criminal responsibility.

The Crown was under no burden of proving intention to cause death or injury. The only intention necessary was that of delivering the kick to Cobby. Nor was foreseeability in issue. It is no defence to a manslaughter charge that the fatality was not anticipated or that death ordinarily would not result from the unlawful act.[*]

In *R. v. Cato et al.* (1975), 62 Cr. App. R. 41, the act supporting the manslaughter conviction was the injection by the accused into another person of morphine which the accused had unlawfully taken into his possession. Attention was directed to causation, and the link alleged to exist between the injection of morphine and the death. The appellant's argument based on the medical evidence of causation and the rejection of that argument by the Court of Appeal are to be found in the following passage, pp. 44-5:

---

[*] Editor's note: This statement of the fault requirement for manslaughter was expressly overruled in *DeSousa*, which was followed by the full Court in *Creighton*, a case we consider later in Chapter 3, "The Fault Requirement (*Mens Rea* or Negligence)".

First of all, he invited us to look at the evidence of causation, and he pointed out that the medical evidence did not at any point say "This morphine killed Farmer"; the actual link of that kind was not present. The witnesses were hesitant to express such a view and often recoiled from it, saying it was not for them to state the cause of death. It is perfectly true, as Mr. Blom-Cooper says, that the expert evidence did not in positive terms provide a link, but it was never intended to do so. The expert witnesses here spoke to factual situations, and the conclusions and deductions therefore were for the jury. The first question was: was there sufficient evidence upon which the jury could conclude, as they must have concluded, that adequate causation was present?

The third sub-question is whether there was evidence from which the jury was entitled to find that it had been established beyond a reasonable doubt that the kick caused the aspiration. It is contended that the burden on the Crown was to prove beyond a reasonable doubt that the kick caused both the vomiting and the aggravated condition of aspiration. I do not agree. A person commits homicide, according to s. 205(1) of the *Code*, when directly or indirectly, by any means, he causes the death of a human being. Once evidence had been led concerning the relationship between the kick and the vomiting, leading to aspiration of stomach contents and asphyxia, the contributing condition of a malfunctioning epiglottis would not prevent conviction for manslaughter. Death may have been unexpected, and the physical reactions of the victim unforeseen, but that does not relieve the appellant.

In *R. v. Garforth*, [1954] Crim. L.R. 936, a decision of the Court of Criminal Appeal of England, the accused, aged 16, and another young man, S, quarrelled with the deceased, aged 18, outside a dance-hall. S kicked the deceased and when he doubled up stabbed him in the neck and heart, then the accused kicked him on the body and legs and S kicked him on the head. S was found guilty of murder and the accused was found guilty of manslaughter. The accused appealed against his conviction on the ground there was no evidence that what he did was a cause of death. It was held, dismissing the appeal, that there was clear evidence that the accused unlawfully assaulted the deceased and inflicted minor injuries which contributed to the death. Had the jury found that the accused intended to do grievous bodily harm, he would have been guilty of murder.

It is a well-recognized principle that one who assaults another must take his victim as he finds him. An extreme example of the application of the principle will be found in the English case of *R. v. Blaue*, [1975] 1 W.L.R. 1411, in which the court upheld a conviction for manslaughter where the victim's wounds were only fatal because of her refusal, on religious grounds, to accept a blood transfusion. The court rejected the argument that the victim's refusal had broken the chain of causation between the stabbing and the death.

Although causation in civil cases differs from that in a criminal case, the "thin skulled man" may appear in the criminal law as in the civil law. The case of *R. v. Nicholson* (1926), 47 C.C.C. 113, 59 N.S.R. 323, will serve as an illustration. In that case, the accused dealt the deceased man two heavy blows. The man who was struck was in poor physical condition. His heart was abnormally small and he was suffering from Bright's disease. An eminent medical specialist was asked if the blow or blows could cause death, given the condition of the body which was described, and he said it was possible. The blow might be one of the causes. Over-indulgence in alcohol, bad health, and the blow and tussle combined, in his opinion, to account for the result. The appeal from conviction was dismissed. Even if the unlawful act, alone, would not have caused the death, it was still a legal cause so long as it contributed in some way to the death. I myself presided at a jury trial in which the accused, one Alan Canada, following an argument, struck his brother lightly on the head with a piece of firewood as a result of which the brother died some time later without regaining consciousness. The medical evidence showed that the bony structure of his skull was unusually thin and fragile. The accused, on the advice of counsel, pleaded guilty to a charge of manslaughter and I have never considered that he was wrong in doing so.

I would conclude this point by saying that although Dr. Hillsdon Smith thought that once vomiting had been induced, aspiration in these circumstances was no more than an accident, both Dr. Brunsdon and Dr. Butt acknowledged that the kick may have contributed to the epiglottal malfunction.

That brings me to the third and final ground of appeal, namely, whether the trial Judge's charge to the jury on the issue of self-defence amounted to misdirection. Although undoubtedly much upset by the actions and language of Cobby during the first ten minutes of play, thereafter the appellant alone was the aggressor. He relentlessly pursued Cobby some 45 minutes later for the purpose of carrying out his threats to "get" Cobby. Despite the frail factual underpinning for such a defence, the trial judge charged fully on self-defence and in a manner which, in my opinion, was not open to criticism.

I would dismiss the appeal.

Appeal dismissed.

PROBLEM

At 9:30 p.m. the accused went to the nearby residence of the victim, angry that his cat had apparently been injured by the victim's cat. The accused stood on the porch of the victim's residence and threatened the cat and the victim, provoking the victim into agreeing to fight with the accused outside. The victim was barefoot and went downstairs to get his shoes. The victim's wife asked the accused to stop and twice pointed out that her husband had had strokes. The victim, who appeared emotionally upset, fetched his shoes and ran or walked quickly some sixty five feet to the sidewalk in front of his house. In a very brief physical encounter, the victim was put or thrown down to the ground by the accused. A short while later that evening the victim suffered an acute heart attack and died at about 11:30 p.m.

The victim had a long history of medical illness. He had diabetes, high blood pressure, a history of strokes, and had suffered at least one prior heart attack. He had triple coronary disease, with high grade calcification and obstruction in all three arteries. He was on disability leave, was inactive and overweight. A stress test had revealed that he was unable to do fundamental tasks such as vacuuming or taking out the garbage.

At the accused's trial on a charge of manslaughter before judge alone, prosecution medical evidence was led that an acute plaque rupture in the right coronary artery ultimately led to the blockage of blood to the victim's heart and, as a result, his death. According to the medical evidence emotional or physical stress or a combination of both may trigger a plaque rupture. It is often difficult to isolate specific triggering events. In cross-examination the cardiologist testified that there was an 80 to 90 per cent probability that the plaque rupture may have occurred even if the physical assault had never taken place. As he put it "I don't think that the actual dropping of the body, the actual fall, the trauma of the fall, had much bearing on the matter".

The trial judge found the accused guilty of unlawful act manslaughter. He found beyond a reasonable doubt that the unlawful act of physical assault, alone, was a contributing cause of death outside the *de minimis* range. The trial judge imposed a sentence of six years imprisonment, emphasizing the need for specific and general deterrence. Do you agree with this ruling and sentence? Compare *R. v. Shanks* (1997), 4 C.R. (5th) 79 (Ont. C.A.) and accompanying annotation by David Tanovich.

The Supreme Court has adopted a stricter approach to causation for the purposes of first degree murder:

R. v. HARBOTTLE

[1993] 3 S.C.R. 306, 24 C.R. (4th) 137, 84 C.C.C. (3d) 1,
1993 CarswellOnt 992, 1993 CarswellOnt 121

The accused together with a companion forcibly confined a young woman. After his companion brutally sexually assaulted her while the accused watched, the accused and his companion discussed ways of killing her. The accused held the victim's legs to prevent her from continuing to kick and struggle while his companion strangled her. The accused was convicted of murder in the first degree. The conviction was upheld at the Court of Appeal where it was conceded that accused was a party to the murder while participating in her forcible confinement and sexual assault. At issue in the Supreme Court of Canada was whether the accused's participation was such that he could be found guilty of first degree murder pursuant to s. 214(5) [s. 231(5)] of the *Criminal Code*. The court dismissed the accused's appeal.

CORY J.: —

. . . .

Object of the Section

In order to provide the appropriate distinctions pertaining to causation that must exist for the different homicide offences, it is necessary to examine the sections in their context while taking into account their aim and object.

At the outset, it is important to remember that when s. 214(5) comes into play it is in essence a sentencing provision. First degree murder is an aggravated form of murder and not a distinct substantive offence. See *R. v. Farrant*, [1983] 1 S.C.R. 124. It is only to be considered after the jury has concluded that the accused is guilty of murder by causing the death of the victim. An accused found guilty of second degree murder will receive a mandatory life sentence. What the jury must then determine is whether such aggravating circumstances exist that they justify ineligibility for parole for a quarter of a century. It is at this point that the requirement of causation set out in s. 214(5) comes into play. The gravity of the crime and the severity of the sentence both indicate that a *substantial and high* degree of blameworthiness, above and beyond that of murder, must be established in order to convict an accused of first degree murder.

Substantial Cause Test

Accordingly, I suggest a restrictive test of substantial cause should be applied under s. 214(5). That test will take into account the consequences of a conviction, the present wording of the section, its history and its aim to protect society from the most heinous murderers.

The consequences of a conviction for first degree murder and the wording of the section are such that the test of causation for s. 214(5) must be a strict one. In my view, an accused may only be convicted under the subsection if the Crown establishes that the accused has committed an act or series of acts which are of such a nature that they must be regarded as a substantial and integral cause of the death. A case which considered and applied a substantial cause test from Australia is *R. v. Hallett*, [1969] S.A.S.R. 141 (S.C. In Banco). In that case, the victim was left beaten and unconscious by the sea and was drowned by the incoming tide. The court formulated the following test of causation, at p. 149, which I find apposite:

> The question to be asked is whether an act or a series of acts (in exceptional cases an omission or series of omissions) consciously performed by the accused is or are so connected with the event that it or they must be regarded as having a sufficiently substantial causal effect which subsisted up to the happening of the event, without being spent or without being in the eyes of the law sufficiently interrupted by some other act or event.

The substantial causation test requires that the accused play a very active role — usually a physical role — in the killing. Under s. 214(5), the actions of the accused must form an essential, substantial and integral part of the killing of the victim. Obviously, this requirement is much higher than that described in *Smithers v. The Queen*, [1978] 1 S.C.R. 506, which dealt with the offence of manslaughter. There it was held at p. 519 that sufficient causation existed where the actions of the accused were "a contributing cause of death, outside the *de minimis* range". That case demonstrates the distinctions in the degree of causation required for the different homicide offences.

The majority of the Court of Appeal below expressed the view that the acts of the accused must physically result in death. In most cases, to cause physically the death of the victim will undoubtedly be required to obtain a conviction under s. 214(5). However, while the intervening act of another will often mean that the accused is no longer the substantial cause of the death under s. 214(5), there will be instances where an accused could well be the substantial cause of the death without physically causing it. For example, if one accused with intent to kill locked the victim in a cupboard while the other set fire to that cupboard, then the accused who confined the victim might be found to have caused the death of the victim pursuant to the provisions of s. 214(5). Similarly an accused who fought off rescuers in order to allow his accomplice to complete the strangulation of the victim might also be found to have been a substantial cause of the death.

Therefore, an accused may be found guilty of first degree murder pursuant to s. 214(5) if the Crown has established beyond a reasonable doubt that:

(1) the accused was guilty of the underlying crime of domination or of attempting to commit that crime;
(2) the accused was guilty of the murder of the victim;
(3) the accused participated in the murder in such a manner that he was a substantial cause of the death of the victim;
(4) there was no intervening act of another which resulted in the accused no longer being substantially connected to the death of the victim; and
(5) the crimes of domination and murder were part of the same transaction; that is to say, the death was caused while committing the offence of domination as part of the same series of events.

It would be appropriate to charge a jury in those terms.

For a comment on *Harbottle* see Allan Manson, "Rethinking Causation: The Implications of *Harbottle*" (1994), 24 C.R. (4th) 153-165.

The approach of *Smithers* was applied as the test for second degree murder but the majority also re-calibrated the *de minimis* language:

R. v. NETTE

[2001] 3 S.C.R. 488, 46 C.R. (5th) 197, 158 C.C.C. (3d) 486,
2001 CarswellBC 2481, 2001 CarswellBC 2482 (S.C.C.)

The accused was charged with first degree murder arising from the death of a 95-year-old widow, who had been the victim of robbery. Her house was entered and her hands and feet bound up. Some clothing was wrapped around her head. She was left on the bed. Some 24 to 48 hours later she died of asphyxiation due to upper airway obstruction. By the time of her death, her dentures had come loose in her mouth and the clothing wrapped around her head had become tightly wound around her neck. She had fallen from the bed.

During an RCMP undercover sting operation, the accused told a police officer that he had been involved in the robbery and death. The accused was charged with first degree murder under s. 231(5) of the *Criminal Code* — murder while committing the offence of unlawful confinement — and tried before a judge and jury. At trial, he claimed that he had fabricated the admission. He testified that he had gone alone to the victim's house only with intent to break and enter, that the back door to the house was open as though someone already had broken into the home, and that he left after finding the victim already dead in her bedroom. The accused was convicted of second degree murder. He appealed, on the basis that the jury was misdirected as to the test of causation applicable to second degree murder.

The Supreme Court dismissed the accused's appeal.

ARBOUR J. (IACCOBUCCI, MAJOR, BINNIE, and LEBEL JJ. concurring): —

In determining whether a person can be held responsible for causing a particular result, in this case death, it must be determined whether the person caused that result both in fact and in law. Factual causation, as the term implies, is concerned with an inquiry about how the victim came to his or her death, in a medical, mechanical, or physical sense, and with the contribution of the accused to that result. Where factual causation is established, the remaining issue is legal causation.

Legal causation, which is also referred to as imputable causation, is concerned with the question of whether the accused person should be held responsible in law for the death that occurred. It is informed by legal considerations such as the wording of the section creating the offence and principles of interpretation. These legal considerations, in turn, reflect fundamental principles of criminal justice such as the principle that the morally innocent should not be punished: see *Re B.C. Motor Vehicle Act*, [1985] 2 S.C.R. 486, at p. 513; *R. v. Vaillancourt*, [1987] 2 S.C.R. 636, at p. 652-53; *R. v. Stinchcombe*, [1991] 3 S.C.R. 326, at p. 336; *R. v. Creighton*, [1993] 3 S.C.R. 3, at p. 17; *Cribbin, supra*, at p. 568. In determining whether legal causation is established, the inquiry is directed at the question of whether the accused person should be held criminally responsible for the consequences that occurred. The nature of the inquiry at the stage of determining legal causation is expressed by G. Williams as follows in his *Textbook of Criminal Law* (2nd ed. 1983), at pp. 381-82, quoted in *Cribbin*, at p. 568:

> When one has settled the question of but-for causation, the further test to be applied to the but-for cause in order to qualify it for legal recognition is not a test of causation but a moral reaction. The question is whether the result can fairly be said to be imputable to the defendant... . If the term "cause" must be used, it can best be distinguished in this meaning as the "imputable" or "responsible" or "blamable" cause, to indicate the value-judgment involved. The word "imputable" is here chosen as best representing the idea. Whereas the but-for cause can generally be demonstrated scientifically, no experiment can be devised to show that one of a number of concurring but-for causes is more substantial or important than another, or that one person who is involved in the causal chain is more blameworthy than another.

In a given case, the jury does not engage in a two-part analysis of whether both factual and legal causation have been established. Rather, in the charge to the jury, the trial judge seeks to convey the requisite degree of factual and legal causation that must be found before the accused can be held criminally responsible for the victim's death.

While causation is a distinct issue from *mens rea*, the proper standard of causation expresses an element of fault that is in law sufficient, in addition to the requisite mental element, to base criminal responsibility. The starting point in the chain of causation which seeks to attribute the prohibited consequences to an act of the accused is usually an unlawful act in itself. When that unlawful act is combined with the requisite mental element for the offence charged, causation is generally not an issue. For example, in the case of murder, where an accused intends to kill a person and performs an act which causes or contributes to that person's death, it is rare for an issue to arise as to whether the accused caused the victim's death. As I discussed in *Cribbin, supra*, where the jury is faced with a charge of murder and is satisfied that the accused intended to kill or intended to cause bodily harm that he knew was likely to cause death and was reckless as to whether death occurred, it will rarely be necessary for the trial judge to charge the jury on the standard of causation. In such a case, the *mens rea* requirement generally resolves any concerns about causation. It would be rare in a murder case where the intention to kill or to cause bodily harm likely to cause death is proven for the accused to be able to raise a doubt that, while he intended the result that occurred, he did not cause the intended result. Where it is established that the accused had the subjective foresight of death or serious bodily harm likely to cause death required to sustain a murder conviction, as opposed to the lower manslaughter requirement of objective foreseeability of serious bodily harm, it would be unusual for an issue of causation to arise. Assuming a case arose where intention was established but causation was not proven, a proper verdict might be attempted murder: *Cribbin*, at p. 564.

The law of causation is in large part judicially developed, but is also expressed, directly or indirectly, in provisions of the *Criminal Code*. For example, s. 225 of the *Code* provides that where a person causes bodily injury that is in itself dangerous and from which death results, that person causes the death notwithstanding that the immediate cause of death is proper or improper treatment. Similarly, ss. 222(5)(c) and 222(5)(d) provide that a person commits culpable homicide where he causes the death of a person by causing that person, by threats, fear of violence or by deception, to do anything that causes his death or by wilfully frightening a child or sick person. These statutory provisions and others like them in the *Code* preempt any speculation as to whether the act of the accused would be seen as too remote to have caused the result alleged, or whether the triggering of a chain of events was then interrupted by an intervening cause which serves to distance and exonerate the accused from any responsibility for the consequences. Where the factual situation does not fall within one of the statutory rules of causation in the *Code*, the common law general principles of criminal law apply to resolve any causation issues that may arise.

In light of the statutory rules mentioned above, and in light of general principles of criminal responsibility, the civil law of causation is of limited assistance. The criminal law does not recognize contributory negligence, nor does it have any mechanism to apportion responsibility for the harm occasioned by criminal conduct, except as part of sentencing after sufficient causation has been found. In the same way it provides for the possibility of attributing responsibility through the law of attempt, which has no equivalent in the civil context. As a result, I do not find the appellant's submissions relating to the civil standard of causation to be helpful in elucidating the applicable criminal standard.

. . . .

In oral argument, the appellant submitted that the *Smithers* test applies to all culpable homicide but that the *Smithers* test should be reformulated and "crystallized" to the specific standard of "significant" or "substantial" rather than using the *Smithers* terminology of "beyond *de minimis*" or "more than trivial". The "crystallized" test of "significant" or "substantial" cause simply clarifies the language of causation so that the jury can properly focus on the correct standard, in the appellant's submission, and does not raise the threshold of causation required. The alleged errors made by the trial judge are first that the jury was instructed on the *Smithers* standard of "more than a trivial cause" rather than the "crystallized" test of "significant" or "substantial" and, second, that the trial judge twice erred in expressing the *Smithers* standard of "more than a trivial cause" by describing it instead as a "slight or trivial cause". The appellant submits that, as a result of these errors, the trial judge incorrectly explained the standard of causation for second degree murder to the jury and the jury may therefore have failed to understand the correct standard of causation.

The position of the respondent and the intervener Attorney General of Ontario is that *Harbottle* did establish an elevated causation threshold with the use of the terminology of "substantial cause" but that this elevated standard only applies to the offence of first degree murder pursuant to s. 231(5) of the *Criminal Code* and possibly also s. 231(6) of the *Code*. With respect to second degree murder and manslaughter, the respondent and intervener submit that the *Smithers* standard continues to apply.

There appears to be an inconsistency in the appellant's argument in the present case. On the one hand, he is arguing that the "substantial cause" terminology of *Harbottle* does not represent a higher standard of causation than the *Smithers* standard and that using the terminology of "substantial cause" in relation to all homicide offences would not raise the causation threshold. On the other hand, however, he is arguing that Wilkinson J.'s use of the *Smithers* terminology instead of the *Harbottle* terminology in charging the jury on second degree murder was an error of law so serious that it justifies overturning the conviction for second degree murder and ordering a new trial. If, as the appellant submits, "substantial cause" is not a higher standard of causation than the *Smithers* formulation of "beyond *de minimis*", it would seem to follow that using the *Smithers* terminology instead of the *Harbottle* terminology could not be an error of law, much less an error so serious that it should result in a new trial.

I agree with the appellant that what *Harbottle* really stresses is not solely or even primarily a higher causation requirement to raise murder to first degree murder under s. 231(5) of the *Code*, but rather the increased degree of participation required before the accused may be convicted of first degree murder under s. 231(5). However, I do not agree that the terminology of "substantial cause" should be used to describe the requisite degree of causation for all homicide offences.

. . . .

Once the jury concludes that the accused has committed murder, *Harbottle* indicates that the jury should then move on to consider whether aggravating circumstances exist that justify the increased sentence and stigma of a first degree murder conviction under s. 231(5). The additional "causation" requirement under s. 231(5) does not refer to factual causation but rather to an increased degree of legal causation. In other words, once the jury has determined that the accused committed murder, which entails a finding that the accused caused the victim's death in both factual and legal terms, it is then necessary to consider whether the moral culpability of the accused, as evidenced by his role in the killing, justifies a verdict of first degree murder. As Cory J. states in *Harbottle*, "[t]he gravity of the crime and the severity of the sentence both indicate that a substantial and high degree of blameworthiness, above and beyond that of murder, must be established in order to convict an accused of first degree murder". Such a high degree of blameworthiness would only be established where the actions of the accused were found to be "an essential, substantial and integral part of the killing of the victim". The terminology of "substantial cause" is used to indicate a higher degree of legal causation but it is a standard that only comes into play at the stage of deciding whether the accused's degree of blameworthiness warrants the increased penalty and stigma of first degree murder.

It is clear from a reading of *Harbottle* that the "substantial cause" test expresses the increased degree of moral culpability, as evidenced by the accused person's degree of participation in the killing, that is required before an accused can be found guilty under s. 231(5) of the *Criminal Code* of first degree murder. The increased degree of participation in the killing, coupled with a finding that the accused had the requisite *mens rea* for murder, justifies a verdict of guilty under s. 231(5) of the *Code*.

. . . .

D. Explaining the Standard of Causation to the Jury

As I discussed earlier, it is important to distinguish between what the legal standard of causation is and how that standard is conveyed to the jury. The difference between these two concepts has been obscured somewhat in the present case by the parties' focus on the terminology used to describe the standard of causation. I agree with the appellant's submission that there is only one standard of causation for all homicide offences, whether manslaughter or murder. However, I do not agree with the appellant that the standard must be expressed for all homicide offences, including second degree murder, as one of "substantial cause" as stated in *Harbottle*. Nor must the applicable standard be expressed with the terminology of "beyond *de minimis*" used in the *Smithers* standard.

. . . .

The causation standard expressed in *Smithers* is still valid and applicable to all forms of homicide. In addition, in the case of first degree murder under s. 231(5) of the *Code*, *Harbottle* requires additional instructions, to which I will return. The only potential shortcoming with the *Smithers* test is not in its substance, but in its articulation. Even though it causes little difficulty for lawyers and judges, the use of Latin expressions and the formulation of the test in the negative are not particularly useful means of conveying an abstract idea to a jury. In order to explain the standard as clearly as possible to the jury, it may be preferable to phrase the standard of causation in positive terms using a phrase such as "significant contributing cause" rather than using expressions phrased in the negative such as "not a trivial cause" or "not insignificant". Latin terms such as "*de minimis*" are rarely helpful.

In deciding how the applicable standard of causation should be articulated to the jury, trial judges have a discretion in choosing the terminology they wish to use to explain the standard. Causation issues are case-specific and fact-driven. For that reason, it is important to afford a trial judge with the flexibility to put issues of causation to the jury in an intelligible fashion that is relevant to the circumstances of the case, including whether or not there are multiple accused persons or parties. As I discussed in *Cribbin, supra,* at pp. 565-66, while different terminology has been used to explain the applicable standard in Canada, Australia and England, whether the terminology used is "beyond *de minimis*", "significant contribution" or "substantial cause", the standard of causation which this terminology seeks to articulate, within the context of causation in homicide, is essentially the same. . . . To the extent that trial judges may find it more useful to express the standard of causation in *Smithers* in a more direct and affirmative fashion, they may find it preferable to express the standard positively as a "significant contributing cause", to use the terminology of Lambert J.A. in the present appeal.

In light of *Harbottle*, where the jury must be instructed on first degree murder under s. 231(5) of the *Code* in addition to manslaughter or second degree murder, the terminology of "substantial cause" should be used to describe the applicable standard for first degree murder so that the jury understands that something different is being conveyed by the instructions concerning s. 231(5) of the *Code* with respect to the requisite degree of participation of the accused in the offence. In such cases, it would make sense to instruct the jury that the acts of the accused have to have made a "significant" contribution to the victim's death to trigger culpability for the homicide while, to be guilty of first degree murder under s. 231(5), the accused's actions must have been an essential, substantial and integral part of the killing of the victim.

E. Is Causation an Issue on the Facts of the Present Appeal?

. . . .

As I mentioned earlier, causation issues rarely arise in murder offences. Thus, in the usual case, it will be unnecessary for the trial judge to explain the applicable standard of causation to the jury in relation to either second degree murder or first degree murder. Causation issues arise more frequently in manslaughter cases, in which the fault element resides in a combination of causing death by an unlawful act, or by criminal negligence, and mere objective foreseeability of death. As the cases illustrate, causation issues tend to arise in factual situations involving multiple parties (e.g. *Harbottle*), thin skull victims (e.g. *Smithers*), intervening events (e.g. *Hallett*) or some combination of these factors.

. . . .

Given that the jury found the accused guilty of second degree murder, we must conclude that the jury found that the appellant had the requisite intent for the offence of murder, namely subjective foresight of death. In light of the jury's conclusion with respect to intent, which in my view could not have been affected by the instructions on causation, it is clear that no reasonable jury could have had any doubt about whether the appellant's actions constituted a significant, operative cause of the victim's death. What is not clear from the verdict is the basis for the acquittal on the charge of first degree murder. The appellant suggests that the jury acquitted on first degree murder because it had a reasonable doubt as to whether the accused caused the victim's death on the *Harbottle* standard of causation, but convicted of second degree murder because it was satisfied the accused caused death on the lower *Smithers* standard. In my view, the conviction for second degree murder was amply supported on the evidence and the jury was correctly charged on the applicable legal requirements of causation. The jury was entitled to have a doubt as to whether the degree of participation of the accused in the underlying offence of unlawful confinement, combined with the need for his substantial contribution to the death of the victim, was sufficient to elevate the murder to first degree. Whatever the jury's reasons for acquitting the appellant of first degree murder, the jury's verdict of second degree murder is unimpeachable.

. . . .

L'HEUREUX-DUBÉ J. (concurring in the result), (MCLACHLIN C.J.C., GONTHIER and BASTARACHE JJ. concurring): — I had the benefit of reading my colleague Madam Justice Arbour's reasons and while I concur in the result she reaches, I do not agree with her suggestion to rephrase the standard of causation for culpable homicide set out by this court in *R. v. Smithers*, [1978] 1 S.C.R. 506, 34 C.C.C. (2d) 427, 75 D.L.R. (3d) 321.

. . . .

In her reasons, my colleague also refers to the English translation of the *Smithers* test when she writes: "Since *Smithers*, the terminology of 'beyond *de minimis*' or 'more than a trivial cause' has been used interchangeably with 'outside the *de minimis* range' to charge juries as to the relevant standard of causation for all homicide offences, be it manslaughter or murder".

. . . .

Having said so, my colleague suggests reformulating the *Smithers* beyond *de minimis* test, i.e., "a contributing cause [of death] that is not trivial or insignificant" in the language of a "significant contributing cause". Evidently, my colleague considers that this rephrasing is merely a matter of semantics and, in her view, it does not alter the current test. I respectfully disagree. In my opinion, this issue is a matter of substance, not semantics. There is a meaningful difference between expressing the standard as "a contributing cause that is not trivial or insignificant" and expressing it as a "significant contributing cause". Changing the terminology of the *Smithers* test in this manner would drastically change its substance. On this point, I share Professor S. Yeo's view in his article "Giving Substance to Legal Causation" (2000), 29 C.R. (5th) 215 at p. 219:

> I submit that there is a material difference between describing something as "not an insignificant cause" on the one hand, and as "a significant cause" on the other. To ignore this difference is to ignore the reason for the use of a double negative in the first place. While the former description focuses the inquiry at the lower end of the scale of degrees of causation, the latter does not invoke such a focus. Using another set of words to illustrate my argument, when Mary says that she does not dislike John, she means, at most, that she is impartial towards him rather than that she likes him.

To claim that something not unimportant is important would be a sophism. Likewise, to consider things that are not dissimilar to be similar would amount to an erroneous interpretation. In the same vein, a substantial difference exists between the terms insignificant" and "significant", and there is no doubt in my mind that to remove the double negative formulation from the *Smithers* causation test would effect a radical change to the law. I therefore agree with the position of both the respondent and the intervener that a "significant contributing cause" calls for a more direct causal relationship than the existing "not insignificant" or "non trivial" test, thus raising the standard from where it currently stands.

. . . .

In conclusion, I reiterate that the causation test in *Smithers* remains the law and to rephrase it in the language of a "significant contributing cause", as my colleague suggests, would draw the line at a different place, thus drastically changing the law. I have found no legitimate reason to reformulate the *Smithers* test, rather it is my opinion that such alteration should be strenuously proscribed since it will elevate the threshold of causation. As a result, I consider the current language of "a contributing cause [of death] that is not trivial or insignificant" to be the correct formulation that trial judges should use when expressing to the jury the standard of causation for all homicide offences.

For comments on *Nette* see Stuart, "*Nette*: Confusing Cause in Reformulating the *Smithers* Test" (2002), 46 C.R. (5th) 230 and Sanjeev Anand, "Determining Causal Standards for First Degree Murder in the Wake of *Nette*: When Does the Substantial Cause Test Apply?" (2002), 46 Crim. L.Q. 282.

R. v. TALBOT

(2007), 44 C.R. (6th) 176, 2007 CarswellOnt 627, 217 C.C.C. (3d) 415 (C.A.)

In the course of an appeal following a jury acquittal following an altercation outside a restaurant, an issue arose as to whether the initial blow or subsequent kick caused the death. In the course of determining that the issue was not necessary to decide the appeal the court reviewed the law since *Nette*.

DOHERTY J.A. (LASKIN and ARMSTRONG J.A. concurring): —

[79] .... Causation in the criminal law has a factual and legal component. The former is concerned with the physical or medical cause of death. A "but for" inquiry answers the factual causation question in most, but not all situations. If the victim would not have died when he or she died but for the act of the accused, that act is a factual cause of death: see Isabel Grant, Dorothy Chunn & Christine Boyle, *The Law of Homicide* (Toronto: Carswell, 1994) at 3-21 to 3-29; Glanville Williams, *Textbook of Criminal Law*, 2d ed. (Agincourt, Ont.: Carswell, 1983) at 380-81; Wayne R. LaFave, *Substantive Criminal Law*, 2d ed. (Eagan, Minn.: Thomson/West, 2003) vol. 1 at 467-68.

[80] Legal causation requires a normative inquiry. It asks who among those who have factually caused a death should be held liable for causing that death in the eyes of the criminal law: see *R. v. Nette*, [2001] 3 S.C.R. 488 at paras. 44-45.

[81] Juries are not asked to determine factual and legal causation separately. Instead, the two inquiries are joined and the jury is asked to decide whether the accused's actions significantly contributed to the victim's death: see *R. v. Nette*, *supra*, at paras. 46-73. A contributing cause can be a cause that exacerbates an existing fatal condition, thereby accelerating death: see *R. v. Munro and Munro* (1983), 8 C.C.C. (3d) 260 at 290-91 (Ont. C.A.); *Criminal Code*, s. 226.

[82] If the Crown sought to rely on the kick as a contributing cause of death, it was incumbent on the Crown to prove beyond a reasonable doubt that the kick was a contributing cause within the meaning of *R. v. Nette*, *supra*. The evidence adduced by the Crown went no further than to suggest there was some unquantifiable possibility that was less than a likelihood that the kick exacerbated the internal head injuries.

This pithy analysis on legal cause cuts through ambiguities left by the Supreme Court in *Nette*. Arbour J. for the majority expressed a preference for the language of "significant contributing cause" but left it open for a trial judge to use the original *Smithers* language of outside the *de minimis* range In *Nette*, L'Heureux Dube dissented on the basis that the language of significant cause would unnecessarily raise the *Smithers* standard. In *Talbot*, the Ontario Court of Appeal rests content with significance being the sole test. This should provide welcome clarity for trial judges, at least in Ontario.

Another ambiguity arising from both *Smithers* and *Nette* is the distinction between factual cause and the normative issue of legal cause. In essence, Justice

Doherty boils down these cause inquiries into the one key test of significant contributing cause. Whether this test will deal satisfactorily with more difficult cause cases, such as those involving other intervening acts and multiple actors, left open by Arbour J. in *Nette* and Dickson J. in *Smithers*, remains to be seen.

(c) *Charter*

The Supreme Court in *Nette* did not address *Charter* issues. Prior to *Nette* in *R. v. Cribbin* (1994), 28 C.R. (4th) 137 (Ont. C.A.) Justice Arbour had determined, when on the Ontario Court of Appeal, that causation is embedded in the section 7 principle of fundamental justice that moral innocence should not be punished. The law should refrain from holding a person responsible for consequences that should not be attributed to the accused. Criminal causation was a legal rule based on concepts of moral responsibility. The morally innocent would be wrongly punished if criminal causation were reduced to a simple *sine qua non* test. However she dismissed arguments that the *Smithers* test was too vague or too broad. She indicated that cases where an independent actor intervened to make matters worse raised more difficult issues. For criticism of *Cribbin* see Jill Presser, "All for a Good Cause: The Need for Overhaul of the *Smithers* Test of Causation" (1984), 28 C.R. (4th) 178.

R. v. F. (D.L.)

(1989), 73 C.R. (3d) 391, 1989 CarswellAlta 195 (Alta. C.A.)

McCLUNG J.A.: — As a result of a pedestrian injury accident in Calgary on December 2, 1986, the respondent, a youth, was tried on a multiple count information which included allegations that he:

1. Did unlawfully operate a motor vehicle within the said city while his ability to operate a motor vehicle was impaired by alcohol or a drug and did thereby cause bodily harm to Alex Primeau, contrary to the *Criminal Code*.
2. Having consumed alcohol in such a quantity that the concentration thereof in his blood exceeded 80 milligrams of alcohol in 100 millilitres of blood, did unlawfully operate a motor vehicle, contrary to the *Criminal Code*.
3. Did unlawfully operate a motor vehicle on a highway within the said city in a manner dangerous to the public, having regard to all the circumstances including the nature, condition and use of such place and the amount of traffic that at the time was or might reasonably be expected to be on such place, and did thereby cause bodily harm to Alex Primeau, contrary to the *Criminal Code*.

D.L.F. was acquitted on all counts by the trial judge after his review of the blameworthy aspects of D.L.F.'s driving as well as his physical condition. That review, which need not be set out in full, satisfied the trial judge that the driving pattern of the accused was dangerous within the meaning assigned by s. 249(1) of the *Code*. However, he was acquitted. The acquittal was gained, and this appeal taken, from the judge's conclusion that there was no culpable connection established between D.L.F.'s driving deficiencies and the bodily harm sustained by a pedestrian who was injured when he was struck by D.L.F.'s vehicle. The acquittal on the count alleging dangerous driving causing bodily harm is all that is under appeal by the Crown.

The trial judge felt that he was obligated to analyze each circumstance alleged by the Crown which, in their totality, were said to establish dangerous driving. The judge did so under the focus of what acts of negligence could be said to be traceable, and therefore contributory to, the bodily harm suffered by the pedestrian. The judge refused any connection arising from the accused's failure to wear corrective lenses to help his driving vision. He rejected any causal relationship arising from speed in excess of the posted limit and the accident. He rejected evidence of inefficient brakes. He rejected the failure of the accused to accommodate his driving to a narrowing of the road at the point of impact. The judge concluded that none of these facts were instrumental in the collision and the injuries that were suffered. He held that the sole factual connection joining the driving conduct and the accident was D.L.F.'s failure to see the pedestrian, who was jaywalking, before the impact. The judge credited this to inattention, not to dangerous driving.

. . . .

We think we are not only bound by, but fully agree with, the trial judge's finding that the driving pattern disclosed in the evidence was dangerous within the prohibition of s. 249(1), the definition section. The nature, condition and use of the highway by the accused and the pedestrian traffic that should have been anticipated, all support the judge's conclusion. However, the trial judge seems to have erred in attempting to analyze each blameworthy facet of the accused's driving pattern and attempting to determine whether those individual components, under separate examination, were an effective cause of the accident.

. . . .

Under the additional responsibility of determining whether bodily injury was *thereby caused* to any person by the dangerous driving (s. 249(3)), other considerations arise. Sections 249(3) and 249(4) codify aggravated acts of dangerous driving. That aggravation is supplied by proof that the accused's unlawful driving caused harm or death to others. The offence becomes indictable and the exposure to gaol, in the case of s. 249(3), is doubled as the maximum sentence becomes ten years. The words "thereby causes" demand some examination of the factual connection between the dangerous driving and the injury or fatality. That, of course, is an inquiry that is not required in prosecutions brought under s. 249(1), a lesser and included offence.

The approach suggested by Rick Libman of the Ontario Crown Attorney Office in his article, "The Requirements of Causation in the New Offences of

Impaired Driving Causing Bodily Harm or Death" (1985), 48 M.V.R. 21, in terms of simplicity, has proved to be a useful and orderly guide for the trial of these aggravated driving cases. Mr. Libman suggests that in cases under s. 249(3) and s. 249(4), the trial court should:

1. Determine whether the driving conduct in question has been proven to be driving in a dangerous manner within the definition assigned by s. 249(1).
2. Determine whether the injuries complained of meet the test of "bodily harm" defined by s. 267(2) — ". . . bodily harm means any hurt or injury to the complainant that interferes with his or her health or comfort and that is more than merely transient or trifling in nature".
3. Where the preceding questions have been answered adversely to the accused, determine what correlative link exists between the dangerous driving and the bodily harm proven.

The difficult question remains: when is bodily harm or death *"thereby caused"* in s. 249(3) or s. 249(4) prosecutions? In my view the words *"thereby caused"* must demand, at least, that the unlawful operation of the accused's vehicle be proven to be a real and truly contributing cause of any ensuing injury or death and the trial court should be chary of allowing speculative inferences alone to stand as the causative link between the driving and the injury accident solely because of the target of the statute. The unlawful driving must still demonstrably influence the actual injury accident beyond serving as its backdrop. Mr. Libman (and Mr. MacDonald for the Crown here), invokes *R. v. Smithers*, [1978] 1 S.C.R. 506, 34 C.C.C. (2d) 427, and urges that the level of proof is "did the activities of the accused contribute in some way to the injury?" That was the Crown's proof commitment in culpable homicide cases, now statutorily defined by s. 222(*a*) of the *Criminal Code*. In *Smithers*, a kicking-death manslaughter prosecution demanding proof of general intent alone, the causation hurdle was described as proof that the unlawful act ". . . was at least a contributing cause of death, outside the *de minimis* range". The "outside *de minimis*" test has been recited in at least four appellate aggravated driving cases since and is now authoritative. *R. v. Laroque* (1988), 5 M.V.R. (2d) 221 (Ont. C.A.); *R. v. Singhal* (1988), 5 M.V.R. (2d) 172 (B.C. C.A.); *R. v. Halkert*, unreported, December 15/88, #4281 (Sask. C.A.) and *R. v. Pinske* (1988), 6 M.V.R. (2d) 19, appeal to S.C.C. dismissed October 12, 1989. Nonetheless, I confess to some difficulty with its fairness in all aggravated driving prosecutions.

I do not wish to flounder in semantics but the application of the "outside *de minimis*" test, as proposed by Mr. Libman, is not easily reconciled with the common understanding of the statutory words "thereby cause". In everyday usage, the latter words convey "resulting in" or "create by that means" — something more, and more onerous, than a mere identifiable contribution which I understand the "outside *de minimis*" test to imply.

The difficulty is twofold; the verb "cause" is particularly troublesome when found in penal statutes requiring full *mens rea* or even none at all. *R. v. Sault Ste. Marie* (1978), 85 D.L.R. (3d) 161, 183 (S.C.C.). Beyond that, a standard of proof related at all to the concept of "*de minimis*" would normally find little philosophical communion within the criminal law.

The distinction would not be a real issue in the majority of s. 249(3) or 249(4) prosecutions but in cases involving parallel or competing causes of an injury accident, one of which may be quite external to the conduct of the accused, it can arise. Two or three car collisions come to mind. See *R. v. Ewart*, Appeal No. 8803-0334-A (Alta. C.A.). Where the facts disclose the preponderant cause of an accident to be divorced from the conduct of the accused, the accused may be substantially blameless for that accident but snared under the criminality of the "outside *de minimis*" rule. In such cases, a finding that the accident which resulted in injury or death was inevitable, whatever the driving deficiencies of the accused, has been taken. *Singhal* (*supra*).

With all respect, there will be cases where it could be argued that the "outside *de minimis*" test is in conflict with the fundamental justice predicate of s. 7 of the *Canadian Charter of Rights and Freedoms*. It is a test of sweeping accountability. In *Smithers* the unlawful link that caused death involved nothing, on even a standard of objective awareness, suggesting the foreseeability of the victim's death. Statutory interpretations, at least those guiding the criminal process, that align with *Charter* values should now prevail. *Hills v. Atty. Gen. of Canada*, [1988] 1 S.C.R. 513. Nonetheless until the Supreme Court chooses to reconsider the matter the broader "outside *de minimis*" rule will govern. For this court the matter is presently resolved by *R. v. Pinske* (*supra*).

These concerns do not arise under the facts of this case and I do not apply them to resolve this appeal. They are only raised under a review of the stages of the approach suggested by Mr. Libman. This prosecution is, I think, determined by the judge's conclusion that there was dangerous driving including the fact that while the pedestrian was jaywalking, D.L.F. should have seen him but did not. In Judge Fitch's assessment of the evidence:

> He should have seen him, and there certainly is a direct causal connection between failing to observe the pedestrian jaywalking and the accident.

> If the charge before me was merely dangerous driving, the section in the *Code* prior to the 1985 amendments, and in the absence of the case law connecting dangerous driving and consequences, my conclusion would be, yes the accused's driving was dangerous within the meaning of the *Code*.

Under those findings a s. 249(3) offence was proven. I would allow the Crown's appeal and direct the entry of a conviction under the third Count of the Information which alleged dangerous driving causing bodily harm contrary to s. 249(3). The respondent is directed to appear, on a date to be forthwith fixed, for sentencing, before the Family and Youth Division of the Provincial Court of Alberta at Calgary.

(d) Cases of Intervening Cause

The Supreme Court in *Smithers, Nette* and *Harbottle* expressly recognise there might be more difficult causation issues especially where new actors intervene. Little guidance is offered as to the approach to be taken.

Note first the four statutory homicide rules where intervening causes are stated not to break the chain of causation: ss. 222(5)(c), 224, 225 and 226. The only way around these rules would be a successful *Charter* challenge.

In other cases, courts are left to struggle. Consider the following approaches, the first two adopted in the United Kingdom and Australia.

R. v. SMITH

[1959] 2 All E.R. 193 (Cts.-Man. App. Ct.)

THE LORD CHIEF JUSTICE: — The appellant in this case was convicted by a General Court-Martial in Germany of murder and was sentenced to imprisonment for life. The matter arose in this way: the appellant was a private soldier in the King's Regiment. At the material time a company of the King's Regiment was sharing barracks with a company of the Gloucestershire Regiment, and on the night of April 13, 1958, a fight developed. As a result of that fight three members of the Gloucesters were stabbed with a bayonet and one of them, Private Creed, subsequently died. It was for his murder that the appellant was convicted.

. . . .

The second ground concerns a question of causation. The deceased man in fact received two bayonet wounds, one in the arm and one in the back. The one in the back, unknown to anybody, had pierced the lung and caused haemorrhage. There followed a series of unfortunate occurrences. A fellow member of his company tried to carry him to the medical reception station. On the way he tripped over a wire and dropped the deceased man. He picked him up again, went a little further, and fell apparently a second time causing the deceased man to be dropped on the ground. Thereafter he did not try a third time, but went for help and ultimately the deceased man was brought into the reception station. There, the medical officer, Captain Millward, and his orderly were trying to cope with a number of other cases, two serious stabbings and some minor injuries, and it is clear that they did not appreciate the seriousness of the deceased man's condition or exactly what had happened. A transfusion of saline solution was attempted and failed. When his breathing seemed impaired, he was given oxygen and artificial respiration was applied, and in fact he died after he had been in the station about an hour, which was about two hours after the original stabbing. It is now known that, having regard to the injuries which the man had in fact suffered, his lung being pierced, the treatment that he was given was thoroughly bad and might well have affected his chances of recovery. There was evidence that there is a tendency for a wound of this sort to heal and for the haemorrhage to stop. No doubt his being dropped on the ground and having artificial respiration applied would halt or at any rate impede the chances of healing. Further, there were no facilities whatsoever for blood transfusion, which would have been the best possible treatment. There was evidence that, if he had received immediate and different treatment, he might not have died. Indeed, had facilities for blood transfusion been available and been administered, Dr. Camps, who gave evidence for the defence, said that his chances of recovery were as high as 75 percent.

In these circumstances Mr. Bowen urges that not only was a careful summing-up required, but that a correct direction to the court would have been that they must be satisfied that the death of Private Creed was a natural consequence and the sole consequence of the wound sustained by him and flowed directly from it. If there was, says Mr. Bowen, any other cause whether resulting from negligence or not, or if, as he contends here, something happened which impeded the chance of the deceased recovering, then the death did not result from the wound. The court is quite unable to accept that contention. It seems to the court that if at the time of death the original wound is still an operating cause and a substantial cause, then the death can properly be said to be the result of the wound, albeit that some other cause of death is also operating. Only if it can be said that the original wounding is merely the setting in which another cause operates can it be said that the death does not result from the wound. Putting it in another way, only if the second cause is so overwhelming as to make the original wound merely part of the history can it be said that the death does not flow from the wound.

There are a number of cases in the law of contract and tort on these matters of causation, and it is always difficult to find a form of words when directing a jury or, as here, a court, which will convey in simple language the principle of causation. It seems to the court enough for this purpose to refer to one passage in the judgment of Lord Wright in *The Oropesa*, reported in [1943] P. 32, where he says (at p. 39):

> To break the chain of causation it must be shown that there is something which I will call ultroneous, something unwarrantable, a new cause which disturbs the sequence of events, something which can be described as either unreasonable or extraneous or extrinsic.

To much the same effect was a judgment on the question of causation given by Denning J., as he then was, in *Minister of Pensions v. Chennel* in [1947] K.B. 250.

Mr. Bowen placed great reliance on a case decided in this court, *Jordan* (1956), 40 Cr. App. R. 152, and in particular on a passage in the headnote which says:

Semble, that death resulting from any normal treatment employed to deal with a felonious injury may be regarded as caused by the felonious injury, but that the same principle does not apply where the treatment employed is abnormal.

Reading those words into the present case, Mr. Bowen says that the treatment that this unfortunate man received from the moment that he was struck to the time of his death was abnormal. The court is satisfied that *Jordan (supra)* was a very particular case depending upon its exact facts. It incidentally arose in this court on the grant of an application to call further evidence, and, leave having been obtained, two well-known medical experts gave evidence that in their opinion death had not been caused by the stabbing, but by the introduction of terramycin after the deceased had shown that he was intolerant to it and by the intravenous introduction of abnormal quantities of liquid. It also appears that at the time when that was done the stab wound which had penetrated the intestine in two places had mainly healed. In those circumstances the court felt bound to quash the conviction, because they could not say that a reasonable jury, properly directed, would not have been able on that to say that there had been a break in the chain of causation; the court could only uphold the conviction in that case if they were satisfied that no reasonable jury could have come to that conclusion.

In the present case it is true that the Judge-Advocate did not, in his summing-up, go into the refinements of causation. Indeed, in the opinion of this court, he was probably wise to refrain from doing so. He did leave the broad question to the court whether they were satisfied that the wound had caused the death in the sense that the death flowed from the wound, albeit that the treatment he received was in the light of after-knowledge a bad thing. In the opinion of this court, that was on the facts of the case a perfectly adequate summing-up on causation; I say "on the facts of the case," because in the opinion of the court they can only lead to one conclusion. A man is stabbed in the back, his lung is pierced and haemorrhage results; two hours later he dies of haemorrhage from that wound; in the interval there is no time for a careful examination and the treatment given turns out in the light of subsequent knowledge to have been inappropriate and, indeed, harmful. In those circumstances no reasonable jury or court could, properly directed, in our view possibly come to any other conclusion than that the death resulted from the original wound. Accordingly, the court dismisses this appeal.

Appeal dismissed.

R. v. BLAUE

[1975] 1 W.L.R. 1411 (C.A.)

July 16. LAWTON L.J. read the following judgment of the court. On October 17, 1974, at Teesside Crown Court after a trial before Mocatta J. the defendant was acquitted of the murder of Jacolyn Woodhead but was convicted of her manslaughter on the ground of diminished responsibility (count 1). He was also convicted of wounding her with intent to do her grievous bodily harm (count 2) and of indecently assaulting her (count 3). He pleaded guilty to indecently assaulting two other women (counts 4 and 5). He was sentenced to life imprisonment on counts 1 and 2 and to concurrent sentences of 12 months' imprisonment on counts 3, 4 and 5.

The defendant appeals with the leave of this court against his conviction on count 1 and, if his appeal is successful, he applies for leave to appeal against his sentence on count 2.

The victim was aged 18. She was a Jehovah's Witness. She professed the tenets of that sect and lived her life by them. During the late afternoon of May 3, 1974, the defendant came into her house and asked her for sexual intercourse. She refused. He then attacked her with a knife inflicting four serious wounds. One pierced her lung. The defendant ran away. She staggered out into the road. She collapsed outside a neighbour's house. An ambulance took her to hospital, where she arrived at about 7.30 p.m. Soon after she was admitted to the intensive care ward. At about 8.30 p.m. she was examined by the surgical registrar who quickly decided that serious injury had been caused which would require surgery. As she had lost a lot of blood, before there could be an operation there would have to be a blood transfusion. As soon as the girl appreciated that the surgeon was thinking of organising a blood transfusion for her, she said that she should not be given one and that she would not have one. To have one, she said, would be contrary to her religious beliefs as a Jehovah's Witness. She was told that if she did not have a blood transfusion she would die. She said that she did not care if she did die. She was asked to acknowledge in writing that she had refused to have a blood transfusion under any circumstances. She did so. The prosecution admitted at the trial that had she had a blood transfusion when advised to have one she would not have died. She did so at 12.45 a.m. the next day. The evidence called by the prosecution proved that at all relevant times she was conscious and decided as she did deliberately, and knowing what the consequences of her decision would be. In his final speech to the jury, Mr. Herrod for the prosecution accepted that her refusal to have a blood transfusion was *a* cause of her death. The prosecution did not challenge the defence evidence that the defendant was suffering from diminished responsibility.

Towards the end of the trial and before the summing up started counsel on both sides made submissions as to how the case should be put to the jury. Counsel then appearing for the defendant invited the judge to direct the jury to acquit the defendant generally on the count of murder. His argument was that her refusal to have a blood transfusion had broken the chain of causation between the stabbing and her death. As an alternative he submitted that the jury should be left to decide whether the chain of causation had been broken. Mr. Herrod submitted that the judge should direct the jury to convict, because no facts were in issue and when the law was applied to the facts there was only one possible verdict, namely, manslaughter by reason of diminished responsibility.

When the judge came to direct the jury on this issue he did so by telling them that they should apply their common sense. He then went on to tell them they would get some help from the cases to which counsel had referred in their speeches. He reminded them of what Lord Parker C.J. had said in *Reg. v. Smith*, [1959] 2 Q.B. 35, 42 and what Maule J. had said 133 years before in *Reg. v. Holland* (1841), 2 Mood. & R. 351, 352. He placed particular reliance on what Maule J. had said. The jury, he said, might find it "most material and most helpful." He continued:

> This is one of those relatively rare cases, you may think, with very little option open to you but to reach the conclusion that was reached by your predecessors as members of the jury in *Reg. v. Holland*, namely, "yes" to the question of causation that the stab was still, at the time of this girl's death, the operative cause of death — or a substantial cause of death. However, that is a matter for you to determine after you have withdrawn to consider your verdict.

Mr. Comyn has criticized that direction on three grounds: first, because *Reg. v. Holland* should no longer be considered good law; secondly, because *Reg. v. Smith*, when rightly understood, does envisage the possibility of unreasonable conduct on the part of the victim breaking the chain of causation; and thirdly, because the judge in reality directed the jury to find causation proved although he used words which seemed to leave the issue open for them to decide.

In *Reg. v. Holland*, 2 Mood. & R. 351, the defendant in the course of a violent assault, had injured one of his victim's fingers. A surgeon had advised amputation because of the danger to life through complications developing. The advice was rejected. A fortnight later the victim died of lockjaw. Maule J. said, at p. 352: "the real question is, whether in the end the wound inflicted by the prisoner was the cause of death." That distinguished judge left the jury to decide that question as did the judge in this case. They had to decide it as juries always do, by pooling their experience of life and using their common sense. They would not have been handicapped by a lack of training in dialectic or moral theology.

Maule J.'s direction to the jury reflected the common-law's answer to the problem. He who inflicted an injury which resulted in death could not excuse himself by pleading that his victim could have avoided death by taking greater care of himself: see *Hale's Pleas of the Crown* (1800 ed.), pp. 427-428. The common-law in Sir Matthew Hale's time probably was in line with contemporary concepts of ethics. A man who did a wrongful act was deemed *morally* responsible for the natural and probable consequences of that act. Mr. Comyn asked us to remember that since Sir Matthew Hale's day the rigour of the law relating to homicide has been eased in favour of the accused. It has been — but this has come about through the development of the concept of intent, not by reason of a different view of causation. Well known practitioner's textbooks, such as *Halsbury's Law's of England*, 3rd ed., vol. 10 (1955), p. 706 and *Russell on Crime*, 12th ed. (1964), vol. 1, p. 30 continue to reflect the common-law approach. Textbooks intended for students in jurisprudence have queried the common-law rule: see Hart and Honoré, *Causation in Law* (1959), pp. 320-321 and Smith and Hogan, *Criminal Law*, 3rd ed. (1973), p. 214.

. . . .

Mr. Comyn tried to overcome this line of reasoning by submitting that the jury should have been directed that if they thought the deceased's decision not to have a blood transfusion was an unreasonable one, then the chain of causation would have been broken. At once the question arises — reasonable by whose standards? Those of Jehovah's Witnesses? Humanists? Roman Catholics? Protestants of Anglo-Saxon descent? The man on the Clapham omnibus? But he might well be an admirer of Eleazar who suffered death rather than eat the flesh of swine (2 Maccabees, ch. 6, vv. 18-31) or of Sir Thomas More who, unlike nearly all his contemporaries, was unwilling to accept Henry VIII as Head of the Church in England. Those brought up in the Hebraic and Christian traditions would probably be reluctant to accept that these martyrs caused their own deaths.

As was pointed out to Mr. Comyn in the course of argument, two cases, each raising the same issue of reasonableness because of religious beliefs, could produce different verdicts depending on where the cases were tried. A jury drawn from Preston, sometimes said to be the most Catholic town in England, might have different views about martyrdom to one drawn from the inner suburbs of London. Mr. Comyn accepted that this might be so: it was, he said, inherent in trial by jury. It is not inherent in the common law as expounded by Sir Matthew Hale and Maule J. It has long been the policy of the law that those who use violence on other people must take their victims as they find them. This in our judgment means the whole man, not just the physical man. It does not lie in the mouth of the assailant to say that his victim's religious beliefs which inhibited him from accepting certain kinds of treatment were unreasonable. The question for decision is what caused her death. The answer is the stab wound. The fact that the victim refused to stop this end coming about did not break the causal connection between the act and death.

If a victim's personal representatives claim compensation for his death the concept of foreseeability can operate in favour of the wrongdoer in the assessment of such compensation: the wrongdoer is entitled to expect his victim to mitigate his damage by accepting treatment of a normal kind: see *Steele v. R. George & Co. (1937) Ltd.*, [1942] A.C. 497. As Mr. Herrod pointed out, the criminal law is concerned with the maintenance of law and order and the protection of the public generally. A policy of the common law applicable to the settlement of tortious liability between subjects may not be, and in our judgment is not, appropriate for the criminal law.

The issue of the cause of death in a trial for either murder or manslaughter is one of fact for the jury to decide. But if, as in this case, there is no conflict of evidence and all the jury has to do is to apply the law to the admitted facts, the judge is entitled to tell the jury what the result of that application will be. In this case the judge would have been entitled to have told the jury that the defendant's stab wound was an operative cause of death. The appeal fails.

Appeal dismissed.

Application to certify point of law of general public importance involved refused.

THE QUEEN v. BINGAPORE

(1974-5), 11 S.A.S.R. 469 (S. Aus. S.C.)

The court (BRIGHT, SANGSTER and JACOBS JJ.) delivered the following judgment: —

This is in part an appeal as of right pursuant to s. 352(*a*) of the *Criminal Law Consolidation Act* 1935-1972 and in part an application for leave to appeal pursuant to placitum (*c*) of the same section and is wholly against the appellant's conviction for murder.

. . . .

The appellant was, admittedly, involved in an assault on the victim, McMillan.

About 11.45 a.m. a business man parked his car in Angas Street near the unoccupied premises; he noticed a man, slumped against the railings outside the unoccupied premises, appearing to be dazed and holding what appeared to be a red coloured rag against his head; that man then moved off towards Police Headquarters further west along Angas Street. Somewhere about that time McMillan arrived at Police Headquarters, was seen to be bleeding profusely, an ambulance was called and McMillan was taken to the Royal Adelaide Hospital and admitted.

. . . .

At the Royal Adelaide Hospital, McMillan's condition was found to include a profusely bleeding wound to the head and, after some trouble, an artery was sutured and the bleeding stopped; internal head injuries were suspected; he was kept at the hospital overnight. On the Saturday at about 12.30 p.m. conversations took place between a resident medical officer, McMillan, and Mrs. McMillan, the brief effect of which was that the medical officer warned both the McMillans of the danger involved in McMillan leaving the hospital, namely the danger of death, notwithstanding which McMillan signed a "risk form" and the McMillans left the hospital. They walked to the new lodgings at McLaren Street and some six hours or thereabouts later Mr. McMillan was brought back to the Royal Adelaide Hospital by ambulance, was seen to be in need of urgent attention, and within four and a half hours was operated on, but unsuccessfully, and he died the next day from brain damage caused by subdural haemorrhage which, in turn, was described in evidence as consistent with trauma to the head within a range of times which included the Friday morning.

. . . .

Three challenges were made to the learned trial judge's directions on causation. On causation we need look no further than *Reg. v. Bristow*, at p. 217 (citing *Reg. v. Smith*) and, in turn, cited with approval in *Reg. v. Hallett*: —

> It seems to the court that, if at the time of death the original wound is still an operating cause and a substantial cause, then the death can properly be said to be the result of the wound, albeit that some other cause of death is also operating. Only if it can be said that the original wounding is merely the setting in which another cause operates can it be said that the death does not result from the wound.

Counsel for the appellant contended that we should add to the law (as it is at present found in the authorities) a new proposition that where the gross negligence/unreasonable conduct/some degree of negligence more than mere negligence, (counsel used all three expressions without limiting his contentions to any one of them) contributed to the death of the victim, the chain of causation was broken. Alternatively, he contended, the learned trial judge's direction that causation was sufficiently established if the acts of the accused was "a" cause, should have been cut down to "the" cause, or alternatively "the most substantial" cause. In so far as we are able to follow his contentions we do not agree with them. In any case, on the evidence as the jury must have viewed it, the chain of causation was violence by the appellant to the victim, subdural haemorrhage from that violence, and death from that subdural haemorrhage, a short and direct chain. The appellant's only complaint is that had an operation on the victim been performed earlier it might have saved him, and that the victim's wanton departure from hospital (to which he was returned at his wife's instance about six hours later) denied him any opportunity for such an earlier operation. That complaint, of course, relates not to a break in the chain of causation, not to a new cause, but to the loss of a possible opportunity of avoiding death from a still operating cause, namely the violence inflicted by the appellant. The act of the appellant causing injuries from which the victim dies does not cease to be a causative act because the victim thereafter acts to his detriment or because some third party is negligent. The case of *Reg. v. Jordan* to which we were referred, is clearly distinguishable, for there the victim did not die from injuries caused by the act of the prisoner, but from some other cause for which the prisoner could not be held responsible.

. . . .

Appeal dismissed.

R. v. MAYBIN

(2010) 81 C.R. (6th) 48 (B.C. C.A.)

Three accused were charged with unlawful act manslaughter. Two brothers assaulted the victim in a bar: TM punched the victim while MM assisted in the attack. As a result the victim was left unconscious on a pool table. The third accused, BG, was a doorman at the bar. He came over to the commotion and saw the victim lying on the pool table. BG punched the victim in the head and then carried him outside. The victim was taken to hospital where he died. The medical evidence indicated that subarachnoid haemorrhage which resulted in the victim's death might have been caused by the blows struck by TM, the blow struck by BG, or an accumulation of both. The trial judge found that the attack on the victim was not a single transaction, and that there were two separate assaults: the first by TM to which MM was a party, and the second by BG. He held that the medical evidence was equivocal and did not establish beyond a reasonable doubt either that the first assault was the cause of the victim's death, nor that the second assault was the cause of the victim's death. As a result he acquitted all three accused of manslaughter.

The Crown appealed. A majority of the Court of Appeal granted the appeal with regard to TM and MM, and a new trial was ordered for them. The acquittal of BG was upheld.

RYAN J.A. (HUDDART J.A. concurring): —

Causation

21 As discussed in *R. v. Nette*, 2001 SCC 78, [2001] 3 S.C.R. 488 ("*Nette*"), when determining responsibility for causing a particular result, the trier of fact must decide whether a person caused that result both in fact and in law. . . .

22 The majority in *Nette* (para. 45) recognized that factual causation is generally (though not always) settled by the "but-for" test. In a manslaughter case the trier of fact should usually ask: But-for the action(s) of the accused, would the death have occurred? The importance of factual cause for legal purposes is that nothing that is not a factual cause can be a legal cause. Once factual causation is established, the legal question becomes whether the wrongdoer should answer for the consequences of his or her act. Alan Brudner puts it this way:

In criminal law the doctrine of proximate cause [i.e. imputable or legal cause] states the conditions under which someone whose act was a factual (but-for) cause of an outcome is legally answerable (rightly subject to punishment) for that outcome. The traditional answer is that someone is responsible for an outcome if he intentionally produced it, recklessly brought it about, or if the ordinarily circumspect person would have foreseen it as likely to result from his act (though the thinskull rule is, on one interpretation, an exception). [Emphasis added.] (Alan Brudner, "Owning Outcomes: On Intervening Causes, Thin Skulls, and Fault-undifferentiated Crimes" (1998) 11 *Can J.L. and Jurisprudence* 89 at 91.)

23 In the case of unlawful act manslaughter, as noted in *Nette* (para. 53), a person will be held legally responsible for the consequences of his unlawful act if it can be said, as was stated in *R. v. Smithers*, [1978] 1 S.C.R. 506 at p. 519 ("*Smithers*"), that his or her unlawful act "was at least a contributing cause of death, outside the de minimis range."

24 In the case at bar, the trial judge failed to fully examine the factual cause of Mr. Brophy's death, ended his factual inquiry early and never reached the question whether anyone should be held legally responsible for the death of Michael Brophy. A reading of the transcript leaves one with the impression that the Crown and defence were pre-occupied with the medical cause of death as if that were the only question in determining factual causation. As a result, the trial judge ended his examination of the factual cause of death once he concluded he could not say which blow or combination of blows administered by the Maybin brothers and Mr. Gains caused the death of Mr. Brophy. This focus was not wrong, but its scope was too narrow. The essential question in determining factual cause in this case was: "but for the actions of the parties, would Michael Brophy have died at that time and place". If the answer to this question was that Michael would not have died but for the actions of the parties, the next question would be whether the parties should be held to be legally responsible for the death.

[The majority concluded that the actions of the accused TM and MM did not simply cause physical injury to the victim; those actions also left the victim unconscious on a pool table where he became a target for BG. But for those actions the accused would not have died, and so factual causation was met, unless the actions of the doorman were an intervening cause.]

28 On this appeal, counsel for the Maybin brothers submits that even if the trial judge had analyzed the causation issues in the manner I have suggested, the verdict would necessarily be the same. Counsel submits that the act of Buddha Gains can only be seen to be an intervening cause, or a novus actus interveniens, which breaks the chain of causation and results in the Maybin brothers no longer being substantially connected to the death of Mr. Brophy.

Novus Actus Interveniens - Intervening Cause

29 Grant, Chunn and Boyle observe in their text, *The Law of Homicide* (Toronto: Thomson Canada Limited, 1994) at 3-37, 38, that the term novus actus interveniens (literally, "new intervening act") is a "conclusory label applied when a judge decides that the intervention should relieve earlier actors of responsibility". As they say, the label "is not particularly helpful in identifying a test to determine which intervening acts break the causal chain."

30 The concept of an intervening cause was discussed in *R. v. Tower*, 2008 NSCA 3, 76 W.C.B. (2d) 685, where Cromwell J.A. (as he then was) said:

> [25] To be convicted of manslaughter, the accused's acts must have been a significant contributing cause of the deceased's death: *R. v. Nette*, [2001] 3 S.C.R. 488. The accused's actions do not have to have been the sole cause of death; there may be other contributing causes. However, the law recognizes that other causes may intervene to "break the chain of causation" between the accused's acts and the death. This is the concept of an "intervening cause", that some new event or events result in the accused's actions not being a significant contributing cause of death: see, e.g., Kent Roach, *Criminal Law*, 3rd ed. (Toronto: Irwin Law, 2004), Chapter 2, section B(2)(d).

> [26] The law of intervening cause is not highly developed in Canada. However, both the Supreme Court of Canada and this Court have said that the effect of the accused's acts must have subsisted up to the happening of the event, without being spent or without being in the eyes of the law sufficiently interrupted by some other act or event: *R. v. Hallett*, [1969] S.A.S.R. 141 (S.C. in banco); *R. v. Harbottle*, [1993] 3 S.C.R. 306 at 324; *R. v. Nette*, 2001 SCC 78, [2001] 3 S.C.R. 488 at para. 78; *R. v. Reid*, 2003 NSCA 104, [2003] N.S.J. No. 360 (C.A.) at paras. 72-73.

31 In his *Textbook of Criminal Law*, 2d ed. (London: Stevens & Sons Limited, 1983), Glanville Williams concludes that where the intervening act is comprised of the action of an independent third party, that act will generally break the chain of causation. This, he says, is because a person ought not to be held responsible for the independent decisions of other responsible actors. Williams says at p. 391:

> The legal attitude is that a man is primarily responsible only for what he himself does or incites. The fact that his own wrongful conduct provided the background for some consequential wrong act by another, and that he should have foreseen the act, does not make him responsible for it.

> Putting the rule in terms of causation, the new intervening act (novus actus interveniens) of a responsible actor, who has full knowledge of what he is doing, and is not subject to mistake or pressure, will normally operate to relieve the defendant of liability for a further consequence, because it makes the consequence "too remote". Underlying this rule there is undoubtedly, a philosophical attitude. Moralists and lawyers regard the individual's will as the autonomous prime cause of his behaviour. What a person does (if he has reached adult years, is of sound mind and is not acting under mistake, intimidation or other similar pressure) is his own responsibility, and is not regarded as having been caused by other people. An intervening act of this kind, therefore, breaks the causal connection that would otherwise have been perceived between previous acts and the forbidden consequence. (An intervening wrongful omission does not break it.)

32 Williams' articulation of the law is often referred to with approval by Canadian courts. (For example see para. 31 of *R. v. J.S.R.,* 2008 ONCA 544, 237 C.C.C. (3d) 305 ("J.S.R.") quoted in the following paragraph). It is useful as an explanatory statement of the application of the rule in cases where an actor can truly be said to be acting independently of the accused. I would suggest, however, that it cannot serve as a contemporary test as to what may constitute a novus actus interveniens when independent actors are involved. This is because Williams places the focus on the independence of the actors, rather than of the acts, and he excludes reasonable foreseeability from the analysis.

33 In their text, *Substantive Criminal Law* (St. Paul: West Publishing, 1986) at 406, Wayne R. Lafave and Austin W. Scott Jr. distinguish between cases where the intervening act is a coincidence in which case it will break the chain of causation unless it is foreseeable, and cases where the intervening act is a response to the conduct of the first actor, which will not break the causal chain unless it is abnormal and thus unforeseeable....

35 In para. [22] of these reasons, I made reference to the observation of Alan Brudner that the criminal law will hold someone legally responsible for an outcome if he [or she] intentionally produced it, recklessly brought it about, or if the ordinarily circumspect person would have seen it as likely to result from his [or her] act. Conversely, the law will not hold someone legally responsible if the ordinarily circumspect person would not have seen the outcome as likely to result from his or her act. In my view, this principle explains the purpose of the novus actus interveniens rule. The application of the rule provides a way of ensuring that a person will not be held responsible for objectively unforeseeable consequences. Recent case law supports this view.

36 The Ontario Court of Appeal case of *R. v. Shilon* (2006), 240 C.C.C. (3d) 401 ("Shilon") and the Manitoba Court of Appeal case of *R. v. Sinclair; R. v. Pruden-Wilson*, 2009 MBCA 71, 240 Man.R. (2d) 135 ("*Pruden-Wilson*") are examples. In those cases, the question was not whether the persons who directly caused the harm (death in both cases) were independent responsible actors, but whether the actions of those actors were foreseeable by the accused persons (Shilon and Pruden-Wilson) who engaged in the dangerous acts leading to the eventual harm.

37 In *Shilon*, the Ontario Court of Appeal applied a reasonable foreseeability of harm test. In that case, a Mr. Trakas allowed a Mr. Chiovitti to test drive a motor cycle he had for sale on condition that Mr. Chiovitti leave behind his pick-up truck for security. No sooner had Mr. Chiovitti taken the motorcycle when one of his accomplices, the accused Shilon, drove off with the pick-up. Mr. Trakas called the police and gave chase to the truck. The pick-up drove dangerously to get away from the pursuing Mr. Trakas. During the course of the chase, Mr. Trakas crashed into a police car, killing a police officer. The driver

of the pick-up, Mr. Shilon, was charged with manslaughter. The Crown sought mandamus after Mr. Shilon's discharge at a preliminary hearing. The Ontario Court of Appeal allowed an appeal from a dismissal of the writ holding that there was some evidence to go to a jury on the issue of causation. In response to an argument that the actions of Mr. Trakas amounted to an intervening cause, Gillese J.A. said this for the Court:

> [43] I accept that independent voluntary human intervention in events started by an accused may break the chain of causation. However, on any realistic appraisal of the facts, and as was found by both levels of court below, Trakas' conduct was directly linked to that of the driver of the pick-up truck. Glanville Williams writes of intervening cause where the responsible actor is not acting under "mistake, intimidation or other similar pressure". Was Trakas acting free of "similar pressure"? It was the conduct of the driver of the pick-up truck that provoked Trakas' driving. It was the driver of the pick-up truck who created and continued the highly charged situation in which Trakas, the victim of a premeditated theft, responded predictably to catch the thief and recover his property. In my view, the question of whether Trakas' actions are sufficiently independent as to sever the chain of causation is a question best left to a properly instructed jury. [Emphasis added.]

38 In *Pruden-Wilson*, the appellant was one of three men who viciously beat a man and left him lying by the roadside. The three men ran off when a vehicle approached. It was early morning and dark when the car drove by. The driver, frightened by what she saw, called 911. Before help could arrive, the beaten man was struck by another driver who had not seen him on the road, who was driving a vehicle that was not roadworthy and who was unable to stop in time to prevent the accident. A medical doctor could only say that the injuries suffered by the victim could be attributable to either event.

39 Mr. Pruden-Wilson's counsel argued that the vehicle that ran over the victim constituted an intervening act so as to break the chain of causation in that case. The Court disagreed. It held that an act could not be said to break the chain of causation unless it was "extraordinary or unusual". Hamilton and Freedman JJ.A. said this for the Court at para. 47:

> [47] While foreseeability of risk is sometimes used in the analysis for the concept of intervening act, we prefer the descriptors extraordinary or unusual. This avoids confusion with the question of foreseeability that arises in the context of the mens rea analysis. As already noted, both Arbour J. in *Nette*, and Cromwell J.A. in *Tower*, referred to *Hallett*, in which the South Australia Supreme Court indicated that "extraordinary" as opposed to the "ordinary" operation of natural forces can constitute an intervening event. Remember that *Hallett* was the case in which the victim of a beating was left on the ocean shore and drowned when the tide came in. The court wrote (at p. 150):
>
>> We are not concerned to deny that there may be cases where the extraordinary as opposed to the ordinary operation of natural forces might be regarded as breaking the chain of causation, as in the case of the earthquake referred to in the passage from Smith and Hogan [*Criminal Law*, 2d ed. (London: Butterworths, 1969)] cited by the learned Judge. So here if the deceased had been placed in a situation safe

from the ordinary operations of the sea and had been engulfed by an extraordinary tidal wave as the result of an earthquake in the sea it may be that the earthquake and not the act of the appellant would be regarded as the cause of death. But we cannot regard the ordinary operations of the tides at Tumby Bay, whether known to the appellant or not, as being such a supervening cause. [Emphasis in the original.]

With regard to TM and MM, the majority decided it was open to a trier of fact to find it reasonably foreseeable that their assault could attract the intervention of others, including bar staff, with the possibility of resulting bodily harm. In that event they would have caused the death of the victim, and so a new trial was ordered.

With regard to BG, expanding consideration of the causation question beyond the medical evidence would not change the result. BG struck the unconscious victim, but the medical evidence left room for reasonable doubt about whether that blow was a contributing cause of death, and so the appeal from the acquittal was dismissed.

Finch C.J.B.C. dissented. The reasons of Ryan J.A. with regard to BG were agreed with. With regard to TM and MM, an accused should not be held responsible for the intentional actions of a third party acting independently. The independent actions of BG legally severed TM and MM from the victim's death. Even if TM and MM could be held responsible for reasonably foreseeable actions, there was no evidence on the record for the claim that it was objectively foreseeable that bar staff would become involved in the altercation.

For a comment on *Maybin* see Steve Coughlan 81 CR (6th) 48, suggesting that although the bright line rule supported by Chief Justice Finch in dissent (that the intentional actions of an independent third party are an intervening cause) has some attractions, nonetheless the majority approach is to be preferred. The question of intervening cause is always a difficult one, and so a simple rule in this particular context would at least narrow the areas of ambiguity. The notion that one cannot be responsible for the choices of other people also has a certain intuitive appeal. However, although such a rule would be simpler, it would not clearly be consistent with the approach taken by the criminal law to liability in other similar situations such as in *Blaue* and *Bingapore*, where actions of others did not break the chain of causation. To ask whether the intervening cause is something extraordinary—whether act of nature or decision by another person—is to set the same test in all circumstances, which in itself, suggests Coughlan, helps simplify matters. **Which approach do you prefer?**

PROBLEMS

1. **An accused is driving with excessive alcohol in his blood but is driving normally. A pedestrian comes out of nowhere and walks into the path of the vehicle. He is killed. The accused is charged with impaired driving causing death. Is there any argument that he did not cause the death?**

Compare *Wilmot* (1940), 74 C.C.C. 1 (Alta. C.A.), affirmed (1940), [1941] S.C.R. 53, 75 C.C.C. 161 (S.C.C.); *Fisher* (1992), 13 C.R. (4th) 222 (B.C. C.A.); *White* (1994), 28 C.R. (4th) 160, 89 C.C.C. (3d) 336 (N.S. C.A.); and *R. v. Horton* (2003), 20 C.R. (6th) 160 (Sask. Q.B.).

2. The accused was charged with criminal negligence causing death. He participated in a high speed race with his friend, J.M., on a residential street in a 60 km/h zone. They both drove Hondas modified for high performance. At a stop the accused revved his engine and J.M. took off at high speed with the accused giving chase. A number of witnesses testified as to their very high speed being side by side at points and changing lanes at excessive speeds. The accused did not pass J.M. At one point the accused dropped back but J.M. continued at speed. Half a mile later J.M. lost control, struck a utility pole and was killed. Is there an argument that the accused is not legally responsible for causing the death?

Compare *R. v. Menezes* (2007), 50 C.R. (5th) 343 (Ont. S.C.).

3. The accused, the victim and two others, all aged 17, decided to play Russian roulette. A single cartridge was placed in the revolver. The accused spun the chamber, pointed the gun to his head and pulled the trigger. Nothing happened. He handed the gun to the victim, who spun it, put it to his head, then pulled the trigger. The cartridge exploded, and he fell over dead. The accused is charged with manslaughter. What result? How about the others? Suppose the game was played where each participant directed the gun not at himself but at another player?

Compare *Commonwealth v. Atencio* (1963), 189 N.E. (2d) 223 (Mass. S.C.).

4. The accused operated a corner store in a run-down area of a large city. One item he stocked was Sterno, a canned heat containing methanol. The label read "Danger. Poison. For use only as a fuel". The accused sold large quantities of Sterno to persons who lived in the neighbourhood. Two of them died. As Crown Attorney, you have been asked by the police whether charges should be laid. Advise.

Compare *Commonwealth v. Feinberg* (1969), 253 A. 2d 636 (Pa. S.C.).

5. The accused owns a tavern at a crossroads in the country. He recognizes that a customer is badly impaired but continues to serve him as he "doesn't want any trouble". After a few more drinks the customer leaves. Shortly thereafter there is the noise of squealing tires and thrown gravel and a collision. The owner rushes to the parking lot where he finds the customer behind the steering wheel of his car, dead. It is clear there would be civil liability for the commercial host although not for any social host serving liquor in such a situation: see *Childs v. Desormeaux*, 2006 SCC 18, [2006] 1 S.C.R. 643 (S.C.C.). How about criminal responsibility?

Chapter 3

THE FAULT REQUIREMENT

(MENS REA OR NEGLIGENCE)

1. INTRODUCTION

J.F. STEPHEN, A HISTORY OF THE CRIMINAL LAW OF ENGLAND

Vol. 2, (1883), 94-95

The maxim, *actus non facit reum nisi mens sit rea*, is sometimes said to be the fundamental maxim of the whole criminal law; but I think that, like many other Latin sentences supposed to form part of the Roman law, the maxim not only looks more instructive than it really is, but suggests fallacies which it does not precisely state.

It is frequently though ignorantly supposed to mean that there cannot be such a thing as legal guilt where there is no moral guilt, which is obviously untrue, as there is always a possibility of a conflict between law and morals.

It also suggests the notion that there is some state of mind called a *mens rea*, the absence of which, on any particular occasion, deprives what would otherwise be a crime of its criminal character. This also is untrue. There is no one such state of mind, as any one may convince himself by considering the definitions of dissimilar crimes. A pointsman falls asleep, and thereby causes a railway accident and the death of a passenger; he is guilty of manslaughter. He deliberately and by elaborate devices produces the same result; he is guilty of murder; if in each case there is a *mens rea*, as the maxim seems to imply, *mens rea* must be a name for two states of mind, not merely differing from but opposed to each other, for what two states of mind can resemble each other less than indolence and an active desire to kill?

The truth is that the maxim about *mens rea* means no more than that the definition of all or nearly all crimes contains not only an outward and visible element, but a mental element, varying according to the different nature of different crimes. Thus, in reference to murder, the *mens rea* is any state of mind which comes within the description of malice aforethought. In reference to theft the *mens rea* is an intention to deprive the owner of his property permanently, fraudulently and without claim of right. In reference to forgery the *mens rea* is anything which can be described as an intent to defraud. Hence the only means of arriving at a full comprehension of the expression *mens rea* is by a detailed examination of the definitions of particular crimes, and therefore the expression itself is unmeaning.

W.S. GILBERT, THE MIKADO, (1885)

That's the pathetic part of it. Unfortunately the fool of an Act says, 'Compassing the death of the heir apparent.' There's not a word about mistake, or not knowing, or having no notion, or not being there. There should be, of course, but there isn't. That's the slovenly way in which these Acts are drawn.

G. MUELLER, ON COMMON LAW MENS REA

(1957-58), 42 Minn. L. Rev. 1043 at 1055, 1061

There has crept into our thinking the idea that there is no singular concept of *mens rea* but that, since every crime has a different *mens rea* requirement, one should talk of *mentes reae* rather than *mens rea*. This is a misconception and it is false to conclude, as some do, that there is no unifying *mens rea* concept. Just as all cars have different wheels, little cars little wheels and big cars big wheels, and we are justified in referring to them collectively under the unifying concept wheels, so all crimes have a different *mens rea* and yet the concept of *mens rea* must be regarded as a unifying concept of various possible frames of mind.

Mens rea, then, is not the mere psychic relation between act and actor, it is, rather, the ethico-legal *negative* value of the deed (appearing in various legally prescribed forms), i.e., it is a *community value of which the perpetrator at the time of the deed knows the existence and that it will materialize when the deed becomes known.*

G.L. WILLIAMS, CRIMINAL LAW: THE GENERAL PART

2nd ed. (1961), 30-31

It may be said that any theory of criminal punishment leads to a requirement of some kind of *mens rea*. The deterrent theory is workable only if the culprit has knowledge of the legal sanction; and if a man does not foresee the consequence of his act he cannot appreciate that punishment lies in store for him if he does it. The retributive theory presupposes moral guilt; incapacitation supposes social danger; and the reformative aim is out of place if the offender's sense of values is not warped.

However, the requirement as we have it in the law does not harmonise perfectly with any of these theories. It does not quite fit the deterrent theory, because a man may have *mens rea* although he is ignorant of the law, . . . Again, the requirement does not quite conform to the retributive theory, because the *mens rea* of English law does not necessarily connote an intention to engage in moral wrongdoing. . . . There are similar difficulties with incapacitation and reform.

What, then, does legal *mens rea* mean? It refers to the mental element necessary for the particular crime, and this mental element may be either *intention* to do the immediate act or bring about the consequence or (in some crimes) *recklessness* as to such act or consequence. . . . Some crimes require intention and nothing else will do, but most can be committed either intentionally or recklessly. Some crimes require particular kinds of intention or knowledge.

Outside the class of crimes requiring *mens rea* there are some that do not require any particular state of mind but do require negligence. Negligence in law is not necessarily a state of mind; and thus these crimes are best regarded as not requiring *mens rea*. However, negligence is a kind of legal fault, and in that respect they are akin to crimes requiring *mens rea*.

Yet other crimes do not even require negligence. They are crimes of strict or vicarious responsibility, and, like crimes of negligence, they constitute exceptions to the adage *Actus non facit reum nisi mens sit rea.*

In the Canadian context, we shall discover that there is a constitutional requirement of fault for any offence threatening the liberty interest. Almost always the only real issue is what the fault requirement actually entails. Jurisprudence on fault is a matter of common law, statutory interpretation and *Charter* standards and is still in a state of flux. There is considerable ambiguity and confusion about definition. A central issue continues to be whether the approach is subjective or objective.

2.   SUBJECTIVE/OBJECTIVE DISTINCTION

The Supreme Court of Canada judgments in *R. v. Creighton*, [1993] 3 S.C.R. 3, 23 C.R. (4th) 189, 83 C.C.C. (3d) 346 and *R. v. Hundal*, [1993] 1 S.C.R. 867, 19 C.R. (4th) 169, 79 C.C.C. (3d) 97, accept that there should be a clear distinction between the subjective standard of whether the accused was actually aware of a risk and the objective standard of whether the accused failed to measure up to the external standard of the reasonable person, irrespective of awareness. On the subjective standard all of the accused's individual factors are taken into account. The objective standard is now clearly much tougher given the ruling by the majority in *Creighton*, to be fully discussed later, that on the objective standard no personal factors, such as age, race, gender, poverty and experience, can be taken into account except where they relate to incapacity. **Should such factors be considered before State punishment?**

How do we determine the accused's state of mind?

"The thought of man is not triable for the devil alone knoweth the thought of man." (Brian C.J., (1477), Year Books, Pasch Ed. IV Fi pl.2.)

"The state of man's mind is as much a fact as the state of his digestion." (Bowen L.J. in *Edington v. Fitzmaurice* (1885), 29 Ch.D. 459.)

The important distinction between a subjective substantive standard and the objective approach to proof is emphasized in the following judgments:

R. v. HUNDAL

[1993] 1 S.C.R. 867, 19 C.R. (4th) 169, 79 C.C.C. (3d) 97,
1993 CarswellBC 489, 1993 CarswellBC 1255

The court was called on to determine the fault requirement for the crime of dangerous driving.

CORY J. (for the majority): —

A truly subjective test seeks to determine what was actually in the mind of the particular accused at the moment the offence is alleged to have been committed. In his very useful text, Professor Stuart puts it in this way in *Canadian Criminal Law* (2nd ed.) at pp. 123-24 and at p. 125:

> What is vital is that *this accused* given his personality, situation and circumstances, actually intended, knew or foresaw the consequence and/or circumstance as the case may be. Whether he "could", "ought" or "should" have foreseen or whether a reasonable person would have foreseen is not the relevant criterion of liability.

> . . . .

> In trying to ascertain what was going on in the accused's mind, as the subjective approach demands, the trier of fact may draw reasonable inferences from the accused's actions or words at the time of his act or in the witness box. The accused may or may not be believed. To conclude that, considering all the evidence, the Crown has proved beyond a reasonable doubt that the accused "must" have thought in the penalized way is no departure from the subjective substantive standard. Resort to an objective substantive standard would only occur if the reasoning became that the accused "must have realized it if he had thought about it". [Emphasis in original.]

On the other hand, the test for negligence is an objective one requiring a marked departure from the standard of care of a reasonable person. There is no need to establish the intention of the particular accused. The question to be answered under the objective test concerns what the accused "should" have known.

R. v. THÉROUX

[1993] 2 S.C.R. 5, 19 C.R. (4th) 194, 79 C.C.C. (3d) 449,
1993 CarswellQue 5, 1993 CarswellQue 156

The court was called on to discuss the fault requirement for the crime of fraud. Justice McLachlin spoke for the majority:

This brings us to the *mens rea* of fraud. What is the guilty mind of fraud? At this point, certain confusions inherent in the concept of *mens rea* itself become apparent. It is useful initially to distinguish between the mental element or elements of a crime and the *mens rea*. The term *mens rea*, properly understood, does not encompass all of the mental elements of a crime. The *actus reus* has its own mental element; the act must be the voluntary act of the accused for the *actus reus* to exist. *Mens rea*, on the other hand, refers to the guilty mind, the wrongful intention, of the accused. Its function in criminal law is to prevent the conviction of the morally innocent — those who do not understand or intend the consequences of their acts. Typically, *mens rea* is concerned with the consequences of the prohibited *actus reus*. Thus in the crimes of homicide, we speak of the consequences of the voluntary act — intention to cause death, or reckless and wilfully blind persistence in conduct which one knows is likely to cause death. In other offences, such as dangerous driving, the *mens rea* may relate to the failure to consider the consequences of inadvertence.

This brings me to the question of whether the test for *mens rea* is subjective or objective. Most scholars and jurists agree that, leaving aside offences where the *actus reus* is negligence or inadvertence and offences of absolute liability, the test for *mens rea* is subjective. The test is not whether a reasonable person would have foreseen the consequences of the prohibited act, but whether the accused subjectively appreciated those consequences at least as a possibility. In applying the subjective test, the court looks to the accused's intention and the facts as the accused believed them to be: G. Williams, *Textbook of Criminal Law* (2nd ed. 1983), at pp. 727-28.

Two collateral points must be made at this juncture. First, as Williams underlines, this inquiry has nothing to do with the accused's system of values. A person is not saved from conviction because he or she believes there is nothing wrong with what he or she is doing. The question is whether the accused subjectively appreciated that certain consequences would follow from his or her acts, not whether the accused believed the acts or their consequences to be moral. Just as the pathological killer would not be acquitted on the mere ground that he failed to see his act as morally reprehensible, so the defrauder will not be acquitted because he believed that what he was doing was honest.

The second collateral point is the oft-made observation that the Crown need not, in every case, show precisely what thought was in the accused's mind at the time of the criminal act. In certain cases, subjective awareness of the consequences can be inferred from the act itself, barring some explanation casting doubt on such inference. The fact that such an inference is made does not detract from the subjectivity of the test.

R. v. MULLIGAN

(1974), 26 C.R.N.S. 179, 18 C.C.C. (2d) 270,
1974 CarswellOnt 11 (Ont. C.A.)

MARTIN J.A.: —

. . . .

The central issue in this case was whether the accused, when he caused the death of his wife by repeatedly stabbing her, meant to cause her death or meant to cause her bodily harm that he knew was likely to cause her death, and was reckless whether death ensued and thereby committed the crime of murder as defined by the *Criminal Code*, R.S.C. 1970, c. C-34, s. 212(*a*)(i), (ii). The accused's intention was a fact in issue and like any other fact in issue it fell to be determined by a consideration of all the evidence including his acts, his utterances and any other circumstances which might shed light on his state of mind. As previously observed, the accused did not testify with respect to his state of mind at the relevant time. Such evidence would have been relevant and admissible. *Rex v. Fitzpatrick* (1926), 19 Cr. App. R. 91; Wigmore on Evidence, 3rd ed., Vol. II, pp. 714-15.

The jury would, of course have been entitled to reject his evidence and conclude that the circumstances were consistent only with the existence of the necessary intent. Although the accused did not testify on his own behalf, the statements made by him to the police contained an assertion that he did not mean to kill the deceased. The jury was properly charged with respect to the use that they could make of those statements and it is perhaps unnecessary to add that the jury was entitled, if it saw fit, to reject his assertion that he did not mean to kill the deceased.

In *Vallance v. The Queen*, [1961] 108 C.L.R. 56, Windeyer J. said at pp. 82-83:

> What a man does is often the best evidence of the purpose he had in mind. The probability that harm will result from a man's act may be so great, and so apparent, that it compels an inference that he actually intended to do that harm. Nevertheless, intention is a state of mind. The circumstances and probable consequences of a man's act are no more than evidence of his intention. For this reason this court has often said that it is misleading to speak of a man

being presumed always to intend the natural and probable consequences of his acts. And this, I do not doubt is so.

and at p. 83 said:

A man's own intention is for him a subjective state, just as are his sensations of pleasure or of pain. But the state of another man's mind, or of his digestion, is an objective fact. When it has to be proved, it is to be probed in the same way as other objective facts are proved. A jury must consider the whole of the evidence relevant to it as a fact in issue. If an accused gives evidence of what his intentions were, the jury must weigh his testimony along with whatever inference as to his intentions can be drawn from his conduct or from other relevant facts. References to a "subjective test" could lead to an idea that the evidence of an accused man as to his intent is more credible than his evidence of other matters. It is not: he may or may not be believed by the jury. Whatever he says, they may be able to conclude from the whole of the evidence that beyond doubt he had a guilty mind and a guilty purpose. But always the questions are what did *he* in fact know, foresee, expect, intend.

R. v. ORTT

(1968), 6 C.R.N.S. 233, [1970] 1 C.C.C. 223, 1968 CarswellOnt 29 (Ont. C.A.)

On appeal from a conviction of non-capital murder, the main ground was that the charge of the trial judge suggested there was an onus on the accused to prove his incapacity to have the specific intent necessary. The trial judge had said to the jury:

The intention of a person *can* be judged by what he says or what he does. *In our law a person is presumed to have intended the natural consequences of his act.* Where a person deliberately strikes another with a lethal weapon an intention to kill will be *presumed* or, at least, an intention to cause bodily harm which is likely to result in death will be *presumed*. If a person strikes another with a knife in the region of the heart, in the region of the abdomen, various parts of the body, as was done to this woman, there would be a *presumption* that the person inflicting those wounds intended to cause the death of that woman or intended to cause bodily harm to her which he knew was likely to cause death and that he was reckless whether death would ensue or not. Where a person does acts calculated to kill a person and does kill that person, that is evidence of intent.

While the appeal was dismissed on the basis that the charge as a whole made it clear that the Crown had the onus of proof on the issue of intent, the court noted:

It has been held by this court that it is error in law to tell a jury it is a presumption of law that a person intends the natural consequences of his acts: *R. v. Giannotti* (1956), 115 C.C.C. 203, 23 C.R. 259. Moreover the word "presumption" alone creates a difficulty in that it may suggest an onus on the accused. I agree with the comment of the authors of *Martin's Annual Criminal Code* (1968), p. 195:

> The difficulty would not arise if the use of the word "presumption" were avoided. A presumption requires that a certain conclusion must be drawn, unless the accused takes steps to make that conclusion unwarranted. An inference, however, is no more than a matter of common sense and merely indicates that a certain conclusion may be drawn if warranted by the evidence.

As was said by Denning L.J. in *Hosegood v. Hosegood* (1950), 66 T.L.R. 735 at p. 738:

> The presumption of intention is not a proposition of law but a proposition of ordinary good sense. It means this: that, as a man is usually able to foresee what are the natural consequences of his acts, so it is, as a rule, reasonable to infer that he did foresee them and intend them. But, while that is an inference which may be drawn, it is not one which must be drawn. If on all the facts of the case it is not the correct inference, then it should not be drawn.

In my opinion, therefore, the word "presumption" is to be avoided in this context and juries simply told that generally it is a reasonable inference that a man intends the natural consequences of his acts so that when, for instance, a man points a gun at another and fires it the jury may reasonably infer that he meant either to cause his death or to cause him bodily harm that he knew was likely to cause death reckless of whether death ensued or not.

The following detailed consideration of the current law on fault will reveal that a low level objective standard is pervasive for public welfare offences and that, while the subjective approach is still required for most crimes, for a significant number of crimes there are now less demanding standards of fault.

3.   FAULT FOR PUBLIC WELFARE (REGULATORY) OFFENCES

(a)   Common Law

Until the pivotal decision in *Sault Ste. Marie*, in the case of some offences that were argued to be not truly criminal the choice for the courts was between requiring the Crown to establish full subjective *mens rea* in the actor or absolute liability. Absolute liability, at that time also called strict liability, rested merely on proof of an act with no requirement of any form of fault. Consider how the Supreme Court made this choice in a still controlling 1957 decision:

BEAVER v. R.

[1957] S.C.R. 531, 26 C.R. 193, 118 C.C.C. 129, 1957 CarswellOnt 10

The accused was appealing convictions on counts of selling and possessing diacetylmorphine.

CARTWRIGHT J. (RAND and LOCKE JJ. concurring): —

. . . .

It is not necessary to set out the facts in detail. There was evidence on which it was open to the jury to find (i) that Max Beaver sold to a police officer, who was working under cover, a package which in fact contained diacetylmorphine, (ii) that the appellant was a party to the sale of the package, (iii) that while the appellant did not have the package on his person or in his physical possession he and Max Beaver were acting jointly in such circumstances that the possession which the latter had of the package was the possession of both of the accused, and (iv) that the appellant had no knowledge that the substance contained in the package was diacetylmorphine and believed it to be sugar of milk.

I do not mean to suggest that the jury would necessarily have made the fourth finding but there was evidence on which they might have done so, or which might have left them in a state of doubt as to whether or not the appellant knew that the package contained anything other than sugar of milk.

The learned trial judge, against the protest of the appellant, charged the jury, in effect, that if they were satisfied that the appellant had in his possession a package and sold it, then, if in fact the substance contained in the package was diacetylmorphine, the appellant was guilty on both counts, and that the questions (i) whether he had any knowledge of what the substance was, or (ii) whether he entertained the honest but mistaken belief that it was a harmless substance were irrelevant and must not be considered. Laidlaw J.A. who delivered the unanimous judgment of the Court of Appeal, [116 Can. C.C. 231], was of opinion that this charge was right in law and that the learned trial judge was bound by the decision in *R. v. Lawrence*, 102 Can. C.C. 121, to direct the jury as he did. The main question on this appeal is whether this view of the law is correct.

The problem is one of construction of the *Opium and Narcotic Drug Act*, R.S.C. 1952, c. 201, and particularly the following sections, which at the date of the offences charged read as follows:

4(1) Every, person who . . .

(*d*) has in his possession any drug save and except under the authority of a licence from the Minister first had and obtained, or other lawful authority; . . .

(*f*) manufactures, sells, gives away, delivers or distributes or makes any offer in respect of any drug, or any substance represented or held out by such person to be a drug, to any person without first obtaining a licence from the Minister, or without other lawful authority;

. . .

is guilty of an offence, and is liable

(i) upon indictment, to imprisonment for any term not exceeding seven years and not less than six months, and to a fine not exceeding one thousand dollars and not less than two hundred dollars, and, in addition, at the discretion of the judge, to be whipped; or

(ii) upon summary conviction, to imprisonment with or without hard labour for any term not exceeding 18 months and not less than six months, and to a fine not exceeding one thousand dollars and not less than two hundred dollars.

. . . .

The judgment in appeal is supported by earlier decisions of Appellate Courts in Ontario, Quebec and Nova Scotia, but a directly contrary view has been expressed by the Court of Appeal for British Columbia. While this conflict has existed since 1948, this is the first occasion on which the question has been brought before this court.

It may be of assistance in examining the problem to use a simple illustration. Suppose X goes to the shop of Y, a druggist, and asks Y to sell him some baking soda. Y hands him a sealed packet which he tells him contains baking soda and charges him a few cents. X honestly believes that the packet contains baking soda but in fact it contains heroin. X puts the package in his pocket, takes it home and later puts it in a cupboard in his bathroom. There would seem to be no doubt that X has had actual manual and physical possession of the package and that he continues to have possession of the package while it is in his cupboard. The main question raised on this appeal is whether, in the supposed circumstances, X would be guilty of the crime of having heroin in his possession?

. . . .

In *Reynolds v. G.H. Austin & Sons Ltd.*, [1951] 2 K.B. 135, Devlin J. says at pp. 147-8:

It has always been a principle of the common law that *mens rea* is an essential element in the commission of any criminal offence against the common law. In the case of statutory offences it depends on the effect of the statute. In *Sherras v. De Rutzen*, [1895] 1 Q.B. 918, 921, Wright, J., in his well-known judgment, laid it down that there was a presumption that *mens rea* was an essential ingredient in a statutory offence, but that that presumption was liable to be displaced either by the words of the statute creating the offence or by the subject-matter with which it dealt. . . . Kennedy, L.J., in *Hobbs v. Winchester Corporation*, [1910] 2 K.B. 471, 483, thought that in construing a modern statute this presumption as to *mens rea* did not exist. In this respect, as he said, he differed from Channell, J., in the court below. But the view of Wright, J., in *Sherras v. De Rutzen* has consistently been followed. I need refer only to the dictum of Lord Goddard, C.J., in *Harding v. Price*, [1948] 1 K.B. 695, 700, "The general rule applicable to criminal cases is *actus non facit reum nisi mens sit rea*, and I venture to repeat what I said in *Brend v. Wood* (1946), 62 T.L.R. 462, 463, 'It is of the utmost importance for the protection of the liberty of the subject that a court should always bear in mind that, unless a statute either clearly or by necessary implication rules out *mens rea* as a constituent part of a crime, the court should not find a man guilty of an offence against the criminal law unless he has a guilty mind.' "

In *R. v. Tolson* (1889), 23 Q.B.D. 168 at p. 188, Stephen J. says:

"I think it may be laid down as a general rule that an alleged offender is deemed to have acted under that state of facts which he in good faith and on reasonable grounds believed to exist when he did the act alleged to be an offence. I am unable to suggest any real exception to this rule, nor has one ever been suggested to me.

And adds at p. 189:

Of course, it would be competent to the legislature to define a crime in such a way as to make the existence of any state of mind immaterial. The question is solely whether it has actually done so in this case.

I adhere to the opinion which, with the concurrence of my brother Nolan, I expressed in *R. v. Rees*, 115 Can. C.C. 1 at p. 11, [1956] S.C.R. 640 at p. 651 that the first of the statements of Stephen J. quoted above should now be read in the light of the judgment of Lord Goddard C.J., concurred in by Lynskey and Devlin JJ. in *Wilson v. Inyang*, [1951] 2 All E.R. 237, which, in my opinion, rightly decides that the essential question is whether the belief entertained by the accused is an honest one and that the existence or non-existence of reasonable grounds for such belief is merely relevant evidence to be weighed by the tribunal of fact in determining that essential question.

In *Watts & Gaunt v. The Queen*, 105 Can. C.C. 193 at p. 199, [1953], 1 S.C.R. 505 at p. 511, Estey J. says:

While an offence of which *mens rea* is not an essential ingredient may be created by legislation, in view of the general rule a section creating an offence ought not to be so construed unless Parliament has, by express language or necessary implication, disclosed such an intention.

. . . .

When the decisions as to the construction of the *Opium and Narcotic Drug Act* on which the respondent relies are examined it appears that two main reasons are assigned for holding that *mens rea* is not an essential ingredient of the offence created by s. 4(1)(*d*), these being (i) the assumption that the subject-matter with which the Act deals is of the kind dealt with in the cases of which *Hobbs v. Winchester Corp.*, [1910] 2 K.B. 471, is typical and which are sometimes referred to as "public welfare offence cases", and (ii) by implication from the wording of s. 17 of the Act.

As to the first of these reasons, I can discern little similarity between a statute designed, by forbidding the sale of unsound meat, to ensure that the supply available to the public shall be wholesome, and a statute making it a serious crime to possess or deal in narcotics; the one is to ensure that a lawful and necessary trade shall be carried on in a manner not to endanger the public health, the other to forbid altogether conduct regarded as harmful in itself. As a necessary feature of his trade, the butcher holds himself out as selling meat fit for consumption; he warrants that quality; and it is part of his duty as trader to see that the merchandise is wholesome. The statute simply converts that civil personal duty into a public duty.

. . . .

Has X possession of heroin when he has in his hand or in his pocket or in his cupboard a package which in fact contains heroin but which he honestly believes contains only baking soda? In my opinion that question must be answered in the negative. The essence of the crime is the possession of the forbidden substance and in a criminal case there is in law no possession without knowledge of the character of the forbidden substance. Just as in *R. v. Ashwell* (1885), 16 Q.B.D. 190, the accused did not in law have possession of the complainant's sovereign so long as he honestly believed it to be a shilling so in my illustration X did not have possession of heroin so long as he honestly believed the package to contain baking soda. The words of Lord Coleridge C.J. in *R. v. Ashwell* at p. 225, quoted by Charles J. delivering the unanimous judgment of the Court of Criminal Appeal in *R. v. Hudson* (1943), 29 Cr. App. R. 65 at p. 71:

"In good sense it seems to me he did not take it till he knew what he had got; and when he knew what he had got, that same instant he stole it."

might well be adapted to my illustration to read: "In good sense it seems to me he did not have possession of heroin till he knew what he had got."

. . . .

If the matter were otherwise doubtful I would be drawn to the conclusion that Parliament did not intend to enact that *mens rea* should not be an essential ingredient of the offence created by s. 4(1)(*d*) by the circumstance that on conviction a minimum sentence of six months' imprisonment plus a fine of $200 must be imposed. Counsel informed us that they have found no other statutory provision which has been held to create a crime of strict responsibility, that is to say, one in which the necessity for *mens rea* is excluded, on conviction for which a sentence of imprisonment is mandatory. The legislation dealt with in *Hobbs v. Winchester, supra*, provided that a sentence of imprisonment might, not must, be imposed on a convicted person.

. . . .

It would, of course, be within the power of Parliament to enact that a person who, without any guilty knowledge, had in his physical possession a package which he honestly believed to contain a harmless substance such as baking soda but which in fact contained heroin, must on proof of such facts be convicted of a crime and sentenced to at least six months' imprisonment; but I would refuse to impute such an intention to Parliament unless the words of the statute were clear and admitted of no other interpretation. To borrow the words of Lord Kenyon in *Fowler v. Padget* (1798), 7 Term R. 509 at p. 514, 101 E.R. 1103: "I would adopt any construction of the statute that the words will bear, in order to avoid such monstrous consequences as would manifestly ensue from the construction contended for by the defendant."

The conclusion which I have reached on the main question as to the proper construction of the word possession makes it unnecessary for me to consider the other points raised by Mr. Dubin in his argument as to the construction of s. 4(1)(*d*). For the above reasons I would quash the conviction on the charge of having possession of a drug.

As to the charge of selling, as is pointed out by my brother Fauteux, the appellant's version of the facts brings his actions within the provisions of s. 4(1)(*f*) since he and his brother jointly sold a substance represented or held out by them to be heroin; and I agree with the conclusion of my brother Fauteux that the conviction on the charge of selling must be affirmed.

. . . .

FAUTEUX J. (dissenting), ABBOTT J. (concurring): —

. . . .

The plain and apparent object of the Act is to prevent, by a rigid control of the possession of drugs, the danger to public health, and to guard society against the social evils which an uncontrolled traffic in drugs is bound to generate. The scheme of the Act is this: The importation, exportation, sale, manufacture, production and distribution of drugs are subject to the obtention of a licence which the Minister of National Health and Welfare may issue, with the approval of the Governor-General in Council, and in which the place where such operations may be carried on is stated. Under the same authority are indicated ports and places in Canada where drugs may be exported or imported, the manner in which they are to be packed and marked for export, the records to be kept for such export, import, receipt, sale, disposal and distribution. The Act also provides for the establishment of all other convenient and necessary regulations with respect to duration, terms and forms of the several licences therein provided. Without a licence, it is an offence to import or export from Canada and an offence for any one who, not being a common carrier, takes or carries, or causes to be taken or carried from any place in Canada to any other place in Canada, any drug. Druggists, physicians, dentists and veterinary surgeons stand, of course, in a privileged class; but even their dealings in drugs for medicinal purposes are the object of a particular control. Under penalties of the law, some of them have to keep records of their operations, while others have the obligation to answer inquiries in respect thereto. Having in one's possession drugs without a licence or other lawful authority, is an offence. In brief, the principle underlying the Act is that possession of drugs covered by it is unlawful; and where any exception is made to the principle, the exceptions themselves are attended with particular controlling provisions and conditions.

The enforcement sections of the Act manifest the exceptional vigilance and firmness which Parliament thought of the essence to forestall the unlawful traffic in narcotic drugs and cope effectively with the unusual difficulties standing in the way of the realization of the object of the statute. Substantive and procedural principles generally prevailing under the *Criminal Code* in favour of the subject are being restricted or excepted. The power to search by day or by night, either premises or the person, is largely extended under s. 19. Special writs of assistance are provided for under s. 22. The consideration of the provisions of ss. 4 and 17 being deferred for the moment, the burden of proof is either alleviated or shifted to persons charged with violations under ss. 6, 11, 13, 16 and 18. Minimum sentences are provided or are made mandatory, under ss. 4 and 6. Deportation of aliens found guilty is also mandatory and this notwithstanding the provisions of the *Immigration Act* [R.S.C. 1952, c. 325] or any other Act, under s. 26. And the application of the *Identification of Criminals Act* [R.S.C. 1952, c. 144], ordinarily limited to the case of indictable offences, is, by s. 27, extended to any offence under the Act.

All of these provisions are indicative of the will of Parliament to give the most efficient protection to public health against the danger attending the uncontrolled use of drugs as well as against the social evils incidental thereto, by measures generally centred and directed to possession itself of the drugs covered by the Act. The subject-matter, the purpose and the scope of the Act are such that to subject its provisions to the narrow construction suggested on behalf of appellant would defeat the very object of the Act.

. . . .

This case, amongst others, such as *R. v. Thomas Wheat, R. v. Marion Stocks*, [1921] 2 K.B. 119, is a clear authority supporting the proposition that the presumption that *mens rea* is an ingredient to an offence, as well as the defence flowing from an honest belief as to the existence of a state of facts may, by reason of the subject-matter of the Act or of the language of its provisions, or of both, cease to obtain. The *Opium and Narcotic Drug Act* comes, in my view, within these classes of Acts referred to by Wright J. in *Sherras v. De Rutzen, supra.*

. . . .

On the plain, literal and grammatical meaning of the words of this section, there is an absolute prohibition to be in possession of drugs, whatever be the various meanings of which the word possession may be susceptible, unless the possession is under the authority of a licence from the Minister, first had and obtained, or under other lawful authority. . . .

Appeal from conviction for possession of drug allowed; appeals from conviction for sale of a drug and finding of being an habitual criminal dismissed.

Although the majority in *Beaver* was only 3-2 it has since been accepted that all drug offences require subjective *mens rea*. In the case of offences based on possession, section 4(3) of the *Criminal Code* now expressly requires knowledge.

R. v. CITY OF SAULT STE. MARIE

[1978] 2 S.C.R. 1299, 3 C.R. (3d) 30, 40 C.C.C. (2d) 353,
1978 CarswellOnt 24, 1978 CarswellOnt 594

DICKSON J.: — In the present appeal the court is concerned with offences variously referred to as "statutory", "public welfare", "regulatory", "absolute liability", or "strict responsibility", which are not criminal in any real sense, but are prohibited in the public interest: *Sherras v. De Rutzen*, [1895] 1 Q.B. 918. Although enforced as penal laws through the utilization of the machinery of the criminal law, the offences are in substance of a civil nature and might well be regarded as a branch of administrative law to which traditional principles of criminal law have but limited application. They relate to such everyday matters as traffic infractions, sales of impure food, violations of liquor laws, and the like. In this appeal we are concerned with pollution.

The doctrine of the guilty mind expressed in terms of intention or recklessness, but not negligence, is at the foundation of the law of crimes. In the case of true crimes there is a presumption that a person should not be held liable for the wrongfulness of his act if that act is without *mens rea*: *R. v. Prince* (1875), L.R. 2 C.C.R. 154; *R. v. Tolson* (1889), 23 Q.B.D. 168; *R. v. Rees*, 115 C.C.C. 1, [1956] S.C.R. 640; *Beaver v. The Queen*, 118 C.C.C. 129, [1957] S.C.R. 531, 26 C.R. 193; *R. v. King*, 133 C.C.C. 1, [1962] S.C.R. 746. Blackstone made the point over two hundred years ago in words still apt: "to constitute a crime against human laws, there must be, first, a vicious will; and secondly, an unlawful act consequent upon such vicious will . . .": see *Commentaries on the Laws of England* (1809), Book IV, 15th ed., c. 15, p. 21. I would emphasize at the outset that nothing in the discussion which follows is intended to dilute or erode that basic principle.

. . . .

The City of Sault Ste. Marie was charged that it did discharge, or cause to be discharged, or permitted to be discharged, or deposited materials into Cannon Creek and Root River, or on the shore or bank thereof, or in such place along the side that might impair the quality of the water in Cannon Creek and Root River, between March 13, 1972 and September 11, 1972. The charge was laid under s. 32(1) of the *Ontario Water Resources Act*, R.S.O. 1970, c. 332, [formerly *Ontario Water Resources Commission Act*, renamed by 1972, c. 1, s. 70(1)] which provides, so far as relevant, that every municipality or person that discharges, or deposits, or causes, or permits the discharge or deposit of any material of any kind into any water course, or on any shore or bank thereof, or in any place that may impair the quality of water, is guilty of an offence and, on summary conviction, is liable on first conviction to a fine of not more than $5,000 and on each subsequent conviction to a fine of not more than $10,000, or to imprisonment for a term of not more than one year, or to both fine and imprisonment.

Although the facts do not rise above the routine, the proceedings have to date had the anxious consideration of five courts. The City was acquitted in Provincial Court (Criminal Division), but convicted following a trial *de novo* on a Crown appeal. A further appeal, by the City, to the Divisional Court was allowed and the conviction quashed. The Court of Appeal for Ontario on yet another appeal directed a new trial. Because of the importance of the legal issues, this court granted leave to the Crown to appeal and leave to the City to cross-appeal.

To relate briefly the facts, the City on November 18, 1970, entered into an agreement with Cherokee Disposal and Construction Co. Ltd., for the disposal of all refuse originating in the City. Under the terms of the agreement, Cherokee became obligated to furnish a site and adequate labour, material and equipment. The site selected bordered Cannon Creek which, it would appear, runs into the Root River. The method of disposal adopted is known as the "area", or "continuous slope" method of sanitary land fill, whereby garbage is compacted in layers which are covered each day by natural sand or gravel.

Prior to 1970, the site had been covered with a number of fresh-water springs that flowed into Cannon Creek. Cherokee dumped material to cover and submerge these springs and then placed garbage and wastes over such material. The garbage and wastes in due course formed a high mound sloping steeply toward, and within 20 ft. of, the creek. Pollution resulted. Cherokee was convicted of a breach of s. 32(1) of the *Ontario Water Resources Act*, the section under which the City has been charged. The question now before the court is whether the City is also guilty of an offence under that section.

In dismissing the charge at first instance, the judge found that the City had had nothing to do with the actual disposal operations, that Cherokee was an independent contractor and its employees were not employees of the City. On the appeal *de novo* Judge Vannini found the offence to be one of strict liability and he convicted. The Divisional Court in setting aside the judgment found that the charge was duplicitous. As a secondary point, the Divisional Court also held that the charge required *mens rea* with respect to causing or permitting a discharge. When the case reached the Court of Appeal that court held that the conviction could not be quashed on the ground of duplicity, because there had been no challenge to the information at trial. The Court of Appeal agreed, however, that the charge was one requiring proof of *mens rea*. A majority of the court (Brooke and Howland JJ.A.) held there was not sufficient evidence to establish *mens rea* and ordered a new trial. In the view of Mr. Justice Lacourcière, dissenting, the inescapable inference to be drawn from the findings of fact of Judge Vannini was that the City had known of the potential impairment of waters of Cannon Creek and Root River and had failed to exercise its clear powers of control.

The divers, and diverse, judicial opinions to date on the points under consideration reflect the dubiety in these branches of the law.

. . . .

The mens rea point

The distinction between the true criminal offence and the public welfare offence is one of prime importance. Where the offence is criminal, the Crown must establish a mental element, namely, that the accused who committed the prohibited act did so intentionally or recklessly, with knowledge of the facts constituting the offence, or with wilful blindness toward them. Mere negligence is excluded from the concept of the mental element required for conviction. Within the context of a criminal prosecution a person who fails to make such inquiries as a reasonable and prudent person would make, or who fails to know facts he should have known, is innocent in the eyes of the law.

In sharp contrast, "absolute liability" entails conviction on proof merely that the defendant committed the prohibited act constituting the *actus reus* of the offence. There is no relevant mental element. It is no defence that the accused was entirely without fault. He may be morally innocent in every sense, yet be branded as a malefactor and punished as such.

Public welfare offences obviously lie in a field of conflicting values. It is essential for society to maintain, through effective enforcement, high standards of public health and safety. Potential victims of those who carry on latently pernicious activities have a strong claim to consideration. On the other hand, there is a generally held revulsion against punishment of the morally innocent.

Public welfare offences evolved in mid-19th century Britain (*R. v. Woodrow* (1846), 15 M. & W. 404, and *R. v. Stephens* (1866), L.R. 1 Q.B. 702) as a means of doing away with the requirement of *mens rea* for petty police offences. The concept was a judicial creation, founded on expediency. That concept is now firmly embedded in the concrete of Anglo-American and Canadian jurisprudence, its importance heightened by the ever-increasing complexities of modern society.

Various arguments are advanced in justification of absolute liability in public welfare offences. Two predominate. Firstly, it is argued that the protection of social interests requires a high standard of care and attention on the part of those who follow certain pursuits and such persons are more likely to be stimulated to maintain those standards if they know that ignorance or mistake will not excuse them. The removal of any possible loophole acts, it is said, as an incentive to take precautionary measures beyond what would otherwise be taken, in order that mistakes and mishaps be avoided. The second main argument is one based on administrative efficiency. Having regard to both the difficulty of proving mental culpability and the number of petty cases which daily come before the courts, proof of fault is just too great a burden in time and money to place upon the prosecution. To require proof of each person's individual intent would allow almost every violator to escape. This, together with the glut of work entailed in proving *mens rea* in every case would clutter the docket and impede adequate enforcement as virtually to nullify the regulatory acts statutes. In short, absolute liability, it is contended, is the most efficient and effective way of ensuring compliance with minor regulatory legislation and the social ends to be achieved are of such importance as to override the unfortunate by-product of punishing those who may be free of moral turpitude. In further justification, it is urged that slight penalties are usually imposed and that conviction for breach of a public welfare offence does not carry the stigma associated with conviction for a criminal offence.

Arguments of greater force are advanced against absolute liability. The most telling is that it violates fundamental principles of penal liability. It also rests upon assumptions which have not been, and cannot be, empirically established. There is no evidence that a higher standard of care results from absolute liability. If a person is already taking every reasonable precautionary measure, is he likely to take additional measures, knowing that however much care he takes, it will not serve as a defence in the event of breach? If he has exercised care and skill, will conviction have a deterrent effect upon him or others? Will the injustice of conviction lead to cynicism and disrespect for the law, on his part and on the part of others? These are among the questions asked. The argument that no stigma attaches does not withstand analysis, for the accused will have suffered loss of time, legal costs, exposure to the processes of the criminal law at trial and, however one may downplay it, the opprobrium of conviction. It is not sufficient to say that the public interest is engaged and, therefore, liability may be imposed without fault. In serious crimes, the public interest is involved and *mens rea* must be proven. The administrative argument has little force. In sentencing, evidence of due diligence is admissible and therefore the evidence might just as well be heard when considering guilt. Additionally, it may be noted that s. 198 of the *Alberta Highway Traffic Act*, R.S.A. 1970, c. 169, provides that upon a person being charged with an offence under this Act, if the Judge trying the case is of the opinion that the offence (a) was committed wholly by accident or misadventure and without negligence, and (b) could not by the exercise of reasonable care or precaution have been avoided, the Judge may dismiss the case. See also s. 230(2) [am. 1976, c. 62, s. 48] of the Manitoba *Highway Traffic Act*, R.S.M. 1970, c. H60, which has a similar effect. In these instances at least, the Legislature has indicated that administrative efficiency does not foreclose inquiry as to fault. It is also worthy of note that historically the penalty for breach of statutes enacted for the regulation of individual conduct in the interests of health and safety was minor, $20 or $25; today, it may amount to thousands of dollars and entail the possibility of imprisonment for a second conviction. The present case is an example.

Public welfare offences involve a shift of emphasis from the protection of individual interests to the protection of public and social interests: see F.B. Sayre, "Public Welfare Offenses", 33 *Columbia Law Rev.* 55 (1933); Hall, *General Principles of Criminal Law* (1947), c. 13, p. 427; R.M. Perkins, "Civil Offense", 100 *U. of Pa. L. Rev.* 832 (1952); Jobson, "Far From Clear", 18 *Crim. L.Q.* 294 (1975-76). The unfortunate tendency in many past cases has been to see the choice as between two stark alternatives: (i) full *mens rea*; or (ii) absolute liability. In respect of public welfare offences (within which category pollution offences fall) where full *mens rea* is not required, absolute liability has often been imposed. English jurisprudence has consistently maintained this dichotomy: see "Criminal Law, Evidence and Procedure", 11 Hals., 4th ed., pp. 20-2, para. 18. There has, however, been an attempt in Australia, in many Canadian Courts, and indeed in England, to seek a middle position, fulfilling the goals of public welfare offences while still not punishing the entirely blameless. There is an increasing and impressive stream of authority which holds that where an offence does not require full *mens rea*, it is nevertheless a good defence for the defendant to prove that he was not negligent.

Dr. Glanville Williams has written: "There is a half-way house between *mens rea* and strict responsibility which has not yet been properly utilized, and that is responsibility for negligence" (*Criminal Law: General Part*, 2nd ed. (1961), p. 262.) Morris and Howard, in *Studies in Criminal Law* (1964), p. 200, suggest that strict responsibility might with advantage be replaced by a doctrine of responsibility for negligence strengthened by a shift in the burden of proof. The defendant would be allowed to exculpate himself by proving affirmatively that he was not negligent. Professor Howard ("Strict Responsibility in the High Court of Australia", 76 *L.Q.R.* 547 (1960)) offers the comment that English law of strict responsibility in minor statutory offences is distinguished only by its irrationality, and then has this to say in support of the position taken by the Australian High Court, at p. 548:

> Over a period of nearly sixty years since its inception the High Court has adhered with consistency to the principle that there should be no criminal responsibility without fault, however minor the offence. It has done so by utilizing the very half-way house to which Dr. Williams refers, responsibility for negligence.

In his work, "Public Welfare Offenses", at p. 78, Professor Sayre suggests that if the penalty is really slight involving, for instance, a maximum fine of $25, particularly if adequate enforcement depends upon wholesale prosecution, or if the social danger arising from violation is serious, the doctrine of basing liability upon mere activity rather than fault, is sound. He continues, however, at p. 79:

> On the other hand, some public welfare offenses involve a possible penalty of imprisonment or heavy fine. In such cases it would seem sounder policy to maintain the orthodox requirement of a guilty mind but to shift the burden of proof to the shoulders of the defendant to establish his lack of a guilty intent if he can. For public welfare offenses defendants may be convicted by proof of the mere act of violation; but, if the offense involves a possible prison penalty, the defendant should not be denied the right of bringing forward affirmative evidence to prove that the violation was the result of no fault on his part.

and at p. 82:

> It is fundamentally unsound to convict a defendant for a crime involving a substantial term of imprisonment without giving him the opportunity to prove that his action was due to an honest and reasonable mistake of fact or that he acted without guilty intent. If the public danger is widespread and serious, the practical situation can be met by shifting to the shoulders of the defendant the burden of proving a lack of guilty intent.

The doctrine proceeds on the assumption that the defendant could have avoided the *prima facie* offence through the exercise of reasonable care and he is given the opportunity of establishing, if he can, that he did in fact exercise such care.

The case which gave the lead in this branch of the law is the Australian case of *Proudman v. Dayman* (1941), 67 C.L.R. 536, where Dixon J., said, at p. 540:

> It is one thing to deny that a necessary ingredient of the offence is positive knowledge of the fact that the driver holds no subsisting licence. It is another to say that an honest belief founded on reasonable grounds that he is licensed cannot exculpate a person who permits him to drive. As a general rule an honest and reasonable belief in a state of facts which, if they existed, would make the defendant's act innocent affords an excuse for doing what would otherwise be an offence.

This case, and several others like it, speak of the defence as being that of reasonable mistake of fact. The reason is that the offences in question have generally turned on the possession by a person or place of an unlawful status, and the accused's defence was that he reasonably did not know of this status: *e.g.*, permitting an unlicensed person to drive, or lacking a valid licence oneself, or being the owner of property in a dangerous condition. In such cases, negligence consists of an unreasonable failure to know the facts which constitute the offence. It is clear, however, that in principle the defence is that all reasonable care was taken. In other circumstances, the issue will be whether the accused's behaviour was negligent in bringing about the forbidden event when he knew the relevant facts. Once the defence of reasonable mistake of fact is accepted, there is no barrier to acceptance of the other constituent part of a defence of due diligence.

The principle which has found acceptance in Australia since *Proudman v. Dayman, supra,* has a place also in the jurisprudence of New Zealand: see *The*

Queen v. Strawbridge, [1970] N.Z.L.R. 909; *The King v. Ewart* (1905), 25 N.Z.L.R. 709.

· · · ·

[The court then reviewed a number of Canadian decisions.]

We have the situation therefore in which many courts of this country, at all levels, dealing with public welfare offences favour (i) *not* requiring the Crown to prove *mens rea*, (ii) rejecting the notion that liability inexorably follows upon mere proof of the *actus reus*, excluding any possible defence. The courts are following the lead set in Australia many years ago and tentatively broached by several English Courts in recent years.

It may be suggested that the introduction of a defence based on due diligence and the shifting of the burden of proof might better be implemented by legislative act. In answer, it should be recalled that the concept of absolute liability and the creation of a jural category of public welfare offences are both the product of the judiciary and not of the Legislature. The development to date of this defence, in the numerous decisions I have referred to, of courts in this country as well as in Australia and New Zealand, has also been the work of judges. The present case offers the opportunity of consolidating and clarifying the doctrine.

The correct approach, in my opinion, is to relieve the Crown of the burden of proving *mens rea*, having regard to *Pierce Fisheries* and to the virtual impossibility in most regulatory cases of proving wrongful intention. In a normal case, the accused alone will have knowledge of what he has done to avoid the breach and it is not improper to expect him to come forward with the evidence of due diligence. This is particularly so when it is alleged, for example, that pollution was caused by the activities of a large and complex corporation. Equally, there is nothing wrong with rejecting absolute liability and admitting the defence of reasonable care.

In this doctrine it is not up to the prosecution to prove negligence. Instead, it is open to the defendant to prove that all due care has been taken. This burden falls upon the defendant as he is the only one who will generally have the means of proof. This would not seem unfair as the alternative is absolute liability which denies an accused any defence whatsoever. While the prosecution must prove beyond a reasonable doubt that the defendant committed the prohibited act, the defendant must only establish on the balance of probabilities that he has a defence of reasonable care.

I conclude, for the reasons which I have sought to express, that there are compelling grounds for the recognition of three categories of offences rather than the traditional two:

1. Offences in which *mens rea*, consisting of some positive state of mind such as intent, knowledge, or recklessness, must be proved by the prosecution

either as an inference from the nature of the act committed, or by additional evidence.

2. Offences in which there is no necessity for the prosecution to prove the existence of *mens rea*; the doing of the prohibited act *prima facie* imports the offence, leaving it open to the accused to avoid liability by proving that he took all reasonable care. This involves consideration of what a reasonable man would have done in the circumstances. The defence will be available if the accused reasonably believed in a mistaken set of facts which, if true, would render the act or omission innocent, or if he took all reasonable steps to avoid the particular event. These offences may properly be called offences of strict liability. Mr. Justice Estey so referred to them in *Hickey's* case.

3. Offences of absolute liability where it is not open to the accused to exculpate himself by showing that he was free of fault.

Offences which are criminal in the true sense fall in the first category. Public welfare offences would, *prima facie*, be in the second category. They are not subject to the presumption of full *mens rea*. An offence of this type would fall in the first category only if such words as "wilfully", "with intent", "knowingly", or "intentionally" are contained in the statutory provision creating the offence. On the other hand, the principle that punishment should in general not be inflicted on those without fault applies. Offences of absolute liability would be those in respect of which the Legislature had made it clear that guilt would follow proof merely of the proscribed act. The over-all regulatory pattern adopted by the Legislature, the subject-matter of the legislation, the importance of the penalty, and the precision of the language used will be primary considerations in determining whether the offence falls into the third category.

Ontario Water Resources Act, s. 32(1)

Turning to the subject-matter of s. 32(1) — the prevention of pollution of lakes, rivers and streams — it is patent that this is of great public concern. Pollution has always been unlawful and, in itself, a nuisance: *Groat v. City of Edmonton*, [1928] 3 D.L.R. 725, [1928] S.C.R. 522. A riparian owner has an inherent right to have a stream of water "come to him in its natural state, in flow, quantity and quality": *Chasemore v. Richards* (1859), 7 H.L. Cas. 349 at p. 382. Natural streams which formerly afforded "pure and healthy" water for drinking or swimming purposes become little more than cesspools when riparian factory owners and municipal corporations discharge into them filth of all descriptions. Pollution offences are undoubtedly public welfare offences enacted in the interests of public health. There is thus no presumption of a full *mens rea*.

There is another reason, however, why this offence is not subject to a presumption of *mens rea*. The presumption applies only to offences which are "criminal in the true sense", as Ritchie J., said in *the Queen v. Pierce Fisheries, supra*, at p. 199 C.C.C., p. 597 D.L.R., p. 13 S.C.R. The *Ontario Water Resources Act* is a provincial statute. If it is valid provincial legislation (and no suggestion was made to the contrary), then it cannot possibly create an offence which is criminal in the true sense.

The present case concerns the interpretation of two troublesome words frequently found in public welfare statutes: "cause" and "permit". These two words are troublesome because neither denotes clearly either full *mens rea* nor absolute liability. It is said that a person could not be said to be permitting something unless he knew what he was permitting. This is an over-simplification. There is authority both ways, indicating that the courts are uneasy with the traditional dichotomy. Some authorities favour the position that "permit" does not import *mens rea*; see *Millar v. The Queen* (1954), 107 C.C.C. 321, 17 C.R. 293; *R. v. Royal Canadian Legion* (1971), 4 C.C.C. (2d) 196; *R. v. Teperman & Sons Ltd.*, [1968] 4 C.C.C. 67; *R. v. Jack Cewe Ltd.* (1975), 23 C.C.C. (2d) 237; *Browning v. J.W.H. Watson (Rochester) Ltd.*, [1953] 1 W.L.R. 1172; *Lyons v. May*, [1948] 2 All E.R. 1062; *Korten v. West Sussex County Council* (1903) , 72 L.J.K.B. 514. For a *mens rea* construction see *James & Son Ltd. v. Smee*, [1955] 1 Q.B. 78; *Somerset v. Hart* (1884), 12 Q.B.C. 360; *Grays Haulage Co. Ltd. v. Arnold*, [1966] 1 All E.R. 896; Smith & Hogan, *Criminal Law*, 3rd ed. (1973), p. 87; Edwards, *Mens Rea and Statutory Offences* (1955), pp. 98-119. The same is true of "cause". For a non-*mens rea* construction, see *R. v. Peconi* (1907), 1 C.C.C. (2d) 213; *Alphacell Ltd. v. Woodward*, [1972] A.C. 824; *Sopp v. Long*, (1969] 1 All E.R. 855; *Laird v. Dobell*, [1906] 1 K.B. 131; *Korten v. West Sussex County Council, supra*; *Shave v. Rosner*, [1954] 2 W.L.R. 1057. Others say that "cause" imports a requirement for a *mens rea*: see *Lovelace v. D.P.P.*, [1954] 3 All E.R. 481; *Ross Hillman Ltd. v. Bond*, [1974] 2 All E.R. 287; Smith and Hogan, *Criminal Law*, pp, 89-90.

The Divisional Court of Ontario relied on these latter authorities in concluding that s. 32(1) created a *mens rea* offence.

The conflict in the above authorities, however, shows that in themselves the words "cause" and "permit" fit much better into an offence of strict liability than either full *mens rea* or absolute liability. Since s. 32(1) creates a public welfare offence, without a clear indication that liability is absolute, and without any words such as "knowingly" or "wilfully" expressly to import *mens rea*, application of the criteria which I have outlined above undoubtedly places the offence in the category of strict liability.

Proof of the prohibited act *prima facie* imports the offence, but the accused may avoid liability by proving that he took reasonable care. I am strengthened in this view by the recent case of *R. v. Servico Ltd.* (1977), 2 Alta. L.R. (2d) 388, in which the Appellate Division of the Alberta Supreme Court held that an offence of "permitting" a person under 18 years to work during prohibited hours was an offence of strict liability in the sense which I have described. It also will be recalled that the decisions of many lower courts which have considered s. 32(1) have rejected absolute liability as the basis for the offence of causing or permitting pollution, and have equally rejected full *mens rea* as an ingredient of the offence.

New trial ordered.

The distinction between crimes and regulatory offences was central to the decision in *Sault Ste. Marie (City)*. It was revisited by Mr. Justice Cory in a minority concurring judgment in *Wholesale Travel Group Inc.* That decision's complex rulings on the issue of fault and reverse onus for regulatory offences will soon be revisited in these materials.

Do you find Mr. Justice Cory's approach to distinguishing regulatory offences persuasive?

R. v. WHOLESALE TRAVEL GROUP INC.

[1991] 3 S.C.R. 154, 8 C.R. (4th) 145, 67 C.C.C. (3d) 193,
1991 CarswellOnt 117, 1991 CarswellOnt 1029

The accused corporation, a travel agency, was charged with various counts of misleading advertising contrary to what is now s. 60(2) of the *Competition Act*. Although that offence carries a sentence on conviction on indictment to a fine in the discretion of the court and to imprisonment for five years or to both and on summary conviction to a fine of $25,000 or to imprisonment for one year or both, Mr. Justice Cory nevertheless characterized it as a regulatory offence as follows:

CORY J. (L'HEUREUX-DUBÉ J. concurring): —

. . . .

The Rationale for the Distinction

It has always been thought that there is a rational basis for distinguishing between crimes and regulatory offences. Acts or actions are criminal when they constitute conduct that is, in itself, so abhorrent to the basic values of human society that it ought to be prohibited completely. Murder, sexual assault, fraud, robbery and theft are all so repugnant to society that they are universally recognized as crimes. At the same time, some conduct is prohibited, not because it is inherently wrongful, but because unregulated activity would result in dangerous conditions being imposed upon members of society, especially those who are particularly vulnerable.

The objective of regulatory legislation is to protect the public or broad segments of the public (such as employees, consumers and motorists, to name but a few) from the potentially adverse effects of otherwise lawful activity. Regulatory legislation involves a shift of emphasis from the protection of individual interests and the deterrence and punishment of acts involving moral fault to the protection of public and societal interests. While criminal offences are usually designed to condemn and punish past, inherently wrongful conduct, regulatory measures are generally directed to the prevention of future harm through the enforcement of minimum standards of conduct and care.

It follows that regulatory offences and crimes embody different concepts of fault. Since regulatory offences are directed primarily not to conduct itself but to the consequences of conduct, conviction of a regulatory offence may be thought to import a significantly lesser degree of culpability than conviction of a true crime. The concept of fault in regulatory offences is based upon a reasonable care standard and, as such, does not imply moral blameworthiness in the same manner as criminal fault. Conviction for breach of a regulatory offence suggests nothing more than that the defendant has failed to meet a prescribed standard of care.

That is the theory, but, like all theories, its application is difficult. For example, is the single mother who steals a loaf of bread to sustain her family more blameworthy than the employer who, through negligence, breaches regulations and thereby exposes his employees to dangerous working conditions, or the manufacturer who, as a result of negligence, sells dangerous products or pollutes the air and waters by its plant? At this stage it is sufficient to bear in mind that those who breach regulations may inflict serious harm on large segments of society. Therefore, the characterization of an offence as regulatory should not be thought to make light of either the potential harm to the vulnerable or the responsibility of those subject to regulation to ensure that the proscribed harm does not occur. It should also be remembered that, as social values change, the degree of moral blameworthiness attaching to certain conduct may change as well.

Nevertheless there remains, in my view, a sound basis for distinguishing between regulatory and criminal offences. The distinction has concrete theoretical and practical underpinnings and has proven to be a necessary and workable concept in our law. Since *Sault Ste. Marie*, this court has reaffirmed the distinction. Most recently, in *Thomson Newspapers Ltd. v. Canada (Director of Investigation and Research*, [1990] 1 S.C.R. 425, 76 C.R. (3d) 129, 54 C.C.C. (3d) 417, at pp. 510-511 [S.C.R., p. 209 C.R.], Justice La Forest adopted the following statement of the Law Reform Commission of Canada (Criminal Responsibility for Group Action, Working Paper No. 16 1976, at p. 12):

> [The regulatory offence] is not primarily concerned with values, but with results. While values necessarily underlie all legal prescriptions, the regulatory offence really gives expression to the view that it is expedient for the protection of society and for the orderly use and sharing of society's resources that people act in a prescribed manner in prescribed situations, or that people take prescribed standards of care to avoid risks of injury. The object is to induce compliance with rules for the overall benefit of society.

B. The Fundamental Importance of Regulatory Offences in Canadian Society

Regulatory measures are the primary mechanisms employed by governments in Canada to implement public policy objectives. What is ultimately at stake in this appeal is the ability of federal and provincial governments to pursue social ends through the enactment and enforcement of public welfare legislation.

Some indication of the prevalence of regulatory offences in Canada is provided by a 1974 estimate by the Law Reform Commission of Canada. The commission estimated that there were, at that time, approximately 20,000 regulatory offences in an average province, plus an additional 20,000 regulatory offences at the federal level. By 1983, the commission's estimate of the federal total had reached 97,000. There is every reason to believe that the number of public welfare offences at both levels of government has continued to increase.

Statistics such as these make it obvious that government policy in Canada is pursued principally through regulation. It is through regulatory legislation that the community seeks to implement its larger objectives and to govern itself and the conduct of its members. The ability of the government effectively to regulate potentially harmful conduct must be maintained.

It is difficult to think of an aspect of our lives that is not regulated for our benefit and for the protection of society as a whole. From cradle to grave, we are protected by regulations; they apply to the doctors attending our entry into this world and to the morticians present at our departure. Every day, from waking to sleeping, we profit from regulatory measures which we often take for granted. On rising, we use various forms of energy whose safe distribution and use are governed by regulation. The trains, buses and other vehicles that get us to work are regulated for our safety. The food we eat and the beverages we drink are subject to regulation for the protection of our health.

In short, regulation is absolutely essential for our protection and well-being as individuals, and for the effective functioning of society. It is properly present throughout our lives. The more complex the activity, the greater the need for and the greater our reliance upon regulation and its enforcement. For example, most people would have no idea what regulations are required for air transport or how they should be enforced. Of necessity, society relies on government regulation for its safety.

II. The Offence in the Present Case

Competition legislation generally

The offence of misleading advertising with which Wholesale Travel is charged is found in the *Competition Act* (the "Act"). This Act, like its predecessor, the *Combines Investigation Act*, is aimed at regulating unacceptable business activity. In *General Motors of Canada Ltd. v. City National Leasing Ltd.*, [1989] 1 S.C.R. 641, Dickson C.J.C. held that the Act embodied a complex scheme of economic regulation, the purpose of which is to eliminate activities that reduce competition in the marketplace.

The nature and purpose of the Act was considered in greater detail in *Thomson Newspapers, supra.* La Forest J. pointed out that the Act is aimed at regulating the economy and business with a view to preserving competitive conditions which are crucial to the operation of a free market economy. He observed that the Act was not concerned with "real crimes" but with regulatory or public welfare offences. He put the position this way, at p. 510 [S.C.R., pp. 199-200 C.R.]:

> At bottom, the Act is really aimed at the regulation of the economy and business, with a view to the preservation of the competitive conditions which are crucial to the operation of a free market economy. This goal has obvious implications for Canada's material prosperity. It also has broad political overtones in that it is aimed at preventing concentration of power . . . It must be remembered that private organizations can be just as oppressive as the state when they gain such a dominant position within their sphere of operations that they can effectively force their will upon others.
>
> *The conduct regulated or prohibited by the Act is not conduct which is by its very nature morally or socially reprehensible. It is instead conduct we wish to discourage because of our desire to maintain an economic system which is at once productive and consistent with our values of individual liberty. It is, in short, not conduct which would be generally regarded as by its very nature criminal and worthy of criminal sanction. It is conduct which is only criminal in the sense that it is in fact prohibited by law.* One's view of whether it should be so proscribed is likely to be functional or utilitarian, in the sense that it will be based on an assessment of the desirability of the economic goals to which combines legislation is directed or its potential effectiveness in achieving those goals. *It is conduct which is made criminal for strictly instrumental reasons.* [Emphasis added.]

These decisions make it clear that the *Competition Act* in all its aspects is regulatory in character.

The Offence of False or Misleading Advertising

Is the offence of false or misleading advertising regulatory in nature? It seems to me that the fact that the provision is located within a comprehensive regulatory framework would ordinarily be sufficient to demonstrate its regulatory nature. Several other considerations point to the same conclusion.

The offence of misleading advertising has existed in Canada since 1914. It is not without significance that it was, in 1969, transferred from the *Criminal Code* to the *Combines Investigation Act*, a step which confirms the regulatory nature of the offence. The provision was amended in 1975 to provide for a defence of due diligence, converting the offence from absolute to strict liability.

It is true that the availability of imprisonment as a sanction for breach of a statute might be taken to indicate that the provision is criminal in nature.

However, this fact is not itself dispositive of the character of an offence. Rather, one must consider the conduct addressed by the legislation and the purposes for which such conduct is regulated. This view was most recently expressed by La Forest J. in *Thomson Newspapers, supra*, at p. 509 [S.C.R., p. 129 C.R.]. He noted that many regulatory offences provide for imprisonment in order to ensure compliance with the terms of the statute and thereby achieve the regulatory goal.

The appellant has argued that conviction for the offence of false advertising carries a stigma of dishonesty, with the inference that the accused falsely advertised for the purposes of obtaining economic advantage. It is said that nothing could be more damaging to a business than the implication that it has made dishonest representations. In my view, however, the offence does not focus on dishonesty but rather on the harmful consequences of otherwise lawful conduct. Conviction suggests only that the defendant has made a representation to the public which was in fact misleading, and that the defendant was unable to establish the exercise of due diligence in preventing the error. This connotes a fault element of negligence rather than one involving moral turpitude. Thus, any stigma that might flow from a conviction is very considerably diminished.

In summary, the offence of false advertising possesses the essential characteristics which distinguish regulatory offences from those which are truly criminal. Accordingly, it should be considered to be a regulatory offence rather than a crime in the ordinary sense.

. . . .

[His Lordship further held that the contextual approach to *Charter* interpretation required that regulatory and criminal offences be treated differently for the purposes of *Charter* review.]

Before proceeding to the substantive analysis, however, it is necessary to consider the justifications for differential treatment. They are two-fold: the first relates to the distinctive nature of regulatory activity, while the second acknowledges the fundamental need to protect the vulnerable through regulatory legislation.

1. *The Licensing Justification*

Those who argue against differential treatment for regulatory offences assert that there is no valid reason to distinguish between the criminal and regulatory accused. Each, it is said, is entitled in law to the same procedural and substantive protections. This view assumes equality of position between criminal and regulatory defendants; that is to say, it assumes that each starts out from a position of equal knowledge, volition and "innocence". The argument against differential treatment further suggests that differentiating between the regulatory and criminal defendants implies the subordination and sacrifice of the regulatory accused to the interests of the community at large. Such a position, it is argued, contravenes our basic concern for individual dignity and our fundamental belief in the importance of the individual. It is these assumptions which the licensing justification challenges.

Criminal law is rooted in the concepts of individual autonomy and free will and the corollary that each individual is responsible for his or her conduct. It assumes that all persons are free actors, at liberty to choose how to regulate their own actions in relation to others. The criminal law fixes the outer limits of acceptable conduct, constraining individual freedom to a limited degree in order to preserve the freedom of others. Thus, the basis of criminal responsibility is that the accused person has made a deliberate and conscious choice to engage in activity prohibited by the *Criminal Code*. The accused person who is convicted of an offence will be held responsible for his or her actions, with the result that the opprobrium of society will attach to those acts and any punishment imposed will be considered to be deserved.

The licensing argument is directed to this question of choice. Thus, while in the criminal context, the essential question to be determined is whether the accused has made the choice to act in the manner alleged in the indictment, the regulated defendant is, by virtue of the licensing argument, assumed to have made the choice to engage in the regulated activity. The question then becomes not whether the defendant chose to enter the regulated sphere but whether, having done so, the defendant has fulfilled the responsibilities attending that decision. Professor Genevra Richardson puts the position this way in "Strict Liability for Regulatory Crime: the Empirical Research," [1987] Crim. L.R. 295, at pp. 295-296:

> [I]t can be argued that the strict liability regulatory offender is not a "blameless innocent". By indulging in the regulated activity she has voluntary adopted the risks of regulatory infraction and her supposed "innocence" flows from the law's traditional tendency to view the criminal act "only in the context of its immediate past".

The licensing concept rests on the view that those who choose to participate in regulated activities have, in doing so, placed themselves in a responsible relationship to the public generally and must accept the consequences of that responsibility. Therefore, it is said, those who engage in regulated activity should, as part of the burden of responsible conduct attending participation in the regulated field, be deemed to have accepted certain terms and conditions applicable to those who act within the regulated sphere. Foremost among these implied terms is an undertaking that the conduct of the regulated actor will comply with and maintain a certain minimum standard of care.

The licensing justification is based not only on the idea of a conscious choice being made to enter a regulated field, but also on the concept of control. The concept is that those persons who enter a regulated field are in the best position to control the harm which may result, and that they should therefore be held responsible for it. A compelling statement of this view is found in the decision of the United States Supreme Court in *Morissette v. United States*, 342 U.S. 246, 72 S.Ct. 240 (Mich., 1952), where the court stated, at p. 256 [U.S.]:

> The accused, if he does not will the violation, usually is in a position to prevent it with no more care than society might reasonably expect and no more exertion than it might reasonably exact from one who assumed his responsibilities.

The licensing justification may not apply in all circumstances to all offenders. That is, there are some cases in which the licensing argument may not apply so as to permit the imputation to an accused of choice, knowledge and implied acceptance of regulatory terms and conditions. This may occur, for instance, where the nature of the regulated conduct is so innocuous that it would not trigger in the mind of a reasonable person the possibility that the conduct was regulated.

The nature of the regulated conduct will itself go far to determining whether the licensing argument applies. It is useful to distinguish between conduct which, by virtue of its inherent danger or the risk it engenders for others, would generally alert a reasonable person to the probability that the conduct would be regulated, from that conduct which is so mundane and apparently harmless that no thought would ordinarily be given to its potentially regulated nature. In the latter circumstances, the licensing argument would not apply.

. . . .

2. *The Vulnerability Justification*

The realities and complexities of a modern industrial society, coupled with the very real need to protect all of society and particularly its vulnerable members, emphasize the critical importance of regulatory offences in Canada today. Our country simply could not function without extensive regulatory legislation. The protection provided by such measures constitutes a second justification for the differential treatment, for *Charter* purposes, of regulatory and criminal offences.

This court has on several occasions observed that the *Charter* is not an instrument to be used by the well-positioned to roll back legislative protections enacted on behalf of the vulnerable. This principle was first enunciated by Dickson C.J.C. for the majority in *R. v. Videoflicks Ltd.*, (sub nom. *R. v. Edwards Books & Art Ltd.*), [hereinafter "*Edwards Books*"], [1986] 2 S.C.R. 713, 55 C.R. (3d) 193, 30 C.C.C. (3d) 385. He wrote, at p. 779 [S.C.R., p. 241 C.R.]:

> In interpreting and applying the *Charter* I believe that the courts must be cautious to ensure that it does not simply become an instrument of better situated individuals to roll back legislation which has as its object the improvement of the condition of less advantaged persons.

The same principle has been repeated and emphasized in *Irwin Toy Ltd. v. Quebec (Attorney General)*, [1989] 1 S.C.R. 927, at p. 993, and in *Slaight Communications Inc. v. Davidson*, [1989] 1 S.C.R. 1038, at p. 1051. This principle recognizes that much government regulation is designed to protect the vulnerable. It would be unfortunate indeed if the *Charter* were used as a weapon to attack measures intended to protect the disadvantaged and comparatively powerless members of society. It is interesting to observe that in the United States, courts struck down important components of the program of regulatory legislation known as "the New Deal". This so-called "*Lochner* era" is now almost universally regarded by academic writers as a dark age in the history of the American Constitution.

Regulatory legislation is essential to the operation of our complex industrial society; it plays a legitimate and vital role in protecting those who are most vulnerable and least able to protect themselves. The extent and importance of that role has increased continuously since the onset of the Industrial Revolution. Before effective workplace legislation was enacted, labourers — including children — worked unconscionably long hours in dangerous and unhealthy surroundings that evoke visions of Dante's *Inferno*. It was regulatory legislation with its enforcement provisions which brought to an end the shameful situation that existed in mines, factories and workshops in the nineteenth century. The differential treatment of regulatory offences is justified by their common goal of protecting the vulnerable.

The importance of the vulnerability concept as a component of the contextual approach to *Charter* interpretation has been recognized in the employer/employee field in *Edwards Books, supra,* and *Slaight Communications, supra,* and in the sphere of commercial advertising in *Irwin Toy, supra.* The same considerations should apply whenever regulatory legislation is subject to *Charter* challenge.

In *R. v. Stucky* (2009), 240 C.C.C. (3d) 141 (Ont. C.A.) the Court noted that in 1999 Parliament had made false or misleading advertising a *mens rea* offence under s. 52 of the federal *Competition Act*. The distinction between regulatory offences and crimes had blurred and in this case criminal law principles applied.

R. v. CHAPIN

[1979] 2 S.C.R. 121, 7 C.R. (3d) 225, 45 C.C.C. (2d) 333,
1979 CarswellOnt 39, 1979 CarswellOnt 1316

DICKSON J.: —

The Facts

Mrs. Loise Chapin went duck hunting in the Balmoral marsh, near Chatham, one windy afternoon in mid-October 1976. She was accompanied by a friend whom she had not seen for some time. As they walked through the marsh they were, she testified, talking a lot and not paying attention to anything but the beautiful day. They reached a dyke road and walked along it a short distance, then along some "duck boards", five or six inches in width, placed over water and leading to a duck blind from which Mrs. Chapin intended to shoot.

Some time, and two ducks, later, Mrs. Chapin was arrested by a conservation officer of the Ontario Ministry of Natural Resources. He had been in the area and heard shots. Leaving his car, he proceeded on foot through two gates, down through a small canal gully, over scrub land and across a corn field, and finally arrived at a road leading to a small pond. The road over which Mrs. Chapin and her friend had passed earlier was approximately 12 feet in width and composed of a mixture of mud and gravel. As the conservation officer approached the pond, he observed, in the centre of the road and about ten feet from the water's edge, a small pile of soy beans, weed seeds and wheat, like the gleanings from a harvesting operation on a farm. The officer said that he was practically on top of the pile before he noticed it. It was a small pile, about a foot to a foot and a half in length, three inches wide and approximately two inches in depth. The blind from which Mrs. Chapin had been shooting was located some distance out from the edge of the pond and about 50 yards from the pile. The officer also noted grain in the water on either side of the boardwalk.

Mrs. Chapin testified that she was unaware of the presence of the grain. It was a very windy day and many things were flying around the marsh. When she walked along the duck boards, in hip waders and carrying a gun, her sole concern was to avoid falling into the water. It seems to be generally accepted that Mrs. Chapin did not know that the grain was there until it was pointed out to her by the conservation officer. Even then, she did not know what it was. She was shooting on private property belonging to the Balmoral Hunt Club, of which her husband was part owner. During the trial, there was vague reference by defence counsel to "spite baiting", but no evidence adduced to indicate by whom or in what circumstances the grain had been deposited.

The Migratory Birds Regulations

Now, it is unlawful to hunt for migratory birds within 1/4 mile of a place where bait has been deposited. Section 14 [am. SOR/73-509; SOR/75-436] of the *Migratory Birds Regulations*, SOR/71-376, reads:

> 14. (1) Subject to subsection (2), no person shall hunt for migratory game birds within one-quarter mile of any place where bait has been deposited.
>
> (2) Subsection (1) does not apply to a place where bait had been deposited, if
>
> (a) a game officer inspects that place and declares that it is clear of bait, and
>
> (b) seven days have elapsed since the inspection referred to in paragraph (a).
>
> (3) Where bait is deposited in a place after an inspection referred to in subsection (2), that subsection ceases to apply to that place for the remainder of the open season.

(4) No person shall deposit bait in any place during the period commencing seven days before the open season applicable in that place and ending on the day immediately following the last day of the open season in that place unless that person, at least thirty days prior to placing the bait,

(a) obtains the consent in writing of

(i) every landowner and every lessee or tenant whose land is located within one-quarter mile of that place, and

(ii) the Director and the Chief Game Officer of a province, and

(b) posts in that place signs of a type and wording satisfactory to, and in a location designated by, the Director,

(5) A consent obtained pursuant to paragraph (4)(a) is valid only in respect of the open season in respect of which it was obtained.

(6) Subsection (4) does not apply to the holder of a permit referred to in section 19 or 20 who places bait

(a) in a confined area specified in his permit, or

(b) at a distance of not less than one-quarter mile from an area where the hunting of migratory birds is permitted for the sole purpose of feeding migratory birds lawfully in his possession.

(7) For the purpose of subsection (1), any area

(a) of standing crops, whether flooded or not,

(b) of harvested crop land that is flooded,

(c) where crops are properly shocked in the field where they grow, or

(d) where grain is scattered solely as a result of normal agricultural or harvesting operations shall not be regarded as a place where bait has been deposited.

Section 12(1) of the *Migratory Birds Convention Act*, R.S.C. 1970, c. M-12, provides:

12. (1) Every person who violates this Act or any regulation is, for each offence, liable upon summary conviction to a fine of not more than three hundred dollars and not less than ten dollars, or to imprisonment for a term not exceeding six months, or to both fine and imprisonment.

. . . .

The case has now, by leave, reached this court. There are two preliminary observations. First, the judicial history of the case, all before the judgment of this court in *R. v. Sault Ste. Marie* (1978), 3 C.R. (3d) 30, 40 C.C.C. (2d) 353, provides an interesting example of the courts attempting to come to grips with the classic sort of regulatory offence. The three courts which have dealt with the matter to date have characterized the offence in three different ways. Walker J. P. treated it as an offence of strict liability, to which the accused could plead that she committed the offence under an honest and reasonable mistake of fact. Beardall Co. Ct. J. considered it to be one of absolute liability. The court of Appeal majority regarded it as a *mens rea* offence, while Houlden J.A. regarded it as one of absolute liability.

In *Sault Ste. Marie* at pp. 53-54, this court recognized three categories of offences.

. . . .

The Crown argues that the offence is one of absolute liability or, in the alternative, strict liability. The respondent contends that it is one requiring full *mens rea* or, if not, a strict liability offence.

Not a Mens Rea Offence

One would be hard pressed to characterize the offence created by s. 14(1) of the *Migratory Birds Regulations* as a "crime in the true sense". Violation is punishable upon summary conviction, and not by indictment. One must note the absence of the usual signals connoting *mens rea*, such as "wilfully" or "with intent". In contrast, to take an example, s. 10 of the *Migratory Birds Convention Act* commences:

> 10. Any person who wilfully refuses to furnish information or wilfully furnishes false information to a game officer. . . .

The *Migratory Birds Convention Act* is a regulatory statute enacted by the Parliament of Canada for the general welfare of the Canadian public, not to mention the welfare of the ducks. The purpose of the legislation is expressed in the preamble to the Migratory Birds Convention, which has been sanctioned, ratified and confirmed by s. 2 of the Act, and which reads in part as follows:

Whereas many species of birds in the course of their annual migrations traverse certain parts of the Dominion of Canada and the United States; and

Whereas many of these species are of great value as a source of food or in destroying insects which are injurious to forests and forage plants on the public domain, as well as to agricultural crops, in both Canada and the United States, but are nevertheless in danger of extermination through lack of adequate protection during the nesting season or while on their way to and from their breeding grounds:

His Majesty the King of the United Kingdom of Great Britain and Ireland and of the British dominions beyond the seas, Emperor of India, and the United States of America, being desirous of saving from indiscriminate slaughter and of insuring the preservation of such migratory birds as are either useful to man or are harmless, have resolved to adopt some uniform system of protection which shall effectively accomplish such objects.

Article I of the Convention, attached as a schedule to the Act, describes the migratory game birds included in the terms of the Convention. Article II provides for closed seasons, "during which no hunting shall be done except for scientific or propagating purposes under permits issued by proper authorities". Article III provides for a continuous close season on certain migratory game birds. Article IV provides for special protection to be given the wood duck and the eider duck.

Article V provides for the prohibition of the taking of nests or eggs, and Art. VI for the prohibition of the shipment or export of migratory birds or their eggs during the continuance of the close season. Finally, Art. VII provides for the issuance of permits to kill migratory birds which, under extraordinary conditions, may become seriously injurious to the agricultural or other interests in any particular community.

The *Migratory Birds Convention Act* authorizes the making of *Migratory Birds Regulations* for the purpose of effecting the public welfare goals of the Migratory Birds Convention. Section 4 of the Act provides, in part:

> 4.(1) The Governor in Council may make such regulations as are deemed expedient to protect the migratory game, migratory insectivorous and migratory nongame birds that inhabit Canada during the whole or any part of the year.
>
> (2) Subject to the provisions of the Convention, the regulations may provide . . .
>
> (*b*) for limiting the number of migratory game birds that may be taken by a person in any specified time during the season when the taking of such birds is legal, and providing the manner in which such birds may then be taken and the appliances that may be used therefor.

It seems clear that the offence of hunting for migratory game birds within 1/4 mile of any place where bait has been deposited contrary to s. 14(1) of the *Migratory Birds Regulations* and s. 12(1) of the *Migratory Birds Convention Act* is legislation designed to protect migratory birds from indiscriminate slaughter for the general welfare of the public. It seems equally clear that s. 14(1) of the *Migratory Birds Regulations* creates a public welfare offence which is not criminal in the true sense, and it is therefore not subject to the presumption of full *mens rea*. Section 14(1) is thus not creating a new crime, but in the public interest is prohibiting an act under a penalty: *Sherras v. De Rutzen*, [1895] 1 Q.B. 918 (D.C.).

Not an Absolute Liability Offence

The language of the offence is straightforward: "No person shall. . . ." Yet there is not a strict prohibition on hunting, rather a hunt controlled within certain limits as to season, methods, and types and numbers of species taken. Nor can one ignore the controls on shipment and export of game, not the stricter controls in certain prescribed geographic areas "for the control and management of such area".

Accepting that this is a public welfare or regulatory offence, neither party mentions the approach taken by this court in *Sault Ste. Marie, supra*, that "public welfare offences would *prima facie* be in the second category" of strict liability. The Crown merely lists the factors suggested as relevant in *Sault Ste. Marie, viz.*, the overall regulatory pattern, the subject matter of the legislation, the importance of the penalty and the precision of the language, in order to move the offence out of the second category and into the third.

The Crown suggests that "the summary conviction nature of the penalty" should carry some weight. Summary conviction it may be, but one could hardly term the penalties minimal. Rather than a "small monetary fine" alone, we find a number of serious consequences upon conviction. Section 12(1) of the Act lays down a minimum fine of $10 and a maximum fine of $300, or up to six months' imprisonment, or both. (The County Court Judge imposed a fine of $100 in this case.) Other serious consequences ensue. Section 22(1) provides for a mandatory prohibition upon conviction of either holding or applying for a migratory game bird hunting permit for a period of one year from date of conviction. Further, as the respondent points out, the court may, under s. 88(2) of the *Game and Fish Act*, R.S.O. 1970, c. 186, cancel "any licence to hunt" — not just a game bird licence — and may further order no obtaining of, or application for, a hunting licence "during the period stated in the order". Nor is that all. The most serious potential consequence comes in s. 7 of the *Migratory Birds Act* itself, permitting the justice of the peace to make an order of forfeiture of the gun and any other equipment used in violation of the Act or Regulations. While the respondent employs these penalties in support of her full *mens rea* position, they certainly support the *prima facie* classification of strict liability.

The best the Crown can do to shift this offence into the category of absolute liability is to suggest that the availability of a defence of reasonable care would considerably weaken the enforcement of the legislation. This may be true, but, as Weatherston J.A. observed, the problems that may be encountered in the administration of a statute or regulation are a very unsure guide to its proper interpretation. Difficulty of enforcement is hardly enough to dislodge the offence from the category of strict liability, particularly when regard is had to the penalties that may ensue from conviction. I do not think that the public interest, as expressed in the Convention, requires that s. 14 of the Regulations be interpreted so that an innocent person should be convicted and fined and also suffer the mandatory loss of his hunting permit and the possible forfeiture of his hunting equipment, merely in order to facilitate prosecution.

The Crown contends that a person found hunting within 1/4 mile of a place where bait is deposited is guilty of an offence, to which no defence is available. On the Crown's submission, proof of making all *reasonable* efforts to ascertain the presence of the bait would be unavailing, as would proof of all *possible* efforts. This, in my view, is an untenable position. Hunting being a permitted sport, it would be a practical impossibility for a hunter to search a circular area having a diameter of 1/2 mile for the presence of illegally deposited bait before hunting. One must bear in mind the nature of the terrain over which hunting is done, as the evidence in this case discloses, and the fact that many hunters hope to get into position before first light. Is one first expected to search through swamp, bog, creeks, corn fields, over land and in water in search of illegal bait?

The case of *R. v. Pierce Fisheries Ltd.*, [1971] S.C.R. 5, 12 C.R.N.S. 272, [1970] 5 C.C.C. 193, was cited, but I do not believe that it assists the Crown. In that case, care had not been taken to acquire knowledge of the facts constituting the offence. Ritchie J. said that it would not have been a difficult matter for some officer or responsible person of the accused company to acquire knowledge of the undersize lobsters, and failure to acquire that knowledge did not afford a defence. Nor does the decision of the Ontario Court of Appeal in *R. v. Hickey*, supra, assist, having regard to the many differences between the *Ontario Highway Traffic Act*, R.S.O. 1970, c. 202, and the legislation here under consideration.

In my view, subs. (1) and (4) of s. 14 of the Regulations must be read together. Together they speak of legal baiting, the obtaining of written consents and the posting of signs to give notice of the presence of bait. Anyone who hunts within such a posted area may be more readily taken to be knowingly or recklessly in breach of the Regulations. The Regulations do not seek to impose an absolute obligation upon a hunter who innocently hunts in an unposted area within 1/4 mile of bait which has been placed illegally by a person unknown. Parliament could not have intended to afford a person hunting within 1/4 mile of an illegally baited area any less protection than that afforded a person hunting within 1/4 mile of a legally baited area. Otherwise, as counsel for Mrs. Chapin argues, an activity which is legal is rendered illegal by the illegal act of someone over whom the accused has no control. We should not assume that punishment is to be imposed without fault.

These considerations incline me to the view that the offence here under study is not one of absolute liability.

Strict Liability Offence

In my view, the offence created by s. 14(1) is one of strict liability. It is a classic example of an offence in the second category delineated in the *Sault Ste. Marie* case, *supra*. An accused may absolve himself on proof that he took all the care which a reasonable man might have been expected to take in all the circumstances or, in other words, that he was in no way negligent.

Conclusion

It remains to consider whether to dispose of the case in this court or send it back for a new trial. The respondent has to date been subjected to two trials and two appeals. She lost her hunting privileges from April to November 1977. Her gun was seized and held under seizure for some time.

The following evidence is undisputed. The hunting was done at a private club, of which the husband of the respondent was part owner and to which she had been going for some eight years. The club had a permit from the Canadian Wildlife Service to bait at the proper season, but the club had never baited ponds. The respondent played no part in the management of the marsh. The day was windy, with matter of all kinds flying about. The pile of grain was not large. It looked like a gleaning after harvesting. It lay on a mud and gravel road. Mrs. Chapin had no reason to be looking down. The conservation officer did not notice the grain until he was practically on top of it. The other grain was in the water on either side of a narrow duck walk which Mrs. Chapin had to navigate to get to the blind. There were no signs indicating that this was a baited area.

After careful reading of all the evidence, I have arrived at the conclusion reached by this count in *Thibodeau v. R.*, [1955] S.C.R. 646, 21 C.R. 265, namely, that on the evidence in the record it would have been unreasonable to convict the respondent, and that we ought not to direct a new trial.

I would accordingly dismiss the appeal. Pursuant to the terms under which leave to appeal was granted, the respondent is entitled to costs on a solicitor-and-client basis.

Appeal dismissed.

(b) *Charter* Standards

Within a mere three years from the date of the entrenchment of the *Canadian Charter of Rights and Freedoms,* the *Sault Ste. Marie* compromise of allowing a due diligence defence for regulatory offences with a reverse onus became a minimum constitutional standard of fault for any offence which threatens the liberty interest.

**REFERENCE RE SECTION 94(2) OF THE
MOTOR VEHICLE ACT (B.C.)**

[1985] S.C.R. 486, 48 C.R. (3d) 289, 23 C.C.C.(3d) 289,
1985 CarswellBC 398, 1985 CarswellBC816

LAMER J. (DICKSON C.J.C., BEETZ, CHOUINARD and LE DAIN JJ. concurring): —

The Facts

On August 16, 1982, the Lieutenant-Governor in Council of British Columbia referred the following question to the Court of Appeal of that province, by virtue of s. 1 of the *Constitutional Question Act,* R.S.B.C. 1979, c. 63.:

> Is s. 94(2) of the *Motor Vehicle Act,* R.S.B.C. 1979, as amended by the *Motor Vehicle Amendment Act, 1982,* consistent with the *Canadian Charter of Rights and Freedoms*?

On February 3, 1983, the Court of Appeal handed down reasons in answer to the question in which it stated that s. 94(2) of the Act is inconsistent with the *Canadian Charter of Rights and Freedoms*: (1983), 4 C.C.C. (3d) 243, 33 C.R.

(3d) 22. The Attorney General for British Columbia launched an appeal to this court.

The Legislation

Motor Vehicle Act, R.S.B.C. 1979, c. 288, s. 94, as amended by the *Motor Vehicle Act Amendment Act, 1982*, S.B.C. 1982 c. 36, s. 19:

> 94.(1) A person who drives a motor vehicle on a highway or industrial road while
>> (a) he is prohibited from driving a motor vehicle under sections 90, 91, 92 or 92.1, or
>> (b) his driver's licence or his right to apply for or obtain a driver's licence is suspended under s. 82 or 92 as it was before its repeal and replacement came into force pursuant to the *Motor Vehicle Amendment Act, 1982*,
>
> commits an offence and is liable,
>> (c) on a first conviction, to a fine of not less than $300 and not more than $2000 and to imprisonment for not less than seven days and not more than six months, and
>> (d) on a subsequent conviction, regardless of when the contravention occurred, to a fine of not less than $300 and not more than $2000 and to imprisonment for not less than 14 days and not more than one year.
>
> (2) Subsection (1) creates an absolute liability offence on which guilt is established by proof of driving, whether or not the defendant knew of the prohibition or suspension.

Canadian Charter of Rights and Freedoms: Constitution Act, 1982:

> S.1 The *Canadian Charter of Rights and Freedoms* guarantees the rights and freedoms set out in it subject only to such reasonable limits prescribed by law as can be demonstrably justified in a free and democratic society.
> S.7 Everyone has the right to life, liberty and security of the person and the right not to be deprived thereof except in accordance with the principles of fundamental justice.

. . . .

The judgment of the Court of Appeal of British Columbia

The court was of the view that the phrase "principles of fundamental justice" was not restricted to matters of procedure, but extended to substantive law, and that the courts were "therefore called upon, in construing the provisions of s. 7 of the *Charter*, to have regard to the content of legislation".

Relying on the decision of this court in *R. v. City of Sault Ste-Marie*, [1978] 2 S.C.R. 1299, the Court of Appeal found "that s. 94(2) of the *Motor Vehicle Act* is inconsistent with the principles of fundamental justice." They did not heed the invitation of counsel opposing the validity of s. 94(2) to declare that, as a result of that decision by our court, all absolute liability offences violated s. 7 of the *Charter* and could not be salvaged under s. 1. Quite the contrary, the court of Appeal said that "there are, and will remain, certain public welfare offences, *e.g.* air and water pollution offences, where the public interest requires that the offences be absolute liability offences." Their finding was predicated on the following reasoning:

> The effect of s. 94(2) is to transform the offence from a mens rea offence to an absolute liability offence hence giving the defendant no opportunity to prove that his action was due to an honest and reasonable mistake of fact or that he acted without guilty intent. Rather than placing the burden to establish such facts on the defendant and thus making the offence a strict liability offence, the legislature has seen fit to make it an absolute liability offence coupled with a mandatory term of imprisonment.

It can therefore be inferred with certainty that, in the court's view, the combination of mandatory imprisonment and absolute liability was offensive to s. 7. It cannot however be ascertained from their judgment whether the violation was triggered by the requirement of minimum imprisonment or solely by the availability of imprisonment as a sentence.

Section 7

[I]n the context of s. 7, and in particular of the interpretation of "principles of fundamental justice" there has prevailed in certain quarters an assumption that all but a narrow construction of s. 7 will inexorably lead the courts to "question the wisdom of enactments", to adjudicate upon the merits of public policy.

From this have sprung warnings of the dangers of a judicial "super-legislature" beyond the reach of Parliament, the provincial Legislatures and the electorate.

. . . .

This is an argument which was heard countless times prior to the entrenchment of the *Charter* but which has in truth, for better or for worse, been settled by the very coming into force of the *Constitution Act, 1982*.

. . . .

The concerns with the bounds of constitutional adjudication explain the characterization of the issue in a narrow and restrictive fashion, *i.e.*, whether the terms "principles of fundamental justice" have a substantive or merely procedural content. In my view, the characterization of the issue in such fashion preempts an open-minded approach to determining the meaning of "principles of fundamental justice".

The substantive/procedural dichotomy narrows the issue almost to an all-or-nothing proposition. Moreover, it is largely bound up in the American experience with substantive and procedural due process. It imports into the

Canadian context American concepts, terminology and jurisprudence, all of which are inextricably linked to problems concerning the nature and legitimacy of adjudication under the U.S. Constitution. That Constitution, it must be remembered, has no s. 52 nor has it the internal checks and balances of sections 1 and 33. We would, in my view, do our own Constitution a disservice to simply allow the American debate to define the issue for us, all the while ignoring the truly fundamental structural differences between the two constitutions. Finally, the dichotomy creates its own set of difficulties by the attempt to distinguish between two concepts whose outer boundaries are not always clear and often tend to overlap. Such difficulties can and should, when possible, be avoided.

. . . .

The task of the court is not to choose between substantive or procedural content *per se* but to secure for persons "the full benefit of the *Charter's* protection" (Dickson C.J.C. in *R. v. Big M Drug Mart Ltd.*, [1985] 1 S.C.R. 295 at 344), under s. 7, while avoiding adjudication of the merits of public policy. This can only be accomplished by a purposive analysis and the articulation (to use the words in *Curr v. The Queen*, [1972] S.C.R. 889, at p. 899) of "objective and manageable standards" for the operation of the section within such a framework.

A number of courts have placed emphasis upon the Minutes of the Proceedings and Evidence of the Special Joint Committee of the Senate and of the House of Commons on the Constitution in the interpretation of "principles of fundamental justice". . .

In particular, the following passages dealing with the testimony of federal civil servants from the Department of Justice have been relied upon:

Mr. Strayer (Assistant Deputy Minister, Public Law):

> Mr. Chairman, it was our belief that the words "fundamental justice" would cover the same thing as what is called procedural due process, that is the meaning of due process in relation to requiring fair procedure. However, it in our view does not cover the concept of what is called substantive due process, which would impose substantive requirements as to policy of the law in question.

> This has been most clearly demonstrated in the United States in the area of property, but also in other areas such as the right to life. The term due process has been given the broader concept of meaning both the procedure and substance. Natural justice or fundamental justice in our view does not go beyond the procedural requirements of fairness.

. . . .

> Mr. Strayer: The term "fundamental justice" appears to us to be essentially the same thing as natural justice.

Mr. Tassé (Deputy Minister) also said of the phrase "principles of fundamental justice" in testimony before the committee:

We assume that the court would look at that much like a court would look at the requirements of natural justice, and the concept of natural justice is quite familiar to courts and they have given a good deal of specific meaning to the concept of natural justice. We would think that the court would find in that phraseology principles of fundamental justice a meaning somewhat like natural justice or inherent fairness.

Courts have been developing the concept of administrative fairness in recent years and they have been able to give a good deal of consideration, certainly to these sorts of concepts and we would expect they could do the same with this.

The Honourable Jean Chrétien, then federal Minister of Justice, also indicated to the Committee that, while he thought "fundamental justice marginally more appropriate than natural justice" in s. 7, either term was acceptable to the government.

. . . .

[T]he simple fact remains that the *Charter* is not the product of a few individual public servants, however distinguished, but of a multiplicity of individuals who played major roles in the negotiating, drafting and adoption of the *Charter*. How can one say with any confidence that within this enormous multiplicity of actors, without forgetting the role of the provinces, the comments of a few federal civil servants can in any way be determinative?

. . . .

Another danger with casting the interpretation of s. 7 in terms of the comments made by those heard at the Special Joint Committee Proceedings is that, in so doing, the rights, freedoms and values embodied in the *Charter* in effect become frozen in time to the moment of adoption with little or no possibility of growth, development and adjustment to changing societal needs.

. . . .

The main sources of support for the argument that "fundamental justice" is simply synonymous with natural justice have been the Minutes of the Proceedings and Evidence of the Special Joint Committee on the Constitution and the *Bill of Rights* jurisprudence. In my view, neither the Minutes nor the *Bill of Rights* jurisprudence are persuasive or of any great force. The historical usage of the term "fundamental justice" is, on the other hand, shrouded in ambiguity. Moreover, not any one of these arguments, taken singly or as a whole, manages to overcome in my respectful view the textual and contextual analyses.

Consequently, my conclusion may be summarized as follows:

The term "principles of fundamental justice" is not a right, but a qualifier of the right not to be deprived of life, liberty and security of the person; its function is to set the parameters of that right.

Sections 8 to 14 address specific deprivations of the "right" to life, liberty and security of the person in breach of the principles of fundamental justice, and as such, violations of s. 7. They are therefore illustrative of the meaning, in criminal or penal law, of "principles of fundamental justice"; they represent principles which have been recognized by the common law, the international conventions and by the very fact of entrenchment in the *Charter*, as essential elements of a system for the administration of justice which is founded upon a belief in the dignity and worth of the human person and the rule of law.

Consequently, the principles of fundamental justice are to be found in the basic tenets and principles, not only of our judicial process, but also of the other components of our legal system.[1]

We should not be surprised to find that many of the principles of fundamental justice are procedural in nature. Our common law has largely been a law of remedies and procedures and, as Frankfurter J. wrote in *McNabb v. U.S.* 318 U.S. 332 (1942) at p. 347, "the history of liberty has largely been the history of observance of procedural safeguards". This is not to say, however, that the principles of fundamental justice are limited solely to procedural guarantees. Rather, the proper approach to the determination of the principles of fundamental justice is quite simply one in which, as Professor Tremblay has written, "future growth will be based on historical roots". ((1984), 18 U.B.C.L. Rev. 201 at 254).

Whether any given principle may be said to be a principle of fundamental justice within the meaning of s. 7 will rest upon an analysis of the nature, sources, rationale and essential role of that principle within the judicial process and in our legal system, as it evolves.

Consequently, those words cannot be given any exhaustive content or simple enumerative definition, but will take on concrete meaning as the courts address alleged violations of s. 7.

I now turn to such an analysis of the principle of *mens rea* and absolute liability offences in order to determine the question which has been put to the court in the present Reference.

Absolute Liability and Fundamental Justice in Penal Law

It has from time immemorial been part of our system of laws that the innocent not be punished. This principle has long been recognized as an essential element of a system for the administration of justice which is founded upon a belief in the dignity and worth of the human person and on the rule of law. It is so old that its first enunciation was in Latin *actus non facit reum nisi mens sit rea.*

As Glanville Williams said:

---

1 Editor's note. Recall that the majority in *Malmo-Levine* later decided that a principle of fundamental justice must be a legal principle for which there is societal consensus and of sufficient precision to be workable in practice.

There is no need here to go into the remote history of *mens rea*; suffice it to say that the requirement of a guilty state of mind (at least for the more serious crimes) had been developed by the time of Coke, which is as far back as the modern lawyer needs to go. "If one shoot at any wild fowl upon a tree, and the arrow killeth any reasonable creature afar off, without any evil intent in him, this is *per infortunium*."

(Glanville Williams, *Criminal Law, The General Part*, Second Edition, London, Stevens and Sons Limited, 1961, p. 30.)

One of the many judicial statements on the subject worth mentioning is of the highest authority, *per* Goddard C.J. in *Harding v. Price*, [1948] 1 K.B. 695 at p. 700, where he said:

The general rule applicable to criminal cases is *actus non facit reum nisi mens sit rea*, and I venture to repeat what I said in *Brend v. Wood* (1946), 62 T.L.R. 462, 463: 'It is of the utmost importance for the protection of the liberty of the subject that a court should always bear in mind that, unless a statute either clearly or by necessary implication rules out *mens rea* as a constituent part of a crime, the court should not find a man guilty of an offence against the criminal law unless he has a guilty mind'.

This view has been adopted by this court in unmistakable terms in many cases, amongst which the better known are *Beaver v. The Queen*, [1957] S.C.R. 531, and the most recent and often quoted judgment of Dickson J. (as he then was), writing for the court in *R. v. City of Sault Ste. Marie*, *supra*.

This court's decision in the latter case is predicated upon a certain number of postulates one of which, given the nature of the rules it elaborates, has to be to the effect that absolute liability in penal law offends the principles of fundamental justice. Those principles are, to use the words of Dickson J., to the effect that "there is a generally held revulsion against punishment of the morally innocent". He also stated that the argument that absolute liability "violates fundamental principles of penal liability" was the most telling argument against absolute liability and one of greater force than those advanced in support thereof.

In my view it is because absolute liability offends the principles of fundamental justice that this court created presumptions against legislatures having intended to enact offences of a regulatory nature falling within that category. This is not to say, however, and to that extent I am in agreement with the Court of Appeal, that, as a result, absolute liability *per se* offends s. 7 of the *Charter*.

A law enacting an absolute liability offence will violate s. 7 of the *Charter* only if and to the extent that it has the potential of depriving of life, liberty, or security of the person.

Obviously, imprisonment (including probation orders) deprives persons of their liberty. An offence has that potential as of the moment it is open to the judge to impose imprisonment. There is no need that imprisonment, as in s. 94(2), be made mandatory.

I am therefore of the view that the combination of imprisonment and of absolute liability violates s. 7 of the *Charter* and can only be salvaged if the authorities demonstrate under s. 1 that such a deprivation of liberty in breach of those principles of fundamental justice is, in a free and democratic society, under the circumstances, a justified reasonable limit to one's rights under s. 7.

As no one has addressed imprisonment as an alternative to the non-payment of a fine, I prefer not to express any views in relation to s. 7 as regards that eventuality as a result of a conviction for an absolute liability offence; nor do I need to address here, given the scope of my finding and the nature of this appeal, minimum imprisonment, whether it offends the *Charter per se* or whether such violation, if any, is dependent upon whether it be for a *mens rea* or strict liability offence. Those issues were not addressed by the court below and it would be unwise to attempt to address them here. It is sufficient and desirable for this appeal to make the findings I have and no more, that is, that no imprisonment may be imposed for an absolute liability offence, and, consequently, given the question put to us, an offence punishable by imprisonment cannot be an absolute liability offence.

. . . .

Administrative expediency, absolute liability's main supportive argument, will undoubtedly under s. 1 be invoked and occasionally succeed. Indeed, administrative expediency certainly has its place in administrative law. But when administrative law chooses to call in aid imprisonment through penal law, indeed sometimes criminal law and the added stigma attached to a conviction, exceptional, in my view, will be the case where the liberty or even the security of the person guaranteed under s. 7 should be sacrificed to administrative expediency. Section 1 may, for reasons of administrative expediency, successfully come to the rescue of an otherwise violation of s. 7, but only in cases arising out of exceptional conditions, such as natural disasters, the outbreak of war, epidemics, and the like.

Of course I understand the concern of many as regards corporate offences, specially, as was mentioned by the Court of Appeal, in certain sensitive areas such as the preservation of our vital environment and our natural resources. This concern might well be dispelled were it to be decided, given the proper case, that s. 7 affords protection to human persons only and does not extend to corporations.

Even if it be decided that s. 7 does extend to corporations, I think the balancing under s. 1 of the public interest against the financial interests of a corporation would give very different results from that of balancing public interest and the liberty or security of the person of a human being.

Indeed, the public interest as regards "air and water pollution offences" requires that the guilty be dealt with firmly, but the seriousness of the offence does not in my respectful view support the proposition that the innocent *human* person be open to conviction, quite the contrary.

Section 94(2)

I do not take issue with the fact that it is highly desirable that "bad drivers" be kept off the road. I do not take issue either with the desirability of punishing severely bad drivers who are in contempt of prohibitions against driving. The bottom line of the question to be addressed here is: whether the Government of British Columbia has demonstrated as justifiable that the risk of imprisonment of a few innocent is, given the desirability of ridding the roads of British Columbia of bad drivers, a reasonable limit in a free and democratic society. That result is to be measured against the offence being one of strict liability open to a defence of due diligence, the success of which does nothing more than let those few who did nothing wrong remain free.

As did the Court of Appeal, I find that this demonstration has not been satisfied, indeed, not in the least.

McIntyre and Wilson JJ. gave separate concurring judgments.

In *R. v. Pontes* (1995), 41 C.R. (4th) 201, 100 C.C.C. (3d) 353, [1995] 3 S.C.R. 44, the Supreme Court reconsidered the constitutionality of the offence of driving while prohibited under s. 94 of the B.C. *Motor Vehicle Act*. This time the court held that the offence was constitutional. A 5-4 majority classified the offence as one of absolute liability but held there was no violation of the right to life, liberty and security of the person as there was no longer any risk of imprisonment. By amendments to the B.C. *Offence Act* a person is no longer liable to imprisonment and non-payment of a fine would not result in imprisonment. The majority did, however, leave open for future consideration the issue of an absolute liability offence punishable by a fine with the possibility of imprisonment for non-payment where the legislation provided a means test for the imposition and collection of any fine. For a critical review of this complex decision see Anne-Marie Boisvert, "Innocence Morale, Diligence Raisonnable et Erreur de Droit" (1995), 41 C.R. (4th) 243 and Jill Presser, "Absolute Liability and Mistakes of Law in the Regulatory Context: *Pontes* Disappoints and Confuses" (1995), 41 C.R. (4th) 249. See also *R. v. Transport Robert*, below.

In *Lévis (Ville) c. Tétreault*, [2006] 1 S.C.R. 420, 36 C.R. (6th) 215, 207 C.C.C. (3d) 1, the Supreme Court held that regulatory vehicle offences of failure to pay registration and license fees by the due date under the Quebec Highway Safety Code were properly classified as strict liability.

In writing for a unanimous court of seven justices, Justice LeBel noted that the sections in question did not place the burden of proving *mens rea* on the prosecution and included no expression of the legislature's intent to create an absolute liability offence. Applying the court's approach in *R. v. Sault Ste. Marie*, there was common law presumption that they should be characterised as strict rather than absolute, thereby affording the accused the chance of proving a due diligence defence. Absolute liability offences still exist, but they have become, said LeBel J. for the court, an exception requiring clear proof of legislative intent.

In deciding between strict and absolute liability LeBel J. expressly rejected the inquiry added by Cory J. in *R. v. Pontes*, [1995] 3 S.C.R. 44 of asking whether the legislature intended to make a due diligence defence available. LeBel J. indicated this made the approach "harder to apply" and it was better to return to the clear framework of *Sault Ste. Marie*.

On the facts the due diligence defence raised had not been made out. Justice LeBel reasoned that the concept of diligence is based on the acceptance of a citizen's civic duty to take action to find out what his or her obligations are. Passive ignorance is not a valid defence. T did no more than state that he expected to receive a renewal notice for his licence and that he had confused the licence expiry date with the due date for paying the fees required to keep the licence valid. He proved no action or attempt to obtain information. The same was true of the company, which did nothing, even though it was aware of the date when the fees relating to the registration of its vehicle would be due. It could and should have been concerned when it did not receive a notice. Christine Boyle and Sam de Groot, "The Responsible Citizen in the City of Levis: Due Diligence and Officially Induced Error" C.R. *ibid.* 249, suggest that this gloss will make it harder for the defence of due diligence to succeed.

The Supreme Court's strong preference for strict liability for regulatory offences is thus alive and well. There has been a tendency in recent jurisprudence for this classification issue to focus more on the *Charter* guarantee of a due diligence defence applying only where there is a risk of imprisonment. For example, in its brief endorsement judgment in *Corporation of the City of London v. Polewsky* (2005), 202 C.C.C. (3d) 257, the Ontario Court of Appeal rejected the possibility of a due diligence defence for speeding charges on the basis that there were no good policy reasons against absolute liability and that the chance of going to jail in default of payment of a fine was too remote. This decision needs to be reconsidered in light of the Supreme Court's emphasis in *City of Levis* on the common law presumption of strict liability. Compare *R. v. Williams* (1992), 14 C.R. (4th) 218 (N.S.C.A.), where speeding offences in Nova Scotia were held to be properly classified as strict to allow for due diligence defences in appropriate cases.

In *R. v. Cancoil Thermal Corp.* (1986), 52 C.R. (3d) 188 (Ont. C.A.) the Ontario Court of Appeal considered the provincial *Occupational Health and Safety Act*, and specifically charges under s. 14 of that Act. The Court noted that the statute included a due diligence defence for subss. 14(1)(b),(c) and (d), but not for subs. 14(1)(a). They took that omission to indicate that the legislature intended subs. 14(1)(a) to be an absolute liability offence. However, since imprisonment was available as a penalty, s. 14(1)(a) had to be read as a strict liability offence despite the legislature's intention, in order to avoid a s. 7 *Charter* violation.

R. v. WHOLESALE TRAVEL GROUP INC.

[1991] 3 S.C.R. 154, 8 C.R. (4th) 145, 67 C.C.C. (3d) 193,
1991 CarswellOnt 117, 1991 CarswellOnt 1029

In a most complex ruling the court determined that a due diligence defence was all that could constitutionally be required in the case of the offence of false advertising under what is now s. 52(1)(*a*) of the *Competition Act*, R.S.C. 1985, c. C-34.

The court also unanimously ruled that the due diligence defence could not be watered down by a more rigorous requirement than that of reasonable care. The court struck down the *Competition Act's* express requirement that there had to have been a prompt retraction of the advertisement before an accused could subsequently successfully rely on the due diligence defence.

The court's conclusion on these issues is found in the judgment of Chief Justice Lamer:

Counsel for Wholesale Travel argued that the stigma attaching to a conviction of false/misleading advertising is akin to the stigma of dishonesty which attaches to a conviction of theft. Given that the stigma attaching to theft was explicitly contemplated in *Vaillancourt* as one which may well necessitate a subjective *mens rea*, it was argued that the offence of false/misleading advertising also requires an element of subjective *mens rea* in order to comply with the principles of fundamental justice. In my view, while a conviction for false/misleading advertising carries some stigma, in the sense that it is not morally neutral behaviour, it cannot be said that the stigma associated with this offence is analogous to the stigma of dishonesty which attaches to a conviction for theft. A conviction for false/misleading advertising will rest on a variety of facts, many of which will not reveal any dishonesty but, rather, carelessness and the conviction of same does not brand the accused as being dishonest. In my opinion, the same cannot be said for a conviction for theft.

Thus, while it is clear that there are some offences for which the special stigma attaching to conviction is such that subjective *mens rea* is necessary in order to establish the moral blameworthiness which justifies the stigma and sentence, the offence of false/misleading advertising is not such an offence. . .

Therefore, an element of subjective *mens rea* is not required by s. 7 of the *Charter* and the provisions in question are not inconsistent with s. 7 on the basis that they do not require intent or knowledge on the part of an accused. I turn now to the question posed above: namely, do paras. (a) through (d) of s. 37.3(2) provide an accused with a defence of due diligence?[2]

---

2 The defence read as follows:

    37.3(2) No person shall be convicted of an offence under section 36 or 36.1, if he establishes that,

        (*a*) the act or omission giving rise to the offence with which he is charged was the result of error;

        (*b*) he took reasonable precautions and exercised due diligence to prevent the occurrence of such error;

        (*c*) he, or another person, took reasonable measures to bring the error to the attention of the class of

Section 37.3(2) (a) through (d) sets out the only defence, under the Act, to false/misleading advertising, once it has been established that the advertisement is objectively false or misleading (i.e., once the actus reus is established). It is clear from the inclusion of the word "and" after s. 37.3(2)(c) that all four components of s. 37.3(2) must be established in order for the accused to be acquitted. While the Crown has suggested that, in certain circumstances, only paras. (a) and (b) must be fulfilled (relying on certain dicta of the Ontario Court of Appeal in *R. v. Consumers Distributing Co.*, *supra*, it is my respectful view that this is an incorrect interpretation of the provision.

Thus, the question becomes whether a situation could arise where an accused would be unable to establish all four components of s. 37.3(2) but would nonetheless be duly diligent (i.e., not negligent). If the answer to this question is yes, it means that the constitutionally required element of negligence is not fulfilled by the statutory defence contained in s. 37.3(2).

The Crown has conceded that the statutory defence afforded by s. 37.3(2) is "more restricted" than the common law defence of due diligence, but nonetheless argues that the limited nature of the statutory defence does not render it unconstitutional. Although paras. (a) and (b) of s. 37.3(2) refer specifically to an "error" and to the exercise of due diligence to prevent an "error", they, in my view, largely correspond to the usual due diligence defence. In other words, paras. (a) and (b) operate so as to provide a defence to an accused who has taken reasonable precautions to prevent false/misleading advertising and who has been duly diligent in ensuring that advertising is not false or misleading in nature. However, the additional requirement of "timely retraction" embodied in paras. (c) and (d) means that the statutory defence is considerably more narrow than the common law defence of due diligence.

An accused who did not realize, and could not reasonably have been expected to realize, that the representation in question was false or misleading until it was too late to comply with paras. (c) and (d) or who was, for some reason, unable to comply with paras. (c) and (d), but who had nonetheless taken reasonable precautions and who had exercised due diligence in preventing false/misleading advertising, would not fall within the statutory defence and would be convicted of false/misleading advertising. I agree with the majority of the Ontario Court of Appeal that paras. (c) and (d) of s. 37.3(2) could have the effect of depriving an accused of the defence of due diligence and could therefore require the conviction of an accused who was not negligent. Paragraphs (c) and (d) make the failure to undertake corrective advertising (a component of the offence of false/misleading advertising) an "offence" of absolute liability. Consequently, the constitutionally required fault level is not present in the false/misleading advertising provisions.

---

persons likely to have been reached by the representation or testimonial; and

(*d*) the measures referred to in paragraph (*c*) . . . were taken forthwith after the representation was made or the testimonial was published.

In light of the above discussion, I agree with the majority of the Court of Appeal that it is the presence of paras. (c) and (d) alone which offends s. 7 of the *Charter*. Thus, unless the limitation on s. 7 can be upheld under s. 1 of the *Charter*, these two paragraphs must be held to be of no force or effect, pursuant to s. 52(1) of the *Constitution Act, 1982*.

[The court held that paragraphs (c) and (d) could not be upheld under s. 1. The court accepted, under the *Oakes* test, that the legislation had a sufficiently important objective. Under the proportionality aspect of the *Oakes* test, however, the court was not convinced that the minimal impairment branch was satisfied.]

The question under this part of the proportionality test is whether the impugned law (in this case, the modified due diligence defence embodied in paras. (c) and (d) of s. 37.3(2)) violates *Charter* rights as little as possible in order to achieve the "pressing and substantial" objectives. In other words, while the means chosen may be rationally connected to the objectives, they may, at the same time, be unnecessarily intrusive on constitutional rights in light of alternative means.

In *R. v. Chaulk, supra*, I stated that while Parliament need not choose the absolutely least intrusive means of attaining its objective, the means chosen must come within a range of means which impair *Charter* rights as little as is reasonably possible. In my view, the modified due diligence defence embodied in paras. (c) and (d) does not fall within the constitutionally acceptable range.

It is not necessary to convict of false/misleading advertising those who did not undertake corrective advertising because they did not realize (and ought not to have realized) that the advertisement was false/misleading, in order to achieve the objectives set out above. If Parliament wished to encourage corrective advertising in order to meet the objectives set out above, it could have:

(a) enacted a separate offence of "failure to correct false/misleading advertising" under which an accused who discovers or who ought to have discovered that an advertisement was false or misleading is required to be duly diligent in taking the corrective measures set out in paras. (c) and (d) in order to come within the statutory defence to this offence;

or

(b) maintained the component of "failure to correct false/misleading advertising" within the existing statutory defence to false advertising, but worded paras. (c) and (d) in such a way that the requirement for corrective advertising would arise upon the accused's discovery that the advertisement was false or misleading (or upon a finding that the accused ought to have discovered that the advertisement was false/misleading).

In my view, either of these alternative means would, without convicting the innocent, achieve the objective of encouraging advertisers to undertake corrective advertising and would therefore achieve the dual objectives of protecting consumers from the effects of false advertising and of preventing advertisers from benefiting from false/misleading representations. Given that these two alternatives were clearly open to Parliament, it can be seen that the existing paragraphs are unnecessarily intrusive on constitutional rights.

While an absolute liability component to the offence of false advertising would perhaps be more effective in facilitating convictions than would the alternatives proposed above, the simple answer to this contention is that Parliament could have retained the absolute liability component and, at the same time, infringed *Charter* rights to a much lesser extent, had it not combined this absolute liability with the possibility of imprisonment. In this sense, removing the possibility of imprisonment and leaving paras. (c) and (d) unchanged was a further less intrusive means which was available to Parliament.

By a narrow majority of 5-4, the Supreme Court further held that placing the persuasive burden of proof on the accused was constitutional. The majority of the court rejected a compromise proposal of the Ontario Law Reform Commission that a more principled solution to strict responsibility offences would be to presume negligence such that the accused would merely have an evidentiary burden. On this issue the following opinions were expressed.

LAMER C.J.C. (SOPINKA, MCLACHLIN and LA FOREST JJ. concurring) (dissenting on this point): —

. . . .

2. *As Little as Possible*

While the imposition of a persuasive burden is rationally connected to the objective, it does not, in my view, infringe constitutionally protected rights as little as is reasonably possible. The Crown has not established that it is necessary to convict those who were duly diligent in order to "catch" those accused who were *not* duly diligent.

Parliament clearly had the option of employing a mandatory presumption of negligence (following from proof of the *actus reus*) which could be rebutted by something *less* than an accused's establishing due diligence on a balance of probabilities. This option was, in fact, recommended by the Ontario Law Reform Commission in its *Report on the Basis of Liability for Provincial Offences* (Toronto, 1990). The Commission stated (at p. 48):

> With respect to the burden of proof for strict liability offences, the Commission proposes a compromise solution that balances the fundamental rights of the accused with the need for effective law enforcement. We recommend the enactment of a mandatory presumption rather than a reverse onus. In other words, *in the absence of evidence to the contrary, negligence will be presumed. The Crown will continue to bear the burden of establishing the physical element or actus reus beyond a reasonable doubt. However, in a strict liability case, it will be necessary that evidence of conduct capable of amounting to reasonable care be adduced, either by the testimony of the accused, through the examination or cross-examination of a Crown or defence witness, or in some other way. The accused will merely have an evidentiary*

burden and will no longer be required to satisfy the persuasive burden of establishing, on a balance of probabilities, that he was not negligent. Where evidence of reasonable care has been adduced, thereby rebutting the presumption, in order to secure a conviction the prosecution should be required to establish the accused's negligence beyond a reasonable doubt. [Emphasis added.]

. . . .

In light of the alternative means open to Parliament, I am of the view that the use of a persuasive burden in s. 37.3(2) cannot be justified under the proportionality part of the *Oakes* test.

In summary, it is my view that the words "he establishes that" contained in s. 37.3(2) limit s. 11(*d*) of the *Charter* and cannot be upheld as a reasonable limit under s. 1. Consequently, the words "he establishes that" must be held to be of no force or effect, pursuant to s. 52(1) of the *Constitution Act, 1982*.

Once the words "he establishes that" are deleted from s. 37.3(2), the question becomes, who proves what under the remaining provision? Parliament may well choose to re-enact the offence of false/misleading advertising within constitutionally acceptable parameters but, until such time, how is this offence to be proven? In my opinion, the answer to this question requires the court to consider this court's judgment in *R. v. Sault Ste. Marie (City), supra*, but this time in light of the *Charter*.

In *R. v. Sault Ste. Marie (City), supra*, this court set out a classification of offences to be followed where the Legislature had not expressly addressed the requirement of fault. The court drew a general distinction between "true crimes" and "public welfare offences". While the court contemplated public welfare offences which carried relatively light sentences, it would seem that the offence of false/misleading advertising would be one which would fall within the "public welfare" classification in *Sault Ste. Marie*. For "public welfare offences", the court held that the standard of fault was that of "strict liability". This meant that conviction would follow proof (by the Crown) of the *actus reus*, unless the accused proved, on a balance of probabilities, that he or she took all reasonable care and was duly diligent.

It is clear to me from the foregoing discussion of this court's judgments in *Oakes, Wigglesworth, Vaillancourt, Whyte*, and *Chaulk, supra*, that where an accused faces imprisonment upon conviction, the presence of the persuasive burden in the *Sault Ste. Marie* category of "strict liability" is inconsistent with the principles of fundamental justice. The previous judgments of this court make clear that, to the extent that imprisonment is a possible penalty, this category of "strict liability", placing a persuasive burden on the accused, cannot withstand *Charter* scrutiny. It follows from this that when imprisonment is a possible punishment for the commission of a "public welfare offence", the persuasive burden contemplated by this court in *R. v. Sault Ste. Marie (City)* cannot be operative; in this sense, the developing *Charter* jurisprudence of this court has, over the last five years, been modifying this holding in *Sault Ste. Marie*. At the same time, the reasons for not imposing a fault requirement of subjective *mens rea* for "public welfare offences", which were discussed at length in *Sault Ste. Marie*, are still compelling. Therefore, I would characterize the modification of *Sault Ste. Marie* as follows: where the Legislature has not expressly addressed the requirement of fault (or where, as here, it has done so in a manner which violates the Constitution), a "public welfare offence" (such as false/misleading advertising) which carries the possibility of imprisonment will be construed as setting up a rebuttable mandatory presumption of negligence. Once the Crown proves the *actus reus*, the accused will carry the evidentiary burden of pointing to some evidence (led either by the Crown or the defence) which is capable of raising a reasonable doubt as to his or her negligence, short of which a conviction will properly ensue.

CORY J. (L'HEUREUX-DUBÉ J. concurring): —

. . . .

It is difficult to conceive of a situation in which a regulated accused would not be able to adduce *some* evidence giving rise to the possibility that due diligence was exercised. For instance, an environmental polluter would often be able to point to *some* measures it had adopted in order to prevent the type of harm which ultimately resulted. This might raise a reasonable doubt that it had acted with due diligence, no matter how inadequate those measures were for the control of a dangerous situation. Similarly, a wholly inadequate effort to ensure that an advertisement was true might nevertheless succeed in raising a reasonable doubt as to due diligence.

To impose such a limited onus is inappropriate and insufficient in the regulatory context. Criminal offences have always required proof of guilt beyond a reasonable doubt; the accused cannot, therefore, be convicted where there is a reasonable doubt as to guilt. This is not so with regulatory offences, where a conviction will lie if the accused has failed to meet the standard of care required. Thus, the question is not whether the accused has exercised *some* care, but whether the degree of care exercised was sufficient to meet the standard imposed. If the false advertiser, the corporate polluter and the manufacturer of noxious goods are to be effectively controlled, it is necessary to require them to show on a balance of probabilities that they took reasonable precautions to avoid the harm which actually resulted. In the regulatory context, there is nothing unfair about imposing that onus; indeed, it is essential for the protection of our vulnerable society.

. . . .

As with the s. 7 challenge, licensing considerations support the conclusion that strict liability does not violate s. 11(*d*) of the *Charter*. The licensing argument attributes to the regulated actor knowledge and acceptance, not only of the standard of reasonable care itself, but also of the responsibility to establish on a balance of probabilities the exercise of reasonable care. Acceptance of this burden is an implied term and a precondition of being allowed to engage in activity falling within the regulated sphere. Regulated actors are taken to understand that, should they be unable to discharge this burden, an inference of negligence will be drawn from the fact that the proscribed result has occurred.

I wish to emphasize, however, that the difference in the scope and meaning of s. 11(*d*) in the regulatory context does not imply that the presumption of innocence is meaningless for a regulated accused. The Crown must still prove the *actus reus* of regulatory offences beyond a reasonable doubt. Thus, the Crown must prove that the accused polluted the river, sold adulterated food, or published a false advertisement. However, once having established this beyond a reasonable doubt, the Crown is presumptively relieved of having to prove anything further. Fault is presumed from the bringing about of the proscribed result, and the onus shifts to the defendant to establish reasonable care on a balance of probabilities.

For these reasons, I conclude that the presumption of innocence as guaranteed in s. 11(*d*) of the *Charter* is not violated by strict liability offences as defined in *Sault Ste. Marie*. The imposition of a reverse persuasive onus on the accused to establish due diligence on a balance of probabilities does not run counter to the presumption of innocence, notwithstanding the fact that the same reversal of onus would violate s. 11(*d*) in the criminal context.

IACOBUCCI J. (GONTHIER and STEVENSON JJ. concurring): — [Agreeing with the result of Justice Cory's judgment, and therefore making up the majority judgment.]

. . . .

With respect to the second requirement of *Oakes*, I agree that there is a rational connection between the desired objective and the means chosen to attain the objective. Removing the burden on the Crown to prove lack of due diligence beyond a reasonable doubt, and instead requiring the accused to establish due diligence on a balance of probabilities, is without a doubt a rational and logical way of attaining the legislative objective.

However, it is with respect to the third requirement of the *Oakes* analysis, that I respectfully disagree with the conclusions of Lamer C.J.C. This step requires a consideration of whether the means chosen impair the right or freedom in question *no more than is necessary to accomplish the desired objective*. Lamer C.J.C. is of the opinion that the use of a persuasive burden in s. 37.3(2) of the *Competition Act* cannot pass this third step of the *Oakes* analysis because of the presence of an alternative means open to Parliament that would be less intrusive on s. 11(*d*) of the *Charter* and would "go a long way" in achieving the objective. The alternative in question is the use of a "mandatory presumption of negligence" (following from the proof of the *actus reus*) which could be rebutted by something less than an accused establishing due diligence on a balance of probabilities, *i.e.*, by raising a reasonable doubt as to due diligence. With respect, I cannot agree that such a means would achieve the stated objective as effectively, nor would it go a long way in achieving it. Such a means would shift to the accused the burden of simply raising a reasonable doubt as to due diligence, and would not thereby allow the effective pursuit of the regulatory objective. It would leave the Crown the legal burden of proving facts largely within the peculiar knowledge of the accused.

For the reasons given by Cory J. in the context of his s. 11(*d*) analysis, such an alternative would in practice make it virtually impossible for the Crown to prove public welfare offences such as the one in question, and would effectively prevent governments from seeking to implement public policy through prosecution. It would also not provide effective inducement for those engaged in regulated activity to comply strictly with the regulatory scheme, including adopting proper procedures and record-keeping and might even have a contrary effect. Though such a result would be clearly advantageous to an accused, it would not be effective in avoiding the loss of convictions because the Crown could not prove facts within the particular knowledge of the accused. In sum, taking into account the particular circumstances described by Cory J. in his reasons, Parliament could *not* "reasonably have chosen an alternative means which would have achieved the identified objective as effectively": *R. v. Chaulk*, [1990] 3 S.C.R. 1303, 2 C.R. (4th) 1, 62 C.C.C. (3d) 193, at p. 1341, [S.C.R., p. 31 C.R.] per Lamer C.J.C. for the majority.

As for the final requirement of the *Oakes* analysis, I would also respectfully disagree with the conclusions of Lamer C.J.C. As noted by Cory J. in his reasons, regulated activity and public welfare offences are a fundamental part of Canadian society. Those who choose to participate in regulated activities must be taken to have accepted the consequential responsibilities and their penal enforcement. One of these consequences is that they should be held responsible for the harm that may result from their lack of due diligence. Unless they can prove on a balance of probabilities that they exercised due diligence, they shall be convicted and in some cases face a possible prison term. These participants are in the best position to prove due diligence, since they possess in most cases the required information. Viewed in this context, and taking into account the fundamental importance of the legislative objective as stated and the fact that the means chosen impair the right guaranteed by s. 11(*d*) as little as is reasonably possible, the effects of the reverse onus on the presumption of innocence are proportional to the objective.

Having found that the reverse onus on the accused to establish due diligence on a balance of probabilities (via the words "he establishes that" in s. 37.3(2) of the *Competition Act*) satisfies all four requirements of the *Oakes* analysis, I conclude that such an onus is saved under s. 1 of the *Charter* as a reasonable limit in a free and democratic society. Accordingly, I would dispose of the appeal in the manner suggested by Cory J.

It has not yet been determined whether the majority's ruling on the question of onus can also apply to the burden of proving due diligence defences in the case of some *Criminal Code* offences. In the context of the following regulatory offence, which was accepted to be one of strict liability, consider whether it was wise that the Supreme Court decided that the accused should bear a persuasive and not merely evidentiary burden of proving due diligence:

> An elevator installation worker, employed by the elevator installation subcontractor, fell down an elevator shaft to his death at a building under construction. He had apparently arrived earlier than expected, unfastened a barrier to the shaft, and either climbed or jumped down to a wooden structure a few feet below the level of the 13th floor. The structure had been temporarily supported but was not sufficiently strong to support a person's weight. Charges were laid under the *Occupational Health and Safety Act*, R.S.O. 1980, c. 321, against the general contractor for failing to ensure that the safety measures set out in the regulations were carried out on its project, and also against the project's superintendent for failing to ensure that workers acted in accordance with the safety measures.

Compare *R. v. Ellis-Don Ltd.* (1990), 2 C.R. (4th) 118 (Ont. C.A.), in which the majority held that the accused should merely have an evidentiary burden. This ruling was reversed without full reasons by the Supreme Court of Canada, applying *Wholesale Travel* (1992), 71 C.C.C. (3d) 63 (S.C.C.). Unlike *Wholesale Travel*, the court had here been presented with full evidence of enforcement patterns seeking to show that the reverse onus was unnecessary.

R. v. TRANSPORT ROBERT,
R. v. WILLIAM CAMERON TRUCKING
(sub. nom. R. v. 1260448 ONTARIO INC.)

(2003), 16 C.R. (6th) 136, 180 C.C.C. (3d) 254 (Ont. C.A.),
leave to appeal refused (2004), 330 N.R. 197 (note) (S.C.C.)

By the court (McMurtry C.J.O., Rosenberg and Moldaver JJ.A.): —

The issue in these two appeals is whether it is open to the Legislature to create an absolute liability offence where there is no possibility of imprisonment or probation if the defendant is convicted. Section 84.1(1) of the *Highway Traffic Act*, R.S.O. 1990, c. H.8 (*HTA*) provides that the owner and operator of a commercial motor vehicle are guilty of an offence where a wheel becomes detached from the vehicle while it is on a highway. Subsection (5) provides that it is no defence to the charge that the defendant exercised due diligence to avoid or prevent the detaching of the wheel. The penalty for the offence is a fine of not less than $2,000 and not more than $50,000, but the defendant is not liable to imprisonment or probation as a result of the conviction or for default in payment of the fine resulting from the conviction (subsection (4)).

The defendants submit that notwithstanding the only possible penalty for this offence is a monetary one, the creation of this absolute liability offence violates the guarantee to security of the person in s. 7 of the *Canadian Charter of Rights and Freedoms* and the presumption of innocence in s. 11(d) of the *Charter*. For the following reasons we have concluded that there is no violation of s. 7 or s. 11(d). We therefore allow the Crown appeal in the *Transport Robert* case and dismiss the appeal by *William Cameron Trucking*.

In view of our conclusion on the constitutional issue, it is unnecessary to review the facts of either prosecution in any great deal. Most of the evidence adduced at the trials was led in an attempt to explain how the wheels became detached and why the defendants nevertheless acted with due diligence.

. . . .

Analysis

Section 11(d)

The argument based on s. 11(d) of the *Charter* can be dealt with quickly. As Professor Hogg points out in *Constitutional Law of Canada*, (Carswell, Toronto, 1997) vol. 2, p. 48-17, while s. 11(d) prohibits the reversal of the burden of proof of a fact that is an element of the offence, that subsection says nothing about elimination of an element. If the offence as drafted includes certain elements or if s. 7 mandates proof of a certain element as a matter of fundamental justice, placing the burden of proof of such elements on the defence may be an unconstitutional violation of s. 11(d) subject to the Crown establishing that the reversal is a reasonable limit under s. 1. However, there is no violation of s. 11(d) because the legislature has defined an offence so as to eliminate an element, or as here, a possible common law defence.

The real and only constitutional issue in this case then is whether, despite the wording of s. 84.1 of the *HTA*, s. 7 mandates that the defendants be able to defend the case on the basis of due diligence. We therefore turn to that issue.

Although the rights guaranteed by s. 7 can only be enjoyed by human beings, a corporation has standing to challenge the constitutionality of a penal provision on the basis that the provision violates the s. 7 rights of a human being: *R. v. Wholesale Travel Group Inc.*, [1991] 3 S.C.R. 154. Thus, it is open to these corporate defendants to challenge the constitutionality of s. 84.1 of the *HTA*.

As the law now stands, a defendant alleging a violation of s. 7 must establish both a violation of the right to life, liberty or security of the person and that the deprivation of that right does not accord with the principles of fundamental justice. The defendants properly concede that since there is no possibility that an individual convicted of the offence can be either imprisoned or placed on probation, s. 84.1 of the *HTA* does not violate any liberty interest protected by s. 7. They do submit, however, that the provision infringes the security of the person of an individual because it allows for the conviction of a person who is without fault. Their submission of an infringement of the security of the person is primarily based on the effect of the stigma attached to a conviction together with the large possible monetary penalty, the highest in the *HTA*.

. . . .

Security of the person and absolute liability

As indicated, the defendants submit that as a result of the combination of the high maximum fine and the stigma attached to the s. 84.1 of the *HTA* offence, a conviction for that offence results in the deprivation of security of the person. They point out that s. 84.1 was enacted in response to a number of highly publicized incidents and recommendations from inquests following the deaths of motorists when wheels came loose from commercial vehicles. They argue that a person convicted of this offence is stigmatized as someone who has exposed innocent motorists or pedestrians to the risk of serious injury or death. They also point out that the offence should be considered, not from the point of view of a large trucking company, but that of an individual, possibly an owner/operator with one commercial vehicle.

In considering the constitutionality of s. 84.1, it is necessary to take into account certain contextual factors. The section applies only to owners and operators of commercial vehicles. These persons operate for profit in a highly regulated industry. In *R. v. Ladouceur* (1990), 56 C.C.C. (3d) 22 at 39 (S.C.C.), Cory J. for the majority of the Supreme Court explained that driving is a privilege and not a right: "[I]t is fitting that governmental action be taken to prevent or at least to lessen this carnage on our highways. Proper laws and regulations are necessary to regulate the privilege of driving a motor vehicle on public thoroughfares."

Although s. 84.1 provides for a maximum fine of $50,000 and a minimum fine of $2,000, under s. 59(2) of the *Provincial Offences Act*, R.S.O. 1990, c. P.33, in exceptional circumstances, the court may impose a fine that is less than the minimum or suspend the sentence. The Crown points out that s. 84.1 has received a narrow interpretation from this court in *Ontario (Minister of Transport) v. Ryder Truck Rental Canada Ltd.* (2000), 47 O.R. (3d) 171 at para. 16 (C.A.), where it was held that the offence only applies if a wheel becomes detached and does not apply where the entire axle, hub, wheel and tire assembly comes off in one piece. The Crown also concedes that although due diligence is not available as a defence, certain other *actus reus* "defences" would be available as where the wheel became detached in a collision caused by a third party.

While the courts have not fully defined the limits of security of the person in s. 7, there are certain propositions established by the cases. In *Blencoe v. British Columbia (Human Rights Commission)*, [2000] 2 S.C.R. 307 at para. 57, Bastarache J., speaking for the majority held that, "[N]ot all state interference with an individual's psychological integrity will engage s. 7. Where the psychological integrity of a person is at issue, security of the person is restricted to 'serious state-imposed psychological stress' ". Thus, "[N]ot all forms of psychological prejudice caused by government will lead to automatic s. 7 violations." Further, there is no "generalized right to dignity, or more specifically, a right to be free from stigma" (para. 57) and, "[d]ignity and reputation are not self-standing rights. Neither is freedom from stigma" (para. 80).

In *Blencoe*, the concern was with the lengthy delay in dealing with a human rights complaint, a proceeding that according to the respondent *Blencoe*, had ruined his reputation. Bastarache J. held at para. 83 that it would only be in "exceptional cases where the state interferes in profoundly intimate and personal choices of an individual that state-caused delay in human rights proceedings could trigger the s. 7 security of the person interest . . . they would not easily include the type of stress, anxiety and stigma that result from administrative or civil proceedings."

There are admittedly distinctions between the *Blencoe* context and the context of these cases. In particular, the defendants here are charged with quasi-criminal offences and required to appear in open court to face the charges. We also take the point that this offence was enacted in response to a serious public safety issue "in the wake of several serious incidents of 'flying truck wheels' ". See *Ryder Truck Rental, supra*, at para. 1.

However, we are not convinced that a prosecution for the s. 84.1 offence engages the kind of exceptional state-induced psychological stress, even for an individual, that would trigger the security of the person guarantee in s. 7. The offence does not create a true crime, and like most regulatory offences, it focuses on the harmful consequences of otherwise lawful conduct rather than any moral turpitude. Thus, in *Wholesale Travel, supra*, at p. 224, Cory J. rejected the accused's claim that conviction for false advertising carried the stigma of dishonesty. In that case, where due diligence was available, the court characterized the fault element as one of "negligence rather than one involving moral turpitude" and thus, "any stigma that might flow from a conviction is very considerably diminished." The same can be said in this case. The s. 84.1 offence focuses on the unintended but harmful consequences of the commercial trucking industry. We reject the proposition that a defendant charged with this offence is stigmatized as a person operating in a wanton manner, heedless of the extreme dangers to life and limb posed by his or her operation. Conviction for the offence at most implies negligence and like the misleading advertising offence considered in *Wholesale Travel*, any stigma is very considerably diminished.

The diminished stigma attached to the s. 84.1 offence is not sufficient to trigger the security interest in s. 7 even when coupled with the possibility of a significant fine. This is simply not the kind of serious state-imposed psychological stress that is intended to be covered by security of the person. It is qualitatively different than the kinds of stresses that have been recognized in the cases. A review of those cases demonstrates a concern with state action that intrudes in an intimate and profound way as in *New Brunswick (Minister of Health and Community Services) v. G.(J.)*, [1999] 3 S.C.R. 46 (attempt to take a child away from its parents); *Rodriguez v. British Columbia (Attorney General)*, [1993] 3 S.C.R. 519 (criminal prohibition on assisting suicide for a desperately ill patient) and *R. v. Morgentaler*, [1988] 1 S.C.R. 30 (regulating abortion).

The right to security of the person does not protect the individual operating in the highly regulated context of commercial trucking for profit from the ordinary stress and anxieties that a reasonable person would suffer as a result of government regulation of that industry. As Lamer C.J.C. said in *G. (J.)* at para 59, "[I]f the right were interpreted with such broad sweep, countless government initiatives could be challenged on the ground that they infringe the right to security of the person, massively expanding the scope of judicial review, and, in the process, trivializing what it means for a right to be constitutionally protected."

Accordingly, s. 84.1 of the *HTA* does not violate s. 7. It is therefore unnecessary to consider whether any violation could be saved by s. 1.

Disposition

The appeal by the defendant William Cameron Trucking is dismissed. The appeal by the Crown in *Transport Robert* is allowed, the order for a new trial set aside and a conviction entered. Particularly in light of the evidence led by the defendant concerning its attempts at preventing the loss of wheels, we agree with the Crown that the proper disposition would be imposition of the minimum fine of $2,000. The defendant will have 30 days to pay the fine.

Is there a a danger that law and order legislatures will now jump on the strategy used in s. 84.1 in Ontario or in B.C. generally to avoid the due diligence *Charter* standard? Will they now routinely expressly impose absolute liability and expressly avoid the possibility of imprisonment even in default?

There are important policy questions to consider. **Is, for example, absolute liability good penal policy for the high profile offence that led to the special**

s. 84.1 regime? There are certainly arguments of law enforcement expediency here relied on by the Ontario Court of Appeal. **But what of the fundamental choice of policy asserted by the Supreme Court in *Sault Ste. Marie*?** If owners and operators of commercial vehicles can prove reasonable maintenance standards for a vehicle that has nevertheless lost a wheel on the highway even at great risk to others, punishment is NOT justly imposed. On the other hand, if due diligence cannot be established, punishment is indeed fully deserved and one wonders why it is limited to a fine, even one as large as $50,000. A large fine would be rational if the offence targeted only corporations but that is not necessarily so considering it could ensnare an individual using his own vehicle for commercial reasons.

See further Stuart, "Is the *Sault Ste. Marie* Approach in Regulatory Offences About to Disappear?" (2004), 16 C.R. (6th) 147.

PROBLEMS

1. **A fishing packaging company is charged with being in possession of lobsters less than three and three sixteenth inches from length of eye socket to the rear of the body, contrary to the minimum length specified in Lobster Fishery Regulations passed under the *Fisheries Act*, R.S.C. 1952, as amended. Inspectors found 26 short lobsters amongst the 50,000 or 60,000 lbs. of lobsters on the premises. The penalty is a fine. Company officials deny any knowledge of the undersized lobsters. Should the offence be defined as absolute or strict liability? Should the company be convicted? What of fisherman who caught them?**

Compare *R. v. Pierce Fisheries Ltd.*, [1969] 4 C.C.C. 163 (N.S. C.A.), reversed (1970), [1971] S.C.R. 5, 12 C.R.N.S. 272, 5 C.C.C. 193.

2. **The accused shot and killed a black bear and three grizzly bears. They had obtained the appropriate hunting licence for each type of bear. A week earlier, after an abortive hunt, they had shot and killed an ailing horse and left it in the area. The bears had been attracted to the carcass. The accused were charged with the offence of using bait for the purpose of hunting big game, contrary to s. 50(1)(*b*) of the *Alberta Wildlife Act*, R.S.A. 1980, c. W-9, which reads: "No person shall for the purpose of hunting or taking big game set out, use or employ . . . any bait of any kind". The penalty is a fine of not less than $100 and not more than $1,500 and, in default of payment, imprisonment for a term of not more than six months.**

How should the offence be classified?

Compare *R. v. Brown* (1982), 29 C.R. (3d) 107, 69 C.C.C. (2d) 301, (Alta. C.A.), leave to appeal to S.C.C. refused (1982), 46 N.R. 85.

3. **The accused was charged with wilfully having evaded or attempted to evade the payment of moneys, contrary to s. 62(*d*) of the *Quebec Revenue Department Act*, S.O. 1972, c. 22. At trial, counsel for the accused admitted**

all the facts charged except that he had acted "wilfully". The prosecution then declared its case closed. Counsel for the accused moved for non-suit, alleging absence of proof of intent, this being a *mens rea* offence.

Rule on the motion

(1) where "wilfully" appears in the section, and

(2) where it does not.

Compare *Pichette v. Quebec (Deputy Minister of Revenne)* (1982), 29 C.R. (3d) 129 (Que. C.A.).

4. The accused, while hunting, shot a deer, then realized that he had left his deer tag at home. He returned home to get his deer tag, but in the meantime a Lands and Forests Officer found the untagged deer. The accused was charged with failing to tag deer contrary to the Deer Regulations made pursuant to the *Nova Scotia Lands and Forests Act*, R.S.N.S. 1967, c. 163. The regulations declare that a licensed hunter on killing a deer "shall immediately affix and securely lock" his tag to the carcass. The penalty is a fine of not less than $100 nor more than $300.

Is the offence absolute or strict? Is it constitutional?

Compare *R. v. Maidment* (1984), 37 C.R. (3d) 387, 10 C.C.C. (3d) 512 (N.S. C.A.).

5. The accused was charged under s. 5(1) of the *Food and Drugs Act*, R.S.C. 1970, c. F-27, which provides:

> 5.(1) No person shall label, package, treat, process, sell or advertise any food in a manner that is false, misleading or deceptive or is likely to create an erroneous impression regarding its character, value, quantity, composition, merit or safety.

An inspector of the Federal Department of Consumer and Corporate Affairs went to the accused's meat market to discuss the purchase of a side of beef. He requested that, after packaging, all bone and trim be returned to him. Subsequent analysis indicated a weight discrepancy of some 15 pounds. Reconstructing the side of beef indicated both the sirloin tip and a sirloin steak were missing. Also, extraneous portions of bone and fat were found that could not have been part of the side purchased. The accused testified that he was not in the store on the day the side was butchered. His employee, who could not specifically recollect the sale, stated that the store was very busy that day. The employee and the accused both testified that no meat was ever deliberately left out of an order but occasionally meat was forgotten or inadvertently left in the freezer. When those incidents occurred and the store was notified the mistakes were always rectified. Section 29 of the Act only provides a defence to any individual dealing with *pre-packaged* material if he can establish that he could not with reasonable diligence ascertain the quality of the goods. Give judgment. Compare *R. v. Grottoli* (1978), 43 C.C.C. (2d) 158 (Ont. C.A.).

6. The possibility of a leakage from the MacMillan Bloedel Ltd.'s underground pipes at its Skidegate operation in the Queen Charlotte Islands came to the company's attention in 1993 when it received a complaint from

the Ministry of the Environment. At that time the pipes, which had been installed in the 1960s, were dug up and tested. No leakage was discovered. The company's equipment supervisor and its manager were of the opinion that the pipes were sound. In September 1995 an environmental inspector with the company's environmental services department prepared a comprehensive report. Amongst other things, the report identified the use of underground fuel lines by the company, including those at Skidegate, as a significant environmental problem. He recommended that the pipes either be installed above ground or in a secondary sleeve to allow early detection of leaks. Company personnel reviewed the report. Underground lines at some locations were replaced as a result. The company had replaced underground lines at some of its operations prior to receiving the report. There was some evidence that where pipes were replaced, they were found to be in good condition. The Skidegate pipes were regarded as low on the company's list of environmental concerns. There was no evidence as to when any action was intended to be taken with respect to them.

On May 16, 1997, diesel fuel was observed by a fisheries officer in Crabapple Creek, adjacent to the Skidegate operation. The accused was charged with an offence contrary to the *Fisheries Act* of depositing or permitting to be deposited a deleterious substance in water frequented by fish contrary to s. 36(3) of the *Fisheries Act* of Canada. At trial it was common cause that the discharge had occurred as a result of a fuel leakage from pipes at the accused's Skidegate facility. The company tendered the opinion of a metallurgical expert that the cause was microbiologically influenced corrosion likely brought about in 1993 by the evacuation of the fuel lines. Has the accused company established the defence of due diligence?

Compare *R. v. MacMillan Bloedel Ltd.* (2002), 5 C.R. (6th) 129 (B.C. C.A.), discussed by Bruce Pardy, "*MacMillan Bloedel*: Progress on Due Diligence" (2002), 5 C.R. (6th) 146.

7. The accused was driving his two sons, aged 12 and 8, to school on April 8, 2004. He was stopped by a police constable and charged with violating s. 106(6) of the *Highway Traffic Act*; under what is now s. 106(4) of the HTA:

> No person shall drive on a highway a motor vehicle in which there is a passenger who is under sixteen years of age and occupies a seating position for which a seat belt assembly has been provided unless that passenger is wearing the complete seat belt assembly and it is properly adjusted and securely fastened.

The accused testified that he had ensured that both boys were wearing their seat belts when he left the family home. He was not aware that his younger son, seated in the back seat, had unfastened his seat belt during the drive. Should the offence be classified as absolute or strict? If the latter should the accused be acquitted on the basis of due diligence?

Compare *R. v. Kanda* (2008), 53 C.R. (6th) 331, 227 C.C.C. (3d) 417 (Ont. C.A.)

8. On April 29, 2008, the accused was driving westbound on Highway 7, a two-lane highway. The speed limit was 80 km/ h. She drove up behind a large tractor trailer that was moving at about 90 km/h and pulled out to pass the truck. She testified that as she attempted to pass the tractor trailer, it seemed longer than it had when she pulled out into the passing lane and the truck seemed to pick up speed as she attempted to pass it. She indicated that she became afraid, and sped up to get around the truck and back into the westbound lane. The police officer who was operating the radar from a police car behind the accused's car testified that there was nothing unsafe or remarkable about her driving apart from the speed. He clocked the accused at between 129 km/h and 131 km/ h as she passed the truck. She slowed to about 110 km/h after she had passed the truck. Based on the single radar reading of 131 km/h, which was 51 km/h over the speed limit, the officer elected to charge the accused with stunt driving contrary to s. 172 of the Ontario *Highway Traffic Act* as amended in 2007. The penalty is a fine of not less than $2,000 and not more than $10,000, imprisonment of up to six months, or to both a fine and a term of imprisonment. In addition to these sanctions, the driver's licence may be suspended for up to two years on a first conviction and for up to ten years on a subsequent conviction. A person charged under s. 172 is required to surrender his or her licence to the police officer at the scene, is subject to an automatic seven-day administrative licence suspension and the vehicle must be impounded for seven days at the cost of and risk to its owner. Does the accused have a defence? See *R. v. Raham* (2010), 74 C.R. (6th) 96 (Ont. C.A.).

(c)   Summary

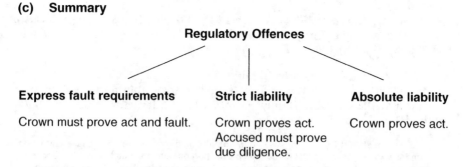

Regulatory Offences

Express fault requirements	Strict liability	Absolute liability
Crown must prove act and fault.	Crown proves act. Accused must prove due diligence.	Crown proves act.

It would appear that all provincial offences, and federal offences which do not incorporate *Criminal Code* standards, may be safely characterized as regulatory. In such cases the approach to fault seems clear. Courts should give full expression to any express legislative fault requirement whether this be subjective *mens rea*, negligence or statutory due diligence defences. In the case of all other regulatory offences, as a matter of common-law presumption or constitutional requirement, where the liberty interest is engaged, the court should read in a defence of due diligence. Under this state of the law absolute liability offences should be very rare unless the legislature, as in B.C., chooses not to enact a penalty of imprisonment, not even in default of payment of a fine.

A few provincial offences expressly invoke subjective m*ens rea*. For example the Ontario *Highway Traffic Act*, s. 134(3):

> Where signs or traffic control devices have been posted or placed under subsection (2), no person shall drive or operate a vehicle on the closed highway or part thereof in intentional disobedience of the signs or traffic control devices.

In such cases the due diligence compromise is irrelevant.

Another example of an express fault requirement in a regulatory statute is the objective test required for provincial offences of careless driving. Typical wording is that found in the *Highway Traffic Act*, R.S.O. 1990, c. H.8, s. 130:

> Every person is guilty of an offence of driving carelessly who drives a vehicle or street car on a highway without due care and attention and without reasonable consideration for other persons using the highway and on conviction is liable to a fine of not less than $200 and not more than $1,000 or to imprisonment for a term of not more than six months, or to both, and in addition his licence or permit may be suspended for a period of not more than two years.

R. v. BEAUCHAMP

(1953), 16 C.R. 270, 106 C.C.C. 6, 1953 CarswellOnt 11 (Ont. C.A.)

The accused was convicted of careless driving. The accused had driven his bus out onto the street from the parking garage. At this time there were no other cars on the street. The accused waited for another bus to leave the garage and then proceeded to back very slowly into a parking position on the street. Unfortunately, in the interim, another car had come down the street and parked in that position. The accused testified he checked his inside mirror, also looked through the back window, but found his outside mirror was loose and, because of the vibration, of no use. The bus crumpled the other car's bumper, grille and fender. The Court of Appeal allowed the accused's appeal.

MacKay J.A.: —

. . . .

My conclusions are that, while the same facts may, and in many cases do, give rise to both civil and criminal proceedings, nevertheless there is no necessity, in dealing with criminal or quasi-criminal conduct in relation to the operation of motor vehicles, for entering into a discussion or consideration of the negligence that would support a civil action. It is also clear that there are different degrees of criminal or quasi-criminal negligence.

Section 29(1) of *The Highway Traffic Act* creates a statutory offence that is quasi-criminal in its nature: *Rex v. Van Leishout* (1943), 80 C.C.C. 361.

A crime is defined in 9 Halsbury, 2nd ed. 1933, p. 9, para. 1, as follows:

A crime is an unlawful act or default which is an offence against the public, and renders the person guilty of the act or default liable to legal punishment. While a crime is often also an injury to a private person, who has remedy in a civil action, it is as an act or default contrary to the order, peace, and well-being of society that a crime is punishable by the State. A civil proceeding has for its object the recovery of money or other property, or the enforcement of a right for the advantage of the person suing, while a criminal proceeding has for its object the punishment of a public offence.

To support a charge under s. 29(1) of *The Highway Traffic Act*, the evidence must be such as to prove beyond reasonable doubt that the accused drove in the manner prohibited by the subsection, namely, without due care and attention or without reasonable consideration for others. The standard of care and skill to be applied has been long established and is not that of perfection. It is, I think, correctly stated in Mazengarb, *op cit.*, at pp. 176-7, as follows:

The law does not require of any driver that he should exhibit "perfect nerve and presence of mind, enabling him to do the best thing possible." It does not expect men to be more than ordinary men. Drivers of vehicles cannot be required to regulate their driving as if in constant fear that other drivers who are under observation, and apparently acting reasonably and properly, may possibly act at a critical moment in disregard of the safety of themselves and other users of the road.

But the law does insist upon a reasonable amount of skill in the handling of a vehicle which is a potential source of danger to other users of the road. . . . The question always is "What would an ordinary prudent person in the position of the plaintiff have done in relation to the event complained of?" (Pollock on Torts uses the term "average man".)

Motor vehicles are now in general use as a common means of transportation and pleasure. If too high a standard of care and skill were demanded, those people who are not capable of attaining such a standard would be deprived of the privilege of driving motor vehicles, and their use would be confined to experts, and even persons who might become experts might well be prevented from qualifying as such by experience. It must also be borne in mind that the test, where an accident has occurred, is not whether, if the accused had used greater care or skill, the accident would not have happened. It is whether it is proved beyond reasonable doubt that this accused, in the light of existing circumstances of which he was aware or of which a driver exercising ordinary care should have been aware, failed to use the care and attention or to give to other persons using the highway the consideration that a driver of ordinary care would have used or given in the circumstances? The use of the term "due care", which means care owing in the circumstances, makes it quite clear that, while the legal standard of care remains the same in the sense that it is what the average careful man would have done in like circumstances, the factual standard is a constantly shifting one, depending on road, visibility, weather conditions, traffic conditions that exist or may reasonably be expected, and any other conditions that ordinary prudent drivers would take into consideration. It is a question of fact, depending on the circumstances in each case.

In this case, and in some of the cases to which I have referred, evidence has been admitted to show that the accused had a good record as a careful driver. Such evidence is not relevant on the issue of guilt or innocence. As was said by Lord Hewart C.J. in *McCrone v. Riding, supra*, at p. 158: "That standard is an objective standard, impersonal and universal, fixed in relation to the safety of other users of the highway. It is in no way related to the degree of proficiency or degree of experience attained by the individual driver."

There is a further important element that must also be considered, namely, that the conduct must be of such a nature that it can be considered a breach of duty to the public and deserving of punishment. This further step must be taken even if it is found that the conduct of the accused falls below the standard set out in the preceding paragraphs. This principle may be somewhat difficult to apply, but I think it might be illustrated by the common example of a motorist attempting to park at the curb in a space between two other parked vehicles. Frequently one or other of the parked vehicles is bumped in the process. Damage seldom arises, because cars are equipped with bumpers, but if damage were caused it might well give rise to a civil action for damages, but it could hardly be said to be such a lack of care or attention as would be considered to be deserving of punishment as a crime or quasi-crime.

The added *Beauchamp* requirement in Ontario that careless driving be deserving of punishment has often resulted in acquittals. In *R. v. Ereddia* (2006), 42 C.R. (6th) 180 (Ont. C.J.) the accused was acquitted for a minor error of judgment in cracking a mirror of a parked garbage truck. This *Beauchamp* requirement was rejected in *R. v. Jacobsen* (1964), 44 C.R. 24 (B.C. C.A.).

Given that the legislature has expressly stated a fault requirement for careless driving without reference to a reverse onus one might have expected that there is no reverse onus on the accused to establish due diligence. Such a reverse onus is, however, frequently required: see especially *R. v. Skorput* (1992), 72 C.C.C. (3d) 294 (Ont. Prov. Div.).

4. FAULT FOR CRIMES

(a)   Murder and the *Charter*

(i)   *Murder under ss. 229(a)(i) and (ii)*

SIMPSON v. R.

(1981), 20 C.R. (3d) 36 at 61-64, 58 C.C.C. (2d) 122 (Ont. C.A.),
1981 Carswell 40

MARTIN J.A.: —

Following the argument of the appeal, and while the decision of the court was under reserve, the court requested counsel to submit argument with respect to the effect of a passage in the judge's charge defining the intent requisite for attempted murder, to which no objection was taken at the trial and which was not a ground of appeal. The court reconvened on 12th February 1981 and heard argument with respect to the passage in question.

The learned trial judge charged the jury as follows:

> Under the *Criminal Code*, anyone who attempts by any means to commit murder is guilty of an indictable offence. In this case, neither victim died, most fortunately. So the charge isn't murder, but attempted murder. What is murder? It is defined in s. 212 of the *Criminal Code*, in part, as follows:
> "Culpable homicide is murder
>> (*a*) where the person who causes the death of a human being
>>> (i) means to cause his death, or
>>> (ii) means to cause him bodily harm that he knows is likely to cause his death and is reckless whether death ensues or not".
>
> Now, "culpable" means "blameworthy". Culpable homicide is death of a human being for which some person may be blamed in law. The definition that I have just read to you, then, is one of murder, and the charge we are dealing with here is attempt to murder. I have earlier told you that proof of the intention of the accused is an essential element in the offence of attempt to murder. The Crown must satisfy you beyond a reasonable doubt that the accused stabbed the victim and that he did so intending to cause the death, or intending to cause the victim bodily harm that he knew or ought to have known was likely to cause death and was reckless whether death ensued or not. I repeat the second part of that definition: If the Crown has, on the evidence, satisfied you beyond a reasonable doubt that the accused was the stabber and that in stabbing he intended to cause bodily harm that he knew or ought to have known was likely to cause death and was reckless whether death ensued or not, then the offence of attempted murder has been proved.

It has now been authoritatively decided that either of the intents specified in s. 212(*a*)(i) and (ii) [now ss. 229(*a*)(i) and (ii)] suffices to constitute the intent required for the offence of attempted murder: see *Lajoie v. R.*, [1974] S.C.R. 399, 20 C.R.N.S. 360; *R. v. Ritchie*, (1970), 16 C.R.N.S. 287, [1970] 5 C.C.C. 336 (C.A.). Unfortunately, the learned trial judge, in paraphrasing the intent specified in s. 212(*a*)(ii) — namely, an intention to cause bodily harm that the offender *knows* is likely to cause death — substituted for the requisite intent an intention to cause bodily harm that the offender knows or *ought to know* is likely to cause death. This incorrect summary of the provision of s. 212(*a*)(ii) constituted a serious error. Liability under s. 212(*a*)(ii) is subjective, and the requisite *knowledge* that the intended injury is likely to cause death must be brought home to the accused subjectively. To substitute for that state of mind an intention to cause bodily harm that the accused knows or *ought* to know is likely to cause death is to impose liability on an objective basis. An intention to cause bodily harm that the offender *ought* to have known was likely to cause death is merely evidence from which, along with all the other circumstances, the jury *may* infer that the accused actually had the requisite intention and knowledge required by s. 212(*a*)(ii). It does not, however, constitute the requisite state of mind.

The effect of the misdirection is magnified by the fact that the incorrect statement of the intention required to be proved was repeated twice in the passage above reproduced. Although the learned trial judge had read the provisions of s. 212(*a*)(i) and (ii) just before the impugned passage, the jury was more likely to remember his clear-cut summary than the provisions of the *Code*: see *R. v. Harrison* (1945), 84 C.C.C. 78 at 82-83 (C.A.).

The error was never corrected by the learned trial judge. It is true that, in putting the case for the Crown, he said:

> The Crown suggests to you that, if you are satisfied that Simpson was the attacker, you should in the circumstances have no doubt that he intended to kill or cause bodily harm knowing that it might result in death and being reckless as to whether death ensued or not.

It is to be observed that even this passage is not entirely correct, as it refers to an intention to cause bodily harm knowing that it *might* result in death, as distinct from an intention to inflict bodily harm that the offender knows is *likely* to cause bodily harm. In any event, the jury would rely on the judge's instruction, as they had previously been told they must, with respect to the elements of the offence of attempted murder.

In my view, the seriousness of the error requires a new trial, unless it is proper to invoke the curative provisions of s. 613(1)(*b*)(iii). In *R. v. Smith* (1977), 33 C.C.C. (2d) 172 (Ont. C.A.), the trial judge, in instructing the jury as to the definition of murder, had on a number of occasions incorrectly summarized the provisions of s. 212(*a*)(ii) by omitting from the definition of the necessary intent the requirement that the person who means to cause bodily harm knows that the bodily harm is likely to cause death. The court in that case was satisfied, in view of the clear direction with respect to this requirement by the trial judge on so many occasions during his charge, that in the context in which the slips occurred they did not result in a substantial wrong or miscarriage of justice. In *R. v. Reynolds* (1978), 44 C.C.C. (2d) 129 (C.A.), the trial judge, in instructing the jury as to the elements of murder under s. 212(*a*)(ii), had made a similar error on a number of occasions in his charge, but on the error being brought to his attention he gave the jury an emphatic and correct instruction which, in the opinion of the court, nullified the earlier errors.

I have not been persuaded, even by Mr. Watt's able argument, that it is appropriate to invoke the provisions of s. 613(1)(*b*)(iii) in relation to the conviction of the appellant on count 2, relating to Cathy Wagenaar. I am not satisfied that a reasonable jury, properly instructed, having found that the appellant was Cathy Wagenaar's assailant, would inevitably have found that he intended to kill her or intended to inflict an injury upon her that he *knew* was likely to kill her. Although it would be open to a properly instructed jury to conclude that the requisite intent to constitute attempted murder had been established, the accompanying circumstances and the assailant's utterances are not such as to inevitably require a reasonable jury to reach that conclusion.

. . . .

New trial ordered.

R. v. EDELENBOS

(2004), 23 C.R. (6th) 350, 187 C.C.C. (3d) 465,
2004 CarswellOnt 2701 (Ont. C.A.)

The accused was charged with first degree murder of E.C. He admitted he had gone to her home and had sexually assaulted and strangled her. His defence to murder was one of intention. His defence was that he strangled her to stop her from screaming and that he did not intend to kill her, and should therefore be convicted of manslaughter. The jury returned a verdict of first degree murder. The accused appealed his conviction *inter alia* on the basis that the trial judge erred in defining the word "likely" in his jury charge regarding the intent requirement for murder; the Ontario Court of Appeal dismissed his appeal.

LANG J.A.: —

[12] For the most part, the trial judge's charge to the jury followed the accepted pattern regarding the intent required for murder, and the difference between murder and manslaughter. However, the trial judge gave the jury a novel explanation of the meaning in s. 229 of "likely" in the clause "means to cause him bodily harm that he knows is likely to cause his death".

[13] As applicable in this case, the current Ontario Specimen Jury Instructions (Criminal) (Toronto: Carswell, 2002), prepared by Watt J. of the Ontario Superior Court of Justice (the "Watt Charges"), would have had the judge tell the jury:

The crime of murder requires proof of a particular state of mind. For an unlawful killing to be murder, Crown counsel must prove that Mr. Edelenbos meant either to kill Ms. Coffey or meant to cause Ms. Coffey bodily harm that Mr. Edelenbos *knew* was likely to kill Ms. Coffey, and was reckless whether Ms. Coffey died or not. The Crown does *not* have to prove *both*. One is enough. All of you do *not* have to agree on the same state of mind, as long as everyone is sure that one of the required states of mind has been proven beyond a reasonable doubt.

If Mr. Edelenbos did *not* mean to do either, Mr. Edelenbos committed manslaughter. (Emphasis in original)

Although the Watt Charges were not distributed until 2002, the charge often used in 2000 was similar in content. It is relevant to observe that the Watt Charges contain no definition of "likely".

[14] Instead of using the standard charge however, the trial judge gave the following definition of "likely":

Likely means more than a possibility. It involves a substantial degree of probability. However, it does not mean more likely than not in the mathematical sense of 51 percent. The phrase is meant to convey the notion of a substantial or real chance, as distinct from a mere possibility. Likely to cause death means could well cause death. A fine calculation that the odds were against death, although the risk was plainly there, is no defence. By using the word "likely" the legislators were trying to get at killings where the risk was subjectively so appreciable that to engage in the conduct would be seen as a virtual equivalent of an intentional killing. A likelihood is a real risk, a substantial risk or something that might well happen.

[15] In choosing this definition, the trial judge relied on Isabel Grant, Dorothy Chunn, and Christine Boyle in *The Law of Homicide*, looseleaf (Scarborough: Carswell, 1994). They argue, at pp. 4-44 to 4-46 that, in some circumstances, the difference between knowing that death is "likely" and that death is "possible" distinguishes murder from manslaughter. They look to foreign case law to support this approach, particularly the New Zealand Court of Appeal decision in *R. v. Piri*, [1987] N.Z.L.R. 66.

[16] No Canadian cases were brought to our attention that discuss the meaning of "likely" in the context of s. 229. It would seem that the need for such a discussion has probably not arisen. In my view, the need did not arise in this case. It was unnecessary and potentially confusing to the jury for the trial judge to engage in a nuanced discussion of the precise meaning of "likely" in the circumstances of this trial. The facts simply did not call for an analysis of where "likely" stands on the spectrum from possible to probable. The jury in this case would have given the word "likely" its common sense plain language meaning, as other juries have across Canada.

[17] The purpose of the Ontario Specimen Criminal Jury Trial Project, chaired by Watt J., was to help judges draft jury instructions in plain language. The resulting Watt Charges do not include a definition of "likely" in the standard

murder instructions. In my view, this is because juries are able to apply "likely", in accordance with its established ordinary meaning, to the particular context.

[18] Where the jury does not need an analysis of a commonplace everyday word, the trial judge should avoid entering into the possible shades of its meaning. I recognize, however, that there may be cases where the trial judge may feel that the circumstances call for elaboration or definition. If so, before providing such an elaboration or definition, particularly one that has apparently not been used in a Canadian context, the trial judge should so advise counsel during the pre-charge conference. Each counsel should then be given an opportunity to make submissions.

[19] No such opportunity was given in this case. The trial judge did not advise counsel about his research in the area or his intention to depart from the standard charge. At the conclusion of the charge, defence counsel objected to the instruction on the meaning of "likely". The trial judge then explained his reasoning. While defence counsel, at that time, did not persist with his objection, he simply was not given an adequate opportunity to consider and research the matter. In any event, the absence of an objection is not fatal to an appeal.

[20] As I have said, the circumstances of this case did not require an analysis of the meaning of "likely"; indeed, in my view, it would be a most exceptional situation that would ever require such an analysis. The issue here, therefore, is whether the definition given by the judge to the jury operated to the prejudice of the defence. I conclude that it did not, for five reasons.

[21] First, the challenged instruction must be considered in context. It comprised three-quarters of a page in a succinct 45-page charge. The jury was not given a copy of the jury charge to take with them into their deliberations. Accordingly, the jury would not have laboured over the precise words of the instruction. Rather, it would have been left with an impression of the judge's definition of "likely".

[22] Second, in the course of his instruction, the judge referred to "likely" as being a "substantial degree of probability", not a "mere possibility", a "substantial risk", and on two occasions, as "something that might well happen". While he spoke of a "real chance" or "real risk", he also said murder was conduct virtually "equivalent to an intentional killing", a definition consistent with the authorities: see *R. v. Cooper*, [1993] 1 S.C.R. 146, 78 C.C.C. (3d) 289.

[23] Third, during the charge, a copy of the relevant provision of the *Criminal Code* was projected onto a screen for the jury, including its reference to "likely" to cause death. That provision does not include a definition of "likely". The trial judge provided the jury with a copy of s. 229 when they retired for their deliberations, while he did not give them a copy of his jury charge.

[24] Fourth, the trial judge himself used the word "likely" repeatedly in his charge, showing that he assumed the term did not need repeated or complex analysis. After he provided the definition of "likely", the trial judge referred simply to "likely" to cause death on 12 further occasions. As well, immediately after the definition, the trial judge instructed the jury that "recklessness" was "redundant" or "almost an afterthought". He said that, "if the Crown establishes the first two elements beyond a reasonable doubt—that an accused person intended to cause bodily harm and that he or she knew that it would likely cause death then this by itself, or these two elements by themselves, meet the test for recklessness."

[25] Finally, the trial judge's instructions following the definition of "likely" made the Crown's burden with respect to intent very clear. The trial judge instructed the jury that the critical issue was whether the Crown had established beyond a reasonable doubt that Mr. Edelenbos meant to cause Ms. Coffey's death or meant to cause her bodily harm that he knew was "likely" to cause her death. He canvassed the evidence of the effect of Mr. Edelenbos's inebriation on the capacity to form intent and the need for the Crown to prove Mr. Edelenbos's appropriate level of subjective intent.

[26] Quite rightly, he omitted the part of the standard jury charge that says it may be inferred, as a matter of common sense, that a sane and sober person usually intends to cause predictable consequences. There was evidence that Mr. Edelenbos had been drinking. The trial judge said:

> The critical issue in this trial is whether or not the prosecutor has established beyond a reasonable doubt that Martin Edelenbos either meant to cause the death of Eileen Coffey, or meant to cause her bodily harm that he knew was likely to cause her death. The intoxicating effect of alcohol is well known. Intoxication which causes a person to cast off restraint and act in a manner in which he or she would not have acted if sober affords no excuse for the commission of an offence while in that state if he or she had the intent required to constitute the offence. A drunken intent is nonetheless an intent. The offence of murder is not committed if the accused lacked the intent to either cause the death of Eileen Coffey, or to cause her bodily harm that he knew was likely to cause her death. Intoxication could compromise the formation of:
>
>   1. The intent to cause death;
>
>   2. The intent to cause bodily harm; or
>
>   3. The appreciation that the intended bodily harm was likely to cause death.
>
> The Crown is entitled to prove either intent beyond a reasonable doubt. If the intent to cause bodily harm for the second type of murder has been so proved, then the Crown must go on and also prove beyond a reasonable doubt that he knew that such bodily harm was likely to cause death. In considering whether the Crown has proved beyond a reasonable doubt either of these scenarios you should take into account Mr. Edelenbos's consumption of alcohol, along with the other facts which throw light on his state of mind at the time the offence was allegedly committed.

[27] The trial judge reviewed the evidence about alcohol consumption and said:

> Once he assaulted Ms. Coffey he only meant to stop her screaming when he put his hands, or hand on her throat. He denies either intending to kill her, or intending to cause her bodily harm. He denies any appreciation that his assault was likely to cause her death. He swore that the lethal nature of his assault was not evident to him because of the extent of his intoxication. He insists that the only intent he had was to stop her from screaming, despite his concession in the sober confines of this courtroom that the obvious purpose of putting one's hands around another's throat is to stop them from breathing.
>
> To prove either the intent to cause death, or the intent to cause bodily harm that Mr. Edelenbos knew was likely to cause death, the Crown relies on [expert evidence].

[28] The judge went on to describe the expert evidence about the severity of the injuries to Ms. Coffey and the evidence that Mr. Edelenbos was in sufficient control to carry out a thorough clean-up after the killing.

[29] Taking into consideration the instructions given by the trial judge after the definition of "likely", and reading the charge as a whole, I conclude that the jury would have appreciated that the Crown was obliged to prove Mr. Edelenbos's subjective intent to cause bodily harm that was likely to cause Ms. Coffey's death.

See further *R. v. Czibulka* (2005), 24 C.R. (6th) 152, 189 C.C.C. (3d) 199 (Ont. C.A.), *R. v. Patterson* (2006), 205 C.C.C. (3d) 171 (Ont. C.A.), *R. v. Moo* (2009), 247 C.C.C. (3d) 34 (Ont. C.A.), *R. v. Brar* (2009), 250 C.C.C. (3d) 198 (B.C. C.A.) and *R. v. Kahnapace* (2010), 76 C.R. (6th) 38 (B.C. C.A.) (instructions referring to foresight of danger or risk rather than likelihood amounting to error). See the further analysis of Gary Trotter, "Instructing Juries on Murder and Intent" (2005), 24 C.R. (6th) 178.

(ii)   Constructive murder: ss. 229(c) and 230

VAILLANCOURT v. R.

[1987] 2 S.C.R. 636, 60 C.R. (3d) 289, 39 C.C.C. (3d) 118,
1987 CarswellQue 18, 1987 CarswellQue 98

LAMER J. (DICKSON C.J.C. and WILSON J. concurring): —

INTRODUCTION

Vaillancourt was convicted of second degree murder following a trial before a Sessions Court judge and jury in Montreal. He appealed to the Quebec Court of Appeal, arguing that the Judge's charge to the jury on the combined operation of ss. 213(*d*) [now s. 230(*d*)] and 21(2) of the *Criminal Code*, R.S.C. 1970, c. C-34, was incorrect. His appeal was dismissed and the conviction was affirmed [31 C.C.C. (3d) 75]. Before this court, he has challenged the constitutional validity of s. 213(*d*), alone and in combination with s. 21(2), under the *Canadian Charter of Rights and Freedoms*.

THE FACTS

For the purposes of this appeal, the Crown does not contest the following statement of the facts.

The appellant and his accomplice committed an armed robbery in a pool hall. The appellant was armed with a knife and his accomplice with a gun. During the robbery, the appellant remained near the front of the hall while the accomplice went to the back. There was a struggle between the accomplice and a client. A shot was fired and the client was killed. The accomplice managed to escape and has never been found. The appellant was arrested at the scene.

In the course of his testimony, the appellant said that he and his accomplice had agreed to commit this robbery armed only with knives. On the night of the robbery, however, the accomplice arrived at their meeting place with a gun. The appellant said that he objected because on a previous armed robbery his gun had discharged accidentally, and he did not want that to happen again. He insisted that the gun be unloaded. The accomplice removed three bullets from the gun and gave them to the appellant. The appellant then went to the bathroom and placed the bullets in his glove. The glove was recovered by the police at the scene of the crime and was found at trial to contain three bullets. The appellant testified that at the time of the robbery he was certain that the gun was unloaded.

CONSTITUTIONAL QUESTIONS

Before this court, the following constitutional questions were formulated:

> 1. Is s. 213(*d*) of the *Criminal Code* inconsistent with the provisions of either s. 7 or s. 11(*d*) of the *Canadian Charter of Rights and Freedoms* and, therefore, of no force or effect?
> 2. If not, is the combination of s. 21 and 213(*d*) of the *Criminal Code* inconsistent with the provisions of either s. 7 or s. 11(*d*) of the *Canadian Charter of Rights and Freedoms* and is s. 21 of the *Criminal Code* therefore of no force or effect in the case of a charge under s. 213(*d*) of the *Criminal Code*?

The Law

Narrowing the issue

The appellant has framed his attack on s. 213(*d*) of the *Code* in very wide terms. He has argued that the principles of fundamental justice require that, before Parliament can impose any criminal liability for causing a particular result, there must be some degree of subjective *mens rea* in respect of that result. This is a fundamental question with far-reaching consequences. If this case were decided on that basis, doubt would be cast on the constitutional validity of many provisions throughout our *Criminal Code*, in particular s. 205(5)(*a*) [now s. 222(5)(*a*)], whereby causing death by means of an unlawful act is culpable homicide, and s. 212(*c*) [now s. 229(*c*)], whereby objective foreseeability of the likelihood of death is sufficient for a murder conviction in certain circumstances.

However, the appellant was convicted under s. 213(*d*) and the constitutional question is limited to this provision. In my opinion, the validity of s. 213(*d*) can be decided on somewhat narrower grounds. In addition, the Attorney General of Canada has seen fit not to intervene to support the constitutionality of s. 213(*d*), which is clearly in jeopardy in this case, though he might have intervened to support ss. 205(5)(*a*) and 212(*c*) and other similar provisions. I will thus endeavour not to make pronouncements the effect of which will be to predispose in *obiter* of other issues more properly dealt with if and when the constitutionality of the other provisions is in issue. I do, however, find it virtually impossible to make comments as regards s. 213(*d*) that will not have some effect on the validity of the rest of s. 213 or that will not reveal to some extent my views as regards s. 212(*c*). However, the validity of those sections and of subs. (*a*) to (*c*) of s. 213 is not in issue here and I will attempt to limit my comments to s. 213(*d*).

The appellant has also challenged the combined operation of ss. 21(2) and 213(*d*). Given my decision on the validity of s. 213(*d*), and in view of the importance of s. 21(2) and the absence of the Attorney General of Canada, I do not find it necessary or advisable to deal with s. 21(2) in this appeal.

Analysis of s. 213(d)

Section 213(*d*) in the context of the murder provisions

It is first necessary to analyze s. 213(*d*) in the context of the other murder provisions in the *Code* in order to determine its true nature and scope. Murder is defined as a culpable homicide committed in the circumstances set out at ss. 212 and 213 of the *Code*. There is a very interesting progression through s. 212 to s. 213 with respect to the mental state that must be proven.

The starting point is s. 212(*a*)(i), which provides:

212. Culpable homicide is murder

(*a*) where the person who causes the death of a human being

(i) means to cause his death . . .

This clearly requires that the accused have actual subjective foresight of the likelihood of causing the death, coupled with the intention to cause that death. This is the most morally blameworthy state of mind in our system.

There is a slight relaxation of this requirement in s. 212(*a*)(ii), which provides:

212. Culpable homicide is murder

(*a*) where the person who causes the death of a human being . . .

(ii) means to cause him bodily harm that he knows is likely to cause his death, and is reckless whether death ensues or not . . .

Here again the accused must have actual subjective foresight of the likelihood of death. However, the Crown need no longer prove that he intended to cause the death, but only that he was reckless whether death ensued or not. It should also be noted that s. 212(*a*)(ii) is limited to cases where the accused intended to cause bodily harm to the victim.

Section 212(*c*) provides:

212. Culpable homicide is murder. . .

(*c*) where a person, for an unlawful object, does anything that he knows or ought to know is likely to cause death, and thereby causes death to a human being, notwithstanding that he desires to effect his object without causing death or bodily harm to any human being.

In part, this is simply a more general form of recklessness, and thus the logical extension of s. 212(*a*)(ii), in that it applies when the accused "does *anything* . . . he knows . . . is likely to cause death" (emphasis added). However, there is also a further relaxation of the mental element required for murder, in that it is also murder where the accused "does *anything that he . . . ought to know* is likely to cause death" (emphasis added). This eliminates the requirement of actual subjective foresight and replaces it with objective foreseeability or negligence.

The final relaxation in the definition of murder occurs at s. 213:

213. Culpable homicide is murder where a person causes the death of a human being while committing or attempting to commit high treason or treason or an offence mentioned in section 52 (sabotage), 76 (piratical acts), 76.1 (hijacking an aircraft), 132 or subsection 133(1) or sections 134 to 136 (escape or rescue from prison or lawful custody), 143 or 145 (rape or attempt to commit rape), 149 or 156 (indecent assault), subsection 246(2) (resisting lawful arrest), 247 (kidnapping and forcible confinement), 302 (robbery), 306 (breaking and entering) or 389 or 390 (arson), whether or not the person means to cause death to any human being and whether or not he knows that death is likely to be caused to any human being, if

(*a*) he means to cause bodily harm for the purpose of
(i) faclitating the commission of the offence, or
(ii) facilitating his flight after committing or attempting to commit the offence,
and the death ensues from the bodily harm;

(*b*) he administers a stupefying or overpowering thing for a purpose mentioned in paragraph (*a*), and the death ensues therefrom;

(*c*) he wilfully stops, by any means, the breath of a human being for a purpose mentioned in paragraph (*a*), and the death ensues therefrom; or

(*d*) he uses a weapon or has it upon his person
(i) during or at the time he commits or attempts to commit the offence, or
(ii) during or at the time of his flight after committing or attempting to commit the offence,
and the death ensues as a consequence.

Under this provision, it is murder if the accused causes the victim's death while committing or attempting to commit one of the enumerated offences if he performs one of the acts in subss. (*a*) to (*d*). Proof that the accused performed one of the acts in subss. (*a*) to (*d*) is substituted for proof of any subjective foresight, or even objective foreseeability, of the likelihood of death.

I should add that there appears to be a further relaxation of the mental state when the accused is a party to the murder through s. 21(2) of the *Code*, as in this case. However, as I have said, it is sufficient to deal with 213(*d*) in order to dispose of this appeal.

The historical development of s. 213

Although the concept of felony murder has a long history at common law, a brief review of the historical development of s. 213 indicates that its legitimacy is questionable.

In the early history of English criminal law, "murdrum", or murder, referred to a secret killing, or the killing of a Dane, or later a Norman, by an Englishman, and to the fine levied on the township where the killing occurred. By the early 14th century, the fines had been abandoned and murder had come to be the name used to describe the worst kind of homicide. The expression "malice aforethought" was subsequently adopted to distinguish murder from manslaughter, which denoted all culpable homicides other than murder. Malice aforethought was not limited to its natural and obvious sense of premeditation, but would be implied whenever the killing was intentional or reckless. In these instances, the malice was present and it is the premeditation which was implied by law.

Coke took this one step further and implied both the malice and the premeditation in cases where the death occurred in the commission of an unlawful act. He wrote in the Third Part of the Institutes of the Laws of England (1817), London, W. Clarke and Sons, at p. 56:

Unlawful. If the act be unlawful it is murder. As if A. meaning to steale a deere in the park of B., shooteth at the deer, and by the glance of the arrow killeth a boy that is hidden in a bush: this is murder, for that the act was unlawfull, although A. had no intent to hurt the boy, nor knew not of him. But if B. the owner of the park had shot at his own deer, and without any ill intent had killed the boy by the glance of his arrow, this had been homicide by misadventure and no felony.

So if one shoot at any wild fowle upon a tree, and the arrow killeth any reasonable creature afar off, without any evill intent in him, this is *per infortunium*: for it was not unlawfull to shoot at the wilde fowle: but if he had shot at a cock or hen, or any tame fowle of another mans, and the arrow by mischance had killed a man, this had been murder, for the act was unlawfull.

Coke's statement of the unlawful act murder rule has been much criticized. Stephen demonstrated that Coke's statement was not supported by the authorities cited: History of the Criminal Law of England (1883), vol. 3, pp. 57-58. Further, a recent author has suggested that Coke's statement was just "a slip of the quill" and that Coke intended to say that accidental killing by an unlawful act was manslaughter: see D. Lanham, "Felony Murder — Ancient and Modern" (1983), 7 Crim. L.J. 90, at pp. 92-94. Other 17th century writers (Dalton, Countrey Justice (1619), pp. 225-26, and Hale, History of the Pleas of the Crown (1736), vol. 1, at p. 475) and cases (*Chichester's Case* (1647), Aleyn 12, and *Hull's Case* (1664), Kel. 40) rejected the unlawful act murder rule as set out by Coke. Despite all of this, Coke's doctrine seems to have been accepted by the writers and the cases in the 18th century, and their only contribution was to limit it to killings in the course of felonies: see *R. v. Plummer* (1702), Kel. 109, 84 E.R. 1103 at 1107; Hawkins Pleas of the Crown (1716), vol. 1, c. 29, s. 11; *R. v. Woodburne* (1722), 16 St. Tr. 53; Foster, Crown Law (1762), p. 258; East, Pleas of the Crown (1803), vol. 1, at p. 255. Of course, at that time both the underlying felony and the murder were punishable by death, so the definition of a homicide in the course of a felony as a murder had little practical effect.

In the 19th century, the felony murder rule was accepted as part of the common law: see *Stephen's Digest of the Criminal Law*, 9th ed. (1950), art. 264(*c*). However, the rule was strongly criticized by Stephen, who labelled it "cruel" and "monstrous": *History of the Criminal Law*, vol. 3, p. 75.

Despite the rule's questionable origins and the subsequent criticisms, s. 175 of the *English Draft Code of 1879* included a restricted form of felony murder, which was subsequently adopted in the first *Canadian Criminal Code*, in 1892. Through subsequent amendments this provision has been widened, and it is now s. 213. It is more restricted than the common-law rule, in that it is limited to deaths occurring in the commission of certain enumerated offences and it requires that the accused have committed one of the acts set out in subss. (*a*) to (*d*).

Section 213 and its predecessors in the *Code* have long been subject to academic criticism: see J. Willis, Comment on *Rowe v. R.* (1951), 29 Can. Bar Rev. 784, at pp. 794-96; J. Ll. J. Edwards, "Constructive Murder in Canadian and English Law" (1961), 3 Cr. L.Q. 481, at pp. 506-509; A. Hooper, "Some

Anomalies and Developments in the Law of Homicide" (1967), 3 Univ. of B.C. L. Rev. 55, at pp. 75-77; P. Burns and R.S. Reid, "From Felony Murder to Accomplice Felony Attempted Murder: The Rake's Progress Compleat?" (1977), 55 Can. Bar Rev. 75, at pp. 103-105; G. Parker, *An Introduction to Criminal Law* (1977), pp. 145-48; D. Stuart, *Canadian Criminal Law: A Treatise* (1982), pp. 222-25; I. Grant and A.W. Mackay, "Constructive Murder and the Charter: In Search of Principle" (1987), 25 Alta. L. Rev. 129; cf. A.W. Mewett and M. Manning, Criminal Law, 2nd ed. (1985), p. 545. It has also been subject to judicial criticism. In *R. v. Farrant*, [1983] 1 S.C.R. 124, 32 C.R. (3d) 289, 4 C.C.C. (3d) 354, Dickson J. (as he then was) wrote that s. 213 seemed harsh (p. 130). In *R. v. Ancio*, [1984] 1 S.C.R. 225, 39 C.R. (3d) 1, 10 C.C.C. (3d) 385, dealing with the *mens rea* of attempted murder, McIntyre J. wrote at pp. 250-51 [S.C.R.]:

> It was argued, and it has been suggested in some of the cases and academic writings on the question, that it is illogical to insist upon a higher degree of *mens rea* for attempted murder, while accepting a lower degree amounting to recklessness for murder. I see no merit in this argument. The intent to kill is the highest intent in murder and there is no reason in logic why an attempt to murder, aimed at the completion of the full crime of murder, should have any lesser intent. *If there is any illogic in this matter, it is in the statutory characterization of unintentional killing as murder.* [Emphasis added.]

Finally, the Law Reform Commission of Canada criticized s. 213 in its working paper 33, Homicide (1984), at pp. 47-51, and excluded the notion of constructive murder from its *Draft Criminal Code* in its report 30, Recodifying Criminal Law (1986), s. 6(3), p. 54.

Felony murder in other jurisdictions

Felony murder is a peculiarly common-law concept which appears to be unknown outside a small circle of common-law jurisdictions, and it has not fared well in those jurisdictions. In the United Kingdom, where the rule originated, it was abolished by the *Homicide Act*, 1957 (5 & 6 Eliz. 2, c. 11). The rule is still quite widespread in the United States, though it is said to be in decline: R.W. Perkins and R.N. Boyce, *Criminal Law*, 3rd ed. (1982), p. 70. The rule has been abolished by statute or by the courts in several jurisdictions (see *People v. Aaron; People v. Thompson; People v. Wright*, 299 N.W. 2d 304, 409 Mich. 672, 13 A.L.R. 4th 1180 (S.C. 1980), and *State v. Doucette*, 470 A. 2d 676 (S.C. Vt., 1983)), and it has been downgraded to manslaughter in others. In addition, the courts and the legislatures have limited the scope of the common-law rule by limiting the felonies to which it is applicable, requiring some degree of *mens rea* with respect to the death, establishing affirmative defences or limiting the punishments available. The rule also exists in New Zealand and certain Australian states, but it is narrower, and abolition has been recommended in some jurisdictions.

Section 213(d) and the Charter

This appeal calls into play two principles of fundamental justice.

The First Principle: The essential elements of certain crimes and s. 7 of the *Charter*

Prior to the enactment of the *Charter*, Parliament had full legislative power with respect to "The Criminal Law" (*Constitution Act, 1867*, s. 91(27)), including the determination of the essential elements of any given crime. It could prohibit any act and impose any penal consequences for infringing the prohibition, provided only that the prohibition served "a public purpose which can support it as being in relation to criminal law": *Ref. re S. 5(a) of the Dairy Indust. Act*, [1949] S.C.R. 1 at 50, affirmed (sub nom. *Cdn. Fed. of Agriculture v. Can. (A.G.)*) [1951] A.C. 179 (P.C.). Once the legislation was found to have met this test, the courts had very little power to review the substance of the legislation. For example, in *R. v. Sault Ste. Marie (City)*, [1978] 2 S.C.R. 1299, 3 C.R. (3d) 30, 40 C.C.C. (2d) 353 [Ont.], Dickson J. (as he then was) held that, when an offence was criminal in the true sense, there was a presumption that the prosecution must prove the *mens rea*. However, it was always open to Parliament expressly to relieve the prosecution of its obligation to prove any part of the *mens rea*, as it is said to have done in s. 213 of the *Criminal Code* with respect to the foreseeability of the death of the victim. It is thus clear that, prior to the enactment of the *Charter*, the validity of s. 213 could not have been successfully challenged.

However, federal and provincial legislatures have chosen to restrict through the *Charter* this power with respect to criminal law. Under s. 7, if a conviction, given either the stigma attached to the offence or the available penalties, will result in a deprivation of the life, liberty or security of the person of the accused, then Parliament must respect the principles of fundamental justice. It has been argued that the principles of fundamental justice in s. 7 are only procedural guarantees. However, in *Ref. re S. 94(2) of Motor Vehicle Act*, [1985] 2 S.C.R. 486, 48 C.R. (3d) 289, 23 C.C.C. (3d) 289, this court rejected that argument and used s. 7 to review the substance of the legislation. As a result, while Parliament retains the power to define the elements of a crime, the courts now have the jurisdiction and, more important, the duty, when called upon to do so, to review that definition to ensure that it is in accordance with the principles of fundamental justice.

This court's decision in *Re Motor Vehicle Act* stands for the proposition that absolute liability infringes the principles of fundamental justice, such that the combination of absolute liability and a deprivation of life, liberty or security of the person is a restriction on one's rights under s. 7 and is *prima facie* a violation thereof. In effect, *Re Motor Vehicle Act* acknowledges that, whenever the state resorts to the restriction of liberty, such as imprisonment, to assist in the enforcement of a law, even, as in *Re Motor Vehicle Act*, a mere provincial regulatory offence, there is, as a principle of fundamental justice, a minimum mental state which is an essential element of the offence. It thus elevated *mens rea* from a presumed element in *Sault Ste. Marie, supra*, to a constitutionally-required element. *Re Motor Vehicle Act* did not decide what level of *mens rea* was constitutionally required for each type of offence, but inferentially decided that even for a mere provincial regulatory offence *at least* negligence was required, in that *at least* a defence of due diligence must *always* be open to an accused who risks imprisonment upon conviction. In *Sault Ste. Marie*, Dickson J. stated at pp. 1309-10:

> Where the offence is criminal, the Crown must establish a mental element, namely, that the accused who committed the prohibited act did so intentionally or recklessly, with knowledge of the facts constituting the offence, or with wilful blindness toward them. Mere negligence is excluded from the concept of the mental element required for conviction. Within the context of a criminal prosecution a person who fails to make such enquiries as a reasonable and prudent person would make, or who fails to know facts he should have known, is innocent in the eyes of the law.

It may well be that, as a general rule, the principles of fundamental justice require proof of a subjective *mens rea* with respect to the prohibited act, in order to avoid punishing the "morally innocent". It must be remembered, however, that Dickson J. was dealing with the *mens rea* to be presumed in the absence of an express legislative disposition, and not the *mens rea* to be required in all legislation providing for a restriction on the accused's life, liberty or security of the person. In any event, this case involves criminal liability for the result of an intentional criminal act, and it is arguable that different considerations should apply to the mental element required with respect to that result. There are many provisions in the *Code* requiring only objective foreseeability of the result or even only a causal link between the act and the result. As I would prefer not to cast doubt on the validity of such provisions *in this case*, I will assume, but only for the purposes of this appeal, that something less than subjective foresight of the result may sometimes suffice for the imposition of criminal liability for causing that result through intentional criminal conduct.

But, whatever the minimum *mens rea* for the act or the result may be, there are, though very few in number, certain crimes where, because of the special nature of the stigma attached to a conviction therefor or the available penalties, the principles of fundamental justice require a *mens rea* reflecting the particular nature of that crime. Such is theft, where, in my view, a conviction requires proof of some dishonesty. Murder is another such offence. The punishment for murder is the most severe in our society, and the stigma that attaches to a conviction for murder is similarly extreme. In addition, murder is distinguished from manslaughter only by the mental element with respect to the death. It is thus clear that there must be some special mental element with respect to the death before a culpable homicide can be treated as a murder. That special mental element gives rise to the moral blameworthiness which justifies the stigma and sentence attached to a murder conviction. I am presently of the view that it is a principle of fundamental justice that a conviction for murder cannot rest on anything less than proof beyond a reasonable doubt of subjective foresight. Given the effect of this view on part of s. 212(*c*), for the reasons I have already given for deciding this case more narrowly, I need not and will not rest my finding that s. 213(*d*) violates the *Charter* on this view, because s. 213(*d*) does not, for reasons I will set out hereinafter, even meet the lower threshold test of objective foreseeability. I will therefore, for the sole purpose of this appeal, go no further than to say that it is a principle of fundamental justice that, absent proof beyond a reasonable doubt of at least objective foreseeability, there surely cannot be a murder conviction.

Section 1

Finding that s. 213 of the *Criminal Code* infringes ss. 7 and 11(*d*) of the *Charter* does not end the inquiry on the constitutional validity of s. 213. Any or all of subss. (*a*) to (*d*) of s. 213 can still be upheld as a reasonable limit "demonstrably justified in a free and democratic society" under s. 1 of the *Charter*.

In this case and at this stage of the inquiry, we need only consider subs. (*d*) of s. 213. The criteria to be assessed under s. 1 have been set out by this court in several cases, particularly *R. v. Big M Drug Mart Ltd.*, [1985] 1 S.C.R. 295, 18 C.C.C. (3d) 385, and *R. v. Oakes, supra*. First, the objective which the measures are designed to serve must be "of sufficient importance to warrant overriding a constitutionally protected right or freedom": *Big M Drug Mart*, at p. 352 [S.C.R.]. Through s. 213(*d*) of the *Code*, Parliament intended to deter the use or carrying of a weapon in the commission of certain offences, because of the increased risk of death. In my view, it is clear that this objective is sufficiently important.

In addition, the measures adopted must be reasonable and demonstrably justified. The measures adopted appear to be rationally connected to the objective: indiscriminately punishing for murder all those who cause a death by using or carrying a weapon, whether the death was intentional or accidental, might well be thought to discourage the use and the carrying of weapons. I believe, however, that the measures adopted would unduly impair the rights and freedoms in question: see *Big M Drug Mart* at p. 352 [S.C.R.]. It is not necessary to convict of murder persons who did not intend to foresee the death and who could not even have foreseen the death in order to deter others from using or carrying weapons. If Parliament wishes to deter the use or carrying of weapons, it should punish the use or carrying of weapons. A good example of this is the minimum imprisonment for using a firearm in the commission of an indictable offence under s. 83 of the *Criminal Code*. In any event, the conviction for manslaughter which would result instead of a conviction for murder is punishable by from a day in jail to confinement for life in a penitentiary. Very stiff sentences when weapons are involved in the commission of the crime of manslaughter would sufficiently deter the use or carrying of weapons in the commission of crimes. But stigmatizing the crime as murder unnecessarily impairs the *Charter* right.

In my view, therefore, s. 213(*d*) is not saved by s. 1.

CONCLUSION

As a result of the foregoing, I would answer the first constitutional question in the affirmative, as s. 213(*d*) violates both s. 7 and s. 11(*d*) of the *Charter*, and I would declare s. 213(*d*) of the *Criminal Code* to be of no force or effect. I would, for the reasons which I have given, decline to answer the second constitutional question. It follows that the appeal must be allowed, the appellant's conviction for murder set aside, and a new trial ordered.

Short concurring opinions of three justices and the dissenting opinion of McIntyre J. are here omitted.

For views on *Vaillancourt*, see the Criminal Reports Forum in (1988), 60 C.R. (3d) 332-345. See also Stuart, "Progress on the Constitutional Requirement of Fault" (1988), 64 C.R. (3d) 352.

In *Martineau* Lamer C.J. went further, finding a majority for the view that under s. 7 of the *Charter* objective foresight is not enough to establish murder. There must be subjective foresight of the likelihood of death.

R. v. MARTINEAU

[1990] 2 S.C.R. 633, 79 C.R. (3d) 129, 58 C.C.C. (3d) 353,
1990 CarswellAlta 143, 1990 CarswellAlta 657

The accused and a companion, armed with a pellet pistol and a rifle respectively, set out to commit a crime. The accused testified that he thought it would only be a break and enter. They forced their way into a trailer and tied up two of its occupants, James and Ann McLean. The companion shot and killed the two people after robbing them and their home. The accused testified that as soon as he heard the first shot, he realized that James McLean had been shot. He testified that he then said or thought, , say your prayers". As they left, the accused asked his companion why he killed them and the companion answered "They saw our faces". The accused responded "But they couldn't see mine 'cause I had a mask on". The accused was convicted of second degree murder. The trial judge charged the jury on s. 213(*a*) and (*d*) (now s. 230(*a*) and (*d*)) and on s. 21(1) and (2) of the *Criminal Code*. The Court of Appeal held that s. 213(*a*) was inconsistent with ss. 7 and 11(*d*) of the *Charter* for reasons given in *R. v. Vaillancourt* and that it was not saved by s. 1 of the *Charter*. The court ordered a new trial and the Crown appealed.

Per LAMER C.J.C. (DICKSON C.J.C. and WILSON, GONTHIER and CORY JJ. concurring): —

This is the first of a series of appeals that raises the constitutionality of s. 213(*a*) of the *Criminal Code*, R.S.C. 1970, c. C-34, (now s. 230(*a*), *Criminal Code*, R.S.C., 1985, c. C-46).

. . . .

In *Vaillancourt* I analyzed a number of matters, including s. 213 of the *Code* in the context of the other murder provisions, the historical development of s. 213, felony murder provisions in other jurisdictions, the essential elements of certain crimes at common law, and the principles of fundamental justice under the *Charter* and their application to s. 213 of the *Code*. As a result of this analysis I concluded that objective foreseeability of death was the minimum threshold test before a conviction for murder could be sustained. I went on to state, however, that it was my view that the principles of fundamental justice require more; they demand that a conviction for murder requires proof beyond a reasonable doubt of subjective foresight of death. The Chief Justice, Estey and Wilson JJ. agreed with that position. I am still of that view today, and indeed, while I agree with the Alberta Court of Appeal and could dispose of this appeal on the basis of objective foreseeability, it is on the basis of the principle of subjective foresight of death that I choose to dispose of this appeal. I choose this route because I would not want this case, a very serious matter, to return to this court once again on the grounds that there is some doubt as to the validity of the portion of s. 212(*c*) of the *Code* that allows for a conviction for murder if the accused "ought to know" that death is likely to result. I need not, therefore, repeat the analysis from *Vaillancourt* here, except to add some brief observations as regards s. 213(*a*) and the principle of fundamental justice that subjective foresight of death is required before a conviction for murder can be sustained.

Section 213(*a*) of the *Code* defines culpable homicide as murder where a person causes the death of a human being while committing or attempting to commit a range of listed offences, whether or not the person means to cause death or whether or not he or she knows that death is likely to ensue if that person means to cause bodily harm for the purpose of facilitating the commission of the offence or flight after committing or attempting to commit the offence. The introductory paragraph of the section, therefore, expressly removes from the Crown the burden of proving beyond a reasonable doubt that the accused had subjective foresight of death. This section stands as an anomaly as regards the other murder provisions, especially in light of the common-law presumption against convicting a person of a true crime without proof of intent or recklessness: *R. v. Sault Ste. Marie (City)*, [1978] 2 S.C.R. 1299 at 1309-10, 3 C.R. (3d) 30, 40 C.C.C. (2d) 353, [Ont.], per Dickson J., (as he then was).

A conviction for murder carries with it the most severe stigma and punishment of any crime in our society. The principles of fundamental justice require, because of the special nature of the stigma attached to a conviction for murder, and the available penalties, a *mens rea* reflecting the particular nature of that crime. The effect of s. 213 is to violate the principle that punishment must be proportionate to the moral blameworthiness of the offender, or as Professor Hart puts it in *Punishment and Responsibility* (1968), at p. 162, the fundamental principle of a morally based system of law that those causing harm intentionally be punished more severely than those causing harm unintentionally. The rationale underlying the principle that subjective foresight of death is required before a person is labelled and punished as a murderer is linked to the more general principle that criminal liability for a particular result is not justified except where the actor possesses a culpable mental state in respect of that result: see *R. v. Bernard*, [1988] 2 S.C.R. 833, 67 C.R. (3d) 113, 45 C.C.C. (3d) 1, per McIntyre J.; and *R. v. Buzzanga* (1979), 49 C.C.C. (2d) 369 (C.A.), per Martin J.A. In my view, in a free and democratic society that values the autonomy and free will of the individual, the stigma and punishment attaching to the most serious of crimes, murder, should be reserved for those who choose to intentionally cause death or who choose to inflict bodily harm that they know is likely to cause death. The essential role of requiring subjective foresight of death in the context of murder is to maintain a proportionality between the stigma and punishment attached to a murder conviction and the moral blameworthiness of the offender. Murder has long been recognized as the "worst" and most heinous of peace time crimes. It is, therefore, essential that to satisfy the principles of fundamental justice, the stigma and punishment attaching to a murder conviction must be reserved for those who either intend to cause death or who intend to cause bodily harm that they know will likely cause death. In this regard, I refer to the following works as support for my position, in addition to those cited in *Vaillancourt*: Cross, "The Mental Element in Crime" (1967), 83 L.Q. Rev. 215; Ashworth, "The Elasticity of *Mens Rea*" in Crime, Proof and Punishment (1981); Williams, The Mental Element in Crime (1965); and Williams, "Convictions and Fair Labelling" [1983] 42 C.L.J. 85.

In sum then, I am of the view that a special mental element with respect to death is necessary before a culpable homicide can be treated as murder. That special mental element gives rise to the moral blameworthiness that justifies the stigma and punishment attaching to a murder conviction. For all the foregoing reasons, and for the reasons stated in *Vaillancourt*, I conclude that it is a principle of fundamental justice that a conviction for murder cannot rest on anything less than proof beyond a reasonable doubt of subjective foresight of death. That was my position when *Vaillancourt* was decided, and that is my position today. Therefore, since s. 213 of the *Code* expressly eliminates the requirement for proof of subjective foresight, it infringes ss. 7 and 11(*d*) of the *Charter*.

As regards s. 1 of the *Charter*, there is no doubt that the objective of deterring the infliction of bodily harm during the commission of certain offences because of the increased risk of death is of sufficient importance to warrant overriding a *Charter* right. Further, indiscriminately punishing for murder all those who cause death irrespective of whether they intended to cause death might well be thought to discourage the infliction of bodily harm during the commission of certain offences because of the increased risk of death. But it is not necessary in order to achieve this objective to convict of murder persons who do not intend or foresee the death. In this regard the section unduly impairs the *Charter* rights. If Parliament wishes to deter persons from causing bodily harm during certain offences, then it should punish persons for causing the bodily harm. Indeed, the conviction for manslaughter that would result instead of a conviction for murder is punishable by, from a day in jail, to confinement for life. Very stiff sentences for the infliction of bodily harm leading to death in appropriate cases would sufficiently meet any deterrence objective that Parliament might have in mind. The more flexible sentencing scheme under a conviction for manslaughter is in accord with the principle that punishment be meted out with regard to the level of moral blameworthiness of the offender. To label and punish a person as a murderer who did not intend or foresee death unnecessarily stigmatizes and punishes those whose moral blameworthiness is not that of a murderer, and thereby unnecessarily impairs the rights guaranteed by ss. 7 and 11(*d*) of the *Charter*. In my view then, s. 213(*a*), indeed all of s. 213, cannot be saved by s. 1 of the *Charter*.

The fact that I have based my reasons on the principle of subjective foresight casts serious if not fatal doubt on the constitutionality of part of s. 212(*c*) of the *Code*, specifically the words "ought to know is likely to cause death". The validity of s. 212(*c*) of the *Code* has not been directly attacked in this appeal, but the court has had the benefit of hearing argument from the Attorney General of Canada and from the Attorneys General for Alberta, British Columbia, Ontario, Quebec, and Manitoba, who chose to intervene, on the issue of whether subjective foresight or objective foreseeability of death is the constitutionally required minimum *mens rea* for murder. In my view, subjective foresight of death must be proven beyond a reasonable doubt before a conviction for murder can be sustained, and as a result, it is obvious the part of s. 212(*c*) of the *Code* allowing for a conviction upon proof that the accused ought to have known that death was likely to result violates ss. 7 and 11(*d*) of the *Charter*. I find further support for this view in the following passage from Professor Stuart's treatise *Canadian Criminal Law: A Treatise*, at pp. 217-18, dealing specifically with the objective element of s. 212(*c*) of the *Code* and the principle of subjective foresight:

> This is a clear instance where our legislation has not kept up with developments in other jurisdictions. We have seen that a similar objective test for murder resorted to by the House of Lords in the notorious decision in *Director of Public Prosecutions v. Smith* (1960) [[1961]

A.C. 290 (H.L.)] was rejected by the British Legislature and by the Australian High Court. Very few jurisdictions, including those in the United States, resort to anything but the subjective approach in defining murder. The only direct parallels to our section 212(c) are to be found in the codes of Queensland, Tasmania, and New Zealand. The wording in these provisions is almost identical to ours except that in New Zealand the words "or ought to have known" were deleted as a result of a quick and firm rejection of *Smith*. The New Zealand section now reads in part:

> . . . if the offender for any unlawful object does an act that he knows to be likely to cause death, and thereby kills any person, though he may have desired that his object should be effected without hurting anyone.

Indeed, Lord Goff in his article "The Mental Element in the Crime of Murder" (1988), 104 L.Q. Rev. 30, at p. 36, had this to say about the *Smith* decision and about objective foreseeability as a test for murder:

> This decision was very much criticised, by Judge and jurist alike. What they disliked about it was that it imposed an objective instead of a subjective test for ascertaining the existence of the relevant mental element for the crime of murder. In due course, it was reversed by statute; later, on an appeal from a jurisdiction where that statute did not apply at the relevant time, *Smith* was, in effect, held by the Judicial Committee of the Privy Council to have been wrongly decided (see *Frankland and Moore v. R.*), [[1987] 2 W.L.R. 1251]). *So the objective test was never part of the common law, properly understood; and we can now forget about it.* [Emphasis added.]

Although it would be open to save that part of s. 212(c) under s. 1 of the *Charter*, it seems to me that the attempt would fail for the reasons I have given in respect of the attempt to similarly save s. 213 of the *Code*. I would therefore answer the constitutional questions as follows:

> Q: Does s. 213(a) of the *Criminal Code* infringe or deny the rights or freedoms guaranteed by s. 7 and/or s. 11(d) of the *Canadian Charter of Rights and Freedoms*?

> A: Yes, the section infringes both ss. 7 and 11(d) of the *Charter*.

> Q: If the answer to question 1 is affirmative, is s. 213(a) justified by s. 1 of the *Canadian Charter of Rights and Freedoms*, and therefore not inconsistent with the *Constitution Act, 1982*?

> A: No.

The only remaining issue is the potential application of s. 613(1)(b)(iii) of the *Criminal Code*. The Court of Appeal for Alberta declined to invoke the section and enter a conviction for the following reason, at p. 279:

> The jury in this case was not instructed on any portion of s. 212. I am unable to say that a properly instructed jury must necessarily have found that the appellant had, at some point, the requisite intention under that section rather than being carried along by events.

I agree. In the present case, the respondent was convicted pursuant to a combination of ss. 213 and 21 of the *Code*. Since in this case the jury was left only with s. 213 which has been declared to be inoperative, a new trial must be ordered. Accordingly, the Court of Appeals decision quashing the convictions and directing a new trial is affirmed. The appeal is, therefore, dismissed.

L'HEUREUX-DUBÉ J. (dissenting): —

. . . .

My colleague concludes that s. 213(*a*) is unconstitutional because it violates ss. 7 and 11(*d*) of the *Charter* and cannot be saved by s. 1. In his opinion, the principles of fundamental justice demand that subjective foresight of death be proven beyond a reasonable doubt before a conviction for murder can be secured. I reach a contrary conclusion on the basis that subjective foresight is not the only appropriate standard that can be applied to conform to ss. 7 and 11(*d*) of the *Charter*. My reasons are as follows: the test of objective foreseeability of death for the crime of murder does not offend the principles of fundamental justice; this Court's decisions, including *R. v. Vaillancourt*, [1987] 2 S.C.R. 636, 60 C.R. (3d) 289, 39 C.C.C. (3d) 118 [Que.], do not commend such a result; the exclusive standard of subjective foresight of death for the crime of murder has found no parallel in other common law jurisdictions; and there are significant policy considerations in favour of upholding the existing legislation.

. . . .

The above analysis indicates that tests of subjective foresight and objective foreseeability cannot be seen as static or distinct concepts. They are certainly not mutually exclusive. In most instances, and certainly in those limited circumstances delineated by s. 213(*a*), discussed below, death will be both objectively and subjectively foreseeable. There is a profound interrelationship between the two, especially when dealing with a crime committed during the execution of a predicate crime. The validity of a provision should not be evaluated on a strict "either-or" approach, and a fastidious adherence to prescribed labels becomes particularly obdurate when gauging the constitutionality of Parliamentary legislation.

. . . .

Vaillancourt held that s. 213(*d*) of the *Criminal Code* violated ss. 7 and 11(*d*) of the *Canadian Charter of Rights and Freedoms*, and could not be saved by s. 1. Paragraph 213(*a*) of the *Criminal Code* is completely different — in its historical development, in its consistency with the objective foreseeability of death test established in *Vaillancourt*, and in the parallel provisions adopted in other common law jurisdictions.

. . . .

(b)   *Section 213(a) Passes the Objective Foreseeability Test*

An exacting combination of factors *must* be proven, all beyond a reasonable doubt, before the accused can be found guilty of murder under this paragraph. The offender must:

(1) cause the death by means of the commission of a "culpable homicide";

(2) cause the death while committing or attempting to commit one of a limited number of very serious crimes all of which are, by their very nature, inherently dangerous;

(3) intentionally inflict bodily harm while committing one of these inherently dangerous offences, all of which are specific intent crimes;

(4) inflict the bodily harm purposefully in order to perpetrate the dangerous underlying crime or for the purpose of facilitating his flight; and

(5) the death must ensue from the bodily harm intentionally inflicted.

It should be noted that in the present case the underlying offence was committed, and the intent to inflict bodily harm was clear. Moreover, this amalgamation of indispensable prerequisites establishes that this crime, as phrased by Lamer J. in *Vaillancourt* is "tantamount to one which has objective foreseeability as an essential element, and, if objective foreseeability is sufficient, then it would not be in violation of s. 7 or s. 11(*d*) in doing so in that way". I am of the view that in light of these requirements, the test of objective foreseeability is sufficient, and that if that test has been met, then no *Charter* violation has taken place. The above list requires that the accused specifically intend to, and actually commit the underlying offence, and specifically intend to, and actually inflict bodily harm. In my view, the inexorable conclusion is that the resulting death is objectively foreseeable.

Those who are critical of all forms of the "felony-murder" rule base their denunciation on the premise that *mens rea* is the exclusive determinant of the level of "stigma" that is properly applied to an offender. This appears to me to confuse some very fundamental principles of criminal law and ignores the pivotal contribution of *actus reus* to the definition and appropriate response to proscribed criminal offences. If both components, *actus reus* as well as *mens rea*, are not considered when assessing the level of fault attributable to an offender, we would see manslaughter and assault causing bodily harm as no more worthy of condemnation than an assault. Mere attempts would become as serious as full offences. The whole correlation between the consequences of a criminal act and its retributive repercussions would become obscured by a stringent and exclusive examination of the accused's own asserted intentions.

As stated in Crump and Crump, "In Defense of the Felony Murder Doctrine" (1985), 8 Harv. J. of L. and P.P. 359, at p. 366:

Scholarly criticisms of felony murder have tended to neglect its relationship to proportionality and grading. The criticisms erroneously tend to regard *mens rea* as the only legitimate determinant of the grade of a homicide resulting from a felony. This reasoning sometimes leads modern writers into the same rigid formalism, divorced from policy, that they rightly reject in historical justifications of the rule. *Mens rea is not a "unified field theory" of homicide, and while such a theory might make the subject artificially "logical" or "consistent", it does not reflect our society's more complex understanding of the nature, function, and purpose of the criminal law. The fallacy of this approach is its denigration of actus reus and its failure to include the result of defendant's conduct as a determinant of just disposition.* [Emphasis added.]

. . . .

(c)   *A Comparative Analysis*

This sudden introduction of a subjective foresight standard for the crime of murder is most novel, and finds no parallel in Great Britain, Australia, New Zealand or the United States. While each of these jurisdictions imposes different requirements for the crime of murder, none has adopted the requirement of subjective foresight of death.

. . . .

IV. POLICY CONSIDERATIONS

During the 27-year period from 1961-87, the evidence reveals that 2,177 homicide offences occurred during the commission of another criminal act. The percentage of homicide offences committed during the commission of another criminal act has varied from 11.9 percent in 1965 to 28.4 percent in 1970. The annual average for the period was 16.7 percent. "Homicide in Canada: Offences Committed During the Commission of Another Criminal Act", statistics provided by R.C.M.P. for the period 1961-87. The homicide offences committed during another criminal act are divided into four categories:

Robbery: includes robbery, theft, and break and enter offences. 1315 victims; 61.7 percent of all homicide offences committed during another criminal act.

Sexual Assault & Rape: includes all sexual attacks on either males or females. 483 victims; 22.3 percent of all homicide offences committed during another criminal act.

Escape: involves attempts to escape from correctional institutions or lawful custody, to avoid arrest, or to escape detection as a parole or probation violator. 346 victims; 14.2 percent of all homicide offences committed during another criminal act.

Other: includes other types of criminal acts such as arson, assault, kidnapping, etc. 33 victims; 1.8 percent of all homicide offences committed during another criminal act.

These statistics reflect a matter of critical public concern, and sustain the Legislature's compulsion to deliver an appropriate response. It is constitutionally permissible under the *Canadian Charter of Rights and Freedoms* to define the mental element required for murder with reference to an intention by the perpetrator to harm or injure the victim, with death resulting. How that harm or injury is to be defined, and what level of harm or injury is required are matters for Parliament to consider and decide.

· · · ·

The fact that the principles embraced by s. 213(*a*) have existed for over 300 years is in itself relevant, though not necessarily determinative, of whether or not a rule of "fundamental justice" has been breached by virtue of their adoption by the Parliament of Canada. In my view, while the guarantee entrenched in s. 7 of the *Charter* is to have broad application, it cannot go so far as to grant the courts judicial licence to modify or strike down legislation in the absence of a constitutional violation.

· · · ·

Section 213(*a*) is intended to carve out certain killings and place them in a category of the most serious culpable homicides, murder. This is a designation which Parliament is entitled to ascribe pursuant to its responsibility for the protection of those under its dominion. This legislative objective can be anchored in Parliament's legitimate attempt to deter persons from conduct which falls within s. 213(*a*). In particular, Parliament is attempting to deter those who commit crimes from intentionally inflicting actual bodily harm on their victims in order to achieve their unlawful purpose. The killings subsumed within s. 213(*a*) are regarded as sufficiently heinous to warrant being placed in the category of the gravest culpable homicides. Parliament felt that this was the appropriate manner to ensure that the criminal law is in accordance with social values as to the gravity of such killings, and that this was an effective method to preserve the lives and safety of Canadians.

In *R. v. Arkell* (1988), 43 C.C.C. (3d) 402, 64 C.R. (3d) 340 (B.C. C.A.), affirmed 79 C.R. (3d) 207, 59 C.C.C. (3d) 65, [1990] 2 S.C.R. 695, at pp. 412-13, McLachlin J.A. (now of this court) considered the validity of s. 214(5) (now s. 231(5)). Writing for the British Columbia Court of Appeal – this court's decision in *Arkell* is being rendered concurrently with the present one – she held that:

> ... it must be recognized that many factors other than the accused's degree of moral blameworthiness must be considered by Parliament in establishing a sentencing scheme. General deterrence, the degree of perceived danger to the public and the prevalence of certain types of offences are only some of the other considerations which Parliament may properly consider. It follows that the mere fact that a harsher sentence may be imposed for one offence

than for another offence which is arguably more blameworthy, does not mean that the scheme that permits the sentence violates s. 7 of the *Charter*.

. . . .

Many factors enter into the determination of an appropriate penalty for a particular offence; the degree of blameworthiness is only one. *The question is one of policy, to be determined by Parliament. So long as Parliament does not act irrationally or arbitrarily or in a manner otherwise inconsistent with the fundamental principles of justice, its choice must be upheld.* [Emphasis added.]

I agree completely, and find that the test applies to s. 213(a) as well. If Parliament chooses to label a crime "murder" and attach commensurate penalties, so long as a *mens rea* requirement is imposed, as it is here, this court should not lightly interfere with that legislative decision. Mewett & Manning, writing before this court's decision in *Vaillancourt*, acknowledged at pp. 544-45 that:

Section 213 [now section 230] and the concept of constructive murder have been much criticized and, in fact, abolished in many jurisdictions. The criticism is that it imposes liability for murder in situations where death was not intended nor even, in some cases, foreseen. *But murder is a legal concept; it does not have to be defined in terms of intentional killing, and even under s. 212 [now s. 229] the definition is not this narrow. The policy behind s. 213 is to put the risk of killing a victim during the course of the commission of certain offences upon the offender to a higher degree than if it were merely classified as manslaughter.* In any case, with the present distinction between murder punishable by death and murder punishable by life imprisonment now abolished, much of the criticism loses its force. It was the thought of someone being executed for a non-intended homicide that led to the feeling that the definition of murder should somehow be limited to the old common law concept of "murder with malice aforethought". [Emphasis added.]

Parliament can abrogate s. 213 in its entirety and pioneer a strict subjective standard for the crime of murder, but the Constitution does not require that it do so. As McIntyre J. said, dissenting in *Vaillancourt*, at p. 663:

The principal complaint in this case is not that the accused should not have been convicted of a serious crime deserving of severe punishment, but simply that Parliament should not have chosen to call that crime "murder". No objection could be taken if Parliament classified the offence as manslaughter or a killing during the commission of an offence, or in some other manner. . . While it may be illogical to characterize an unintentional killing as murder, *no principle of fundamental justice is offended only because serious criminal conduct, involving the commission of a crime of violence resulting in the killing of a human being, is classified as murder and not in some other manner.* [Emphasis added.]

In *R. v. Smith*, [1987] 1 S.C.R. 1045, 34 C.C.C. (3d) 97, 58 C.R. (3d) 193, Lamer J. cited numerous examples of curial deference to Parliamentary enactments. My colleague then adopted, at p. 1070, the following passage of Borins Dist. Ct. J. from *R. v. Guiller*, Ont. Dist. Ct., Sept. 23, 1985, unreported:

It is not for the court to pass on the wisdom of Parliament with respect to the gravity of various offences and the range of penalties which may be imposed upon those found guilty of committing the offences. *Parliament has broad discretion in proscribing conduct as criminal and in determining proper punishment.* While the final judgment as to whether a punishment exceeds constitutional limits set by the *Charter* is properly a judicial function the court should be reluctant to interfere with the considered views of Parliament and then only in the clearest of cases where the punishment prescribed is so excessive when compared with the punishment prescribed for other offences as to outrage standards of decency. [Emphasis added.]

In the present appeal, my colleague's justification for insisting on the narrowest of all possible definitions for the crime of murder is that [pp. 106-107]:

> A conviction for murder carries with it the most severe stigma and punishment of any crime in our society. . . . [and] should be reserved for those who choose to intentionally cause death or who choose to inflict bodily harm that they know is likely to cause death.

The menacing component of "stigma" was discussed in *Vaillancourt* as well. As Lindsay pointed out in "The Implications of *R. v. Vaillancourt*: Much Ado About Nothing?" (1989), 47 U. of Toronto Fac. L. Rev. 465, at p. 472:

> It should also be noted that Lamer J. justified a requirement of a "special mental element" based on *either* the stigma associated with a crime or the penalties available. A murder conviction qualified on both grounds. However, theft can involve penalties as low as an absolute discharge. *Thus, the inclusion of theft in Lamer J.'s list of crimes requiring a "special mental element" must have been based on stigma rather than available penalties.* [Emphasis added.]

I find this concentration on social "stigma" to be overemphasized, and in the great majority of cases, completely inapplicable. The facts in the present appeals reveal the truly heinous nature of the criminal acts at issue. The concern that these offenders not endure the Mark of Cain is, in my view, an egregious example of misplaced compassion. If the apprehension is that the offenders in question will suffer from their "murderer" label, I suspect they will fare little better tagged as "manslaughterers". Accidental killings cannot, after *Vaillancourt*, result in murder prosecutions. Only killings resulting from circumstances in which death is, at a minimum, objectively foreseeable will be prosecuted under s. 213(*a*). Furthermore, the duration of imprisonment, if at all different, will not attenuate the "stigma". To the extent that any such "stigma" can be said to exist, it is at least as palpable upon release to the outside world as it is within the prison environment itself.

. . . .

Section 213(*a*) does not deal with accidental killings, but rather with killings that are objectively foreseeable as a result of the abominable nature of the predicate crimes, committed with specific intent, coupled with the intentional infliction of bodily harm. Given the dual subjective requirement already in place, the deterrence factor is most cogent in these circumstances. Whatever the competing arguments may be with respect to deterring the merely negligent, here we are dealing with those who have already expressly acted with the intent to commit at least two underlying serious crimes. If deterrence is to ever have any application to the criminal law, and in my view it should, this is the place.

Deterrence can neither be analyzed in the abstract nor in isolation from the context of the provision in question. Section 213(a) deals with one who has already proven to be a "hijacker", a "kidnapper", a "rapist", or an "arsonist". Furthermore, this person has already proven willing to cause bodily harm to commit the offence or to enable himself to escape after having committed the offence. In these circumstances, it is certainly appropriate for Parliament to put this person on notice, that if these purposeful acts result in death, you will be charged as a "murderer" as well.

This notion of Parliamentary autonomy cannot be displaced unless a *Charter* violation has occurred. In my view that has not taken place here. Repeating my colleagues own test, as articulated in *Vaillancourt* at p. 657, if the legislation is "tantamount to one which has objective foreseeability as an essential element, and, if objective foreseeability is sufficient, then it would not be in violation of s. 7 or s. 11(d) in doing so in that way."

V. Conclusion

Policy considerations in Canada as well as in other jurisdictions have inspired legislation that considers objective foreseeability sufficient as the minimum *mens rea* requirement for murder. While it may not be the very best test for all cases, it is certainly a constitutionally valid one. Parliament did not have to enact s. 213(a), but that is not the question before this court. The issue is whether it could. In my view, the answer rests on what level of foreseeability will be required before a conviction for murder can be returned. Based on this court's precedents, and the principles of fundamental justice, I believe that the objective foreseeability of death test for the crime of murder is constitutionally valid. The additional mandatory elements demanded by s. 213(a) lend even greater force to this conclusion.

Striking down the legislation simply because some other scheme may be preferable would be an unwarranted intrusion into Parliament's prerogative, and would undermine the means it has chosen to protect its citizens. The *Charter* is not designed to allow this court to substitute preferable provisions for those already in place in the absence of a clear constitutional violation. Such a task should be reserved for the Law Reform Commission or other advisory bodies. This court's province is to pronounce upon the constitutionality of those provisions properly before it. The *Charter* does not infuse the courts with the power to declare legislation to be of no force or effect on the basis that they believe the statute to be undesirable as a matter of criminal law policy. For the aforementioned reasons, I do not believe that s. 213(a) offends the *Canadian Charter of Rights and Freedoms*.

. . . .

SOPINKA J. (concurring in the result): — I have had the advantage of reading the reasons of Lamer C.J.C. and L'Heureux-Dubé J. [appeal from (1988), 43 C.C.C. (3d) 417]. I agree with Lamer C.J.C. that there must be a new trial in this case. I would give the same answers to the constitutional questions as Lamer C.J.C. but, with respect, I cannot agree with his reasons.

In my view, the issue of subjective foresight of death should be addressed only if it is necessary to do so in order to decide this case or if there is an overriding reason making it desirable to do so. Overbroad statements of principle are inimical to the tradition of incremental development of the common law. Likewise, the development of law under the *Canadian Charter of Rights and Freedoms* is best served by deciding cases before the courts, not by anticipating the results of future cases.

The first inquiry is whether ruling on the issue of subjective foresight is necessary for the disposition of this case. In my view, the case at bar is governed by the reasons given in this court's decision in *R. v. Vaillancourt*, [1987] 2 S.C.R. 636, 60 C.R. (3d) 289, 39 C.C.C. (3d) 118 [Que.]. The court need go no further.

For diverging comments on *Martineau* see Stuart, "Further Progress on the Constitutional Requirement of Fault, But Stigma is Not Enough" (1990), 79 C.R. (3d) 247 and Rosemary Cairns Way, "Constitutionalizing Subjectivism: Another View" (1990), 79 C.R. (3d) 260.

In *R. v. Sit* (1991), 9 C.R. (4th) 126 (S.C.C.), the Supreme Court made it clear that the constructive murder category under what was s. 213(*c*) [later s. 230(*c*)] was also unconstitutional since it resorts to a test of objective foresight and therefore does not involve proof beyond a reasonable doubt that the accused had subjective foresight of the death of the victim.

For over ten years after *Vaillancourt*, prosecutors appeared reluctant to test the possible interpretation that the unlawful object murder category under s. 229(*c*) was still partially constitutional. However, in *Meiler* (1999), 25 C.R. (5th) 161, 136 C.C.C. (3d) 11 (Ont. C.A.), the Ontario Court of Appeal confirmed a murder conviction where a trial judge had instructed the jury it could convict on the basis of s. 229(*c*) if it found that the accused for an unlawful object did anything knowing that it was likely to cause someone's death. The decision can be criticized for not adopting a narrower interpretation limiting s. 229(*c*) to a person who had a subjective awareness of the likelihood of the actual victim's death: see, further, R.J. Delisle, "Unlawful Object Murder Is Alive and Well" (1995), 25 C.R. (5th) 179. In *Meiler*, on the accused's evidence, he was carrying a loaded and cocked shotgun with intent to kill a particular person and the gun discharged during a struggle and accidentally killed another. The particular application of s. 229(*c*) in *Meiler* appears to resurrect a type of constructive murder the Supreme Court had declared unconstitutional.

R. v. SHAND

80 C.R. (6th) 199, 266 C.C.C. (3d) 137, 2011 CarswellOnt 14 (Ont. C.A.)

The accused and two others went to the home of a local drug dealer planning to steal marihuana. The drug dealer indicated that he did not have the quantity of marihuana they were asking for. They noticed the dealer's girlfriend holding a bag a marihuana and pursued her into the basement. There was disputed evidence to what occurred there. It was clear that the accused pulled out a gun and that it discharged killing a male, F. The dispute was as to whether the gun was discharged accidentally or deliberately. On the second degree murder charge the trial judge directed the jury on s. 229(a)(i), 229(a)(ii) and also s.229(c). The defence objected to an instruction on s.229(c) arguing that liability under that section was incompatible with an accidental charge. The jury convicted of second degree murder.

On appeal the accused, supported by intervenors, challenged the constitutionality of s. 229 (c) on the basis that s. 7 of the *Charter* demanded a minimum *mens rea* of intent to cause serious bodily harm to the victim to found a conviction for murder and, in the alternative, that the section violated s.7 on the basis of vagueness and overbreadth.

ROULEAU J.A.: —

[Before considering whether s. 229(c) is constitutional, Justice Rouleau found it first necessary to determine the proper interpretation and application of the section. Though its wording had undergone little change in over 100 years, its context had changed greatly. There have been amendments to the *Criminal Code*, the phrase "ought to know" was read out of s. 229(c) by the Supreme Court in *R. v. Martineau* [1990] 2 S.C.R. 633 and the Supreme Court held that constructive murder provisions in s. 230 which permitted conviction with objective foresight of death were unconstitutional. The new context dictated a narrower reading of s. 229(c), clearly focussed on the requirement that, when the act causing the death is carried out, the accused subjectively foresaw that some person's death is likely. It was important that s. 229(c) be given a meaning distinct from ss. 229(a)(i) and (ii) (para. 129)].

138. In *DeWolfe* [(1976) 130 O.R. (2d) 302 (Ont.C.A.)] , this court commented that courts must be careful about engaging in the unrealistic dissection of the unlawful object in order to fit the facts of the case into s. 229(c). This will arise in situations in which the accused commits an act or series of acts with one general purpose, and the fundamental question facing the trier of fact is whether or not the accused intended to kill or to cause grievous bodily harm to the victim. In these cases, decision makers should be careful not to search out additional and tenuous unlawful objects that the accused carried out, in order to apply s. 229 (c)

141. As gatekeeper, the trial judge must be cautious not to instruct juries on s. 229(c) in situations which fit squarely within ss. 229(a) or (b). The unlawful

object must be a genuine object, and not simply one aspect of the same "general purpose" of causing death or bodily harm that is likely to cause death.

142. This caution also addresses the concern that section 229 (c) might be used by the Crown as a substitute to ss. 229(a) or (b), in an attempt to somehow lessen the burden of proving intent. . .

3) THE CONSTITUTIONALITY OF s. 229(c)

155 Relying largely on *Vaillancourt* and *Martineau*, the appellant and interveners contend that it is unconstitutional to label an unintentional killing "murder". They argue that s. 229(c) imposes an impermissibly low mens rea requirement for murder, the most serious offence in the *Criminal Code*. In their submission, nothing short of intentionally killing or causing bodily harm knowing that it is likely to cause death, is sufficient to meet the constitutional minimum for murder. Harm caused unintentionally should not be dealt with as harshly as these intentional acts.

156 The appellant and interveners argue that in *Martineau*, the Supreme Court of Canada did not rule on the constitutionality of s. 229(c). In their submission, *Martineau* should be read as establishing the principle that subjective foresight of death is a necessary, but not a sufficient condition to meet the constitutional minimum for murder.

. . .

158 The Crown submits that, based on existing Supreme Court jurisprudence, the constitutional issue raised by the appellant and interveners has already been decided. A proper reading of Martineau and its companion cases, as well as subsequent decisions of that court, establishes subjective foresight of death as a sufficient constitutional standard of mens rea for murder. The respondent argues that s. 229(c) is, in substance, no different from s. 229(a)(ii). Neither provision requires an intention to cause death. Section 229(a)(ii) requires an intent to cause bodily harm and the subjective foresight of death, while s. 229(c) simply replaces the intent to cause bodily harm with an intent to pursue another unlawful object.

159 The respondent contends that an accused who, engaged in an unlawful pursuit, chooses to commit a dangerous act knowing that another person is likely to die as a result, is as morally blameworthy as the person who intends to cause death or to cause bodily harm knowing that death is likely.

160 In my view, the issue as to whether the *mens rea* for murder under s. 229(c) is constitutionally sufficient has been resolved in past Supreme Court jurisprudence. As I will explain, I agree with the respondent's submission that,

in *Martineau* and its companion cases, the Supreme Court of Canada decided the issue, and found s. 229(c) to be constitutional.

. . .

4) APPLYING THE PRINCIPLES TO THE FACTS OF THIS CASE

188 As explained earlier, s. 229(c) will be satisfied where the following elements are present:

(a) the accused must pursue an unlawful object other than to cause the death of the victim or bodily harm to the victim knowing that death is likely;

(b) the unlawful object must itself be an indictable offence requiring *mens rea* [applying *R. v. Vasil* [1981] 1 S.C.R. 459;

(c) in furtherance of the unlawful object, the accused must intentionally commit a dangerous act;

(d) the dangerous act must be distinct from the unlawful object, but as stated above, only in the sense that the unlawful object must be something other than the likelihood of death, which is the harm that is foreseen as a consequence of the dangerous act;

(e) the dangerous act must be a specific act, or a series of closely related acts, that in fact results in death, though the dangerous act need not itself constitute an offence; and

(f) when the dangerous act is committed, the accused must have subjective knowledge that death is likely to result.

189 In applying the principles outlined above to the facts of this case, the unlawful object was robbery. Although the appellant carried a gun to the robbery, and this is also unlawful, this was not his purpose or goal, so it is not an unlawful object in the sense used in s. 229(c). In all probability, the appellant was hoping to carry out the theft with little violence and no likelihood of death.

190 In identifying the dangerous act, as explained earlier, it is important not to frame the dangerous act too broadly. A broad and vague characterization of what constitutes the dangerous act does not fit well into the causation framework and may skew the subsequent mens rea analysis.

191 It would, for example, be wrong to frame the dangerous act as entering a home with a loaded gun or engaging in a home invasion with a gun. Although these "acts", in a sense, led to the events in the basement bedroom, they were not the acts that actually caused the death.

192 When Brisbois fled to the basement with the marijuana and the appellant and J.B. pursued her, the situation changed significantly.

193 In my view, it is upon entering the basement bedroom that the appellant committed the dangerous act. The act was drawing and using his gun in an attempt to subdue the occupants of the room. This act was clearly done in furtherance of the unlawful object, being the robbery. Whether the gun was intentionally or accidently discharged, it was the choice to use the gun in order to subdue the occupants that caused the death.

194 The critical issue, then, is whether the appellant possessed the necessary mens rea at the time that he committed the dangerous act. If, when he pulled out the gun and used it in the confined space of the basement bedroom, the appellant knew that it was likely to cause death, but did so nonetheless in pursuance of the theft, this would satisfy the mens rea component of s. 229(c).

195 If, however, he did not then know that death was likely, the necessary mens rea would be absent. It is critical that the appellant's state of mind at this particular point in time is ascertained. That determination is a subjective one. The question is not what he ought to have known. The question is what he actually knew and foresaw. Surrounding facts, including the appellant's prior conduct, can be considered to determine what the appellant actually knew. What his state of mind may have been before or after committing the dangerous act is not determinative.

196 In determining the appellant's subjective knowledge, relevant facts could include: the appellant's knowledge of whether the gun was loaded and whether the safety of the gun was on or off; the appellant's knowledge of the presence and location of a person or persons who could be hurt if the gun discharged; whether the appellant was acting in panic or out of fear; the conduct of the appellant as observed by others; whether the appellant drew the gun or had already drawn it; and whether the appellant was using the gun to press or force others to submit or using it in an attempt to extricate himself from a dangerous situation. All of these facts may shed light on the mental state of the appellant at the critical moment in time.

197 The appellant argues that s. 229(c) had no application to the facts of this case, as it requires that there be a dangerous act distinct from the unlawful object. At trial, the theory of the defence was that the appellant brought the gun in order to carry out the robbery and that it discharged accidentally, killing the victim. On the appellant's view, there was no dangerous act separate and distinct from the unlawful object of robbery, as the gun and its use were an integral part of the robbery. In other words, this was a robbery gone wrong.

198 As I explained earlier, the dangerous act need not be distinct in the sense of being unrelated to the acts carrying out the unlawful object. In fact, as the text of s. 229(c) requires that the dangerous act be committed for or in pursuance of the unlawful object, the dangerous act must be associated with the unlawful

object to fall within the provision. In the present case, the dangerous act was the choice to draw and use the gun in order to subdue the occupants of the basement bedroom and take the bag of marijuana. The fact that the gun may have discharged accidently while being used to that end does not remove these facts from the ambit of s. 229(c).

199 In my view, therefore, there was an adequate factual basis for the trial judge to charge the jury on s. 229(c).

The *Shand* court, in its re-evaluation of s. 229(c) since the *Charter* rulings in *R. v. Martineau*, [1990] 2 S.C.R. 633, makes a strong case through meticulous analysis of Supreme Court jurisprudence that the constitutionality of s. 229(c) purged of the object foresight limb has already been decided by the Supreme Court.

Key aspects of the re-evaluation of s. 229(c) in *Shand* are the emphasis that the dangerous act be intentional, that the act cause the death and that there be subjective foresight of the likelihood of death. These requirements are important and welcome vehicles for restraint, remembering that murder carries a mandatory sentence of life imprisonment. This restraint is not as evident in *R. v. S. (J.)* (2008), 237 C.C.C. (3d) 305 (Ont. C.A.), where the Court of Appeal (per Doherty, Moldaver and Watt JJ.A.) decided that s. 229(c) but not the transferred intent s. 229(b) could be applied to convict one of murder who shot over the heads of a Boxing Day sale crowd in a public street at a rival gang member whose return shot killed an innocent bystander. The *Shand* court at various points goes out of its way to ensure that trial judges do not unduly stretch the ambit of s. 229(c) and indeed do not instruct on it where the issue should focus on whether the accused meant to cause death or bodily harm to the victim and knew of the likelihood of death.

There are, however, some troubling aspects. In its ruling on the facts in *Shand* the Court of Appeal finds that s. 229(c) was applicable even if the discharge of the gun was accidental. This is difficult to square with the Court's strong assertion that the dangerous act must be intentional and that the key mental element is subject foresight of the likelihood of death, not just of a possibility or a danger of death. In this application we appear to be back to a form of constructive murder held unconstitutional in *Martineau*.

Professor Kent Roach "The Problematic Revival of Murder under Section 229(c) of the Criminal Code" (2010) 47 *Alta. L. Rev.* 675 shows how the resurgent use of s. 229(c) since *R. v. Meiler* (1999), 25 C.R. (5th) 161 (Ont. C.A.), especially in Ontario, has resulted in accidental killings being held to constitute s. 229(c) murder. He is especially critical of several arson cases. The Court in *Shand* does try to avoid this result in its discussion of arson examples where it emphasises the requirement of knowledge of the likelihood of death. Roach questions the judicial reluctance to resort to the transferred intent provision in s. 229(b) in cases like *J.S. R.* and questions whether the approach in *J.S.R.* is consistent with the

Charter standard in *Martineau* that intentional conduct must be punished more severely than negligent conduct. Neither of these issues was addressed in *Shand*.

Although the Court in *Shand* has tried hard to achieve clarity, the six elements it requires for s. 229 (c) liability are hugely complex and a nightmare to try to explain to juries; even more so where they have to be combined with a charge on party liability such as under s. 21(2). Where there has been a fatal attack on a person who died as a result, pragmatic judges may wish to keep matters relatively simple and take the Court of Appeal's hint in *Shand* to stick to directions on s. 229(a)(i) and (ii).

There is also a real danger that the Court's reference to a "dangerous act" requirement for s. 229(c) will be hard for the judge or jury to distinguish from unlawful act manslaughter, which presently only requires a dangerous unlawful act and normally no marked departure from the objective norm (*R. v. Creighton*, [1993] 3 S.C.R. 3).

Parliament has not got round to deleting the unconstitutional objective "ought to have foreseen" element from s. 229(c). On three occasions embarrassing for the justice system, s. 229(c) in its unconstitutional form was left with juries. This necessitated new trials in B.C, Ontario and New Brunswick (see the detailed discussion by Roach). In *R. v. Townsend*, 2010 BCCA 400, Justice Chiasson speaking for the Court said:

> I cannot leave these reasons without wondering why steps have not been taken to amend the Criminal Code to conform to the now 20-year-old decision of the Supreme Court of Canada in *Martineau* determining that language in s. 229(c) is unconstitutional. The law that is recorded in the statute, on which every citizen is entitled to rely, is not the law of the land. An issue such as arose in this case should not occur. It creates the risk of a miscarriage of justice and the potential need to incur significant costs addressing an error in an appellate court with the possible costs of a new trial, assuming one is practical. In my view, failure to deal appropriately with such matters by updating the *Criminal Code* to remove provisions that have been found to offend the Constitution is not in the interests of justice. [para 43]

The Ontario Court of Appeal adopted a strict approach to the fault element for s. 229(c) in the arson case of *R. v. Roks* (2011), 87 C.R. (6th) 144 (Ont. C.A.). The accused was guilty of a conspiracy to commit arson of a building to defraud insurers. The conspirators had hired expert arsonists but they had used too much gasoline and one of the arsonists had died in the explosion. Justice Watt decided the trial judge had reached an unreasonable verdict in finding the accused guilty of murder under s. 229(c). Considering the requirements set out in *Shand*, the unlawful object was fraud on the insurers and the act of setting the store premises on fire was a dangerous, unlawful act committed intentionally that was distinct from the unlawful object. However, the evidence did not support the conclusion that the accused knew that the death of a human being would likely occur. Justice Watt defined the requisite fault element as follows:

> The accused must know that the death of a human being is a *likely* consequence of the dangerous act. The term "likely" refers to the probability of a consequence. Proof that an accused was aware of the risk, possibility, danger or chance of death as a consequence of a dangerous act is inadequate to establish the mental or fault element in s. 229(c) [para 134]

Justice Watt noted that the accused was not involved in the setting of the fire and knew that the fire was to be set on Christmas Eve to minimise the risk to others. Foresight of death was not enough. At points the trial judge wrongly spoke of foresight of harm. She also proceeded backwards from the fact that someone died to the conclusion the accused must have known someone would die. She relied heavily on the "common sense proposition" that "harm or death is a natural and even likely consequence of spreading accelerants in a building then setting fire to them". Her analysis essentially substituted a test of objective foreseeability, which was constitutionally infirm. A verdict of manslaughter was substituted.

Roks was a judge-alone case where we see the trier of fact's reasoning process. Justice Watt decided that knowledge of likelihood is to be interpreted as knowledge of a probability. We have seen that courts have long not required that gloss to be automatically included in jury directions on the meaning of knowledge of likelihood of death for s. 229(a)(ii) purposes. That view should now be reconsidered for reasons of consistency and proper jury comprehension. The meaning of likelihood is not self-evident. Jury instructions on the meaning of reasonable doubt have long found it important to explain distinctions between possibilities, probabilities and certainty.

(iii) First degree murder: s. 231

The punishment for both first and second degree murder is fixed at life imprisonment. The significance of the distinction relates to parole eligibility: see s. 745.

R. v. SMITH

(1979), 51 C.C.C. (2d) 381, 1979 CarswellSask 193 (Sask. C.A.)

CULLITON C.J.S.: — Gerald Thomas Smith was charged that he, on July 9, 1978, at the Edenwold District, Saskatchewan, did cause the death of Darryl Wayne Skwarchuk and thereby commit first degree murder contrary to s. 218 [now s. 231] [rep. & sub. 1974-75-76, c. 93, s. 5] of the *Criminal Code*.

After a jury trial presided over by MacLeod J., he was found guilty as charged and was sentenced to life imprisonment without eligibility for parole until he has served 25 years of his sentence.

While he has appealed in respect of conviction and sentence, his counsel conceded both at the trial and on the appeal that there were only three verdicts open to the jury, namely, guilty of first degree murder, guilty of second degree murder or guilty of manslaughter. I am satisfied the evidence fully supported that position.

The argument that a verdict of manslaughter was open to the jury was founded on the plea of provocation. That defence was rejected by the jury and, in my view, rightly so. Thus, the sole question on the appeal is simply whether or not there was evidence of planning and deliberation upon which the jury could properly find the appellant guilty of first degree murder.

For the court to consider this question, it is not necessary to review all of the evidence adduced at trial. The evidence upon which the Crown relied in its contention that a finding of first degree murder was a proper finding, was the evidence of William Mitchel Massier. I think it is evident the jury accepted his evidence and it is the only evidence in respect of the actual killing.

Massier was a young man 18 years of age, who, at the time he gave evidence, was also charged with the murder of Skwarchuk. He said he knew Smith and first met him in October, 1977, while working at MacDonald's. He said, he also knew Skwarchuk and met him in November, 1977, while Skwarchuk was working at a laundromat. He said that he, Smith and Skwarchuk became friends. He said they partied together and jointly engaged in a number of breaking and entering offences in the spring of 1978. He said from time to time they went hunting together and probably did so some 20 or 25 times. They always went north of the city and usually had a rented car or Skwarchuk's car. On occasion he said they had a friend's car.

Massier said that on July 9, 1978, he had a .12 gauge shot-gun. He said he had possessed that gun for three or four months having obtained it from an apartment which they broke and entered. He said Skwarchuk also had a .22 gun and that Smith owned a .22 semi-automatic rifle and a pellet gun.

Smith lived at 201 Branew Apts. at the corner of St. John St. and Victoria Ave. Massier testified they used to party there. These parties consisted of drinking liquor and at times smoking marijuana and taking pills. Skwarchuk lived on Osler St.

On Sunday, July 9, 1978, at about 11:00 or 11:30 a.m., Massier said Smith telephoned to him and asked if they should keep the rented car that day. According to Massier, Smith had possession of a car which they had rented the previous day. He told Smith to keep the car.

About 12 noon, Smith arrived at Massier's place in the car accompanied by Skwarchuk. Massier said he went out and was told they were going hunting and he said he would go with them. They then went to Smith's apartment and picked up a .22 ruger with a scope, a .12 gauge shot-gun and a pellet pistol. The shot-gun had been sawed off and was owned by Massier. Smith also brought some shot-gun shells. They then went to Skwarchuk's and obtained 50 rounds of .22 ammunition.

After this, they drove to MacDonald's where they had something to eat. According to Massier, Smith and Skwarchuk were taking valium pills. After eating, they returned to Massier's place and picked up some tools and a pair of gloves. According to Massier, they obtained the tools and gloves because Smith said he wanted to break into a drug store. At the same time, they picked up more .22 ammunition.

Following this, they drove north on Highway 6. After travelling some 10 or 15 miles they turned west off of the highway. Massier said, from time to time, thereafter, they stopped to shoot birds, ducks and mail boxes. Finally they arrived at an abandoned farmhouse and stopped there. Smith shot off the door knob with the shot-gun.

According to the evidence of Massier, while driving from Regina, Smith had consumed the best part of a mickey of rye. He said during the drive there was considerable conversation about girl friends but no unfriendliness was shown by anyone.

After Smith had shot off the door knob, Massier said he broke down the inside door and they all went into the house. He said Smith and Skwarchuk were shooting up the house and windows with the shot-gun and he smashed a couple of windows with a beer bottle. He said he also shot a few rounds with the .22.

Massier said after about 15 minutes, Smith and Skwarchuk said they wanted to leave. They then all left the house. He said they went to the car and there he obtained a pair of leather gloves. He said he put the gloves on and returned to the house and started smashing windows with a board. He said he smashed two front windows and then smashed a window on the west side. He jumped through this window and was then at the back of the house. He broke two more windows there and then went around the corner where he saw Smith and Skwarchuk and heard an argument between them.

Massier said he was some distance away and could not understand exactly what they were saying. He said it seemed to him Smith was telling Skwarchuk to put down his gun and he would do the same. He said Smith had the shot-gun and Skwarchuk the .22 and they were pointing the guns at each other.

Massier said he did not think the situation was serious so he returned to his window breaking activity. He said he was on the east side of the house when he heard a shot. He testified he then immediately came to the front of the house and saw Smith standing at the front of the car, on the driver's side, and Skwarchuk was about three yards from the rear bumper on the passenger side. He saw Smith with the shot-gun in his hand and Skwarchuk's gun was on the ground. He said Skwarchuk had been shot in the left elbow, and his arm was hanging and blood was squirting on the ground. He said Skwarchuk was running away; that he ran some distance, stopped and faced the car. Massier testified Skwarchuk was screaming and yelling and said he was bleeding to death and should be taken to a hospital.

When Skwarchuk stopped, Massier said he went to the car and asked Smith what was going on and Smith told him to shut up. He said he asked Smith if he was going to shoot Skwarchuk and Smith did not answer. He said he then asked Smith if he was going to shoot him and Smith told him to shut up and get behind him. According to Massier, this episode lasted from one to three minutes. During this time, Smith reloaded the shot-gun. He put in five shells. According to Massier, Smith then called Skwarchuk's name. Following this Skwarchuk took a step towards the car and when Smith pumped the shell into the chambers of the gun, Skwarchuk turned and ran. He said Smith shot from long range and he could not tell whether Skwarchuk had been hit. He said Smith shot again. It appeared some pellets hit Skwarchuk in the back. Massier said Skwarchuk continued to run but before he stopped, Smith shot him again and he fell down and stayed down.

According to Massier, Smith then walked up to Skwarchuk who was sitting with his knees up and his head resting on his knees. He said Smith held the gun three or four inches from the back of Skwarchuk's head and then fired the same. Skwarchuk fell back and appeared to be dead. Massier said this episode took about 30 seconds.

After this, Massier said he asked Smith if he was going to shoot him, to which Smith replied: "No, you are my friend: don't worry about it". Massier testified Smith told him to go back to the car and get the .22. He said he went to the car and was followed by Smith. Massier said when he went to load the .22, the clip was not in the gun. He said Smith gave him the clip which he loaded with four shells and gave it to Smith. Smith put the clip in the gun. When asked by Massier what he was going to do, Smith answered he was going to shoot Skwarchuk with the .22 and that would be his insurance: if he got caught, he would say Massier shot him. Massier testified he followed Smith who went to where Skwarchuk was lying and shot him in the head three times.

According to Massier, he was told to take Skwarchuk's watch; that he did so and threw it into a pond. They heard a truck approach and Smith said that they should take off. Smith put the .22 and the shot-gun in the car and they returned to the city. They were subsequently arrested and charged with the murder of Skwarchuk.

Section 214(2) [rep. & sub. 1974-75-76, c. 105, s. 4] of the *Code* reads:

214(2) [now s. 231(2)] Murder is first degree murder when it is planned and deliberate.

In *More v. The Queen*, [1963] 3 C.C.C. 289, [1963] S.C.R. 522, the Supreme Court of Canada considered the meaning of the words "planned" and "deliberate". The court made it clear that the accused could not be found guilty of first degree murder unless it was proved beyond a reasonable doubt, not only that the murder was planned but also that it was deliberate. Fauteux J. (later C.J.C.), accepted as a meaning of "planned" — "arranged beforehand".

In so far as the word "deliberate" is concerned Cartwright J. (later C.J.C.). said at p. 291 C.C.C., p. 534 S.C.R.:

The learned trial judge also rightly instructed the jury that the word "deliberate", as used in s. 202A(2)(a), means "considered, not impulsive".

Other meanings of the adjective given in the Oxford Dictionary are "not hasty in decision", "slow in deciding" and "intentional". The word as used in the subsection cannot have simply the meaning "intentional" because it is only if the accused's act was intentional that he can be guilty of murder and the subsection is creating an additional ingredient to be proved as a condition of an accused being convicted of capital murder.

Similar views were expressed by the Supreme Court in *McMartin v. The Queen*, [1965] 1 C.C.C. 142, [1964] S.C.R. 484. In *R. v. Mitchell*, [1965] 1 C.C.C. 155, 43 C.R. 391, Spence J., in delivering the majority judgment of the

Supreme Court, after referring to *More v. The Queen, supra*, and *McMartin v. The Queen, supra*, said at p. 162 C.C.C., pp. 393-4 C.R.:

> I am of the opinion that the judgment in these two cases have as their *ratio decidendi* the principle that in determining whether the accused committed the crime of capital murder in that it was "planned and deliberate on the part of such person" the jury should have available and should be directed to consider all the circumstances including not only the evidence of the accused's actions but of his condition, his state of mind as affected by either real or even imagined insults and provoking actions of the victim and by the accused's consumption of alcohol. There is no doubt this is a finding of fact. The questions which the jury must decide and decide beyond reasonable doubt before they may convict the accused of capital murder under the relevant subsection — s. 202A(2)(*a*) — are: Was the murder which he committed planned and was it deliberate? I separate the jury's problem in that form because I am in complete agreement with Whittaker J.A., when he said [[1964] 2 C.C.C. at p. 16]: "It is possible to imagine a murder to some degree planned and yet not deliberate." Therefore, to determine whether the charge to the jury delivered by the learned trial Judge was adequate in submitting to them the issue of planning and deliberation the charge must be examined with some care.

In *R. v. Widdifield*, Gale J. (later C.J.O.), in charging the jury on planned and deliberate, as reported in 6 *Crim. L.Q.* 152 at p. 153 (1963-64), said:

> I think that in the Code "planned" is to be assigned, I think, its natural meaning of a calculated scheme or design which has been carefully thought out, and the nature and consequences of which have been considered and weighed. But that does not mean, of course, to say that the plan need be a complicated one. It may be a very simple one, and the simpler it is perhaps the easier it is to formulate.

The foregoing direction was approved by the Ontario Court of Appeal in *R. v. Reynolds* (1978), 44 C.C.C. (2d) 129. See particulary the comments of Martin J.A., speaking for the court at p. 137.

I realize it is both difficult and unwise to attempt to give an exhaustive meaning to the word "planned". It is a common word and to it should be attributed its meaning as understood in everyday life. Clearly, planning must not be confused with intention as the planning would only occur after the intent to murder had been formed. There must be some evidence the killing was the result of a scheme or design previously formulated or designed by the accused and the killing was the implementation of that scheme or design. It is obvious a murder committed on a sudden impulse and without prior consideration, even though the intent to kill is clearly proven, would not constitute a planned murder.

In the present case, there is not the slightest evidence the appellant had given any consideration to the murder of Skwarchuk until after he and Skwarchuk had left the house. In instructing the jury, the learned trial judge said:

> So without beating it more than that, the Crown must establish to establish first degree murder that the accused caused the death, he intended to do so and that he planned and deliberated. Now, I think you can say without any doubt that there was no plan to kill prior to arriving at the farm. There's no evidence of that, nor any suggestion of that. Equally there was no plan or intention to kill the first while at the farm. If the accused planned to kill, deliberated this,

it must have been started, at the earliest, about the time of the altercation. There is no evidence that it would have started earlier than that, and then the question that you must weigh and consider is did he have the time to deliberate under the circumstances; did he have time to plan, and if so, did he? If you can say beyond a reasonable doubt that from the circumstances that you see and the facts that you find that it was planned and deliberate, then you should return a verdict of guilty of first degree murder. If you have a reasonable doubt about any of those things, then you should not bring a verdict of first degree murder.

To the foregoing instruction, no objection was taken by counsel either for the Crown or for the appellant. As a matter of fact, learned counsel for the Crown, in his address to the jury relied entirely on the evidence of Massier to establish "planned" and "deliberate".

I am satisfied there was no evidence whatever to support the conclusion that the actions of the appellant, cruel and sadistic as they were, in killing Skwarchuk was the implementation of a previously determined design or scheme. I think it is obvious his actions were the result of a sudden impulse. It would be pure speculation to try and determine what triggered that impulse.

It may well be that the killing was deliberate. However, even if it was, there could only be a verdict of first degree murder if the evidence established as well that the murder was planned.

Whether or not there was evidence the murder was planned was a question of law for the judge. In my respectful view, as there was no such evidence, the learned trial judge erred in law in instructing the jury there was evidence upon which a verdict of first degree murder could be found. In these circumstances, therefore, I direct that the verdict of first degree murder be set aside and a conviction of second degree murder be substituted therefore.

In *R. v. Travers* (2007), 51 C.R. (6th) 105 (Que. S.C.) Champagne J. required first degree murder to be well ordered and based on consideration, prudence and reflection. In *R. v. K. (M.M.)* (2006), 213 C.C.C. (3d) 538 (Alta. C.A.) it was held that the trial judge had wrongly equated wilful with deliberation, which required more.

R. v. NYGAARD AND SCHIMMENS

(1989), 72 C.R. (3d) 257, 51 C.C.C. (3d) 417,
1989 CarswellAlta 621, 1989 CarswellAlta 152 (S.C.C.)

M bought a car stereo from the accused N for $100. Payment was made by means of a cheque signed jointly by T and H. The cheque bounced. N came to M's motel and told him that, if the matter was not cleared up that day, M could expect trouble. Later that day N, the accused S, and another man, went to the apartment. S struck M several times on the forehead with a baseball bat and broke his arm, which was raised to protect his face. S then asked who had signed the cheque. When told it was H, he proceeded to attack H with the bat, hitting him three times between the eyes with full two-handed swings. H died in hospital of multiple skull fractures. S and N were charged with first degree murder. Following trial before judge and jury they were convicted.

When the matter reached the Supreme Court of Canada a new trial was ordered respecting a misdirection on a point of evidence. In the course of the judgment the court unanimously held that the trial judge had not erred in directing the jury that they could return a verdict of first degree murder on the basis of a combination of sections 229(*a*)(ii) and 231(2):

CORY J.: —

Throughout history the idea that one human being could cold-bloodedly plan and deliberate upon the killing of another has been repugnant to all civilized societies and has tended to be considered as the most reprehensible of violent crimes. In *Droste v. R.*, Dickson C.J.C. noted that it is the element of planning and deliberation of the murder which makes the crime of murder in the first degree more culpable and justifies the harsher sentence.

It remains then to consider what is the specific *mens rea* required by s. 212(*a*)(ii) to which the element of planning and deliberation must be related. The section requires that the Crown prove that the accused meant to cause the victim such bodily harm that he knew that it was likely to cause the death of the victim and was reckless whether death ensued or not as a result of causing that bodily harm. The essential element is that of intending to cause bodily harm of such a grave and serious nature that the accused knew that it was likely to result in the death of the victim. The aspect of recklessness is almost an afterthought insofar as the basic intent is concerned.

In *Sansregret v. R.*, [1985] 1 S.C.R. 570, 45 C.R. (3d) 193, 18 C.C.C. (3d) 223, recklessness was defined as being the attitude of one who was aware of the danger the prohibited conduct could bring about yet nevertheless persisted in that conduct despite the knowledge of the risk. Thus the section requires the accused to intend to cause the gravest of bodily harm that is so dangerous and serious that he knows it is likely to result in death and to persist in that conduct despite the knowledge of the risk.

In my view, the vital element of the requisite intent is that of causing such bodily harm that the perpetrator knows that it is likely to cause death and yet persists in the assault. There can be no doubt that a person can plan and deliberate to cause terrible bodily harm that he knows is likely to result in death. Nothing is added to the aspect of planning and deliberation by the requirement that the fatal assault be carried out in a reckless manner, that is to say, by heedlessly proceeding with the deadly assault in the face of the knowledge of the obvious risks. The planning and deliberation to cause the bodily harm which is likely to be fatal must of necessity include the planning and deliberating to continue and to persist in that conduct despite the knowledge of the risk. The element of recklessness does not exist in a vacuum as a sole *mens rea* requirement, but rather it must act in conjunction with the intentional infliction of terrible bodily harm. I therefore conclude that planning and deliberation may well be coupled with the *mens rea* requirements of s. 212(*a*)(ii) and that a first degree murder conviction can be sustained by virtue of the combined operation of ss. 214(2) and 212(*a*)(ii). This ground of appeal must therefore fail.

As well, the appellant argued it was wrong to label an offence under s. 212(*a*)(ii) as murder. It was said that the requisite *mens rea* is such that it is not as grave a crime as that defined in s. 212(*a*)(i), where the requisite intent is to cause the death of someone. I cannot accept that contention. The variation in the degree of culpability is too slight to take into account. Let us consider the gravity of the crime described by s. 212(*a*)(ii) in the light of three examples which, pursuant to the section, would be murder. First, an accused forms the intent to inflict multiple stab wounds in the abdomen and chest of a person knowing that the wounds are likely to kill the victim and, heedless of the known probable result, proceeds with the stabbing. Second, an accused forms the intent to shoot a former associate in the chest knowing that death is likely to ensue and, uncaring of the result, shoots the victim in the chest. Third, two accused form the intent to repeatedly and viciously strike a person in the head with a baseball bat realizing full well that the victim will probably die as a result. Nonetheless they continue with the bone-splintering, skull-shattering assault. The accused in all these examples must have committed as grave a crime as the accused who specifically intends to kill. Society would, I think, find the drawing of any differentiation in the degree of culpability an exercise in futility. The difference in the calibration on the scale of culpability is too minute to merit a distinction. I would conclude that the crime defined in s. 212(*a*)(ii) can properly be described as murder and on a "culpability scale" it varies so little from s. 212(*a*)(i) as to be indistinguishable.

I find some support for this position in *R. v. Vaillancourt*, [1987] 2 S.C.R. 636, 60 C.R. (3d) 289, 39 C.C.C. (3d) 118 [Que.]. There Lamer J., giving the reasons for the court, stated at pp. 644-45:

> There is a very interesting progression through s. 212 to s. 213 with respect to the mental state that must be proven.
>
> The starting point is s. 212(*a*)(i) . . .
>
> This clearly requires that the accused have actual subjective foresight of the likelihood of causing the death coupled with the intention to cause that death. This is the most morally blameworthy state of mind in our system.
>
> There is a slight relaxation of this requirement in s. 212(*a*)(ii) . . .
>
> Here again the accused must have actual subjective foresight of the likelihood of death. However, the Crown need no longer prove that he intended to cause the death but only that he was reckless whether death ensued or not. It should also be noted that s. 212(*a*)(ii) is limited to cases where the accused intended to cause bodily harm to the victim.

He went on to note that there is still a greater relaxation of the requisite mental element in s. 212(*c*), a provision which "eliminates the requirement of actual subjective foresight and replaces it with objective foreseeability or negligence" (pp. 645-46). It is clear from these observations that the court in that case concluded that there was but a slight relaxation of the requisite intent in s. 212(*a*)(ii) from that required by s. 212(*a*)(i). Section 212(*a*)(ii) demands a highly subjective mental element to be present, that of the intent to cause the gravest of bodily injuries that are known to the accused to be likely to cause death to the victim. It is to this intent that the s. 214(2) requirement of planning and deliberation can be properly applied.

For comment on *Nygaard* see Stuart (1989), 72 C.R. (3d) 259-261.

R. v. COLLINS

69 C.R. (3d) 235, 48 C.C.C. (3d) 343, 1989 CarswellOnt 83 (Ont. C.A.)

GOODMAN J.A.: —

. . . .

There can be no doubt that the onus was on the Crown to establish beyond a reasonable doubt the *actus reus* and *mens rea* of the substantive offence of murder under s. 212. I am of the view, however, that under s. 214(4)(*a*) [now s. 231(4)(*a*)] there is an onus on the Crown to establish beyond a reasonable doubt that the victim was a person who falls within the designation of the occupations set forth in that subsection acting in the course of his duties to the knowledge of the accused or with recklessness on his part as to whether the victim was such a person so acting.

In my opinion there is no binding authority to the contrary. It seems clear to me that the object of the classification of first degree murder in s. 214 is to require a more severe punishment for the offence of murder in circumstances that involve an added degree of moral culpability or to act as a more effective deterrent in the prevention of the murder of persons engaged in the preservation, prevention of infringement and enforcement of the law or of persons who have fallen under the domination of an offender.

It is my view that s. 214(4)(*a*) should be interpreted in such a manner that requires proof of the facts which give rise to the added moral culpability or which would act as an additional deterrent. It is clear to me that to fulfil such interpretation it is necessary that the Crown prove that the murderer had knowledge of the identity of the victim as one of the persons designated in the subsection and that such person was acting in the course of his duties or was reckless as to such identity and acts of the victim.

The section could, of course, be interpreted to simply require that the Crown prove that the occupation of the victim was one of those set forth in the subsection and that the person was acting in the course of his duties without proof of knowledge thereof on the part of the murderer. The subsection does not refer to proof of such knowledge.

I am satisfied that if the latter interpretation is adopted, it would offend s. 7 of the *Charter*. If, for example, a gunman sees two persons on the street dressed in plain clothes of whom one is a merchant walking home and the other is a detective on his way to investigate or in the process of investigating a break-in, and if the gunman decides without planning and deliberation to shoot and kill one of them and does, so he would be guilty of murder no matter which person he killed. In the case of the killing of the ordinary citizen he would be guilty of second degree murder with a sentence of life imprisonment with a possibility of parole eligibility after 10 years but in the case of the killing of the detective he would be guilty of first degree murder with a sentence of life imprisonment with a possibility of parole in no less than 25 years, being the minimum period before parole eligibility (subject of course to the provisions of s. 745 of the *Code* (formerly s. 672)).

Although the crime of murder is deserving of the heavy sentence involved, it seems to me that there would be no difference in moral culpability in the example set forth above no matter which person was the victim, nor would there be any additional deterrent provided under s. 214(4)(*a*) in those circumstances if proof of knowledge that the detective was indeed a detective acting in the course of his duty were not required. There would then be no rational or logical reason for imposing a heavier penalty in the case where the murderer killed the person whom he did not know and had no reason to know was a police officer acting in the course of his duties.

On the other hand, if s. 214(4)(*a*) is interpreted to require proof of such knowledge before the murder can be classified as first degree murder, then a heavier sentence can be justified on the basis of added moral culpability or as additional deterrent on the grounds of public policy. In such event, it is my opinion that the subsection would not contravene the provisions of s. 7 of the *Charter*.

I am of the opinion that, where a statutory provision is open to two interpretations, one of which will contravene the *Charter* and the other of which will not, the provision should be interpreted in such a manner as will not contravene the *Charter*: see *R. v. Corbett*, [1988] 1 S.C.R. 670, 64 C.R. (3d) 1 at 23, 41 C.C.C. (3d) 385, per Beetz J.

I conclude that the onus was on the Crown to prove that the appellant knew that the victim was a police officer who was acting in the course of his duty and I find, accordingly, that the provisions of s. 214(4)(*a*) do not contravene s. 7 of the *Charter*. In the present case the trial judge charged the jury in accordance with this conclusion. There was evidence to support a finding of knowledge on the part of the appellant. (And see *R. v. Prevost* (1988), 64 C.R. (3d) 188, 42 C.C.C. (3d) 314 at 318 (C.A.).) This ground of appeal, therefore, fails.

R. v. ARKELL

[1990] 2 S.C.R. 695, 79 C.R. (3d) 207, 59 C.C.C. (3d) 65,
1990 CarswellBC 197, 1990 CarswellBC 758

The accused was convicted, pursuant to now s. 231(5), of first degree murder. It was the theory of the Crown that the victim was killed while he attempted to sexually assault her. One of the the constitutional questions for the court was whether s. 231(5) contravened s. 7 of the *Charter.*

LAMER C.J.C. (DICKSON C.J.C. and WILSON, GONTHIER and CORY JJ. concurring): —

The main argument of the appellant, as regards his constitutional challenge of the section, is that it is arbitrary and irrational and thereby offends s. 7 of the *Charter.*

. . . .

The argument of the appellant suggests that the sentencing scheme is flawed and in violation of s. 7 of the *Charter* because it results in the punishment of individuals that is not proportionate to the seriousness of the offences giving rise to the sentences. First, I must note that as a result of this court's decision in *Martineau*, released concurrently, it can no longer be said that s. 214(5) has the potential to classify unintentional killings as first degree murder. A conviction for murder requires proof beyond a reasonable doubt of subjective foresight of death. Therefore, when we reach the stage of classifying murders as either first or second degree, we are dealing with individuals who have committed the most serious crime in our *Criminal Code*, and who have been proven to have done so with the highest level of moral culpability, that of subjective foresight. Section 214(5) represents a decision by Parliament to impose a more serious punishment on those found guilty of murder while committing certain listed offences.

This leads me to a second point, namely, a consideration of the underlying rationale of s. 214(5). Again, I refer to the decision of this court in *R. v. Paré*, [1987] 2 S.C.R. 618, at pp. 632-33:

All murders are serious crimes. Some murders, however, are so threatening to the public that Parliament has chosen to impose exceptional penalties on the perpetrators. One such class of murders is that found in s. 214(5), murders done while committing a hijacking, a kidnapping and forcible confinement, a rape, or an indecent assault. . .

The offences listed in s. 214(5) are all offences involving the unlawful domination of people by other people. Thus an organizing principle for s. 214(5) can be found. This principle is that where a murder is committed by someone already abusing his power by illegally dominating another, the murder should be treated as an exceptionally serious crime. Parliament has chosen to treat these murders as murders in the first degree.

I can find no principle of fundamental justice that prevents Parliament, guided by the organizing principle identified by this court in *Paré*, from classifying murders done while committing certain underlying offences as more serious, and thereby attaching more serious penalties to them. In the case of the distinction between first and second degree murder, the difference is a maximum extra 15 years that must be served before one is eligible for parole. This distinction is neither arbitrary nor irrational. The section is based on an organizing principle that treats murders committed while the perpetrator is illegally dominating another person as more serious than other murders. Further, the relationship between the classification and the moral blameworthiness of the offender clearly exists. Section 214 only comes into play when murder has been proven beyond a reasonable doubt. In light of *Martineau*, this means that the offender has been proven to have had subjective foresight of death. Parliament's decision to treat more seriously murders that have been committed while the offender is exploiting a position of power through illegal domination of the victim accords with the principle that there must be a proportionality between a sentence and the moral blameworthiness of the offender and other considerations such as deterrence and societal condemnation of the acts of the offender. Therefore, I conclude that in so far as s. 214(5) is neither arbitrary nor irrational, it does not infringe upon s. 7 of the *Charter*.

L'Heureux-Dubé J. and Sopinka J. concurred in the result.

For critical comments, see Allan Manson, "The Easy Acceptance of Long Term Confinement in Canada" (1990), 79 C.R. (3d) 265.

In *R. v. Strong* (1990), 2 C.R. (4th) 239 (Alta. C.A.), the court held that first degree murder under s. 231(5) did not include murder in the course of robbery. Not all offences involving illegal domination of one person by another had been included in the list of offences. However in *R. v. Pritchard* (2008), 61 C.R. (6th) 254 (S.C.C.) the Supreme Court held that killing in the course of unlawful confinement met the requirement even if this was for purpose of robbery. **Doesn't this make the section arbitrary and irrational, contrary to section 7 of the *Charter*?**

(b)   Subjective Awareness Guaranteed by *Charter* for Few Crimes

When the Supreme Court struck down the constructive murder rule in s. 230(*d*) of the *Criminal Code* in *Vaillancourt*, Justice Lamer left the impression that the court might one day decide that subjective *mens rea* was constitutionally required for all crimes. It is now clear that the Supreme Court is only likely to declare such a requirement for a very few offences. At present the Supreme Court has required subjective fault for murder, *i.e.*, *Martineau*, attempted murder; *R. v. Logan*, [1990] 2 S.C.R. 731, 79 C.R. (3d) 169, 58 C.C.C. (3d) 391, accessory liability to an offence constitutionally requiring a subjective test, *Logan*; and war crimes and crimes against humanity, *R. v. Finta*, [1994] 1 S.C.R. 701, 28 C.R. (4th) 265, 88 C.C.C. (3d) 417. There is also *obiter* recognition in *Vaillancourt* and *Martineau* that theft requires subjective awareness.

It is important to be clear what this *Charter* rule means, and what it does not mean. That only a few crimes are *guaranteed* subjective fault does not displace the common law presumption from *R. v. Beaver*, [1957] S.C.R. 531, 26 C.R. 193, 118 C.C.C. 129 that all crimes as a matter of fact have subjective fault unless Parliament has clearly expressed a contrary intention. What the *Martineau* rule establishes is that for a few crimes, even if Parliament *does* clearly express a contrary intention, the offence must have subjective fault nonetheless. See the further discussion of this point under subheading 5(a)(i) Common Law Presumption.

The *Charter* analysis is still turning on the unruly criterion of stigma criticized by most commentators as unreliable and potentially circular. See, for example, Isabel Grant and Christine Boyle, "Equality, Harm and Vulnerability: Homicide and Sexual Assault Post-*Creighton*" (1993), 23 C.R. (4th) 252 at 258-259 and Rosemary Cairns Way, "Constitutionalizing Subjectivism: Another View" (1990), 79 C.R. (3d) 260. The Supreme Court has decided that the stigma necessary to require subjective *mens rea* does not follow from a conviction of the *Criminal Code* offences of unlawful act causing bodily harm, *R. v. DeSousa*, [1992] 2 S.C.R. 944, 15 C.R. (4th) 66, 76 C.C.C. (3d) 124; dangerous driving, *R. v. Hundal*, [1993] 1 S.C.R. 867, 19 C.R. (4th) 169, 79 C.C.C. (3d) 97; manslaughter, *R. v. Creighton*, [1993] 3 S.C.R. 3, 23 C.R. (4th) 189, 83 C.C.C. (3d) 346; failing to provide necessaries of life, *R. v. Naglik*, [1993] 3 S.C.R. 122, 23 C.R. (4th) 335, 83 C.C.C. (3d) 526, and careless use of a firearm, *R. v. Finlay*, [1993] 3 S.C.R. 103, 23 C.R. (4th) 321, 83 C.C.C. (3d) 513 and *R. v. Gosset*, [1993] 3 S.C.R. 76, 23 C.R. (4th) 280, 83 C.C.C. (3d) 494.

Provincial Courts of Appeal have also been unreceptive to *Charter* arguments to entrench subjective tests. Challenges have been rejected for offences of causing bodily harm in committing assault, *R. v. Brooks* (1988), 64 C.R. (3d) 322, 41 C.C.C. (3d) 157 (B.C. C.A.); criminal negligence, *R. v. Nelson* (1990), 75 C.R. (4th) 70, 54 C.C.C. (3d) 285 (Ont. C.A.) and *R. v. Gingrich* (1991), 6 C.R. (4th) 197, 65 C.C.C. (3d) 188 (Ont. C.A.); and arson, *R. v. Peters* (1991), 11 C.R. (4th) 48, 69 C.C.C. (3d) 461 (B.C. C.A.).

5.   THREE TYPES OF FAULT FOR CRIMES SINCE *CREIGHTON*

Given *Creighton*, *Criminal Code* offences are, for the determination of fault, divided into three categories as follows:

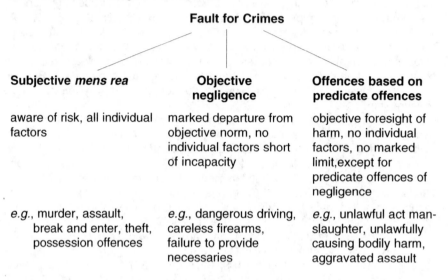

Fault for Crimes

Subjective *mens rea*	Objective negligence	Offences based on predicate offences
aware of risk, all individual factors	marked departure from objective norm, no individual factors short of incapacity	objective foresight of harm, no individual factors, no marked limit,except for predicate offences of negligence
e.g., murder, assault, break and enter, theft, possession offences	*e.g.*, dangerous driving, careless firearms, failure to provide necessaries	*e.g.*, unlawful act man-slaughter, unlawfully causing bodily harm, aggravated assault

(a)   Crimes Requiring Subjective Awareness

(i)   Common law presumption

We have just seen that subjective *mens rea* is only a *Charter* requirement in the case of a few very serious crimes.

Where the *Criminal Code* definitions of an offence include a clear *mens rea* word, such as "intentionally", "wilfully", or "knowingly", Parliament has made its choice of the subjective test clear.

Where the definition of the crime contains no *mens rea* words, and there is no language indicating the crime is to be interpreted as one of objective negligence, it should be interpreted as an offence of subjective *mens rea*. Decisions reading in subjective fault requirements for drug offences, *R. v. Beaver*, [1957] S.C.R. 531, 26 C.R. 193 and the former offence of rape, *R. v. Pappajohn*, [1980] 2 S.C.R. 120, 52 C.C.C. (2d) 481 and *R. v. Sansregret*, [1985] 1 S.C.R. 570, 45 C.R. (3d) 193, are still authoritative. McLachlin J., who delivered the majority judgment in *R. v. Creighton*, also authored the majority judgment in *R. v. Théroux*, [1993] 2 S.C.R. 5, 19 C.R. (4th) 194, 79 C.C.C. (3d) 449, in which the court interpreted the ambiguous word "fraudulent" to require a subjective *mens rea* requirement for theft and fraud. In *R. v. Clemente*, [1994] 2 S.C.R. 758, 31 C.R. (4th) 28, 91 C.C.C. (3d) 1, the Supreme Court read into the offence of threatening to cause death or serious harm the requirement of an intent to intimidate or instill fear or an intent to be taken seriously.

However, in *R. v. Hinchey* (1996), 3 C.R. (5th) 187, 111 C.C.C. (3d) 353 (S.C.C.), L'Heureux-Dubé J., speaking for four of seven justices, appeared reluctant to adopt an approach of a common law presumption of subjective *mens rea*. Her Ladyship also noted that some offences have been interpreted to have both subjective and objective fault requirements. She gave *Lohnes* as an example. Her remarks are *obiter*, as she agreed that the crime in question, s. 121(1)(c) of the *Criminal Code* prohibiting the giving or receiving a benefit by a government official or employee, did require subjective *mens rea*. See the comment by Don Stuart, "Corruption in Hinchey: Scrambling *Mens Rea* Principles" (1997), 3 C.R. (5th) 238.

A more recent pronouncement from the Supreme Court of Canada asserts a common law presumption of subjective *mens rea*. In *Lucas*, [1998] 1 S.C.R. 439, 14 C.R. (5th) 237, 123 C.C.C. (3d) 97 (S.C.C.), the court held that the crime of defamatory libel under ss. 298-300 of the *Criminal Code* was a demonstrably justified limit on the freedom of expression guaranteed by s. 2(b) of the *Charter.* Cory J., for a full court unanimous on this point, declared the need for a requirement of an intent to defame based on the principle that:

> . . . in the absence of an express legislative provision, it should be presumed that proof of subjective *mens rea* is a requirement of criminal offences (C.R., para. 64).

The court cited *City of Sault Ste. Marie* and, surprisingly, *Vaillancourt.* The court went on to enunciate a test of whether the accused knew that the message, as it would be understood by a reasonable person, was false (C.R., para.102). Allan Manson, Annotation to *Lucas* (1998), 14 C.R. (5th) 237 at 241, argues that this wrongly incorporates an objective standard and that the test should be "whether the accused knows that the message, as he or she believes it will be understood, is false" (C.R. at 242).

In *R. v. Boulanger* (2006), 39 C.R. (6th) 1, [2006] 2 S.C.R. 49, 210 C.C.C. (3d) 1 (S.C.C.) the Court acquitted on a charge under s. 122 of the *Criminal Code* of breach of trust by an official. The court read in a subjective *mens rea* requirement of intent for an offence which contains no express *mens rea* words such as wilful, purpose, or intent.

Courts have recently applied a presumption of subjective *mens rea* to acquit on charges of breach of probation (*R. v. Eby* (2007), 47 C.R. (6th) 289 (Alta. Prov.Ct.)), abandoning a newly born infant in a toilet not knowing the baby was alive (*R. v. H. (A.D.)* (2009), 68 C.R. (6th) 74 (Sask. Q.B.)), criminal harassment (*R. v. Eltom* (2010), 258 C.C.C. (3D) 224 (Ont. S.C.J.)) and contempt of court by an inexperienced lawyer (*R. v.Devost* (2010), 256 C.C.C. (3d) 374 (Ont. C.A.)).

(ii) *Motive*

> THOMAS. Now is my way clear, now is the meaning plain:
> Temptation shall not come in this kind again.
> The last temptation is the greatest treason:
> To do the right deed for the wrong reason.
>
> (T.S. Eliot, *Murder in the Cathedral*)

At common law courts have often said that a requirement of intent does not require proof of a motive.

J. HALL, GENERAL PRINCIPLES OF CRIMINAL LAW

2nd ed. (1960), 104

. . . .

In sum: (1) the professional literature, especially beginning with Hale, distinguished *mens rea* from motive. *Mens rea*, a fusion of cognition and volition, is the mental state expressed in the *voluntary* commission of a proscribed harm. (2) The exclusion of motive, as not essential in *mens rea*, does not deny the importance of motive in determining the culpability ("guilt") of the defendant. Instead, the reason for doing that is the necessity to preserve the objectivity of the principle of *mens rea* and the principle of legality, *i.e.* to signify some degree of culpability regardless of how good the motive was. Thus questions of motivation and mitigating circumstances are allocated to administration which can explore such issues thoroughly. (3) Implied in the above conclusions is that the principle of *mens rea* must be given an objective ethical meaning — the premise being that actual harms (disvalues) are proscribed. Accordingly, neither the offender's conscience nor the personal code of ethics of the judge or the jury can be substituted for the ethics of the penal law. The insistence that guilt should be personal must be interpreted to accord with the paramount value of the objectivity of the principle of *mens rea*.

LEWIS v. R.

[1979] 2 S.C.R. 821, 10 C.R. (3d) 299, 47 C.C.C. (2d) 24,
1979 CarswellBC 520, 1979 CarswellBC 531

The accused and one Tatlay were jointly charged with the murder of Tatlay's daughter and son-in-law. The accused admitted mailing a package to the victims on behalf of Tatlay but denied any knowledge that the package contained a bomb.

DICKSON J.: —

. . . .

During their deliberations, the jury asked to have read back: (i) the evidence of Brabant with regard to whether or not Lewis had written something down while in the telephone booth; and (ii) the cross-examination of Crown counsel dealing with the financial situation of Lewis. Defence counsel did not request that the judge at this time charge the jury on the concept of motive.

At the end of the day, the critical question in Lewis' case was whether or not at the time he mailed the package he knew that it contained a bomb.

Appeal

On appeal, a number of grounds were relied upon. All were rejected by a unanimous Court of Appeal. With respect to motive, the court had this to say:

> Counsel for Lewis also submitted that the charge was deficient in failing to include a definition of "motive" and a direction regarding the absence of proof of motive on Lewis's part. There was some evidence, inconclusive, that Lewis' objective was money. In any event, the jury, as intelligent people, could not fail to consider the matter. That they were concerned is evidenced from the fact that they interrupted their deliberations to return to the courtroom and have read to them the cross-examination of Lewis dealing with his financial situation. This was done in a manner satisfactory to counsel. The defence of Lewis was, on the whole, adequately and fairly put before the jury by the judge.

Motive in law

In ordinary parlance, the words "intent" and "motive" are frequently used interchangeably, but in the criminal law they are distinct. In most criminal trials the mental element, the *mens rea* with which the court is concerned, relates to "intent", *i.e.*, the exercise of a free will to use particular means to produce a particular result, rather than with "motive", *i.e.*, that which precedes and induces the exercise of the will. The mental element of a crime ordinarily involves no reference to motive: 11 Hals. (4th) 17, para. 11.

. . . .

Accepting the term "motive" in a criminal law sense, as meaning "ulterior intention", it is possible, I think, upon the authorities, to formulate a number of propositions.

(1) As evidence, motive is always relevant and hence evidence of motive is admissible.

. . . .

(2) Motive is no part of the crime and is legally irrelevant to criminal

responsibility. It is not an essential element of the prosecution's case as a matter of law.

. . . .

(3) Proved absence of motive is always an important fact in favour of the accused and ordinarily worthy of note in a charge to the jury.

. . . .

(4) Conversely, proved presence of motive may be an important factual ingredient in the Crown's case, notably on the issues of identity and intention, when the evidence is purely circumstantial.

. . . .

(5) Motive is therefore always a question of fact and evidence and the necessity of referring to motive in the charge to the jury falls within the general duty of the trial Judge not only to outline the theories of the prosecution and defence but to give the jury matters of evidence essential in arriving at a just conclusion.

. . . .

(6) Each case will turn on its own unique set of circumstances. The issue of motive is always a matter of degree.

. . . .

The Present Case

In the light of the foregoing propositions, I examine the case at bar. One of the points to note is that the Crown put forward two alternative theories as to the transaction between Tatlay and Lewis. The dominant theory of the Crown was that Tatlay, enraged at his daughter's defiance, instigated Lewis to fashion and mail the kettle-bomb which killed the couple. Alternatively, the Crown suggested that Tatlay or some other person might have made the bomb, and that Lewis mailed the parcel, knowing it to contain a bomb. The broad theory related to both Tatlay and Lewis, the narrow theory related only to Lewis. Thus Lewis would stand convicted, as the trial judge pointed out in his charge, if the jury accepted either theory:

> Now, if you were satisfied beyond a reasonable doubt that Lewis made this bomb and that Tatlay procured him to do it, that is, enlisted his services to do it, then I say — and I will tell you the law more particularly in a few moments — that you would have evidence upon

> which you could find — that you are satisfied beyond a reasonable doubt that these men were guilty of murder.
>
> Alternatively, it seems to me that even if you found that Lewis did not fashion the lethal weapon but he was the courier, that is, he is the one who mailed it, and that he mailed it with the realization of what he was mailing, again I would say that would be evidence if you are satisfied beyond a reasonable doubt of that fact, to justify finding that he was guilty of murder.

The *actus reus* of the narrow theory is identified by the Crown as the mailing of the parcel. This removes the materiality of motive as to proof of identity, and thus narrows the necessary mental element, or *mens rea*, to knowledge that the parcel contained a bomb, the requisite specific intent following as a matter of inference.

. . . .

Applying the propositions which I have outlined earlier, it will be seen that motive was not proven as part of the Crown's case, nor was absence of motive proven by the defence. There was therefore no clear obligation in law to charge on motive. Whether or not to charge became, therefore, a matter of judgment for the trial judge, and his decision should not be lightly reversed. As Coyne J.A. said in *R. v. Malanik (No. 2)* (1951), 13 C.R. 160, 101 C.C.C. 182 (Man. C.A.), at p. 164:

> The summing-up must not be examined microscopically in a critical spirit to make *post facto* fault-finding (*R. v. Stoddart* (1909), 2 Cr. App. R. 217, approved in *Preston v. R.*, [1949] S.C.R. 156 at 162, 7 C.R. 72, 93 C.C.C. 81), but solely to determine whether the summing-up as a whole in the light of all the proceedings was such as to enable the jury to appreciate the case before them and their powers and duty and to afford some reasonable assistance to the exercise and performance of them in the case.

Every summing-up must be regarded in the light of the conduct of the trial and the questions which have been raised by the counsel for the prosecution and for the defence respectively: per Alverstone L.C.J. in *R. v. Stoddart, supra*, at p. 246.

Counsel at trial did not ask the judge to instruct on motive, and the judge obviously felt that such instruction was not called for in the light of the entire trial. Although evidence of Brabant was important to the case against Lewis, there was really very little conflict between the evidence of Brabant and that of Lewis.

. . . .

In the result, I am unable to find error on the part of the trial judge and I therefore reach the same conclusion as the Court of Appeal of British Columbia.

I would accordingly dismiss the appeal.

Appeal dismissed.

The Court here says in *Lewis* that motive is not an essential element of the prosecution's case. However, we will see that criminal law distinguishes between two types of intent: specific intent and general intent. *Lewis* describes motive as "ulterior intention", which is also how specific intent is described in some decisions. Is the court consistent in how it deals with ulterior intention?

―――――――――

Canada's Anti-terrorist Bill C-36, rushed through Parliament in 2001 following the horror of the 9/11 attacks in the United States, contains broad and controversial definitions of terrorist activity. These are now to be found in s. 83.01 of the *Criminal Code*. One such definition requires that acts or omissions have been committed "in whole or in part for a political, religious or ideological purpose, objective or cause".

Are there particular dangers in requiring proof of such motives?

The controversial anti-terrorist measures are considered in detail below in Chapter 10.

R. v. KHAWAJA

(2011), 82 C.R. (6th) 122, 273 C.C.C. (3d) 415, 2010 CarswellOnt 9672 (Ont. C.A.)

Per curiam:

88 Motive refers to the reason, or at least one of the reasons, that a person chooses to engage in conduct intending to bring about a certain consequence. One's reason for choosing to bring about that consequence is one's "motive": *R. v. Lewis*, [1979] 2 S.C.R. 821, at pp. 831-32; D. Stuart, *Canadian Criminal Law: A Treatise*, 5th ed. (Toronto: Thomson Carswell, 2007), at p. 225. We agree with the trial judge that s. 83.01(1)(b)(i)(A) requires proof of motive, in that it requires proof that one of the reasons for engaging in the proscribed conduct was "a political, religious or ideological purpose, objective or cause". In fact, there are two motive clauses in the definition of "terrorist activity". Section 83.01(1)(b)(i)(B), which we have described as the ulterior intention clause, also requires proof of motive, in that it requires proof of a reason for which the person brought about the intended consequence: see K. Roach, "Terrorism Offences and the *Charter*: A Comment on *R. v. Khawaja*" (2007) 11 *Can. Crim. L.R.* 272, at p. 292.

89 While we agree that s. 83.01(1)(b)(i)(A) is properly described as a motive clause, we attribute no significance in the constitutional argument to the fact

that the section requires proof of motive. The mental processes that precede and generate conduct are multi-faceted and interrelated. They can be parsed and labeled in a variety of ways. Conduct may have one or many motives. The same state of mind may be described as motive, intention or purpose. None of the labels is intrinsically more accurate than the others. The distinction between motive and other mental states is often one of terminology rather than substance: B. Fisse, *Howard's Criminal Law*, 5th ed. (Sydney: Law Book Co., 1990), at pp. 485-86.

90 For example, the offence of break and enter with intent to steal can be described as requiring proof of the reason or motive that precipitated the break-in - an intention to steal. However, if one wishes to avoid using the word "motive" to describe an element of the *mens rea*, one can refer to the intention to steal as the burglar's ulterior intention and describe the burglar's motive as his or her desire for financial gain, a state of mind that is irrelevant to criminal culpability.

91 The aphorism that "motive is no part of a crime" does not express a criminal law principle referable to the permitted scope of criminal liability, much less a principle of fundamental justice protected by s. 7 of the Charter. The aphorism refers to the interpretive rule that, ordinarily, when interpreting the mens rea required for criminal culpability, and absent statutory language to the contrary, the reason or reasons that cause an accused to engage in prohibited conduct or to choose to bring about a prohibited consequence are irrelevant to culpability: *United States of America v. Dynar*, [1997] 2 S.C.R. 462, at pp. 496-97. The aphorism is also a reflection of the nomenclature used to describe the fault component of crimes and, more specifically, to distinguish between states of mind that are relevant to culpability as described in the statute creating the offence (e.g., intent, purpose), and states of mind that are not relevant to that definition (e.g., motive): Colvin & Anand, at pp. 192-93. Professor G. Williams in his *Textbook of Criminal Law*, 2nd ed. (London: Stevens & Sons, 1983) puts it this way, at p. 75:

> In ordinary speech, "intention" and "motive" are often convertible terms. For the lawyer, the word "motive" generally refers to some further intent which forms no part of the legal rule.

92. Nor do we accept that treating motive as relevant to criminal culpability is foreign to Canadian criminal law. Motive plays a part in many aspects of the substantive criminal law, including the definition of the fault component of some crimes and the definition of exculpatory justifications and excuses: M. Plaxton, "Irruptions of Motive in the War on Terror" (2007) 11 Can. Crim. L.R. 233; Colvin & Anand, at pp. 192-93. For example, there are many Criminal Code offences that require that the prohibited conduct be done for a specified purpose that is ulterior to the conduct component of the crime (e.g., s. 23(1) (accessory after the fact), s. 51 (intimidating Parliament or the legislature), s. 52 (sabotage),

s. 53 (inciting to mutiny), s. 57(2) (false statement in relation to passport), s. 151 (sexual interference), s. 152 (invitation to sexual touching)). The requirement that the Crown prove "purpose" can refer to different states of mind, including the requirement of proof of the reason that precipitated the conduct that brought about the intended consequence. When purpose is used in this sense, it is effectively indistinguishable from the concept of motive: *R. v. Hibbert*, [1995] 2 S.C.R. 973, at para. 27; *R. v. Kerr*, [2004] 2 S.C.R. 371, at paras. 26-27.

The Ontario Court of Appeal has itself earlier found it useful to distinguish motive from intent in its decision in *R. v. Priestap* (2006), 39 C.R. (6th) 391 (Ont. C.A.). The offence of prowling at night was held to have been introduced to criminalise "peeping tom" conduct and the Crown did not have to prove motive or an underlying specific evil purpose.

Was the distinction between intent and motive satisfactorily made in the following decision allowing a defence of prank?

R. v. MATHE

(1973), 11 C.C.C. (2d) 427, 1973 CarswellBC 103 (B.C. C.A.)

BRANCA J.A.: — The appellant was charged

for that he the said Eugene William Mathe on the 29th day of September 1972 at the City of Victoria, County aforesaid in the Province of British Columbia did unlawfully attempt to steal cash from Kathleen Hadley and at the time thereof did use threats of violence to the said Kathleen Hadley contrary to the *Criminal Code*.

The facts involved were very short and the material part of the narrative was testified to by Mrs. Hadley, a teller at the Canada Permanent Trust Company office at 1125 Douglas St. in the City of Victoria.

She stated that the appellant came into the building to her wicket at about 10:15 a.m. on September 29, 1972, alone, and said, "I have a 38 in my pocket. Hand over the cash." and then added, "Quickly hand over the cash." She went to her cash drawer and started getting out twenties at which time he said, "That's not what I want." and added that he was only joking and that he was a security guard and did not want the cash. He then shook her hand and left the building, walking north on Douglas St. in the company of a man named John Fuller, who was a customer of the bank and who was known to Mrs. Hadley.

She was very scared but when she took out the twenties from her cash drawer she set off a buzzer which was soundless and nothing went on which might indicate that fact to the appellant. He was apprehended later at 11:10 a.m. by the police, standing by the fountain at Centennial Square, only a couple of blocks from the police station in Victoria by Constable Dibden, who testified as follows:

> I approached Mr. Mathe and asked him to accompany me to the City Police Station as he answered the description of a person of — who had earlier been broadcast by the Police Department. He agreed to go along with me, at this time I said, "Were you at Canada Trust Building on Douglas Street this morning" and he stated he was. I said, "Did you tell the girl this was a holdup"? He stated, "I was only fooling, I didn't mean to hold the place up". I said, "Where's the gun that you told her you had"? He stated, "Did I say that, she'll have to prove that". By this time we approached on foot at the Police Station. I took him inside to the main floor of the Police Station where I turned him over to Detective Horsman.

The officer said the appellant had been drinking but did not believe he was intoxicated.

Horsman, a detective of the Victoria City Police Force, saw the appellant at 1:25 p.m. and charged and warned the appellant. He answered certain questions and the answers were at variance with what I have said. The detective said he felt that the appellant had been drinking excessively.

. . . .

It is true, as the learned trial Judge said, that his explanation might well yield an inference that the appellant at the time he uttered the words had a change of heart for some reason and decided to abandon the transaction or not to proceed with an apparent act of robbery. The action, however, plus the words were equally consistent with and confirmed a conclusion that the appellant very stupidly went into the office and uttered his words as a joke and then to show that, in fact it was a joke, he uttered the words, "That's not what I want" as she started sorting the twenties out and he added that he was only joking. The inference that the whole thing was a farce is as strong as the inference that it indicated a change of plan.

If, in fact, the transaction amounted to a joke, there was no crime. If on the other hand he was serious initially but decided to abandon the transaction, then there could be a crime. The accused was protected at all times by the presumption of innocence and by the fact that the Crown was under an obligation to prove guilt beyond a reasonable doubt.

The evidence, therefore, if it yields to an inference of guilt but likewise to an inference of innocence, cannot result in proof of the crime beyond a reasonable doubt.

In *R. v. Wilkins*, [1965] 2 C.C.C. 189, 44 C.R. 375, Wilkins was charged with the theft of a motor-cycle belonging to a policeman which was parked and running while the policeman was writing out a parking ticket. He took the motor-cycle to drive it for only a short distance and for the purpose of playing a joke on the policeman. He was convicted of theft and appealed.

The conviction was quashed on appeal and Roach J.A., who delivered a majority judgment stated at p. 195 as follows:

> In the instant case the facts could not possibly justify a conviction of theft. The accused did not intend to steal the vehicle, that is, to convert the property in it to his own use but only to drive it as contemplated by s. 281. His intention was merely to play a joke on Nichol and the Judge so found. The intention to perpetrate this joke, stupid though it was, is incompatible with the evil intent which is inherent in the crime of theft.

In *R. v. Kerr*, [1965] 4 C.C.C. 37, 47 C.R. 268, the accused was a prominent businessman, who with others was celebrating the winning of a dog trial championship show and while at the airport with his friends, being highly intoxicated, he behaved quite foolishly and made off with a 30-lb. ashtray, while the custodian was present and witnessing the whole transaction. The custodian notified the police, who then found it on Kerr's lawn in front of his house the next morning and Kerr then said to them that he was going to return it and was not aware, in fact, that he had taken it.

Miller C.J.M., with whom Guy J.A., concurred, stated at p. 41:

> In his reasons for judgment the learned Magistrate obviously thought that drunkenness was the main defence advanced, and he directed his mind almost entirely to the question of drunkenness and whether the accused was so drunk that he did not know what he was doing. The evidence as to drinking was led to show not only his condition but as an explanation of his mental attitude towards this silly, stupid, removal of the ashtray and in proof of the fact that it was a prank and not a theft. The learned Magistrate said taking the ashtray as a prank is not a defence to a charge of stealing. That may be so in some cases, but when all the circumstances of this case are considered it must be deemed that it was only a question of an ill-considered prank (if it were considered at all) and that the elements of intent and *animus furandi* were completely absent. Certainly, if the learned Magistrate had properly directed himself he would, in my opinion, have had at least a reasonable doubt as to the intent of the accused.

See also *Handfield v. The Queen* (1953), 109 C.C.C. 53, 17 C.R. 343, [1953] Que. Q.B. 584*n*, where a conviction dealing with the theft of an election banner belonging to one candidate was removed by the appellants and taken to a location down the road and placed on a tree in front of the home of the uncle of one of the accused who was not a political friend of the candidate from whom the banner was taken. The appellants were convicted and the conviction quashed in the Court of Appeal on the basis that it was done as a trick.

This court, of course, is in as good a position to draw inferences from the uncontradicted facts proved in evidence by the Crown as was the trial Judge in the court below: see *R. v. Rusnak (Alias Ross)*, [1963] 1 C.C.C. 143. In my judgment the evidence was such that it raised a substantial reasonable doubt in reference to the guilt of the appellant on the charge which should have been resolved in his favour and which I so resolve. The same reasoning would preclude a conviction for any included lesser offences.

The appeal must he allowed, the conviction quashed and a verdict of acquittal entered.

The concurring judgments of Maclean and Seaton JJ.A. are omitted.

Similar reasoning led to an acquittal on a charge of break, enter and theft in *R. v. Dewit and Sierens* (1981), 62 C.C.C. (2d) 176 (Man. Prov. Ct.). Sometimes a court will reject "the defence of no *animus furandi*" and mitigate the penalty by imposing a light fine, *Paris v. R.* (1971), 15 C.R.N.S. 111 (Que. C.A.), or by granting a discharge, *Bogner v. R.* (1975), 33 C.R.N.S. 348 (Que. C.A.) and *R. v. Duggan* (1975), 38 C.R.N.S. 25 (N.S. Co. Ct.).

Which approach do you prefer?

PROBLEM

The accused stopped his vehicle on a street corner and had a conversation with a female police officer, who was posing as a prostitute. He indicated he wanted a "lay" but that he only had $20 as he was a student. The officer agreed and asked him to pull around the block. The accused drove off in the opposite direction. On his arrest he was found to have only $14 in his possession. Charged with communicating for the purpose of obtaining the sexual services of a prostitute contrary to s. 213 of the *Criminal Code*, his defence is that he was merely "fooling around" to satisfy his curiousity. Give judgment. Compare *Pake* (1995), 45 C.R. (4th) 117, 103 C.C.C. (3d) 524 (Alta. C.A.).

Although motive is normally considered not part of the fault inquiry, we will see much later, when we turn to Justifications and Excuse, that motive is often central to such defences as self-defence.

(iii)   Desire/Purpose

R. v. HIBBERT

[1995] 2 S.C.R. 973, 40 C.R. (4th) 141, 99 C.C.C. (3d) 193,
1995 CarswellOnt 117, 1995 CarswellOnt 530

In the context of a major ruling on duress (considered later), Chief Justice Lamer for the court considered the meaning of the word "purpose" in s. 21(1)(b) of the Code. That section imposes criminal liability for an offence on anyone who "does or omits to do anything for the purpose of aiding any person to commit it". The court held that purpose is not the same as desire. In an earlier ruling, *R. v. Paquette* (1976), [1977] 2 S.C.R. 189, 39 C.R.N.S. 257, 30 C.C.C. (2d) 417, the court had concluded that a person who, out of fear, assisted another person to commit a crime did not have a "common intention" with that person, and so would not be liable as a party under s. 21(2). In *Hibbert* the court decides not to adopt that same approach to s. 21(1)(b), and indeed to abandon it with regard to s. 21(2).

LAMER C.J.: —

. . . .

It is impossible to ascribe a single fixed meaning to the term "purpose". In ordinary usage, the word is employed in two distinct senses. One can speak of an actor doing something "on purpose" (as opposed to by accident) thereby equating purpose with "immediate intention". The term is also used, however, to indicate the ultimate ends an actor seeks to achieve, which imports the idea of "desire" into the definition. This dual sense is apparent in the word's dictionary definition. For instance, the Oxford English Dictionary (2nd ed., 1989), defines "purpose" alternatively as "[t]hat which one sets before oneself as a thing to be done or attained; the object which one has in view" and as "[t]he action or fact of intending or meaning to do something; intention, resolution, determination". The first of these definitions reflects the notion of one's "purpose" as relating to one's ultimate object or desire, while the latter conveys the notion of "purpose" as being synonymous with "intention".

Commentators who have considered the meaning of "purpose" in definitions of criminal offences have come to differing conclusions on the question of which of these alternate meanings is more appropriate in this context. Professor E. Colvin, for instance, argues on behalf of the "purpose as desire" interpretation in his text *Principles of Criminal Law*, 2nd ed. (Toronto: Carswell, 1991). He states (at pp. 121-22):

> The terms "direct intention" and "desire" are sometimes used instead of purpose. The latter term, however, best describes the relevant state of mind. In ordinary language descriptions of action, the concept of purpose usually refers to an actor's *reasons* for doing what he did . . . [Emphasis in original.]

According to Colvin, "an actor's purpose was to accomplish something if the prospect of its occurrence played a causal role in his decision to do what he did" (p. 122). The actor's knowledge that his actions will result in the occurrence, however, is not determinative. As Colvin states (at p. 123):

> If it is to be concluded that an actor's purpose in doing something did not include an outcome which was foreseen, then the actor must have been genuinely opposed or indifferent to it. Purpose is not negatived where an actor *chose* to bring about the outcome as a means of attaining some further objective. [Emphasis in original.]

Other commentators, however, have questioned this equation of "purpose" with "desire", arguing instead that a person who consciously performs an act knowing the consequences that will (with some degree of certainty) flow from it "intends" these consequences or causes them "on purpose", regardless of whether he or she *desired* them. As Mewett and Manning state:

... the distinction between purpose/intent and knowledge/intent does not work, because if there is, given an awareness of the consequences of an act, a freedom of choice as to whether one acts or not, by choosing to act those consequences have been chosen. If intent is the choosing of consequences, it does not make any difference to the existence of the intent whether the accused wants those consequences to follow or merely knows that they will follow, without necessarily desiring them to do so.

"Intent", is not a very descriptive word. *Mens rea* connotes volition on the part of the accused, that is to say, given an awareness that certain consequences will follow (or will probably follow) if he acts, an accused who chooses to act when he has the alternative of not acting "intends" those consequences in the sense of choosing to bring them about. It seems not only unnecessary but positively misleading to attempt to distinguish between purpose/ intent and knowledge/intent.

(*Criminal Law* (2nd ed., 1985), at p. 113.)

A similar argument is made by the English authors J. C. Smith and B. Hogan:

... person may know that he cannot achieve his purpose, A, without bringing about some other result, B. If he is to bring about A, he knows he must also, at the same time or earlier, bring about B. It may be that, in any other circumstances, he would much rather B did not happen, indeed its occurrence may be abhorrent to him. But, the choice being between going without A and having A and B, he decides to have A and B. It seems fair to say that he intends to cause B as well as A.

(*Criminal Law* (7th ed., 1992), at p. 55.)

As this debate reveals, the term "purpose" is capable of bearing two distinct meanings, both of which can be supported by reasoned arguments. In a case, such as this one, where an interpretation of the term in a specific statutory context is required, the court's task is to determine which of the two possible meanings best accords with Parliament's intention in drafting the particular statutory provision at issue. In other words, our task in the present case is to consider the meaning of "purpose" as it is employed in s. 21(1)(*b*) of the *Code* in light of the Parliamentary objective underlying the subsection. It must be emphasized, however, that the word "purpose" is employed in many different sections of the *Criminal Code*, in a number of distinct contexts. My conclusions in the present case on the proper interpretation of the word "purpose" as it is employed in s. 21(1)(*b*) of the *Code* are thus restricted to this particular subsection. It may well be that in the context of some other statutory provision a different interpretation of the term will prove to be the most appropriate.

... As I will explain, I am of the view that in the context of s. 21(1)(*b*) of the *Code*, the second of the two meanings of "purpose" discussed above — that is, the interpretation that equates "purpose" with "intention" — best reflects the legislative intent underlying the subsection. In contrast, adopting the first interpretation of "purpose" (the "purpose" equals "desire" interpretation) to describe the mens rea for aiding in s. 21(1)(*b*) would, in my view, create a number of theoretical and practical difficulties that Parliament is unlikely to have envisioned or intended.

The problems associated with the "purpose equals desire" interpretation are several. First, incorporating the accused's feelings about the desirability of the commission of an offence by the principal into the definition of the mens rea for "aiding" can result in distinctions being made which appear arbitrary and unreasonable in light of the policy underlying s. 21(1)(b). As Professor Colvin notes, under the "purpose equals desire" interpretation a person would not be guilty of aiding in the commission of an offence if he or she were "genuinely opposed or indifferent to it" (p. 123). The reason for the aider's indifference or opposition would be immaterial. The perverse consequences that flow from this are clearly illustrated by the following hypothetical situation described by Mewett and Manning:

> If a man is approached by a friend who tells him that he is going to rob a bank and would like to use his car as the getaway vehicle for which he will pay him $100, when that person is . . . charged under s. 21 for doing something for the purpose of aiding his friend to commit the offence, can he say "My purpose was not to aid the robbery but to make $100"? His argument would be that while he knew that he was helping the robbery, his desire was to obtain $100 and he did not care one way or the other whether the robbery was successful or not.

(*Criminal Law, supra*, at p. 112.)

I agree with the authors' conclusion that "[t]hat would seem an absurd result" (p. 112). As I noted in *McIntosh, supra*, at pp. 704-5, "[a]bsurdity is a factor to consider in the interpretation of ambiguous statutory provisions". That is, to quote the words of La Forest J.A. (as he then was) in *Re Estabrooks Pontiac Buick Ltd.* (1982), 44 N.B.R. (2d) 201, at p. 210, "[t]he fact that the words as interpreted would give an unreasonable result . . . is certainly ground for the courts to scrutinize a statute carefully to make abundantly certain that those words are not susceptible of another interpretation". In my view, the absurdity that would flow from the equation of "purpose" with "desire" cannot legitimately be ascribed to Parliamentary intention. This serves to cast considerable doubt on the correctness of this interpretation of the word "purpose" in this context, especially when one recalls that there exists an alternative interpretation of the word that can just as accurately be said to reflect its "plain meaning", under which this absurdity would be avoided.

. . . .

Finally, I am satisfied that the interpretation of the mens rea for liability under s. 21(1)(b) that I am proposing will not result in unjust convictions in cases involving coercion by threats of death or bodily harm, since in these cases the common law defence of duress will remain available to the accused. As I will explain shortly, this defence, properly understood, provides an excuse to persons who assist in the commission of offences as a result of threats of serious violence. On the other hand, interpreting "purpose" as equivalent to "desire" in

s. 21(1)(*b*) would result in the introduction of unnecessary complication into the law. Under such an interpretation, juries in duress cases would have to be provided with extremely complex instructions that would, in the end, have very little, if any, impact on the final determination of guilt or innocence. As a matter of logic, the issue of whether an accused can invoke an excuse or justification arises only after the Crown has proven the existence of all the elements of the offence, including mens rea. Thus, if "purpose" were understood as incorporating "desire", and hence as being susceptible to "negation" by duress, trial judges would have to instruct juries accordingly. This would require judges, and juries, to delve into the arcane issue of whether a person who intentionally commits an offence in order to save his or her own skin commits the offence "on purpose" — a question of some philosophical significance, perhaps, but no easy matter for a judge to explain succinctly, or for a jury to comprehend readily.

Furthermore, as was the case with s. 21(1)(b), the interpretation of s. 21(2)'s *mens rea* requirement that was adopted by the court in *Paquette* is not essential as a means of ensuring the avoidance of unjust convictions in duress cases, since here, as in cases involving s. 21(1)(b), accused persons who act under duress have recourse to the protection from criminal liability provided by the common law defence of duress. At the same time, it can be seen that the interpretation of s. 21(2) adopted in *Paquette* significantly complicates the law of duress, in so far as it requires juries to be instructed on both the manner in which duress might "negate" *mens rea* and on the common law defence of duress itself, notwithstanding the fact that both cover essentially the same ground. This problem would be exacerbated if the interpretation of s. 21(2) in *Paquette* was preserved alongside the interpretation of s. 21(1)(b) that we are adopting in the present appeal. In a significant number of cases, the two subsections will be presented to the jury as alternative bases for liability. In such cases, a trial judge who was required to follow both the holding in this case and *Paquette* would have to instruct the jury that the accused's subjective view as to the desirability of the commission of the offence was not relevant to s. 21(1)(b), but that it was relevant to s. 21(2), and that the existence of duress might "negate" *mens rea* under the latter (but not the former) provision. He or she would then have to go on to charge the jury, in the alternative, on the common law defence of duress. While complex jury instructions are sometimes unavoidable if justice is to be done, I am of the view that unnecessary complexity is something that courts should strive to avoid. The Canadian justice system places considerable faith in jurors' ability to follow the trial judge's instructions. In exchange, I believe it is incumbent on the courts to do what they can to ease, rather than add to, the difficult burden we call upon jurors to bear, subject, of course, to the overriding imperative that trial fairness be preserved.

In *Hibbert*, the court concludes that a "purpose" could in some sections of the *Code* involve asking what an accused desired, though s. 21(1)(b) was not one of those sections. The *Hibbert* approach is the more usual one: see for example *R. v. Buzzanga* (1979), 49 C.C.C. (2d) 369 (Ont. C.A.) below. However, subsequent to *Hibbert*, the court was required to consider the guilt or innocence of Jason Kerr, a prisoner who carried a knife in a prison in which it was accepted that warring gangs were in control. Kerr was threatened by another inmate, Garon, and warned that he would be attacked the next day. The next morning he armed himself with a homemade knife and used it to defend himself against Garon. In fact, Kerr killed Garon with the knife, but he was acquitted on murder charges on the basis of self-defence. Kerr was also charged, though, under s. 88 of the *Criminal Code* with "possession of a weapon for a purpose dangerous to the public peace". The question of whether Kerr's possession of the weapon prior to the assault made him guilty of this offence reached the Supreme Court of Canada.

In the Supreme Court, the seven judges gave four separate sets of reasons. Six of the seven held that Kerr should be acquitted, but for three different sets of reasons. In particular, the judges disagreed over how the particular element of "purpose dangerous to the public peace" could be proven, and whether it was proven on the facts of the case. Justice Bastarache indicates that he believes the same "objective/subjective" approach as in *Hibbert* should be adopted. Justice LeBel states very clearly that the test is purely subjective. **What approach do the other judges adopt?**

Subjective *Mens Rea* (Awareness of Risk)

| Intent | Recklessness |
| Knowledge | Wilful blindness |

(iv) Intention or knowledge

Our *Code* uses a variety of terms e.g. "means to" (murder: s. 229(a)), "intentionally" (assault: s. 265), "with intent" (theft: s. 322), "purpose" (possessing weapon for a purpose dangerous to the public peace: s. 88 and "knowingly" (possessing: s. 4(3)).

In modern Criminal Codes, such as those found in the United States, such terms are statutorily defined. Since 1892, our *Criminal Code* has left this task of general definition to judges. Our courts have been heavily influenced by the writings of Professor Glanville Williams of Cambridge University. When our courts invoke subjective *mens rea* we shall see below that they are now usually satisfied with *mens rea* in any of the forms of intent, knowledge, recklessness or wilful blindness.

However there is uncertain jurisprudence that limits the *mens rea* required for certain offences to intent rather than allowing extensions to recklessness or wilful blindness. The leading decision is that in *Buzzanga and Durocher*, which is also the leading authority on the definition of intent as conscious purpose or foresight of a certainty:

R. v. BUZZANGA and DUROCHER

(1979), 49 C.C.C. (2d) 369 (Ont. C.A.)

The defendants were active in promoting the construction of a French language high school in Essex County. They caused to be printed and circulated the following document:

WAKE UP CANADIANS

YOUR FUTURE IS AT STAKE!

IT IS YOUR TAX DOLLARS THAT SUBSIDIZE THE ACTIVITIES OF THE FRENCH MINORITY OF ESSEX COUNTY.

DID YOU KNOW THAT THE ASSOCIATION CANADIAN FRANCAIS DE L'ONTARIO HAS INVESTED SEVERAL HUNDREDS OF THOUSANDS OF DOLLARS OF YOUR TAX MONEY IN QUEBEC?

AND THAT NOW THEY ARE STILL DEMANDING 5 MILLION MORE OF YOUR TAX DOLLARS TO BUILD A FRENCH LANGUAGE HIGH SCHOOL?

YOU ARE SUBSIDIZING SEPARATISM WHETHER IN QUEBEC OR ESSEX COUNTY.

IF WE GIVE THEM A SCHOOL, WHAT WILL THEY DEMAND NEXT . . . INDEPENDENT CITY STATES? CONSIDER THE ETHNIC PROBLEM OF THE UNITED STATES AND TAKE HEED.

DID YOU KNOW THAT THOSE OF THE FRENCH MINORITY WHO SUPPORT THE BUILDING OF THE FRENCH LANGUAGE HIGH SCHOOL ARE IN FACT A SUBVERSIVE GROUP AND THAT MOST FRENCH CANADIANS OF ESSEX COUNTY ARE OPPOSED TO THE BUILDING OF THAT SCHOOL?

WHO WILL RID US OF THIS SUBVERSIVE GROUP IF NOT OURSELVES?

WE MUST STAMP OUT THE SUBVERSIVE ELEMENT WHICH USES HISTORY TO JUSTIFY ITS FREELOADING ON THE TAXPAYERS OF CANADA, NOW.

THE BRITISH SOLVED THIS PROBLEM ONCE BEFORE WITH THE ACADIANS, WHAT ARE WE WAITING FOR . . . ?

MARTIN J.A.: —

. . . .

The statement was composed by the appellant Durocher whose facility with the English language was greater than that of Buzzanga.

The appellant Durocher testified that the francophone community seemed to be "fed up" with the issue of the French-language high school and was becoming apathetic. He said that although economics was the stated reason for not building the school, this was merely an excuse and the real reason was prejudice. The appellant Buzzanga shared Durocher's feeling in this respect.

Both appellants testified as to their purpose in preparing and distributing the pamphlet. The appellant Durocher testified that his purpose was to show the prejudice directed towards French Canadians and expose the truth about the real problem that existed with respect to the French-language school. He said that the statement was largely composed from written material he had seen and from experiences he had had, although the paragraph: "WHO WILL RID US OF THIS SUBVERSIVE GROUP, IF NOT OURSELVES?" was pure theatrics and has its origin in the quotation "Who will rid me of this meddlesome priest", attributed to Henry II. He testified in some detail as to the origin of various parts of the document and endeavoured to show that it reflected statements contained in such sources as letters to the editor of the Windsor Star, a document alleged to have been circulated by a member of the Essex County Ratepayers Association, a paid advertisement published in several newspapers, a book entitled "Bilingual Today, French Tomorrow", and the like. He said that he thought the pamphlet would be a catalyst that would bring a quick solution to the problem of the French-language school by provoking a Government reaction and thereby put pressure on the school board. He thought that by stating these things people would say: "This is ridiculous." A fair reading of his evidence is that he did not want to promote hatred against the "French people", for to do so would be to promote hatred against himself.

The appellant Buzzanga, too, said that he wanted to expose the situation, to show the things that were being said so that intelligent people could see how ridiculous they were. The pamphlet was intended as a satire. He wanted to create a furor that would reach the "House of Commons" and compel the Government to do something that would compel the opposing factions on the school question to reopen communications. He said it was not his intention "to raise hatred towards anyone".

The appellant Buzzanga arranged for the printing and distribution of the document. He placed the order for the printing of the document in the name of Wilfred Fortowsky, the president of the Essex County Ratepayers Association, but asked the printer to delete the name of Mr. Fortowsky when he picked up the material, leaving, however, the name of the Essex County Ratepayers Association on the order form. Neither Mr. Fortowsky nor the Essex County Ratepayers Association were, of course, aware that their names had been so used.

. . . .

The threshold question to be determined is the meaning of "wilfully" in the term "wilfully promotes hatred" in s. 281.2(2) [now s. 319(2)] of the *Criminal Code*. It will, of course, be observed that the word "wilfully" modifies the words "promotes hatred", rather than the words "communicating statements".

The word "wilfully" has not been uniformly interpreted and its meaning to some extent depends upon the context in which it is used. Its primary meaning is "intentionally", but it is also used to mean "recklessly": see Glanville Williams, *Criminal Law, The General Part*, 2nd ed. (1961), pp. 51-2; Glanville Williams, *Text book of Criminal Law* (1978), p. 87; Smith and Hogan, *Criminal Law*, 4th ed. (1978), pp. 104-5. The term "recklessly" is here used to denote the subjective state of mind of a person who foresees that his conduct may cause the prohibited result but, nevertheless, takes a deliberate and unjustifiable risk of bringing it about: see Glanville Williams, *Textbook of Criminal Law*, pp. 70 and 76; Smith and Hogan, *Criminal Law*, 4th ed., pp. 52-3.

The word "wilfully" has, however, also been held to mean no more than the accused's act is done intentionally and not accidentally. In *R. v. Senior*, [1899] 1 Q.B. 283, Lord Russell of Killowen C.J., in interpreting the meaning of the words "wilfully neglects" in s. 1 of the *Prevention of Cruelty to Children Act*, 1894 (U.K.), c. 41, said at pp. 290-1: " 'Wilfully' means that the act is done deliberately and intentionally, not by accident or inadvertence, but so that the mind of the person who does the act goes with it."

On the other hand, in *Rice v. Connolly*, [1966] 2 Q.B. 414, where the accused was charged with wilfully obstructing a constable in the execution of his duty, Lord Parker L.C.J., said at p. 419: "'Wilful' in this context not only in my judgment means 'intentional' but something which is done without lawful excuse. . .".

In *Willmott v. Atack*, [1976] 3 All E.R. 794, the appellant was convicted on a charge of wilfully obstructing a peace officer in the execution of his duty. A police officer, acting in the execution of his duty, arrested a motorist who struggled and resisted. The appellant, who knew the motorist, intervened with the intention of assisting the officer but, in fact, his conduct obstructed the officer. The Queen's Bench Divisional Court quashed the conviction and held that it was not sufficient to prove the appellant intended to do what he did, and which resulted in an obstruction, but that the prosecution must prove that the appellant intended to obstruct the officer.

The judgment of the Court of Criminal Appeal of Queensland in *R. v. Burnell*, [1966] Qd. R. 348, also illustrates that, depending on its context, the word "wilfully" may connote an intention to bring about a proscribed consequence. In that case the appellant was charged with arson in having set fire to a shed. Section 461 of the Queensland *Criminal Code* provides that ". . . any person who wilfully and unlawfully sets fire to . . . any building or structure is guilty of a crime. . .". The accused had deliberately set fire to some mattresses in a shed whereby the shed was set on fire. The trial Judge instructed the jury that "wilfully" connoted no more than a willed and voluntary act as distinguished from the result of an accident or mere negligence. The Queensland Court of Criminal Appeal, in setting aside the conviction, held that in the context of the section "wilfully" required proof that the accused did an act which resulted in setting fire to the building with the intention of bringing about that result. Gibbs J. (with whom Douglas J. concurred), said at p. 356:

Under s. 461 it is not enough that the accused did the act which resulted in setting fire to the building foreseeing that his act might have that effect but recklessly taking the risk; it is necessary that the accused did the act which resulted in setting fire to the building with the intention of bringing about that result.

Mr. Manning conceded that in some cases the element of wilfulness is supplied by recklessness but he contended that in its context in s. 281.2(2) of the *Criminal Code* "wilfully" means with the intention of promoting hatred. In the course of his argument, Mr. Manning stressed the definition of "wilfully" contained in s. 386(1) [now s. 429(1)] of the *Code*, which reads:

386(1) Every one who causes the occurrence of an event by doing an act or by omitting to do an act that it is his duty to do, knowing that the act or omission will probably cause the occurrence of the event and being reckless whether the event occurs or not, shall be deemed, for the purposes of this Part, wilfully to have caused the occurrence of the event.

Mr. Manning emphasized that s. 386(1) provides that wilfully is to have the meaning specified in that section for the purposes of Part IX [now Part XI] of the *Code*. He argued with much force that the state of mind specified in s. 386(1) is recklessness and that where Parliament intends to extend the meaning of wilfully to include recklessness it does so expressly. In *R. v. Rese*, [1968] 1 C.C.C. 363 at p. 366, 2 C.R.N.S. 99, Laskin J.A. (as he then was), referred to the definition now contained in s. 386(1) as an extended meaning of "wilfully".

As previously indicated, the word "wilfully" does not have a fixed meaning, but I am satisfied that in the context of s. 281.2(2) it means with the intention of promoting hatred, and does not include recklessness. The arrangement of legislation proscribing the incitement of hatred, in my view, leads to that conclusion.

Section 281.2(1), unlike s. 281.2(2), is restricted to the incitement of hatred by communicating statements in a public place where such incitement is likely to lead to a breach of the peace. Although no mental element is expressly mentioned in s. 281.2(1), where the communication poses an immediate threat to public order, *mens rea* is, none the less, required since the inclusion of an offence in the *Criminal Code* must be taken to import *mens rea* in the absence of a clear intention to dispense with it: see *R. v. Prue; R. v. Baril* (1979), 46 C.C.C. (2d) 257 at pp. 260-1, 96 D.L.R. 577 at pp. 580-1, 8 C.R. (3d) 68 at p. 73. The general *mens rea* which is required and which suffices for most crimes where no mental element is mentioned in the definition of the crime, is either the intentional or reckless bringing about of the result which the law, in creating the offence, seeks to prevent and, hence, under s. 281.2(1) is either the intentional or reckless inciting of hatred in the specified circumstances.

The insertion of the word "wilfully" in s. 281.2(2) was not necessary to import *mens rea* since that requirement would be implied in any event because of the serious nature of the offence: see *R. v. Prue, supra*. The statements, the communication of which are proscribed by s. 281.2(2), are not confined to statements communicated in a public place in circumstances likely to lead to a breach of the peace and they, consequently, do not pose such an immediate threat to public order as those falling under s. 281.2(1); it is reasonable to assume, therefore, that Parliament intended to limit the offence under s. 281.2(2) to the intentional promotion of hatred. It is evident that the use of the word "wilfully" in s. 281.2(2), and not in s. 281.2(1), reflects Parliament's policy to strike a balance in protecting the competing social interests of freedom of expression on the one hand, and public order and group reputation on the other hand.

Having concluded that proof of an intention to promote hatred is essential to constitute the offence: under s. 281.2(2), it is necessary to consider the mental attitude which must be established to constitute an intention to promote hatred. The state of mind connoted by "intention", where an intention to bring about a certain result is an element of the offence, has been the subject of much discussion, and writers on jurisprudence, as well as Judges, have not always been in agreement as to its meaning.

. . . .

There are cases which appear to provide support for the proposition that where an intention to produce a particular consequence is essential to constitute the offence, an act is not done with intent to produce the prohibited consequence unless it is the actor's conscious purpose to bring it about, and that the actor's foresight of the certainty of the consequence is not synonymous with an intention to produce it: see *R. v. Miller* (1959), 125 C.C.C. 8 at p. 30, 31 C.R. 101; *R. v. Ahlers*, [1915] 1 K.B. 616; *Sinnasamy Selvanayagam v. The King*, [1951] A.C. 83; *R. v. Steane*, [1947] 1 K.B. 997. Most of these cases are subjected to critical examination by Dr. Glanville Williams in *Criminal Law, The General Part*, 2nd ed. (1961), pp. 40-2.

There is, however, substantial support for the proposition that in the criminal law a person intends a particular consequence not only when his conscious purpose is to bring it about, but also when he foresees that the consequence is certain or substantially certain to result from his conduct: see Glanville Williams, *Criminal Law, The General Part*, 2nd ed. (1961), p. 38; Walter Wheeler Cook, *Act, Intention, and Motive in the Criminal Law* (1916-17), 26 Yale L.J. 645 at pp. 654-8; Rollin Perkins, *A Rationale of Mens Rea*, 52 Harv. L. Rev. 905 at pp. 910-1 (1938-39).

Smith and Hogan, the learned authors of *Criminal Law*, 4th ed., state at p. 51, that the authorities referred to by them:

> suggest that in the criminal law generally, though not universally, a person intends a consequence if it is his purpose to achieve it or if he knows that the achievement of some other purpose is certain, or "morally" certain, to produce the consequence in question.

In *R. v. Lemon; R. v. Gay News Ltd.*, *supra*, Lord Diplock, however, defined intention in much wider terms. He said that where intention to produce a particular result is a necessary element of an offence, no distinction is to be drawn in law between the state of mind of one who does an act because he desires to produce that particular result, and the state of mind of one who, when he does the act, is aware that it is likely to produce that result but is prepared to take the risk that it may do so in order to achieve some other purpose. He considered that the law has been settled by *Hyam v. Director of Public Prosecutions, supra*, "that both states of mind constitute 'intention' in the sense in which that expression is used in the definition of a crime whether at common law or in a statute" (at p. 905).

Hyam v. Director of Public Prosecutions, supra, was concerned with the mental element required to constitute "malice aforethought". It may well be that either an intention to kill or cause serious bodily harm, or foresight that death or serious bodily harm is a highly probable consequence of an act done for some other purpose, is a sufficient *mens rea* for murder at common law. I do not consider, however, that the actor's foresight that a consequence is highly probable, as opposed to substantially certain, is the same thing as an intention to bring it about: see *Hyam v. Director of Public Prosecutions, supra, per* Lord Hailsham at p. 75; *R. v. Belfon*, [1976] 3 All E.R. 46; Smith and Hogan, *Criminal Law*, 4th ed., pp. 47-51; Commentary on *R. v. Lemon et al.*, [1979] Crim. L.R. 311 at p. 314. In my view, the mental attitude described by Lord Diplock is a form of recklessness.

I agree, however (assuming without deciding that there may be cases in which intended consequences are confined to those which it is the actor's conscious purpose to bring about), that, as a general rule, a person who foresees that a consequence is certain or substantially certain to result from an act which he does in order to achieve some other purpose, intends that consequence. The actor's foresight of the certainty or moral certainty of the consequence resulting from his conduct compels a conclusion that if he, none the less, acted so as to produce it, then he decided to bring it about (albeit regretfully), in order to achieve his ultimate purpose. His intention encompasses the means as well as to his ultimate objective.

I conclude, therefore, that the appellants "wilfully" (intentionally) promoted hatred against the French Canadian community of Essex County only if: (a) their conscious purpose in distributing the document was to promote hatred against that group, or (b) they foresaw that the promotion of hatred against that group was certain or morally certain to result from the distribution of the pamphlet, but distributed it as means of achieving their purpose of obtaining the French-language high school.

Whether the trial judge misdirected himself as to the meaning of wilfully?

The learned trial judge in comprehensive reasons first considered whether the document objectively promoted hatred and concluded that the cumulative effect of the document rendered it a communication that promoted hatred against the French-speaking community of Essex County. He then said:

> It is, however, incumbent upon the Crown to prove beyond a reasonable doubt that the two accused wilfully promoted such hatred. In other words, has the Crown established the necessary element of *mens rea*. In considering the meaning to be given to the word "wilfully" in this section the court must distinguish between what has been described by learned writers as primary and secondary intent; or to phrase it in a more understanding way, the distinction between intent and motive. I have earlier discussed the purpose or motive as explained by the accused themselves. They wished to create a situation that would require the intervention of senior levels of Government and result in the construction of the high school. It is in evidence that the handbill was, in fact, shown to a mediator representing the Minister of Education who was in this area attempting to resolve the school issue. It is, of course, a matter of judicial notice that the Province did pass special legislation requiring the construction of the school. It is extremely doubtful, however, that this document played any part in the formulation of that decision. It was also their desire to unify the French Canadian community. As Father Vincent stated, opposition from outside often cements an ethnic group and tends to strengthen people rather than weaken them.
>
> This is what the court would refer to as the purpose or motive of the accused.
>
> Wilful in this section, however, means intentional as opposed to accidental. Miss Susan Moylan who testified for the accused was involved in the early discussions between the accused in the preparation of the handbill. She testified that the document was not to create strong feelings but to create strong actions and strong reactions. How one can do the latter without the former is beyond the comprehension of this court. The accused themselves testified they wished to create controversy, furor and an uproar. What better way of describing active dislike, detestation, enmity or ill will. The motives of the accused may or may not be laudable. The means chosen by the accused was the wilful promotion of hatred.

. . . .

I am not persuaded that the learned trial judge fell into the error of detaching the word "wilfully" from the words "promotes hatred" and applied it only to the distribution of the pamphlet. I am of the view, however, that the learned trial judge erred in holding that "wilfully" means only "intentional as opposed to accidental". Although, as previously indicated, "wilfully" has sometimes been used to mean that the accused's act, as distinct from its consequences, must be intended and not accidental (as in *R. v. Senior*, [1899] 1 Q.B. 283), it does not have that meaning in the provisions under consideration.

The learned trial judge's view of the meaning of "wilfully" inevitably caused him to focus attention on the intentional nature of the appellants' conduct, rather than on the question whether they actually intended to produce the consequence of promoting hatred.

. . . .

In some cases the inference from the circumstances that the necessary intent existed may be so strong as to compel the rejection of the accused's evidence that he did not intend to bring about the prohibited consequence. The learned trial judge did not, however, state that he disbelieved the appellants' evidence that they did not intend to promote hatred. He appears to have treated the appellants' testimony that they wished to create "controversy, furor and an uproar" as a virtual admission that they had the state of mind requisite for guilt.

I am, with deference to the learned trial judge, of the view that an intention to create "controversy, furor and an uproar" is not the same thing as an intention to promote hatred, and it was an error to equate them. I would, of course, agree that if the appellants intentionally promoted hatred against the French-speaking community of Essex County as a means of obtaining the French-language high school, they committed the offence charged. The appellants' evidence, if believed, does not, however, as the learned trial judge appears to have thought, inevitably lead to that conclusion. The learned trial judge, not having disbelieved the appellants' evidence, failed to give appropriate consideration to their evidence on the issue of intent and, in the circumstances, his failure so to do constituted self-misdirection.

In view of the conclusion which I have reached it is necessary to refer only briefly to the other grounds of appeal which we regard as requiring discussion.

. . . .

Conclusion

I have concluded that the self-misdirection with respect to the meaning of the word "wilfully", and the failure to appreciate the significance of the appellants' evidence on the issue of intent requires a new trial. The outrageous conduct of the appellants in preparing and distributing this deplorable document was evidence to be weighed in determining their intent, but in the peculiar circumstances of this case I am not satisfied that the inferences to be drawn from it are such as to inevitably lead to a conclusion that they had the requisite intent or that the trial judge would inevitably have reached that conclusion but for his self-misdirection.

In the result, I would allow the appeal, set aside the convictions and order new trials.

Appeal allowed; new trial ordered.

This interpretation was later adopted by the Supreme Court in *R. v. Keegstra*, [1990] 3 S.C.R. 697, 1 C.R. (4th) 129, 61 C.C.C. (3d) 1, a decision holding that s. 319(2) was constitutional. Although the offence violated freedom of expression guaranteed by s. 2(*b*) of the *Charter* the limit was held to be demonstrably justified as a reasonable limit under s. 1. One of the reasons given by Chief Justice Dickson for the majority was that:

> The interpretation of "wilfully" in *Buzzanga* has great bearing upon the extent to which s. 319(2) limits the freedom of expression. This mental element, requiring more than merely negligence or recklessness as to result, significantly restricts the reach of the provision, and thereby reduces the scope of the targeted expression (at 193).

In *R. v. Harding* (2001), 48 C.R. (5th) 1 (Ont. C.A.), the court, after referring to *Buzzanga*, nevertheless decided that "wilfully" in s. 319(2) should be extended to the subjective concept of wilful blindness.

In two high profile wilful obstruction of justice charges, lack of proof of intent was the basis for acquittals. In *Kirkham* (1998), 17 C.R. (5th) 250, 126 C.C.C. (3d) 397 (Sask. Q.B.), a Crown Attorney had arranged for a police questionnaire to obtain information about the background of potential jurors for a mercy killing murder trial, *Latimer*, which he did not disclose to defence counsel. In *Murray* (2000), 34 C.R. (5th) 290, 144 C.C.C. (3d) 289 (Ont. S.C.J.), a defence counsel in the double murder case of *Bernardo* had withheld incriminating videotapes of sexual abuse of murder victims by his client and co-accused for 17 months. Such a definitional quagmire concerning so basic a crime as obstruction of justice speaks volumes about a need for a General Part with clear fault definitions.

R. v. Chartrand (1994), 31 C.R. (4th) 1 (S.C.C.), concerning the crime of abduction of a child under 14, is now strong authority for the view that where an offence has an express "with intent" element this requires proof of intent or actual foresight of certainty. Madam Justice L'Heureux-Dubé for the court relied on *Buzzanga*. The court implicitly decided recklessness would not do but there is no discussion of why this should be so.

In the case of so-called incomplete or inchoate crimes (see Chapt. 9 below) Canadian courts have usually limited the *mens rea* to intent and not extended to recklessness and wilful blindness; see, for example, *Ancio* (1984), 39 C.R. (3d) 1 (S.C.C.) (attempts) but in *R. v. Hamilton*, [2005] 2 S.C.R. 432, 198 C.C.C. (3d) 1, 30 C.R. (6th) 243 a 6-3 majority extended the offence of counselling an offence that was not committed to recklessness. See Chapter 9.

Even if the word "knowing" is not included in a criminal provision, the Crown must prove knowledge of the relevant circumstance. Further, the presence of the word "knowing" in a criminal provision can sometimes point to the existence of a corresponding external element. In *United States v. Dynar*, [1997] 2 S.C.R. 462 (which will also be considered below under "Attempts") the accused was charged with laundering money "knowing" that it was the proceeds of crime. The money in question was provided by the FBI as part of a "sting" operation and was not, in fact, the proceeds of crime. The Supreme Court held that this meant the accused could not be found guilty; the requirement in the statute that he "know" the money was the proceeds of crime (as opposed to simply believing that) meant that the money had to actually be the proceeds of crime:

> 41 Because it is not possible to know what is false, no one who converts money that is not in fact the proceeds of crime commits these offences. This is clear from the meaning of the word "know". In the Western legal tradition, knowledge is defined as true belief: "The word 'know' refers exclusively to true knowledge; we are not said to 'know' something that is not so" (Glanville Williams, *Textbook of Criminal Law* (2nd ed. 1983), at p. 160).

Although use of the word "knowing" points to the presence of a corresponding external element, use of the word "intent" or similar language does not necessarily have the same effect. There are many offences in the *Criminal Code* which require that the accused have a particular intent, but where it is irrelevant whether the accused succeeds in this attempt. See, for example, s. 348(1):

348. (1) Every one who
    (a) breaks and enters a place with intent to commit an indictable offence therein,
    (b) breaks and enters a place and commits an indictable offence therein. . .
is guilty [of an offence].

Under s. 348(1)(b) it would be necessary to show that the accused actually committed an indictable offence; under s. 348(1)(a) it is only necessary to show the intent to do so.

The term most often associated with such a "free-floating" fault element is "with intent to". That is not the only possible language, however, and so it is a matter of reading the provision grammatically to determine what is intended. See, for example, s. 249.1:

249.1 (1) Every one commits an offence who, operating a motor vehicle while being pursued by a peace officer operating a motor vehicle, fails, without reasonable excuse and in order to evade the peace officer, to stop the vehicle as soon as is reasonable in the circumstances.

(v) Recklessness or wilful blindness

There are occasions where our *Criminal Code* expressly relies on recklessness as fault.

    1.   murder under s. 229(a)(ii);

    2.   "wilful" as defined in s. 429 for all Part XI offences (mostly property offences such as mischief, damage to property and arson);

    3.   criminal harassment (s. 264); and

    4.   offences based on criminal negligence (s. 219) (considered separately as *sui generis* later).

There are no examples where Parliament has expressly resorted to wilful blindness, a concept invented by Glanville Williams.

Whether or not there is an express extension to recklessness or wilful blindness the following two leading decisions in *Theroux* and *Sansregret* show the normal willingness in our courts to extend subjective *mens rea* beyond actual intent or knowledge to recklessness and wilful blindness. The central concept is actual awareness of risk in one of these forms.

R. v. THÉROUX

[1993] 2 S.C.R. 5, 19 C.R. (4th) 194, 79 C.C.C. (3d) 449,
1993 CarswellQue 5, 1993 CarswellQue 156

The accused, the directing mind of a company involved in residential construction, was charged with fraud. The company entered into contracts and received deposits on the basis of a false representation by the company that the deposits were insured. The company became insolvent, the project was not completed and most of the depositors lost their money. The trial judge found that the accused, as directing mind of the company, was responsible for the misrepresentations that the deposits were guaranteed. The accused knew at the time that the insurance was not in place but nevertheless made misrepresentations to induce potential home purchasers to sign a contract and give a deposit. The trial judge also found that the accused sincerely believed that the residential project would be completed and hence that the deposits would not be lost. The accused was convicted of fraud pursuant to s. 380(1)(a) of the *Criminal Code* and the Court of Appeal upheld the conviction. The issue for the Supreme Court was whether the fact that the accused honestly believed that the project would be completed negated the *mens rea* of the offence of fraud.

McLachlin J.: —

There is no doubt that the appellant deliberately practised a deceitful act, constituting the *actus reus* of the offence of fraud. The issue is whether the fact that he honestly believed that the projects would be completed negates the guilty mind or *mens rea* of the offence. This requires this court to examine the question of what constitutes the *mens rea* for the offence of fraud.

. . . .

The prohibited act is deceit, falsehood, or some other dishonest act. The prohibited consequence is depriving another of what is or should be his, which may, as we have seen, consist in merely placing another's property at risk. The *mens rea* would then consist in the subjective awareness that one was undertaking a prohibited act (the deceit, falsehood or other dishonest act) which could cause deprivation in the sense of depriving another of property or putting that property at risk. If this is shown, the crime is complete. The fact that the accused may have hoped the deprivation would not take place, or may have felt there was nothing wrong with what he or she was doing, provides no defence. To put it another way, following the traditional criminal-law principle that the mental state necessary to the offence must be determined by reference to the external acts which constitute the *actus* of the offence (see Williams, *supra*, c. 3), the proper focus in determining the *mens rea* of fraud is to ask whether the accused intentionally committed the prohibited acts (deceit, falsehood, or other dishonest act) knowing or desiring the consequences proscribed by the offence (deprivation, including the risk of deprivation). The personal feeling of the accused about the morality or honesty of the act or its consequences is no more relevant to the analysis than is the accused's awareness that the particular acts undertaken constitute a criminal offence.

This applies as much to the third head of fraud, "other fraudulent means", as to lies and acts of deceit. Although other fraudulent means have been broadly defined as means which are "dishonest", it is not necessary that an accused personally consider these means to be dishonest in order that he or she be convicted of fraud for having undertaken them. The "dishonesty" of the means is relevant to the determination whether the conduct falls within the type of conduct caught by the offence of fraud; what reasonable people consider dishonest assists in the determination whether the *actus reus* of the offence can be made out on particular facts. That established, it need only be determined that an accused knowingly undertook the acts in question, aware that deprivation, or risk of deprivation, could follow as a likely consequence.

I have spoken of knowledge of the consequences of the fraudulent act. There appears to be no reason, however, why recklessness as to consequences might not also attract criminal responsibility. Recklessness presupposes knowledge of the likelihood of the prohibited consequences. It is established when it is shown that the accused, with such knowledge, commits acts which may bring about these prohibited consequences, while being reckless as to whether or not they ensue.

These doctrinal observations suggest that the *actus reus* of the offence of fraud will be established by proof of:

1. the prohibited act, be it an act of deceit, a falsehood or some other fraudulent means; and

2. deprivation caused by the prohibited act, which may consist in actual loss or the placing of the victim's pecuniary interests at risk.

Correspondingly, the *mens rea* of fraud is established by proof of:

1. Subjective knowledge of the prohibited act; and

2. Subjective knowledge that the prohibited act could have as a consequence the deprivation of another (which deprivation may consist in knowledge that the victim's pecuniary interests are put at risk).

Where the conduct and knowledge required by these definitions are established, the accused is guilty whether he actually intended the prohibited consequence or was reckless as to whether it would occur.

The inclusion of *risk* of deprivation in the concept of deprivation in *Olan* requires specific comment. The accused must have subjective awareness, at the very least, that his or her conduct will put the property or economic expectations of others at risk. As noted above, this does not mean that the Crown must provide the trier of fact with a mental snapshot proving exactly what was in the accused's mind at the moment the dishonest act was committed. In certain cases, the inference of subjective knowledge of the risk may be drawn from the facts as the accused believed them to be. The accused may introduce evidence negating that inference, such as evidence that his deceit was part of an innocent prank, or evidence of circumstances which led him to believe that no one would act on his lie or deceitful or dishonest act. But in cases like the present one, where the accused tells a lie knowing others will act on it and thereby puts their property at risk, the inference of subjective knowledge that the property of another would be put at risk is clear.

R. v. BOULANGER

(2006), 39 C.R. (6th) 1, [2006] 2 S.C.R. 49, 210 C.C.C. (3d) 1, 2006 CarswellQue 5739, 2006 CarswellQue 5740 (S.C.C.)

The accused was charged with breach of trust under s. 122 of the *Criminal Code*. The accused was director of public security for a municipality, and his daughter was involved in an automobile accident. After a report had been filed the accused ordered a subordinate officer to prepare a supplementary accident report on the accident. The supplementary report concluded that his daughter was not at fault; the accused forwarded the report to his insurance company and as a result did not have to pay the insurance deductible of $250.

Justice McLachlin, for a unanimous Court, observed that the offence of breach of trust had existed at common law and had been in the *Criminal Code* since 1892, but that nonetheless the elements of the offence remained uncertain. She concluded, after a thorough review, that the Crown was required to prove the following elements:

1. The accused is an official;

2. The accused was acting in connection with the duties of his or her office;

3. The accused breached the standard of responsibility and conduct demanded of him or her by the nature of the office;

4. The conduct of the accused represented a serious and marked departure from the standards expected of an individual in the accused's position of public trust; and

5. The accused acted with the intention to use his or her public office for a purpose other than the public good, for example, for a dishonest, partial, corrupt or oppressive purpose.

It is the Court's discussion of the final element, the *mens rea* for the offence, which is important to us here. Is the Court's approach here to the relevance of the accused's subjective purpose consistent with their approach in *Theroux*?

2.4.2 *Mens Rea*

55 In the early common law cases, the mental element of misfeasance in public office was imprecise and varied from case to case. However, common law judges

consistently insisted on the presence of some variant of nefarious or dishonest intent. This was described using different terms: dishonesty, corruption, partiality and oppression. All reflected a central concern: that public officials, entrusted with duties for the benefit of the public, carry out those duties honestly and for the benefit of the public, and that they not abuse their offices for corrupt or improper purposes.

56 Consistent with fundamental criminal law principles, the bar for mental culpability for the offence of public misfeasance was an elevated one. Mistakes did not suffice. Nor did errors of judgment. To quote Abbott C.J. in *Borron*:

> ... the question has always been, not whether the act done might, upon full and mature investigation, be found strictly right, but from what motive it had proceeded; whether from a dishonest, oppressive, or corrupt motive, under which description, fear and favour may generally be included, or from mistake or error. In the former case, alone, they have become the objects of punishment. [pp. 721-22]

In principle, the *mens rea* of the offence lies in the intention to use one's public office for purposes other than the benefit of the public. In practice, this has been associated historically with using one's public office for a dishonest, partial, corrupt or oppressive purpose, each of which embodies the non-public purpose with which the offence is concerned.

57 As with any offence, the *mens rea* is inferred from the circumstances. An attempt by the accused to conceal his or her actions may often provide evidence of an improper intent: *Arnoldi*. Similarly, the receipt of a significant personal benefit may provide evidence that the accused acted in his or her own interest rather than that of the public. However, the fact that a public officer obtains a benefit is not conclusive of a culpable *mens rea*. Many legitimate exercises of public authority or power by a public servant confer incidental advantages on the actor. As Widgery J. (as he then was) stated in *R. v. Llewellyn-Jones* (1966), 51 Cr. App. R. 4, at p. 7:

> ... I would not be prepared to say that it would be misconduct for this purpose for a registrar to make a decision which did affect his personal interests, merely because he knew that his interests were so involved, if the decision was made honestly and in a genuine belief that it was a proper exercise of his jurisdiction so far as the beneficiaries and other persons concerned came into it. [Cited by Widgery L.C.J. in *Dytham*, at p. 394.]

Conversely, the offence may be made out where no personal benefit is involved.

. . .

63 I turn first to *mens rea*. The question is whether the evidence establishes an intention to use his public office for a purpose other than the public good, for example, for a dishonest, partial, corrupt or oppressive purpose. The trial judge found that the evidence supported the good faith of both Mr. Boulanger and

Constable Stephens (para. 100). Specifically, she concluded that the report accorded with the preponderance of evidence relating to the accident, that it was not falsified, and that the accused did not ask or obtain a supplementary report with the intent of misleading the insurance company (paras. 97-99). Indeed, she expressly labelled Mr. Boulanger's conduct as an error in judgment (para. 108). Moreover, as Dalphond J.A. noted, the facts as found demonstrate no attempt whatsoever to conceal.

64 It is true that Mr. Boulanger knew that he would benefit from Constable Stephens' report. This alone does not, however, establish a culpable state of mind. For example, as discussed, it is not misconduct to make a decision knowing it furthers one's personal interests, if the decision is made honestly and in the belief that it is a proper exercise of the public power the official enjoys: *Dytham*. Mr. Boulanger's private purpose did not seek to undermine the public good. Had Mr. Boulanger instructed Constable Stephens to put a particular content into the report, that might have amounted to using his office in a way that betrayed the public trust. But Mr. Boulanger did not do this. Constable Stephens testified that the report contained his own opinion about the responsibility of Alexandra Boulanger for the accident (trial judgment, at para. 51). He further testified that he never felt any pressure or obligation to write the report (trial judgment, at para. 52). As noted, the trial judge concluded that the report accorded with the preponderance of evidence relating to the accident, that it was not falsified, and that Mr. Boulanger did not ask or obtain a supplementary report with the intent of misleading the insurance company (paras. 97-99). In these circumstances, it is not clear that Mr. Boulanger's intention was to betray the public trust reposed in him.

65 As a check, it may be asked whether Mr. Boulanger's intention rose to the level of culpability traditionally required by the common law for the offence of breach of trust — for example, whether he acted for a dishonest, partial, corrupt or oppressive purpose. Dishonesty, corruption and oppression were clearly not made out. Nor, arguably, was partiality. "Partiality" denotes an "unfair bias in favour of one thing . . . compared with another": *The New Oxford Dictionary of English* (1998), at p. 1352. Mr. Boulanger's intention was to have Constable Stephens make a complete report, not to skew it in one direction or another.

66 I conclude that the facts as found raise a reasonable doubt that the *mens rea* necessary for conviction under s. 122 of the *Criminal Code* was established.

SANSREGRET v. R.

[1985] 1 S.C.R. 570, 45 C.R. (3d) 193, 18 C.C.C. (3d) 223,
1985 CarswellMan 176, 1985 CarswellMan 380

Sansregret is a leading decision on the crime of rape, to be considered later in the chapter on "Sexual Assault". During the course of his unanimous judgment for the Supreme Court, Mr. Justice McIntyre authoritatively defined and distinguished the concepts of recklessness and wilful blindness as follows:

. . . .

The concept of recklessness as a basis for criminal liability has been the subject of much discussion. Negligence, the failure to take reasonable care, is a creature of the civil law and is not generally a concept having a place in determining criminal liability. Nevertheless, it is frequently confused with recklessness in the criminal sense and care should be taken to separate the two concepts. Negligence is tested by the objective standard of the reasonable man. A departure from his accustomed sober behaviour by an act or omission which reveals less than reasonable care will involve liability at civil law but forms no basis for the imposition of criminal penalties. In accordance with well-established principles for the determination of criminal liability, recklessness, to form a part of the criminal *mens rea*, must have an element of the subjective. It is found in the attitude of one who, aware that there is danger that his conduct could bring about the result prohibited by the criminal law, nevertheless persists, despite the risk. It is, in other words, the conduct of one who sees the risk and who takes the chance. It is in this sense that the term "recklessness" is used in the criminal law and it is clearly distinct from the concept of civil negligence.

. . . .

The idea of wilful blindness in circumstances such as this has been said to be an aspect of recklessness. While this may well be true, it is wise to keep the two concepts separate because they result from different mental attitudes and lead to different legal results. A finding of recklessness in this case could not override the defence of mistake of fact. The appellant asserts an honest belief that the consent of the complainant was not caused by fear and threats. The trial judge found that such an honest belief existed. In the facts of this case, because of the reckless conduct of the appellant, it could not be said that such a belief was reasonable but, as held in *Pappajohn*, the mere honesty of the belief will support the "mistake of fact" defence, even where it is unreasonable. On the other hand, a finding of wilful blindness as to the very facts about which the honest belief is now asserted would leave no room for the application of the defence because, where wilful blindness is shown, the law presumes knowledge on the part of the accused, in this case knowledge that the consent had been induced by threats.

Wilful blindness is distinct from recklessness because, while recklessness involves knowledge of a danger or risk and persistence in a course of conduct which creates a risk that the prohibited result will occur, wilful blindness arises where a person who has become aware of the need for some inquiry declines to make the inquiry because he does not wish to know the truth. He would prefer to remain ignorant. The culpability in recklessness is justified by consciousness of the risk and by proceeding in the face of it, while in wilful blindness it is justified by the accused's fault in deliberately failing to inquire when he knows there is reason for inquiry. Cases such as *Wretham v. R.* (1971), 16 C.R.N.S. 124 (Ont. C.A.); *R. v. Blondin* (1971), 2 C.C.C. (2d) 118, affirmed [1971] S.C.R. v, 4 C.C.C. (2d) 566; *R. v. Currie* (1976), 24 C.C.C. (2d) 292 (Ont. C.A.); *R. v. McFall* (1976), 26 C.C.C. (2d) 181 (B.C. C.A.); *R. v. Aiello* (1978), 38 C.C.C. (2d) 485 (Ont. C.A.); *Taylor's Central Garages (Exeter) Ltd. v. Roper*, [1951] 2 T.L.R. 284 (Div. Ct.), among others, illustrate these principles. The textwriters have also dealt with the subject, particularly Glanville Williams, *Criminal Law: The General Part*, 2nd ed. (1961), at pp. 157-60. He says, at p. 157:

> Knowledge, then, means either personal knowledge or (in the licence cases) imputed knowledge. In either event there is someone with actual knowledge. To the requirement of actual knowledge there is one strictly limited exception. Men readily regard their suspicions as unworthy of them when it is to their advantage to do so. To meet this, the rule is that if a party has his suspicion aroused but then deliberately omits to make further enquiries, because he wishes to remain in ignorance, he is deemed to have knowledge.

He then referred to the words of Lord Sumner in *Re The Zamora*, [1921] 1 A.C. 801 at 811-12 (P.C.), which was a case wherein a ship and cargo were condemned in the Prize Court as contraband. The managing director of the shipping company denied knowledge of the contraband carried by the ship, and on this subject Lord Sumner said, at pp. 811-12:

> Lord Sterndale [the president of the Prize Court] thus expressed his final conclusion: "I think the true inference is that, if Mr. Banck did not know this was a transaction in contraband, it was because he did not want to know, and that he has not rebutted the presumption arising from the fact of the whole cargo being contraband."
>
> Their Lordships have been invited to read this as saying that Mr. Banck is not proved to have known the contraband character of the adventure; that if he did not know, because he did not want to know, he was within his rights and owed no duty to the belligerents to inform himself; and that the *Zamora* is condemned contrary to the passage above cited from *The Hakan* upon a legal presumption arising solely and arbitrarily from the fact that the whole cargo was contraband. It may be that in his anxiety not to state more than he found against Mr. Banck, the learned President appeared to state something less, but there are two senses in which a man is said not to know something because he does not want to know it. A thing may be troublesome to learn, and the knowledge of it, when acquired, may be uninteresting or distasteful. To refuse to know any more about the subject or anything at all is then a wilful but a real ignorance. On the other hand, a man is said not to know because he does not want to know, where the substance of the thing is borne in upon his mind with a conviction that full details or precise proof may be dangerous, because they may embarrass his denials or compromise his protests. In such a case he flatters himself that where ignorance is safe, 'tis

folly to be wise, but there he is wrong, for he has been put upon notice and his further ignorance, even though actual and complete, is a mere affectation and disguise.

Glanville Williams, however, warns that the rule of deliberate blindness has its dangers and is of narrow application. He says, at p. 159:

> The rule that wilful blindness is equivalent to knowledge is essential, and is found throughout the criminal law. It is, at the same time, an unstable rule, because Judges are apt to forget its very limited scope. A court can properly find wilful blindness only where it can almost be said that the defendant actually knew. He suspected the fact; he realised its probability; but he refrained from obtaining the final confirmation because he wanted in the event to be able to deny knowledge. This, and this alone, is wilful blindness. It requires in effect a finding that the defendant intended to cheat the administration of justice. Any wider definition would make the doctrine of wilful blindness indistinguishable from the civil doctrine of negligence in not obtaining knowledge.

This subject is also dealt with by Professor Stuart in *Canadian Criminal Law* (1982), at p. 130 et seq., where its relationship to recklessness is discussed.

In *R. v. Hamilton*, [2005] 2 S.C.R. 432, 198 C.C.C. (3d) 1, 30 C.R. (6th) 243 (a case on counselling, considered later under Chapter 9. Incomplete Crimes) Fish J. for the majority remarked as follows:

> Finally, a brief word on *R. v. Sansregret*, [1985] 1 S.C.R. 570, 45 C.R. (3d) 193, 18 C.C.C. (3d) 223. The court in that case defined recklessness as the conduct of "one who, aware that there is danger that his conduct could bring about the result prohibited by the criminal law, nevertheless persists, despite the risk. . . . in other words, the conduct of one who sees the risk and who takes the chance" (p. 582). The court, in *Sansregret*, did not set out the degree of risk required to attract criminal sanction. As Don Stuart points out, courts have arbitrarily endorsed varying standards: "uncertainty, probability, likelihood [and] possibility" - and, in some instances, "probability" and "possibility" in the very same case (*Canadian Criminal Law: A Treatise* (4th ed. 2001), at pp. 225-26).
>
> We have not been invited in this case to revisit *Sansregret* or to consider afresh the governing principles of recklessness as a fault element under the criminal law of Canada. And I should not be taken to have done so.

In *R. v. Jorgensen* (1996), 43 C.R. (4th) 137 (S.C.C.) J was the sole officer of a company which owns and operates an adult video store in Scarborough, Ontario. Undercover police officers bought eight videotapes from that store. Jorgensen and the company were charged with eight counts of knowingly selling obscene material without lawful justification or excuse contrary to s. 163(2)(*a*) of the *Criminal Code*. The trial judge found that three of the eight videos were obscene within the meaning of s. 163(8) of the *Criminal Code* due to their portrayal of sex coupled with violence and coercion, or subordination which created the risk of harm. The Ontario Court of Appeal upheld the convictions: (1993) 26 C.R. (4th) 75 (Ont. C.A.) (reported *sub. nom. R. v. Ronish*).

On appeal the Supreme Court substituted an acquittal. Sopinka J. spoke for the court on the issue of *mens rea*. The court struck a middle position. The Crown had argued that to prove that the accused "knowingly" sold obscene material it should be sufficient to prove that the accused knew that he was selling sex films. The court rejected this argument, since this would amount to convicting the accused of a crime when the only intent proven was to do something legal:

88 Having reviewed these cases, I would suggest that the jurisprudence supports the conclusion that for the Crown to convict on a charge of "knowingly" selling obscene materials, it must show more than that the accused had a general knowledge of the nature of the film as a sex film. Although the cases have been few and are by no means clear on this point, cases such as *McFall* and *Metro News* illustrate that courts have looked for some indication that the seller of the obscene material was aware of the relevant facts that made the material obscene. In the case of displaying paintings or posters, it could be inferred that the person selling these paintings or posters had knowledge of what made them obscene. The obscene material is plainly in view and its contents and knowledge of the specific nature of its contents can be assumed "known". The same cannot be said concerning films, videos and other media involving a collection of images and where it takes some time and active steps to observe and "know" the contents. In the case of pornographic films and videos, it cannot be easily inferred that those selling these materials "know" their contents. As noted above, it may be inferred that the retailer is aware that the materials are erotic or pornographic and deal with the exploitation of sex. But selling films which deal with the exploitation of sex is not an illegal activity in itself. There must be something in the material that transports it into the realm of obscenity. Not only must the dominant characteristic of the material be the exploitation of sex, but the exploitation of sex must be undue.

But although the Crown is required to prove more than the sexual nature of the films, it is not required to prove that the retailer actually knows that the films meet the legal definition of obscenity:

97 This is not, of course, to suggest that a retailer must know that the materials being sold were obscene in law. If the retailer says he viewed the films and saw the particular spanking or noticed the underlying degradation but thought that it was harmless and inoffensive, this will not provide a defence. The retailer will not be immune from charges merely because he or she does not know how the law defines obscenity. Nor will a retailer be immune from conviction because he or she is unaware that there are any laws against selling obscene material. This would amount to the defence of mistake of law and it is well established that ignorance of the law is no defence. What is required is that the Crown prove beyond a reasonable doubt the retailer's knowledge that the materials being sold have the qualities or contain the specific scenes which render such materials obscene in law.

R. v. CURRIE

(1975), 24 C.C.C. (2d) 292 (Ont. C.A.)

GALE C.J.O. (dissenting): — The accused was charged and convicted for uttering a forged document. I need not go into the circumstances of the case because it is my judgment that, although not expressing himself in his judgment as clearly as he might have, the judge made sufficient findings to support the decision that the appellant was guilty on the ground of wilful blindness.

I base my conclusion on the finding of the judge that the appellant "deliberately or knowingly" neglected to make the inquiries which he ought to have made. Such a finding plainly suggests that the judge decided that the appellant was in fact suspicious of the authenticity of the cheque, for otherwise he could not have "deliberately" failed to make the necessary inquiries.

My brothers do not agree with me.

ARNUP J.A.: — I agree with the conclusions reached by my brother Martin. To his recitation of the facts I would add only two points. In his statement to the police, the accused said: "I didn't think anything was wrong." In his evidence at trial, he gave this evidence:

A. I didn't think I was going against the law, I thought I was helping somebody.
Q. Why did you feel this man needed help?
A. He'd been drinking a lot.
Q. Was he a clean cut fellow?
A. Yes.
Q. What was the impression he gave you?
A. Honest type, respectable person.
Q. Did you have any suspicion that that wasn't his cheque?
A. No.

The trial judge did not, in his reasons for judgment, indicate that he declined to accept this evidence.

MARTIN J.A.: — The appellant appeals from his conviction before a Provincial Court Judge sitting under Part XVI of the *Criminal Code*, on December 5, 1974, on a charge that:

on or about the 8th day of April, 1974, at the Regional Municipality of Niagara ... did unlawfully and knowingly utter a forged document, to wit: a cheque payable to Edward Gerada in the amount of $478.15 at the Canadian Imperial Bank of Canada, Main and Hellems in the City of Welland, with intent to use same as if it were genuine. Contrary to the provisions of the *Criminal Code of Canada*.

The appellant was 19 years of age at the time of the events giving rise to this charge. On April 8, 1974, he presented for payment, at a branch of the Canadian Imperial Bank of Commerce, at Welland, a cheque payable to one Edward Gerada, in the amount of $478.15. There was endorsed, on the back of the cheque at that time, a signature which purported to be that of the payee of the cheque, Edward Gerada. The cheque in fact had been stolen from Mr. Gerada's mailbox and the endorsement on the cheque was a forgery.

The appellant had a bank account at that branch with a small balance. He had had an account there for some months and was known to the teller of the bank. When he presented the cheque for payment he signed his own name on the back of the cheque, together with his address and telephone number.

When Mr. Gerada failed to receive the cheque which he was expecting, he communicated with the police who arrested the appellant. At that time the appellant made a statement to the police, which in substance was this: that he was sitting in the Reeta Hotel in Welland, having a beer with a friend of his, Mr. Gilbert Davidson, when a man whom he had never seen before asked him to cash the cheque for him, and said that he would pay the appellant $5 for cashing it. The appellant then took the cheque, cashed it and gave the proceeds to this unknown man.

The appellant gave evidence at his trial and he gave the same explanation as that contained in his statement to the police. His evidence on this point was confirmed by Mr. Davidson, who was with him.

The learned trial judge did not reject the evidence of the appellant. However, he registered a conviction and based his finding of guilt upon his conclusion that the appellant was "wilfully blind" as to the forged nature of the endorsement. The trial judge in convicting the appellant said:

> The Crown has submitted very strongly the doctrine of wilful blindness, said to be in this set of circumstances. [*sic*] That the accused must take on some responsibility, make some inquiries as to the validity of the cheque from whom he was obtaining it, before he voluntarily proceeded to cash that cheque through his bank. I am of the opinion that these responsibilities do fall upon the accused, that for some reason either deliberately or knowingly he neglected to make these inquiries which I believe he should have in the circumstances. And therefore that he wilfully blinded himself to the situation he was entering upon and he should have been suspicious of the circumstances, the manner in which the cheque was handed to him from an unknown person and he had a responsibility before his placing that cheque through his banking authorities to make some investigation as to the authenticity of the cheque and the person from whom he was receiving it from.

It is the view of my brother Arnup and myself, that this passage in the trial judge's reasons for judgment is not free from ambiguity and is reasonably open to the conclusion that the learned trial judge was of the view that the doctrine of wilful blindness applied because the accused should have been suspicious in all the circumstances of the forged endorsement on the cheque when he received it and should have made further inquiry.

This was a misconception on the part of the trial judge as to the doctrine of wilful blindness, which he purported to apply. I accept the statements of that doctrine as set out in Williams on *Criminal Law, the General Part*, 2nd ed. (1961), at p. 157, where the following is stated:

> To meet this, the rule is that if a party has his suspicion aroused but then deliberately omits to make further enquiries, because he wishes to remain in ignorance, he is deemed to have knowledge.

He further states at p. 158:

> In other words, there is a suspicion which the defendant deliberately omits to turn into certain knowledge. This is frequently expressed by saying that he "shut his eyes" to the fact, or that he was "wilfully blind". Lord Hewart, C.J., expressed it by saying that "the respondent deliberately refrained from making inquiries the result of which he might not care to have".

I refer also to the judgment of this court in *R. v. F.W. Woolworth Co. Ltd.* (1974), 18 C.C.C. (2d) 23, where Kelly J.A., speaking for the court pointed out at p. 30 that, generally speaking, the doctrine of constructive knowledge has no application in criminal law. The fact that a person ought to have known that certain facts existed, while it may, for some purposes in civil proceedings, be equivalent to actual knowledge, does not constitute knowledge for the purpose of criminal liability, and does not by itself form a basis for the application of the doctrine of wilful blindness.

For these reasons we are of the opinion that the appeal must be allowed, the conviction quashed and a verdict of acquittal directed to be entered.

Appeal allowed.

———————

Canadian courts generally draw a clear line between objectively determined negligence and the subjective test for recklessness or wilful blindness; for example in decisions that negligence is not enough to convict for failing to appear offences: *Weishar* (2003), 13 C.R. (6th) 59 (Ont. S.C.J.) and *Mullin* (2003), 13 C.R. (6th) 54 (Y.T. Terr. Ct.).

R. v. BRISCOE

[2010] 1 S.C.R. 411, 2010 CarswellAlta 589, 2010 CarswellAlta 588, 73 C.R. (6th) 224, 253 C.C.C. (3d) 140

In a very disturbing case on the facts, the issue was whether the accused had aided in the first degree murder of two teenage girls by driving them to a secluded location where they were raped and killed by others. We will return to that issue under "Parties". Here we consider the ruling that the requirement of "knowledge of the likelihood of death" can be satisfied by wilful blindness. *Briscoe* is now the controlling authority defining wilful blindness as "deliberate ignorance".

CHARRON J.: —

21 Wilful blindness does not define the mens rea required for particular offences. Rather, it can substitute for actual knowledge whenever knowledge is a component of the mens rea. The doctrine of wilful blindness imputes knowledge to an accused whose suspicion is aroused to the point where he or she sees the need for further inquiries, but deliberately chooses not to make those inquiries. See *Sansregret v. The Queen*, [1985] 1 S.C.R. 570, and *R. v. Jorgensen*, [1995] 4 S.C.R. 55. As Sopinka J. succinctly put it in *Jorgensen* (at para. 103), "[a] finding of wilful blindness involves an affirmative answer to the question: Did the accused shut his eyes because he knew or strongly suspected that looking would fix him with knowledge?"

22 Courts and commentators have consistently emphasized that wilful blindness is distinct from recklessness. The emphasis bears repeating. As the Court explained in *Sansregret* (at p. 584):

> . . . while recklessness involves knowledge of a danger or risk and persistence in a course of conduct which creates a risk that the prohibited result will occur, wilful blindness arises where

a person who has become aware of the need for some inquiry declines to make the inquiry because he does not wish to know the truth. He would prefer to remain ignorant. The culpability in recklessness is justified by consciousness of the risk and by proceeding in the face of it, while in wilful blindness it is justified by the accused's fault in deliberately failing to inquire when he knows there is reason for inquiry. [Emphasis added.]

23 It is important to keep the concepts of recklessness and wilful blindness separate. Glanville Williams explains the key restriction on the doctrine:

> The rule that wilful blindness is equivalent to knowledge is essential, and is found throughout the criminal law. It is, at the same time, an unstable rule, because judges are apt to forget its very limited scope. A court can properly find wilful blindness only where it can almost be said that the defendant actually knew. He suspected the fact; he realised its probability; but he refrained from obtaining the final confirmation because he wanted in the event to be able to deny knowledge. This, and this alone, is wilful blindness. It requires in effect a finding that the defendant intended to cheat the administration of justice. Any wider definition would make the doctrine of wilful blindness indistinguishable from the civil doctrine of negligence in not obtaining knowledge. [Emphasis added.]

(*Criminal Law: The General Part* (2nd ed. 1961), at p. 159 (cited in *Sansregret* at p. 586.)

24 Professor Don Stuart makes the useful observation that the expression "deliberate ignorance" seems more descriptive than "wilful blindness", as it connotes "an actual process of suppressing a suspicion". Properly understood in this way, "the concept of wilful blindness is of narrow scope and involves no departure from the subjective focus on the workings of the accused's mind" (*Canadian Criminal Law: A Treatise* (5th ed. 2007), at p. 241). While a failure to inquire may be evidence of recklessness or criminal negligence, as for example, where a failure to inquire is a marked departure from the conduct expected of a reasonable person, wilful blindness is not simply a failure to inquire but, to repeat Professor Stuart's words, "deliberate ignorance".

How far does an accused have to go in making inquiries?

R. v. LAGACE

(2003), 181 C.C.C. (3d) 12, 2003 CarswellOnt 4509 (Ont. C.A)

DOHERTY J.A. (for the Court): —

27 Counsel for the appellant also argues that as a matter of law, the doctrine of wilful blindness could not operate against the appellant because he made an inquiry after his suspicion was aroused.28 I disagree. Culpability on the basis of wilful blindness rests on a finding of deliberate ignorance. An accused who suspects that property is stolen but declines to make the inquiries that will confirm that suspicion, preferring instead to remain ignorant is culpable. Where

an accused makes some inquiry, the question remains whether that accused harboured real suspicions after that inquiry and refrained from making further inquiries because she preferred to remain ignorant of the truth. Where some inquiry is made, the nature of that inquiry will be an important consideration in determining whether the accused remained suspicious and chose to refrain from further inquiry because she preferred to remain deliberately ignorant of the truth. For example, a finding that an accused took all reasonable steps to determine the truth would be inconsistent with the conclusion that the accused was wilfully blind: *R. v. Mara*, [1997] 2 S.C.R. 630 at para. 51.29 I, of course, do not suggest that there is any onus on the accused to demonstrate that all reasonable steps were taken. In any case where the Crown relies on the doctrine of wilful blindness and some inquiry has been made, the trier of fact will have to decide whether the Crown has proved beyond a reasonable doubt that despite that inquiry the accused remained suspicious and refrained from making any further inquiry because she preferred to remain ignorant of the truth. As I read the trial judge's reasons, he held that the appellant's inquiry did not remove his suspicion and that no further inquiry was made because the appellant chose not to confirm his suspicion, preferring ignorance over the truth.

R. v. BLONDIN

(1971), 2 C.C.C. (2d) 118, 1970 CarswellBC 72 (B.C. C.A.)

ROBERTSON J.A.: — The respondent ("Blondin") was charged:

that he . . . between the 27th day of August A.D. 1969 and the 29th day of August A.D. 1969, at the Municipality of Richmond, in the County of Vancouver, in the Province of British Columbia, did unlawfully import into Canada a narcotic, to wit: Cannabis resin, contrary to the provisions of the *Narcotic Control Act*.

He was tried by a judge and jury in the County Court and was found not guilty. Against that acquittal the Crown has appealed. Blondin did not give evidence.

Having returned to Canada from Japan, Blondin went to the premises of Canadian Pacific Air Lines in the air terminal in Richmond to collect baggage that he had shipped from Japan, namely, a scuba-diving outfit. The weight of the tank that was part of the outfit aroused suspicion. At one time while it was being examined there were present, among others, Blondin, a Customs official named Montgomery and a constable of the R.C.M.P. named Kennedy. Kennedy was not in uniform and at that time did not identify himself to Blondin as a member of the R.C.M.P. Attempts to remove the valve stem from the tank having proved fruitless, Blondin voluntarily accompanied Montgomery and Kennedy to the Aquatic Shop in Vancouver to try to have the valve stem removed from the tank. At the Aquatic Shop the valve stem was removed, but not much could be seen inside the tank. In the course of the operation the harness was removed from the tank and this revealed that the tank had been cut in half and that the two halves had been put together again; they were kept together by a sleeve inside. When the two halves were separated, Kennedy saw inside a number of brown wafer-like objects; he immediately had the tank closed. Later analysis showed that the objects were cannabis resin, or hashish; they weighed about 23 lbs. After the tank was closed Kennedy, who had not yet made it known to Blondin that he was a police officer, approached Blondin. As Kennedy approached him, Blondin volunteered "I guess I am in for it". Kennedy then identified himself and gave the usual warning. I shall refer to these exchanges as the first conversation. Kennedy then took Blondin, Montgomery and the tank to the R.C.M.P. barracks in Montgomery's car. In the car what I shall call the second conversation occurred. Kennedy asked Blondin if he was aware of what was in the tank and Blondin replied that he did not know. Blondin then asked Kennedy what was in the tank and Kennedy replied that it was hashish. Kennedy asked Blondin if he knew what hashish was and Blondin replied that he did not. On arrival at the barracks Blondin, Montgomery and Kennedy went upstairs to the drug squad office, where a third conversation took place. Kennedy asked Blondin if he was aware that the tank contained narcotics and Blondin said that he knew that there was something in the tank and that it was illegal. He went on to say that he had been paid to bring the tank over. Kennedy asked him who had paid him and Blondin replied that he did not think it was right for him to say. Kennedy asked Blondin to whom he was delivering the tank, and Blondin replied that he did not wish to say.

I am of the respectful opinion that the learned trial judge erred when he instructed the jury that, in order to find Blondin guilty, they must find that he knew that the substance in the tank was cannabis resin. It would be sufficient to find, in relation to a narcotic, *mens rea* in its widest sense.

It remains to decide whether the judge could properly instruct the jury that, if they were satisfied beyond a reasonable doubt that Blondin knew that it was illegal to import the substance in the tank, they might find him guilty, even though he did not know that the substance was a narcotic. I am not prepared so to hold. An essential ingredient of the offence is the importation of a narcotic and I do not consider that *mens rea qua* that offence is proven by an intention to commit an offence which, so far as Blondin's admitted knowledge went, might have been one against the *Customs Act*, R.S.C. 1952, c. 58.

These reasons will, I fear, dispose of this case inadequately if I do not indicate how I think the jury could properly have found *mens rea* in the circumstances of this case. They could have done so if they had found that Blondin had been paid to smuggle a substance illegally into Canada and either was reckless about what it was or wilfully shut his eyes to what it was, inferring therefrom that he suspected that it might be a narcotic. It follows that the learned judge ought to have told the jury that they might convict if they found that Blondin brought the substance into Canada from Japan and knew that it was a narcotic. He should also have instructed the jury that they might convict if they found that he had brought the substance into Canada illegally and had either been reckless about what it was or wilfully shut his eyes to what it was, and then drew the inference that he suspected that it might be a narcotic.

I would allow the appeal, set aside the verdict and order a new trial.

MacFARLANE J.A.: —

I agree with my brother Robertson that the learned trial judge was wrong in instructing the jury that the Crown must prove beyond reasonable doubt that the respondent knew the substance was cannabis resin. I agree also it would be wrong to instruct the jury that proof of knowledge that the substance was one which it would be unlawful to import is itself sufficient to support a conviction. The offence of smuggling goods which may be imported lawfully on disclosure and payment of customs duty is, for this purpose, I think, essentially different from that of importing a narcotic, which Parliament has declared to be a serious offence. I refer to the statement by Cartwright J., as he then was, in *Beaver v. The Queen*, [1957] S.C.R. 531 at 539, 26 C.R. 193, 118 C.C.C. 129, that Parliament regards dealing in narcotics as conduct "harmful in itself". The importation of narcotics has been forbidden except by licence issued under authority of the Governor in Council pursuant to s. 12 of the statute [the *Narcotic Control Act*, 1960-61 (Can.), c. 35].

I therefore agree with my brother Robertson that the jury should have been instructed that the onus on the Crown was to prove beyond reasonable doubt that the respondent knew the substance was a narcotic, although not necessarily cannabis resin.

In *Beaver v. The Queen, supra,* the Supreme Court was dealing with a case of unlawful possession of a narcotic. Delivering the judgment of the majority of the court, Cartwright J. (as he then was) said at p. 541:

> The essence of the crime is the possession of the forbidden substance and in a criminal case there is in law no possession without knowledge of the character of the forbidden substance. . . .
>
> In my view the law is correctly stated in the following passage in the judgment of O'Halloran J.A., with whom Robertson J.A. concurred, in *Rex v. Hess* (1949) 8 C.R. 42, 94 C.C.C. 48 at 50-1 (B.C. C.A.):
>
> "To constitute 'possession' within the meaning of the criminal law it is my judgment that where, as here, there is manual handling of a thing, it must be co-existent with knowledge of what the thing is, and both these elements must be co-existent with some act of control (outside public duty). When those three elements exist together, I think it must be conceded that under sec. 4(1)(*d*) it does not then matter if the thing is retained for an innocent purpose."

I think that on a fair interpretation I must treat this decision as being applicable to a case of importing a narcotic. It follows that knowledge that the substance being imported is a narcotic is an essential ingredient of that offence.

As to proof of knowledge, I think the following extract from the speech of Lord Reid in *Warner v. Metropolitan Police Commissioner*, [1969] 2 A.C. 256 at 279-80 (a possession case) is apt and I respectfully adopt it:

> The object of this legislation is to penalise possession of certain drugs. So if mens rea has not been excluded what would be required would be the knowledge of the accused that he had prohibited drugs in his possession: it would be no defence, though it would be a mitigation, that he did not intend that they should be used improperly. And it is a commonplace that, if the accused had a suspicion but deliberately shut his eyes, the court or jury is well entitled to hold him guilty. Further it would be pedantic to hold that it must be shown that the accused knew precisely which drug he had in his possession. Ignorance of the law is no defence and in fact virtually everyone knows that there are prohibited drugs. So it would be quite sufficient to prove facts from which it could properly be inferred that the accused knew that he had a prohibited drug in his possession. That would not lead to an unreasonable result. In a case like this Parliament, if consulted, might think it right to transfer the onus of proof so that an accused would have to prove that he neither knew nor had any reason to suspect that he had a prohibited drug in his possession. But I am unable to find sufficient grounds for imputing to Parliament an intention to deprive the accused of all right to show that he had no knowledge or reason to suspect that any prohibited drug was in his premises or in a container which was in his possession.

I accordingly agree that it would be correct to instruct a jury that the existence of that knowledge may be inferred as a fact, with due regard to all the circumstances, if the jury finds that the accused has recklessly or wilfully shut his eyes or refrained from inquiry as to the nature of the substance he imports.

I would, therefore, allow the appeal, set the verdict of acquittal aside and order a new trial.

The brief concurring judgment of Davey J.A. is omitted.

A further appeal to the Supreme Court of Canada was dismissed without reasons (1972), 4 C.C.C. (2d) 566 (S.C.C.).

(b)   Crimes of Objective Fault

The *Criminal Code* has long contained a wide variety of offences which expressly adopt an objective standard such as "ought to", "reasonable care", "good reason", "reasonable ground", "reasonably expected" or "reasonable steps". Such offences included, until declared unconstitutional by the Supreme Court, unlawful object murder. The current list includes the doctrine of common intent for accessories, s. 21(2), careless use of firearms or ammunition, s. 86(2), and a strange assortment of other offences including counselling another to be a party to an offence, s. 22(2), treason, s. 46(2)(*b*), failure to use reasonable care to prevent injury from an explosive substance, ss. 79-80, bigamy as a result of a mistaken and unreasonable belief that a spouse is dead, s. 290, publishing defamatory material, s. 303 and criminal breach of trust, s. 422. Another important example is Parliament's declaration that there can be no mistaken belief in consent defence to a sexual assault charge unless reasonable steps were taken: see below Chapter 4 "Rape and Sexual Assault". The anomalous list of offences clearly indicates a haphazard approach.

Sometimes our courts have resorted to an objective standard for a *Criminal Code* offence where such an approach is not expressly required. Sometimes courts read in objective fault where the crime involves a duty to act, as in the case of failing to provide necessaries of life (see *Naglik*). This has long been the approach for unlawful act manslaughter, discussed *infra*, and also respecting offences requiring "criminal negligence". The jurisprudence respecting the latter has been conflicting and complex and requires separate treatment.

(i)   Criminal negligence: s. 219

Since 1955 the *Criminal Code* has provided:

219.(1) Every one is criminally negligent who
    (a) in doing anything, or
    (b) in omitting to do anything that it is his duty to do,
shows wanton or reckless disregard for the lives or safety of other persons.
(2) For the purposes of this section, "duty" means a duty imposed by law.

220. Every person who by criminal negligence causes death to another person is guilty of an indictable offence and liable

    (a) where a firearm is used in the commission of the offence, to imprisonment for life and to a minimum punishment of imprisonment for a term of four years; and
    (b) in any other case, to imprisonment for life.

221. Every one who by criminal negligence causes bodily harm to another person is guilty of an indictable offence and liable to imprisonment for a term not exceeding ten years.

222.(1) A person commits homicide when, directly or indirectly, by any means, he causes the death of a human being.
(2) Homicide is culpable or not culpable.
(3) Homicide that is not culpable is not an offence.
(4) Culpable homicide is murder or manslaughter or infanticide.
(5) A person commits culpable homicide when he causes the death of a human being,
    (a) by means of an unlawful act;
    (b) by criminal negligence;
    (c) by causing that human being, by threats or fear of violence or by deception, to do anything that causes his death; or
    (d) by wilfully frightening that human being, in the case of a child or sick person.

. . . .

234. Culpable homicide that is not murder or infanticide is manslaughter.

. . . .

236. Every person who commits manslaughter is guilty of an indictable offence and liable
    (a) where a firearm is used in the commission of the offence, to imprisonment for life and to a minimum punishment of imprisonment for a term of four years; and
    (b) in any other case, to imprisonment for life.

O'GRADY v. SPARLING

[1960] S.C.R. 804, 33 C.R. 293, 128 C.C.C. 1 at 808,
1960 CarswellMan 41

The appellant, charged with careless driving contrary to provincial legislation, argued that such legislation was inoperative as being in relation to criminal law and also because Parliament had occupied the field by its enactment (s. 233(1) of the *Criminal Code*, repealed in 1985) proscribing criminally negligent driving. For the majority, Judson J. dismissed the appeal, in part on the basis that criminal negligence according to what is now s. 219 of the *Criminal Code* is a form of recklessness which connotes advertence. The court adopted the following passage from Kenny's *Outlines of Criminal Law*, 17th ed.:

> The difference between recklessness and negligence is the difference between advertence and inadvertence; they are opposed and it is a logical fallacy to suggest that recklessness is a degree of negligence. The common habit of lawyers to qualify the word "negligence" with some moral epithet such as "wicked", "gross", or "culpable" has been most unfortunate since it has inevitably led to great confusion of thought and of principle.

There was, however, an overwhelming tendency for provincial courts to ignore *O'Grady* in adopting an objective standard for criminal negligence under s. 219. Many, however, assert a requirement of a gross departure from the objective norm.

R. v. TUTTON and TUTTON

[1989] 1 S.C.R. 1392, 69 C.R. (3d) 289, 48 C.C.C. (3d) 129,
1989 CarswellOnt 959, 1989 CarswellOnt 84

The accused were charged with manslaughter respecting the death of their five-year-old son. The charge and particulars alleged that they had caused the death of their son by criminal negligence through omitting to provide him necessaries of life, in failing to provide insulin and to obtain timely medical assistance. Their son had been diagnosed as a diabetic more than two years earlier. At the time, his parents were advised of his need to have insulin on a daily basis for the rest of his life and thorough instructions were given as to what was required for his care. For some time, both parents followed the instructions for the administration of insulin and observed the necessary dietary controls. They were members of a religious sect which believed in faith healing, believing that God can perform miracles and cure ailments in response to prayer. The sect was not opposed to seeking medical advice and taking medicine, but believed that God can cure ailments which are beyond the purview of medical science. The parents' primary concern was for a cure for their son which would relieve him of the necessity of a lifetime daily intake of insulin. On one occasion the mother ceased administering insulin because she firmly believed that her son was being healed through the power of the Holy Spirit. His health immediately failed and he was taken to hospital, where the parents were strongly advised to continue with the insulin. They did so, but later the mother received a further vision from God which she believed advised her that her son was in fact cured of diabetes and no longer required insulin treatment. As a result of this the mother, with the agreement of the father, stopped the insulin "by God's authority". The son rapidly became ill. He died shortly after being admitted to hospital, his death being attributed to complications of diabetic hyperglycemia. Following a trial by judge and jury, the accused were convicted of manslaughter. On appeal, the Ontario Court of Appeal set aside the conviction and ordered a new trial. The court held that there had been a reversible error as the trial judge had not clearly explained to the jury that the reverse onus in respect of proving a lawful excuse on a balance of probabilities applied only in the case of the included offence of failing to provide the necessaries of life under s. 197(2) [now s. 215(2)] of the *Criminal Code*. The court further held that, although in some cases criminal negligence consisted of a marked and substantial departure from the standard of a reasonable person in the circumstances, in this case of criminal negligence through omission the jury had to be satisfied that the accused knew that there was a risk to the life or safety of their son and unjustifiably took that risk or closed their minds to any such risk with disregard for either his life or his safety. The Crown appealed.

After reserving for some 18 months, the Supreme Court of Canada unanimously confirmed the order of a new trial on the basis that there had been a reversible error in the charge respecting onus of proof. The court also took the opportunity to consider the test for criminal negligence. On this issue, there was an inconclusive three-three split.

McINTYRE J. (L'HEUREUX-DUBÉ J. concurring): —

. . . .

In reaching a conclusion as to whether the conduct of an accused person has shown, within the meaning of s. 202 [now s. 219] of the *Criminal Code*, wanton or reckless disregard for the lives or safety of other persons, the authorities dictate an objective test: see the review of the authorities on this subject by Cory J.A. for the Court of Appeal in *R. v. Waite* (1986), 52 C.R. (3d) 355, 28 C.C.C. (3d) 326, approved in this court (judgment given concurrently) [post, p. 323]. Indeed, in the Court of Appeal, Dubin J.A. accepted the objective test as one of general application, but made an exception in cases where the conduct complained of consisted of an act or acts of omission, as opposed to those of commission. In such cases, it was his view that occasions would arise where a subjective test would be required where acts of omission were under consideration. He considered that this was such a case. It is my view, however, that no such distinction as Dubin J.A. would adopt may be made. I am wholly unable to see any difference in principle between cases arising from an omission to act and those involving acts of commission. Indeed, the words of s. 202 of the *Criminal Code* make it clear that one is criminally negligent who, *in doing anything* or *in omitting to do anything* that it is his duty to do, shows wanton or reckless disregard for the lives or safety of other persons. The objective test must, therefore, be employed where criminal negligence is considered, for it is the conduct of the accused, as opposed to his intention or mental state, which is examined in this inquiry.

Our concept of criminal culpability relies primarily upon a consideration of the mental state which accompanies or initiates the wrongful act, and the attribution of criminal liability without proof of such a blameworthy mental state raises serious concerns. Nonetheless, negligence has become accepted as a factor which may lead to criminal liability and strong arguments can be raised in its favour. Section 202 of the *Criminal Code* affords an example of its adoption. In choosing the test to be applied in assessing conduct under s. 202 of the *Criminal Code*, it must be observed at once that what is made criminal is negligence. Negligence connotes the opposite of thought-directed action. In other words, its existence precludes the element of positive intent to achieve a given result. This leads to the conclusion that what is sought to be restrained by punishment under s. 202 of the *Code* is conduct, and its results. What is punished, in other words, is not the state of mind but the consequence of mindless action. This is apparent, I suggest, from the words of the section, which make criminal conduct which *shows* wanton or reckless disregard. It may be observed as well that the words "wanton or reckless" support this construction, denying as they do the existence of a directing mental state. Nor can it be said that criminal negligence, as defined in s. 202, imports in its terms some element of malice or intention. This point was made in the Crown's factum in para. 41, which provided, in part:

> The plain and ordinary meaning of the terms "wanton" and "reckless" when used in connection with the concept of negligence would seem to include a state of being heedless of apparent danger. Section 202(1) does not use the term "reckless" as an extended definition of intention or malice, but rather employs the term as part of a definition of conduct which amounts to "negligence" in a criminal context.

In my view, then, an objective standard must be applied in determining this question because of the difference between the ordinary criminal offence, which requires proof of a subjective state of mind, and that of criminal negligence. In criminal cases, generally, the act coupled with the mental state or intent is punished. In criminal negligence, the act which exhibits the requisite degree of negligence is punished. If this distinction is not kept clear, the dividing line between the traditional *mens rea* offence and the offence of criminal negligence becomes blurred. The difference, for example, between murder and manslaughter, both unlawful killings, is merely one of intent. If the question of an accused's intent had to be considered and separately proved in offences under s. 202 of the *Criminal Code*, the purpose of the section would be defeated because intentional conduct would perforce be considered under other sections of the *Code* and s. 202, aimed at mindless but socially dangerous conduct, would have no function. For these reasons, the objective test should be employed and, in my view, the Court of Appeal was in error in concluding in this case that a subjective test would be required. The test is that of reasonableness, and proof of conduct which reveals a marked and significant departure from the standard which could be expected of a reasonably prudent person in the circumstances will justify a conviction of criminal negligence.

In reaching this conclusion, I am not overlooking the comments I made in *Sansregret v. R.*, [1985] 1 S.C.R. 570 at 581-82, 45 C.R. (3d) 193, 23 C.C.C. (3d) 223, which were cited by counsel for the appellant. In *Sansregret*, I expressed the view that "recklessness, to form a part of the criminal *mens rea*, must have an element of the subjective." I then went on to say that "It is in this sense that the term 'recklessness' is used in the criminal law and it is clearly distinct from the concept of civil negligence." It was argued upon the basis of these words and later comments on the nature of negligence in relation to the criminal law that a subjective test should therefore be applied in considering the existence of criminal negligence under s. 202 of the *Code*. I would reject that argument on the basis that the concept of recklessness there described is not applicable in a case under s. 202 of the *Code*. Sansregret was charged with rape, a crime which involves positive mind-directed conduct on the part of the accused which aims at the accomplishment of a specific result. It is a traditional *mens rea* offence and a mental state must be proved, in that case an intention to persist with his purpose despite the fact that the complainant's consent has been extorted by threats and fear. Recklessness on his part forms a part of the *mens rea* (the blameworthy state of mind) and has to be proved on a subjective basis as part of the mental element of the offence. In this sense, the words in *Sansregret* are apposite. Section 202, on the other hand, has created a separate offence; an offence which makes negligence — the exhibition of wanton or reckless behaviour — a crime in itself and has thus defined its own terms. As noted by Cory J.A. in *R. v. Waite*, s. 202 of the *Criminal Code* was enacted in its present form as a codification of the offence which had emerged in Canadian jurisprudence, and in respect of which the necessary *mens rea* may be inferred on an objective basis from the acts of the accused.

The application of an objective test under s. 202 of the *Criminal Code*, however, may not be made in a vacuum. Events occur within the framework of other events and actions and, when deciding on the nature of the questioned conduct, surrounding circumstances must be considered. The decision must be made on a consideration of the facts existing at the time and in relation to the accused's perception of those facts. Since the test is objective, the accused's perception of the facts is not to be considered for the purpose of assessing malice or intention on the accused's part but only to form a basis for a conclusion as to whether or not the accused's conduct, in view of his perception of the facts, was reasonable. This is particularly true where, as here, the accused have raised the defence of mistake of fact. If an accused under s. 202 has an honest and reasonably held belief in the existence of certain facts, it may be a relevant consideration in assessing the reasonableness of his conduct. For example, a welder, who is engaged to work in a confined space, believing on the assurance of the owner of the premises that no combustible or explosive material is stored nearby, should be entitled to have his perception, as to the presence or absence of dangerous materials, before the jury on a charge of manslaughter when his welding torch causes an explosion and a consequent death.

As noted earlier, the Tuttons raised the defence of mistake of fact at trial. They argued that the failure to supply insulin was based upon the belief that the child had been cured by divine intervention and that the failure to provide medical care in timely fashion was based upon the belief that the child was not seriously ill, so medical assistance was not necessary. The trial Judge, it was argued, was in error in telling the jury that for any such belief to be effective as a defence it must have been reasonably held. It was held in this court in *Pappajohn v. R.*, [1980] 2 S.C.R. 120, 14 C.R. (3d) 243, 19 C.R. (3d) 97, 52 C.C.C. (2d) 481 [B.C.], that an honest, though mistaken, belief in the existence of circumstances which, if present, would make the questioned conduct non-culpable would entitle an accused to an acquittal. It was also held in *Pappajohn* that the honest belief need not be reasonable, because its effect would be to deny the existence of the requisite *mens rea*. The situation would be different, however, where the offence charged rests upon the concept of negligence, as opposed to that of the guilty mind or blameworthy mental state. In such case, an unreasonable though honest belief on the part of the accused would be negligently held. The holding of such a belief could not afford a defence when culpability is based on negligent conduct. I would therefore conclude that the trial Judge made no error in charging the jury to the effect that any mistaken belief which could afford a defence in a charge of criminal negligence would have to be reasonable.

In the case at bar, then, the assertion of the Tuttons that they believed a cure had been effected by divine intervention and that insulin was not necessary for the preservation of the child's life would have to be considered by the jury. The jury would have to consider whether such belief was honest and whether it was reasonable. In this, they would be required to consider the whole background of the case. They would have to take into account the experience of the Tuttons with the child's illness; the fact that they had seen the result of the withdrawal of insulin on one occasion and that they had been informed of its necessity for the continued care of the child; and the fact that Mrs. Tutton had received some formal instruction or training in dealing with diabetes and diabetics. They would, as well, have to consider whether the belief in a miraculous cure leading to the conclusion that insulin and medical care were not required, though honest, was reasonable. Upon these facts and all others concerning the matter which were revealed in the evidence, the jury would be required to decide whether the refusal of insulin and medical attention represented a marked and significant departure from the standard to be observed by reasonably prudent parents.

I would dismiss the appeal and confirm the direction for a new trial.

LAMER J.: — I have read the reasons of my colleague, Mr. Justice McIntyre, and I am in agreement with them, subject to the following remarks. I am of the view that, when applying the objective norm set out by Parliament in s. 202 [now s. 219] of the *Criminal Code* [R.S.C. 1970, c. C-34; now R.S.C. 1985, c. C-46], there must be made "a generous allowance" for factors which are particular to the accused, such as youth, mental development and education: see Don Stuart, *Canadian Criminal Law: A Treatise*, 2nd ed. (1987), Toronto, Carswell, p. 194; see also Toni Pickard, "Culpable Mistakes and Rape: Relating *Mens Rea* to the Crime" (1980), 30 Univ. of Toronto L.J. 75. When this is done, as we are considering conduct which is likely to cause death, that is, high risk conduct, the adoption of the subjective or of an objective test will, in practice, nearly if not always produce the same result: see Eric Colvin, "Recklessness and Criminal Negligence" (1982), 32 Univ. of Toronto L.J. 345.

I should note that Parliament, when enacting s. 202, did not purport to determine the nature of the negligence which is required when grounding criminal liability thereupon. My understanding of s. 202 is that Parliament has in that section simply defined the expression "criminal negligence" whenever used in the *Criminal Code*.

I should finally mention that in this case the constitutionality of s. 205(5)(*b*) [now s. 222(5)(*b*)] was not in issue. Indeed, assuming without now deciding that it is a principle of fundamental justice that knowledge of a likely risk or deliberate ignorance thereof (foresight or wilful blindness) is an essential element of the offence of manslaughter, the issue as to whether proof of the substituted element of "criminal negligence" as defined by Parliament and interpreted by this court satisfies the test set out in *R. v. Vaillancourt*, [1987] 2 S.C.R. 636, 60 C.R. (3d) 289, 39 C.C.C. (3d) 118 [Que.], does not arise. I therefore do not by my concurrence feel precluded or limited when addressing such a constitutional challenge, of course, if and when called upon to do so.

WILSON J. (DICKSON C.J.C. and LAFOREST J. concurring): —

. . . .

I do not, however, agree with my colleagues' conclusion that criminal negligence under s. 202 [now s. 219] of the *Criminal Code*, R.S.C. 1970, c. C-34 [now R.S.C. 1985, c. C-46], consists only of conduct in breach of an objective standard and does not require the Crown to prove that the accused had any degree of guilty knowledge. I also have reservations concerning the approach my colleagues suggest is available in order to relieve against the harshness of the objective standard of liability which they find in s. 202 and to ensure that the morally innocent are not punished for the commission of serious criminal offences committed through criminal negligence.

. . . .

I wish to deal first with the implications of my colleagues' approach in this case. By concluding that s. 202 of the *Criminal Code* prohibits conduct and the consequences of mindless action absent any blameworthy state of mind, they have, in effect, held that the crime of criminal negligence is an absolute liability offence. Conviction follows upon proof of conduct which reveals a marked and substantial departure from the standard expected of a reasonably prudent person in the circumstances regardless of what was actually in the accused's mind at the time the act was committed.

. . . .

This court made clear in *Sault Ste. Marie* and other cases that the imposition of criminal liability in the absence of proof of a blameworthy state of mind, either as an inference from the nature of the act committed or by other evidence, is an anomaly which does not sit comfortably with the principles of penal liability and fundamental justice.

. . . .

This is particularly so in the case of offences carrying a substantial term of imprisonment which by their nature, severity and attendant stigma are true criminal offences aimed at punishing culpable behaviour as opposed to securing the public welfare. In the absence of clear statutory language and purpose to the contrary, this court should, in my view, be most reluctant to interpret a serious criminal offence as an absolute liability offence.

. . . .

Section 202 of the *Criminal Code* is, in my view, notorious in its ambiguity. Since its enactment in its present form in the 1955 amendments to the *Criminal Code* it has bedevilled both courts and commentators who have sought out its meaning. The interpretation put upon it usually depends upon which words are emphasized. On the one hand, my colleague's judgment demonstrates that emphasizing the use of the words " and "negligence" can lead to the conclusion that an objective standard of liability was intended and that proof of unreasonable conduct alone will suffice. On the other hand, if the words "wanton or reckless disregard for the lives or safety of other persons" are stressed along with the fact that what is prohibited is not negligence simpliciter but "criminal" negligence, one might conclude that Parliament intended some degree of advertence to the risk to the lives or safety of others to be an essential element of the offence. When faced with such fundamental ambiguity, it would be my view that the court should give the provision the interpretation most consonant not only with the text and purpose of the provision but also, where possible, with the broader concepts and principles of the law: see also *R. v. Paré*, [1987] 2 S.C.R. 618, 60 C.R. (3d) 346, 38 C.C.C. (3d) 97.

. . . .

The expression *wanton* disregard for the lives and safety of others is perhaps less clear. The word *wanton* taken in its acontextual sense could signal an element of randomness or arbitrariness more akin to an objective standard but, given the context in which it appears, coupled with the adjective "reckless", and its clear use to accentuate and make more heinous the already serious matter of disregard for the lives or safety of others, I would think that the preferable interpretation is that the word "wanton" was intended to connote wilful blindness to the prohibited risk: see P.J.T. O Hearn, "Criminal Negligence: An Analysis in Depth — Part II" (1965), 7 Cr. L.Q. 407, at p. 411.

In short, the phrase "wanton or reckless disregard for the lives or safety of other persons" signifies more than gross negligence in the objective sense. It requires some degree of awareness or advertence to the threat to the lives or safety of others or alternatively a wilful blindness to that threat which is culpable in light of the gravity of the risk that is prohibited.

. . . .

As I have suggested above, the words of the section can reasonably bear an interpretation which leaves room for the mental element of awareness or advertence to a risk to the lives or safety of others or wilful blindness to such risk. Conduct which shows a wanton or reckless disregard for the lives and safety of others will by its nature constitute *prima facie* evidence of the mental element, and in the absence of some evidence that casts doubt on the normal degree of mental awareness, proof of the act and reference to what a reasonable person in the circumstances must have realized will lead to a conclusion that the accused was aware of the risk or wilfully blind to the risk.

. . . .

I would add that the importance of what the reasonable person would have foreseen to the determination of whether a particular accused would have become aware or wilfully blind to the prohibited risk will vary with the context. For example, in the case of a licensed driver engaging in high-risk motoring, I am in general agreement with Morden J.A. in *R. v. Sharp* (1984), 39 C.R. (3d) 367, 12 C.C.C. (3d) 428 at 434-35 (C.A.), that it is open to the jury to find the accused's blameworthy state of mind from driving which shows wanton or reckless disregard for the lives or safety of others, subject to an explanation in the evidence which would account for the deviant conduct, such as a sudden mechanical malfunction or a bee sting or other accident beyond the accused's control. I would think that in the driving context, where risks to the lives and safety of others present themselves in a habitual and obvious fashion, the accused's claim that he or she gave no thought to the risk or had simply a negative state of mind would in most, if not all, cases amount to the culpable positive mental state of wilful blindness to the prohibited risk.

The minimal nature of the requirement of a blameworthy state of mind and the relevance of the objective standard as a rebuttable mode of proof suggests to me that a holding that s. 202 requires proof of the mental element of advertence to the risk or wilful blindness to the risk will not undermine the policy objectives of the provision. The loss in terms of deterrence and social protection would seem to be negligible when the retention of a subjective standard would at most offer protection for those who due to some peculiarity or unexpected accident commit conduct which, although it shows a reckless or wanton disregard for the lives or safety of others, can be explained as inconsistent with any degree of awareness of or wilful blindness to such a risk. Should social protection require the adoption of an objective standard it is open to Parliament to enact a law which clearly adopts such a standard. In my respectful view this court should not do it for them.

. . . .

In recognition of the harshness of a uniform application of an objective standard of criminal liability, much of the recent work in criminal jurisprudence has canvassed the possibility of introducing a subjective dimension into the objective standard in order to relieve the harshness of imposing an objective standard on those who, because of their peculiar characteristics, could not fairly be expected to live up to the standard set by the reasonable person. H.L.A. Hart was perhaps the first to explore this possibility, in his essay "Negligence, *Mens Rea* and Criminal Responsibility" in Oxford Essays in Jurisprudence (1961), c. 2. He recognized the dangers of the use of an objective standard at p. 47:

> If our conditions of liability are invariant and not flexible *i.e.* if they are not adjusted to the capacities of the accused, then some individuals will be held liable for negligence though they could not have helped their failure to comply with the standard. In *such* cases, indeed, criminal responsibility will be made independent of any "subjective element": since the accused could not have conformed to the required standard.

In response to this most legitimate fear, Professor Hart proposed the following two-pronged test for criminal negligence:

> (i) Did the accused fail to keep those precautions which any reasonable man with normal capacities would in the circumstances have taken?
>
> (ii) Could the accused, given his mental and physical capacities, have taken those precautions?

A similar approach has been taken by the criminal law theorist George Fletcher. Professor Fletcher also proposed that criminal liability for negligent conduct be determined in a two-step process, the first being the determination of wrongdoing, which in the case of the prohibition of negligence would proceed on the basis of breach of an objective standard, and the second being the process by which the court determines whether it would be fair to hold a particular accused responsible for the act of wrongdoing. Professor Fletcher notes in *Rethinking Criminal Law* (1978), at p. 511:

> If the law ignored the question of attribution, namely, the question whether individuals were properly held accountable for their wrongful acts, the criminal law undoubtedly would generate some unjust decisions. If it were true that the only relevant norms of the legal system were those of wrongdoing, injustice would be inescapable in cases in which individuals could not but violate the law.

See also G. Fletcher, "The Theory of Criminal Negligence: A Comparative Analysis" (1971), 119 Univ. of Pa. L. Rev. 401; A. Stalker, "Can George Fletcher Help Solve The Problem of Criminal Negligence?" (1981), 7 Queen's L.J. 274. Professor Toni Pickard has also adopted an approach to this issue similar to that of Professors Hart and Fletcher. She proposes in "Culpable Mistakes and Rape? Relating *Mens Rea* to the Crime" (1980), 30 Univ. of Toronto L.J. 75, at p. 79, to modify an objective standard of unreasonableness so that "the relevant characteristics of the particular actor, rather than those of the ordinary person" will be "the background against which to measure the reasonableness of certain conduct or beliefs". Professor Pickard elaborates:

> This individualized standard is neither "subjective" nor "objective". It partakes of the subjective position because the inquiry the fact finder must conduct is about the defendant himself, not about some hypothetical ordinary person. It partakes of the objective position because the inquiry is not limited to what was, in fact, in the actor's mind, but includes an inquiry into what could have been in it, and a judgment about what ought to have been in it.

In their judgments in this case my colleagues McIntyre and Lamer JJ. seem to have adopted variations of the above developments. McIntyre J., for example, states [pp. 302-303]:

> The application of an objective test under s. 202 of the *Criminal Code*, however, may not be made in a vacuum. Events occur within the framework of other events and actions and, when deciding on the nature of the questioned conduct, surrounding circumstances must be considered. The decision must be made on a consideration of the facts existing at the time and in relation to the accused's perception of those facts. Since the test is objective, the accused's perception of the facts is not to be considered for the purpose of assessing malice or intention on the accused's part but only to form a basis for a conclusion as to whether or not the accused's conduct, in view of his perception of the facts, was reasonable.

My colleague then, however, goes on to suggest that the factual perceptions of the accused must be not only honest but reasonable in order to be factored into the assessment of the objective standard. For example, he suggests that the appellants in this case should not be held to the standard of honest but mistaken belief in circumstances which would render their conduct not culpable, as set out in *Pappajohn, supra*, but rather that their beliefs and perceptions in order to be considered must not be negligently or unreasonably held. To my mind, when the offence charged is criminal negligence the distinction from *Pappajohn* lies not in the introduction of an overriding standard of reasonableness, as this in effect holds the accused simply to the standards of what would be expected from the reasonable person, but rather in the degree of guilty knowledge that must be proven. Although a person may have an honest yet unreasonable view of the circumstances which would render him or her in the large sense blameless, this would not necessarily decide the relevant question of whether he or she had any awareness of the prohibited risk or at some time during the relevant transaction wilfully blinded him or herself to an otherwise obvious risk. To require, as does my colleague, that all misperceptions be reasonable will, in my view, not excuse many of those who through no fault of their own cannot fairly be expected to live up to the standard of the reasonable person.

My colleague Justice Lamer takes a somewhat different approach. He suggests [at p. 304] that courts when applying the objective standard in s. 202 should make " 'a generous allowance' for factors which are particular to the accused, such as youth, mental development and education". I do not doubt that an expansive application of this approach could relieve some of the harshness of applying an objective standard to those who could not fairly be expected to meet the standard and I am cautiously sympathetic to attempts to integrate elements of subjective perception into criminal law standards that are clearly objective: see *R. v. Vasil*, [1981] 1 S.C.R. 469, 20 C.R. (3d) 193, 58 C.C.C. (2d) 97 [Ont.]; *R. v. Hill*, [1986] 1 S.C.R. 313, 51 C.R. (3d) 97, 25 C.C.C. (3d) 322. Despite this, the test proposed by my colleague suffers, in my respectful view, from the various degrees of over- and underinclusiveness that would be expected from a test which is only a rough substitute for a finding of a blameworthy state of mind in each case. For example, an instruction to the trier of fact that they are to hold a young accused with modest intelligence and little education to a standard of conduct that one would expect from the reasonable person of tender years, modest intelligence and little education sets out a fluctuating standard which in my view undermines the principles of equality and individual responsibility which should pervade the criminal law. It tells the jury simply to lower the standard of conduct expected from such people regardless of whether in the particular case the accused attained the degree of guilty knowledge that I have set out above. Professor Fletcher in "The Theory of Criminal Negligence: A Comparative Analysis" has termed the decision whether to make the standard of liability more or less objective by including or excluding specific personal characteristics a "policy question", "a low visibility device for adjusting the interests of competing classes of litigants", and I respectfully agree with the following criticism he makes of this process at pp. 407-408:

> The question in the criminal context is not one of adjusting the interests of competing classes of litigants, but of justifying the state's depriving an individual of his liberty.

Professor Fletcher's solution to this problem, the introduction of a comprehensive range of individualized excuses, is in my view far from realization in Canadian criminal law jurisprudence and, as such, the concern he identifies of the culpability of the individual is still, in my view, best served by continued adherence to subjective standards of liability.

One problem with attempts to individualize an objective standard is that regard for the disabilities of the particular accused can only be applied in a general fashion to alter the objective standard. It seems preferable to me to continue to address the question of whether a subjective standard (a standard, I might add, that in its form is applied equally to all and consistent with individual responsibility) has been breached in each case than to introduce varying standards of conduct which will be only roughly related to the presence or absence of culpability in the individual case. Varying the level of conduct by factoring in some personal characteristics may be unavoidable if the court is faced with a clearly objective standard but it should, in my opinion, be avoided if the more exacting subjective test is available as a matter of statutory interpretation. I have no doubt that factors such as the accused's age and mental development will often be relevant to determining culpability, but under a subjective test they will be relevant only as they relate to the question of whether the accused was aware of or wilfully blind to the prohibited risk and will not have to be factored in wholesale in order to adjust the standard of conduct that is expected from citizens.

Attempts to introduce subjective elements into objective standards not only risk being overinclusive in the sense that they mandate a lowering of the objective standard of liability on a characteristic by characteristic basis, they also risk the danger of being underinclusive for those accused who have idiosyncracies that cannot be articulated ex ante into the necessarily limited list of personal characteristics which can be grafted on to an objective standard. For example, the characteristics listed by my colleague Lamer J. would not relieve the harshness of the application of an objective standard for a driver who, because of a sudden injury or ailment, drove a motor vehicle in a fashion which showed a reckless or wanton disregard for the lives and safety of others. It would not matter that the particular accused was not capable of adverting or wilfully closing his or her eyes to the prohibited risk; the conduct in itself would have breached the objective standard.

The limited range of personal characteristics which can be imported into a modified objective standard is often justified by the notion that a thoroughly subjective approach will allow those who deprive themselves of normal awareness through voluntary intoxication or fits of temper to be exempted from criminal liability. My answer to this (it was also my answer in the cases of *Bernard, supra,* and *R. v. Quin,* [1988] 2 S.C.R. 825, 67 C.R. (3d) 162, 44 C.C.C. (3d) 570) is that greater attention must be paid to the minimal levels of guilty knowledge that are required for conviction of many offences of violence under the *Criminal Code.* It is, in my respectful view, perfectly permissible for the trier of fact to reason from an objective standard and ask the question: must not the accused have had the minimal awareness of what he or she was doing? The important point is that this question is rebuttable and leaves room for acquitting an accused who, for whatever reason, lacked the minimal awareness that would normally accompany the commission of high-risk or violent acts.

I am in complete agreement with what my colleague Justice Lamer has to say concerning the issue of constitutionality.

WAITE v. R.

[1989] 1 S.C.R. 1436, 69 C.R. (3d) 323, 48 C.C.C. (3d) 1,
1989 CarswellOnt 85, 1989 Carswell 960

The accused, who had been drinking, struck and killed four young people taking part in a hayride and injured a fifth. The hayride involved three tractors each towing a wagon with bales of hay along a public road. Four or five of the young people had been running alongside the wagons or had been running from one wagon to another when the accused came upon the hayride. The accused drove behind the hayride, passed it, turned around and deliberately approached the hayride at high speed on the wrong side of the road. The accused testified that he had said to his companions, "Let's see how close we can get". Estimates of the speed varied from 50 to 90 m.p.h. He was driving without headlights.

Following trial before a judge and jury, the accused was found not guilty of four counts of causing death by criminal negligence and one count of causing bodily harm by criminal negligence, but guilty of five counts of the included offence of dangerous driving. The charge to the jury did not specifically mention the objective test for criminal negligence but did convey that the *mens rea* required for proof of the commission of the offence could be found in the accused's conduct. While the jury were deliberating, they returned to ask the judge the difference between dangerous driving and criminal negligence. The judge advised them that in dangerous driving they should look objectively at the manner of driving but that in the case of criminal negligence they had to look at a subjective element and find a "deliberate and wilful assumption of the risk involved in driving in the manner in which he was driving". The Ontario Court of Appeal allowed the Crown's appeal. It held that where allegations of criminal negligence are based upon the manner of driving or some other act of commission, the test is the objective one of whether the driving or the act of commission constitutes a marked and substantial departure from the conduct expected of a reasonable man in the same circumstances. A new trial was directed on the criminal negligence charges. The accused appealed.

The accused's appeal to the Supreme Court was heard at the same time as *Tutton*. The court unanimously dismissed the accused's appeal. The objective McIntyre wing repeated their views in *Tutton* justifying an objective test of a marked and substantial departure from the standard of behaviour expected of reasonably prudent persons in the circumstances. In agreeing to dismiss the appeal, the subjective wing reasoned as follows:

WILSON J.: —

In my view the trial judge's final instruction to the jury was in error as to the degree of *mens rea* required under s. 202 [now s. 219] of the *Criminal Code*, R.S.C. 1970, c. C-34 [now R.S.C. 1985, c. C-46]. When the jury asked the trial Judge to explain the moral difference between dangerous driving and causing death by criminal negligence, the trial judge instructed the jury that the subjective element in criminal negligence was "a deliberate and wilful assumption of the risk involved in driving in the manner in which he was driving". Later in his reply to the jury he repeated that the subjective element in criminal negligence was "assumption and deliberate assumption of the risk". Although I believe there is a subjective element to criminal negligence, the Judge in this case placed much too high an onus on the Crown to prove elements of deliberation and wilfulness. For the reasons I gave in *Tutton* I am of the view that the mental element in criminal negligence is the minimal intent of awareness of the prohibited risk or wilful blindness to the risk.

The trial judge's erroneous instructions to the jury were given near the close of the trial and they were crucial because they were in response to a question from the jury. The facts of the case also suggest that, had the jury been instructed as to the minimal intent requirements of awareness or wilful blindness to the prohibited risk, they would not necessarily have returned the verdict of acquittal on the charges of causing death by criminal negligence: see *Vézeau v. R.*, [1977] 2 S.C.R. 277, 34 C.R.N.S. 309, 28 C.C.C. (2d) 81 [Que.].

Is this a proper application of the subjective test? Compare Stuart, "Criminal Negligence: Deadlock and Confusion in the Supreme Court" (1989), 69 C.R. (3d) 331.

R. v. ANDERSON

[1990] 1 S.C.R. 265, 75 C.R. (3d) 50, 53 C.C.C. (3d) 481,
1990 CarswellMan 190, 1990 CarswellMan 375

The accused was charged with criminal negligence causing death. He had been thinking of something else, ran a red light and a passenger in the car he hit died as a result of injuries suffered in the accident. There was no evidence of any erratic driving apart from driving through the red traffic light. The accused, although legally impaired, showed little sign of impairment. The trial judge found that the Crown had failed to prove the charge beyond a reasonable doubt. During the course of his reasons the trial judge stated that neither the *mens rea* nor the consequences of the manner of driving were material in making a decision as to guilt or innocence. An appeal was allowed by the Court of Appeal. The accused appealed. The sole issue was whether the trial judge's comments relating to the relevance of consequences and intention affected the outcome.

The judgment of the seven-person court was delivered by SOPINKA J.: —

. . . .

In approaching the critique of a trial judgment dealing with a charge of criminal negligence, one can only have profound sympathy for the plight of the trial judge. This area of the law, both here and in other common law countries, has proved to be one of the most difficult and uncertain in the whole of the criminal field. The sections of the *Criminal Code*, R.S.C. 1970, c. C-34, under consideration here are relatively simple.

The use of the word "negligence" suggests that the impugned conduct must depart from a standard objectively determined. On the other hand, the use of the words "wanton and reckless disregard" suggests that an ingredient of the offence includes a state of mind or some moral quality to the conduct which attracts the sanctions of the criminal law. The section makes it clear that the conclusion that there is a wanton or reckless disregard is to be drawn from the conduct which falls below the standard. The major disagreement in the cases centers around the manner in which this conclusion is to be drawn.

On the one hand, there are the cases that hold that it is to be done on an objective basis. If the conduct is a marked departure from the norm, then, based on the standard of an ordinary prudent individual, the accused ought to have known that his actions could endanger the lives or safety of others. On the other hand, there are cases that apply a subjective standard and require some degree of advertence to the risk to be proved. This may be done by inferring advertence from the nature of the conduct in the context of the surrounding circumstances. A refinement on the latter view is that a marked departure constitutes a *prima facie* case of negligence. The trier of fact may but it is not obliged to infer the necessary mental element from the conduct which is found to depart substantially from the norm.

In both the objective and subjective approaches, the court is determining foreseeability of consequences. In a civil negligence case concerned with adjustment of losses, the connection between conduct and consequences is often quite tenuous. The mythical reasonable man has been equipped with a great deal of clairvoyance in order to compensate the innocent victim. Often the defendant will not, in fact, have foreseen the consequences of his negligent acts for which he is held accountable on an objective basis. In a criminal case the connection must be more substantial. To establish recklessness, the consequences must be more obvious. That is the rationale for the requirement of a marked departure from the norm. The greater the risk created, the easier it is to conclude that a reasonably prudent person would have foreseen the consequences. Equally, it is easier to conclude that the accused must have foreseen the consequences. It is apparent, therefore, that as the risk of harm increases, the significance of the distinction between the objective and subjective approaches decreases. The ultimate in this process of reasoning is reached when the risk is so high that the consequences are the natural result of the conduct creating the risk. The conduct in such circumstances can be characterized as intentional.

A finding that the impugned conduct is a marked departure from the standard is, accordingly, central to both the objective and subjective approaches. In *R. v. Tutton*, [1989] 1 S.C.R. 1392, this court was divided as to which approach is correct.

. . . .

Criminal Negligence — Application to This Case

In this case as in most of these cases there is no direct evidence of the state of mind of the appellant. The conclusion that he had a wanton or reckless disregard for the lives and safety of others must be drawn from the conduct which is alleged to be a marked departure from the norm. If an objective standard is employed, this will be determined on the basis of the state of mind of an ordinary prudent person in the circumstances. If the subjective standard or its refinement are applied, then the conclusion, if drawn, must be drawn from the conduct of the appellant.

The conduct relied on in this case is (a) the combination of drinking and driving, and (b) the breach of a traffic light regulation. Clearly the trial judge considered both. He concluded that the conduct was not a marked departure from the norm. That being the case, a conclusion that the appellant had a wanton or reckless disregard for the lives and safety of others could not be drawn on either a subjective or objective basis.

The trial judge specifically addressed the question of the drinking and driving. The Court of Appeal agreed that this was so. Nevertheless he was not prepared to find that this, together with the traffic violation, was sufficient. It left him in a state of doubt. No doubt setting out to drive after drinking in some circumstances may be sufficient to conclude either objectively or subjectively that there is a wanton or reckless disregard for the lives and safety of others. It will not be so, however, in every case. The contrary conclusion would render redundant subss. (2) and (3) of s. 237 [now s. 255] of the *Criminal Code* which provides specific penalties for causing death or bodily harm through the operation of a motor vehicle while impaired. The decision, however, in each case is one of fact, and in this case the trial judge was not prepared to so conclude.

Was this finding affected by the reference to intention? The statement in context is as follows: "nor is *mens rea*, or the intention required to be proved by the Crown. It matters not what the man's intention was when he entered the automobile to put it into use." I do not read this statement to mean that the evidence that the appellant chose to drive his car knowing he had been drinking was not relevant. Such an interpretation would constitute too microscopic an approach to the trial judge's reasons. Clearly, the trial judge went on to consider the relevance of this evidence. What the trial judge was dealing with here was the Crown's obligation. Intention need not be proved by the Crown. From the Crown's point of view, it did not matter that the appellant intended to drive safely when he entered the automobile. The sentence following the above-quoted passage emphasizes that this is the context in which the statement is made: "Nevertheless, of course, the Crown must carry its burden. . . ."

The trial judge's statement that the consequences are not relevant must also be dealt with in the context in which it was made. This reference is undoubtedly one to the tragic death of the passenger in the other vehicle involved in the collision. The death of the passenger was a necessary ingredient of the *actus reus*. It was not otherwise relevant unless a conclusion could be drawn from it with respect to whether there was a wanton and reckless disregard for the lives and safety of other persons. It was not suggested by the Crown that it was a circumstance from which such a conclusion could be drawn either on an objective or subjective basis.

In the circumstances of this case, the unfortunate fact that a person was killed added nothing to the conduct of the appellant. The degree of negligence proved against the appellant by means of the evidence that he drove after drinking and went through a red light was not increased by the fact that a collision occurred and death resulted. If driving and drinking and running a red light was not a marked departure from the standard, it did not become so because a collision occurred. In some circumstances, perhaps, the actions of the accused and the consequences flowing from them may be so interwoven that the consequences may be relevant in characterizing the conduct of the accused. That is not the case here.

In my opinion, the trial Judge came to the conclusion on the evidence that there was a reasonable doubt that the conduct of the accused constituted criminal negligence. He was entitled to do so on the facts. Although he made some general remarks that perhaps should not have been made without elaboration, I am satisfied that no error of law resulted. In any event, the statements to which I have alluded did not affect the outcome. The respondent has not satisfied me that the verdict would not necessarily have been the same. The Court of Appeal ought not to have set aside the acquittal.

In view of this conclusion, it is unnecessary to deal with the appellant's submissions with respect to *R. v. Caldwell*, [1981] All E.R. 961, nor the appellant's submissions that the judgment of the Manitoba Court of Appeal is inconsistent with the principle in *R. v. Vaillancourt* (1987), 39 C.C.C. (3d) 118.

Disposition

In the result, the appeal is allowed, the judgment of the Court of Appeal set aside and the acquittal restored.

See comment by Patrick Healy, "*Anderson:* Marking Time or a Step Back on Criminal Negligence?" (1990), 75 C.R. (3d) 58.

We shall see in the next section that recently the Supreme Court in *F. (J.)* appears, after 20 years, to have resolved the division in *Tutton* in favour of the objective standard. However we shall see that they added a requirement of a marked *and substantial* departure from the objective norm for offences based on "criminal negligence".

(ii)   Marked departure test

In *Tutton*, Justice Lamer argued that the objective test should include a generous allowance for characteristics particular to the accused. Justice Wilson (preferring to adopt a subjective approach to *mens rea*) expressed concerns over such a "modified objective" test, arguing that it could be both over-inclusive and under-inclusive. The Court continued the debate over whether an objective test ought to set a uniform standard or be a modified objective test in *R. v. Hundal*, [1993] 1 SCR 867.

Writing for the majority, Justice Cory held that dangerous driving was an objective fault crime, but that it should be judged on a modified objective standard:

40 A modified objective test was aptly described by McIntyre J. in *R. v. Tutton, supra,* at p. 1413. Although he was dealing with criminal negligence, his words, at p. 1432, are apt in considering the dangerous driving section which is essentially concerned with negligent driving that constitutes a marked departure from the norm:

> The application of an objective test under s. 202 of the *Code,* however, may not be made in a vacuum. Events occur within the framework of other events and actions and when deciding on the nature of the questioned conduct surrounding circumstances must be considered. The decision must be made on a consideration of the facts existing at the time and in relation to the accused's perception of those facts. Since the test is objective, the accused's perception of the facts is not to be considered for the purpose of assessing malice or intention on the accused's part but only to form a basis for a conclusion as to whether or not the accused's conduct, in view of his perception of those facts, was reasonable. If an accused under s. 202 has an honest and reasonably held belief in the existence of certain facts, it may be a relevant consideration in assessing the reasonableness of his conduct. For example, a welder, who is engaged to work in a confined space believing on the assurance of the owner of the premises that no combustible or explosive material is stored nearby, should be entitled to have his perception, as to the presence or absence of dangerous materials, before the jury on a charge of manslaughter when his welding torch causes an explosion and a consequent death.

Justice McLachlin (Chief Justice Lamer concurring) agreed with the substance of the majority's conclusion about how to judge whether an accused was guilty of dangerous driving, but expressed doubts about their use of terminology:

6 This brings me to the modified objective test. The label "modified objective test" might be taken to suggest an amalgam of objective and subjective factors; a test that looks at what ought to have been in the accused's mind, but goes on to consider what was actually there or not there. If this is what it means, it runs afoul of Professor Stuart's sensible admonition that jurists should be very clear about whether they are convicting on the basis of the subjective test or the objective test. On the objective test, the Crown is not required to establish what was in the accused's mind as a matter of fact.

7 Consideration of the context in which the term has been used suggests that the phrase "modified objective test" was introduced in an effort to ensure that jurists applying the objective test take into account all relevant circumstances in the events surrounding the alleged offence and give the accused an opportunity to raise a reasonable doubt as to what a reasonable person would have thought in the particular situation in which the accused found himself or herself. Thus Cory J. in discussing the modified objective test at p. 883 stresses that "personal factors" may be raised and affirms at p. 886 that "it will remain open to the accused to raise a reasonable doubt that a reasonable person would have been aware of the risks in the accused's conduct". He goes on to say, "The test must be applied with some measure of flexibility. That is to say the objective test should not be applied in a vacuum but rather in the context of the events surrounding the incident."

8 If, as my colleague suggests, McIntyre J. was describing a modified objective test in *R. v. Tutton*, [1989] 1 S.C.R. 1392, at p. 1432, the language and example used indicate that his concern too was to ensure that in applying the objective test all relevant circumstances, including those personal to the accused be considered. He reaffirms the objective test by asserting that only "an honest and reasonably held belief" can exonerate the accused. In other words, it is no defence to say, on the subjective level, "I was being careful", or "I believed I could do what I did without undue risk". The defence arises only if that belief was reasonably held. McIntyre J. goes on to offer the example of a welder who is engaged to work in a confined space believing on the assurance of the owner of the premises that no combustible or explosive material is nearby. The welder charged in connection with a subsequent explosion, McIntyre J. asserts, should be allowed to introduce evidence that he believed there were no combustible or explosive materials on the premises. This is an objective test; the fact that the welder had been told there were no combustible or explosive materials on the site is one of the circumstances which a jury should take into account in determining what a reasonable person would have thought and done. Was it reasonable for the welder in these circumstances to turn his torch on in the enclosed space? The answer, on the objective test, is "of course".

9 Nor does Cory J.'s example of "a totally unexpected heart attack, epileptic seizure or detached retina" (at p. 886), which renders an accused unable to control his or her motor vehicle, require the introduction of an element of subjectivity. The better analysis, in my view, is that the onset of a "disease or disability" makes the act of losing control of the motor vehicle involuntary, with the result that there is no *actus reus*. Thus we do not reach the question of what a reasonable person would have been thinking or adverting to as the car goes off the road, much less what the accused was in fact thinking or not thinking. Alternatively, if the *actus reus* were taken as established in these examples, the heart attack or epileptic seizure might be viewed as a circumstance which negates the ordinary inference of want of care which flows from the fact of having lost control of a motor vehicle.

The Supreme Court in *Creighton* and its companion cases adopted a new approach to the interpretation of all objective crimes. The court was unanimous in requiring a marked departure from the standard of care of a reasonable person. The court however divided 5:4 over the question whether personal factors could be considered in applying an objective standard. McLachlin J. for the majority decided that no individual factors short of incapacity could be considered. **Which opinion do you prefer?**

R. v. CREIGHTON

[1993] 3 S.C.R. 3, 23 C.R. (4th) 189, 83 C.C.C. (3d) 346,
1993 CarswellOnt 115, 1993 CarswellOnt 989

On a charge of manslaughter, defence counsel conceded at trial that the injection into the deceased's body of cocaine constituted trafficking within the definition set out in s. 4(1) of the *Narcotic Control Act*. The Crown argued that the accused was guilty of manslaughter as the death was the direct consequence of that unlawful act, contrary to s. 222(5)(*a*) of the *Criminal Code*. The accused was convicted, and the Court of Appeal upheld the conviction. The common law had decided that where the accused had committed an unlawful act, objective foreseeability of the risk of bodily harm which is neither trivial nor transitory was sufficient and foreseeability of the risk of death was not required. The Supreme Court was called on to determine whether the common law definition of unlawful act manslaughter contravened s. 7 of the *Charter*. In deciding that it did not the court expressed some thoughts on the meaning of negligence in the criminal law.

Lamer C.J. (Sopinka, Iacobucci and Major JJ. concurring): — The Crown bears the burden of proving beyond a reasonable doubt that a reasonable person in the context of the offence would have foreseen the risk of death created by his or her conduct. As I explain in more detail in *R. v. Gosset*, S.C.C., No. 22523, released this same day, the reasonable person will be invested with any enhanced foresight the accused may have enjoyed by virtue of his or her membership in a group with special experience or knowledge related to the conduct giving rise to the offence. For example, in *Gosset* the accused police officer's experience and training in the handling of firearms is relevant to the standard of care under s. 86(2) of the *Criminal Code* concerning the careless use of firearms. In the present case, the reasonable person should be deemed to possess Mr. Creighton's considerable experience in drug use. Once the Crown has established beyond a reasonable doubt that this reasonable person in the context of the offence would have foreseen the risk of death created by his or her conduct, the focus of the investigation must shift to the question of whether a reasonable person in the position of the accused would have been capable of foreseeing such a risk. The objective test cannot, to reiterate, relieve the accused of criminal liability simply because he or she did not, in fact, foresee creating the risk of death. I wish to reiterate that the standard of care remains uniform and unchanging irrespective of the particular accused — the prosecution must demonstrate a marked departure from the standard of a reasonable person; rather, it is in the determination of what is reasonable that the skill and expertise of the accused may be considered.

The objective test can be best understood when stated as a "checklist" for the trier of fact to apply to the accused's conduct in a particular case. Where the accused is charged with the offence of unlawful act manslaughter, the trier of fact must ask:

(1) Would a reasonable person in the same circumstances have been aware that the likely consequences of his or her unlawful conduct would create the risk of death?

This question provides the threshold to the objective test. If the answer to this question is No, then the accused must be acquitted. If the answer is Yes, however, the trier must then ask:

(2) Was the accused unaware

(a) because he or she did not turn his or her mind to the consequences of the conduct and thus to the risk of death likely to result; or

(b) because he or she lacked the capacity to turn his or her mind to the consequences of the conduct and thus to the risk of death likely to result, due to human frailties?

If the answer is (a), the accused must be convicted, since the criminal law cannot allow the absence of actual awareness to be an excuse to criminal liability. An important distinction must be maintained within the objective test between the capacity to decide to turn one's mind to a risk, and the decision not to turn one's mind to it. As Colvin, *Principles of Criminal Law* (2nd ed. 1991), notes, at p. 155:

As long as attention is directed to the individual's own capabilities, a judgment of fault can be made on the ground that there was a fair opportunity to have recognized the risks and harm of conduct.

A key element of the objective test is that of the control an accused could have exercised over the frailty which rendered him or her incapable of acting as the reasonable person would in the same circumstances. The notion of control is related to that of moral responsibility; if one is able to act prudently and not endanger the life of others, one will be held liable for failing to do so. One must be morally — and criminally — responsible to act according to his or her capacities not to inflict harm, even unintentional harm. By contrast, the inability to control a particular frailty which resulted in the creation of the risk may offer a moral excuse for having brought about that risk. Therefore, if the answer to the second branch of the objective test is (b), the third and final stage of the inquiry is required:

(3) In the context of the particular offence, would the reasonable person with the capacities of the accused have made him or herself aware of the likely consequences of the unlawful conduct and the resulting risk of death?

In this inquiry, the accused's behaviour is still measured against the standard of the reasonable person, but the reasonable person is constructed to account for the accused's particular capacities and resulting inability to perceive and address certain risks. This test is similar to that advocated by Hart, in "Negligence, *Mens Rea* and Criminal Responsibility", *supra*, at p. 154:

(i) Did the accused fail to take those precautions which any reasonable man with normal capacities would in the circumstances have taken?

(ii) Could the accused, given his mental and physical capacities, have taken those precautions?

It must be emphasized that this is not a subjective test: if a reasonable person with the frailties of the accused would nevertheless have appreciated the risk, and the accused did not in fact appreciate the risk, the accused must be convicted.

The rationale of incorporating capacity into the objective determination of fault is analogous to the rationale underlying the defence of mistake of fact in criminal law, where an accused who has an honest and reasonably held belief in an incorrect set of facts, and acts on the basis of those facts, is excused from punishment for the resulting harm. Human frailties which may affect the capacity of an accused to recognize the risks of unlawful conduct must be considered, however, not because they result in the accused believing in an incorrect set of facts, but rather because they render the accused incapable of perceiving the correct set of facts. It is, however, only those human frailties which relate to an accused's capacity to appreciate the risk in question that may be considered in this inquiry.

I shall now turn to elaborating what "human frailties" may factor into the objective test. It is perhaps best to begin by stating clearly what is not included. Intoxication or impairment through drug use which occurs as a result of voluntary consumption cannot serve to vitiate liability for the risks created by the negligent conduct of an accused. Additionally, a sudden and temporary incapacity to appreciate risk due to exigent circumstances (an emergency which diverts one's attention from an activity, for example) is not properly considered under the third part of the test, but may well result in an acquittal under the first part of the test, that is, would a reasonable person's attention in the same circumstances of the accused have been diverted from that activity.

Human frailties encompass personal characteristics habitually affecting an accused's awareness of the circumstances which create risk. Such characteristics must be relevant to the ability to perceive the particular risk. For example, while illiteracy may excuse the failure to take care with a hazardous substance identifiable only by a label, as the accused may be unable, in this case, to apprehend the relevant facts, illiteracy may not be relevant to the failure to take care with a firearm. This attention to the context of the offence and the nature of the activity is explored in greater detail below.

It should be emphasized that the relevant characteristics must be traits which the accused could not control or otherwise manage in the circumstances. For example, while a person with cataracts cannot be faulted for having reduced vision, he or she may be expected to avoid activity in which that limitation will either create risk or render him or her unable to manage risk which is inherent in an activity (driving, for example). The reasonable person is expected to compensate for his or her frailties, to the extent he or she is conscious of them and able to do so.

This general discussion is not intended to set out an exhaustive definition, but rather to lay the groundwork for examining the different factual contexts which may arise. Two central criteria in this regard are (1) the gravity of the offence, and (2) the inherent purposefulness of the conduct involved. With respect to the gravity of the offence, there may be a significant gulf between neglecting to safely store a bottle containing a prescription drug, and neglecting to unload a firearm and return it to its cabinet. In these different contexts, the behaviour of the reasonable person who possesses all of the accused's limitations may be very different, and therefore the answer to the third question regarding the ability of an accused to control or compensate for his or her frailties may be different as well.

McLACHLIN J. (L'HEUREUX-DUBÉ, GONTHIER and CORY JJ. concurring): —

The Nature of the Objective Test

I respectfully differ from the Chief Justice on the nature of the objective test used to determine the *mens rea* for crimes of negligence. In my view, the approach advocated by the Chief Justice personalizes the objective test to the point where it devolves into a subjective test, thus eroding the minimum standard of care which Parliament has laid down by the enactment of offences of manslaughter and penal negligence.

By way of background, it may be useful to restate what I understand the jurisprudence to date to have established regarding crimes of negligence and the objective test. The *mens rea* of a criminal offence may be either subjective or objective, subject to the principle of fundamental justice that the moral fault of the offence must be proportionate to its gravity and penalty. Subjective *mens rea* requires that the accused has intended the consequences of his or her acts, or that knowing of the probable consequences of those acts, the accused has proceeded recklessly in the face of the risk. The requisite intent or knowledge may be inferred directly from what the accused said or says about his or her mental state, or indirectly from the act and its circumstances. Even in the latter case, however, it is concerned with "what was actually going on in the mind of this particular accused at the time in question": L'Heureux-Dubé J. in *R. v. Martineau, supra*, at p. 655, quoting Stuart, *Canadian Criminal Law* (2nd ed. 1987), at p. 121.

Objective *mens rea*, on the other hand, is not concerned with what the accused intended or knew. Rather, the mental fault lies in failure to direct the mind to a risk which the reasonable person would have appreciated. Objective *mens rea* is not concerned with what was actually in the accused's mind, but with what should have been there, had the accused proceeded reasonably.

It is now established that a person may be held criminally responsible for negligent conduct on the objective test, and that this alone does not violate the principle of fundamental justice that the moral fault of the accused must be commensurate with the gravity of the offence and its penalty: *R. v. Hundal*, [1993] 1 S.C.R. 867.

However, as stated in *Martineau*, it is appropriate that those who cause harm intentionally should be punished more severely than those who cause harm inadvertently. Moreover, the constitutionality of crimes of negligence is also subject to the caveat that acts of ordinary negligence may not suffice to justify imprisonment: *R. v. City of Sault Ste. Marie*, [1978], 2 S.C.R. 1299; *R. v. Sansregret*, [1985] 1 S.C.R. 570. To put it in the terms used in *Hundal*: The negligence must constitute a "marked departure" from the standard of the reasonable person. The law does not lightly brand a person as a criminal. For this reason, I am in agreement with the Chief Justice in *R. v. Finlay, supra*, that the word "careless" in an underlying firearms offence must be read as requiring a marked departure from the constitutional norm.

It follows from this requirement, affirmed in *Hundal*, that in an offence based on unlawful conduct, a predicate offence involving carelessness or negligence must also be read as requiring a "marked departure" from the standard of the reasonable person. As pointed out in *DeSousa*, the underlying offence must be constitutionally sound.

To this point, the Chief Justice and I are not, as I perceive it, in disagreement. The difference between our approaches turns on the extent to which personal characteristics of the accused may affect liability under the objective test. Here we enter territory in large part uncharted. To date, debate has focused on whether an objective test for *mens rea* is ever available in the criminal law; little has been said about how, assuming it is applicable, it is to be applied. In *R. v. Hundal*, *supra*, it was said that the *mens rea* of dangerous driving should be assessed objectively in the context of all the events surrounding the incident. But the extent to which those circumstances include personal mental or psychological frailties of the accused was not explored in depth. In these circumstances, we must begin with the fundamental principles of criminal law.

1. Underlying Principles

The debate about the degree to which personal characteristics should be reflected in the objective test for fault in offences of penal negligence engages two fundamental concepts of criminal law.

The first concept is the notion that the criminal law may properly hold people who engage in risky activities to a minimum standard of care, judged by what a reasonable person in all the circumstances would have done. This notion posits a uniform standard for all persons engaging in the activity, regardless of their background, education or psychological disposition.

The second concept is the principle that the morally innocent not be punished (*Re B.C. Motor Vehicle Act*, [1985] 2 S.C.R. 486, at p. 513; *R. v. Gosset*, S.C.C., No.22523, reasons of Lamer C.J. at p. 20). This principle is the foundation of the requirement of criminal law that the accused must have a guilty mind, or *mens rea*.

I agree with the Chief Justice that the rule that the morally innocent not be punished in the context of the objective test requires that the law refrain from holding a person criminally responsible if he or she is not capable of appreciating the risk. Where I differ from the Chief Justice is in his designation of the sort of educational, experiential and so-called "habitual" factors personal to the accused which can be taken into account. The Chief Justice, while in principle advocating a uniform standard of care for all, in the result seems to contemplate a standard of care which varies with the background and predisposition of each accused. Thus an inexperienced, uneducated, young person, like the accused in

R. v. Naglik, S.C.C., Nos. 22490 and 22636, September 9, 1993, could be acquitted, even though she does not meet the standard of the reasonable person (reasons of the Chief Justice, at p. 24). On the other hand, a person with special experience, like Mr. Creighton in this case, or the appellant police officer in *R. v. Gosset*, S.C.C., No. 22523 (reasons released concurrently), will be held to a higher standard than the ordinary reasonable person.

I must respectfully dissent from this extension of the objective test for criminal fault. In my view, considerations of principle and policy dictate the maintenance of a single, uniform legal standard of care for such offences, subject to one exception: incapacity to appreciate the nature of the risk which the activity in question entails.

This principle that the criminal law will not convict the morally innocent does not, in my view, require consideration of personal factors short of incapacity. The criminal law, while requiring mental fault as an element of a conviction, has steadfastly rejected the idea that a person's personal characteristics can (short of incapacity) excuse the person from meeting the standard of conduct imposed by the law.

. . . .

The Chief Justice relies on Professor H.L.A. Hart in support of importing what Wilson J. calls "individualized excusing conditions" into the objective test for offences of manslaughter and penal negligence. In fact, Professor Hart sees the principle of preventing the punishment of the morally innocent as dictating only that people should not be punished when they lacked the capacity to appreciate the consequences of their conduct. He reasons that no one should be held blameworthy and punished for criminal conduct if he or she acted without free will (H. Hart, *Punishment and Responsibility* (1968), at pp. 35-40). He states that "the need to inquire into the 'inner facts' is dictated ... by the moral principle that no one should be punished who could not help doing what he did" (p. 39) (emphasis added).

In summary, I can find no support in criminal theory for the conclusion that protection of the morally innocent requires a general consideration of individual excusing conditions. The principle comes into play only at the point where the person is shown to lack the capacity to appreciate the nature and quality or the consequences of his or her acts. Apart from this, we are all, rich and poor, wise and naive, held to the minimum standards of conduct prescribed by the criminal law. This conclusion is dictated by a fundamental proposition of social organization. As Justice Oliver Wendell Holmes wrote in *The Common Law* (1881), at p. 108: "when men live in society, a certain average of conduct, a sacrifice of individual peculiarities going beyond a certain point, is necessary to the general welfare."

It may be that in some cases educational deficiencies, such as illiteracy on the part of a person handling a marked bottle of nitroglycerine in the Chief

Justice's example, may preclude a person from being able to appreciate the risk entailed by his or her conduct. Problems of perception may have the same effect; regardless of the care taken, the person would have been incapable of assessing the risk, and hence been acquitted. But, in practice, such cases will arise only exceptionally.

. . . .

This is not to say that the question of guilt is determined in a factual vacuum. While the legal duty of the accused is not particularized by his or her personal characteristics short of incapacity, it is particularized in application by the nature of the activity and the circumstances surrounding the accused's failure to take the requisite care. As McIntyre J. pointed out in *R. v. Tutton*, [1989] 1 S.C.R. 1392, the answer to the question of whether the accused took reasonable care must be founded on a consideration of all the circumstances of the case. The question is what the reasonably prudent person would have done in all the circumstances. Thus a welder who lights a torch causing an explosion may be excused if he has made an enquiry and been given advice upon which he was reasonably entitled to rely, that there was no explosive gas in the area. . . .

The matter may be looked at in this way. The legal standard of care is always the same—what a reasonable person would have done in all the circumstances. The *de facto* or applied standard of care, however, may vary with the activity in question and the circumstances in the particular case.

. . . .

A person may fail to meet an elevated *de facto* standard of care in either of two ways. First, the person may undertake an activity requiring special care when he or she is not qualified to give that care. Absent special excuses like necessity, this may constitute culpable negligence. An untrained person undertaking brain surgery might violate the standard in this way. Second, a person who is qualified may negligently fail to exercise the special care required by the activity. A brain surgeon performing surgery in a grossly negligent way might violate the standard in this second way. The standard is the same, although the means by which it is breached may differ.

Just as the adoption of a uniform standard of care which is blind to personal characteristics of the accused short of incapacity precludes lowering the standard for deficiencies of experience and temperament, so it precludes raising the standard for special experience or training. Since the criminal law is concerned with setting minimum standards for human conduct, it would be inappropriate to hold accused persons to a higher standard of care by reason of the fact that they may be better informed or better qualified than the person of reasonable prudence. Some activities may impose a higher de facto standard than others; brain surgery requires more care than applying an antiseptic. But as discussed earlier, this flows from the circumstances of the activity, not from the expertise of the actor.

. . . .

LA FOREST J.: —

. . . .

There are important educative and psychological differences between the two approaches that have led me to prefer the subjective view of *mens rea*. That view underlines that no one will be punished for anything he or she did not intend or at least advert to, and its use supports one's feeling that a morally innocent person will not be punished.

The objective view, however qualified, does not fully serve these ends. It is true that the qualified objective view would theoretically protect some of the individuals the subjective view would protect, but by no means all; see *Tutton, supra*, per Wilson J., at p. 1419. And it does not respond to the educative and psychological ends sought to be attained by those advocating subjective *mens rea*. Indeed, it introduces a differentiation between individuals in criminal proceedings that, however well-meant, seems foreign to our law. What is more, the qualified objective approach loses most of the practical advantages sought to be attained by the objective approach. Indeed, some of the difficulties that have been perceived to result from the adoption of the subjective view would be exacerbated. I think, in particular, of the difficulties of instructing a jury. On this question, too, I find McLachlin J.'s reasons more persuasive.

Creighton stands firmly against any development of a cultural defence: see Charmaine M. Wong, "Good Intentions, Troublesome Applications: The Cultural Defence and Other Uses of Cultural Evidence in Canada" (1999), 42 Crim. L.Q. 367. The author fully explores the possibilities and drawbacks to such a defence but, surprisingly, makes no mention of *Creighton*. See, too, Stephen Coughlan, "The Omission of Provocation from a General Part" in Stuart, Delisle and Manson (eds.), *Towards a Clear and Just Criminal Law* (1999), 243 at 244-245, who argues against the defence and suggests debate seems to exist only in the United States. See also Jennifer Choi, "The Viability of a 'Cultural Defence' in Canada" (2003), 8 Can. Crim. L.R. 93.

As to the issue of incapacity, it has been held that severe mental retardation can be taken into account for criminal negligence, *Ubhi* (1994), 27 C.R. (4th) 332 (B.C. C.A.), leave to appeal refused (1994), 31 C.R. (4th) 405 (note) (S.C.C.), but not religious beliefs in an exorcism case involving the death of an infant, *Canhoto* (1999), 140 C.C.C. (3d) 321, 29 C.R. (5th) 170 (Ont. C.A.).

Creighton was seemingly ignored on the issue of no individual factors in *Brocklebank* (1996), 106 C.C.C. (3d) 234 (Can. Ct. Martial App. Ct.). The standard for negligent performance of military duty was adjusted to take into account accused's rank, degree of responsibility and exigencies of operation.

In *R. v. L. (J.)* (2006), 204 C.C.C. (3d) 324 (Ont. C.A.) a conviction for criminal negligence causing death was overturned in part because the trial judge had not taken into account the factor of youthfulness.

R. v. BEATTY

54 C.R. (6th) 1, 2008 CarswellBC 307, 2008 CarswellBC 308, [2008] 1
S.C.R. 49,
228 C.C.C. (3d) 225

The accused was charged with three counts of dangerous operation of a motor vehicle causing death under s. 249(4) of the *Criminal Code*. The accused's pick up truck, for no apparent reason, suddenly crossed the solid centre line into the path of an oncoming vehicle, killing all three occupants. Witnesses driving behind the victims' car observed the accused's vehicle being driven in a proper manner prior to the accident. An expert inspection concluded that the accused's vehicle had not suffered from mechanical failure. Intoxicants were not a factor. The accused stated that he was not sure what happened but that he must have lost consciousness or fallen asleep due to heat stroke from working in the sun all day. The trial judge concluded that these few seconds of negligent driving could, without more, fall within the continuum that would attract civil negligence but could not support a finding of a marked departure from the standard of care of a reasonably prudent driver for a conviction.

The British Columbia Court of Appeal set aside the acquittals and ordered a new trial. The accused's conduct of crossing the centre line into the path of oncoming traffic at 90 kilometres per hour on a well travelled road could only be viewed as objectively dangerous and a "marked departure" from the requisite standard of care.

In the Supreme Court, although three separate opinions were delivered, the court was unanimous in the result in deciding that the appeal should be allowed and the acquittals restored.

CHARRON J. (BASTARACHE, DESCHAMPS, ABELLA, and ROTHSTEIN JJ. concurring):

[20] It is well established that dangerous driving is based on a form of negligent conduct. [The court reviewed the rationale established in *Hundal*.]

. . . .

3.3.2 First Modification to the Objective Test: The Marked Departure

[33] The court in *Hundal*, however, made it clear that the requisite *mens rea* may only be found when there is a "marked departure" from the standard of care expected of a reasonable person in the circumstances of the accused. This

modification to the usual civil test for negligence is mandated by the criminal setting. It is only when there is a "marked departure" that the conduct demonstrates sufficient blameworthiness to support a finding of penal liability. One aspect of driving, "the automatic and reflexive nature of driving," particularly highlights the need for the "marked departure" requirement in a criminal setting. Cory J. described this aspect as follows (at p. 884-85):

> Second, the nature of driving itself is often so routine, so automatic that it is almost impossible to determine a particular state of mind of a driver at any given moment. Driving motor vehicles is something that is familiar to most adult Canadians. It cannot be denied that a great deal of driving is done with little conscious thought. It is an activity that is primarily reactive and not contemplative. It is every bit as routine and familiar as taking a shower or going to work. Often it is impossible for a driver to say what his or her specific intent was at any moment during a drive other than the desire to go from A to B.

[34] Therefore, as noted by Cory J., the difficulty of requiring positive proof of a particular subjective state of mind lends further support to the notion that *mens rea* should be assessed by objectively measuring the driver's conduct against the standard of a reasonably prudent driver. In addition, I would note that the automatic and reflexive nature of driving gives rise to the following consideration. Because driving, in large part, is automatic and reflexive, some departures from the standard expected of a reasonably prudent person will inevitably be the product, as Cory J. states, of "little conscious thought". Even the most able and prudent driver will from time to time suffer from momentary lapses of attention. These lapses may well result in conduct that, when viewed objectively, falls below the standard expected of a reasonably prudent driver. Such automatic and reflexive conduct may even pose a danger to other users of the highway. Indeed, the facts in this case provide a graphic example. The fact that the danger may be the product of little conscious thought becomes of concern because, as McLachlin J. (as she then was) aptly put it in *R. v. Creighton*, [1993] 3 S.C.R. 3, at p. 59: "The law does not lightly brand a person as a criminal." In addition to the largely automatic and reflexive nature of driving, we must also consider the fact that driving, although inherently risky, is a legal activity that has social value. If every departure from the civil norm is to be criminalized, regardless of the degree, we risk casting the net too widely and branding as criminals persons who are in reality not morally blameworthy. Such an approach risks violating the principle of fundamental justice that the morally innocent not be deprived of liberty.

[35] In a civil setting, it does not matter how far the driver fell short of the standard of reasonable care required by law. The extent of the driver's liability depends not on the degree of negligence, but on the amount of damage done. Also, the mental state (or lack thereof) of the tortfeasor is immaterial, except in respect of punitive damages. In a criminal setting, the driver's mental state does matter because the punishment of an innocent person is contrary to fundamental principles of criminal justice. The degree of negligence is the determinative

question because criminal fault must be based on conduct that merits punishment.

[36] For that reason, the objective test, as modified to suit the criminal setting, requires proof of a marked departure from the standard of care that a reasonable person would observe in all the circumstances. As stated earlier, it is only when there is a marked departure from the norm that objectively dangerous conduct demonstrates sufficient blameworthiness to support a finding of penal liability. With the marked departure, the act of dangerous driving is accompanied with the presence of sufficient *mens rea* and the offence is made out. The court, however, added a second important qualification to the objective test — the allowance for exculpatory defences.

3.3.3 Second Modification to the Objective Test: The Allowance for Exculpatory Defences

[37] The underlying premise for finding fault based on objectively dangerous conduct that constitutes a marked departure from the norm is that a reasonable person in the position of the accused would have been aware of the risk posed by the manner of driving and would not have undertaken the activity. However, there will be circumstances where this underlying premise cannot be sustained because a reasonable person in the position of the accused would not have been aware of the risk or, alternatively, would not have been able to avoid creating the danger. Of course, it is not open to the driver to simply say that he or she gave no thought to the manner of driving because the fault lies in the failure to bring to the dangerous activity the expected degree of thought and attention that it required. As Cory J. explained (at p. 885 of *Hundal*):

> It would be a denial of common sense for a driver, whose conduct was objectively dangerous, to be acquitted on the ground that he was not thinking of his manner of driving at the time of the accident.

However, because the accused's mental state is relevant in a criminal setting, the objective test must be modified to give the accused the benefit of any reasonable doubt about whether the reasonable person would have appreciated the risk or could and would have done something to avoid creating the danger. On these occasions, even when the manner of driving viewed objectively will clearly be dangerous, the accused cannot be convicted. Cory J., in *Hundal*, gave some useful examples (at p. 887):

> Take for example a driver who, without prior warning, suffers a totally unexpected heart attack, epileptic seizure or detached retina. As a result of the sudden onset of a disease or physical disability the manner of driving would be dangerous yet those circumstances could provide a complete defence despite the objective demonstration of dangerous driving. Similarly, a driver who, in the absence of any warning or knowledge of its possible effects,

takes a prescribed medication which suddenly and unexpectedly affects the driver in such a way that the manner of driving was dangerous to the public, could still establish a good defence to the charge although it had been objectively established.

[38] We can readily appreciate the injustice of branding the driver in each of these examples as a criminal. In the same vein, a reasonably held mistake of fact may provide a complete defence if, based on the accused's reasonable perception of the facts, the conduct measured up to the requisite standard of care. It is therefore important to apply the modified objective test in the context of the events surrounding the incident. In *Tutton*, McIntyre J. provided the following useful example in the context of a criminal negligence charge (at p. 1432, repeated in *Hundal*, at pp. 887-88):

> If an accused under s. 202 has an honest and reasonably held belief in the existence of certain facts, it may be a relevant consideration in assessing the reasonableness of his conduct. For example, a welder, who is engaged to work in a confined space believing on the assurance of the owner of the premises that no combustible or explosive material is stored nearby, should be entitled to have his perception, as to the presence or absence of dangerous materials, before the jury on a charge of manslaughter when his welding torch causes an explosion and a consequent death.

[39] It is important however not to confuse the personal characteristics of the accused with the context of the events surrounding the incident. In the course of the earlier debate on whether to adopt a subjective or objective test, Lamer J. favoured an objective approach but, in an attempt to alleviate its potential harshness, he would have made generous allowances for factors particular to the accused, such as youth, mental development and education: see for example, *Tutton*, at p. 1434. Under this approach, the young and inexperienced driver's conduct would be measured against the standard expected of a reasonably prudent but young and inexperienced driver. This approach, however, was not favoured by other members of the court. As Wilson J. stated in *Tutton*, this individualized approach 'sets out a fluctuating standard which in my view undermines the principles of equality and individual responsibility which should pervade the criminal law" (p. 1418).

3.4 Restatement of the Test in *Hundal*

[41] In *Hundal*, Cory J. summarized the analytical framework for applying the modified objective test in the following oft-quoted passage (at pp. 888-89):

> It follows then that a trier of fact may convict if satisfied beyond a reasonable doubt that, viewed objectively, the accused was, in the words of the section, driving in a manner that was "dangerous to the public, having regard to all the circumstances, including the nature, condition and use of such place and the amount of traffic that at the time is or might reasonably be expected to be on such place". In making the assessment, the trier of fact should be satisfied that the conduct amounted to a marked departure from the standard of care that a reasonable person would observe in the accused's situation.

Next, if an explanation is offered by the accused, such as a sudden and unexpected onset of illness, then in order to convict, the trier of fact must be satisfied that a reasonable person in similar circumstances ought to have been aware of the risk and of the danger involved in the conduct manifested by the accused.

[42] In reviewing a number of cases that have applied this test, I have observed two common difficulties. First, there appears to be some confusion on the distinction, if any, between "objectively dangerous driving" on one hand, and "a marked departure from the standard of care" on the other. This difficulty is quite understandable because some departures from the reasonable standard of care may not be "marked" or "significant" but are nonetheless undeniably dangerous. As we shall see, this case is one example. Second, there appears to be much uncertainty in the case law on how to deal with evidence about the accused's mental state. In particular, when is evidence about the accused's actual mental state relevant? Is it relevant in determining whether the conduct constitutes a "marked departure" from the norm or, as the courts below in this case have done, should it be considered only as part of a distinct analysis on potential exculpatory defences?

[43] As we have seen, the requisite *mens rea* for the offence of dangerous driving was the sole issue before the court in *Hundal*, and the test was expressed accordingly. In order to clarify the uncertainties I have mentioned, it may assist to restate the summary of the test in terms of both the *actus reus* and the *mens rea* of the offence. I respectfully disagree with the Chief Justice that the test for the *actus reus* is defined in terms of a marked departure from the normal manner of driving (para. 67). The *actus reus* must be defined, rather, by the words of the enactment. Of course, conduct that is found to depart markedly from the norm remains necessary to make out the offence because nothing less will support the conclusion that the accused acted with sufficient blameworthiness, in other words with the requisite *mens rea*, to warrant conviction. In addition, it may be useful to keep in mind that while the modified objective test calls for an objective assessment of the accused's manner of driving, evidence about the accused's actual state of mind, if any, may also be relevant in determining the presence of sufficient *mens rea*. I would therefore restate the test reproduced above as follows:

(a) The Actus reus

The trier of fact must be satisfied beyond a reasonable doubt that, viewed objectively, the accused was, in the words of the section, driving in a manner that was "dangerous to the public, having regard to all the circumstances, including the nature, condition and use of the place at which the motor vehicle is being operated and the amount of traffic that at the time is or might reasonably be expected to be at that place".

(b) The Mens rea

The trier of fact must also be satisfied beyond a reasonable doubt that the accused's objectively dangerous conduct was accompanied by the required *mens rea*. In making the objective assessment, the trier of fact should be satisfied on the basis of all the evidence, including evidence about the accused's actual state of mind, if any, that the conduct amounted to a marked departure from the standard of care that a reasonable person would observe in the accused's circumstances. Moreover, if an explanation is offered by the accused, then in order to convict, the trier of fact must be satisfied that a reasonable person in similar circumstances ought to have been aware of the risk and of the danger involved in the conduct manifested by the accused.

[44] I wish to elaborate on certain aspects of this test before applying it to the facts of this case.

3.4.1 Determining the Actus reus

[45] I deal firstly with the *actus reus*. The offence is defined by the words of the legislative provision, not by the common law standard for civil negligence. In order to determine the *actus reus*, the conduct must therefore be measured as against the wording of s. 249. Although the offence is negligence-based, this is an important distinction. As we have seen, conduct that constitutes dangerous operation of a motor vehicle as defined under s. 249 will necessarily fall below the standard expected of a reasonably prudent driver. The converse however is not necessarily true – not all negligent driving will constitute dangerous operation of a motor vehicle. If the court is satisfied beyond a reasonable doubt that the manner of driving was dangerous to the public within the meaning of s. 249, the *actus reus* of the offence has been made out. Nothing is gained by adding to the words of s. 249 at this stage of the analysis.

[46] As the words of the provision make plain, it is the manner in which the motor vehicle was operated that is at issue, not the consequence of the driving. The consequence, as here where death was caused, may make the offence a more serious one under s. 249(4), but it has no bearing on the question whether the offence of dangerous operation of a motor vehicle has been made out or not. Again, this is also an important distinction. If the focus is improperly placed on the consequence, it almost begs the question to then ask whether an act that killed someone was dangerous. The court must not leap to its conclusion about the manner of driving based on the consequence. There must be a meaningful

inquiry into the manner of driving. The consequence, of course, may assist in assessing the risk involved, but it does not answer the question whether or not the vehicle was operated in a manner dangerous to the public. This court explained this distinction in *R. v. Anderson*, [1990] 1 S.C.R. 265, as follows:

> In the circumstances of this case, the unfortunate fact that a person was killed added nothing to the conduct of the appellant. The degree of negligence proved against the appellant by means of the evidence that he drove after drinking and went through a red light was not increased by the fact that a collision occurred and death resulted. *If driving and drinking and running a red light was not a marked departure from the standard, it did not become so because a collision occurred.* In some circumstances, perhaps, the actions of the accused and the consequences flowing from them may be so interwoven that the consequences may be relevant in characterizing the conduct of the accused. That is not the case here. [Emphasis added; p. 273.]

3.4.2 Determining the Mens rea

[47] In determining the question of *mens rea*, the court should consider the totality of the evidence, including evidence, if any, about the accused's actual state of mind. As discussed at length above, the *mens rea* requirement for the offence of dangerous driving will be satisfied by applying a modified objective test.[3] This means that, unlike offences that can only be committed if the accused possesses a subjective form of *mens rea*, it is not necessary for the Crown to prove that the accused had a positive state of mind, such as intent, recklessness or wilful blindness. Of course, this does not mean that the actual state of mind of the accused is irrelevant. For example, if proof is made that a driver purposely drove into the path of an oncoming vehicle in an intentionally dangerous manner for the purpose of scaring the passengers of that vehicle or impressing someone in his own vehicle with his bravado, the requirement of *mens rea* will easily be met. One way of looking at it is to say that the subjective *mens rea* of intentionally creating a danger for other users of the highway within the meaning of s. 249 of the *Criminal Code* constitutes a "marked departure" from the standard expected of a reasonably prudent driver. Doherty J.A. similarly equates such deliberate action with a "(marked and substantial" departure from the norm in the context of a criminal negligence charge in *R. v. Willock* (2006), 210 C.C.C. (3d) 60 (Ont. C.A.), where he states, at para. 32:

> I think the appellant's conduct during the two or three seconds in issue could only reasonably be said to constitute a marked and substantial departure from the conduct expected of a reasonable driver if the appellant deliberately jerked the steering wheel to cause the vehicle to swerve, presumably to either show off or frighten his young passengers. If that finding was reasonably open on the evidence, then the appellant could properly have been convicted of

---

3 This reference to a "modified objective test" cannot, it seems, be meant to reverse the rejection of such a test in *Creighton*. Rather, it appears to be an unfortunate ambiguity, and is merely intended to refer to the fact that the objective test in this context is a marked departure from the norm, not merely a departure.

criminal negligence, as he was unable to retain control of the vehicle before it crossed the median and collided with the westbound vehicle. As indicated, I read the trial judge as making that finding. With respect, I do not think that finding was reasonably available on the totality of the evidence.

I agree with the Chief Justice (at para. 75 of her reasons) that the analysis in *Willock* does not have the effect of imposing on the Crown the burden of proving the subjective intention of the accused in order to make out the offence. Doherty J.A. specifically held at para. 31 that "conduct occurring in a two to three second interval can amount to a marked departure from the standard of a reasonable person and demonstrate a wanton or reckless disregard for the life or safety of others." Doherty J.A. simply recognizes, as I do, that evidence about the actual intention of an accused is relevant to a court's objective assessment of whether or not conduct constitutes a marked departure from the norm.

[48] However, subjective *mens rea* of the kind I have just described need not be proven to make out the offence because the mischief Parliament sought to address in enacting s. 249 encompasses a wider range of behaviour. Therefore, while proof of subjective *mens rea* will clearly suffice, it is not essential. In the case of negligence-based offences such as this one, doing the proscribed act with the absence of the appropriate mental state of care may instead suffice to constitute the requisite fault. The presence of objective *mens rea* is determined by assessing the dangerous conduct as against the standard expected of a reasonably prudent driver. If the dangerous conduct constitutes a "marked departure" from that norm, the offence will be made out. As stated earlier, what constitutes a "marked departure" from the standard expected of a reasonably prudent driver is a matter of degree. The lack of care must be serious enough to merit punishment. There is no doubt that conduct occurring in a few seconds can constitute a marked departure from the standard of a reasonable person. Nonetheless, as Doherty J.A. aptly remarked in *Willock*, "conduct that occurs in such a brief time frame in the course of driving, which is otherwise proper in all respects, is more suggestive of the civil rather than the criminal end of the negligence continuum" (para. 31). Although *Willock* concerned the offence of criminal negligence, an offence which is higher on the continuum of negligent driving, this observation is equally apt with respect to the offence of dangerous operation of a motor vehicle.

[49] If the conduct does not constitute a marked departure from the standard expected of a reasonably prudent driver, there is no need to pursue the analysis. The offence will not have been made out. If, on the other hand, the trier of fact is convinced beyond a reasonable doubt that the objectively dangerous conduct constitutes a marked departure from the norm, the trier of fact must consider evidence about the actual state of mind of the accused, if any, to determine whether it raises a reasonable doubt about whether a reasonable person in the

accused's position would have been aware of the risk created by this conduct. If there is no such evidence, the court may convict the accused.

4. Application to this Case

[50] First, did Mr. Beatty commit the *actus reus* of the offence? Did he operate his motor vehicle "in a manner that is dangerous to the public, having regard to all the circumstances, including the nature, condition and use of the place at which the motor vehicle is being operated and the amount of traffic that at the time is or might reasonably be expected to be at that place"? I repeat here the Court of Appeal's analysis of the circumstances for convenience:

> However, the evidence showed that there was only one lane for travel in each direction, the traffic was proceeding at or near the posted speed limit of 90 kilometres per hour, the highway was well-travelled, there was limited visibility approaching the curve, and the collision occurred within a split second of the respondent's crossing onto the oncoming lane of traffic.
>
> Viewed objectively, the respondent's failure to confine his vehicle to its own lane of travel was in "all the circumstances" highly dangerous to other persons lawfully using the highway, and in particular those approaching in a westerly direction on their own side of the road. [paras. 23, 24]

[51] Up to this point in the analysis, I would agree with the Court of Appeal. In all the circumstances, Mr. Beatty's failure to confine his vehicle to his own lane of traffic was dangerous to other users of the highway. Further, no suggestion was made at trial that Mr. Beatty was in a state of non-insane automatism at the time. However, this conclusion only answers the *actus reus* part of the offence. The more difficult question is whether Mr. Beatty had the necessary *mens rea*. There is no evidence here of any deliberate intention to create a danger for other users of the highway that could provide an easy answer to that question. Indeed, the limited evidence that was adduced about the actual state of mind of the driver suggested rather that the dangerous conduct was due to a momentary lapse of attention. Hence, the trial judge was correct in finding that the question of *mens rea* in this case turns on whether Mr. Beatty's manner of driving, viewed on an objective basis, constitutes a marked departure from the norm.

[52] In my respectful view, the Court of Appeal erred in faulting the trial judge for addressing her attention to Mr. Beatty's "momentary lack of attention" and his "few seconds of lapsed attention". The trial judge appropriately focussed her analysis on Mr. Beatty's manner of driving in all the circumstances. She noted that there was no evidence of improper driving before the truck momentarily crossed the centre line and that the "few seconds of clearly negligent driving" was the only evidence about his manner of driving (para. 36). She appropriately considered the totality of the evidence in finding that "the only reasonable inference" was that "he experienced a loss of awareness" that caused him to

drive straight instead of following the curve in the road (para. 36). In her view, this momentary lapse of attention was insufficient to found criminal culpability. She concluded that there was "insufficient evidence to support a finding of a marked departure from the standard of care of a prudent driver" (para. 37).

[53] Based on the totality of the evidence, I see no reason to interfere with the trial judge's assessment of Mr. Beatty's conduct in this case and her conclusion on Mr. Beatty's criminal liability. By contrast, it is my respectful view that the Court of Appeal leaped too quickly to the conclusion that the requisite *mens rea* could be made out from the simple fact of the accident occurring, leaving no room for any assessment of Mr. Beatty's conduct along the continuum of negligence.

[54] For these reasons, I would allow the appeal and restore the acquittals.

Chief Justice McLachlin (Binnie and LeBel JJ. concurring) would have preferred the analysis that the "marked departure" requirement applies to both the *actus reus* and the *mens rea* of the offence of dangerous operation of a motor vehicle. She added that a momentary lapse of attention without more cannot establish the *actus reus* and *mens rea* of the offence of dangerous driving. The heavy sanctions and stigma that follow from a criminal offence should not be visited upon a person for a momentary lapse of attention. Provincial regulatory offences appropriately and adequately deal with this sort of conduct. However, additional evidence might show that a momentary lapse is part of a larger pattern that, considered as a whole, establishes the marked departure from the norm required for the offence of dangerous driving.

In a separate opinion Fish J. expressed the view that the *mens rea* for dangerous driving could be established in two ways. In rare cases, the prosecution would be able to establish that the accused drove in a deliberately dangerous manner. In such cases it was not necessary to establish that the conduct was a marked departure from the norm. The fault element can be established, and generally is, by demonstrating that the accused failed to meet the objective standard of a reasonable person in the circumstances. In such cases, the fault element was not the marked departure from the norm of a reasonably prudent driver, but the fact that a reasonably prudent driver in the accused's circumstances would have been aware of the risk of that conduct, and if able to do so, would have acted to avert it.

Reviewing the ruling in *Beatty*

This major ruling on dangerous driving is written in language which applies to any crime requiring objective fault where there is a risk of imprisonment. For such crimes the court holds that, in contrast to civil liability for negligence or the due diligence standard for regulatory offences, principles of fundamental justice under s. 7 of the *Charter* require proof of a marked departure from the objective norm. A uniquely Canadian *Charter* standard is now firmly in place for crimes based on objective fault. The court also determines that sometimes it may be necessary to consider the accused's mental state to decide whether the reasonable person would have been aware of the risk. **Do you agree with the court's approach?**

Do you agree with the decision in *Beatty* that causing three deaths on the basis of a momentary lack of attention was not a marked departure from the objective norm? Given *Beatty* expect defences of momentary inattention to be frequently advanced against dangerous driving charges. It should be remembered, though, that in *Beatty* there was no evidence of any other bad driving.

However, most major vehicle accidents happen in a flash and proof of a pattern of bad driving that day will often be hard to come by with witnesses long gone down the highway. Given the lenient ruling on the facts one can expect that many serious accidents on highways, even those involving fatalities, will now almost always have to be dealt with by charges of careless driving under provincial laws where the maximum penalties are typically as low as six months imprisonment. Dangerous driving acquittals resulted in *R. v. McCaughan* (2009), 65 C.R. (6th) 360 (Man. C.A.), *R. v. Desbiens* (2010), 73 C.R. (6th) 97 (Que. C.A.) and *R. v. Delorey* (2011), 78 C.R. (6th) 66 (N.S. C.A.) (tire conditions of loaner vehicle from car dealership causing accident). See too *R. v. Jiang* (2007), 48 C.R. (6th) 49 (B.C. C.A.) (medical evidence of chronic sleep disorder). However, evidence of prior drinking was sufficient to convict in *R. v. Settle* (2010), 261 C.C.C. (3d) 45 (B.C. C.A.).

The Court decides that no personal factors can be considered on an objective fault test on the basis that this had been determined in *R. v. Creighton*, [1993] 3 S.C.R. 3, 23 C.R. (4th) 189, 83 C.C.C. (3d) 346. We shall see in later chapters that the court itself has consistently decided since that decision that, in the context of defences such as self-defence, necessity and duress, the objective approach must be modified to require that individual factors be considered so that the reasonable person is considered in the context of the accused's situation and experience. In the law of the tort of negligence the court has no problem taking into account personal factors. In establishing the tort of negligent investigation in *Hill v. Hamilton-Wentworth (Regional Municipality) Police Services Board*, 50 C.R. (6th) 279, [2007] 3 S.C.R. 129 Chief Justice McLachlin writing for the 6-3 majority observes that:

> The general rule is that the standard of care in negligence is that of the reasonable person in similar circumstances. In cases of professional negligence, this rule is qualified by an additional principle: the defendant must "live up to the standards possessed by persons of reasonable skill and experience in that calling". (para. 69)

Why then are we not to take into account the experience and situation of the driver in a dangerous driving case? Are we, for example, to hold a driver of a large transport truck, or a police officer at the wheel of a cruiser, criminally responsible for bad driving only on the standard of the average, reasonable driver? The approach appears quite unrealistic and will likely be ignored in trial courts with live witnesses, as has been the case with this aspect of the *Creighton* ruling. Can a trier of fact really overlook such obvious factors as age and experience? In *R. v. Tayfel* (2009), 72 C.R. (6th) 45 (Man. C.A.) the Court understandably, and contrary to *Creighton*, took into account the experience of bush pilots in deciding upon the amount of fuel needed. The accused miscalculated the amount of fuel in his tanks and did not use the flight standard for non-visual flying. He ran out of fuel and crash-landed near Winnipeg, injuring four persons and killing a passenger. The Court of Appeal found him guilty of dangerous operation of an aircraft but not guilty of criminal negligence charges.

For various views on *Beatty* see Stuart "*Beatty: Charter* Standard of Marked Departure for All Crimes of Negligence" (2008) 54 C.R. (6th) 33, David Tanovich, "The Implications of *Beatty* for Criminal Negligence" (2008) 54 C.R. (6th) 38 and Hamish Stewart, "*Beatty:* Towards a Coherent Law of Penal Negligence" (2008) 54 C.R. (6th) 45.

At one point in *Beatty* the court speaks of the offence of criminal negligence under s. 216 as an offence "higher on the continuum of negligent driving" (para. 48). There is no longer a specific crime of negligent driving but a motorist could still be charged with criminal negligence causing bodily harm, criminal negligence causing death or manslaughter. We have seen that the court was infamously equally divided in *R. v. Tutton*, [1989] 1 S.C.R. 1392, 69 C.R. (3d) 289, 48 C.C.C. (3d) 129 on what to make of this special fault element of "criminal negligence" requiring proof of conduct showing wanton or reckless disregard for lives or safety. Most provincial courts before and after *Tutton* have applied the marked departure from the objective norm test (see, for example, *R. v. Rajic* (1993), 21 C.R. (4th) 208, 80 C.C.C. (3d) 533 (Ont. C.A.), leave to appeal refused 24 C.R. (4th) 404n, 83 C.C.C. (3d) vi (note), [1993] 3 S.C.R. viii. Yet some courts insist that this a form of fault higher than dangerous driving (see *R. c. Palin* (1999), 135 C.C.C. (3d) 119 (Que. C.A.), leave to appeal refused (1999), 243 N.R. 196 (note) (S.C.C.) and *R. v. L. (J.)* (2006), 204 C.C.C. (3d) 324 (Ont. C.A.)).

It took a stunning period of some 20 years for the Supreme Court to resolve the impasse in *Tutton* respecting the meaning of criminal negligence under s. 219:

R. v. F. (J.)

(2008), 60 C.R. (6th) 205, 2008 CarswellOnt 6339, 2008 CarswellOnt 6340, 236 C.C.C. (3d) 421 (S.C.C.)

The split verdict in *Tutton* has since seemingly been resolved by the court in *F. (J.)*, though that decision was actually considering a technical appeal based on inconsistent jury verdicts rather than directly addressing the issue of the fault requirement for criminal negligence. In the course of that decision Justice Fish for a majority of the court stated:

[7] The fault element required for conviction at trial was essentially common to both counts of manslaughter. On count 1, the requisite fault element was that of the underlying offence of criminal negligence; on count 2, the requisite fault element was that of failure to provide the necessaries of life. Neither criminal negligence nor failure to provide the necessaries of life requires proof of

intention or actual foresight of a prohibited consequence. Under both counts, the jury was required to determine not what the respondent knew or intended, but what he ought to have foreseen.

[8] On the count alleging failure to provide necessaries, the Crown was bound to establish that the respondent's failure to protect his foster child represented "a *marked departure* from the conduct of a reasonably prudent parent in circumstances where it was objectively foreseeable that the failure to provide the necessaries of life would lead to a *risk* of danger to the life, or a *risk* of permanent endangerment to the health, of the child": *R. v. Naglik*, [1993] 3 S.C.R. 122, at p. 143 (emphasis added). It will later become apparent why I have emphasized the word "risk" in this description of the offence by the Chief Justice, speaking for the court on this point.

[9] On the count alleging criminal negligence, the Crown was bound to show that the respondent's very same omission represented a marked and substantial departure (as opposed to a marked departure) from the conduct of a reasonably prudent parent in circumstances where the accused either recognized and ran an obvious and serious risk to the life of his child or, alternatively, gave no thought to that risk: *R. v. Tutton*, [1989] 1 S.C.R. 1392, at pp. 1430-31; *R. v. Sharp* (1984),12 C.C.C. (3d) 428 (Ont. C.A.).

Note that in this passage Justice Fish has done more than decide that criminal negligence in s. 222(5)(b) is based on objective fault. He has also drawn a distinction between a "marked and substantial" departure from the required level of care, which is required for a conviction of criminal negligence, as opposed to a mere "marked departure" from that standard, required as a *Charter* standard for other objective fault crimes. As a practical matter, this is likely to be a hard line for courts to draw. This normative distinction between degrees of gross negligence seems likely to confuse and cause head-scratching by lawyers, judges and jurors. Be that as it may, until otherwise advised there are now three degrees of objective fault requirements:

1. Due diligence with the onus reversed for regulatory offences (as a matter of common law presumption under *Sault Ste. Marie* or as a *Charter* standard where there is a risk of imprisonment) .This is a standard of simple negligence like that long applied for the tort of negligence.

2. A marked departure from the objective norm as a *Charter* standard for crimes with objective fault requirements (*Beatty*) (gross negligence).

3. A marked and substantial departure from the objective norm for offences bases on criminal negligence under s. 219 *F. (J.)* (worse than gross negligence)

It may have been preferable for the court to have rested content with the notion that the fault requirements for criminal negligence and failing to provide necessities of life are essentially the same: a marked departure from the objective norm, and then to have pointed to the higher stigma and especially the higher penalties declared by Parliament for criminal negligence. So jurors could then in future have been advised that criminal negligence is the more serious offence carrying a larger penalty. The particular problem here making *F. (J.)* a hard case is that the two counts charged were both forms of manslaughter where the maximum penalty of life is the same whatever the underlying offence. It is not clear why the Crown chose to complicate matters by charging the two counts.

The majority in *F. (J.)* confirmed, as did the majority in *Beatty*, that negligence is a form of fault, not *actus reus*. This is consistent with the definition of forms of fault in modern *Criminal Codes*, and also with the *Charter* standard that intentional conduct must be punished more than negligent conduct: *R. v. Martineau.*

(c) Crimes Based on Predicate Offences

On the authority of *Creighton* and *DeSousa* there are some offences based on predicate offences where the fault requirement regarding the consequence of the underlying offence is much reduced but constitutional. The problem will be how to identify them. Thus far there are three recognized by the Supreme Court: *DeSousa* concerns the offence of unlawful act causing harm (s. 269); *Creighton* the manslaughter category of unlawful act causing death (s. 222(5)(a)); and *R. v. Godin*, [1994] 2 S.C.R. 484, 31 C.R. (4th) 33, 89 C.C.C. (3d) 574, aggravated assault (s. 268). In each case the unlawful act is interpreted to require objective foresight of harm. *DeSousa* also held that the unlawful act must be a provincial or federal offence, that the fault for the predicate offence must be proved and that this cannot be absolute liability. There is no requirement of a marked departure from the objective norm beyond proof of the underlying offence. However where the predicate, or underlying offence is one of negligence the gross departure limit must be applied to it. See *R. v. Gosset* (1993), 23 C.R. (4th) 280 (S.C.C.) at 284.

Beatty requires a marked departure for all objective crimes. Logically, this should include those based on predicate offences given the reduced fault requirement of an objectively dangerous act. On this view the offence of unlawful act manslaughter, for example, may well now always require a marked departure from the norm. See further L.Wilson, "Too Many Manslaughters" (2007) 52 Crim. L.Q. 433. In the view of the majority in *F. (J.)* manslaughter by criminal negligence would require a marked and substantial departure from the objective norm.

R. v. DeSOUSA

[1992] 2 S.C.R. 944, 15 C.R. (4th) 66, 76 C.C.C. (3d) 124, 1992 CarswellOnt 100, 1992 CarswellOnt 1006F

A fight broke out at a New Year's Eve party. The accused was involved in the fight. A bystander was injured on the arm when a bottle, allegedly thrown by the accused, broke against a wall and a glass fragment struck the bystander. The accused was charged with unlawfully causing bodily harm contrary to s. 269 of the *Criminal Code*. At the outset of the trial, before any evidence was heard, the accused brought a motion to have s. 269 declared of no force or effect on the ground that it violated s. 7 of the *Charter*. The trial judge granted the motion and quashed the indictment. He found that s. 269 created criminal responsibility for causing bodily harm by way of an unlawful act. The unlawful act could be a violation of a federal or provincial statute, including an offence of absolute liability. Since the section also allowed the possibility of imprisonment, it contravened s. 7 of the *Charter* and was not justified under s. 1. On appeal, the Court of Appeal overturned the motion judgment and set aside the order quashing the indictment. The accused appealed. Notice that an assault is not an essential element of the offence charged in this case; if an assault caused bodily harm the accused would be culpable under s. 267(1)(*b*).

Sopinka J. (Cory, Gonthier, McLachlin, and Iacobucci JJ. concurring):

. . . .

B. Section 269 of the *Criminal Code* —

To be brought within the ambit of s. 269, an accused must have committed an underlying unlawful offence (otherwise referred to as the predicate offence) and have caused bodily harm to another person as a result of committing that underlying offence. For liability to be imposed for unlawfully causing bodily harm, the harm caused must have sufficient causal connection to the underlying offence committed (see *R. v. Wilmot*, (1940), 74 C.C.C. 1 (Alta. C.A.), at pp. 17 and 26-27 [C.C.C.], appeal dismissed for want of jurisdiction [1941] S.C.R. 53, 75 C.C.C. 161. The requirement of an underlying "unlawful" offence includes at its most general, and subject to the restrictions discussed below, only offences prohibited by federal or provincial legislation.

. . . .

(1)   The Mental Element Requirement of Section 269

The major issue raised in this appeal concerns the mental element required by s. 269 of the *Code*. After delineating the statutorily required mental element, the question of the constitutional sufficiency of this element will then be addressed to determine whether it passes constitutional muster.

It is axiomatic that in criminal law there should be no responsibility without personal fault. A fault requirement was asserted to be a fundamental aspect of our common law by this court in *R. v. Sault Ste. Marie (City)*, [1978] 2 S.C.R. 1299, 3 C.R. (3d) 30, 40 C.C.C. (2d) 353, and as a matter of constitutional law under s. 7 of the *Charter* in *Reference re s. 94(2) of the Motor Vehicle Act (British Columbia)*, [1985] 2 S.C.R. 486, 48 C.R. (3d) 289, 23 C.C.C. (3d) 289, (sub nom. *Constitutional Question Act, R.S.B.C. 1979, Chap. 63*) [1986] D.L.Q. 90 (headnote) [hereafter *Re B.C. Motor Vehicle Act.*] As a matter of statutory interpretation, a provision should not be interpreted to lack any element of personal fault unless the statutory language mandates such an interpretation in clear and unambiguous terms. Unlike most offences, the mental element of s. 269 is composed of two separate requirements. The first requirement is that the mental element of the underlying offence of s. 269 be satisfied. The second requirement is that the additional fault requirement supplied by the wording of s. 269, discussed more fully, *infra*, also be satisfied.

(a) *The mental element of the underlying offence*

To be convicted under s. 269, the prosecution must first satisfy the mental element requirement of the underlying offence. In interpreting the ambit of the underlying offences covered by s. 269 it is important to recognize the abhorrence of the criminal law for offences of absolute liability. While not all underlying offences will have a possibility of imprisonment and despite the fact that s. 269 has a fault requirement in addition to that supplied by the underlying offence, as a matter of statutory interpretation, underlying offences of absolute liability are excluded from forming the basis for a prosecution under s. 269. For the reasons given by this court in *Sault Ste. Marie, supra,* and *Re B.C. Motor Vehicle Act, supra,* s. 269 should not be interpreted so as to bootstrap underlying offences of absolute liability into the criminal law. The criminal law is based on proof of personal fault and this concept is jealously guarded when a court is asked to interpret criminal provisions, especially those with potentially serious penal consequences. This statutory conclusion is mandated by the general presumption in the interpretation of criminal statutes against absolute liability and the absence of clear words to the contrary to rebut this presumption. Thus, the concept of "unlawful" as it is used in s. 269 does not include any underlying offence of absolute liability. The inclusion of such offences would be contrary to the general canons of criminal interpretation quite apart from any *Charter* considerations (see particularly *R. v. Baril,* [1979] 2 S.C.R. 547, 8 C.R. (3d) 68, 46 C.C.C. (2d) 257, at p. 553 [S.C.R.], and *Beaver v. R.,* [1957] S.C.R. 531, 26 C.R. 193, 118 C.C.C. 129, at pp. 537-538 and 542-543 [S.C.R.]). Although not relying on constitutional requirements in foreclosing the possibility of absolute liability offences forming the predicate offences of s. 269, certainly principles of fundamental justice require no less.

In addition to satisfying the statutorily required mental element of the underlying offence, the mental element of the underlying offence must also be constitutionally sufficient in its own right. If the underlying offence contains a constitutionally insufficient mental element, it is of no force or effect and thus cannot form the basis for a prosecution under s. 269. The underlying offence must be valid in law on its own before it can be used to support a charge under s. 269.

(b) *The meaning of "unlawful" in section 269*

In addition to the mental element required by the underlying offence, the wording of s. 269, and particularly the case law interpreting the term "unlawfully", imports an additional aspect to the mental element of s. 269. The case law interpreting the use of this term in similar provisions has focused on the offence most commonly known as unlawful act manslaughter. While manslaughter is not the offence at issue in this appeal, the case law which seeks to interpret the term "unlawful" in that context is instructive.

The leading English authority on the issue of the meaning of "unlawful" in this area is *R. v. Larkin* (1942), 29 Cr. App. R. 18, where the Court of Criminal Appeal held that:

> Where the act which a person is engaged in performing is unlawful, then if at the same time it is a dangerous act, that is, an act which is likely to injure another person, and quite inadvertently the doer of the act causes the death of that other person by that act, then he is guilty of manslaughter. (At p. 23 [Cr. App. R.].)

English authority has consistently held that the underlying unlawful act required by its manslaughter offence requires proof that the unlawful act was "likely to injure another person" or in other words put the bodily integrity of others at risk. . . . This position has also been adopted by most Canadian courts. [citations omitted.]

. . . .

Despite ample authority that the underlying act must be objectively dangerous in order to sustain a conviction under what is now s. 222(5)(*a*), the law in this area is not entirely free from doubt. In *R. v. Smithers*, [1978] 1 S.C.R. 506, 40 C.R.N.S. 79, 34 C.C.C. (2d) 427, Dickson J. (as he then was) adopted certain comments made by G. Arthur Martin (later Martin J.A.) in a short case note on the English *Larkin* case. The adopted comments included the following:

> There are many unlawful acts which are not dangerous in themselves and are not likely to cause injury which, nevertheless if they cause death, render the actor guilty of culpable homicide. . .

. . . .

> In the case of so-called intentional crimes where death is an unintended consequence the actor is always guilty of manslaughter at least.

> ("Criminal Law — Voluntary and Involuntary Manslaughter — Lawful and Unlawful Acts" (1943), 21 Can. Bar. Rev. 503, at pp. 504-505; cited in *Smithers, supra,* at p. 519. [S.C.R.])

This passage appears to raise doubt as to whether the "unlawful act" must be inherently dangerous to sustain a manslaughter conviction. This issue was not addressed in *Smithers*, however, as the assault which occurred in that case was clearly an intentional, dangerous, act. As well, *Smithers* was a case concerned with the issue of causation and not the meaning to be given to the term "unlawful act". Finally, *Smithers* was not argued under the *Charter*. In the absence of a more definitive statement or a more extensive analysis of the issue, I am reluctant to freeze the meaning of "unlawful" for the purposes of s. 269 based on the 1943 comments of even as persuasive a source as G. Arthur Martin. More telling, and also more considered, authority was provided by Martin J.A. in *Tennant, supra,* which predates *Smithers* but was not discussed by Dickson J. in the latter decision. In *Tennant,* a Court of Appeal panel composed of Gale C.J.O. and Brooke and Martin JJ.A. rendered a *per curiam* judgment which concluded that:

> When death is accidentally caused by the commission of an unlawful act which any reasonable person would inevitably realize must subject another person to, at least, the risk of some harm resulting therefrom, albeit not serious harm, that is manslaughter. (At p. 96 [C.C.C., p. 19 C.R.N.S.].)

The court later noted that:

> . . . if death was caused by the *accidental discharge* of the fire-arm in the commission of such unlawful act and if the jury were satisfied beyond a reasonable doubt that the *unlawful act* was such as any reasonable person would inevitably realize must subject another to the risk of, at least, some harm, albeit not serious harm, the death would amount to manslaughter. [Emphasis in original.] (At p. 96. [C.C.C., p. 19 C.R.N.S.].)

The court thus substantially adopted the English position as articulated in *Larkin.*

In accordance with the English law and in furtherance of the developing Canadian case law, the most principled approach to the meaning of "unlawful" in the context of s. 269 is to require that the unlawful act be at least objectively dangerous. This conclusion is both supported by the meaning given to the word "unlawful act" by virtually all of the lower courts and also is in accord with the emerging jurisprudence of this court in regard to personal fault.

Objective foresight of bodily harm should be required for both criminal and non-criminal unlawful acts which underlie a s. 269 prosecution. I can see no reason why there should be a difference between the two categories of acts. There is no need to differentiate between criminal and non-criminal unlawful acts when one unifying concept is available. Thus the test is one of objective foresight of bodily harm for all underlying offences. The act must be both unlawful, as described above, *and* one that is likely to subject another person to danger of harm or injury. This bodily harm must be more than merely trivial or transitory in nature and will in most cases involve an act of violence done deliberately to another person. In interpreting what constitutes an objectively dangerous act, the courts should strive to avoid attaching penal sanctions to mere inadvertence. The contention that no dangerousness requirement is required if the unlawful act is criminal should be rejected. The premise on which this proposition is based is that most, if not all, criminal acts are inherently dangerous. This premise is an overstatement inasmuch as a large part of the criminal law is concerned with offences against property and other interests which are not inherently dangerous. But, even if this premise were accepted, the difference between the two positions would be simply one of semantics. To maintain the correct focus it is preferable to inquire whether a reasonable person would inevitably realize that the underlying unlawful act would subject another person to the risk of bodily harm rather than getting sidetracked on a question regarding the classification of the offence.

(2) Constitutional Sufficiency

The mental element of s. 269 has two separate aspects. The first aspect of the mental element is the requirement that an underlying offence with a constitutionally sufficient mental element has been committed. Additionally, s. 269 requires that the prosecution prove that the bodily harm caused by the underlying unlawful act was objectively foreseeable. This latter requirement insures that all prosecutions under s. 269 contain *at least* a fault requirement based on an objective standard. As this court has not indicated that fundamental justice requires fault based on a subjective standard for all offences, the mental element required by s. 269 passes constitutional muster unless s. 269 is one of those few offences which due to its stigma and penalty require fault based on a subjective standard. I agree with the respondent and intervenors that s. 269 has neither the stigma nor criminal sanction to require a more demanding mental element than it already has. The criminal sanction is flexible and thus can be tailored to suit the circumstances of the case. The stigma associated with conviction will generally reflect the degree of opprobrium which the underlying offence attracts. The stigma attached to the underlying offence will in turn influence the minimum mental requirement for that offence.

Unless a minimum mind state of subjective intention in regard to consequences is constitutionally required, the test discussed above satisfies the dictates of s. 7 of the *Charter*. I will now consider that issue.

C. Foresight of Consequences

Although I have concluded by means of statutory interpretation that s. 269 requires objective foresight of the consequences of an accused's unlawful act, the appellant argues that s. 7 of the *Charter* requires subjective foresight of all consequences which comprise part of the *actus reus* of an offence. The appellant notes that in *R. v. Martineau*, [1990] 2 S.C.R. 633, 79 C.R. (3d) 129, 58 C.C.C. (3d) 353, Lamer C.J.C., speaking for the majority of the court, discussed a:

> general principle that criminal liability for a particular result is not justified except where the actor possesses a culpable mental state in respect of that result: . . . At p. 645 [S.C.R.].)

The appellant also relies on *R. v. Metro News Ltd.* (1986), 53 C.R. (3d) 289, 29 C.C.C. (3d) 35 (C.A.), leave to appeal refused, [1986] 2 S.C.R. viii, 64 C.R. (3d) xxx (note), 29 C.C.C. (3d) 35n, for a similar proposition that:

The minimum and necessary mental element required for criminal liability for most crimes is knowledge of the circumstances which make up the *actus reus* of the crime and foresight or intention with respect to any consequence required to constitute the *actus reus* of the crime. (At pp. 54-55 [C.C.C.], p. 309 C.R.].)

The appellant submits that this authority supports a requirement that the minimum mental element required by s. 7 of the *Charter* for s. 269 includes an intention to cause bodily harm. In isolation, it is true that the language used in some earlier decisions of this court could be interpreted as suggested by the appellant. This proposition draws additional support from statements such as those of Wilson J. in *R. v. Docherty*, [1989] 2 S.C.R. 941, 72 C.R. (3d) 1, 51 C.C.C. (3d) 1, where she infers that proof of intention is required in regard to *each* of the elements of the *actus reus*. Wilson J. states:

A full *mens rea* offence under the *Criminal Code* demands that the accused have an intent to perform the acts that constitute the *actus reus* of the offence. (At p. 958 [S.C.R.].)

As one of the elements of the *actus reus* in this appeal is that bodily harm be produced, it is arguable that the case law of this court has implied that foresight of the consequences of an act must be proved when such consequences constitute an essential element of the offence. This argument, however, misconstrues and overgeneralizes the language used by this court in these earlier judgments (see also *R. v. Rees*, [1956] S.C.R. 640, 24 C.R. 1, 115 C.C.C. 1, and *R. v. Pappajohn*, [1980] 2 S.C.R. 120, 14 C.R. (3d) 243, 19 C.R. (3d) 97, 52 C.C.C. (2d) 481, at p. 139 [S.C.R.]). In the circumstances of *Docherty*, the offence definition itself required intention in regard to all aspects of the *actus reus* and thus this proposition was not meant to be set down as an overriding principle of criminal law. Equally, in *Martineau* it was only as a result of the stigma and penal consequences of a murder conviction that subjective foresight of death was required. Here again, it was not meant to be stated as a general principle of criminal law. As far back as Blackstone's *Commentaries*, it was recognized that criminal guilt did not always require foresight of the consequences of an unlawful act:

If a man be doing any thing *unlawful*, and a consequence ensues which he did not foresee or intend, as the death of a man or the like, his want of foresight shall be no excuse; for, being guilty of one offence, in doing antecedently what is in itself unlawful, he is criminally guilty of whatever consequence may follow the first misbehaviour.

(Blackstone, *Commentaries on the Laws of England* (1769), Book IV, at p. 27.)

In *R. v. Nguyen*, [1990] 2 S.C.R. 906, 79 C.R. (3d) 332, (sub nom. *R. v. Nguyen; R. v. Hess*) 59 C.C.C. (3d) 161 [hereinafter *Hess*], the court concluded that a meaningful mental element was required in regard to a *blameworthy* element of the *actus reus*. Provided that there is a sufficiently blameworthy element in the *actus reus* to which a culpable mental state is attached, there is no additional requirement that any other element of the *actus reus* be linked to this mental state or a further culpable mental state. As inferred by Blackstone, *supra*, provided that the actor is already engaged in a culpable activity, foresight of consequences is not required in order to hold that actor responsible for the results of his or her unlawful activity. Lamer C.J.C. stated in *Martineau* that "[i]f Parliament wishes to deter persons from causing bodily harm during certain offences, then it should punish persons for causing the bodily harm" (p. 647 [S.C.R.]). This is exactly what s. 269 attempts to do. In this particular provision the mental element requirement is composed of both the mental element of the underlying unlawful act *and* the additional requirement of objective foresight of bodily harm. There is, however, no constitutional requirement that intention, either on an objective or a subjective basis, extend to the consequences of unlawful acts in general.

The absence of a constitutional requirement that intention extend to all aspects of an unlawful act was discussed by Wilson J. in *R. v. Bernard*, [1988] 2 S.C.R. 833, 67 C.R. (3d) 113, 45 C.C.C. (3d) 1, at pp. 888-889 [S.C.R.], where she concludes that the minimal element of the application of force is sufficient for a conviction for sexual assault causing bodily harm. She inferentially confirms that s. 7 of the *Charter* does not mandate intention in regard to all of the consequences required by the offence. The contrary position, that intention must extend to all of the required consequences of an offence, is not supported by the case law and should not be adopted as a constitutional requirement.

There are many provisions where one need not intend all of the consequences of an action. As was pointed out in *Hess, supra*, there must be an element of personal fault in regard to a culpable aspect of the *actus reus*, but not necessarily in regard to each and every element of the *actus reus*. The requirement of fault in regard to a meaningful aspect of the *actus reus* is necessary to prevent punishing the mentally, and morally innocent and is in keeping with a long line of cases of this court including *Rees, supra*, and *Pappajohn, supra*. In many offences, such as assault or dangerous driving, the offence is made out regardless of the consequences of the act but the consequences can be used to aggravate liability for the offence. For example, both assault and assault causing bodily harm have identical *mens rea* requirements and the element of causing bodily harm is merely used to classify the offence. No principle of fundamental justice prevents Parliament from treating crimes with certain consequences as more serious than crimes which lack those consequences.

A number of *Criminal Code* offences call for a more serious charge if certain consequences follow. To require intention in relation to each and every consequence would bring a large number of offences into question including manslaughter (s. 222(5)), criminal negligence causing bodily harm (s. 221), criminal negligence causing death (s. 220), dangerous operation causing bodily harm (s. 249(3)), dangerous operation causing death (s. 249(4)), impaired driving causing bodily harm (s. 255(2)), impaired driving causing death (s. 255(3)), assault causing bodily harm (s. 267(1)(*b*)), aggravated assault (s. 268), sexual assault causing bodily harm (s. 272(*c*)), aggravated sexual assault (s. 273), mischief causing danger to life (s. 430(2)) and arson causing bodily harm (s. 433(*b*)). As noted by Professor Colvin, "[i]t would, however, be an error to suppose that *actus reus* and *mens rea* always match in this neat way" (E. Colvin, *Principles of Criminal Law*, 2nd ed. (Toronto: Carswell, 1991), at p. 55).

Conduct may fortuitously result in more or less serious consequences depending on the circumstances in which the consequences arise. The same act of assault may injure one person but not another. The implicit rationale of the law in this area is that it is acceptable to distinguish between criminal responsibility for equally reprehensible acts on the basis of the harm that is actually caused. This is reflected in the creation of higher maximum penalties for offences with more serious consequences. Courts and legislators acknowledge the harm actually caused by concluding that in otherwise equal cases a more serious consequence will dictate a more serious response.

There appears to be a general principle in Canada and elsewhere that, in the absence of an express legislative direction, the mental element of an offence attaches only to the underlying offence and not to the aggravating circumstances (Colvin, *supra*, at p. 57). This has been confirmed by this court in a number of cases including those which have held that sexual assault requires intention simply in relation to the assault and not any aggravating circumstance (see *R. v. Chase*, [1987] 2 S.C.R. 293, 59 C.R. (3d) 193, 37 C.C.C. (3d) 97, and *R. v. Bernard*, *supra*, at pp. 888-889) [S.C.R.]. To require fault in regard to each consequence of an action in order to establish liability for causing that consequence would substantially restructure current notions of criminal responsibility. Such a result cannot be founded on the constitutional aversion to punishing the morally innocent. One is not morally innocent simply because a particular consequence of an unlawful act was unforeseen by that actor. In punishing for unforeseen consequences the law is not punishing the morally innocent but those who cause injury through avoidable unlawful action. Neither basic principles of criminal law, nor the dictates of fundamental justice require, by necessity, intention in relation to the consequences of an otherwise blameworthy act.

DISPOSITION

On a proper interpretation of s. 269 of the *Code*, the concept of an unlawful act as it is used in that section includes only federal and provincial offences. Excluded from this general category of offences are any offences which are based on absolute liability and which have constitutionally insufficient mental elements on their own. Additionally, the term "unlawfully", as it is used in this section requires an act which is at least objectively dangerous. Interpreted in this way s. 269 complies with the requirements of s. 7 of the *Charter*. In the absence of a violation of s. 7, there is no violation of s. 11(*d*).

For a critical comment on *DeSousa* see Stuart, "The Supreme Court Drastically Reduces the Constitutional Requirement of Fault: A Triumph of Pragmatism and Law Enforcement Expediency" (1992), 15 C.R. (4th) 88.

R. v. CREIGHTON

[1993] 3 S.C.R. 3, 23 C.R. (4th) 189, 83 C.C.C. (3d) 346,
1993 CarswellOnt 115, 1993 CarswellOnt 989

The court divided 5-4 on the issue of whether the objective test for unlawful act manslaughter required reasonable foresight of death (Lamer C.J. for the minority) or merely reasonable foresight of bodily harm (McLachlin J. for the majority).

LAMER C.J. (SOPINKA, IACOBUCCI and MAJOR JJ. concurring): —

18 It is now well established that there is a group of offences, albeit a small group, that requires a subjectively determined culpable mental state in relation to the prohibited result.

. . . .

20 The only basis upon which subjective foresight of death or the risk of death could be found to be constitutionally required in the case of unlawful act manslaughter, therefore, would be to find that the offence is one of those crimes for which "because of the special nature of the stigma attached to a conviction therefore or the available penalties, the principles of fundamental justice require a *mens rea* reflecting the particular nature of that crime": see *R. v. Vaillancourt*, per Lamer J., at p. 653.

21 There are two main branches to the analysis of social stigma. First the court must look to the conduct being punished to determine if it is of sufficient gravity to import significant moral opprobrium on the individual found guilty of engaging in such conduct. In the case of manslaughter under s. 222(5)(a), the conduct in question consists of killing someone as a consequence of committing an unlawful act. In this respect, there may well be no difference between the *actus reus* of manslaughter and that of murder; arguably both give rise to the stigma of being labelled by the state and the community as responsible for the wrongful death of another. Clearly, there can be no conduct in our society more grave than taking the life of another without justification.

22 The second branch of the stigma test concerns the moral blameworthiness not of the offence, but of the offender found guilty of committing it. As a general proposition, more stigma will attach to those who knowingly engage in wrongful

conduct than to those who recklessly or inadvertently engage in the same conduct. . .

23 In my view, the stigma which attaches to a conviction for unlawful act manslaughter is significant, but does not approach the opprobrium reserved in our society for those who knowingly or intentionally take the life of another. It is for this reason that manslaughter developed as a separate offence from murder at common law.

[Chief Justice Lamer then went on to hold that although objective fault was sufficient, the stigma associated with manslaughter required symmetry between the external and fault elements:]

29 Thus, as I stated, unlawful act manslaughter falls into the class of offences where a mental element in relation to the consequence must be established, but in any event, I find the stigma attached to a conviction for culpable homicide, albeit culpable homicide which is not murder, to be significant enough to require, at a minimum, objective foresight of the risk of death in order for the offence to comply with s. 7 of the *Charter*.

MCLACHLIN J. (L'HEUREUX-DUBÉ, GONTHIER and CORY JJ. concurring) (and LAFOREST concurring separately): — The *Criminal Code* defines three general types of culpable homicide. There is murder, the intentional killing of another human being. There is infanticide, the intentional killing of a child. All other culpable homicides fall into the residual category of manslaughter.

Manslaughter is a crime of venerable lineage. It covers a wide variety of circumstances. Two requirements are constant: (1) conduct causing the death of another person; and (2) fault short of intention to kill. That fault may consist either in committing another unlawful act which causes the death, or in criminal negligence. The common-law classification of manslaughter is reflected in the definition of culpable homicide in s. 222(5) of the *Criminal Code*.

. . . .

The structure of the offence of manslaughter depends on a predicate offence of an unlawful act or criminal negligence, coupled with a homicide. It is now settled that the fact that an offence depends upon a predicate offence does not render it unconstitutional, provided that the predicate offence involves a dangerous act, is not an offence of absolute liability, and is not unconstitutional: *R. v. DeSousa*, [1992] 2 S.C.R. 944. But a further objection is raised in this case. It is said that the offence of manslaughter is unconstitutional because it requires only foreseeability of the risk of bodily harm and not foreseeability of death, and that the trial judge erred in requiring only foreseeability of bodily harm.

The cases establish that in addition to the *actus reus* and *mens rea* associated with the underlying act, all that is required to support a manslaughter conviction is reasonable foreseeability of the risk of bodily harm. While s. 222(5)(*a*) does not expressly require foreseeable bodily harm, it has been so interpreted: see *R. v. DeSousa, supra*. The unlawful act must be objectively dangerous, that is likely to injure another person. The law of unlawful act manslaughter has not, however, gone so far as to require foreseeability of death. The same is true for manslaughter predicated on criminal negligence; while criminal negligence, *infra*, requires a marked departure from the standards of a reasonable person in all the circumstances, it does not require foreseeability of death.

. . . .

In more recent times, the prevailing view has been that foreseeability of bodily harm is required for manslaughter. In England, it was said in *R. v. Larkin*, [1943] 1 All E.R. 217 (C.A.), at p. 219, that the act must be "a dangerous act, that is, an act which is likely to injure another person". In *R. v. Tennant* (1975), 23 C.C.C. (2d) 80, at p. 96, the Ontario Court of Appeal stated that the unlawful act must be "such as any reasonable person would inevitably realize must subject another to the risk of, at least, some harm, albeit not serious harm". Similarly, in *R. v. Adkins* (1987), 39 C.C.C. (3d) 346 (B.C. C.A.), at p. 348, Hutcheon J.A. wrote, "the unlawful act was such as any reasonable person would inevitably realize must subject another to the risk of at least some harm."

This court in *R. v. DeSousa, supra*, confirmed that a conviction for manslaughter requires that the risk of bodily harm have been foreseeable. After referring to the statement in *Larkin, supra*, that a "dangerous act" is required, Sopinka J. stated that English authority has consistently held that the underlying unlawful act required for manslaughter requires "proof that the unlawful act was 'likely to injure another person' or in other words put the bodily integrity of others at risk" (at p. 959). Moreover, the harm must be more than trivial or transitory. The test set out by Sopinka J. (at p. 961) for the unlawful act required by s. 269 of the *Criminal Code* is equally applicable to manslaughter:

> . . . the test is one of objective foresight of bodily harm for all underlying offences. The act must be both unlawful, as described above, *and* one that is likely to subject another person to danger of harm or injury. This bodily harm must be more than merely trivial or transitory in nature and will in most cases involve an act of violence done deliberately to another person. In interpreting what constitutes an objectively dangerous act, the courts should strive to avoid attaching penal sanctions to mere inadvertence. The contention that no dangerousness requirement is required if the unlawful act is criminal should be rejected. [Emphasis in original.]

So the test for the *mens rea* of unlawful act manslaughter in Canada, as in the United Kingdom, is (in addition to the *mens rea* of the underlying offence) objective foreseeability of the risk of bodily harm which is neither trivial nor transitory, in the context of a dangerous act. Foreseeability of the risk of death is not required. The question is whether this test violates the principles of fundamental justice under s. 7 of the *Charter*.

. . . .

2. Constitutionality of the "Foresight of Bodily Harm" Test for Manslaughter

Before venturing on analysis, I think it appropriate to introduce a note of caution. We are here concerned with a common-law offence virtually as old as our system of criminal law. It has been applied in innumerable cases around the world. And it has been honed and refined over the centuries. Because of its residual nature, it may lack the logical symmetry of more modern statutory offences, but it has stood the practical test of time. Could all this be the case, one asks, if the law violates our fundamental notions of justice, themselves grounded in the history of the common law? Perhaps. Nevertheless, it must be with considerable caution that a 20th century court approaches the invitation which has been put before us: to strike out, or alternatively, rewrite, the offence of manslaughter on the ground that this is necessary to bring the law into conformity with the principles of fundamental justice.

As I read the reasons of the Chief Justice, his conclusion that the offence of manslaughter as it stands is unconstitutional, rests on two main concerns. First, it is his view that the gravity or seriousness of the offence of manslaughter, and in particular the stigma that attaches to it, requires a minimum *mens rea* of foreseeability of death. Second, considerations of symmetry between the element of mental fault and the consequences of the offence mandate this conclusion. I will deal with each concern in turn.

(a) Gravity of the Offence

A number of concepts fall under this head. Three of them figure among the four factors relevant to determining the constitutionality of a *mens rea* requirement, as set out by this court in *R. v. Martineau*, [1990] 2 S.C.R. 633:

1. The stigma attached to the offence, and the available penalties requiring a *mens rea* reflecting the particular nature of the crime;

2. Whether the punishment is proportionate to the moral blameworthiness of the offender; and

3. The idea that those causing harm intentionally must be punished more severely than those causing harm unintentionally.

The Chief Justice in his reasons places considerable emphasis on the first factor of stigma. He argues that "there may well be no difference between the *actus reus* of manslaughter and murder; arguably both give rise to the stigma of being labelled by the state and the community as responsible for the wrongful death of another" (p. 11). But later in his reasons (at p. 12) he concedes that "the stigma which attaches to a conviction for unlawful act manslaughter", while "significant, . . . does not approach the opprobrium reserved in our society for those who *knowingly* or *intentionally* take the life of another" (emphasis is original). The Chief Justice goes on to observe that "[i]t is for this reason that manslaughter developed as a separate offence from murder at common law." Nevertheless, in the end the Chief Justice concludes that the "constitutional imperative", taken with other factors, requires a minimum *mens rea* of foreseeability of the risk of death, suggesting that stigma may remain an important factor in his reasoning.

To the extent that stigma is relied on as requiring foreseeability of the risk of death in the offence of manslaughter, I find it unconvincing. The most important feature of the stigma of manslaughter is the stigma which is not attached to it. The *Criminal Code* confines manslaughter to non-intentional homicide. A person convicted of manslaughter is not a murderer. He or she did not intend to kill someone. A person has been killed through the fault of another, and that is always serious. But by the very act of calling the killing manslaughter the law indicates that the killing is less blameworthy than murder. It may arise from negligence, or it may arise as the unintended result of a lesser unlawful act. The conduct is blameworthy and must be punished, but its stigma does not approach that of murder.

To put it another way, the stigma attached to manslaughter is an appropriate stigma. Manslaughter is not like constructive murder, where one could say that a person who did not in fact commit murder might be inappropriately branded with the stigma of murder. The stigma associated with manslaughter is arguably exactly what it should be for an unintentional killing in circumstances where risk of bodily harm was foreseeable.

. . . .

It would shock the public's conscience to think that a person could be convicted of manslaughter absent any moral fault based on foreseeability of harm. Conversely, it might well shock the public's conscience to convict a person who has killed another only of aggravated assault — the result of requiring foreseeability of death — on the sole basis that the risk of death was not reasonably foreseeable. The terrible consequence of death demands more. In short, the *mens rea* requirement which the common law has adopted — foreseeability of harm — is entirely appropriate to the stigma associated with the offence of manslaughter. To change the *mens rea* requirement would be to risk the very disparity between *mens rea* and stigma of which the appellant complains.

I come then to the second factor mentioned in *Martineau*, the relationship between the punishment for the offence and the *mens rea* requirement. Here again, the offence of manslaughter stands in sharp contrast to the offence of murder. Murder entails a mandatory life sentence; manslaughter carries with it no minimum sentence. This is appropriate. Because manslaughter can occur in a wide variety of circumstances, the penalties must be flexible. An unintentional killing while committing a minor offence, for example, properly attracts a much lighter sentence than an unintentional killing where the circumstances indicate an awareness of risk of death just short of what would be required to infer the intent required for murder. The point is, the sentence can be and is tailored to suit the degree of moral fault of the offender. It follows that the sentence attached to manslaughter does not require elevation of the degree of *mens rea* for the offence.

. . . .

This brings me to the third factor relating to the gravity of the offence set out in *Martineau*, the principle that those causing harm intentionally must be punished more severely than those causing harm unintentionally. As noted, this principle is strictly observed in the case of manslaughter. It is by definition an unintentional crime. Accordingly, the penalties imposed are typically less than for its intentional counterpart, murder.

I conclude that the standard of *mens rea* required for manslaughter is appropriately tailored to the seriousness of the offence.

b)   *Symmetry Between the Element of Fault and the Consequences of the Offence*

The Chief Justice correctly observes that the criminal law has traditionally aimed at symmetry between the *mens rea* and the prohibited consequences of the offence. The *actus reus* generally consists of an act bringing about a prohibited consequence, *e.g.*, death. Criminal-law theory suggests that the accompanying *mens rea* must go to the prohibited consequence. The moral fault of the accused lies in the act of bringing about that consequence. The Chief Justice reasons from this proposition that since manslaughter is an offence involving the prohibited act of killing another, a *mens rea* of foreseeability of harm is insufficient; what is required is foreseeability of death.

The conclusion that the offence of manslaughter is unconstitutional because it does not require appreciation of the consequential risk of death rests on two propositions: (1) that risk of bodily harm is appreciably different from risk of death in the context of manslaughter; and (2) that the principle of absolute symmetry between *mens rea* and each consequence of a criminal offence is not only a general rule of criminal law, but a principle of fundamental justice which sets a constitutional minimum. In my view, neither of these propositions is free from doubt.

I turn first to the distinction between appreciation of the risk of bodily harm and the risk of death in the context of manslaughter. In my view, when the risk of bodily harm is combined with the established rule that a wrong-doer must take his victim as he finds him and the fact that death did in fact occur, the distinction disappears. The accused who asserts that the risk of death was not foreseeable is in effect asserting that a normal person would not have died in these circumstances, and that he could not foresee the peculiar vulnerability of the victim. Therefore, he says, he should be convicted only of assault causing bodily harm or some lesser offence. This is to abrogate the thin-skull rule that requires that the wrong-doer take his victim as he finds him. Conversely, to combine the test of reasonable foreseeability of bodily harm with the thin-skull rule is to mandate that in some cases, foreseeability of the risk of bodily harm alone will properly result in a conviction for manslaughter.

What the appellant asks us to do, then, is to abandon the "thin-skull" rule. It is this rule which, on analysis, is alleged to be unjust. Such a conclusion I cannot accept. The law has consistently set its face against such a policy. It decrees that the aggressor must take his victim as he finds him. Lord Ellenborough C.J. discussed the principle nearly two centuries ago:

> He who deals in a perilous article must be wary how he deals; otherwise, if he observe not proper caution, he will be responsible . . . It is a universal principle that, when a man is charged with doing an act, of which the probable consequence may be highly injurious, the intention is an inference of law, resulting from the doing of the act. (*R. v. Dixon* (1814), 3 M. & S. 11; approved, per Blackburn J., *R. v. Hicklin* (1868), L.R. 3 Q.B. 375, and per Amphlett J., *R. v. Aspinall* (1876), 2 Q.B.D. 48, 65).

Stephen J. illustrated the principle in similar fashion in *R. v. Serné* (1887), 16 Cox 311, at p. 313:

> . . . when a person began doing wicked acts for his own base purposes, he risked his own life as well as that of others. That kind of crime does not differ in any serious degree from one committed by using a deadly weapon, such as a bludgeon, a pistol, or a knife. If a man once begins attacking the human body in such a way, he must take the consequences if he goes further than he intended when he began.

The principle that if one engages in criminal behaviour, one is responsible for any unforeseen actions stemming from the unlawful act, has been a well-established tenet for most of this century in Canada, the U.S. and U.K. . . . . In *Smithers v. The Queen*, [1978] 1 S.C.R. 506 at pp. 521-22, Dickson J., writing for a unanimous court, confirmed this principle:

> It is a well-recognized principle that one who assaults another must take his victim as he finds him. . . .
>
> Although causation in civil cases differs from that in a criminal case, the "thin-skulled man" may appear in the criminal law as in the civil law . . . Even if the unlawful act, alone, would not have caused the death, it was still a legal cause so long as it contributed in some way to the death.

The thin-skull rule is a good and useful principle. It requires aggressors, once embarked on their dangerous course of conduct which may foreseeably injure others, to take responsibility for all the consequences that ensue, even to death. That is not, in my view, contrary to fundamental justice. Yet the consequence of adopting the amendment proposed by the Chief Justice would be to abrogate this principle in cases of manslaughter.

In fact, when manslaughter is viewed in the context of the thin-skull principle, the disparity diminishes between the *mens rea* of the offence and its consequence. The law does not posit the average victim. It says the aggressor must take the victim as he finds him. Wherever there is a risk of harm, there is also a practical risk that some victims may die as a result of the harm. At this point, the test of harm and death merge.

The second assumption inherent in the argument based on symmetry between *mens rea* and each consequence of the offence is that this is not only a general rule of criminal law, but a principle of fundamental justice — a basic constitutional requirement. I agree that as a general rule the *mens rea* of an offence relates to the consequences prohibited by the offence. As I stated in *R. v. Théroux*, [1993] 2 S.C.R. 5, at p. 17, "[t]ypically, *mens rea* is concerned with the consequences of the prohibited *actus reus*." Yet our criminal law contains important exceptions to this ideal of perfect symmetry. The presence of these exceptions suggests that the rule of symmetry is just that — a rule — to which there are exceptions. If this is so, then the rule cannot be elevated to the status of a principle of fundamental justice which must, by definition, have universal application.

It is important to distinguish between criminal law theory, which seeks the ideal of absolute symmetry between *actus reus* and *mens rea*, and the constitutional requirements of the *Charter*. As the Chief Justice has stated several times, "the Constitution does not always guarantee the 'ideal'" (*R. v. Lippé*, [1991] 2 S.C.R. 114 at p. 142; *R. v. Wholesale Travel Group Inc.*, [1991] 3 S.C.R. 154, at p. 186; *R. v. Finlay*, S.C.C. No. 22596, released concurrently, at p. 12).

I know of no authority for the proposition that the *mens rea* of an offence must always attach to the precise consequence which is prohibited as a matter of constitutional necessity. The relevant constitutional principles have been cast more broadly. No person can be sent to prison without *mens rea*, or a guilty mind, and the seriousness of the offence must not be disproportionate to the degree of moral fault. Provided an element of mental fault or moral culpability is present, and provided that it is proportionate to the seriousness and consequences of the offence charged, the principles of fundamental justice are satisfied.

. . . .

Thus when considering the constitutionality of the requirement of foreseeability of bodily harm, the question is not whether the general rule of symmetry between *mens rea* and the consequences prohibited by the offence is met, but rather whether the fundamental principle of justice is satisfied that the gravity and blameworthiness of an offence must be commensurate with the moral fault engaged by that offence. Fundamental justice does not require absolute symmetry between moral fault and the prohibited consequences. Consequences, or the absence of consequences, can properly affect the seriousness with which Parliament treats specified conduct.

The trial judge properly found that Mr. Creighton committed the unlawful act of trafficking in cocaine. He also found that he was guilty of criminal negligence, using the standard which I view as correct, the standard of the reasonable person. The only remaining question, on the view I take of the law, was whether the reasonable person in all the circumstances would have foreseen the risk of bodily harm. I am satisfied that the answer to this question must be affirmative. At the very least, a person administering a dangerous drug like cocaine to another has a duty to inform himself as to the precise risk the injection entails and to refrain from administering it unless reasonably satisfied that there was no risk of harm. That was not the case here, as the trial judge found.

The issue of symmetry between *actus reus* and *mens rea* was in issue in an unsuccessful *Charter* challenge to Parliament's new criminal harassment offence in s. 264.

R. v. KRUSHEL

(2000), 31 C.R. (5th) 295, 142 C.C.C. (3d) 1,
2000 CarswellOnt 325 (Ont. C.A.)

CATZMAN J.A. (CARTHY and WEILER JJ.A. concurring): —

. . . .

All three appellants were convicted of criminal harassment under s. 264 of the *Criminal Code*. That section provides, in relevant part:

264.(1) No person shall, without lawful authority and knowing that another person is harassed or recklessly as to whether the other person is harassed, engage in conduct referred to in subsection (2) that causes that other person reasonably, in all the circumstances, to fear for their safety or the safety of anyone known to them.

(2) The conduct mentioned in subsection (1) consists of

(a) repeatedly following from place to place the other person or anyone known to them;

(b) repeatedly communicating with, either directly or indirectly, the other person or anyone known to them;

(c) besetting or watching the dwelling-house, or place where the other person, or anyone known to them, resides, works, carries on business or happens to be; or

(d) engaging in threatening conduct directed at the other person or any member of their family.

. . . .

The appellant Krushel was convicted of criminal harassment under s. 264 by engaging in the conduct referred to in s. 264(2)(c). The victim was his former common law spouse. He was sentenced to 90 days, to be served intermittently, and two years probation.

. . . .

(i)   Section 7

Counsel for Krushel submitted that s. 264 infringed s. 7 of the *Charter* for two reasons: first, that the section was impermissibly vague in that it fails to give sufficient notice of what conduct is prohibited; and second, that it allows the morally innocent to be punished, specifically, in its failure to require that the accused have the intention to cause the victim to fear for their safety or the safety of anyone known to them (the "constructive liability argument").

The constructive liability argument was considered by the Alberta Court of Appeal in *R. v. Sillipp* (1997), 120 C.C.C. (3d) 384 (Alta. C.A.), leave to appeal to S.C.C. refused (1998), 219 A.R. 107 (S.C.C.). In that case, as in this, the appellant argued that s. 264 allowed the morally innocent to be punished because it lacked a *mens rea* requirement attaching to the consequence of reasonable fear. That court concluded that s. 7 was not infringed by the provisions of s. 264. At pp. 397-398, Berger J.A., speaking for the court, described the operation of the section in the following terms:

> In my view, the *actus reus* of the offence of criminal harassment is constituted by volitional subsection (2) conduct which meets discernible standards of nature, cause and effect, with the *mens rea* requirement being that of an intention to engage in that conduct or, at minimum, recklessness or wilful blindness, relative to that conduct.
>
> That which is prohibited is a person engaging in subsection (2) conduct with knowledge (reckless or wilful blindness) that *such conduct* is causing the complainant to be harassed. The *mens rea* of the offence is the intention to engage in the prohibited conduct with the knowledge that the complainant is thereby harassed.
>
> . . . .
>
> A conviction under s. 264 requires that the accused have "known" that his subsection (2)

conduct was causing the complainant to be harassed, or that he was aware of such risk and was reckless or wilfully blind as to whether or not the person was harassed. The Appellant's "morally innocent accused" who honestly believed that his subsection (2) behaviour was not known to the complainant, and who was not reckless or wilfully blind, would escape criminal liability.

In the result, Berger J.A. concluded, at p. 399:

> The Appellant's argument that it is a matter of constitutional necessity that the element of mental culpability be linked to the prohibited consequence of causing actual fear in the complainant is unfounded. Clearly Parliament has created a new kind of culpable activity — subsection (2) conduct which, by objective standards (as described earlier in this judgment), is of a nature and extent as to reasonably cause fear. Such conduct is deemed by s. 264 to be criminal activity. Thus, in accordance with the principle set out in *DeSousa (supra)*, given that there is in s. 264 a sufficiently blameworthy element in the *actus reus* to which the culpable mental state attaches, foresight of the prohibited consequence of causing actual fear is not required in order to hold the accused responsible for the results of his or her unlawful activity.

In reaching this conclusion, Berger J.A. noted (at pp. 396-398) that the contention that there must be symmetry between *mens rea* and each consequence of an offence had been expressly rejected by McLachlin J. in *R. v. Creighton* (1993), 83 C.C.C. (3d) 346 (S.C.C.) and (at p. 399) that there need only be a sufficiently blameworthy element in the *actus reus* to which the culpable mental state attaches: *R. v. DeSousa* (1992), 76 C.C.C. (3d) 124 (S.C.C.). I agree with Berger J.A., and I would reject the constructive liability argument.

The argument that s. 264 is impermissibly vague was not considered by the Alberta Court of Appeal. However, in an earlier challenge to s. 264, the Alberta Court of Queen's Bench rejected that argument: *R. v. Sillipp* (1995), 99 C.C.C. (3d) 394 (Alta. Q.B.). In that proceeding, Murray J. dismissed an application to declare s. 264 to be of no force and effect, finding, *inter alia*, that the section did not suffer from vagueness. His reasons on this point appear at p. 406:

> In my opinion, s. 264 does not suffer from vagueness. Certainly there are many facets of it that will have to be interpreted by the court. I have no doubt that as time progresses it will be given a constant and settled meaning. I have no problem interpreting s. 264 so as to understand that certain conduct is subject to legal restrictions and the area of risk is set out, namely, if you intentionally behave in certain ways knowing that by doing so you are harassing another person, then if your conduct causes that person to reasonably fear for his or her safety, you run the risk of being criminally sanctioned. I would think that anyone reading the section would receive that message loud and clear. I do not believe that it has the effect of permitting a "standardless sweep" so as to allow the police, or for that matter, the judiciary, to simply use its discretion in how they interpret it or apply its provisions which was the concern of Lamer C.J.C. in *Morales, supra*. I have listened to argument by Crown and defence counsel and I am satisfied that the legislation permits the framing of a meaningful legal debate with respect to the objectives contained in the legislation. In my view, it provides "an adequate basis for reaching a conclusion as to its meaning by reasoned analysis applying legal criteria".

I agree with Murray J., and I would reject the appellant's argument that s. 264 violates s. 7 because it is impermissibly vague.

On the above state of the law, do you think that the following accused, each charged with manslaughter, should be convicted?

1. The accused pointed a rifle at his friend and discharged it, killing him. The accused and the victim were friends who had been hunting the day before. The accused had, only moments before, pulled the trigger and the gun had not discharged. He thought that the gun was not loaded and that it would not discharge. There was evidence that the firing mechanism on the gun was faulty. Note that under s. 87(1) of the *Criminal Code* it is an offence to point a firearm at another whether or not it is loaded.
Compare *R. v. Jakubowych* (1968), 66 W.W.R. 755 (Alta. S.C.).

2. During a hunting trip a woman shot and killed her husband, mistaking him for a bear. The shooting occurred after it was no longer fully daylight, but the Crown did not show that it occurred after hunting was still legally permitted or that it was too dark to permit an appropriate method of identification of a target. The accused would have been expecting her husband to be with a guide, who was not in fact walking beside the deceased. The deceased was walking on uneven ground, which would have required him to be walking bent over to some degree, and would have caused him to appear to be bobbing up and down. The deceased was dressed in dark clothing and was walking in an area of tall grass, which would have made him appear to be shorter than he actually was. The deceased did not signal in any way, though he knew that the accused might be expecting game to be flushed out in the area where he was walking. The accused expected that there would be a bear in the area of the shooting, and she knew what a bear looked like and how it moved. She was originally unable to identify the object she saw appear, but after looking at it for a short period of time she determined it was a bear, based on its rounded shape and what she perceived to be its head. She thought it was clear that it was a bear and shot it from 200 feet, which was not a long shot.
Compare *R. v. Harshbarger* (2010), 79 C.R. (6th) 373 (N.L. T.D.).

3. The accused had intravenously injected a quantity of prescription asthma pills mixed with water into a friend's arm. That friend later bought a large quantity of pyribenzamine pills and requested the accused to crush six of them and mix them with water and inject them as before. He did not want to but she insisted, so he did so. In a short time she lapsed into unconsciousness and underwent convulsive spasms. She encountered difficulty in breathing. The accused summoned an ambulance only when she seemed to stop breathing. She was already dead. Pyribenzamine can be lawfully purchased at any drug store without a prescription.
Compare *R. v. Davis* (1978), 37 C.C.C. (2d) 114 (Sask. C.A.).

4. Justice Ewaschuk of the Ontario Superior Court found the following:
"In 1980 the accused's mother died of cancer, leaving him an orphan. As a result he lived with his grandmother.

On 20th October 1983 the grandmother left Hamilton to visit friends. She left her then 16-year-old grandson in the charge of his aunt. The accused later lied to his aunt and told her that he would be staying at the home of Roberto Fidanza, a fellow classmate. Instead these two, and others, on Saturday, 22nd October 1983, met at the grandmother's home to party and have a general good time.

Initially, in fact, at about 7:00 p.m. that evening, three other male friends dropped over with a case of beer, which was eventually drunk. At about 8:00 p.m. two more male friends, among them the deceased, Roberto Fidanza, 16 years old, arrived with two girlfriends and another case of beer, also eventually consumed.

Between 10:30 and 11:00 p.m., Fidanza and another male teenager came up from downstairs, where they had been with the two girls. The two young girls remained downstairs. The accused, Barron, suggested that the boys "streak" the girls by disrobing themselves. All declined to do so except Fidanza and Barron, the author of the escapade.

The deceased and the accused thereupon undressed themselves to their underwear. The deceased eventually reached the landing above the downstairs with the accused directly behind him, when the deceased apparently changed his mind. He hesitated and said, , I don't want to do it." The accused then stated, "Come on, Roberto, let's go," and with that statement gave the deceased a slight push on the back.

Unfortunately the push or shove was substantial enough for the deceased to lose his balance and fall down the stairs to his eventual death.

In fact, he died on 1st November 1983 of a pneumonic infection of his lungs brought on as a direct result of the head injuries suffered from the fall. The blood-alcohol reading of this rather small 120-pound boy proved to be 131 milligrams at the time of his death.

The events that followed the fall proved bizarre. Seemingly out of character, the accused panicked and acted callously. He struck a friend who tried to telephone for an ambulance. He then ordered everyone out of his grandmother's home, compelling the others to carry his unconscious classmate outside. In fact, the deceased never regained consciousness. Eventually, the other teenagers were able to get an ambulance and hail down a police car.

The accused himself fled the scene. Eventually he returned but denied pushing his friend. It was not until the police told him that one of the other boys claimed that the accused pushed the deceased that he admitted it. However, even then he falsely claimed that someone else pushed him from behind."

Compare *R. v. Barron* (1984), 39 C.R. (3d) 379 (Ont. H.C.), reversed (1985), 48 C.R. (3d) 334, 23 C.C.C. (3d) 544 (Ont. C.A.).

5. A group of friends spent the night stealing cars and joyriding. K, aged 13 at the time, while standing on a boulevard, threw a metal shovel at a car three or four times, as the driver of the car deliberately drove past him. On the last throw the shovel hit a 14-year-old youth, who was then

hanging half out of the car window. The car was going at 80-90 kilometers per hour. The boy was hit and killed by the blow.
Compare *R. v. T. (K.)* (2003), 31 C.R. (6th) 187 (Man. C.A.).

One would have expected that since *Creighton* the Supreme Court would be applying *DeSousa* with caution, especially in the case of a very serious crime such as that of aggravated assault. The crime of aggravated assault under what is now s. 268(1) is the most serious form of assault and carries a maximum penalty of 14 years' imprisonment. Under s. 268(1):

> Every one commits an aggravated assault who wounds, maims, disfigures or endangers the life of the complainant.

Prior to *DeSousa* and *Creighton* most Courts of Appeal had interpreted the offence of aggravated assault to merely require proof of an intent to assault and of an act which in fact caused the aggravated consequences complained of. See *Leclerc* (1991), 7 C.R. (4th) 282 (Ont. C.A.), *Lucas* (1987), 34 C.C.C. (3d) 28 (Que. C.A.), *Carriere* (1987), 56 C.R. (3d) 57 (Alta. C.A.) and *Scharf* (1988), 42 C.C.C. (3d) 378 (Man. C.A.). This meant a form of absolute liability respecting that consequence. Only the New Brunswick Court of Appeal in *Parish* (1990), 60 C.C.C. (3d) 350 (N.B. C.A.) had related the intent to the consequences prohibited in their determination that the Crown would have to prove not just an intent to assault but an intent to wound, maim, disfigure or endanger life.

In *Godin* (1993), 22 C.R. (4th) 265 (N.B. C.A.), Angers J.A. for the majority of the New Brunswick Court of Appeal persisted with this approach. He persuasively pointed out that the offence was distinguishable from the offence of unlawfully causing bodily harm at issue in *DeSousa* in that it was not defined as wounding, maiming, etc. in the course of assault nor expressly as an offence which caused certain consequences. It followed that there would have to be subjective foresight of the forbidden acts. The majority pointed out that a life might be endangered without the commission of an assault. When *Godin* reached the Supreme Court, [1994] 2 S.C.R. 484, 31 C.R. (4th) 33, 89 C.C.C. (3d) 574, the court took but a few lines in an oral endorsement to reverse the New Brunswick Court of Appeal. The court did not fully justify its position. It merely remarked that the section "pertains to an assault that has the consequence of wounding, maiming or disfiguring". Intent was not required respecting those consequences and the fault element was objective foresight of bodily harm. This was said to flow from *DeSousa* and *Creighton*. On the above analysis of *Creighton* can this be correct? The reference to "bodily harm" may have been a slip of the tongue. The express *mens rea* required for an assault under s. 265 (1) is applying force intentionally and there is no mention of bodily harm. However the *Godin* test has now been applied in *R. v. Williams* (see earlier under Commission of an Unlawful Act.)

The Supreme Court in *Godin* did not consider *L. (S.R.)* (1992), 16 C.R. (4th) 311, 76 C.C.C. (3d) 502 (Ont. C.A.), in which there was a careful attempt by the Ontario Court of Appeal to apply *DeSousa* to aggravated assault. This necessitated a reversal of that court's previous decision in *Leclerc*. The crime of aggravated assault was now to be interpreted, per Justice Doherty for the court, as requiring not only proof of the *mens rea* required for assault, applying force intentionally, but also objective foresight of the risk of wounding, maiming, disfiguring or endangering life. The Ontario Court saw that the further pronouncement in *Desousa* that a fault element need not relate to the consequence was *obiter* and decided not to follow it. Compare *Reyat* (1993), 20 C.R. (4th) 149 (B.C. C.A.).

The Ontario Court of Appeal's interpretation was most welcome, and had the Supreme Court accepted it, would have done much to undo the Supreme Court's unnecessary and unprincipled attempt to separate the fault requirement from its factual context. However, especially since *Creighton*, there is even more to be said for the approach of the New Brunswick Court of Appeal which sought to keep objective tests out of the law of assault and to apply the usual principle of relating fault to the prohibited consequence. The effect of *Godin* is that the crime of aggravated assault has been added to the uncertain list of so-called predicate offences for which the fault requirement is much reduced.

At present the *Criminal Code* attempts through its maximum penalties to distinguish in seriousness between assault, assault with a weapon or causing bodily harm and aggravated assault. Not surprisingly, given the inconsistency and confusion in the Supreme Court, Courts of Appeal are in disarray as to how *DeSousa, Creighton* and *Godin* are to determine the *mens rea* required for assault causing bodily harm. The Saskatchewan Court of Appeal, *Swenson* (1994), 91 C.C.C. (3d) 541 (Sask. C.A.), merely requires the basic assault element of intent to apply force. There is no requirement of foresight of bodily harm. Criminal responsibility for the more serious offence of assault causing bodily harm will result even if bodily harm resulted in an unforeseen or unforeseeable way. This amounts to absolute liability as to the consequence. This is even less of a requirement than the objective foresight of harm *DeSousa* required for unlawfully causing bodily harm. In contrast the Ontario Court of Appeal, *Nurse* (1993), 83 C.C.C. (3d) 546 and *Emans* (2000), 35 C.R. (5th) 386, (*sub nom. R. v. E. (A.)*) 146 C.C.C. (3d) 449 (Ont. C.A.), and the Alberta Court of Appeal, *Dewey* (1998), 21 C.R. (5th) 232, 132 C.C.C. (3d) 348 (Alta. C.A.), assert for assault causing bodily harm a test of reasonable foresight of harm but not the specific type of harm.

Our law of assault is in urgent need of rethinking by the Supreme Court or Parliament. Crimes of assault should be based on actual foresight of the type of harm caused or risked and should carry higher penalties than those crimes based on a failure to reasonably foresee the risk, such as the present crime of criminal negligence causing bodily harm. It would be more workable to distinguish between only two types of assault based on the seriousness of the harm caused or risked. So too with crimes of criminal negligence.

6.   NORMATIVE THEORIES

G.P. FLETCHER, RE-THINKING CRIMINAL LAW

(1978), 367

When used normatively, "criminal" refers to the type of person who by virtue of his deeds deserves to be branded and punished as a criminal. When used descriptively, as in the phrase "criminal act" it may refer simply to any act that the legislature has declared to be "criminal".

G.P. FLETCHER, THE THEORY OF CRIMINAL NEGLIGENCE: A COMPARATIVE ANALYSIS

(1970-71), 119 U. of Penn. L. Rev. 401 at 414-415

We require *mens rea* as an essential condition for criminal liability, not because we suppose that mental states are essential to criminality, but because we realize intuitively that the condemnatory sanctions should apply only to those who are justly condemned for their conduct. And men are not justly condemned and deprived of their liberty unless they are personally culpable in violating the law. That is the point of Coke's saying: the act is not culpable under the law (*actus non facit reum*) unless the actor is culpable for acting as he did (*nisi mens sit rea*).

The proper construction of Coke's embezzlement case is that if the actor lacks the intent required by the law as it existed in the 17th century, he is not culpable for violating the law: there is neither an act prohibited by the law nor personal culpability for engaging in the prohibited act. It does not follow, inversely, that if the actor intended to steal at the time he received possession of the goods that the maxim *actus facit reum nisi mens sit rea* would be satisfied. The actor might be *non compos mentis*, and Coke demonstrably would say that he lacked *mens rea* even though he intentionally took the goods of another. Similarly, the actor might have performed the act under duress or necessity, and in these situations, his conduct should be treated the same as the conduct of an actor *non compos mentis*. In all of these cases, the actor acts with the subjective state prohibited by law, namely, the intention to take the goods of another. But he is not personally culpable — he lacks *mens rea* — if he is insane, or if his conduct is rendered involuntary by duress or necessity.

. . . .

Once the normative status of *mens rea* comes into focus, the problem of negligence as a form of *mens rea* is tractable. If *mens rea* refers not to a specific subjective state, but to the actor's moral culpability in acting as he does, then there might logically be a way to establish personal culpability without referring to a state of mind. In the normal case of intentional conduct, where the actor is sane and his conduct is not excused by duress or necessity, it might be sufficient in establishing *mens rea* to show that the actor acted intentionally. But surely it does not follow that intentional conduct, or something like it, is a necessary condition for criminal culpability. Structural differences between negligence and intentional conduct do not preclude treating negligence as a form of *mens rea*. Nor is the issue settled by the characteristic externality of negligent conduct. Whether negligence constitutes *mens rea* depends on whether negligent conduct is a ground for justly blaming another.

ANNE STALKER, CAN GEORGE FLETCHER HELP SOLVE THE PROBLEM OF CRIMINAL NEGLIGENCE?

(1982), 7 Queen's L.J. 274 at 291-292

A normative test is one that applies directly to the underlying policy, without translating it into measurable and consistent components. A descriptive test, on the other hand, would specify identifiable elements that are consistent from case to case. The problem with a normative test is that it is discretionary and can change from judge to judge and day to day. The problem with a descriptive test is that it is rigid and may not accurately reflect the underlying principle or policy in every situation.

J.M. WEILER, R. V. KUNDEUS: THE SAGA OF TWO SHIPS PASSING IN THE NIGHT

(1976), 14 Osgoode Hall L.J. 457 at 470

[Brett] asks whether there is any reason for holding the accused free from blame, rather than whether the prosecution has proved the mental element of the crime. He rejects the latter approach since he does not believe that it is possible to identify in advance all of the possible excuses that might serve to absolve the accused from blame. In his judgment, the search for the conditions of imputability which requires a precise *a priori* analysis of *mens rea* is never successful.

Something is always left out. We cannot anticipate and enumerate all of the conditions of blameworthiness in advance: better not to try. Instead we can recognize blame when we see it, and should have no need for an *a priori* definition.

ROSEMARY CAIRNS WAY, THE CHARTER, THE SUPREME COURT AND THE INVISIBLE POLITICS OF FAULT: A CRITICAL ANALYSIS OF THE CONSTITUTIONALIZATION OF FAULT

LL.M. thesis for the Faculty of Law, Queen's University, October 1992.

The political nature of subjectivism however, remains largely unexamined in the court's judgments. Although I am concerned about the implications of subjectivism, this thesis is not an argument for objectivism. It is a plea for a multidimensional, contextualized approach to fault, and it questions whether such an approach is possible or likely within a constitutionalized discourse of rights. A great deal of energy in criminal law theory is devoted to the objective/subjective debate, which is understood as one of the fundamental conundrums of the criminal law. In my view, the current construction of the objective/subjective debate as irreconcilable polarities submerges the complexity of the question of blame. The risk of unidimensional, decontextualized approaches to law is magnified when complex concepts like fault are elevated to constitutional status. The implications of a decision to view constitutional culpability through the lens of objectivism, although different in kind from those which flow from a commitment to subjectivism would be equally grave.

. . . .

Decisions about responsibility should invoke a rich and multifaceted debate about the nature and appropriate allocation of blame, the assumption of free will and the efficacy of the criminal law as a mechanism of social control. To act without engaging in this debate is at once to impoverish our jurisprudence about the criminal law and to limit the possibilities for change.

TONI PICKARD AND PHIL GOLDMAN, DIMENSIONS OF CRIMINAL LAW

(1992), 402-405.

The basis in fairness for an objective standard. An "objective" standard presupposes the possibility of agreeing on what is reasonable or natural in any given situation. That possibility, in turn, presupposes both shared understandings, perceptions, and values among the fact finders, and shared understandings between those who are finding facts and the population subject to the law. (Remember that, in law, whether a belief is reasonable or not is conceived to be a question of fact, not a choice of values or perspectives.)

. . . .

Loss of centre and the problem of fairness. Whatever may be true of distant cultures, people in Canada, though differently situated and subject to marked disparities in power, do seem to share at least some understandings across the divisions. Indeed, if we did not think people in our culture shared some understandings, we would hardly be able to use phrases like "our culture" meaningfully. There is, however, a growing acknowledgment that people of different classes, races, ages, genders, religions, sexual orientations, ethnic backgrounds, physical abilities, political visions, and so on, not only have different and sometimes conflicting values, but that their perceptions of facts, of cause and effect, of what is natural, and of what is meant by certain words and gestures are significantly shaped by those differing and sometimes conflicting values.

Increasingly, people believe that facts (even scientific facts) and (more obviously) meanings are not out there in the world in any absolute sense, independent of the observer (that is, objectively), but that, on the contrary, a fact or a meaning — even whether something is perceived as a fact, or heard as a meaning — is in large part a function of the observer's beliefs (and hence, of social place). This insight seriously undermines our ability to believe that the way a decision maker or fact finder sees things is in fact "how things are" or "objectively true". Still more radically affected is our sense that it is fair to impose some people's judgments of what is reasonable on others.

7. GENERAL REVIEW QUESTIONS

1. **Emotions are running high outside a courthouse. A crowd of student protestors is awaiting the outcome of a controversial trial of acquaintance rape charges alleged to have occurred on campus.**

The group is chanting "Justice for women". One member of the group, Andrew, is challenged by another student, Bob, a supporter of the accused. Bob shouts "Vigilantes go home". At this point Andrew shakes a clenched fist at Bob and says "Let's sort it out". Bob promptly lands a blow on Andrew's jaw. The punch is hard enough to knock Andrew off balance. He falls over, hits his forehead on a granite pillar of the courthouse steps and loses consciousness. He quickly comes to and is unharmed. A nearby police officer asks Bob for his name and address. Bob gives his name but is so flustered he can't remember the number of his temporary apartment. He gives it as No. 314 Portsmouth House. It is in fact No. 217. The officer indicates Bob will be charged with assault.

At this point, Andrew's friends take him to an ambulance stationed in the courthouse parking lot. The ambulance driver, Chris, aged 60, agrees to take Andrew to be checked at the Hotel Dieu. Chris has been an ambulance driver for 30 years. This is his very last shift and he is tired. He drives down West Street with his emergency lights and siren activated. It is cold but roads are dry and visibility is fine. As he approaches an intersection the traffic signal turns red. He slows to about 5 k.p.h. but proceeds through the intersection. He collides with a Pyke milk truck which enters the intersection on a green light at about 30 k.p.h. Neither driver saw the other vehicle until it was too late. Both vehicles were damaged. Furthermore, Andrew was jolted from the stretcher and broke his leg. He was attended to in the hospital where he was pronounced fit except for the broken bone. It healed satisfactorily within six weeks.

You are serving your articles with a 65-year-old judge who is to preside over the upcoming trial arising from these events. She asks you for a legal memorandum identifying viable legal issues and their possible resolution. She requests careful reference to appropriate case and statutory authority.

There are <u>three</u> charges to consider.

    <u>Bob</u> is charged with:

1. assault causing bodily harm to Andrew (to wit, a broken leg) contrary to s. 267(1)(*b*) of the *Criminal Code*, and
2. wilful obstruction of a police officer, by giving a false address contrary to s. 129(*a*) of the *Criminal Code*.

    <u>Chris</u> is charged with:

3. failing to stop at a red light contrary to s. 124(16) of the *Highway Traffic Act* of Ontario.

Respecting this third charge, note that under s. 124:

(16) Every driver approaching a traffic control signal showing a circular red indicator and facing the indication shall stop his vehicle and shall not proceed until a green indication is shown.

(18) Notwithstanding subsection (16), a driver of an emergency vehicle, after stopping the vehicle, may proceed without a green indication being shown if it is safe to do so.

Pursuant to s. 188(1) of the Act, anyone convicted of an offence under s. 124 is subject to a minimum fine of $60 and a maximum fine of $500.

2. Hemophilia is a hereditary disorder that interferes with blood clotting in about one male in 5,000. Until the early 70's the accepted treatment was blood transfusions. The development of blood-factor concentrates allowed patients to receive treatment quickly at home by simple injection. In Canada, it has always been necessary to import a large quantity of such concentrates from the United States. Each sample injected will come from a number of separate donors.

In 1982, following the death of four hemophiliacs from AIDS in the United States, the Canadian Blood Committee, a committee of civil servants appointed from each province to implement the policy of blood distribution, were warned of the "theoretical risk" that an unknown transmissible agent present in blood-factor concentrates might cause AIDS. The Committee decided that this was too speculative a risk to cause them to change their policy and such concentrates were continued to be used. In 1984, it was widely reported that a United States agency had confirmed that there was an AIDS risk from contaminated blood and that it could be eliminated by a high-heat treatment of the blood product. The Canadian Blood Committee decided, after consultation with doctors, users and manufacturers, to use up existing inventory and phase in heat-treated blood over an eight-month period ending in July 1984.

In October 1992, Alex, a hemophiliac, dies after a debilitating illness. His wife of 20 years, Barbara, only learned that he died from AIDS from the coroner, who asked her whether the cause was contaminated blood. Barbara is devastated. Doctor Cain has been the family physician for both Alex and Barbara since 1975. Neither Doctor Cain nor Alex ever told her that Alex had the HIV virus. Doctor Cain says he was bound by a professional oath of confidentiality and, anyhow, Alex insisted that he did not trouble his wife with the bad news. Alex and Barbara never used a condom. Barbara now has her blood tested and is found to have the HIV virus herself. The HIV virus will usually lead to full-blown AIDS within six to seven years. Thereafter death will occur within three years. Barbara is 100 percent sure that Alex got the virus from contaminated blood he started to inject in January of 1984 and that the only way she could have got the virus herself is from Alex.

She consults a Crown Attorney who lays three charges.

Each member of the Blood Committee is charged, based on the Committee's delay in stopping the distribution of contaminated blood in 1984, with criminal negligence causing death of Alex and criminal negligence causing bodily harm to Barbara contrary, respectively, to ss. 220 and 221 of the *Criminal Code*. Dr. Cane is charged, based on his failure to warn Barbara of Alex's AIDS, with criminal negligence causing her bodily harm contrary to s. 221 of the *Criminal Code*.

The Crown Attorney asks you for a legal memorandum in which you discuss, with reference to appropriate authority, possible defences to each charge assessing the chances of her obtaining convictions. Indicate what further evidence, if any, may be useful in the upcoming trials.

3. The accused, Cain, is charged, pursuant to s. 221 of the *Criminal Code*, with causing bodily harm by criminal negligence. Cain is also charged with a violation of s. 8 of the *Explosives Act* of Ontario. That section provides:

> 8. Every one who allows explosives to be stored in a manner which endangers the lives or safety of others is guilty of an offence punishable by a fine of up to $25,000 or imprisonment of six months or both.

Cain, aged 40, has just been promoted to foreman for a construction company charged with the task of excavating for a new library being erected by the University. The construction site is immediately opposite the building housing the law faculty. The task has proved more difficult than expected and Cain is finding his new job quite stressful. On the evening of December 1, 1992, the accused placed a case of explosives in a storage container on the construction site. For the last several weeks of blasting he had assumed the container was one of the type that automatically locks when the lid is closed. That was the sort of container in use at his former job. Unfortunately the container was not of that type and the explosives were left accessible to anyone who cared to lift the lid. Cain had previously delegated the storage of explosives to a particular worker. On the day in question that worker had caused trouble and Cain had told him to leave the site. Cain remembers being angry and preoccupied with that altercation. He did not notice a padlock on the container.

Arthur Able, a young law student, was disappointed with the quality of instruction in his criminal law class and also with the underground classrooms where he gained such instruction. On the evening of December 1 he decided to bury the classrooms. He climbed the fence and found the explosives left by the accused. He fashioned a crude demolition device and set the time for the beginning of the Criminal Law class. The blast destroyed the premises and the learned law professor was injured as a result.

Write a legal memorandum advising, with reference to appropriate authority, as to all the possible defences to the two charges against Cain.

4. Alec is a large, athletic young man. He always wears a Hells Angels biker jacket and has many visible tattoos. During a routine medical check-up it is discovered that he is HIV positive. When the young Public Health nurse, Betty, advises him of the results he immediately says "No problem, they have this thing licked, right?" Betty knows that her medical protocol is to clearly and strongly advise him that he should register for treatment and to inform all his sexual partners, past, present or future, as to his HIV status and to now always use a condom. However Betty is scared of him and is also exhausted after a very long shift. She says nothing. Driving herself home she is preoccupied by the thought that she did not do the right thing. She approaches an intersection with traffic lights. She believes the green light has turned orange and she slides through. In fact the orange light was malfunctioning and she has gone through a red light. There is a minor "fender bender" accident as she collides with someone commencing on green. No one is injured.

Alec later has unprotected sexual intercourse with a new partner, Claire. He told Claire he is HIV positive but before he said anything more, she said "No problem. Don't bother with a condom. I don't like them". Two months later she tests HIV positive. She has had no sexual relations with anyone since that one occasion with Alec. A year later she develops full blown AIDS. She proves severely allergic to anti-AIDS drugs and is in the process of dying.

You are articled to a Crown Attorney who asks you for a legal memorandum. He wants to go for broke. He is contemplating six charges and wants your advice on the legal issues that he might anticipate arising on those charges and advice as to his chances of obtaining convictions.

The six contemplated charges are as follows:

In the case of Alec,

> 1. aggravated assault endangering life contrary to s. 268.1 of the *Criminal Code*, and
> 2. if Claire dies, second degree murder or
> 3. first degree murder.

In the case of Betty,

4. aggravated assault endangering life contrary to s. 268.1 of the *Criminal Code*, and

5. "failing to stop at an intersection" contrary to s. 125A of the Ontario *Highway Traffic Act*, and

6. careless driving contrary to s. 130 of the Ontario *Highway Traffic Act*.

The penalty for the s. 125A traffic offence is a fixed $200 fine. For s. 130 it is a fine of not less than $200 and not more than $1000 or to imprisonment of not more than 6 months or both. Both could result in a license suspension.

Chapter 4

RAPE AND SEXUAL ASSAULT

1. RAPE LAWS IN CONTEXT[1]

> Sexual violence is about power and control, not sexual desire. It is about exerting power and aggression over someone else.[2]

It is submitted that sexual assault is an equality issue. Children are singled out for sexual assault because of their age and sex, that is, because of their vulnerability, accessibility, powerlessness, and lack of credibility. Women are singled out for sexual assault and their accusations of sexual assault are systematically disbelieved because of their gender, that is, because they are relegated to an inferior social status as female, including being socially defined as appropriate targets for forced sex. As a result of these perceptions, women are made vulnerable to sexual assault.[3]

Sexual assault is endemic. According to the Badgley Committee's Report,[4] about one in two females and one in three males have been subjected to unwanted sexual acts. About four in five of these incidents first happened when these persons were children.[5]

Sexual assault is a highly gendered crime that is disproportionately perpetrated by men against women. According to 2007 police-reported data, rates of sexual victimization were more than five times higher for women than for men while 97% of those accused of sexual offences were male.[6] Almost 40% of women report having experienced some kind of sexual violence since the age of 16.[7]

---

1 We acknowledge with thanks the updating of this introduction by Pam Hrick, a second-year law student at Queen's.

2 Ontario, *Changing Attitudes, Changing Lives: Ontario's Sexual Violence Action Plan* (Toronto: Ontario Women's Directorate, 2011) at 4 <http://www.citizenship.gov.on.ca/owd/english/women/svap2011.pdf>.

3 Affidavit filed to gain intervener status in the Supreme Court of Canada for the Legal Education and Action Fund (LEAF) in the case of *Seaboyer v. R.*, on appeal from the Ontario Court of Appeal.

4 *Sexual Offences Against Children* (Ottawa: Minister of Supply and Services, 1984) Volume 1 at 175 and 186.

5 A thorough discussion of child sexual abuse is beyond the scope of this chapter. However, for further comment, see Nicholas Bala, "Double Victims: Child Sexual Abuse and the Canadian Criminal Justice System" (1980), 15 *Queen's L. J.* 3 and Institute for the Prevention of Child Abuse, Update Child Sex Abuse and the Law (1992).

6 Shannon Brennan and Andrea Taylor-Butts, *Sexual Assault in Canada 2004 and 2007* (Ottawa: Statistics Canada, Canadian Centre for Justice Statistics, 2008) at 12-13.

7 Canadian Panel on Violence Against Women, *Changing the Landscape: Ending Violence – Achieving Equality* (Ottawa: Minister of Supply and Services, 1993). For controversial views in both Canada and the United Kingdom that recent research on the extent of violence against women and children is based on faulty methodologies and has exaggerated the problem, see John Fekete, *Moral Panic: Biopolitics Rising* (1994) and Christina Hoff Sommers, *Who Stole Feminism? How Women Have Betrayed Women* (1994).

Women in marginalized demographics often experience a higher rate of sexual violence. For example, it is estimated that 83% of women with disabilities will be sexually assaulted in their lifetime.[8] Aboriginal women are also three-and-a-half times more likely than other women to experience violence, including sexual assault.[9]

The myth, that the "worst rapes" are committed by strangers, should be dispelled. The danger is that only these types of sexual assaults will be taken seriously by the police and eventually the courts. In reality, many women experience sexual violence in intimate partner relationships or at the hands of individuals known to them. Only 18% of sexual assaults conform to the stereotype of the accused being a stranger in an alleyway, while 31% are committed by family members and 28% are committed by acquaintances.[10]

A brutal violation by a stranger may be less devastating than a brutal violation by one who the survivor loved and trusted. LEAF points out the very real harm that women who have been sexually violated suffer. They experience "the dissolution of the foundations, values and pleasures which previously gave their life meaning and stability. . .and can include trust in relationships, a sense of security in one's home and one's bedroom,. . .control over one's physical and emotional functions, self-confidence,"[11] etc. The myth about the identity of perpetrators is probably based on the notion that once consent has been given it cannot be withdrawn. This is clearly offensive. The devastation of those who are sexually assaulted can be significant.

Notwithstanding the frequency of this crime, it is estimated that fewer than 10% of sexual assaults are reported to the police. Sexual offences are less likely to be cleared by police than other types of violent crimes, with charges being laid in just over a third of sexual assault cases as compared to almost half of other types of violent offences. The conviction rate in sexual assault cases in adult courts is also lower than for other types of violent crime.[12] The majority of sexual assault survivors never report the assault because of mistrust of the system that is trying them, not their attackers:

> Our files are filled with poignant examples of women who are twice punished. They have lived through the violation of a sexual assault and then the violation of the courtroom experience, where often they – the victims – are put on trial. These women undergo the humiliating and painful process of relating the story of their assault to a room full of strangers, of reliving the trauma, their responses directed by questions over which they have no control. Their reward often is to see their assaulter acquitted.[13]

---

8 Liz Stimpson and Margaret C. Best, "Courage Above All: Sexual Assault Against Women with Disabilities" (Toronto: DisAbled Women's Network, 1991) cited in Ontario, *Sexual Assault: Dispelling Myths* (Toronto: Ontario Women's Directorate, 2009) <http://www.citizenship.gov.on.ca/owd/english/resources/publications/dispelling/dispellingthemyth.pdf>.

9 Jodi-AnneBrzozowski, Andrea Taylor-Butts and Sara Johnson, *Victimization and Offending Among the Aboriginal Population in Canada* (Ottawa: Statistics Canada, Canadian Centre for Justice Statistics, Juristat. Vol. 26, no. 3, 2006) at 5.

10 *Supra* note 5 at 13.

11 *Supra* note 2 at 13.

12 *Supra* note 5 at 10-11.

13 Pat Marshall, "Sexual Assault, The Charter and Sentencing Reform", 63 C.R. (3d) 216 at 217.

The crime of sexual assault is unique in that it is overwhelmingly perpetrated against women and children. The law has responded to these groups in a particular way due to their unique role in society. Historically, women were considered chattels and the law responded to crimes against women from this viewpoint. Consider the following roots of our sexual assault laws, as they formed part of the Laws from Alfred, King of the West Saxons, 871-900:

> If anyone seizes by the breast a young woman belonging to the commons, he shall pay her 5 shillings compensation.
>
> s. 1. If he throws her down but does not lie with her, he shall pay [her] 10 shillings compensation
>
> s. 2. If he lies with her, he shall pay [her] 60 shillings compensation.
>
> s. 3. If another man has previously lain with her, then the compensation shall be half this [amount].
>
> s. 4. If she is accused [of having previously lain with a man], she shall clear herself by [an oath of] 60 hides, or lose half the compensation due to her.
>
> s. 5. If this [outrage] is done to a woman of higher birth, the compensation to be paid shall increase according to the wergeld.[14]

The underlying rationale behind such laws is clearly rooted in viewing women as possessions.

> Rape was originally seen as a crime of theft of sexual property. A rapist would often have to pay money in damages to the woman's husband or father because the woman was seen as having lost the value of a marriageable daughter or of a pure wife.[15]

This point of view—of women as sexual possessions—has been reflected in certain aspects of Canadian criminal law. For example, until 1983 it was not an offence under the *Criminal Code* for a man to rape his wife. Attitudes toward the crime of rape developed from these roots and produced pernicious myths:

> Many people believed that if a woman got raped it was her own fault. They thought that only certain kinds of women got raped. These attitudes meant that women who were raped did not want to tell people because they were afraid of being blamed. Because women did not tell, many people thought that rape did not happen very often.[16]

Other myths concerned women who did report their rape. Often they were not believed and were suspected of having provoked the attack. Again, the attitude was that women were at fault. These propositions were not held in isolation, but were also reflected in many powerful segments of society, including within the criminal justice system, which accepted a number of harmful propositions, such as:

---

14 The Laws of the Earliest English Kings, 71 (F.L. Altenborough trans. & ed., 1922).

15 Megan Ellis, *Surviving Procedures After a Sexual Assault*, (Vancouver: Press Gang Publishers, 1985) at 4. See, too, Constance Backhouse, "Nineteenth Century Canadian Rape Law: 1800-1892" in David Flaherty, *Essays in the History of the Criminal Law* (1983, Osgoode Soc.), vol. II, 200.

16 *Ibid* at 5.

A (good) woman cannot be raped against her will, and will mount fierce resistance before yielding her virtue. She should have injuries to corroborate her claims of having been forced. . .Absent overt resistance that is recognized as such by a sexual aggressor and by the trier of fact, silence can be taken as a yes; no may mean yes; drinking or dancing with, humouring, accepting a ride or working late with, faking sleep, rolling over in one's sleep, wearing particular clothes or few clothes or sex-appropriate clothes, being unescorted by a man – all may mean yes if a man who wants sex wants it to mean yes or can persuade a judge or jury that there is some air of reality to the logic by which his wish becomes her desire.[17]

Such attitudes were reflected in the way courts treated rape cases and the clearly discriminatory evidentiary rules which were fashioned regarding women who were raped. Women were often questioned about their past sexual history for two reasons. There was the belief that sexual history or reputation was clearly relevant to the issue of consent, as well as being related to whether or not the woman was telling the truth. Also, if the woman had not reported the rape immediately, it was suggested that in the interim she had fabricated the charge of rape. In rape prosecutions the jury was warned that it was dangerous to convict on the evidence of the woman alone if there was not other corroborating evidence, independent of her, implicating the accused. In other instances the statute provided that no conviction could be had without corroboration even if the jury was satisfied of guilt beyond a reasonable doubt.

(a)   Prior Sexual History

Courts have long focused on the previous sexual history of the primary witness in a sexual assault case as relevant to the outcome of the trial. Unchastity was considered relevant both to the issue of consent and to the credibility of the testimony of the witness. It was not uncommon to read judicial expressions such as that "no impartial mind can resist the conclusion that a female who had been in the recent habit of illicit intercourse with others will not be so likely to resist as one spotless and pure."[18] Even Wigmore believed that such information was relevant. A sexually active victim was suspect since "[t]he unchaste ... mentality finds incidental but direct expression in the narration of imaginary sex incidents of which the narrator is the heroine or the victim."[19] An unrestricted right to cross-examine a rape victim as to her previous sexual history with others was perhaps the practice that was most responsible for trials being seen as trials of the victim rather than trials of the accused.

(b)   Doctrine of Recent Complaint

The doctrine of recent complaint was embodied in the common law. It meant that a complaint by a victim of a sexual assault had to be made at the first

---

17 Sheila McIntyre, "Tracking and Resisting Backlash Against Equality Gains in Sexual Offence Law" (2000)· 20(3) *Canadian Woman Studies* 72 at 73.

18 *Lee v. State* (1915), 132 Tenn. 655 at 658, 179 S.W. 145.

19 John Henry Wigmore, *Evidence in Trials at Common Law*, rev. ed. James H. Chadbourn (Boston: Little, Brown, 1970), vol. 3A, sec. 924a, p. 736 (originally published in 1904).

reasonable opportunity and it had to be made spontaneously.[20] This was an exception to the general common-law rule that a witness' previous statements are inadmissible since they constitute self-confirmation of one's own version of the event.[21]

The justification for the fresh-complaint rule was clearly due to the distrust of women. As was stated in the Model Penal Code, the "requirement of prompt complaint springs in part from a fear that unwanted pregnancy or bitterness at a relationship gone sour might convert a willing participant in sexual relations into a vindictive complainant."[22] This was the "logic" behind the doctrine of recent complaint.

Such views were integral in the judicial consideration of sexual assault charges, and resulted in the establishment of certain presumptions. As was held by one court, it "is so natural as to be almost inevitable that a female upon whom the crime has been committed will make immediate complaint."[23] Since the presumption existed that a sexual assault would lead immediately to a complaint, judges often commented on the absence of a complaint at the first reasonable opportunity, inviting juries to draw an adverse or negative inference about the victim's credibility.[24]

(c) Corroboration

The requirement for corroboration of a woman's evidence in sexual matters was established by early authorities and "justified" by writers. As Wigmore stated:

> Modern psychiatrists have amply studied the behaviour of errant young girls and women coming before the courts in all sorts of cases. Their psychic complexes are multifarious, distorted partly by inherent defects, partly by diseased derangements or abnormal instincts, partly by bad social environment, partly by temporary physiological or emotional conditions. One form taken by these complexes is that of contriving false charges of sexual offences by men.... The real victim, however, too often in such cases is the innocent man ... (and) a plausible tale by an attractive, innocent-looking girl may lead to a life-sentence for the accused, because the rules of Evidence (and the Judge's unacquaintance with modern psychiatry) permit no adequate probing of the witness' veracity.... No Judge should ever let a sex-offence charge go to the jury unless the female complainant's social history and mental make-up have been examined and testified to by a qualified physician.[25]

The justification for this rule was very explicitly laid out in the *Columbia Law Review*:

> Surely the simplest, and perhaps the most important reason not to permit conviction for rape on the uncorroborated word of the prosecutrix is that that word is very often false ... Since stories

---

20 *R. v. Lillyman* (1896), 2 L.R. 167; *R. v. Osbourne*, [1905] 1 K.B. 551 (C.C.R.); *Thomas v. The Queen*, [1952] 2 S.C.R. 344; *R. v. Kulak* (1979), 46 C.C.C. (2d) 30 (Ont. C.A.).

21 *Cross on Evidence*, (6th ed., 1979) p. 258.

22 *Model Penal Code and Commentaries*, (The American Law Institute, 1985) s. 213.6, Comment 5, p. 421.

23 *State v. Connelly* (1894), 57 Minn. 482, 59 N.W. 479, at 481.

24 See *R. v. Kistendey* (1975), 29 C.C.C. (2d) 382 (Ont. C.A.); *R. v. Boyce* (1974), 28 C.R.N.S. 336 (Ont. C.A.).

25 *Supra* note 19 at sec. 924a, p. 736-7.

of rape are frequently lies or fantasies, it is reasonable to provide that such a story, in itself, should not be enough to convict a man of a crime.[26]

This view was also reflected in court decisions. Without a corroboration requirement, "every man is in danger of being prosecuted and convicted on the testimony of a base woman, in whose testimony there is no truth".[27] And as a court quoting Glanville Williams found, "sexual cases are particularly subject to the danger of deliberately false charges, resulting from sexual neurosis, fantasy, jealousy, spite, or simply a girl's refusal to admit that she consented to an act of which she is now ashamed".[28] This reflects the state the common law was in.

While in this day and age, the propositions Wigmore espoused seem patently unreasonable, no one can doubt the influence that Wigmore had and does have in law. For this reason, it seems important to examine his assumptions:

> Wigmore ... omitted material from ... case histories which might undermine or contradict his hypothesis that young girls who report sexual assault or abuse are lying about the charge....
>
> Wigmore's unequivocal assertion that young girls who complain of sexual assault are likely to be lying is not supported by recent clinical experience or by survey research data. Surveys conducted during the period of the 1950's through the 1970's suggest that a significant portion of the female population has had some type of childhood sexual encounter with an adult male, many with relatives....
>
> Historically, the Wigmore doctrine has survived because it appealed to society's traditional distrust and general hostility towards women, which was embodied in the law ... . When Wigmore passionately expressed his view about the threatening nature of complaints of sexual assault made by female children, he articulated and memorialized an attitude which was apparently widely shared. By documenting his case, however, he has allowed later readers to discover the inherent flaw — or call it a 'blind spot' — which lay behind his ostensibly objective presentation of scientific evidence.[29]

ALAN N. YOUNG, WHEN TITANS CLASH: THE LIMITS OF CONSTITUTIONAL ADJUDICATION
(1995), 44 C.R. (4th) 152 at 153-155

In a comment on the Supreme Court's controversial decision in *R. v. O'Connor* (1995), 44 C.R. (4th) 1, 103 C.C.C. (3d) 1, [1995] 4 S.C.R. 411, which set out a two-part procedure for determining defence access to therapeutic and medical records of sexual assault complainants, Professor Alan Young described the following "battlefield":

In the last five years we have seen an ever-increasing defence strategy of requesting production of psychiatric and therapeutic records relating to sexual assault complainants. Stripped of its ideological and political context, this phenomena is no different than the flurry of breathalyzer production requests

---

26 "Corroborating Charges of Rape" (1967), 67 *Colum. L. Rev.* 1137-1138.

27 *Davis v. State* (1904), 120 Ga. 433, 48 S.E. 180, at 181.

28 *State v. Anderson* (1965), 272 Minn. 384, 137 N.W. 2d 781, at 783, quoting Glanville Williams, "Corroboration — Sexual Cases" October 1962, *Crim. L. Rev.* 662-671.

29 L.B. Bienen, "A Question of Credibility: John Henry Wigmore's Use of Scientific Authority" (1983), 19 *Cal. Western L. Rev.* 235 at 253.

which followed upon the *Bourget* decision in 1987. Ultimately, the breathalyzer production strategy faded into oblivion as the courts imposed an "air of reality" restriction on the applications and indicated that they would not be inclined to order stays of proceedings for failure to produce alcohol standard solutions, representative ampoules and breathalyzer mouthpieces.

Unlike the breathalyzer experience, the issue of producing sensitive and confidential records of complainants is animated by deeply held ideological and political beliefs, and, as such, this issue would not fade into oblivion notwithstanding the "likely to be relevant" threshold restriction which the courts placed upon these applications for production. In this context, battle lines appeared to be carved in stone with little incentive to adopt a compromise settlement. In fact, complainants and custodians of sensitive records have appeared willing to disregard court orders. Beyond the unprofessional conduct of the Crown in *R. v. O'Connor*, reported *ante*, p. 1, in failing to properly comply with an order of production, we have seen cases in which the records have been destroyed and shredded in an attempt to thwart the request for production. To date, the courts have turned a blind eye to this extra-legal obstruction and have concluded that a stay of proceeding is not warranted upon proof of an intent to obstruct but is only warranted if the obstruction truly impaired full answer and defence in a material way.

[Since Professor Young wrote this piece the Supreme Court of Canada has ordered a stay when documents were shredded on the basis that they might have been helpful to the accused. See *R. v. Carosella*, (1997), 112 C.C.C. (3d) 289 (S.C.C.).]

To understand the intensity of this battle one must recognize that, historically, sexual assault victims have been re-victimized by an insensitive and patriarchal criminal justice system. Fuelled by Freud's assertion that women and children are hysterical by nature, we find countless examples of statutory and common law evidentiary rules which treated the evidence of sexual assault victims with great suspicion and skepticism. In *Wigmore's Treatise on Evidence*, the eminent commentator noted that "no judge should ever let a sexual offence charge go to the jury unless the female complainant's social history and mental makeup have been examined and testified to by a qualified physician."

The ghosts of the past still haunt the criminal justice system, and, as Madam Justice L'Heureux-Dubé, noted, "uninhibited disclosure of complainants' private lives indulges the discriminatory suspicion that women and children's reports of sexual victimization are uniquely likely to be fabricated." Therefore, it is not surprising that complainants and custodians of sensitive records would view almost all production requests as a form of character assassination which is premised upon the dangerous Freudian and Wigmorian stereotype of half the population being prone to fabrication.

On the other hand, we have a defence lawyer poised for battle because his/ her client has denied the accusation. In most cases of sexual assault, there is an absence of confirmatory evidence and independent witnesses, and this raises the spectre of false accusations. This fear of false accusation is somewhat supported by a recent study by the Canadian Centre for Justice Statistics which revealed that the "unfounded"[30] rate for sexual assault was 14 per cent, 9 per cent and 14 per cent for sexual assault level I (s. 271), level II (s. 272) and level III (s. 273) respectively. These figures were compared to the unfounded rate for non-sexual assault which varied from 8 per cent with respect to assault level I (s. 266) to 3 per cent with respect to assault level II and III (ss. 267 and 268).[31] Furthermore, a recent study by an American sociologist demonstrated that 40 per cent of all rape charges investigated by city police turned out to be false as determined by recantation by the accuser and supported by other evidence.[32] Although it is conceded that further study must be given in order to explain this high unfounded rate, it is not surprising that defence counsel will search for whatever effective tools may be available to fully explore an accusation of sexual assault in order to ensure that his or her client is in the category of the unfounded complaint.

There are other offences which have higher unfounded rates than sexual assault (arson — 23.8 per cent; trespass at night — 14.3 per cent; abduction of person under 14 - 42.3 per cent),[33] yet we do not see the mad rush to impeach the credibility of Crown witnesses in these cases by resort to psychiatric and therapeutic records. This apparent inconsistency in defence strategy may suggest that defence lawyers still cling to and believe in the Wigmorian assessment of sexual assault complainants. However, it is equally plausible that the reliance on production requests in sexual assault trials is more a reflection of the nature of these trials, which turn largely on credibility battles without the luxury of independent evidence of a confirmatory nature. Regardless of which explanation is correct, it is apparent that both sides to this battle view the other with much suspicion and some disdain.

2. DEFINITION OF THE CRIME OF RAPE

Until it was replaced by the crime of sexual assault in 1982 [S.C. 1980-81-82, c. 125, s. 19], the offence of rape was defined by what was then s. 143 of the *Criminal Code* as follows:

---

30 "Unfounded" does not necessarily mean frivolous or false. It is defined as follows: "if the preliminary enquiry conducted by the police reveals that a reported crime has not been committed, this incident is to be classified as unfounded."

31 *Juristat*, "Canadian Justice Processing of Sexual Assault Cases" (Ottawa: Centre for Justice Statistics, March 1994), vol. 14, no. 7 at p. 10.

32 E. Kanin, *False Rape Accusations (1994) Archives of Sexual Behavior* (New York: Plenum Press, 1994), at pp. 81-92.

33 Statistics Canada, *Canadian Crime Statistics 1993* (Ottawa: Centre for Justice Statistics, 1993).

A male person commits rape when he has sexual intercourse with a female person who is not his wife,

(a) without her consent, or
(b) with her consent if the consent
     (i) is extorted by threats or fear of bodily harm,
     (ii) is obtained by personating her husband, or
     (iii) is obtained by false and fraudulent representations as to the nature and quality of the act.

Note the absolute immunity for the man who raped his wife. Note also the requirement of proof of sexual intercourse, defined elsewhere to be "penetration to even the slightest degree". This aspect often became the focal point of the trial and the reason why a prosecution might fail despite it being clear that a forced sexual encounter had occurred.

Section 143 contained no express *mens rea* requirement. That requirement and the possibility of a defence of mistaken belief was the issue in the controversial cases of *Pappajohn* and *Sansregret* which follow.

PAPPAJOHN v. R.

[1980] 2 S.C.R. 120, 14 C.R. (3d) 243, 52 C.C.C. (2d) 481,
1980 CarswellBC 446, 1980 CarswellBC 546

McIntyre J. (Pigeon, Beetz and Chouinard JJ. concurring): — The appellant appeals his rape conviction, which was affirmed in the Court of Appeal for British Columbia [5 C.R. (3d) 193, 45 C.C.C. (2d) 67] with one dissent, upon the ground that the trial Judge failed to put to the jury the defence of mistake of fact. That ground is expressed in the appellant's factum in these words:

> Did the learned trial Judge err in failing to instruct the jury on the question of honest belief by the accused that the Complainant consented to intercourse and thus on the facts of this case, failed to put properly before the jury a defence, such failure being a non-direction amounting to mis-direction?

A consideration of the facts of the case is vital to a resolution of the problem it poses. The complainant was a real estate saleswoman employed by a well-known and well-established real estate firm in Vancouver. She was successful in her work. The appellant is a businessman who was anxious to sell his home in Vancouver, and he had listed it for sale with the real estate firm with which the complainant was associated. She was to be responsible for the matter on her firm's behalf. On 4th August 1976 at about 1:00 p.m. she met the appellant by appointment at a downtown restaurant for lunch. The purpose of the meeting was to discuss the house sale. The lunch lasted until about 4:00 or 4:30 p.m. During this time a good deal of liquor was consumed by both parties. The occasion became convivial, the proprietor of the restaurant and his wife joined the party and estimates of the amount of alcohol consumed varied in retrospect, as one would expect. It does seem clear, however, that, while each of the parties concerned had a substantial amount to drink, each seemed capable of functioning normally.

At about 4:00 p.m. or shortly thereafter they left the restaurant. The appellant drove the complainant's car while she sat in the front passenger seat. They went to the appellant's house, the one which was listed for sale, to further consider questions arising in that connection. Up to the time of arrival at the home, at about 4:30 or 5:00 p.m., there is no significant variation in their accounts of events. From the moment of arrival, however, there is a complete divergence. She related a story of rape completely against her will and over her protests and struggles. He spoke of an amorous interlude involving no more than a bit of coy objection on her part and several acts of intercourse with her consent. Whatever occurred in the house, there is no doubt that at about 7:30 p.m. the complainant ran out of the house naked with a man's bow tie around her neck and her hands tightly tied behind her back with a bathrobe sash. She arrived at the door of a house nearby and demanded entry and protection. The occupant of the house, a priest, admitted her. She was in an upset state and exhibited great fear and emotional stress. The police were called, and these proceedings followed. More detailed reference to the facts will be made later.

When the defence closed its case, and before the trial Judge commenced his charge, the jury was excluded while counsel for the appellant argued that, on the facts of the case as it appeared from the evidence, the trial Judge should have put the defence of mistake of fact to the jury. He contended that the appellant was entitled to have the Judge tell the jury that, if the appellant entertained an honest though mistaken belief that the complainant was consenting to the acts of intercourse as they occurred, the necessary *mens rea* would not be present and the appellant would be entitled to an acquittal. Reliance for this proposition was placed upon *D.P.P. v. Morgan*; *D.P.P. v. McDonald*; *D.P.P. v. McLarty*; *D.P.P. v. Parker*, [1976] A.C. 182 (H.L.), and *R. v. Plummer* (1975), 31 C.R.N.S. 220, 24 C.C.C. (2d) 497 (Ont. C.A.). The trial judge refused to accede to defence counsel's request and, in disposing of the motion, had this to say:

> In this case, the complainant has testified that the accused had intercourse with her during a three-hour period some five times without her consent. The accused has testified that the acts of intercourse that he had with the complainant were all with her consent and that the only resistance to his amorous advances was of a token variety, and that orally, along the lines of; "Oh George, what are you doing?"
>
> There are many conflicts in the evidence during the critical period of time when the acts of sexual intercourse took place, and the jury will have to be directed to accept either the complainant's or the accused's version of the facts.
>
> The essence of the case, as I see it, is essentially: Has the Crown negatived the complainant's consent?

. . . .

In the Court of Appeal this ruling found support in the majority judgment of Farris C.J.B.C., with whom Craig J.A. agreed. The majority adopted the view that the issue emerging from the evidence was a simple one of consent or no consent. In a dissenting judgment, Lambert J.A. was of the opinion that there was sufficient evidence to put the defence to the jury. He would have directed the jury that the accused was entitled to an acquittal if the jury found that he entertained an honest and *reasonably held* mistaken belief in the existence of consent. This is a view which I cannot share, in view of the pronouncement in this court in *Beaver v. R.*, [1957] S.C.R. 531 at 538, 118 C.C.C. 129.

It is well-established that it is the duty of a trial judge, in giving directions to a jury, to draw to their attention and to put before them fairly and completely the theory of the defence. In performing this task, it is also clear that the trial judge must put before the jury any defences which may be open to the accused upon the evidence, whether raised by the accused's counsel or not. He must give all necessary instructions on the law relating to such defences, review the relevant evidence and relate it to the law applicable. This, however, does not mean that the trial judge becomes bound to put every defence suggested to him by counsel. Before any obligation arises to put defences, there must be in the evidence some basis upon which the defence can rest, and it is only where such an evidentiary basis is present that a trial judge must put a defence. Indeed, where it is not present he should not put a defence, for to do so would only be to confuse.

. . . .

McIntyre J. then reviewed the evidence in greater detail and continued:

In summary, then, this was the state of evidence when the trial judge was called upon to make his ruling. It became his task to apply the rule enunciated above. In assessing his resolution of the matter, we must consider the situation as it presented itself to him at the time. Speculation as to what the jury did, or would have done after being charged, is not relevant here.

With that thought in mind, and bearing in mind that the object of the judicial search must be evidence of a mistaken but honest belief in the consent of the complainant, one must first ask the question "Where is this evidence to be found?" It cannot be found in the evidence of the complainant. She denies actual consent, and her evidence cannot provide any support for a mistaken belief in consent. Her conduct, according to her description, is that of a terrified, hysterical, non-consenting woman who resisted the appellant's advances, albeit unsuccessfully, and when able fled from his house in search of assistance. Turning then to the evidence of the appellant, it immediately becomes apparent that his evidence speaks of actual consent, even co-operation, and leaves little, if any, room for the suggestion that she may not have been consenting but he thought she was. The two stories are, as has been noted before, diametrically opposed on this vital issue. It is not for the trial judge to weigh them and prefer one to the other. It is for him in this situation, however, to recognize the issue which arises on the evidence for the purpose of deciding what defences are open. In this situation the only realistic issue which can arise is the simple issue of consent or no consent. In my opinion, the trial judge was correct in concluding that there simply was not sufficient evidence to justify the putting of the defence of mistake of fact to the jury. He left the issue of consent, and that was the only one arising on the evidence.

In reaching this conclusion, I am not unmindful of the evidence of surrounding circumstances which were said to support the appellant's contention. I refer to the absence of serious injury suffered by the complainant and the absence of damage to clothing, as well as to the long period of time during which the parties remained in the bedroom. These matters may indeed be cogent on the issue of actual consent but, in my view, they cannot by themselves advance a suggestion of a mistaken belief. The finding of the clothes at the foot of the bed and the necklace and the keys in the living room are equally relevant on the issue of actual consent and, in my view, cannot affect the issue, which was clearly framed by the opposing assertions of consent and non-consent.

It would seem to me that, if it is considered necessary in this case to charge the jury on the defence of mistake of fact, it would be necessary to do so in all cases where the complainant denies consent and an accused asserts it. To require the putting of the alternative defence of mistaken belief in consent, there must be, in my opinion, some evidence beyond the mere assertion by counsel for the appellant of belief in consent. This evidence must appear from or be supported by sources other than the appellant in order to give it any air of reality. In *R. v. Plummer, supra*, Evans J.A. (as he then was), speaking for the Ontario Court of Appeal, considered that there was such evidence as far as Brown was concerned, and directed a new trial because the defence had not been put. In that case, the complainant had gone to Plummer's "pad", where she had been raped by Plummer. Brown entered the room where the rape occurred after Plummer had gone. Apparently he had arrived at the house separately from Plummer. It was open on the evidence to find that he was unaware then that Plummer had threatened the complainant and terrorized her into submission. He had intercourse with her, and she said that because of continuing fear from Plummer's threats, she submitted without protest. In these special circumstances the defence was required. The facts clearly established at least an air of reality to Brown's defence. In *Morgan, supra*, there was evidence of an invitation by the complainant's husband to have intercourse with his wife and his assurance that her show of resistance would be a sham. In other words, there was evidence explaining, however preposterous the explanation might be, a basis for the mistaken belief. In the case at bar, there is no such evidence.

Where the complainant says rape and the accused says consent, and where on the whole of the evidence, including that of the complainant, the accused and the surrounding circumstances, there is a clear issue on this point, and where, as here, the accused makes no assertion of a belief in consent, as opposed to an actual consent, it is unrealistic, in the absence of some other circumstance or circumstances, such as are found in the *Plummer* and *Morgan* cases, *supra*, to consider the judge bound to put the mistake of fact defence. In my opinion, the trial judge was correct in refusing to put the defence on the evidence before him.

I might add that I have had the advantage of reading the reasons of my brother Dickson and, while it is apparent that I am unable to accept his view on the evidentiary question, I am in agreement with that part of his judgment dealing with the availability as a defence to a charge of rape in Canada of what is generally termed the defence of mistake of fact. I would dismiss the appeal.

[Martland J. concurred with McIntyre J. but held that the mistaken belief would have to be honest and reasonable.]

DICKSON J. (dissenting) (ESTEY J. concurring): —

. . . .

It will be convenient to identify the pivotal issues on which the appellant's case turns:

(1) What is the *mens rea* of rape?

(2) Is a mistaken belief in consent available in defence to the charge of rape?

(3) If so, does mistake afford a defence only where the mistake is one which is held both honestly *and on reasonable grounds*?

(4) Did the trial judge err in the case at bar in ruling that there was not sufficient basis of fact to justify leaving the defence of mistake of fact to the jury?

I

Mens Rea

There rests now, at the foundation of our system of criminal justice, the precept that a man cannot be adjudged guilty and subjected to punishment unless the commission of the crime was voluntarily directed by a willing mind. Blackstone spoke of a "vicious act" consequent upon a "vicious will" (Commentaries on the Laws of England (1765), vol. 4, p. 21). Proof of the mental element is an essential and constituent step in establishing criminal responsibility. Parliament can, of course, by express words, create criminal offences for which a guilty intention is not an essential ingredient. Equally, *mens rea* is not requisite in a wide category of statutory offences which are concerned with public welfare, health and safety. Subject to these exceptions, *mens rea*, consisting of some positive state of mind, such as evil intention or knowledge of the wrongfulness of the act or reckless disregard of consequences, must be proved by the prosecution. The mental element may be established by inference from the nature of the act committed, or by additional evidence.

The *mens rea* which is required, and its nature and extent, will vary with the particular crime; it can be determined only by detailed examination of the *actus reus* of the offence. Speaking generally, at least where the circumstance is not "morally indifferent", the mental element must be proved with respect to all circumstances and consequences that form part of the *actus reus*. It follows that, in a case of alleged rape, where a fact or circumstance is not known to, or is misapprehended by, the accused, leading to a mistaken but honest belief in the consent of the woman, his act is not culpable in relation to that element of the offence: Glanville Williams, *Criminal Law, The General Part*, 2nd ed. (1961), p. 52:

> For if the *actus reus* includes surrounding circumstances, it cannot be said to be intentional unless *all its elements*, including those circumstances, are known. (The italics are mine.)

Taking these principles, then, what is the mental element required under s. 143 of the *Criminal Code*, R.S.C. 1970, c. C-34, on a charge of rape? This crime was historically regarded as an offence of physical violence. Blackstone defined rape as "the carnal knowledge of a woman forcibly and against her will" (Commentaries, p. 210). A more comprehensive definition of rape at common law is found in Archbold, *Pleading, Evidence and Practice in Criminal Cases*, 38th ed. (1973), para. 2871:

> Rape consists in having unlawful sexual intercourse with a woman without her consent by force, fear or fraud [citing East's Pleas of the Crown (1803), vol. 1, p. 434, and Hale's Pleas of the Crown (1736), vol. 1, p. 627].

Section 143 of our *Code*, in brief, defines rape as an act of sexual intercourse with a female person without her consent, or with consent if that consent is extorted by threats or fear of bodily harm. It will be seen that the statutory definition does not depart in any significant way from the common law definition. For all practical purposes, the *Criminal Code* merely codifies the common law. The essence of the crime consists in the commission of an act of sexual intercourse where a woman's consent, or genuine consent, has been withheld.

. . . .

In summary, intention or recklessness must be proved in relation to all elements of the offence, including absence of consent. This simply extends to rape the same general order of intention as in other crimes.

II

Mistake of Fact

Belief by an accused in a mistaken set of facts has not always afforded an answer to a criminal charge. By the early criminal law, the only real defence that could be raised was that an act had not been voluntary and therefore could not be imputed to the accused. Thus it was possible in some cases to excuse a man who had acted under a mistake by the argument that his conduct was not truly voluntary: Russell On Crime, 12th ed. (1964), vol. 1, p. 71. In the 17th century, Hale wrote: "But in some cases *ignorantia facti* doth excuse, for such an ignorance many times makes the act itself morally involuntary." (Pleas of the Crown (1736), vol. 1, p. 42).

The leading English cases on mistake of fact are, of course, *R. v. Prince* (1875), 13 Cox C.C. 138 (C.C.R.), and *R. v. Tolson* (1889), 23 Q.B.D. 168 (C.C.R.). In the *Prince* decision (p. 152), Brett J. cited from Blackstone's Commentaries, p. 27:

> *Ignorance* or *mistake* is another defect of will, when a man, intending to do a lawful act, does that which is unlawful. For here, the deed and the will acting separately, there is not that conjunction between them which is necessary to form a criminal act.

Brett J. held that mistake as a defence applies whenever facts are present, in which an accused believes and has reasonable ground to believe, which if true would render his act innocent and not a crime. The *Tolson* case, following *Prince*, considered the extent to which a mistaken, though honest and reasonable, belief that the first spouse was dead could afford a defence to a charge of bigamy. The classic statement is that of Cave J. (p. 181):

> At common law an honest and reasonable belief in the existence of circumstances, which, if true, would make the act for which the prisoner is indicted an innocent act has always been held to be a good defence.

An honest and reasonable mistake of fact is on the same footing as the absence of a reasoning faculty, as with infants, or impairment of the faculty, as in lunacy (*Tolson*, p. 181). Culpability rests upon commission of the offence with knowledge of the facts and circumstances comprising the crime. If, according to an accused's belief concerning the facts, his act is criminal, then he intended the offence and can be punished. If, on the other hand, his act would be innocent, according to facts as he believed them to be, he does not have the criminal mind and ought not to be punished for his act. (See E.R. Keedy, "Ignorance and Mistake in the Criminal Law" (1908), 22 Harvard L. Rev. 75, p. 82).

As stated by Dixon J., as he then was, in *Thomas v. R.*, 59 C.L.R. 279 at 299-300 (H.C.):

> States of volition are necessarily dependant upon states of fact, and a mistaken belief in the existence of circumstances cannot be separated from the manifestation of the will which it prompts ... the nature of an act of volition may be of an entirely different description if it is based on mistake of fact. The state of facts assumed must often enter into the determination of the will. It would be strange if our criminal law did not contain this principle and treat it as fundamental.

Mistake is a defence, then, where it prevents an accused from having the *mens rea* which the law requires for the very crime with which he is charged. Mistake of fact is more accurately seen as a negation of guilty intention than as the affirmation of a positive defence. It avails an accused who acts innocently, pursuant to a flawed perception of the facts, and nonetheless commits the *actus reus* of an offence. Mistake is a defence, though, in the sense that it is raised as an issue by an accused. The Crown is rarely possessed of knowledge of the subjective factors which may have caused an accused to entertain a belief in a fallacious set of facts.

If I am correct that: (i) s. 143 of the *Criminal Code* imports a *mens rea* requirement; and (ii) the *mens rea* of rape includes intention, or recklessness as to non-consent of the complainant, a mistake that negatives intention or recklessness entitles the accused to an acquittal. Glanville Williams notes in *Criminal Law, The General Part*, para. 65, p. 173:

> It is impossible to assert that a crime requiring intention or recklessness can be committed although the accused laboured under a mistake negativing the requisite intention or recklessness. Such an assertion carries its own refutation.

Howard (Criminal Law, 3rd ed. (1977)), points out that rape is aimed at the protection of women from forcible subjection to non-marital sexual intercourse, but that the facts of life not infrequently impede the drawing of a clean line between consensual and non-consensual intercourse (p. 149):

> it is easy for a man intent upon his own desires to mistake the intentions of a woman or girl who may herself be in two minds about what to do. Even if he makes no mistake it is not unknown for a woman afterwards either to take fright or for some other reason to regret what has happened and seek to justify herself retrospectively by accusing the man of rape.

I do not think the defence of mistaken belief can be restricted to those situations in which the belief has been induced by information received from a third party. That was the situation in the *Morgan* case, *supra*. In *Morgan*, the belief in consent was induced by information related by the complainant's husband, who spoke of his wife's sexual propensities. The foundation for the defence, incredible as it turned out to be, in view of the violence, was the misinformation of the husband. Had the defendants believed that information and had the wife's overt conduct been relatively consistent with it, the defendants would have had a defence. That is the effect of the dicta of the House of Lords in the *Morgan* case.

In principle, the defence should avail when there is an honest belief in consent or an absence of knowledge that consent has been withheld. Whether the mistake is rooted in an accused's mistaken perception or is based upon objective but incorrect facts confided to him by another should be of no consequence. The kind of mistaken fact pleaded by the *Morgan* defendants, however, is more likely to be believed than a bald assertion of mistaken belief during a face-to-face encounter. In any event, it is clear that the defence is available only where there is sufficient evidence presented by an accused, by his testimony or by the circumstances in which the act occurred, to found the plea.

III

Honest and Reasonable Mistake

The next question which must be broached is whether a defence of honest, though mistaken, belief in consent must be based on reasonable grounds.

. . . .

In Canada, the *Tolson* rule has already been rejected by this court in favour of the honest belief standard. Unless this court wishes to overrule *Beaver v. R.*, [1957] S.C.R. 531, 118 C.C.C. 129, it is difficult to see how the minority in *Morgan* can decide this appeal.

In *R. v. Rees*, [1956] S.C.R. 640, 24 C.R. 1, 115 C.C.C. 1, the issue was whether there is *mens rea* for the offence of knowingly or wilfully contributing to juvenile delinquency. Cartwright J. set out the *Tolson* test and then held as follows (p. 11 C.R.):

> The first of the statements of Stephen J. quoted above should now be read in the light of the judgment of Lord Goddard C.J., concurred in by Lynskey and Devlin JJ. in *Wilson v. Inyang* [*supra*], which, in my opinion, rightly decides that the essential question is whether the belief entertained by the accused is an honest one and that the existence or non-existence of reasonable grounds for such belief is merely relevant evidence to be weighed by the tribunal of fact in determining such essential question.

One year later, in *Beaver v. R.*, *supra*, a narcotics case, the opinion of Cartwright J. was accepted by a majority of the court. He adopted the paragraph quoted above from *Rees*. *Beaver* has since been regarded as an authoritative contribution to the law as to mental element, and mistaken belief, in true crimes.

It is not clear how one can properly relate reasonableness (an element in offences of negligence) to rape (a "true crime" and not an offence of negligence). To do so, one must, I think, take the view that the *mens rea* goes only to the physical act of intercourse and not to non-consent, and acquittal comes only if the mistake is reasonable. This, upon the authorities, is not a correct view, the intent in rape being not merely to have intercourse but to have it with a non-consenting woman. If the jury finds that mistake, whether reasonable or unreasonable, there should be no conviction. If, upon the entire record, there is evidence of mistake to cast a reasonable doubt upon the existence of a criminal mind, then the prosecution has failed to make its case. In an article by Professor Colin Howard, "The Reasonableness of Mistake in the Criminal Law" (1961), 4 University of Queensland L.J. 45, the following is offered (p. 47):

> To crimes of *mens rea*, or elements of a crime which requires *mens rea*, mistake of fact *simpliciter* is a defence; to crimes of negligence, or elements of an offence which requires only negligence, mistake of fact is a defense only if the mistake was in all the circumstances a reasonable one to make.

The same analysis is expressed by Glanville Williams, *Criminal Law, The General Part*, para. 71, p. 202.

. . . .

. . .With respect, there is no compelling reason for extending to rape the misapprehension, having its genesis in *Tolson* and now endemic in English law, that makes bigamy a crime of negligence and would have a like effect if applied to statutory rape.

Lambert J.A. recognized that, while his conclusion was directed by precedent rather than logic, he also found it to be supported, in relation to rape, by policy and practical sense [p. 212]:

> Why should a woman who is sexually violated by such a man have to defend herself by screams or blows in order to indicate her lack of consent, or have to consent through fear, for a charge of rape to be sustained? Surely a firm oral protest, sufficient to deny any reasonable grounds for belief in consent, should be a sufficient foundation in these circumstances for a charge of rape.

I am not unaware of the policy considerations advanced in support of the view that if mistake is to afford a defence to a charge of rape it should, at the very least, be one of a reasonable man might make in the circumstances. There is justifiable concern over the position of the woman who alleges that she has been subjected to a non-consensual sexual act; fear is expressed that subjective orthodoxy should not enable her alleged assailant to escape accountability by advancing some cock-and-bull story. The usual response of persons accused of rape is: "She consented." Are such persons now to be acquitted simply by saying: "Even if she did not consent, I believed she consented"? The concern is legitimate and real. It must, however, be placed in the balance with other relevant considerations. First, cases in which mistake can be advanced in answer to a charge of rape must be few in number. People do not normally commit rape per incuriam. An evidential case must exist to support the plea. Second, if the woman in her own mind withholds consent but her conduct and other circumstances lend credence to belief on the part of the accused that she was consenting, it may be that it is unjust to convict. I do not think it will do to say that in those circumstances she in fact consented. In fact, she did not, and it would be open to a jury to so find. Third, it is unfair to the jury and to the accused to speak in terms of two beliefs, one entertained by the accused, the other by a reasonable man, and to ask the jury to ignore an actual belief in favour of an attributed belief. The mind with which the jury is concerned is that of the accused. By importing a standard external to the accused, there is created an incompatible mix of subjective and objective factors. If an honest lack of knowledge is shown, then the subjective element of the offence is not proved. The following passage from the Heilbron Report is, however, apposite:

> 66. *Morgan's* case did not decide, as some critics seem to have thought, than an accused person was entitled to be acquitted, however ridiculous his story might be, nor did it decide that the reasonableness or unreasonableness of his belief was irrelevant. Furthermore it is a mistaken assumption that a man is entitled to be acquitted simply because he asserts this belief, without more.

Perpetuation of fictions does little for the jury system or the integrity of criminal justice. The ongoing debate in the courts and learned journals as to whether mistake must be reasonable is conceptually important in the orderly development of the criminal law, but, in my view, practically unimportant, because the accused's statement that he was mistaken is not likely to be believed unless the mistake is, to the jury, reasonable. The jury will be concerned to consider the reasonableness of any grounds found, or asserted to be available, to support the defence of mistake. Although "reasonable grounds" is not a precondition to the availability of a plea of honest belief in consent, those grounds determine the weight to be given the defence. The reasonableness or otherwise of the accused's belief is only evidence for or against the view that the belief was actually held and the intent was therefore lacking.

Canadian juries, in my experience, display a high degree of common sense and an uncanny ability to distinguish between the genuine and the specious.

The words of Dixon J. in *Thomas, supra*, at p. 309, bear repeating:

> a lack of confidence in the ability of a tribunal correctly to estimate evidence of states of mind and the like can never be sufficient ground for excluding from inquiry the most fundamental element in a rational and humane criminal code.

In *Textbook Of Criminal Law* (1978), p. 102, Professor Glanville Williams states the view, with which I am in agreement, that it is proper for the trial Judge to tell the jury "that if they think the alleged belief was unreasonable, that may be one factor leading them to conclude that it was not really held; but they must look at the facts as a whole". It will be a rare day when a jury is satisfied as to the existence of an unreasonable belief. If the claim of mistake does not raise a reasonable doubt as to guilt and all other elements of the crime have been proved, then the trier of fact will not give effect to the defence. But if there is any evidence that there was such an honest belief, regardless of whether it is reasonable, the jury must be entrusted with the task of assessing the credibility of the plea.

To apply the reasonable standard in this appeal, the court, in my view, would have to: (a) accept the minority decision in *Morgan, supra*; (b) overrule *Beaver, supra*, or find a means of distinguishing the offence of rape; and (c) defy accepted and sound principles of criminal law.

IV

The Plea and the Evidence

I come now to what is perhaps the most difficult part of this case, namely, whether there was an evidential base sufficient to require the trial judge to place before the jury the defence of mistaken belief in consent.

. . . .

Leaving aside the possibility of post-bondage intercourse, the jury could have reached any one of three alternative conclusions: (1) the appellant was telling the truth and the complainant did consent; (2) he was not telling the truth, she did not consent and he was aware of that fact or reckless to it; or (3) though he did not plead mistake, he believed she was consenting, notwithstanding token resistance. His defence of consent is rejected and that of honest belief accepted. I think there was sufficient evidence to put that third alternative to the jury.

Because the case turns on evidential matters, detailed reference thereto is unavoidable.

. . . .

There is circumstantial evidence supportive of a plea of belief in consent: (1) Her necklace and car keys were found in the living room. (2) She confirmed his testimony that her blouse was neatly hung in the clothes closet. (3) Other items of folded clothing were found at the foot of the bed. (4) None of her clothes were damaged in the slightest way. (5) She was in the house for a number of hours. (6) By her version, when she entered the house the appellant said he was going to break her. She made no attempt to leave. (7) She did not leave while he undressed. (8) There was no evidence of struggle. (9) She suffered no physical injuries, aside from three scratches.

The Heilbron Report contains the following observations which seem pertinent to the case at bar. The crime of rape involves an act— sexual intercourse — which is not in itself either criminal or unlawful and can indeed be both desirable and pleasurable; whether it is criminal depends on complex considerations, since the mental states of both parties and the influence of each upon the other, as well as their physical interaction, have to be considered and are sometimes difficult to interpret — all the more so since normally the act takes place in private; there can be many ambiguous situations in sexual relationships; hence, however precisely the law may be stated it cannot always adequately resolve these problems; in the first place, there may well be circumstances where each party interprets the situation differently, and it may be quite impossible to determine with any confidence which interpretation is right.

Toy J. gave a full, fair and accurate summary of the testimony by the complainant and appellant. There can be no criticism of the instructions in this respect. He did not, however, charge the jury on the defence of mistaken belief, as he earlier ruled that there was not "in the evidence any sufficient basis of fact to leave the defence of mistake of fact to this jury".

In my view, with respect, the judge erred in failing to instruct the jury: (a) that, as to pre-bondage intercourse, the issues were consent and belief in consent; and (b) that, as to post-bondage intercourse, the issue was whether an act of intercourse occurred or not. If the answer to (b) was negative, a conviction could not be founded upon the post-bondage period. If the answer was in the affirmative, a conviction would almost of necessity follow, because there was admittedly no consent or belief in consent after the "bondage". That the case gave the jury difficulty is clear from the fact that the charge was delivered about noon on a Friday and the verdict was not rendered until about 5:00 p.m. on Saturday.

I am mindful of the comment of Pigeon J. in *Leary, supra,* that consideration should be given to the plight of a complainant, who should not be subjected to the humiliation of having to testify again unless justice makes it imperative. The possibility of a mistaken belief in consent in the pre-bondage phase was an issue that should have been placed before the jury; the judge's failure to do so makes it imperative, in my opinion, in the interests of justice, that there be a new trial. It was open to the jury to find only token resistance prior to the "bondage"incident, which the appellant may not have perceived as withholding of consent. The accused was convicted of that which, perhaps, he did not intend to do had he known of no consent. It does not follow that, by simply disbelieving the appellant on consent, in fact, the jury thereby found that there was no belief in consent and that the appellant could not reasonably have believed in consent.

I would allow the appeal, set aside the judgment of the British Columbia Court of Appeal and direct a new trial.

Appeal dismissed.

For a view that mistaken beliefs in consent are mistakes of law rather than fact, see Lucinda Vandervort, "Mistake of Law and Sexual Assault: Consent and *Mens Rea*" (1987-88), 2 C.J.W.L. 233.

ROBIN WEINER, SHIFTING THE COMMUNICATION BURDEN: A MEANINGFUL CONSENT STANDARD IN RAPE

(1983), 6 Harv. Women's L.J. 143 at 147, 149

Robin Weiner has commented on the potential difficulties of applying an objective approach.

> If women and men always communicated their sexual interests and desires in the same manner, or if they understood each other's communications, they could, in fact, be represented by the same hypothetical person.... Behavior is not so accurately perceived, however; a gender gap in sexual communications exists.
>
> . . . .
>
> Courts do not clarify the perspective from which the 'reasonableness' standard should be applied. They vary dramatically in what must be reasonable — the perpetrator's behavior, the victim's fear, or the perpetrator's perception of the victim's behavior as an indication of lack of consent.

SANSREGRET v. R.

[1985] 1 S.C.R. 570, 45 C.R. (3d) 193, 18 C.C.C. (3d) 223,
1985 CarswellMan 176, 1985 CarswellMan 380

McIntyre J.: — This appeal [from (1984), 37 C.R. (3d) 45, 10 C.C.C. (3d) 164] raises once more the issue of the application of the defence of mistake of fact in a rape case. On this occasion its relevance on a charge laid under s. 143(*b*)(i) of the *Criminal Code*, now repealed but in force when this case arose, is questioned. In view of the significant changes made in this branch of the law by the amendments in 1980-81-82-83 (Can.), c. 125, it may be thought that this question has become of minor importance, but it would appear that similar cases involving similar defence claims may well arise under the new *Code* provisions and the applicable principles will still require consideration.

The appellant, a man in his early 20s, and the complainant, a woman of 31 years, had lived together in the complainant's house for about a year before the events of 15th October 1982. Their relationship had been one of contention and discord with violence on the part of the appellant: "slappings" or "roughing up" in his description, "blows" in hers. The appellant had left the house for short periods and in September 1982 the complainant decided to end the affair. She told the appellant to leave and he did.

On 23rd September 1982, some days after his dismissal, the appellant broke into the house at about 4:30 a.m. He was "raging" at her and furious because of his expulsion. He terrorized her with a file-like instrument with which he was armed. She was fearful of what might occur, and in order to calm him down she held out some hope of a reconciliation and they had intercourse. A report was made to the police of this incident, the complainant asserting she had been raped, but no proceedings were taken. The appellant's probation officer became involved and there was evidence than he had asked the complainant not to press the matter, presumably because it would interfere with the appellant's probation.

On 15th October 1982, again at about 4:30 a.m., the appellant broke into the complainant's house through a basement window. She was alone, and awakened by the entry she seized the bedroom telephone in an effort to call the police. The appellant picked up a butcher knife in the kitchen and came into the bedroom. He was furious and violent. He accused her of having another boyfriend; pulled the cord of the telephone out of the jack and threw it into the living room; threatened her with the knife and ordered her to take off her nightdress and made her stand in the kitchen doorway, naked save for a jacket over her shoulders, so he could be sure where she was while he repaired the window to conceal his entry from the police, should they arrive. He struck her on the mouth with sufficient force to draw blood, and on three occasions rammed the knife blade into the wall with great force, once very close to her. He told her that if the police came he would put the knife through her, and added that if he had found her with a boyfriend he would have killed them both. At one point he tied her hands behind her back with a scarf. The complainant said she was in fear for her life and sanity.

By about 5:30 a.m., after an hour of such behaviour by the appellant, she tried to calm him down. She pretended again that there was some hope of a reconciliation if the appellant would settle down and get a job. This had the desired effect. He calmed down and after some conversation he joined her on the bed and they had intercourse. The complainant swore that her consent to the intercourse was solely for the purpose of calming him down, to protect herself from further violence. This, she said, was something she had learned from earlier experience with him. In her evidence she said:

> I didn't consent at any time.
>
> I was very afraid. My whole body was trembling. I was sure I would have a nervous breakdown. I came very, very close to losing my mind. All I knew was I had to keep this man calm or he would kill me.

At about 6:45 a.m., after further conversation with the appellant, she got dressed and prepared to leave for work. She had a business appointment at 8:00 a.m. She drove the appellant to a location which he chose, and in the course of the journey he returned her keys and some money that he had taken from her purse upon his arrival in the early morning. Upon dropping him off she drove immediately to her mother's home, where she made a complaint of rape. The police were called and the appellant was arrested that evening.

The appellant was charged with rape, unlawful confinement, robbery, breaking and entering with intent to commit an indictable offence, and possession of a weapon. At trial, before Krindle Co. Ct. J. in the County Court of Winnipeg without a jury, he was acquitted on the charge of rape but was convicted of breaking and entering and unlawful confinement [34 C.R. (3d) 162]. The Court of Appeal (Matas, Huband and Philp JJ.A., Philp J.A. dissenting) allowed the Crown's appeal on the charge of rape and entered a conviction as well as imposing a sentence of five years' imprisonment. The unlawful confinement count was held to be subsumed in the rape. The appellant appealed to this Court asserting that the defence of mistake of fact, in this case a belief by the appellant that the complainant consented to intercourse, is open to an accused under s. 143(*b*)(i) of the *Criminal Code* as well as under subs. (*a*), and that it is the honesty of such belief that is determinative in considering the defence, not its reasonableness. Reliance was placed on *Pappajohn v. R.*, [1980] 2 S.C.R. 120, 14 C.R. (3d) 243, 19 C.R. (3d) 97, 52 C.C.C. (2d) 481.

The indictment set out the rape count in these terms:

> 1. THAT he, the said John Henry Sansregret, a male person, on or about the fifteenth day of October, in the year of our Lord one thousand nine hundred and eighty-two, at the City of Winnipeg in the Eastern Judicial District in the Province of Manitoba, did unlawfully have sexual intercourse with [T.W.], a female person who was not his wife, with her consent, which consent was extorted by threats or fear of bodily harm.

It clearly falls within s. 143(*b*)(i) of the *Criminal Code*. On the facts of this case, briefly summarized above, at first glance it may appear strange indeed that a defence of mistake of fact could be suggested, let alone made out. To appreciate how the issue arises, reference must be made to the findings of fact made at trial and to the judgments given in the Court of Appeal.

The trial judge described the complainant as a bright, sophisticated woman, articulate, capable, and well-employed. She considered that the appellant was neither particularly intelligent nor "verbal" and expressed surprise that any intimate relationship had ever arisen between them. She described the events of 23rd September 1982, a month before the events in question, and she considered that there was no evidence that the appellant knew she had complained of rape as a result of that incident. Comment will be made on this question later. She then referred to the defence of mistake of fact, and said [at p. 164]:

> If there were any evidence before me that the accused was aware on 15th October that the complainant had considered the sexual relations of 23rd September 1982 to have been non-consensual, I would have rejected this defence out of hand. There is no such evidence. I can speculate, but that is not proof.

She described in detail the events of 15th October and said that she accepted the complainant's version insofar as it differed from the appellant's, but she observed that in many respects his evidence confirmed hers. She continued [at p. 166):

> I am satisfied beyond any doubt that the accused broke and entered the complainant's residence on 15th October motivated primarily by jealousy and I do not doubt for a moment that, had the complainant had a man there, the knife would have been used aggressively. Having not found another man, he was bound and determined to make the complainant hear what he had to say to her by confining her unlawfully. He certainly broke and entered the dwelling-house with the intent to commit an indictable offence therein, and he certainly took possession of the butcher knife for purposes dangerous to the public peace.

Having entered the house and discovering that the complainant was on the telephone, being unsure about whether or not she had called the police, two things became paramount. One was to cover up the evidence of his break-in so that it would not be visible from the street, and to cover up his presence in the house by reducing it to darkness. The second was to prevent the escape of the complainant, or her use of the telephone, particularly probable events while he was outside putting the basement window back on the house. What better way to confine her than to take her car keys, her house keys and her money, to strip her naked, to bind her hands and to force her to stand by the back door and whistle so he could hear where she was.

I find that the accused forced the complainant to strip and tied her hands, not by way of preliminaries to an intended rape, but by way of confining the complainant. I similarly find the forced taking of her keys and money to part of the unlawful confinement.

She said that once the appellant became satisfied that the police would not come he set out to convince the complainant to reconcile. She accepted the evidence of the complainant that she was absolutely terrified, and that her consent was given solely to protect herself from further violence or death. She told him the things he wanted to hear regarding reconciliation, and she assured him that no other man was of interest to her. Then the trial judge continued [at pp. 167-68]:

As I said, no rational person could have been under any honest mistake of fact. However, people have an uncanny ability to blind themselves to much that they do not want to see, and to believe in the existence of facts as they would wish them to be. The accused says that, notwithstanding the reign of terror which preceded their chat, notwithstanding that he held a knife while they talked, notwithstanding that he did most of the talking and that the complainant's answers were clearly equivocal, he presumed and believed that everything between them was peachy, this notwithstanding that three weeks earlier, on a replay of the same sort of evening, his probation officer became involved and the complainant moved out of her house. Very honestly, despite my confidence in the ability of people to blind themselves to reality, and even if the accused had not lied about other parts of his testimony, I would have been hard pressed to credit the honesty of his belief.

However, his honest belief finds support in the testimony of the complainant. She knows him and, in her opinion, notwithstanding all the objective facts to the contrary, he did believe that everything was back to normal between them by the time of the sexual encounter. His subsequent behaviour as well attests to that fact.

I do not like the conclusion which this leads me to. There was no real consent. There was submission as a result of a very real and justifiable fear. No one in his right mind could have believed that the complainant's dramatic about-face stemmed from anything other than fear. But the accused did. He saw what he wanted to see, heard what he wanted to hear, believed what he wanted to believe.

The facts in *R. v. Pappajohn*, [1980] 2 S.C.R. 120, 14 C.R. (3d) 243, 19 C.R. (3d) 97, 52 C.C.C.(2d) 481, are quite dissimilar to those in this case. The dictum of the Supreme Court of Canada, however, is clear and broad and in no way seems to limit itself to the peculiar circumstances of that case. Perhaps the Crown will appeal this decision to obtain some direction from the Supreme Court on whether it was that court's intention to cover situations where an accused who demonstrates the clarity and shrewdness this accused showed in securing his own safety at the outset can turn around and, because it does not suit his wishes, can go wilfully blind to the obvious shortly thereafter. In any event, the ratio of *Pappajohn* is clear and it leaves me no alternative but to acquit.

To summarize, the trial judge found that the appellant did not enter the house with intent to make a sexual assault on the complainant; that the complainant consented to intercourse only because of the fear engendered by the threats of the appellant and to save herself, and that the appellant honestly believed that the complainant was giving a free and genuine consent to intercourse. She found as well that the complainant, who knew the appellant, also believed in the honesty of his belief.

. . . .

Rape, as defined in s. 143(*a*) of the *Criminal Code*, is of course the act of having sexual intercourse without consent. The issue with which we are concerned arises directly in a charge under subs. (*a*). The question will be: Did the accused have an honest belief that the woman gave her consent? It is in this form that the issue arose in *Pappajohn*, in *Morgan, supra*, and in *R. v. Plummer* (1975), 31 C.R.N.S. 220, 24 C.C.C. (2d) 497 (Ont. C.A.). While those cases provide authority for the existence of the defence and for its application where the consent is in issue, in my view they do not cover a charge under s. 143(*b*)(i) where consent is assumed from the outset. In other words, the existence of the consent is established and only its nature, that is, whether it was freely given or procured by threats, is in issue. Where the accused in a case arising under s. 143(*b*)(i) asserts an honest belief in consent, the honest belief must encompass more than the fact of consent. It must include a belief that it has been freely given and not procured by threats. I agree in this respect with Huband J.A. The defence would apply then, subject to what is said later about wilful blindness, in favour of an accused who had an honest belief that the consent was not the result of threats but one freely given.

. . . .

I would conclude then that the *mens rea* for rape under s. 143(*a*) of the *Code* must involve knowledge that the woman is not consenting, or recklessness as to whether she is consenting or not, and, for s. 143(*b*)(i), knowledge that the consent was given because of threats or fear of bodily harm, or recklessness as to its nature. It would follow, as has been held by the majority of this court in *Pappajohn*, that an honest belief on the part of the accused, even though unreasonably held, that the woman was consenting to intercourse freely and voluntarily and not because of threats would negate the *mens rea* under s. 143(*b*)(i) of the *Code* and entitle the accused to an acquittal.

The concept of recklessness as a basis for criminal liability has been the subject of much discussion. Negligence, the failure to take reasonable care, is a creature of the civil law and is not generally a concept having a place in determining criminal liability. Nevertheless, it is frequently confused with recklessness in the criminal sense and care should be taken to separate the two concepts. Negligence is tested by the objective standard of the reasonable man.

A departure from his accustomed sober behaviour by an act or omission which reveals less than reasonable care will involve liability at civil law but forms no basis for the imposition of criminal penalties. In accordance with well-established principles for the determination of criminal liability, recklessness, to form a part of the criminal *mens rea*, must have an element of the subjective. It is found in the attitude of one who, aware that there is danger that his conduct could bring about the result prohibited by the criminal law, nevertheless persists, despite the risk. It is, in other words, the conduct of one who sees the risk and who takes the chance. It is in this sense that the term "recklessness" is used in the criminal law and it is clearly distinct from the concept of civil negligence.

On the face of it, one would have thought that a man who intimidates and threatens a woman and thereafter obtains her consent to intercourse would know that the consent was obtained as a result of the threats. If specific knowledge of the nature of the consent was not attributable to him in such circumstances, then one would think that at the very least recklessness would be. It might be said then that this case could have been disposed of on the basis of recklessness. The trial judge, however, did not do so because of her application of the "mistake of fact" defence.

There was indeed an abundance of evidence before the trial judge upon which a finding of recklessness could have been made. After a stormy period of cohabitation, the complainant dismissed the appellant from her house in September 1982, thus demonstrating her rejection of him. He broke into the house on 23rd September and there went through a performance which led to an act of intercourse with a consent given by the complainant out of fear for her life. This incident led to a report to the police and the involvement of the appellant's probation officer. In the early morning hours of 15th October he again broke into the house and repeated his earlier performance, which provided the basis for the present charges.

There was also evidence from which the clear inference can be drawn that the appellant knew a complaint of rape had been made in respect of the first incident. Though the complainant complained to the police about that incident, no charges were laid. She was persuaded not to pursue the matter by the appellant's probation officer, who had approached her and told her that he would find a job for Sansregret if she did not press the charges. A police officer testified as to a conversation which occurred between himself and Sansregret after the latter's arrest. In response to a question as to why he ran from the police when they approached him on the evening of 16th October, the appellant replied: "From before, that time she phoned the police on me before."This reply was confirmed by Sansregret on direct examination but then denied on cross-examination. Sansregret admitted that he knew his probation officer had called the complainant with respect to the September incident and that he knew that he was not welcome in her house. There was then evidence that the appellant knew of her attitude towards him; knew that she had complained to the police with respect to the 23rd September incident; and knew that it was only the intervention of his parole officer which prevented charges from being laid after that incident. I therefore disagree with the trial Judge, who, in my opinion, was in error in not drawing the inference that the appellant knew that the complainant had complained of rape as a result of the incident on 23rd September.

It is evident that the trial judge would have convicted the appellant of rape had it not been for the defence of mistake of fact. She considered that the belief in the consent expressed by the appellant was an honest one and therefore on the basis of *Pappajohn, supra*, even if it were unreasonably held, as it is clear she thought it was, he was entitled to his acquittal. This application of the defence of mistake of fact would be supportable were it not for the fact that the trial judge found in addition that the appellant had been wilfully blind to reality in his behaviour on 15th October. Such a finding would preclude the application of the defence and lead to a different result. It is my opinion then that the trial Judge erred in this matter in that, though she made the requisite findings of fact that the appellant was wilfully blind to the consequences of his acts, she did not apply them according to law.

The idea of wilful blindness in circumstances such as this has been said to be an aspect of recklessness. While this may well be true, it is wise to keep the two concepts separate because they result from different mental attitudes and lead to different legal results. A finding of recklessness in this case could not override the defence of mistake of fact. The appellant asserts an honest belief that the consent of the complainant was not caused by fear and threats. The trial judge found that such an honest belief existed. In the facts of this case, because of the reckless conduct of the appellant, it could not be said that such a belief was reasonable but, as held in *Pappajohn*, the mere honesty of the belief will support the "mistake of fact" defence, even where it is unreasonable. On the other hand, a finding of wilful blindness as to the very facts about which the honest belief is now asserted would leave no room for the application of the defence because, where wilful blindness is shown, the law presumes knowledge on the part of the accused, in this case knowledge that the consent had been induced by threats.

Wilful blindness is distinct from recklessness because, while recklessness involves knowledge of a danger or risk and persistence in a course of conduct which creates a risk that the prohibited result will occur, wilful blindness arises where a person who has become aware of the need for some inquiry declines to make the inquiry because he does not wish to know the truth. He would prefer to remain ignorant. The culpability in recklessness is justified by consciousness of the risk and by proceeding in the face of it, while in wilful blindness it is justified by the accused's fault in deliberately failing to inquire when he knows there is reason for inquiry. Cases such as *Wretham v. R.* (1971), 16 C.R.N.S. 124 (Ont. C.A.); *R. v. Blondin*, 2 C.C.C. (2d) 118, affirmed [1971] S.C.R. v, 4 C.C.C. (2d) 566; *R. v. Currie* (1976), 24 C.C.C. (2d) 292 (Ont. C.A.); *R. v. McFall* (1976), 26 C.C.C. (2d) 181 (B.C.C.A.); *R. v. Aiello* (1978), 38 C.C.C. (2d) 485 (Ont. C.A.); *Taylor's Central Garages (Exeter) Ltd. v. Roper*, [1951]

2 T.L.R. 284 (Div. Ct.), among others, illustrate these principles. The textwriters have also dealt with the subject, particularly Glanville Williams, *Criminal Law: The General Part*, 2nd ed. (1961), at pp. 157-60. He says, at p. 157:

> Knowledge, then, means either personal knowledge or (in the licence cases) imputed knowledge. In either event there is someone with actual knowledge. To the requirement of actual knowledge there is one strictly limited exception. Men readily regard their suspicions as unworthy of them when it is to their advantage to do so. To meet this, the rule is that if a party has his suspicion aroused but then deliberately omits to make further enquiries, because he wishes to remain in ignorance, he is deemed to have knowledge.

He then referred to the words of Lord Sumner in *Re The Zamora*, [1921] 1 A.C. 801 at 811-12 (P.C.), which was a case wherein a ship and cargo were condemned in the Prize Court as contraband. The managing director of the shipping company denied knowledge of the contraband carried by the ship, and on this subject Lord Sumner said, at pp. 811-12:

> Lord Sterndale [the president of the Prize Court] thus expressed his final conclusion: "I think the true inference is that, if Mr. Banck did not know this was a transaction in contraband, it was because he did not want to know, and that he has not rebutted the presumption arising from the fact of the whole cargo being contraband."
>
> Their Lordships have been invited to read this as saying that Mr. Banck is not proved to have known the contraband character of the adventure; that if he did not know, because he did not want to know, he was within his rights and owed no duty to the belligerents to inform himself; and that the *Zamora* is condemned contrary to the passage above cited from *The Hakan* upon a legal presumption arising solely and arbitrarily from the fact that the whole cargo was contraband. It may be that in his anxiety not to state more than he found against Mr. Banck, the learned President appeared to state something less, but there are two senses in which a man is said not to know something because he does not want to know it. A thing may be troublesome to learn, and the knowledge of it, when acquired, may be uninteresting or distasteful. To refuse to know any more about the subject or any, thing at all is then a wilful but a real ignorance. On the other hand, a man is said not to know because he does not want to know, where the substance of the thing is borne in upon his mind with a conviction that full details or precise proofs may be dangerous, because they may embarrass his denials or compromise his protests. In such a case he flatters himself that where ignorance is safe, 'tis folly to be wise, but there he is wrong, for he has been put upon notice and his further ignorance, even though actual and complete, is a mere affectation and disguise.

Glanville Williams, however, warns that the rule of deliberate blindness has its dangers and is of narrow application. He says, at p. 159:

> The rule that wilful blindness is equivalent to knowledge is essential, and is found throughout the criminal law. It is, at the same time, an unstable rule, because judges are apt to forget its very limited scope. A court can properly find wilful blindness only where it can almost be said that the defendant actually knew. He suspected the fact; he realised its probability; but he refrained from obtaining the final confirmation because he wanted in the event to be able to deny knowledge. This, and this alone, is wilful blindness. It requires in effect a finding that the defendant intended to cheat the administration of justice. Any wider definition would make the doctrine of wilful blindness indistinguishable from the civil doctrine of negligence in not obtaining knowledge.

This subject is also dealt with by Professor Stuart in *Canadian Criminal Law* (1982), at p. 130 et seq., where its relationship to recklessness is discussed.

This case reveals, in my view, an appropriate set of circumstances for the application of the "wilful blindness" rule. I have outlined the circumstances which form the background. I have referred to the findings of the trial Judge that the appellant blinded himself to the obvious and made no inquiry as to the nature of the consent which was given. If the evidence before the court was limited to the events of 15th October, it would be difficult indeed to infer wilful blindness. To attribute criminal liability on the basis of this one incident would come close to applying a constructive test to the effect that he should have known she was consenting out of fear. The position, however, is changed when the evidence reveals the earlier episode and the complaint of rape which it caused, knowledge of which, as I have said, had clearly reached the accused. Considering the whole of the evidence, then, no constructive test of knowledge is required. The appellant was aware of the likelihood of the complainant's reaction to his threats. To proceed with intercourse in such circumstances constitutes, in my view, self-deception to the point of wilful blindness.

In my view, it was error on the part of the trial judge to give effect to the "mistake of fact" defence in these circumstances where she had found that the complainant consented out of fear and the appellant was wilfully blind to the existing circumstances, seeing only what he wished to see. Where the accused is deliberately ignorant as a result of blinding himself to reality the law presumes knowledge, in this case knowledge of the nature of the consent. There was therefore no room for the operation of this defence.

This is not to be taken as a retreat from the position taken in *Pappajohn*, *supra*, that the honest belief need not be reasonable. It is not to be thought that any time an accused forms an honest though unreasonable belief he will be deprived of the defence of mistake of fact. This case rests on a different proposition. Having wilfully blinded himself to the facts before him, the fact that an accused may be enabled to preserve what could be called an honest belief, in the sense that he has no specific knowledge to the contrary, will not afford a defence because, where the accused becomes deliberately blind to the existing facts, he is fixed by law with actual knowledge and his belief in another state of facts is irrelevant.

I would dismiss this appeal.

A. MANSON, ANNOTATION

(1985), 45 C.R. (3d) 194

McIntyre J. clarifies much of the confusion apparent in the lower court judgments by accurately characterizing the issue as whether the accused believed, not just in the existence of consent, but that the consent had been freely given and not procured by threats. The trial judge found as a fact that "the appellant honestly believed that the complainant was giving a free and genuine consent to intercourse" (p. 200). McIntyre J. states at p. 206 that a "finding of recklessness in this case could not override the defence of mistake of fact". However, he ultimately concludes (p. 208) that the accused's mistaken honest belief cannot exonerate him, since he "was wilfully blind to the existing circumstances, seeing only what he wished to see". In so doing, McIntyre J. seems to misunderstand the relationship between recklessness, wilful blindness and mistaken honest belief when knowledge of some factual element is an essential issue. In the result, he effectively reverses the finding of fact made by the trial judge.

Let us assume that a case involves as an essential element the issue of whether the accused knew that a thing was black or white. The accused would be guilty if he knew that the thing was black. If the offence can be committed recklessly, then the accused would be reckless as to this essential element if he recognized that it was a question whether the thing was black or white but acted in the face of this issue without resolving it. The accused would be wilfully blind if he had a strong suspicion that the thing was black and had steps available which would confirm the suspicion, but deliberately chose not to take the steps. In other words, where knowledge is an element, wilful blindness is tantamount to knowledge, in that the accused virtually knows but insulates himself from perfect knowledge. By comparison, an accused could be said to have an honest but mistaken belief only if he in fact believed that the thing was white. A finding of recklessness as to the colour, or wilful blindness about blackness cannot coexist with a finding that the accused had an honest belief in whiteness. Regardless of the reasonableness of the conclusion, a finding of honest belief can arise only if the accused has resolved the question of colour, albeit erroneously. Of course, the question is not answered simply by listening to the accused's version of what he knew or believed, but by examining and weighing all of the evidence. At the end of the day, however, if the trial judge finds that the accused honestly believed that the thing was white, then there is no room any longer for a question of wilful blindness or recklessness.

Rape is committed when the accused intentionally acts without the free consent of the complainant or is reckless as to the issue of consent. Thus, both knowledge of non-consent and recklessness as to this element would result in a conviction. Because knowledge is incorporated into the calculus, then wilful blindness is necessarily also applicable, since it is tantamount to knowledge. McIntyre J. may be correct when he assesses the evidence and indicates that there was substantial support for a finding of wilful blindness given the antecedent relations between the accused and the complainant. Nonetheless, as a matter of fact, the trial judge found an honest belief in freely given consent. An exculpatory mistake of fact requires a finding of honest belief, which cannot coexist with a concomitant conclusion that the accused was wilfully blind as to the element in issue. The former is an honest but mistaken belief in whiteness, while the latter is a strong suspicion — deliberately unconfirmed — of blackness.

McIntyre J. obviously doubts whether the accused in fact had an honest belief in freely given consent. That, however, was the trial judge's finding (p. 168): "No one in his right mind could have believed that the complainant's dramatic about-face stemmed from anything other than fear. *But the accused did*." (The italics are mine.) The question of the accused's belief in the impact of the threats was clearly within the trial judge's contemplation. In the circumstances, the finding certainly appears dubious. However, the Crown did not dispute it, nor did the Manitoba Court of Appeal reverse it: see 36 C.R. (3d) 45.

The jurisdiction of the Supreme Court of Canada is limited to questions of law alone: see *R. v. Warner*, [1960] S.C.R. 144, 34 C.R. 246, 128 C.C.C. 366; *Hobbins v. R.*, [1982] 1 S.C.R. 553, 27 C.R. (3d) 289, 66 C.C.C. (2d) 289 at 291. In the absence of a power to reverse the finding of fact, the appeal should have been allowed.

3. CRIMES OF SEXUAL ASSAULT (1983)

In 1983 the crime of rape was replaced by a three-tier structure of sexual assault offences, now ss. 271, 272 and 273. The aim was to reflect the violent rather than the sexual nature of the offence. Heavy reliance was placed on the study by L. Clark and D. Lewis, *Rape: The Price of Coercive Sexuality*.[34] The House of Commons Debates reflect the impetus and the result of ten years of protest from rape crisis centres, women's groups and many others:

> [T]he current laws relating to rape and indecent assault are being changed to emphasize the violence as opposed to the sexual aspects to these crimes. In other words, we will no longer have the term 'rape' in law.
>
> This legislation has a long history. Individual women and groups of women all across the country have been pushing for years to change the rape laws. It was apparent that this section of the *Criminal Code* cried out for reform. The number of reported rape cases was far below the actual number of offences. It has been estimated that only one in ten cases of rape was reported. That was due largely to the stigma which surrounded the rape victim — the idea that nice girls do not get raped and the belief that she must have asked for it.... The conviction rate for rape has traditionally been much lower than the conviction rate for other serious crimes — only 52 percent conviction rate for rape, compared with an 82 percent conviction rate in the case of other indictable offences. As a result, women's groups such as the National Action Committee on the Status of Women and the National Council of Women began calling for a complete removal of the existing rape sections from the *Criminal Code*. They wanted, instead, the enactment of a new offence dealing with rape as a type of assault.
>
> The government responded with Bill C-52 some four years ago, and that had one major beneficial effect. It brought together all women's groups calling for four basic principles which they wanted to see embodied in the law: treatment of rape as a type of assault, creating tiers of sexual assault to parallel existing assault offences, abolishing spousal immunity, and limiting admissibility of past sexual history ....

---

34 (Toronto: The Women's Press, 1977).

We now have a bill which provides that the assault and sexual assault structure of the *Criminal Code* will have three tiers. The Minister has outlined those three tiers. The women's groups which appeared before the committee were unanimous in their desire that the new law would be modeled on existing assault provisions in the *Criminal Code*, so that there would be a firm foundation for the new sexual assault provisions. This was the reason our party insisted in committee on three tiers of assault and sexual assault....

I know the bill before us is not perfect, but indeed it is a great step forward and it is of particular significance to women. I believe this piece of legislation will mark a new beginning in the way society views coercive sexual acts.[35]

Along with this new, gender neutral definition of the offence came the abolition of spousal immunity, restrictions on the cross-examination of the primary witness as to her previous sexual history, ss. 276-277, the abrogation of the doctrine of recent complaint, s. 275, (see *R. v. Page* (1984), 40 C.R. (3d) 85, 12 C.C.C. (3d) 250 (Ont. H.C.) and accompanying Annotation criticizing the same) and the repeal of corroboration requirements and warnings, s. 274. It is clear that these legislative changes have answered some of the complaints of legal bias against victims of sexual assault. To what extent *attitudes* have changed remains to be seen.

Since 'rape' was replaced with the term 'sexual assault', there has been some confusion over the definition of the crime since Parliament did not define the term in the *Criminal Code*. The Supreme Court of Canada had to grapple with the issue in the following case.

R. v. CHASE

[1987] 2 S.C.R. 293, 59 C.R. (3d) 193, 37 C.C.C. (3d) 97,
1987 CarswellNB 25, 1987 CarswellNB 315

McINTYRE J.: — This appeal concerns the meaning of the term 'sexual assault', as it is used in ss. 244 and 246.1 of the *Criminal Code*.

. . . .

The facts may be briefly described. The respondent, Chase, was a neighbour of the complainant, a 15-year-old girl. They lived in a small hamlet near Fredericton, New Brunswick. On October 22, 1983, Chase entered the home of the complainant without invitation. The complainant and her 11-year-old brother were in the downstairs portion of the house, playing pool. Their 83-year-old grandfather was upstairs sleeping. Their parents were absent. The respondent seized the complainant around the shoulders and arms and grabbed her breasts. When she fought back, he said: "Come on dear, don't hit me, I know you want

35 Hon. Flora MacDonald, reported in *House of Commons Debates*, Official Reporter Vol. XVII, First Session, *Thirty-Second Parliament.*(Quebec: Supply and Services Canada) p. 20041 (4 August, 1982).

it." The complainant said at trial that: "He tried to grab for my private, but he didn't succeed because my hands were too fast." Eventually, the complainant and her brother were able to make a telephone call to a neighbour and the respondent left. Prior to leaving, he said that he was going to tell everybody that she had raped him. The whole episode lasted little more than half an hour. The respondent was charged with the offence of sexual assault and was found guilty after trial in the Provincial Court. He appealed to the Court of Appeal for New Brunswick where his appeal was dismissed, a verdict of guilty of the included offence of common assault under s. 245(1) of the *Criminal Code* was substituted, and a sentence of six months' imprisonment was imposed.

. . . .

In the Court of Appeal, Angers J.A., speaking for a unanimous Court (Stratton C.J.N.B., Ryan and Angers JJ.A.), expressed the view that the principles developed with respect to rape and indecent assault were of little assistance in approaching the question of sexual assault. In his view, the modifier "sexual" should be taken to refer to parts of the body, particularly the genitalia. He considered that a broader definition of the term could lead to absurd realities if it encompassed other portions of the human anatomy described as having "secondary sexual characteristics". He also expressed the view that sexual assault did not require or involve a specific intent. Because there was no contact with the complainant's genitals, the conviction at trial was set aside and a conviction for common assault substituted. It becomes evident from the recital of these facts that the only question arising on the appeal is that of the definition of the offence of sexual assault.

The new sexual assault provisions of the *Criminal Code* were enacted in the Act to amend the *Criminal Code* in relation to sexual offences and other offences against the person and to amend certain other Acts in relation thereto or in consequence thereof, S.C. 1980-81-82-83, c. 125. They replace the previous offences of rape, attempted rape, sexual intercourse with the feeble-minded, and indecent assault on a female or male. It is now for the courts to endeavour to develop a realistic and workable approach to the construction of the new sections. The key sections are 244 and 246.1 [now ss. 265 and 271], *supra*. Section 246.1 creates the offence of sexual assault, an expression nowhere defined in the *Criminal Code*. To determine its nature, we must first turn to the assault section 244(1), where an assault is defined in terms similar, if not identical, to the concept of assault at common law. Section 244(2) provides that the section applies to sexual assaults. It was suggested in argument by the respondent that paras. (a), (b) and (c) of s. 244(1) are to be read disjunctively so that only para. (a) could be applicable to the offence of sexual assault. This, it was said, must have been the position taken by the New Brunswick Court of Appeal because, in its consideration of s. 244, it dealt only with para. (a), apparently considering that contact was necessary to complete a sexual assault.

I would dispose of this argument by simply referring to the specific words of s. 244(2) which make the section applicable to sexual assaults. In my view, however sexual assault may be defined, its definition cannot be limited to the provisions of s. 244(1)(a).

Since judgment was given in this case in the New Brunswick Court of Appeal, other appellate courts have dealt with the problem. As far as I am able to determine, none has followed the approach of the Court of Appeal in this case. In *R. v. Alderton* (1985), 49 O.R. (2d) 257, the matter was presented to the Ontario Court of Appeal. In that case, the accused gained entry to an apartment building at night, wearing a face mask. He entered the apartment of the complainant who was alone and asleep in her bedroom. He seized her and forced her back upon the pillows but after a struggle she managed to escape. The Court of Appeal dismissed an appeal from a conviction of sexual assault made at trial. Martin J.A., speaking for a unanimous court (Martin, Lacourcière and Finlayson JJ.A.), said at p. 263:

> We are, with the greatest deference, unable to accept the views of the court expressed in that case [*Chase*]. Without in any way attempting to give a comprehensive definition of a "sexual assault" we are all satisfied that it includes an assault with the intention of having sexual intercourse with the victim without her consent, or an assault made upon a victim for the purpose of sexual gratification.
>
> We are all of the view that in the circumstances of the present case, there was ample evidence upon which the jury could find that the appellant committed a sexual assault upon the complainant and, indeed, we think the evidence did not permit of any other conclusion.

As he said, in these words, Martin J.A. was not attempting a comprehensive definition of sexual assault, nor was he saying that the concept of sexual assault was limited to an assault with the intention of having sexual intercourse or for the purposes of sexual gratification. His view was that, where these elements were present, it would be sufficient to categorize the assault as sexual. They do not constitute the sole basis for a finding of sexual assault, nor may this reference to them be taken as a finding that a specific intent is required for the completion of the offence.

In *R. v. Taylor* (1985), 44 C.R. (3d) 263, the matter was considered in the Alberta Court of Appeal. The accused, in seeking to discipline a teenage girl placed in his care, tied the girl's wrists to an overhead metal support and made her stand naked for periods of ten to fifteen minutes and, on one occasion, administered several blows with a wooden paddle on the buttocks. There were no other acts which could have been described as sexual in nature. The accused was acquitted at trial. The Crown's appeal was allowed and a new trial was ordered. Laycraft C.J.A., for a unanimous court (Laycraft C.J.A., Haddad and Belzil JJ.A.), said, at p. 268:

> The new provisions do not define "sexual assault". However, "assault" is defined and thus the new offences are an assault with some additional meaning required by the modifier "sexual". In the offences which were replaced this was also true of "indecent assault", a term

which gave no difficulty in judicial interpretation. For decades, juries were charged that indecent assault was an assault in circumstances of indecency (*R. v. Louie Chong* (1914), 32 O.L.R. 66, 23 C.C.C. 250 (C.A.); *R. v. Quinton*, [1947] S.C.R. 234, 3 C.R. 6, 88 C.C.C. 231). Though this approach was susceptible to the comment that it was simply an assertion that an assault is indecent if it is indecent, it was nevertheless an approach perfectly understandable by generations of juries, and eminently practicable in the administration of the criminal law.

He then went on to discuss various authorities and rejected the *Chase* approach with its reliance on the specific involvement of areas of body and the dictionary definitions of the term "sexual". He noted that all the decisions he discussed rejected the *Chase* approach and he spoke approvingly of the position of Martin J.A. in the Ontario Court of Appeal in *Alderton, supra*, saying, at p. 269:

> Without joining a battle of dictionaries, it is my view that these words were intended to comprehend a wide range of forcible acts within the definition of "assault" to which, in the circumstances disclosed by the evidence, there is a carnal aspect. "Sexual assault" is therefore an act of force in circumstances of sexuality as that can be seen in the circumstances. Like Martin J.A. I would not attempt a comprehensive definition of "sexual assault". The term includes, however, an act which is intended to degrade or demean another person for sexual gratification. Nothing in the new sections of the *Code* in my view restricts the carnal or sexual aspect only to acts of force involving the sexual organs and I respectfully disagree with the restricted meaning expressed in *R. v. Chase, supra*.

It was his view that the carnal aspect was to be judged objectively: "Viewed in the light of all the circumstances, is the sexual or carnal context of the assault visible to a reasonable observer?"

In the British Columbia Court of Appeal, the matter was considered in *R. v. Cook* (1985), 20 C.C.C. (3d) 18. In this case, on facts which clearly revealed conduct which would qualify as sexual assaults, the *Chase* approach was again rejected. Lambert J.A. did not attempt to give a precise definition of sexual assault where Parliament had declined to do so, but he did consider that the characteristic which made a simple assault into a sexual assault was not solely a matter of anatomy. He considered that a real affront to sexual integrity and sexual dignity may be sufficient.

It will be seen from this brief review of the cases that the approach taken by the New Brunswick Court of Appeal in the case at bar has found little, if any, support. All the cases cited have recognized the need for a broader approach and all have recognized the difficulty in formulating one. While I would agree that it is difficult and probably unwise to attempt to develop a precise and all-inclusive definition of the new offence of sexual assault at this stage in its development, it seems to me to be necessary to attempt to settle upon certain considerations which may be of assistance to the courts in developing on a case-to-case basis a workable definition of the offence.

To begin with, I agree, as I have indicated, that the test for the recognition of sexual assault does not depend solely on contact with specific areas of the human anatomy. I am also of the view that sexual assault need not involve an attack by a member of one sex upon a member of the other; it could be perpetrated upon one of the same sex. I agree as well with those who say that the new offence is truly new and does not merely duplicate the offences it replaces. Accordingly, the definition of the term "sexual assault" and the reach of the offence it describes is not necessarily limited to the scope of its predecessors. I would consider as well that the test for its recognition should be objective.

While it is clear that the concept of a sexual assault differs from that of the former indecent assault, it is nevertheless equally clear that the terms overlap in many respects and sexual assault in many cases will involve the same sort of conduct that formerly would have justified a conviction for an indecent assault. The definitional approach to indecent assault also an offence not defined in the *Criminal Code*, therefore offers a guide in our approach to the new offence, as recognized by Laycraft C.J.A. After many years of dealing with the concept of indecent assault, the courts developed the definition, "an assault in circumstances of indecency". This, of course, was in imprecise definition but everyone knew what an indecent assault was. The law in that respect was reasonably clear and there was little difficulty with its enforcement. In my view then, a similar approach may be adopted in formulating a definition of sexual assault.

Applying these principles and the authorities cited, I would make the following observations. Sexual assault is an assault within any one of the definitions of that concept in s. 244 (1) of the *Criminal Code* which is committed in circumstances of a sexual nature, such that the sexual integrity of the victim is violated. The test to be applied in determining whether the impugned conduct has the requisite sexual nature is an objective one: "Viewed in the light of all the circumstances, is the sexual or carnal context of the assault visible to a reasonable observer" (*Taylor, supra*, per Laycraft C.J.A., at p. 269). The part of the body touched, the nature of the contact, the situation in which it occurred, the words and gestures accompanying the act, and all other circumstances surrounding the conduct, including threats which may or may not be accompanied by force will be relevant (see S.J. Usprich, "A New Crime in Old Battles: Definitional Problems with Sexual Assault" (1987), 29 Crim. L.Q. 200, at p. 204) The intent or purpose of the person committing the act, to the extent that this may appear from the evidence, may also be a factor in considering whether the conduct is sexual. If the motive of the accused is sexual gratification, to the extent that this may appear from the evidence, it may be a factor in determining whether the conduct is sexual. It must be emphasized, however, that the existence of such a motive is simply one of many factors to be considered, the importance of which will vary depending on the circumstances.

Implicit in this view of sexual assault is the notion that the offence is one requiring a general intent only. This is consistent with the approach adopted by this court in cases such as *Leary v. The Queen*, [1978] 1 S.C.R. 29, and *Swietlinski v. The Queen*, [1980] 2 S.C.R. 956, where it was held that rape and indecent assault were offences of general intent. I am unable to see any reason why the same approach should not be taken with respect to sexual assault. The factors which could motivate sexual assault are said to be many and varied (see C. Boyle, *Sexual Assault* (1984), at p. 74). To put upon the Crown the burden of proving a specific intent would go a long way toward defeating the obvious purpose of the enactment. Moreover, there are strong reasons in social policy which would support this view. To import an added element of specific intent in such offences, would be to hamper unreasonably the enforcement process. It would open the question of the defence of drunkenness, one which has always been related to the capacity to form a specific intent and which has generally been excluded by law and policy from offences requiring only the minimal intent to apply force (see *R. v. Bernard* (1985), 18 C.C.C. (3d) 574 (Ont. C.A., per Dubin J.A.)) For these reasons, I would say that the offence will be one of general rather than specific intent.

Turning to the case at bar I have no difficulty in concluding, on the basis of the principles I have discussed above, that there was ample evidence before the trial Judge upon which he could find that sexual assault was committed. Viewed objectively in the light of all the circumstances, it is clear that the conduct of the respondent in grabbing the complainant's breasts constituted an assault of a sexual nature. I would therefore allow the appeal, set aside the conviction of common assault recorded by the Court of Appeal and restore the conviction of sexual assault made at trial. The sentence of six months should stand.

Appeal allowed.

PROBLEM

The accused is charged with sexually assaulting his three-year-old son. He admits that he grabbed his son's testicles on three occasions as a disciplinary response to the child having engaged in similar activity with others, including the accused. He wanted to show him how much it hurt. There is evidence of bruising. Has the accused committed a sexual assault?
Compare *R. v. V. (K.B.)* (1993), 22 C.R. (4th) 86, 82 C.C.C. (3d) 382, [1993] 2 S.C.R. 857.

In the 1983 amendments, Parliament changed the provisions concerning coerced consent (s. 265(3), considered earlier in Chapter 2). It also codified for the first time a defence of mistake as to consent applicable to all assaults, including sexual assaults. See s. 265(4). **Does the section continue the *Pappajohn* interpretation?**

R. v. BULMER

[1987] 1 S.C.R. 782, 58 C.R. (3d) 48, 33 C.C.C. (3d) 385,
1987 CarswellBC 702, 1987 CarswellBC 149

On the trial of the accused on charges of rape, attempted rape and indecent assault, the evidence indicated that the complainant, a prostitute, agreed to provide her services to the accused L. for a certain price. She testified that they went to a hotel room and, on entering, she discovered the two other accused, B. and I., and objected to their presence. I. sought to engage her services. She quoted her price and told him to come back in 20 minutes. B. and I. then left, but returned shortly after. A discussion followed, and I. told the complainant that she would have to provide her services without payment. Frightened, she performed various sexual acts with all three. She denied giving consent and receiving payment. There was no physical violence other than the various sexual acts. B. did not give evidence. L. and I. testified that price was discussed with the complainant after B. and I. returned to the room and that she finally agreed to have sex with them for $20 each. No threats were made. The occupant of an adjoining room testified that he heard two persons leave and return. He also heard a woman complaining about their presence. Her voice seemed normal at first, but as time passed it took on a whining, wheedling tone. There was also discussion about price.

In defence, the accused took the position that the complainant had consented to the acts. Counsel made the alternative submission that L. had held an honest but mistaken belief in consent. The trial judge left the defence to the jury and told them that all three could rely upon the defence. The jury returned verdicts of guilty of rape against both L. and I. B. was acquitted of rape, but convicted of indecent assault. The majority of the British Columbia Court of Appeal having dismissed their appeals, the accused appealed further.

The Supreme Court agreed that there was evidence of the mistake defence fit to go to the jury but ordered a new trial on the basis that the trial judge had wrongly instructed, in his supplementary charge, that the belief had to be both honest and reasonable.

McINTYRE J. (DICKSON C.J., WILSON, LE DAIN, and LA FOREST JJ. concurring): —

In discussing the application of the "air of reality" test in the *Pappajohn* case, I said, at p. 133:

> To require the putting of the alternative defence of mistaken belief in consent, there must be, in my opinion some evidence beyond the mere assertion of belief in consent by counsel for the appellant. This evidence must appear from or be supported by sources other than the appellant in order to give it any air of reality.

These words appear, on occasion, to have been misunderstood, but I do not withdraw them. There will not be an air of reality about a mere statement that "I thought she was consenting" not supported to some degree by other evidence or circumstances arising in the case. If that mere assertion were sufficient to require a trial Judge to put the "mistake of fact" defence, it would be a simple matter in any rape case to make such an assertion and, regardless of all other circumstances, require the defence to be put. It must be remembered that at this stage of the proceedings the trial judge is not in any way concerned with the question of guilt or innocence. He is not concerned with the weight of evidence or with the credibility of evidence. The question he must answer is this. In all the circumstances of this case, is there any reality in the defence? To answer this question, he must consider all the evidence, all the circumstances. The statement of the accused alleging a mistaken belief will be a factor but will not by itself be decisive, and even in its total absence, other circumstances might dictate the putting of the defence. This view finds support in the passage from the Heilbron Report (Great Britain, Report of the Advisory Group on the Law of Rape (1975)) referred to by Dickson J., at p. 155 in *Pappajohn*, in these terms:

> 66. *Morgan's* case did not decide, as some critics seem to have thought, that an accused person was entitled to be acquitted, however ridiculous his story might be, nor did it decide that the reasonableness or unreasonableness of his belief was irrelevant. *Furthermore it is a mistaken assumption that a man is entitled to be acquitted simply because he asserts his belief, without more.* [Emphasis added.]

When the defence of mistake of fact — or for that matter any other defence — is raised, two distinct steps are involved. The first step for the trial judge is to decide if the defence should be put to the jury. It is on this question, as I have said, that the "air of reality" test is applied. It has nothing to do with the jury and is not a factor for its consideration. If it is decided to put the defence, the second step requires the trial judge to explain the law to the jury, review the relevant evidence, and leave the jury with the issue of guilt or innocence. The jury must consider all the evidence, and they must be satisfied beyond a reasonable doubt in the case of a rape charge that there was no consent before they may convict. Where they find there was consent or honest belief in consent or if they have a doubt on either issue, they must acquit. They should be told as well that the belief, if honestly held, need not be based on reasonable grounds. Before going further, it should be observed that since the decision of this court in *Pappajohn*, the *Criminal Code* has been amended by the addition of s. 244(4) [now s. 265(4)], which provides:

> (4) Where an accused alleges that he believed that the complainant consented to the conduct that is the subject-matter of the charge, a Judge, if satisfied that there is sufficient evidence and that, if believed by the jury, the evidence would constitute a defence, shall instruct the jury, when reviewing all the evidence relating to the determination of the honesty of the accused's belief, to consider the presence or absence of reasonable grounds for that belief.

This section, in my view, does not change the law as applied in *Pappajohn*. It does not require that the mistaken belief be reasonable or reasonably held. It simply makes it clear than in determining the issue of the honesty of the asserted belief, the presence or absence of reasonable grounds for the belief are relevant factors for the jury's consideration. This approach was, I suggest, foreshadowed in *Pappajohn* by Dickson J., at pp. 155-56, where he said:

> Perpetuation of fictions does little for the jury system or the integrity of criminal justice. The ongoing debate in the courts and learned journals as to whether mistake must be reasonable is conceptually important in the orderly development of the criminal law, but in my view, practically unimportant because the accused's statement that he was mistaken is not likely to be believed unless the mistake is, to the jury, reasonable. The jury will be concerned to consider the reasonableness of any grounds found, or asserted to be available, to support the defence of mistake. Although "reasonable grounds" is not a precondition to the availability of a plea of honest belief in consent, those grounds determine the weight to be given the defence. The reasonableness, or otherwise, of the accused's belief is only evidence for, or against, the view that the belief was actually held and the intent was, therefore, lacking.

The jury should then be instructed, in accordance with s. 244(4) of the *Code*, that when considering all the evidence relating to the question of the honesty of the accused's asserted belief in consent they must consider the presence or absence of reasonable grounds for that belief.

. . . .

LAMER J. — I have read the reasons for judgment of my colleague Justice McIntyre and, for the reasons he sets out, I agree that this appeal should succeed. I wish to add, however, the following qualifications to certain statements made in his reasons.

I agree with McIntyre J. that "a trial judge is not bound to put every defence suggested by counsel in the absence of some evidentiary base" (at p. 789), and that "to put a wholly unsupported defence would only cause confusion" (at p. 790) amongst the jurors. In addition I do not take issue with the "air of reality" test referred to in *Pappajohn v. The Queen*, [1980] 2 S.C.R. 120 by McIntyre J.

With respect, however, I have difficulties with his application of the "air of reality" test. In *Pappajohn*, he said, at p. 133:

> To require the putting of the alternative defence of mistaken belief in consent, there must be, in my opinion, some evidence beyond the mere assertion of belief in consent by counsel for the appellant. This evidence must appear from or be supported by sources other than the appellant in order to give it any air of reality.

In his reasons in this case, he says (at p. 790):

> These words [air of reality] appear, on occasion, to have been misunderstood, but I do not withdraw them. There will not be an air of reality about a mere statement that "I thought she was consenting" not supported to some degree by other evidence or circumstances arising in the case. If that mere assertion were sufficient to require a trial judge to put the mistake of fact defence, it would be a simple matter in any rape case to make such an assertion and, regardless of all other circumstances, require the defence to be put.

If this means that the trial judge is not required to put the defence to the jury merely because the accused's lawyer has referred to the defence in argument, then I agree. There must be some evidence supporting the defence before it is to be put to the jury. However, I must respectfully take issue with the "air of reality" norm if it is to be understood as going so far as enabling the trial judge to choose not to leave the defence of honest belief with the jury even in a case where the accused has taken the stand and asserted under oath that he or she honestly believed in consent. An accused's oath to the effect that he or she honestly believed in consent is always some evidence, and its probative value in any given case belongs to the jury and not to the trial judge. It is, of course, open to the trial Judge to comment on the probative value of the evidence, but the jury remains the master of the facts. The trial judge must not usurp the role of the jury by removing the evidence from the jury's consideration on the ground that, in his or her view, the defence lacks an "air of reality".

. . . .

The old common-law rule in sexual assault cases that the trial judge must instruct the jury that it is unsafe to convict in the absence of corroboration of the complainant's testimony (which was abolished by s. 246.4 of the *Criminal Code*) would in effect be replaced by a rule requiring corroboration of the accused's testimony. Such a requirement will often work an injustice to the accused. Clearly the best, and quite often the only, evidence of the accused's subjective belief will be his or her testimony, and there is no basis in law or in principle for requiring corroboration. In addition, this court decided in *Pappajohn* that the accused's belief must be honest but need not be reasonable. As a result, there clearly cannot be a requirement that the accused's belief be supported by the circumstances before it can be submitted to the jury. As Dickson J., as he then was, wrote, at p. 156:

> It will be a rare day when a jury is satisfied as to the existence of an unreasonable belief. If the claim of mistake does not raise a reasonable doubt as to guilt, and all other elements of the crime have been proved, then the trier of fact will not give effect to the defence. But, it there is any evidence that there was such an honest belief, regardless of whether it is reasonable, the jury must be entrusted with the task of assessing the credibility of the plea.

I should, in passing, add that in my view the issue of mistaken belief in consent should also be submitted to the jury in all cases where the accused testifies at trial that the complainant consented. The accused's testimony that the complainant consented must be taken to mean that he believed that the complainant consented. As a result, if the jury believes the complainant and concludes that the complainant did not consent, that does not end the matter, for the accused's assertion cannot be disposed of completely unless consideration is then given to his or her being honestly mistaken in believing that the complainant consented.

Finally, I wish to add that I do not believe that this view of the "air of reality" test will open the floodgates to claims of honest mistake as to consent in sexual assault cases. An accused who wishes to raise the defence in the absence of any other evidence supporting an honest mistake will be required to take the stand and will run the risks of cross-examination. In addition, I do not think that the jury will be fooled by false claims of the defence. Juries are constantly assessing and then discarding defences because they lack an air of reality and do not raise a reasonable doubt. Sexual offence cases are no different.

Subject to these reservations, I agree with McIntyre J.'s reasons and would accordingly allow the appeal and direct a new trial.

Appeal allowed and new trial ordered.

In *R. v. Reddick*, [1991] 1 S.C.R. 1086, 5 C.R. (4th) 389, 64 C.C.C. (3d) 257, the majority adopted and applied the *Pappajohn* requirement of sources other than the accused. It seems clear that this special "air of reality" ruling in *Pappajohn* accounted for the reality that the mistaken belief defence has rarely been put to juries. Since *Pappajohn* there have been very few decisions with written reasons where an acquittal has been based on a mistaken belief defence and only one such acquittal confirmed by a Court of Appeal; see *R. v. Weaver* (1990), 80 C.R. (3d) 396 (Alta. C.A.).

The pattern seemed likely to change with the decision in *R. v. Osolin*, [1993] 4 S.C.R. 595, 26 C.R. (4th) 1, 86 C.C.C. (3d) 481. The court in *Osolin* unanimously decided that the air of reality test declared in s. 265(4) did not violate the presumption of innocence of s. 11(*d*) of the *Charter* nor the right to trial by jury under s. 11(*f*). Mr. Justice Cory reached this conclusion by changing or reading down. He expressly rejected the McIntyre view that there must be a source of evidence other than the accused:

> In my view, this proposition cannot be correct. There is no requirement that there be evidence independent of the accused in order to have the defence put to the jury. However, the mere assertion by the accused that "I believed she was consenting" will not be sufficient. What is required is that the defence of mistaken belief be supported by evidence beyond the mere assertion of a mistaken belief.

The court was unanimous on this point. McLachlin J. expressly adopted Cory J.'s "resolution of the confusion which existed in the earlier cases". This is as close as Her Ladyship gets to acknowledging that her previous position for the court in *Reddick* has changed.

The court in *Osolin* did not accept all of the Lamer position in *Bulmer*. The mistaken belief defence need not always be put where the accused testifies as to mistaken belief. Like any other defence, the trial judge must assess whether there is an evidentiary basis for the defence to be considered by the jury.

In a complex series of split opinions the Supreme Court has now reached further agreement on this issue of air of reality. This was summarized by Chief Justice Lamer for a unanimous court in *Davis*.

R. v. DAVIS

[1999] 3 S.C.R. 759, 29 C.R. (5th) 1, 139 C.C.C. (3d) 193,
1999 CarswellNfld 291, 1999 CarswellNfld 292

LAMER C.J.C. (L'HEUREUX-DUBÉ, GONTHIER, CORY, MCLACHLIN, MAJOR and BINNIE JJ. concurring): —

. . . .

The defence of honest but mistaken belief in consent is simply a denial of the *mens rea* of sexual assault: *R. v. Ewanchuk*, [1999] 1 S.C.R. 330 (S.C.C.) at para. 43; *R. v. Pappajohn*, [1980] 2 S.C.R. 120 (S.C.C.) at p. 148. The *actus reus* of sexual assault requires a touching, of a sexual nature, without the consent of the complainant. The *mens rea* requires the accused to intend the touching and to know of, or to be reckless or wilfully blind as to the complainant's lack of consent: *Ewanchuk, supra,* at paras. 25 and 42. In some circumstances, it is possible for the complainant not to consent to the sexual touching but for the accused to honestly but mistakenly believe that the complainant consented. In these circumstances, the *actus reus* of the offence is established, but the *mens rea* is not.

Before the defence can be considered, there must be sufficient evidence for a reasonable trier of fact to conclude that (1) the complainant did not consent to the sexual touching, and (2) the accused nevertheless honestly but mistakenly believed that the complainant consented: see *R. v. Osolin,* [1993] 4 S.C.R. 595 (S.C.C.) at p. 648, per McLachlin J. In other words, given the evidence, it must be *possible* for a reasonable trier of fact to conclude that the *actus reus* is made out but the *mens rea* is not. In these circumstances, the defence is said to have an "air of reality", and the trier of fact, whether a judge or jury, must consider it. Conversely, where [page795] there is no air of reality to the defence, it should not be considered, as no reasonable trier of fact could acquit on that basis: see *R. v. Park*, [1995] 2 S.C.R. 836 (S.C.C.) at para. 11.

In determining whether there is an air of reality to the defence, the trial judge should consider the totality of the evidence: see *Osolin, supra,* at p. 683, per Cory J.; *Park, supra,* at para. 16. The role of the judge in making this determination was set out by Major J. in *Ewanchuk, supra,* at para. 57. He held that the judge should make "no attempt to weigh the evidence". The sole concern is "with the facial plausibility of the defence", and the judge should "avoid the risk of turning the air of reality test into a substantive evaluation of the merits of the defence". Care should be taken not to usurp the role of the trier of fact. Whenever there is a possibility that a reasonable trier of fact could acquit on the basis of the defence, it must be considered.

It is not necessary for the accused to specifically assert a belief that the complainant consented. By simply asserting that the complainant consented, either directly under oath or through counsel, the accused is also asserting a *belief* that the complainant consented: see *Park, supra*, at para. 17. However, the accused's mere assertion will not give the defence an air of reality: see *R. v. Bulmer*, (*sub nom. R. v. B.*) [1987] 1 S.C.R. 782 (S.C.C.) at p. 790.

While this is evidence of a belief in consent, it is not sufficient evidence of an *honest but mistaken* belief in consent. Sexual assault is not a crime that is generally committed by accident: see *Pappajohn*, at p. 155, *per* Dickson J.; *Osolin*, at pp. 685-86, *per* Cory J. In most cases, the issue will be simply one of "consent or no consent", and there will be only one of two possibilities. The first is that the complainant consented, in which case there is no *actus reus*. The second is that the complainant did not consent, and the accused had subjective knowledge of this fact. Here, the *actus reus* [page796] is made out, and the *mens rea* follows straightforwardly.

For example, suppose the complainant and the accused relay diametrically opposed stories. The complainant alleges a brutal sexual assault and vigorous resistance, whereas the accused claims consensual intercourse. Suppose further that it is impossible to splice together the evidence to create a third version of events in which the accused honestly but mistakenly believed the complainant consented. In such circumstances, the trial becomes, essentially, a pure question of credibility. If the complainant is believed, the *actus reus* is made out and the *mens rea* follows straightforwardly. If the accused is believed, or if there is a reasonable doubt as to the complainant's version of events, there is no *actus reus*. There is no third possibility of an honest but mistaken belief in consent, notwithstanding the accused's assertion that the complainant consented: *Park, supra*, at paras. 25-26.

Although the accused's mere assertion that the complainant consented will not be sufficient evidence to raise the defence, the requisite evidence may nevertheless come from the accused: see *Park, supra*, at pp. 852-53, paras. 19-20, per L'Heureux-Dubé J.; *Osolin, supra*, at pp. 686-87, *per* Cory J., and pp. 649-50, *per* McLachlin J. It may also come from the complainant, other sources, or a combination thereof. In *R. v. Esau*, [1997] 2 S.C.R. 777 (S.C.C.). McLachlin J., dissenting in the result, accurately conveyed the nature of this evidence at para. 63:

> There must be evidence not only of non-consent and belief in consent, but in addition evidence capable of explaining how the accused could honestly have mistaken the complainant's lack of consent as consent. Otherwise, the defence cannot reasonably arise. There must, in short, be evidence of a situation of ambiguity in which the accused could honestly have misapprehended that the complainant was consenting to the sexual activity in question.

Finally, the court has held that there will be no air of reality where the evidence shows that the accused was reckless or wilfully blind as to whether the complainant consented. In those circumstances, the accused has subjectively adverted to the absence of consent, and therefore cannot have an *honest* but mistaken belief that the complainant consented.

I note that the appellant was charged with offences allegedly committed prior to the introduction of s. 273.2 in August of 1992. Consequently, the statutory amendments to the defence of honest but mistaken belief in consent do not apply to this appeal.

PROBLEM

The accused was charged with the sexual assault of V, a 15-year-old girl. V and her young friend, T, had willingly gone with the accused and another man, both aged 28. The men had picked them up in the accused's car at 1:30 a.m. The accused drove to a parking lot where the four consumed some beer. The other man kissed V in the back seat. They then went to a second parking lot, where the two girls exchanged seats at the request of the other man. They drove to a third lot, where the accused had sexual intercourse with V. The accused then drove the two girls to T's home. V testified that she resisted the accused throughout. She said she told him no during intercourse and tried to push him away. She testified that, although the accused was not violent and the windows were open and the doors unlocked, she was afraid to scream. V stated that when they arrived at T's apartment, the accused hugged her. V said that it was possible that she had hugged him back, before saying "bye". When asked by counsel for the accused why, on returning to T's apartment building, she didn't run into the apartment with T to escape, she stated that she didn't because she didn't want the men "to know that anything was wrong". The accused testified that V had been a willing partner while they mutually kissed and touched each other and that he climbed over the gear shift onto her side of the car after she touched his leg and penis. He stated that V hugged him before she left the car. The accused stated that he gave a slip of paper to T on which he had written his name and telephone number before she and V switched places in the car. He also argued that, in light of V's denial that she had consented, circumstances were such that he had entertained an honest but mistaken belief in consent. The trial judge put both defences to the jury. The accused was acquitted.

Was there an air of reality to the mistaken belief defence? Compare *Livermore*, [1995] 4 S.C.R. 123, 43 C.R. (4th) 1, 102 C.C.C. (3d) 212 (S.C.C.) and *Esau*, [1997] 2 S.C.R. 777, 7 C.R. (5th) 357, 116 C.C.C. (3d) 289 (S.C.C.).

In *Livermore* a new trial was ordered on the basis of misdirections on the issue of consent. In sole dissent on this point, Major J. concluded as follows:

> The circumstances giving rise to the complaint were decisive in this case. The alleged sexual assault took place in the bucket seat of a sports car. The cramped quarters were such that on the facts of this case some co-operation, if not the consent, of the complainant was necessary for the alleged offence to have occurred. This was consistent with the accused's testimony and inconsistent with that of the complainant. The errors of the trial judge such as they were would not have changed the result.

What do you think of Major J.'s reasoning?

SUSAN ESTRICH, TEACHING RAPE LAW

(1992), 102 Yale L.J. 509

I know many students, and even a few professors, who believe that the women are always right and the men are always wrong; that if she didn't consent fully and voluntarily, it is rape, no matter what she said or did, or what he did or did not realize. Everything about his past should be admitted, and nothing about hers. And that's what they want to hear in class.

This kind of orthodoxy is not only bad educationally but, in the case of rape, it also misses the point. Society is not so orthodox in its views. There is a debate going on in courthouses and prosecutors' offices, and around coffee machines and dinner tables, about whether Mike Tyson was guilty or not, and whether William Kennedy Smith ever should have been prosecuted; about when women should be believed, and what counts as consent. There's a debate going on in America as to what is reasonable when it comes to sex. Turn on the radio and you will hear it. To silence that debate in the classroom is to remove the classroom from reality, and to make ourselves irrelevant. It may be hard for some students, but ultimately the only way to change things — and that's usually the goal of those who find the discussions most difficult — is to confront the issues squarely, not to pretend that they don't exist. Besides, the purpose of education, in my classes anyway, is to prepare our students to participate in the controversies that animate the law, not to provide them with a shelter from reality.

. . . .

When I first started teaching rape, the hard questions were whether and when "no means yes," whether nonconsent meant more than saying no, and whether force required more than a push onto the bed and a heavy caress. In those days, it was possible to argue that both the man and the woman in a typical acquaintance rape case were telling the truth: that she said no and did not consent, and that he thought he was engaging in consensual intercourse. The question was not just who to believe, but what standard to apply — male or female, objective or subjective — and how to define it. Is the reasonable man the average man, or the man most reasonable women would like to date? And who is the reasonable woman?

Today, the old questions seem a little easier, but there is a new set that is, in many respects, even more difficult. In the William Kennedy Smith trial, for example, the defense lawyers took pains to point out that they were not arguing that no means yes, or that necking constitutes presumptive consent or even that going to a man's house in the middle of the night entitles him to make any assumptions. Rather, they argued that the complainant said yes.

The Smith defence strategy, I think, reflects an accurate assumption that judges and juries these days are less inclined to accept male conduct that only a few years ago was tolerated as understandably macho. I don't find as many students in my classes these days who believe that a man has the right to ignore the fact that a woman is saying no. And I don't think the reason for this change is that feminists have defined what is "politically correct" in the classroom; I think instead that most of my students, male and female, actually believe that a man should listen to a woman's words, and take her at her word.

This shift in our thinking about the elements of culpability leaves credibility as the only defense game in town. After all, rapes rarely take place in front of witnesses. If no doesn't mean yes, if bruises aren't necessary, and if no unusual force is required, then in many cases there's not going to be much physical evidence to rely on. She gives her version and he gives his. If you are the defense attorney, your job is to convince the jury not to believe what she says — which means that the only way to defend may be to destroy the credibility of the victim.

The key question in many acquaintance rape cases today thus becomes not what counts as rape but rather what we need to know about the victim, and the defendant, in order to decide who is telling the truth.

. . . .

It is one thing to exclude evidence of a woman's sexual past or of psychiatric treatment when she has been beaten and burned; it is easy to argue there that admitting such evidence does almost nothing except to deter legitimate prosecutions and to victimize the victim. But it is surely a harder case when there have been no weapons and no bruises, and when the man's liberty depends on convincing a jury not to believe a woman who appears at least superficially credible.

Many of the traditional rules of rape liability were premised on the notion that women lie; Wigmore went so far as to view rape complainants as fundamentally deranged. I don't buy that for a moment nor, I expect, do most of my students. Yet even if only one of a hundred men, or one of a thousand, is falsely accused, the question is still how we can protect that man's right to disprove his guilt. Assume for a moment, I tell my students, that it was you, or your brother, or your boyfriend or your son, who was accused of rape by a casual date with a history of psychiatric problems, or by a woman he met in a bar who had a history of one-night stands. Would you exclude that evidence? What else can the man do to avoid a felony conviction and a ruined life? Where do you draw the line? But if you don't exclude the evidence, will some women as a result become unrapable, at least as a matter of law? That is, will women who have histories of mental instability or of "promiscuity" ever be able to convince juries who know those histories that they really were raped? Similar issues arise with respect to the man's credibility. The first question many people asked when Anita Hill charged that Clarence Thomas had harassed her was whether there were other women who had been similarly mistreated. The first significant ruling in the Smith case, indeed the decisive ruling, was the judge's pretrial decision to exclude the testimony of three other women who claimed that they had been sexually abused by the defendant. If the testimony of only one woman cannot be believed — unless she is a Sunday school teacher, camera in hand, as Desiree Washington was, and the defendant is a black man who has made a host of inconsistent statements, as Mike Tyson did — is it fair to exclude the testimony of the other women? And if the testimony is not excluded, do we risk convicting a defendant for being a bad man, indeed being a rapist, rather than committing the particular act charged?

One answer is to say that we need symmetry: exclude all the evidence about both of them. That's the approach the judge followed in the William Kennedy Smith case. On the surface, it is neat and appealing. The only problem is that it's a false symmetry that is being enforced. After all, evidence that a man has abused other women is much more probative of rape than evidence that a woman has had consensual sex with other men is probative of consent. Most women have had sexual experiences, and unless those experiences fall into some kind of unusual pattern, the mere fact that a woman has had lovers tells us almost nothing about whether she consented on the particular occasion that she is charging as rape. But won't we all look at a defendant differently if three other women have also come forward to say they were abused? The danger with such evidence is not that it proves so little, but that it may prove too much. Symmetry won't get you out of this hole, at least not in my classroom.

Thus, even if most students can agree these days that no means no, and that force can be established if you push a woman down, there's very little agreement about what we need to know about her or him before deciding whether she in fact said yes or no, and whether he actually pushed her down or just lay down with her. The consensus on what counts as rape is more apparent than real. These days, society's continued ambivalence towards acquaintance rape is increasingly being expressed in evidentiary rules and standards of credibility rather than in the definitions of force and consent. The questions have shifted; answering them is no easier.

R. v. SEABOYER; R. v. GAYME

[1991] 2 S.C.R. 577, 7 C.R. (4th) 117, 66 C.C.C. (3d) 321,
1991 CarswellOnt 1022, 1991 CarswellOnt 109

The rape shield provisions inserted into the *Criminal Code* in 1983 were ss. 276 and 277. The former section dealt with evidence of the complainant's sexual activity as referable to the issue of consent and the latter as referable to the credibility of the complainant. The court, by a majority of 7:2, decided s. 277 was constitutional but not s. 276.

MCLACHLIN J. (LAMER C.J.C., LAFOREST, SOPINKA, CORY, STEVENSON and IACOBUCCI JJ. concurring): — These cases raise the issue of the constitutionality of ss. 276 and 277 of the *Criminal Code*, R.S.C. 1985, c. C-46 (formerly ss. 246.6 and 246.7), commonly known as the "rape-shield" provisions. The provisions restrict the right of the defence on a trial for a sexual offence to cross-examine and lead evidence of a complainant's sexual conduct on other occasions. The question is whether these restrictions offend the guarantees accorded to an accused person by the *Canadian Charter of Rights and Freedoms*.

My conclusion is that one of the sections in issue, s. 276, offends the *Charter*. While its purpose — the abolition of outmoded, sexist-based use of sexual conduct evidence — is laudable, its effect goes beyond what is required or justified by that purpose. At the same time, striking down s. 276 does not imply reversion to the old common law rules, which permitted evidence of the complainant's sexual conduct even though it might have no probative value to the issues on the case and, on the contrary, might mislead the jury. Instead, relying on the basic principles that actuate our law of evidence, the courts must seek a middle way that offers the maximum protection to the complainant compatible with the maintenance of the accused's fundamental right to a fair trial.

. . . ..

I deal first with *Seaboyer*. The accused was charged with sexual assault of a woman with whom he had been drinking in a bar. On the preliminary inquiry the judge refused to allow the accused to cross-examine the complainant on her sexual conduct on other occasions. The appellant contends that he should have been permitted to cross-examine as to other acts of sexual intercourse which may have caused bruises, and other aspects of the complainant's condition which the Crown had put in evidence. While the theory of the defence has not been detailed at this early stage, such evidence might arguably be relevant to consent, since it might provide other explanations for the physical evidence tendered by the Crown in support of the use of force against the complainant.

The *Gayme* case arose in different circumstances. The complainant was 15, the appellant 18. They were friends. The Crown alleges that the appellant sexually assaulted her at his school. The defence, relying on the defences of consent and honest belief in consent, contends that there was no assault and that the complainant was the sexual aggressor. In pursuance of this defence, the appellant at the preliminary inquiry sought to cross-examine and present evidence of prior and subsequent sexual conduct of the complainant.

. . . .

It should be noted that the admissibility of the evidence sought to be tendered in the two cases is not at issue. In neither case did the preliminary inquiry judge consider whether the evidence would have been relevant or admissible in the absence of ss. 276 or 277 of the *Criminal Code.*

RELEVANT LEGISLATION

Criminal Code, s. 276:

276. (1) In proceedings in respect of an offence under section 271, 272 or 273, no evidence shall be adduced by or on behalf of the accused concerning the sexual activity of the complainant with any person other than the accused unless
> (*a*) it is evidence that rebuts evidence of the complainant's sexual activity or absence thereof that was previously adduced by the prosecution;
> (*b*) it is evidence of specific instances of the complainant's sexual activity tending to establish the identity of the person who had sexual contact with the complainant on the occasion set out in the charge; or
> (*c*) it is evidence of sexual activity that took place on the same occasion as the sexual activity that forms the subject-matter of the charge, where that evidence relates to the consent that the accused alleges he believed was given by the complainant.

(2) No evidence is admissible under paragraph (1)(*c*) unless
> (*a*) reasonable notice in writing has been given to the prosecutor by or on behalf of the accused of his intention to adduce the evidence together with particulars of the evidence sought to be adduced; and
> (*b*) a copy of the notice has been filed with the clerk of the court.

(3) No evidence is admissible under subsection (1) unless the judge, provincial court judge or justice, after holding a hearing in which the jury and the members of the public are excluded and in which the complainant is not a compellable witness, is satisfied that the requirements of this section are met.

Criminal Code, s. 277:

277. In proceedings in respect of an offence under section 271, 272 or 273, evidence of sexual reputation, whether general or specific, is not admissible for the purpose of challenging or supporting the credibility of the complainant.

. . . .

Everyone, under s. 7 of the *Charter*, has the right to life, liberty and security of person and the right not to be deprived thereof except in accordance with the principles of fundamental justice.

. . . .

The real issue under s. 7 is whether the potential for deprivation of liberty flowing from ss. 276 and 277 takes place in a manner that conforms to the principles of fundamental justice.

. . . .

All the parties agree that the right to a fair trial — one which permits the trier of fact to get at the truth and properly and fairly dispose of the case — is a principle of fundamental justice. Nor is there any dispute that encouraging reporting of sexual offences and protection of the complainant's privacy are legitimate goals, provided they do not interfere with the primary objective of a fair trial. Where the parties part company is on the issue of whether ss. 276 and 277 of the *Criminal Code* in fact infringe the right to a fair trial. The supporters of the legislation urge that it furthers the right to a fair trial by eliminating evidence of little or no worth and considerable prejudice. The appellants, on the other hand, say that the legislation goes too far and in fact eliminates relevant evidence which should be admitted notwithstanding the possibility of prejudice.

. . . .

This court has affirmed the trial judges' power to exclude Crown evidence the prejudicial effect of which outweighs its probative value in a criminal case, but a narrower formula than that articulated by McCormick has emerged. In *Wray, supra*, at p. 293, [[1971] S.C.R.] the court stated that the judge may exclude only "evidence gravely prejudicial to the accused, the admissibility of which is tenuous, and whose probative force in relation to the main issue before the court is trifling". More recently, in *R. v. Sweitzer*, [1982] 1 S.C.R. 949, at p. 953, an appeal involving a particularly difficult brand of circumstantial evidence offered by the Crown, the court said that "admissibility will depend upon the probative effect of the evidence balanced against the prejudice caused to the accused by its admission." In *Morris, supra*, at p. 193 [[1983] 2 S.C.R.], the court without mentioning *Sweitzer* cited the narrower *Wray* formula. But in *R. c. Potvin*, [1989] 1 S.C.R. 525, 68 C.R. (3d) 193, 47 C.C.C. (3d) 289, La Forest J. (Dickson C.J.C. concurring) affirmed in general terms "the rule that the trial Judge may exclude admissible evidence if its prejudicial effect substantially outweighs its probative value" (p. 531 [S.C.R.]).

I am of the view that the more appropriate description of the general power of a judge to exclude relevant evidence on the ground of prejudice is that articulated in *Sweitzer* and generally accepted throughout the common law world.

. . . .

The Canadian cases cited above all pertain to evidence tendered by the Crown against the accused. The question arises whether the same power to exclude exists with respect to defence evidence. Canadian courts, like courts in most common-law jurisdictions, have been extremely cautious in restricting the power of the accused to call evidence in his or her defence, a reluctance founded in the fundamental tenet of our judicial system that an innocent person must not be convicted. It follows from this that the prejudice must substantially outweigh the value of the evidence before a judge can exclude evidence relevant to a defence allowed by law.

. . . .

Section 277 excludes evidence of sexual reputation for the purpose of challenging or supporting the credibility of the plaintiff. The idea that a complainant's credibility might be affected by whether she has had other sexual experience is today universally discredited. There is no logical or practical link between a woman's sexual reputation and whether she is a truthful witness. It follows that the evidence excluded by s. 277 can serve no legitimate purpose in the trial. Section 277, by limiting the exclusion to a purpose which is clearly illegitimate, does not touch evidence which may be tendered for valid purposes, and hence does not infringe the right to a fair trial.

I turn then to s. 276. Section 276, unlike s. 277, does not condition exclusion on use of the evidence for an illegitimate purpose. Rather, it constitutes a blanket exclusion, subject to three exceptions — rebuttal evidence, evidence going to identity, and evidence relating to consent to sexual activity on the same occasion as the trial incident. The question is whether this may exclude evidence which is relevant to the defence and the probative value of which is not substantially outweighed by the potential prejudice to the trial process. To put the matter another way, can it be said a priori, as the Attorney-General for Ontario contends, that any and all evidence excluded by s. 276 will necessarily be of such trifling weight in relation to the prejudicial effect of the evidence that it may fairly be excluded?

In my view, the answer to this question must be negative. The Canadian and American jurisprudence affords numerous examples of evidence of sexual conduct which would be excluded by s. 276 but which clearly should be received in the interests of a fair trial, notwithstanding the possibility that it may divert a jury by tempting it to improperly infer consent or lack of credibility in the complainant.

Consider the defence of honest belief. It rests on the concept that the accused may honestly but mistakenly (and not necessarily reasonably) have believed that the complainant was consenting to the sexual act. If the accused can raise a reasonable doubt as to his intention on the basis that he honestly held such a belief, he is not guilty under our law and is entitled to an acquittal. The basis of the accused's honest belief in the complainant's consent may be sexual acts performed by the complainant at some other time or place. Yet s. 276 would preclude the accused leading such evidence.

Another category of evidence eliminated by s. 276 relates to the right of the defence to attack the credibility of the complainant on the ground that the complainant was biased or had motive to fabricate the evidence. In *State v. Jalo*, 27 Or. App. 845, 557 P.2d 1359 (1976), a father accused of sexual acts with his young daughter sought to present evidence that the source of the accusation was his earlier discovery of the fact that the girl and her brother were engaged in intimate relations. The defence contended that when the father stopped the relationship, the daughter, out of animus toward him, accused him of the act. The father sought to lead this evidence in support of his defence that the charges were a concoction motivated by animus. Notwithstanding its clear relevance, this evidence would be excluded by s. 276. The respondent submits that the damage caused by its exclusion would not be great, because all that would be forbidden would be evidence of the sexual activities of the children, and the father could still testify that his daughter was angry with him. But surely the father's chance of convincing the jury of the validity of his defence would be greatly diminished if he were reduced to saying, in effect, "My daughter was angry with me, but I can't say why or produce any corroborating evidence." As noted above, to deny a defendant the building blocks of his defence is often to deny him the defence itself.

Other examples abound. Evidence of sexual activity excluded by s. 276 may be relevant to explain the physical conditions on which the Crown relies to establish intercourse or the use of force, such as semen, pregnancy, injury or disease — evidence which may go to consent. . . . In the case of young complainants, where there may be a tendency to believe their story on the ground that the detail of their account must have come from the alleged encounter, it may be relevant to show other activity which provides an explanation for the knowledge.

. . . .

Even evidence as to pattern of conduct may on occasion be relevant. Since this use of evidence of prior sexual conduct draws upon the inference that prior conduct infers similar subsequent conduct, it closely resembles the prohibited use of the evidence and must be carefully scrutinized. . . . Yet such evidence might be admissible in non-sexual cases under the similar fact rule. Is it fair, then, to deny it to an accused, merely because the trial relates to a sexual offence?

. . . .

These examples leave little doubt that s. 276 has the potential to exclude evidence of critical relevance to the defence. Can it honestly be said, as the Attorney-General for Ontario contends, that the value of such evidence will always be trifling when compared with its potential to mislead the jury? I think not. The examples show that the evidence may well be of great importance to getting at the truth and determining whether the accused is guilty or innocent under the law — the ultimate aim of the trial process. They demonstrate that s. 276, enacted for the purpose of helping judges and juries arrive at the proper and just verdict in the particular case, overshoots the mark, with the result that it may have the opposite effect of impeding them in discovering the truth.

. . . .

2. Is s. 276 Saved by s. 1 of the *Charter*?

Is s. 276 of the *Criminal Code* justified in a free and democratic society, notwithstanding the fact that it may lead to infringements of the *Charter*?

The first step under s. 1 is to consider whether the legislation addresses a pressing and substantial objective.

. . . .

The second requirement under s. 1 is that the infringement of rights be proportionate to the pressing objective. . . . In creating exceptions to the exclusion of evidence of the sexual activity of the complainant on other occasions, Parliament correctly recognized that justice requires a measured approach, one which admits evidence which is truly relevant to the defence notwithstanding potential prejudicial effect. Yet Parliament at the same time excluded other evidence of sexual conduct which might be equally relevant to a legitimate defence and which appears to pose no greater danger of prejudice than the exceptions it recognizes. To the extent the section excludes relevant defence evidence whose value is not clearly outweighed by the danger it presents, the section is overbroad.

I turn finally to the third aspect of the proportionality requirement — the balance between the importance of the objective and the injurious effect of the legislation. The objective of the legislation, as discussed above, is to eradicate the erroneous inferences from evidence of other sexual encounters that the complainant is more likely to have consented to the sexual act in issue or less likely to be telling the truth. The subsidiary aims are to promote fairer trials and increased reporting of sexual offences and to minimize the invasion of the complainant's privacy. In this way the personal security of women and their right to equal benefit and protection of the law are enhanced. The effect of the legislation, on the other hand, is to exclude relevant defence evidence, the value of which outweighs its potential prejudice. As indicated in the discussion of s. 7, all parties agree that a provision which rules out probative defence evidence which is not clearly outweighed by the prejudice it may cause to the trial strikes the wrong balance between the rights of complainants and the rights of the accused. The line must be drawn short of the point where it results in an unfair trial and the possible conviction of an innocent person. Section 276 fails this test.

I conclude that s. 276 is not saved by s. 1 of the *Charter*.

. . . .

4.   What Follows From Striking Down s. 276?

The first question is whether the striking down of s. 276 revives the old common-law rules of evidence permitting liberal and often inappropriate reception of evidence of the complainant's sexual conduct.

. . . .

The answer to this question is no. The rules in question are common-law rules. Like other common-law rules of evidence, they must be adapted to conform to current reality. As all counsel on these appeals accepted, the reality in 1991 is that evidence of sexual conduct and reputation in itself cannot be regarded as logically probative of either the complainant's credibility or consent. Although they still may inform the thinking of many, the twin myths which s. 276 sought to eradicate are just that — myths — and have no place in a rational and just system of law. It follows that the old rules which permitted evidence of sexual conduct and condoned invalid inferences from it solely for these purposes have no place in our law.

The inquiry as to what the law is in the absence of s. 276 of the *Code* is thus remitted to consideration of the fundamental principles governing the trial process and the reception of evidence. Harking back to Thayer's maxim, relevant evidence should be admitted, and irrelevant evidence excluded, subject to the qualification that the value of the evidence must outweigh its potential prejudice to the conduct of a fair trial. Moreover, the focus must be not on the evidence itself, but on the use to which it is put. As Professor Galvin puts it, our aim is "to abolish the outmoded, sexist-based use of sexual conduct evidence while permitting other uses of such evidence to remain": at p. 809 [70 Minn. L. Rev.].

This definition of the problem suggests an approach which abolishes illegitimate uses and inferences, while preserving legitimate uses. There is wide agreement that the approach of a general exclusion supplemented by categories of exceptions is bound to fail because of the impossibility of predicting in advance what evidence may be relevant in a particular case: see Galvin, Doherty, and Elliott. On the other hand, judges are not free to act on whim. As Professor Vivian Berger puts it in her article "Man's Trial, Woman's Tribulation: Rape Cases in the Courtroom" (1977), 77 Colum. L. Rev. 1, at p. 69:

> The problem is to chart a course between inflexible legislative rules and wholly untrammelled judicial discretion: The former threatens the rights of defendants; the latter may ignore the needs of complainants.

Professor Galvin, after a comprehensive review of the various approaches to rape-shield legislation which have been adopted in different jurisdictions, proposes a prohibition on illegitimate uses of the evidence, combined with case-by-case judgment exercised with the aid of guidelines.

. . . .

Galvin's proposal, with some modification, reflects an appropriate response to the problem of avoiding illegitimate inferences from evidence of the complainant's sexual conduct, while preserving the general right to a fair trial. It is, moreover, a response which is open to trial judges in the absence of legislation. It reflects, in essence, an application of the fundamental common-law notions which govern the reception of evidence on trials. The general prohibition on improper use of evidence of sexual conduct reflects the fact that it is always open to a judge to warn against using a particular piece of evidence for an inference on an issue for which that evidence has no probative force. Similarly, the mandate to the judge to determine when the evidence may be properly receivable is a reflection of the basic function of the trial judge of determining the relevance of evidence and whether it should be received, bearing in mind the balance between its probative value and its potential prejudice.

As for the procedures which should govern the determination of whether the sexual conduct evidence should be admitted, Galvin proposes a written motion followed by an in camera hearing (p. 904). The devices of a preliminary affidavit and an in camera hearing are designed to minimize the invasion of the complainant's privacy. If the affidavit does not show the evidence to be relevant, it will not be heard at all. Where this threshold is met, the evidence will be heard in camera so that, in the event the judge finds its value is outweighed by its potential prejudice, it will not enter the public domain. Such procedures do not require legislation. It has always been open to the courts to devise such procedures as may be necessary to ensure a fair trial. The requirements of a *voir dire* before a confession can be admitted, for example, is judge-made law.

While accepting the premise and the general thrust of Galvin's proposal, I suggest certain modifications. There seems little purpose in having separate rules for the use of sexual conduct evidence for illegitimate inferences of consent and credibility in the Canadian context. Again, I question whether evidence of other sexual conduct with the accused should automatically be admissible in all cases; sometimes the value of such evidence might be little or none. The word "complainant" is more compatible with the presumption of innocence of the accused than the word "victim". Professor Galvin's reference to the defence of reasonable belief in consent must be adapted to meet Canadian law, which does not require reasonableness. And the need to warn the jury clearly against improper uses of the evidence should be emphasized, in my view.

In the absence of legislation, it is open to this court to suggest guidelines for the reception and use of sexual conduct evidence. Such guidelines should be seen for what they are — an attempt to describe the consequences of the application of the general rules of evidence governing relevance and the reception of evidence — and not as judicial legislation cast in stone.

In my view, the trial judge under this new regime, shoulders a dual responsibility. First, the judge must assess with a high degree of sensitivity whether the evidence proffered by the defence meets the test of demonstrating a degree of relevance which outweighs the damages and disadvantages presented by the admission of such evidence. The examples presented earlier suggest that while cases where such evidence will carry sufficient probative value will exist, they will be exceptional. The trial judge must ensure that evidence is tendered for a legitimate purpose, and that it logically supports a defence. The fishing expeditions which unfortunately did occur in the past should not be permitted. The trial judge's discretion must be exercised to ensure that neither the *in camera* procedure nor the trial become forums for demeaning and abusive conduct by defence counsel.

The trial judge's second responsibility will be to take special care to ensure that, in the exceptional case where circumstances demand that such evidence be permitted, the jury is fully and properly instructed as to its appropriate use. The jurors must be cautioned that they should not draw impermissible inferences from evidence of previous sexual activity. While such evidence may be tendered for a purpose logically probative of the defence to be presented, it may be important to remind jurors that they not allow the allegations of past sexual activity to lead them to the view that the complainant is less worthy of belief, or was more likely to have consented for that reason. It is hoped that a sensitive and responsive exercise of discretion by the judiciary will reduce and even eliminate the concerns which provoked legislation such as s. 276, while at the same time preserving the right of an accused to a fair trial.

I would summarize the applicable principles as follows:

1. On a trial for a sexual offence, evidence that the complainant has engaged in consensual sexual conduct on other occasions (including past sexual conduct with the accused) is not admissible solely to support the inference that the complainant is by reason of such conduct:
   (a) more likely to have consented to the sexual conduct at issue in the trial;
   (b) less worthy of belief as a witness.

2. Evidence of consensual sexual conduct on the part of the complainant may be admissible for purposes other than an inference relating to the consent or credibility of the complainant, where it possesses probative value on an issue in the trial and where that probative value is not substantially outweighed by the danger of unfair prejudice flowing from the evidence.

By way of illustration only, and not by way of limitation, the following are examples of admissible evidence:

(A) Evidence of specific instances of sexual conduct tending to prove that a person other than the accused caused the physical consequences of the rape alleged by the prosecution;

(B) Evidence of sexual conduct tending to prove bias or motive to fabricate on the part of the complainant;
(C) Evidence of prior sexual conduct, known to the accused at the time of the act charged, tending to prove that the accused believed that the complainant was consenting to the act charged (without laying down absolute rules, normally one would expect some proximity in time between the conduct that is alleged to have given rise to an honest belief and the conduct charged);
(D) Evidence of prior sexual conduct which meets the requirements for the reception of similar act evidence, bearing in mind that such evidence cannot be used illegitimately merely to show that the complainant consented or is an unreliable witness.
(E) Evidence tending to rebut proof introduced by the prosecution regarding the complainant's sexual conduct;

3. Before evidence of consensual sexual conduct on the part of a victim is received, it must be established on a *voir dire* (which may be held in camera) by affidavit or the testimony of the accused or third parties, that the proposed use of the evidence of other sexual conduct is legitimate.
4. Where evidence that the complainant has engaged in sexual conduct on other occasions is admitted on a jury trial, the judge should warn the jury against inferring from the evidence of the conduct itself, either that the complainant might have consented to the act alleged, or that the complainant is less worthy of credit.

. . . .

L'HEUREUX-DUBÉ J. (GONTHIER J. concurring) (dissenting in part): —

[She agreed to allow the appeal on jurisdictional grounds but held that, in any event, there had been no *Charter* violation and that any violation could have been justified under section 1.]

. . . .

Sexual assault is not like any other crime. In the vast majority of cases the target is a woman and the perpetrator is a man. . . . Unlike other crimes of a violent nature, it is for the most part unreported. Yet, by all accounts, women are victimized at an alarming rate, and there is some evidence that an already frighteningly high rate of sexual assault is on the increase. The prosecution and conviction rates for sexual assault are among the lowest for all violent crimes. Perhaps more than any other crime, the fear and constant reality of sexual assault affects how women conduct their lives and how they define their relationship with the larger society. Sexual assault is not like any other crime.

. . . .

There are a number of reasons why women may not report their victimization: fear of reprisal, fear of a continuation of their trauma at the hands of the police and the criminal justice system, fear of a perceived loss of status and lack of desire to report due to the typical effects of sexual assault such as depression, self-blame or loss of self-esteem. Although all of the reasons for failing to report are significant and important, more relevant to the present inquiry are the numbers of victims who choose not to bring their victimization to the attention of the authorities due to their perception that the institutions, with which they would have to become involved, will view their victimization in a stereotypical and biased fashion.

The woman who comes to the attention of the authorities has her victimization measured against the current rape mythologies, *i.e.*, who she should be in order to be recognized as having been, in the eyes of the law, raped; who her attacker must be in order to be recognized, in the eyes of the law, as a potential rapist; and how injured she must be in order to be believed. If her victimization does not fit the myths, it is unlikely that an arrest will be made or a conviction obtained. As prosecutors and police often suggest, in an attempt to excuse their application of stereotype, there is no point in directing cases toward the justice system if juries and judges will acquit on the basis of their stereotypical perceptions of the "supposed victim" and her "supposed" victimization.

. . . .

More specifically, police rely in large measure upon popular conceptions of sexual assault in order to classify incoming cases as "founded" or "unfounded". It would appear as though most forces have developed a convenient shorthand regarding their decisions to proceed in any given case. This shorthand is composed of popular myth regarding rapists (distinguishing them from men as a whole), and stereotype about women's character and sexuality. Holmstrom and Burgess, at pp. 174-199, conveniently set out and explain the most common of these myths and stereotypes:

1. *Struggle and Force: Woman as Defender of Her Honour.* There is a myth that a woman cannot be raped against her will, that if she really wants to prevent a rape she can.

The prosecution attempts to show that she did struggle, or had no opportunity to do so, while the defence attempts to show that she did not.

Women know that there is no response on their part that will assure their safety. The experience and knowledge of women is borne out by the *Canadian Urban Victimization Survey: Female Victims of Crime* (1985). At p. 7 of the report, the authors note:

> Sixty percent of those who tried reasoning with their attackers, and 60 percent of those who resisted actively by fighting or using weapon [sic] were injured. Every sexual assault incident is unique and so many factors are unknown (physical size of victims and offenders, verbal or physical threats, etc.) that no single course of action can be recommended unqualifiedly.

2. *Knowing the Defendant: The Rapist as a Stranger.* There is a myth that rapists are strangers who leap out of bushes to attack their victims. . . . [T]he

view that interaction between friends or between relatives does not result in rape is prevalent.

The defence uses the existence of a relationship between the parties to blame the victim. . . .

3. *Sexual Reputation: The Madonna-Whore Complex.* . . . [W]omen . . . are categorized into one-dimensional types. They are maternal or they are sexy. They are good or they are bad. They are madonnas or they are whores.

The legal rules use these distinctions.

4. *General Character: Anything Not 100 Percent Proper and Respectable.* . . . Being on welfare or drinking or drug use could be used to discredit anyone, but where women are involved, these issues are used to imply that the woman consented to sex with the defendant or that she contracted to have sex for money.

5. *Emotionality of Females.* Females are assumed to be "more emotional" than males. The expectation is that if a woman is raped, she will get hysterical during the event and she will be visibly upset afterward. If she is able to "retain her cool," then people assume that "nothing happened".

6. *Reporting Rape.* Two conflicting expectations exist concerning the reporting of rape. One is that if a woman is raped she will be too upset and ashamed to report it, and hence most of the time this crime goes unreported. The other is that if a woman is raped, she will be so upset that she will report it. Both expectations exist simultaneously.

7. *Woman as Fickle and Full of Spite.* Another stereotype is that the feminine character is especially filled with malice. Woman is seen as fickle and as seeking revenge on past lovers.

8. *The Female Under Surveillance: Is the Victim Trying to Escape Punishment?* . . . It is assumed that the female's sexual behaviour, depending on her age, is under the surveillance of her parents or her husband, and also more generally of the community. Thus, the defense argues, if a woman says she was raped, it must be because she consented to sex that she was not supposed to have. She got caught, and now she wants to get back in the good graces of whomever's surveillance she is under.

9. *Disputing That Sex Occurred.* That females fantasize rape is another common stereotype. Females are assumed to make up stories that sex occurred when in fact nothing happened. . . . Similarly, women are thought to fabricate the sexual activity not as part of a fantasy life, but out of spite.

10. *Stereotype of the Rapist.* One stereotype of the rapist is that of a stranger who leaps out of the bushes to attack his victim and later abruptly leaves her. . . .

[S]tereotypes of the rapist can be used to blame the victim. She tells what he did. And because it often does not match what jurors *think* rapists do, his behaviour is held against her.

. . . .

This list of stereotypical conceptions about women and sexual assault is by no means exhaustive. Like most stereotypes, they operate as a way, however flawed, of understanding the world and, like most such constructs, operate at a level of consciousness that makes it difficult to root them out and confront them directly. This mythology finds its way into the decisions of the police regarding their "founded"/"unfounded" categorization, operates in the mind of the Crown when deciding whether or not to prosecute, influences a judge's or juror's perception of guilt or innocence of the accused and the "goodness" or "badness" of the victim, and finally, has carved out a niche in both the evidentiary and substantive law governing the trial of the matter.

. . . .

Absolutely pivotal to an understanding of the nature and purpose of the provisions and constitutional questions at issue in this case is the realization of how widespread the stereotypes and myths about rape are, notwithstanding their inaccuracy.

The appellants argue that we, as a society, have become more enlightened, that prosecutors, police, judges and jurors can be trusted to perform their tasks without recourse to discriminatory views about women manifested through rape myth. Unfortunately, social science evidence suggests otherwise. Rape myths still present formidable obstacles for complainants in their dealings with the very system charged with discovering the truth. Their experience in this regard is illustrated by the following remarks of surprisingly recent vintage:

> Women who say no do not always mean no. It is not just a question of saying no, it is a question of how she says it, how she shows and makes it clear. If she doesn't want it she has only to keep her legs shut and she would not get it without force and there would be marks of force being used.

> (Judge David Wild, Cambridge Crown Court, 1982, quoted in Elizabeth Sheehy, "Canadian Judges and the Law of Rape: Should the *Charter* Insulate Bias?" (1989) 21 Ottawa L. Rev. 741, at p. 741.)

> Unless you have no worldly experience at all, you'll agree that women occasionally resist at first but later give in to either persuasion or their own instincts.

> (Judge Frank Allen, Manitoba Provincial Court, 1984, quoted in Sheehy at p. 741.)

> [I]t is easy for a man intent upon his own desires to mistake the intentions of a woman or girl who may herself be in two minds about what to do. Even if he makes no mistake it is not

unknown for a woman afterwards either to take fright or for some other reason to regret what has happened and seek to justify herself retrospectively by accusing the man of rape.

(Colin Howard, *Criminal Law*, 3d ed. (Sydney: Law Book Co., 1977), at p. 149.)

Modern psychiatrists have amply studied the behaviour of errant young girls and women coming before the courts in all sorts of cases. Their psychic complexes are multifarious, distorted partly by inherent defects, partly by diseased derangements or abnormal instincts, partly by bad social environment, partly by temporary physiological or emotional conditions. One form taken by these complexes is that of contriving false charges of sexual offenses by men.

(J.H. Wigmore, *Evidence in Trials at Common Law*, Vol. 3A, rev. J.H. Chadbourn (Boston: Little, Brown, 1970), at p. 736.)

Regrettably, these remarks demonstrate that many in society hold inappropriate stereotypical beliefs, and apply them when the opportunity presents itself.

. . . .

It is thus clear that, from the making of the initial complaint down to the determination of the issue at trial, stereotype and mythology are at work, lowering the number of reported cases, influencing police decisions to pursue the case, thereby decreasing the rates of arrest, and, finally, distorting the issues at trial and necessarily, the results. Professor Catharine MacKinnon asserts that in the United States:

It is not only that women are the principal targets of rape, which by conservative definition happens to almost half of all women at least once in their lives. It is not only that over one-third of all women are sexually molested by older trusted male family members or friends or authority figures as an early, perhaps initiatory, interpersonal sexual encounter. . . . All this documents the extent and terrain of abuse and the effectively unrestrained and systematic sexual aggression by less than one-half of the population against the other more than half. It suggests that it is basically allowed.

(Catharine MacKinnon, *Toward a Feminist Theory of the State* (Cambridge, Mass.: Harvard, University Press, 1989), at pp. 142-143.)

. . . .

Under the guise of a principled application of the legal concept of relevance, the common law allowed the accused to delve at great length into the moral character of the complainant by adducing "relevant" sexual history. The prejudicial impact of such an inquiry has already been discussed at length. The true nature and purpose of the inquiry into sexual history is revealed by the resulting prejudice and by the fact that these concepts were only applicable in respect of sexual offences and, in addition, were not deemed relevant to the credibility of the male accused.

Application of the relevance concept was not the only way in which the common law integrated stereotype and myth into trials of sexual offences. Also part of the unique body of evidentiary law surrounding sexual offences were, among other things, the doctrine of recent complaint and corroboration rules. These evidentiary concepts were also based upon stereotypes of the female complainant requiring independent evidence to support her evidence and, in addition, evidence that she raised a "hue and cry" after her assault. It is noteworthy that both recent complaint and corroboration rules formed exceptions to general rules of evidence.

. . . .

Relevance and Admissibility at Common Law and Under the Legislative Provisions

Like many of the other legal rules and principles that are brought to bear in trials of persons charged with sexual offences, the concept of relevance has been imbued with stereotypical notions of female complainants and sexual assault. That this is so is plain from the common law, which held that evidence of "unchasteness" was relevant to both consent and credibility. Any connection between the evidence sought to be adduced and the fact or matter of which it was supposedly probative must be bridged by stereotype (that "unchaste" women lie and "unchaste" women consent indiscriminately), otherwise the propositions make no sense. While some may think that these represent egregious examples of the use of stereotype, it is well to remember that relevancy determinations such as this are still being made, though the myth which drives the particular determination may be better obscured or, due to the entrenchment of these beliefs, more automatically made.

Traditional definitions of what is relevant include "whatever accords with common sense" (Peter K. McWilliams, *Canadian Criminal Evidence*, 3d ed. (Aurora, Ont.: Canada Law Book, 1990), at p. 35); "'relevant' means that any two facts to which it is applied are so related to each other that according to the common course of events one either taken by itself or in connection with other facts proves or renders probable the past, present or future existence or non-existence of the other" (Sir James Fitzjames Stephen's *Digest of the Law of Evidence* 12th ed. (London: Macmillan, 1936), art. 1), and finally Thayer's "logically probative" test with relevance as an affair of logic and not of law, a test adopted by this court in *Morris*.

. . . .

Whatever the test, be it one of experience, common sense or logic, it is a decision particularly vulnerable to the application of private beliefs. Regardless of the definition used, the content of any relevancy decision will be filled by the particular judge's experience, common sense and/or logic. For the most part there will be general agreement as to that which is relevant, and the determination will not be problematic. However, there are certain areas of inquiry where experience, common sense and logic are informed by stereotype and myth. As I have made clear, this area of the law has been particularly prone to the utilization of stereotype in determinations of relevance and, again, as was demonstrated earlier, this appears to be the unfortunate concomitant of a society which, to a large measure, holds these beliefs. It would also appear that recognition of the large role that stereotype may play in such determinations has had surprisingly little impact in this area of the law.

. . . .

Once the mythical bases of relevancy determinations in this area of the law are revealed (discussed at greater length later in these reasons), the irrelevance of most evidence of prior sexual history is clear. Nevertheless, Parliament has provided broad avenues for its admissibility in the setting out of the exceptions to the general rule in s. 246.6 (now s. 276). Moreover, *all* evidence of the complainant's previous sexual history with the accused is *prima facie* admissible under those provisions. Evidence that is excluded by these provisions is simply, in a myth- and stereotype-free decision-making context, irrelevant.

For comments on *Seaboyer* see Christine Boyle and Marilyn MacCrimmon, "*R. v. Seaboyer:* A Lost Cause?" (1992), 7 C.R. (4th) 225 and a reply by Anthony Allman in (1992), 10 C.R. (4th) 153.

Most would agree that receiving evidence of the complainant's previous sexual history on a trial of sexual assault will so prejudice the trial that the same should rarely be admitted. **Has the court drawn the proper line?**

While striking down the complainant's statutory protection, the court recognized the possibility that the then existing common-law rules could permit the inappropriate reception of evidence of the complainant's sexual conduct and the majority therefore changed the common law. The majority said it was suggesting "guidelines for the reception of sexual conduct evidence" and these were not to be seen as "judicial legislation cast in stone". Rather they were "an attempt to describe the consequences of the application of the general rules of evidence governing relevance and the reception of evidence". While the majority wrote that it was not legislating but only offering "guidelines", if the "guidelines" are the Supreme Court of Canada's thoughts on the common law of today, their expression differs little from the exercise of legislating. There will surely be no different result waiting for the trial judge who decides not to follow the guidelines.

The new regime announced in *Seaboyer* offers greater protection to the complainant than did the legislative provision that was struck down. The old s. 276 forbade the introduction of evidence "concerning the sexual activity of the complainant with *any person other than the accused*". The common law had always recognized that previous sexual conduct with the accused was relevant to the issue of whether the complainant consented on the occasion under review. The majority's opinion "question(ed) whether evidence of other sexual conduct with the accused should automatically be admissible in all cases; sometimes the value of such evidence might be little or none". While sometimes the value of such evidence will be little or none the majority decided to exclude it in all cases: "evidence that the complainant has engaged in consensual sexual conduct on other occasions (*including past sexual conduct with the accused*) is not admissible solely to support the inference that (she) was more likely to have consented".

Suppose A and B have been living together for a year. The evidence is clear and undisputed that the parties regularly engaged in consensual sexual intercourse. On the evening brought into question before the court sexual intercourse occurred. A says it was consensual and B says it was not. The court in *Seaboyer* says that evidence of the previous consensual activity is not admissible. Such evidence cannot come in if the sole purpose is to show consent. No one, of course, would suggest that such previous conduct would be determinative of the issue, but is it relevant and at least worth considering along with the other evidence?

The commonly accepted meaning of relevance, we noted earlier, bespeaks a very low threshold: does the evidence offered render the desired inference more probable than it would be without the evidence? Consider the absolute nature of the prohibition which operates regardless of whether the probative value of the evidence outweighs the potential prejudice to the proper outcome of the trial. There is no discretion in the trial Judge to receive the evidence if, in her opinion, the probative value outweighs the prejudice.

The majority in *Seaboyer* cited frequently and quoted heavily from Professor Galvin's article, "Shielding Rape Victims in the State and Federal Courts: A Proposal for the Second Decade".[36] Galvin's proposed rape shield law, however, was confined to the exclusion of evidence of sexual conduct with persons other than the accused. The majority in *Seaboyer* wrote "Galvin's proposal, with some modification, reflects an appropriate response to the problem."[37] One "modification" eliminates the distinction regarding sexual conduct with the accused. This is a major modification. Professor Galvin wrote:

> Even the most ardent reformers acknowledged the high probative value of past sexual conduct in at least two instances. The first is when the defendant claims consent and establishes prior consensual relations between himself and the complainant. . . . Although the evidence is offered to prove consent, its probative value rests on the nature of the complainant's specific mindset toward the accused rather than on her general unchaste character. . . . All 25 statutes adopting the Michigan approach (to rape shield laws) allow the accused to introduce evidence of prior sexual conduct between himself and the complainant. The high probative value and minimal prejudicial effect of this evidence have been discussed.[38]

---

36 (1986), 70 Minn. L. Rev. 763.
37 *Ibid.*, at 156.
38 *Supra* note 14 at 807-880.

Another article quoted by the majority in *Seaboyer* is Professor Vivian Berger's *"Man's Trial, Woman's Tribulation"*.[39] Professor Berger justified the reception of evidence of sexual conduct with the accused in this way:

> The inference from past to present behaviour does not, as in cases of third party acts, rest on highly dubious beliefs about "women who do" and "women who don't" but rather relies on common sense and practical psychology. Admission of the proof supplies the accused with a circumstance making it probable that he did not obtain by violence what he might have secured by persuasion.[40]

Another *major* modification to Galvin's proposal is with respect to so-called similar fact evidence. Galvin proposed that "evidence of a pattern of sexual conduct so distinctive and so closely resembling the accused's version of the alleged encounter with the victim as to tend to prove that the victim consented to the act charged" could be received. The majority in *Seaboyer* wrote that "similar fact evidence . . . cannot be used illegitimately merely to show that the complainant consented" and where evidence of sexual conduct on other occasions is admitted, the trial judge should warn the jury against this prohibited use. Why? This major modification of Galvin's proposal is not explained unless we are to take it as a given that previous sexual conduct of the complainant can never be indicative of a propensity, a disposition, a willingness, to have sexual intercourse, from which a trier could infer that she acted in conformity with that character.

Suppose the evidence is that the accused and complainant met in Sam's Bar one Saturday night and left to go to her apartment. It's agreed that sexual intercourse occurred but the parties disagree on the issue of consent. The accused's evidence is that he was sitting at the bar when complainant approached him, offered him a drink and propositioned him. Should the accused be able to call Sam to testify that every Saturday night for the previous four weeks the complainant came into his bar, offered a stranger a drink, propositioned him and left in his company?

On the issue of receiving similar fact evidence tendered by the accused, Professor Berger wrote:

> What if the accused were offering to show that the victim habitually goes to bars on Saturday nights, picks up strangers and takes them home to bed with her, and that over the past 12 months she has done so on more than 20 occasions. Now could one assert with assurance that this particular sexual record does not substantially reinforce the defendant's version of the night's events? And if it does, should he not be permitted as a matter of constitutional right to place this evidence before the jury?[41]

---

39 (1977), 77 Colum. L. Rev. 1.
40 *Ibid.*, at 58-59.
41 *Ibid.*

4.   PARLIAMENT'S RESPONSE TO *SEABOYER* (1992)

(a)   Rape Shield

Seaboyer produced an immediate outcry on the basis that it would mean that women and children would be even less likely to pursue charges of sexual assault given that there would be unrestricted cross-examination of their prior sexual history. Such comments were quite unfair to the majority of the Supreme Court of Canada. For the majority, Madam Justice McLachlin had been quite alive to the dangers of leaving this crucial issue to unfettered judicial discretion and had crafted what she considered to be careful guidelines as to the admissibility of such evidence. She had also extended the protection to prior sexual conduct *with the accused.* One of the sources of the vehement reaction was that the majority took but a line to hold that, although victims might have equality rights, these had to give way to the accused's right to make full answer and defence.

The response from the Minister of Justice, the Honourable Kim Campbell, was swift. She announced that Parliament would better respond to protect women and children. She called a meeting of national and regional women's groups and thereafter worked very closely with them in drafting and revising a Bill.[42] The coalition of some 60 women's groups reached unanimity at each point and agreed to oppose any attempt to water down the Bill.

Bill C-49 was tabled on December 12, 1991. It was referred to committee after second reading on April 16, 1992. It quickly passed through the House of Commons and Senate and received Royal Assent on June 23, 1992. Bill C-49 was proclaimed to be in force on August 15, 1992.

The new s. 276, regarding the admissibility of evidence of the complainant's sexual activity, provides:

> **276.** (1) In proceedings in respect of an offence under section 151, 152, 153, 155 or 159, subsection 160(2) or (3) or section 170, 171, 172, 173, 271, 272 or 273, evidence that the complainant has engaged in sexual activity, whether with the accused or with any other person, is not admissible to support an inference that, by reason of the sexual nature of that activity, the complainant
>> (a) is more likely to have consented to the sexual activity that forms the subject-matter of the charge; or
>> (b) is less worthy of belief.
>
> (2) In proceedings in respect of an offence referred to in subsection (1), no evidence shall be adduced by or on behalf of the accused that the complainant has engaged in sexual activity other than the sexual activity that forms the subject-matter of the charge, whether with the accused or with any other person, unless the judge, provincial court judge or justice determines, in accordance with the procedures set out in sections 276.1 and 276.2, that the evidence
>> (a) is of specific instances of sexual activity;
>> (b) is relevant to an issue to be proved at trial; and
>> (c) has significant probative value that is not substantially outweighed by the danger of prejudice to the proper administration of justice.

---

42   *Proceedings of the Standing Senate Committee on Legal and Constitutional Affairs,* 3rd Sess., 34 Parl. 1991-92 (June 22, 1992): 29-31. See, too, Sheila McIntyre, "Redefining Reformism: The Consultations that Shaped Bill C-49" in J. Roberts and R. Mohr, eds., *Confronting Sexual Assault. A Decade of Legal and Social Change* (1994), chapter 12.

(3) In determining whether evidence is admissible under subsection (2), the judge, provincial court judge or justice shall take into account

    (*a*) the interests of justice including the right of the accused to make a full answer and defence;

    (*b*) society's interest in encouraging the reporting of sexual assault offences;

    (*c*) whether there is a reasonable prospect that the evidence will assist in arriving at a just determination in the case;

    (*d*) the need to remove from the fact-finding process any discriminatory belief or bias;

    (*e*) the risk that the evidence may unduly arouse sentiments of prejudice, sympathy or hostility in the jury;

    (*f*) the potential prejudice to the complainant's personal dignity and right of privacy;

    (*g*) the right of the complainant and of every individual to personal security and to the full protection and benefit of the law; and

    (*h*) any other factor that the judge, provincial court judge or justice considers relevant.

The new s. 276.1 imposes a requirement of written notice for a hearing to determine admissibility under s. 276(2). Section 276.2 provides for the exclusion of the public at the hearing and the non-compellability of the complainant. The new s. 276.4 requires the trial judge to instruct the jury as to the proper use of the evidence received.

Does the new legislation give more or less discretion to judges than did *Seaboyer*? What are the differences?

Section 276(1) seems to contain an express blanket prohibition on what is commonly referred to as the "twin myths" reasoning. It prohibits the use of prior sexual history of the complainant on the issue of consent or to show that the complainant was less worthy of belief. This seemed to make it unconstitutional because *Seaboyer* had called for discretion (see Delisle, "Potential Charter Challenges to the New Rape Shield Law" (1992), 13 C.R. (4th) 309).

However, Professor David Paciocco, "The New Rape Shield Provision Should Survive Charter Challenge" (1993), 21 C.R. (4th) 223, suggested that the legislation could be read down. Section 276(1) only prohibited general stereotypical inferences. Evidence of prior sexual history with the accused could be admitted under s. 276(2) where the defence could establish that a specific inference can be drawn from such evidence to an issue relevant in the trial. In *Charter* challenges in lower courts the Paciocco position carried the day and was increasingly relied on as the proper interpretation.

When the Supreme Court finally considered the constitutionality of the "new" statutory scheme in *Darrach* a unanimous court had little difficulty in declaring the "new" rape shield provisions constitutional.

R. v. DARRACH

[2000] 2 S.C.R. 443, 36 C.R. (5th) 223, 148 C.C.C. (3d) 97,
2000 CarswellOnt 3321, 2000 CarswellOnt 3322

The accused was charged with sexual assault and, at his trial, attempted to introduce evidence of the complainant's sexual history. He unsuccessfully challenged the constitutionality of s. 276.1(2)(*a*) of the *Criminal Code* (which requires that the affidavit contain "detailed particulars" about the evidence), ss. 276(1) and 276(2)(c) (which govern the admissibility of sexual conduct evidence generally), and s. 276.2(2) (which provides that the complainant is not a compellable witness at the hearing determining the admissibility of evidence of prior sexual activity). After a *voir dire*, the trial judge refused to allow the accused to adduce the evidence of the complainant's sexual history. The accused was convicted and the Court of Appeal dismissed the accused's appeal, concluding that the impugned provisions did not violate the accused's right to make full answer and defence, his right not to be compelled to testify against himself or his right to a fair trial as protected by ss. 7, 11(c) and 11(d) of the *Canadian Charter of Rights and Freedoms*. Here we consider the accused's argument that s. 276 (1) was unconstitutional.

GONTHIER J. (MCLACHLIN C.J.C., L'HEUREUX-DUBÉ, IACOBUCCI, MAJOR, BASTARACHE, BINNIE, ARBOUR and LEBEL J.J. concurring): —

. . . .

The current s. 276 categorically prohibits evidence of a complainant's sexual history only when it is used to support one of two general inferences. These are that a person is more likely to have consented to the alleged assault and that she is less credible as a witness by virtue of her prior sexual experience. Evidence of sexual activity may be admissible, however, to substantiate other inferences.

. . . .

The current version of s. 276 is carefully crafted to comport with the principles of fundamental justice. It protects the integrity of the judicial process while at the same time respecting the rights of the people involved. The complainant's privacy and dignity are protected by a procedure that also vindicates the accused's right to make full answer and defence. The procedure does not violate the accused's s. 7 *Charter* right to a fair trial nor his s. 11(c) right not to testify against himself or his s. 11(d) right to a fair hearing.

. . . .

[T]he court's jurisprudence . . . has consistently held that the principles of fundamental justice enshrined in s. 7 protect more than the rights of the accused.

. . . .

One of the implications of this analysis is that while the right to make full answer and defence and the principle against self-incrimination are certainly core principles of fundamental justice, they can be respected without the accused being entitled to "the most favourable procedures that could possibly be imagined" (*R. v. Lyons*, [1987] 2 S.C.R. 309 (S.C.C.) at p. 362; cited in *Mills, supra*, at para. 72). Nor is the accused entitled to have procedures crafted that take only his interests into account. Still less is he entitled to procedures that would distort the truth-seeking function of a trial by permitting irrelevant and prejudicial material at trial.

In *Seaboyer*, the court found that the principles of fundamental justice include the three purposes of s. 276 identified above: protecting the integrity of the trial by excluding evidence that is misleading, protecting the rights of the accused, as well as encouraging the reporting of sexual violence and protecting "the security and privacy of the witnesses" (p. 606). This was affirmed in *Mills*, *supra*, at para. 72. The court crafted its guidelines in *Seaboyer* in accordance with these principles, and it is in relation to these principles that the effects of s. 276 on the accused must be evaluated.

The court in *Mills* upheld the constitutionality of the provisions in the *Criminal Code* that control the use of personal and therapeutic records in trials of sexual offences. The use of these records in evidence is analogous in many ways to the use of evidence of prior sexual activity, and the protections in the *Criminal Code* surrounding the use of records at trial are motivated by similar policy considerations. L'Heureux-Dubé J. has warned that therapeutic records should not become a tool for circumventing s. 276: "[w]e must not allow the defence to do indirectly what it cannot do directly" (*R. v. O'Connor*, [1995] 4 S.C.R. 411 (S.C.C.), at para. 122, and *R. v. Osolin*, [1993] 4 S.C.R. 595, at p. 624). Academic commentators have observed that the use of therapeutic records increased with the enactment of s. 276 nonetheless (see K. Kelly, "'You must be crazy if you think you were raped': Reflections on the Use of Complainants' Personal and Therapy Records in Sexual Assault Trials" (1997), 9 *C.J.W.L.* 178, at p. 181).

. . . .

[T]he test for admissibility in s. 276(2) requires not only that the evidence be relevant but also that it be more probative than prejudicial. *Mills* dealt with a conflict among the same three *Charter* principles that are in issue in the case at bar: full answer and defence, privacy and equality (at para. 61). The court defined these rights relationally: "the scope of the right to make full answer and defence must be determined in light of privacy and equality rights of complainants and witnesses" (paras. 62-66 and 94). The exclusionary rule was upheld. The privacy and equality concerns involved in protecting the records justified interpreting the right to make full answer and defence in a way that did not include a right to all relevant evidence.

. . . .

In the case at bar, I affirm the reasons in *Seaboyer* and find that none of the accused's rights are infringed by s. 276 as he alleges. *Seaboyer* provides a basic justification for the legislative scheme in s. 276, including the determination of relevance as well as the prejudicial and probative value of the evidence. *Mills* and *White* show how the impact of s. 276 on the principles of fundamental justice relied on by the accused should be assessed in light of the other principles of fundamental justice that s. 276 was designed to protect. The reasons in *Mills* are apposite because they demonstrate how the same principles of equality, privacy and fairness can be reconciled. I shall show below how the procedure created by s. 276 to protect the trial process from distortion and to protect complainants is consistent with the principles of fundamental justice. It is fair to the accused and properly reconciles the divergent interests at play, as the court suggested in *Seaboyer*.

. . . .

Section 276(1) — The Exclusionary Rule

The accused objects to the exclusionary rule itself in s. 276(1) on the grounds that it is a "blanket exclusion" that prevents him from adducing evidence necessary to make full answer and defence, as guaranteed by ss. 7 and 11(*d*) of the *Charter*. He is mistaken in his characterization of the rule. Far from being a "blanket exclusion", s. 276(1) only prohibits the use of evidence of past sexual activity when it is offered to support two specific, illegitimate inferences. These are known as the myths", namely that a complainant is more likely to have consented or that she is less worthy of belief "by reason of the sexual nature of the activity" she once engaged in.

This section gives effect to McLachlin J.'s finding in *Seaboyer* that the "twin myths" are simply not relevant at trial. They are not probative of consent or credibility and can severely distort the trial process. Section 276(1) also clarifies *Seaboyer* in several respects. Section 276 applies to all sexual activity, whether with the accused or with someone else. It also applies to non-consensual as well as consensual sexual activity, as this court found implicitly in *R. v. Crosby*, [1995] 2 S.C.R. 912 (S.C.C.), at p. 924. Although the *Seaboyer* guidelines referred to "consensual sexual conduct" (pp. 634-35), Parliament enacted the new version of s. 276 without the word "consensual". Evidence of non-consensual sexual acts can equally defeat the purposes of s. 276 by distorting the trial process when it is used to evoke stereotypes such as that women who have been assaulted must have deserved it and that they are unreliable witnesses, as well as by deterring people from reporting assault by humiliating them in court. The admissibility of evidence of non-consensual sexual activity is determined by the procedures in s. 276. Section 276 also settles any ambiguity about whether the "twin myths" are limited to inferences about "unchaste" women in particular; they are not (as discussed by C. Boyle and M. MacCrimmon, "The Constitutionality of Bill C-49: Analyzing Sexual Assault As If Equality Really Mattered" (1998), 41 *Crim. L.Q.* 198, at pp. 231-32).

The *Criminal Code* excludes all discriminatory generalizations about a complainant's disposition to consent or about her credibility based on the *sexual nature* of her past sexual activity on the grounds that these are improper lines of reasoning. This was the import of the court's findings in *Seaboyer* about how sexist beliefs about women distort the trial process. The text of the exclusionary rule in s. 276(1) diverges very little from the guidelines in *Seaboyer*. The mere fact that the wording differs between the court's guidelines and Parliament's enactment is itself immaterial. In *Mills, supra,* the court affirmed that "[t]o insist on slavish conformity" by Parliament to judicial pronouncements "would belie the mutual respect that underpins the relationship" between the two institutions (para. 55). In this case, the legislation follows the court's suggestions very closely.

The phrase "by reason of the sexual nature of the activity" in s. 276 is a clarification by Parliament that it is inferences from the *sexual nature* of the activity, as opposed to inferences from other potentially relevant features of the activity, that are prohibited. If evidence of sexual activity is proffered for its non-sexual features, such as to show a pattern of conduct or a prior inconsistent statement, it may be permitted. The phrase "by reason of the sexual nature of the activity" has the same effect as the qualification "solely to support the inference" in *Seaboyer* in that it limits the exclusion of evidence to that used to invoke the "twin myths" (p. 635).

. . . .

An accused has never had a right to adduce irrelevant evidence. Nor does he have the right to adduce misleading evidence to support illegitimate inferences: "the accused is not permitted to distort the truth-seeking function of the trial process" (*Mills, supra,* at para. 74). Because s. 276(1) is an evidentiary rule that only excludes material that is not relevant, it cannot infringe the accused's right to make full answer and defence. Section 276(2) is more complicated, and I turn to it now.

Section 276(2) — "Significant Probative Value"

If evidence is not barred by s. 276(1) because it is tendered to support a permitted inference, the judge must still weigh its probative value against its prejudicial effect to determine its admissibility. This essentially mirrors the common law guidelines in *Seaboyer* which contained this balancing test (at p. 635). The accused takes issue with the fact that s. 276(2)(*c*) specifically requires that the evidence have "significant probative value". The word "significant" was added by Parliament but it does not render the provision unconstitutional by raising the threshold for the admissibility of evidence to the point that it is unfair to the accused.

. . . .

The context of the word "significant" in the provision in which it occurs substantiates this interpretation. Section 276(2)(c) allows a judge to admit evidence of "*significant* probative value that is not *substantially* outweighed by the danger of prejudice to the proper administration of justice" (emphasis added). The adverb "substantially" serves to protect the accused by raising the standard for the judge to exclude evidence once the accused has shown it to have significant probative value. In a sense, both sides of the equation are heightened in this test, which serves to direct judges to the serious ramifications of the use of evidence of prior sexual activity for all parties in these cases.

In light of the purposes of s. 276, the use of the word "significant" is consistent with both the majority and the minority reasons in *Seaboyer*. Section 276 is designed to prevent the use of evidence of prior sexual activity for improper purposes. The requirement of "significant probative value" serves to exclude evidence of trifling relevance that, even though not used to support the two forbidden inferences, would still endanger the "proper administration of justice". The court has recognized that there are inherent "damages and disadvantages presented by the admission of such evidence" (*Seaboyer, supra,* at p. 634). As Morden A.C.J.O. puts it, evidence of sexual activity must be significantly probative if it is to overcome its prejudicial effect. The *Criminal Code* codifies this reality.

By excluding misleading evidence while allowing the accused to adduce evidence that meets the criteria of s. 276(2), s. 276 enhances the fairness of trials of sexual offences. Section 11(d) guarantees a fair trial. Fairness under s. 11(d) is determined in the context of the trial process as a whole (*R. v. Stoddart* (1987), 37 C.C.C. (3d) 351 (Ont. C.A.), at pp. 365-66). As L'Heureux-Dubé J. wrote in *Crosby, supra,* at para. 11, "[s]ection 276 cannot be interpreted so as to deprive a person of a fair defence." At the same time, the accused's right to make full answer and defence, as was held in *Mills, supra,* at para. 75, is not "automatically breached where he or she is deprived of relevant information." Nor is it necessarily breached when the accused is not permitted to adduce relevant information that is not "significantly" probative, under a rule of evidence that protects the trial from the distorting effects of evidence of prior sexual activity.

. . . .

Thus the threshold criteria that evidence be of "significant" probative value does not prevent an accused from making full answer and defence to the charges against him. Consequently his *Charter* rights under ss. 7 and 11(d) are not infringed by s. 276(2)(c).

The Procedural Sections to Determine Relevance: The Affidavit and Voir Dire

The constitutionality of the procedure that must be followed to introduce evidence of prior sexual activity has also been challenged. It requires that whoever seeks to introduce it "by or on behalf of the accused" must present an affidavit and establish on a *voir dire* that the evidence is admissible in accordance with the criteria in the *Criminal Code*.

[The court determined that the procedural provisions were not violative of the accused's constitutional rights. In the course of its analysis the court later commented on relevance and probative value of evidence of previous sexual activity.]

Although the Supreme Court has determined the issue of constitutionality, it seems very likely that *Darrach* has not resolved the question of the proper application of ss. 276 (1) and (2), especially in the context of prior sexual history with the accused where the issue is consent. We have seen that the court in *Darrach* at one point says that such evidence is not relevant, then in the next breath it says it may be admitted. Towards the end of the judgment this is put in yet another way:

> Evidence of prior sexual activity will rarely be relevant to support a denial that sexual activity took place or to establish consent (C.R., para. 58).

That judges have different views on the issue of the relevance and probative value of evidence of prior sexual history with the accused on the issue of consent is reflected in the views of the Ontario Court of Appeal in the court below in *Darrach*, which were not addressed in the Supreme Court. According to Morden A.C.J.O. for the court (1998), 13 C.R. (5th) 283, 122 C.C.C. (3d) 225 (Ont. C.A.), (Osborne and Doherty JJ.A. concurring):

> It will likely be that evidence of previous sexual activity with the accused will satisfy the requirements of admissibility in s. 276(2) more often than that relating to sexual activity with others. This does not mean that this evidence should always be admitted (C.R. at 299).

Trial judges appear to regularly admit evidence of a prior or ongoing relationship where there is a viable issue of consent. That is not to say that such evidence is determinative. Otherwise the trial would be devoid of context and potentially unfair to accused. See, for example, *Termertzoglou* (2002), 11 C.R. (6th) 179 (Ont. S.C.J.) and *Strickland* (2007), 45 C.R. (6th) 183 (Ont. S.C.J.).

Most of the rape shield provisions in the United States allow the admission of prior sexual history with the accused. In the United Kingdom the House of Lords in *R. v. A. (No. 2)*, [2001] 3 All E.R. 1 decided, referring to *Darrach*, that a new U.K. rape shield law should not be applied to preclude evidence of prior sexual history with the accused. This would violate the right to a fair trial under the European Convention of Human Rights.

(b)   Consent

The new s. 273.1 seeks to define consent in the case of sexual assault but, consistent with *R. v. Jobidon*, is expressly not exhaustive:

> **273.1**(1) Subject to subsection (2) and subsection 265(3), "consent" means, for the purposes of sections 271, 272 and 273, the voluntary agreement of the complainant to engage in the sexual activity in question.
>
> (2) No consent is obtained, for the purposes of sections 271, 272 and 273, where
> - (*a*) the agreement is expressed by the words or conduct of a person other than the complainant;
> - (*b*) the complainant is incapable of consenting to the activity;
> - (*c*) the accused induces the complainant to engage in the activity by abusing a position of trust, power or authority;
> - (*d*) the complainant expresses, by words or conduct, a lack of agreement to engage in the activity; or
> - (*e*) the complainant, having consented to engage in sexual activity, expresses, by words or conduct, a lack of agreement to continue to engage in the activity.
>
> (3) Nothing in subsection (2) shall be construed as limiting the circumstances in which no consent is obtained.

These provisions clearly set out to give courts better guidance as to situations in which consent can be held to have been not genuine and therefore not consent in law. Subsections (*b*), (*c*) and (*e*) were amended as the bill passed through committee. The amendments were largely inconsequential, merely clarifying rather than changing the original intent. Subsection (*b*) had read that the complainant was incapable of consenting to the activity "by reason of intoxication or other condition". The provision was criticized as being vague, especially in its reference to "other condition". Parliament clearly decided to leave the matter to the discretion of trial judges while preserving the common-law principle that one incapable of giving consent cannot be considered to have consented.

These new consent provisions seem adequately drafted and a welcome assertion of the "No Means No" philosophy. With the exception of subs. (*c*), which will require judicial interpretation, the provisions appear to merely restate existing legal principles.

Some interpreted subs. (*d*) as preserving the existing common law that consent can be express or implied. A suggestion by the women's coalition that consent should be limited to unequivocal expressions[43] was rejected. Critics of Bill C-49 suggested that in future written consent will be needed in advance for any sexual conduct, that there is an onus of proof on the accused[44] or that Bill C-49 criminalizes seduction.[45]

---

43 The Coalition's rejected proposal of November 27, 1991, had the following definition: "For the purposes of sections 271, 272 and 273 consent shall be sought and obtained and shall mean words or gestures which unequivocally express or manifest voluntary agreement to the sexual activity": see, further, Sheila McIntyre, "Redefining Reformism: The Consultations that Shaped Bill C-49" in J. Roberts and R. Mohr (eds.), *Sexual Assault. A Decade of Legal and Social Change* (1994), Chapter 12.

44 This was the position of an editorial in *The Globe and Mail*, May 19, 1992: "An assault on the law, not to say common sense", effectively rebutted by the Minister of Justice in a letter published in *The Globe and Mail*, May 27, 1992.

45 *Ibid.*

(c) Mistaken Belief in Consent

While Bill C-49 does not remove a belief in consent defence to a charge of sexual assault it substantially restricts it. Under s. 273.2 belief in consent is not a defence to any sexual assault charge where

(*a*) the accused's belief arose from the accused's
   (i) self-induced intoxication, or
   (ii) recklessness or wilful blindness; or

(*b*) the accused did not take reasonable steps, in the circumstances known to the accused at the time, to ascertain that the complainant was consenting.

Sections 273.1 and 273.2 were authoritatively interpreted by the Supreme Court.

R. v. EWANCHUK

[1999] 1 S.C.R. 330, 22 C.R. (5th) 1, 131 C.C.C. (3d) 481,
1999 CarswellAlta 99, 1999 CarswellAlta 100

The accused initiated a number of touching incidents, each progressively more intimate although the complainant clearly said "no" on each occasion. He stopped each time she said "no" but persisted shortly afterwards. The accused was charged with sexual assault.

At a trial before a judge of the Alberta Court of Queen's Bench the accused did not testify, leaving only the complainant's evidence as to what took place between them. The accused was acquitted. The trial judge found that the complainant was a credible witness. He found that in her mind she had not consented to any of the sexual touching which took place, that she had been fearful throughout the encounter, that she didn't want the accused to know she was afraid and that she had actively projected a relaxed and unafraid visage. He concluded that the failure of the complainant to communicate her fear, including her active efforts to the contrary, rendered her subjective feelings irrelevant. He characterized the defence as one of "implied consent". On the totality of the evidence, provided solely by the Crown's witnesses, the trial judge concluded that the Crown had not proven the absence of consent beyond a reasonable doubt and acquitted the accused.

A majority of the Alberta Court of Appeal dismissed the Crown appeal. Each of the three justices of the Court of Appeal issued separate reasons. McClung and Foisy JJ.A. both dismissed the appeal on the basis that it was a fact-driven acquittal from which the Crown could not properly appeal. In addition, McClung J.A. concluded that the Crown had failed to prove beyond a reasonable doubt that the accused had intended to commit an assault upon the complainant. Fraser C.J. delivered a lengthy dissent.

The Supreme Court allowed the Crown appeal, substituting a conviction and remitting the matter for sentence.

MAJOR J. (LAMER C.J., CORY, IACOBUCCI, BASTARACHE and BINNIE JJ.
concurring): —

. . . The trial judge relied on the defence of implied consent. This was a
mistake of law as no such defence is available in assault cases in Canada. This
mistake of law is reviewable by appellate courts . . .

1. Facts

The complainant was a 17-year-old woman living in the city of Edmonton.
She met the accused respondent Ewanchuk on the afternoon of June 2, 1994,
while walking through the parking lot of the Heritage Shopping Mall with her
roommate. The accused, driving a red van towing a trailer, approached the two
young women. He struck up a conversation with them. He related that he was
in the custom wood-working business and explained that he displayed his work
at retail booths in several shopping malls. He said that he was looking for staff
to attend his displays, and asked whether the young women were looking for
work. The complainant's friend answered that they were, at which point the
accused asked to interview her friend privately. She declined, but spoke with
the accused beside his van for some period of time about the sort of work he
required, and eventually exchanged telephone numbers with the accused.

The following morning the accused telephoned the apartment where the
complainant and her friend resided with their boyfriends. The complainant
answered the phone. She told the accused that her friend was still asleep. When
he learned this, the accused asked the complainant if she was interested in a job.
She indicated that she was, and they met a short time later, again in the Heritage
Mall parking lot. At the accused's suggestion, the interview took place in his
van. In the words of the complainant, a "very business-like, polite" conversation
took place. Some time later, the complainant asked if she could smoke a
cigarette, and the accused suggested that they move outside since he was allergic
to cigarette smoke. Once outside the van, he asked the complainant if she would
like to see some of his work, which was kept inside the trailer attached to his
van, and she indicated that she would.

The complainant entered the trailer, purposely leaving the door open behind
her. The accused followed her in, and closed the door in a way which made the
complainant think that he had locked it. There is no evidence whether the door
was actually locked, but the complainant stated that she became frightened at
this point. Once inside the trailer, the complainant and the accused sat down
side-by-side on the floor of the trailer. They spoke and looked through a portfolio
of his work. This lasted 10 to 15 minutes, after which the conversation turned
to more personal matters.

During the time in the trailer the accused was quite tactile with the
complainant, touching her hand, arms and shoulder as he spoke. At some point

the accused said that he was feeling tense and asked the complainant to give him a massage. The complainant complied, massaging the accused's shoulders for a few minutes. After she stopped, he asked her to move in front of him so that he could massage her, which she did. The accused then massaged the complainant's shoulders and arms while they continued talking. During this mutual massaging the accused repeatedly told the complainant to relax, and that she should not be afraid. As the massage progressed, the accused attempted to initiate more intimate contact. The complainant stated that, "he started to try to massage around my stomach, and he brought his hands up around — or underneath my breasts, and he started to get quite close up there, so I used my elbows to push in between, and I said, "No".

The accused stopped immediately, but shortly thereafter resumed non-sexual massaging, to which the complainant also said, "No". The accused again stopped, and said, "See, I'm a nice guy. It's okay."

The accused then asked the complainant to turn and face him. She did so, and he began massaging her feet. His touching progressed from her feet up to her inner thigh and pelvic area. The complainant did not want the accused to touch her in this way, but said nothing as she said she was afraid that any resistance would prompt the accused to become violent. Although the accused never used or threatened any force, the complainant testified that she did not want to "egg [him] on". As the contact progressed, the accused laid himself heavily on top of the complainant and began grinding his pelvic area against hers. The complainant testified that the accused asserted, "that he could get me so horny so that I would want it so bad, and he wouldn't give it to me because he had self-control".

The complainant did not move or reciprocate the contact. The accused asked her to put her hands across his back, but she did not; instead she lay "bone straight". After less than a minute of this the complainant asked the accused to stop. "I said, Just please stop. And so he stopped". The accused again told the complainant not to be afraid, and asked her if she trusted that he wouldn't hurt her. In her words, the complainant said, "Yes, I trust that you won't hurt me." On the stand she stated that she was afraid throughout, and only responded to the accused in this way because she was fearful that a negative answer would provoke him to use force.

After this brief exchange, the accused went to hug the complainant and, as he did so, he laid on top of her again, continuing the pelvic grinding. He also began moving his hands on the complainant's inner thigh, inside her shorts, for a short time. While still on top of her the accused began to fumble with his shorts and took out his penis. At this point the complainant again asked the accused to desist, saying, "No, stop."

Again, the accused stopped immediately, got off the complainant, smiled at her and said something to the effect of, "It's okay. See, I'm a nice guy, I stopped." At this point the accused again hugged the complainant lightly before opening up his wallet and removing a $100 bill, which he gave to the complainant. She testified that the accused said that the $100 was for the massage and that he told her not to tell anyone about it. He made some reference to another female employee with whom he also had a very close and friendly relationship, and said that he hoped to get together with the complainant again.

Shortly after the exchange of the money the complainant said that she had to go. The accused opened the door and the complainant stepped out. Some further conversation ensued outside the trailer before the complainant finally left and walked home. On her return home the complainant was emotionally distraught and contacted the police.

At some point during the encounter the accused provided the complainant with a brochure describing his woodwork and gave her his name and address, which she wrote on the brochure. The investigating officer used this information to locate the accused at his home, where he was arrested.

B. The Components of Sexual Assault

A conviction for sexual assault requires proof beyond reasonable doubt of two basic elements, that the accused committed the *actus reus* and that he had the necessary *mens rea*. The *actus reus* of assault is unwanted sexual touching. The *mens rea* is the intention to touch, knowing of, or being reckless of or wilfully blind to, a lack of consent, either by words or actions, from the person being touched.

(1) *Actus Reus*

The crime of sexual assault is only indirectly defined in the *Criminal Code*, R.S.C., 1985, c. C-46. The offence is comprised of an assault within any one of the definitions in s. 265(1) of the *Code*, which is committed in circumstances of a sexual nature, such that the sexual integrity of the victim is violated: see *R. v. S. (P.L.)*, [1991] 1 S.C.R. 909.

. . . .

The *actus reus* of sexual assault is established by the proof of three elements: (i) touching, (ii) the sexual nature of the contact, and (iii) the absence of consent. The first two of these elements are objective. It is sufficient for the Crown to prove that the accused's actions were voluntary. The sexual nature of the assault is determined objectively; the Crown need not prove that the accused had any *mens rea* with respect to the sexual nature of his or her behaviour: see *R. v. Litchfield*, [1993] 4 S.C.R. 333, and *R. v. Chase*, [1987] 2 S.C.R. 293.

The absence of consent, however, is subjective and determined by reference to the complainant's subjective internal state of mind towards the touching, at the time it occurred: see *R. v. Jensen* (1996), 106 C.C.C. (3d) 430 (Ont. C.A.), at pp. 437-38, aff'd [1997] 1 S.C.R. 304, *R. v. Park*, [1995] 2 S.C.R. 836, at p. 850, per L'Heureux-Dubé J., and D. Stuart, Canadian Criminal Law (3rd ed. 1995), at p. 513.

. . . .

While the complainant's testimony is the only source of direct evidence as to her state of mind, credibility must still be assessed by the trial judge, or jury, in light of all the evidence. It is open to the accused to claim that the complainant's words and actions, before and during the incident, raise a reasonable doubt against her assertion that she, in her mind, did not want the sexual touching to take place. If, however, as occurred in this case, the trial judge believes the complainant that she subjectively did not consent, the Crown has discharged its obligation to prove the absence of consent.

. . . .

(a) "Implied Consent"

Counsel for the respondent submitted that the trier of fact may believe the complainant when she says she did not consent, but still acquit the accused on the basis that her conduct raised a reasonable doubt. Both he and the trial judge refer to this as "implied consent". It follows from the foregoing, however, that the trier of fact may only come to one of two conclusions: the complainant either consented or not. There is no third option. If the trier of fact accepts the complainant's testimony that she did not consent, no matter how strongly her conduct may contradict that claim, the absence of consent is established and the third component of the *actus reus* of sexual assault is proven. The doctrine of implied consent has been recognized in our common law jurisprudence in a variety of contexts but sexual assault is not one of them. There is no defence of implied consent to sexual assault in Canadian law.

(b) Application to the Present Case

In this case, the trial judge accepted the evidence of the complainant that she did not consent. That being so, he then misdirected himself when he considered the actions of the complainant, and not her subjective mental state, in determining the question of consent. As a result, he disregarded his previous finding that all the accused's sexual touching was unwanted. Instead he treated what he perceived as her ambiguous conduct as a failure by the Crown to prove the absence of consent.

As previously mentioned, the trial judge accepted the complainant's testimony that she did not want the accused to touch her, but then treated her conduct as raising a reasonable doubt about consent, described by him as "implied consent". This conclusion was an error. See D. Stuart, Annotation on *R. v. Ewanchuk* (1998), 13 C.R. (5th) 330, where the author points out that consent is a matter of the state of mind of the complainant while belief in consent is, subject to s. 273.2 of the *Code*, a matter of the state of mind of the accused and may raise the defence of honest but mistaken belief in consent.

The finding that the complainant did not want or consent to the sexual touching cannot co-exist with a finding that reasonable doubt exists on the question of consent. The trial judge's acceptance of the complainant's testimony regarding her own state of mind was the end of the matter on this point.

. . . .

(c) Effect of the Complainant's Fear

To be legally effective, consent must be freely given. Therefore, even if the complainant consented, or her conduct raises a reasonable doubt about her non-consent, circumstances may arise which call into question what factors prompted her apparent consent. The *Code* defines a series of conditions under which the law will deem an absence of consent in cases of assault, notwithstanding the complainant's ostensible consent or participation. As enumerated in s. 265(3), these include submission by reason of force, fear, threats, fraud or the exercise of authority, and codify the longstanding common law rule that consent given under fear or duress is ineffective: see G. Williams, *Textbook of Criminal Law* (2nd ed. 1983), at pp. 551-61.

. . . .

The words of Fish J.A. in *Saint-Laurent v. Hétu*, [1994] R.J.Q. 69 (C.A.), at p. 82, aptly describe the concern which the trier of fact must bear in mind when evaluating the actions of a complainant who claims to have been under fear, fraud or duress:

> "Consent" is . . . stripped of its defining characteristics when it is applied to the submission, non-resistance, non-objection, or even the apparent agreement, of a deceived, unconscious or compelled will.

In these instances the law is interested in a complainant's reasons for choosing to participate in, or ostensibly consent to, the touching in question. In practice, this translates into an examination of the choice the complainant believed she faced. The courts' concern is whether she freely made up her mind about the conduct in question. The relevant section of the *Code* is s. 265(3)(b), which states that there is no consent as a matter of law where the complainant believed that she was choosing between permitting herself to be touched sexually or risking being subject to the application of force.

. . . The trier of fact has to find that the complainant did not want to be touched sexually and made her decision to permit or participate in sexual activity as a result of an honestly held fear. The complainant's fear need not be reasonable, nor must it be communicated to the accused in order for consent to be vitiated. While the plausibility of the alleged fear, and any overt expressions of it, are obviously relevant to assessing the credibility of the complainant's claim that she consented out of fear, the approach is subjective.

Section 265(3) identifies an additional set of circumstances in which the accused's conduct will be culpable. The trial judge only has to consult s. 265(3) in those cases where the complainant has actually chosen to participate in sexual activity, or her ambiguous conduct or submission has given rise to doubt as to the absence of consent. If, as in this case, the complainant's testimony establishes the absence of consent beyond a reasonable doubt, the *actus reus* analysis is complete, and the trial judge should have turned his attention to the accused's perception of the encounter and the question of whether the accused possessed the requisite *mens rea*.

(2) *Mens Rea*

Sexual assault is a crime of general intent. Therefore, the Crown need only prove that the accused intended to touch the complainant in order to satisfy the basic *mens rea* requirement. See *R. v. Daviault*, [1994] 3 S.C.R. 63.

However, since sexual assault only becomes a crime in the absence of the complainant's consent, the common law recognizes a defence of mistake of fact which removes culpability for those who honestly but mistakenly believed that they had consent to touch the complainant. To do otherwise would result in the injustice of convicting individuals who are morally innocent: see *R. v. Creighton*, [1993] 3 S.C.R. 3. As such, the *mens rea* of sexual assault contains two elements: intention to touch and knowing of, or being reckless of or wilfully blind to, a lack of consent on the part of the person touched. See *Park*, supra, at para. 39.

The accused may challenge the Crown's evidence of *mens rea* by asserting an honest but mistaken belief in consent. The nature of this defence was described in *Pappajohn v. The Queen*, [1980] 2 S.C.R. 120, at p. 148, by Dickson J. (as he then was) (dissenting in the result):

> Mistake is a defence . . . where it prevents an accused from having the mens rea which the law requires for the very crime with which he is charged. Mistake of fact is more accurately seen as a negation of guilty intention than as the affirmation of a positive defence. It avails an accused who acts innocently, pursuant to a flawed perception of the facts, and nonetheless commits the actus reus of the offence. Mistake is a defence though, in the sense that it is raised as an issue by an accused. The Crown is rarely possessed of knowledge of the subjective factors which may have caused an accused to entertain a belief in a fallacious set of facts.

The defence of mistake is simply a denial of *mens rea*. It does not impose any burden of proof upon the accused (see *R. v. Robertson*, [1987] 1 S.C.R. 918, at p. 936) and it is not necessary for the accused to testify in order to raise the issue. Support for the defence may stem from any of the evidence before the court, including the Crown's case-in-chief and the testimony of the complainant. However, as a practical matter, this defence will usually arise in the evidence called by the accused.

(a) Meaning of "Consent" in the Context of an Honest but Mistaken Belief in Consent

As with the *actus reus* of the offence, consent is an integral component of the *mens rea*, only this time it is considered from the perspective of the accused. Speaking of the *mens rea* of sexual assault in *Park*, supra, at para. 30, L'Heureux-Dubé J. (in her concurring reasons) stated that:

> . . . the mens rea of sexual assault is not only satisfied when it is shown that the accused knew that the complainant was essentially saying "no", but is also satisfied when it is shown that the accused knew that the complainant was essentially not saying "yes".

In order to cloak the accused's actions in moral innocence, the evidence must show that he believed that the complainant communicated consent to engage in the sexual activity in question. A belief by the accused that the complainant, in her own mind wanted him to touch her but did not express that desire, is not a defence. The accused's speculation as to what was going on in the complainant's mind provides no defence.

For the purposes of the *mens rea* analysis, the question is whether the accused believed that he had obtained consent. What matters is whether the accused believed that the complainant effectively said "yes" through her words and/or actions. The statutory definition added to the *Code* by Parliament in 1992 is consistent with the common law:

> 273.1 (1) Subject to subsection (2) and subsection 265(3), "consent" means, for the purposes of sections 271, 272 and 273, the voluntary agreement of the complainant to engage in the sexual activity in question.

There is a difference in the concept of "consent" as it relates to the state of mind of the complainant vis-à-vis the *actus reus* of the offence and the state of mind of the accused in respect of the *mens rea*. For the purposes of the *actus reus*, "consent" means that the complainant in her mind wanted the sexual touching to take place.

In the context of *mens rea* — specifically for the purposes of the honest but mistaken belief in consent — "consent" means that the complainant had affirmatively communicated by words or conduct her agreement to engage in sexual activity with the accused. This distinction should always be borne in mind and the two parts of the analysis kept separate.

(b) Limits on Honest but Mistaken Belief in Consent

Not all beliefs upon which an accused might rely will exculpate him. Consent in relation to the *mens rea* of the accused is limited by both the common law and the provisions of ss. 273.1(2) and 273.2 of the *Code*.

. . . .

For instance, a belief that silence, passivity or ambiguous conduct constitutes consent is a mistake of law, and provides no defence: see *R. v. M. (M.L.)*, [1994] 2 S.C.R. 3. Similarly, an accused cannot rely upon his purported belief that the complainant's expressed lack of agreement to sexual touching in fact constituted an invitation to more persistent or aggressive contact. An accused cannot say that he thought "no meant yes". As Fraser C.J. stated at p. 272 of her dissenting reasons below:

> One "No" will do to put the other person on notice that there is then a problem with "consent". *Once a woman says "No" during the course of sexual activity, the person intent on continued sexual activity with her must then obtain a clear and unequivocal "Yes" before he again touches her in a sexual manner.* [Emphasis in original.]

I take the reasons of Fraser C.J. to mean that an unequivocal "yes" may be given by either the spoken word or by conduct.

Common sense should dictate that, once the complainant has expressed her unwillingness to engage in sexual contact, the accused should make certain that she has truly changed her mind before proceeding with further intimacies. The accused cannot rely on the mere lapse of time or the complainant's silence or equivocal conduct to indicate that there has been a change of heart and that consent now exists, nor can he engage in further sexual touching to "test the waters". Continuing sexual contact after someone has said "No" is, at a minimum, reckless conduct which is not excusable. In *R. v. Esau*, [1997] 2 S.C.R. 777, at para. 79, the court stated:

> An accused who, due to wilful blindness or recklessness, believes that a complainant . . . in fact consented to the sexual activity at issue is precluded from relying on a defence of honest but mistaken belief in consent, a fact that Parliament has codified: Criminal Code, s. 273.2(a)(ii).

(c) Application to the Facts

In this appeal the accused does not submit that the complainant's clearly articulated "No's" were ambiguous or carried some other meaning. In fact, the accused places great reliance on his having stopped immediately each time the complainant said "no" in order to show that he had no intention to force himself upon her. He therefore knew that the complainant was not consenting on four separate occasions during their encounter.

. . . .

As the accused did not testify, the only evidence before the court was that of the complainant. She stated that she immediately said "NO" every time the accused touched her sexually, and that she did nothing to encourage him. Her evidence was accepted by the trial judge as credible and sincere. Indeed, the accused relies on the fact that he momentarily stopped his advances each time the complainant said "NO" as evidence of his good intentions. This demonstrates that he understood the complainant's "NO's" to mean precisely that. Therefore, there is nothing on the record to support the accused's claim that he continued to believe her to be consenting, or that he re-established consent before resuming physical contact. The accused did not raise nor does the evidence disclose an air of reality to the defence of honest but mistaken belief in consent to this sexual touching.

The trial record conclusively establishes that the accused's persistent and increasingly serious advances constituted a sexual assault for which he had no defence. But for his errors of law, the trial judge would necessarily have found the accused guilty. In this case, a new trial would not be in the interests of justice.

In her reasons, Justice L'Heureux-Dubé makes reference to s. 273.2(b) of the *Code*. Whether the accused took reasonable steps is a question of fact to be determined by the trier of fact only after the air of reality test has been met. In view of the way the trial and appeal were argued, s. 273.2 (b) did not have to be considered.

. . . .

Cases involving a true misunderstanding between parties to a sexual encounter infrequently arise but are of profound importance to the community's sense of safety and justice. The law must afford women and men alike the peace of mind of knowing that their bodily integrity and autonomy in deciding when and whether to participate in sexual activity will be respected. At the same time, it must protect those who have not been proven guilty from the social stigma attached to sexual offenders.

L'HEUREUX-DUBÉ (GONTHIER J. concurring): —

. . . So pervasive is violence against women throughout the world that the international community adopted in December 18, 1979 (Res. 34/180), in addition to all other human rights instruments, the Convention on the Elimination of All Forms of Discrimination Against Women, Can. T.S. 1982 No. 31, entered into force on September 3, 1981, to which Canada is a party, which has been described as "the definitive international legal instrument requiring respect for and observance of the human rights of women."(R. Cook, "Reservations to the

Convention on the Elimination of All Forms of Discrimination Against Women" (1990), 30 Va. J. Int'l L. 643, at p. 643).

. . . .

Our *Charter* is the primary vehicle through which international human rights achieve a domestic effect (see *Slaight Communications Inc. v. Davidson*, [1989] 1 S.C.R. 1038; *R. v. Keegstra*, [1990] 3 S.C.R. 697). In particular, s. 15 (the equality provision) and s. 7 (which guarantees the right to life, security and liberty of the person) embody the notion of respect of human dignity and integrity.

. . . .

I have had the benefit of the reasons of Justice Major in this appeal and I agree generally with his reasons on most issues and with the result that he reaches. However, I wish to add some comments and discuss some of the reasoning of the trial judge and of the majority of the Court of Appeal.

. . . .

This case is not about consent, since none was given. It is about myths and stereotypes . . .

The trial judge believed the complainant and accepted her testimony that she was afraid and he acknowledged her unwillingness to engage in any sexual activity. In addition, there is no doubt that the respondent was aware that the complainant was afraid since he told her repeatedly not to be afraid. The complainant clearly articulated her absence of consent: she said no. Not only did the accused not stop, but after a brief pause, as Fraser C.J. puts it, he went on to an "increased level of sexual activity" to which twice the complainant said no. What could be clearer?

. . . .

In the circumstances of this case, it is difficult to understand how the question of implied consent even arose. Although he found the complainant credible, and accepted her evidence that she said "no" on three occasions and was afraid, the trial judge nonetheless did not take "no" to mean that the complainant did not consent. Rather, he concluded that she implicitly consented and that the Crown had failed to prove lack of consent. This was a fundamental error. As noted by Professor Stuart in Annotation on *R. v. Ewanchuk* (1998), 13 C.R. (5th) 330, at p. 330:

> Both the trial judgment and that of Justice McClung do not make the basic distinction that consent is a matter of the state of mind of the complainant and belief in consent is, subject to s. 273.2 of the Criminal Code, a matter of the state of mind of the accused.

This error does not derive from the findings of fact but from mythical assumptions that when a woman says "no" she is really saying "yes," "try again," or "persuade me." To paraphrase Fraser C.J. at p. 263, it denies women's sexual autonomy and implies that women are "walking around this country in a state of constant consent to sexual activity".

In the Court of Appeal, McClung J.A. compounded the error made by the trial judge. At the outset of his opinion, he stated at p. 245 that "it must be pointed out that the complainant did not present herself to Ewanchuk or enter his trailer in a bonnet and crinolines." He noted, at pp. 245-46, that "she was the mother of a six-month-old baby and that, along with her boyfriend, she shared an apartment with another couple".

Even though McClung J.A. asserted that he had no intention of denigrating the complainant, one might wonder why he felt necessary to point out these aspects of the trial record. Could it be to express that the complainant is not a virgin? Or that she is a person of questionable moral character because she is not married and lives with her boyfriend and another couple? These comments made by an appellate judge help reinforce the myth that under such circumstances, either the complainant is less worthy of belief, she invited the sexual assault, or her sexual experience signals probable consent to further sexual activity. Based on those attributed assumptions, the implication is that if the complainant articulates her lack of consent by saying "no," she really does not mean it and even if she does, her refusal cannot be taken as seriously as if she were a girl of "good" moral character. "Inviting" sexual assault, according to those myths, lessens the guilt of the accused . . .

McClung J.A. writes, at p. 247:

> There is no room to suggest that Ewanchuk knew, yet disregarded, her underlying state of mind as he furthered his *romantic intentions*. He was not aware of her true state of mind. Indeed, his ignorance about that was what she wanted. The facts, set forth by the trial judge, provide support for the overriding trial finding, couched in terms of consent by implication, that the accused had no proven preparedness to assault the complainant to get what he wanted. [Emphasis added.]

On the contrary, both the fact that Ewanchuk was aware of the complainant's state of mind, as he did indeed stop each time she expressly stated "no," and the trial judge's findings reinforce the obvious conclusion that the accused knew there was no consent. These were two strangers, a young 17-year-old woman attracted by a job offer who found herself trapped in a trailer and a man approximately twice her age and size. This is hardly a scenario one would characterize as reflective of "romantic intentions." It was nothing more than an effort by Ewanchuk to engage the complainant sexually, not romantically.

The expressions used by McClung J.A. to describe the accused's sexual assault, such as "clumsy passes" (p. 246) or "would hardly raise Ewanchuk's stature in the pantheon of chivalric behaviour" (p. 248), are plainly inappropriate in that context as they minimize the importance of the accused's conduct and the reality of sexual aggression against women.

McClung J.A. also concluded that "the sum of the evidence indicates that Ewanchuk's advances to the complainant were far less criminal than hormonal" (p. 250) having found earlier that "every advance he made to her stopped when she spoke against it" and that "[t]here was no evidence of an assault or even its threat" (p. 249). According to this analysis, a man would be free from criminal responsibility for having non-consensual sexual activity whenever he cannot control his hormonal urges. Furthermore, the fact that the accused ignored the complainant's verbal objections to any sexual activity and persisted in escalated sexual contact, grinding his pelvis against hers repeatedly, is more evidence than needed to determine that there was an assault.

Finally, McClung J.A. made this point: "In a less litigious age going too far in the boyfriend's car was better dealt with on site — a well-chosen expletive, a slap in the face or, if necessary, a well directed knee" (p. 250). According to this stereotype, women should use physical force, not resort to courts to "deal with" sexual assaults and it is not the perpetrator's responsibility to ascertain consent, as required by s. 273.2(b), but the women's not only to express an unequivocal "no," but also to fight her way out of such a situation. In that sense, Susan Estrich has noted that "rape is most assuredly not the only crime in which consent is a defense; but it is the only crime that has required the victim to resist physically in order to establish nonconsent" ("Rape" (1986), Yale L.J. 1087, at p. 1090).

. . . .

This case has not dispelled any of the fears I expressed in *Seaboyer*, supra, about the use of myths and stereotypes in dealing with sexual assault complaints (see also Bertha Wilson, "Will Women Judges Really Make a Difference?" (1990), 28 Osgoode Hall L.J. 507). Complainants should be able to rely on a system free from myths and stereotypes, and on a judiciary whose impartiality is not compromised by these biased assumptions. The *Code* was amended in 1983 and in 1992 to eradicate reliance on those assumptions; they should not be permitted to resurface through the stereotypes reflected in the reasons of the majority of the Court of Appeal. It is part of the role of this court to denounce this kind of language, unfortunately still used today, which not only perpetuates archaic myths and stereotypes about the nature of sexual assaults but also ignores the law.

. . . .

I agree entirely with Chief Justice Fraser that, unless and until an accused first takes reasonable steps to assure that there is consent, the defence of honest but mistaken belief does not arise (see *R. v. Daigle*, [1998] 1 S.C.R. 1220; *Esau*, supra, per McLachlin J. dissenting; and J. McInnes and C. Boyle, "Judging

Sexual Assault Law against a Standard of Equality" (1995), 25 U.B.C. L. Rev. 341). In this case, the accused proceeded from massaging to sexual contact without making any inquiry as to whether the complainant consented. Obviously, interpreting the fact that the complainant did not refuse the massage to mean that the accused could further his sexual intentions is not a reasonable step. The accused cannot rely on the complainant's silence or ambiguous conduct to initiate sexual contact. Moreover, where a complainant expresses non-consent, the accused has a corresponding escalating obligation to take additional steps to ascertain consent. Here, despite the complainant's repeated verbal objections, the accused did not take any step to ascertain consent, let alone reasonable ones. Instead, he increased the level of his sexual activity. Therefore, pursuant to s. 273.2(b) Ewanchuk was barred from relying on a belief in consent.

. . . .

MᴄLᴀᴄʜʟɪɴ J.: — I agree with the reasons of Justice Major. I also agree with Justice L'Heureux-Dubé that stereotypical assumptions lie at the heart of what went wrong in this case. The specious defence of implied consent (consent implied by law), as applied in this case, rests on the assumption that unless a woman protests or resists, she should be "deemed" to consent (see L'Heureux-Dubé J.). On appeal, the idea also surfaced that if a woman is not modestly dressed, she is deemed to consent. Such stereotypical assumptions find their roots in many cultures, including our own. They no longer, however, find a place in Canadian law.

L'Heureux-Dubé J.'s rebuke to McLung J. led him to protest in press statements. These in turn were the subject of a formal complaint to the Canadian Judicial Council. On May 9, 1999, a panel chaired by Constance Glube, Chief Justice of Nova Scotia, issued a report expressing strong disapproval of the judge's conduct. It did not recommend his removal from office.

What do you think of each of the new limits the court imposes on the mistaken belief defence?

For a critical review see Stuart, Canadian Criminal Law. A Treatise (5th ed., 2010) Chapter 4. See too Deborah Hatch, "Culpability and Capitulation: Sexual Assault and Consent in the Wake of *R. v. Ewanchuk*" (1999), 43 Crim. L.Q. 551.

The Supreme Court in *Ewanchuk* substituted a conviction of sexual assault and remitted the matter back for sentencing. The sentencing judge rejected the Crown submission for a five year sentence. Noting the accused's prior criminal record of four convictions for sexual offences, including rape, the judge nevertheless held that this offence was not flagrant and the accused was now in a stable relationship. The judge imposed a sentence of one year imprisonment. On the further Crown appeal the sentence was increased to two years less one day: (2003), 6 C.R. (6th) 88 (Alta. C.A.).

The acid test of the new *Ewanchuk* tests will be in borderline cases. A rapist does not have consent and makes no mistake. So, too, with any other sexual predator. But the key question is how the assault doctrines of consent and mistake work out when the situation between the two parties was ambiguous and there is a real issue of whether a sexual assault occurred.

In *Ewanchuk*, Major J. expressed the opinion that ambiguous situations are rare in sexual assault cases:

> Cases involving a true misunderstanding between parties to a sexual encounter infrequently arise but are of profound importance to the community's sense of safety and justice (para. 66).

This assessment may be contrasted with that of Justice Casey Hill of the Ontario Court of Justice, General Division, who wrote in an unreported judgment in *T.S.*, [1999] O.J. No. 268, (January 25, 1999), Doc. Brampton 2084/98 (Ont. Gen. Div.) as follows:

> Ordinarily, people communicate things like consent or no-consent simply and effectively: *The Queen v. Esau, per* McLachlin J. Be that as it may, however, we have also acknowledged "the complex and diverse nature of consent" (*The Queen v. Currier, per* McLachlin J.) and that the dynamics of a sexual encounter are not infrequently far from simple. In *Regina v. Welch* (1995), 25 O.R. (3d) 665 (C.A.) at 674, Griffiths J.A. referred to "the varying and private nature of sexual relations". As Dickson J. stated in dissent in *Pappajohn v. The Queen* (1980), 52 C.C.C. (2d) 481 (S.C.C.) at 505, there can be many "ambiguous situations" in sexual relationships and there may well be circumstances where each party interprets the situation differently. It has been said that it is difficult to draw clear bright lines in defining human relations particularly those of a consenting sexual nature: *The Queen v. Currier, per* Cory J. at para. 102.

It has always seemed obvious that extending the reach of sexual assault laws to include such conduct as unwanted touching would inevitably embroil trial courts in deciding whether to criminalize conduct where the parties actually miscommunicated. This is especially likely in situations where there was first consensual conduct and later, according to the complainant, a withdrawal of consent. The acquittal rates for sexual assault are unknown but widely believed to be relatively high. This also suggests triers of fact are finding ambiguity.

It is strange that the duty to take reasonable steps in s. 273.2(*b*) was not considered when *Darrach* reached the Supreme Court or by the majority in *Ewanchuk*. There are undoubted difficulties in interpreting s. 273.2(*b*), which clearly has subjective and objective elements and was drafted to demand that reasonable steps be taken but not necessarily all steps that could be imagined. In *Malcolm* (2000), 35 C.R. (5th) 365, 147 C.C.C. (3d) 34 (Man. C.A.), Madam Justice Helper, speaking for the Manitoba Court of Appeal, recently carefully reviewed case law and writings on s. 273.2(*b*) and arrived at a commendably clear test:

> Section 273.2(b) requires the court to apply a quasi-objective test to the situation. First, the circumstances known to the accused must be ascertained. Then, the issue which arises is, if a reasonable man was aware of the same circumstances, would he take further steps before proceeding with the sexual activity? If the answer is yes, and the accused has not taken further steps, then the accused is not entitled to the defence of honest belief in consent. If the answer is no, or even maybe, then the accused would not be required to take further steps and the defence will apply. (C.R. at 373, para. 24.)

The court held that a new trial had to be ordered where a trial judge had acquitted on the basis of a mistaken belief defence without considering the reasonable steps requirement. After a night of partying and drinking, without any invitation to so do, the accused entered the complainant's bedroom while she was sleeping, knowing that she was married to a close friend. He did not engage in any conversation with her. He stated that by her conduct, he believed she wanted to have sexual intercourse with him. Surely in such a situation, the court would need to be satisfied that the accused took reasonable steps to ascertain that the complainant was consenting to that sexual activity.

R. v. CORNEJO

(2003), 18 C.R. (6th) 124, 181 C.C.C. (3d) 206 CarswellOnt 4679
(Ont. C.A.), leave to appeal refused (2004), 2004 CarswellOnt 4086,
2004 CarswellOnt 4087 (S.C.C.)

The accused was charged with sexual assault. The jury acquitted and the Crown appealed, arguing that the trial erred in leaving the defence of honest but mistaken belief in consent for the jury's consideration when there was no air of reality to that defence.

Per ABELLA J.A. (CATZMAN and GILLESE JJ.A. concurring): —

The complainant and Luis Cornejo were co-workers. They appeared to have a moderately friendly casual relationship which included bantering with a sexual aspect . . . [She had twice said no to his sexual advances.] . . . . On the day of the events that gave rise to the charges, both the complainant and Mr. Cornejo were at a company golf tournament. They did not speak to each other at the tournament and left separately. They had both been drinking.

Mr. Cornejo testified that he called the complainant at home at about 12:30 a.m. and that she sounded as if she had been sleeping. He spoke to her very briefly, during which time she told him she wanted to get off the telephone because she was expecting a telephone call from her boyfriend. Several minutes later, Mr. Cornejo called the complainant again and was informed that her boyfriend had not called so she needed the line to call her boyfriend. Mr. Cornejo called a third time, and asked what had occurred between the complainant and her boyfriend. The complainant told him that her boyfriend was not coming over. Mr. Cornejo said he asked if he could come over, and the complainant's response, according to the transcript, was "mm-hmm". Mr. Cornejo testified that he took this to be an affirmative response to his request.

He arrived at the complainant's apartment at about 1:30 a.m. When he got no response after knocking on her door, he tried the door, found it unlocked and entered the apartment. The complainant had left the door unlocked for her boyfriend. The complainant was sleeping on her couch. Mr. Cornejo testified that he said "hello" to the complainant, at which point the complainant woke up and asked "What the hell are you doing here?" He then sat beside her on the couch, ran his fingers through her hair, and kissed her on the forehead and on her mouth. He testified that she put her finger on his mouth and said "no, not on the mouth". He asked "why not" and she responded "because I don't love you". He then began kissing her on the neck and removed the blanket that was covering her.

His evidence was that she did not touch him in return, and that she remained lying on the couch with her eyes closed throughout the entire encounter. Mr. Cornejo said that when he tried to take her jeans off, she lifted her pelvis. Shortly thereafter, he took her underwear off and indicated that once again she had lifted her pelvis. When he tried to position the complainant for intercourse, she said "no". Mr. Cornejo sat up and said "I thought that you wanted it". She told him to get out. He then noticed he had blood on his hand and asked her if she had her period. She did not respond. He went to the washroom. She told him that she wanted him to leave, at which point he left.

According to the complainant, although she rarely drank, on the day of the golf tournament she drank nine beers and was very drunk. She fell asleep on her couch at home and awoke to find Mr. Cornejo on top of her, naked and attempting to penetrate her. Her underwear and pants had been removed. She tried unsuccessfully to push him off and asked him repeatedly what he was doing. She was explicit in asserting that she did not consent to the sexual activity. She does not remember any of the facts that Mr. Cornejo relies on, and has no memory of him entering the apartment or telephoning her that night. She was wearing a tampon when Mr. Cornejo attempted to penetrate her.

When ruling on whether the air of reality threshold was met, the trial judge relied solely on the pelvic movements of the complainant as evidence satisfying the air of reality threshold:

> And with respect to the summation of the decision in *Ewanchuk*, it states that a belief that one, silence; two, facility; or three, ambiguous conduct constitutes consent is not the defence.
>
> It would seem to me that, if the accused's testimony is believed, there is conduct on the complainant's part that goes beyond any of those three listed items, and would constitute unambiguous consent and that is co-operation in the removal of clothing. And that I take to be the gist of part of the accused's testimony.
>
> Therefore, I think that there is sufficient evidence to permit this defence to go to the jury.

With respect, I believe that the trial judge erred in concluding in these circumstances that the movements of the complainant's pelvis were a sufficient evidentiary basis to allow the defence to go to the jury.

Analysis

In *R. v. Cinous*, [2002] 2 S.C.R. 3, the Supreme Court of Canada discussed the air of reality test, albeit not in the context of a sexual assault. This judgment confirmed that a trial judge has a duty to keep from the jury any defences lacking an evidentiary foundation or an air of reality. As explained by McLachlin C.J.C. at p. 29, the "test is whether there is evidence on the record upon which a properly instructed jury acting reasonably could acquit". Further, the trial judge must consider the "totality of the evidence" and assume the evidence relied upon by the accused to be true.

In *R. v. Livermore*, [1995] 4 S.C.R. 123 at 135, McLachlin J. explained that the defence of honest but mistaken belief in consent "involves two elements: (1) that the accused *honestly believed* the complainant consented; and (2) that the accused have been *mistaken* in this belief" [original emphasis].

In *Ewanchuk*, [1999] 1 S.C.R. 330 at p. 354, Major J. stated:

> In order to cloak the accused's action in moral innocence, the evidence must show that he believed that the complainant *communicated consent to engage in the sexual activity in question*. A belief by the accused that the complainant in her own mind, wanted him to touch her, but did not express desire, is not a defence . . . . What matters is whether the accused believed that the complainant effectively said "yes" through words and/or actions [original emphasis].

He also observed, at p. 356, that "belief that silence, passivity or ambiguous conduct constitutes consent is a mistake of law, and provides no defence".

In my view, based on Mr. Cornejo's own testimony, the evidence points to an absence of consent on the complainant's part and a giant leap of imagination on his. The lifting of her pelvis by a woman who has been drinking, is asleep, and, as Mr. Cornejo well knew, is totally uninterested in any kind of intimate relationship, cannot give rise to an assumption that the woman is consenting to sexual activity. In these circumstances, I cannot, with respect, see any air of reality to Mr. Cornejo's assertion that he honestly believed the complainant was consenting to his presence in her apartment, let alone to the sexual activity he engaged in with her there.

In these circumstances, other than Mr. Cornejo's assertion that he believed the complainant was consenting and the movement of her pelvis significantly after he had already initiated the sexual activity, there was overwhelming evidence that she either did not consent or was incapable of consenting. Mr. Cornejo took advantage of a passive and unclear response.

During his testimony, Mr. Cornejo explained that the complainant's eyes were closed while he was kissing her and while he removed her clothing, and admitted that it was possible that she was asleep during the encounter. He testified that when she said "no", she suddenly seemed very awake and there was a big difference in the way she was acting.

The facts do not provide an evidentiary foundation for the assertion that when Mr. Cornejo commenced sexual activity with the complainant, he believed she was consenting. After entering a person's home, late at night without permission, an individual cannot commence sexual activity with a person who has been drinking and was asleep, and then rely on the mistake defence solely on the basis that at one point late in the encounter, the woman moved her body. The trial judge failed to make reference to any facts other than the movement of the complainant's body after the sexual activity had begun. In these circumstances, the movement of the complainant's pelvis was simply an insufficient basis to allow the defence to go the jury.

These circumstances called for Mr. Cornejo to take reasonable steps to ascertain consent, and as he took no steps, s. 273.2(b) statutorily bars the defence. As explained by Don Stuart in *Canadian Criminal Law*, (6th ed.) (Scarborough: Carswell, 2011) at p. 295:

> The accused still has to pass the air of reality test for a mistake of defence . . . . He now will never have the defence open where his mistaken belief arose from self-induced intoxication, recklessness or wilful blindness, or, more importantly, where he did not take reasonable steps in the circumstances known to him to ascertain that the complainant was consenting.

Therefore, given Mr. Cornejo's failure to take any steps, in the words of McLachlin J. in *Cinous* at p. 31, there was no 'real issue' for the jury to decide.

. . . .

The requirement to provide evidence of reasonable steps being taken is explained by Professor Kent Roach in *Criminal Law*, 2nd ed. (Toronto: Irwin Law, 2000) at pp. 157-158 as follows:

> The denial in section 273.2(b) of the mistake of fact unless the accused takes reasonable steps in the circumstances known to him at the time to ascertain whether the complainant was consenting to the activity in question combines subjective and objective fault elements in a novel and creative manner. . . . The accused's obligation to take reasonable steps is only based on what he subjectively knows at the time. On the other hand, section 273.2(b) requires the accused to act as a reasonable person would in the circumstances by taking reasonable steps to ascertain whether the complainant was consenting. Much will depend on the court's view of what reasonable steps are necessary to ascertain consent. Some judges may find that positive steps are required in most, if not all, situations regardless of the accused's subjective perception of the circumstances. Others may only require such steps if the complainant has indicated resistance or lack of consent in some way that is subjectively known to the accused.[46]

---

46 It is indeed now clear that judges differ as to what reasonable steps are required. See, for example, *R. v. Williams* (2009), 67 C.R. (6th) 363 (Ont. S.C.J.) (no positive steps required to ascertain consent in face of passive behaviour where parties were friends; criticized in C.R. annotation by Janine Benedet) and see *R. v. Millar*, (2008), 59 C.R. (6th) 39 (Ont. S.C.J.) (accused acquitted on basis of mistaken belief where intoxicated complainant allowed accused to touch and kiss her). However, courts found failures to take reasonable steps where an identical twin initiated sexual intercourse with the sleeping complainant, who co-operated until she found out he wasn't her partner (*R. v. Crangle* (2010), 256 C.C.C. (3d) 234 (Ont. C.A.)) or where a massage

. . . .

They did not speak at the golf tournament that day, and she had given him no indication that she was interested in seeing him, let alone engaging in sexual activity with him. On the night in question, Mr. Cornejo telephoned the complainant three times after midnight. Knowing that the complainant had been waiting for her boyfriend to visit her, Mr. Cornejo decided to drive to her apartment on the strength of what can only be described as an ambiguous groan on her part. When he arrived, he knocked on the door and she did not answer. Mr. Cornejo testified that he had no right to enter her apartment that night and that the complainant was sound asleep when he arrived. When he awoke the complainant, she asked, "What the hell are you doing here", an unambiguous comment and a clear reflection that she had not agreed to his coming to her apartment.

The only words Mr. Cornejo said the complainant expressed were "what the hell are you doing here", "no, not on the mouth", and "because I don't love you". Either in isolation or taken together, these are phrases of rejection. They are not ambiguous. It is hard to see how these statements could be interpreted as enticement entitling Mr. Cornejo to assume that he could proceed with his sexual activity. These were circumstances crying out for reasonable steps to ascertain consent. The complainant's prior rejections of his sexual advances, his apology to her in the past for his inappropriate sexual advances, her request to him that he hang up during the first two telephone calls so she could speak to her boyfriend, her ambiguous response to his third phone call, her failure to answer the door, his entering the apartment without permission and finding the complainant sleeping and shocked by his presence, all required that he take reasonable steps to clarify whether she was consenting to sexual activity. She never touched him, her eyes were closed, he knew she had been drinking that day, and every rejection by her that evening, even according to his own evidence, resulted in more aggressive sexual conduct on his part.

Mr. Cornejo's counsel pointed to the following as reasonable steps taken to ascertain consent: he ran his fingers through her hair; he kissed her on the forehead; he kissed her on the mouth; the complainant lifted her pelvis when he removed her clothing. But this is a submission that permits Mr. Cornejo to transform his own acts into reflections of consent. In these circumstances, Mr. Cornejo ought to have taken steps before he engaged in any sexual activity to ascertain whether she was consenting. In *R. v. Darrach* (1998), 122 C.C.C. (3d) 225 (Ont. C.A.), affirmed [2002] 2 S.C.R. 443, Morden A.C.J.O. explained at para. 90 that s. 273.2(b) requires that "a person about to engage in sexual activity take reasonable steps . . . to ascertain that the complainant was consenting." In my view, no steps of any kind, let alone reasonable ones, were taken.

---

therapist who obtained consent to massage the patient's chest then proceeded to massage her breasts (*R. v. Zacher* (2009), 71 C.R. (6th) 141 (Alta. Prov. Ct.), confirmed on appeal).

On the basis of Mr. Cornejo's own evidence, the complainant said no and physically stopped him from kissing her on the mouth. This could not be interpreted as a reasonable step in ascertaining consent to sexual activity or as providing him with confidence that he had thus secured her consent to proceed further. Any reasonable person in Mr. Cornejo's position, who was aware of these same circumstances, would have taken further steps to ascertain consent before proceeding with sexual activity. No reasonable person, on the other hand, when being told that someone was uninterested in being kissed because she did not love him, would assume that she would, in the alternative, be interested in having her clothes removed and engaging in sexual intercourse.

As a result, the trial judge erred in leaving the defence of honest but mistaken belief in consent with the jury. Accordingly, I would allow the appeal, set aside the acquittals, and direct a new trial.

In the United Kingdom the recent Canadian *Criminal Code* amendments have had a direct impact in the decision of the U.K. Parliament to finally reverse the subjective approach required by *D.P.P. v. Morgan*: see The Home Office Document "Setting the Boundaries: Reforming the law on sex offences": http://www.homeoffice.gov.uk/docs/vol1main/pdf. The new *Sexual Offences Act* of 2003, in force as of May, 2004, limits the mistaken belief defence to a reasonable belief to be determined having regard to all the circumstances, including any steps taken to ascertain consent. By requiring that the belief be reasonable, the U.K. position is tougher than the subjective/objective compromise in s. 273.2(*b*) in Canada.

To assess whether the Supreme Court has got the balance right consider the *Ewanchuk* tests in the following problems.

PROBLEMS

1. Two teenagers, Jack and Jill, have their first date at the movies. After the movies they go to Jack's apartment for coffee. They talk. Jill tells Jack that she has a boyfriend but also that she is an open, friendly, and affectionate person; and that she often likes to touch people. Jack tells her that he is an open, friendly, and affectionate person; and that he often likes to touch people. They talk more. They touch each other; they hug. At some point Jack kisses Jill. Jack thinks she has responded positively to his sexual advance although nothing was said. Jill did not welcome the kiss and felt she did nothing to encourage Jack. She was not scared of him. She admits that at that point she opened two buttons of her blouse but this was because she felt claustrophobic and nothing else. Jack felt he was being encouraged by her action and touched her breasts. Jill slaps him.

2. The same as problem 1, except that it was Jill who kissed Jack.

3. The accused is charged with sexual assault. The accounts of the complainant and the accused varied significantly. The complainant was 15 years old, a ward of the Children's Aid Society and living in a group home. The accused was 23 years old, and lived in a bachelor apartment. They met at a bus stop, chatted briefly and then agreed to walk to the accused's apartment and drink beer together. On the way from the beer store the accused made flirtatious and sexually suggestive remarks. When the two returned to the apartment, they sat and drank beer for some time. The complainant testified that she became increasingly withdrawn and uncomfortable as the evening progressed and that this frustrated the accused. The accused denied this.

At one point, the complainant got up to go to the bathroom, and when she returned she found the accused lying on the bed. At his urging she joined him on the bed, although she said she felt awkward. The accused testified that the complainant had gone to get massage oil and then allowed him to massage her, which the complainant denied. The accused then began to play with the complainant's hair, and used his hand to lay her down on the bed. They then began to have intercourse and, at some time during that intercourse, he asked her whether he should use a condom, and, according to the accused, the complainant said that that would be a good idea. He then went into the bathroom to put on a condom and returned. However, on his account, he had difficulty sustaining an erection and no further intercourse took place. He then manually stimulated himself and he and the complainant went to sleep. The complainant testified that there was an initial brief period of intercourse, followed by her becoming quiet and withdrawn, followed by a second encounter. On cross-examination, the accused acknowledged that at some time the complainant had said "No", but he took that as meaning "No" without a condom. The accused also testified that he told the complainant, at some point, that he knew when a woman said no, she meant no. The complainant testified that she said "No" on the earlier occasion as the accused was trying to take her pants off, but the accused testified that she took off her own pants. The trial judge found that "it is common ground that she did say 'No' at one stage, although, on the evidence, it is not clear to me just when that was said and under what circumstances". The trial judge found that the complainant was not an active participant in the sexual activity and that in her mind, she had decided she didn't want to have sexual relations with the accused that night. Compare *O. (M.)* (2000), 36 C.R. (5th) 258 (S.C.C.).

4. The accused is charged with sexual assault. The accused and the complainant went to a birthday party at a private residence.

The complainant arrived at the party at about 12:30 a.m. with a male friend. At around 4 a.m. she felt she was intoxicated and unable to drive. She decided to stay the night and lay down on a couch in the living-room. She testified she later "woke up to intercourse". The person with whom she was having intercourse was behind her. At first she thought it was the friend with whom she had come to the party and with whom she had a relationship. When she turned round and saw it was the accused, she was in shock. She got up and left. She testified that when she awoke her pants and underwear had been pulled down. She was unable to provide an explanation as to how this had occurred or whether she had assisted.

The accused testified that he too tried to go to sleep on the couch at about 4 a.m. He testified that the complainant, some time after daylight, started to rub herself against him. He asked her if she wanted to have sex and she said "yes". According to the accused she pulled down her clothes and consented to intercourse. He was surprised she got up and left the house without saying anything.

Is there an air of reality to the accused's alternative defences of consent and mistaken belief? If so, should the defence or defences succeed? Are you satisfied with result?

Compare *R. v. Osvath* (1996), 46 C.R. (4th) 124 (Ont. C.A.), appeal quashed by the majority of the Supreme Court on the basis that the decision did not involve an error of law: (1997), 5 C.R. (5th) 329 (S.C.C.).

5. The accused was charged with sexual assault after he and another man publicly fondled the breasts of an unconscious woman. Early one afternoon, the two men were lying on a sidewalk in downtown Edmonton with the woman between them. A passing motorist observed the sexual touching and called police. The men, who were intoxicated but able to answer questions, were still touching the woman's breasts when police arrived. The complainant was taken to hospital. The police left before she regained consciousness and she was never interviewed.

At trial, the Crown called the driver and the two attending officers. The woman was not called as a witness, and the defence called no evidence. There was no evidence about how the woman came to be lying between the men or about anything she might have said or done before losing consciousness. Is the accused guilty of sexual assault?

Compare *R. v. Ashlee* (2006), 40 C.R. (6th) 125, 212 C.C.C. (3d) 477 (Alta. C.A.), leave to appeal refused (2006), 404 W.A.C. 396 (note) (S.C.C.) and see annotation by Janine Benedet, C.R. ibid. 126-127.

6. In *R. v. V. (R.)* (2004), 20 C.R. (6th) 346 (Ont. S.C.J.) a husband had persisted in sexual advances on three occasions over a weekend although his wife had clearly said no. He did not proceed to the point of sexual intercourse. The trial judge acquitted on the basis of a mistaken belief in consent. He went as far as to say:

> Within the confines of a viable marriage, the Crown must prove beyond a reasonable doubt that the conduct of the accused was subjectively outside the norms of tolerated sexual behaviour in that particular couple's sexual relationship within their marriage...[The] Crown must establish not that the complainant said "no" on that particular occasion, but that in the context of the parties' entire marital relationship, and in the context of the particular situation, her saying "no" differed from the way they historically interacted for a sexual purpose and that the accused , thereby, should have known from such different behaviour that her "no" or her rejection of the accused's advances in fact was different from the way the parties interacted sexually in the past (at 2612).

After deliberating well over a year, the summary conviction appeal judge, Thomas J. of the Ontario Superior Court, dismissed the Crown appeal. He rejected the Crown position that a criminal assault occurred once there was physical touching without express consent of his wife in advance. The Crown's position was held to be wrong in law, erroneous in principle and offending common sense. Do you agree with the Crown or Justice Thomas? See Christine Boyle, "Sexual Assault as Foreplay: Does Ewanchuk Apply to Spouses?" (2004) 20 C.R. (6th) 359-367. The Ontario Court of Appeal dismissed the appeal in a brief endorsement judgement. It was an error to find a mistaken belief defence nor was there implied consent. However the trial judge had made inconsistent findings so there was no proof beyond reasonable doubt: (2004) CarswellOnt 5287 (Ont. C.A.).

A 6-3 majority of the Supreme Court recently re-asserted its *Seaboyer* and *Ewanchuk* principles in the course of a controversial ruling that a person cannot validly consent to sexual activity in advance:

R. v. A. (J.)

2011 CarswellOnt 3515, 2011 CarswellOnt 3516, 84 C.R. (6th) 1, 271 C.C.C. (3d) 1, [2011] 2 S.C.R. 440 (S.C.C.)

One evening, in the course of sexual relations, J.A. placed his hands around the throat of his long-term partner, K.D., and choked her until she was unconscious. At trial, K.D. estimated that she was unconscious for "less than three minutes". She testified that she consented to J.A. choking her, and understood that she might lose consciousness. She stated that she and J.A. had experimented with erotic asphyxiation, and that she had lost consciousness before. When K.D. regained consciousness, she was on her knees with her hands tied behind her back, and J.A. was inserting a dildo into her anus. K.D. gave conflicting testimony about whether this was the first time J.A. had inserted a dildo in her anus. K.D. testified that J.A. removed the dildo 10 seconds after she regained consciousness. The two then had vaginal intercourse. When they finished, J.A. cut K.D.'s hands loose.

K.D. made a complaint to the police two months later and stated that while she consented to the choking, she had not consented to the sexual activity that had occurred. She later recanted her allegation, claiming that she made the complaint because J.A. threatened to seek sole custody of their young son. The trial judge found that K.D. had consented to being choked into unconsciousness but had not suffered bodily harm. However, she found that K.D. had not consented to the insertion of a dildo and convicted J.A. of sexual assault. In the alternative she could not legally consent to sexual activity while unconscious.

The Ontario Court of Appeal allowed the appeal, set aside the conviction and dismissed the charges against J.A. The Court was unanimous that there had not been proof beyond reasonable doubt that K.D. had not consented to the insertion of the dildo in advance of unconsciousness. A 2-1 majority (per Simmons J.A., Juriancz J.A. concurring, LaForme J.A. dissenting) further decided that such consent would have been legally valid. The Crown appealed.

A 6-3 majority of the Supreme Court allowed the appeal and restored the conviction for sexual assault.

McLACHLIN C.J. (DESCHAMPS, ABELLA, CHARRON, ROTHSTEIN and CROMWELL JJ. concurring): —

[3] Our task on this appeal is to determine whether the *Criminal Code* defines consent as requiring a conscious, operating mind throughout the sexual activity. I conclude that the *Code* makes it clear that an individual must be conscious throughout the sexual activity in order to provide the requisite consent. Parliament requires ongoing, conscious consent to ensure that women and men are not the victims of sexual exploitation, and to ensure that individuals engaging in sexual activity are capable of asking their partners to stop at any point.

...

[21] The only question before this Court is whether consent for the purposes of sexual assault requires the complainant to be conscious throughout the sexual activity. This is because the Crown appeals to this Court as of right on the basis of "any question of law on which a judge of the court of appeal dissents": *Criminal Code*, s. 693(1)(*a*). Accordingly, whether the complainant consented in fact or suffered bodily harm are not at issue; nor is the Court of Appeal's holding that for reasons of procedural fairness, the Crown in this case cannot rely on bodily harm to vitiate consent since it did not formally allege that bodily harm occurred. Since the issue of bodily harm is not before this Court, I take no position on whether or in which circumstances individuals may consent to bodily harm during sexual activity. In my view, it would be inappropriate to decide the matter without the benefit of submissions from interested groups.

B. *Framework of Sexual Assault*

[22] Before turning to the issue in this case, it is useful to consider the framework of the law of sexual assault.

[23] A conviction for sexual assault under s. 271(1) of the *Criminal Code* requires proof beyond a reasonable doubt of the *actus reus* and the *mens rea* of the offence. A person commits the *actus reus* if he touches another person in a sexual way without her consent. Consent for this purpose is actual subjective consent in the mind of the complainant at the time of the sexual activity in question: *Ewanchuk*. As discussed below, the *Criminal Code*, s. 273.1(2), limits this definition by stipulating circumstances where consent is not obtained.

[24] A person has the required mental state, or *mens rea* of the offence, when he or she knew that the complainant was not consenting to the sexual act in question, or was reckless or wilfully blind to the absence of consent. The accused may raise the defence of honest but mistaken belief in consent if he believed that the complainant communicated consent to engage in the sexual activity. However, as discussed below, ss. 273.1(2) and 273.2 limit the cases in which the accused may rely on this defence. For instance, the accused cannot argue that he misinterpreted the complainant saying "no" as meaning "yes" (*Ewanchuk*, at para. 51).

[25] The issue in this case is whether the complainant consented, which is relevant to the *actus reus*; the Crown must prove the absence of consent to fulfill the requirements of the wrongful act. However, the provisions of the *Criminal Code* with respect to the *mens rea* defence of honest but mistaken belief also shed light on the issue of whether consent requires the complainant to have been conscious throughout the duration of the sexual activity.

[26] The relevant provisions of the *Criminal Code* are ss. 265, 273.1 and 273.2.

C. *The Concept of Consent under the Criminal Code*

[31] The foregoing provisions of the *Criminal Code* indicate that Parliament viewed consent as the conscious agreement of the complainant to engage in every sexual act in a particular encounter.

[32] The proper approach to statutory interpretation was summarized in *Canada Trustco Mortgage Co. v. Canada*, 2005 SCC 54, [2005] 2 S.C.R. 601: "The interpretation of a statutory provision must be made according to a textual, contextual and purposive analysis to find a meaning that is harmonious with the Act as a whole." The Court emphasized that while "[t]he relative effects of ordinary meaning, context and purpose on the interpretive process may vary, . . . in all cases the court must seek to read the provisions of an Act as a harmonious whole" (para 10).

[33] It follows that we must seek to interpret the provisions that deal with consent in a harmonious way. Applying this approach, we see that Parliament defined consent in a way that requires the complainant to be conscious throughout the sexual activity in question. The issue is not whether the Court should identify a new exception that vitiates consent to sexual activity while unconscious (see Fish J., at para. 95), but whether an unconscious person can qualify as consenting under Parliament's definition.

[34] Consent for the purposes of sexual assault is defined in s. 273.1(1) as "the voluntary agreement of the complainant to engage in the sexual activity in question". This suggests that the consent of the complainant must be specifically

directed to each and every sexual act, negating the argument that broad advance consent is what Parliament had in mind. As discussed below, this Court has also interpreted this provision as requiring the complainant to consent to the activity "at the time it occur[s]" (*Ewanchuk*, at para. 26).

[35] Section 273.1(2) provides a non-exhaustive list of circumstances in which no consent is obtained. These examples shed further light on Parliament's understanding of consent.

[36] Section 273.1(2)(*b*) provides that no consent is obtained if "the complainant is incapable of consenting to the activity". Parliament was concerned that sexual acts might be perpetrated on persons who do not have the mental capacity to give meaningful consent. This might be because of mental impairment. It also might arise from unconsciousness: see *R. v. Esau*, [1997] 2 S.C.R. 777; *R v. Humphrey* (2001), 143 O.A.C. 151, at para. 56, *per* Charron J.A. (as she then was). It follows that Parliament intended consent to mean the conscious consent of an operating mind.

[37] The provisions of the *Criminal Code* that relate to the *mens rea* of sexual assault confirm that individuals must be conscious throughout the sexual activity. Before considering these provisions, however, it is important to keep in mind the differences between the meaning of consent under the *actus reus* and under the *mens rea*: *Ewanchuk*, at paras. 48-49. Under the *mens rea* defence, the issue is whether the accused believed that the complainant *communicated consent*. Conversely, the only question for the *actus reus* is whether the complainant was subjectively consenting in her mind. The complainant is not required to *express* her lack of consent or her revocation of consent for the *actus reus* to be established.

[38] With this caution in mind, I come to the three provisions that relate to the *mens rea* that are relevant to the issue in this case: s. 273.1(2)(*d*), s. 273.1(2)(*e*) and s. 273.2(*b*).[39] Section 273.1(2)(*d*) provides that there can be no consent if the "complainant expresses, by words or conduct, a lack of agreement to engage in the activity". Since this provision refers to the expression of consent, it is clear that it can only apply to the accused's *mens rea*. The point here is the linking of lack of consent to any "activity". This suggests a present, on-going conception of consent, rather than advance consent to a suite of activities.

[40] Section 273.1(2)(*e*) establishes that it is an error of law for the accused to believe that the complainant is still consenting after she "expresses . . . a lack of agreement [to continue] to engage in the activity". Since this provision refers to the expression of consent, it is clear that it can only apply to the accused's *mens rea*. Nonetheless, it indicates that Parliament wanted people to be capable of revoking their consent at any time during the sexual activity. This in turn supports the view that Parliament viewed consent as the product of a conscious

mind, since a person who has been rendered unconscious cannot revoke her consent. As a result, the protection afforded by s. 273.1(2)(*e*) would not be available to her.

[41] According to my colleague, Fish J., s. 273.1(2)(*e*) "suggests that the complainant's consent *can* be given in advance, and remains operative unless and until it is subsequently revoked" (para. 104 (emphasis in original)). With respect, I cannot accept this interpretation. The provision in question establishes that the accused must halt all sexual contact once the complainant expresses that she no longer consents. This does not mean that a failure to tell the accused to stop means that the complainant must have been consenting. As this Court has repeatedly held, the complainant is not required to express her lack of consent for the *actus reus* to be established. Rather, the question is whether the complainant subjectively consented in her mind: *Ewanchuk*; *R. v. M. (M.L.)*, [1994] 2 S.C.R. 3.

[42] Section 273.2 sheds further light on Parliament's conception of consent. Section 273.2 (*b*) states that a person wishing to avail himself of the *mens rea* defence must not only believe that the complainant communicated her consent (or in French, "*l'accusé croyait que le plaignant avait consenti*"), but must also have taken reasonable steps to ascertain whether she "was consenting" to engage in the sexual activity in question at the time it occurred. How can one take reasonable steps to ascertain whether a person is consenting to sexual activity while it is occurring if that person is unconscious? Once again, the provision is grounded in the assumption that the complainant must consciously consent to each and every sexual act. Further, by requiring the accused to take reasonable steps to ensure that the complainant "was consenting", Parliament has indicated that the consent of the complainant must be an ongoing state of mind.

[43] The question in this case is whether Parliament defined consent in a way that extends to advance consent to sexual acts committed while the complainant is unconscious. In my view, it did not. J.A.'s contention that advance consent can be given to sexual acts taking place during unconsciousness is not in harmony with the provisions of the *Code* and their underlying policies. These provisions indicate that Parliament viewed consent as requiring a "capable" or operating mind, able to evaluate each and every sexual act committed. To hold otherwise runs counter to Parliament's clear intent that a person has the right to consent to particular acts and to revoke her consent at any time. Reading these provisions together, I cannot accept the respondent's contention that an individual may consent in advance to sexual activity taking place while she is unconscious.

[46] The only relevant period of time for the complainant's consent is while the touching is occurring: *Ewanchuk*, at para. 26. The complainant's views towards the touching before or after are not directly relevant. An offence has not occurred

if the complainant consents at the time but later changes her mind (absent grounds for vitiating consent). Conversely, the *actus reus* has been committed if the complainant was not consenting in her mind while the touching took place, even if she expressed her consent before or after the fact.

[47] The jurisprudence of this Court also establishes that there is no substitute for the complainant's actual consent to the sexual activity at the time it occurred. It is not open to the defendant to argue that the complainant's consent was implied by the circumstances, or by the relationship between the accused and the complainant. There is no defence of implied consent to sexual assault: *Ewanchuk*, at para. 31.

[57] . . .. In the case of non-sexual assaults, consent may, where appropriate, be implied at common law: *R. v. Cuerrier*, [1998] 2 S.C.R. 371, *per* McLachlin J. (as she then was), at para. 52; *R. v. Jobidon*, [1991] 2 S.C.R. 714, *per* Gonthier J., at p. 743. This Court, applying the common law, has recognized cases in which the social setting and the relationship between the parties implies consent to non-sexual touching, such as shaking hands at a business meeting or colliding with a hockey player on the ice. Conversely, in interpreting the provisions of the *Criminal Code* that relate to sexual assault, this Court has expressly rejected the notion of implied consent: *Ewanchuk*, at para. 31.

[58] The respondent also argues that requiring conscious consent to sexual activity may result in absurd outcomes. He cites the example of a person who kisses his sleeping partner. In that situation, he argues, the accused would be guilty of sexual assault unless he is permitted to argue that his sleeping partner consented to the kiss in advance.

[59] The first difficulty with altering the definition of consent to deal with the respondent's hypothesis is that it would only provide a defence where the complainant specifically turns her mind to consenting to the particular sexual acts that later occur before falling asleep. The respondent's position is that there is no sexual assault in this case because the complainant consented to both being rendered unconscious and to engaging in the sexual activity that occurred while she was unconscious. If a hypothetical complainant did not expect her partner to kiss her — or whatever other acts are at issue — while she was asleep, the respondent's approach would not provide a defence.

[60] The second difficulty is the risk that the unconscious person's wishes would be innocently misinterpreted by his or her partner. Sexual preferences may be very particular and difficult for individuals to precisely express. If the accused fails to perform the sexual acts precisely as the complainant would have wanted — by neglecting to wear a condom for instance — the unconscious party will be unintentionally violated. In addition to the risk of innocent misinterpretation, the respondent's position does not recognize the total vulnerability of the

unconscious partner and the need to protect this person from exploitation. The unconscious partner cannot meaningfully control how her person is being touched, leaving her open to abuse: *R. v. Osvath* (1996), 46 C.R. (4th) 124 (Ont. C.A.), *per* Abella J.A. (as she then was), dissenting.

[61] A third difficulty is evidentiary. If the complainant is unconscious during the sexual activity, she has no real way of knowing what happened, and whether her partner exceeded the bounds of her consent. Only one person really knows what happened during the period of unconsciousness, leaving the unconscious party open for exploitation. The complainant may never discover that she was in fact the victim of a sexual assault. Fish J. correctly points out that in some cases, there may be forensic evidence that establishes conclusively that the accused exceeded the bounds of the consent given. However, if the complainant never suspects that a sexual assault has occurred, no forensic evidence will be gathered. Moreover, many acts of sexual assault leave no forensic evidence.

[62] A fourth difficulty is jurisprudential. Recognizing exceptions to the requirement of conscious consent would not only run counter to the definition of consent in the *Criminal Code*, but would impose on the courts the task of determining how consent to unconscious sexual activity can be proven. The respondent suggests that the court could ask if the complainant consented before losing consciousness to the sexual acts that subsequently occurred — pre-unconsciousness authorization. This would require the court to determine what the unconscious party wanted just prior to going unconscious, and then assess if this is what indeed occurred. This inquiry would be objective, contrary to the subjective inquiry required by the *Criminal Code*. The only other option — post-unconsciousness determination of consent where the complainant decides when she regains consciousness if she would have consented to all the acts that occurred — is also problematic. A *post facto* determination runs contrary to the rule that the complainant's post-act sentiments are irrelevant; if a complainant consents to sexual activity while it is taking place, but later decides that she should not have, the accused should be acquitted on the *actus reus* of the offence.

[63] The Crown suggested that this Court could allow for mild sexual touching that occurs while a person is unconscious by relying on the *de minimis* doctrine, based on the Latin phrase "*de minimis non curat lex*", or the "law does not care for small or trifling things": *Canadian Foundation for Children, Youth and the Law v. Canada (Attorney General)*, 2004, SCC 4, [2004] 1 S.C.R. 76, at para. 200, *per* Arbour J., dissenting. Without suggesting that the *de minimis* principle has no place in the law of sexual assault, it should be noted that even mild non-consensual touching of a sexual nature can have profound implications for the complainant.

[64] Running through the arguments in favour of carving out particular circumstances as exceptions to the conscious consent paradigm of the *Criminal*

Code is the suggestion that the strict approach Parliament has adopted toward consent in the context of sexual assault has no place in relationships of mutual trust, like marriage. However, accepting this view would run counter to Parliament's clear rejection of defences to sexual assault based on the nature of the relationship. The *Criminal Code* does not establish a different inquiry into consent depending on the relationship between the accused and the complainant. Their relationship may be evidence for both the *actus reus* and the *mens rea,* but it does not change the nature of the inquiry into whether the complainant consented, as conceived by the *Criminal Code.*

[65] In the end, we are left with this. Parliament has defined sexual assault as sexual touching without consent. It has dealt with consent in a way that makes it clear that ongoing, conscious and present consent to "the sexual activity in question" is required. This concept of consent produces just results in the vast majority of cases. It has proved of great value in combating the stereotypes that historically have surrounded consent to sexual relations and undermined the law's ability to address the crime of sexual assault. In some situations, the concept of consent Parliament has adopted may seem unrealistic. However, it is inappropriate for this Court to carve out exceptions when they undermine Parliament's choice. In the absence of a constitutional challenge, the appropriate body to alter the law on consent in relation to sexual assault is Parliament, should it deem this necessary.

IV. Summary

[66] The definition of consent for sexual assault requires the complainant to provide actual active consent throughout every phase of the sexual activity. It is not possible for an unconscious person to satisfy this requirement, even if she expresses her consent in advance. Any sexual activity with an individual who is incapable of consciously evaluating whether she is consenting is therefore not consensual within the meaning of the *Criminal Code.*

Fish J. (Binnie and LeBel JJ.concurring) (dissenting)

[68] It is a fundamental principle of the law governing sexual assault in Canada that no means "no" and only yes means "yes".

[69] K.D., the complainant in this case said yes, not no. She consented to her erotic asphyxiation by the respondent, J.A., her partner at the time. Their shared purpose was to render K.D. unconscious and to engage in sexual conduct while she remained in that state. It is undisputed that K.D.'s consent was freely and voluntarily given — in advance and while the conduct was still in progress. Immediately afterward, K.D. had intercourse with J.A., again consensually.

[70] K.D. first complained to the police nearly two months later when J.A. threatened to seek sole custody of their two-year-old child. She later recanted.

[71] We are nonetheless urged by the Crown to find that the complainant's *yes in fact* means *no in law*. With respect for those who are of a different view, I would decline to do so.

[72] The provisions of the *Criminal Code*, R.S.C. 1985, c. C-46, regarding consent to sexual contact and the case law (including *R. v. Ewanchuk* [1999] 1 S.C.R. 330) relied on by the Crown were intended to protect women against abuse by others. Their mission is not to "protect" women *against themselves* by limiting their freedom to determine autonomously when and with whom they will engage in the sexual relations of their choice. Put differently, they aim to safeguard and enhance the sexual autonomy of women, and not to make choices for them.

[73] The Crown's position, if adopted by the Court, would achieve exactly the opposite result. It would deprive women of their freedom to engage by choice in sexual adventures that involve no proven harm to them or to others. That is what happened here.

[74] Adopting the Crown's position would also require us to find that cohabiting partners across Canada, including spouses, commit a sexual assault when either one of them, *even with express prior consent*, kisses or caresses the other while the latter is asleep. The absurdity of this consequence makes plain that it is the product of an unintended and unacceptable extension of the *Criminal Code* provisions upon which the Crown would cause this appeal to rest.

[75] Lest I be misunderstood to suggest otherwise, I agree that consent will be vitiated where the contemplated sexual activity involves a degree of bodily harm or risk of fatal injury that cannot be condoned under the common law, or on grounds of public policy. Asphyxiation to the point of unconsciousness may well rise to that level, but the contours of this limitation on consent have not been addressed by the parties. Nor has the matter been previously considered by the Court. For procedural reasons as well, the issue of bodily harm must be left for another day.

[76] I agree as well that prior consent affords no defence where it is later revoked or where the ensuing conduct does not comply with the consent given.

[77] Applying these principles here, I would dismiss the appeal.

[78] Finally, I think it helpful to set out succinctly the issue on this appeal.

[79] According to the Chief Justice, the question is "whether an unconscious person can qualify as consenting [to sexual activity]" (at para. 33). With respect, that is not the question at all: *No one* has suggested in this case that an unconscious person can validly consent to sexual activity.

[80] Rather, the question is whether a *conscious* person can freely and voluntarily consent in advance to agreed sexual activity that will occur while he or she is briefly and consensually rendered unconscious. My colleague would answer that question in the negative; I would answer that question in the affirmative, absent a clear prohibition in the *Criminal Code*, absent proven bodily harm that would vitiate consent at common law, and absent any evidence that the conscious partner subjected the unconscious partner to sexual activity beyond their agreement.

[81] In this case, J.A. engaged with K.D. in sexual activity to which K.D. freely consented while conscious. The Chief Justice would nonetheless convict J.A. of sexual assault, a serious crime. I oppose this result. In my respectful view, it is unwarranted as a matter of statutory interpretation, prior decisions of the Court, or considerations of policy. And it is wrong on the facts of this case.

[82] That is what divides us. The rest is commentary.

[95] The Chief Justice finds that Parliament has created a statutory exception to the well-established general principle that the complainant's genuine consent precludes a finding of sexual assault. In my colleague's view, the purpose and effect of this perceived exception is to vitiate consent to "unconscious sexual activity" — that is, sexual contact that is expected to occur while the consenting adult is asleep or unconscious. With respect, nothing in the *Criminal Code* indicates that Parliament has considered, let alone adopted, an exception of this sort.

[96] Section 273.1(1) of the *Code* defines consent for the purposes of the sexual assault provisions as "the voluntary agreement of the complainant to engage in the sexual activity in question". Nothing in this definition refers to the timing of consent or otherwise excludes advance consent to unconscious sexual contact. And it is important to remember that, on this appeal, neither the voluntariness nor the specificity of the complainant's consent is in issue before us.

[97] On the contrary, as the Court of Appeal found, there is no basis in the evidence to support a finding that the complainant did not freely and consciously consent to "the sexual activity in question": erotic asphyxiation involving anal penetration during the contemplated period of transitory unconsciousness, followed by vaginal intercourse.

[101] Section 273.1(2)(*b*) provides that "[n]o consent is obtained . . . where . . . the complainant is incapable of consenting to the activity". I agree that unconsciousness qualifies as "incapa[city]" within the meaning of this provision. But it is apparent from the ordinary meaning of the words used by Parliament and from their context that s. 273.1(2)(*b*) has no application here. It simply confirms that consent cannot be *obtained* from a person who is at the time

incapable of consenting. It does not contemplate consent given in advance at a time when the complainant, as in this case, was *capable* — not *incapable* — of giving her free and knowing consent.

[102] Section 273.1(2)(*e*), the second exception invoked by the Crown, provides that no consent is obtained where "the complainant, having consented to engage in sexual activity, <u>expresses, by words or conduct, a lack of agreement to continue to engage in the activity</u>". The Crown submits, and the Chief Justice accepts, that this provision is inconsistent with the possibility of advance consent to unconscious sexual touching because Parliament intended people engaged in sexual activity to have the right to revoke consent at any time during the activity and "[a] person who has been rendered unconscious cannot revoke her consent" (reasons of the Chief Justice, at para. 40).

[103] I agree that prior consent to sexual activity can later be revoked. And I agree that a person cannot while unconscious consent or revoke consent. It hardly follows, in my respectful view, that consenting adults cannot, as a matter of law, willingly and consciously agree to engage in a sexual practice involving transitory unconsciousness — on the ground that, during the brief period of that consensually induced mental state, they will be unable to consent to doing what they have already consented to do.

[104] If anything, the wording of s. 273.1(2)(*e*) suggests that the complainant's consent *can* be given in advance, and remains operative unless and until it is subsequently revoked: It provides that "the complainant, <u>having consented</u> to engage in sexual activity", may later revoke his or her consent. I agree with the respondent that revocation is a question of fact. In this regard, I again mention that the complainant, upon regaining consciousness, did not revoke her prior consent to the sexual conduct in issue — which was then still ongoing. And it has not been suggested that she had earlier revoked her consent by words or conduct, or even in her own mind.

[105] With respect, there is no factual or legal basis for holding that K.D.'s prior consent, otherwise operative throughout, was temporarily rendered inoperative during the few minutes of her voluntary unconsciousness. In my view, it was not suspended by the fact that she had rendered herself incapable of revoking the consent she had chosen, freely and consciously, *not to revoke* either immediately before or immediately after the brief interval of her unconsciousness. Nothing in s. 273.1(2)(*e*) creates a legal requirement, or a binding legal fiction, that warrants convicting the complainant's partner of sexual assault in these circumstances.

[106] Finally, the Chief Justice relies on s. 273.2(*b*), which precludes a defence of honest but mistaken belief in consent where "the accused did not take reasonable steps, in the circumstances known to the accused at the time, to

ascertain that the complainant was consenting". The Chief Justice finds that, "by requiring the accused to take reasonable steps to ensure that the complainant 'was consenting', Parliament has indicated that the consent of the complainant must be an ongoing state of mind" (para. 42).

[107] With respect, I read s. 273.2 differently. It provides that a belief in consent is not a defence where "the accused believed that the complainant consented to the activity [in question]" and failed to take reasonable steps "to ascertain that the complainant was consenting". Any doubt whether "was consenting" and "consented" refer to prior consent is dispelled by the corresponding French text of the provision: "*Ne constitue pas un moyen de défense . . . le fait que l'accusé croyait que le plaignant avait consenti à l'activité à l'origine de l'accusation . . . [et] n'a pas pris les mesures raisonnables . . . pour s'assurer du consentement.*"

[108] Lest I be misunderstood in this regard, I hasten to add that K.D.'s prior consent to the "activity in question" constituted a valid consent only to the contemplated activity. In the absence of any evidence that J.A.'s conduct exceeded the scope of K.D.'s consent, I am unable to find in the mentioned provisions of the *Criminal Code* any basis for concluding that K.D.'s consent in fact was not a valid consent in law.

[In particular, the minority held that the right of women to make decisions about their bodies, and whether to engage in sexual activity, was better respected by allowing advance consent, not by forbidding it.]

IV

[110] First, the provisions in question were enacted to address policy concerns that are entirely different from those before us here. The preamble to Bill C-49 and the Parliamentary debates preceding its enactment demonstrate that the consent provisions were intended to protect women from sexual violence and to protect and enhance their freedom to choose when, and with whom, they will engage in sexual relations of their choice.

[111] The dominant theme throughout the debates was that women have "the right to make decisions about their bod[ies], including whether or not to engage in sexual activity" and that "[n]o in every conceivable circumstance means no" (*House of Commons Debates*, vol. VIII, 3rd Sess., 34th Parl., April 8, 1992, at p. 9507, and vol. IX, June 15, 1992, at p. 12045). Legislative changes were required to ensure that a woman who previously said "yes" to sexual activity could subsequently say "no" and be taken seriously, first by her sexual partner and, failing that, by the police and the courts.

[112] These policy concerns are simply not engaged on the facts before us: *This is not a case about a woman who said no — at any time*. Rather, the complainant

described herself as a willing and enthusiastic participant throughout all stages of the sexual activity in question. She consented to the sexual activity leading up to her unconsciousness and to the unconsciousness itself. The Court of Appeal found, as we have seen, that nothing in the record supports a finding that she did not consent to the sexual activity that occurred while she was unconscious.

[113] Moreover, we have no idea how long the anal penetration had gone on when she awoke — she may in fact have awoken as soon as it began — but we do know that she did not ask the accused to stop when she was awake and knew exactly what was going on.

[114] I am unable to conclude that Parliament, in protecting the right to say no, restricted the right of adults, female or male, consciously and willingly to say yes to sexual conduct in private that neither involves bodily harm nor exceeds the bounds of the consent freely given. The right to make decisions about one's own body clearly comprises both rights.

[115] Although this right to choose is not absolute, I agree that private, consensual sexual behaviour "should only give rise to criminal sanctions where there is a compelling principle of fundamental justice that constitutes a reasonable limit on the right to personal and sexual autonomy" (D. M. Tanovich, "Criminalizing Sex At The Margins" (2010), 74 C.R. (6th) 86 at p. 90.). I agree as well that "it would be a significant limit on the sexual autonomy of each individual to say that, as a matter of law, no-one can consent in advance to being sexually touched while asleep or unconscious" (Hamish Stewart, *Sexual Offences in Canadian Law* (loose-leaf), at p. 3-25.

[116] Respect for the privacy and sexual autonomy of consenting adults has long been embraced by Parliament as a fundamental social value and an overarching statutory objective: "Keeping the state out of the bedrooms of the nation" is a legislative policy, and not just a political slogan.

[117] The approach advocated by the Chief Justice would also result in the criminalization of a broad range of conduct that Parliament cannot have intended to capture in its definition of the offence of sexual assault. Notably, it would criminalize kissing or caressing a sleeping partner, however gently and affectionately. The absence of contemporaneous consent, and therefore the *actus reus*, would be conclusively established by accepted evidence that the complainant was asleep at the time. Prior consent, or even an explicit request — "kiss me before you leave for work" — would not spare the accused from conviction....

[119] The Crown acknowledges that, on its view of the law, anyone who engages in amorous expressions of affection while his or her partner is asleep would be guilty of sexual assault. In response to the implausibility of the suggestion that

Parliament intended to criminalize such conduct, the Crown has identified only two safeguards, more aptly characterized as palliatives that should give us little comfort: prosecutorial discretion and the doctrine of *de minimis non curat lex* (the law is not concerned with trifling matters).

[120] As for prosecutional discretion, I think it is sufficient to recall that this Court, in dealing with the delicate issue of nullifying consent at law, has in the past demonstrated a "healthy reluctance to endorse the exercise of prosecutorial discretion as a legitimate means of narrowing the applicability of a criminal section" (*R. v. Cuerrier*, [1998] 2 S.C.R. 371, at para. 136, *per* Cory J.). And Justice McLachlin (as she then was), in agreement on this point, made clear that "[p]rosecutorial deference cannot compensate for overextension of the criminal law; it merely replaces overbreadth and uncertainty at the judicial level with overbreadth and uncertainty at both the prosecutorial level and the judicial level" (para. 53).

[121] And, as for reliance on the *de minimis* doctrine, I do not view sexual assault of any kind as a trifling matter. It is a serious crime with serious consequences both for the complainant and for an accused. I agree with the Chief Justice (at para. 63) that "even mild non-consensual touching of a sexual nature can have profound implications for the complainant". For public policy reasons, the Ontario Court of Appeal has held that it would be inappropriate to apply this principle in the context of domestic assaults (*R. v. Carson* (2004), 185 C.C.C. (3d) 541, at para. 25).

[122] Finally, even if one accepts that s. 273.1(3) "authorizes the courts to identify additional cases in which no consent is obtained" (reasons of the Chief Justice, at para. 29), identifying a *new* exception in this case would go well beyond what *Jobidon* permits.

[127] Nor is the rejection of the defence of implied consent in *Ewanchuk* dispositive of the issue before us. We are not asked by the respondent to *infer* the complainant's consent. Her actual subjective consent w*as established through her own testimony*. *Ewanchuk* decided that if the complainant testifies that she did *not* subjectively consent — and she is believed — then the *actus reus* will be made out regardless of her outward conduct. That is not our case.

[128] As we shall presently see, this Court has stressed that consent should only be vitiated by judges in limited circumstances and on a case-by-case basis. The broad nullification of consent now proposed by my colleague can hardly be said to have been decided in *Ewanchuk*, a case in which the possibility of advance consent to unconscious sexual touching was not even remotely in issue.

...

V

[129] In *Jobidon*, this Court stressed that "[t]he law's willingness to vitiate consent on policy grounds is <u>significantly limited</u>" (at p. 766 (emphasis added)). As Gonthier J. took care to explain, the Court's decision in that case was narrowly restricted to situations in which adults intentionally apply force to each other during the course of a fist fight or brawl and serious hurt or non-trivial bodily harm is both intended and caused.

[130] Since *Jobidon* was decided, the vitiation of consent on grounds of public policy has been limited to situations in which actual bodily harm was both intended *and* caused. In *R. v. Paice*, 2005 SCC 22, [2005] 1 S.C.R. 339, the majority of the Court insisted that both constraints remain operative. To remove either requirement, the Court held, would risk the criminalization — "by judicial fiat" — of "numerous activities that were never intended by Parliament to come within the ambit of the assault provisions" (para. 12).

[131] The policy concerns identified by the Crown do not warrant the extension of the "significantly limited" principle invoked in *Jobidon* to a situation in which bodily harm was neither intended nor caused. As I have explained, the record before us does not permit us to revisit the issue of bodily harm addressed in the courts below. Our mandate is circumscribed by the question of law before us, which is whether unconsciousness *alone* is sufficient to nullify consent.

[145] For all of these reasons, I would affirm the judgment of the Court of Appeal and dismiss the present appeal to this Court.

With which position do you agree? Identify policy considerations favouring each side. Do you think that consent and mistaken belief principles in the *Criminal Code* and *Ewanchuk* should apply equally to cases where there was prior consensual sexual conduct? Do you think that the doctrine of *de minimis non curat lex* has any application to sexual assault cases? For markedly divergent views see Janine Benedet, "*J.A.*: Consent to Sexual Activity Cannot Be Irrevocable" (2011) 84 C.R. (6th) 35 and Don Stuart, "*J.A.*: Asserting Dogma Over Reality" (2011) 84 C.R. (6th) 38. For criticism of the Ontario Court of Appeal ruling see Hilary Young, "*R. v. A. (J.)* and the Risks of Advance Consent to Unconscious Sex", (2010) 14 Can. Crim. L. Rev. 253.

Much of the debate in *J.A.* focuses around the possibility of the morally innocent being charged with sexual assault for kissing a sleeping spouse. The majority opinion seems to mean that such a person would in fact be guilty. On the one hand it seems counter-intuitive that such behaviour should be criminal, but on the other hand it seems unlikely that any charges would ever be laid in such circumstances. **To what extent should the law worry about conceptual purity as opposed to crafting a law which is in fact applied fairly?**

For example, the decision in *Ewanchuk* was criticised on the grounds that it had the potential to criminalise the behaviour of morally innocent people who were engaged in typical sexual overtures. Elaine Craig "Ten Years After *Ewanchuk* The Art of Seduction is Alive and Well: An Examination of the Mistaken Belief in Consent Defence" (2009) 13 *Can. Crim. L. Rev.* 3 has published a comprehensive review of reported and unreported mistaken belief decisions since *Ewanchuk*. She argues that situations of ambiguity arising from harmless sexual overtures do not in fact result in criminal charges: rather, a claim of mistaken belief in consent is most typically argued in cases where the complainant is unconscious and intoxicated.

'Ambiguity' arises in these cases not from a pubescent and gendered confusion over the complainant's (lack of) sexual interest but rather from a sleeping or barely conscious complainant who moans, rolls over or lifts her hips slightly while the accused is disrobing, fondling or penetrating her. She suggests that the fear of over-criminalisation has been misplaced and that, properly applied, *Ewanchuk* can reach fair results in cases of ambiguous communications. She applauds the courts for applying these principles to respect the sexual integrity of the intoxicated party-goer but suggests that they have not been properly applied to protect wives and girlfriends where consensual sexual acts have escalated and exceeded the initial consent.

A contrary view is that the judicial record suggests that *Ewanchuk* principles too often result in the mistaken belief issue having no air of reality to be considered by judge or jury. Especially where there was a prior sexual relationship, trial judges sometimes find the *Seaboyer* and *Ewanchuk* principles unjust and won't apply their full rigour. Where both accused and the complainant were heavily intoxicated, *Charter* issues have not been resolved (see below).

5. *CHARTER* ARGUMENTS

After *Creighton*, challenges based on assertion of a constitutional requirement of fault now seem far less likely to succeed. There would nevertheless appear to be at least four possible *Charter* challenges to Bill C-49's substantive regime. Of course, given the seriousness of the problem of sexual violence, if any of these challenges were accepted the court might well wish to consider saving Parliament's scheme as a demonstrably justified reasonable limit under s. 1.

(1) Section 273.2's exclusion of any intoxication defence imposes absolute liability which threatens the liberty interest.

It is quite clear that any penal law that imposes absolute liability will violate s. 7 of the *Charter* and be declared of no force and effect where there is a potential deprivation of the liberty interest. Absolute liability occurs where a conviction can be based on mere proof of the act without any necessity to prove any form of fault on the part of the accused. Absolute liability seems to occur where the extreme drunkenness of the accused is said to be irrelevant but that of the victim determinative. Such a challenge succeeded in the controversial decision of the Supreme Court in *Daviault*, considered later under the defence of intoxication.

(2) Sexual assault is one of those few offences requiring a minimum degree of *mens rea* in the form of subjective foresight.

The Supreme Court has identified a few offences which have a constitutional requirement of subjective foresight. It placed considerable emphasis on the special nature of the stigma attached and the penalties available. Thus far the list of offences is short. The criterion of stigma has been often criticized as an inadequate and unreliable test but if it remains the discriminating factor, is sexual assault an offence calling for such special treatment?

(3) The duty to take reasonable steps in s. 273.2 is an objective standard which is unconstitutional because the legislation does not require a marked departure from the objective norm.

This argument flows from *Creighton* and *Beatty*. Of course, the offence could be read down as requiring the marked departure standard. There could also be a strong argument that one engaging in sexual conduct without taking reasonable steps to ascertain whether there was consent has necessarily markedly departed from the expected norm. Furthermore, the section refers to "in the circumstances known to the accused at the time" and this would appear to allow for some individual factors and thus be a less severe objective standard than that imposed by the majority in *Creighton*.

(4) Section 273.2 is unconstitutional because it violates the constitutional principle that those causing harm intentionally must be punished more severely than those causing harm unintentionally.

This principle, acknowledged and applied in *Creighton*, is sound and should be boldly asserted by all judges. In *Creighton*, the flexible penalty for manslaughter was held to satisfy the *Charter* requirement. This suggests that the new sexual assault scheme will also survive. However, there may be a difference. While the maximum penalty for sexual assault remains the same, Parliament has criminalized, in the same prohibition carrying the same penalty, one who is deliberately aware of a risk and one who was acting unreasonably. The new sexual assault scheme could be struck down or at least read down to ensure that these fundamental principles are respected. The key determination of whether the actor was deliberate or negligent should be made at trial and not left to the uncertain exercise of sentencing.

Do you think that any of these *Charter* arguments should succeed?

Prior to *Ewanchuk*, the Ontario Court of Appeal interpreted s. 273.2(*b*) and held it to be constitutional:

R. v. DARRACH

(1998), 122 C.C.C. (3d) 225, 13 C.R. (5th) 283, 1998 CarswellOnt 684 (Ont. C.A.), affirmed [2000] 2 S.C.R. 443, 36 C.R. (5th) 223, 148 C.C.C. (3d) 97, 2000 CarswellOnt 3321, 2000 CarswellOnt 3322

MORDEN A.C.J.O. (OSBORNE and DOHERTY JJ.A. concurring): —

With respect to the challenge [to s. 273.2(b)] based on s. 7, I am far from satisfied that sexual assault is one of those "very few" offences (*R. v. Vaillancourt*, [1987] 2 S.C.R. 636 (S.C.C.), at 653) which carries such a stigma that its *mens rea* component must be one of subjectivity. See Hogg, *Constitutional Law of Canada* (1992), loose-leaf ed., Vol. 2 at pp. 44-34 to 44-35. I say this because: it is an offence of general intent; it can be prosecuted by way of summary conviction; it is a generic offence which covers a broad range of conduct, some of which may be very minor compared to other offences; there is no minimum penalty, the maximum penalty is 10 years, and within this range the sentence can be tailored to reflect the moral opprobrium of both the offence and the offender. See *R. v. Creighton*, [1993] 3 S.C.R. 3 (S.C.C.), particularly at pp. 48-49, with respect to the offence of manslaughter. Further, I accept that the stigma characterization has been fairly criticized as being a most unstable one for making important constitutional decisions on the applicability of s. 7 of the *Charter* to the substantive elements of offences. See, for example, Hogg, *Constitutional Law of Canada* (1992) loose-leaf ed., at p. 44-35 and Stuart, *Charter Justice in Canadian Criminal Law*, 2nd ed. (1996) at p. 74.

Notwithstanding the foregoing reservations, I am prepared to decide this issue on the basis that the offence of sexual assault carries with it a sufficient social stigma as to require a subjective fault requirement on the part of the accused person. In my view, notwithstanding s. 273.2(b), the offence is still largely one based on subjective fault — at least to a level that would satisfy constitutional requirements.

No doubt, the provision can be regarded as introducing an objective component into the mental element of the offence but it is one which, in itself, is a modified one. It is personalized according to the subjective awareness of the accused at the time. The accused is to "take reasonable steps, *in the circumstances known to the accused at the time*, to ascertain that the complainant was consenting". In other words, the accused is not under an obligation to determine all the relevant circumstances — the issue is what he actually knew, not what he ought to have known.

In addition, while the provision requires reasonable steps, it does not require that *all* reasonable steps be taken, as it did in the first version of the bill (Bill C-49, s. 1) that resulted in s. 273.2 and as does s. 150.1(4) of the *Criminal Code*, which is referred to in the judgment of the Supreme Court of Canada in *R. v. Nguyen*, [1990] 2 S.C.R. 906 (S.C.C.) at 922 and 925. Clearly, "all reasonable steps" imposes a more onerous burden than that in s. 273.2(b). I, of course, do not intend to express any view on the constitutionality of s. 150.1(4).

The subjective *mens rea* component of the offence remains largely intact. The provision does not require that a mistaken belief in consent must be reasonable in order to exculpate. The provision merely requires that a person about to engage in sexual activity take "reasonable steps . . . to ascertain that the complainant was consenting." Were a person to take reasonable steps, and nonetheless make an unreasonable mistake about the presence of consent, he or she would be entitled to ask the trier of fact to acquit on this basis.

The extent to which the provision alters principles of liability underlying the offence of sexual assault is indicated in the reasons of McLachlin J. in *R. v. Esau* (1997), 116 C.C.C. (3d) 289 (S.C.C.) at 314. Although the statement is in a dissenting judgment I do not think that there is any proposition in the majority judgment of Major J. at variance with it. McLachlin J. said:

> A person is not entitled to take ambiguity as the equivalent of consent. If a person, acting honestly and without wilful blindness, perceives his companion's conduct as ambiguous or unclear, his duty is to abstain or obtain clarification on the issue of consent. This appears to be the rule at common law. In this situation, to use the words of Lord Cross of Chelsea in *Morgan, supra*, [[1976] A.C. 182] at p. 203, "it is only fair to the woman and not in the least unfair to the man that he should be under a duty to take reasonable care to ascertain that she is consenting to the intercourse and be at risk of a prosecution if he fails to take such care". As Glanville Williams, *Textbook of Criminal Law* (London: Stevens & Sons, 1978), at p. 101, put it: "the defendant is guilty if he realized the woman might not be consenting and took no steps to find out".

Following this quotation, she said at pp. 314-15:

> I note that Parliament has affirmed this common sense proposition in enacting s. 273.2 of the *Criminal Code* of Canada which states that "[i]t is not a defence to a charge [of sexual assault] that the accused believed that the complainant consented to the activity that forms the subject-matter of the charge, where . . . the accused did not take reasonable steps, in the circumstances known to the accused at the time, to ascertain that the complainant was consenting". See also *R. v. Darrach* (1994), 17 O.R. (3d) 481 (Prov. Div.) [the judgment under appeal before this court]. The question is whether the defendant at bar, properly attentive to the issue of consent (i.e., not wilfully blind), could have, in light of the ambiguity, honestly concluded that the complainant had the capacity and was consenting to the sexual activity.

Finally, having regard to the basic rationale underlying constitutionally mandated fault requirements that it is wrong to punish a person who is "morally innocent" (*Reference re s. 94(2) of the Motor Vehicle Act (British Columbia)* (1985), 23 C.C.C. (3d) 289 (S.C.C.) at 311), it is difficult to contemplate that a man who has sexual intercourse with a woman who has not consented is morally innocent if he has not taken reasonable steps to ascertain that she was consenting.

. . . .

This *Charter* issue was not brought before the Supreme Court of Canada when the decision was appealed.

In its controversial decision in *R. v. O'Connor* (1995), 44 C.R. (4th) 1, 103 C.C.C. (3d) 1, [1995] 4 S.C.R. 411, respecting defence access to medical records of sexual assault complaints, the court unanimously decided that the right of the accused to full answer and defence should be weighed against the privacy rights of complainants which were constitutionally protected under ss. 7 and 8 of the *Charter*. However a 5-4 majority refused to recognize s. 15 equality rights for such complainants. Parliament, in Bill C-49, and in Bill C-72 in response to *Daviault*, see later, and in its Bill in response to *O'Connor* which introduced ss. 276.1-278.91 into the *Criminal Code*, invokes in aid in preambles, equality rights of women and children.

Recognition of equality rights for sexual assault complainants came with a revised composition of the court in *Mills*, [1999] 3 S.C.R. 668, 28 C.R. (5th) 207, 139 C.C.C. (3d) 321 (S.C.C.). When it came to establish a s. 15 right to equality, the court proceeded by mere assertion. Particularly stunning is the lack of any reference to the ten-part test for judging s. 15 claims established in *Law v. Canada (Minister of Human Resources Development)*, [1999] 1 S.C.R. 497 (S.C.C.), by Justice Iacobucci J. for a unanimous court, only a few month earlier. The court in *Law* set out to describe basic principles under which courts are to analyze claims of discrimination under s. 15. The essence of the *Law* test is that there is in fact no *Charter* guarantee of equality *per se*. The guarantee is against discrimination within the meaning of s. 15. This is set out in part 3 of *Law* as follows:

> (3) Accordingly, a court that is called upon to determine a discrimination claim under s. 15(1) should make the following three broad inquiries:
>
> A. Does the impugned law (a) draw a formal distinction between the claimant and others on the basis of one or more personal characteristics, or (b) fail to take into account the claimant's already disadvantaged position within Canadian society resulting in substantively differential treatment between the claimant and others on the basis of one or more personal characteristics?
>
> B. Is the claimant subject to differential treatment based on one or more enumerated and analogous grounds?
>
> and
>
> C. Does the differential treatment discriminate, by imposing a burden upon or withholding a benefit from the claimant in a manner which reflects the stereotypical application of presumed group or personal characteristics, or which otherwise has the effect of perpetuating or promoting the view that the individual is less capable or worthy of recognition or value as a human being or as a member of Canadian society, equally deserving of concern, respect, and consideration? (para 88).

The Court in *Law* also requires careful identification of "one or more relevant comparators", discrimination on an enumerated or analogous ground and a consideration of context. Why then did the court in *Mills* not apply any of this careful analysis? In *Law*, Iacobucci J. did indicate that they were guidelines for analysis and not to be interpreted as a rigid test. He certainly didn't suggest they could be ignored. It would clearly be an error of law for lower courts to do so. Is the comparator group in *Mills* all other victims of crime or is it male victims of sexual assault? It surely couldn't be the accused given that the context is a criminal trial where the issue is punishment rather than compensation. Is the violation discrimination by gender or age or is it an analogous ground because complainants in sexual assault cases have been discriminated against through myths and stereotypical views?

The implications of an enforceable s. 15 claim for complainants in sexual assault cases is left unexplored. The policy issues are far wider than establishing rights for protection of therapeutic and other records of complainants. Can complainants now seek status to be represented throughout a sexual assault trial? How about rights to cross-examine the accused, to challenge the similar fact evidence rule or to reverse the presumption of innocence?

See, further, Stuart, *Charter Justice in Canadian Criminal Law* (5th ed., 2010) Chapters 1 and 10.

In *R. v. Shearing* (2002), 2 C.R. (6th) 213 (S.C.C.), a case involving multiple sexual offence charges, the defence counsel had been given the diary of one of the complainants. The trial judge allowed him to cross-examine on the inconsistencies between that document and her present testimony. The trial judge, however, refused to permit cross-examination on the failure by the complainant to mention anything about sexual abuse by the accused. When the matter reached the Supreme Court, a 7-2 majority ordered a new trial to allow such cross-examination. Binnie J., writing for the majority, saw the issue as one of the right to cross-examine rather than production. *Seaboyer* was the controlling authority. The majority also speaks of equality "interests" rather than equality rights. L'Heureux-Dubé J. (Gonthier J. concurring) dissented on the basis that the defence should hand back the diary and seek production under the *Criminal Code* provisions. She also considered that the majority had wrongly returned to the doctrine of recent complaint. For a comment on *Shearing* see Stuart, "*Shearing*: Admitting Similar Fact Evidence and Re-asserting the Priority of Rights of Accused in Sexual Assault Trials" (2002), 2 C.R. (6th) 268.

In *R. v. Kapp*, 2008 SCC 41, 58 C.R. (6th) 1 (S.C.C.) , a decision on the affirmative action clause section 15(2), the court was unanimous in backing away from the *Law* tests. Chief Justice McLachlin and Justice Abella, speaking for the court, re-emphasised its approach in *Andrews v. Law Society of British Columbia*, [1989] 1 S.C.R. 143. In particular the court now holds that dignity of the person is no longer a test of discrimination and that the *Law* factors need not be slavishly followed. The court cites but does not analyse numerous scholarly criticisms of the *Law* test, which in general suggest that the approach in *Law* was too complicated, too confusing and made s. 15 claims much harder to establish. The exact significance of the court's retreat remains to be seen in future cases but its promise of a new and simpler path will likely be widely applauded.

6. OTHER SUBSTANTIVE OPTIONS

Would it have been preferable for Parliament to have created a separate offence of negligent sexual assault penalizing unreasonable behaviour in a sexual context with a maximum penalty of five years' imprisonment? Would the possibility of guilty pleas to this lesser offence be an advantage? Should

the distinction between deliberate and negligent conduct be left to sentencing? Should it make a difference?

For the case for a separate negligent sexual assault offence see Stuart, "Sexual Assault Substantive Issues Before and After Bill C-49" (1993), 35 Crim. L.Q. 1. and Helen Power, "Towards a Redefinition of the Mens Rea of Rape" (2003), 23 Oxford J. Legal Stud. 381.

Some commentators express concern that placing rape in the same category as sexual touching, including an unwanted kiss, has trivialized rape. Some view rape as more than a crime of violence:

CATHERINE MCKINNON, FEMINISM, MARXISM AND THE STATE: TOWARDS FEMINIST JURISPRUDENCE

(1983), 8 Signs: Journal of Women in Culture and Society 635 at 646-647

Feminists have reconceived rape as central to women's condition in two ways. Some see rape as an act of violence, not sexuality, the threat of which intimidates all women. Others see rape, including its violence, as an expression of male sexuality, the social imperatives of which define all women. . . . The more feminist view to me, one which derives from victims' experiences, sees sexuality as a social sphere of male power of which forced sex is paradigmatic. Rape is not less sexual for being violent: to the extent that coercion has become integral to male sexuality, rape may be sexual to the degree that, and because, it is violent.

The point of defining rape as "violence not sex" or "violence against women" has been to separate sexuality from gender in order to affirm sex (heterosexuality) while rejecting violence (rape). The problem remains what it has always been: telling the difference. The convergence of sexuality with violence, long used at law to deny the reality of women's violation, is recognized by rape survivors, with a difference: where the legal system has seen the intercourse in rape, victims see the rape in intercourse. The uncoerced context for sexual expression becomes as elusive as the physical acts come to feel indistinguishable. Instead of asking, what is the violation of rape, what if we ask, what is the nonviolation of intercourse? To tell what is wrong with rape, explain what is right about sex. If this, in turn, is difficult, the difficulty is as instructive as the difficulty men have in telling the difference when women see one. Perhaps the wrong of rape has proven so difficult to articulate because the unquestionable starting point has been that rape is definable as distinct from intercourse, when for women it is difficult to distinguish them under conditions of male domination.

KATIE ROIPHE, RAPE HYPE BETRAYS FEMINISM

New York Times Magazine, June 13, 1993

People have asked me if I have ever been date-raped. And thinking back on complicated nights, on too many glasses of wine, on strange and familiar beds, I would have to say yes. With such a sweeping definition of rape, I wonder how many people there are, male or female, who haven't been date-raped at one point or another. People pressure and manipulate and cajole each other into all sorts of things all of the time.

With their expansive version of rape, rape-crisis feminists are inventing a kinder, gentler sexuality. Beneath the broad definition of rape, these feminists are endorsing their own utopian vision of sexual relations: sex without struggle, sex without power, sex without persuasion, sex without pursuit. If verbal coercion constitutes rape, then the word rape itself expands to include any kind of sex a woman experiences as negative.

Experience since 1983 suggests that rape prosecutions are now routinely prosecuted at the lowest level of sexual assault, as sexual assault *simpliciter*. The problem is that the second category under s. 272 requires proof of bodily harm, a threat or the use of a weapon. This may be difficult to prove in many acquaintance-rape situations where there may be no physical injury such as bruises.

In *B. (W.P.)* (1992), 13 C.R. (4th) 281 (Ont. Prov. Ct.), Judge Cole decided on his own motion to commit an accused charged with sexual assault *simpliciter* to trial on the more serious offence of sexual assault causing bodily harm. He utilized the ruling in *R. v. McCraw*, [1991] 3 S.C.R. 72, where the Supreme Court of Canada interpreted bodily harm to include psychological injury. Judge Cole recognizes that *McCraw* was reached in the different context of s. 264.1(1)(*a*), involving the crime of threatening serious bodily harm, but holds that the Supreme Court clearly intended to make a general pronouncement.

There would appear to be dangers in the approach of Judge Cole. He holds that judges at preliminary inquiries and at trial must be satisfied that there is evidence of psychological harm and that it is non-trivial. This may well have the indirect effect of compelling victims to testify as to the consequences of the assault and to be submitted to cross-examination as to the extent of injury. In this sense, the victim will be back on trial once again. Another problem is that it is difficult to see how any form of sexual assault will not involve at least some psychological harm. If this is true, sexual assault *simpliciter* will have ceased to exist by judicial fiat.

Should any form of attempted penetration of any orifice become a new category placed in the second level of sexual assault, where the maximum penalty is raised from 10 to 14 years? What shall the offence be called?

The amendment would emphasize the seriousness of all rapes and make it unnecessary and indeed irrelevant to hear evidence as to the consequences for the victim. If rapists were again singled out for special legal treatment it would be much easier to track and assess responses to rape. At present rape statistics are not separated from those for other types of sexual assault.

Chapter 5

MISTAKE

1. MISTAKE OF FACT

(a) General Principles

On the issue of whether a mistake of fact is a defence, *Pappajohn v. R.* (see previous chapter) is still the leading decision. Chief Justice Dickson there decided for the majority that a mistake of fact defence constitutes a denial that the Crown has proved the fault element. It follows that, in the absence of statutory wording to the contrary:

1. Where there is a subjective *mens rea* requirement the mistake need merely be honestly held with reasonableness only relevant to assessment of credibility;
2. Where the fault element requires objective negligence, the mistake must be both honest and reasonable;
3. Where there is a due diligence defence, the mistake must be both honest and reasonable, with an onus of proof on the accused in the case of regulatory offences; and
4. Where the offence is one of absolute liability, mistake of fact is not a defence.

(b) *Charter* Standards

The fourth situation may raise a constitutional challenge.

Until repealed in 1988 it was an offence, often known as statutory rape, to have sexual intercourse with a girl under 14 even if she consented or, indeed, even if she was the initiating partner. The provision was as follows:

> 146. (1) Every male person who has sexual intercourse with a female person who
> > (a) is not his wife, and
> > (b) is under the age of 14 years,
> whether or not he believes that she is 14 years of age or more, is guilty of an indictable offence and is liable to imprisonment for life. [am. 1972, c. 13, s. 70]

The express exclusion of the defence of mistake as to age of the victim was challenged under s. 7 of the *Charter.*

R. v. HESS; R. v. NGUYEN

[1990] 2 S.C.R. 906, 79 C.R. (3d) 332, 59 C.C.C. (3d) 161,
1990 CarswellMan 223, 1990 CarswellMan 437

H and N were both charged with sexual intercourse with a female person under the age of 14 under what was then s. 146(1) of the *Criminal Code* (since repealed). In the case of H, the trial judge quashed the indictment on the ground that s. 146(1) violated s. 15 of the *Charter*. The Ontario Court of Appeal reversed the decision and ordered a new trial. In the case of N, the trial judge convicted. The conviction was upheld by the Manitoba Court of Appeal which found that there had been no violation of s. 15 and that although s. 146(1) breached s. 7 of the *Charter*, that breach was saved by s. 1. The accused appealed and the appeals were heard together.

WILSON J. (LAMER C.J.C., LA FOREST and L'HEUREUX-DUBÉ JJ. concurring): — I have had the advantage of reading the reasons of my colleague Justice McLachlin. While I agree that s. 146(1) of the *Criminal Code of Canada* (as it read in May 1985) infringes s. 7 of the *Canadian Charter of Rights and Freedoms*, in my view the impugned provision is not saved by s. 1 of the *Charter*. I am also of the view that s. 146(1) does not trigger s. 15(1) of the *Charter*.

. . . .

Section 146(1) of the *Code* makes it an indictable offence punishable by a maximum of life imprisonment for a man to have sexual intercourse with a female under the age of 14 who is not his wife. The provision expressly removes the defence that the accused bona fide believed that the female was 14 years of age or older. An accused may not resort to the defence of mistake of fact, a defence which the principles set out in *R. v. Sault Ste. Marie (City)* ... and *Pappajohn v. R.* ..., make clear would normally be available. These cases provide that absent a legislative decision to eliminate the *mens rea* requirement, where one is dealing with a "true" criminal offence as opposed to a "public welfare" offence of the kind seen in *Sault Ste. Marie*, the Crown must prove *mens rea* (*i.e.*, "some positive state of mind such as intent, knowledge or recklessness") either by an inference from the nature of the act committed or by additional evidence (per Dickson J. (as he then was) in *Sault Ste. Marie*, at p. 1325).

. . . .

[I]t seems to me particularly important to reiterate that long before the *Charter* was enacted our system of law had a profound commitment to the principle that the innocent should not be punished.

Even the most cursory review of the history of the doctrine of *mens rea* confirms this observation and reveals that the doctrine is an integral and indispensable feature of our criminal law.

. . . .

The doctrine of *mens rea* reflects the conviction that a person should not be punished unless that person knew that he was committing the prohibited act or would have known that he was committing the prohibited act if, as Stroud put it, "he had given to his conduct, and to the circumstances, that degree of attention which the law requires, and which he is capable of giving".

Our commitment to the principle that those who did not intend to commit harm and who took all reasonable precautions to ensure that they did not commit an offence should not be imprisoned stems from an acute awareness that to imprison a "mentally innocent" person is to inflict a grave injury on that person's dignity and sense of worth. Where that person's beliefs and his actions leading up to the commission of the prohibited act are treated as completely irrelevant in the face of the state's pronouncement that he must automatically be incarcerated for having done the prohibited act, that person is treated as little more than a means to an end. That person is in essence told that because of an overriding social or moral objective he must lose his freedom even although he took all reasonable precautions to ensure that no offence was committed.

Prior to the *Charter*, Parliament had to use express statutory language in order to displace the requirement that the prosecutor prove *mens rea*. With the advent of the *Charter*, Parliament must now be prepared to show that a provision that purports to make it unnecessary for the Crown to prove *mens rea* and that does not provide an accused, at a minimum, with a due diligence defence is a reasonable limit that can be demonstrably justified in a free and democratic society. I therefore turn to s. 1 of the *Charter*.

. . . .

(iii) *Minimal Impairment and Proportionality*

When the respondents turn to the question whether the impugned provision impairs the right as little as possible, they assert that the defence of due diligence or reasonable belief would not provide as effective a deterrent to men who might wish to engage in sexual intercourse with a female under 14 as the removal of all defences based on the accused's lack of knowledge of the victim's age. They also submit that the fact that Parliament has chosen to replace s. 146(1) with a provision that allows for a due diligence defence does not mean that one cannot justify s. 146(1) as a reasonable limit on s. 7 of the *Charter*. I note that Justice McLachlin not only accepts these submissions but that she is also of the view that in those instances where an accused is truly mentally innocent this factor may be taken into account in the sentence [p. 327]: "if . . . persuaded that the accused was truly morally blameless, he may be set free: see s. 663 (now s. 737) of the *Criminal Code*".

I think it useful to consider these arguments under three separate headings.

(a) The Deterrence Argument

The respondents place a great deal of weight on arguments about deterrence in their analysis of whether the impugned provision is rationally connected to the legislative objective and in their submissions with respect to the proportionality test set out in *Oakes*. . . . [T]he premise on which the deterrence arguments are based is not a strong one since it assumes that before having sexual intercourse with a young girl the accused, including a teen-aged accused, will in fact address his mind to a fairly obscure provision of the *Code*.

But if I am wrong in this, it seems to me that any deterrence value that s. 146(1) might have would only protect a narrow sub-set of the group that s. 146(1) addresses. Whatever deterrence value the fear of making a mistake might have would only protect that group of young females close enough to the age of 14 that a mistake as to whether they were under or over 14 was a realistic possibility.

. . . .

More importantly, the deterrent effect of the rule cannot readily be documented and the respondents have not submitted *any* evidence to support their deterrence argument. Where one is dealing with the potential for life imprisonment it is not good enough, in my view, to rely on intuition and speculation about the potential deterrent effect of an absolute liability offence. We need concrete and persuasive evidence to support the argument.

. . . .

The respondents contend that all that a person need do to avoid the risk of conviction is to refrain from having sex with a young girl unless he is sure that she is over fourteen. But this begs the question: what if he is sure that she is over 14 but turns out to be wrong? This argument boils down to the proposition that all that a person who has made a mistake of fact needs to do to avoid the risk of conviction is to make sure that he is not making a mistake of fact. The argument would appear to be somewhat circular.

This point leads me to another, more fundamental, problem with the deterrence argument, one that Dickson J. identified in *Sault Ste. Marie*. I noted in connection with my s. 7 analysis that the criminal law has come to recognize that punishing the mentally innocent with a view to advancing particular objectives is fundamentally unfair. It is to use the innocent as a means to an end. While utilitarian reasoning may at one time have been acceptable, it is my view that when we are dealing with the potential for life imprisonment it has no place in a free and democratic society. Thus, even if there were some substance to the premise on which the deterrence argument is based, the argument would still, in my opinion, lead to a fundamentally unfair state of affairs.

(b) Sentencing

Justice McLachlin recognizes that there *is* something troubling about subjecting someone who has made a genuine mistake of fact to life imprisonment. She feels that mental innocence may be taken into account when sentencing the accused. It seems to me that her discomfort with the idea of incarcerating the mentally innocent for as extended a period as the mentally guilty is entirely natural. But in my view, rather than work in favour of s. 146(1), this serves to highlight the weaknesses of arguments upholding the linking of life imprisonment to an absolute liability offence. Indeed, it seems to me that my colleague implicitly accepts that there *should* be some correlation between moral blame and punishment.

But one cannot leave questions of mental innocence to the sentencing process. The legislature must take into account the implications of the distinction between the mentally innocent and the mentally guilty when drafting legislation. Any flaws in the provision cannot be justified by arguments that ask us to have faith that the prosecutor and judge will take these flaws into account when deciding how the accused will be punished. Reliance on prosecutorial or judicial discretion to mitigate the harshness of an unjust law will provide little comfort to the mentally innocent and cannot, in my view, serve to justify a fundamentally unsound provision.

(c) Section 150.1(4) of the *Criminal Code*, R.S.C., 1985, c. C-46

In 1987, Parliament repealed s. 146(1) and put in place a series of measures that include a provision that allows a person who would previously have been charged under s. 146(1) the defence of due diligence [An Act to amend the *Criminal Code* and the *Canada Evidence Act*, R.S.C. 1985, c. 19 (3rd Supp.)]. Sections 151 and 152 of the current *Code* create the new substantive offences of sexual interference and invitation to sexual touching. Both of these provisions apply to sexual conduct with a person under the age of 14. Section 150.1(4) limits the range of defences available to an accused charged under these sections, removing the defence of consent but allowing a due diligence defence:

150.1 . . .

(4) It is not a defence to a charge under section 151 or 152, subsection 160(3) or 173(2), or section 271, 272 or 273 that the accused believed that

the complainant was fourteen years of age or more at the time the offence is alleged to have been committed *unless the accused took all reasonable steps to ascertain the age of the complainant.* [Emphasis added.]

. . . .

Sections 151 and 152 seek to protect young people from a broad range of sexual activity. These provisions continue to protect young females from the physical and emotional trauma of premature sexual intercourse. . . . Parliament has concluded that it can effect its objective of protecting young females from the undesirable consequences of premature sexual intercourse in a manner that does not restrict an accused's right as much as s. 146(1).

I am therefore of the view that s. 146(1) does not satisfy the proportionality test set out in *Oakes*. The potential benefits flowing from the retention of absolute liability are far too speculative to be able to justify a provision that envisages the possibility of life imprisonment for one who is mentally innocent. At a minimum the provision must provide for a defence of due diligence.

. . . .

While it is not, strictly speaking, necessary for me to consider s. 15(1) of the *Charter*, it may be useful to address the question whether in addition to a s. 7 violation there is also a s. 15(1) violation, particularly since I cannot agree with Justice McLachlin's conclusion that s. 146(1) of the *Code* infringes s. 15(1) of the *Charter*.

The appellants Hess and Nguyen submit that s. 146(1) of the *Code* creates a distinction that violates s. 15(1) of the *Charter*. They say that s. 146(1) distinguishes between potential accused on the basis of a ground enumerated in s. 15(1) of the *Charter* in that only men may be charged under the provision. They point out, moreover, that the provision clearly envisages that only females may be complainants. The question arises therefore whether it is open to the Legislature to create an offence that applies only to accused of one sex and to victims of one sex.

. . . .

In these appeals we are asked to consider when a distinction drawn on the basis of sex may legitimately be made and when it may not. In the context of the criminal law it seems to me that the answer to this question will depend on the nature of the offence in issue. If the impugned provision creates an offence that can, as a matter of fact, be committed by either sex but goes on to specify that it is only an offence when committed by one sex, then there may well be an infringement of s. 15(1) that would have to be justified under s. 1 of the *Charter*.

. . . .

It seems to me that the first question that we face in these appeals is whether s.146(1) addresses an offence that as a matter of biological fact can only be committed by males.

I note that s. 3(6) of the *Code* states:

> (6) For the purposes of this Act, sexual intercourse is complete upon penetration to even the slightest degree, notwithstanding that seed is not emitted.

In addition, s. 147 states that only males over 14 may commit the offence envisaged in s. 146, a provision that reflects the common law's rather artificial assumption that boys under 14 are not physically capable of sexual intercourse. . . . When s. 146(1) is read in light of ss. 147 and 3(6), it becomes clear that the legislature was of the opinion that, because only males over a certain age were physically capable of penetrating another person, only they needed to be listed as potential accused. . . . In my view, we are therefore dealing with an offence that involves an act that as a matter of biological fact only men over a certain age are capable of committing. And given that only men may be the penetrators, it is as absurd to suggest that the provision discriminates against males because it does not include women in the category of potential offenders as it is to suggest that a provision that prohibits self-induced abortion is discriminatory because it does not include men among the potential class of offenders.

. . . .

[I]t is appropriate to issue a declaration to the effect that the words in s. 146(1) "whether or not he believes that she is 14 years of age or more" are of no force and effect. The section shorn of its offensive words therefore reads:

> **146.** (1) Every male person who has sexual intercourse with a female person who
>   (*a*) is not his wife, and
>   (*b*) is under the age of 14 years,
>
> is guilty of an indictable offence and is liable to imprisonment for life.

McLACHLIN J. (dissenting) (GONTHIER J. concurring): —

. . . .

An accused can be convicted under s. 146(1) although he lacks a guilty mind. He clearly must intend to have intercourse. But that is not an offence. Without wishing to commit the crime or intending to commit the crime of having intercourse with a girl of less than 14 years, an accused may stand convicted. It follows from the principles laid down by this in *Re B.C. Motor Vehicle Act* and *Vaillancourt* that s. 146(1) violates s. 7 of the *Charter*.

2. *Does s. 146(1) of the Criminal Code violate s. 15 of the Charter?*

It is argued that s. 146(1) violates s. 15 of the *Charter* in two ways.

The first is that only men can be convicted under s. 146(1). Men are thus deprived of a benefit or advantage enjoyed by women. The second is that only young women are protected by s. 146(1). Thus males of 14 years or less are not given the same benefit as females.

Two requirements must be met to establish infringement of s. 15 of the *Charter*. First, an inequality or distinction in the treatment of members of groups must be established. Second, this distinction must constitute discrimination: *Andrews v. Law Soc. of B.C.*, [1989] 1 S.C.R. 143.

The alleged violations of s. 15 raised in this case both involve distinctions on the basis of sex, one of the categories enumerated in s. 15. Thus the first condition for a violation of s. 15 is met. The question is whether the second requirement, discrimination, is established.

. . . .

In my view, the essential requirements for discrimination under s. 15 remain as set forth in *Andrews*.

Applying that test, I find that s. 146(1) constitutes discrimination under s. 15 of the *Charter*. It makes distinctions on the enumerated ground of sex. It burdens men as it does not burden women. It offers protection to young females which it does not offer to young males. It is discriminatory.

. . . .

3. *Are the violations of ss. 7 and 15 saved under s. 1 of the Charter?*

(a) Is the Breach of s. 7 Saved by s. 1 of the *Charter*?

(i) *The objective of the proposed limit*

. . . .

Section 146(1) represents the Canadian equivalent of a provision which is known throughout the western democratic world. The offence has long been part of the criminal law of England which we in Canada inherited. It has survived innumerable constitutional challenges in the United States. . . . It is not an exaggeration to say that the offence of "statutory rape", as it is commonly referred to, is embedded in our social consciousness.

These facts attest to the importance of the objective served by the offence.

. . . .

What then is the objective of s. 146(1)? It has two aspects. The first is the protection of female children from the harms which may result from premature sexual intercourse and pregnancy. The second is the protection of society from the impact of the social problems which sexual intercourse with children may produce.

. . . .

[T]he protection of children from the evils of intercourse is multi-faceted and so obvious as not to require formal demonstration. Children merit this protection for three primary reasons. The first is the need to protect them from the consequences of pregnancies with which they are ill-equipped to deal from the physical, emotional and economic point of view. The second is the need to protect them from the grave physical and emotional harm which may result from sexual intercourse at such an early age. The third is the need to protect them from exploitation by those who might seek to use them for prostitution and related nefarious purposes.

. . . .

I conclude that the objectives of s. 146(1) of the *Criminal Code* are of great importance — sufficient importance to justify overriding a constitutionally protected right.

(ii) *Are the means chosen to effect the objective reasonable and demonstrably justified in a free and democratic society?*

A. Rational Connection

Is there a rational connection between the imposition of strict liability and deterrence of men from intercourse with young girls? In my view, there is. Were the defence of reasonable belief available, a man could escape conviction simply by saying that he believed the girl to be older than 14. The defence of due diligence would require him to make inquiries to avoid conviction, but still leaves open the possibility that the girl may lie as to her age or even produce false identification, not an uncommon practice in the world of juvenile prostitution.

The imposition of strict liability eliminates these defences. In doing so, it effectively puts men who are contemplating intercourse with a girl who might be under 14 years of age on guard. They know that if they have intercourse without being certain of the girl's age, they run the risk of conviction, and many conclude that they will not take the chance. That wisdom forms part of the substratum of consciousness with which young men grow up, as exemplified by terms such as "jailbait". There can be no question but that the imposition of absolute liability in s. 146(1) has an additional deterrent effect.

B. Degree of Impairment

The limit should impair the right or freedom "as little as possible" . . . The infringement would not extend beyond what is reasonably necessary to achieve the legislative objective. This is because a measure which infringes more than necessary is to that extent infringing a right without justification. That is inconsistent with s. 1 of the *Charter*.

In dealing with this point, I find it useful to ask whether there is another way the same objective could be achieved without infringement of the right or with a lesser infringement of the right. In the case of s. 146(1), the answer to this question must be negative for the reasons I discussed under A. Rational Connection.

. . . .

I cannot leave this aspect of the analysis without adverting to the fact that Parliament has repealed s. 146(1) and adopted a provision allowing the defence of due diligence. In my opinion, the fact that Parliament has chosen to do this does not establish that the objectives of s. 146(1) can be accomplished with a lesser infringement of the accuseds rights. An equally viable explanation is that Parliament has chosen, for whatever reasons, to reduce its objective.

. . . .

C. Proportionality Between the Effect of the Limit and the Objective

We arrive at the point where we must weigh the impact of the infringement of the accused's constitutional right against the importance of what is achieved by the legislation. In the case at bar, what hangs in the balance is the public and private interest in protecting very young girls from intercourse on the one hand, and on the other the right of a person charged with an offence not to be convicted if he did not intend to commit the offence.

In the abstract, both considerations are of high importance.

. . . .

The question in the case at bar is whether deviation from the principle which requires *mens rea* can *ever* be tolerated in our society. The submission put before us was essentially that in no case could a measure which violated the requirement for *mens rea* be justified under s. 1 of the *Charter*.

. . . .

I cannot accept this submission.

As a matter of construction, to hold that s. 1 can never as a matter of law be applicable to *Charter* rights falling within certain categories is to rewrite the *Charter*. The framers of the *Charter* expressly subjected all the rights and freedoms which it guarantees to the override of s. 1.

. . . .

I therefore proceed on the premise that important as the right not to be convicted in the absence of *mens rea* is, one must nevertheless proceed to s. 1 of the *Charter* to determine if s. 146(1) can be saved as a reasonable measure justified in a free and democratic society.

The first point is that many societies which we would regard as free and democratic, such as England and the United States, consider the offence of statutory rape to be both reasonable and justifiable notwithstanding its elimination of *mens rea*.

. . . .

The second is that the elimination of *mens rea* from s. 146(1) of the *Criminal Code* may be viewed as less offensive than, for example, the elimination of *mens rea* from the offence of murder.

. . . .

Although one may postulate the case of a "morally blameless" person being convicted under s. 146(1), however rare that case may be, one must also remember that all that a person need do to avoid the risk of this happening is to refrain from having sex with girls of less than adult age unless he knows for certain that they are over 14. Viewed thus, the infringement on the freedom imposed by s. 146(1) of the *Criminal Code* does not appear unduly Draconian, considering the great harms to which the section is directed.

. . . .

The actual effect of the absence of *mens rea* in s. 146(1) is much less serious than it may be in other cases.

. . . .

These considerations, coupled with the fact that the lack of *mens rea* in s. 146(1) is less intrusive of the accused's rights than is the case in other absolute liability offences, lead me to conclude that the intrusion on the accused's right not to be convicted in the absence of a guilty mind represented by s. 146(1) is reasonable and demonstrably justifiable in a free and democratic society.

(b) Is the breach of s. 15 saved by s. 1 of the *Charter*?

. . . .

I need not expatiate further on the objective of s. 146(1); it is clearly capable of overriding other *Charter* rights, provided the means used are appropriate and proportionate. The rational link between the objective and the measure and impairment to a minimum degree are likewise established. The only question is whether the infringement of s. 15 is justified, given the objectives of s. 146(1).

I am satisfied that the means represented by s. 146(1) are proportionate and justified when weighed against the seriousness of the infringement of the rights of equality of accused persons and victims under s. 15 of the *Charter*. The singling out of males as the only offenders is justified given the fact that only males can cause pregnancies, one of the chief evils addressed by s. 146(1). The protection of female children to the exclusion of male children may be justified on the same ground; only females are likely to become pregnant.

Justice Sopinka agreed with the majority that the section contravened s. 7 and could not be saved by s. 1. He also agreed with the minority that the section infringed s. 15 of the *Charter* but he believed it was saved by s. 1.

For commentary, see William Black and Isabel Grant, "Equality and Biological Differences" (1990), 79 C.R. (3d) 372.

In the twenty years that have passed since *Hess and Nguyen,* Parliament has created a number of new offences to protect against abuse directed at the young and vulnerable, and has also raised the age of protection to 16. In each case the accused is given a mistaken belief in age defence but this will only avail if the accused took *all* reasonable steps to find out the complainant's age. The standard of all reasonable steps has generally proved to be a tough standard to meet in cases of internet luring,[1] child pornography,[2] and sexual assault and sexual interference where the complainant is under age.[3]

---

1 *R. v. Legare* (2009), 70 C.R. (6th) 1 (S.C.C.) and *R. v. Levigne* (2010), 77 C.R. (6th) 1 (S.C.C.) (in absence of evidence to contrary provision not shifting burden of proof). See, too, *R. v. Alicandro* (2009), 246 C.C.C. (3d) 1 (Ont. C.A.). But see *R. v. Thain* (2009), 243 C.C.C. (3d) 230 (Ont. C.A.) (new trial ordered), *R. v. Hoffart* (2010), 76 C.R. (6th) 182 (Alta. Prov. Ct.) (acquittal), and *R. v. Pengelley*, Ont. S.C.J. (acquittal).

2 *R. v. Morelli* (2010), 72 C.R. (6th) 208 (S.C.C.).

3 *R. v. Mastel* (2011), 84 C.R. (6th) 405 (Sask. C.A.), *R. v. O. (J.M.)* (1992), 17 C.R. (4th) 350 (Nfld. C.A.) but see *R. v. P. (L.T.)* (1997), 113 C.C.C. (3d) 42 (B.C. C.A.).

PROBLEM

At the time of the alleged offences of sexual assault and sexual interference, the accused was 43 and the complainant was 15 years old. They had known each other for about two years. Their interactions were limited to the local hockey arena, where the complainant had tickets in the "kids zone." The two would often talk at the rink or outside in the smoking area. The complainant testified that she never lied about her age, that the accused knew that she was in middle school when they met and that she was in grade 10 at the time of the sexual activity giving rise to the charge. The complainant snuck away from a friend's home and met the accused at his house at midnight. He gave her three or four vodka coolers. He refused to provide the complainant with his last name when asked. He asked her to go into the bedroom and they had sexual intercourse. The friend who picked her up testified that she appeared drunk and upset.

The accused testified that the complainant looked older than 15, that she always dressed in high heels and low cut shirts, and that she had once told him she was 17, although he could provide no details of when that occurred. He also testified that the complainant told him she had a part-time job and that she took birth control pills.

The trial judge acquitted. While he rejected the accused's evidence that the complainant had told him she was 17, he found that the accused believed the complainant to be 16 years or older and that he had taken all reasonable steps in the circumstances to ascertain her age. Should this decision be reversed?

Compare *R. v. Mastel* (2011), 84 C.R. (6th) 405 (Sask. C.A.).

In her C.R. comment Janine Benedet suggests that any

"visual observation" standard is of particular concern since it can amount to relying on signs of early sexualisation that may itself be the result of abuse, so as to justify further sexual exploitation. Girls who develop physically at an earlier age and who conform to cultural expectations to dress in a sexualized way are at particular risk under this approach. Given the magnitude of the potential harm and the reference to "all" reasonable steps in the subsection, the approach of the Newfoundland Court of Appeal in *R. v. Osborne* (1992) 17 C.R. (4th) 350 is to be preferred. There the court noted that the requirement is "more than a casual requirement. There must be an earnest inquiry or some other *compelling* factor that obviates the need for an inquiry." [emphasis added] Smoking and high heels are not compelling factors. Where, as here, the accused knows that the complainant is an adolescent, the need for active inquiry is overwhelming.

Should there be a successful *Charter* challenge on the basis that the "all steps" requirement is placing a limit on the minimum *Charter* fault standard of due diligence? The Supreme Court in *Wholesale Travel*, considered earlier, held that that standard cannot be limited, even for regulatory offences. We have seen that Parliament did not require that high standard for the mistaken belief defence to sexual assault.

(c) As to Nature of Offence

The remainder of this chapter addresses the issue of how courts determine whether a mistake of fact exonerates, and whether it should be thought of as a "defence" or not.

On the one hand one might think of "mistake of fact" as just a failure on the part of the Crown to prove an element of the offence. That is the approach adopted by Justice Dickson in *R. v. Pappajohn,* who indicated it was wrong to view the mistaken belief in consent issue as a defence; it was rather a denial of proof of *mens rea*. In *R. v. Beaver*, [1957] S.C.R. 531 the Supreme Court established that one cannot knowingly possess something without knowledge of the character of the substance possessed. More simply, what of an accused who takes an item mistaking it for her own? That mistake would seem to mean that the Crown cannot prove an element of the offence (that the accused knew the property belonged to another) and so the accused should be found not guilty.

On the other hand, "mistake of fact" is also sometimes spoken of in the case law as a defence.

A particularly difficult issue arises where on the accused's version of the facts he is committing a particular offence but, had he not been mistaken, he would be guilty of another offence. May the fault for the other offence be transferred to find guilt? Courts have not been consistent. The traditional approach is from the old English case of *R. v. Tolson* (1889), 23 Q.B.D. 168 (Eng. Q.B.), which only allows the defence if, on the accused's view, he was innocent of any offence whatsoever. On that approach, an accused who believes he is committing a relatively less serious offence (trafficking in mescaline) could be found guilty of a more serious offence (trafficking in LSD) despite his mistake: see *R. v. Kundeus*, following. However, other cases seem to apply the rule that the accused can be guilty of an offence despite a mistake of fact only if, on the accused's view, he was committing an offence of equal seriousness: see *R. v. Blondin* (1970), 2 C.C.C. (2d) 118 (B.C. C.A.).

These different approaches can lead to different results on the same facts.

PROBLEM

A plainclothes police officer intervenes to stop a fight between two youths. An onlooker, not knowing that he was a police officer, tries to pull him away telling him to mind his own business. The officer punched the onlooker in the nose and the onlooker punched him back. The officer then drew his revolver and gained control of the situation. The onlooker is charged with assault of a police officer contrary to s. 270 of the *Criminal Code*. This offence carries a maximum penalty on indictment of 5 years imprisonment. The maximum penalty for assault under s. 266 is the same although in practice the offence of assault of a police officer is considered more serious and attracts a higher penalty. Consider whether the mistake defence should succeed on the *Tolson* and *Beaver* tests. Which result do you prefer and why?

Compare **R. v. McLeod** (1954), 20 C.R. 281 (B.C. C.A.) and **R. v. Collins** (1989), 69 C.R. (3d) 235, 48 C.C.C. (3d) 343 (Ont. C.A.).

What test was applied in the following two decisions. Do you agree with the results?

R. v. LADUE

[1965] 4 C.C.C. 264, 45 C.R. 287, 1965 CarswellYukon 2 (Y.T. C.A.)

DAVEY J.A.: — Ladue either copulated or attempted to copulate with a dead woman and was convicted under s. 167(*b*) [now s. 182(*b*)] of the *Criminal Code* of indecently interfering with a dead human body. The material part of the section reads as follows:

167. Every one who

. . . .

(*b*) improperly or indecently interferes with or offers any indignity to a dead human body or human remains, whether buried or not,

is guilty of an indictable offence and is liable to imprisonment for five years.

The only point of substance in Ladue's appeal against his conviction is whether the learned trial judge was right in holding that it was not open to the appellant to contend that he was not guilty because he did not know the woman was dead. There was considerable evidence upon which the learned judge might have held, if he had not considered the defence untenable in law, that while Ladue knew what he was doing physically, he was so intoxicated that he did not realize the woman was dead. Subject to what I have to say later that would have been a good defence.

In his oral reasons the learned trial judge, in dealing with the effect of intoxication upon the appellant's understanding, said this:

What does the argument amount to? The only way you can make it, the only way in which you could make this argument — certainly I don't know. She was dead. He thought she was unconscious. Because she was dead? No. That is about it. At the time of the incident can a person be heard to say "that it didn't occur to me she was dead, and I am therefore innocent." I will tell you, I will not listen to such an argument. That would be an admission he was having intercourse with a person.

It is a fundamental principle of criminal law that, unless excluded by statute, *mens rea*, that is guilty intention, is necessary to constitute a crime, and that a person doing an act is not guilty of a crime if his mind be innocent: *R. v. Prince* (1875), L.R. 2 C.C.R. 154; *R. v. Tolson* (1889), 23 Q.B.D. 168, *per* Willis J., at pp. 171-2. I see nothing in s. 167(*b*) to exclude that principle. Accordingly it was open to the appellant to attempt to rebut the inference of *mens rea* flowing from what he deliberately did to the body by proving that he did not know the woman was dead.

But in attempting to defend himself in that way the appellant runs into the insuperable difficulty alluded to by the learned trial judge. The appellant could not have failed, even in his drunken state, to perceive that the woman was unconscious, and incapable of giving her consent to copulation. Indeed the appellant does not suggest that he thought he had her consent to the act. So if the woman was alive he was raping her. Therefore it is impossible for him to argue that, not knowing her to be dead, he was acting innocently. An intention to commit a crime, although not the precise crime charged, will provide the necessary *mens rea* under a statute in the form of s. 167(*b*): *R. v. Tolson per* Willis J., at p. 172, Stephen J., at pp. 189-90; *R. v. Prince, per* Brett J., at pp. 169-170, because in those circumstances an accused cannot contend he was acting lawfully or innocently.

It follows that in my respectful opinion the learned trial judge was right in the particular circumstances of this case in saying that he would not entertain an argument that appellant was innocent because he did not know the woman was dead.

. . . .

The nature of the offence under s. 167(*b*) and the language of that section would not seem to require knowledge that the body is dead as a specific ingredient of an offence under that section, because in most cases that fact would be clear, and proof of a deliberate act improperly or indecently interfering with a body that was in fact dead would be sufficient proof of a criminal intention or *mens rea*. It would be only in the most exceptional case where the offender might have any doubt whether a body was quick or dead, and in such a case he might defend himself by showing that he did not know the body was dead and that according to his understanding he was acting lawfully and innocently. That is what the appellant cannot show in this case, because if the woman was alive he was raping her.

I would dismiss the appeal.

Appeal dismissed.

R. v. KUNDEUS

[1976] 2 S.C.R. 272, 32 C.R.N.S. 129 at 135, 24 C.C.C. (2d) 276,
1975 CarswellBC 181, 1975 CarswellBC 285

26th June 1975. DE GRANDPRÉ J. (MARTLAND, JUDSON, RITCHIE, PIGEON, DICKSON and BEETZ JJ. concurring): — With leave of this Court, the Crown appeals the unanimous judgment of the British Columbia Court of Appeal, ante

p. 133, setting aside the conviction of respondent. In the words of the indictment, Kundeus was charged that he did:

> on the 24th day of August A.D. 1972, unlawfully traffic in a restricted drug, to wit: Lysergic Acid Diethylamide (LSD), contrary to the provisions of the *Food and Drugs Act.*

The facts are stated in the reasons for judgment of the trial judge [p. 132]:

> Police Constable MacKay-Dunn testified that on 24th August 1972 at about 10:15 p.m., the constable, acting undercover in the Gastown area, and the accused were at a table in the Travellers Hotel, 57 West Cordova in the City of Vancouver. The police constable testified the accused was calling out, "Speed, acid, MDA or hash" to passers-by in the beer parlor. The police constable asked for hash or acid. The accused said they were all sold out. The accused offered mescaline at $2. The police constable accepted the offer, requested two "hits" and paid $4 to the accused for same. The accused left, returned in about five minutes, and handed two capsules, Ex. 1, to the police constable. Exhibit 1 was, in fact, two capsules of L.S.D. (see Ex. 2).

The trial judge adds that [p. 132]: "The accused elected not to adduce any evidence in defence."

After having stated that the sole issue was *mens rea*, the trial judge examined the relevant parts of the *Food and Drugs Act*, R.S.C. 1970, c. F-27, and the regulations thereunder, as well as the cases of *Regina v. Blondin* (1971), 2 C.C.C. (2d) 118, affirmed (1972), 4 C.C.C. (2d) 566n (Can.); *Regina v. Burgess*, [1970] 3 C.C.C. 268 (Ont. C.A.); and *Regina v. Custeau*, 17 C.R.N.S 124, 6 C.C.C. (2d) 179 (Ont. C.A.), and concluded:

> The court has considered the evidence in this trial and the able submissions of respective counsel.
> The court concludes that the prosecution has proved, beyond a reasonable doubt, the guilt of the accused.

Respondent inscribed an appeal alleging an error involving a question of law upon the following ground:

> The learned trial judge misdirected himself in law in holding that if he was satisfied beyond a reasonable doubt that the accused knew it was illegal to sell the drug mescaline, although said drug is not a restricted drug as defined in the *Food and Drugs Act*, and in fact intended to sell the drug mescaline, he should convict the accused of trafficking in L.S.D., a restricted drug under the *Food and Drugs Act*, when the substance sold as mescaline was analyzed to be L.S.D., even if the accused did not know that the substance was in fact the restricted drug L.S.D.

The Court of Appeal disagreed with the conclusion reached by the trial judge and specifically refused to follow *Regina v. Custeau*. The conviction was consequently set aside.

Mens rea cannot, of course, be examined without reference to *Beaver v. The Queen*, 26 C.R. 193, [1957] S.C.R. 531, 118 C.C.C. 129.

. . . .

Our facts are different. They are very simple and uncontradicted. One reading of them is that Kundeus was offering L.S.D. for sale, actually sold L.S.D. and received payment therefor. On that reading, it is obvious that the conviction should have been affirmed.

Another reading is that adopted by the Court of Appeal and expressed by McFarlane J.A., speaking for the Court (*ante* p. 133):

> The evidence disclosed, and the trial judge found, that the appellant offered to sell mescaline at $2 to a police constable acting undercover. The constable accepted the offer and paid the appellant $4 for two "hits". The appellant left, returned in about five minutes and handed the constable two capsules which were found, on analysis, to contain L.S.D.
>
> I think I must interpret the reasons for judgment of the trial judge as a finding that although the appellant did in fact sell L.S.D. he thought he was selling, and intended to sell, mescaline and that the constable also thought he was purchasing mescaline.

Assuming that this reading of the trial judgment is the proper one, was the Court of Appeal right in holding that the necessary *mens rea* had not been proved? I do not believe so.

In *Regina v. Blondin, supra*, a case dealing with the importation of narcotics, the Crown succeeded on the following ground of its appeal [p. 6]:

> (e) THAT the learned trial Judge misdirected the jury in instructing it that the Crown was obliged to prove beyond a reasonable doubt that the accused knew that the contents of the scuba diving tank (Exhibit 1) was a narcotic drug as alleged in the Indictment herein, namely, Cannabis Resin.

After a full review of the authorities, Robertson J.A. concluded (pp. 13-14):

> Basing my opinion upon what I understand to be the principle enunciated in the several passages I have quoted, I am of the respectful opinion that the learned trial Judge erred when he instructed the jury that, in order to find Blondin guilty, they must find that he knew that the substance in the tank was cannabis resin. It would be sufficient to find, in relation to a narcotic, *mens rea* in its widest sense.

An appeal to this Court by the accused was dismissed by the full bench in the following terms: "We agree that the Court of Appeal rightly allowed the appeal and directed a new trial on ground (e) of the notice of appeal to that Court."

That judgment must be read with another decision of this Court, namely, *Regina v. King*, 38 C.R. 52, [1962] S.C.R. 746, 133 C.C.C. 1, where the facts, the question submitted to this Court and the holding are expressed in the [S.C.R.] headnote:

> The accused went to his dentist by appointment to have two teeth extracted. He was injected with a drug known as sodium pentothal, a quick-acting anaesthetic. Earlier, he had been required to sign a printed form containing a warning not to drive after the anaesthetic until his head had cleared. After he regained consciousness, the nurse in attendance, to whom

he appeared to be normal, warned him not to drive until his head was "perfectly clear". He replied that he intended to walk. The accused said that he heard no such warning and did not remember signing any form containing a warning. He remembered getting into his car and that while driving he became unconscious. His car ran into the rear of a parked vehicle. Medical evidence was given that his mental and physical condition (he was staggering and his co-ordination was poor) was consistent with the after-effects of the drug in question which may induce a state of amnesia accompanied by a period during which the subject may feel competent to drive a car and in the next second be in a condition in which he would not know what was happening. The accused stated that he did not know anything about this drug.

He was charged and convicted of the offence of driving a motor vehicle while his ability to do so was impaired by a drug, contrary to s. 223 of the *Criminal Code*. After a trial *de novo* before a County Court judge under s. 720 of the *Code*, his conviction was affirmed. The Court of Appeal granted him leave to appeal and quashed the conviction. The Crown was granted leave to appeal to this Court on the question as to whether *mens rea* relating to both the act of driving and to the state of being impaired was an essential element of the offence.

I refer particularly to a paragraph of the reasons of Ritchie J., speaking also for the Chief Justice and for Martland J., at p. 763:

> The existence of *mens rea* as an essential ingredient of an offence and the method of proving the existence of that ingredient are two different things, and I am of the opinion that when it has been proved that a driver was driving a motor vehicle while his ability to do so was impaired by alcohol or a drug, then a rebuttable presumption arises that his condition was voluntarily induced and that he is guilty of the offence created by s. 223 and must be convicted unless other evidence is adduced which raises a reasonable doubt as to whether he was, through no fault of his own, disabled when he undertook to drive and drove, from being able to appreciate and know that he was or might become impaired.

In the case at bar, such a rebuttable presumption has arisen. No evidence having been tendered by the accused, it is not possible to find that he had an honest belief amounting to a non-existence of *mens rea* and the Court of Appeal was in error in its conclusion.

The quality of respondent's conduct is not to be determined by the existence or non-existence of a binding civil agreement as to the purchase of L.S.D. between him and the constable. That is not the test. In *Poitras v. The Queen* (1973), 12 C.C.C. (2d) 337 (Can.), where the question was to determine the exact meaning of "trafficking" under the *Narcotic Control Act*, R.S.C. 1970, c. N-1, Dickson J., speaking for the majority, wrote at pp. 416-17:

> It was argued on behalf of the appellant that the words "to buy" do not appear in the definition of "trafficking" under the *Narcotic Control Act*; therefore, a mere purchaser does not traffic and an agent for the purchaser comes under the same protective umbrella. I do not agree. One cannot apply the civil law of "agency" in this context. "Agency" does not serve to make non-criminal an act which would otherwise be attended by criminal consequences. Even if the appellant could be said to be the "agent" of Constable Arsenault for the purposes of civil responsibility, his acts may, none the less, amount to trafficking in narcotics or aiding in such trafficking. If, as the trial Judge would seem to have found, the evidence was consistent with the accused delivering or selling or trading in drugs or offering to do so, the fact that he may have been acting as an agent for Arsenault would not exculpate him.

In my view, the result in *Regina v. Custeau* was the proper one and this notwithstanding the error committed by the Court of Appeal of Ontario and underlined by the Court of Appeal of British Columbia in the case at bar, mescaline having been described as a controlled drug when it is a drug mentioned in the regulations under the Act which cannot be sold without a prescription.

I would allow the appeal, set aside the order of the Court of Appeal of British Columbia and restore the judgment at trial together with the sentence imposed thereat.

LASKIN C.J.C. (SPENCE J. concurring) (dissenting): —

. . . .

The scheme of the *Food and Drugs Act* is of considerable relevance in this case. Sections 40 and 42, on which the prosecution was based, are in Pt. IV of the Act dealing with "restricted drugs", which are those included in Sched. H, and L.S.D. is one of those mentioned. Part III of the Act deals with "controlled drugs" which are those included in Sched. G, and among them are amphetamine and methamphetamine.

. . . .

It is common ground that any offence under the Act or regulations relating to the sale of mescaline would be punishable under s. 26. On the other hand, this provision would have no application to controlled or restricted drugs in the face of the penalty provisions of ss. 34 and 42 which alone govern illegal dealing in them. A comparison of the respective penalty provisions governing mescaline and L.S.D. shows how much heavier the penalty is in respect of illegal dealing in the latter than in the former, both where the prosecution is on summary conviction and on indictment.

. . . .

It was the contention of the appellant Crown that the required proof of *mens rea* was furnished by evidence showing what Crown counsel called a general intention to traffic in drugs; and, this being shown, it was immaterial that the accused did not intend to traffic in the specific drug which was named in the charge but thought (as did his purchaser) that he was trafficking in another drug. Crown counsel thus takes the position to which I referred earlier in these reasons, and he stated in this connection that the accused could meet the case against him only by relying on mistake of fact which must be an honest mistake on reasonable grounds that the facts believed by him to be true would not attract culpability of any drug offence. That, according to Crown counsel, was not this case.

There are, in my opinion, three issues that stem from this submission. The first is whether mistake of fact arises at all as a separate defence for the accused in the face of the burden on the Crown to prove *mens rea* as an element of the offence charged. The offence charged was trafficking in a restricted drug, namely, L.S.D.; and although I would agree that proof of knowledge by the accused that he was trafficking in a drug of that class might be enough, even if it be not L.S.D., the question that must be faced is whether it is enough for the Crown to offer proof of trafficking in any drug or, as here, in a drug that is in a lower scale of prohibition and regulation.

Having regard to the evidence adduced at the trial and to the findings of fact on that evidence, I do not think it necessary in the present case to consider the relationship between the Crown's burden of proof, where *mens rea* is an element of the offence charged, and mistake of fact as an affirmative defence. Clearly enough, mistake of fact in that sense does not arise where proof of *mens rea* is an element of proof of the offence charged and the evidence adduced by the Crown does not establish it. If mistake is put forward in this context by evidence offered by or on behalf of the accused, it is only by way of meeting an evidentiary burden and raising a reasonable doubt that the Crown has met the persuasive burden of proof resting upon it. What we are concerned with here, on the record, is whether evidence by the Crown going to show that the accused intended to commit a lesser offence than that charged is enough to support the conviction entered after trial.

The second issue which arises on the Crown's submissions is whether the mistake of fact must be objectively reasonable or whether it is enough that it be based upon an honest belief. Leaving to one side cases of strict criminal liability (on which the judgment of Dixon J. in *Proudman v. Dayman* (1941), 67 C.L.R. 536 at 539-41, is specially instructive), where serious criminal charges are involved, this Court put the matter as follows in *Beaver v. The Queen*, *supra*, where Cartwright J. said this (at p. 538):

> the essential question is whether the belief entertained by the accused is an honest one and . . . the existence or non-existence of reasonable grounds for such belief is merely relevant evidence to be weighed by the tribunal of fact in determining that essential question.

See also *D.P.P. v. Morgan*, [1975] 2 All E.R. 347.

The third issue, which is tied in with the first, is whether mistake of fact is shown on proof that, on the facts as the accused honestly believed them to be, he was innocent of the offence charged, albeit guilty of another offence, or whether he must show that he was innocent of any offence. This last matter invites consideration of a proposition advanced in *Regina v. Prince* (1875), L.R. 2 C.C.R. 154, by the one dissenting judge of the 16 who heard the case in the Court of Crown Cases Reserved. The majority of that court held that *mens rea* was not an essential ingredient of the offence charged, which was unlawfully taking any unmarried girl under age 16 out of the possession and against the will of her father or mother. (The word "knowingly" was not in the charge.) The accused reasonably believed that the girl he had abducted was over age 16. One of the points made by Brett J., who dissented on the ground that *mens rea* was an ingredient of the offence as it related to age, was that where *mens rea* must be proved it would suffice to show, if the facts were as the accused believed them to be, that he would still be guilty of a crime, albeit one of a lesser degree than that charged as a result of the *actus reus*.

I do not think that this view is any longer sustainable. The requirement that where the *actus reus* of an offence is proved there must also be proof of the *mens rea* of the same crime is now basic in our criminal law. Williams, *Criminal Law: The General Part*, 2nd ed. (1961), at p. 129, makes the point when dealing with the question of "transferred malice" as follows:

> The accused can be convicted where he both has the *mens rea* and commits the *actus reus* specified in the rule of law creating the crime, though they exist in respect of different objects. He cannot be convicted if his *mens rea* relates to one crime and his *actus reus* to a different crime, because that would be to disregard the requirement of an appropriate *mens rea*.

And again at p. 131:

> What are different crimes for the purpose of the rule depends primarily upon the arrangement of the statute; each section presumptively creates a different crime or group of crimes. It is possible for a single sentence of a section to create a number of different crimes, as is shown by the decisions on duplicity in pleading. If a section is thus held to create different crimes, it would not he possible to transfer the malice from one crime to another even within the same section.

See also Smith and Hogan, *Criminal Law*, 3rd ed. (1973), at pp. 49-51.

This is apt for the statutory situation which exists here and to which I have referred earlier in these reasons. Even if it be proper to describe trafficking in controlled drugs, whatever be the drug, or trafficking in restricted drugs, whatever be the drug, as being, in each case, a description of the same crime, I think it is impossible to bring mescaline within either category when it stands entirely outside the group of controlled or restricted drugs and is governed by other statutory provisions than those governing controlled or restricted drugs. I am unable to agree that where *mens rea* is an element of an offence, as it is here, it can be satisfied by proof of its existence in relation to another offence unless, of course, the situation involves an included offence of which the accused may be found guilty on his trial of the offence charged.

A different class of case, raising the question of *mens rea* referable to a more serious crime than that charged, is *Regina v. Ladue*, 45 C.R. 287, [1965] 4 C.C.C. 264, a judgment of the Yukon Territory Court of Appeal which is staffed by members of the British Columbia Court of Appeal. The charge was indecently interfering with a dead human body, and the evidence showed copulation or attempted copulation with a woman who was then dead, albeit the accused testified that by reason of his intoxication he did not know that she was dead. The Court held that knowledge that the woman was dead was not an ingredient of the offence and hence, I take it, not an element requiring proof by the Crown. The Court also appears to have held, somewhat inconsistently, that proof that he did not know the woman was dead could be offered in defence by the accused, but it added that here he would be in the dilemma of admitting to rape (there being no question of consent), a more serious offence than that charged. It does occur to me, however, that the facts being what they were, the proper charge ought to have been attempted rape.

Is any general principle deducible from the foregoing catalogue of instances? Certainly, it cannot be said that, in general, where *mens rea* is an ingredient of an offence and the *actus reus* is proved it is enough if an intent is shown that would support a conviction of another crime, whether more or less serious than the offence actually committed. Coming to the particular, to the case before this Court, where proof is made of an *actus reus* that, in a general sense, is common to a range or variety of offences which require *mens rea* but those offences differ as to gravity by reason of different classifications and different penalties, is a charge of a more serious offence established by proof only that the accused intended to commit and could have been found guilty of a less serious, a lesser offence? The matter, in terms of principle, depends on how strict an observance there should be of the requirement of *mens rea*. If there is to be a relaxation of the requirement, should it not come from Parliament, which could provide for the substitution of a conviction of the lesser offence, in the same way as provision now exists in our criminal law for entering a conviction on an included offence?

Kundeus is a pre-*Charter* decision. Given the proportionality requirement articulated in *R. v. Martineau*, would the same result be reached today?

2. MISTAKE OF LAW

(a) Policy Considerations

Section 19 of the *Criminal Code* declares:

> Ignorance of the law by a person who commits an offence is not an excuse for committing that offence.

O.W. HOLMES, THE COMMON LAW

Howe, ed., (1963), 40-41

Ignorance of the law is no excuse for breaking it. This substantive principle is sometimes put in the form of a rule of evidence, that every one is presumed to know the law. It has accordingly been defended by Austin and others, on the ground of difficulty of proof. If justice requires the fact to be ascertained, the difficulty of doing so is no ground for refusing to try. But every one must feel that ignorance of the law could never be admitted as an excuse, even if the fact could be proved by sight and hearing in every case. Furthermore, now that parties can testify, it may be doubted whether a man's knowledge of the law is any harder to investigate than many questions which are gone into. The difficulty, such as it is, would be met by throwing the burden of proving ignorance on the law-breaker.

The principle cannot be explained by saying that we are not only commanded to abstain from certain acts, but also to find out that we are commanded. For if there were such a second command, it is very clear that the guilt of failing to obey it would bear no proportion to that of disobeying the principal command if known, yet the failure to know would receive the same punishment as the failure to obey the principal law.

The true explanation of the rule is the same as that which accounts for the law's indifference to a man's particular temperament, faculties, and so forth. Public policy sacrifices the individual to the general good. It is desirable that the burden of all should be equal, but it is still more desirable to put an end to robbery and murder. It is no doubt true that there are many cases in which the criminal could not have known that he was breaking the law, but to admit the excuse at all would be to encourage ignorance where the law-maker has determined to make men know and obey, and justice to the individual is rightly outweighed by the larger interests on the other side of the scales.

P.K. RYU, H. SILVING, ERROR JURIS: A COMPARATIVE STUDY

(1957), 24 U. of Chic. L. Rev. 421 at 466-471

There is a noticeable trend toward increasing recognition of error of law as a defense in several legal systems.

. . . .

Within the concept of responsibility, conceived to imply a basic freedom of choice, knowledge of the law is essential for there can be no choice without knowledge. In answering the crucial question — For what is man responsible? — Binding, the most ardent advocate of the defense of legal error, stated that criminality was defiance of the legal prohibition, a contempt of the law or a rebellion against its commands. The idea that the essence of law violation is "rebellion against the law," however, implies that every lawbreaker is a revolutionary. We believe that in a free society the sanction of the community is imposed neither for "rebellion" nor for "disobedience" but simply for violation of a duty toward the community — the actor's duty, as a member of the community, to abide by its rules. To be subject to a sanction thus conceived, the actor, as a free agent, must know the rule which he violates.

The duty of free men, however, is not exhausted merely by compliance with known law. They must also exert their conscience to ascertain what the law is.

. . . .

Lastly, the difficulty of proving legal knowledge is not in itself greater than is the difficulty of showing the presence of any other mental element. When a man shoots another in broad daylight from a distance of five feet, he will not, in the absence of special circumstances, be heard to say that he believed the target to be a hare. Nor would any man — in legal systems which admit error of law as a defense — be heard to say that he did not know the killing of a human being to be unlawful. The problem of proof changes with circumstances. A man who shoots another might well be heard to say he thought the target a hare if he had shot, in a place reserved for hunting, at great distance and under unfavorable light conditions. So might a man be heard to say that he believed he did no wrong in abbreviating the life of a friend who had but a short time to live, in order to save him from extreme suffering. As in the case of the hunter it might be deemed significant that his companions shared his optical illusion, so in the case of the mercy killer it might be considered relevant that many other persons of his environment shared his legal illusion. Thus a significant question in judging a claim of legal error is: "Is he alone ignorant of that which everybody in the State knows?"

. . . .

The policy suggested in this article may be summarized thus: Any restraint imposed upon man is, in a sense, offensive to human dignity. The aim of free society is hence to reduce legal restraint to the minimum required in a given situation. Restraint is less undignified when imposed upon conscious nonconformance with law. Subjection of man to sanctions under a law which is unknown and unknowable to him and which he has no opportunity to accept or to reject expresses the view that he is a mere object of the law. We believe, however, that in a democratic society man is the ultimate end of the law.

R. v. ESOP

(1836), 173 E.R. 203

The prisoner was indicted for an unnatural offence, committed on board of an East India ship, lying in St. Katherine's Docks. It appeared that he was a native of Bagdad.

Chambers, for the prisoner. — In the country from which the prisoner comes, it is not considered an offence; and a person who comes into this country and does an act, believing that it is a perfectly innocent one, cannot be convicted according to the law of England. A party must know that what he does is a crime. This is the principle upon which infants, idiots, and lunatics are held not to be answerable. If a person is unconscious that he is doing a wrong act, or believes that it is a right or innocent act, he is exonerated. Where one man kills another under the persuasion that he is doing a good action, he is not liable to punishment, for he knows not the distinction between right and wrong, and upon that point is insane.

Bosanquet, J. — I am clearly of opinion that this is no legal defence.

Vaughan, J. — Where is the evidence that it is not a crime in the prisoner's own country? But if it is not a crime there, that does not amount to a defence here. Numbers have been most improperly executed if it is a defence.

The prisoner, after the examination of some witnesses on his behalf, from whose statements it appeared that the witnesses for the prosecution acted under the influence of spite and ill will, was found

Not guilty.

R. v. CAMPBELL AND MLYNARCHUK

21 C.R.N.S. 273, 10 C.C.C. (2d) 26, 1972 CarswellAlta 125 (Alta. Dist. Ct.)

KERANS D.C.J. (orally): — This is an appeal by Darlene Agatha Campbell from conviction and sentence.

. . . .

On a charge before the Summary Conviction Court that she did, between February 9, 1972, and February 21, 1972, at the City of Edmonton, in the Province of Alberta, unlawfully take part as a performer in an immoral performance at Chez Pierre's situated at 10615 Jasper Ave., Edmonton, contrary to s. 163(2) [now s. 167(2)] of the *Criminal Code*.

This matter, therefore, comes before me by way of a trial *de novo*. That section provides, in s-s. (2):

> (2) Everyone commits an offence who takes part or appears as an actor, performer, or assistant in any capacity, in an immoral, indecent or obscene performance, entertainment or representation in a theatre.

The facts before me are relatively straightforward. On the dates in question, at the place in question, the appellant danced on stage, before an audience. At the start of her performance, she was wearing some clothes. By the end of her performance, she was not wearing any clothes. The dance was described to me as a "go-go dance" which, I understand, is a violent movement of almost all parts of the body, more or less in time to strongly rhythmic music.

I have no doubt in coming to the conclusion that this is a performance within the meaning of the section, and that, in doing what she did, the appellant took part as a performer in that performance. On the question of whether or not the performance was immoral, both counsel have agreed that I am bound to follow the recent decision of the Appellate Division of the Supreme Court of Alberta in *R. v. Johnson (No. 1)*, 8 C.C.C. (2d) 1. This was a stated case before the learned Riley J. [(1972), 6 C.C.C. (2d) 462], and appealed from him to the Appellate Division.

In that case, McDermid J.A., speaking for the Court, said, after drawing attention to the fact that s. 170 of the *Criminal Code* makes it a crime for anyone to appear nude in a public place, that he understood the enactment of that offence, by the Parliament of Canada, and, I quote, "declared that it is a breach of a moral standard in Canada". And he goes on,

> We know of no better way of establishing a moral standard than a declaration by the Parliament of Canada, and so the Provincial Judge was justified in accepting this as his standard in finding that the dance by the respondent in the nude was an immoral performance.

I understand, therefore, that since, to be nude in a public place is itself an offence; to perform in the nude, therefore, is an immoral performance within the meaning of the charging section. Therefore, I must conclude that the performance here was immoral within the meaning of that section.

. . . .

The next argument raised on behalf of the appellant is that the appellant lacked the necessary *mens rea* for this offence. The facts in this respect were these: she engaged to do this performance, where, earlier, she had refused to engage to do this performance, because she relied upon the statement made to her, by Pierre Couchard, that he, in turn, had been informed that a Supreme Court Judge had, to use his words because he also gave evidence, "Ruled that we could go ahead with bottomless dancing." That decision arose out of a charge in the City of Calgary, of a business acquaintance of Couchard, who was the manager of the place where this performance took place. Ironically, the decision to which Couchard and the appellant referred is the decision at the Trial Division level in *R. v. Johnson (No. 1)*, to which I earlier referred, and which, the witnesses tell me, obtained some newspaper publicity. It was a decision then, that subsequently was reversed on appeal.

Mistake of fact is a defence to a criminal charge, where it can be said that the facts believed by the accused, if true, would have afforded him a defence. It is also said that a mistake of mixed fact and law is a defence. I understand that proposition to be correct, simply because, if there is a mistake of mixed fact and law, then there is a mistake of fact. In my view, there was no mistake of fact by the appellant here. What she was told had happened, in fact, did happen.

Her mistake, if she made any mistake, was in concluding that a statement of law, expressed by the learned Riley J., was the law. That is not a mistake of fact, that is a mistake of law. It is a mistake of law to misunderstand the significance of the decision of a judge, or of his reasons. It is also a mistake of law to conclude that the decision of any particular judge correctly states the law, unless that Judge speaks on behalf of the ultimate Court of Appeal.

This is not a situation like others, where a mistake of law can be a defence, not because a mistake of law is a defence, but because a mistake of law can negative a malicious intent required for that crime. Thus, for example, where the law requires that a person wilfully, or maliciously, or knowingly, does something wrong, it could conceivably be a defence as negativing intention, to show that, because of the mistake in the understanding of the law, there was no wilful intent or malice. This is not one of those situations, as no such special intention is required for this offence. The only *mens rea* required here is that the appellant intended to do that which she did. And there is no suggestion, for a moment, that she lacked that *mens rea*.

This statement, that mistake of law is no defence, is contained in the *Criminal Code*, in s. 19, under the old numbering, which says:

> 19. Ignorance of the law by a person who commits an offence is not an excuse for committing that offence.

Excuse, or legal justification, is a defence at law, and I understand that defence to mean that it is a defence to a criminal charge to show that the act complained of was authorized by some other law. Section 19 says that defence is not available, in effect, when a person has made a mistake as to whether or not this act is excused by another law or authorized by another law.

Properly understood, in my view, the section removing ignorance of the law as a defence, in criminal matters, is not a matter of justice, but a matter of policy. There will always be cases, not so complicated as this, where honest and reasonable mistakes as to the state of the law will be the explanation of the conduct of an accused. In such a circumstance, one cannot help but have sympathy for the accused. But that situation, traditionally, is not a defence. It is not a defence, I think, because the first requirement of any system of justice, is that it work efficiently and effectively. If the state of understanding of the law of an accused person is ever to be relevant in criminal proceedings, we would have an absurd proceeding. The issue in a criminal trial would then not be what the accused did, but whether or not the accused had a sufficiently sophisticated understanding of the law to appreciate that what he did offended against the law. There would be a premium, therefore, placed upon ignorance of the law.

Our courts, following the traditions of English jurisprudence, have closed that avenue from consideration in the criminal court-room. I respectfully disagree with the learned American judges in those cases cited by the counsel for the appellant.

The defence should not be allowed as a matter of public policy, contrary to the statement of those learned judges. Indeed, it cannot be allowed because of public policy. This is the case, notwithstanding the sympathy evoked by the situation of an accused person.

Kenny, in his book, *Outlines of Criminal Law*, and I am quoting from the first edition, said at p. 69:

> although mistakes of law, unreasonable or even reasonable, thus leave the offender punishable for the crime which he has blundered into, they may of course afford good grounds for inflicting on him a milder punishment.

That is the only relevance, in my view, of the situation in which the appellant finds herself.

I have given some consideration as to whether or not this position varies at all, because of the unique circumstances here, where the appellant relied upon a specific judgment of a very immediate in terms of time and place, as opposed to a solicitor's opinion or some understanding as to the law. There is no question that there is something of an anomaly here. Reliance on a specific order, of a specific judge, granted at a specific time and place, seems, at first sight, not to be ignorance of the law, but knowledge of the law. If it turns out that that judge is mistaken, then, of course, the reliance on that Judge's judgment is mistaken. The irony is this: people in society are expected to have a more profound knowledge of the law than are the Judges. I am not the first person to have made that comment about the law, and while it is all very amusing, it is really to no point.

The principle that ignorance of the law should not be a defence in criminal matters is not justified because it is fair, it is justified because it is necessary, even though it will, sometimes produce an anomalous result.

When this appellant relied on the decision of the learned trial judge, she relied on his authority for the law. As it turns out, that reliance was misplaced, as misplaced as reliance on any statement as to the law I might make. Less so, I am sure.

Like counsel, I have had difficulty finding any authorities on this point. I was referred to *Conway v. The King* (1943), 81 C.C.C. 189, by counsel for the appellant. I have read that case. This issue, in my view, is not discussed in that case.

I have also read *R. v. Brinkley* (1907), 12 C.C.C. 454, in which the matter is discussed, although not this specific situation. In that case, a man had received advice from his counsel that a decree of divorce, made by a foreign court, validly dissolved his marriage in the eyes of the courts of Canada, and that he was, therefore, free to remarry without fear of bigamy. That opinion was mistaken. He was charged with bigamy, and he was convicted, notwithstanding his reliance on that opinion.

I have also read *Kokoliades v. Kennedy* (1911), 18 C.C.C. 495, which, to me, comes as close as can be to the situation here. This was a case in the Quebec Supreme Court, and arose in 1911. In that case, the accused was charged in the City of Montreal, with selling candy on a Sunday, contrary to a provision in a federal statute. His defence was that he relied on a municipal by-law licensing him to sell candy on a Sunday.

It would appear that this strange situation arose because there was some doubt as to the validity of the federal legislation which had been removed from the revised statutes, although not repealed. Subsequently, the Province of Quebec and the City of Montreal passed regulatory legislation purporting to permit in certain cases sales on the Lord's Day forbidden in the federal statute. The magistrate hearing the trial heard argument from the Crown that the federal legislation was constitutionally valid, and the Montreal City by-law was constitutionally invalid, and therefore an excuse was not available to the accused because the law authorizing him to do what he did, and upon which he relied, although enacted by a Legislature, or under the authority of the Legislature, was *ultra vires*.

The learned magistrate in that case, found that the Montreal by-law was *ultra vires*, and the federal statute *intra vires*; a decision which, in another case, was subsequently confirmed by the Privy Council, as we all know.

The learned magistrate went on to say that, because the law upon which the accused relied was unconstitutional, it was no law at all. He had nothing to rely upon, and he was guilty. This matter was appealed to Quebec Supreme Court. The Supreme Court Judge said that a statute authorizing an act should give rise to the defence of excuse, even though that statute may be *ultra vires*, and that the defence of excuse should be available in such a situation until there has been a judgment declaring the statute to be *ultra vires* spoken by a Court of high jurisdiction "after the gravest consideration". That is a strange remark. I would have thought that courts of high or low jurisdiction give every case grave consideration.

The situation there is not unlike the situation here. The accused there, saw a city by-law, seemingly authorizing him to do what he did, and relied upon it. It turned out the by-law had no validity. But it would take sophistication in the law to appreciate that.

Similarly, here, the appellant relied upon a statement of law, by a Supreme Court Judge in Alberta. It would take the greatest of sophistication of knowledge of the law to conclude that he was or might be mistaken. In the first case, a judge, on appeal, held that the defence of excuse ought to be allowed.

I respectfully disagree with the judge in that case, for the reasons I have mentioned.

. . . .

I, therefore, conclude that the mistake of law of the appellant affords no defence to her on this charge. There being no other defences, and the facts necessary having been made out, the conviction of the below, in my opinion, was correct. The appeal as to conviction is dismissed.

. . . .

I should have been more careful in my language a moment ago, when I said the appeal as to conviction was dismissed. Under the new law, I should have more properly said that I find the appellant guilty of the charge, and will hear argument as to whether or not to allow or dismiss the appeal as to conviction.

. . . .

Well, I have already indicated, in a quotation from Kenny, that, in this awkward situation, the matter does not afford a defence, but should certainly be considered in mitigation of sentence. Indeed, there are several cases, not as awkward as this, in the law reports, involving a person who had an honest and reasonable mistake in belief as to the law, and for whom the courts expressed sympathy, and, in respect of whom, sentence was mitigated.

It is at this stage where the scales of justice are balanced. Clothed with very recent power to refuse to enter a conviction, I can now balance the scales of justice even more delicately. I have read a note in vol. 14 of the English and Empire Digest, at p. 51 of an old case, *R. v. Bailey* (1800), Russ & Ry. 1. It goes back to 1800. In that case, the Government of England had passed a statute, making something a crime which was not previously a crime. Subsequently, the accused did the forbidden act. The court found that, in fact, in the district in which this crime was committed, no news had yet reached anyone of the passage of this Act. Nor could any news have reached this district of the passage of this Act. And that the accused, therefore, had to be convicted of an offence which he did not and could not have known was an offence. And they said there that the proper way of dealing with the matter was to give a pardon, which I understand to be a conviction followed immediately by the wiping out of a conviction.

I have no power to give a pardon, but I do have power to give an absolute discharge. In my view, this is the proper case.

Ironically, the decision of Riley J. in *Johnson*, relied on by Campbell to her detriment, was later upheld on final appeal: *Johnson v. R.* (1974), 23 C.R.N.S. 273, 13 C.C.C. (2d) 402 (S.C.C.).

(b)   Distinguishing Mistake of Law and Fact

R. v. PRUE; R. v. BARIL

[1979] 2 S.C.R. 547, 8 C.R. (3d) 68 , 46 C.C.C. (2d) 257,
1979 CarswellBC 689, 1979 CarswellBC 524 (S.C.C.)

LASKIN C.J. (SPENCE, DICKSON and ESTEY JJ. concurring): —

The facts relevant to the disposition of these two appeals are set out in the reasons prepared by my brother Ritchie which I have had the advantage of reading. The basic fact, common to both cases, is that the two accused suffered an automatic suspension of their driving licences under s. 86D of the Motor-vehicle Act, R.S.B.C. 1960, c. 253, as amended by 1976 (B.C.), c. 35, s. 20, and by 1977 (B.C.), c. 41, s.3. They thereafter drove motor vehicles notwithstanding such suspension, and were then charged not for a violation of the provincial statute under which the suspension was made but rather under s. 238(3) of the federal Criminal Code. There was a finding on the trials of this charge that neither accused knew that his licence to drive had been suspended. Despite this finding they were convicted at first instance, but on appeal by way of stated case, their convictions were set aside by Gould J. who held that proof of *mens rea* was essential to a conviction of an offence under s. 238(3). The British Columbia Court of Appeal affirmed. I hold the same view.

Section 238(3) [now s. 259(4)] of the *Criminal Code* is as follows:

> 238(3) Every one who drives a motor vehicle in Canada while he is disqualified or prohibited from driving a motor vehicle by reason of the legal suspension or cancellation, in any province, of his permit or licence or of his right to secure a permit or licence to drive a motor vehicle in that province is guilty of
>
> (a) an indictable offence and is liable to imprisonment for two years; or
>
> (b) an offence punishable on summary conviction.

What Parliament has done is to create a criminal offence merely by reason of a violation of a provincial sanction against driving while one's licence is suspended, save that it applies its own sanction throughout Canada. It needs no extensive citation of authority to say that Parliament does not acquire legislative jurisdiction simply by making its legislation operative throughout Canada: see *Toronto Electric Commissioners v. Snider* [[1925] A.C. 396], at p. 401. There must be a substantive non-geographical basis for federal legislation, and where the criminal law is concerned, and especially where an offence is included in the Criminal Code, it is generally found in a requirement of proof of *mens rea*.

This Court expressed this general principle in *Beaver v. The Queen* [[1957] S.C.R. 531], and it was expressed many years ago in England in *Sherras v. De*

Rutzen [[1895] 1 Q.B. 918], at p. 921. If *mens rea* is not a requirement for proof of an offence under s. 238(3), I would have serious doubt as to its validity on the principle expressed in *Johnson v. Attorney-General of Alberta* [[1954] S.C.R. 127], namely, that just as it is not open to a Province to supplement by additional sanctions the provisions of the *Criminal Code*, it is not open to Parliament to add a sanction, without more, to a violation of a provincial penal statute.

Much of the argument in this Court by the Crown appellant proceeded on the basis that ignorance of the suspension was ignorance of law and not of fact, and hence there was no defence to the charge under s. 238(3). The effect, if this is a correct appraisal, is to make s. 238(3) an offence of absolute liability where the provincial suspension of a driving licence is automatic under the provincial enactment (proof of such suspension being made), but not if the provincial suspension does not take effect without a requirement of notice. In either case, the consequence is to govern the operation of the federal statute by what is prescribed by the provincial enactment, and hence to create a variable type of federal offence which may have a different operation in different provinces according to the character of the relevant provincial legislation.

This cannot be. Criminality under the *Criminal Code* must depend on what Parliament independently proscribes; it risks the vulnerability of its enactment if it simply applies a sanction to a violation of a provincial statute. In my opinion, the issue of ignorance of fact or ignorance of law is properly applicable to the enforcement of the provincial enactment under which the suspension from driving is made and not to the enforcement of s. 238(3) of the *Criminal Code*. Thus, in the present case reference should properly be made to the British Columbia *Motor-vehicle Act*, s. 18, as amended and to ss. 98 and 99, as amended, if it is to be invoked against persons who claim to be unaware of the suspension of their driving licences.

So far as the operation of s. 238(3) is concerned, the existence of a suspension from driving is a question of fact underlying the invocation of that provision, and so too is proof that an accused charged thereunder drove while his licence to do so was under suspension. That was the view taken by Culliton C.J.S. in *Regina v. Ooms* [[1973] 4 W.W.R. 767], by the Ontario Court of Appeal in *Regina v. Finn* [[1972] 3 O.R. 509], and earlier in Nova Scotia in *Regina ex rel. Ross v. Jollimore* [(1961), 131 C.C.C. 319]. I do not see how this position is affected by whether the provincial legislation operates to make a suspension automatic or whether it arises only upon some notice or other action to be taken thereunder. For the purpose of the *Criminal Code*, whether there has been an effective suspension is simply a question of fact. In my opinion, therefore, *Regina v. Villeneuve* [[1968] 1 C.C.C. 267], a judgment of O'Hearn Co.Ct.J. in Nova Scotia, was wrongly decided.

This brings me back to the essentiality of *mens rea* to found a conviction under s. 238(3). I should have thought that the fact that the offence may be prosecuted by indictment and carries in that respect a maximum two-year term of imprisonment would support the application of the general principle laid down in *Beaver v. The Queen, supra.* I need not repeat the constitutional consideration which I have mentioned earlier and which leads to the same conclusion. Indeed, the inclusion of an offence in the *Criminal Code* by that very fact must be taken to import *mens rea*, and there would have to be clear indication against it before a would be justified in denying its essentiality. The *Criminal Code* is a code of outright prohibitions, distinguishable from regulatory offences created by other kinds of federal legislation. In this last-mentioned class, it is understandable that there should be questions raised about the requirement of *mens rea*. The judgment of this Court in *Regina v. Pierce Fisheries Ltd.* [[1971] S.C.R. 5] is illustrative.

The encompassing judgment of my brother Dickson in *Regina v. City of Sault Ste. Marie* [[1978] 2 S.C.R. 1299], does not lead to a different conclusion in the present case. It must be remembered that in wrestling, as he so admirably did, with whether there were two or (as he concluded) three categories of offences, he was dealing with the operation of provincial legislation, namely, The *Ontario Water Resources Commission Act*, R.S.O. 1970, c. 332, and was not concerned with evaluating offences under the *Criminal Code*. Several passages in his reasons make clear that *mens rea* continued to be essential to prove commission of a *Criminal Code* offence. I refer particularly to the following passage (at p. 1309):

> The distinction between the true criminal offence and the public welfare offence is one of prime importance. Where the offence is criminal, the Crown must establish a mental element, namely, that the accused who committed the prohibited act did so intentionally or recklessly, with knowledge of the facts constituting the offence, or with wilful blindness toward them.

Justice Dickson's classification would be an appropriate reference point for assessing the thrust of the provincial *Motor-vehicle Act* in its effect upon a person who drove in the Province while his licence to do so was suspended, but I see no need here to go further than to say with him that s. 238(3) falls clearly within his first category of offences requiring *mens rea*.

I would dismiss the two appeals.

RITCHIE J. (PIGEON J. concurring) (dissenting): —

... It will be readily apparent that a wide difference exists between the case of a man who acts in ignorance of the provision for automatic suspension and is therefore acting under a mistake of law, and a man who resides in a province where the imposition of such a suspension can only be effected as the result of the intervention of some administrative act by the authorities. The latter situation is evidenced in jurisdictions where provision is made for the clerk of the court, the presiding magistrate or some other official giving notice to the accused of the suspension of his licence before that suspension can be effective. In the latter type of case when the requisite administrative step or steps have not been taken and the accused can show that he was therefore ignorant of the fact of his suspension, his ignorance is one of fact and not of law, and in this event it has been consistently held that he has a valid defence to the charge. The cases in support of this proposition are collected and form the subject of comment in the reasons for judgment of Mr. Justice Martin of the Court of Appeal of Ontario in *R. v. Lock* [(1974), 18 C.C.C. (2d) 477], and they are referred to with approval in the reasons for judgment of Mr. Justice Seaton in these cases. These cases turn on the finding that the failure to give notice or to take such other administrative step as is required is a question of fact and that the accused's failure to know of the suspension is not a mistake of law.

In the present cases the respondents' lack of knowledge of the suspension of their licences was not occasioned by any mistake of fact but rather by ignorance of the law attendant upon failure to be aware of the automatic suspension for which provision is made in s. 86D of the *Motor-vehicle Act* (*supra*). In this latter regard I share the view expressed by His Honour Judge Peter O'Hearn of the County Court in Nova Scotia, in *R. v. Villeneuve, supra,* where conviction under s. 221 of the *Criminal Code* (now s. 236) resulted in automatic revocation of the licence and the defence was advanced that the accused was ignorant of the fact that his licence had been revoked. Judge O'Hearn, in referring to *Regina ex rel. Ross v. Jollimore* [(1961), 131 C.C.C. 319], said of the charge before him (at pp. 270-1):

> Of what was he ignorant? In *Jollimore* it could be said that the defendant did not know whether the Magistrate had forwarded a record of the original conviction to the Registrar, or whether the Registrar had acted thereupon by revoking the licence. These are administrative acts; they are matters of fact. In the instant case, the accused was ignorant of the fact that his licence was revoked but this was a direct consequence of his ignorance of the legal effect of conviction under *Cr. Code* s. 221. That is, his ignorance of the fact of revocation is not independent of his ignorance of the law, but directly dependent upon it, and his ignorance is essentially ignorance of the law. There is no independent factual error to make it a mistake of mixed law and fact.

I am satisfied that the mistake made by the accused in the present cases is nothing more than a mistake as to the legal consequences of a conviction under s. 236 of the *Criminal Code* involving as they do the automatic suspension of the operator's licence under s. 86D of the *Motor-vehicle Act*.

Once the mistake is recognized as being founded in ignorance of the law the respondents are faced with the provisions of s. 19 of the *Criminal Code* which read as follows:

> 19. Ignorance of the law by a person who commits an offence is not an excuse for committing that offence.

What we have here is a plain statement of the law in British Columbia, as contained in s. 86D of the *Motor-vehicle Act*, requiring the automatic suspension of an operator's licence upon breach of certain sections of the *Criminal Code* dealing with the operation of motor vehicles and a disregard of the provisions of this section which involved the accused in a breach of s. 238 of the *Criminal Code*. There is no evidence that either of the respondents made any effort to determine whether their licences had been suspended or not and this is not a case involving ignorance of some regulation or technicality which might have been understandably unknown to the driving public and thus to the respondents.

For all these reasons I would allow these appeals, set aside the judgment of the Court of Appeal for British Columbia and direct the conviction of the two respondents for the offences with which they were charged.

[The dissenting judgment of Beetz J. has been omitted.]

Appeals dismissed.

Where the mistake or ignorance relates to law, s. 19 must be applied. There are, however, two major exceptions — colour of right, which is a statutory exception applying to certain property offences, and that of officially induced error of law, a common law defence.

R. v. CUSTANCE

2005 MBCA 23, 2005 CarswellMan 30, 194 C.C.C. (3d) 225, 28 C.R. (6th) 357 (Man. C.A.)

The accused was charged with breach of a recognizance, after he had been released on bail. One of the conditions of his bail was that he reside at a particular address, in an apartment that a friend of his claimed to have rented. When the accused arrived at 9:00 p.m. Friday night he discovered that his friend had not in fact rented the apartment yet. In an attempt not to be in breach of his bail conditions the accused stayed in a car in the parking lot of the apartment building until Monday morning when he went to court. In the meantime the police had discovered that he had not stayed in the apartment he had indicated, and on the Monday morning he was arrested and charged with the breach. The Court of Appeal held that he had been properly convicted, because he had made a mistake of law, not of fact.

STEEL J.A.: —

16   A typical mistake of fact that occurs in these types of situations is an accused writing the date of his trial down incorrectly and thus failing to appear. See *R. v. Hutchinson (K.)* (1994), 160 A.R. 58 (Prov. Ct.), and *R. v. Daoud* (1988), 65 Sask.R. 308 (Q.B.), which explained at para. 7:

> Evidence of a general mistake of fact can negative *mens rea* and thus defeat the Crown's attempts to prove guilt beyond a reasonable doubt.

17   In this case, the accused appeared to rely on two mistakes. The first was that Mr. Gaudet had secured an apartment at the address specified. That was a reasonable mistake of fact. Mr. Gaudet gave the address in open court. There was no reason the accused should not have relied on that representation. On the evening he was released, the accused became aware of a possible problem, but still was hopeful that the problem could be resolved. However, once he arrived at the apartment, he was told that the keys to the apartment were not available and would not be available within the next little while. It was at this point that the second mistake occurred. Instead of giving himself up to the police as being unable to comply with his recognizance and waiting in custody for another residence to be obtained, he stayed in a car in the parking lot under the mistaken belief that such action would constitute compliance with his recognizance order. This was a mistake of law, and such a mistake, unlike mistake of fact, does not negative *mens rea*. By residing in his car in the parking lot all weekend (in an attempt to comply with the recognizance), the accused was mistaken about the legal consequences of his actions and was therefore operating under a mistake of law.

18   The Supreme Court of Canada commented on mistake of law in *R. v. Forster*, [1992] 1 S.C.R. 339, a case involving a member of the Canadian Armed Forces who tendered her resignation in writing to her commander the day before she was obliged to begin a new posting. She did not report to that posting. She was charged with being absent without leave contrary to s. 90 of the *National Defence Act*, R.S.C., 1985, c. N-5, since s. 23(1) of that Act provided that a person's enrollment in the Armed Forces "binds the person to serve in the Canadian Forces until the person is, in accordance with regulations, lawfully released." Notwithstanding her resignation, the accused had not been lawfully released under s. 23(1). While the accused did not argue that her resignation was lawfully effective, she did claim that she honestly believed that she had resigned from the Forces and thus that she did not possess the requisite *mens rea* for the offence under s. 90 of being absent without leave. Speaking for the unanimous court on this point, Lamer C.J.C. observed at p. 346:

> . . . . Even if we take the appellant's assertions about her beliefs at face value, she did not labour under any mistake about what she in fact did: she deliberately refrained from reporting to her new posting in Ottawa. Instead, she was mistaken about the legal consequences of her actions, because of her failure to understand that she was under a continuing legal obligation to report for duty notwithstanding her purported resignation by letter from the Forces. Thus, while she may not have intended to commit any offence under military law, this lack of intention flowed from her mistake as to the continuing legal obligation to report for duty which that regime imposed upon her until properly released . . . .
>
> It is a principle of our criminal law that an honest but mistaken belief in respect of the legal consequences of one's deliberate actions does not furnish a defence to a criminal charge, even when the mistake cannot be attributed to the negligence of the accused: *Molis v. The Queen*, [1980] 2 S.C.R. 356. . . . .

The Court of Appeal held that the accused's sentence of "time served" was appropriate in the circumstances.

(c) Colour of Right for Property Offences

R. v. DOROSH

20 C.R. (6th) 368, 183 C.C.C. (3d) 224, 2004 CarswellSask 55 (Sask. C.A.)

1   BAYDA C.J.S.: — The appellant (defendant) was charged with stealing a trailer, the property of Randy Zayshley of a value not exceeding $5,000, contrary to s. 334(b) of the *Criminal Code*. He was tried and convicted by a judge of the Provincial Court, whereupon, pursuant to s. 813 of the *Code*, he appealed from his conviction to the Court of Queen's Bench. His appeal was dismissed. Then, pursuant to s. 839(1) of the *Code*, he applied to this court for leave to appeal, and if leave be granted, he requested this court to hear his appeal. At the conclusion of the hearing, this court granted the application for leave, allowed the appeal and directed a new trial, with reasons to follow. These are those reasons.

2   The ground of appeal raised by the defendant before the Court of Queen's Bench, and before this Court, involved the question whether the learned Provincial Court judge (the trial judge) erred in his interpretation of the phrase "without colour of right" appearing in s. 322 of the *Code* and in his application of the law embodied by that phrase to the facts of this case.

3   The facts are essentially not in dispute. (Although the trial judge did not explicitly make findings of fact, it is implicit in his ruling that he accepted the testimonies of the defendant and the other witnesses and found no contradiction that required resolution.) The defendant purchased from Mr. Zayshley a "1988 Dodge Van with Carpet Cleaning Unit as is condition, no warranty's." No purchase price was stipulated in the bill of sale. Instead, the document contemplated as consideration for the sale, the delivery by the defendant to Mr. Zayshley of three items, namely, a cargo trailer, a roto tiller, and a power plant together with the payment to Mr. Zayshley of $1,200 cash and $1,300 "in thirty days." The document went on to state "All items as is and free and clear of all debts." The defendant delivered the three items to Mr. Zayshley and paid him the $1,200 cash. He has not paid the remaining $1,300.

4   Shortly after he acquired the van and cleaning unit, the defendant concluded that the cleaning unit "was not operational". He testified that Mr. Zayshley orally undertook that the van and unit were operational. The unit, he contends, needs "major repairs" estimated to cost "several thousand dollars." He

went on to say that he "tried reaching Mr. Zayshley and could not get a hold of him." He became "suspicious" about the transaction and contacted his lawyer. The lawyer made a search of the Personal Property Registry and determined that there were writs of execution registered against Mr. Zayshley's name. (It turned out that the writs were actually registered against the name of Mr. Zayshley's son who happens to have the name: Randy Zayshley Jr.)

5   Based on the information he received from his lawyer, the defendant concluded that "there were liens against the van." In addition, the defendant felt that Mr. Zayshley failed to honour his undertaking to train the defendant in the use of the cleaning equipment. All of this put together lead the defendant to conclude that "the deal was dead." He went to Mr. Zayshley's home and picked up the trailer that he had originally delivered to Mr. Zayshley as part of the consideration for the purchase of the van. Mr. Zayshley was not at home at the time. The defendant in his testimony explained:

> I felt I was picking up my own trailer, and I tried reaching them to get a hold of them to tell them that, look, there was problems with the van, that - like I stressed so strongly, over and over to him, with the deal, the van had to be operational because I knew nothing about carpet cleaning; I needed help in the training. I stressed that very strongly and he agreed, and nothing, and nothing came through with the training or the van was not operational, that it needed major repairs, there were liens against it. Like it was - I felt like I was being rooked into this deal. [Transcript pp. 46, line 25 -47, line 9]

6   He then advertised the trailer for sale and sold it to a person by the name of Donald Heisler who responded to the advertisement. When asked in his examination-in-chief about his "state of mind" when he sold the trailer to Mr. Heisler, he testified:

> Well as far as I was concerned, I hadn't - Mr. Zayshley, I tried repeatedly phoning Mr. Zayshley. In fact I had talked to his wife or girlfriend once on the phone and I told her to have Randy phone me back, there was a problem with the van. I got no replies back. And as far as I was concerned the deal was dead, and the trailer was mine. And this is like a month later, so I decided to resell the trailer. [Transcript p. 47, lines 13-20]

7   The police arranged to have the trailer returned to Mr. Zayshley and charged the defendant with theft.

. . . .

9   During the trial, in one of his exchanges with counsel, the trial judge referred to colour of right in these terms:

> Like to me colour of right is when I say I'm going to sell this pen to you for a dollar and you say here's a dollar, I'll pick up the pen later, and now, unbeknownst to you there's pen number 2, and you come up and you get this pen. Now the pen that, you know, you thought you were buying is worth so much and the other pen is worth a totally different amount. And you thought you were taking the pen you bought, so now you thought you had a colour of right to take the pen that you picked up, when all of a sudden I say, no, no, this is the one that you

bought. So that to me is the criminal law issue of colour of right. But to acknowledge an issue of colour of right when somebody is grabbing something because they think they have a civilly justifiable claim, that may well not hold water. [Transcript p. 29, lines 8-23]

. . . .

11   In my respectful view the trial judge neither properly interpreted the phrase "without colour of right" as used in s. 322 of the *Code*, nor properly applied the law embodied by that phrase to the facts of this case. The summary appellate court judge erred in failing to redress those errors.

12   The relevant provisions of s. 322 of the *Code* are subsections (1)(a), (2) and (3):

322.(1) Every one commits theft who fraudulently and without colour of right takes, or fraudulently and without colour of right converts to his use or to the use of another person, anything, whether animate or inanimate, with intent

(a) to deprive, temporarily or absolutely, the owner of it, or a person who has a special property or interest in it, of the thing or of his property or interest in it;

. . . .

(2) A person commits theft when, with intent to steal anything, he moves it or causes it to move or to be moved, or begins to cause it to become movable.

(3) A taking or conversion of anything may be fraudulent notwithstanding that it is effected without secrecy or attempt at concealment.

13   The *actus reus* of the offence charged consisted of the taking by the defendant of the trailer (an animate thing). There is no dispute that the Crown established this element of the offence beyond a reasonable doubt. Indeed, the defendant admitted the taking.

14   The *mens rea* element is another matter. The Crown needed to prove, beyond a reasonable doubt, the three requirements of this element, namely, (i) a fraudulent intent on the part of the defendant at the time of the taking of the trailer; (ii) an absence of any colour of right asserted by the defendant, and (iii) an intent on the part of the defendant to deprive, temporarily or absolutely, the owner, Mr. Zayshley, of the trailer.

15   The parties and the trial judge focussed their attention on the second of these requirements and made no reference to the first or the third.

16   The jurisprudential history surrounding the phrase "colour of right" indicates that the meaning of the phrase has a certain quality of elusiveness (see *The Law of Theft and Related Offences* by Winifred H. Holland (Toronto: Carswell, 1998) at pp. 150-170). The definition of the phrase by Martin J.A., speaking for the Court (including Gale C.J.O. and Estey J.A.), in *R. v. DeMarco*

(1973), 13 C.C.C. (2d) 369 (Ont. C.A.) at 372 may be taken to have settled many, if not all, of the contentious issues raised by earlier Canadian cases where the phrase was considered. He said:

> The term "colour of right" generally, although not exclusively, refers to a situation where there is an assertion of a proprietary or possessory right to the thing which is the subject-matter of the alleged theft. One who is honestly asserting what he believes to be an honest claim cannot be said to act "without colour of right", even though it may be unfounded in law or in fact: see *R. v. Howson*, [1966] 3 C.C.C. 348, 55 D.L.R. (2d) 582, [1966] 2 O.R. 63. The term "colour of right" is also used to denote an honest belief in a state of facts which, if it actually existed would at law justify or excuse the act done: *R. v. Howson*. The term when used in the latter sense is merely a particular application of the doctrine of mistake of fact.

17 Since *DeMarco* was decided, the Supreme Court of Canada has dealt with the "colour of right" issue in two cases: *R. v. Lilly*, [1983] 1 S.C.R. 794; and *R. v. Jones*, [1991] 3 S.C.R. 110. Nothing said in the judgments in either of those cases in any way detracts from Martin J.A.'s definition. If anything, the court's decision in *Lilly* may be said to impliedly support the definition. In two other cases, *R. v. Lafrance*, [1975] 1 S.C.R. 201 and *R. v. Milne*, [1992] 1 S.C.R. 697 the "colour of right" issue arose only incidentally and not as a principal issue. These judgments as well contain nothing that detracts from the DeMarco definition.

18 A colour of right can have its basis in either a mistake of civil law (a colour of right provides an exception to s. 19 of the *Code*; see: *The Law of Theft and Related Offences* p. 153) or in a mistake in a state of facts. The mistake in each case must give rise to either an honest belief in a proprietary or possessory right to the thing which is the subject matter of the alleged theft or an honest belief in the state of facts which if it actually existed would at law justify or excuse the act done.

19 In my respectful view the trial judge erred when, in essence, he found that a colour of right can have a basis only in a mistake in a state of facts. The "pen" example he gave in his exchange with counsel during the course of the proceedings that I quoted earlier is a clear acknowledgement of his acceptance that a mistake in a state of facts can serve as a basis for a colour of right. But in that same exchange he essentially rejected a mistake of civil law as a basis when he said:

> But to acknowledge an issue of colour of right when somebody is grabbing something because they think they have a civilly justifiable claim that may well not hold water. [Emphasis added, Transcript p. 29, lines 20-23]

20 The judge obviously carried this thinking into his final ruling.

21 Even if it can be said that the judge did not reject the first basis - a mistake in civil law - as a basis for colour of right, then he clearly erred in applying to

the facts of this case the law embraced by a properly defined colour of right concept. I say that for these reasons: The judge appears to have acknowledged that the defendant had a belief he had a claim to the trailer. But, instead of asking himself: Did the defendant have an honest belief in his claim even though the claim may be unfounded in law and in fact?, the judge, in effect, asked himself the question: Was the defendant's claim unfounded in law? The judge then proceeded to answer the latter question in the negative and on that premise concluded the defendant had no colour of right.

22   Parenthetically, I note that counsel (counsel for the Crown before us did not appear as counsel at trial) and the judge appeared to treat the absence of a colour of right not as a requirement of *mens rea* for the Crown to prove beyond a reasonable doubt, but as a defence for the defendant to establish. I again note that no attention - not even casual - was paid to the other two requirements of *mens rea*, namely, the fraudulent intent and the specific intent contemplated by clause 322(1)(a). I do not propose to deal with these aspects of the case as they were not argued before us.

. . . .

25   It is for these reasons that we directed a new trial.

R. v. DRAINVILLE

(1991), 5 C.R. (4th) 38, 1991 CarswellOnt 88 (Ont. Prov. Div.)

The accused, a priest and elected member of the provincial Legislature, was charged with mischief contrary to s. 430(1)(*c*) of the *Criminal Code*. With others he had blocked a parcel of land to protest the construction of a road. Although the province had title to the land, the protestors believed that the aboriginal rights to the lands should prevail. The Ontario Supreme Court and the Court of Appeal had ruled that the aboriginal rights were extinguished by an 1850 treaty. The accused and other protestors had to be taken away from the land by the police. The incident resulted in a delay of approximately one hour.

FOURNIER PROV. DIV. J.: —

. . . .

On Civil Disobedience & The Rule of Law

Another line of defence advanced on behalf of the accused, is that his actions constitute at best passive resistance, a type of civil disobedience which ought not result in his conviction. It is said that his involvement was indeed minimal, that his motives and intentions were noble and good, and that in fact, he has contributed in his own small way to a just and honourable political solution. In referring to a "political solution", counsel is no doubt alluding to the memorandum of agreement dated April 23, 1990, entered into by the representatives of the Teme-Augama Anishnabai Nation and those of the Ontario Government. Though the issue of title is now before the Supreme Court of Canada, though the actual title is still with the Ontario Government, it seems that this agreement provides for a stewardship arrangement covering some four Townships; over the next 10 to 25 years, it seems that this "stewardship management" approach could be expanded gradually so that, ultimately, all of the contested lands known to the Teme-Augama Anishnabai Nation as N'Daki Mena will be so governed. It seems that indeed a viable political solution may be been found after a long period of hardship and legal complications. It seems that the protestors and the accused in this case may have had a valid point; and what can we make of that within the context of this case?

As I pointed out in my decision *R. v. Gary Potts* (unreported) this is certainly mindful, that civil disobedience is a time-honoured method of drawing public attention to claims of fundamental freedoms and human rights. I mentioned such notable examples as Rev. Martin Luther King and Mahatma Ghandhi.

Ironically enough Father Drainville, during the course of his examination in chief, cited a passage from a book entitled "The Words of Gandhi" a selection of Richard Attenborough, released by Newmarket Press, 1982. At p. 57 thereof he quotes:

> Civil disobedience is the inherent right of a citizen. He dare not give it up without ceasing to be a man. Civil disobedience is never followed by anarchy. Criminal disobedience can lead to it. Every state puts down criminal disobedience by force. It perishes, if it does not. But to put down civil disobedience is to attempt to imprison conscience.

Father Drainville would no doubt qualify his actions in obstructing the roadway as "civil disobedience", which presumably should be condoned by this. In order to gain a better insight as to what Gandhi had in mind when he wrote these words, I took the liberty of referring to a book entitled *The Life of Mahatma Ghandhi* by Louis Fischer (New York: Harper & Row, 1st Harper Paperback ed., 1983). It seems that Gandhi was significantly influenced by the writings of Henry David Thoreau, a poet and essayist, born in 1817, and referred to as a "New England rebel" who hated Negro slavery, the individual's slavery to the Church, the State, property, customs and traditions (see p. 88). At one point, Thoreau allegedly refused to pay his taxes and was sent to jail until a friend of his bailed him out. That experience apparently evoked his most provoking political essay entitled "Civil Disobedience". In this essay he wrote:

> The only obligation which I have a right to assume, is to do at any time what I think right. To be right, is more honourable than to be *law-abiding*. [Emphasis added.]

It is said that Mahatma Ghandhi referred to this essay as a "masterly treatise" and that "it left a deep impression on me".

In that light, it is clear that Mahatma Ghandhi was more concerned with doing what he felt in his conscience to be right, rather than observe the legislated provisions of a government. One cannot assume that what he meant by "civil disobedience" was lawful activity as we know it in our judicial system, and that "criminal disobedience" was unlawful. It is clear that he had his own standards, that he was a self-appointed judge of what was acceptable and not acceptable, that he arrogated himself with the power and ability to determine what was criminal and what was not!

Surely, this approach is not exactly consistent with what we commonly refer to as the "rule of law"; and anyone relying on such ideology, conceivably does so at his peril. This also illustrates the great wisdom behind the expression: "don't believe everything you read"!

In an unreported decision of the Provincial Court of Saskatchewan, *R. v. Pratt*, Judge Nutting is quoted as follows [p. 126, [1990] 3 C.N.L.R. 120]:

> The adoption of civil disobedience methods in the promotion of a just cause does not transform illegal actions into legal ones. Certainly, the motives and idealism of those who commit an act of civil disobedience are to be weighed in the balance in regard to any penal sanctions; however, no honourable or just cause justifies the breaking of an acceptable and reasonable law.

In the unreported case of *R. v. Potts*, this Court made its views known with respect to civil disobedience. I had occasion to quote Mr. Chief Justice Howland, as he then was, when he addressed the government at the opening of Courts ceremony, in Toronto, in January 1990. He said:

> It is one of the fundamental principles of our democratic society that no one is above the law, and everyone is equal before the law. The rule of law is based on the fact that our current laws represent the will of the majority of the people. If a law no longer represents the will of the majority, then it should be changed but until it is changed by lawful means, it must be obeyed. Defiance of the law is not the answer.

Finally, let me reiterate this Court's position. Is "civil disobedience" or even "passive resistance" such a small infraction, or such a minimal use of force, that the "*actus reus*" ought to be overlooked? Should such activity as obstructing a road be justified by some sort of approval by the s on the grounds that the motives are good and noble, or that the situation is really a "political" one? In light of the existing circumstances of this case, where it seems a just and appropriate political solution appears to have been found, this might be a tempting proposition. But certainly that would be tantamount to a declaration that, in some instances, at the discretion of some judge, and irrespective of the "rule of law", there are times when "the ends justify the means". Even in this case, where it appears that the government of Ontario may be about to change its policies and perhaps admit to a previous error in judgment, where it appears that a memorandum of agreement termed a viable "political solution" is now in place and that those protestors may have been morally right, surely, the process of legitimizing previously unlawful acts, after the fact is an inherently dangerous concept which is simply not acceptable as an alternative to the "rule of law".

To permit this process to replace the "rule of law" would be to grant permission to anyone to arrogate himself with the powers of a judge and determine for himself or herself, and from time to time, what is acceptable or just, and what is not, on behalf of the majority. As such anyone could adjudicate himself or herself above the law, and no one would be equal before the law. Such a situation would surely lead to anarchy, and very quickly so.

For these reasons, this court is of the view that an apparently insignificant or harmless step taken without respect for the "rule of law" is indeed one which is made of the very same substance that disrespect, insult, mischief, filibuster, insurrection, mutiny and ultimately, outright war, are all made of. For these reasons "civil disobedience" cannot be condoned. Those who wish to resort to it as a means of expression are able to do so in our free and democratic society, but they must also suffer the consequences of their actions. They must be made to suffer the sanctions which are provided for as Mr. Chief Justice Howland stated: "defiance of the law is not the answer!"

Accordingly, and for the reasons just given, that line of defence cannot succeed.

Colour of Right:

The defence places most of its emphasis on this line of defence. In determining whether Father Drainville might benefit from this approach, a quick review of the law and pertinent cases is useful.

Firstly, s. 429(2) of the *Code* provides that:

> No person shall be convicted of an offence under sections 430 to 446 where he proves that he acted with legal justification or excuse and with colour of right.

A correct interpretation of this section provides a successful defence to anyone able to demonstrate "legal justification or excuse" or "colour of right". See *R. v. Creaghan* (1982), 31 C.R. (3d) 277, 1 C.C.C. (3d) 449 (Ont. C.A.). Furthermore, "colour of right" is defined as:

> an honest belief in the existence of a state of facts which, if it actually existed, would at law justify or excuse the act done."

It is also a fair statement of the law that a successful defence can arise from a mistake of fact or law, or mixed law and fact, and that the test to be used by the presiding judge in the determination of the presence of an honest belief, is a "subjective test". See *R. v. Howson*, [1966] 2 O.R. 63, 47 C.R. 322, [1966] 3 C.C.C. 348 (C.A.).

There is further direction in the *Howson* decision, to the effect that the word "right" should be construed broadly, and that it is in its ordinary sense, charged with legal implications. Finally, it seems that "reasonableness" is not a necessary element in these considerations. (See *Howson, supra*)

In *R. v. Nundah* (1916), 16 N.S.W. R. 482 referred to by Mr. Justice Porter in the *Howson* decision, at p. 482, Cullen C.J.C. in dealing with the questions of honesty on the part of the accused in his belief in his ownership said:

> The question whether he honestly believed the property to be his is that which is material. Possibly some of the stronger beliefs held by human beings might be found by other minds to be completely destitute of reasonable grounds. . . . A man may be ever so much mistaken in his reasoning processes and yet be honest, though you would not accept his mere statement of opinion unless there was some colour in the circumstances for his entertaining the opinion he claims to have had.

And still on the subject of "reasonableness" Mr. Justice Laskin in *R. v. Howson* goes on to say at p. 79 [O.R.]:

> Although the unreasonableness of a belief, when objectively considered, does not necessarily destroy the honesty of the belief, it may be considered, along with other evidence in determining whether the Crown has established that a taking or a conversion was without colour of right. Certainly, it cannot alone be a ground for establishing that there was no colour of right. The issue requires, however, some evidence from the accused although the ultimate burden is on the Crown.

In this case, as I ruled in *R. v. Potts* recently, using an "objective" test, it could not be said that Mr. Drainville harboured an honest belief that the Teme-Augama Anishnabai Nation had title to the lands, where the road blockade and obstruction took place. In the absence of an explanation of some sort, the court would certainly draw a very adverse inference in the circumstances at hand. In the case of *R. v. Potts*, the court ruled in favour of the accused, as it was left with a reasonable doubt as to Mr. Potts' state of mind, relating to colour of right. It could be said that Chief Gary Potts had a point of view as to the ownership of the contested lands, which was based in part on certain very strong moral convictions, but also based on a belief in a state of mixed law and fact, which if it actually had existed, would at law have justified or excused his actions. In fact he would have been obstructing a roadway which belonged to him and his people, a clear defence to allegations pursuant to s. 430(1)(c) of the *Criminal Code*.

This brings us to another consideration, not brought up in the *Gary Potts* trial, and that is the distinction between an honest belief in a "moral" as opposed to a "legal or lawful" right. It is clear that in Ontario, at least, an honest belief in a moral as opposed to legal right cannot constitute a colour of right defence. See *R. v. Hemmerly* (1976), 30 C.C.C. (2d) 141 (Ont. C.A.). Martin J.A. at p. 145 writes:

Even if the appellant believed that he had a moral claim to the money (which I am far from holding), a belief in a moral claim could not constitute a colour of right: see Glanville Williams' *Criminal Law* (*the General Part*, 2nd ed. (1961), p. 322, Harris v. Harrison [1963] Crim. L.R. 497, and commentary.)

Glanville Williams in his well-known work, referred to above, expresses the view that while belief in a moral right as distinct from a legal right is irrelevant to the question of a claim of right, belief in a moral right in exceptional circumstances may show that the act is not done fraudulently.

It is true that the *Canadian Charter of Rights and Freedoms* starts off as follows:

Whereas Canada is founded upon principles that recognize the supremacy of God and the rule of law:

But one must recognize that this is perhaps an ideal which we as a nation would like to achieve, but without being successful necessarily all the time. This great declaration seems to assume that both the supremacy of God and the rule of law are consistent with each other, without there being any conflicts between the two. One need only consider for a moment our great struggles with the law as it pertains to contentious issues such as "abortion" to realize that we have, at times, great conflicts between what we accept as "legal" and what we accept as "moral". Perhaps in an imperfect world such as ours, such conflicts are inevitable.

However one thing is certain; when there have been conflicts between our "legal" rules, and our "moral" rules, the courts invariably have ruled in favour of change along the lines provided by the "rule of law".

Though we strive as much as we can towards as near perfect a legal system as is possible, one which hopefully might be in perfect harmony with our "moral values", our real life experience is full of instances where from time to time there are difficult conflicts for us to accept between the "legal" and the "moral". Judging from developments enunciated in *R. v. Hemmerly, supra,* the "rule of law" must prevail.

Accordingly, this has been an area of grave concern for Father Drainville, the accused in these proceedings. A brief review of his evidence before this court convinces us that certainly he has a great and deep moral conviction as the basis for his belief that the Teme-Augama Anishnabai Nation has a good claim to the lands — subject of these proceedings.

As noble and honourable as his motives might be, they are really irrelevant in our considerations pertaining to "colour of right". Unless it can be demonstrated to this court that his honest belief in the existence of a state of facts, in this case title to the subject lands, is based on a mistake of fact or law, his defence cannot succeed on moral conviction alone. Moral convictions though deeply and honestly held cannot transform illegal actions into legal ones; only the "rule of law" must prevail.

. . . .

Father Drainville did not find himself inextricably caught in a conflict as such between "moral rules of God" and the "rule of law"; his moral convictions, or his devotion to God did not entail his obstructing of a roadway, but only that he stand in solidarity perhaps with his brothers and sisters of the Teme-Augama Anishnabai Nation. That could have been done "lawfully" without offence pursuant to the *Criminal Code* of Canada, and certainly without offence to God! On the contrary he purposely and deliberately placed himself at peril, perhaps indeed for the sake of emphasis or additional media coverage of his "message" in support of a cause which could be termed "noble". However, having chosen that path, he must now walk it to its very end!

This of course places this court in a somewhat difficult position as enunciated by my brother Judge Michel in his unreported decision in this court on July 16, 1990 of *R. v. Smith*. However, the court cannot and must not become emotionally or politically involved in such disputes. The court must apply the law of the land as it existed at the relevant time according to the principles of the "rule of law".

Accordingly, by virtue of the principles enunciated in *R. v. Hemmerly*, a belief in a moral claim of right such as demonstrated by Father Drainville in these proceedings cannot constitute a defence of "colour of right". His defence must fail. There will be a finding of guilt.

So, too, the defence did not avail an environmental protester against a mischief charge resulting from the throwing of acid at a ship to stop it fishing: *Watson* (1999), 27 C.R. (5th) 139, 137 C.C.C. (3d) 422 (Nfld. C.A.). Three reasons were given for holding a mistaken belief that Canadian law did not apply beyond a 200-mile limit did not constitute a colour of right defence. There were no cases in which colour of right had been an answer to ignorance of the jurisdiction of the *Criminal Code*. It is no part of the *mens rea* of the offence of mischief that one intends to commit the crime within the jurisdiction of the *Criminal Code* of Canada. Thirdly, the basis of the defence of colour of right as it relates to law is the misunderstanding of the law respecting private rights. **Are these reasons convincing?**

In *R. v. Manuel* (2008), 231 C.C.C. (3d) 468 (B.C. C.A.) the Court rejected the idea that in aboriginal land claims what is being asserted is belief in a moral right as opposed to a legal right belief. The Court, however, found no honest belief on that case.

(d)   Officially Induced Error of Law

LÉVIS (CITY) v. TÉTREAULT;
LÉVIS (CITY) v. 2629-4470 QUÉBEC INC.

[2006] 1 S.C.R. 420, 36 C.R. (6th) 215, 2006 SCC 12, 207 C.C.C. (3d) 1,
2006 CarswellQue 2911, 2006 CarswellQue 2912

In these two cases, the City of Lévis appealed acquittals entered by the Quebec Municipal Court on charges brought against T and a numbered company under the *Highway Safety Code*, R.S.Q., c. C-24.2. T was charged with driving a motor vehicle without a valid driver's licence contrary to s. 93.1. He raised the defence of due diligence, stating that he was unaware that the date appearing on his licence was the date the licence expired rather than a payment due date. The numbered company was charged with operating a motor vehicle for which the fees relating to its registration had not been paid contrary to s. 31.1. It raised the defences of due diligence and officially induced error, alleging that a representative of the Société de l'assurance automobile du Québec ("SAAQ") had had it pay registration fees corresponding to a 15-month period and had told it that a renewal notice would be sent to it before the period expired. Because of an error, the SAAQ sent the notice to the company with an incomplete address and the postal service returned it to the sender. The Municipal Court of the City of Lévis found that both offences were offences of strict liability. The defences of due diligence were accepted and the accused acquitted.

When the matter finally reached the Supreme Court, the Court confirmed that the offences were properly classified as strict liability. On the facts the Court however held that the defence of due diligence had not been established. Both accused had simply remained passive rather than attempting to discover the nature of their legal obligation to pay. The Supreme Court allowed the appeal, entered convictions and imposed minimum fines.

In the course of dismissing the appeals the Court also finally decided that the defence of officially induced error of law is available for any offence.

LeBel J.: —

. . . .

D. Defence of Officially Induced Error

20.   Because the respondent company argues that it was misled by erroneous information obtained from an SAAQ official regarding the procedure for paying the fees relating to the registration of its vehicle, we must now consider the nature and availability of the defence of officially induced error. This Court has never clearly accepted this defence, although several decisions by Canadian courts have recognized it to be relevant and legitimate.

21.   First of all, to place the nature and limits of this defence in the proper perspective, it should be noted that ignorance of the law is not accepted in Canadian criminal law as a means to erase or mitigate criminal liability, despite occasional criticism of the inflexibility of this rule (D. Stuart, *Canadian Criminal Law: A Treatise* (4th ed. 2001), at pp. 322-31). Section 19 of the *Criminal Code*, R.S.C. 1985, c. C-46, states that ignorance of the law is not an excuse for committing an offence. Pursuant to art. 60 C.P.P., this principle applies to regulatory offences created by Quebec legislation. As a result of art. 60, the rules and principles of Canadian criminal law relating to the definition and conduct of available defences against criminal charges apply in Quebec penal law (G. Létourneau and P. Robert, *Code de procédure pénale du Québec annoté* (6th ed. 2004), at pp. 8-9 and 88).

22.   This Court has firmly and consistently applied the principle that ignorance of the law is no defence. It has given effect to this principle not only in the context of the criminal law itself, but also in cases involving regulatory offences (*Molis v. The Queen*, [1980] 2 S.C.R. 356; *Pontes*). However, the inflexibility of this rule is cause for concern where the error in law of the accused arises out of an error of an authorized representative of the state and the state then demands, through other officials, that the criminal law be applied strictly to punish the conduct of the accused. In such a case, regardless of whether it involves strict liability or absolute liability offences, the fundamental fairness of the criminal process would appear to be compromised. Although the Court has not ruled on this point, Lamer C.J. responded to these concerns, in concurring reasons in *Jorgensen* (*R. v. Jorgensen*, [1995] 4 S.C.R. 55), by proposing to recognize the defence of officially induced error and attempting to define the conditions under which the defence would be allowed.

23.   In that case, which involved a charge of selling obscene material, Lamer C.J. carefully reviewed the development of this defence by the courts. He pointed out that the defence had surfaced gradually in criminal law and had been applied by trial and appeal courts to both crimes and regulatory offences: *Jorgensen*, at paras. 12-24). He noted that the judges of this Court, including Ritchie J. in *R. v. MacDougall*, [1982] 2 S.C.R. 605, at p. 613, had at times appeared to acknowledge the appropriateness of such a defence (*Jorgensen*, at para. 17). Later, Gonthier J. too, discussed the framework and nature of the defence of officially induced error in his dissenting reasons in *Pontes*, at p. 88 (*Jorgensen*, at para. 23).

24.   In Lamer C.J.'s view, this defence constituted a limited but necessary exception to the rule that ignorance of the law cannot excuse the commission of a criminal offence:

> Officially induced error of law exists as an exception to the rule that ignorance of the law does not excuse. As several of the cases where this rule has been discussed note, the

complexity of contemporary regulation makes the assumption that a responsible citizen will have a comprehensive knowledge of the law unreasonable. This complexity, however, does not justify rejecting a rule which encourages a responsible citizenry, encourages government to publicize enactments, and is an essential foundation to the rule of law. Rather, extensive regulation is one motive for creating a limited exception to the rule that *ignorantia juris neminem excusat*.

(*Jorgensen*, at para. 25)

25.   Lamer C.J. equated this defence with an excuse that has an effect similar to entrapment. The wrongfulness of the act is established. However, because of the circumstances leading up to the act, the person who committed it is not held liable for the act in criminal law. The accused is thus entitled to a stay of proceedings rather than an acquittal (*Jorgensen*, at para. 37).

26.   After his analysis of the case law, Lamer C.J. defined the constituent elements of the defence and the conditions under which it will be available. In his view, the accused must prove six elements:

(1) that an error of law or of mixed law and fact was made;
(2) that the person who committed the act considered the legal consequences of his or her actions;
(3) that the advice obtained came from an appropriate official;
(4) that the advice was reasonable;
(5) that the advice was erroneous; and
(6) that the person relied on the advice in committing the act.

(*Jorgensen*, at paras. 28-35).

27.   Although the Court did not rule on this issue in *Jorgensen*, I believe that this analytical framework has become established. Provincial appellate courts have followed this approach to consider and apply the defence of officially induced error (*R. v. Larivière* (2000), 38 C.R. (5th) 130 (Que. C.A.); *Maitland Valley Conservation Authority v. Cranbrook Swine Inc.* (2003), 64 O.R. (3d) 417 (C.A.)). I would also note that, in this appeal, neither the prosecution nor the intervener, the Attorney General of Canada, has questioned the existence of this defence in Canadian criminal law as it presently stands. At most, the Attorney General of Canada has suggested another condition in addition to those enumerated by Lamer C.J., namely that the act was committed contemporaneously with the reception of the information. I do not think this addition is necessary. The Attorney General of Canada's concerns relate more to the need to demonstrate that the advice was reasonable and that the accused relied on it. It should be noted, as the Ontario Court of Appeal has done, that it is necessary to establish the objective reasonableness not only of the advice, but also of the reliance on the advice (*R. v. Cancoil Thermal Corp.* (1986), 27 C.C.C. (3d) 295; *Cranbrook Swine*). Various factors will be taken into consideration in the course of this assessment, including the efforts made by the accused to obtain information, the clarity or obscurity of the law, the position and role of the

official who gave the information or opinion, and the clarity, definitiveness and reasonableness of the information or opinion (*Cancoil Thermal*, at p. 303). It is not sufficient in such cases to conduct a purely subjective analysis of the reasonableness of the information. This aspect of the question must be considered from the perspective of a reasonable person in a situation similar to that of the accused.

31.　In the case of the [accused company], a due diligence defence has not been made out, and it has not been demonstrated that all the conditions under which the defence of officially induced error is available have been met.

. . . .

33.　In my view, the respondent's allegations of fact do not show conduct that meets the standard of due diligence. The respondent was aware of the date when the fees relating to the registration of its vehicle would be due and, accordingly, the date when the registration would cease to be valid. It could and should have been concerned when it failed to receive a notice. Instead, it did nothing. It had a duty to do more. The acquittal was therefore unjustified.

34.　Nor has the respondent established that the conditions under which the defence or excuse of officially induced error is available have been met in this case and justified a stay of proceedings. The issues raised related at most to administrative practices, not to the legal obligation to pay the fees by the prescribed date. Two fundamental conditions that must be met for this defence to be available were therefore missing. In the circumstances, the respondent could not have considered the legal consequences of its conduct on the basis of advice from the official in question, nor could it have acted in reliance on that opinion, since no information regarding the nature and effects of the relevant legal obligations had been requested or obtained.

Do you agree with the Supreme Court that this defence should be established with a remedy of a judicial stay rather than an acquittal on the merits, as is the case with most defences?

In *Canada (Attorney General) v. Charles* (2005), 30 C.R. (6th) 316 (Sask. C.A.) farmers selling wheat in protest of the monopoly of the Canadian Wheat Board were held to have a defence of officially induced error of law to a charge of failing to report their export to customs officials. The customs officials had no legal basis for refusing to accept documentation other than the Wheat Board export license. However, in *R. v. Shiner* (2007), 46 C.R. (6th) 268 (N.L. C.A.) the defence did not succeed in the case of sealers catching blueback seal and selling their pelts. The fact that the ban against such hunting had not been enforced in previous years, and that a Department of Fisheries and Oceans Officer was present at the hunt and did nothing, was not a sufficient basis for the defence. Their acquittals were reversed.

For an argument that a rigid division of legally significant error into ignorance of law and mistake of fact is contrary to s. 7 of the *Charter*, see Hamish Stewart, "Mistake of Law Under the *Charter*" (1998), 34 Crim. L.Q. 476.

1. A motorist is stopped by the police and requested to provide a breathalyzer sample at the police station. At the police station he refuses to provide a sample and is charged with failing to provide a breath sample without reasonable excuse contrary to the *Criminal Code*. Consider whether he has a defence

> **(1) If he refused because he had heard of a Provincial Court ruling that the breathalyzer provisions are unconstitutional. That decision was reversed by the Court of Appeal before the accused's trial on the refusal charge.**

In *R. v. MacIntyre* (1983), 24 M.V.R. 67, leave to appeal to S.C.C. refused 2 O.A.C. 400, the Ontario Court of Appeal dismissed the defence without reasons being given.

> **(2) If the situation is the same but before the refusal a lawyer advised the accused, in error, that the provincial court judge's decision was still valid law.**

Compare *R. v. Dunn* (1977), 21 N.S.R. (2d) 334 (C.A.) and *R. v. Whelan* (2002), 170 C.C.C.(3d) 151 (N.L.C.A.).

> **(3) Would your answer to (2) differ if the advice had been that of the Registrar of Motor Vehicles?**

2. The accused were operating a laboratory in which they were manufacturing various chemicals. Unknown to the accused a police investigation discovered that one of these drugs was M.D.M.A., which was not an illegal drug under any of the schedules of the *Food and Drugs Act*, R.S.C. 1970, c. F-27. However the police suspected it could be used in combination with others to produce illegal drugs. The police managed to have M.D.M.A. added to the schedule of restricted drugs under the *Food and Drugs Act*. This amendment was published in the *Canada Gazette*. The accused continued to produce M.D.M.A. and, two months later, were charged with trafficking in that drug. Can the accused rely on ignorance of the law?

Compare *Molis v. R.*, [1980] 2 S.C.R. 356, 55 C.C.C. (2d) 558.

3. The accused is charged with possession of a prohibited weapon contrary to s. 90(1) of the *Criminal Code*. When stopped by the police he was wearing a knife sheath attached to his belt. The officer examined the knife and, with a forceful downward motion of his arm and wrist, while holding the handle of the knife, was able to open its blade. The accused immediately indicated that he was unaware that the knife could be opened

in this manner. Section 84(1)(b) of the *Criminal Code* defines a prohibited weapon in part as "any knife that has a blade that opens automatically by gravity or centrifugal force or by hand pressure applied to a button, spring or other device in or attached to the handle of the knife". Has the accused made a mistake of law or fact?

Compare *R. v. Archer* (1983), 6 C.C.C. (3d) 129 (Ont. C.A.).

4. The accused were charged with unlawfully conducting a bingo contrary to s. 206(1)(*d*) of the *Criminal Code*. The charges arose out of gaming operations on a reserve. The accused maintained that they were entitled to be acquitted by reason of a defence of colour of right. That right was the belief that s. 206 did not apply to their activities since they were carried out on a reserve which they thought was not subject to the laws of Canada relating to gaming. Is this a mistake of fact or law? Is there a colour of right defence?

Compare *R. v. Jones* (1991), 8 C.R. (4th) 137 (S.C.C.).

5. The accused relied on the information of a firearms officer that a permit was not required for a garage sale. He was charged with the *Criminal Code* offence of selling firearms without a permit.

Compare *R. v. Dubeau* (1993), 80 C.C.C. (3d) 54 (Ont. Gen. Div.).

6. The accused is charged with contravening a municipal bylaw by using a family dwelling as a professional office. On first conviction the penalty is a fine of not more that $25,000. The accused, a registered denture therapist, and the co-accused, her husband, opened an office for some of her work at their place of resi dence. Before doing so the husband purchased a copy of the relevant bylaw at the city offices and asked a city planner whether he could open a business in his place. The planner advised that his wife could open the office as she qualified as a drugless practitioner. Should there be a defence of officially induced error of law? Would it matter if the offence was one of absolute liability?

Compare *R. v. Bauman* (1994), 32 C.R. (4th) 176 (Ont. Prov. Ct.).

GENERAL REVIEW QUESTIONS

1. Al Capone is charged with speeding contrary to s. 109 of the *Highway Traffic Act*, R.S.O. 1980, c. 198, in that he drove a motor vehicle in excess of 50 k.p.h. in a 50 k.p.h. zone. If he is convicted the penalty is mandatory: a fine of $18.75.

The uncontested evidence is that the accused was driving at 65 k.p.h. in a 50 k.p.h. zone and that he was knowingly exceeding that speed limit as he genuinely believed he was in a 70 k.p.h. zone. The source of the mistake was a sign reading "70 k.p.h. limit ahead" which Al interpreted to immediately raise the speed limit, whereas this was in reality only achieved 300 metres further along the street, by a sign reading "70 k.p.h. limit". Al, a school principal, had been troubled about this ambiguity before and had telephoned the local police detachment. A sergeant had unambiguously informed him (in error) that the speed limit was raised by the first sign.

You are articled to the defence lawyer. She requests a memorandum discussing all possible defences and the authorities on which they would be based. In each case assess the likelihood of success.

2. Kevin owns a bar. A customer, Susan, comes into the bar and orders a double whisky. Kevin asks her how old she is, to which she answers in unambiguous terms that he should mind his own business. Kevin is pretty confident that she is about 16 years of age. The problem is that he is not sure whether the recent raising of the drinking age from 16 to 18 is in effect. He asks a lawyer in the bar who advises, "The Act comes into effect next week". Kevin serves Susan. Susan's seemingly younger companion, Gordon, then also orders whisky. Kevin, suspecting Gordon is underage, asks him for his driver's licence. Gordon produces the driver's licence of one Ross, whose age is shown as 18, Kevin is surprised but gives no thought to whether the licence is really that of the customer. He serves Gordon.

In fact the new provincial *Liquor Act* is already in force. Section 10 reads:

> Every one who supplies liquor to a person under the age of 18 is guilty of an offence and liable to a fine of not less than $300.

Kevin is facing two charges under s. 10 since Susan is 17 and Gordon 15. Write a legal memorandum on his possible defences, discussing appropriate authorities and assessing his chances of acquittal.

Chapter 6

INCAPACITY

1. AGE

Until 1982 the age of absolute exemption from criminal responsibility was set by the *Criminal Code* at seven. That a child under seven committed the *actus reus* with the requisite *mens rea* made no difference. Furthermore children over seven and under 14 were likewise exempt unless the prosecutor could show that the child was "competent to know the nature and consequence of his conduct and to appreciate that it was wrong". In 1982 this latter so-called *doli incapax* presumption was abolished and the age of criminal responsibility was raised from seven to twelve years in a new s. 13 [en. 1980-81-82, c. 110, s. 72] of the *Criminal Code*. The *Young Offenders Act*, S.C. 1980-81-82, c. 110, replaced the *Juvenile Delinquents Act*. It governs the trials of all children over the age of 11 but under the age of 18. The *Young Offenders Act* was itself replaced by the *Youth Criminal Justice Act*, S.C. 2002, c. 1, which came into force in April 1, 2003.

Consideration of the special procedural and dispositional alternatives dealt with in this new Act are beyond the scope of this book. For our purposes it is sufficient to observe that the substantive law principles that we are exploring apply equally in Youth Court. See, generally, Corrado, Bala, Linden and LeBlanc, *Juvenile Justice in Canada* (Butterworths, 1992), Nicholas Bala, *Young Offenders Law* (Irwin Law, 1997) and Nicholas Bala, *Youth Justice Criminal Law* (Irwin Law, 2003).

In *R. v. B. (D.)*, 2008 SCC 25, 231 C.C.C. (3d) 338, 56 C.R. (6th) 203, [2008] 2 S.C.R. 3 (S.C.C.) the Supreme Court recognised a new principle of fundamental justice that young people who engage in criminal conduct should be presumed to have less moral blameworthiness and culpability than adults. The majority constitutionalized a presumption of lower sentences for young offenders. Contrast the ruling in *Canadian Foundation for Children v. Canada (A.G.)*, [2004] 1 S.C.R. 76, 16 C.R. (6th) 203 (the spanking case considered above in Chapter 1) that the common law principle of acting in the best interests of the child was not a principle of fundamental justice as there was insufficient consensus for that principle and it was not workable.

2. INSANITY (MENTAL DISORDER)

(a) Psychiatric Classification: Limited Truths

Psychiatric Classification of Mental Disorder

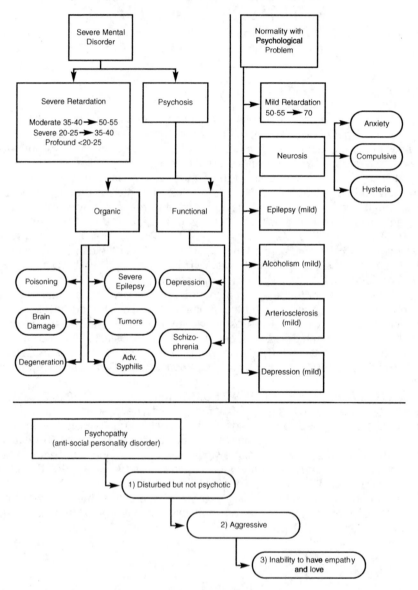

This diagram is derived from the work of Dr. N.D. Walker of Cambridge University,

Crime and Punishment in Britain (1968) and D.S.M. IV). Thanks to Adam Wygodny, a former Queen's law student, for the computer graphics.

There are problems inherent in any classifications that make expertise in diagnosis elusive in all but the most obvious cases. In particular, each psychiatric label is a shorthand expression of relative rather than absolute conditions which are difficult to define; any one individual can present the conditions more strongly at some times rather than others, and each individual can present symptoms of more than one psychiatric label at any one time.

These limits are recognized in the influential DSM-III classification announced by the American Psychiatric Association in 1980. The classification is now known as DSM-IV to reflect changes made up until 1994.[1] This divides "mental disorder" into, *inter alia*, "mental retardation", psychoses,[2] "anxiety disorders" and "personality disorders". It is, for example, stated at the outset:

> In DMS-IV there is no assumption that each category of mental disorder is a completely discrete entity with absolute boundaries dividing it from other mental disorders or from no mental disorder.[3]

Clinicians are encouraged to assign more than one label whenever appropriate. The DSM-IV "personality disorder" label includes "Anti-social Personality Disorder"[4] as a form of mental disorder. This has also been known as the concept of "psychopathy" or "sociopathy". The label appears frequently in the criminal law and is highly controversial.

The classic description of "psychopathic syndrome" is provided by the McCords[5] in their exhaustive study:

> The psychopath is asocial. His conduct often brings him into conflict with society. The psychopath is driven by primitive desires and an exaggerated craving for excitement. In his self-centred search for pleasure, he ignores restrictions of his culture. The psychopath is highly impulsive. He is a man for whom the moment is a segment of time detached from all others. His actions are unplanned and guided by his whims. The psychopath is aggressive. He has learned few socialized ways of coping with frustration. The psychopath feels little, if any, guilt. He can commit the most appalling acts, yet view them without remorse. The psychopath has a warped capacity for love. His emotional relationships, when they exist, are meager, fleeting, and designed to satisfy his own desires. These last two traits, guiltlessness and lovelessness, conspicuously mark the psychopath as different from other men.[6]

The World Health Organization's 1978 International Classification of Diseases[7] similarly describes a "personality disorder with predominantly sociopathic or asocial manifestation" as a:

---

1 *Diagnostic and Statistical Manual of Mental Disorders*, 4th ed. (1994) (DSM-IV).

2 The classification avoids the umbrella "psychosis" label but has a category of "psychotic disorders not elsewhere specified".

3 At xxii.

4 At 649-650.

5 W. and J. McCord, *The Psychopath: An Essay on the Criminal Mind*, (1964).

6 Above note 5, 16-17.

7 W.H.O., *Mental Disorders: Glossary and Guide to Their Classification in Accordance with the Ninth Revision of the International Classification of Diseases*, (1978), point 301.7.

Personality disorder characterized by disregard for social obligations, lack of feeling for others, and impetuous violence or callous unconcern. There is a gross disparity between behaviour and the prevailing social norms. Behaviour is not readily modifiable by experience, including punishment. People with this personality are often affectively cold and may be abnormally aggressive or irresponsible. Their tolerance to frustration is low; they blame others or offer plausible rationalizations for the behaviour which brings them into conflict with society.

The DSM-IV classification avoids abstraction and instead identifies[8] a host of "diagnostic criteria":

Diagnostic criteria for 301.7 Anti-social Personality Disorder

A. There is a pervasive pattern of disregard for and violation of the rights of others occurring since age 15 years, as indicated by three (or more) of the following:

    (1) failure to conform to social norms with respect to lawful behaviours as indicated by repeatedly performing acts that are grounds for arrest
    (2) deceitfulness, as indicated by repeated lying, use of aliases, or conning others for personal profit or pleasure
    (3) impulsivity or failure to plan ahead
    (4) irritability and aggressiveness, as indicated by repeated physical fights or assaults
    (5) reckless disregard for safety of self or others
    (6) consistent irresponsibility, as indicated by repeated failure to sustain consistent work behaviour or honor financial obligations
    (7) lack of remorse, as indicated by being indifferent to or rationalizing having hurt, mistreated, or stolen from another.

B. The individual is at least age 18 years.

C. There is evidence of Conduct Disorder ... with onset before age 15 years.

D. The occurrence of anti-social behaviour is not exclusively during the course of Schizophrenia or a Manic Episode.

Conduct disorders are defined[9] as involving repetitive and persistent patterns of violations of social norms falling into four categories: aggression to people and animals, destruction of property, deceitfulness or theft and serious violation of rules.

The DSM guide highlights the glaring deficiencies of the label "psychopathic syndrome". Surely the criteria, based on consensus, rather than being verified by research, are arbitrary, extremely ambiguous, over inclusive and, above all, circular. A startling example of the process occurred in 1973 where it took a vote of the trustees and a 60 percent vote of the membership by ballot to remove homosexuality from the Manual's list of mental disorders.[10] The criteria were even vaguer in the 1980 classification. In 1987 they were changed because in constructing questions for use by clinicians "it was found that many of those criteria were imprecise and in need of further specification". This label seems to be a ragbag description of a persistent recidivist who carries on committing crimes

---

8 At 649-650. Reproduced by permission of the American Psychiatric Association.
9 At 85, 646.
10 See Eric H. Marcus, "Unbiased Medical Testimony: Reality or Myth?" (1985), 6 Am. J. For. Psych. 3.

for no apparent reason. There is a strong body of opinion in England[11] but less so in Canada[12] that the label "obliterates more information than it conveys".[13] It tells us nothing about causation, prognosis or treatment. Changing the label to "sociopath", "personality disorder", "character disorder" or the like will not address these criticisms.[14] With any psychiatric label, and this one in particular, lawyers should request that psychiatrists be as precise as possible in their descriptions of the actual behaviour of the individual before the court rather than hide behind imperfect abstractions. Clearly they are too imprecise for use as legal criteria of responsibility.

Some psychiatrists accept this perspective. Professor Orchard,[15] for example, recognizes that the issue of legal insanity,

> ultimately must be decided by the judge and jury. This conclusion is consistent with the important legal principle that expert opinion, including medical and psychiatric opinion, should be used to assist the court in arriving at a finding, but that the responsibility of making this finding is, and must remain, in the hands of the triers of fact. Doctors may not enjoy the obvious questioning of the validity of their diagnosis and opinions which this entails. However, as no one, not even a doctor, sad to say, is infallible, it is most important that any judge or jury look at all the evidence, including the psychiatric opinion and the data upon which it is based, with the utmost of careful scrutiny. In the light of the serious consequences that may ensue, this means vigorous examination and cross-examination are necessary.

T.S. SZASZ, PSYCHIATRY, ETHICS AND THE CRIMINAL LAW

(1958), 58 Col. L. Rev. 183 at 190

The controversial sceptic of psychology and author of *The Manufacture of Madness* and *The Myth of Mental Illness*, displays his usual boisterous style in condemning the *Durham* rule:

According to the *Durham* decision, if the defence of insanity has been raised in a criminal trial, it is considered to be a "matter of fact" for the jury to decide whether the offender suffered from a "mental illness" at the time of the commission of the act with which he is charged.

This is unadulterated nonsense. It could come about only as a result of the great prestige which the medical profession commands in our present-day society, and is, in fact, an expression of that prestige. Disregarding even the most

---

11 See especially Walker, *Crime and Punishment in Britain*, rev. ed. (1968), 82-8 and (with S. McCabe) *Crime and Insanity in England*, (1973), vol. 2, chapter 10.

12 J. Nemeth, "Psychopathic Personality. Its Relevance in the Correctional After-Care Agency" (1961), 3 Can. J. Corr. 128, but compare H.H.A. Cooper, "The Inadequate Psychopath: Some Medico-Legal Problems and a Clinical Profile" (1973), 21 Chitty's L.J. 325, R.D. Hare, Manual for the Revised Checklist (1991) and G.T. Harris, M.E. Rice and C.A. Cormier, "Psychopathy and Violent Recidivism" (1991), 15 *Law and Human Behaviour* at 625-637.

13 Walker, above note 11.

14 Walker, above, note 11, but see *contra* the *Report of the Butler Committee on Mentally Abnormal Offenders*, (1975) (Cmnd. 6244), which recommends the term "personality disorder".

15 B.C.L. Orchard, "Insanity — A Psychiatrist's View of the Recent Rulings of the Supreme Court of Canada" (1981), 2 Sup. Crt. L. Rev. 405.

obvious doubt concerning exactly what the expression "mental illness" is supposed to denote, it denotes a *theory* (if it denotes anything) and not a fact. This would be true, of course, for any disease, and especially for a bodily disease, after which the notion of "mental disease" is fashioned. Thus, it may be a fact that a patient is jaundiced, that is, that his skin appears to be yellow to the average observer. But being jaundiced is not the same as having a "disease". And whether this hypothetical patient with yellow skin has a gall stone, infectious hepatitis, or whatever, his "disease" is a *theory* which physicians (or others) form in order to explain his yellow skin. Accordingly, it would be a perversion of our language and thought to refer to a "disease" (or "illness", which I use as a synonym) as if it were a "fact".

To speak of "mental illness" is, epistemologically, very much worse than it is to speak of diseases of the body. Yet the jury is supposed to determine, as a matter of *fact*, whether the accused has or has not a "mental illness". Of course, it is quite possible for a group of people (a jury) to decide that someone is "crazy" or "mentally ill". But this is then *their theory* of why he has acted the way he did. It is no more — or less — a fact than it would be to assert that the accused is possessed by the devil; that is another "theory", now discarded. To believe that one's own theories are facts is considered by many contemporary psychiatrists as a "symptom" of schizophrenia. Yet this is what the language of the *Durham* decision does. It rectifies some of the shakiest and most controversial aspects of contemporary psychiatry (*i.e.*, those pertaining to what is "mental disease" and the classification of such alleged diseases) and by legal fiat seeks to transform inadequate theory into "judicial fact".

Further, *Durham* takes the notion of "mental illness" and requires the psychiatrist and the jury to determine whether the criminal act in question was committed as a result of such "illness". This, too, is supposed to be a "fact". Unfortunately, this not only cannot be a fact, but it cannot even be a theory. For, if the notion of "mental illness" means anything, it means that it is the theory by means of which we "explain" how the events in question might have occurred.

In 1999 the APA began work on its fifth revision of DSM scheduled to be published in 2013. Modern critics complain that the DSM categories are still not the subject of scientifically verified research, have grown exponentially, that psychiatrists too often tend to blindly rely on them to prescribe psychoactive drugs, and that psychiatrists have become too beholden to the pharmaceutical industry: see Marcia Angell. "The Illusions of Psychiatry", *The New York Review of Books,* July 14, 2011. She notes that DSM V will broaden diagnostic boundaries by including precursors of disorders such as "psychosis risk syndrome" and "mild cognitive impairment", the use of the term spectrum, such as "autism spectrum disorder", and adding new entities such as "hypersexual disorder", "restless leg syndrome" and "binge eating".

(b) Mental Disorder under *Criminal Code*

In February, 1992, Bill C-30 came into force. It enacted a new Part XXI of the *Criminal Code*, which declares a comprehensive legal regime to deal with accused who suffer from mental disorder. The law is sometimes concerned with the accused's state of mind at the time of his trial. The accused must be both mentally and physically present. There are detailed provisions in Part XXI relating to remands for observation and for determinations whether an accused is fit to stand his trial. Our concern here, however, is with an accused who is fit to stand trial and who seeks a verdict under s. 672.45 of not criminally responsible on account of mental disorder. Such an inquiry relates to the accused's state of mind at the time of the alleged act.

Until Bill C-30, such a verdict had been called an acquittal on account of insanity. The key provisions were as follows:

16. (1) No person shall be convicted of an offence in respect of an act or omission on his part while he was insane.

(2) For the purposes of this section a person is insane when he is in a state of natural imbecility or has disease of the mind to an extent that renders him incapable of appreciating the nature and quality of an act or omission or of knowing that an act or omission is wrong.

(3) A person who has specific delusions, but is in other respects sane, shall not be acquitted on the ground of insanity unless the delusions caused him to believe in the existence of a state of things that, if it existed, would have justified or excused his act or omission.

(4) Every one shall, until the contrary is proved, be presumed to be and to have been sane.

. . . .

614. (1) Where, upon the trial of an accused who is charged with an indictable offence, evidence is given that the accused was insane at the time the offence was committed and the accused is acquitted,

(a) the jury, or

(b) the Judge or Magistrate, where there is no jury, shall find whether the accused was insane at the time the offence was committed and shall declare whether he is acquitted on account of insanity.

(2) Where the accused is found to have been insane at the time the offence was committed, the Court, Judge or Magistrate before whom the trial is held shall order that he be kept in strict custody in the place and in the manner that the Court, Judge or Magistrate directs, until the pleasure of the lieutenant governor of the province is known.

Section 16 was a Canadian version of the famous *M'Naghten* rules, whose history is described in the following decision.

U.S. v. FREEMAN

(1966), 357 F. (2d) 606 (2nd. Circ.)

KAUFMAN J.: —

. . . .

M'Naghten and its antecedents can, in many respects, be seen as examples of the law's conscientious efforts to place in a separate category, people who cannot be justly held "responsible" for their acts. As far back as 1582, William Lambard of Lincolns' Inn set forth what can be viewed as the forerunner of the M'Naghten test as we know it: "If a man or a natural fool, or a lunatic in the time of his lunacy, or a child who apparently has no knowledge of good or evil do kill a man, this is no felonious act . . . for they cannot be said to have any understanding will." By 1724, the language had shifted from "good or evil" to the more familiar emphasis on the word "know." Thus, in *Rex v. Arnold*, 16 How. St. Tr. 695, 764 the "Wild Beast" test was enunciated. It provided for exculpation if the defendant "doth not *know* what he is doing, no more than . . . a wild beast." (Emphasis added.)

By modern scientific standards the language of these early tests is primitive. In the 18th century, psychiatry had hardly become a profession, let alone a science. Thus, these tests and their progeny were evolved at a time when psychiatry was literally in the Dark Ages.

In the pre-M'Naghten period, the concepts of phrenology and monomania were being developed and had significant influence on the right and wrong test. Phrenologists believed that the human brain was divided into 35 separate areas, each with its own peculiar mental function. The sixth area, for example, was designated "destructiveness." It was located, we are told, above the ear because this was the widest part of the skull of carnivorous animals. Monomania, on the other hand, was a state of mind in which one insane idea predominated while the rest of the thinking processes remained normal.

Of course, both phrenology and monomania are rejected today as meaningless medical concepts since the human personality is viewed as a fully integrated system. But, by an accident of history, the rule of M'Naghten's case froze these concepts into the common law just at a time when they were becoming obsolete. A discussion of M'Naghten's case will demonstrate how this came about. Daniel M'Naghten suffered from what now would be described as delusions of persecution. Apparently, he considered his major persecutor to be Robert Peel, then Prime Minister of England, for M'Naghten came to London with the intention of assassinating the chief of the Queen's government. His plan would have succeeded but for the fact that Peel chose to ride in Queen Victoria's carriage because of her absence from the city, while Drummond, his secretary, rode in the vehicle which normally would have been occupied by Peel.

M'Naghten, believing that the Prime Minister was riding in his own carriage, shot and killed Drummond in error.

After a lengthy trial in 1843, M'Naghten was found "not guilty by reason of insanity." M'Naghten's exculpation from criminal responsibility was most significant for several reasons. His defense counsel had relied in part upon Dr. Isaac Ray's historic work, Medical Jurisprudence of Insanity which had been published in 1838. This book, which was used and referred to extensively at the trial, contained many enlightened views on the subject of criminal responsibility in general and on the weaknesses of the right and wrong test in particular. Thus, for example, the jury was told that the human mind is not compartmentalized and that a defect in one aspect of the personality could spill over and affect other areas. As Chief Judge Biggs tells us in his Isaac Ray lectures compiled in The Guilty Mind, the court was so impressed with this and other medical evidence of M'Naghten's incompetency that Lord Chief Justice Tindal practically directed a verdict for the accused.

For these reasons, M'Naghten's case could have been the turning point for a new approach to more modern methods of determining criminal responsibility. But the Queen's ire was raised by the acquittal and she was prompted to intervene. Mid-19th century England was in a state of social upheaval and there had been three attempts on the life of the Queen and one on the Prince Consort. Indeed, Queen Victoria was so concerned about M'Naghten's acquittal that she summoned the House of Lords to "take the opinion of the judges on the law governing such cases." Consequently, the 15 judges of the common-law courts were called in a somewhat extraordinary session under a not too subtle atmosphere of pressure to answer five prolix and obtuse questions on the status of criminal responsibility in England. Significantly, it was Lord Chief Justice Tindal who responded for 14 of the 15 judges, and thus articulated what has come to be known as the M'Naghten Rules or M'Naghten test. Rather than relying on Dr. Ray's monumental work which had apparently impressed him at M'Naghten's trial, Tindal, with the Queen's breath upon him, reaffirmed the old restricted right-wrong test despite its 16th century roots and the fact that it, in effect, echoed such uninformed concepts as phrenology and monomania.

Under s. 614(2) where an accused was acquitted on account of insanity, the trial judge had to order that the accused be kept in strict custody "until the pleasure of the lieutenant governor of the province is known". The trial judge had no discretion or power in this matter. In practice, it was up to provincial Mental Health Review Boards to decide if, when and how the accused should be detained. This amounted to indeterminant detention at the discretion of the mental health authorities .

In *R. v. Swain* (1991), 5 C.R. (4th) 253 (S.C.C.), the Supreme Court held that the mandatory detention of an insane acquittee under s. 614(2) without any chance of a hearing offended s. 7 of the *Charter* and also that detention without criteria constituted arbitrary detention under s. 9. Neither violation could be saved by s. 1. The court ordered a six-month period of temporary validity for s. 614(2). The Minister of Justice obtained one extension. Finally, Bill C-30 was passed as a general reform package and also to respond to *Swain*.

The 1991 amendments abandoned the legalistic terminology of "insanity" in favour of "mental disorder" now used by most psychologists and psychiatrists. However, the change is not as significant as first appears given that s. 2 defines "mental disorder" as "a disease of the mind" and that the tests remain tests of legal irresponsibility derived from the M'Naghten rules. There is thus a descriptive advantage in continuing to refer to the defence of insanity at trial. It is still clear that the issue is still not determined by modern psychology and psychiatry. The revised s. 16 reads as follows:

> **16.**(1) No person is criminally responsible for an act committed or an omission made while suffering from a mental disorder that rendered the person incapable of appreciating the nature and quality of the act or omission or of knowing that it was wrong.
>
> (2) Every person is presumed not to suffer from a mental disorder so as to be exempt from criminal responsibility by virtue of subsection (1), until the contrary is proved on the balance of probabilities.
>
> (3) The burden of proof that an accused was suffering from a mental disorder so as to be exempt from criminal responsibility is on the party that raises the issue.

Parliament has made it clear that the accused has the burden of proving the exemption on a balance of probabilities. It will be recalled that in *Chaulk* (1991), 2 C.R. (4th) 1 (S.C.C.), the Supreme Court of Canada, over the sole dissent of Wilson J., held that this was the effect of the former presumption of sanity. The majority further ruled that the onus of proof on the accused could be demonstrably justified as a reasonable limit under s. 1.

The verdict is now "not criminally responsible on account of mental disorder" (s. 672.34). Following such a verdict the trial judge now has a discretion, and an obligation on application by the accused or the Crown, to hold a disposition hearing (s. 672.45). Such disposition may be an absolute or conditional discharge or detention in custody in a hospital (s. 672.54). See Laura Burt, "The Mental Disorder Provisions: Community Residence and Dispositions Under Section 672.54 (*c*)" (1993), 36 Crim. L.Q. 40. Subject to such a court order, detention or release is in the jurisdiction of Provincial Review Boards, which are now mandatory and subject to detailed procedural requirements. See ss. 672.38-672.94 and see, generally, A.J.C. O'Marra, "*Hadfield* To *Swain*: The *Criminal Code* Amendments Dealing With the Mentally Disordered Accused" (1993), 36 Crim. L.Q. 49. This includes a right of appeal to a Court of Appeal. See *R. v. Peckham* (1994), 33 C.R. (4th) (C.A.), where the court held that in applying the test of reasonableness the court "must be cognizant of the Board's expertise and show that expertise appropriate curial deference". Parliament also enacted caps on detention such as life for first or second degree murder and ten years for certain designated offences and two years for other offences, see s. 672.64. However the capping provision has not been proclaimed. Unless and until such proclamation there would appear to have been little change to the former reality of indeterminate detention especially as trial judges may wish to defer to mental health authorities.

The new legal regime survived *Charter* review in *Winko v. Forensic Psychiatric Institute*, [1999] 2 S.C.R. 625. For a court unanimous on the issues of constitutionality, McLachlin J. held that the provisions did not violate s. 7 protections. The scheme was premised on treatment and assessment, and balanced the rights of the offender and society. The offender found not criminally responsible by reason of mental disorder had to be discharged absolutely unless the board or the court found that the offender was a significant threat to public safety. This meant a real risk of physical or psychological harm beyond the trivial or annoying. The provisions were not vague or overbroad and did not impose a burden on the offender. The regime did not violate the equality guarantee under s. 15. Although there was differential treatment based on the personal characteristic of medical illness it was not discriminatory. At every stage of Part XX.1 the assessment was based on the individual's situation and needs and was subject to the overriding rule of the least restrictive avenue and annual review.

Regrettably, the court in *Winko* did not address the significance of the non-proclamation of the capping provisions. This had prompted the Manitoba Court of Appeal to declare that ss. 672.54 and 672.81(1) violated s. 7 and were of no force or effect: *Hoeppner* (1999), 25 C.R. (5th) 91 (Man. C.A.), reconsideration refused (1999), 145 Man. R. (2d) 160 (note) (S.C.C.). In *Winko*, McLachlin J., in the course of deciding that the new scheme was not overbroad, indicated baldly that "I cannot agree with the contrary decision" in *Hoeppner* (at para. 71, C.R.).

Where the defence of lack of responsibility through mental disorder has not been raised or has been rejected, upon conviction the trial judge has the normal range of sentencing options. These powers do not include the jurisdiction to order the place and type of imprisonment although the prison regime can be determined by setting the length at two years or more, federal, or less than two years, provincial. The judge has no power to order psychiatric treatment in a prison or that the accused be transferred from a prison to a psychiatric facility; see *R. v. Deans* (1977), 37 C.C.C. (2d) 221 (Ont. C.A.); *R. v. Trecroce* (1980), 55 C.C.C.(2d) 202 (Ont. C.A.) at 218. Judicial recommendations do not have to be followed by prison authorities. There is no sentence alternative in Canada, as there is in England, of a hospital order where a judge may sentence directly to a mental institution. A power to order detention in a psychiatric facility for up to 60 days in acute cases was contained in the 1992 amendments, s. 736.11, but this provision has not been proclaimed. Provincial psychiatric hospitals appear reluctant to accept more mentally-disordered persons sent from the criminal justice system. In *R. v. Knoblauch* (2001), 37 C.R. (5th) 349 (S.C.C.), however, the Supreme Court decided that sections 742.1 and 742.3 of the *Criminal Code* do not preclude a conditional sentence that requires all or part of a sentence to be served in a locked psychiatric unit with consent.

It would appear that even under the new *Criminal Code* regime there are limited dispositional options. A defence based on mental disorder will still likely result in indeterminate detention at the discretion of health authorities. The defence is therefore likely to be rare except in those cases where the accused faces the option of a long prison sentence and would prefer secure custody in a mental facility.

COOPER v. R.

(1979), [1980] 1 S.C.R. 1149, 13 C.R. (3d) 97, 51 C.C.C. (2d) 129,
1979 CarswellOnt 60, 1979 CarswellOnt 74

The accused was charged with the murder of a patient at a psychiatric hospital (the detailed facts and the accused's psychiatric history are considered below). At the trial the defence of insanity was not raised by the accused but the trial judge nevertheless put it to the jury. The accused's appeal to the Ontario Court of Appeal was dismissed. Only the dissenting judge, Dubin J.A., would have ordered a new trial on the ground of misdirection as to defence of insanity.

DICKSON J. (LASKIN C.J.C., BEETZ, ESTEY and MCINTYRE JJ. concurring): — Issues fundamental to the design and range of the "insanity defence" and to notions of responsibility in our criminal justice system are before the court in this appeal.

The case opens up the broad and difficult question of the obligation of a trial Judge to charge on insanity in circumstances where an accused has a lengthy psychiatric history but the medical evidence is that he does not suffer from "disease of the mind".

The appellant, Gary Albert Cooper, was charged with the murder of one Denise Hobbs, at the time an in-patient at the Hamilton Psychiatric Hospital. The appellant was an out-patient at the same institution. There was evidence that the appellant had been drinking during the day of 8th October 1975. That evening he arrived at a regularly scheduled dance held at a nearby church for patients of the hospital, and there met Denise Hobbs, with whom he was acquainted. At his invitation, the two left the dance to seek a bottle of pop and cigarettes. Ultimately, after an unsuccessful attempt at sexual intercourse the appellant choked the deceased. The cause of death was asphyxiation by strangulation.

At trial, counsel for the defence directed argument to raising a doubt on the issue of intent, and did not plead the "defence" of insanity. Nonetheless, the trial judge, Van Camp J., charged the jury on insanity, though in a manner vigorously challenged in this appeal. The jury found the appellant guilty of non-capital murder, and an appeal was dismissed without written reasons, Dubin J.A. dissenting. At a later date Dubin J.A. delivered lengthy reasons in dissent [40 C.C.C. (2d) 145].

. . . .

The question raised by this appeal is whether there was evidence from which a properly charged jury could conclude, on a balance of probabilities, that the appellant had disease of the mind to an extent that rendered him incapable of appreciating the nature and quality of the act of which he was charged or of knowing that it was wrong. "Wrong" means legally wrong: *Schwartz v. R.*, [1977] 1 S.C.R. 673, 34 C.R.N.S. 138, 29 C.C.C. (2d) 1. Before turning to the evidence adduced at trial, it will be convenient to consider this question at some length, for it raises two distinct legal issues fundamental to our defence of insanity under s. 16(2). First, the meaning to be ascribed to the phrase "disease of the mind" and, second, the interpretation to be given the words "incapable of appreciating the nature and quality of an act".

I
DISEASE OF THE MIND

Let me say by way of commencement that, to date, the phrase "disease of the mind" has proven intractable and has eluded satisfactory definition by both medical and legal disciplines. It is not a term of art in either law or psychiatry. Indeed, Glanville Williams (*Textbook of Criminal Law* (1978), p. 592) says that the phrase is no longer in medical use. "It is a mere working concept, a mere abstraction, like sin" (Wily and Stallworthy, Mental Abnormality and the Law (1962), p. 20). Although the term expresses a legal concept, and a finding is made according to a legal test, psychiatric knowledge is directly linked to the legal conclusion, for medical testimony forms part of the evidence on which the trier of fact must reach its decision. But medical and legal perspectives differ.

. . . .

In *R. v. Kemp*, [1957] 1 Q.B. 339, an oft-cited decision, the primary issue was whether arteriosclerosis came within the meaning of "disease of the mind". Devlin J. agreed that there was an absence of medical opinion as to the categories of malfunction properly to be termed "diseases of the mind", and rejected the idea that, for legal purposes, a distinction should be made between diseases physical and mental in origin. In his view, arteriosclerosis is a disease of the mind and can provide a defence to a criminal charge. He reviewed the relationship between medical evidence and the legal conclusions to be drawn therefrom (p. 406):

> Doctors' personal views, of course, are not binding on me. I have to interpret the rules according to the ordinary principles of interpretation, but I derive help from their interpretations inasmuch as they illustrate the nature of the disease and the matters which from the medical point of view have to be considered in determining whether or not it is a disease of the mind.

In *Bratty v. A.G. for Northern Ireland*, [1963] A.C. 386, [1961] 3 All E.R. 523 (H.L.), Lord Denning agreed that the question of whether an accused suffers from a disease of the mind is properly resolved by the Judge. He acknowledged that "The major mental diseases, which the doctors call psychoses . . . are clearly diseases of the mind" and that "any mental disorder which has manifested itself in violence and is prone to recur is a disease of the mind" (p. 534).

. . . .

Support for a broad and liberal legal construction of the words, "disease of the mind" will be found in the writings of the renowned jurist Sir Owen Dixon, formerly Chief Justice of Australia, who wrote in "A Legacy of Hadfield, M'Naghten and Maclean" (1957), 31 A.L.J. 225 at 260:

> The reason why it is required that the defect of reason should be "from disease of the mind", in the classic phrase used by Sir *Nicholas Tindal*, seems to me no more than to exclude drunkenness, conditions of intense passion and other transient states attributable either to the fault or to the nature of man. In the advice delivered by Sir *Nicholas Tindal* no doubt *the words "disease of the mind" were chosen because it was considered that they had the widest possible meaning. He would hardly have supposed it possible that the expression would be treated as one containing words of the law to be weighed like diamonds. I have taken it to include, as well as all forms of physical or material change or deterioration, every recognizable disorder or derangement of the understanding whether or not its nature, in our present state of knowledge, is capable of explanation or determination.* (The italics are mine.)

To the learned authors of Smith and Hogan, *Criminal Law*, 4th ed. (1978), p. 164: "It seems that any disease which produces a malfunction is a disease of the mind."

Recently, in Canada, the Ontario Court of Appeal contributed judicial direction in this area of the law in the cases of *R. v. Rabey* (1977), 40 C.R.N.S. 46, 37 C.C.C. (2d) 461, and *R. v. Simpson* (1977), 35 C.C.C. (2d) 337, both of which were decided subsequent to the trial of the appellant. Judgment in *Rabey* postdates the decision of the Court of Appeal in the case at bar, and is presently on appeal to this court on an issue unrelated to those raised herein. Martin J.A., who wrote for the court in both *Rabey* and *Simpson*, was not among the members of the court who heard the *Cooper* appeal.

Simpson has greater significance for the present appeal. There, the accused appealed the finding of not guilty by reason of insanity on two charges of attempted murder. The facts, which indicate two incidents of stabbing, are not remarkable. As framed by Martin J.A., the issue was whether a personality disorder is a disease of the mind within the meaning of s. 16 of the *Code*. He held that, notwithstanding the psychiatric evidence, the question raised must be resolved as a question of law. But the legal position, as I understand it, is properly expressed in the following passage (pp. 349-50):

> The term "disease of the mind" is a legal concept, although it includes a medical component, and what is meant by that term is a question of law for the Judge. . . . It is the

function of the psychiatrist to describe the accused's mental condition and how it is considered from the medical point of view. It is for the Judge to decide whether the condition described is comprehended by the term "disease of the mind."

As a matter of practice, the trial judge can permit the psychiatrist to be asked directly whether or not the condition in question constitutes a disease of the mind. Concerning the controversy over the classification of a "psychopathic personality", Martin J.A. found implicit recognition in Canadian and British authorities for the proposition that such a disorder can constitute a disease.

The general principles, not in issue on the further appeal to this court, were reiterated by Martin J.A. in *R. v. Rabey*. Disease of the mind is a legal term. It is within the province of the judge to determine what mental conditions are within the meaning of that phrase and whether there is any evidence that an accused suffers from an abnormal mental condition comprehended by that term. More importantly, he held that, if there is any evidence that the accused did suffer from such a disease, in legal terms, the question of fact must be left with the jury.

I think Dubin J.A. correctly characterizes the decision in *Simpson* as holding that "personality disorder" has been recognized as "being capable of constituting a 'disease of the mind' ". I share his view that "there is no reason to give a narrow or limited interpretation to the term 'disease of the mind' ". Admittedly, in *Simpson* both of the psychiatrists stated that the personality disorder there in question did or could constitute a disease of the mind. While Martin J.A. in that case had little difficulty finding evidence that the appellant suffered from a "disease of the mind", the case foundered upon the second segment of s. 16(2). It should also be kept in mind that *Simpson* presented an odd situation, in which the Crown successfully raised the insanity defence against the wishes of the accused, who appealed the verdict of not guilty by reason of insanity.

What is interesting in these two cases, for our purposes, is the maintenance of a clear distinction between the weight to be given medical opinions expressed in evidence, however relevant, and the task of the trial Judge to form an independent conclusion as to whether the mental condition falls within the legal concept.

In summary, one might say that, in a legal sense, "disease of the mind" embraces any illness, disorder or abnormal condition which impairs the human mind and its functioning, excluding, however, self-induced states caused by alcohol or drugs, as well as transitory mental states such as hysteria or concussion. In order to support a defence of insanity, the disease must, of course, be of such intensity as to render the accused incapable of appreciating the nature and quality of the violent act or of knowing that it is wrong.

Underlying all of this discussion is the concept of responsibility and the notion that an accused is not legally responsible for acts resulting from mental disease or mental defect.

. . . .

With great respect, in the case at bar, the trial judge, in her charge to the jury, which I will discuss shortly, fell into error, in that she confused the legal issue of whether the appellant's disorder could constitute disease of the mind with the factual issue of whether the appellant was suffering from disease of the mind at the relevant time. Once the evidence is sufficient to indicate that an accused suffers from a condition which could, in law, constitute disease of the mind, the judge must leave it open to the jury to find, as a matter of fact, whether the accused had disease of the mind at the time the criminal act was committed. The more troublesome issue, where a defence of insanity has been pleaded, concerns the second criterion to be applied in determining criminal responsibility. As Martin J.A. pointed out in *Rabey* (p. 474):

> In many, if not most cases involving the defence of insanity, the question whether the accused suffered from a disease of the mind is not the critical issue; the pivotal issue is whether a condition which, admittedly, constitutes a disease of the mind rendered the accused incapable of appreciating the nature and quality of the act or of knowing that it was wrong.

The real question in this case, in my view, is not whether the accused was suffering from a disease of the mind but whether he was capable of appreciating the nature and quality of the act. That second question ought to have been left to the jury in clear terms.

II
APPRECIATE

In contrast to the position in England under the M'Naghten Rules, where the words used are "knows the nature and quality of his act", s. 16 of the *Code* uses the phrase "appreciating the nature and quality of an act or omission". The two are not synonymous. The draftsman of the *Code*, as originally enacted, made a deliberate change in language from the common-law rule in order to broaden the legal and medical considerations bearing upon the mental state of the accused and to make it clear that cognition was not to be the sole criterion. Emotional as well as intellectual awareness of the significance of the conduct is in issue. The Report of the Royal Commission on the law of Insanity as a Defence in Criminal Cases (McRuer Report) (1956), contains a useful discussion on the point (p. 12):

> The word "appreciating", not being a word that is synonymous with "knowing", requires far-reaching legal and medical consideration when discussing Canadian law. It had its origin in the Stephen Draft Code. Not infrequently judicial reference is made to the New Oxford Dictionary for the definition of words used in Canadian statutes. The New Oxford Dictionary gives five different uses of the word 'appreciate', depending on the context. The one applicable to this statute is:

"2. To estimate aright, to perceive the full force of.
"b. esp. to be sensitive to, or sensible of, any delicate impression or distinction.
" 'Until the truth of any thing . . . be appreciated, its error, if any, cannot be detected.' "

An examination of the civil law of England and Canada shows that there is an important difference between "know" or "knowledge" on the one hand and "appreciate" or "appreciation" on the other when used and applied to a given set of circumstances. This is best illustrated by the principles of law underlying those cases in which the maxim *volenti non fit injuria* is involved. There is a clear distinction between mere knowledge of the risk and appreciation of both the risk and the danger.

To "know" the nature and quality of an act may mean merely to be aware of the physical act, while to "appreciate" may involve estimation and understanding of the consequences of that act. In the case of the appellant, as an example, in using his hands to choke the deceased he may well have known the nature and quality of that physical act of choking. It is entirely different to suggest, however, that in performing the physical act of choking he was able to appreciate its nature and quality, in the sense of being aware that it could lead to or result in her death. In the opinion of the medical expert who testified at the trial, the appellant could have been capable of intending bodily harm and of choking the girl, but not of having intended her death.

Our *Code* postulates an independent test, requiring a level of understanding of the act, which is more than mere knowledge that it is taking place; in short, a capacity to apprehend the nature of the act, and its consequences. The position in law is well expressed in the McRuer Report at p. 12:

> Under the Canadian statute law a disease of the mind that renders the accused person incapable of an appreciation of the nature and quality of the act must necessarily involve more than mere knowledge that the act is being committed; there must be an appreciation of the factors involved in the act and a mental capacity to measure and foresee the consequences of the violent conduct.

It should be noted that the issue of appreciation of the nature and quality of the act was not before this court in *Schwartz v. R., supra*. The sole issue was the meaning of the word "wrong". The decision in *Schwartz* should not be taken as authority for the proposition that "appreciating" the nature and quality of an act is synonymous with "knowing" the physical character of that act.

The test proposed in the McRuer Report, which I would adopt (save for deletion of the "fully" in the fourth line) is this (p. 13):

> The true test necessarily is, was the accused person at the very time of the offence — not before or after, but at the moment of the offence — by reason of disease of the mind, unable fully to appreciate not only the nature of the act but the natural consequences that would flow from it? In other words, was the accused person, by reason of disease of the mind, deprived of the mental capacity to foresee and measure the consequences of the act?

The legally relevant time is the time when the act was committed.

In *R. v. O'Brien, supra*, Ritchie J.A. referred to the McRuer Report and stated at pp. 301-302:

> If an accused person is to be deprived of the protection of s. 16, he must, at the time of committing the offence, have had an *appreciation of the factors involved in his act and the mental capacity to measure and foresee the consequences of it.*

In the *Simpson* decision, *supra*, Martin J.A. offered the view that s. 16(2) exempts from liability an accused who, due to a disease of the mind, has no real understanding of the nature, character and consequences of the act at the time of its commission. I agree. With respect, I accept the view that the first branch of the test, in employing the word "appreciates", imports an additional requirement to mere knowledge of the physical quality of the act. The requirement, unique to Canada, is that of perception, an ability to perceive the consequences, impact and results of a physical act. An accused may be aware of the physical character of his action (*i.e.*, in choking) without neccessarily having the capacity to appreciate that, in nature and quality, that act will result in the death of a human being. This is simply a restatement, specific to the defence of insanity, of the principle that *mens rea*, or intention as to the consequences of an act, is a requisite element in the commission of a crime.

III
EVIDENCE — NON-MEDICAL

It will now be convenient to turn to the evidence, because, as I understand him, counsel for the Crown concedes that, if there was sufficient evidence to go to the jury on the question of insanity, the trial judge failed to deal adequately with insanity in her charge and effectively withdrew the insanity defence from the jury.

It is important to observe at the outset that the trial judge did charge the jury on insanity, although, as I have stated, the defence was not raised by the appellant's counsel. The judge felt the evidence sufficient to warrant an instruction to the jury on the issue, whatever the posture of defence counsel. In my opinion, she was correct in doing so, having regard to the evidence upon this issue, which I will now endeavour to summarize.

The Crown adduced evidence that before 7:00 p.m. on the night in question a resident nursing assistant, present at the church where the dance was being held, addressed the appellant upon his arrival. The appellant had a "faraway", "dazed", "blank" look in his eyes, and appeared unresponsive. The appellant's father testified that he received a telephone call at approximately 8:15 p.m. from his son, who seemed excited and out of breath. The appellant, trying to speak quickly, was having difficulty "getting his words out". He told his father, "Hello dad, how are you doing? Dad I just killed somebody ... on James Street Mountain steps ... I was coming down the steps and thought somebody was following me . . . I jumped over the railing . . . I jumped out and grabbed hold of them." In response to the question "Is he dead'." the appellant said: "Yes. I felt for a heartbeat and a pulse. I dragged her out in the bushes."

Constable Slote of the Hamilton police force testified that he received a call at 8:39 p.m. from the appellant, who attested to having "just seen a murder". The conversation was recorded on the police dispatcher:

> I seen somebody kill a girl. I don't know if he dragged her in the bushes or not . . . I was just coming down the James Street stairs and I heard a screams [sic]; I don't know, I'd just turned around and seen somebody grab some girl and drag her into the bushes . . . I don't know, you know, if she's dead or alive or what.

Constable Slote considered it a crank call, as there was a lack of emotion in the caller's voice. A police cruiser dispatched to the telephone booth, and thereafter to Cooper's apartment, was unable to locate the appellant.

The deceased was discovered the following morning, 9th October, in the bushes near the James Street steps. Her upper body and part of her face were covered by her jacket, and her brassiere, unfastened, was in place. Her slacks, also unfastened, were about her hips. Soil and leaves adhered to her back. There was no evidence of sexual intercourse. However, she had been undressed and an attempt made to redress her. There was no evidence of struggle, and the deceased was neither battered nor badly bruised. Her strangulation was by hand, without the use of a rope or weapon.

At 11:35 a.m. that morning the appellant was apprehended and detained by police officers until 12:10 p.m., at which time an interrogation commenced. At the time he was true to his story of having seen a murder committed by another person. To both officers in attendance, the appellant appeared mentally slow and spoke slowly.

The officers left the appellant to continue the investigation and returned to the interview at 7:25 p.m. Upon their confronting him with additional facts and indicating that he would be charged with murder, the appellant said, "Hold it. Hold it. I didn't mean to kill her." The appellant offered to give a full statement (which I have paraphrased, except where in quotes):

> I went to the church and bumped into Denise Hobbs. . . . we went for a walk down the James Street stairs then I kissed her then she wanted to go back up then I grabbed her around the throat and choked her [with] my hands. Then I got scared and tried to feel for pulse or something and got none so I ran downstairs for a phone booth.
>
> ". . . we were in the bushes standing up, I kissed her and I grabbed her around the throat and choked her *I was afraid she would go back and tell them I was kissing her*."(The italics are mine.)

The appellant did testify at trial. Defence counsel attempted to establish a lack of intention to commit the murder, supported by the evidence of the appellant's intoxication and susceptibility to abnormal behaviour.

The appellant was 31 years of age. His father, Albert Cooper, testified that, as a young boy, the appellant was subject to seizures, convulsions and sudden mood changes — he would quickly become very excited for no apparent reason and then quickly calm down. Often the appellant would seem to be "far away" and his "mind was elsewhere". Sometimes he would have blackouts and fall down. He heard things which were not there to be heard. His condition worsened as he got older. The appellant was first seen by psychiatrists at age 7. At age 10 or 12 he was treated for auditory hallucinations. He experienced a great deal of difficulty at school, and at age 16 had progressed only as far as Grade V at a trade school. He held a series of menial jobs, from which he was discharged after short periods of time. In his testimony the appellant stated that he had been admitted to the Hamilton Psychiatric Hospital in 1965 (it was in fact in 1962) and remained until 1971, after which time he was an out-patient and still had contact with the doctors at the hospital. He married in April 1972 (he had met his wife at the psychiatric hospital) and had two children. He returned to the hospital for a period of 15 days in 1974.

IV
EVIDENCE — MEDICAL

Medical evidence relating to the appellant's mental and behavioural problems is offered in testimony of Dr. Sim. I think it useful to break down his evidence, reorganized slightly from the sequence in which it was given at trial, as follows:

(a) *General history*

The hospital records indicated that the appellant was first seen at age 7, as he was failing at school and exhibited disturbing behaviour. A condition of borderline mental deficiency was diagnosed at that time. He was re-examined at age 8 and described as being wild and hyperactive and having a poor sense of reality. At 10, an abnormal E.E.G. reading was discovered upon examination for his problem of narcolepsy (sleep seizures). At 11, further I.Q. testing disclosed borderline deficiency, and at age 12 the appellant was treated by a psychiatrist for mental confusion and auditory hallucinations. He was admitted to the Hamilton Psychiatric Hospital as a young man and diagnosed as "without psychosis — borderline intelligence". In 1965 his condition was described as "psychosis with mental deficiency". Dr. Sim described "psychosis" in this way:

> Psychosis, basically, involves a break with reality in which the person may or may not be confused, and have other symptoms like hallucinations of his hearing, seeing, tasting, or smelling, feeling things that are not actually around, or can have such symptoms as delusions.

And delusion is usually described as a false belief which cannot be changed by persuasion and/or reason.

In 1965 there was a bizarre episode wherein the appellant was reported to have swallowed part of a lighter, his belt buckle, buttons from his clothing and a zipper from his trousers. In 1967 he swallowed part of a disassembled cigarette lighter. In 1967 he was re-diagnosed as "mental deficiency without psychosis". Since, he has also been described medically as having "personality disorder, anti-social type with borderline mental retardation". Other evidence indicated that the appellant was released from the hospital in 1971 and returned subsequently in 1974 for a period of 15 days.

(b) *Electroencephalogram*

Dr. Sim reviewed the medical history of abnormal brainwave patterns (electrical discharges from the brain). All such tests (from March 1962 to June 1974) showed generalized abnormality, and in one or two of the E.E.G. tests there was abnormality in brainwaves from the temporal lobe. However, the E.E.G. tests were suggestive, at most, of an "epileptic diathesis" (tendency or propensity to epilepsy, without necessarily resulting in seizures). Dr. Sim could say only that it is possible that Cooper could experience epileptic seizures.

(c) *Intelligence*

The appellant's intellectual ability was measured on a number of occasions according to the full-scale intelligence quotient. His I.Q. ranged from 69 to 79 and was usually between 71 and 79. The normal I.Q. reading is in the region of 90 to 110. In Dr. Sim's opinion, the appellant is of borderline intelligence (*i.e.*, bordering on retardation or classification as an "outright mentally defective person"). The changeover is at an I.Q. of 70. To quote the doctor:

> In summary we are dealing with a male who has shown evidence of breaking with reality in the past. He has a long history of unstable, aggressive and inadequate behaviour. He was unable to adjust at school, academically, socially, economically, in his marriage. He has some brainwave abnormalities which could more readily make this man more irritable and aggresive by alcohol than a person without these abnormalities. He is also of limited intelligence, having a borderline to high-grade defective level of I.Q. Putting all this together, and bringing the stress — the fact that he was under stress financially and so forth, plus the alcohol and under the circumstances which are described as having occurred at the time, it would be my opinion that he would be in such a state of clouded consciousness that he would not be able to form the intent to kill.

Dr. Sim agreed with the diagnosis of other psychiatrists of 26th March 1976 that the appellant had "personality disorder, mixed type, showing schizoid, anti-social explosive and inadequate features, borderline mental retardation".

However, on direct examination Dr. Sim was of the view that at the time of the offence the appellant was *not* suffering from a disease of the mind.

(d) *Intention*

Dr. Sim expressed the opinion that, although the appellant probably knew he was causing bodily harm, he was incapable of forming an intent to kill and he could not have known that any harm he was causing might result in death.

. . . .

V
THE CHARGE

The charge on insanity was sketchy in the extreme. It was introduced with these words:

> However, I do have to consider one further defence with you, I would prefer not to, but, as I look at it, it seems to me that the question will be in your minds, and so I must discuss with you the question of insanity.

And concluded with these words:

> With that evidence before you, again it would seem to be impossible for you to bring in a finding of not guilty by reason of insanity, but the evidence is yours to consider, and it is your finding.

In the course of the charge on insanity, the following was said:

> The reason I have been reluctant to put this before you but have considered I should is that the evidence of Dr. Sim was that this man did not have a disease of the mind. However, if there is other evidence before you, you are entitled to weigh the evidence of Dr. Sim with the other evidence. The other evidence that you had was the evidence of his father as to the nature of the convulsions, the mood changes, the faraway looks, the low I.Q., the rapid speech, the blackouts, the falls, the hearing of things throughout his early life.

Crown counsel, commenting upon the charge, objected that it was unnecessary to put the insanity defence to the jury, as that defence was not available to the accused. The judge replied:

> I do agree that the charge on insanity was sparse: little attention was drawn to the evidence. I considered that it had to be put before the jury. I had hoped that by indicating that the evidence was so weak that [sic] it would not form a major part of their concern.

At the time of sentencing, counsel for the accused said:

> In light of that, my Lady, I think his problem is more a psychiatric one than a penal system is geared to handle, and I ask your Ladyship not to make a recommendation, or, I should say, an order, beyond the minimum period of ten years.

The judge replied:

> I would agree that this is a matter in which, if there is any provision for psychiatric help, it should be obtained, and I will endeavour to make such a recommendation.

VI
CONCLUSIONS

In my opinion, there was evidence sufficient to require the judge to fully instruct the jury on the issue of insanity. The judge was of the opinion that that issue should go to the jury. With respect, the trial judge erred:

(1) In treating Dr. Sim's reply to the judge's isolated question as virtually determinative of the issue of whether the appellant had a "disease of the mind". Although in practice it is often convenient to do so, in strictness a medical witness is not entitled to state that a particular condition is or is not a disease of the mind, since this is a legal question. Mental disease is not purely a matter of psychiatric definition. It is for the jury, and not for medical men, of whatever eminence, to determine the issue: *R. v. Rivett* (1950), 34 Cr. App. R. 87 at 94 (C.A.). The entire psychiatric history, if accepted by the jury, was such as would have entitled the jury to hold that the accused suffered from a disease of the mind, within its legal meaning, regardless of whether one isolates the personality disorder. Personality disorders such as the appellant displayed at various stages in his life can constitute a disease of the mind. The real question before the jury was the extent to which the accused's appreciation of the nature and quality of his act was impaired. Included in the evidence on this point was the evidence of Dr. Sim that the appellant lacked the capacity to form the intent to cause death.

(2) In failing to review adequately the evidence bearing upon the insanity issue and in failing to relate the evidence of the accused's capacity to intend certain acts to the issue of insanity. The judge did not analyze the evidence of Dr. Sim or the other evidence as it may have related to the defence of insanity on the issue of whether the appellant appreciated the nature and quality of his act. Failure before the jury on the issues of intent and intoxication did not preclude success on the issue of insanity. The insanity question should have been put to the jury in such a way as to ensure their due appreciation of the value of the evidence: *R. v. Laycock*, [1952] O.R. 908, 15 C.R. 292, 104 C.C.C. 274 (C.A.).

(3) In concluding this portion of the charge in language which, to all intents, withdrew from the jury the essential determination of fact which it was its province to decide. If the issue was to go to the jury, then, in fairness to the

accused, a much more careful charge was warranted. The issue should have been clearly left with the jury to decide. On a matter of such importance, and having regard to the strong evidence of personality disorder, s. 613 [am. 1974-75-76, c. 93, s. 75] of the *Code* should not be applied in this case.

Before concluding, I should state that Dubin J.A. discussed at some length "natural imbecility". I have refrained from doing so, as I believe the present appeal can be decided without broaching that aspect of the case.

I would allow the appeal and order a new trial.

The dissenting judgment of Martland J., Pratte J. concurring, is omitted.

Appeal allowed; new trial ordered.

KJELDSEN v. R.

[1981] 2 S.C.R. 617, 24 C.R. (3d) 289, 64 C.C.C. (2d) 161,
1981 CarswellAlta 311, 1981 CarswellAlta 94

McIntyre J., on behalf of the court, held that psychopathy was a disease of the mind within the meaning of *Criminal Code*, s. 16, and also adopted the further analysis of Martin J.A. in *R. v. Simpson* (1977), 35 C.C.C. (2d) 337 at 355 (Ont. C.A.):

Emotional disturbance caused by disease of the mind may be so severe as to deprive the accused of the use of his understanding at the time of the act, rendering him incapable of appreciating the nature and quality of the act or of knowing that it was wrong, and thus exempting him from liability under s. 16(2) of the *Code*: see *R. v. Gorecki* (1976), 32 C.C.C. (2d) 135, a judgment of this court . . . I do not, however, read the psychiatric evidence to be that the accused was by reason of emotional turmoil produced by disease of the mind incapable of understanding or realizing what he was doing, but rather that he lacked normal emotions and was therefore incapable of experiencing normal feelings concerning the acts assuming he committed them.

While I am of the view that s. 16(2) exempts from liability an accused who by reason of disease of the mind has no real understanding of the nature, character and consequences of the act at the time of its commission, I do not think the exemption provided by the section extends to one who has the necessary understanding of the nature, character and consequences of the act, but merely lacks appropriate feelings for the victim or lacks feelings of remorse or guilt for what he has done, even though such lack of feeling stems from "disease of the mind". Appreciation of the nature and quality of the act does not import a requirement that the act be accompanied by appropriate feeling about the effect of the act on other people: see *Willgoss v. R.* (1960), 105 C.L.R. 295 (Aust. H.C.); *R. v. Leech*, 21 C.R.N.S. 1, 10 C.C.C. (2d) 149 (Alta. T.D.); *R. v. Craig* (1975), 22 C.C.C. (2d) 212, affirmed 28 C.C.C. (2d) 311 (Alta. C.A.). No doubt the absence of such feelings is a common characteristic of many persons who engage in repeated and serious criminal conduct.

R. v. ABBEY

[1982] 2 S.C.R. 24, 29 C.R. (3d) 193, 68 C.C.C. (2d) 394,
1982 CarswellBC 230, 1982 CarswellBC740

The accused was charged with importing cocaine and unlawfully possessing cocaine for the purpose of trafficking. Upon his arrival at Vancouver International Airport from Lima, Peru, the accused's shoulder bag was searched and found to contain two plastic bags with 5.5 ounces of 50 percent pure cocaine. When asked what was in the bags, the accused answered, "Naturally, cocaine", and advised the police in a written statement about the events leading to his arrest. In his defence the accused raised insanity. The psychiatric evidence suggested that he suffered a disease of the mind which, although not rendering him incapable of appreciating the nature and quality of his act, involved a delusional belief that he was committed to a course of action, no harm would come to him and he would not be punished. The trial judge acquitted the accused by reason of insanity, ruling that he was insane within the meaning of *Code*, s. 16(2) because he failed to appreciate the penal consequences of his act. When the matter reached the Supreme Court it was held that this was one of the errors necessitating a new trial.

DICKSON J.: —

. . . .

. . . . As the court observed in *Cooper, supra*, the requirement that the accused be able to perceive the consequences of a physical act is a restatement, specific to the defence of insanity, of the principle of *mens rea*, or intention as to the consequences of an act, as a requisite element in the commission of a crime. The mental element must be proved with respect to all circumstances, and consequences, that form part of the *actus reus*. As the Crown in this case correctly points out, "while punishment may be a *result* of the commission of a criminal act it is not an *element* of the crime itself". A delusion which renders an accused "incapable of appreciating the nature and quality of his act" goes to the *mens rea* of the offence and brings into operation the "first arm" of s. 16(2): he is not guilty by reason of insanity. A delusion which renders an accused incapable of appreciating that the penal sanctions attaching to the commission of the crime are applicable to him does not go to the *mens rea* of the offence, does not render him incapable of appreciating the nature and quality of the act, and does not bring into operation the "first arm" of the insanity defence.

Abbey was charged with importing and trafficking in cocaine. There is no dispute as to the fact that he carried cocaine into the country. In his statement to police, it was his admitted intention to import cocaine for the purposes of trafficking. In other words, Abbey appreciated that the *actus reus* of each of the offences charged was being committed. Both the psychiatrist called for the defence and the psychiatrist who testified on behalf of the Crown stated that Abbey appreciated the nature and quality of his act. The judge erred, in my view, in going on to say that a failure to appreciate the penal sanctions ("consequences of punishment") brought the accused within the ambit of the "first arm" of the insanity defence of s. 16(2).

The second arm of s. 16(2)

Should the question of "personal penal consequences" be relevant at all, it is more appropriately discussed within the context of the second arm of s. 16(2), *i.e.*, "knowing that an act is wrong". Glanville Williams in his *Criminal Law, The General Part*, at p. 478 says:

> "It has been determined that this phrase ['nature and quality'] refers to the physical character of the act, not its legal quality: legal right and wrong are cared for by the second question [citing *R. v. Codere, supra*, at p. 27]."

This court having decided in *Schwartz v. R., supra*, that "wrong" means wrong according to law, and it being established that Abbey knew his act was "wrong", his inability to "appreciate" the penal consequences is really irrelevant to the question of legal insanity. There seems to be no doubt on the evidence, and on the judge's findings, that Abbey knew that he was doing an act forbidden by law.

With respect, the trial judge homogenized the first and second arms of s. 16(2), collapsing the one into the other in, for example, the following passage from his judgment:

> "As I understand the evidence and the submissions of counsel, the accused had the capacity to appreciate the nature of the act of importing and of possessing the cocaine. He also had the capacity to appreciate the immediate consequences of those acts, that is to say, that they were illegal, that he should not commit them overtly . . ."

In *Schwartz v. R.*, [1977] I S.C.R. 673, 34 C.R.N.S. 138, 29 C.C.C. (2d) 1, Justice Martland, for a 5:4 majority of the court, adopted the interpretation of the English Court of Criminal Appeal in *R. v. Windle*, [1952] 2 Q.B. 826, that "wrong" in s. 16(2) of the *Criminal Code* means "contrary to law". In fact the majority specified criminal law. The four dissenting judges, through Dickson J., would have adopted the opinion of the Australian High Court in *Stapleton v. R.* (1952), 86 C.L.R. 358, that "wrong" means morally wrong. In determining which interpretation of the word "wrong" should be adopted, the court relied more on traditional legal sources than on assessment of the social policy considerations. Justice Martland was unwilling to acquit an insane person who knew that his act was illegal but considered it morally justifiable, pointing out that this would not acquit a sane person. He was also of the view that the interpretation of morally wrong required a subjective test of insanity which would be dangerous. Justice Dickson in dissent held that "moral wrong" was "not to be judged by the personal standards of the offender but by his awareness that society regards the act as wrong". Justice Dickson used an historical and contextual approach to statutory construction in reasoning that, if a wrong meant contrary to law, Parliament would have used the word "unlawful" as it had done elsewhere in the *Code*, that the law in 1843 dealt with insanity in terms of rightness and wrongness, and that the McRuer Report concluded that "wrong" means "something that would be condemned in the eyes of mankind".

R. v. CHAULK

[1990] 3 S.C.R. 1303, 2 C.R. (4th) 1, 62 C.C.C. (3d) 193,
1990 CarswellMan 385, 1990 CarswellMan 239

The Supreme Court overruled *Schwartz*.

LAMER C.J.C. (DICKSON C.J.C. and WILSON, LA FOREST, GONTHIER and CORY JJ.): —

[I]t is plain to me that the term "wrong" as used in s. 16(2) must mean more than simply legally wrong. In considering the capacity of a person to know whether an act is one that he ought or ought not to do, the inquiry cannot terminate with the discovery that the accused knew that the act was contrary to the formal law. A person may well be aware that an act is contrary to law but, by reason of "natural imbecility" or disease of the mind, is at the same time incapable of knowing that the act is morally wrong in the circumstances according to the moral standards of society. This would be the case, for example, if the person suffered from a disease of the mind to such a degree as to know that it is legally wrong to kill but, as described by Dickson J. in *Schwartz*, kills "in the belief that it is in response to a divine order and therefore not morally wrong" (p. 678).

. . . .

[T]he insanity defence should not be made unavailable simply on the basis that an accused knows that a particular act is contrary to law and that he knows, generally, that he should not commit an act that is a crime. It is possible that a person may be aware that it is ordinarily wrong to commit a crime but, by reason of a disease of the mind, believes that it would be "right" according to the ordinary morals of his society to commit the crime in a particular context. In this situation, the accused would be entitled to be acquitted by reason of insanity.

McLachlin J. (L'Heureux-Dubé and Sopinka JJ. concurring): —

Lamer C.J.C. has accepted the appellants' invitation to reconsider this court's earlier conclusion that the capacity to know the act or omission was *legally* wrong suffices. In his view, an accused who is capable of knowing an act or omission is legally wrong is not subject to the criminal process, if mental illness rendered him or her incapable of knowing the act or omission was morally wrong. I, on the other hand, take the view that it does not matter whether the capacity relates to legal wrongness or moral wrongness — all that is required is that the accused be capable of knowing that the act was in some sense "wrong". If the accused has this capacity, then it is neither unfair nor unjust to submit the accused to criminal responsibility and penal sanction.

. . . .

[W]hat is essential is that the accused know that he or she ought not to do the act in question. This condition is met if the accused knows that the act is legally wrong.

. . . .

To hold that absence of moral discernment due to mental illness should exempt a person who knows that legally he or she ought not to do a certain act is, moreover, to introduce a lack of parallelism into the criminal law; generally absence of moral appreciation is no excuse for criminal conduct. When the moral mechanism breaks down in the case of an individual who is sane, we do not treat that as an excuse for disobeying the law; for example, in the case of a psychopath. The rationale is that an individual either knows or is presumed to know the law, and the fact that his or her moral standards are at variance with those of society is not an excuse. Why, if the moral mechanism breaks down because of disease of the mind, should it exempt the accused from criminal responsibility where he or she knows, or was capable of knowing, that the act was illegal and hence one which he or she "ought not to do"? Why should deficiency of moral appreciation due to mental illness have a different consequence than deficiency of moral appreciation due to a morally-impoverished upbringing, for example? I see no reason why the policy of the law should differ in the two cases.

. . . .

The problem with making capacity to appreciate moral wrong the test for criminal responsibility where the incapacity is caused by mental illness, is that of determining what society's moral judgment will be in every situation. What result is to obtain on those occasions where an accused claims an incapacity to know that his or her unlawful act was morally wrong and, objectively, the act was one for which the moral wrongfulness can be disputed? Certainly a court is in no position to make determinations on questions of morality, nor is it fair to expect a jury to be able to agree on what is morally right or morally wrong. The prospect of greater certainty, and the avoidance of metaphysical arguments on right and wrong is the chief advantage of adhering to the traditional *M'Naghten* test for criminal responsibility where causative disease of the mind exists — whether the accused, for whatever reason, was capable of appreciating that his or her act is wrong.

The importance of certainty in the criminal law cannot be over-estimated. It should be relatively clear when criminal responsibility attaches and when it does not if the criminal law is to have the requisite deterrent effect, and if it is to be seen to function fairly and equitably to all. A person's criminal responsibility should not hinge on questions of whether an act would be generally perceived as immoral.

In *R. v. Oommen*, [1994] 2 S.C.R. 507, 30 C.R. (4th) 195, 91 C.C.C. (3d) 8, the court applied the new *Chaulk* test in holding that an insanity defence had been wrongly rejected by the trial judge in a murder case. Late one night the accused shot and killed, without apparent motive, a young female friend at his apartment. He had long suffered from a mental disorder described as "a psychosis of a paranoid delusional type". His specific belief at the time of the shooting was that members of a local union had conspired to "destroy" him and that they had given a commission to the victim to kill him.

At his murder trial before judge alone the accused raised the defence of insanity. The trial judge rejected it. Although the accused had had a compulsive fear that the young girl would kill him, it was more probable than not that at the time of the killing the accused was capable of knowing that he was doing wrong according to moral standards of society. The evidence of medical witnesses was that his delusion would not prevent him from being aware of what he was doing in the sense that he knew his discharge of the firearm was a death-threatening act. His subjective belief that the act was not wrong would not, according to the trial judge, assist him.

The Supreme Court unanimously confirmed the Alberta Court of Appeal's order of a new trial. The court confirmed that under s. 16(1) of the *Criminal Code* a person who lacks capacity to know that the act he is committing is wrong is exempt from criminal responsibility. The inquiry is to focus not on general capacity to know right from wrong but rather on the ability to know that a particular act was wrong in the circumstances. The question is whether the accused lacks the capacity to rationally decide whether the act is right or wrong and hence to make a rational choice about whether to do it or not. Does the accused possess the capacity present in the ordinary person to know that the act was wrong having regard to the everyday standards of the ordinary person? Since s. 16 is an independent condition of criminal responsibility the Supreme court decided that it was not necessary to show that a defence such as self-defence would apply; this rejected the view of the Alberta Court of Appeal in the court below (1993), 21 C.R.

(4th) 117 (Alta. C.A.). The findings of the trial judge were consistent with the conclusion that the accused's mental disorder deprived him of the capacity to know his act was wrong by the standards of the ordinary person.

(c) Mental Disorder Negativing *Mens Rea*

In *R. v. Swain*, [1991] 1 S.C.R. 933, Mr. Justice Lamer, for the majority, held that the common-law rule allowing the Crown to adduce evidence of insanity over and above the accused's wishes was not in accordance with principles of fundamental justice under s. 7 and could not be saved by s. 1. His Lordship referred to the relaxation of the *Oakes* test to require merely that the violation infringed rights as "little as is reasonably possible", but however determined that consideration of judicial deference had no place respecting common-law violations for which only the "least intrusive" alternative would do. The majority went on to fashion a new common-law rule which would only allow the Crown to independently raise the issue of insanity after the trier of fact had concluded that the accused was otherwise guilty. The issue of insanity would be tried after a finding of guilt, but before a conviction was entered. The court also recognized that the Crown could adduce evidence of insanity during the trial, if the accused had put his or her mental state in issue.

The court in *Swain* refers to evidence of mental impairment short of insanity negativing the requisite mental element, for example, planning and deliberation in the case of first degree murder or the specific intent required for murder. This ruling was *obiter* but was accepted as the law in *Jacquard* (1997), 113 C.C.C. (3d) 1 (S.C.C.), the court dividing only on whether the judge's direction had been sufficiently clear. Thus the Supreme Court has recognized that evidence of mental disorder short of a full-blown defence under s.16 may be admitted on the issue of *mens rea*.

In *R. v. Wade* (1995), 41 C.R. (4th) 100, 98 C.C.C. (3d) 97, [1995] 2 S.C.R. 737, the majority of the Supreme Court rejected the view of the Ontario Court of Appeal that a trial judge should have put the possibility of manslaughter to a jury in a case where the husband killed his wife in extreme rage. The Ontario Court of Appeal had accepted that the jury had rejected the defence of automatism in their verdict of second degree murder but had pointed to evidence that he was in some form of altered mental state when he attacked his wife.

3. AUTOMATISM

R. v. RABEY

(1977), 40 C.R.N.S. 46, 37 C.C.C.(2d)461,
1977 CarswellOnt 24 (Ont. C.A.)

The accused was charged with causing bodily harm with intent to wound and possessing a weapon for the purpose of committing an offence. The trial judge acquitted. On appeal the Ontario Court of Appeal ordered a new trial on the charge of wounding on the basis that the defence of sane automatism was not available. Any defence would be that of insanity or lack of *mens rea*. The acquittal on the weapons charge was confirmed on the basis of lack of proof of *mens rea*. On further appeal the majority of the Supreme Court adopted the approach of Martin J.A. in the Court of Appeal. Reproduced first is the review of the evidence in the Court of Appeal:

MARTIN J.A.: —

Factual background

On 1st March 1974 the respondent, Wayne Kenneth Rabey, then aged 20, was a third-year student at the University of Toronto at Erindale College where he was enrolled in the honours science course, majoring in geology. Miss X was also a third-year student at Erindale College.

An association between Miss X and the respondent began in September 1973 when, in their third year, they commenced to have most of their classes together. Along with two classmates, John Lund and Rick Hampel, they studied together in their spare periods, lunched together and went to the "pub" together.

Miss X and the respondent had also gone for walks together and visited each other's homes. During the Christmas holidays in 1973, along with John Lund they had gone with a group of students to Quebec to ski.

It is clear that the respondent was emotionally attached to Miss X, but his feelings were not reciprocated, and she described her relationship with the respondent as "just a friend". On Miss X's initiative, her association with the respondent lessened after their return from the trip to Quebec.

Miss X on 28th February 1974, during a lecture, wrote a letter to a girlfriend. She put the letter in her notebook which she placed in her locker. The letter referred to another student, a young man by whose sexual experience Miss X was impressed and in whom she expressed a sexual interest. The letter also stated that even though she insulted Wayne and Rick they still "bugged" her in class, and she implied that they were "nothings".

The respondent, whose evidence was accepted by the trial Judge, testified that he was sitting outside the library on the afternoon of 28th February when Miss X came out of the library and asked him to help her with some problems. He said that they went inside the library to work on the problems, and when flipping through Miss X's notebook to find some equations, during her absence for a few minutes, he came across the letter mentioned above. He read part of the letter, was interested in its contents, and put it in his pocket. The respondent read the letter that evening at home and underlined certain passages. He said that he was upset, confused and angry at the time.

The following day, 1st March 1974, the respondent went to the geology lab to review some problems posted on the board, and while there he took a piece of Galena rock, wrapped it in paper towelling and put it in his pocket. He testified that he intended to take the rock home to study it, as he had previously done with other samples of rock with the consent of his professor.

There was a class starting at 11:00 a.m. but the respondent decided not to take it as he wanted to study for an examination that he had in the afternoon. He testified that later that morning he met another student who said that he was going to be playing squash at 12:00 o'clock, and the respondent said he would go and watch him play. The respondent said that, quite by chance, while on the way to the squash courts, he met Miss X in the locker area. He said that when he first saw her he felt strange for a second but that this feeling passed. He invited Miss X to go with him to watch the game, and she accepted the invitation.

When they reached the observation gallery no one was playing in any of the squash courts. Miss X said the respondent seemed surprised to find the courts empty. They then returned downstairs; the respondent seemed his normal self. When they had reached the foot of the stairs he asked Miss X what she thought of "Gord", a mutual friend, and she replied that he was "just a friend". The respondent then asked her what she thought of him, referring to himself. She said he was a friend too. They then started to go through a set of fire doors located near the bottom of the stairs, which, being heavy, were hard to push open. Before Miss X could get the door on her side open she heard a crash and a "crumbling sound", and she thought something was falling down from the roof. She turned around to see what was happening, and the respondent grabbed her around the arms and struck her on the head twice. She then became unconscious, and when she recovered consciousness the respondent was on his knees, leaning forward and choking her. She asked him why he was doing this, and he yelled, "You bitch, you bitch", after which she again lost consciousness.

Kenneth Turner, a student at Erindale College, was walking down the stairs on his way to the gymnasium when he noticed the respondent crouched at the bottom of the stairs near some books and a red puddle. As Turner continued down the stairs, the respondent apparently noticed him and came up the stairs towards him. The respondent said there had been a terrible accident. Turner noticed the respondent was very pale, sweating, glassy-eyed and had a frightened expression, and Turner endeavoured to reassure him. Turner also noticed that there was a trail which led under the stairwell from the pool of blood which he had first noticed. He looked over the railing and saw Miss X's head, her body being under the stairs.

At this time the respondent said, "I've killed her and I am going to kill you too." The respondent then seized Turner, who freed himself and then went for assistance. Turner met Professor Houston in the hall and requested Professor Houston to accompany him. On the way to the area where Turner had seen Miss X they encountered the respondent, whom Professor Houston sought to restrain momentarily by placing his hand on the respondent's wrist. The respondent said he had to get a nurse, and continued on his way. Professor Houston noticed that the respondent was very pale and seemed bewildered.

The respondent appeared in the office of Mrs. Degutis, a nurse employed at the college health centre, and asked her to come quickly to help him; that he thought he had killed someone. Mrs. Degutis said he looked very upset and seemed filled with fear and anxiety. His pulse was very fast and was not strong; he had a limp, "clammy" appearance. As a result of her observation of the respondent she placed him in a room by himself. In subsequent contacts with the respondent after Miss X had been found, Mrs. Degutis was unable to convince him that Miss X was not dead.

In the meantime, Professor Houston had found Miss X in an unconscious condition "under" the stairwell. She soon recovered consciousness and was taken to the college health centre and then to a hospital. She was found to have three puncture wounds in her head in which fragments of rock were embedded and which required 20 stitches to close. She also had a reddish mark on her throat. She, however, made a complete recovery within a short time.

Two quantities of black rock, which fragmented easily, were found at two different sites in the area of the bottom of the stairwell. The largest piece of rock, some school books and a purse were found in the vicinity of a pool of blood near the foot of the stairwell. There was a smear of blood, some 14 feet long, leading from the pool of blood at the bottom of the stairwell to another pool of blood beside the stairwell. The physical findings support the inference that Miss X was struck near the foot of the stairs and then dragged to the position, partly underneath the stairs, where she was found.

William Huggett, Associate Dean of Erindale College, shortly after 12:00 o'clock on 1st March 1974, was requested to go to the nursing station, and on arriving there he found the respondent in an inner room. The respondent appeared depressed or dazed; he recognized Dean Huggett and said, "I don't know why I started or why I stopped", and also said that he "liked her better than anyone he had ever known".

Constable Pollitt arrived at the college shortly after 1:00 o'clock and went to the nursing station where he arrested the respondent at about 1:25 p.m. After being cautioned by Constable Pollitt the respondent said: "I did it, I know I did it, I just couldn't stop hitting her."

The letter written by Miss X the day before was found in the pocket of the respondent's jacket. Detective Price took a statement from the respondent between 4:30 and 4:45 p.m. The statement reads, in part, as follows:

> I was asking her about the ballet, then I asked her if she liked this guy Gord. She said something about just as a friend. Then I guess I hit her right then on the head. She was bleeding from the head and the next thing I remember it all happened so fast she was on the floor and I was sitting on top of her and choking her. I thought she was dead, there was blood everywhere. I just don't know what happened.

The respondent, of whom a number of character witnesses spoke highly, recounted how he obtained Miss X's letter, his chance meeting with her in the locker area and their fruitless visit to the squash courts, as previously outlined.

He testified that he remembered asking Miss X what she thought of a mutual friend, and her replying that he was just a friend. The next thing he remembered was choking her; that her face was a "funny" colour. He remembered seeing a lot of blood and stopped choking her. The next thing he remembered was being on the bottom of the steps and seeing Turner coming down. He thought he remembered asking Turner to go for help, but he did not remember Turner answering. He remembered grabbing Turner but did not remember Turner running away; he was "just gone". He remembered seeing Turner's face and a lady's face; the next thing he remembered was being at the nurse's office and telling her that he had killed someone, or he thought that he had killed someone. He recalled talking to Dean Huggett and the nurse, calling his mother on the telephone and being arrested.

The psychiatric evidence

The respondent was admitted, on 5th March 1974, to the Lakeshore Psychiatric Hospital for psychiatric assessment on a warrant of remand by the Provincial Court, and was discharged on 1st April 1974. A detailed neurological examination of the respondent disclosed no neurological disease. Dr. Slyfield's report to the Provincial Court stated that if the respondent was telling the truth about his amnesia for most of the incident, then it was probable that his consciousness was dissociated at the time but that such a psychological mechanism need not indicate mental illness.

The medical reports of the Lakeshore Psychiatric Hospital with respect to the psychiatric assessment of the respondent were admitted in evidence by the consent of both counsel.

Dr. Orchard, assistant professor of psychiatry at the University of Toronto, examined the respondent on 18th May 1974.

Dr. Orchard testified that, in his opinion, the respondent entered into a complete dissociative state at the foot of the stairs. The dissociative state is a recognized diagnosis and is a disorder of consciousness which occurs as a result of part of the nervous system shutting off. Dr. Orchard said that a person in a severe dissociative state may be capable of performing physical actions without consciousness of such actions. In Dr. Orchard's opinion, when the respondent entered the dissociative state near the foot of the stairs his mind "shut off", and the return of consciousness was gradual; he returned to some awareness when he found his hands around Miss X's neck. The clouding of consciousness did not completely lift, however, until later when he spoke to his mother and the police.

Dr. Orchard said that the dissociative state which occurred was caused by a powerful emotional shock which resulted from the shattering of the respondent's image of Miss X; he was unable to tolerate seeing her as she revealed herself in the letter, and because the reality was not tolerable for him the dissociative state occurred as a psychological defence mechanism. The conversation at the foot of the stairs as to how she regarded "Gord" and himself, against the background of the letter, "triggered" the dissociative state. In Dr. Orchard's opinion the dissociative state which occurred was comparable to that produced by a physical blow; it was caused by a blow" which produced certain physical effects as observed by Turner, Professor Houston, Mrs. Degutis and Dean Huggett. Dr. Orchard did not consider that the subsequent statements made by the respondent, indicating that he was aware that he had struck Miss X, were inconsistent with the respondent being in a dissociative state that was total at the time he struck Miss X with the rock and, by a process of reconstruction, realizing what he had done when some awareness returned to him and he found himself choking Miss X while she was lying on the floor with blood around her.

Dr. Orchard said that the respondent was a young man of average health, or better than average health, with no pre-disposition to dissociate. Dr. Orchard distinguished between the dissociative state and dissociation which may occur as a result of a major pathological condition, such as schizophrenia, manic-depressive psychosis or injury to the brain. The severe dissociative state, such as the respondent suffered, usually occurs in persons within the category of normal people where the mind is unable to cope with stress in an area that is important to that individual, and it is more severe than the dissociation which occurs as a symptom of other conditions. He said that it is rare for the severe dissociative state not caused by some underlying pathology to recur, and that there was only a very slight possibility that the respondent would suffer from a recurrence of this disorder of consciousness.

Dr. Orchard said that he could find no evidence that the respondent suffered from any pathological condition which he defined as a "diseased condition or abnormally sick condition". He testified that the dissociative state itself is an occurrence, is not a mental illness and is not a "disease of the mind". There are three main groups of mental disorders, which he categorized as follows:

(1) The psychoses which are the major mental illnesses involving a loss of contact with reality.

(2) The neuroses which are the minor mental illnesses which do not involve loss of contact with reality.

(3) The personality or character disorders which are neither psychoses nor neuroses but are a "maladaptive pattern or life-style".

Dr. Orchard agreed that in the medical literature the dissociative state is included as one of the neuroses in the subdivision of hysteria. Although, in cross-examination, Dr. Orchard rejected as authoritative a number of textbooks on psychiatry to which he was referred, he acknowledged that in a textbook, which he accepted as generally authoritative, the dissociative state is classified as a neurosis. It was Dr. Orchard's view that the dissociative state is not "fully categorizable"; it is not a psychosis because there is no ongoing pathological condition, and it occurs without a pre-disposing personality; it is not a neurosis, which by definition is a minor mental illness without loss of contact with reality, since in the dissociative state there is a loss of contact with reality.

Dr. Rowsell, who, like Dr. Orchard, is a psychiatrist of eminence, examined the respondent on 16th May 1975. He had available to him, as Dr. Orchard had, the reports of the Lakeshore Psychiatric Hospital.

It was the opinion of Dr. Rowsell that the respondent did not go into a dissociative state; that he is a controlled young man who went into an extreme state of rage at that moment and while in that state, struck Miss X on the head and choked her; he had good reason to think from the amount of blood that he had killed her. Dr. Rowsell testified that, in his opinion, the respondent was aware that he was hitting Miss X, being then in a state of rage. Dr. Rowsell testified that if, contrary to his opinion, the respondent was in a dissociative state, he suffered from "disease of the mind". Dr. Rowsell said that consciousness is the distinguishing feature of mental life; the dissociative state is, by definition, a subdivision of hysterical neurosis, which is a definite mental illness. It is, by definition, a disorder of the mind.

Dr. Rowsell was of the opinion that the "blotting out" of parts of the incident by the respondent occurred after the event. Dr. Rowsell, unlike Dr. Orchard, was of the opinion that the respondent still had a psychiatric problem for which he required treatment to help him face up to what had occurred. He considered that the treatment would take six months to a year and could be undertaken on an out-patient basis. The prognosis was excellent.

RABEY v. R.

[1980] 2 S.C.R. 513, 15 C.R. (3d) 225, 54 C.C.C. (2d) 1,
1980 CarswellOnt 35, 1980 CarswellOnt 71

RITCHIE J. (MARTLAND, PIGEON and BEETZ JJ. concurring): —

. . . .

It should be observed also that the appellant was subjected to a number of interviews with psychiatrists, with the result that the courts have found themselves involved in the shadowy area of mental disorders, concerning which it is not surprising to find that there are wide differences in opinion amongst the "experts". The meaning of the word "automatism" — in any event so far as it is employed in the defence of non-insane automatism — has in my opinion been satisfactorily defined by Lacourcière J. (as he then was) of the Ontario High Court of Justice in the case of *R. v. K.* (1971), 3 C.C.C. (3d) 84 at 84:

> Automatism is a term used to describe unconscious, involuntary behaviour, the state of a person who, though capable of action, is not conscious of what he is doing. It means an unconscious, involuntary act, where the mind does not go with what is being done.

The defence of automatism, as used in the present case, of course involves a consideration of the provisions of s. 16.

. . . .

What is said here is that at the relevant time the appellant was in a state where, though capable of action, he was not conscious of what he was doing, and more particularly that he was not suffering from a disease of the mind and was therefore not insane. The central question in deciding any case involving the defence of automatism is whether or not the accused was suffering from a disease of the mind. The opinions of psychiatrists go no further than characterizing the condition in which the appellant was found as being "a dissociative state", but it is clear, at least since the case of *Bratty v. A.G. Northern Ireland*, [1963] A.C. 386, 46 Cr. App. R. 1, [1961] 3 All E.R. 523 (H.L.), that the question of whether or not such a state amounts to "a disease of the mind" is a question of law for the judge to determine. The general rule is that it is for the judge as a question of law to decide what constitutes a "disease of the mind", but that the question of whether or not the facts in a given case disclose the existence of such a disease is a question to be determined by the trier of fact. I think it would be superfluous for me to retrace the line of authorities in this area, as they have been so exhaustively discussed by my brother Dickson and also by Martin J.A. of the Court of Appeal and by the learned trial judge. I am satisfied in this regard to adopt the following passages from the reasons for judgment of Martin J.A. at pp. 62-63:

> In general, the distinction to be drawn is between a malfunctioning of the mind arising from some cause that is primarily internal to the accused, having its source in his psychological or emotional makeup, or in some organic pathology, as opposed to a malfunctioning of the mind, which is the transient effect produced by some specific external factor such as, for example, concussion. Any malfunctioning of the mind or mental disorder having its source primarily in some subjective condition or weakness internal to the accused (whether fully understood or not) may be a "disease of the mind" if it prevents the accused from knowing what he is doing, but transient disturbances of consciousness due to certain specific external factors do not fall within the concept of disease of the mind. (For an interesting and helpful discussion see "The Concept of Mental Disease In Criminal Law Insanity Tests" 33 University of Chicago L. Rev. 229, by Herbert Fingarette.) Particular transient mental disturbances may not, however, be capable of being properly categorized in relation to whether they constitute "disease of the mind" on the basis of a generalized statement and must be decided on a case-by-case basis.

The same learned judge later stated in the same judgment at p. 68:

> In my view, the ordinary stresses and disappointments of life which are the common lot of mankind do not constitute an external cause constituting an explanation for a malfunctioning of the mind which takes it out of the category of a "disease of the mind". To hold otherwise would deprive the concept of an external factor of any real meaning. In my view, the emotional stress suffered by the respondent as a result of his disappointment with respect to Miss X cannot be said to be an external factor producing the automatism within

the authorities, and the dissociative state must be considered as having its source primarily in the respondent's psychological or emotional makeup. I conclude, therefore, that, in the circumstances of this case, the dissociative state in which the respondent was said to be constituted a "disease of the mind". I leave aside, until it becomes necessary to decide them, cases where a dissociative state has resulted from emotional shock without physical injury, resulting from such causes, for example, as being involved in a serious accident although no physical injury has resulted; being the victim of a murderous attack with an uplifted knife, notwithstanding that the victim has managed to escape physical injury; seeing a loved one murdered or seriously assaulted, and like situations. Such extraordinary external events might reasonably be presumed to affect the average normal person without reference to the makeup of the person exposed to such experience.

For the above reasons I am of the opinion, with deference, that the learned trial Judge erred in holding that the so-called "psychological blow", which was said to have caused the dissociative state, was, in the circumstances of this case, an externally originating cause, and she should have held that if the respondent was in a dissociative state at the time he struck Miss X he suffered from "disease of the mind". A new trial must, accordingly, be had on count 2.

In my view a possible key to the cause of the malfunctioning of the appellant's mind at the time of the alleged assault is to be found in para. 5 of the agreed statement of facts, to which I have already referred, and where it is said of him:

5. The Appellant had never dated any other girl for any length of time, and had only a minimal amount of sexual experience. An introvert, he was infatuated with the attractive, outgoing. . . .

It seems to me that his infatuation with this young woman had created an abnormal condition in his mind, under the influence of which he acted unnaturally and violently to an imagined slight to which a normal person would not have reacted in the same manner.

It was contended on behalf of the appellant that a finding of disease of the mind and consequently of insanity in the present case would involve gross unfairess to the appellant, who could be subject to the provisions of s. 545 [re-en. 1972, c. 13, s. 45; am. 1974-75-76, c. 93, s. 69] of the *Criminal Code* and thus detained at the pleasure of the Lieutenant-Governor of the province. That such a result does not carry with it the hardship contended for is illustrated by the following passage from the reasons for judgment of Martin J.A. at p. 69:

It would, of course, be unthinkable that a person found not guilty on account of insanity because of a transient mental disorder constituting a disease of the mind, who was not dangerous and who required no further treatment, should continue to be confined. The present provisions of s. 545(1)(*b*) [re-en. 1972, c. 13, s. 45], however, authorize the Lieutenant-Governor to make an order if, in his opinion, it would be in the best interest of the accused and not contrary to the interest of the public for the discharge of a person found not guilty on account of insanity, either absolutely or subject to such conditions as he prescribes. In addition to the periodic reviews required to be made by a board of review appointed pursuant to s. 547(1) of the *Code*, the Lieutenant-Governor under s. 547(6) of the *Code* may request the board of review to review the case of any person found not guilty on account of insanity, in which case the board of review is required to report forthwith whether such person has recovered and, if so, whether in its opinion it is in the interest of the public and of that person for the Lieutenant-Governor to order that he be discharged absolutely or subject to such conditions as the Lieutenant-Governor may prescribe.

For all these reasons, as well as for those expressed by Martin J.A. in the Court of Appeal for Ontario, I would dismiss the appeal and dispose of the matter in the manner proposed by him.

DICKSON J., dissenting (ESTEY and McINTYRE JJ. concurring): — The automatism "defence" has come into considerable prominence in recent years. Although the word "automatism" made its way but lately to the legal state, it is basic principle that absence of volition in respect of the act involved is always a defence to a crime. A defence that the act is involuntary entitles the accused to a complete and unqualified acquittal. That the defence of automatism exists as a middle ground between criminal responsibility and legal insanity is beyond question. Although spoken of as a defence, in the sense that it is raised by the accused, the Crown always bears the burden of proving a voluntary act.

The issue in this appeal is whether automatism resulting from a "psychological blow" is available to an accused in answer to a charge of causing bodily harm with intent to wound. The appellant, Wayne Kenneth Rabey, suddenly and without warning assaulted a fellow student and friend, causing her injury. The theory of the defence was that his behaviour was caused by a psychological blow, an intense emotional shock which induced a "dissociative state", during which, for a time, the appellant was neither conscious of nor able to control his conduct, so that it was involuntary. This is sometimes spoken of as non-insane automatism, to distinguish it from cases in which the state of automatism is attributable to disease of the mind.

At common law a person who engaged in what would otherwise have been criminal conduct was not guilty of a crime if he did so in a state of unconsciousness or semi-consciousness. Nor was he responsible if he was, by reason of disease of the mind or defect of reason, unable to appreciate the nature and quality of an act or that its commission was wrong. The fundamental precept of our criminal law is that a man is responsible only for his conscious, intentional acts. Devlin J. summed up the position in *R. v. Kemp*, [1956] 3 All E.R. 249 at 251:

In the eyes of the common law if a man is not responsible for his actions he is entitled to be acquitted by the ordinary form of acquittal, and it matters not whether his lack of responsibility was due to insanity or to any other cause.

In order to protect the public from the dangerous criminally insane the common law was changed by statute, long ago. By the *Criminal Lunatics Act*, 1800 (39 & 40 Geo. 3), c. 94, and the *Trial of Lunatics Act*, 1883 (46 & 47 Vict.), c. 38, and in Canada by the *Criminal Code*, [now] R.S.C. 1970, c. C-34, a verdict of not guilty by reason of insanity results in committal to an institution.

The purpose of the qualified verdict of acquittal is, of course, to ensure custody and treatment for those who might pose a continuing threat to society by reason of mental illness. In Canada, an accused who is acquitted on the ground of insanity is kept in strict custody in the place and in the manner that the court directs, until the pleasure of the Lieutenant-Governor of the province is known [s. 542(2) of the *Code*].

The term "automatism" first appeared in the cases and in the periodical literature about 30 years ago. It is seen with increasing frequency. The defence of automatism is successfully invoked in circumstances of a criminal act committed unconsciously, and, in the past, has generally covered acts done while sleepwalking or under concussional states following head injuries.

The defence of automatism is, in some respects, akin to that of insanity. In both instances, the issue is whether an accused had sufficient control over or knowledge of his criminal act to be held culpable. The two defences are, however, separate and distinct. As Professor J. Ll. J. Edwards observed in "Automatism and Criminal Responsibility" (1958), 21 Mod. L. Rev. 375 at 384:

> Both circumstances are concerned to prove mental irresponsibility, the essential difference . . . being that in the case of insanity the defect of the understanding must originate in a disease of the mind, whereas in the defence of automatism *simpliciter* the criminal law is not concerned with any question of the disease of the mind.

Although separate, the relationship between the two defences cannot be discounted. Automatism may be subsumed in the defence of insanity in cases in which the unconscious action of an accused can be traced to, or rooted in, a disease of the mind. Where that is so, the defence of insanity prevails. This is all felicitously expressed by Gresson P. in *R. v. Cottle*, [1958] N.Z.L.R. 999 at 1007 (C.A.):

> It would appear that automatism raised as a defence to a criminal charge may be something quite different and distinct from insanity. In a particular case, it may be that the automatism relied on is due to some "disease of the mind" but is not necessarily so. Automatism, which strictly means action without conscious volition, has been adopted in criminal law as a term to denote conduct of which the doer is not conscious — in short doing something without knowledge of it, and without memory afterwards of having done it — a temporary eclipse of consciousness that nevertheless leaves the person so affected able to exercise bodily movements. In such a case, the action is one which the mind in its normal functioning does not control. This may be due to some "disease of the mind" or it may not; it may happen with a perfectly healthy mind (*e.g.* in somnambulism which may be unaccompanied by an abnormality of mind), or it may occur where the mind is temporarily affected as the result of a blow, or by the influence of a drug or other intoxication. It may on the other hand be caused by an abnormal condition of the mind capable of being designated a mental disease. What are known as the M'Naghten Rules can have no application unless there is some form of "disease of the mind", which is not necessarily present in all cases of automatism.

. . . .

This case raises interesting issues, and the judicial conclusion, in my view, should be guided by general principles of criminal responsibility. Before alluding to those principles, it is useful to recall s. 16(4) of the *Criminal Code*, which reads:

> (4) Every one shall, until the contrary is proved, be presumed to be and to have been sane.

In the usual case in which an accused pleads insanity, he has the burden of overcoming the presumption of sanity. In the present case the appellant is not seeking to establish that he was insane on 1st March 1974. The Crown is asserting the insanity in answer to the defence of automatism raised by the appellant. The presumption of sanity runs in the appellant's favour.

We turn to s. 16(2): a person is insane when he is in a state of natural imbecility or has a disease of the mind to an extent that renders him incapable of appreciating the nature and quality of an act or omission or of knowing that an act or omission is wrong. The important words, for present purposes, are "disease of the mind".

The first principle, fundamental to our criminal law, which governs this appeal is that no act can be a criminal offence unless it is done voluntarily. Consciousness is a sine qua non to criminal liability.

The prosecution must prove every element of the crime charged. One such element is the state of mind of the accused, in the sense that the act was voluntary. The circumstances are normally such as to permit a presumption of volition and mental capacity. That is not so when the accused, as here, has placed before the court, by cross-examination of Crown witnesses or by evidence called on his own behalf, or both, evidence sufficient to raise an issue that he was unconscious of his actions at the time of the alleged offence. No burden of proof is imposed upon an accused raising such defence beyond pointing to facts which indicate the existence of such a condition: *R. v. Berger* (1975), 27 C.C.C. (2d) 357 at 379, leave to appeal to the Supreme Court of Canada refused 27 C.C.C. (2d) 357n. Whether lack of consciousness relates to *mens rea* or to *actus reus* or both may be important in a case in which the offence charged is one of absolute liability, but the conceptual distinction does not concern us in the case at bar.

The second principle is that no person should be committed to a hospital for the criminally insane unless he suffers from disease of the mind in need of treatment or likely to recur.

The Ontario Court of Appeal held that the excusing factor was insanity. This finding was reached though the appellant exhibited no pathological symptoms indicative of a previously existing, or ongoing, psychiatric disorder. On medical evidence accepted by the trial judge, the prospect of a recurrence of dissociation is extremely remote. There was no finding that the appellant suffered from psychosis, neurosis or personality disorder. He does not have an organic disease of the brain. This was an isolated event. The appellant has already spent several weeks in a mental institution undergoing psychiatric, neurological and psychological assessment, the result of which did not indicate need for treatment.

There are undoubtedly policy considerations to be considered. Automatism as a defence is easily feigned. It is said the credibility of our criminal justice system will be severely strained if a person who has committed a violent act is allowed an absolute acquittal on a plea of automatism arising from a psychological blow. The argument is made that the success of the defence depends upon the semantic ability of psychiatrists, tracing a narrow path between the twin shoals of criminal responsibility and an insanity verdict. Added to these concerns is the in terrorem argument that the floodgates will be raised if psychological blow automatism is recognized in law.

There are competing policy interests. Where the condition is transient rather than persistent, unlikely to recur, not in need of treatment and not the result of self-induced intoxication, the policy objectives in finding such a person insane are not served. Such a person is not a danger to himself or to society generally.

The Ontario Court of Appeal in the present case focused upon "external cause". The "ordinary stresses and disappointments of life" were held not to constitute an external cause. The court considered that the "emotional stress" suffered by the appellant could not be said to be an external factor producing the automatism; the dissociative state had its source primarily in the psychological or emotional makeup of the appellant.

There is no evidence to support Martin J.A.'s statement attributing the dissociated state to the psychological or emotional makeup of the appellant. To exclude the defence of automatism it lay upon the Crown to establish that the appellant suffered from a disease of the mind at the time of the attack. The existence of the mental disease must be demonstrated in evidence. Here there is no such evidence from any of the expert or other witnesses with reference to the crucial period of the assault. Moreover, as earlier noted, s. 16(4) presumes sanity. The Court of Appeal's conclusion was directly contrary to the testimony of Dr. Orchard, accepted by the trial judge, and finds no support in the testimony of Dr. Rowsell.

Martin J.A. left open the question whether it is possible to dissociate as a result of emotional shock rather than physical injury. The effect of the appellate court judgment was to differ from the trial judge's finding that the dissociation was brought about by an externally operating cause. In the circumstances, I do not think it is open to this court to disturb the findings of fact at trial.

If the effect of the appellate court judgment is that, as a matter of law, emotional stress can never constitute an external factor then, with respect, I disagree. Indeed, in the passage quoted below the court seems to concede as much. If the controlling factor is one of degree of emotional stress, and the application of some form of quantitative test, then the question becomes one of fact for the trier of fact and not one of law for an appellate court.

It is not clear to me why, as a matter of law, an emotional blow — which can be devastating — should be regarded as an external cause of automatism in some circumstances and an internal cause in others, as the Court of Appeal would seem to propose in this passage [p. 68]:

> I leave aside, until it becomes necessary to decide them, cases where a dissociative state has resulted from emotional shock without physical injury, resulting from such causes, for example, as being involved in a serious accident although no physical injury has resulted; being the victim of a murderous attack with an uplifted knife, notwithstanding that the victim has managed to escape physical injury; seeing a loved one murdered or seriously assaulted, and the like stiuations. Such extraordinary external events might reasonably be presumed to affect the average normal person without reference to the subjective makeup of the person exposed to such experience.

I cannot accept the notion that an extraordinary external event, *i.e.*, an intense emotional shock, can cause a state of dissociation or automatism if and only if all normal persons subjeccted to that sort of shock would react in that way. If I understood the quoted passage correctly, an objective standard is contemplated for one of the possible causes of automatism, namely, psychological blow, leaving intact the subjective standard for other causes of automatism, such as physical blow or reaction to drugs.

As in all other aspects of the criminal law (except negligence offences) the inquiry is directed to the accused's actual state of mind. It is his subjective mental condition with which the law is concerned. If he has a brittle skull and sustains a concussion which causes him to run amok, he has a valid defence of automatism. If he has an irregular metabolism which induced an unanticipated and violent reaction to a drug, he will not be responsible for his acts. If he is driven into shock and unconsciousness by an emotional blow, and was susceptible to that reaction but has no disease, there is no reason in principle why a plea of automatism should not be available. The fact that other people would not have reacted as he did should not obscure the reality that the external psychological blow did cause a loss of consciousness. A person's subjective reaction, in the absence of any other medical or factual evidence supportive of insanity, should not put him into the category of persons legally insane. Nor am I prepared to accept the proposition, which seems implicit in the passage quoted, that whether an automatic state is an insane reaction or a sane reaction may depend upon the intensity of the shock.

M.E. Schiffer, in his text *Mental Disorder and the Criminal Trial Process* (1978), states that psychological blow automatism is described as a reaction to a shock (p. 101):

> However, in cases where the psychological stress has taken the form of a sudden jolt or blow to the accused, the court may be more willing to treat a short-lived bout of automatism as sane. Because the automatism, in order to be a defence in itself, must be an "on the sudden" reaction to psychological stress, the defence of "psychological blow automatism" may be seen as somewhat analogous to the defence of provocation.

I agree with the requirement that there be a shock precipitating the state of automatism. Dissociation caused by a low stress threshold and surrender to anxiety cannot fairly be said to result from a psychological blow. In a recent decision of the British Columbia Court of Appeal, *R. v. MacLeod* (1980), 52 C.C.C. (2d) 193, Craig J.A. adopted the judgment of Martin J.A. in *Rabey*. The facts of *MacLeod* cannot be compared with those in the instant appeal. There, the accused absorbed four double drinks of liquor prior to entering the alleged state of dissociation. His loss of consciousness cannot be traced to an immediate emotional shock. He had been subject to ongoing stress for some time, which was heightened by his wife's recent departure. "Though unwilling to classify it a disease of the mind, the accused's medical witness described it as a "neurotic disorder" which could be induced by an "anxiety reaction". The Court of Appeal held that non-insane automatism was not available.

Dr. Glanville Williams' new book, *Textbook of Criminal Law* (1978), is helpful in this discussion, in particular c. 27. The author cites, as the main instances of automatism, "sleepwalking, concussion, some cases of epilepsy, hypoglycaemia and dissociative states". Williams says (pp. 608-609) that "automatism" has come to express "any abnormal state of consciousness (whether confusion, delusion or dissociation) that is regarded as incompatible with the existence of *mens rea*, while not amounting to insanity", adding:

> It would better be called "impaired consciousness", but the orthodox expression can be used if we bear in mind that it does not mean what it says.

And in a footnote [on p. 609]:

> Because automatism is a legal concept, a psychiatrist should be asked to testify to the mental condition as psychiatrically recognized, not to "automatism". It is for the Judge to make the translation. In most of the conditions referred to legally as automatism the psychiatrist would speak of an altered state of consciousness.

The *Parnerkar* case is discussed at some length and the following observations made with respect thereto [p. 613]:

> The decision illustrates the difficulty that can be caused to the courts by over-enthusiastic psychiatrists. If such evidence were regularly given and accepted a considerable breach would be made in the law of homicide. A medical witness who proclaims that the defendant, though awake, did not know that he was stabbing a person because of his dissociated state invites incredulity, particularly where it is shown that the defendant immediately afterwards telephoned for an ambulance and the police. Further, to assert that this medical condition amounts to insanity ignores the distinction that has been developed between sane and non-sane automatism. *If Parnerkar was in a state of automatism at all it was of the non-insane variety, since there was no evidence of psychosis or brain damage or continuing danger.* (The italics are mine.)

At the conclusion of the discussion on *Parnerkar*, Williams makes the following comment, particularly apt in the present case [p. 613]:

It may also be remarked that commitment to hospital is inappropriate in a case of hysterical dissociation, since once the episode is over the patient does not need to be detained.

Under the heading "Insanity versus Automatism" Williams states that before the decision in *Quick, supra*, Lord Denning's view in *Bratty, supra*, was generally accepted. The test of insanity was the likelihood of recurrence of danger. In *Quick* the Court of Appeal adopted what might seem at first sight to be a different test for insane versus non-insane automatism. But the real question is whether the violence is likely to be repeated. Williams concludes that "on the whole, it would be much better if the courts kept to Lord Denning's plain rule; the rule in *Quick* adds nothing to it" (p. 615).

This view, which the Ontario Court of Appeal appears to have rejected, finds ample support in the legal literature. See S.M. Beck, "Voluntary Conduct: Automatism, Insanity and Drunkenness" (1966-67), 9 Cr. L.Q. 315 at 321: "The cause of the automatic conduct, and the threat of recurrence, are plainly factors that determine the line between sane and insane automatism"; F.A. Whitlock, *Criminal Responsibility and Mental Illness* (1963), p. 120: "The test of whether or not an episode of automatism is to be judged as sane or insane action seems to rest on the likelihood of its repetition"; Professor J. Ll J. Edwards, "Automatism and Criminal Responsibility", at p. 385: "Where evidence is available of recurrent attacks of automatism during which the accused resorts to violence . . . . [this] inevitably leads to consideration of the imposition of some restraint"; S. Prevezer, "Automatism and Involuntary Conduct", [1958] Crim. L.R. 440 at 441: "If . . . it can safely be predicted that his conduct is not likely to recur, having regard to the cause of the automatism, there can be no point in finding him insane and detaining him in Broadmoor"; G.A. Martin, "Insanity as a Defence" (1965-66), 8 Cr. L.Q. 240 at 253: "Perhaps the distinction lies in the likelihood of recurrence and whether the person suffering from it is prone to acts of violence when in that state."

In principle, the defence of automatism should be available whenever there is evidence of unconsciousness throughout the commission of the crime that cannot be attributed to fault or negligence on his part. Such evidence should be supported by expert medical opinion that the accused did not feign memory loss and that there is no underlying pathological condition which points to a disease requiring detention and treatment.

I would add only that s. 16 determines the consequences of the finding of "no consciousness" on the basis of a legal conclusion guided by the medical evidence of the day. What is disease of the mind in the medical science of today may not be so tomorrow. The court will establish the meaning of disease of the mind on the basis of scientific evidence as it unfolds from day to day. The court will find as a matter of fact in each case whether a disease of the mind, so defined, is present.

The circumstances in this case are highly unusual, uncomplicated by alcohol or psychiatric history. The real question in the case is whether the appellant should be confined in an institution for the criminally insane. The trial Judge negated an act of passion, lack of self-control or impulsiveness. The medical evidence negated a state of disease or disorder or mental disturbance arising from infirmity. Save what was said by Dr. Rowsell, whose evidence as to *ex post facto* hysterical amnesia was rejected by the trial judge, the medical experts gave the appellant a clean mental bill of health. I can see no possible justification for sending the case back for a new trial.

I would allow the appeal, set aside the judgment of the Ontario Court of Appeal and restore the verdict of acquittal.

Appeal dismissed.

R. v. PARKS

[1992] 2 S.C.R. 871, 15 C.R. (4th) 289, 75 C.C.C. (3d) 287,
1992 CarswellOnt 107, 1992 CarswellOnt 996

The accused was experiencing serious personal problems, including the loss of his job, which made it difficult for him to sleep. One night he fell asleep in the living room, but a few hours later he got up, put on a jacket and running shoes, grabbed his car keys and the keys to his in-laws' home and drove 23 kilometres to their home. Some of this distance is a multi-lane high-speed highway, and the trip takes 20 minutes in moderate traffic. He then parked in a somewhat confined underground parking area, took a tire iron from his car and entered the home. He got a knife from the kitchen and went to his in-laws' bedroom, where they were sleeping. He strangled his father-in-law until he was unconscious and at some stage inflicted cuts to his head and chest. The father-in-law was hospitalized but recovered. The accused repeatedly stabbed his mother-in-law and brutally beat her with a blunt instrument. She died. The accused then drove to a nearby police station, taking the knife with him. He arrived at the police station with badly-cut hands. He was agitated and in great distress. He made various exclamations to the effect that he had just killed two people with his bare hands. He indicated that these people were his mother and father-in-law. The accused had previously had a good relationship with both of his wife's parents. He was charged with murder and attempted murder.

At his murder trial, he raised the defence of sleepwalking and was acquitted by a jury. The trial judge ruled that his defence should be left to the jury as non-insane automatism, entitling him to an acquittal, rather than as a form of the defence of insanity which, if accepted, would result in the special verdict of not guilty by reason of insanity. At the subsequent trial for attempted murder, the trial judge acquitted the accused on the basis that the doctrine of issue estoppel required him to accept the previous jury's determination that the defence of sleepwalking had been made out.

The Crown appealed these acquittals. The Ontario Court of Appeal [(1990) 78 C.R. (3d) 1] dismissed the appeals on the basis that there was no evidence of a disease of the mind and that, while the facts of the case stretched credulity, an appellate court had to guard against the temptation to usurp the jury's function. The Crown appealed further. The Supreme Court dismissed the appeal. The court was in agreement that, on this evidence, the trial judge had not erred in leaving the jury the defence of automatism rather than that of insanity.

CHIEF JUSTICE LAMER (for the court on this point): —

This court has only ruled on sleepwalking in an *obiter dictum* in *R. v. Rabey*, [1980] 2 S.C.R. 513, 15 C.R. (3d) 225. The court found that sleepwalking was not a "disease of the mind" in the legal sense of the term and gave rise to a defence of automatism. Should the court maintain this position?

In *Black's Law Dictionary*, 5th ed. (St. Paul, Minn.: West Publishing Co., 1979) automatism is defined as follows:

> Behaviour performed in a state of mental unconsciousness or dissociation without full awareness, *i.e.*, somnambulism, fugues. Term is applied to actions or conduct of an individual apparently occurring without will, purpose, or reasoned intention on his part; a condition sometimes observed in persons who, without being actually insane, suffer from an obscuration of the mental faculties, loss of volition or of memory, or kindred affections. . . .

In *Rabey* this court affirmed the judgment of the Ontario Court of Appeal (1977), 40 C.R.N.S. 46, 37 C.C.C. (2d) 461, in which Martin J.A. defined the expression "disease of the mind" at pp. 472-473 [C.C.C., p. 57 C.R.N.S.]:

> "Disease of the mind" is a legal term, not a medical term of art; although a legal concept, it contains a substantial medical component as well as a legal or policy component.

> The legal or policy component relates to (a) the scope of the exemption from criminal responsibility to be afforded by mental disorder or disturbance, and (b) the protection of the public by the control and treatment of persons who have caused serious harms while in a mentally disordered or disturbed state. The medical component of the term, generally, is medical opinion as to how the mental condition in question is viewed or characterized medically. Since the medical component of the term reflects or should reflect the state of medical knowledge at a given time, the concept of "disease of the mind" is capable of evolving with increased medical knowledge with respect to mental disorder or disturbance.

As Martin J.A. pointed out at p. 477 [C.C.C., p. 62 C.R.N.S.], Canadian and foreign courts and authors have recognized that sleepwalking is not a disease of the mind:

> Sleepwalking appears to fall into a separate category. Unconscious behaviour in a state of somnambulism is non-insane automatism....

In Canada, see also *R. v. Hartridge* (1966), 48 C.R. 389, [1967] 1 C.C.C. 346 (Sask. C.A.).

In Britain, Lord Denning in *Bratty v. Attorney General for Northern Ireland*, [1963] A.C. 386 (H.L.), at p. 409, recognized that sleepwalking gave rise to a defence of automatism:

No act is punishable if it is done involuntarily: and an involuntary act in this context — some people nowadays prefer to speak of it as "automatism" — means an act which is done by the muscles without any control by the mind, such as a spasm, a reflex action or a convulsion; or an act done by a person who is not conscious of what he is doing, such as an act done whilst suffering from concussion or whilst sleepwalking.

Other foreign decisions have recognized the same principle: *Ryan v. R.*, [1967] A.L.R. 577; *R. v. Cottle*, [1958] N.Z.L.R. 999; *R. v. Ngang*, [1960] 3 S.A.L.R. 363; *R. v. Tolson* (1889), 23 Q.B.D. 168 (C.C.R.); *H.M. Advocate v. Fraser* (1878), 4 Couper 70.

However, two British decisions seem to go against this line of authority: *R. v. Sullivan*, [1984] A.C. 156, [1983] 2 All E.R. 673 (H.L.), and *R. v. Burgess*, [1991] 2 Q.B. 92 (C.A.). The comment in *Sullivan* at p. 677 [All E.R.] was *obiter*, since the case concerned epilepsy:

If the effect of a disease is to impair these faculties so severely as to have either of the consequences referred to in the latter part of the [*M'Naghten*] rules, it matters not whether the aetiology of the impairment is organic, as in epilepsy, or functional, or whether the impairment itself is permanent or is transient and intermittent, provided that it subsisted at the time of commission of the act.

Some writers have interpreted this *obiter* as an indication that future cases of sleepwalking would only lead to a defence of insanity:

Although sleepwalkers have always received an absolute acquittal for what they do, no social inconvenience has hitherto resulted. There seems to be no recorded instance of a sleepwalker doing injury a further time after being acquitted. However, since the decision in *Sullivan*, to be discussed in the next section, it seems very likely that sleepwalkers will in future find themselves saddled with an insanity verdict. [Williams, *supra*, at p. 666.]

However, the evidence in the case at bar does not indicate the presence of an illness. Accordingly, I do not believe that this *obiter* can be applied to sleepwalking cases such as that of Mr. Parks. *Burgess* cannot be applied here for the same reason, but we will return to it later.

. . . .

In the case at bar the trial judge first reviewed the case law and scholarly analysis and said he did not intend to go against it:

In *Rabey*, *supra*, Martin J.A. considered somnambulism or sleepwalking to be a special category or case of non-insane automatism, one that perhaps could not be justified in accordance with a strict application of principles invoked to determine whether a condition from which an accused suffers amounts to "a disease of the mind" within s-s. 16(2) of the *Criminal Code*. Quite simply put, and notwithstanding that the observations concerning the legal characterization of sleepwalking as a separate category of non-insane automatism would not appear to have been necessary to a decision of the issue on appeal in *Rabey*, *supra*, I am not prepared to depart from the pronouncement of such an eminent authority as Martin J.A. on matters concerning the scope of criminal responsibility. The statement there made is, as one might expect, amply supported by the jurisprudence and academic writings upon the issue.

He then considered the facts of the instant case:

> In the circumstances of the present case, it is doubtful whether the sleep disorder from which the accused suffers would constitute a disease of the mind under s-s. 16(2) in accordance with general principle.

I therefore propose to review the evidence in this matter. A large part of the defence evidence in this case was medical evidence. Five physicians were heard: Dr. Roger James Broughton, a neurophysiologist and specialist in sleep and sleep disorders, Dr. John Gordon Edmeads, a neurologist, Dr. Ronald Frederick Billings, a psychiatrist, Dr. Robert Wood Hill, a forensic psychiatrist, and finally, Dr. Frank Raymond Ervin, a neurologist and psychiatrist.

The medical evidence in the case at bar showed that the respondent was in fact sleepwalking when he committed the acts with which he is charged. All the expert witnesses called by the defence said that in their opinion Parks was sleepwalking when the events occurred. This is what Dr. Broughton said:

> Q. ... assuming for a moment that Mr. Parks caused the death of Barbara Woods, did you, sir, reach an opinion as to his condition at the time he caused that death?
>
> A. Yes. My opinion is that he did it during a sleepwalking episode.

Though sceptical at the outset, the expert witnesses unanimously stated that at the time of the incidents the respondent was not suffering from any mental illness and that, medically speaking, sleepwalking is not regarded as an illness, whether physical, mental or neurological.

. . . .

They also unanimously stated that a person who is sleepwalking cannot think, reflect or perform voluntary acts.

. . . .

The evidence also disclosed that sleepwalking was very common, almost universal, among children, and that 2 to 2.5 percent of "normal" adults had sleepwalked at least once. Dr. Hill further noted that he found it significant that there were several sleepwalkers in the respondent's family:

> Thirdly, I think, as I indicated, it turns out, as enquiries are made more and more, that there is a significant history in the background family of Mr. Parks of difficulties, of bedwetting difficulties, of sleeptalking and sleepwalking, that is in keeping with what we know about the phenomena of sleepwalking. We know that there are often family members so affected and that was present.

Dr. Broughton, for his part, indicated that he had never known of sleepwalkers who had acted violently who had repeated this kind of behaviour:

Q. Yes. Now, with respect to Mr. Parks, do you have any opinion, sir, as to the probability of a recurrence of an event of sleepwalking with serious aggression involving physical harm to others?

A. I think the risk of that is infinitesimal, I don't think it would exceed the risk of the general population almost. He has the family predisposition to sleepwalk, but it would only be in the likelihood of all precipitating and extenuating and so forth factors that built up to this crisis that would theoretically have to almost reappear.

Q. And even if they were to reappear, would there be any probability of another homicidal event?

A. It would still — As I say, there are no reported cases in the literature, so there is essentially — The probability of it occurring is not statistically significant. It is just absolutely improbable.

In cross-examination he also added that sleepwalking episodes in which violent acts are committed are not common:

Q. And does that, in fact, agree with your own experience with respect to people that you have dealt with at the sleep lab and have seen over the years, that the majority of sleepwalking episodes generally involve what you call trivial behaviour?

A. It is well known that aggression during sleepwalking is quite rare.

Q. How many cases of aggression during sleepwalking have you personally deal[t] with or been involved with at your sleep lab?

A. In the last — Perhaps a total of five or six. In the last five years we have seen three.

Further, on being questioned about a cure or treatment, Dr. Broughton answered that the solution was sleep hygiene, which involved eliminating factors that precipitated sleepwalking such as stress, lack of sleep and violent physical exercise.

. . . .

Three very important points emerge from this testimony: (1) the respondent was sleepwalking at the time of the incident; (2) sleepwalking is not a neurological, psychiatric or other illness — it is a sleep disorder very common in children and also found in adults; (3) there is no medical treatment as such, apart from good health practices, especially as regards sleep. It is important to note that this expert evidence was not in any way contradicted by the prosecution, which as the trial judge observed, did have the advice of experts who were present during the testimony given by the defence experts and whom it chose not to call.

The Crown, for its part, relied on a decision of the English Court of Appeal, *R. v. Burgess, supra,* in which the court held that sleepwalking was a mental illness. It is worth noting here, however, that the evidence in *Burgess* was completely different from or even contradictory to that presented in the case at bar.

The facts in *Burgess* are more or less similar to those at issue here. Burgess and a friend fell asleep watching a video. The friend woke up when she felt a blow on the head. Burgess was facing her, holding the video recorder in the air, about to strike her on the head with it, and he did so. Burgess, who woke up immediately after the incident, testified that he did not remember having hit her. He presented a defence of automatism, which the judge rejected. He was acquitted on grounds of insanity and appealed this judgment. Nevertheless, while the facts are similar the medical evidence was very different. Expert witnesses were called. The first witness, a Dr. D'Orban, agreed that Burgess was sleepwalking, but regarded this as a pathological condition. Another expert, called by the Crown, Dr. Fenwick, said that in his opinion this was not sleepwalking but a "hysterical dissociative state". The following is a passage from this judgment at pp. 775-776 [All E.R.], which states the situation very clearly:

> One turns then to examine the evidence upon which the Judge had to base his decision and for this purpose the two medical experts called by the defence are the obvious principal sources. Dr. d'Orban in examination-in-chief said:
>
>> "On the evidence available to me, and subject to the results of the tests when they became available, I came to the same conclusion as Dr. Nicholas and Dr. Eames, whose reports I had read, and that was that (the appellant's) actions had occurred during the course of a sleep disorder."
>
> He was asked . . . in cross-examination:
>
>> "Q. Would you go so far as to say that it was liable to recur?
>>
>> A. It is possible for it to recur, yes.
>>
>> *Judge Lewis.* Is this a case of automatism associated with a pathological condition or not?
>>
>> A. I think the answer would have to be Yes, because it is an abnormality of the brain function, so it would be regarded as a pathological condition."
>
> .   .   .   .
>
> The prosecution, as already indicated, called Dr Fenwick, whose opinion was that this was not a sleepwalking episode at all. If it was a case where the appellant was unconscious of what he was doing, the most likely explanation was that he was in what is described as a hysterical dissociative state. . . .
>
> He then went on to describe features of sleepwalking. This is what he said:
>
> .   .   .   .

"Finally, should a person be detained in hospital? The answer to that is: Yes, because sleepwalking is treatable. Violent night terrors are treatable. There is a lot which can be done for the sleepwalker, so sending them to hospital after a violent act to have their sleepwalking sorted out, makes good sense."

In my view, therefore, that case is clearly distinguishable from the one at bar. I am of the view that in the instant case, based on the evidence and the testimony of the expert witnesses heard, the trial judge did not err in leaving the defence of automatism rather than that of insanity with the jury, and that the instant appeal should be dismissed. For a defence of insanity to have been put to the jury, together with or instead of a defence of automatism, as the case may be, there would have had to have been in the record evidence tending to show that sleepwalking was the cause of the respondent's state of mind. As we have just seen, that is not the case here. This is not to say that sleepwalking could never be a disease of the mind, in another case on different evidence.

LA FOREST J. (five justices concurring): — I have had the advantage of reading the reasons of the Chief Justice. I agree with him that the trial judge was correct in leaving only the defence of non-insane automatism with the jury. I am also in agreement with what the Chief Justice has to say on that issue, but I wish to add the following comments concerning the distinction in law between insane and non-insane automatism, particularly as it relates to somnambulism.

In his reasons, the Chief Justice finds that the evidence and expert testimony from the trial of the accused support the trial judge's decision to instruct the jury on non-insane automatism. I agree with this finding, but in my view that is not the end of the matter. In distinguishing between automatism and insanity the trial judge must consider more than the evidence; there are overarching policy considerations as well. Of course, the evidence in each case will be highly relevant to this policy inquiry.

Automatism occupies a unique place in our criminal law system. Although spoken of as a "defence", it is conceptually a subset of the voluntariness requirement, which in turn is part of the *actus reus* component of criminal liability. A useful introduction is found in the dissenting reasons of Dickson J. (as he then was) in *R. v. Rabey*, [1980] 2 S.C.R. 513, 15 C.R. (3d) 225, at p. 522 [S.C.R.]:

Although the word "automatism" made its way but lately to the legal stage, it is basic principle that absence of volition in respect of the act involved is always a defence to a crime. A defence that the act is involuntary entitles the accused to a complete and unqualified acquittal. That the defence of automatism exists as a middle ground between criminal responsibility and legal insanity is beyond question. Although spoken as a defence, in the sense that it is raised by the accused, the Crown always bears the burden of proving a voluntary act.

One qualification to this statement should be noted. When the automatistic condition stems from a disease of the mind that has rendered the accused insane, then the accused is not entitled to a full acquittal, but to a verdict of insanity;

see *Bratty v. Attorney General for Northern Ireland*, [1963] A.C. 386 (H.L.), at pp. 403-404 and 414 [A.C.]. The condition in that instance is referred to as insane automatism, and the distinction between it and non-insane automatism is the crucial issue in this appeal.

When a defence of non-insane automatism is raised by the accused, the trial judge must determine whether the defence should be left with the trier of fact. This will involve two discrete tasks. First, he or she must determine whether there is some evidence on the record to support leaving the defence with the jury. This is sometimes referred to as laying the proper foundation for the defence; see *Bratty, supra*, at pp. 405 and 413 [A.C.]. Thus an evidential burden rests with the accused, and the mere assertion of the defence will not suffice; see *Bratty*, at p. 414 [A.C.]. Dickson J. summarized the point in comprehensive fashion in the following passage in *Rabey*, at p. 545 [S.C.R.]:

> The prosecution must prove every element of the crime charged. One such element is the state of mind of the accused, in the sense that the act was voluntary. The circumstances are normally such as to permit a presumption of volition and mental capacity. That is not so when the accused, as here, has placed before the court, by cross-examination of Crown witnesses or by evidence called on his own behalf, or both, evidence sufficient to raise an issue that he was unconscious of his actions at the time of the alleged offence. No burden of proof is imposed upon an accused raising such defence beyond pointing to facts which indicate the existence of such a condition.

If the proper foundation is present the judge moves to the second task: he or she must consider whether the condition alleged by the accused is, in law, non-insane automatism. If the trial judge is satisfied that there is some evidence pointing to a condition that is in law non-insane automatism, then the defence can be left with the jury; see *Rabey*, per Ritchie J., at p. 519 [S.C.R.]. The issue for the jury is one of fact: did the accused suffer from or experience the alleged condition at the relevant time? Because the Crown must always prove that an accused has acted voluntarily, the onus rests on the prosecution at this stage to prove the absence of automatism beyond a reasonable doubt.

In the present case, there is no question that the accused has laid the proper foundation for the defence of automatism. The expert testimony reviewed by the Chief Justice is more than adequate on that score. At issue here is the question of law: is sleepwalking properly classified as non-insane automatism, or does it stem from a disease of the mind, thereby leaving only the defence of insanity for the accused? When considering this question, s. 16(4) of the *Criminal Code*, R.S.C., 1985, c. C-46, should be recalled: "Every one shall, until the contrary is proved, be presumed to be and to have been sane." If the accused pleads automatism, the Crown is then entitled to raise the issue of insanity, but the prosecution then bears the burden of proving that the condition in question stems from a disease of the mind; see *Rabey, supra*, at pp. 544-545 [S.C.R.].

In Canada, the approach to distinguishing between insane and non-insane automatism was settled by this court's judgment in *Rabey*.

. . . .

In part because of the imprecision of medical science in this area, the legal community reserves for itself the final determination of what constitutes a "disease of the mind". This is accomplished by adding the "legal or policy component" to the inquiry.

A review of the cases on automatism reveals two distinct approaches to the policy component of the disease of the mind inquiry. These may be labelled the "continuing danger" and "internal cause" theories; see E. Colvin, *Principles of Criminal Law,* 2d ed. (Toronto: Carswell, 1991), at p. 293. At first glance these approaches may appear to be divergent, but in fact they stem from a common concern for public safety. This was recognized by Martin J.A. who referred to "protection of the public" as a focus of the policy inquiry. More recently, the Chief Justice had occasion to comment on this aspect of the insanity provisions of the *Criminal Code*, albeit in a division of powers context, in *R. v. Swain,* [1991] 1 S.C.R. 933, 5 C.R. (4th) 253, 63 C.C.C. (3d) 481, at p. 998 [S.C.R.]:

> It is true that the dominant characteristic of these provisions is not punishment; however, neither is it treatment. The "pith and substance" of the legislative scheme dealing with individuals acquitted by reason of insanity is the protection of society from dangerous people who have engaged in conduct proscribed by the *Criminal Code* through the prevention of such acts in the future. While treatment may be incidentally involved in the process, it is not the dominant objective of the legislation.

The continuing danger theory holds that any condition likely to present a recurring danger to the public should be treated as insanity. The internal cause theory suggests that a condition stemming from the psychological or emotional makeup of the accused, rather than some external factor, should lead to a finding of insanity. The two theories share a common concern for recurrence, the latter holding that an internal weakness is more likely to lead to recurrent violence than automatism brought on by some intervening external cause.

It would appear that the internal cause approach has gained a certain ascendancy in both Canadian and English jurisprudence. The theory was the basis for deciding *Rabey*.

. . . .

The theory has also been adopted in England, first in *R. v. Quick; R. v. Paddison,* [1973] 3 All E.R. 347 (C.A.) [hereafter *R. v. Quick*], at p. 356 [All E.R.], and most recently in *R. v. Hennessy,* [1989] 2 All E.R. 9 (C.A.), where Lord Lane C.J. stated the approach as follows, at p. 13 [All E.R.]:

> The question in many cases, and this is one such case, is whether the function of the mind was disturbed on the one hand by disease or on the other hand by some external factor.

The judgments in both *Rabey* and *Hennessy* are careful to state that the internal cause theory is not a universal approach to the disease of the mind inquiry.

Indeed Martin J.A., at p. 477 [C.C.C., p. 62 C.R.N.S.], appears to suggest that sleepwalking is one of those conditions that is not usefully assessed on this basis.

The internal cause approach has been criticized as an unfounded development of the law, and for the odd results the external/internal dichotomy can produce; see G. Williams, *Textbook of Criminal Law* 2d ed. (London: Sweet & Maxwell, 1983), at pp. 671-676; D. Stuart, *Canadian Criminal Law* 2d ed. (Toronto: Carswell, 1987), at pp. 92-94; Colvin, *supra*, at p. 291. These criticisms have particular validity if the internal cause theory is held out as the definitive answer to the disease of the mind inquiry. However, it is apparent from the cases that the theory is really meant to be used only as an analytical tool, and not as an all-encompassing methodology. As Watt J. commented in his reasons in support of his charge to the jury in this case, the dichotomy "constitutes a general, but not an unremitting or universal, classificatory scheme for 'disease of the mind'".

As Martin J.A. suggested in *Rabey*, somnambulism is an example of a condition that is not well suited to analysis under the internal cause theory. The poor fit arises because certain factors can legitimately be characterized as either internal or external sources of automatistic behaviour. For example, the Crown in this case argues that the causes of the respondent's violent sleepwalking were entirely internal, a combination of genetic susceptibility and the ordinary stresses of everyday life (lack of sleep, excessive afternoon exercise, and a high stress level due to personal problems). These "ordinary stresses" were ruled out as external factors by this court in *Rabey* (although by a narrow majority). However, the factors that for a waking individual are mere ordinary stresses can be differently characterized for a person who is asleep, unable to counter with his conscious mind the onslaught of the admittedly ordinary strains of life. One could argue that the particular amalgam of stress, excessive exercise, sleep deprivation and sudden noises in the night that causes an incident of somnambulism is, for the sleeping person, analogous to the effect of a concussion upon a waking person, which is generally accepted as an external cause of non-insane automatism; see Williams, *supra*, at p. 666. In the end, the dichotomy between internal and external causes becomes blurred in this context, and is not helpful in resolving the inquiry.

The continuing danger approach stems from an *obiter* comment of Lord Denning in *Bratty*, *supra*, where he proposes the following test for distinguishing between insane and non-insane automatism, at p. 412 [A.C.]:

> It seems to me that any mental disorder which has manifested itself in violence and is prone to recur is a disease of the mind. At any rate it is the sort of disease for which a person should be detained in hospital rather than be given an unqualified acquittal.

Lord Denning's causal proposition has not been universally accepted, although some elements of the theory remain today. It was questioned in *R. v. Quick*, *supra*, at pp. 351-352 [All E.R.], and legal academics have questioned the utility of the test; see Stuart, *supra*, at pp. 94-95; Colvin, *supra*, at p. 294. As well, medical authorities have doubted the ability of their profession to predict recurrent dangerousness; see Roth, "Modern Psychiatry and Neurology and the Problem of Responsibility", in S.J. Hucker, C. Webster and M. Ben-Aron, eds., *Mental Disorder and Criminal Responsibility* (Toronto: Butterworths, 1981), at pp. 104-109. In *Rabey*, Martin J.A. doubted the merit of Lord Denning's test, noting, at p. 476 [C.C.C., p. 60 C.R.N.S.], that the converse of Denning's proposition was surely not good law. He stated:

> It would be quite unreasonable to hold that a serious mental disorder did not constitute a disease of the mind because it was unlikely to recur. To so hold would be to exclude from the exemption from responsibility afforded by insanity, persons, who by reason of a severe mental disorder were incapable of appreciating the nature and quality of the act or of knowing that it was wrong, if such mental disorder was unlikely to recur.

The majority of this court approved these comments, and Dickson J. in dissent conceded the point, at p. 533 [S.C.R.]:

> A test of proneness to recur does not entail the converse conclusion, that if the mental malady is not prone to recur it cannot be a disease of the mind. A condition, organic in nature, which causes an isolated act of unconscious violence could well be regarded as a case of temporary insanity.

Nonetheless, Dickson J. sought to revive Lord Denning's basic formulation...

. . . .

While Dickson J.'s views did not carry the day in *Rabey*, nothing in the majority judgment precludes the consideration of a continuing danger as a factor at the policy stage of the inquiry.

Since *Rabey*, the House of Lords has revisited the question of disease of the mind, in *R. v. Sullivan*, [1984] A.C. 156, Lord Diplock, speaking for a unanimous court, commented, at p. 172 [A.C.], as follows:

> The nomenclature adopted by the medical profession may change from time to time; Bratty was tried in 1961. But the meaning of the expression "disease of the mind" as the cause of "a defect of reason", remains unchanged for the purposes of the application of the M'Naghten Rules. I agree with what was said by Devlin J. in *Reg. v. Kemp* [1957] 1 Q.B. 399, 407, that "mind" in the M'Naghten Rules is used in the ordinary sense of the mental faculties of reason, memory and understanding. If the effect of a disease is to impair these faculties so severely as to have either of the consequences referred to in the latter part of the rules, it matters not whether the aetiology of the impairment is organic, as in epilepsy, or functional, or whether the impairment itself is permanent or is transient and intermittent, provided that it subsisted at the time of commission of the act. *The purpose of the legislation relating to the defence of insanity, ever since its origin in 1800, has been to protect society against recurrence of the dangerous conduct. The duration of a temporary suspension of the mental faculties of reason, memory and understanding, particularly if, as in Mr. Sullivan's case, it is recurrent, cannot on any rational ground be relevant to the application by the courts of the M'Naghten Rules*, though it may be relevant to the course adopted by the

> Secretary of State, to whom the responsibility for how the defendant is to be dealt with passes after the return of the special verdict of "not guilty by reason of insanity." [My emphasis.]

This passage, while not entirely clear, appears to endorse the consideration of recurrence as a non-determinative factor in the insanity inquiry. Lord Diplock states that the *duration* of the condition in question is not a relevant consideration: a disease of the mind can be temporary or permanent. He also suggests that the relative impermanence of a condition is particularly inconsequential *if the condition is prone to recur*. A necessary corollary of these statements is the more general proposition that recurrence suggests insanity, but the absence of recurrence does not preclude it. This view of the law was stated explicitly in *R. v. Burgess*, [1991] 2 All E.R. 769 (C.A.), at p. 774 [All E.R.]:

> It seems to us that if there is a danger of recurrence that may be an added reason for categorising the condition as a disease of the mind. On the other hand, the absence of the danger of recurrence is not a reason for saying that it cannot be a disease of the mind. Subject to that possible qualification, we respectfully adopt Lord Denning's suggested definition.

In my view, the Court of Appeal has properly stated the law on this point. Recurrence is but one of a number of factors to be considered in the policy phase of the disease of the mind inquiry. Moreover, the absence of a danger of recurrence will not automatically exclude the possibility of a finding of insanity.

In this case, then, neither of the two leading policy approaches determines an obvious result. It is clear from the evidence that there is almost no likelihood of recurrent violent somnambulism. A finding of insanity is therefore less likely, but the absence of a continuing danger does not mean that the respondent must be granted an absolute acquittal. At the same time, the internal cause theory is not readily applicable in this case. It is therefore necessary to look further afield.

In his dissenting reasons in *Rabey*, at p. 546, [S.C.R.] Dickson J. enumerates certain additional policy considerations that are relevant to the distinction between insanity and automatism:

> There are undoubtedly policy considerations to be considered. Automatism as a defence is easily feigned. It is said the credibility of our criminal justice system will be severely strained if a person who has committed a violent act is allowed an absolute acquittal on a plea of automatism arising from a psychological blow. The argument is made that the success of the defence depends upon the semantic ability of psychiatrists, tracing a narrow path between the twin shoals of criminal responsibility and an insanity verdict. Added to these concerns is the *in terrorem* argument that the floodgates will be raised if psychological blow automatism is recognized in law.

These factors are raised by Dickson J. as arguments against a finding of non-insane automatism. In the present case, however, none of these arguments is persuasive. It seems unlikely that the recognition of somnambulism as non-insane automatism will open the floodgates to a cascade of sleepwalking defence claims. First of all, the defence of somnambulism has been recognized, albeit in *obiter* discussion, in an unbroken line of cases stretching back at least a century, yet I am unaware of any current problem with specious defence claims of somnambulistic automatism. Indeed, this case and *Burgess* are among the few appellate decisions in which the status of somnambulism was a question to be decided. Moreover, it is very difficult to feign sleepwalking — precise symptoms and medical histories beyond the control of the accused must be presented to the trier of fact, and as in this case the accused will be subjected to a battery of medical tests. Finally, a comprehensive listing of the indicia of sleepwalking can be consulted by both the court and the medical experts; see P. Fenwick, "Somnambulism and the Law: A Review" (1987), 5 Behavioral Sciences and the Law 343, at p. 354.

It may be that some will regard the exoneration of an accused through a defence of somnambulism as an impairment of the credibility of our justice system. Those who hold this view would also reject insane automatism as an excuse from criminal responsibility. However, these views are contrary to certain fundamental precepts of our criminal law: only those who act voluntarily with the requisite intent to commit an offence should be punished by criminal sanction. The concerns of those who reject these underlying values of our system of criminal justice must accordingly be discounted.

In the end, there are no compelling policy factors that preclude a finding that the accused's condition was one of non-insane automatism. I noted earlier that it is for the Crown to prove that somnambulism stems from a disease of the mind; neither the evidence nor the policy considerations in this case overcome the Crown's burden in that regard. Committal under s. 614(2) of the *Criminal Code* is therefore precluded, and the accused should be acquitted.

As I noted at the outset, it is apparent that the medical evidence in this case is not only significant in its own right, but also has an impact at several stages of the policy inquiry. As such, I agree with the Chief Justice that in another case, on different evidence, sleepwalking might be found to be a disease of the mind. As Dickson J. commented in *Rabey*, at p. 552 [S.C.R.]:

> What is disease of the mind in the medical science of today may not be so tomorrow. The court will establish the meaning of disease of the mind on the basis of scientific evidence as it unfolds from day to day. The court will find as a matter of fact in each case whether a disease of the mind, so defined, is present.

The Supreme Court split over whether, notwithstanding the confirmation of the acquittal, the matter should be referred to the trial judge to consider a common-law peace bond. This issue had been raised by Chief Justice Lamer when the case was argued in the Supreme Court. The Chief Justice (Cory J. concurring) held that the matter should be remitted for a consideration of such an order. However, the other six justices rejected such a possibility, each expressing agreement with three separate opinions given by Sopinka, McLachlin and La Forest JJ.

LAMER C.J.C. (dissenting on this point): —

As I see it, however, that does not end the matter. Although the expert witnesses were unanimous in saying that sleepwalkers are very rarely violent, I am still concerned by the fact that as the result of an acquittal in a situation like this (and I am relieved that such cases are quite rare), the accused is simply set free without any consideration of measures to protect the public, or indeed the accused himself, from the possibility of a repetition of such unfortunate occurrences. In the case of an outright acquittal, should there not be some control? And if so, how should this be done? I am of the view that such control could be exercised by means of the common-law power to make an order to keep the peace vested in any judge or magistrate. This power of "preventive justice" has been recognized in England for centuries and has its origin in one or more sources:

> The cases do, however, in tracing the history of the law, suggest that it is derived from one or more sources:
>
> (i) The common law;
>
> (ii) The statute law, being the Justices of the Peace Act, 1361 (Imp.), c. 1 (hereinafter the "Statute of Edward III"); and/or
>
> (iii) The form of commission which the justice of the peace is required to take in England.

In Canada this power has already been used in Ontario and British Columbia and was recognized by this court in 1954 in *Mackenzie v. Martin*, [1954] S.C.R. 361, 108 C.C.C. 305, at pp. 368-369 [S.C.R.]:

> In my view the common-law preventive justice was in force in Ontario; s-s. [(2)] of s. 748, or any other provision of the *Criminal Code* to which our attention was directed, does not interfere with the use of that jurisdiction, and the respondent was intending to exercise it. He, therefore, had jurisdiction over the subject-matter of the complaint, and did not exceed it.

In exercising this power, the rules of natural justice must be observed and in this regard the more recent decision of the Ontario Court of Appeal, *Broomes v. R.* (1984), 12 C.C.C. (3d) 220, is of particular interest for these purposes. A judge who acquitted an accused of assault decided, however, to exercise this "preventive justice" and made an order binding over the accused to keep the peace on certain conditions. On appeal, the accused argued that he had been denied the rules of natural justice because he was not told in advance that such an order would be made. Steele J. of the Ontario High Court of Justice dismissed the appeal, relying on an English decision (at p. 221):

> I accept the decision in *R. v. Woking Justices, Ex p. Gossage*, [1973] 2 All E.R. 621 at p. 623 (Eng. C.A.), where Lord Widgery C.J. stated as follows:

It seems to me that a very clear distinction is drawn between, on the one part, persons who come before the justices as witnesses, and on the other, persons who come before the justices as defendants. Not only do the witnesses come with no expected prospect of being subjected to any kind of penalty, but also the witnesses as such, although they may speak in evidence, cannot represent themselves through counsel and cannot call evidence on their own behalf. *By contrast*, the defendant comes before the court knowing that allegations are to be made against him, knowing that he can be represented if appropriate, and knowing that he can call evidence if he wishes. It seems to me that a rule which requires a witness to be warned of the possibility of a binding-over should not necessarily apply to a defendant in that different position.

I think from the extracts from Lord Parker C.J.'s judgment that I have read, Lord Parker C.J. would have taken the same view; but, be that as it may, it seems to me to be putting it far too high in the case of an acquitted defendant to say that it is a breach of the rules of natural justice not to give him an indication of the prospective binding-over before the binding-over is imposed. That is not to say that it would not be wise, and indeed courteous in these cases for justices to give such a warning; there certainly would be absolutely no harm in a case like the present if the justices, returning to court, had announced they were going to acquit, but had immediately said "We are however contemplating a binding-over; what have you got to say?" *I think it would be at least courteous and perhaps wise that that should be done, but I am unable to elevate the principle to the height at which it can be said that a failure to give such a warning is a breach of the rules of natural justice.* [Emphasis added.]

Accordingly, such a power exists. The question remains whether it should be exercised in the case of the respondent Parks, or at least whether its exercise should be considered. I am of the view that this approach should be considered. As I have already said, despite the unanimous and uncontradicted evidence that the chances of such an occurrence taking place again are for all practical purposes nil, I feel that all necessary measures should be taken to ensure that such an event does not recur. After all, before this tragic incident occurred, the probability of Mr. Parks killing someone while in a somnambulistic state was infinitesimal. Yet this is precisely what took place. Furthermore, the evidence at trial was not adduced with a view to determining whether an order would be justified and to determine the appropriate conditions of such an order. Thus, for example, an order might be made requiring Parks to do certain things suggested by a specialist in sleep disorders, for example to report to him periodically. In appropriate cases of outright acquittals on grounds of automatism measures that would reinforce sleep hygiene and thereby provide greater safety for others should always be considered. If the trial judge considers that making such an order would be in the interest of the public, he should so advise the parties and consider whatever evidence and submissions are tendered. In those situations where an order is made, it should be complied with in the same way as any other order of the court.

If conditions should be imposed on Mr. Parks they will restrict his liberty. It follows that the decision to impose such conditions and the terms of those conditions should not violate the rights guaranteed under s. 7 of the *Canadian Charter of Rights and Freedoms*. However, such a hearing is justified, as the sleepwalker has, although innocently, committed an act of violence which resulted in the death of his mother-in-law. Members of the community may quite reasonably be apprehensive for their safety. In those circumstances it cannot be said that the court has unduly intruded upon the liberty of the accused by exploring, on notice to the accused, the possibility of imposing some minimally intrusive conditions which seek to assure the safety of the community. If conditions are imposed, then they obviously must be rationally connected to the apprehended danger posed by the person and go no further than necessary to protect the public from this danger.

I would therefore refer this matter back to the trial judge so that he can hear the parties on this point and decide, upon the evidence before him, whether such an order is appropriate. If this proves to be the case, it will be up to the trial judge to determine the content of the order.

I would accordingly dismiss this appeal and uphold the acquittal of the respondent but refer the matter back to the trial judge for him to decide on the making of an order to keep the peace on certain conditions, pursuant to the "preventive justice" power which he possesses.

SOPINKA J.: —

. . . .

This court has recognized the existence of a common-law preventative justice power in addition to the specific statutory power to make an order to keep the peace pursuant to an information laid under what is now s. 810 of the *Criminal Code*, R.S.C., 1985, c. C-46: *Mackenzie v. Martin*, [1954] S.C.R. 361, 108 C.C.C. 305. However even at common law this power has significant limits. In *Mackenzie*, Kerwin J. quoted from Blackstone on the nature of the power:

> This preventative justice consists in obliging those *persons, whom there is probable ground to suspect of future misbehaviour*, to stipulate with and to give full assurance to the public, that *such offence as is apprehended* shall not happen; by finding pledges or securities for keeping the peace, or for their good behaviour. [At p. 368 [S.C.R.], emphasis added.]

Several lower court decisions have similarly recognized that this common-law power cannot be exercised on the basis of mere speculation, but requires a proven factual foundation which raises a probable ground to suspect of future misbehaviour. See: *R. v. Chohan* (1968), 5 C.R.N.S. 30, (sub nom. *R. v. White*) [1969] 1 C.C.C. 19 (B.C. S.C.); *R. v. Shaben* (1972), 19 C.R.N.S. 35, 8 C.C.C. (2d) 422 (H.C.); *Stevenson v. Saskatchewan (Minister of Justice)*, (June 8, 1987), (Q.B.), unreported [now reported (1987), 61 Sask. R. 91 (Q.B.)].

The uncontroverted expert evidence in this case is wholly inconsistent with such a conclusion. The Chief Justice characterizes that evidence as indicating that "the chances of such an occurrence taking place again are for all practical purposes nil" (at p. 322, poste).

Moreover the extent and continued validity of this common-law power has yet to be considered in light of the *Canadian Charter of Rights and Freedoms*. Restrictions on an individual's liberty can only be effected in accordance with principles of fundamental justice or must be justified under s. 1. This applies to deprivations of liberty following a criminal conviction as well as those effected in other circumstances.

Our criminal justice system is premised on the requirement that the Crown must prove all the elements of an offence in accordance with legal principles. Leaving aside the question of a lack of criminal responsibility on account of mental disorder, the failure to prove the guilt of the accused beyond a reasonable doubt in accordance with such principles will result in an acquittal. That is exactly what has happened in this case. The respondent has been acquitted in accordance with ordinary criminal law principles.

Turning to the common law power relied upon by the Chief Justice, I have grave doubts as to whether a power that can be exercised on the basis of "probable ground[s] to suspect future misbehaviour" without limits as to the type of "misbehaviour" or potential victims, would survive *Charter* scrutiny. If such a power allowed the imposition of restrictive conditions following an acquittal on the basis of a remote possibility of recurrence, it may well be contrary to s. 7.

Furthermore the potential implications of the course of action contemplated by the Chief Justice are significant not only for the respondent, but also in other cases. Consider an individual who is convicted of a violent crime at trial, but on appeal a stay is entered on the basis that his right to be tried within a reasonable time has been violated. Would the court nonetheless impose restrictions on his liberty in an attempt to ensure that such an event does not recur? Such restrictions would be a significant departure from fundamental principles of criminal law, yet there is nothing in the authorities relied upon by the Chief Justice which limits the consideration of an order to keep the peace to cases such as the one at bar.

I note that there still exists the possibility of an information being laid pursuant to s. 810 of the *Criminal Code*. This, of course, is subject to the evidentiary basis required under that section, "that the informant has reasonable grounds for his fears" (s. 810(3)), and to constitutional challenge. If such a proceeding is to be initiated, it should not be done so by this court acting *proprio motu*.

Finally I observe that the respondent cross-appealed on the ground that if this court were inclined to interfere with the decision of the Court of Appeal, a stay should be entered by reason of the violation of his rights under s. 11(*b*) of the *Charter*. If the respondent remains subject to the criminal justice system and potential restraints on his liberty, it would be necessary to deal with this cross-appeal.

McLachlin J.: —

. . . .

I share the Chief Justice's concern that notwithstanding the justice of an acquittal in this case and the evidence that a recurrence is highly unlikely, great care should be taken to avoid the possibility of a similar episode in the future. However, I also have concerns about the appropriateness of referring the matter back at this stage for a supervisory order in the circumstances of this case.

In addition to the difficult issues raised by an order restricting a person's liberty on account of an act for which he has been acquitted, I have concerns whether further proceedings are appropriate in the circumstances before us. Mr. Parks has been living in the shadow of these charges since May 24, 1987, over five years. His acquittal is now confirmed. We are told he has been making courageous efforts to re-establish his life. Should he now be embroiled in a further set of proceedings concerned, not with his guilt or innocence, but with the maintenance of his liberty?

Generally, the courts do not grant remedies affecting the liberty of the subject unless they are asked to do so by the Crown, which is charged with instituting such legal processes as it deems appropriate having regard to the public interest and fairness to the individual involved. In the absence of an application by the Crown, I hesitate to remit the case for consideration of further measures against the accused.

I add that the possibility of supervisory orders in this situation may be a matter which Parliament would wish to consider in the near future.

La Forest J.: —

. . . .

To be effective, any order to keep the peace would have to be permanent. This would violate established practice (if not the law) regarding peace orders, which requires a defined period for the order; see *R. v. Edgar* (1913), 9 Cr. App. R. 13 (C.C.A.). Of course, the courts could impose a succession of limited-term orders that would amount to a permanent injunction governing the respondent. However, even this course of action may not be feasible in light of concerns over enforcement of the orders, to which I now turn.

Generally, there are two mechanisms for the enforcement of a traditional order to keep the peace. First, any complainant who seeks an order will return to court to complain of any breach of the peace. Thus the complainant acts as a watchdog much like the plaintiff in a civil injunction action. In the instant case, however, there is no "complainant" as such. Only the respondent's immediate family would have a vested interest in the order and an ability to monitor compliance with it, and it would be unrealistic to expect them to complain of any breach of the peace.

A second enforcement mechanism is the imposition of a bond with a guarantee from some third person. This is the standard procedure under the *Magistrate's Courts Act* 1952, c. 55, in England, where the courts require a surety to guarantee the recognizance; see *Halsbury's Laws of England* 4th ed., vol. 29 (London: Butterworths, 1979, para. 444). The surety is entitled to complain to the court if the principal has been or is about to be in breach of the conditions of the recognizance, and as such the surety becomes the court's watchdog. Such an arrangement is feasible over a short term, as the cost of the surety can reasonably be imposed upon the accused. But with a permanent order, the costs of a life-long surety would be onerous, and it would be unreasonable to require the respondent to bear this cost.

It appears, then, that the judiciary is not practically equipped to administer a "keep the peace order" in the circumstances of this case. For this reason, along with the reasons of my colleagues, I would not remit this case back to the trial judge for the consideration of such an order. I would accordingly dismiss the appeal and uphold the acquittal of the respondent.

R. v. STONE

[1999] 2 S.C.R. 290, 24 C.R. (5th) 1, 134 C.C.C. (3d) 353, 1999 CarswellBC 1064, 1999 CarswellBC 1065

The accused decided to visit his sons from a previous marriage. His current wife insisted on accompanying him and expressed her objections to the visit before and after the accused saw his sons for some 15 minutes. According to the accused his wife raised the issue of divorce, told him she had falsely reported to the police that he was abusing her and that they were ready to arrest him, that she would stay in the house and have him support her and their children, and that "she couldn't stand to listen to me whistle, that every time I touched her, she felt sick, that I was a lousy fuck and that I had a small penis and that she's never going to fuck me again". He testified he felt a "whoosh" sensation washing over him from his feet to his head. When his eyes focused again, he was staring straight ahead and felt something in his hand. He was holding a six-inch hunting knife. He looked over and saw his wife slumped over on the seat. She was dead. It was later established she had been stabbed 47 times. He put the body in his truck tool box, cleaned up, drove home, prepared a note for his stepdaughter, packed, checked into a hotel for a shower and shave, collected a debt, sold a car and flew to Mexico. While in Mexico, he awoke one morning to the sensation of having his throat cut. In trying to recall his dream, he remembered stabbing his wife twice in the chest before experiencing a "whooshing" sensation. On his return to Canada he surrendered to police and was charged with murder.

At his trial before judge and jury the accused admitted stabbing his wife. His defences were insane automatism, non-insane automatism, lack of intent, and alternatively, provocation. The trial judge found that there was evidence of unconsciousness throughout the commission of the crime but ruled the defence had laid a proper evidentiary foundation for insane but not non-insane automatism. Accordingly, he instructed the jury on insane automatism, intention in relation to second degree murder and provocation.

The accused was found guilty of manslaughter and sentenced to four years imprisonment. In imposing this sentence, the trial judge took into account the 18 month pre-trial period as the equivalent of three years imprisonment.

The Supreme Court accepted that this was a proper case for provocation to go to the jury and also dismissed the Crown appeal against sentence. The 5-4 division in the court came on the issue of whether sane automatism should have been left with the jury. Justice Bastarache determined that the judge had been correct in not putting the defence to the jury. The majority also decided to reverse the onus of proof. Bastarache J. also offered detailed guidance on how this burden can be discharged and how to distinguish cases of sane automatism from those of insanity which are subsumed by the defence of mental disorder under s. 16.

BINNIE J., dissenting (LAMER C.J., IACOBUCCI and MAJOR JJ. concurring): — A fundamental principle of the criminal law is that no act can be a criminal offence unless it is performed or omitted voluntarily. In this case the appellant acknowledges that he killed his wife. He stabbed her 47 times with his knife in a frenzy. His defence was that he lost consciousness when his mind snapped under the weight of verbal abuse which the defence psychiatrist characterized as "exceptionally cruel" and "psychologically sadistic". The trial judge ruled in favour of the appellant that "there is evidence of unconsciousness throughout the commission of the crime", and the British Columbia Court of Appeal agreed ((1997), 86 B.C.A.C. 169, at p. 173) that "a properly instructed jury, acting reasonably, could find some form of automatism".

The appellant had elected trial by jury. He says he was entitled to have the issue of voluntariness, thus properly raised, determined by the jury. He says that there was no proper legal basis for the courts in British Columbia to deprive him of the benefit of an evidentiary ruling which put in issue the Crown's ability to prove the *actus reus* of the offence.

The trial judge ruled that the evidence of involuntariness was only relevant (if at all) to a defence of not criminally responsible by reason of mental disorder (NCRMD). This was upheld by the Court of Appeal. When it is appreciated that all of the experts agreed the appellant did not suffer from any condition that medicine would classify as a disease of the mind, it is perhaps not surprising that the jury found the accused to be sane. He was convicted of manslaughter. The contention of the appellant that the act of killing, while not the product of a mentally disordered mind, was nevertheless involuntary, was never put to the jury.

The appellant argues that the judicial reasoning that effectively took the issue of voluntariness away from the jury violates the presumption of his innocence and his entitlement to the benefit of a jury trial guaranteed by s. 11(*d*) and (*f*) and is not saved by s. 1 of the Canadian *Charter of Rights and Freedoms*.

. . . .

In my view, it follows from the concurrent findings in the courts below (that the appellant successfully put in issue his consciousness at the time of the offence) that he was entitled to the jury's verdict on whether or not his conduct, though sane, was involuntary. That issue having been withdrawn from the jury, and the Crown thereby having been relieved of the one real challenge to its proof, the appellant is entitled to a new trial.

. . . .

The jury in this case, for example, had before it the testimony of the Crown psychiatrist that the appellant's violent response to his wife's verbal attack was entirely too purposeful and the loss of memory entirely too convenient to be considered "involuntary". The members of the jury could, I think, have been counted on to exhibit powerful scepticism about such evidence. Anyone who thinks a jury of bus drivers, office workers and other practical people will be less sceptical than members of the bench or professors of law has perhaps spent insufficient time in buses or around office coffee machines.

(5) Conclusion on the Automatism Issue

In the result, I believe the appellant was entitled to have the plea of non-mental disorder automatism left to the jury in this case in light of the trial judge's evidentiary ruling that there was evidence the appellant was unconscious throughout the commission of the offence, for the following reasons.

Firstly, I do not accept the Crown's argument that a judge-made classification of situations into mental disorder automatism and non-mental disorder automatism can relieve the Crown of the obligation to prove all of the elements of the offence, including voluntariness. As stated, such an interpretation encounters strong objections under s. 7 and s. 11(*d*) of the *Charter*, and there has been no attempt in this case to provide a s. 1 justification.

Secondly, imposition of a persuasive burden of proof on the appellant to establish "involuntariness" on a balance of probabilities, in substitution for the present evidential burden, runs into the same *Charter* problems, and no attempt has been made in the record to justify it.

Thirdly, the "internal cause" theory, on which the Crown rested its argument, cannot be used to deprive the appellant of the benefit of the jury's consideration of the voluntariness of his action, once he had met the evidential onus, without risking a violation of s. 11(*f*) of the *Charter*. *Rabey*'s treatment of the internal cause theory has to be looked at in light of the decision of this court in *Parks, supra*, which signalled some serious reservations about the usefulness of the "internal cause" theory, except as an "analytical tool". *Rabey*, as clarified in *Parks*, does not impose a presumption that a lack of voluntariness must be attributed to the existence of a mental disorder any time there is no identification of a convincing external cause. Once the appellant in this case had discharged his evidential onus, he was entitled to have the issue of voluntariness go to the jury.

Fourthly, it was wrong of the courts to require the appellant to substitute for his chosen defence of involuntariness the conceptually quite different plea of insanity. One of the few points of agreement between the defence and Crown experts at trial was that the appellant did not suffer from anything that could be described medically as a disease of the mind. He was either unconscious at the time of the killing or he was not telling the truth at the time of the trial. This was a question for the jury. The statutory inquiry into whether he was "suffering from a mental disorder" that rendered him "incapable of appreciating the nature and quality of the act or omission or of knowing that it was wrong" are qualitative questions that are not really responsive to his allegation that he was not conscious of having acted at all.

Finally, the evidence established that there *are* states of automatism where perfectly sane people lose conscious control over their actions. At that point, it was up to the jury, not the judge, to decide if the appellant had brought himself within the physical and mental condition thus identified. As Dickson C.J. observed in *Bernard, supra,* at p. 848, the jurors were "perfectly capable of sizing the matter up".

BASTARACHE J. (L'HEUREUX-DUBÉ, GONTHIER, CORY, and MCLACHLIN JJ. concurring): — The present case involves automatism, and more specifically, "psychological blow" automatism. The appellant claims that nothing more than his wife's words caused him to enter an automatistic state in which his actions, which include stabbing his wife 47 times, were involuntary. How can an accused demonstrate that mere words caused him to enter an automatistic state such that his actions were involuntary and thus do not attract criminal law sanction? This is the issue raised in this appeal.

. . . .

Nature and Origin of the Burdens Applied in Cases Involving Claims of Automatism

This court has stated on many occasions that it is a fundamental principle of criminal law that only voluntary actions will attract findings of guilt. [Citations omitted.]

In *Parks, supra,* La Forest J. classified automatism as a sub-set of the voluntariness requirement, which he too recognized as part of the *actus reus* component of criminal responsibility. I agree and would add that voluntariness, rather than consciousness, is the key legal element of automatistic behaviour since a defence of automatism amounts to a denial of the voluntariness component of the *actus reus*.

The law presumes that people act voluntarily. Accordingly, since a defence of automatism amounts to a claim that one's actions were not voluntary, the accused must rebut the presumption of voluntariness. An evidentiary burden is thereby imposed on the accused. The nature of this evidentiary burden stems from the legal burden imposed in cases involving claims of automatism. Generally, the legal burden in such cases has been on the Crown to prove voluntariness, a component of the *actus reus*, beyond a reasonable doubt — hence Dickson J.'s contention in *Rabey* that an accused claiming automatism need only raise evidence sufficient to permit a properly instructed jury to find a reasonable doubt as to voluntariness in order to rebut the presumption of voluntariness. The Crown then has the legal burden of proving voluntariness beyond a reasonable doubt to the trier of fact. If the Crown fails to satisfy this burden, the accused will be acquitted.

. . . .

In her 1993 *Proposals to amend the Criminal Code (General Principles)*, the Minister of Justice recommended that the legal burden of proof in all cases of automatism be on the party that raises the issue on a balance of probabilities. This is the same legal burden that this court applied to a claim of extreme intoxication akin to a state of automatism in *Daviault, supra*. It is also the legal burden Parliament assigned to the defence of mental disorder in s. 16 of the *Code*, which, as mentioned above, is equally applicable to voluntary and involuntary actions stemming from a disease of the mind and therefore applies to mental disorder automatism.[16] As I explained above, different legal approaches to claims of automatism, whether based on the context in which the alleged automatism arose or on the distinction between mental disorder and non-mental disorder automatism, is problematic and should be avoided.

. . . .

An appropriate legal burden applicable to all cases involving claims of automatism must reflect the policy concerns which surround claims of automatism.

. . . .

The foregoing leads me to the conclusion that the legal burden in cases involving claims of automatism must be on the defence to prove involuntariness on a balance of probabilities to the trier of fact. This is the same burden supported

---

16 Elsewhere in his judgment, Justice Bastarache says "the terms 'mental disorder' automatism and 'non-mental disorder' automatism rather than 'insane' automatism and 'non-insane' automatism more accurately reflect the recent changes to s. 16 of the *Code*, and the addition of Part XX.1 of the *Code*."

by Lord Goddard, dissenting in *Hill v. Baxter*, [1958] 1 Q.B. 277, at pp. 282-83, and imposed in some American jurisdictions; see for example *State v. Caddell*, 215 S.E.2d 348 (N.C. 1975); *Fulcher v. State*, 633 P.2d 142 (Wyo. 1981); *Polston v. State*, 685 P.2d 1 (Wyo. 1984); *State v. Fields*, 376 S.E.2d 740 (N.C. 1989).

In *Chaulk* and *Daviault* this court recognized that although placing a balance of probabilities burden on the defence with respect to an element of the offence constitutes a limitation of an accused person's rights under s. 11(*d*) of the *Charter*, it can be justified under s. 1. In my opinion, the burden is also justified in the present case. The law presumes that people act voluntarily in order to avoid placing the onerous burden of proving voluntariness beyond a reasonable doubt on the Crown. Like extreme drunkenness akin to automatism, genuine cases of automatism will be extremely rare. However, because automatism is easily feigned and all knowledge of its occurrence rests with the accused, putting a legal burden on the accused to prove involuntariness on a balance of probabilities is necessary to further the objective behind the presumption of voluntariness. In contrast, saddling the Crown with the legal burden of proving voluntariness beyond a reasonable doubt actually defeats the purpose of the presumption of voluntariness. Thus, requiring that an accused bear the legal burden of proving involuntariness on a balance of probabilities is justified under s. 1. There is therefore no violation of the Constitution.

. . . .

To sum up, in order to satisfy the evidentiary or proper foundation burden in cases involving claims of automatism, the defence must make an assertion of involuntariness and call expert psychiatric or psychological evidence confirming that assertion. However, it is an error of law to conclude that this defence burden has been satisfied simply because the defence has met these two requirements. The burden will only be met where the trial judge concludes that there is evidence upon which a properly instructed jury could find that the accused acted involuntarily on a balance of probabilities. In reaching this conclusion, the trial judge will first examine the psychiatric or psychological evidence and inquire into the foundation and nature of the expert opinion. The trial judge will also examine all other available evidence, if any. Relevant factors are not a closed category and may, by way of example, include: the severity of the triggering stimulus, corroborating evidence of bystanders, corroborating medical history of automatistic-like dissociative states, whether there is evidence of a motive for the crime, and whether the alleged trigger of the automatism is also the victim of the automatistic violence. I point out that no single factor is meant to be determinative. Indeed, there may be cases in which the psychiatric or psychological evidence goes beyond simply corroborating the accused's version of events, for example, where it establishes a documented history of automatistic-like dissociative states. Furthermore, the ever advancing state of medical knowledge may lead to a finding that other types of evidence are also indicative of involuntariness. I leave it to the discretion and experience of trial judges to weigh all of the evidence available on a case-by-case basis and to determine whether a properly instructed jury could find that the accused acted involuntarily on a balance of probabilities.

Step 2: Determining Whether to Leave Mental Disorder or Non-Mental Disorder Automatism with the Trier of Fact

. . . .

The determination of whether mental disorder or non-mental disorder automatism should be left with the trier of fact must be undertaken very carefully since it will have serious ramifications for both the individual accused and society in general. As mentioned above, mental disorder automatism is subsumed by the defence of mental disorder as set out in the *Code*. Accordingly, a successful defence of mental disorder automatism will result in a verdict of not criminally responsible on account of mental disorder as dictated by s. 672.34 of the *Code*. Under s. 672.54, an accused who receives this qualified acquittal may be discharged absolutely, discharged conditionally or detained in a hospital. In contrast, a successful defence of non-mental disorder automatism will always result in an absolute acquittal.

. . . .

Taken alone, the question of what mental conditions are included in the term disease of the mind is a question of law. However, the trial judge must also determine whether the condition the accused claims to have suffered from satisfies the legal test for disease of the mind. This involves an assessment of the particular evidence in the case rather than a general principle of law and is thus a question of mixed law and fact. See *Southam, supra*, at paras. 35 and 36. The question of whether the accused actually suffered from a disease of the mind is a question of fact to be determined by the trier of fact. See *Rabey* (S.C.C.), *supra*, at p. 519, *per* Ritchie J.; *Parks, supra*, at p. 897, *per* La Forest J.; and *Bratty, supra*, at p. 412, *per* Lord Denning.

In response to the above-mentioned proposed revisions to the *Code* regarding automatism, the Canadian Psychiatric Association submitted a Brief to the House of Commons Standing Committee on Justice and the Solicitor General. In this brief, the Association, on behalf of its 2,400 members nationwide, suggested that from a medical perspective, all automatism necessarily stems from mental disorder. Accordingly, the Association recommended that non-mental disorder automatism be eliminated and all claims of automatism be classified as mental disorders.

Since mental disorder is a legal term, the opinion of the Canadian Psychiatric Association, while relevant, is not determinative of whether two distinct forms of automatism, mental disorder and non-mental disorder, should continue to be recognized at law. In my opinion, this court should not go so far as to eliminate the defence of non-mental disorder automatism as the Association suggests. However, I take judicial notice that it will only be in rare cases that automatism is not caused by mental disorder. Indeed, since the trial judge will have already concluded that there is evidence upon which a properly instructed jury could find that the accused acted involuntarily on a balance of probabilities, there is a serious question as to the existence of an operating mind by the time the disease of the mind issue is considered. The foregoing lends itself to a rule that trial judges start from the proposition that the condition the accused claims to have suffered from is a disease of the mind. They must then determine whether the evidence in the particular case takes the condition out of the disease of the mind category. This approach is consistent with this court's decision in *Rabey, supra*.

Determining Whether the Conditions the Accused Claims to Have Suffered from is a Disease of the Mind

In *Parks*, La Forest J. recognized that there are two distinct approaches to the disease of the mind inquiry: the internal cause theory and the continuing danger theory. He recognized the internal cause theory as the dominant approach in Canadian jurisprudence but concluded, at p. 902, that this theory "is really meant to be used only as an analytical tool, and not as an all-encompassing methodology". This conclusion stemmed from a finding that somnambulism, the alleged trigger of the automatism in *Parks*, raises unique problems which are not well-suited to analysis under the internal cause theory. I agree that the internal cause theory cannot be regarded as a universal classificatory scheme for "disease of the mind". There will be cases in which the approach is not helpful because, in the words of La Forest J., at p. 903, "the dichotomy between internal and external causes becomes blurred". Accordingly, a new approach to the disease of the mind inquiry is in order. As I will explain below, a more holistic approach, like that developed by La Forest J. in *Parks*, must be available to trial judges in dealing with the disease of the mind question. This approach must be informed by the internal cause theory, the continuing danger theory and the policy concerns raised in this court's decisions in *Rabey* and *Parks*.

[The Court then described the jurisprudence surrounding the Internal Cause Theory and the Continuing Danger Theory and concluded.]

In my opinion, trial judges should continue to consider the continuing danger theory as a factor in the determination of whether a condition should be classified as a disease of the mind. However, I emphasize that the continuing danger factor should not be viewed as an alternative or mutually exclusive approach to the internal cause factor. Although different, both of these approaches are relevant factors in the disease of the mind inquiry. As such, in any given case a trial judge may find one, the other or both of these approaches of assistance. To reflect this unified, holistic approach to the disease of the mind question, it is therefore more appropriate to refer to the internal cause factor and the continuing danger factor, rather than the internal cause theory and the continuing danger theory.

. . . .

(3) Other Policy Factors

There may be cases in which consideration of the internal cause and continuing danger factors alone does not permit a conclusive answer to the disease of the mind question. Such will be the case, for example, where the internal cause factor is not helpful because it is impossible to classify the alleged cause of the automatism as internal or external, and the continuing danger factor is inconclusive because there is no continuing danger of violence. Accordingly, a holistic approach to disease of the mind must also permit trial judges to consider other policy concerns which underlie this inquiry. As mentioned above, in *Rabey* and *Parks*, this court outlined some of the policy concerns which surround automatism. I have already referred to those specific policy concerns earlier in these reasons. I repeat that I do not view those policy concerns as a closed category. In any given automatism case, a trial judge may identify a policy factor which this court has not expressly recognized. Any such valid policy concern can be considered by the trial judge in order to determine whether the condition the accused claims to have suffered from is a disease of the mind. In determining this issue, policy concerns assist trial judges in answering the fundamental question of mixed law and fact which is at the centre of the disease of the mind inquiry: whether society requires protection from the accused and, consequently, whether the accused should be subject to evaluation under the regime contained in Part XX.1 of the *Code*.

Application to the Present Case

. . . .

Turning to the disease of the mind stage of the automatism analysis, I note that the evidence in this case raised *only one alleged cause* of automatism, Donna Stone's words. Based on this evidence, the trial judge found that only mental disorder automatism should be left with the jury. This conclusion was based primarily on a finding that the present case is indistinguishable from *MacLeod*, *supra*. Such reliance on precedent fails to reveal what effect, if any, the internal cause factor, the continuing danger factor and other policy factors had on the decision to leave only mental disorder automatism with the jury. This is not in accordance with the holistic approach to the disease of the mind question set out in these reasons. However, the internal cause factor and the continuing danger factor, as well as the other policy factors set out in this court's decisions in *Rabey* and *Parks* all support the trial judge's finding that the condition the appellant alleges to have suffered from is a disease of the mind in the legal sense. In particular, the trigger in this case was not, in the words of Martin J.A. quoted in this court's decision in *Rabey*, at p. 520, "extraordinary external events" that would amount to an extreme shock or psychological blow that would cause a normal person, in the circumstances of the accused, to suffer a dissociation in the absence of a disease of the mind. Accordingly, I find that the trial judge nevertheless reached the correct result on the disease of the mind question. As previously noted, in such a case, only mental disorder automatism must be put to the jury. There is no reason to go beyond the facts of this case in applying the rules discussed above.

In the end, I must conclude that no substantial wrong or miscarriage of justice occurred in the present case.

It is usually regarded as a wise proposition that a judge should not pronounce on matters that were not in issue between the parties and accordingly were not argued. Should the court have considered reversing the onus of proof although the Crown and no intervenor addressed the issue? Are you satisfied with the majority's authority and justification of a presumption of voluntariness and requiring the accused to prove sane automatism on a balance of probabilities? What are the onus implications for other defences such as intoxication and self-defence? Wasn't the presumption of innocence under s. 11(*d*) implicated? What of *Laba* concerning s. 1 justification? The court in *Laba* held that an evidentiary burden should be considered before justifying a persuasive burden for an accused. See critical comments by Delisle, "*Stone:* Judicial Activism Gone Awry to Presume Guilt" (1999), 24 C.R. (5th) 91; David Paciocco, "Death by *Stone*-ing: The Demise of the Defence of Simple Automatism" (1999), 24 C.R. (5th) 273 and "Editorial, Rewriting Automatism" (1999), 4 *Can. Crim. L.R.* 119.

For the view that psychological blow automatism is not based on sound psychological assumptions, see James D. Livingston and Simon N. Verdun-Jones, "Sidebar Psychology:Discussing the Defence of Psychological-Blow Automatism" (2002), 47 *Crim. L.Q.* 79.

R. v. LUEDECKE

2008 ONCA 716, 61 C.R. (6th) 139, 236 C.C.C. (3d) 317, 2008 CarswellOnt
6024 (Ont. C.A.)

The accused and the complainant were guests at a large house party in Toronto where an annual croquet tournament was being held. The complainant attended the party with some friends. At around 2 a.m. she fell asleep on an L-shaped couch while waiting for her friends to depart. At about 5 a.m. she was awakened by a man who was having intercourse with her. He had pulled down her underwear and pushed up her skirt. She pushed him off her, shouted at him "Who are you, what are you doing?". She had no idea who he was. She screamed and pushed him away. He looked dazed and grabbed her belongings. When she came back to get her keys, she found the man still standing in the living room. When she asked who he was, he identified himself as "Jan." She did not recognize him. The complainant went to the hospital and later called police.

The accused, a landscaper, gave a voluntary videotaped statement to police. He stated that the day prior to the party he had been drinking and consuming magic mushrooms at a friend's cottage on Georgian Bay. He arose at dawn, swam, and then drove back to Toronto, where he attended the party. At the party he consumed eight to twelve beers, a couple of drinks of rum and Coke, and a couple of vodkas. By the time he fell asleep on the same couch as the complainant he was very drunk and had been awake for 22 hours. The next thing he remembered was being pushed off the couch by a woman onto the floor. He drove to his parents' house and fell asleep again. When he awoke he saw that he was wearing a condom, which he flushed down the toilet. He went back to sleep and awoke with a vague recollection that something had happened. The defence advanced the defence of non-insane automatism.

The accused testified that he had probably had sexual intercourse with the complainant without her consent, although he could not remember what had happened. The defence called a sleep disorder expert. The expert diagnosed the accused with parasomnia, a disorder in which a person experiences a sudden unexplained arousal from deep sleep, where people are not aware of what they are doing and behave in abnormal ways. He testified that this behaviour could include acts as simple as hand gestures, talking or walking and more rarely acts as complicated as eating, sexual acts or driving a car. He relied on the accused's past history of sleep problems, his statements that he had four prior incidents of what he termed "sexsomnia" with former girlfriends and brainwave measurements of the accused taken in a sleep laboratory. The defence expert also testified that physical activity, sleep deprivation, alcohol and stress increase the likelihood of triggering a parasomnistic episode. He further testified that the parasomnia was not a mental illness or disease of the mind. There was no cure but it could be controlled with good sleep habits, limiting alcohol consumption and medication.

A witness proffered by the Crown to give expert evidence on sleep disorders was not qualified by the court and not permitted to testify. The Crown argued that the defence evidence was based on hearsay, and that the evidence of parasomnistic behaviour did not support a conclusion that the accused could carry out fine motor skills while asleep. This incident was an attack on a stranger and was therefore dissimilar to the alleged previous incidents which, if they occurred, took place in the context of consensual relationships. The Crown argued that the accused was not in a state of automatism when he removed his and the complainant's clothes, put on a condom, and sexually assaulted the complainant.

The trial judge, relying mainly on the uncontradicted evidence of the defence expert found that the accused's actions were involuntary, that he had no control over his actions and that they were not the product of a mental disorder. He acquitted. The Crown appealed.

DOHERTY J.A. (BORINS and LANG JJ.A. concurring): —

. . . .

E. ANALYSIS

[52] Before testing the trial judge's characterization of the respondent's parasomnia as non-mental disorder automatism against the binding jurisprudence, I will sketch in the necessary legal background.

(i) Automatism Claims

[53] Conduct that is not voluntary cannot be criminal: *Rabey*, per Ritchie J. (majority) at p. 6, per Dickson J. (dissenting on other grounds) at p. 26; *Parks*. The voluntariness requirement is a principle of fundamental justice protected by s. 7 and s. 11(d) of the *Charter*: *R. v. Daviault* (1994), 93 C.C.C. (3d) 21 (S.C.C.), at pp. 48-49, 69.

[54] A claim by an accused that his or her conduct was involuntary and should result in an acquittal for that reason can arise in a variety of very different circumstances. Automatism is the legal term used to describe one specific kind of involuntary action: see *Bratty v. Attorney General for Northern Ireland*, (1963) 3 All E.R. 523 (H.L.), per Lord Denning at pp. 408-409; *Parks*, per La Forest J. at p. 302. Automatism refers to involuntary conduct that is the product of a mental state in which the conscious mind is disassociated from the part of the mind that controls action. A person in a state of automatism may perform acts, sometimes complicated and apparently purposeful acts, but have no control over those actions: William Wilson, et al., "Violence, Sleepwalking and the Criminal Law: (2) The Legal Aspects" (2005) Crim. L.R. 614, at pp. 615-16. North P. put it this way in *R. v. Burr*, [1969] N.Z.L.R. 736 (C.A.), at p. 744:

> In my opinion then there is now clear judicial authority for the view that in order for a defence of automatism to succeed, *the person whose conduct is under review must be unconscious of what he was doing. In short that what he did was an unconscious involuntary act... [I]n my opinion, the evidence must be sufficient to lay a proper foundation for the plea that the accused person acted through his body and without the assistance of his mind, in the sense that he*

was not able to make the necessary decisions and to determine whether or not to do the act.
[Emphasis added.]

[55]   The disassociative state that is the hallmark of automatism can be caused by many things including disease, mental illness, concussion, drugs, and parasomnia. Each of these conditions can produce a condition in which an accused, while capable of complex, apparently goal-oriented conduct, is incapable of exercising any control over those actions. As will be discussed below, the cause of the automatism is an important consideration in characterizing the nature of the automatism.

[56]   The automatism "defence" is not a defence in the true sense but is a denial of the commission of the *actus reus* of the crime. Absent the commission of the prohibited act, there can be no crime and hence no criminal liability. A person who is unable to decide whether to perform an act and unable to control the performance of the act cannot be said, in any meaningful sense, to have committed the act. Nor can it be appropriate in a criminal justice system in which liability is predicated on personal responsibility to convict persons based on conduct which those persons have no ability to control: see *Stone*, per Bastarache J. at p. 417, per Binnie J. (dissent) at pp. 378-79; Don Stuart, *Canadian Criminal Law: A Treatise*, 5th ed. (Toronto: Carswell, 2007), at pp. 107-110; David Ormerod, Smith & Hogan *Criminal Law*, 11th ed. (New York: Oxford University Press, 2005), at pp. 44-46; Andrew Ashworth, *Principles of Criminal Law*, 5th ed. (New York: Oxford University Press, 2006), at pp. 98-100; Stanley Yeo, "Putting Voluntariness Back Into Automatism" (2001) 32 V.U.W.L.R. 15.

[57]   Automatism claims raise legitimate questions about an accused's mental status and his or her potential danger to the public. These claims are almost always advanced in cases where the accused has caused serious personal injury or at least put members of the public at serious risk. It hardly seems controversial that persons who engage in what would otherwise be regarded as serious criminal conduct and claim to have had absolutely no control over that conduct should have their mental health and their right to remain at liberty scrutinized. Automatism claims, which by their very nature assert that the accused acted while in an abnormal and impaired mental state, inevitably bring into play the exemption to criminal liability created by s. 16 of the *Criminal Code*.

[58]   Section 16 exempts persons from criminal responsibility if, as a result of a "mental disorder", they were incapable of appreciating the nature and quality of their acts or of knowing that their acts were wrong. As Binnie J. observed in dissent in *Stone*, at paras. 78-83, s. 16 does not speak to the voluntariness of one's actions but instead addresses cognitive functions that assume voluntary conduct. It is, however, accepted in Canada, and throughout the Commonwealth, that a person whose conduct is involuntary because of a condition that is the product of a mental disorder falls exclusively within the purview of the

"insanity" defence: see *R. v. Revelle* (1979), 48 C.C.C. (2d) 267 (Ont. C.A.), at p. 271, aff'd (1981), 61 C.C.C. (2d) 575; *Rabey* (Ont. C.A.), at p. 472, (S.C.C.), at p. 6; *Stone*, per Bastarache J., for the majority, at paras. 160-161; *Attorney-General's Reference* (No. 2 of 1992), [1994] Q.B. 91 (C.A.), at pp. 104-105; *R. v. Falconer* (1990), 171 C.L.R. 30 (H.C.); *The Queen v. Cottle*, [1958] N.Z.L.R. 999 (C.A.).

[59]   If an accused's automatism is rooted in a mental disorder, the accused will not be acquitted but will be found NCR-MD. Under Part XX.I of the *Criminal Code*, a person found NCR-MD is subject to a post-verdict disposition hearing before either the trial judge or a Review Board. Section 672.54 of the *Criminal Code* lists the dispositions available. These range from an absolute discharge to confinement in a hospital. A person found NCR-MD must be granted an absolute discharge if the court or review board is not satisfied that he or she poses a "significant risk": see *Winko v. British Columbia (Forensic Psychiatric Institute)* (1999), 135 C.C.C. (3d) 129 (S.C.C.).

[60]   The distinction between non-mental disorder automatism and mental disorder automatism depends on whether the automatistic state is the product of a "mental disorder". That term is defined in s. 2 of the *Criminal Code* as a "disease of the mind". That phrase, which is almost as old as the insanity defence itself, describes a legal and not a medical concept, the purpose of which is normative, not diagnostic: *Rabey*, per Martin J.A. at pp. 473-74; *Parks*, per La Forest J. at p. 304. I will use the two phrases interchangeably.

[61]   The broader the definition of mental disorder, the narrower the ambit of the "defence" of non-mental disorder automatism. Canadian courts have adopted a very broad definition. In *R. v. Cooper* (1980), 51 C.C.C. (2d) 129 (S.C.C.), at p. 144, Dickson J. said:

> In summary, one might say that in a legal sense "disease of the mind" embraces any illness, disorder or abnormal condition which impairs the human mind and its functioning, excluding however, self-induced states caused by alcohol or drugs, as well as transitory mental states such as hysteria or concussion.

[62]   Professor Brudner has described the effect of this broad definition in these terms:

> Clearly the definition of mental disease elaborated by the courts in the aforementioned cases bears little resemblance to any that a psychiatrist might proffer. *It is a legal rather than a medical definition – one carefully crafted with a view to a policy of controlling persons thought to be dangerous.* This definition ensures, first of all, that anyone accused of a crime who lacked conscious choice because of a dangerous and potentially recurrent disorder or event will not go free but will be subject to continued detention and confinement after acquittal. Obversely, it ensures that only those whose lack of conscious choice was caused by an external and probably non-recurrent event will have the benefit of a defence that leads to an absolute acquittal and a return to society. [Emphasis added.]

[63]   The broad definition of the term "mental disorder" has led to the channelling of most automatism claims into the NCR-MD pool. That trend reached its high water mark in *Stone*. Bastarache J., for the majority, went so far as to take judicial notice "that it will only be in rare cases that automatism is not caused by mental disorder". Bastarache J. further observed, at para. 199, that trial judges should start with the assumption that the condition constitutes a disease of the mind. Trial judges should then look to the evidence to determine whether that presumption has been rebutted. After *Stone*, many argue that successful claims of non-mental disorder automatism will be limited to those very rare "one off" cases in which an accused suffers a single incident of automatism, and where the accused can point to some specific external event that precipitated that event, can demonstrate that the event is unlikely to reoccur, and finally, can show that the event could have produced a disassociative state in an otherwise "normal" person.

.   .   .   .

[90]   *Stone* alters the approach to the characterization of automatism as non-mental disorder automatism or mental disorder automatism in at least two significant ways. First, after *Stone* the trial judge must begin from the premise that the automatism is caused by a disease of the mind and look to the evidence to determine whether it convinces him or her that the condition is not a "disease of the mind". This approach is in direct contrast with *Parks* where the non-mental disorder automatism claim succeeded because the Crown failed to prove that the condition was caused by a disease of the mind.

[91]   Second, although *Stone* accepts the multi-factored approach to the policy component of the characterization of the automatism set out in *Parks*, it refocuses the continuing danger aspect of that approach. After *Stone*, in evaluating the risk of repetition and hence the danger to the public, trial judges must not limit their inquiry only to the risk of further violence while in an automatistic state. Rather, trial judges must examine the risk of the recurrence of the factors or events that triggered the accused's automatistic state. Commenting on this refinement of the continuing danger inquiry Professor Paciocco observes in "Death by *Stone*-ing: The Demise of the Defence of Simple Automatism" at p. 281:

> This part of the judgment effectively reverses *Parks*. The triggers for Parks' somnambulism or sleep-walking included stress, fatigue, insomnia and exercise. There is no point in speaking of the likelihood of such triggers being present in the future. It is a veritable certainty that they will be. *It is clear that had Parks been tried using the Stone test, the only defence that would have been left to the jury would be "mental disorder automatism".* [Emphasis added.]

[92]   Professor Paciocco's prediction is largely borne out by the Canadian parasomnia cases that post-date Stone. I am aware of five including this case. In the other four cases, the automatistic states flowing from the parasomnia were

held to constitute diseases of the mind: see *Canada v. Campbell* (2000), 35 C.R. (5th) 314 (Ont. S.C); *R. v. Balenko*, [2000] Q.J. No. 717 (C.Q. (Crim. Div.)); *R. v. Romas* (2002), 6 M.V.R. (5th) 101 (B.C. Prov. Ct.); and *R. v. Churchyard*, an unreported decision of Smith J. released November 19, 2003 (Ont. S.C.).

[93]   The majority position in *Stone* signals a strong preference for a finding of NCR-MD in cases where an accused establishes that he or she was in a disassociative state and acted involuntarily. Social defence concerns, inevitably present in such cases, must to a large degree drive the analysis in automatism cases after *Stone*.

[94]   The strong preference for an NCR-MD verdict expressed in *Stone* is explained in part by the very different treatment accorded those found NCR-MD compared to the historical treatment provided to those found not guilty by reason of insanity, as was the case at the time of the trial in *Parks*. Prior to 1991, persons found not guilty by reason of insanity were detained indefinitely at the pleasure of the Lieutenant Governor in Council. The provisions of Part XX.I of the *Criminal Code* not only disposed of the insanity nomenclature but completely changed the post-verdict treatment of those found NCR-MD: S.C. 1991, c. 43.

[95]   I do not think it is coincidental that *Stone* and *Winko*, the leading case on the interpretation of Part XX.I of the *Criminal Code*, were heard by the same nine judges about ten days apart, and decided about three weeks apart several months later. It is hard to resist the inference that *Stone* was written having in mind what the court would say three weeks later when it released its decision in *Winko*.

[96]   In *Winko*, McLachlin J. explained the operation of Part XX.I this way at para. 43:

> In summary, the purpose of Part XX.I is to replace the common law regime for the treatment of those who offend while mentally ill with a new approach emphasizing individualized assessment and the provision of opportunities for appropriate treatment. Under Part XX.I, the NCR accused is neither convicted nor acquitted. Instead, he or she is found not criminally responsible by reason of illness at the time of the offence. This is not a finding of dangerousness. *It is rather a finding that triggers a balanced assessment of the offender's possible dangerousness and of what treatment-associated measures are required to offset it. Throughout the process the offender is to be treated with dignity and accorded the maximum liberty compatible with Part XX.I's goals of public protection and fairness to the NCR accused.* [Emphasis added.]

[97]   *Winko* provides a detailed examination of s. 672.54, the provision governing the dispositions available with respect to persons found NCR-MD. As interpreted in *Winko*, s. 672.54 requires the absolute discharge of anyone found NCR-MD unless the court or the Review Board determines that the

individual poses "a significant threat to the public". McLachlin J. said at para. 52:

> This interpretation of s. 672.54 eliminates any need for the NCR accused to prove lack of dangerousness and relieves him or her of any legal or evidentiary burden. If the evidence does not support the conclusion that the NCR accused is a significant risk, the NCR accused need do nothing; the only possible order is an absolute discharge.

[98]   The risk determination required by s. 672.54 cannot not be based on speculation or assumptions about how persons with mental disorders behave. There must be evidence establishing the significant risk. That risk must be a real risk of criminal conduct involving physical or psychological harm to individuals in the community. A risk of trivial harm or miniscule risk of significant harm will not suffice to deprive the individual of his or her liberty: *Winko*, at para. 57.

[99]   As explained in *Winko*, there are also significant procedural safeguards built into Part XX.I of the *Criminal Code*. A person found NCR-MD must receive a timely disposition hearing before either the court or the Review Board. He or she has full access to the bail provisions pending that hearing. The disposition hearing is not adversarial but provides for a full and wide-ranging inquiry into all factors relevant to the appropriate disposition. The disposition hearing allows for the input of medical professionals who will have had a chance to assess the person found NCR-MD and to develop opinions based on an up-to-date assessment of that person's condition. Where, as in most cases, the disposition hearing is before the Review Board, the panel will include a psychiatrist.

[100]   A combined reading of *Stone* and *Winko* yields a comprehensive response to automatism claims. At the pre-verdict stage, social defence concerns dominate. Those concerns focus on the risk posed by the potential recurrence of the conduct in issue. Where that risk exists, the risk combined with the occurrence of the conduct that led to the criminal proceedings will almost always justify further inquiry into the accused's dangerousness so as to properly protect the public.

[101]   In the post-verdict stage, however, the emphasis shifts to an individualized assessment of the actual dangerousness of the person found NCR-MD. Where that personalized assessment does not demonstrate the requisite significant risk, the person found NCR-MD must receive an absolute discharge. Even where a significant risk exists, the disposition order must be tailored to the specific circumstances of the individual and must, to the extent possible, minimize the interference with that individual's liberty.

[102]   *Re Romas*, [2002] B.C.R.B.D. No. 66 (British Columbia Review Board), provides an example of the integration of the *Stone* approach to

automatism and the *Winko* approach to Part XX.I of the *Criminal Code*. At trial (*R. v. Romas*), the accused was charged with an assault-related offence and claimed to have acted as a result of Confusional Sleep Arousal, a sleep disorder. Applying *Stone*, the accused was found NCR-MD. The trial judge referred the matter to the British Columbia Review Board for disposition. About six weeks later the Board, by a majority vote, ordered the accused absolutely discharged. In so ordering, the Board referred to several factors, all of which would seem applicable to the respondent assuming his current condition is consistent with that described at trial.

(ii) The Trial Judge's Application of the Principles in *R. v. Stone*

[103]   I am satisfied that the trial judge failed to appreciate the significance of the hereditary nature of the respondent's condition, failed to give effect to the respondent's well established history of sexsomnia, and failed to appreciate the significance of the strong likelihood of the recurrence of the events that triggered his sexsomnia. The trial judge also failed to appreciate that Dr. Shapiro's medical opinion that parasomnia did not constitute a mental disorder was largely irrelevant to the determination of whether, for policy reasons, the condition should be classified legally as a disease of the mind. These errors led to a failure to apply the proper legal standard when characterizing the respondent's automatism.

[104]   When addressing the cause of the respondent's condition, the trial judge acknowledged that causes internal to the accused, be they physical or mental, were generally treated as indicative of a disease of the mind, while causes external to the accused were generally indicative of a non-mental disorder automatism. The trial judge then said at para. 46:

> The jurisprudence recognizes that somnambulism, as in the *Parks* case, is not suitable to this kind of analysis. Somnambulism is not a disease of the mind.

[105]   The trial judge was wrong to categorically indicate that somnambulism is not a disease of the mind. As *Parks* made clear, it may or may not be depending on the evidence. More significantly to the outcome of this case, I think the trial judge erred in dismissing the potential significance of the causes of the respondent's condition by referring to jurisprudence that had dismissed the internal/external cause distinction as being of no assistance in parasomnia cases. The trial judge should have considered whether, on the evidence, the causes of the parasomnia as explained by Dr. Shapiro offered any insight into the risk of recurrence and hence the potential danger to the public.

[106]   While the cause of parasomnia may not fit within the "external/internal" causal dichotomy described in the case law, Dr. Shapiro's evidence establishes that the predisposition for parasomnia, found in some three per cent of the adult population, is hereditary. A genetic predisposition is the epitome of

an internal cause. Although that disposition does not cause the particular automatistic event, it does predispose the individual to that condition thereby increasing the risk of recurrence. The trial judge erred in discounting the significance of this internal cause of the respondent's condition. He did so based on a misapprehension of the "sleepwalking" case law and a failure to consider evidence relevant to the causal inquiry.

[107]   The trial judge's treatment of the "continuing danger" component of the meaning of "disease of the mind" reveals two errors. First, he found that prior sexsomnia incidents did not assist in assessing the danger to the public because those incidents did not involve criminal conduct. While technically the conduct did involve non-consensual sexual activity, I certainly accept that it was not conduct that should attract a criminal charge.

[108]   Even though the incidents involving former girlfriends did not lead to criminal charges, they were important in assessing the risk posed by the respondent's conduct. These events correspond to the psychiatric history of prior automatistic episodes stressed in *Stone*. The respondent's prior sexsomnia episodes demonstrate that his conduct toward L.O. was not an isolated, "one-off" incident. There were episodes both prior to and subsequent to the attack on L.O. during which the respondent engaged in sexual activity at a time when he was unaware of what he was doing and unable to control himself. In that condition the respondent could not distinguish between a consenting partner and a non-consenting victim. The identity of the subject of the sexual activity was a matter of chance, not a matter of choice.

[109]   I accept that it is perhaps more probable that the respondent would be asleep with or near someone with whom he had a relationship involving consensual sexual relations. It cannot, however, be unexpected that the respondent will find himself asleep in the vicinity of persons with whom he has no relationship. One thinks of an airport or train station waiting room or the sleeping arrangements at a friend's cottage. There is also nothing in the evidence to suggest that the respondent could not move from room to room while in a parasomniac state and engage in non-consensual sexual activity with someone who happens to be in same building but in a different room.

[110]   With respect to the trial judge, his rejection of the prior sexsomnia incidents as having no value in considering whether the respondent posed a risk runs contrary to the fundamental nature of the defence advanced by the respondent. It was central to his position that he had no awareness of what he was doing and no control over his actions. It must follow that he was incapable of distinguishing between a consensual or non-consensual situation while in a parasomniac state. The trial judge should not have relied on a distinction that the accused was incapable of making to diminish the risk posed by the respondent.

[111]   The second error made by the trial judge in examining the "continuing danger" factor arises from his failure to consider the likelihood that the respondent would encounter the events or circumstances that triggered his parasomnia. *Stone*, at p. 440, explicitly directs trial judges to look to the likelihood of the recurrence of the triggering events and not just the likelihood of the recurrence of acts of violence while in an automatistic state.

[112]   The triggers in this case included alcohol, fatigue and stress. These are common place in most people's lives, particularly in the life of a busy, socially active, young man. Had the trial judge addressed the likelihood of the recurrence of the triggering events he would no doubt have found that it was virtually inevitable that some combination of these events would recur and recur with some frequency. On the analysis in *Stone*, the likelihood of recurrence of these triggering events offers significant support for a finding that the respondent's parasomnia should be characterized as a disease of the mind.

[113]   The trial judge also placed considerable emphasis on the firmness of Dr. Shapiro's evidence that the respondent's parasomnia did not constitute a disease of the mind. Dr. Shapiro's opinion that parasomnia did not constitute a disease of the mind, as opposed to his explanation of parasomnia and his opinion that the respondent was in a parasomniac state, had little or no evidentiary value. Nor was the force with which he held that opinion of any significance. As Martin J.A. observed in *Rabey*, at p. 474:

> Indeed, in strictness, a medical witness is not entitled to state that a particular condition is or is not a disease of the mind since that is a legal question. In practice, however, it is often convenient and permissible, in the discretion of the Judge, for a medical witness to testify in those terms.

[114]   The trial judge should not have been influenced by Dr. Shapiro's opinion as to the proper categorization of the respondent's medical condition when deciding whether as a matter of law and for policy reasons that condition should or should not be characterized as a disease of the mind.

[115]   Mr. Addario for the respondent ably, although ultimately unsuccessfully, defended the reasoning of the trial judge. Near the end of his oral submissions he opened a second front in support of his position that the appeal must be dismissed. Mr. Addario submitted that even if a strict application of the analysis set out in *Stone* might suggest an NCR-MD verdict, it would be grossly unfair and unjust to the respondent to label him NCR-MD. Mr. Addario submitted that as wrongheaded as it no doubt is, there is a very strong negative stereotype of persons found to be NCR-MD. Mr. Addario submits that the reality of the respondent's medical condition and his life in general could not be further from that stereotype. He contends that the respondent's parasomnia would not be regarded by any reasonable member of the community as the kind of mental disorder associated with a finding of NCR-MD. Mr. Addario forcefully argues

that, just as the criminal justice system must be concerned with illegitimate automatism claims, it must be concerned that verdicts in automatism cases bear some resemblance to the community's concept of those who should or should not be found NCR-MD.

[116]   There is considerable force in Mr. Addario's submissions. Clearly no reasonable member of the community would, or should, regard the respondent as mentally ill. Indeed, the inappropriateness of labelling persons with parasomnia as mentally ill was acknowledged by Chief Justice Lane in *Burgess*, at p. 776.

[117]   I agree with Mr. Addario's contention that the result in criminal proceedings should, at least on a general level, reflect the community's perception of the appropriate result. Proper labelling is important to the maintaining of the integrity of the criminal justice process. It would be preferable if the *Criminal Code* allowed the court, where it was deemed necessary, to specifically identify in its verdict the condition that caused the involuntary actions, e.g. not criminally responsible on account of parasomnia: see *Ebrahim*, et al., at p. 612. Unfortunately the *Criminal Code* does not provide for that flexibility. Arguably, neither of the available verdicts, not guilty or NCR-MD, would be regarded by the community as particularly apt labels for the respondent.

[118]   The second part of Mr. Addario's submission would have the court accept the negative stereotyping of those found NCR-MD and decline to impose that verdict on the respondent because he does not fit that stereotype. No one should deny the existence of this negative stereotype and the harm it can do to those found NCR-MD. To give effect to Mr. Addario's submission would, however, promote this negative stereotype. Were the court to decline to find the respondent NCR-MD because he does not fit the negative stereotype of persons so found, the court could be taken as accepting that those who are found NCR-MD do fit that stereotype.

[119]   The new mental disorder regime introduced into the *Criminal Code* in 1991 is intended to overcome the improper stereotyping of persons found NCR-MD and to provide for individualized assessment and treatment of those individuals: see *Winko*, at paras. 35-40. The courts can best play a role in the important task of overcoming the negative stereotypes associated with mental illness, not by shaping their verdicts to conform to those stereotypes, but by emphasizing both the basis for a finding of NCR-MD and by explaining what the verdict means. An NCR-MD verdict signals that an accused cannot be held responsible for what would otherwise be his or her criminal act. At the same time, it rejects any suggestion that the accused represents an automatic danger to the public. Instead, the NCR-MD verdict triggers an individualized, careful,

current assessment of the accused's condition leading to a disposition tailored to the individual accused.

Doherty J.A. decided that, given *Criminal Code* limits on the powers of the court in the case of crown appeals against an acquittal, the appropriate order was a new trial limited to the determination of whether the automatism constituted automatism resulting in an acquittal or mental disorder resulting in an NCR-MD verdict. If the evidence remained the same Doherty J.A. indicated that the NCR-MD verdict was the only reasonable verdict available on the current state of the law.

At his new trial, the Crown and defence agreed that the appropriate verdict was NCR-MD. The Ontario Review Board held a disposition hearing and decided that Luedecke should be released absolutely as he no longer posed a significant threat to public safety. The Crown subsequently tried to have Luedecke comply with the provisions of the *Sex Offender Information Registration Act*. That application was dismissed because the Crown had failed to bring it in a timely fashion. See *R. v. Luedecke* (2010), 252 C.C.C. (3d) 542 (Ont. C.J.).

Justice Doherty is impeccably careful in his analysis and he clarifies the law of sane automatism in the light of *Stone*. On the issue of the so-called sexsomnia defence, in this case Luedecke got away lightly. See too Janine Benedet, Annotation to *Luedecke* (trial judgment) (2005) 35 C.R. (6th) 205 (Ont. C.J.) at 206-207. In contrast, Holly Phoenix, "Automatism : A Fading Defence" (2010) 56 Crim. L.Q. 328, is strongly critical. She argues that Luedecke was unnecessarily labelled and presented no significant threat as was found by the subsequent Review Board. This case shows again that in real life the evidence often presents in ways that engage more than one legal doctrine and that this may lead to difficulty and to an unsatisfactory result. Even accepting the evidence that the accused had problems with parasomnia on the night in question, it is hard to look beyond the fact that he was very drunk. The Court of Appeal does not detail the trial finding that at the party Luedecke consumed eight to twelve beers, a couple of drinks of rum and Coke, and a couple of vodkas. So if he was acting in an involuntary way this was to a large extent self-induced. The Court notes that although he had seen a sleep doctor he was not under treatment. So presumably the sleep disorder was not seen to be serious. Was the problem then more the alcohol? And on the issue of involuntariness itself, can the putting on of the condom really be discounted?

R. v. BOUCHARD-LEBRUN

2011 CarswellQue 12785, 2011 SCC 58 (S.C.C.)

Two young men, the accused and another, purchased ecstasy pills of a type known as "*poire bleue*", which they took during the night of October 24. Hours later they decided to go and beat up L for the real or imagined reason that he wore an "upside-down cross" around his neck. Around 5:00 a.m., they illegally entered the building where L lived. They brutally attacked him by punching and kicking him many times. Another occupant of the building, D, went to L's aid but the accused threw D down steps and then stomped his head as he lay on the floor. The assault left D disabled and he will have to spend the rest of his life in hospital.

The trial judge accepted psychiatric evidence that at the material time the accused was suffering from toxic psychosis caused by the voluntary consumption of the ecstasy pills. Two witnesses testified that he had been acting "weirdly" after taking the pills. There were signs of religious delirium during the attack with the accused making references to the Apocalypse, God and the devil. It was accepted that he was in a serious psychotic condition which disappeared days later. He had never experienced a psychotic episode before and was not an addict. The trial judge found that, because of that state of extreme intoxication, the accused had to be acquitted on the counts of breaking and entering with intent to commit a criminal offence, and attempting to break and enter. He then convicted the accused on the counts of aggravated assault on D and assault on L, on the basis that s. 33.1 of the *Criminal Code* provides that self-induced intoxication cannot be a defence to an offence against the bodily integrity of another person. The accused was sentenced to imprisonment for five years.

On appeal against his convictions, the accused argued that his psychosis should have led to a verdict of not criminally responsible on account of mental disorder under s. 16 of the *Criminal Code*. The Quebec Court of Appeal rejected the appeal as did the Supreme Court on the further appeal. We here consider the Court's determination that this was not a case for s. 16. We will revisit the judgment later on its ruling on the issue of intoxication.

LeBel J.: —

[61] For the purposes of the *Criminal Code*, "disease of the mind" is a legal concept with a medical dimension. Although medical expertise plays an essential part in the legal characterization exercise, it has long been established in positive law that whether a particular mental condition can be characterized as a "mental disorder" is a question of law to be decided by the trial judge. In a jury trial, the judge decides this question, not the jury. As Martin J.A. stated in an oft-quoted passage from *Simpson*, "[i]t is the function of the psychiatrist to describe the accused's mental condition and how it is considered from the medical point of view. It is for the Judge to decide whether the condition described is comprehended by the term 'disease of the mind'" (p. 350). If the judge finds as a matter of law that the mental condition of the accused is a "mental disorder", it will ultimately be up to the jury to decide whether, on the facts, the accused was suffering from such a mental disorder at the time of the offence.

[62] Thus, the trial judge is not bound by the medical evidence, since medical experts generally take no account of the policy component of the analysis required by s. 16 *Cr. C.* (*Parks*, at pp. 899-900). Moreover, an expert's opinion on the legal issue of whether the mental condition of the accused constitutes a "mental disorder" within the meaning of the *Criminal Code* has "little or no

evidentiary value" (*R. v. Luedecke*, 2008 ONCA 716, 269 O.A.C. 1, at para. 113).

[63] The respective roles of the expert, the judge and the jury were summarized in *R. v. Stone*, [1999] 2 S.C.R. 290. Writing for the majority, Bastarache J. stated the following:

> Taken alone, the question of what mental conditions are included in the term "disease of the mind" is a question of law. However, the trial judge must also determine whether the condition the accused claims to have suffered from satisfies the legal test for disease of the mind. This involves an assessment of the particular evidence in the case rather than a general principle of law and is thus a question of mixed law and fact. . . . The question of whether the accused actually suffered from a disease of the mind is a question of fact to be determined by the trier of fact. [Citation omitted; para. 197.]

[64] The central issue in this appeal is a question of law within the meaning of *Stone*. It is common ground that the appellant was in a psychotic condition that prevented him from distinguishing right from wrong. The main issue is whether a toxic psychosis caused exclusively by a single episode of intoxication constitutes a "mental disorder" within the meaning of s. 16 *Cr. C.*

[65] It can be seen at this point that the appellant's position poses a serious problem. To argue that toxic psychosis must always be considered a "mental disorder" is to say that the legal characterization exercise under s. 16 *Cr. C.* depends exclusively on a medical diagnosis. If the appellant's position were accepted, psychiatric experts would thus be responsible for determining the scope of the defence of not criminally responsible on account of mental disorder. This argument conflicts directly with this Court's consistent case law over the past three decades and cannot succeed. It would shift the responsibility for deciding whether the accused is guilty from the judge or jury to the expert.

E.   *Specific Problem of a Toxic Psychosis that Results From the Voluntary Consumption of Alcohol or Drugs*

[69] When confronted with a difficult fact situation involving a state of toxic psychosis that emerged while the accused was intoxicated, a court should start from the general principle that temporary psychosis is covered by the exclusion from *Cooper*. This principle is not absolute, however: the accused can rebut the presumption provided for in s. 16(2) *Cr. C.* by showing that, at the material time, he or she was suffering from a disease of the mind that was unrelated to the intoxication-related symptoms. To determine whether an accused has discharged the burden of proof in this respect, the court should adopt the "more holistic approach" described by Bastarache J. in *Stone* (para. 203). As the Attorney General of Ontario ("AGO") suggested in this Court, it is ultimately this "more holistic approach" that will enable a court to determine whether the mental

condition of an accused at the material time constitutes a "mental disorder" for the purposes of s. 16 *Cr. C.* (I.F., at paras. 22-23).

[70] In *Stone*, Bastarache J. proposed a flexible approach structured around two analytical tools and certain policy considerations. The purpose of the approach is to help the courts distinguish mental conditions that fall within the scope of s. 16 *Cr. C.* from those covered by *Cooper*'s exclusion of "self-induced states caused by alcohol or drugs" (p. 1159). In other words, a court should use this approach to determine whether a medically diagnosed disease of the mind constitutes a mental disorder in the legal sense.

[71] The *internal cause factor*, the first of the analytical tools described in *Stone*, involves comparing the accused with a normal person. In that case, Bastarache J. noted that "the trial judge must consider the nature of the trigger and determine whether a normal person in the same circumstances might have reacted to it by entering an automatistic state as the accused claims to have done" (para. 206). The comparison between the circumstances of the accused and those of a normal person will be objective and may be based on the psychiatric evidence. The more the psychiatric evidence suggests that a normal person, that is, a person suffering from no disease of the mind, is susceptible to such a state, the more justified the courts will be in finding that the trigger is external. Such a finding would exclude the condition of the accused from the scope of s. 16 *Cr. C.* The reverse also holds true.

[72] Although the trigger associated with the internal cause factor often involves a "psychological blow", there is no reason why it cannot consist of alcohol or drug use contemporaneous with the offence. What must therefore be determined is what state a normal person might have entered after consuming the same substances in the same quantities as the accused. Since certain factors such as fatigue and the pace of consumption may influence the effects of drugs, this comparison must take account of all the circumstances in which the accused consumed the drugs that triggered the psychotic condition. If a normal person might also have reacted to similar drug use by developing toxic psychosis, it will be easier for the court to find that the mental disorder of the accused was purely external in origin (*Rabey*, at pp. 519 and 533; see also *Moroz*, at para. 46) and was not a disease of the mind within the meaning of the *Criminal Code*.

[73] The second analytical tool, the *continuing danger factor*, is directly related to the need to ensure public safety. The purpose of this factor is to assess the likelihood of recurring danger to others. Where a condition is likely to present a recurring danger, there is a greater chance that it will be regarded as a disease of the mind. To assess this danger, the court must consider, among other factors, "the psychiatric history of the accused and the likelihood that the trigger alleged to have caused the automatistic episode will recur" (*Stone*, at para. 214).

[74] Although Bastarache J.'s reasons were not explicit in this regard, it stands to reason that danger will be recurring only if it is likely to arise again independently of the exercise of the will of the accused. The recurrence of danger is not a factor linked to voluntary behaviour by the accused. This conclusion is consistent with the idea that the effect of the defence provided for in s. 16 *Cr. C.* is to exempt from criminal responsibility an accused whose actions are morally involuntary. The purpose of the defence of mental disorder is to ascertain whether the mental condition of the accused poses an *inherent* danger, that is, a danger that persists despite the will of the accused. As a corollary to this principle, a danger to public safety that might be voluntarily *created* by the accused in the future by consuming drugs would not be the result of a mental disorder for the purposes of s. 16 *Cr. C.*

[75] In *Stone*, Bastarache J. also stated that "a holistic approach to disease of the mind must also permit trial judges to consider other policy concerns which underlie this inquiry" (para. 218). The main policy consideration continues to be the need to protect society from the accused through the special procedure set out in Part XX.1 of the *Criminal Code.* Thus, if the circumstances of a case suggest that a pre-existing condition of the accused does not require any particular treatment and is not a threat to others, the court should more easily hold that the accused was not suffering from a disease of the mind at the time of the alleged events.

[76] The contextual approach required by *Stone* makes it possible to define the scope of this appeal. The purpose of the appeal is not to identify a rule to be applied to every case of toxic psychosis. And because every case has distinctive characteristics, it would be counterproductive to try to formulate an exhaustive definition of the mental conditions covered by *Cooper*'s exclusion of "self-induced states caused by alcohol or drugs". The instant case concerns just one type of toxic psychosis, namely one that resulted *exclusively* from a single episode of self-induced intoxication.

[77] Although the courts can seek assistance from the existing case law, it would be preferable for them to engage in an individualized analysis that takes account of the specific circumstances of each case. This means that the courts should determine on a case-by-case basis, applying the "more holistic approach" from *Stone*, whether the mental condition of each accused is included in or excluded from the definition of "disease of the mind" proposed by Dickson J. in *Cooper*. This approach is consistent with the line of authority based on *Rabey*, in which this Court endorsed Martin J.A.'s opinion that "[p]articular transient mental disturbances may not . . . be capable of being properly categorized in relation to whether they constitute 'disease of the mind' on the basis of a generalized statement and must be decided on a case-by-case basis" (pp. 519-20).

F. *Application of the Principles to This Appeal*

[78] In accordance with the approach set out above, I must now determine whether the appellant was suffering from a mental disorder within the meaning of s. 16 *Cr. C.* at the material time. To do this, it will be helpful to begin by referring to the trial judge's main findings of fact. Judge Decoste found that the appellant, who was highly intoxicated at the material time, was in a psychotic condition caused by the voluntary consumption of drugs. He wrote that [TRANSLATION] "the psychotic condition the accused was in when he committed these criminal acts originated in his drug use during the moments leading up to them" (para. 41). I would also note that the appellant's central argument is based on the contention that toxic psychosis is necessarily a "mental disorder" within the meaning of s. 16 *Cr. C.* because it is an "abnormal effect" of intoxication that affects only those who have a psychological predisposition or whose psyches are particularly fragile.

[79] The evidence in the record does not support the distinction drawn by the appellant between "normal effects" and "abnormal effects" of intoxication. Nor is it compatible with the argument that only persons who are predisposed to a mental disorder are likely to develop toxic psychosis as a result of drug use. For example, Dr. Faucher testified at trial that he saw cases of toxic psychosis [TRANSLATION] "every week" (A.R., at p. 967). As Thibault J.A. noted, the same witness also stated that half (50 percent) of subjects who take drugs containing PCP are likely to develop a psychotic condition when intoxicated. It thus appears that toxic psychosis is unfortunately a fairly frequent phenomenon that seems to result from the high toxicity of chemical drugs.

[80] The application of the first factor from *Stone* thus suggests that the taking of one *"poire bleue"* pill is a specific external factor that contradicts the appellant's argument, since it seems likely that the reaction of a normal person to such a pill would indeed be to develop toxic psychosis. This strongly suggests that the appellant was not suffering from a mental disorder at the time he committed the impugned acts.

[81] The rapid appearance of psychotic symptoms generally indicates that the delusions of the accused can be attributed to a specific external factor. Dr. Faucher's expert assessment, which the trial judge preferred to that of Dr. Turmel, an expert called by the defence, revealed that the rapid reversal of symptoms is characteristic of a toxic psychosis caused by an episode of self-induced intoxication (A.R., at pp. 954-59). Moreover, Professor Parent has written on this topic that [TRANSLATION] "delusions that subside at the same rate as the drug are usually signs of *Substance Intoxication*" ("Les *Troubles psychotiques induits par une substance* en droit pénal canadien: analyse médicale et juridique d'un concept en pleine évolution", at p. 123). Such

delusions therefore do not result from a disease of the mind within the meaning of the *Criminal Code*.

[82] In the instant case, the psychotic symptoms experienced by the appellant began to diminish shortly after he took the *"poire bleue"* pill and continued to do so until they disappeared completely on October 28, 2005. The Court of Appeal held that the disappearance of the symptoms showed that the symptoms of toxic psychosis coincided with the duration of the appellant's intoxication. Thibault J.A. could thus say that [TRANSLATION] "[t]he appellant suffered from no [disease of the mind] before committing the crimes, and once the effects of the drug consumption had passed, he was entirely sane" (para. 77). I see no valid reason to depart from this conclusion.

[83] As for the second factor from *Stone*, there is no evidence indicating that the mental condition of the accused is inherently dangerous in any way. Provided that the appellant abstains from such drugs in the future, which he is capable of doing voluntarily, it would seem that his mental condition poses no threat to public safety. Although I will not adopt a definitive position on this question, I might have concluded otherwise if the appellant had a dependency on drugs that affected his ability to stop using them voluntarily. The likelihood of recurring danger might then be greater.

[84] Finally, after considering all the circumstances of this case, I am satisfied that there is no valid reason to initiate the special procedure provided for in Part XX.1 of the *Criminal Code*. An accused whose mental condition at the material time can be attributed exclusively to a state of temporary self-induced intoxication and who poses no threat to others is not suffering from a mental disorder for the purposes of s. 16 *Cr. C.* The scheme of Part XX.1 applies only if the accused actually suffered from a disease of the mind at the material time. It is not intended to apply to accused persons whose temporary madness was induced artificially by a state of intoxication.

[85] In this context, I conclude that the appellant was not suffering from a "mental disorder" for the purposes of s. 16 *Cr. C.* at the time he committed the assault. He has failed to rebut the presumption that his toxic psychosis was a "self-induced stat[e] caused by alcohol or drugs" in accordance with the definition in *Cooper*. A malfunctioning of the mind that results *exclusively* from self-induced intoxication cannot be considered a disease of the mind in the legal sense, since it is not a product of the individual's inherent psychological makeup. This is true even though medical science may tend to consider such conditions to be diseases of the mind. In circumstances like those of the case at bar, toxic psychosis seems to be nothing more than a symptom, albeit an extreme one, of the accused person's state of self-induced intoxication. Such a state cannot justify exempting an accused from criminal responsibility under s. 16 *Cr. C.*

[88] In light of the case law, it is plausible to expect that the courts will have to perform this legal characterization exercise in circumstances much more difficult than the ones in the case at bar. One example would be a case in which the mental condition of the accused indicates an underlying mental disorder but the evidence also shows that the toxic psychosis was triggered by the consumption of drugs of a nature and in a quantity that could have produced the same condition in a normal person. In such circumstances, the courts should be especially meticulous in applying the "more holistic approach" from *Stone*.

Premenstrual Syndrome

On December 16, 1980, a 36 year-old English woman ended a love affair by deliberately running down her lover with her car and killing him. At trial she pled guilty to manslaughter because of diminished responsibility. She was discharged from custody and had her driver's licence revoked for one year. In a separate decision decided one day earlier, Sandie Smith, an East London barmaid, was placed on probation for carrying a knife and threatening to kill a policeman, though she was already on probation for having stabbed a fellow barmaid to death. In both of these cases the English courts found that the defendants were suffering from premenstrual syndrome (PMS), and as a result recognized PMS as a mitigating factor in sentencing these women. "Criminal Law: Premenstrual Syndrome in the courts?" (1984), 24 Washburn Law Journal 54-77.

PMS can be defined as "The recurrence of symptoms in the premenstruum with complete absence of symptoms in the postmenstruum". Symptoms of PMS occur in the same phase of the cycle each month: irritability, anxiety, tension, depression, hostility, decreased self-esteem, indecision, mood swings, impulsive behaviour, difficulty concentrating, social isolation, etc. The symptoms range from mild inconvenience to complete, although temporary, debilitation.

In most instances a woman with PMS understands her actions and the consequences but is simply powerless to control those actions.

Could PMS be a defence under existing Canadian law? Should it be a defence?

See, further, E. Meehan and K. MacRae, "Legal Implications of Premenstrual Syndrome: A Canadian Perspective" (1986), 135 C.M.A.J. 601 and a reply by Dr. Robinson in (1986), 135 C.M.A.J. 1340 ("the association between PMS and violent, impulsive or criminal acts is by no means firmly established").

In 1994 a more debilitating form of PMS called PMDD (Premenstrual Dysphoric Disorder) was added to the DSM-IV.

PROBLEMS

1. The accused is charged with second degree murder. The victim, who was known to be gay, died from 79 knife wounds, including a cut throat.

The accused stated to the police that he had had a few drinks with the victim, felt sick and laid down on a bed. He woke up suddenly and saw the victim naked, standing near him. He ran to the kitchen, grabbed the knife, killed the victim and simulated a theft. The accused's defence was that he was in a state of automatism caused by psychological shock. As a trial judge, rule as to the whether the defence of automatism should be left with the jury. Compare *Fournier v. R.* (1982), 30 C.R. (3d) 346, 70 C.C.C. (2d) 351 (Que. C.A.).

2. The accused is charged with the attempted murder of a police officer. He sat astride the officer who was lying on the sidewalk, and choked him with his hands. The police officer was rescued by a bystander, who struck the accused three times on the head before rendering him unconscious. The altercation between the accused and the officer had occurred when a car driven by the accused's brother, in which the accused was the passenger, had been stopped and the accused's brother arrested for impaired driving. The police evidence was that the accused had started the fight by karate-kicking the police officer in the chest. The defence was that, after some verbal abuse and physical resistance by the accused, the police officer had struck him in the face and the accused had no further recollection until he woke up in the hospital. An independent eye-witness testified that the police officer had struck the accused forcefully in the face. Should the defence of automatism succeed? Compare *R. v. Bartlett* (1983), 33 C.R. (3d) 247, 5 C.C.C. (3d) 321 (Ont. H.C.).

3. The accused was charged with aggravated assault upon her 7-year-old child. The defence introduced expert evidence to suggest that the accused may, as a result of depression, have suffered from intermittent explosive disorder, which may result in a dissociative state. The Crown expert testified to the contrary, citing the fact that the accused had some memory of the incident and the attack had purposive elements. Should the defence of sane automatism succeed? Compare *R. v. Bergamin* (1996), 3 C.R. (5th) 140, 111 C.C.C. (3d) 550 (Alta. C.A.).

4. The accused is charged with attempted murder of H contrary to s. 239 of the *Criminal Code* and assaulting H with a weapon contrary to s. 267(a). The accused visited H, a friend, one morning. He pulled a knife out of a drawer and stabbed H repeatedly. In the struggle he also stabbed H with a screwdriver. The testimony of the victim was that the accused was not intoxicated but was not himself, looked totally blank and was in a robotic state. After the stabbing the accused stole a vehicle and was involved in an accident. A defence forensic psychiatrist testified that the accused was in a dissociated state. The accused is a heroin addict. There was no apparent motive for the attack. He testified that he was suffering from depression and acute pain from heroin withdrawal. On the day in question the accused consumed approximately 52 Clonidine pills and 20 Imovane pills, mind altering drugs which in sufficient quantity may produce disorders together with hallucinations. There was no evidence that the accused received any

warnings about this medication, either via the containers or the doctor. The drugs had been prescribed for his addiction. As trial judge you are satisfied the accused did not consume any heroin that day. The defence was automatism. Give judgment. Compare *R. v. Vickberg* (1998), 16 C.R. (5th) 164 (B.C. S.C.).

5. The accused was charged with second-degree murder for having caused the death of her husband. Her defence at trial was that she had acted in a state of non-mental disorder automatism. In this regard, two expert witnesses were called by the defence and one expert was called in reply by the Crown. All three experts agreed that the accused had no memory of the shooting. The defence experts concluded that she had acted in a state of automatism brought on shortly before the shooting by her traumatic relationship with her husband and the surrounding circumstances. The Crown's expert was of a different view. He agreed that the accused's amnesia was genuine but, in his opinion, it followed rather than preceded the shooting.

At the very outset of the trial, before any evidence had been called, defence counsel told the jury that he would be leading evidence to establish that the accused had been the victim of terrible abuse, mental and physical, for some 30 years. That assertion was not disputed. Defence counsel stated as well, that as a result of this abuse, the accused suffered at the time of the shooting from "battered wife syndrome". It was not disputed that she did.

The jury acquitted. Is there any ground of appeal for the Crown? Compare *R. v. Graveline* (2006), 38 C.R. (6th) 42 (S.C.C.).

4. INTOXICATION

(a) Common Law

S.M. BECK AND G.E. PARKER, THE INTOXICATED OFFENDER — A PROBLEM OF RESPONSIBILITY

(1966), 44 Can. Bar Rev. 563 at 570-573

What happens when an individual becomes intoxicated? The rather surprising answer, in view of the social and scientific interest in the problem, is that, in behavioural terms, we do not yet know with any degree of precision. An analysis of the experimental literature in 1940 evoked the following comment:

> In view of the psychiatric as well as lay interest in the effect of alcohol on these aspects [changes in volition, emotion and personality] of the individual, it is surprising how little attention they have received from experimental psychologists.

Another review in 1962 indicated little change:

A review of the psychological literature since 1940 suggests that little progress has been made in developing a knowledge of how and in what way alcohol affects behaviour. It appears that a reformulation of the concepts that guide thinking about the action of alcohol in all areas is needed. Except in a few areas . . . , little creative effort appears to have been spent in research on the effect of alcohol on human behaviour. The exploratory experiment to find out what alcohol does, rather than to confirm some hypothesis, is rare.

It would be easy to conclude that because experimental psychology has so far told us little about the effects of alcohol on behaviour, the criminal law would not be justified in altering the criteria of responsibility. Medical science does know, in broad terms, what effects alcohol has on the individual, and this knowledge might well justify a change in the degree of responsibility attributed to the intoxicated offender.

It is certain that intoxication impairs perception, judgment and muscular coordination. Along with this impairment goes an increase in self-confidence, a lessening of inhibitions, and a release of sexual and aggressive impulses. The fact that an individual's repressed instincts may break through and manifest themselves in overt acts during intoxication has led some commentators to the incorrect conclusion that drunken offenders intend their acts in the same manner as do sober men. Their argument is as follows: all men have repressed desires — repressed intents — which they usally manage to control. The drunk is freed from his inhibitions and acts out these desires. His intent while drunk is thus his real intent and his acts are as purposive, or end-directed, as those of a sober man.

Psychoanalysts tell us, however, that people have repressed instincts, sexual and aggressive, not intents. Intents refer to cognitive functions. Alcohol brings about a diminution of the repressive mechanisms, allowing the instinctual to occur in behaviour. These repressive mechanisms are of emotional, not intellectual, origin. In simple terms, the emotional brakes which act as the restraint in all of us are released, and inhibited or self-controlled desires are converted into action. Striking confirmation of this effect of alcohol is provided by a recently published study of the sex offender by the Institute for Sex Research at Indiana University. The study, the most extensive of its kind ever undertaken, is a statistical analysis of interviews with 1,356 men convicted of rape, homosexuality, offences against children and a variety of other sexual crimes. The report shows that 67 percent of the men who threatened or used force on little girls were intoxicated at the time of their offences, as were 40 percent of the rapists whose victims were over 15. The report states that ". . . in very few cases does intoxication seem to do more than simply release pre-existing desires".

The same argument about "real" intent can be made in regard to the actions of a psychotic. Suppose the case of a person who, acting under the delusion that he has been commanded by God to make a sacrifice, kills his child. Certainly it could not be said that such a person's action was not purposive. In fact such a person might realize that ordinary people regard his act as wrong. Consequently he could be held responsible on a strict application of the M'Naghten rules. He would probably be declared insane, however, as most juries are not hindered by the rigidity of the rules when evidence of disease of the mind is so great. Few, if any, would object to that verdict as it would be clear that the offender had lost his power of self-control; that he was incapable of appreciating the moral quality of his act; and that he was incapable of exercising any, rational judgment in the matter.

But an acutely intoxicated person has also lost his power of self-control; his ability to make judgments is impaired, and he might be quite incapable of foreseeing the consequences of his acts.

> This effect of alcohol in depressing the inhibitory centres of the brain is of considerable medico-legal importance. It may lead to a failure to realize that a contemplated act is fraught with danger to oneself or others, or even if the possibility of danger be realized it may result in recklessness, that is, disregard of risk.

Indeed, the language of the report of the Royal Commission on the Law of Insanity in delineating the important differences between the wording of the M'Naghten rules and s. 16 of the *Canadian Criminal Code*, points up the similarity between the state of mind of a person who falls within the ambit of s. 16 and that of one who is acutely intoxicated.

Section 16 speaks of being "incapable of appreciating the nature and quality of an act". The M'Naghten rules say "as not to know the nature and quality of the act he was doing". The Commissioners concluded that:

> there is an important distinction to be drawn under Canadian law between a mental capacity, whether caused by drunkenness or disease of the mind, to "know" what is being done and a mental capacity to "foresee and measure the consequences of the act".
>
> The true test necessarily is, was the accused person at the very time of the offence . . . by reason of disease of the mind, unable fully to appreciate not only the nature of the act but the natural consequences that would flow from it? In other words, was the accused person, by reason of disease of the mind, deprived of the mental capacity to foresee and measure the consequences of the act?

Medical science clearly indicates that one who is acutely intoxicated might also fit within the above test, with the exception, of course, that his incapacity is not due to a disease of the mind (unless the individual is suffering from delirium tremens which is an alcoholic psychosis). The issue then comes back to voluntariness, for the truth is that the acutely intoxicated offender may have no more appreciation of the nature of an act and its consequences than the psychotic offender who may be excused from responsibility under s. 16(2) of the *Criminal Code*. Society, however, refuses to accept the plea of lack of responsibility from one who commits a crime in an intoxicated state. The act of becoming acutely intoxicated is itself judged as irresponsible and the consequences must be paid for. The result is a compromise between the requirement of the criminal law for a responsible or voluntary act, and the judgment of society that a wrongdoer not be exonerated simply because he was drunk. It is that compromise that we shall next examine.

R. v. BERNARD

[1988] 2 S.C.R. 833, 67 C.R. (3d) 113, 45 C.C.C. (3d) 1,
1988 CarswellOnt 93, 1988 CarswellOnt 971

The accused was charged with sexual assault causing bodily harm, contrary to s. 246.2(*c*) [now s. 272(c)] of the *Criminal Code*. The complainant testified that she had been forced to have sexual intercourse in her apartment without her consent and had then been subjected to serious bodily injury by the accused. There was evidence that the accused had punched the complainant twice with a closed fist, once above the eye, causing the eyelid to bleed profusely, and that he had threatened to kill her. The complainant testified that the accused had been drinking but was able to walk, to see everything, to talk clearly and to put albums on the record player. One of the accused's friends testified that he had been drinking on the night in question and, though he became rowdy, he was walking straight and talking. When the police arrived at the apartment he was awakened from a deep sleep and seemed to be suffering somewhat from his drinking. The accused stated that his drunkenness caused the attack on the complainant.

At trial before judge and jury, the accused did not testify. However, the Crown read evidence of a statement made to the police in which the accused admitted forcing the complainant to have sexual intercourse with him. He stated that he did know why he had done it, because he was drunk, and that "When I realized what I was doing, I got off." The trial judge directed the jury that there was no evidence of drunkenness except the accused's statement and, even if they found that he was drunk, drunkenness would be no defence to the charge alleged. The jury returned a verdict of guilty. The Ontario Court of Appeal dismissed an appeal from conviction, holding that the offence of sexual assault causing bodily harm was an offence of general intent, to which the defence of drunkenness did not apply. The accused appealed.

MᶜIɴᴛʏʀᴇ J. (Bᴇᴇᴛᴢ J. concurring): —

. . . .

There are two issues which arise in this appeal. The first is whether sexual assault causing bodily harm (*Criminal Code* s. 246.2(c)) is an offence requiring proof of specific or of general intent, and the second is whether evidence of self-induced drunkenness is relevant to the issue of guilt or innocence in an offence of general intent. Before dealing in detail with these questions, it will be helpful to make certain observations.

A distinction has long been recognized in the criminal law between offences which require the proof of a specific intent and those which require only the proof of a general intent. This distinction forms the basis of the defence of drunkenness and it must be understood and kept in mind in approaching this case. In *R. v. George*, [1960] S.C.R. 871, Fauteux J. said, at p. 877:

> In considering the question of *mens rea*, a distinction is to be made between (i) intention as applied to acts considered in relation to their purposes and (ii) intention as applied to acts considered apart from their purposes. A general intent attending the commission of an act is, in some cases, the only intent required to constitute the crime while, in others, there must be, in addition to that general intent, a specific intent attending the purpose for the commission of the act.

This statement makes the distinction clear. The general intent offence is one in which the only intent involved relates solely to the performance of the act in question with no further ulterior intent or purpose. The minimal intent to apply force in the offence of common assault affords an example. A specific intent offence is one which involves the performance of the *actus reus*, coupled with an intent or purpose going beyond the mere performance of the questioned act. Striking a blow or administering poison with the intent to kill, or assault with intent to maim or wound, are examples of such offences.

This distinction is not an artificial one nor does it rest upon any legal fiction. There is a world of difference between the man who in frustration or anger strikes out at his neighbour in a public house with no particular purpose or intent in mind, other than to perform the act of striking, and the man who strikes a similar blow with intent to cause death or injury. This difference is best illustrated by a consideration of the relationship between murder and manslaughter. He who kills intending to kill or cause bodily harm is guilty of murder, whereas he who has killed by the same act without such intent is convicted of manslaughter. The proof of the specific intent, that is, to kill or to cause bodily harm, is necessary in murder because the crime of murder is incomplete without it. No such intent is required, however, for the offence of manslaughter because it forms no part of the offence, manslaughter simply being an unlawful killing without the intent required for murder. The relevance of intoxication which could deprive an accused of the capacity to form the necesary specific intent in murder and its irrelevance in the crime of manslaughter can readily be seen.

The present law relating to the drunkenness defence has developed in this court from the application of principles set out in *Director of Public Prosecutions v. Beard*, [1920] A.C. 479 (H.L.), discussed and adapted in other United Kingdom cases, including *Attorney General for Northern Ireland v. Gallagher*, [1961] 3 All E.R. 299 (H.L.), *Bratty v. Attorney General for Northern Ireland*, [1961] 3 All E.R. 523 (H.L.), and *Director of Public Prosecutions v. Majewski*, [1977] A.C. 443 (H.L.). In this court, the matter has been dealt with in *R. v. George, supra*, and other cases, but particularly in *Leary v. The Queen* (1978), 1 S.C.R. 29. where Pigeon J., speaking for the majority of the court, said, at p. 57, that rape is a crime of general intention as distinguished from specific intention, a crime therefore "in which the defence of drunkenness can have no application". This may be said to have confirmed the law as it stands in Canada on this question and the appellant's principal attack in this court is upon that decision. It is not necessary for the purposes of this judgment to review in detail the authorities in this court on the question. It will be sufficient to summarize their effect in the following terms. Drunkenness in a general sense is not a true defence to a criminal act. Where, however, in a case which involves a crime of specific intent, the accused is so affected by intoxication that he lacks the capacity to form the specific intent required to commit the crime charged it may apply. The defence, however, has no application in offences of general intent.

The criticism of the law with respect to the defence of drunkenness is based on two propositions. It is said, firstly, that the distinction between the general intent and specific intent offences is artificial and is little more than a legal fiction. Secondly, it is said that it is illogical, because it envisages a defence of drunkenness in certain situations and not in others; it is merely a policy decision made by judges and not based on principle or logic. It will be evident from what I have said that I reject the first ground of criticism. As to the second criticism that it is based upon grounds of policy, I would say that there can be no doubt that considerations of policy are involved in this distinction. Indeed, in some cases, principally *Majewski, supra,* the distinction has been defended on the basis that it is sound social policy. The fact, however, that considerations of policy have influenced the development of the law in this field cannot, in my view, be condemned. In the final analysis all law should be based upon and consistent with sound social policy. No good law can be inconsistent with or depart from sound policy.

If the policy behind the present law is that society condemns those who, by the voluntary consumption of alcohol, render themselves incapable of self-control so that they will commit acts of violence causing injury to their neighbours, then in my view no apology for such policy is needed, and the resulting law affords no affront to the well established principles of the law or to the freedom of the individual. Furthermore, the existing law is not divorced from logical underpinnings as suggested in some academic writings. Not all the academic literature has been critical. A strong statement in support of the law on utilitarian or policy grounds made shortly after *Majewski* is by Sir Rupert Cross in *"Blackstone v. Bentham"* (1976), 92 L.Q.R. 516, where he said, at pp. 525-6:

> In reply to Bentham and the academics I would ask why it is "hard and unthinking" to refuse to allow people to exempt themselves from criminal responsibility for harm done by their bodies by incapacitating their minds from controlling them. Why should the requirement that intention or recklessness must be proved in order to establish liability for an assault not be subject to what appears to be the wholly reasonable retributive principle that it is unjust to those who remain sober to allow those who become drunk to allege that they were unaware of consequences of their bodily movements of which all sober people would have been aware? This is what Blackstone meant when he said that the law would not suffer any man "to privilege one crime by another." ... Punishment is an evil and the less of it the better. But the evil of inflicting punishment is justified if the harm which is thus avoided is greater than that caused by the punishment. It may be asceticism to blame people for simply getting drunk,

but it is sound utilitarianism to seek to prevent people from doing certain kinds of harm while they are drunk. In so far as this object can be achieved by punishment, it is achieved most economically by singling out for punishment those who commit the kind of harm which the law seeks to prevent while they are drunk.

A.J. Ashworth ("Reason, Logic and Criminal Liability" (1975), 91 L.Q.R. 102) says, at p. 130:

> Moreover, it is hardly appropriate to regard a defence of acute intoxication as a simple denial of *mens rea*; it has been suggested that defences should not be classified solely according to the effect of the accused's condition, without reference to their cause. The criminal law permits reason to override the logical application of the traditional doctrines in cases of deliberately self-induced incapacities; to do otherwise would be tantamount to allowing a fraud on the law. It is submitted that, if the law provides no other means of imposing criminal liability in the cases of "voluntarily-induced" incapacities discussed in this article, then there are sufficient reasons for restricting the scope of the defences as the English Judges have done.

. . . .

In my view, the common law rules on the defence of drunkenness, though frequently the subject of criticism, have a rationality which not only accords with criminal law theory, but has also served society well. It is not questioned in this case that the defence of drunkenness, as it applies to specific intent offences, is supportable. It is submitted, however, that it should be extended to include all criminal charges. It is my view that this proposition is not sustainable.

Turning now to the issues raised, the first one is to consider whether the offence of sexual assault causing bodily harm is an offence requiring a general or specific intent. In *Swietlinski v. The Queen*, [1980] 2 S.C.R. 956, this court held that indecent assault, then an offence under the *Criminal Code*, was an offence of general intent. The indecent character of the assault was to be judged upon an objective view of the facts and not upon the mental state of the accused. It was said, at p. 968:

> What acts are indecent and what circumstances will have that character are questions of fact that will have to be decided in each case, but the determination of those questions will depend upon an objective view of the facts and circumstances in relation to the actual assault, and not upon the mental state of the accused.

and later at pp. 970-71:

> Because indecent assault is an offence of general or basic intent, the defence of drunkenness cannot apply where a person is charged with that offence.

This court dealt with the question of sexual assault *simpliciter* under s. 246(1)(*a*) in *R. v. Chase*, [1987] 2 S.C.R. 293.

. . . .

It would therefore be my view that the mental element of the offence in s. 246.2(*c*) is only the intention to commit the assault. The surrounding circumstances must be considered for evidence of its sexual nature and of the resulting bodily harm. The Crown need not show any further mental element (see J.D. Watt, *The New Offences Against the Person* (1984), at p. 113).

In my view, the comments in *Chase, supra*, are equally applicable to an offence under s. 246.2(*c*) which merely adds to the sexual assault *simpliciter* the requirement of bodily harm to the complainant. The resulting interference with the physical integrity of the complainant aggravates the seriousness of a sexual assault but the mental element remains the same. I would conclude that s. 246.2(*c*) creates an offence of general rather than specific intent.

The second issue, whether the defence of drunkenness applies to an offence of general intent includes the question of whether the court should overrule its earlier decision in *Leary*. The attack on *Leary* was based on its rejection of the defence for crimes of general intent. As already mentioned, nobody has suggested that it should not apply in cases of specific intent. The Chief Justice has expressed the view that evidence of self-induced intoxication should be a relevant consideration in determining whether the *mens rea* of any particular offence has been proved by the Crown. As I have indicated, I am unable to agree with this conclusion. The effect of such a conclusion would be that the more drunk a person becomes by his own voluntary consumption of alcohol or drugs, the more extended will be his opportunity for a successful defence against conviction for the offences caused by such drinking, regardless of the nature of the intent required for those offences.

The appellant made two principal arguments in seeking the reversal of the *Leary* rule. He contended that it relieves the Crown from the burden of proving *mens rea* in cases of general intent and, in effect, imposes strict liability upon proof of the *actus reus*. He also contended that the *Leary* rule violates s. 7 and s. 11(*d*) of the *Canadian Charter of Rights and Freedoms*.

In my opinion, both of these submissions must be rejected. I would say at the outset that in crimes of general intent the Crown is not relieved from proving any element of the offence. The effect of excluding the drunkenness defence from such offences is merely to prevent the accused from relying on his self-imposed drunkenness as a factor showing an absence of any necessary intent. While this court has consistently recognized the basic proposition that an accused person should not be subject to criminal sanction unless the Crown shows the existence of a blameworthy or criminal mental state associated with the *actus reus* of the crime, it does not follow that a person who so deprives himself by the voluntary consumption of alcohol or a drug of the normal power of self-restraint that a crime results, should be entitled to an acquittal. Compelling reasons grounded in logic, common sense, and sound social policy dictate otherwise.

As I indicated earlier, it is not necessary to review all of the authorities which have dealt with this issue. It is clear from a review of the cases, however, that until the early years of the nineteenth century drunkenness was considered "rather an aggravation than a defence": see Lord Birkenhead in *D.P.P. v. Beard, supra*, at p. 494. The early principle of the common law was that a voluntary destruction of will power would entitle a person to no more favourable treatment with regard to criminal conduct than a sober person. By the latter part of the 19th century this earlier rule was "mercifully relaxed" (see Lawton LJ. in *Majewski*, [1975] 2 All E.R. 296 (C.A.), at p. 305) in respect of crimes of specific intent where the capacity to form the required specific intent was not present because of intoxication: see the early cases such as *R. v. Doherty* (1887), 16 Cox. C.C. 306, per Stephen J., at p. 308. This new approach was given approval in *Beard's* case and the more modern authorities have been based upon it. This relaxation stems no doubt from a recognition of the severity of the penal consequence of most of the specific intent offences, as compared with the generally lesser penalties associated with the general intent offences. Therefore, the exclusion of the defence from general intent offences was not an exception to the general rule. The exception was the allowance of the defence in specific intent cases adopted to recognize the more complicated mental processes required for the crimes of special intent and the greater penalties involved. Some measure of relief for such cases was therefore provided. Otherwise, the common law preserved the general rule that a person may not by voluntary intoxication render himself immune from the consequences of his conduct.

. . . .

In *Leary*, this court followed the approach taken in the House of Lords in *Majewski*, where the House of Lords unanimously approved the distinction between general and specific intent on the basis that the rule had evolved to protect the community and that voluntary intoxication was a sufficient substitute for the fault element in crimes of general intent.

. . . .

This court in *Leary* approved the *Majewski* approach which has long been accepted in the law of Canada and, for the reasons which I have set out, it is my opinion that this court's judgment in *Leary* ought not to be overruled. I must re-emphasize that the *Leary* rule does not relieve the Crown from its obligation to prove the *mens rea* in a general intent offence. The fact that an accused may not rely on voluntary intoxication in such offences does not have that effect because of the nature of the offence and the mental elements which must be shown. The requisite state of mind may be proved in two ways. Firstly, there is the general proposition that triers of fact may infer *mens rea* from the *actus reus* itself: a person is presumed to have intended the natural and probable consequences of his actions. For example, in an offence involving the mere application of force, the minimal intent to apply that force will suffice to constitute the necessary *mens rea* and can be reasonably inferred from the act itself and the other evidence. Secondly, in cases where the accused was so intoxicated as to raise doubt as to the voluntary nature of his conduct, the Crown may meet its evidentiary obligation respecting the necessary blameworthy mental state of the accused by proving the fact of voluntary self-induced intoxication by drugs or alcohol. This was the approach suggested in *Majewski*. In most cases involving intoxication in general intent offences, the trier of fact will be able to apply the first proposition, namely, that the intent is inferable from the *actus reus* itself. As Fauteux J. observed in *George, supra*, at p. 879, it is almost metaphysically inconceivable for a person to be so drunk as to be incapable of forming the minimal intent to apply force. Hence, only in cases of the most extreme self-intoxication does the trier of fact need to use the second proposition, that is, that evidence of self-induced intoxication is evidence of the guilty mind, the blameworthy mental state.

The result of this two-fold approach is that for these crimes accused persons cannot hold up voluntary drunkenness as a defence. They cannot be heard to say: "I was so drunk that I did not know what I was doing". If they managed to get themselves so drunk that they did not know what they were doing, the reckless behaviour in attaining that level of intoxication affords the necessary evidence of the culpable mental condition. Hence, it is logically impossible for an accused person to throw up his voluntary drunkenness as a defence to a charge of general intent. Proof of his voluntary drunkenness can be proof of his guilty mind.

As I have endeavoured to show, the exclusion of the drunkenness defence in general intent cases is not without logical underpinnings but, whatever the logical weaknesses may be, an overwhelming justification for the exclusion may rest on policy, policy so compelling that it possesses its own logic. Intoxication, whether by alcohol or drugs, lies at the root of many if not most violent assaults: intoxication is clearly a major cause of violent crime. What then is preferable, a recognition of this fact and the adoption of a policy aimed at curbing the problem, or the application of what is said to be logic by providing in law that he who voluntarily partakes of that which is the cause of the crime should for that reason be excused from the consequences of his crime? If that is logic, I prefer policy.

It was argued by the appellant that the *Leary* rule converts the offence of sexual assault causing bodily harm into a crime of absolute liability in that the Crown need not prove the requisite intention for the completion of the offence. Therefore, it is said that *Leary* violates s. 7 and s. 11(*d*) of the *Charter*. In *Re Motor Vehicle Act Reference*, [1985] 2 S.C.R. 486 and in *R. v. Vaillancourt*, [1987] 2 S.C.R. 636, it was held that the requirement for a minimum mental state before the attachment of criminal liability is a principle of fundamental justice. Criminal offences, as a general rule, must have as one of their elements the requirement of a blameworthy mental state. The morally innocent ought not to be convicted. It is said that the *Leary* rule violates this fundamental premise. In my opinion, the *Leary* rule clearly does not offend this essential principle of criminal law but rather upholds it. The *Leary* rule recognizes that accused persons who have voluntarily consumed drugs or alcohol, thereby depriving themselves of self-control leading to the commission of a crime, are not morally innocent and are, indeed, criminally blameworthy. While the rule excludes consideration of voluntary intoxication in the approach to general intent offences, it nonetheless recognizes that it may be a relevant factor in those generally more serious offences where the *mens rea* must involve not only the intentional performance of the *actus reus* but, as well, the formation of further ulterior motives and purposes. It therefore intrudes upon the security of the person only in accordance with sound principle and within the established boundaries of the legal process. For these reasons, I would say that the *Charter* is not violated.

. . . .

I would therefore conclude that the courts below made no error and I would dismiss the appeal.

In any event, should it be considered that I am wrong in my approach to the *Leary* case, this is nonetheless a case in which the provisions of s. 613(1)(*b*)(iii) of the *Criminal Code* should be applied. ... It is my view that there is no sufficient evidence of drunkeness to form any basis whatever for the defence of drunkenness.

WILSON J. (L'HEUREUX-DUBÉ J. concurring): — I have had the benefit of the reasons of the Chief Justice and of my colleagues McIntyre and La Forest JJ. I agree with McIntyre JJ. for the reasons given by him that sexual assault causing bodily harm is an offence of general intent requiring only the minimal intent to apply force. I agree with him also that in most cases involving general intent offences and intoxication the Crown will be able to establish the accused's blameworthy mental state by inference from his or her acts. I think that is the case here. The evidence of intoxication withheld from the trier of fact in this case could not possibly have raised a reasonable doubt as to the existence of the minimal intent to apply force. It is accordingly not necessary in this case to resort to self-induced intoxication as a substituted form of *mens rea*. And, indeed, I have some real concerns as to whether the imposition of criminal liability on that basis would survive a challenge under the *Canadian Charter of Rights and Freedoms*.

The facts are fully set out in the reasons of the Chief Justice and I refer to them only to underline why I agree with my colleague, McIntyre J., that the rule in *Leary v. The Queen*, [1978] 1 S.C.R. 29, should be preserved and applied in this case.

Sexual assault is a crime of violence. There is no requirement of an intent or purpose beyond the intentional application of force. It is first and foremost an assault. It is sexual in nature only because, objectively viewed, it is related to sex either on account of the area of the body to which the violence is applied or on account of words accompanying the violence. Indeed, the whole purpose, as I understand it, of the replacement of the offence of rape by the offence of sexual assault was to emphasize the aspect of violence and put paid to the benign concept that rape was simply the act of a man who was "carried away" by his emotions.

The appellant in his statement to the police admitted that he had forced the complainant to have sexual intercourse with him but claimed that because of his drunkenness he did not know why he had done this and that when he realized what he was doing he off" the complainant. There was evidence that the appellant had punched the complainant twice with his closed fist and had threatened to kill her. The doctor who examined the complainant testified that the complainant's right eye was swollen shut and that three stitches were required to close the wound. It is clear from this that there was intentional and voluntary, as opposed to accidental or involuntary, application of force.

The evidence of the appellant's intoxication consisted of his own statements to the police that he was drunk; the complainant's testimony that, while the appellant was acting out of character in making advances to her, he was able to walk, talk and put albums on the record player; a friend's testimony that prior to the incident the appellant had been drinking at a bar and had become "very rowdy" although still capable of talking and walking straight. By his own admission the appellant had sufficient wits about him after the violent assault to hide a bloodied towel and pillowcase from the police. There is no evidence that we are dealing here with extreme intoxication, verging on insanity or automatism, and as such capable of negating the inference that the minimal intent to apply force was present: see *R. v. Swietlinski*, (1978) 44 C.C.C. (2d) 267 (Ont. C.A.), at p. 294, aff'd [1980] 2 S.C.R. 956. The evidence of intoxication in this case was simply not capable of raising a reasonable doubt as to the existence of the minimal intent required. In this I agree with McIntyre J.

I am less confident about the proposition accepted by my colleague that self-induced intoxication may substitute for the mental element required to be present at the time the offence was committed although I realize that there are statements in judgments of this court to that effect. I do not believe, however, that the court has clearly adopted that proposition. The decision of the House of Lords in *Director of Public Prosecutions v. Majewski*, [1977] A.C. 443, may stand for the rather harsh proposition that even self-induced intoxication producing a state of automatism cannot constitute a defence to an offence of general intent such as assault but I doubt that our Canadian jurisprudence goes that far.

. . . .

I believe that the *Leary* rule is perfectly consistent with an onus resting on the Crown to prove the minimal intent which should accompany the doing of the prohibited act in general intent offences. I view it as preferable to preserve the *Leary* rule in its more flexible form as Pigeon J. applied it, *i.e.*, so as to allow evidence of intoxication to go to the trier of fact in general intent offences only if it is evidence of extreme intoxication involving an absence of awareness akin to a state of insanity or automatism. Only in such a case is the evidence capable of raising a reasonable doubt as to the existence of the minimal intent required for the offence. I would not overrule *Leary*, as the Chief Justice would, and allow evidence of intoxication to go to the trier of fact in every case regardless of its possible relevance to the issue of the existence of the minimal intent required for the offence.

It was argued by the appellant and indeed accepted by the Chief Justice in his reasons that the *Leary* rule converts the offence of sexual assault causing bodily harm into a crime of absolute liability in that the Crown need not prove any mental element. This is said to offend s. 7 of the *Charter* as interpreted in *Re B.C. Motor Vehicle Act*, [1985] 2 S.C.R. 486 and in *R. v. Vaillancourt*, [1987] 2 S.C.R. 636. With all due respect to those who think differently I do not believe that the Crown is relieved from proving the existence of the required minimal intent by the operation of *Leary*. In *R. v. Sault Ste. Marie*, [1978] 2 S.C.R. 1299, Dickson J., as he then was, stated at p. 1310:

> In sharp contrast, "absolute liability" entails conviction on proof merely that the defendant committed the prohibited act constituting the *actus reus* of the offence. There is no relevant mental element. It is no defence that the accused was entirely without fault. He may be morally innocent in every sense, yet be branded as a malefactor and punished as such.

When the *Leary* rule is applied in this case the Crown must still prove beyond a reasonable doubt the existence of the required mental element of the intentional application of force. The offence cannot be said to be one of absolute liability in the sense that no mental element has to be proved in order to obtain a conviction. As Alan Mewett and Morris Manning write in *Criminal Law* (2nd ed. (1985)), at p. 210:

> The courts are not saying that crimes of general or basic intent do not require *mens rea*. Rather they are saying that those crimes have a *mens rea* of a type directed solely to the present and that drunkenness is not sufficient to negate that type of thought process.

Similarly, Glanville Williams argues in his *Textbook of Criminal Law* (2nd ed. (1983)), at pp. 475-76, that it is a misunderstanding to read even *Majewski, supra*, as transforming general intent offences into absolute liability offences because "even on a charge of a crime of basic intent the jury must have regard to all the evidence except the evidence of intoxication in determining the defendant's intention." In short, when evidence of intoxication is withheld from the jury the Crown still bears the burden of proving a blameworthy state of mind.

It was also argued by the appellant and accepted by the Chief Justice that the application of the *Leary* rule violates s. 11(*d*) of the *Charter* by allowing an accused to be convicted even although the trier of fact might well have a reasonable doubt as to the existence of the essential mental element of the offence or as to the availability of a defence which could raise a reasonable doubt as to the guilty of the accused: see *Vaillancourt, supra; R. v. Whyte*, [1988] 2 S.C.R. 3. Again I find myself in respectful disagreement with the Chief Justice and the appellant on this issue. To my mind, the operation of the *Leary* rule in this case does not have that result because the Crown still must prove that the accused applied force intentionally and the evidence of intoxication is withheld from the jury only because it is incapable of raising a reasonable doubt as to the accused's guilt. This is not a case in which self-induced intoxication is being resorted to as a substituted *mens rea* for the intentional application of force.

It is, my view, not strictly necessary in this case to address the constitutionality of substituting self-induced intoxication of general intent offences. The issue would, in my view, only arise in those rare cases in which the intoxication is extreme enough to raise doubts as to the existence of the minimal intent which characterizes conscious and volitional conduct. However, as both the Chief Justice and McIntyre J. have addressed the issue, I will express my own somewhat tentative views upon it.

This court has affirmed as fundamental the proposition that a person should not be exposed to a deprivation of liberty unless the Crown proves the existence of a blameworthy or culpable state of mind: see *Re B.C. Motor Vehicle Act, supra*, at pp. 513-20. It does not follow from this, however, that those who, through the voluntary consumption of alcohol or drugs incapacitate themselves from knowing what they are doing, fall within the category of the "morally innocent" deserving of such protection. This is not to say that such persons do not have a right under s. 7n or s. 12 of the *Charter* to be protected against punishment that is disproportionate to their crime and degree of culpability: see *Re B.C. Motor Vehicle Act, supra*, at pp. 532-34; *R. v. Smith*, [1987] 1 S.C.R. 1045. They do, especially if the consequences of their becoming intoxicated were not intended or foreseen.

The real concern over the substituted form of *mens rea* arises, it seems to me, under s. 11(*d*) of the *Charter*. While this court has recognized that in some cases proof of an essential element of a criminal offence can be replaced by proof of a different element, it has placed stringent limitations on when this can happen.

· · · ·

In my tentative view, it is unlikely that in those cases in which it is necessary to resort to self-induced intoxication as the substituted element for the minimal intent, proof of the substituted element will "inexorably" lead to the conclusion that the essential element of the minimal intent existed at the time the criminal act was committed. But I prefer to leave this question open as it is unnecessary to decide it in order to dispose of this appeal.

I agree with my colleagues McIntyre and La Forest JJ. that, had there been error in the court below, no substantial wrong or miscarriage of justice resulted from it and that it would accordingly be appropriate to apply s. 613(1)(*b*)(iii) of the *Criminal Code*. I would dismiss the appeal.

DICKSON C.J. (LAMER J. concurring) (dissenting): —

. . . .

DRUNKENNESS AND *MENS REA*

In my view, the only issue the court needs to address may be put as follows: should evidence of self-induced intoxication be considered by the trier of fact, along with all other relevant evidence, in determining whether the prosecution has proved beyond a reasonable doubt the *mens rea* required to constitute the offence? I am of the opinion that the court should answer that question in the affirmative.

I wish to make clear at the outset, however, that nothing in these reasons is intended to apply with respect to the quite distinct issues raised by offences, such as driving while impaired, where intoxication or the consumption of alcohol is itself an ingredient of the offence. The *mens rea* of such offences can be left for consideration another day.

In *Leary v. The Queen*, [1978] 1 S.C.R. 29, Pigeon J. for the majority of the court, held that rape was an offence requiring proof of only "basic" or "general" intent rather than "specific" intent. Under that categorization, the court held, the jury should be instructed that evidence that drunkenness may have deprived the accused of the capacity to form the requisite intent should not be taken into account when considering whether the Crown had satisfied the burden of proving beyond a reasonable doubt that the accused had acted with the requisite intent. (See also *Swietlinski v. The Queen*, [1980] 2 S.C.R. 956, dealing with the offence of indecent assault). The offence of rape has now been removed from the *Criminal Code* and in its place are the sexual assault provisions. More recently, in *R. v. Chase*, [1987] 2 S.C.R. 293, the court held that sexual assault was a crime of "basic" or "general" intent. In *Chase*, however, drunkenness was not in issue and the propriety of maintaining the distinction between general and specific intent for purposes of evidence regarding intoxication was not considered. The present case raises that much more basis issue which, in my view, the court should reconsider.

In my dissent in *Leary*, I sought to advance the view that respect for basic criminal law principles required that the legal ficiton, the artificial "specific" intent threshold requirement, be abandoned. I do not intend in these reasons to repeat what I said in *Leary*. With due regard for *stare decisis*, as to which I will have more to say in a moment, and with the greatest of respect for those of a contrary view, I would only add that nothing I have heard or read since the judgment in *Leary* has caused me to abandon or modify in the slightest degree the views of dissent which I there expressed. Analysis of the *Leary* dissent may be summarized as follows.

First of all, one must recognize the fundamental nature of the *mens rea* requirement. To warrant the condemnation of a conviction and the infliction of punishment, one who has caused harm must have done so with a blameworthy state of mind. It is always for the Crown to prove the existence of a guilty mind beyond a reasonable doubt. Intoxication affects one's mental state, one's ability to perceive the circumstances in which one acts, and to appreciate possible consequences. In principle, therefore, intoxication is relevant to the mental element in crime, and should be considered, together with all other evidence, in determining whether the Crown has proved the requisite mental state beyond a reasonable doubt.

It is quite wrong, I think, to characterize the issue as whether the "defence of drunkeness" should apply to this or that offence. While this expression is commonly used, it is misleading and perhaps even unduly emotive. It suggests that those who would otherwise be liable for their criminal conduct will escape because they were drunk at the time the offence was committed. But, of course, no one suggests that special concessions should be made to drunken offenders. The issue is really whether the Crown should be relieved of the usual burden of proving the requisite mental element for the offence, because the accused was intoxicated. Should the jury be entitled to assess all of the evidence relevant to intent and be entitled to decide on the basis of all of the evidence whether the Crown has satisfied that burden?

The categories of "specific" intent on the one hand and "basic" or "general" intent on the other have evolved as an artificial device whereby evidence, otherwise relevant, is excluded from the jury's consideration. This court, in *Swietlinski*, has recognized that intoxication may as a matter of fact deprive an accused of "basic" or "general" intent. It is said, however, by those who support the classificiton that as a matter of policy, consideration of evidence of intoxication must be excluded. Indeed, a notable feature to be found in the analysis of many of those who support restricting the jury's use of evidence relating to drunkenness is the concession that while principle and logic lead in an opposite direction, the policy of protection of the public requires that principle and logic should yield: see, *e.g. Director of Public Prosecutions v. Majewski*, [1976] 2 All E.R. 142, at pp. 167-8 per Lord Edmund-Davies, quoted by Pigeon J. in *Leary, supra*, at pp. 52-3.

In my view, there are two fundamental problems with this approach. First, if the law is to be altered in the name of policy over principle, that is surely a task for Parliament rather than the courts. As Barwick C.J. of the High Court of Australia concluded in *O'Connor* (1980), 4 A. Crim. R. 348, at pp. 363-64:

It seems to me to be completely inconsistent with the principles of the common law that a man should be conclusively presumed to have an intent which, in fact, he does not have, or to have done an act which, in truth, he did not do.

I can readily understand that a person who has taken alcohol or another drug to such an extent that he is intoxicated thereby to the point where he has no will to act or no capacity to form an intent to do an act is blameworthy and that his act of having ingested or administered the alcohol or other drug ought to be visited with severe consequences. The offence of being drunk and disorderly is not maintained these days in all systems of the common law. In any case it has not carried a sufficient penalty properly to express the public opprobrium which should attach to one who, by the taking of alcohol or the use of drugs, has become intoxicated to the point where he is the vehicle for unsocial or violent behaviour. But, though blameworthy for becoming intoxicated, I can see no ground for presuming his acts to be voluntary and relevantly intentional. For what is blameworthy there should be an appropriate criminal offence. But it is not for the Judges to create an offence appropriate in the circumstances: cf. *Knuller (Publishing, Printing & Promotions) Ltd. v. D.P.P.*, [1973] A.C. 435, at pp. 457-458, 464-465 and 490). It must be for the Parliament.

Secondly, even if it were appropriate for the courts to bend principle in the name of policy, so far as I am aware, there is no evidence that the artificiality of the specific intent requirement is actually required for social protection.

An unrestrained application of basic *mens rea* doctrine would not, in my opinion, open a gaping hole in the criminal law inimical to social protection. There are several reasons for this. To the extent that intoxication merely lowers inhibitions, removes self-restraint or induces unusal self-confidence or aggressiveness, it would be of no avail to an accused, as such effects do not relate to the *mens rea* requirement for volitional and intentional or reckless conduct. Similarly, intoxication would be of no avail to an accused who got drunk in order to gain the courage to commit a crime or to aid in his defence. Thirdly, one can trust in the good sense of the jury and that of our trial Judges to weigh all the evidence in a fair and responsbile manner, and they are unlikely to acquit too readily those who have committed offences while intoxicated.

The High Court of Australia held in *O'Connor, supra*, that the distinction between specific and general intent should not be followed and that in all cases, evidence of drunkenness should be left with the jury along with all other evidence relative to the issue of intent. The New Zealand Court of Appeal also rejected the artificial specific intent distinction: *R. v. Kamipeli*, [1975] 2 N.Z.L.R. 610.

. . . .

The experience in New Zealand and Australia, where the specific intent has been abandoned, suggests that the public will be adequately protected if the issue is left to the good sense of the jury. *O'Connor* was preceded in the State of Victoria by *R. v. Keogh*, [1964] V.R. 400. In *O'Connor*, Stephen J. explained as follows, at 358:

A distrust of jurors and an anxiety that they may too readily be persuaded to an acquittal if evidence of the result of self-induced intoxication, particularly by drugs other than alcohol, were allowed, may have formed some part of the public policy on which the decision rests. I may say at once that I have, of course, no experience of English juries: but I have of juries in New South Wales. Starke J., a most experienced Judge in the hearing of criminal charges in Victoria, having had as well a long and distinguished career as an advocate, expressed himself in the present case in relation to the impact of evidence of intoxication upon Victoria jurors. He said:

> "I, of course, have no knowledge of how English juries react. But over nearly 40 years' experience in this State I have found juries to be very slow to accept a defence based on intoxication. I do not share the fear held by many in England that if intoxication is accepted as a defence as far as general intent is concerned the floodgates will open and hordes of guilty men will descend on the community."

I share his views, as if they had been expressed about jurors in New South Wales. In my opinion, properly instructed jurors would be scrupulous and not indulgent in deciding an issue of voluntariness or of intention. Indeed, I am inclined to think that they may tend to think that an accused who had taken alchohol and particularly other drugs to the point of extreme intoxication had brought on himself what flowed from that state of intoxication.

The empirical evidence is to the same effect: see George Smith J., "Footnote to O'Connor's Case" (1981), 5 Crim. L.J. 270, reviewing the effects of the *O'Connor* decision in Australia, and concluding, after review of over 500 trials held in the District Court of New South Wales, that the actual impact on the acquittal rate was minimal (at p. 277):

> Certainly my inquiries would indicate that the decision in *O'Connor's* case, far from opening any floodgates has at most permitted an occasional drip to escape from the tap.

. . . .

III

STARE DECISIS

The real issue in this appeal, it seems to me, is whether the court should now overrule *Leary*. Let me say immediately that, even if a case were wrongly decided, certainty in the law remains an important consideration. There must be compelling circumstances to justify departure from a prior decision. On the other hand, it is clear that this court may overrule its own decisions and indeed, it has exercised that discretion on a number of occasions. . . .

There are at least four separate factors which find support in the jurisprudence of the court which in my submission lead to the conclusion that *Leary* should be overruled.

A. *Canadian Charter of Rights and Freedoms*

Since *Leary* was decided, the *Canadian Charter of Rights and Freedoms* has come into force. This court has held that legislation which imposes the sanction of imprisonment without proof of a blameworthy state of mind violates the guarantee of fundamental justice contained in s. 7 of the *Charter* and must be struck down unless it can meet the exacting test of s. 1 (see *Re B.C. Motor Vehicle Act*, [1985] 2 S.C.R. 486, *R. v. Vaillancourt*, [1987] 2 S.C.R. 636).

The appellant submits that *Leary* runs counter to s. 7 by providing that intoxication is no defence to a crime of general intent. In circumstances where the requisite mental intent is lacking due to an intoxicated condition, a general intent offence is converted into one of absolute liability in which proof of the commission of the actus reus by itself mandates conviction. It is also submitted that *Leary* runs counter to the presumption of innocence and the right to a fair hearing as guaranteed by s. 11(*d*) of the *Charter*, in so far as wrongful intent is irrebuttably presumed upon the showing of intoxication.

. . . .

In *Leary*, I expressed the opinion that the fundamental rationale for the *mens rea* presumption could be framed in the following terms, at p. 34:

> The notion that a court should not find a person guilty of an offence against the criminal law unless he has a blameworthy state of mind is common to all civilized penal systems. It is founded upon respect for the person and for the freedom of human will. A person is accountable for what he wills. When, in the exercise of the power of free choice, a member of society chooses to engage in harmful or otherwise undesirable conduct proscribed by the criminal law, he must accept the sanctions which that law has provided for the purpose of discouraging such conduct. Justice demands no less. But, to be criminal, the wrongdoing must have been consciously committed. To subject the offender to punishment, a mental element as well as a physical element is an essential concomitant of the crime. The mental state basic to criminal liability consists in most crimes in either (a) an intention to cause the *actus reus* of the crime, *i.e.* an intention to do the act which constitutes the crime in question, or (b) foresight or realization on the part of the person that his conduct will probably cause or may cause the *actus reus*, together with assumption of or indifference to a risk, which in all of the circumstances is substantial or unjustifiable. This latter mental element is sometimes characterized as recklessness.

In my view, that same principle is now given constitutional force in *Re B.C. Motor Vehicle Act*, *supra*, *Vaillancourt*, *supra*. In *Re B.C. Motor Vehicle Act*, *supra*, the court held, at p. 514, that "absolute liability in penal law offends the principles of fundamental justice." In *Vaillancourt*, Justice Lamer stated that the *B.C. Motor Vehicle Act Reference* "elevated *mens rea* from a presumed element in *Sault Ste. Marie*, *supra* to a constitutionally required element" (p. 652). While the court has not yet dealt directly with the extent to which objective foreseeability may suffice for the imposition of criminal liability (*Vaillancourt* at pp. 653-54), that issue is not raised in the present context.

The effect of the majority holding in *Leary* is to impose a form of absolute liability on intoxicated offenders, which is entirely inconsistent with the basic requirement for a blameworthy state of mind as a prerequisite to the imposition of the penalty of imprisonment mandated by the above-cited authorities. I agree with the observation of Professor Stuart in *Canadian Criminal Law* (2nd ed. 1987) that s. 7 of the *Charter* mandates the reversal of *Leary* and the assertion of "the fundamental principles of voluntariness and fault" in relation to intoxication and the criminal law (at p. 378). If the constitutional guarantee empowers the court to strike down legislation as in the two cases cited above, surely it provides a sufficient basis for overruling a prior decision of the court which fails to respect constitutionally entrenched values.

The majority holding in *Leary* also runs counter to the s. 11(*d*) right to be presumed innocent until proven guilty. With respect to crimes of general intent, guilty intent is in effect presumed upon proof of the fact of intoxication. Moreover, the presumption of guilt created by the *Leary* rule is irrebuttable.

The same argument made in the context of s. 7 can be made in relation to s. 11(*d*). By providing that intoxication is no defence to a crime of general intent, *Leary* renders the offence one of absolute liability and runs counter to the presumption of innocence by presuming an essential element required by s. 7 upon the proof of the fact of intoxication.

In my view, the *Leary* rule cannot be upheld by reference to s. 1, as it cannot survive the "proportionality" inquiry. While the protection of the public, said to underlie the *Leary* rule, could serve as an important objective, in my view the *Leary* rule does not achieve that objective in a manner consistent with the proportionality test of *Oakes, supra. Oakes* requires that "the measures adopted must be carefully designed to achieve the objective in question." As I have noted, there is no agreement in the case law as to how to distinguish between crimes of "general intent" and crimes of "specific intent". This distinction was plainly not in the minds of the *Code* drafters, and the mental elements of many crimes are not readily classified into one category or the other. There is no rational reason for protecting the public against some drunken offenders but not against others, particularly where the distinction is not based upon the gravity of the offence or the availability of included offences. If the public protection does require special measures, that should be accomplished through comprehensive legislation rather than ad hoc judicial recasting of some offences. For a recent review of possible legislative schemes, see Quigley, "Reform of the Intoxication Defence" (1987), 33 McGill L.J. 1.

The *Leary* rule in effect treats the deliberate act of becoming intoxicated as culpable in itself, but inflicts punishment measured by the unintended consequences of becoming intoxicated. Punishment acts as a deterrent where the conduct is intended or foreseen. There is no evidence to support the assertion that the *Leary* rule deters the commission of unintended crimes. Hence, there is no warrant for violating fundamental principles and convicting those who would otherwise escape criminal liability.

The *Leary* rule fails to satisfy the second branch of the proportionality test as well, namely, that the means chosen should impair as little as possible the right or freedom in question. In general intent offences, the jury is to be instructed to excise from their minds any evidence of drunkenness with the result that the Crown, because the accused is intoxicated, is relieved of proving *mens rea*, thereby placing the intoxicated person in a worse position than a sober person. Alternatively, the jury is required to examine the mental state of the accused, without reference to the alcohol ingested, and consequently find a fictional intent. In my view, imposition of this form of absolute liability goes well beyond what is required to protect the public from drunken offenders. As I have already indicated, striking down the artificial rule which precludes the trier of fact from considering evidence of intoxication in relation to *mens rea* has not produced an increase in the threat to public safety from drunken offenders in Australia, and there is no evidence to suggest that it would do so in Canada.

Finally, it is my view that there is a disproportionality between the effects of *Leary* on rights protected by the *Charter* and the objective of public safety. To paraphrase Lamer J. in *Re B.C. Motor Vehicle Act, supra*, at p. 521, it has not been demonstrated that risk of imprisonment of a few innocent persons is required to attain the goal of protecting the public from drunken offenders.

As stated in *R. v. Holmes*, [1988] 1 S.C.R. 914, at p. 940: "This effect, given the range of alternative legislative devices available to Parliament, is too deleterious to be justified as a reasonable limit under s. 1 of the *Charter*. Simply put, the provision exacts too high a price to be justified in a free and democratic society."

B. *Leary* Attenuated by Subsequent Cases

Since *Leary* there have been developments in the jurisprudence of the court which, in my submission, seriously undermine the view taken by the majority in *Leary*. The court has held that where the holding of a case has been "attenuated" by subsequent decisions, it may be appropriate to overrule that earlier decision: *Reference re the Agricultural Products Marketing Act*, [1978] 2 S.C.R. 1198.

In my view, *Leary* has also been undermined quite independently of the *Charter*. The court has consistently held that an honest but unreasonable mistaken belief in consent will negate the *mens rea* required for rape, indecent assault or sexual assaut: see *Pappajohn v. The Queen* [1980] 2 S.C.R. 120; *Sansregret v. The Queen*, [1985] 1 S.C.R. 570; *R. v. Bulmer*, [1987] 1 S.C.R. 782, and *R. v. Robertson*, [1987] 1 S.C.R. 918 at pp. 939-40. While the reasonableness of the accused's belief is a factor for the jury to consider in determining whether or not the belief was honestly held, a mistaken belief in consent need not be reasonable.

The *Leary* rule fits most awkwardly with that enunciated in *Pappajohn*. Lower courts have held that in the light of *Leary*, where intoxication is a factor in inducing a mistaken belief in consent, the jury must be instructed that while an honest but unreasonable belief will negate *mens rea* (*Pappajohn*) they are to disregard the effect that intoxication might have had in inducing that mistake (*Leary*). In *R. v. Moreau* (1986), 26 C.C.C. (3d) 359 (Ont. C.A.), at pp. 386-7, Martin J.A. described the task of the jury as follows:

> It does not follow that the defence of honest belief in consent is unavailable on a charge of sexual assault to an accused who is voluntarily intoxicated. Where an issue arises on the evidence as to the accused's honest belief in consent, the defence of honest belief in consent must be put to the jury, notwithstanding the accused's self-induced intoxication. There may be a basis in the evidence for the accused's honest belief in consent apart altogether from his intoxication; there may even be reasonable grounds for that belief even though he was intoxicated. The intoxication may not be the cause of the mistaken belief. However, the accused cannot rely on his self-induced intoxication as the basis for his belief that the complainant consented. As Mayrand J.A. said in *R. v. Bresse, Vallieres and Theberge* (1978), 48 C.C.C. (2d) 78 at p. 87, 7 C.R. (3d) 50 (Que. C.A.):

> > One must distinguish the case in which, because of one's voluntary inebriation, a man takes no account of the refusal manifested by a woman from the case in which a man, because of the ambiguous conduct of the woman, believes sincerely that she consented to sexual relations. This *error of fact committed for reasons other than one's voluntary inebriation* is, in my opinion, a valid ground of defence. (Emphasis added.)

> In those circumstances the jury is required to engage in the difficult, and perhaps somewhat artificial task, of putting out of their minds the evidence of intoxcation on the issue whether the accused honestly believed that the complainant consented. The test is not whether a reasonable and sober person would have made the same mistake but whether the accused would have made the same mistake if he had been sober; see Glanville Williams, *Textbook on Criminal Law*, 2nd ed. (1983) at pp. 481-2. However, to hold that evidence of self-induced intoxication is relevant to the honesty of the accused's belief in consent where his belief is founded on his mistaken appreciation, due to intoxication, of the facts relating to the complainant's consent is, in my view, incompatible with the rule laid down in *Leary*, and would completely negate the policy rule that self-induced intoxication is not a defence in crimes of general intent.

In my view, the *Leary* qualification on the criminal law principle of general application with respect to mistake of fact unnecessarily and unduly complicates the jury's task. Indeed, I find it difficult to imagine how it is humanly possible to follow the jury instruction apparently mandated by the combination of *Leary* and *Pappajohn*. This confusing and anomalous result is entirely the product of the deviation from basic criminal-law principles which occurred in *Leary* and accordingly there is much to support the view that it should be overruled.

The inconsistency between *Leary* and *Pappajohn* has not gone unnoticed in the literature. In *Canadian Criminal Law* (2nd ed. 1987), at p. 378, Professor Stuart describes the collision between *Leary* and *Pappajohn* as a "glaring inconsistency". In "Regina v. O'Connor: *Mens Rea* Survives in Australia" (1981), 19 U.W.O. L. Rev. 281, at pp. 300-301, David H. Doherty observes:

The two judgments are clearly inconsistent. *Pappajohn* confirms the essential requirement of a subjective mental culpability as a prerequisite to criminal liability. *Leary* creates a fundamental exception to that requirement. The facts of *Pappajohn* show that the judgments will inevitably come into conflict. The Supreme Court of Canada chose to avoid dealing with the confict in *Pappajohn* by ignoring the evidence of drinking by the accused. It is to be hoped that in a later case the court will seek a more positive resolution to the problem. In seeking that resolution the majority position in *O'Connor* deserves emulation. After reading the opinions expressed in *O'Connor*, one concludes as did the minority in *Leary*, that the position taken in *Majewski* and adopted by the majority in *Leary* constitutes an illogical, unwarranted, and detrimental departure from the contemporary trend in criminal law which recognizes subjective mental blameworthiness at the time of the doing of the prohibited act as the sine qua non of criminal liability. The creation of exceptions to the principle compelled by considerations of public policy must be left to Parliament.

See also Peter J. Connelly, "Drunkenness and Mistake of Fact: Pappajohn v. The Queen; Swietlinski v. The Queen" (1981), 24 Crim. L.Q. 49; Christine Boyle, *Sexual Assault* (1984), at pp. 89-90.

C. *Leary* Creates Uncertainty

The third general consideration justifying the court in overruling *Leary* is the principle established in *Minister of Indian Affairs and Northern Development v. Ranville, supra*, where the court overruled its previous decision in *Commonwealth of Puerto Rico v. Hernandez*, [1975] 1 S.C.R. 228, on the ground that continued recognition of the *persona designata* category could only have the effect of creating doubt as to which procedure a party should follow. The prior decision itself was a cause of uncertainty, and therefore following the prior decision because of *stare decisis* would be contrary to the underlying value behind that doctrine, namely, clarity and certainty in the law. Similarly, in *Vetrovec, supra*, the court overruled previous decisions relating to corroboration and stated, "The law of corroboration is unduly and unnecessarily complex and technical".

I have already indicated the confusion created by the combination of *Leary* and *Pappajohn*. I suggest that the distinction between "general" and "specific" intent which *Leary* mandates and the notorious difficulty in articulating a clear and workable definition of specific intent falls squarely within the principle enunciated in *Ranville* and *Vetrovec*. Because that category is based on policy rather than principle, classification of offences as falling within or without the specific intent category is necessarily an ad hoc, unpredictable exercise.

The situation with respect to the offence of break and enter, raised by the companion case, *R. v. Quin* (reasons being delivered contemporaneously) provides an example. In *R. v. Campbell* (1974), 17 C.C.C. (2d) 320 (Ont. C.A.), the accused was charged with breaking and entering with intent pursuant to s. 306(1)(*a*). The Ontario Court of Appeal held that offence to be a crime of specific intent and hence drunkenness was relevant to the issue of intention. In *Quin*, the accused was charged with breaking and entering and committing an indictable offence pursuant to s. 306(1)(*b*). The same court held that under that subsection, the break and enter offence was one requiring only proof of general intent and hence evidence of intoxication could not be considered. A legal category which creates distinctions of this king, in my view, complicates and confuses the law to an unacceptable degree and, absent some compelling need for its retention, should be abandoned.

Another example of the complexity and uncertainty caused by the specific/ general intent dichotomy is provided by *Swietlinski, supra*. In that case, the accused was charged with murder pursuant to s. 213(*d*) of the *Criminal Code*. The enumerated offence the accused was alleged to have committed was indecent assault. *Leary* had held that rape was an offence of general intent and in *Swietlinski*, the court applied *Leary* to the offence of indecent assault. However, because of the constructive murder provision, this would have led to a situation where the accused would be convicted of murder without any criminal intent. To avoid that result, the court held that where indecent assault formed the ingredient of constructive murder pursuant to s. 213, evidence of drunkenness could be taken into account in determining whether in fact the accused had the requisite intent for the offence of indecent assault. In other words, the court held quite explicitly that intoxication did logically bear upon the issue of intent to commit indecent assault, and that the only issue was whether, as a matter of policy, the jury should be told to put that evidence out of mind. In the light of *Vaillancourt, Swietlinski* is no longer significant for its result. Indeed, *Vaillancourt* and *Swietlinski* have this in common: both cases demonstrate the court's aversion to the imposition of liability without *mens rea*. In my view, to hold that evidence of intoxication can be taken into account with reference to an offence for certain purposes but not for other purposes is further reflection of the confusion, uncertainty, and lack of principle which motivates the specific/ general intent dichotomy.

D. *Leary* Unfavourable to Accused

The fourth factor which bears directly upon whether or not the court should overrule *Leary* in my view, is that the *Leary* rule is one which operates against the accused by expanding the scope of criminal liability beyond normal limits. Respect for the principle of certainty and the institutional limits imposed upon the law-making function of the courts should constrain the court from overruling a prior decision where the effect would be to expand criminal liability. It is not for the courts to create new offences, or to broaden the net of liability, particularly as changes in the law through judicial decision operate retrospectively. The same argument does not apply, however, where the result of overruling a prior decision is to establish a rule favourable to the accused. In my submission, this principle underlies the decision of the court in *Paquette v.*

The Queen, supra, at p. 197, where the court overruled its previous decision in *Dunbar v. The King, supra*, which had held that an accused who was a party to murder, but who had not himself committed the act, could not rely upon the defence of duresss. (See also *R. v. Santeramo* (1976), 32 C.C.C. (2d) 35 (Ont. C.A.), at p. 46 per Brooke J.A. "I do not feel bound by a judgment of this court where the liberty of the subject is in issue if I am convinced that that judgment is wrong.")

IV

DISPOSITION

The trial judge made no reference in his charge to the jury to the requirement that the Crown prove that the accused acted with the requisite intent. In my view, this is fatal to the conviction. Although the Crown presented a strong case against the accused at trial, no request was made by the respondent that this court apply the provision of s. 613(1)(*b*)(iii) of the *Criminal Code*, and in any event, it is not for this court to speculate as to the likely result had the jury been properly instructed.

It follows that the appeal should be allowed, the conviction set aside, and a new trial ordered.

LA FOREST J. (concurring in the result only): — I have had the advantage of reading the opinions prepared by the Chief Justice and Mr. Justice McIntyre. The requirement of *mens rea* in truly criminal offences is, as the Chief Justice had demonstrated, so fundamental that it cannot, since the *Charter*, be removed on the basis of judicially developed policy. It would be anomalous if the courts could infringe such a fundamental right on the basis of such policies when not demonstrated to be essential, while any attempt by Parliament to do so would be subjected to searching scrutiny under s. 1 as established by this court.

In my dissenting reasons in *R. v. Landry*, [1986] 1 S.C.R. 145, at p. 187, I set forth my views regarding the general issue posed here. I there observed that in the changed constitutional environment brought about by the *Charter*, if incursions are to be made upon fundamental legal values, it is for Parliament to do so, not the courts. It is the duty of Parliament to respond to the challenge of criminal activities. While the courts must sensitively consider actions taken by Parliament for the protection of the public generally, they must be forever diligent to prevent undue intrusions on our liberty. The courts are the protectors of our rights. It does not sit well for them to make rules intruding on fundamental rights even when this may appear to them to be desirable in a properly balanced system of criminal justice. That is Parliament's work. I added, at p. 189 of *Landry*:

If Parliament in its wisdom finds it necessary to adjust the balance, it can do so. It is in a better position to provide for the precise balance and has a far better access to the knowledge required to achieve that balance than the courts. The courts can then perform their duty of scrutinizing Parliament's laws both in their general tenor and in their particular application to safeguard our traditional values.

Established common-law rules should not, it is true, lightly be assumed to violate the *Charter*. As a repository of our traditional values they may, in fact, assist in defining its norms. But when a common-law rule is found to infringe upon a right or freedom guaranteed by the *Charter*, it must be justified in the same way as legislative rules. No adequate justification was made here.

Accordingly, I am in general agreement with the law as stated by the Chief Justice. However, I agree with McIntyre J. that on the particular facts of this case no substantial wrong or miscarriage of justice has occurred and it is, therefore, a proper case to apply s. 613(1)(*b*)(iii) of the *Criminal Code*. For this reason, I would dispose of the case in the manner proposed by McIntyre J.

For comments on *Bernard*, see T. Quigley and A. Manson in 67 C.R. (3d) 168-182 and K. Campbell, "Intoxicated Mistakes" (1989), 32 Crim. L.Q. 110.

In *Daviault* a 6:3 majority of the Supreme Court adopted the Wilson compromise that extreme intoxication akin to automatism or insanity had, under the *Charter*, to be a defence to general intent crimes such as sexual assault. The majority, however, likening the defence to insanity, reversed the onus of proof.

(b) *Charter* Standards

R. v. DAVIAULT

[1994] 3 S.C.R. 63, 33 C.R. (4th) 165, 93 C.C.C. (3d) 21,
1994 CarswellQue 10, 1994 CarswellQue 118

The accused was charged with sexual assault. The complainant was a 65-year-old woman who was partially paralyzed and thus confined to a wheelchair. She knew the accused through his wife. At approximately 6 p.m. the accused, at her request, went to her home. He brought a 40-ounce bottle of brandy. The accused, aged 69, was a chronic alcoholic. He would later testify that he had already consumed seven or eight bottles of beer in a bar. The complainant drank part of a bottle of brandy and then fell asleep in her wheelchair. When she awoke during the night to go to the bathroom, the accused appeared, grabbed her chair, wheeled her into the bedroom, threw her on the bed and sexually assaulted her. The accused left the apartment at about 4 a.m. The trial judge found that he had drunk the rest of the bottle of brandy between 6 p.m. and 3 a.m. The accused testified he had no recollection of the events until he awoke nude in the complainant's bed. He denied sexually assaulting her. A pharmacologist called as an expert witness for the accused testified that the accused's alcoholic history made him less susceptible to the effects of alcohol. He estimated that if the accused had consumed seven or eight beers and 35 ounces of brandy his blood alcohol level would be between 400 and 600 milligrams per 100 millilitres of blood. That ratio would cause death or a coma in an ordinary person. According to the expert an individual with this level of alcohol in his blood might suffer an episode of amnesia-automatism or ". In such a state the individual loses contact with reality and the brain is temporarily dissociated from normal functioning. The individual has no awareness of his actions and likely no memory of them the next day. According to the witness it is difficult to distinguish between a person in a blackout and one simply acting while intoxicated. The latter state is more likely if the person has departed from his normal behaviour to act in a gratuitous or violent manner.

The trial judge found that the accused had committed the offence described by the complainant. However, he acquitted because he had a reasonable doubt about whether the accused, by virtue of extreme intoxication to the point of automatism within the meaning of the judgment of Wilson J. in *Bernard*, had possessed the minimal intent necessary to commit the offence. The Quebec Court of Appeal allowed the Crown appeal and substituted a conviction. The Quebec Court of Appeal decided the majority of the Supreme Court in *Bernard* had not held that self-induced intoxication resulting in a state akin to automatism or insanity was available as a defence to sexual assault. The accused appealed.

The majority of the Supreme Court allowed the appeal and ordered a new trial.

CORY   J.   (L'HEUREUX-DUBÉ,   MCLACHLIN   and   IACOBUCCI   JJ. concurring): —

Can a state of drunkenness which is so extreme that an accused is in a condition that closely resembles automatism or a disease of the mind as defined in s. 16 of the *Criminal Code*, R.S.C., 1985, c. C-46, constitute a basis for defending a crime which requires not a specific but only a general intent? That is the troubling question that is raised on this appeal.

. . . .

Categorization of Crimes as Requiring Either a Specific Intent or a General Intent

The distinction between crimes of specific and general intent has been acknowledged and approved by this court on numerous occasions.... On this issue, I am in general agreement with Sopinka J.'s presentation. The categorization of crimes as being either specific or general intent offences and the consequences that flow from that categorization are now well-established in this court. However, as he observes, we are not dealing here with ordinary cases of intoxication but with the limited situation of very extreme intoxication and the need, under the *Charter*, to create an exception in situations where intoxication is such that the mental element is negated. Sopinka J. sees no need for such an exception. This is where I must disagree with my colleague.

. . . .

The passage of the *Charter* makes it necessary to consider whether the decision in *Leary* contravenes s. 7 or 11(*d*) of the *Charter*. There have been some statements by this court which indicate that one aspect of the decision in *Leary* does infringe these provisions of the *Charter*. The first occurred in *R. v. Bernard.* ... Wilson J. (L'Heureux-Dubé J. concurring), agreed with the conclusion reached by McIntyre and Beetz JJ. However, she advocated a modification of the rule set out in *Leary*. Her reasoning proceeds in this way. Sexual assault causing bodily harm is an offence of general intent which requires only a minimal intent to apply force. Ordinarily the Crown can establish the requisite mental state by means of the inferences to be drawn from the actions of the accused. Wilson J. found that the *Leary* rule was perfectly consistent with an onus resting upon the Crown to prove the minimal intent which should accompany the doing of the prohibited act in general intent offences, but she would have applied it in a more flexible form. In her view, evidence of intoxication could properly go before a jury in general intent offences if it demonstrated such extreme intoxication that there was an absence of awareness which was akin to a state of insanity or automatism. Only in such cases would she find that the evidence was capable of raising a reasonable doubt as to the existence of the minimal intent required for a general intent offence.

. . . .

The Alternative Options

What options are available with regard to the admissibility and significance of evidence of drunkenness as it may pertain to the mental element in general intent offences? One choice would be to continue to apply the *Leary* rule. Yet, as I will attempt to demonstrate in the next section, the rule violates the *Charter* and cannot be justified. Thus this choice is unacceptable.

Another route would be to follow *O'Connor* [(1980), 4 A. Crim. R. 348.] Evidence relating to drunkenness would then go to the jury along with all other relevant evidence in determining whether the mental element requirement had been met. It is this path that is enthusiastically recommended by the majority of writers in the field. Yet it cannot be followed. It is now well-established by this court that there are two categories of offences. Those requiring a specific intent and others which call for nothing more than a general intent. To follow

O'Connor would mean that all evidence of intoxication of any degree would always go to the jury in general intent offences. This, in my view, is unnecessary. Further, in *Bernard, supra*, the majority of this court rejected this approach.

A third alternative, which I find compelling, is that proposed by Wilson J. in *Bernard*. I will examine the justifications for adopting this position in more detail shortly, but before doing that it may be helpful to review the nature of the *Charter* violations occasioned by a rigid application of the *Leary* rule.

How the Leary Rule Violates Sections 7 and 11(d) of the Charter

What then is the rule of law established by the decision in *Leary*? The conclusion of the majority in that case establishes that, even in a situation where the level of intoxication reached by the accused is sufficient to raise a reasonable doubt as to his capacity to form the minimal mental element required for a general intent offence for which he is being tried, he still cannot be acquitted. In such a situation, self-induced intoxication is substituted for the mental element of the crime. The result of the decision in *Leary*, applied to this case, is that the intentional act of the accused to voluntarily become intoxicated is substituted for the intention to commit the sexual assault or for the recklessness of the accused with regard to the assault. This is a true substitution of *mens rea*. First, it would be rare that the events transpiring from the consumption of alcohol through to the commission of the crime could be seen as one continuous series of events or as a single transaction. Secondly, the requisite mental element or *mens rea* cannot necessarily be inferred from the physical act or *actus reus* when the very voluntariness or consciousness of that act may be put in question by the extreme intoxication of the accused.

It has not been established that there is such a connection between the consumption of alcohol and the crime of assault that it can be said that drinking leads inevitably to the assault. Experience may suggest that alcohol makes it easier for violence to occur by diminishing the sense of what is acceptable behaviour. However, studies indicate that it is not in itself a cause of violence.

. . . .

In my view, the strict application of the *Leary* rule offends both ss. 7 and 11(*d*) of the *Charter* for a number of reasons. The mental aspect of an offence, or *mens rea*, has long been recognized as an integral part of crime. The concept is fundamental to our criminal law. That element may be minimal in general intent offences; nonetheless, it exists. In this case, the requisite mental element is simply an intention to commit the sexual assault or recklessness as to whether the actions will constitute an assault. The necessary mental element can ordinarily be inferred from the proof that the assault was committed by the accused. However, the substituted *mens rea* of an intention to become drunk cannot establish the *mens rea* to commit the assault.

R. v. Whyte, [1988] 2 S.C.R. 3, dealt with the substitution of proof of one element for proof of an essential element of an offence and emphasized the strict limitations that must be imposed on such substitutions. The position is put in this way at pp. 18-19:

> In the passage from *Vaillancourt* quoted earlier, Lamer J. recognized that in some cases substituting proof of one element for proof of an essential element will not infringe the presumption of innocence if, upon proof of the substituted element, it would be unreasonable for the trier of fact not to be satisfied beyond a reasonable doubt of the existence of the essential element. This is another way of saying that a statutory presumption infringes the presumption of innocence if it requires the trier of fact to convict in spite of a reasonable doubt. *Only if the existence of the substituted fact leads inexorably to the conclusion that the essential element exists, with no other reasonable possibilities, will the statutory presumption be constitutionally valid.* [Emphasis added.]

The substituted *mens rea* set out in *Leary* does not meet this test. The consumption of alcohol simply cannot lead inexorably to the conclusion that the accused possessed the requisite mental element to commit a sexual assault, or any other crime. Rather, the substituted *mens rea* rule has the effect of eliminating the minimal mental element required for sexual assault. Furthermore, *mens rea* for a crime is so well-recognized that to eliminate that mental element, an integral part of the crime, would be to deprive an accused of fundamental justice. See *R. v. Vaillancourt*, [1987] 2 S.C.R. 636.

. . . .

Sopinka J. refers to the common law rules of automatism in order to support his position that voluntariness is not a requirement of fundamental justice. With respect I cannot agree. The decision of this court in *Revelle v. The Queen*, [1981] 1 S.C.R. 576, predates the *Charter*. The rule that self-induced automatism cannot be a defence has never been subjected to a *Charter* analysis. In my view, automatism raises the same concerns as those presented in this case. Thus, to state that the rule in *Leary*, which precludes the accused from negating the mental element of voluntariness on the basis of an extreme state of intoxication, does not violate the *Charter* because the same principle has been developed in the context of the defence of automatism begs the very question which is now before this court. The presumption of innocence requires that the Crown bear the burden of establishing all elements of a crime. These elements include the mental element of voluntariness. That element cannot be eliminated without violating s. 11(*d*) and s. 7 of the *Charter*.

It was argued by the respondent that the "blameworthy" nature of voluntary intoxication is such that it should be determined that there can be no violation of the *Charter* if the *Leary* approach is adopted. I cannot accept that contention. Voluntary intoxication is not yet a crime. Further, it is difficult to conclude that such behaviour should always constitute a fault to which criminal sanctions should apply. However, assuming that voluntary intoxication is reprehensible, it does not follow that its consequences in any given situation are either voluntary or predictable. Studies demonstrate that the consumption of alcohol is not the cause of the crime. A person intending to drink cannot be said to be intending to commit a sexual assault.

Further, self-induced intoxication cannot supply the necessary link between the minimal mental element or *mens rea* required for the offence and the *actus reus*. This must follow from reasoning in *R. v. DeSousa*, [1992] 2 S.C.R. 944, and *R. v. Theroux, supra*. Here, the question is not whether there is some symmetry between the physical act and the mental element but whether the necessary link exists between the minimal mental element and the prohibited act; that is to say that the mental element is one of intention with respect to the *actus reus* of the crime charged. As well, as Sopinka J. observes, the minimum *mens rea* for an offence should reflect the particular nature of the crime. See *R. v. Creighton*, [1993] 3 S.C.R. 3. I doubt that self-induced intoxication can, in all circumstances, meet this requirement for all crimes of general intent.

In summary, I am of the view that to deny that even a very minimal mental element is required for sexual assault offends the *Charter* in a manner that is so drastic and so contrary to the principles of fundamental justice that it cannot be justified under s. 1 of the *Charter*. The experience of other jurisdictions which have completely abandoned the *Leary* rule, coupled with the fact that under the proposed approach, the defence would be available only in the rarest of cases, demonstrate that there is no urgent policy or pressing objective which need to be addressed. Studies on the relationship between intoxication and crime do not establish any rational link. Finally, as the *Leary* rule applies to all crimes of general intent, it cannot be said to be well-tailored to address a particular objective and it would not meet either the proportionality or the minimum impairment requirements.

. . . .

Far more writers have supported the approach advocated by Dickson J. in *Leary*, and adopted in *O'Connor*. In my view, the most vehement and cogent criticism of both *Majewski* and *Leary* is that they substitute proof of drunkenness for proof of the requisite mental element. The authors deplore the division of crimes into those requiring a specific intent and those which mandate no more than a general intent. They are also critical of the resulting presumption of recklessness, and of the loss of a requirement of a true *mens rea* for the offence. They would prefer an approach that would permit evidence of drunkenness to go to the jury together with all the other relevant evidence in determining whether the requisite *mens rea* had been established.

. . . .

I find further support for adopting the approach suggested by Wilson J. in studies pertaining to the effect of the *O'Connor* and *Kamipeli* decisions which have been undertaken in Australia and New Zealand. (Reference to these studies can be found in the English Law Commission's *Intoxication and Criminal Liability, supra,* at pp. 60-63.) One of these studies was conducted in New South Wales, by means of a survey of approximately 510 trials (see Judge G. Smith, "Footnote to *O'Connor's* Case", *supra.* The author, Judge George Smith, concluded, at p. 277, that:

> Those figures disclose that a "defence" of intoxication which could not have been relied upon pre-*O'Connor* was raised in 11 cases or 2.16 percent of the total. Acquittals followed in three cases or 0.59 percent of the total, but only in one case or 0.2 percent of the total could it be said with any certainty that the issue of intoxication was the factor which brought about the acquittal.

. . . .

> It seems to me that no one with any experience of the criminal courts should be greatly surprised at this result for the simple practical reason that any "defence" of drunkenness poses enormous difficulties in the conduct of a case. To name but one, if the accused has sufficient recollection to describe relevant events, juries will be reluctant to believe that he acted involuntarily or without intent whereas, if he claims to have no recollection, he will be unable to make any effective denial of facts alleged by the Crown.

. . . .

> Certainly my inquiries would indicate that the decision in *O'Connor's* case, far from opening any floodgates has at most permitted an occasional drip to escape from the tap.

That study clearly indicates that the *O'Connor* decision has not had an effect of any significance on trials or on the numbers of acquittals arising from evidence of severe intoxication.

. . . .

It is obvious that it will only be on rare occasions that evidence of such an extreme state of intoxication can be advanced and perhaps only on still rarer occasions is it likely to be successful. Nonetheless, the adoption of this alternative would avoid infringement of the *Charter.*

I would add that it is always open to Parliament to fashion a remedy which would make it a crime to commit a prohibited act while drunk.

. . . .

It should not be forgotten that if the flexible "Wilson" approach is taken, the defence will only be put forward in those rare circumstances of extreme intoxication. Since that state must be shown to be akin to automatism or insanity, I would suggest that the accused should be called upon to establish it on the balance of probabilities. This court has recognized, in *R. v. Chaulk*, [1990] 3 S.C.R. 1303, that although it constituted a violation of the accused's rights under s. 11(*d*) of the *Charter*, such a burden could be justified under s. 1. In this case, I feel that the burden can be justified. Drunkenness of the extreme degree required in order for it to become relevant will only occur on rare occasions. It is only the accused who can give evidence as to the amount of alcohol consumed and its effect upon him. Expert evidence would be required to confirm that the accused was probably in a state akin to automatism or insanity as a result of his drinking.

. . . .

Should it be thought that the mental element involved relates to the *actus reus* rather than the *mens rea* then the result must be the same. The *actus reus* requires that the prohibited criminal act be performed voluntarily as a willed act. A person in a state of automatism cannot perform a voluntary willed act since the automatism has deprived the person of the ability to carry out such an act. It follows that someone in an extreme state of intoxication akin to automatism must also be deprived of that ability. Thus a fundamental aspect of the *actus reus* of the criminal act is absent. It would equally infringe s. 7 of the *Charter* if an accused who was not acting voluntarily could be convicted of a criminal offence. Here again the voluntary act of becoming intoxicated cannot be substituted for the voluntary action involved in sexual assault. To do so would violate the principle set out in *Vaillancourt, supra*. Once again to convict in the face of such a fundamental denial of natural justice could not be justified under s. 1 of the *Charter*.

Summary of Proposed Remedy

In my view, the *Charter* could be complied with, in crimes requiring only a general intent, if the accused were permitted to establish that, at the time of the offence, he was in a state of extreme intoxication akin to automatism or insanity. Just as in a situation where it is sought to establish a state of insanity, the accused must bear the burden of establishing, on the balance of probabilities, that he was in that extreme state of intoxication. This will undoubtedly require the testimony of an expert. Obviously, it will be a rare situation where an accused is able to establish such an extreme degree of intoxication. Yet, permitting such a procedure would mean that a defence would remain open that, due to the extreme degree of intoxication, the minimal mental element required by a general intent offence had not been established. To permit this rare and limited defence in general intent offences is required so that the common law principles of intoxication can comply with the *Charter*.

In light of the experience in Australia or New Zealand, it cannot be said that to permit such a defence would open the floodgates to allow every accused who had a drink before committing the prohibited act to raise the defence of drunkenness. As observed earlier, studies made in Australia and New Zealand indicate that there has not been any significant increase in the number of acquittals following the *O'Connor* and *Kamipelli* decisions.

Disposition

In the result, I would allow the appeal, set aside the order of the Court of Appeal and direct a new trial.

LAMER C.J.: — I have read the reasons of my colleagues, Justice Sopinka and Justice Cory. My views of the matter were enunciated through my concurrence in the reasons of Dickson C.J. in *R. v. Bernard*, [1988] 2 S.C.R. 833. While I now prefer characterizing the mental element involved as relating more to the *actus reus* than the *mens rea*, so that the defence clearly be available in strict liability offences, my views have not changed. I agree with my colleague Cory J.'s position on the law and, given my position in *Bernard*, which goes much further, I would of course support carving out, as he does, an exception to the rule laid down in *Leary v. The Queen*, [1978] 1 S.C.R. 29. I would accordingly allow the appeal and direct a new trial.

LA FOREST J.: — In *R. v. Bernard*, [1988] 2 S.C.R. 833, as well as in *R. v. Quin*, [1988] 2 S.C.R. 825, I, along with the Chief Justice, shared the view of then Chief Justice Dickson which strongly challenged the rule in *Leary v. The Queen*, [1978] 1 S.C.R. 29. While the majority of the court differed as to the specific interpretation of *Leary*, what is clear is that they rejected the view espoused by Dickson C.J. I am, therefore, left to choose between the approach set forth in McIntyre J.'s reasons in that case, developed here by Justice Sopinka, and those of Wilson J., developed here by Justice Cory. Of the two, I prefer the latter and accordingly (though I would be inclined to attribute the mental element he describes as going to the *actus reus*) I concur in the reasons of Cory J. and would dispose of this appeal in the manner proposed by him.

SOPINKA J. (GONTHIER and MAJOR JJ. concurring) (dissenting): —

. . . .

Central to [the *Charter*'s] values are the integrity and dignity of the human person. These serve to define the principles of fundamental justice. They encompass as an essential attribute and are predicated upon the moral responsibility of every person of sound mind for his or her acts. The requirement of *mens rea* is an application of this principle. To allow generally an accused who is not afflicted by a disease of the mind to plead absence of *mens rea* where he has voluntarily caused himself to be incapable of *mens rea* would be to undermine, indeed negate, that very principle of moral responsibility which the requirement of *mens rea* is intended to give effect to.

The second requirement of the principles of fundamental justice is that punishment must be proportionate to the moral blameworthiness of the offender. This was held to be a principle of fundamental justice in *R. v. Martineau*, [1990] 2 S.C.R. 633, and *R. v. Creighton, supra*. There are a few crimes in respect of which a special level of *mens rea* is constitutionally required by reason of the stigma attaching to a conviction and by reason of the severity of the penalty imposed by law. Accordingly, murder and attempted murder require a *mens rea* based on a subjective standard. No exception from the principle of fundamental justice should be made with respect to these offences and, as specific intent offences, drunkenness is a defence.

By contrast, sexual assault does not fall into the category of offences for which either the stigma or the available penalties demand as a constitutional requirement subjective intent to commit the *actus reus*. Sexual assault is a heinous crime of violence. Those found guilty of committing the offence are rightfully submitted to a significant degree of moral opprobrium. That opprobrium is not misplaced in the case of the intoxicated offender. Such individuals deserve to be stigmatized. Their moral blameworthiness is similar to that of anyone else who commits the offence of sexual assault and the effects of their conduct upon both their victims and society as a whole are the same as in any other case of sexual assault. Furthermore, the sentence for sexual assault is not fixed. To the extent that it bears upon his or her level of moral blameworthiness, an offender's degree of intoxication at the time of the offence may be considered during sentencing. Taking all of these factors into account, I cannot see how the stigma and punishment associated with the offence of sexual assault are disproportionate to the moral blameworthiness of a person like the appellant who commits the offence after voluntarily becoming so intoxicated as to be incapable of knowing what he was doing. The fact that the *Leary* rule permits an individual to be convicted despite the absence of symmetry between the *actus reus* and the mental element of blameworthiness does not violate a principle of fundamental justice.

It is further contended that the *Leary* rule violates the presumption of innocence because it permits an individual to be convicted despite the existence of a reasonable doubt as to whether or not that individual performed the *actus reus* of his or her own volition. This argument is premised upon the assumption that voluntariness is a constitutionally required element of the *actus reus* of an offence of universal application. Again, I do not think that this assumption is warranted.

. . . .

It is true that as a general rule, an act must be the voluntary act of an accused in order for the *actus reus* to exist. See *R. v. Parks*, [1992] 2 S.C.R. 871, at p. 896, per La Forest J., and *R. v. Theroux*, [1993] 2 S.C.R. 5, at p. 17, per McLachlin J. This, as in the case of *mens rea*, is a general rule of the criminal law, but when elevated to a principle of fundamental justice it too, exceptionally, is not absolute. One well-recognized exception is made relating to the defence of non-insane automatism. As I explain below, automatism does not apply to excuse an offence if the accused's state is brought on by his or her own fault. The condition of automatism deprives the accused of volition to commit the offence but the general rule gives way to the policy that, in the circumstances, the perpetrator who by his or her own fault brings about the condition should not escape punishment. An accused person who voluntarily drinks alcohol or ingests a drug to the extent that he or she becomes an automaton is in the same position. The rules of fundamental justice are satisfied by a showing that the drunken state was attained through the accused's own blameworthy conduct.

Another criticism of the current rules governing the availability of the intoxication defence is that the distinction between offences of specific and general intent is illogical. Critics of the rule contend that there is no principled basis for distinguishing between offences of general and specific intent and thus there is no logical reason why intoxication should be a defence to offences of specific intent but not to offences of general intent.

The appellant does not, however, take issue with the proposition that in general the distinction between offences of specific and general intent is a valid one. His submission is that when drunkenness reaches the stage of automatism, the distinction should no longer apply. This essentially was the tentative view of Wilson J. as expressed in her *obiter* statement in *R. v. Bernard* to which I referred above.

Notwithstanding the position of the appellant, I propose to briefly address the criticism of the rule that it is illogical. In my view, the concept has strong policy underpinnings which, despite the fact that its definition and application may have produced some illogical results, have permitted it to survive for over 150 years in England and to be adopted in Canada and most states of the United States.

. . . .

The principles that emerge from the cases which serve as guidelines in classifying offences as specific or general intent offences are as follows. General intent offences as a rule are those which require the minimal intent to do the act which constitutes the *actus reus*. Proof of intent is usually inferred from the commission of the act on the basis of the principle that a person intends the natural consequences of his or her act. Without attempting to exhaust the policy reasons for excluding the defence of drunkenness from this category of offences, I would observe that it is seldom, even in cases of extreme drunkenness, that a person will lack this minimal degree of consciousness. Moreover, these are generally offences that persons who are drunk are apt to commit and it would defeat the policy behind them to make drunkenness a defence.

Specific intent offences are as a rule those that require a mental element beyond that of general intent offences and include "those generally more serious offences where the *mens rea* must involve not only the intentional performance of the *actus reus* but, as well, the formation of further ulterior motives and purposes" (per McIntyre J. in *R. v. Bernard, supra*, at p. 880). These are often referred to as "ulterior intent" offences. See *Majewski, supra*. Professor Colvin, in "A Theory of the Intoxication Defence" (1981), 59 Can. Bar Rev. 750, correctly points out that it is the further intent in addition to the basic intent that is the hallmark of ulterior intent offences. The policy behind this classification is in part the importance of the mental element over and above the minimal intent required for general intent offences. This distinction demands that the accused not be convicted if the added important mental state is negated by the drunken condition of the accused. Failure to prove the added element will often result in conviction of a lesser offence for which the added element is not required. One example is the offence of assault to resist or prevent arrest which is a specific intent offence. Absent the intent to resist arrest, the accused would be convicted of assault *simpliciter*, a general intent offence.

In addition to the ulterior intent offences there are certain offences which by reason of their serious nature and the importance of the mental element are classed as specific intent offences notwithstanding that they do not fit the criteria usually associated with ulterior intent offences. The outstanding example is murder. This is the most serious of criminal offences which carries a fixed penalty. By reason of the importance of the required mental element and the fixed penalty, this offence is classified as a specific intent offence. The defence of drunkenness is allowed so as to reduce the crime to manslaughter tempering the harshness of the law which precludes drunkenness as a consideration as to sentence. The classification of murder as a specific intent offence illustrates the proper application of policy in a case in which the application of the normal criteria might lead to a different result.

I accept that the application of the terms "specific" and "general" may lead to some illogical results. This is not surprising in light of the circumstances outlined above. Moreover, even the clearest unifying principle will in its application not produce perfect harmony. I am, however, convinced that the underlying policy of the *Leary* rule is sound. I am of the opinion that the criticism of the rule on the grounds of illogicality has been overdone. Applying criteria similar to the above, Professor Colvin has been able to explain "the broad pattern of the decisions emanating from the courts". See Colvin, *supra*, at p. 768.

. . . .

Conclusion

For all of these reasons, in my opinion the best course is for the court to reaffirm the traditional rule that voluntary intoxication does not constitute a defence to an offence of general intent, subject to the comments I have made with respect to improvements in the definition and application of the distinction between offences of specific and general intent. If a different approach is considered desirable because the *Leary* approach does not comport with social policy, Parliament is free to intervene. I note that this observation was made by McIntyre J. in *R. v. Bernard* but Parliament has not intervened. It has been suggested that Parliament should create a new offence of dangerous intoxication. Such a recommendation was made by the Butler Committee in England and by the Law Reform Commission in Canada. (See Butler Committee Report on Mentally Abnormal Offenders (1975) (Cmnd. 6244, paras. 18.51-18.59) and Law Reform Commission of Canada, Recodifying Criminal Law, Report 30, vol. 1 (1986), at pp. 27-28.) Such legislation could be coupled with amendments to the *Criminal Code* to extend the defence of drunkenness to some or all offences to which it does not apply. Such changes, however, are for Parliament and not for this court to make.

In *Majewski*, Lord Elwyn-Jones L.C. summed up the situation in words with which I fully agree. He stated, at p. 475:

> It may well be that Parliament will at some future time consider, as I think it should, the recommendation in the Butler Committee Report on Mentally Abnormal Offenders (Cmnd. 6244, 1975) that a new offence of "dangerous intoxication" should be created. But in the meantime it would be irresponsible to abandon the common-law rule, as "mercifully relaxed," which the courts have followed for a century and a half.

Disposition

The trial judge stated that but for his opinion that the appellant's extreme state of drunkenness constituted a defence, he would have convicted the appellant. I agree with the Court of Appeal that the trial judge erred in law in this regard. The Court of Appeal was right, therefore, to substitute a conviction. I would dismiss the appeal.

The only description of the facts provided by the Supreme Court appears in the judgment of Sopinka J., who indicates that they were "not in dispute". The record appears incomplete. For further details gathered from the Crown factum and from communications with both counsel, see Patrick Healy, "Another Round on Intoxication", published in the Criminal Reports Forum issue on *Daviault*.

> He threw her from the chair onto the bed, began to fondle her under her dressing-gown, and then attempted to rape her. The victim struggled and demanded twice to go to the toilet. The accused

insisted that they have sex. He said several times "We are going to make love". He spoke of going to Florida with the victim and more than once he called the victim by a name that was neither hers nor his wife's. He prevented her from going to the toilet and she urinated on him in the bed. When she attempted to call 911 for assistance, he struck her several times in the face with full force. He also struck the telephone from her hand. He pulled her up by her hair and demanded that she perform *fellatio*, at which point she squeezed and twisted his testicles. She testified that he showed no reaction to this. He then fell onto the bed. She dragged herself along the floor and pulled herself into the wheelchair. All this occurred over a period of about an hour. At about 4 a.m. he searched about to find the shirt that he had been wearing when he arrived. He found it, dressed himself and went home.

The victim testified that during the assault the accused did not appear to be drunk but she did state that the bottle of brandy and the glass from which she had been drinking were empty. The wife of the accused testified that Daviault came home at about 4:20 and did not appear to be drunk. He let himself into the house with his key, walked entirely straight, undressed and went to bed. She said that when he came home very drunk he was usually unable to open the door and slept fully dressed after passing out. On this occasion he also appeared quite calm and not "agitated or tormented" as he normally was after drinking strong liquor. She later noticed that his testicles had turned black.

On *Daviault*, see also, in the Criminal Reports, comments by Isabel Grant, Tim Quigley and Don Stuart. See also Martha Shaffer, "Criminal Responsibility and the *Charter:* The Case of *R. v. Daviault*" in Cameron (ed.), *The Charter's Impact on the Criminal Justice System* (1996) pp. 313-325.

The new trial ordered in *Daviault* resulted in a judicial stay of proceedings: (1995), 39 C.R. (4th) 269 (C.Q.). The complainant by then was deceased and disclosure of statements made originally to the police revealed inconsistencies such that the cross-examination would have been quite different. It was held that to proceed would be a denial of natural justice. See comment by Patrick Healy in (1995), 39 C.R. (4th) 272.

Public reaction to *Daviault* was swift. The Minister of Justice, Allan Rock, was reported to be "deeply troubled" by the ruling because of its "tremendous ramifications in sexual assault cases". It was widely condemned as giving the wrong message to those who drink and harm. Commentators used extravagant hypotheticals of rapists getting off on the basis of having had a few drinks. That such views were misreadings of the majority opinion is quite clear.

The number of acquittals that followed *Daviault* was wildly exaggerated.

Later, Martha Drassinower and Don Stuart, "Nine Months of Judicial Application of the *Daviault* Defence" (1995), 39 C.R. (4th) 280, surveyed reported and unreported judgments in the nine months following the Supreme Court's ruling. Eleven *Daviault* defences were considered at trial. Five were successful but two were subsequently reversed on appeal. Given what must have been thousands of criminal cases involving intoxicated accused over that period, the survey provides some validation of Justice Cory's prediction that the defence would be rarely used and would rarely succeed.

On February 24, 1995, the Minister of Justice, Allan Rock, tabled Bill C-72 in the House of Commons, purporting to provide that "extreme intoxication is not a defence to crimes of violence". **Is this amendment wise? Is it constitutional?**

Bill C-72

An Act to amend the *Criminal Code* (self-induced intoxication)

Preamble

WHEREAS the Parliament of Canada is gravely concerned about the incidence of violence in Canadian society;

WHEREAS the Parliament of Canada recognizes that violence has a particularly disadvantaging impact on the equal participation of women and children in society and on the rights of women and children to security of the person and to the equal protection and benefit of the law as guaranteed by sections 7, 15 and 28 of the *Canadian Charter of Rights and Freedoms*;

WHEREAS the Parliament of Canada recognizes that there is a close association between violence and intoxication and is concerned that self-induced intoxication may be used socially and legally to excuse violence, particularly violence against women and children;

WHEREAS the Parliament of Canada recognizes that the potential effects of alcohol and certain drugs on human behaviour are well-known to Canadians and is aware of scientific evidence that many intoxicants, including alcohol, may not cause a person to act involuntarily;

WHEREAS the Parliament of Canada shares with Canadians the moral view that people who, while in a state of self-induced intoxication, violate the physical integrity of others are blameworthy in relation to their harmful conduct and should be held criminally accountable for it;

WHEREAS the Parliament of Canada desires to promote and help to ensure the full protection of the rights guaranteed under sections 7, 11, 15 and 28 of the *Canadian Charter of Rights and Freedoms* for all Canadians, including those who are or may be victims of violence;

WHEREAS the Parliament of Canada considers it necessary to legislate a basis of criminal fault in relation to self-induced intoxication and general intent offences involving violence;

WHEREAS the Parliament of Canada recognizes the continuing existence of a common-law principle that intoxication to an extent that is less than that which would cause a person to lack the ability to form the basic intent or to have the voluntariness required to commit a criminal offence of general intent is never a defence at law;

AND WHEREAS the Parliament of Canada considers it necessary and desirable to legislate a standard of care, in order to make it clear that a person who, while in a state of incapacity by reason of self-induced intoxication, commits an offence involving violence against another person, departs markedly from the standard of reasonable care that Canadians owe to each other and is thereby criminally at fault;

NOW, THEREFORE, Her Majesty, by and with the advice and consent of the Senate and House of Commons of Canada, enacts as follows:

Self-induced Intoxication

When defence not available

33.1 (1) It is not a defence to an offence referred to in subsection (3) that the accused, by reason of self-induced intoxication, lacked the basic intent or the voluntariness required to commit the offence, where the accused departed markedly from the standard of care as described in subsection (2).

Criminal fault by reason of intoxication

(2) For the purposes of this section, a person departs markedly from the standard of reasonable care generally recognized in Canadian society and is thereby criminally at fault where the person, while in a state of self-induced intoxication that renders the person unaware of, or incapable of consciously controlling, their behaviour, voluntarily or involuntarily interferes or threatens to interfere with the bodily integrity of another person.

Application

(3) This section applies in respect of an offence under this Act or any other Act of Parliament that includes as an element an assault or any other interference or threat of interference by a person with the bodily integrity of another person.

The effect of this most complex provision is to use a deemed fault provision to remove the *Daviault* defence to most general intent offences. Most such offences involve at least threats to bodily integrity so as to come within the ambit of subs. (3). However, s. 33.1 does not affect the common law defence of drunkenness available to specific intent crimes such as murder and robbery.

Whether s. 33.1 will survive *Charter* review remains to be seen. Lower courts have accepted that s. 33.1 flies in the face of the determination in *Daviault* that principles of fundamental justice require a defence of intoxication where this is akin to automatism. But they are divided on the further question of whether the s. 7 violation can be saved under s. 1 as a demonstrably justified reasonable limit. Rulings of constitutionality were reached in *Vickberg* (1998), 16 C.R. (5th) 164 (B.C. S.C.) and *Decaire* (September 11, 1998), (Ont. Gen. Div.). Section 33.1 was ruled unconstitutional in *Dunn* (1999), 28 C.R. (5th) 295 (Ont. Gen. Div.) and

Brenton (1999), 28 C.R. (5th) 308 (N.W.T. S.C.). These rulings are fully discussed by Kelly Smith, "Section 33.1: Denial of *Daviault* Defence Should Be Held Constitutional" (2000), 28 C.R. (5th) 350. Lower courts in Ontario now accept that section 33.1 is unconstitutional: see *R. v. Jensen*, [2000] O.J. No. 4870 (Ont. S.C.) and *R. v. Cedeno* (2005), 27 C.R. (6th) 251 (Ont. C.J.). The Ontario Court of Appeal (see *R. v. Jensen* (2005), 27 C.R. (6th) 240 (Ont. C.A.)) and the Supreme Court of Canada have so far declined to rule on this question. The Supreme Court is not yet on record as justifying a s. 7 violation.

On the other hand, in *Mills* (2000), 28 C.R. (5th) 207 (S.C.C.), the court spoke of a need for dialogue with Parliament which should allow for deference to legislative schemes. Furthermore, *Mills* also recognized that complainants in sexual assault cases have enforceable s. 15 rights which must be balanced not just as a matter of principles of fundamental justice. Isabel Grant, "Second Chances: Bill C-72 and the *Charter*" (1995), 33 Osgoode Hall L.J. 381, argues sex equality considerations should determine that s. 33.1 does not offend s. 7. The clear subtext to the negative reaction and Parliamentary response to *Daviault* was clearly grounded in that context. In *R. v. Dow* (2010), 261 C.C.C. (3d) 399 (Que. S.C.) Hout J. decided in a comprehensive ruling that s. 33.1 was demonstrably justified under s. 1. It was a reasonable alternative and protected vulnerable targets, in particular women and children. Another complication is that evidence was tendered at the Parliamentary committee hearings leading to Bill C-72 refuting the *Daviault* view that intoxication can lead to a state of automatism. See review by Smith, above, at 362-364. See, too, Joseph Wilkinson, "The Possibility of Alcoholic Automatism: Some Empirical Evidence" (1997), 2 Can. Crim. L. Rev. 217. Even if s. 33.1 survives *Charter* review in the Supreme Court, fundamental questions will remain as to the wisdom of the current legal regime for intoxication, rooted, as it still is, in the distinction between specific and general intent.

R. v. DALEY

52 C.R. (6th) 221, 2007 CarswellSask 707, 2007 CarswellSask 708, 226 C.C.C. (3d) 1, [2007] 3 S.C.R. 523

The court makes it clear that where drunkenness is raised as a defence to a specific intent crime the issue is one of intent in fact rather than incapacity. In his lengthy judgment for the majority (four justices dissented on the basis the trial judge had in his direction to the jury not sufficiently related the law to the evidence) Justice Bastarache introduced new terminology for the different types of intoxication defences:

BASTARACHE J.:—

5.1.2.2 THE LEGALLY RELEVANT DEGREES OF INTOXICATION

41 Our case law suggests there are three legally relevant degrees of intoxication. First, there is what we might call "mild" intoxication. This is where there is

alcohol-induced relaxation of both inhibitions and socially acceptable behaviour. This has never been accepted as a factor or excuse in determining whether the accused possessed the requisite *mens rea*. See *Daviault*, at p. 99. Second, there is what we might call "advanced" intoxication. This occurs where there is intoxication to the point where the accused lacks specific intent, to the extent of an impairment of the accused's foresight of the consequences of his or her act sufficient to raise a reasonable doubt about the requisite *mens rea*. The court in *Robinson* noted that this will most often be the degree of intoxication the jury will grapple with in murder trials:

> In most murder cases, the focus for the trier of fact will be on the foreseeability prong of s. 229(a)(ii) of the *Criminal Code*, R.S.C. 1985, c. C 46, that is, on determining whether the accused foresaw that his or her actions were likely to cause the death of the victim. For example, consider the case where an accused and another individual engage in a fight outside a bar. During the fight, the accused pins the other individual to the ground and delivers a kick to the head, which kills that person. In that type of a case, the jury will likely struggle, assuming they reject any self defence or provocation claim, with the question of whether that accused foresaw that his or her actions would likely cause the death of the other individual. [para. 49]

A defence based on this level of intoxication applies only to specific intent offences.

42 It is important to recognize that the extent of intoxication required to advance a successful intoxication defence of this type may vary, depending on the type of offence involved. This was recognized by this court in *Robinson*, at para. 52, in regards to some types of homicides:

> [I]n cases where the only question is whether the accused intended to kill the victim (s. 229(a)(i) of the *Code*), while the accused is entitled to rely on any evidence of intoxication to argue that he or she lacked the requisite intent and is entitled to receive such an instruction from the trial judge (assuming of course that there is an "air of reality" to the defence), it is my opinion that intoxication short of incapacity will in most cases rarely raise a reasonable doubt in the minds of jurors. For example, in a case where an accused points a shotgun within a few inches of someone's head and pulls the trigger, it is difficult to conceive of a successful intoxication defence unless the jury is satisfied that the accused was so drunk that he or she was not capable of forming an intent to kill.

Although I would hesitate to use the language of capacity to form intent, for fear that this may detract from the ultimate issue (namely, actual intent), the point of this passage, it seems to me, is that, for certain types of homicides, where death is the obvious consequence of the accused's act, an accused might have to establish a particularly advanced degree of intoxication to successfully avail himself or herself of an intoxication defence of this type.

43 The third and final degree of legally relevant intoxication is extreme intoxication akin to automatism, which negates voluntariness and thus is a complete defence to criminal responsibility. As discussed above, such a defence

would be extremely rare, and by operation of s. 33.1 of the *Criminal Code*, limited to non-violent types of offences.

The issue of the constitutionality of s. 33.1 was not before the court in *Daley*.

R. v. BOUCHARD-LEBRUN

2011 CarswellQue 12785, 2011 SCC 58 (S.C.C.)

We earlier considered the ruling that toxic psychosis exclusively resulting from the voluntary consumption of ecstasy pills could not result in a finding of not criminally responsible on account of mental disorder. The Court indicated that no *Charter* challenge had been made to s. 33.1, "which means that only the interpretation and application of that provision are in issue" (para. 28).

LeBel J.: —

[35] In a general sense, the appellant can reasonably argue that Parliament implicitly endorsed Sopinka J.'s dissent in *Daviault* by enacting s. 33.1 *Cr. C.* However, the enactment of that provision did not revive the *Leary* rule. It did not actually codify the position taken by the dissenting judges in *Daviault*; rather, it limited the scope of the rule stated by the majority. This means that the principles set out in *Daviault* still represent the state of the law in Canada, subject, of course, to the significant restriction set out in s. 33.1 *Cr. C. Daviault* would still apply today, for example, to enable an accused charged with a property offence to plead extreme intoxication. Indeed, the fact that the appellant was acquitted at trial on the charges against him under ss. 348(1)(*a*) and 463 *Cr. C.* affords an eloquent example of this.

G.   *Section 33.1 Cr. C. Applies in This Case*

[89] The foregoing conclusion leads to the question whether s. 33.1 *Cr. C.* is applicable. This provision applies where three conditions are met: (1) the accused was intoxicated at the material time; (2) the intoxication was self-induced; and (3) the accused departed from the standard of reasonable care generally recognized in Canadian society by interfering or threatening to interfere with the bodily integrity of another person (see generally *R. v. Vickberg* (1998), 16 C.R. (5th) 164 (B.C.S.C.); *R. v. Chaulk*, 2007 NSCA 84, 257 N.S.R. (2d) 99). Where these three things are proved, it is not a defence that the accused lacked the general intent or the voluntariness required to commit the offence.

[90] The self-induced intoxication to which s. 33.1 *Cr. C.* refers is limited in time. It corresponds to the period during which the substance consumed by the

accused produced its effects. Section 33.1(2) *Cr. C.* leaves no doubt about this. It provides that a person "is . . . criminally at fault where the person, <u>while in a state of self-induced intoxication that renders the person</u> unaware of, or <u>incapable</u> of consciously controlling, their behaviour, voluntarily or involuntarily interferes or threatens to interfere with the bodily integrity of another person". Section 33.1 *Cr. C.* is intended to prevent an accused from avoiding criminal liability on the ground that his or her state of intoxication at the material time *rendered the accused incapable* of forming the mental element or having the voluntariness required to commit the offence.

[91] Section 33.1 *Cr. C.* therefore applies to any mental condition that is a direct extension of a state of intoxication. It is also important to understand that no distinction based on the seriousness of the effects of self-induced intoxication is drawn in this provision. The appellant's suggestion that it applies only to the "normal effects" of intoxication is wrong. There is no threshold of intoxication beyond which s. 33.1 *Cr. C.* does not apply to an accused, which means that toxic psychosis can be one of the states of intoxication covered by this provision. It is so covered in the case at bar. The Court of Appeal therefore did not err in law in holding that s. 33.1 *Cr. C.* was applicable rather than s. 16 *Cr. C.*

It is startling that the Supreme Court proceeds to apply s. 33.1 which Parliament enacted to remove the *Daviault* defence of "extreme intoxication akin to insanity or automatism" from offences of general intent which affect bodily integrity. The Court simply noted the lack of a *Charter* challenge and proceeded to apply the section. Since the Court's majority decision in *Daviault* was squarely based on the view that this limited and rare defence was required by the *Charter* it seems too deferential and meek for the Court to have avoided the issue in this way. **Should the Court have ordered a new hearing with intervenors to consider this controversial issue and to decide whether the Court is still committed to the *Daviault* principles it declared 15 years ago?**

Chapter 7

JUSTIFICATIONS AND EXCUSES

1. WHY ALLOW COMMON LAW DEFENCES?

The reason for preserving common-law defences in s. 8(3) in 1955 seems to lie in the acceptance of the pragmatic rationale of the English Royal Commission of 1880 which considered it "if not absolutely impossible, at least not practicable" to anticipate with acceptable precision every future defence. In the following extract Stephen raises another pragmatic consideration with considerable force.

J.F. STEPHEN, THE NINETEENTH CENTURY . . .

Quoted in G.L. Williams, "Necessity" (1978), Crim. L. Rev. 128 at 129-130

It appears to me that the two proposed enactments stand on entirely different principles. After the experience of centuries, and with a Parliament sitting every year, and keenly alive to all matters likely to endanger the public interests, we are surely in a position to say the power of declaring new offences shall henceforth be vested in Parliament only. The power which has at times been claimed for the judges of declaring new offences cannot be useful now, whatever may have been its value in earlier times.

On the other hand it is hardly possible to foresee all the circumstances which might possibly justify or excuse acts which might otherwise be crimes. A long series of authorities have settled certain rules which can be put into a distinct and convenient form, and it is of course desirable to take the opportunity of deciding by the way minor points which an examination of the authorities shows to be still open. In this manner rules can be laid down as to the effect of infancy, insanity, compulsion, and ignorance of law, and also as to the cases in which force may lawfully be employed against the person of another; but is it therefore wise or safe to go so far as to say that no other circumstances than those expressly enumerated shall operate by way of excuse or justification for what would otherwise be a crime? To do so would be to run a risk, the extent of which it is difficult to estimate, of producing a conflict between the *Code* and the moral feelings of the public. Such a conflict is upon all possible grounds to be avoided. It would, if it occurred, do more to discredit codification than anything which would possibly happen, and it might cause serious evils of another kind. Cases sometimes occur in which public opinion is at once violently excited and greatly divided, so that conduct is regarded as criminal or praiseworthy according to the sympathies of excited partisans. If the *Code* provided that nothing should amount to an excuse or justification which was not within the express words of the *Code*, it would, in such a case, be vain to allege that the conduct of the accused person was normally justifiable; that, but for the *Code*, it would have been legally justifiable; that every legal analogy was in its favour; and that the omission of an express provision about it was probably an oversight. I think such a result would be eminently unsatisfactory. I think the public would feel that the allegations referred to ought to have been carefully examined and duly decided upon.

To put the whole matter very shortly, the reason why the common-law definitions of offences should be taken away, whilst the common-law principles as to justification and excuse are kept alive, is like the reason why the benefit of a doubt should be given to a prisoner. The worst result that could arise from the abolition of the common-law offences would be the occasional escape of a person morally guilty. The only result which can follow from preserving the common law as to justification and excuse is, that a man morally innocent, not otherwise protected, may avoid punishment. In the one case you remove rusty spring-guns and man-traps from unfrequented plantations, in the other you decline to issue an order for the destruction of every old-fashioned drag or life-buoy which may be found on the banks of a dangerous river, but is not in the inventory of the Royal Humane Society.

This indeed does not put the matter strongly enough. The continued existence of the undefined common-law offences is not only dangerous to individuals, but may be dangerous to the administration of justice itself. By allowing them to remain, we run the risk of tempting the judges to express their disapproval of conduct which, upon political, moral, or social grounds, they consider deserving of punishment, by declaring upon slender authority that it constitutes an offence at common law; nothing, I think, could place the bench in a more invidious position, or go further to shake its authority.

. . . .

Besides the well-known matters dealt with by the *Code*, there are a variety of speculative questions which have been discussed by ingenious persons for centuries, but which could be raised only by such rare occurrences that it may be thought pedantic to legislate for them expressly beforehand, and rash to do so without materials which the course of events has not provided. Such cases are the case of necessity (two shipwrecked men on one plank), the case of a choice of evils (my horses are running away, and I can avoid running over A only by running over B), and some others which might be suggested.

. . . .

Any ingenious person may divert himself, as Hecato did, by playing with such questions. The Commission acted on the view that in practice the wisest answer to all of them is to say, "When the case actually happens it shall be decided;" and this is effected by the preservation of such parts of the common law as to justification and excuse as are not embodied in the *Code*. Fiction apart, there is at present no law at all upon the subject, but the judges will make one under the fiction of declaring it, if the occasion for doing so should ever arise.

2. AIR OF REALITY FOR DEFENCES

R. v. CINOUS

[2002] 2 S.C.R. 3, 49 C.R. (5th) 209, 162 C.C.C. (3d) 129, 2002 CarswellQue 261, 2002 CarswellQue 262 (S.C.C.)

Per McLACHLIN C.J.C. and BASTARACHE J. (L'HEUREUX-DUBE, GONTHIER, BINNIE, LeBEL JJ. concurring): —

Air of Reality

The key issue is whether there was an air of reality to the defence of self-defence in this case. It is our view that there is no air of reality to the defence: a properly instructed jury acting reasonably could not acquit the accused on the ground of self-defence, even if it accepted his testimonial evidence as true. Since the defence should never have been put to the jury, any errors made in the charge to the jury relating to that defence are irrelevant. The curative proviso of s. 686(1)(b)(iii) should be applied, and the conviction upheld.

This court has considered the air of reality test on numerous occasions. The core elements of the test, as well as its nature and purpose, have by now been clearly and authoritatively set out. See *R. v. Osolin*, [1993] 4 S.C.R. 595, 86 C.C.C. (3d) 481, 109 D.L.R. (4th) 478; *R. v. Park*, [1995] 2 S.C.R. 836, 99 C.C.C. (3d) 1; *R. v. Davis*, [1999] 3 S.C.R. 759, 139 C.C.C. (3d) 193, 179 D.L.R. (4th) 385. Nevertheless, a controversy has arisen in this case concerning the extent of a trial judge's discretion to keep from a jury defences that are fanciful or far-fetched. More narrowly, the contentious issue is the correct evidential standard to be applied in determining whether there is an air of reality to the defence of self-defence on the facts of this case.

In our view, the controversy can be resolved on the basis of existing authority, which we consider to be decisive. The correct approach to the air of reality test is well established. The test is whether there is evidence on the record upon which a properly instructed jury acting reasonably could acquit. See *Wu v. The King*, [1934] S.C.R. 609, 62 C.C.C. 90, [1934] 4 D.L.R. 459, *infra*; *R. v. Squire*, [1977] 2 S.C.R. 13, 29 C.C.C. (2d) 497, 69 D.L.R. (3d) 312; *Pappajohn v. The Queen*, [1980] 2 S.C.R. 120, 52 C.C.C. (2d) 481, 111 D.L.R. (3d) 1; *Osolin, supra; Park, supra; R. v. Finta*, [1994] 1 S.C.R. 701, 88 C.C.C. (3d) 417, 112 D.L.R. (4th) 513. This long-standing formulation of the threshold question for putting defences to the jury accords with the nature and purpose of the air of reality test. We consider that there is nothing to be gained by altering the current state of the law, in which a single clearly-stated test applies to all defences. See *Osolin, supra; Park, supra; Finta, supra*. There is no need to invent a new test, to modify the current test, or to apply different tests to different classes of cases.

(1) The Basic Features of the Air of Reality Test

The principle that a defence should be put to a jury if and only if there is an evidential foundation for it has long been recognized by the common law. This venerable rule reflects the practical concern that allowing a defence to go to the jury in the absence of an evidential foundation would invite verdicts not supported by the evidence, serving only to confuse the jury and get in the way of a fair trial and true verdict. Following *Pappajohn, supra*, the inquiry into whether there is an evidential foundation for a defence is referred to as the air of reality test. See *Park, supra*, at para. 11.

The basic requirement of an evidential foundation for defences gives rise to two well-established principles. First, a trial judge must put to the jury all defences that arise on the facts, whether or not they have been specifically raised by an accused. Where there is an air of reality to a defence, it should go to the jury. Second, a trial judge has a positive duty to keep from the jury defences lacking an evidential foundation. A defence that lacks an air of reality should be kept from the jury. *Wu, supra; Squire, supra; Pappajohn, supra; Osolin, supra; Davis, supra*. This is so even when the defence lacking an air of reality represents the accused's only chance for an acquittal, as illustrated by *R. v. Latimer*, [2001] 1 S.C.R. 3, 2001 SCC 1, 150 C.C.C. (3d) 129, 193 D.L.R. (4th) 577.

It is trite law that the air of reality test imposes a burden on the accused that is merely evidential, rather than persuasive. Dickson C.J. drew attention to the distinction between these two types of burden in *R. v. Schwartz*, [1988] 2 S.C.R. 443 at p. 466, 45 C.C.C. (3d) 97, 55 D.L.R. (4th) 1:

> Judges and academics have used a variety of terms to try to capture the distinction between the two types of burdens. The burden of establishing a case has been referred to as

the "major burden," the "primary burden," the "legal burden" and the "persuasive burden". *The burden of putting an issue in play has been called the "minor burden," the "secondary burden," the "evidential burden," the "burden of going forward," and the "burden of adducing evidence."* [Emphasis added.]

The air of reality test is concerned only with whether or not a putative defence should be "put in play", that is, submitted to the jury for consideration. This idea was crucial to the finding in *Osolin* that the air of reality test is consistent with the presumption of innocence guaranteed by s. 11(d) of the *Canadian Charter of Rights and Freedoms.*

In applying the air of reality test, a trial judge considers the totality of the evidence, and assumes the evidence relied upon by the accused to be true. See *Osolin, supra; Park, supra.* The evidential foundation can be indicated by evidence emanating from the examination-in-chief or cross-examination of the accused, of defence witnesses, or of Crown witnesses. It can also rest upon the factual circumstances of the case or from any other evidential source on the record. There is no requirement that the evidence be adduced by the accused. See *Osolin, supra; Park, supra; Davis, supra.*

The threshold determination by the trial judge is not aimed at deciding the substantive merits of the defence. That question is reserved for the jury. See *Finta, supra; R. v. Ewanchuk,* [1999] 1 S.C.R. 330, 131 C.C.C. (3d) 481, 169 D.L.R. (4th) 193. The trial judge does not make determinations about the credibility of witnesses, weigh the evidence, make findings of fact, or draw determinate factual inferences. See *R. v. Bulmer,* [1987] 1 S.C.R. 782, 33 C.C.C. (3d) 385, 39 D.L.R. (4th) 641; *Park, supra.* Nor is the air of reality test intended to assess whether the defence is likely, unlikely, somewhat likely, or very likely to succeed at the end of the day. The question for the trial judge is whether the evidence discloses a real issue to be decided by the jury, and not how the jury should ultimately decide the issue.

Whether or not there is an air of reality to a defence is a question of law, subject to appellate review. It is an error of law to put to the jury a defence lacking an air of reality, just as it is an error of law to keep from the jury a defence that has an air of reality. See *Osolin, supra; Park, supra; Davis, supra.* The statements that "there is an air of reality" to a defence and that a defence "lacks an air of reality" express a legal conclusion about the presence or absence of an evidential foundation for a defence.

The considerations discussed above have led this court to reject unequivocally the argument that the air of reality test licenses an encroachment by trial judges on the jury's traditional function as arbiter of fact. As Cory J. stated in *Osolin, supra,* at p. 682:

> This is no more than an example of the basic division of tasks between judge and jury. It is the judge who must determine if evidence sought to be adduced is relevant and admissible. In the same way, it is the judge who determines if there is sufficient evidence adduced to give rise to the defence. If there has been sufficient evidence put forward, then the jury must be

given the opportunity to consider that defence along with all the other evidence and other defences left with them in coming to their verdict.

Indeed, the air of reality inquiry has been found not only to be consistent with the traditional division of labour as between judge and jury, but actually to enhance the jury's ability to carry out its task. Again, Cory J.'s statement in *Osolin, supra*, at p. 683, is apposite:

> The jury system has in general functioned exceptionally well. Its importance has been recognized in s. 11(f) of the *Charter*. *One of the reasons it has functioned so very well is that trial judges have been able to direct the minds of jurors* to the essential elements of the offence and *to those defences which are applicable*. That process should be maintained. The charge to the jury must be directed to the essential elements of the crime with which the accused is charged and defences to it. *Speculative defences that are unfounded should not be presented to the jury. To do so would be wrong, confusing, and unnecessarily lengthen jury trials.* [Emphasis added.]

This court has held on many occasions that a single air of reality test applies to all defences. *Osolin, supra; Park, supra*, at para. 12. The test has been applied uniformly to a wide range of defences over the years. These include the defence of honest but mistaken belief in consent in sexual assault cases (*Pappajohn, supra; Bulmer, supra; Osolin, supra; Park, supra; R. v. Esau*, [1997] 2 S.C.R. 777, 116 C.C.C. (3d) 289, 148 D.L.R. (4th) 662; *Ewanchuk, supra; Davis, supra*), and other defences such as intoxication (*R. v. Robinson*, [1996] 1 S.C.R. 683, 105 C.C.C. (3d) 97, 133 D.L.R. (4th) 42; *R. v. Lemky*, [1996] 1 S.C.R. 757, 105 C.C.C. (3d) 137), necessity (*Latimer, supra*), duress (*R. v. Ruzic*, [2001] 1 S.C.R. 687, 2001 SCC 24, 153 C.C.C. (3d) 1, 197 D.L.R. (4th) 577), provocation (*R. v. Thibert*, [1996] 1 S.C.R. 37, 104 C.C.C. (3d) 1, 131 D.L.R. (4th) 675), and self-defence (*Brisson v. The Queen*, [1982] 2 S.C.R. 227, 69 C.C.C. (2d) 97, 139 D.L.R. (3d) 685; *R. v. Hebert*, [1996] 2 S.C.R. 272, 107 C.C.C. (3d) 42, 135 D.L.R. (4th) 577). Adopting different evidential standards for different classes of cases would constitute a sharp break with the authorities.

In dissent Arbour J. (Iacobucci and Major JJ. concurring) sought to revise the approach of the Supreme Court, mainly on her detailed analysis that the air of reality test developed in the context of the mistaken belief defence in sexual assault cases had departed from the common law "no evidence" test for withdrawal from the jury in favour of one of sufficiency of evidence which had usurped the fact-finding function of juries. The "no evidence" test should be adopted for defences such as self-defence especially where there were no special technical or policy considerations, no alternative defences and where it was the accused's only defence. See comment by Stuart, "*Cinous*: The Air of Reality Test Requires Weak Defences to be Withdrawn from Juries" (2002), 49 C.R. (5th) 392.

Whether the defence of self-defence should have been put to the jury in *Cinous* is canvassed later under self-defence.

3. DEFENCE OF PERSON

See sections 34-37 of the *Criminal Code*.

R. v. PINTAR

(1996), 2 C.R. (5th) 151, 110 C.C.C. (3d) 402,
1996 CarswellOnt 3229 (Ont. C.A.)

The accused was charged with two counts of second degree murder. One of the deceased, R, blamed the accused for the break-up of his marriage, and threatened on many occasions to kill him. G, the other deceased, was a stranger to the accused. He had been working for R for a brief time prior to the offence.

On the day of the shooting, R and the other deceased, G, were drinking at a dance and were overheard agreeing to attack the accused. The accused was awakened at daybreak by noises outside his bedroom. He went to investigate and found R standing in the hallway and told him to leave. R refused, saying that he was there to "finish this off" and took a swing at the accused. The accused knocked R out onto the front porch and went back into the house to get dressed. R screamed that he had killed the accused's dog and the accused was next. R continued to yell threats at him while G, who had been waiting in R's truck, got out of the vehicle. The accused got his rifle and went outside with it held across his chest. G and R advanced towards the accused, while R said that he would kill the accused and other members of his family. R grabbed the gun, a struggle ensued and the two deceased were shot by the accused during the struggle. The jury found the accused guilty of two counts of manslaughter. The accused appealed, raising several objections to the trial judge's charge to the jury on the issue of self-defence, including whether the charge on this issue was unnecessarily confusing and complex. The trial judge instructed the jury on ss. 34(1), 34(2), 35 and 37.

MOLDAVER J.A.: — This is yet another case where the court is faced with difficult issues arising out of the complex and confusing self-defence regime in the *Criminal Code*.

. . . .

It is no secret that many trial judges consider their instructions on the law of self-defence to be little more than a source of bewilderment and confusion to the jury. Regardless of their efforts to be clear, trial judges often report glazed eyes and blank stares on the faces of the jury in the course of their instructions on self-defence. Disheartening as this may be, most judges tend to believe that juries are extremely adept at assessing legitimate cases of self-defence and are therefore likely to come to the right result in spite of the confusion created by the charge. While this may be true, it provides little comfort to an accused who has been convicted in the face of legal instruction so complex and confusing that it may well have diverted the jury's attention away from the real basis upon which the claim to self-defence rests.

. . . .

Unquestionably, trial judges do encounter difficulties in explaining the self-defence provisions to juries for the reasons expressed by the Chief Justice. In my opinion, these difficulties are compounded by the standards which appellate courts have imposed, or are perceived to have imposed, when assessing the adequacy of self-defence instructions. Trial judges are often heard to say that 90 per cent of their legal instruction on self-defence is for the Court of Appeal and 10 per cent for the jury. Expressed somewhat differently, fear of under-charging has led to over-charging.

. . . .

To give effect to the functional approach, I would urge trial judges to consider the following guidelines when faced with the prospect of charging a jury on the law of self-defence:

(1) Consider the evidence carefully with a view to determining the essence of the claim to self-defence and the *Code* provision(s) realistically available to that claim.

(2) To the extent that the evidence fails the air of reality test in respect of one or more of the constituent elements of a particular provision, that provision should not be left with the jury.

(3) To the extent that the evidence clearly establishes one or more of the constituent elements of a particular provision, Crown counsel should be encouraged to admit the underlying facts and thereby avoid unnecessary legal instruction.

(4) Where a particular provision affords the accused a wider scope of justification than a companion provision, the narrower provision should only be put to the jury if the evidence lends an air of reality to the factual underpinnings of that provision, and the provision somehow fills a gap unaccounted for in the justification afforded by the wider provision.

. . . .

Experience reveals that it is not uncommon, particularly in murder cases, that even though the primary claim to self-defence rests upon s. 34(2), s. 34(1) remains marginally relevant and theoretically available. This type of situation generally arises when, despite evidence to the contrary, the Crown has made out a strong case that the accused either provoked the initial assault, or intended to kill or cause grievous bodily harm, or both. Nonetheless, since provocation and intent are matters of fact for the jury, s. 34(1) cannot be ruled out, even though the scope of its justification is much narrower than that provided by s. 34(2).

On a practical level, in those cases where s. 34(1) remains theoretically available, it is often difficult, if not impossible, to imagine a scenario wherein the jury would reject the wider justification afforded by s. 34(2) and apply s. 34(1) to acquit. The question then becomes whether the risk of confusing the jury and complicating the charge justifies the inclusion of instruction on s. 34(1), when its application is at best tenuous and its scope of justification narrower than that available under s. 34(2).

For my part, I am of the view that when trial judges are faced with situations like this, they should call upon counsel to justify instruction on the narrower provision. If the results of that exercise reveal either the lack of an evidentiary base for putting the narrower provision, or an inability to demonstrate how the narrower provision might be available to fill a gap not provided for by the broader one, the narrower provision should be discarded. Once again, let me be clear that the underlying purpose of this exercise is not to remove self-defence from the jury's consideration. Rather it is designed to focus the jury's attention on the essence of the claim to self-defence and the available *Code* provision(s) most relevant to it.

New trial ordered.

For at least the last 15 years successive Ministers of Justice have been very active in amending a *Criminal Code* that is growing increasingly unwieldy. The strong trend is to only move to widen the net of the criminal sanction. Reforms that might make it easier for those accused of crime are resisted. This may explain but not justify why calls by the Law Reform Commission of Canada to clarify the law of self-defence in 1987 (*Report No. 31: Recodify Criminal Law* (rev. ed., 1987) p. 36) and by Chief Justice Lamer in *R. v. McIntosh* (1995), 36 C.R. (4th) 171, 95 C.C.C. (3d) 481, [1995] 1 S.C.R. 686 at 180, have been ignored. It is time for a flexible defence that abandons the *Criminal Code*'s present arbitrary and complex distinctions between situations of fatal and non-fatal self-defence, defence of those under protection and defence of strangers, and self-defence by an aggressor and simple self-defence. See, now, "Final Report: Self Defence Review" (Ratushny Report) (1997) and Department of Justice Consultation Paper, "Reforming Criminal Code Defences: Provocation, Self-defence and Defence of Property" (1998).

In the meantime the courts must soldier on trying to make sense out of ss. 34(1), 34(2), 35 and 37. In *R. v. McIntosh*, above, the majority of the Supreme Court decided that s. 34(2) is also available to an initial aggressor. The words "without having provoked" were not to be read in so as to trigger the more restrictive s. 35. The decision of the Ontario Court of Appeal in *Pintar* provides further welcome relief against boilerplate directions dealing at length with all these conflicting sections at great risk of being incomprehensible to jurors. The major pronouncement of Justice Moldaver is that a narrower provision must not be put where there is an air of reality in the evidence for a wider provision. That is a very sensible pronouncement. The particular message of *Pintar* is that s. 34(2) and not s. 34(1) should be put in all murder cases whether or not the accused intended to kill or cause grievous bodily harm. The court relies on the analysis that s. 34(2) is wider than s. 34(1) as it applies on present interpretations even if the accused provoked the assault, even if the accused intended to kill or cause grievous bodily harm and the question is not whether more force was used than was necessary but whether the accused believed on reasonable grounds that he could not otherwise preserve himself from death or grievous bodily harm.

It is certainly debatable whether s. 34(2) is indeed wider as the proportionality test for s. 34(1) has always been interpreted not as a strict mechanical test but one under which a person defending against an attack need not weigh to a nicety the exact measure of necessary defence. Justice Martin for the Ontario Court of Appeal in *R. v. Baxter* (1975), 27 C.C.C. (2d) 96 (Ont. C.A.), viewed ss. 34(1) and (2) as *not* mutually exclusive. The words in s. 34(2) "who causes death or grievous bodily harm" had to mean "even though he intentionally causes death or grievous bodily harm". The court reasoned that any other interpretation would leave unprotected one who, using no more force than was necessary to defend himself against an unprovoked assault, accidentally killed or caused bodily harm to his attacker but did not meet the requirements of s. 34(2). That Justices Martin and Moldaver differ again points to the need for legislative reform. For criticism of both *McIntosh* and *Pintar* see Gerry Ferguson, "Self-Defence: Selecting the Applicable Provisions" (2000) 5 Can. Crim. L.R. 179.

See, now, Gary Trotter, "*R. v. Pawliuck*: Further Efforts to Clarify Self-Defence" (2001) 40 C.R. (5th) 55 and David Paciocco, "Applying the Law of Self-Defence" (2007) 12 Can. Crim. L.Rev. 25.

For a complex divided opinion as to how self-defence operates where the consent has been vitiated for policy reasons in a situation of a fatal bar room brawl reminiscent of *Jobidon,* see *R. v. Paice* (2005), 29 C.R. (6th) 1 (S.C.C.), and critical annotations by Gary Trotter and Steve Coughlan, C.R., *ibid.*, pp. 2 and 5.

Is there an absolute duty to retreat?

In December 2011 Parliament gave second reading to Bill C-26, An Act to amend the Criminal Code (citizen's arrest and the defences of property and persons). If it becomes law, it will replace all of the current self-defence provisions with a single provision, the essence of which is this:

34. (1) A person is not guilty of an offence if
    (a) they believe on reasonable grounds that force is being used against them or another person or that a threat of force is being made against them or another person;
    (b) the act that constitutes the offence is committed for the purpose of defending or protecting themselves or the other person from that use or threat of force; and
    (c) the act committed is reasonable in the circumstances.

Factors

(2) In determining whether the act committed is reasonable in the circumstances, the court may consider, among other factors,
  a) the nature of the force or threat;
  b) the extent to which the use of force was imminent and whether there were other means available to respond to the potential use of force;
  c) the person's role in the incident;
  d) whether any party to the incident used or threatened to use a weapon;
  e) the size, age and gender of the parties to the incident;
  f) the nature, duration and history of any relationship between the parties to the incident, including any prior use or threat of force and the nature of that force or threat;
  g) the nature and proportionality of the person's response to the use or threat of force; and
  h) whether the act committed was in response to a use or threat of force that the person knew was lawful.

No defence

(3) Subsection (1) does not apply if the force is used or threatened by another person for the purpose of doing something that they are required or authorized by law to do in the administration or enforcement of the law, unless the person who commits the act that constitutes the offence believes on reasonable grounds that the other person is acting unlawfully.

This Bill responds to the need for radical simplification. It does, however, introduce some unnecessary complexity. See too Kent Roach, "Reforming Self-Defence and Defence of Property: Choices to be Made" (2011) 57 *Crim. L. Q.* 151. In the context of self-defence there is no need to complicate matters by reference to issues of *actus reus* and purpose as the Bill does in s. 34(b). It seems patronising to list in s. 34(2) a long list of factors for judges to consider in assessing reasonableness. Including a long list of factors with no guidance as to how they should be applied or whether any take priority over others is to invite inconsistency. If the list is maintained it would be important to add the now entrenched common law requirement that proportionality in the context of self-defence must be flexibly applied and that no one is expected to measure with nicety the degree of force needed to repel the reasonably apprehended unlawful force. Furthermore, it needs to be made clear that the response element of reasonable in the circumstances must be judged according to the accused's reasonable belief. See similarly David Paciocco, "Applying the Law of Self-Defence" (2007) 12 *Can. Crim. L. Rev.* 26 and Stanley Yeo, "Streamlining the Response Element of Self-defence" (2010) 14 *Can. Crim. L. Rev.* 231. The Supreme Court rejected a purely objective approach in *Kong*.

Note that this provision does more than create a new self-defence provision. It makes a person not guilty of "an offence" for performing an "act", not merely for applying force to repel force. Certainly striking a blow to defend against an assault would be included, but potentially so too could be theft (commandeering a car to escape an assault), destruction of property (breaking into a building to escape an assault) or other offences.

R. v. DEEGAN

(1979), 49 C.C.C. (2d) 417 at 440-1, 1979 CarswellAlta 236 (Alta. C.A.)

HARRADENCE J.A.: —

. . . .

In *R. v. Stanley*, [(1977), 36 C.C.C. (2d) 216] Branca J.A. said at p. 226:

> Ever since *Semaynes Case* (1605), 5 Co. Rep. 91a, at p. 91b, 77 E.R. 194, it was said:
> "That the house of every one is to him as his (*a*) castle and fortress, as well for his
> defence against injury and violence as for his repose. . .".
> That is something that people who live in our country have been told to understand is the law
> of our land. The precept that a man's home is his castle is as true today as it was then.

I am in complete agreement with this statement.

In *R. v. Hussey* (1924), 18 Cr. App. R. 160, Lord Hewart said at p. 161:

> No sufficient notice had been given to appellant to quit his room, and therefore he was
> in the position of a man who was defending his house. In Archbold's *Criminal Pleading,
> Evidence and Practice*, 26th ed. p. 887, it appears that: "In defence of a man's house, the
> owner or his family may kill a trespasser who would forcibly dispossess him of it, in the same
> manner as he might, by law, kill in self-defence a man who attacks him personally; with this
> distinction, however, that in defending his home he need not retreat, as in other cases of self-
> defence, for that would be giving up his house to his adversary." That is still the law, but not
> one word was said about that distinction in the summing-up, which proceeded on the
> foundation that the defence was the ordinary one of self-defence.

Even if the appellant were not in his home, I do not accept that retreat is
imperative if a defence of self-defence is to be relied on; rather, I adopt the
statement of Dixon C.J. in *R. v. Howe* (1958), 100 C.L.R. 448 at pp. 462-3:

> The view of the Supreme Court appears also to be correct as to the position which the
> modern law governing a plea of self-defence gives to the propriety of a person retreating in
> face of an assault or apprehended assault before resorting to violence to defend himself. The
> view which the Supreme Court has accepted is that to retreat before employing force is no
> longer to be treated as an independent and imperative condition if a plea of self-defence is to
> be made out.

Dixon C.J. then referred to the judgment of Holmes J. in *Brown v. United
States of America* (1920), 256 U.S. 335 at p. 343;

> Holmes J. pronounced upon the question in a way which one may well be content to adopt:
> "Rationally, the failure to retreat is a circumstance to be considered with all the others in order
> to determine whether the defendant went farther than he was justified in doing; not a
> categorical proof of guilt. The law has grown, and even if historical mistakes have contributed
> to its growth, it has tended in the direction of rules consistent with human nature. Many
> respectable writers agree that if a man reasonably believes that he is in immediate danger of
> death or grievous bodily harm from his assailant, he may stand his ground, and that if he kills
> him, he has not exceeded the bounds of lawful self-defence. That has been the decision of

this court. *Beard v. United States*. Detached reflection cannot be demanded in the presence of an uplifted knife. Therefore, in this court, at least, it is not a condition of immunity that one in that situation should pause to consider whether a reasonable man might not think it possible to fly with safety, or to disable his assailant rather than to kill him": *Brown v. United States of America*.

I am quite content to adopt the pronouncement of Holmes J.

R. v. LAVALLEE

[1990] 1 S.C.R. 852, 76 C.R. (3d) 329, 55 C.C.C. (3d) 97,
1990 CarswellMan 198, 1990 CarswellMan 377

The accused was a battered woman in a volatile common-law relationship who killed her partner late one night by shooting him in the back of the head as he left her room. A psychiatrist with extensive professional experience in the treatment of battered wives, Dr. Shane, prepared a psychiatric assessment of the accused which was used in support of her defence of self-defence. The accused was acquitted at trial but the Manitoba Court of Appeal ordered a new trial. On the accused's appeal the Supreme Court of Canada was faced with the decision of the Nova Scotia Court of Appeal in *R. v. Whynot*. That court followed what was then considered to be the law, that it was inherently unreasonable to apprehend death or grievous bodily harm unless and until the physical assault was actually in progress. The Supreme Court of Canada announced a change in the law. It was informed by the expert opinion led at the trial and by books and articles which it read for itself. Notice how the court reasons; how it judicially notices legislative facts; how it decides the case; how it creates law.

WILSON J. (DICKSON C.J.C. and LAMER, L'HEUREUX-DUBÉ, SOPINKA, GONTHIER and MCLACHLIN JJ. concurring): —

The appellant did not testify but her statement made to police on the night of the shooting was put in evidence. Portions of it read as follows:

Me and Wendy argued as usual and I ran in the house after Kevin pushed me. I was scared, I was really scared. I locked the door. Herb was downstairs with Joanne and I called for Herb but I was crying when I called him. I said, "Herb come up here please."Herb came up to the top of the stairs and I told him that Kevin was going to hit me actually beat on me again. Herb said he knew and that if I was his old lady things would be different, he gave me a hug. OK, we're friends, there's nothing between us. He said "Yeah, I know" and he went outside to talk to Kevin leaving the door unlocked. I went upstairs and hid in my closet from Kevin. I was so scared. . . My window was open and I could hear Kevin asking questions about what I was doing and what I was saying. Next thing I know he was coming up the stairs for me. He came into my bedroom and said "Wench, where are you?" And he turned on my light and he said "Your purse is on the floor" and he kicked it. OK then he turned and he saw me in the closet. He wanted me to come out but I didn't want to come out because I was scared. I was so scared. [The officer who took the statement then testified that the appellant started to cry at this point and stopped after a minute or two.] He grabbed me by the arm right there. There's a bruise on my face also where he slapped me. He didn't slap me right then, first he yelled at me then he pushed me and I pushed him back and he hit me twice on the right hand side of my head. I was scared. All I thought about was all the other times he used to beat me, I was scared, I was shaking as usual. The rest is a blank, all I remember is he gave me the gun and a shot was fired through my screen. This is all so fast. And then the guns were in another room and he loaded it the second shot and gave it to me. And I was going to shoot myself. I pointed it to myself, I was so upset. OK and then he went and I was sitting on the bed and he started going like this with his finger [the appellant made a shaking motion with an index finger] and said something like "You're my old lady and you do as you're told" or something like that. He said "wait till everybody leaves, you'll get it then" and he said something to the effect of "either you kill me or I'll get you" that was what it was. He kind of smiled and then he turned around. I shot him but I aimed out. I thought I aimed above him and a piece of his head went that way.

. . . .

Expert evidence on the psychological effect of battering on wives and common-law partners must, it seems to me, be both relevant and necessary in the context of the present case. How can the mental state of the appellant be appreciated without it? The average member of the public (or of the jury) can be forgiven for asking: Why would a woman put up with this kind of treatment? Why should she continue to live with such a man? How could she love a partner who beat her to the point of requiring hospitalization? We would expect the woman to pack her bags and go. Where is her self-respect? Why does she not cut loose and make a new life for herself? Such is the reaction of the average person confronted with the so-called "battered wife syndrome". We need help to understand it and help is available from trained professionals.

The gravity, indeed, the tragedy of domestic violence can hardly be overstated. Greater media attention to this phenomenon in recent years has revealed both its prevalence and its horrific impact on women from all walks of life. Far from protecting women from it, the law historically sanctioned the abuse of women within marriage as an aspect of the husband's ownership of his wife and his "right" to chastise her. One need only recall the centuries old law that a man is entitled to beat his wife with a stick "no thicker than his thumb".

Laws do not spring out of a social vacuum. The notion that a man has a right to "discipline" his wife is deeply rooted in the history of our society. The woman's duty was to serve her husband and to stay in the marriage at all costs "till death do us part" and to accept as her due any "punishment" that was meted out for failing to please her husband. One consequence of this attitude was that "wife battering" was rarely spoken of, rarely reported, rarely prosecuted, and even more rarely punished. Long after society abandoned its formal approval of spousal abuse, tolerance of it continued and continues in some circles to this day.

Fortunately, there has been a growing awareness in recent years that no man has a right to abuse any woman under any circumstances. Legislative initiatives designed to educate police, judicial officers and the public, as well as more aggressive investigation and charging policies, all signal a concerted effort by the criminal justice system to take spousal abuse seriously. However, a woman who comes before a judge or jury with the claim that she has been battered and suggests that this may be a relevant factor in evaluating her subsequent actions still faces the prospect of being condemned by popular mythology about domestic violence. Either she was not as badly beaten as she claims or she would have left the man long ago. Or, if she was battered that severely, she must have stayed out of some masochistic enjoyment of it.

. . . .

In my view, there are two elements of the defence under s. 34(2) of the *Code* which merit scrutiny for present purposes. The first is the temporal connection in s. 34(2)(*a*) between the apprehension of death or grievous bodily harm and the act allegedly taken in self-defence. Was the appellant "under reasonable apprehension of death or grievous bodily harm" from Rust as he was walking out of the room? The second is the assessment in s. 34(2)(*b*) of the magnitude of the force used by the accused. Was the accused's belief that she could not "otherwise preserve herself from death or grievous bodily harm" except by shooting the deceased based "on reasonable grounds"?

The feature common to both s. 34(2)(*a*) and s. 34(2)(*b*) is the imposition of an objective standard of reasonableness on the apprehension of death and the need to repel the assault with deadly force. . . .

If it strains credulity to imagine what the "ordinary man" would do in the position of a battered spouse, it is probably because men do not typically find themselves in that situation.

. . . .

It will be observed that subsection 34(2)(*a*) does not actually stipulate that the accused apprehend *imminent* danger when he or she acts. Case law has, however, read that requirement into the defence. . . . The sense in which "imminent" is used conjures up the image of "an uplifted knife" or a pointed gun. The rationale for the imminence rule seems obvious. The law of self-defence is designed to ensure that the use of defensive force is really necessary. It justifies the act because the defender reasonably believed that he or she had no alternative but to take the attacker's life. If there is a significant time interval between the original unlawful assault and the accused's response, one tends to suspect that the accused was motivated by revenge rather than self-defence. In the paradigmatic case of a one-time barroom brawl between two men of equal size and strength, this inference makes sense. How can one feel endangered to the point of firing a gun at an unarmed man who utters a death threat, then turns his back and walks out of the room? One cannot be certain of the gravity of the threat or his capacity to carry it out. Besides, one can always take the opportunity to flee or to call the police. If he comes back and raises his fist, one can respond in kind if need be. These are the tacit assumptions that underlie the imminence rule.

All of these assumptions were brought to bear on the respondent in *R. v. Whynot* (1983), 37 C.R. (3d) 198, 9 C.C.C. 449 (N.S.C.A.). The respondent, Jane Stafford, shot her sleeping common-law husband as he lay passed out in his truck. The evidence at trial indicated that the deceased "dominated the household and exerted his authority by striking and slapping the various members and from time to time administering beatings to Jane Stafford and the others" (at p. 452). The respondent testified that the deceased threatened to kill all of the members of her family, one by one, if she tried to leave him. On the night in question he threatened to kill her son. After he passed out, the respondent got one of the many shotguns kept by her husband and shot him. The Nova Scotia Court of Appeal held that the trial judge erred in leaving s. 37 (preventing assault against oneself or anyone under one's protection) with the jury. The court stated at p. 464:

> I do not believe that the trial Judge was justified in placing s. 37 of the *Code* before the jury any more than he would have been justified in giving them s. 34. Under s. 34 the assault must have been underway and unprovoked, and under s. 37 the assault must be such that it is necessary to defend the person assaulted by the use of force. No more force may be used than necessary to prevent the assault or the repetition of it. In my opinion, no person has the right in anticipation of an assault that may or may not happen, to apply force to prevent the imaginary assault.

The implication of the court's reasoning is that it is inherently unreasonable to apprehend death or grievous bodily harm unless and until the physical assault is actually in progress, at which point the victim can presumably gauge the requisite amount of force needed to repel the attack and act accordingly. In my view, expert testimony can cast doubt on these assumptions as they are applied in the context of a battered wife's efforts to repel an assault.

The situation of the appellant was not unlike that of Jane Stafford in the sense that she too was routinely beaten over the course of her relationship with the man she ultimately killed. According to the testimony of Dr. Shane these assaults were not entirely random in their occurrence.

. . . .

The cycle described by Dr. Shane conforms to the Walker Cycle Theory of Violence named for clinical psychologist, Dr. Lenore Walker, the pioneer researcher in the field of the battered wife syndrome. Dr. Shane acknowledged his debt to Dr. Walker in the course of establishing his credentials as an expert at trial. Dr. Walker first describes the cycle in the book *The Battered Woman* (1979). In her 1984 book, *The Battered Woman Syndrome*, Dr. Walker reports the results of a study involving 400 battered women. Her research was designed to test empirically the theories expounded in her earlier book. At pp. 95-96 of *The Battered Woman Syndrome* she summarizes the Cycle Theory as follows:

A second major theory that was tested in this project is the Walker Cycle Theory of Violence (Walker, 1979). This tension reduction theory states that there are three distinct phases associated in a recurring battering cycle: (1) tension building, (2) the acute battering incident, and (3) loving contrition. During the first phase, there is a gradual escalation of tension displayed by discrete acts causing increased friction such as name-calling, other mean intentional behaviours, and/or physical abuse. The batterer expresses dissatisfaction and hostility but not in an extreme or maximally explosive form. The woman attempts to placate the batterer, doing what she thinks might please him, calm him down, or at least, what will not further aggravate him. She tries not to respond to his hostile actions and uses general anger reduction techniques. Often she succeeds for a little while which reinforces her unrealistic belief that she can control this man . . .

The tension continues to escalate and eventually she is unable to continue controlling his angry response pattern. "Exhausted from the constant stress, she usually withdraws from the batterer, fearing she will inadvertently set off an explosion. He begins to move more oppressively toward her as he observes her withdrawal. . . . Tension between the two becomes unbearable" (Walker, 1979, p. 59). The second phase, the acute battering incident, becomes inevitable without intervention. Sometimes, she precipitates the inevitable explosion so as to control where and when it occurs, allowing her to take better precautions to minimize her injuries and pain.

"Phase two is characterized by the uncontrollable discharge of the tensions that have built up during phase one" (p. 59). The batterer typically unleashes a barrage of verbal and physical aggression that can leave the woman severely shaken and injured. In fact, when injuries do occur it usually happens during this second phase. It is also the time police become involved, if they are called at all. The acute battering phase is concluded when the batterer stops, usually bringing with its cessation a sharp physiological reduction in tension. This in itself is naturally reinforcing. Violence often succeeds because it does work.

In phase three which follows, the batterer may apologize profusely, try to assist his victim, show kindness and remorse, and shower her with gifts and/or promises. The batterer himself may believe at this point that he will never allow himself to be violent again. The woman wants to believe the batterer and, early in the relationship at least, may renew her hope in his ability to change. This third phase provides the positive reinforcement for remaining in the relationship, for the woman. In fact, our results showed that phase three could also be characterized by an absence of tension or violence, and no observable loving-contrition behaviour, and still be reinforcing for the woman.

Dr. Walker defines a battered woman as a woman who has gone through the battering cycle at least twice. As she explains in her introduction to The Battered Woman at p. xv, "Any woman may find herself in an abusive relationship with a man once. If it occurs a second time, and she remains in the situation, she is defined as a battered woman".

Given the relational context in which the violence occurs, the mental state of an accused at the critical moment she pulls the trigger cannot be understood except in terms of the cumulative effect of months or years of brutality.

. . . .

Another aspect of the cyclical nature of the abuse is that it begets a degree of predictability to the violence that is absent in an isolated violent encounter between two strangers. This also means that it may in fact be possible for a battered spouse to accurately predict the onset of violence before the first blow is struck, even if an outsider to the relationship cannot. Indeed, it has been suggested that a battered woman's knowledge of her partner's violence is so heightened that she is able to anticipate the nature and extent (though not the onset) of the violence by his conduct beforehand. In her article "Potential Uses for Expert Testimony: Ideas Toward the Representation of Battered Women Who Kill" (1986), 9 Women's Rights Law Reporter 227, psychologist Julie Blackman describes this characteristic at p. 229:

> Repeated instances of violence enable battered women to develop a continuum along which they can "rate" the tolerability or survivability of episodes of their partner's violence. Thus, signs of unusual violence are detected. For battered women, this response to the ongoing violence of their situations is a survival skill. Research shows that battered women who kill experience remarkably severe and frequent violence relative to battered women who do not kill. They know what sorts of danger are familiar and which are novel. They have had myriad opportunities to develop and hone their perceptions of their partner's violence. And, importantly, they can say what made the final episode of violence different from the others: they can name the features of the last battering that enabled them to know that this episode would result in life-threatening action by the abuser.

. . . .

Where evidence exists that an accused is in a battering relationship, expert testimony can assist the jury in determining whether the accused had a "reasonable" apprehension of death when she acted by explaining the heightened sensitivity of a battered woman to her partner's acts. Without such testimony I am skeptical that the average fact-finder would be capable of appreciating why her subjective fear may have been reasonable in the context of the relationship. After all, the hypothetical "reasonable man" observing only the final incident may have been unlikely to recognize the batterer's threat as potentially lethal. Using the case at bar as an example the "reasonable man" might have thought, as the majority of the Court of Appeal seemed to, that it was unlikely that Rust would make good on his threat to kill the appellant that night because they had guests staying overnight.

The issue is not, however, what an outsider would have reasonably perceived but what the accused reasonably perceived, given her situation and her experience.

Even accepting that a battered woman may be uniquely sensitized to danger from her batterer, it may yet be contended that the law ought to require her to wait until the knife is uplifted, the gun pointed or the fist clenched before her apprehension is deemed reasonable. This would allegedly reduce the risk that the woman is mistaken in her fear, although the law does not require her fear to be correct, only reasonable. In response to this contention, I need only point to the observation made by Huband J.A. that the evidence showed that when the appellant and Rust physically fought the appellant "invariably got the worst of it". I do not think it is an unwarranted generalization to say that due to their size, strength, socialization and lack of training, women are typically no match for men in hand-to-hand combat. The requirement imposed in *Whynot* that a battered woman wait until the physical assault is "underway" before her apprehensions can be validated in law would, in the words of an American Court, be tantamount to sentencing her to "murder by installment". . . . I share the view expressed by M.J. Willoughby in "Rendering Each Woman Her Due: Can a Battered Woman Claim Self-Defense When She Kills Her Sleeping Batterer" (1989), 38 Kan. L. Rev. 169, at p. 184, that "society gains nothing, except perhaps the additional risk that the battered woman will herself be killed, because she must wait until her abusive husband instigates another battering episode before she can justifiably act".

. . . .

Subsection 34(2) requires an accused who pleads self-defence to believe "on reasonable grounds" that it is not possible to otherwise preserve him or herself from death or grievous bodily harm. The obvious question is if the violence was so intolerable, why did the appellant not leave her abuser long ago? This question does not really go to whether she had an alternative to killing the deceased at the critical moment. Rather, it plays on the popular myth already referred to that a woman who says she was battered yet stayed with her batterer was either not as badly beaten as she claimed or else she liked it. Nevertheless, to the extent that her failure to leave the abusive relationship earlier may be used in support of the proposition that she was free to leave at the final moment, expert testimony can provide useful insights. Dr. Shane attempted to explain in his testimony how and why, in the case at bar, the appellant remained with Rust:

> She had stayed in this relationship, I think, because of the strange, almost unbelievable, but yet it happens, relationship that sometimes develops between people who develop this very disturbed, I think, very disturbed quality of a relationship. Trying to understand it, I think, isn't always easy and there's been a lot written about it recently, in the recent years, in psychiatric literature. But basically it involves two people who are involved in what appears to be an attachment which may have sexual or romantic or affectionate overtones.

> And the one individual, and it's usually the women in our society, but there have been occasions where it's been reversed, but what happens is the spouse who becomes battered, if you will, stays in the relationship probably because of a number of reasons.

> One is that the spouse gets beaten so badly — so badly — that he or she loses the motivation to react and becomes helpless and becomes powerless. And it's also been shown sometimes, you know, in — not that you can compare animals to human beings, but in laboratories, what you do if you shock an animal, after a while it can't respond to a threat of its life. It becomes just helpless and lies there in an amotivational state, if you will, where it feels there's no power and there's no energy to do anything.

> So in a sense it happens in human beings as well. It's almost like a concentration camp, if you will. You get paralyzed with fear.

> The other thing that happens often in these types of relationships with human beings is that the person who beats or assaults, who batters, often tries — he makes up and begs for forgiveness. And this individual, who basically has a very disturbed or damaged self-esteem, all of a sudden feels that he or she — we'll use women in this case because it's so much more common — the spouse feels that she again can do the spouse a favour and it can make her feel needed and boost her self-esteem for a while and make her feel worthwhile and the spouse says he'll forgive her and whatnot.

Apparently, another manifestation of this victimization is a reluctance to disclose to others the fact or extent of the beatings. For example, the hospital records indicate that on each occasion the appellant attended the emergency department to be treated for various injuries she explained the cause of those injuries as accidental. Both in its address to the jury and in its written submissions before this court the Crown insisted that the appellant's injuries were as consistent with her explanations as with being battered and, therefore, in the words of Crown counsel at trial, "the myth is, in this particular case, that Miss Lavallee was a battered spouse". In his testimony Dr. Shane testified that the appellant admitted to him that she lied to hospital staff and others about the cause of her injuries. In Dr. Shane's opinion this was consistent with her overall feeling of being trapped and helpless.

. . . .

The account given by Dr. Shane comports with that documented in the literature. Reference is often made to it as a condition of "learned helplessness", a phrase coined by Dr. Charles Seligman, the psychologist who first developed the theory by experimenting on animals in the manner described by Dr. Shane in his testimony. A related theory used to explain the failure of women to leave battering relationships is described by psychologist and lawyer Charles Patrick Ewing in his book, Battered Women Who Kill (1987). Ewing describes a phenomenon labelled "traumatic bonding" that has been observed between hostages and captors, battered children and their parents, concentration camp prisoners and guards, and batterers and their spouses.

. . . .

I emphasize at this juncture that it is not for the jury to pass judgment on the fact that an accused battered woman stayed in the relationship. Still less is it entitled to conclude that she forfeited her right to self-defence for having done so. I would also point out that traditional self-defence doctrine does not require a person to retreat from her home instead of defending herself: *R. v. Antley*, (1964), 42 C.R. 384, [1964] 2 C.C.C. 142 (C.A.). A man's home may be his castle but it is also the woman's home even if it seems to her more like a prison in the circumstances.

If, after hearing the evidence (including the expert testimony), the jury is satisfied that the accused had a reasonable apprehension of death or grievous bodily harm and felt incapable of escape, it must ask itself what the "reasonable person" would do in such a situation. The situation of the battered woman as described by Dr. Shane strikes me as somewhat analogous to that of a hostage. If the captor tells her that he will kill her in three days time, is it potentially reasonable for her to seize an opportunity presented on the first day to kill the captor or must she wait until he makes the attempt on the third day? I think the question the jury must ask itself is whether, given the history, circumstances and perceptions of the appellant, her belief that she could not preserve herself from being killed by Rust that night except by killing him first was reasonable. To the extent that expert evidence can assist the jury in making that determination, I would find such testimony to be both relevant and necessary.

. . . .

Obviously the fact that the appellant was a battered woman does not entitle her to an acquittal. Battered women may well kill their partners other than in self-defence. The focus is not on who the woman is, but on what she did. In "The Meaning of Equality for Battered Women Who Kill Men in Self-Defense" (1985), 8 *Harv. Women's L. J.* 121, at 149, Phyllis Crocker makes the point succinctly:

> The issue in a self-defence trial is not whether the defendant is a battered woman, but whether she justifiably killed her husband. The defendant introduces testimony to offer the jury an explanation of reasonableness that is an alternative to the prosecution's stereotypic explanations. It is not intended to earn her the status of a battered woman, as if that would make her not guilty.

The trial judge, to his credit, articulated the same principle when introducing Dr. Shane's testimony in the course of his instructions to the jury. After referring to "the so-called battered spouse syndrome", he cautions:

> Let me say at the outset that I think it is better that we try not to attach labels to this. It doesn't matter what we call it. What is important is the evidence itself and how it impacts on the critical areas of the intent of the accused and the issue of self-defence.

. . .

I would accordingly allow the appeal, set aside the order of the Court of Appeal, and restore the acquittal.

For comments by Donna Martinson, Marilyn MacCrimmon, Isabel Grant and Christine Boyle see "A Forum on Lavallee v. R.: Women and Self-Defence" (1991), 25 U.B.C. Law Rev. 23-68.

Although *Lavallee* has been widely-heralded there have been some concerns expressed. Some question the reliability of the opinion of the expert given that it was based on so much hearsay evidence and that the trial Crown expected to have an opportunity to cross-examine the accused, but she was not called. The heavy reliance on the expert testimony as to the "cycle of learned helplessness" has produced the criticism that the particular research relied upon is suspect and unduly restrictive: see Neil Vidmar, "One or Many Words for a Camel? An Overview on Judicial Evaluation of Social Science Evidence", a paper presented to a Canadian Institute for the Administration of Justice conference, October 13-16, 1993. There is also the perspective that resting on expert medical opinion potentially medicalizes the problem and discounts the voice of the particular woman. This is very well-expressed by Professor Isabel Grant:

> A fundamental problem with developing a category like the "battered woman syndrome" is that we risk transforming the reality of this form of gender oppression into a psychiatric disorder. The victim of spousal violence becomes the abnormal actor, the one whose conduct must be explained by the expert. When a woman uses force to defend herself, it is evaluated with reference to a male standard of reasonableness or to an exceptional standard for certain women, *i.e.*, those who are "battered women". The focus is on the irrationality of a woman's response and on the need for medical terminology to transform that irrational response into a reasonable one for a "battered woman". She must either be reasonable "like a man" or reasonable "like a battered woman". Trapped in this dichotomy, the "reasonable" woman may disappear.

The research of Dr. Lenore Walker, relied on by the court in *Lavallee*, has been scathingly denounced:

> The battered woman syndrome illustrates all that is wrong with the law's use of science. The working hypothesis of the battered woman syndrome was first introduced in Lenore Walker's 1979 book, *The Battered Woman*. When it made its debut, this hypothesis had little more to support it beyond the clinical impressions of a single researcher. Five years later, Walker published a second book that promised a more thorough investigation of the hypothesis. However, this book contains little more than a patchwork of pseudo-scientific methods employed to confirm a hypothesis that its author and participating researchers never seriously doubted.

(Faigman and Wright, "The Battered Woman Syndrome in the Age of Science" (1997), 39 Arizona L. Rev. 67. See, further, Alan Gold's Netletter (ADGN/97-253 and ADGN/97-038). See, too, David Paciocco, *Getting Away with Murder; the Canadian Criminal Justice System* (Irwin Law, 1999), who dismisses the battered women's syndrome theory as "junk science" and little more than public interest advocacy dressed in the imposing garb of "study, experimentation and psychobabble" that imperils justice (p. 306).

R. v. PETEL

[1994] 1 S.C.R. 3, 26 C.R. (4th) 145, 87 C.C.C. (3d) 97,
1994 CarswellQue 3, 1994 CarswellQue 10

The accused was charged with the second degree murder of R. R and E were involved in drug-trafficking. E's girlfriend was the accused's daughter. The accused testified as to the terrible existence caused by E moving into her house and engaging in drug-trafficking from the house. She said he was always angry, threatened her frequently and beat her daughter. The accused moved to put an end to E's presence in her house but this was unsuccessful as E continued to go to her home to conduct his drug-trafficking operations. On the day in question E went to the accused's home with a revolver, cocaine and scales. He asked her to hide the weapon. He forced her to weigh some cocaine and suggested he would kill her, together with her daughter and granddaughter. Shortly after the daughter arrived with R. On the accused's testimony she consumed a small amount of drugs, got the weapon she had hidden in the bathroom, and fired at E who fell. Seeing that R was lunging at her she also fired at him. E survived but R died of his injuries. The accused admitted to police that she had fired at both E and R and that she wished both of them dead.

In his charge to the jury on self-defence the trial judge identified the elements of the defence under s. 34(2) of the *Criminal Code*, emphasized that the jury had to base its decision on the accused's assessment of the situation and summarized the evidence. After the jury had begun its deliberations they returned with a question of whether self-defence concerned threats or acts over several months or only that evening. The trial judge answered that the threat or act giving rise to self-defence had to occur on the evening of the crime and that the previous threats or acts were only relevant to assessing the assault that evening. The accused was convicted of second degree murder.

The Quebec Court of Appeal allowed the appeal and ordered a new trial. On further appeal the majority of the Supreme Court dismissed the appeal holding that the trial judge had erred in answering the jury's question.

LAMER C.J. (SOPINKA, CORY, MCLACHLIN and IACOBUCCI JJ. concurring): —

. . . .

Issue

As this is an appeal as of right, the only issue before this court is the one on which there was a dissent, namely whether the trial judge erred in his answer to the jury's question in differentiating the threats made on the evening of the incident from the previous threats and in relating the latter only to whether there had been an assault.

. . . .

In a case involving self-defence, it is the accused's state of mind that must be examined, and it is the accused (and not the victim) who must be given the benefit of a reasonable doubt. The question that the jury must ask itself is therefore not "was the accused unlawfully assaulted?" but rather "did the accused reasonably believe, in the circumstances, that she was being unlawfully assaulted?".

Moreover, *Lavallee, supra*, rejected the rule requiring that the apprehended danger be imminent. This alleged rule, which does not appear anywhere in the text of the *Criminal Code*, is in fact only a mere assumption based on common sense. As Wilson J. noted in *Lavallee*, this assumption undoubtedly derives from the paradigmatic case of self-defence, which is an altercation between two persons of equal strength. However, evidence may be presented (in particular expert evidence) to rebut this presumption of fact. There is thus no formal requirement that the danger be imminent. Imminence is only one of the factors which the jury should weigh in determining whether the accused had a reasonable apprehension of danger and a reasonable belief that she could not extricate herself otherwise than by killing the attacker.

. . . .

The question asked by the jury was specific, as the jury had identified its concern: the threats made by the victim in the months preceding the incident and those made on the day itself and, it can be assumed, the distinction that should be made between the two types of threat or act. The question was general, however, in the sense that the jury did not indicate whether its concern related only to one element of self-defence. The question concerned the "definition of self-defence", without more detail. The judge nonetheless limited his answer to only one of the elements, the existence of an assault and the assailant's ability to carry it out. This led him to make two errors.

First, the judge's answer suggested that the only relevance of the threats prior to July 21 was in enabling the jury to determine whether there had actually been an assault on the evening of July 21, that is, in the present case, death threats, and whether the assailant was in a position to carry out those threats. In a way the judge treated the earlier threats like similar fact evidence of the present threats. Their only use would then be to make it more plausible that Edsell also made threats in the minutes preceding the shots fired by the accused. This in my view diverted the jury from the question it really should have been considering, namely the reasonable belief of the accused in the existence of an assault. Emphasizing the victim's acts rather than the accused's state of mind has the effect of depriving the latter of the benefit of any error, however reasonable. The jury's attention should not be diverted from its proper concern, the guilt of the accused, by an inquiry into the guilt of the victim.

Secondly, and this is the crucial point, the judge's answer might have led the jury to believe that the threats made before July 21 could serve no other purpose than to determine the existence of the assault and the assailant's ability, thus denying their relevance to reasonable apprehension of a danger of death or grievous bodily harm and to the belief that there was no solution but to kill the attacker. The judge said that the previous threats served to [Translation] "assess the assault on the evening of July 21". He then explained what "assess the assault" meant:

> [Translation] . . . these previous acts or threats help you to determine whether Alain Raymond and Serge Edsell attempted or threatened . . . to apply force to Mrs. Pétel . . . whether the assailant had or caused . . . *the alleged victim to believe on reasonable grounds that he had present ability to effect his purpose*. [Emphasis added.]

The judge was in fact here repeating almost exactly the wording of s. 265(1)(*b*) of the *Criminal Code*. Although it is true that the previous threats can help the jury to decide whether threats were made immediately before the respondent shot Edsell and Raymond, they are also very relevant in determining what the respondent believed, not only concerning the existence of the threats, but also concerning her apprehension of the risk of death and her belief in the need to use deadly force. By failing to mention these two elements in his answer, the trial judge seriously limited the relevance of the earlier threats. In explaining how these threats could be used he should actually have referred not only to s. 265(1)(*b*) but also, most importantly, to s. 34(2) of the *Code*.

The importance of failing to relate the earlier threats to the elements of self-defence cannot be underestimated. The threats made by Edsell throughout his cohabitation with the respondent are very relevant in determining whether the respondent had a reasonable apprehension of danger and a reasonable belief in the need to kill Edsell and Raymond. The threats prior to July 21 form an integral part of the circumstances on which the perception of the accused might have been based. The judge's answer to this question might thus have led the jury to disregard the entire atmosphere of terror which the respondent said pervaded her house. It is clear that the way in which a reasonable person would have acted cannot be assessed without taking into account these crucial circumstances. As Wilson J. noted in *Lavallee*, at p. 883:

> The issue is not, however, what an outsider would have reasonably perceived but what the accused reasonably perceived, given her situation and her experience.

By unduly limiting the relevance of the previous threats the judge in a sense invited the jury to determine what an outsider would have done in the same situation as the respondent.

VI. Conclusion

The undisputed evidence that Edsell, her alleged attacker, handed over his weapon and asked his future victim to hide it, conduct that is odd to say the least for someone intending to kill, must have had a clear effect on the jury, indeed on any jury composed of reasonable individuals. In the Court of Appeal and in this court, however, counsel for the Crown did not argue that, given the evidence in this case, no substantial wrong or miscarriage of justice occurred, and that s. 686(1)(*b*)(iii) of the *Criminal Code* should thus be applied. The Crown has the burden of showing that this provision is applicable: *Colpitts v. The Queen*, [1965] S.C.R. 739. This court cannot apply it *proprio motu*. Having found an error of law in the judge's answer to the question by the jury, I must accordingly dismiss the appeal and affirm the order for a new trial.

GONTHIER J. (LA FOREST, L'HEUREUX-DUBÉ, and MAJOR JJ. concurring): — I have had the benefit of reading the reasons of the Chief Justice. I agree with his statement of the applicable principles of law and his explanation of those principles. However, I cannot concur in his reading of the answer given by the trial Judge to the question asked by the jury regarding previous threats or acts and the threats of the evening of July 21, 1989 as they affect the definition of self-defence. In my view the judge's answer did not overlook the very important element of the accused's belief. In his answer to the jury the judge clearly said:

> In other words, these previous acts or threats help you to determine whether Alain Raymond and Serge Edsell attempted or threatened . . . on the evening of July 21, by an act or a gesture, to apply force to Mrs. Pétel, to her daughter or to her granddaughter, whether the assailant had or caused the alleged victim to believe on reasonable grounds that he had present ability to effect his purpose.

It is true that the judge did not elaborate on the accused's belief, nor did he elaborate on the elements of the definition of self-defence other than the relative importance of the previous threats and the threats at the time of the crime, which was all that the question asked by the jury dealt with.

However, he emphasized and pointed to each of the elements of this defence by three times re-reading s. 265(1)(*b*) of the *Criminal Code*, R.S.C., 1985, c. C-46. He could not have done this any better or any more succinctly and clearly. This re-reading, which he characterized as such, repeated his reading of the paragraph in his general charge the day before, which was immediately followed by clear and complete explanations of the essential criterion of the accused's state of mind at the time she caused the death, including her apprehension of death or grievous bodily harm from which she could not preserve herself except by the force she used.

There could be no doubt as to the "purpose" in question. Only one thing was discussed, the purpose to kill on the part of the victim. The belief on reasonable grounds that the victim had present ability to effect this purpose could mean nothing other than the accused's belief that the victim was capable of killing the accused, thus leaving her no alternative but to act first. With all due respect, I cannot conclude that the judge's answer could have been understood by the jury or could have led it to make a finding other than on the basis of a reasonable belief by the accused in a danger of death which she could not avoid except by killing her attacker. In my opinion, the judge's answer contained no error and was adequate.

I would therefore allow the appeal. I would set aside the Court of Appeal's judgment and restore the guilty verdict.

Is *Petel* inconsistent with *Creighton*?

R. v. MALOTT

[1998] 1 S.C.R. 123, 121 C.C.C. (3d) 456,
1998 CarswellOnt 419, 1998 CarswellOnt 420

The accused was charged with murder. The accused and the deceased had lived as common law spouses for almost 20 years. The deceased abused the accused physically, sexually, psychologically and emotionally. On the day of the shooting the accused was scheduled to go to a medical centre with the deceased to get prescription drugs for use in his illegal drug trade. She took a pistol from the deceased's gun cabinet. After driving to the medical centre she shot him to death. She then took a taxi to the deceased's girlfriend's home, shot her and stabbed her with a knife.

At trial, the accused testified to the extensive abuse which she had suffered and led expert evidence to show that she suffered from battered woman syndrome.

The jury found her guilty of second degree murder in the death of the deceased and of attempted murder of his girlfriend. The majority of the Court of Appeal affirmed the convictions. There was no air of reality to the defence of self-defence as it related to the charge of attempted murder. With respect to the deceased, the jury was clearly instructed that the perception of the accused developed against the background of her abuse, was required to be assessed in determining if her actions were reasonable self-defence. The accused appealed, complaining about the adequacy of the trial judge's charge to the jury on the murder charge on the issue of battered woman syndrome as a defence.

The Supreme Court was unanimous in dismissing the appeal on the basis that the trial judge's charge on self-defence and the evidence of abuse while not perfect was adequate. There was a noteworthy *obiter* by the two female members of the court.

L'HEUREUX-DUBÉ J. (McLACHLIN J. concurring): —

. . . [G]iven that this court has not had the opportunity to discuss the value of evidence of "battered woman syndrome" since *R. v. Lavallee*, [1990] 1 S.C.R. 852 (S.C.C.), and given the evolving discourse on "battered woman syndrome" in the legal community, I will make a few comments on the importance of this kind of evidence to the just adjudication of charges involving battered women.

First, the significance of this court's decision in *Lavallee*, which first accepted the need for expert evidence on the effects of abusive relationships in order to properly understand the context in which an accused woman had killed her abusive spouse in self-defence, reaches beyond its particular impact on the law of self-defence. A crucial implication of the admissibility of expert evidence in *Lavallee* is the legal recognition that historically both the law and society may have treated women in general, and battered women in particular, unfairly. *Lavallee* accepted that the myths and stereotypes which are the products and the tools of this unfair treatment interfere with the capacity of judges and juries to justly determine a battered woman's claim of self-defence, and can only be dispelled by expert evidence designed to overcome the stereotypical thinking. The expert evidence is admissible, and necessary, in order to understand the reasonableness of a battered woman's perceptions, which in *Lavallee* were the accused's perceptions that she had to act with deadly force in order to preserve herself from death or grievous bodily harm. Accordingly, the utility of such evidence in criminal cases is not limited to instances where a battered woman is pleading self-defence, but is potentially relevant to other situations where the reasonableness of a battered woman's actions or perceptions is at issue (e.g. provocation, duress or necessity). See *R. v. Hibbert*, [1995] 2 S.C.R. 973 (S.C.C.), at p. 1021.

It is clear from the foregoing that "battered woman syndrome" is not a legal defence in itself such that an accused woman need only establish that she is suffering from the syndrome in order to gain an acquittal. As Wilson J. commented in *Lavallee*, at p. 890: "Obviously the fact that the appellant was a battered woman does not entitle her to an acquittal. Battered women may well kill their partners other than in self-defence." Rather, "battered woman syndrome" is a psychiatric explanation of the mental state of women who have been subjected to continuous battering by their male intimate partners, which can be relevant to the legal inquiry into a battered woman's state of mind. Second, the majority of the court in *Lavallee* also implicitly accepted that women's experiences and perspectives may be different from the experiences and perspectives of men. It accepted that a woman's perception of what is reasonable is influenced by her gender, as well as by her individual experience, and both are relevant to the legal inquiry. This legal development was significant, because it demonstrated a willingness to look at the whole context of a woman's experience in order to inform the analysis of the particular events. But it is wrong to think of this development of the law as merely an example where an objective test — the requirement that an accused claiming self-defence must *reasonably* apprehend death or grievous bodily harm — has been modified to admit evidence of the subjective perceptions of a battered woman. More important, a majority of the court accepted that the perspectives of women, which have historically been ignored, must now equally inform the "objective" standard of the reasonable person in relation to self-defence.

When interpreting and applying *Lavallee*, these broader principles should be kept in mind. In particular, they should be kept in mind in order to avoid a too rigid and restrictive approach to the admissibility and legal value of evidence of a battered woman's experiences. Concerns have been expressed that the treatment of expert evidence on battered women syndrome, which is itself admissible in order to combat the myths and stereotypes which society has about battered women, has led to a new stereotype of the "battered woman": see, e.g., Martha Shaffer, "The Battered Woman Syndrome Revisited: Some Complicating Thoughts Five Years After *R. v. Lavallee*" (1997), 47 U.T.L.J. 1, at p. 9; Sheila Noonan, "Strategies of Survival: Moving Beyond the Battered Woman Syndrome", in Ellen Adelberg and Claudia Currie, eds., *In Conflict with the Law: Women and the Canadian Justice System* (1993), 247, at p. 254; Isabel Grant, "The 'Syndromization' of Women's Experience", in Donna Martinson, et al., "A Forum on *Lavallee v. R.:* Women and Self-Defence" (1991), 25 U.B.C.L. Rev. 23, at pp. 53-54; and Martha R. Mahoney, "Legal Images of Battered Women: Redefining the Issue of Separation" (1991), 90 Mich. L. Rev. 1, at p. 42.

It is possible that those women who are unable to fit themselves within the stereotype of a victimized, passive, helpless, dependent, battered woman will not have their claims to self-defence fairly decided. For instance, women who have demonstrated too much strength or initiative, women of colour, women who are professionals, or women who might have fought back against their abusers on previous occasions, should not be penalized for failing to accord with the stereotypical image of the archetypal battered woman. See, e.g., Julie Stubbs and Julia Tolmie, "Race, Gender, and the Battered Woman Syndrome: An Australia Case Study" (1995), 8 C.J.W.L. 122. Needless to say, women with these characteristics are still entitled to have their claims of self-defence fairly adjudicated, and they are also still entitled to have their experiences as battered women inform the analysis. Professor Grant, *supra*, at p. 52, warns against allowing the law to develop such that a woman accused of killing her abuser must either have been "reasonable 'like a man' or reasonable 'like a battered woman'". I agree that this must be avoided. The "reasonable woman" must not be forgotten in the analysis, and deserves to be as much a part of the objective standard of the reasonable person as does the "reasonable man".

How should the courts combat the "syndromization", as Professor Grant refers to it, of battered women who act in self-defence? The legal inquiry into the moral culpability of a woman who is, for instance, claiming self-defence must focus on the *reasonableness* of her actions in the context of her personal experiences, and her experiences as a woman, not on her status as a battered woman and her entitlement to claim that she is suffering from "battered woman syndrome". This point has been made convincingly by many academics reviewing the relevant cases: see, e.g., Wendy Chan, "A Feminist Critique of Self-Defense and Provocation in Battered Women's Cases in England and Wales" (1994), 6 Women & Crim. Just. 39, at pp. 56-57; Elizabeth M. Schneider, "Describing and Changing: Women's Self-Defense Work and the Problem of Expert Testimony on Battering" (1992), 14 Women's Rts. L. Rep. 213, at pp. 216-17; and Marilyn MacCrimmon, "The Social Construction of Reality and the Rules of Evidence", in Donna Martinson et al., *supra*, at pp. 48-49. By emphasizing a woman's "learned helplessness", her dependence, her victimization, and her low self-esteem, in order to establish that she suffers from "battered woman syndrome", the legal debate shifts from the objective rationality of her actions to preserve her own life to those personal inadequacies which apparently explain her failure to flee from her abuser. Such an emphasis comports too well with society's stereotypes about women. Therefore, it should be scrupulously avoided because it only serves to undermine the important advancements achieved by the decision in *Lavallee*.

There are other elements of a woman's social context which help to explain her inability to leave her abuser, and which do not focus on those characteristics most consistent with traditional stereotypes. As Wilson J. herself recognized in *Lavallee*, at p. 887, "environmental factors may also impair the woman's ability to leave — lack of job skills, the presence of children to care for, fear of retaliation by the man, etc. may each have a role to play in some cases." To this list of factors I would add a woman's need to protect her children from abuse, a fear of losing custody of her children, pressures to keep the family together, weaknesses of social and financial support for battered women, and no guarantee that the violence would cease simply because she left. These considerations necessarily inform the reasonableness of a woman's beliefs or perceptions of, for instance, her lack of an alternative to the use of deadly force to preserve herself from death or grievous bodily harm.

How should these principles be given practical effect in the context of a jury trial of a woman accused of murdering her abuser? To fully accord with the spirit of *Lavallee*, where the reasonableness of a battered woman's belief is at issue in a criminal case, a judge and jury should be made to appreciate that a battered woman's experiences are both individualized, based on her own history and relationships, as well as shared with other women, within the context of a society and a legal system which has historically undervalued women's experiences. A judge and jury should be told that a battered woman's experiences are generally outside the common understanding of the average judge and juror, and that they should seek to understand the evidence being presented to them in order to overcome the myths and stereotypes which we all share. Finally, all of this should be presented in such a way as to focus on the reasonableness of the woman's actions, without relying on old or new stereotypes about battered women.

My focus on women as the victims of battering and as the subjects of "battered woman syndrome" is not intended to exclude from consideration those men who find themselves in abusive relationships. However, the reality of our society is that typically, it is women who are the victims of domestic violence, at the hands of their male intimate partners. To assume that men who are victims of spousal abuse are affected by the abuse in the same way, without benefit of the research and expert opinion evidence which has informed the courts of the existence and details of "battered woman syndrome", would be imprudent.

The accused and his co-accused were inmates in a penitentiary. There had been considerable tension between the accused and a group of other inmates. The group had made threats that the accused took seriously. Fearing for his safety and anticipating an attack, the accused armed himself

with knuckledusters and a stick. The co-accused got a knife. When one of the group members walked by, the accused hit him on the head repeatedly with the knuckledusters, while the co-accused stabbed him in the stomach. The injuries were fatal. The accused and co-accused were charged with first degree murder. In his charge to the jury the trial judge stated that the accused and the co-accused could not claim the defence of self-defence under s. 34(2) unless they believed that they were in imminent danger of death or serious bodily harm from the victim at the time they attacked him. The jury convicted the accused of manslaughter and the co-accused of second degree murder. On appeal the accused argued that the trial judge erred in his direction on s. 34(2). They argued they suffered from "prison environment syndrome" which was analogous to battered wife syndrome in that they lived in an environment in which inmates had to "kill or be killed". Should there be a new trial to consider such a defence? Should it succeed?

Compare *R. v. McConnell* (1996), 48 C.R. (4th) 199, [1996] 1 S.C.R. 1075 and see annotation by Christine Boyle (1996), 48 C.R. (4th) 200.

In *R. v. Cinous* (2002), 49 C.R. (5th) 209 (S.C.C.), the leading pronouncement on how the air of reality standard needs to be met before defences are put to juries (see earlier), the court divided 6-3 (in a judgment over 100 printed pages(!)) over whether or not there was an air of reality to the defence of self-defence in the following circumstance.

The accused was charged with the first degree murder of a criminal accomplice, Mike. The accused testified that he and a friend had been involved in the theft and resale of computers along with Mike and another accomplice, Ice. About one month before the killing, he became convinced that Mike had stolen his gun. He told Mike and Ice that he wanted no more to do with them but they kept calling about doing thefts. He also testified that shortly after the gun went missing he began to hear rumours that Mike and Ice wanted to kill him, and that he was warned by a friend to watch out for them. One morning Mike and Ice called and asked the accused to participate in a computer theft. He agreed to meet with them that evening at his apartment. The accused testified that when they arrived, they kept their jackets on and whispered to one another as they sat in the living room. He saw Ice constantly placing his hand inside his coat. That made him suspect they were armed. The accused said he decided to participate in the theft to see if they really intended to kill him. They left the apartment and got into the accused's van to drive to the location of the theft. The accused said that he knew Mike and Ice wanted to kill him when he saw they had changed their gloves. Neither had changed to the black woollen gloves kept in the van compartment for computer thefts. Mike was wearing surgical latex gloves the accused associated with situations where bloodshed was expected. He had twice before seen them used on "burns" —attacks on criminals by other criminals. The accused drove. Ice sat next to him and Mike sat behind Ice. The accused testified Ice avoided making eye contact with him and kept touching his jacket as if he had a gun. He said he interpreted Ice's hand inside his jacket as a threat. The accused admitted that no other threats were made. The accused testified that he was sure that he was going to be killed and that the shot would more than likely come from behind — from Mike. Since he was driving, he could not get to his own gun quickly enough, were anything to happen. He felt trapped. He pulled into a populated and well-lit gas station to "release the pressure" and get himself out of this bad situation. He bought a bottle of windshield washer after returning to the van to get money from Ice. He poured the fluid in under the hood and brought the bottle back around to the back of the van. He opened the back door, "saw the opportunity", pulled out his gun and shot Mike in the back of the head. The accused testified that this was an instinctive reaction to a situation of danger. It did not occur to him to run away or to call the police.

Was there an air of reality to the defence under s. 34(2)?

The leading judgment on s. 34(1) is now that of Wittman J.A. of the Alberta Court of Appeal in *Kong*. Although he was the dissenting judge in the Alberta Court of Appeal the Supreme Court later enigmatically agreed with his "conclusion" and reversed that of the majority: (2006), 40 C.R. (6th) 231 (S.C.C.)

R. v. KONG

200 C.C.C. (3d) 19, 40 C.R. (6th) 225, 2005 CarswellAlta 1089 (C.A.), reversed 2006 CarswellAlta 1134, 2006 CarswellAlta 1135, 211 C.C.C. (3d) 1, 40 C.R. (6th) 221, [2006] 2 S.C.R. 347

Kong was charged with second degree murder following a stabbing death when two groups got in a late night fight. A young man, Miu, aged 18 and small of stature, was stabbed to death in an alley behind an after hours nightclub. The stabbing occurred during a fight between two groups of friends. Miu's brother hit a member of the accused's group over the head with a bottle. The accused and others in his group drew their knives. Miu ran back towards his brother to help. Miu was fatally stabbed by one blow to his stomach. The accused was charged with second degree murder. At trial, Kong's main defence was that he did not stab the victim. In the alternative he submitted that he did not have the intent required for murder, and that the jury should be charged with self-defence under s. 34(2). The Crown's view was that the accused had administered the fatal stab wound. The evidence of witnesses to the fight conflicted. Kong testified that he waved the knife as a scare tactic, but when the two kept running towards him, he stepped forward and made a horizontal motion with his knife to stop Miu and protect himself and his friend. He admitted that his knife may have caught Miu's clothing but that he did not stab him. The trial judge ruled that the accused's defence of self-defence had no air of reality and was not to be left with the jury. The jury found that Kong was guilty of manslaughter. The accused appealed.

The majority of the Alberta Court of Appeal dismissed the appeal after deliberating for a year. In a lengthy judgment Fraser C.J.A. held that the trial judge had correctly rejected Kong's claim for self-defence as it lacked an air of reality under s. 34(1) or 34(2). Respecting s. 34(1) there was no air of reality to Kong's assertion that he did not intend to cause grievous harm when he stabbed the victim. The verdict of the jury supported that conclusion because the verdict was that he was the person who had stabbed the victim. Nor was there any air of reality to Kong's claim that he used no more force than was necessary to defend himself. The test had to be judged entirely on an objective standard. Chief Justice Fraser offered several policy reasons for this tough standard and invoked in aid the ruling of the Supreme Court in *Latimer* that the proportionality test for necessity had to be tested on a strictly objective basis. Russell J.A. agreed that there was no air of reality for self-defence to be put to the jury.

However Wittmann J.A. disagreed and it was his conclusion that was accepted by the Supreme Court. In his view, considering all the circumstances of this case the defence of self-defence under s. 34(1), although not that under s. 34(2), had an air of reality and should have been put to the jury for its consideration. It should have been left to the jury to determine whether the force used by the accused, in using the knife, was done in self-defence and whether it was proportional or no more than was necessary in the circumstances to protect himself. The appeal should be allowed, the conviction set aside and a new trial ordered.

WITTMAN J.A.: —

The elements of ss. 34(1) and 34(2)

177   The air of reality test must be applied to each of the elements set out under s. 34(1) or s. 34(2) as each element must each be established for self-defence to succeed: *R. v. Hebert*, [1996] 2 S.C.R. 272 at para. 23.

178   As stated in numerous cases, including this court in *R. v. McConnell* (1995), 169 A.R. 321, rev'd [1996] 1 S.C.R. 1075, the wording of s. 34(1) sets out four elements necessary for self-defence: 1) an unlawful assault, 2) the assault was not provoked, 3) lack of intent to kill or cause grievous bodily harm, and 4) the force used be no more than is necessary for self-defence.

179   Self-defence under s. 34(2) depends on three elements: 1) an unlawful assault, 2) the accused has a reasonable apprehension of death or grievous bodily harm, and 3) reasonably believes that he cannot otherwise preserve himself from death or grievous bodily harm unless he repels the unlawful assault in kind.

180   Section 34(1) and 34(2) are for very different situations. Dickson J. (as he then was) explained the differences in *R. v. Brisson*, [1982] 2 S.C.R. 227 at 258:

> Section 34(1) may only be invoked if there is no intention to cause death or grievous harm and no more force than is necessary is used. Section 34(2) is invoked where death or grievous harm has resulted but (i) the accused reasonably apprehended his own death or grievous harm and (ii) he believed on reasonable grounds that he had no other means of avoiding his own death or grievous harm. Section 34(1) affords justification in circumstances where the force used was not intended to cause death or grievous harm and is not excessive. Section 34(2)

affords justification where there was an intention to cause death but under circumstances where objectively it was reasonable that the person accused believed he was going to be killed and subjectively he did so believe. Section 34(2) obviously provides for acquittal, despite the fact that the accused means to cause death or bodily harm that he knows is likely to cause death.

181   The lack of intention to cause death or grievous bodily harm is a significant difference between the two sections. It is required for s. 34(1), but not required under s. 34(2). Whether death has resulted is not a difference between the two sections; the distinction is whether or not the accused intended to cause death or serious bodily harm: see, for example, *R. v. Baxter* (1975), 27 C.C.C. (2d) 96 at 111 (Ont. C.A.); *R. v. Martin* (1985), 47 C.R. (3d) 342 (Que. C.A.).

182   The lack of evidence that the accused is under a reasonable apprehension of death or grievous bodily harm is another significant difference. It is a required element under s. 34(2), but not s. 34(1). The absence of such an apprehension makes s. 34(2) inapplicable, but s. 34(1) may still apply subject to the presence of the other required elements: *R. v. Setrum* (1976), 32 C.C.C. (2d) 109 (Sask. CA).

183   The lack of excessive force is also a key difference. Under s. 34(1), the force used cannot be excessive, but is not an element required under s. 34(2).

184   The Quebec Court of Appeal in *Martin* at para. 28 made clear the distinctions and possible verdicts under ss. 34(1) and (2):

1. If the accused had not been attacked by Dazé and had stabbed him intending to cause death or intending to cause bodily harm that he knew was likely to cause death, then he was guilty of murder. The question of self-defence does not arise here.

2. Similarly, if the accused had not been attacked and had stabbed Dazé but without intending to cause death or serious bodily harm likely to cause death, then he was guilty of manslaughter. Here again there is no question of self-defence.

3. If the accused was attacked by Dazé and, in defending himself, stabbed Dazé without intending to cause death or grievous bodily harm and used no more force than was necessary to defend himself, then he was not guilty.

4. If the accused was attacked by Dazé and, in defending himself, caused Dazé's death but the accused (a) reasonably feared his own death or grievous harm, and (b) believed, on reasonable grounds, that he had no other way of avoiding his own death or grievous harm, then even if the accused intended to cause death or grievous harm to Dazé he was not guilty.

5. Finally, if the accused was attacked and, in defending himself against Dazé's attack, used more force than was necessary to repel the attack so that he had no justification for the killing on the basis of self-defence, he was not automatically guilty of murder. If he intended to cause death or grievous bodily harm likely to cause death, he was guilty of murder. If he did not have this intention, he was guilty of manslaughter.

185   In this case, apprehension of death or grievous bodily harm was not raised in the facts. Section 34(2) does not apply. Intention and the use of force, however, were clearly issues in this case. Thus, the defence under s. 34(1) is potentially applicable, provided the air of reality test is met.

Unlawful assault

186   Does the evidence in this case pass the air of reality test for each of the elements of s. 34(1)? The first two elements are not in issue in this appeal. The first element, an unlawful assault is satisfied by the reasonable perception of an unlawful assault: *R. v. Pétel*, [1994] 1 S.C.R. 3. Where there is evidence which would support a finding that the accused believed on reasonable grounds that he was being assaulted, a jury must be instructed that such a belief will satisfy this element of the defence: *R. v. Proulx* (1998), 110 B.C.A.C. 62. The existence of an actual assault is not a prerequisite for self-defence; it is enough that the accused reasonably believed in the circumstances that he was being, or was about to be, unlawfully assaulted: *Cinous* at para. 107; *McConnell* at paras. 50-51, and 74. Thus, an accused does not have to wait until he is actually attacked.

187   In this case, the appellant's perception of an attack of some sort by Miu as Miu ran towards him could be concluded in the circumstances.

Unprovoked assault

188   On the second element, lack of provocation, no arguments were made by either party nor was there any evidence to suggest the assault was provoked.

Lack of intention to cause death or grievous bodily harm

189   The third element is whether in using force, the appellant intended to cause death or grievous bodily harm. The application of the air of reality test to the third and fourth elements of s. 34(1) can be seen in two decisions where the circumstances were similar to this appeal.

190   In *R. v. Kandola* (1993), 27 B.C.A.C. 226, the accused's home had been surrounded and was being attacked by the deceased and four other men, all of whom were armed with weapons (hockey sticks and possibly a rifle). There were 16 people present in the accused's home, including four or five women and two children. The accused and his family were all terrified as the deceased had made repeated and "terrible" threats over the previous several days. The deceased telephoned the accused, conveying his intent to do violence to the accused and his family. The accused called the police three times, but before they arrived, he retrieved a handgun he had purchased (albeit illegally), crawled to the window of a top floor bedroom at the front of the house. While lying on the floor, he put his arm out the window and fired blindly several times down toward the ground in an effort to scare off the attackers. One of bullets he fired hit and

killed the deceased, who was then attempting to gain access to the house through the front door.

191   As in the present case, the accused in *Kandola* was charged with second degree murder but was convicted of manslaughter. His only defence at trial was self-defence. A further similarity is that the key questions in *Kandola* were whether or not there was intent to cause death or grievous bodily harm and whether the force used by the accused was no more than necessary.

192   In *Kandola*, the court concluded that all the relevant statutory elements for a successful defence of self-defence under s. 34(1) were made out on the evidence. It was held that the trial judge had erred in concluding that the lawfulness of the act of shooting to warn was "negated" because of the recklessness with which that "force" was applied. Wood J.A., in addressing the issue of the force that is justified under s. 34(1), stated at para. 25,

> ... recklessness is not mentioned as a relevant state of mind in s. 34(1). Logically, of course, force which is so recklessly applied in self-defence as to be excessive, will be unnecessary force and by that finding the defence will fail. *But what deprives the accused of the defence in that circumstance is his recklessness as to the measure of force necessary, not recklessness as to the consequences, or the risk of consequences, flowing from the application of that force.* While that may seem somewhat subtle, it is an important distinction which flows from the previously mentioned fact that it is the force itself, and not the consequences of its use, which is justified on a successful defence of self-defence. [Emphasis added]

193   The second reason the trial judge erred in his approach was due to the "long recognized need for a tolerant approach to the objective measurement of proportionate force in genuine self-defence cases": *Kandola* at para. 27.

194   The court in *Kandola* further held at para. 35 that "once the force used in self-defence has been determined to be necessary, the resulting unintended death will not be a culpable homicide". In that case, the trial judge clearly found the force used - firing a warning shot without aiming - was no more than was necessary to enable the accused to defend himself. Once that finding was made, there was no proper basis on which to further consider the recklessness of the manner in which the force was used. As the trial judge had found the force used by the accused was necessary, the inescapable conclusion was that the act of shooting to warn was justified and thus, not an unlawful act.

195   One other case is also illustrative. In *R. v. W.W.R.* (1998), 115 B.C.A.C. 311, the accused was awakened by the complainant, who was sexually assaulting him. The accused, a wood carver, grabbed the closest object, a carving knife, stabbed the complainant once and pushed him away. He admitted the stabbing, but claimed he did so in self-defence. The trial judge convicted him of aggravated assault by wounding because the force he used was not reasonably necessary as all that was really required was the pushing. The appeal was allowed and the accused was acquitted.

196   The court found the accused's evidence was consistent with an instinctive reaction and used the knife as the first thing that came to hand to repel the assault. The trial judge found the explanation for the knife's presence next to the bed was innocent. The court, citing *Kandola*, reiterated that it was the force itself, and not the consequences of the force, which was justified under s. 34(1). The consequences of the use of force were relevant only to the extent that they were intended, and the consequences were not intended in that case.

197   In this case, where the appellant's intent cannot be proven by direct evidence, it must be inferred from the circumstantial evidence. Both *Cinous* at para. 90 and *Arcuri* at para. 23 describe the approach to be followed by the trial judge as one of "limited weighing". The judge must assess whether the evidence is reasonably capable of supporting the inferences that the jury is being asked to draw. "The judge does not draw determinate factual inferences, but rather comes to a conclusion about the field of factual inferences that could reasonably be drawn from the evidence.": *Cinous* at para. 91.

198   In this case, the appellant's testimony was that he pulled out the knife to scare Miu and the other male as they ran towards him. He made a motion with the knife once to try to stop Miu and the other male from continuing to run towards him. The record does not show whether he indicated a stabbing or swinging motion when he demonstrated what he did.

199   There was conflicting evidence about the appellant's motions with the knife. Some witnesses, including the appellant, testified he made a swinging horizontal motion. One witness, Peter, one of the combatants from Miu's group, testified that the appellant was swinging the knife looking like he was trying to keep a perimeter around himself and John. Others testified he made a punching or stabbing motion.

200   The autopsy report and testimony of Dr. Denmark contained relevant evidence of the circumstances surrounding intent. His testimony and report showed that the wound was about one inch in length and went in deep enough to notch the spinal disk.

201   From this evidence, the trial judge must make inferences. However, in deciding whether there is an air of reality, the trial judge is not to determine the appellant's claim that he lacked intent. The evidence is not to be weighed in order to conclude that the appellant made punching or stabbing motions with the knife, not swinging motions, and therefore, he used the knife intending to cause grievous bodily harm. As the majority in *Cinous* stated at para. 87:

> The trial judge must review the evidence and determine whether, if believed, it could permit a properly instructed jury acting reasonably to acquit. It follows that the trial judge cannot consider issues of credibility. Further, the trial judge must not weigh evidence, make findings of fact, or draw determinate factual inferences.

202   Whether and how far to believe the evidence is a matter for the jury: *Cinous* at para. 88.

203   Nor are the consequences of the appellant's actions to be determinative of his intention. As the decisions in *Kandola* and *W.W.R.* illustrate, there is a crucial distinction between intention and consequences. As the evidence relied on by the accused is assumed to be true, there is an evidentiary basis to support the appellant's testimony that he did not intend to cause death or grievous bodily harm, he only intended to defend himself. The consequence of the use of that force - the death of Miu - should only be relevant to the extent it was intended.

204   The jury, not the trial judge, is to decide which motion the appellant made with the knife and whether he could have been intending only to defend himself yet inflict the fatal wound to Miu.

205   The latter conclusion is reasonably capable of belief in this case given that the jury found the appellant guilty of manslaughter, and not murder. The jury found either that the appellant did not have the requisite intention for murder, or that there was a reasonable doubt that he did. In other words, the jury found the appellant did not intend to cause grievous bodily harm knowing it was likely to cause death. While this does not equate to finding no intent to cause grievous bodily harm, it also does not equate to the jury finding that the appellant intended to cause grievous bodily harm. The instructions given to the jury did not leave them with that question. Finding that the appellant intended to use the knife, but did not intend to cause grievous bodily harm was never an option left to the jury. Thus, all the required elements under s. 34(1) are satisfied, save the final one.

Proportionate force

206   The fourth and final element is whether the force used by the appellant was no more than he reasonably believed was necessary to defend himself in the circumstances. As noted above, it is the force applied in self-defence, and not the consequences of that force, that may be justified under s. 34(1): *Kandola* at para. 23. Thus, the question to be determined in this case is not whether stabbing and killing Miu was necessary in order to defend himself; that was the consequence of the force used. Rather, the question is whether the use of the knife, as an application of force, was reasonably necessary in the circumstances, or its use amounted to excessive force.

207   Asking whether the force was no more than was necessary to enable the accused to defend himself, requires, according to some authorities, both an subjective and an objective test. First, whether the accused believed the force used was necessary is a subjective inquiry: *R. v. Cadwallader*, [1996] 1 C.C.C. 380 at 387-88 (Sask. C.A.). Second, whether the accused's belief was a

reasonable belief is an objective inquiry. Alternatively, the Chief Justice suggests a modified objective test applies to the threat assessment by the accused, while an objective test applies to the responsive force used.

208   None of the tests, however framed, requires a precisely calculated response. Under s. 34(1), a person is not expected to "weigh to a nicety" the exact measure of a defensive action or to stop and reflect upon the risk of deadly consequences from such action: *Kandola* at paras. 27 and 28 citing *Palmer v. The Queen* (1971), 55 Cr. App. R. 223 at 242. The principle has also been adopted and applied in *R. v. Ogal* (1928), 50 C.C.C. 71 (Alta. S.C.A.D.); *R. v. Preston* (1953), 106 C.C.C. 135 at 140 (B.C.C.A.); *R. v. Antley*, [1964] 2 C.C.C. 142 at 147 (Ont. C.A.), and *Baxter*.

209   The accused may be mistaken about the nature and extent of force necessary for self-defence provided the mistake was reasonable in the circumstances: *R. v. Nelson* (1992), 71 C.C.C. (3d) 449 at 468-9 (Ont. C.A.). In deciding whether the appellant's use of force was reasonable, the jury is to look to the circumstances to consider what a reasonable person in the accused's situation might do given the threatening attack and the force necessary to defend himself against that apprehended attack: *Baxter* at 110. The objective measurement of proportionate force in self-defence cases requires a tolerant approach: *Kandola* at para. 27.

210   In his text *Canadian Criminal Law*, 4th ed. (Scarborough, Ont: Carswell, 1997), Don Stuart summarized the present state of the law at 442:

> The Canadian judicial attitude to self-defence is now entrenched. It is one of flexibility. Apart from the recognition that strict proportionality is not demanded there are no automatic rules that the defender cannot strike the first blow or cannot succeed in the defence of self-defence if he could have retreated.

211   Again, using the approach of limited weighing, the evidence relied on by the appellant in this case was reasonably capable of supporting the inferences required for the fourth element of s. 34(1), thus, satisfying the air of reality test.

The Supreme Court agreed with Justice Wittman's conclusion. It is unfortunate that they did not give their full imprimatur to his reasons which provide a clear and full review of current jurisprudence under s. 34(1). Integral to his conclusion is that the majority had unduly weighed the evidence and usurped the function of the jury, and that strict objective proportionality test the Chief Justice of Alberta sought to assert should be rejected.

4. DEFENCE OF PROPERTY

In December 2011 Parliament gave second reading to Bill C-26, which would repeal the defence of property provisions in ss. 38-42 and replace them with the following:

35. (1) A person is not guilty of an offence if

    (a) they either believe on reasonable grounds that they are in peaceable possession of property or are acting under the authority of, or lawfully assisting, a person whom they believe on reasonable grounds is in peaceable possession of property;

    (b) they believe on reasonable grounds that another person

        (i) is about to enter, is entering or has entered the property without being entitled by law to do so,

        (ii) is about to take the property, is doing so or has just done so, or

        (iii) is about to damage or destroy the property, or make it inoperative, or is doing so;

    (c) the act that constitutes the offence is committed for the purpose of

        (i) preventing the other person from entering the property, or removing that person from the property, or

        (ii) preventing the other person from taking, damaging or destroying the property or from making it inoperative, or retaking the property from that person; and

    (d) the act committed is reasonable in the circumstances.

The cases below were decided under ss. 38-42 of the *Criminal Code*.

R. v. BAXTER

(1975), 33 C.R.N.S. 22 at 40-3, 27 C.C.C. (2d) 96,
1975 CarswellOnt 54 (Ont. C.A.)

MARTIN J.A.: —

. . . .

The grounds of appeal based upon the judge's charge with respect to the use of force to remove a trespasser may be conveniently dealt with together.

Counsel for the appellant contended that the trial judge erred in instructing the jury that killing or causing grievous bodily harm to a trespasser was not justifiable unless the circumstances were such as to give rise to the defence of self-defence under s. 34(2) of the *Code*, and should have left with the jury, as a separate defence, the provisions of s. 4.1(1) of the *Code* authorizing the use of force to prevent any person from trespassing on a dwelling house or real property if he uses no more force than is necessary.

. . . .

Complaint is also made with respect to the following instruction to the jury by the trial judge. The learned trial judge, after reading s. 41 of the *Code* to the jury, said:

So that in the circumstances here, one, if you are satisfied that either generally or on this occasion the people who were hurt had been ordered from the property then, and were still on it, not getting off it, then they were trespassers if they did not get off when they were asked to get off; if you find that in the evidence, then that was an assault, but the difficulty about that assault under s. 34(2) that I have read to you is that it is very hard to say that; that assault deemed to be such under s. 41(2) of the *Criminal Code* is a violent assault.

The sections of the *Code* authorizing the use of force in defence of a person or property, to prevent crime, and to apprehend offenders, in general, express in greater detail the great principle of the common-law that the use of force in such circumstances is subject to the restriction that the force used is necessary; that is, that the harm sought to be prevented could not be prevented by less violent means and that the injury or harm done by, or which might reasonably be anticipated from the force used, is not disproportioned to the injury or harm it is intended to prevent: see Report of Criminal Code Bill Commission, 1879, referred to in Russell, at p. 432.

Mr. Cooper referred the court to authorities holding that the use of firearms is justified, even though death ensues, in order to prevent burglary or arson: see 1 Hale P.C. 487. The common law cast a special protection around the dwelling. In such cases there is, of course, an element of personal danger which may justify the use even of extreme force in self-defence. Moreover, s. 27 of the *Criminal Code* authorizes the use of as much force as is reasonably necessary to prevent the commission of any offence, for which the offender may be arrested without warrant, and that would be likely to cause immediate and serious injury to the person or property of anyone or to prevent anything being done that, on reasonable and probable grounds, the person using such force believes would, if it were done, constitute such an offence.

The sections of the *Code* authorizing the use of force in defence of a person or property or to prevent the commission of certain serious crimes overlap, and the use of force in particular circumstances may be justified under more than one section. There was, however, in this case no evidence of a reasonable apprehension on the part of the appellant of serious injury to the property of anyone, and his right to use force to prevent reasonably apprehended serious injury to himself was dealt with under self-defence. I should also add that the trial judge was not requested to charge the jury with respect to s. 27.

· · · ·

Firing at a mere trespasser is, of course, not justifiable, and the trial judge in the circumstances of this case correctly charged the jury that killing or causing grievous bodily harm to a trespasser could only be justified in self-defence: *Rex v. Meade and Belt* (1823), 1 Lew. C.C. 184; *Rex v. Scully* (1824), 1 Car & P. 319; *Regina v. McKay*, [1957] V.R. 560; Lanham, supra.

I now turn to the ground of appeal relating tqcthe judge's charge with respect to s. 41(2). Under s. 41(2) a trespasser who resists an attempt by a person in peaceable possession of a dwelling house or real property to prevent his entry or to remove him is deemed to commit an assault without justification or provocation.

The meaning of this subsection is not entirely clear. I am disposed to think that its effect is not to convert mere passive resistance into an assault but merely to provide that if any *force* is used by the wrongdoer in resisting an attempt to prevent his entry or to remove him, such force is unlawful, and hence an assault. The amount of force that may be used to prevent or defend against any assault actually committed by the wrongdoer depends upon the ordinary principles of self-defence as set out in s. 34 of the *Code*. So regarded, s. 41(2) does not alter the common law as stated by Stephen H.C.L., vol. III, p. 15, who says:

> For instance, he may put a trespasser out of his house, or out of his field by force, but he may not strike him, still less may he shoot or stab him. If the wrongdoer resists, the person who is on the defensive may overcome his resistance, and may proportion his efforts to the violence which the wrongdoer uses. If the wrongdoer assaults the person who is defending his property, that person is in the position of a man wrongfully assaulted, and may use whatever violence may become necessary for the protection of his person.

In *Pockett v. Pool* (1896), 11 Man. R. 275 (C.A.), after referring to s. 53 of the then *Code* (now s. 41), Killam J. said at p. 286:

> The latter part of the section does not, in my opinion, apply until there is an overt act in the direction of prevention or removal and an overt act in resistance. . . . Similarly, in the present case, if the defendant had used force to remove the plaintiff and the latter had merely remained passive and allowed himself to be pushed or dragged out of the field, there would have been no assault.

Does s. 41 of the *Criminal Code* entitle a tenant in an apartment building to eject a person from the common hallway of the building? See *R. v. Spencer* (1977), 38 C.C.C. (2d) 303, 1977 CarswellBC 449 (B.C.S.C.).

R. v. GUNNING

[2005] 1 S.C.R. 627, 29 C.R. (6th) 17, 196 C.C.C. (3d) 123,
2005 CarswellBC 1181, 2005 CarswellBC 1182 (S.C.C.)

The accused hosted a party to which an uninvited guest, Mr. Charlie, showed up. Gunning asked Charlie to leave, but Charlie refused, responding in an insulting and intimidating fashion. Gunning, who had drunk quite a lot of alcohol, obtained and loaded his shotgun and returned to tell Charlie to leave once more. During the ensuing conversation the gun went off, killing Charlie. Gunning was charged with murder, based on having killed Charlie while committing the unlawful act of careless use of a firearm. Gunning pleaded not guilty, arguing that he was not guilty of murder because the gun had gone off by accident. He also argued that he was not guilty of careless use of a firearm because his "use" of it, taking it with him to scare away Charlie (as opposed to firing it) was justified on the basis of defence of property. The trial judge misunderstood this argument and directed the jury that the accused had committed the unlawful act of careless use of a firearm. The Supreme Court held that the trial judge had erred in removing this decision from the jury.

CHARRON J.: —

. . . .

B. The Defence of House or Property

23   In the circumstances of this case, the defence of house or real property was intrinsically connected to the underlying offence of careless use of a firearm. Mr. Gunning alleged that he took out his shotgun, loaded it and carried it upstairs to confront Mr. Charlie in the hope of intimidating or scaring him into leaving the house. He argued that he was justified in doing so as he was legitimately defending his property within the meaning of the *Criminal Code*.

24   Mr. Gunning relies on the provisions of s. 41(1) of the *Criminal Code*. It reads as follows:

> 41. (1) Every one who is in peaceable possession of a dwelling-house or real property, and every one lawfully assisting him or acting under his authority, is justified in using force to prevent any person from trespassing on the dwelling-house or real property, or to remove a trespasser therefrom, if he uses no more force than is necessary.

25   There are four elements to the defence raised by Mr. Gunning: (1) he must have been in possession of the dwelling-house; (2) his possession must have been peaceable; (3) Mr. Charlie must have been a trespasser; and (4) the force used to eject the trespasser must have been reasonable in all the circumstances. Only the fourth element was really contentious in this case — the reasonableness of the force used. Where the defence arises on the facts, the onus is on the Crown to prove beyond a reasonable doubt that Mr. Gunning did not act in defence of property.

26   It is common ground between the parties that the intentional killing of a trespasser could only be justified where the person in possession of the property is able to make out a case of self-defence: see *R. v. Baxter* (1975), 27 C.C.C. (2d) 96 (Ont. C.A.), at pp. 114-15; *R. v. Clark* (1983), 5 C.C.C. (3d) 264 (Alta. C.A.), at pp. 272-73; *R. v. Bacon*, [1999] Q.J. No. 19 (QL) (C.A.), at para. 24. Mr. Gunning does not raise self-defence in respect of the shooting; he raises the defence of accident. Rather, the defence of property is raised in justification of his use of the shotgun prior to its discharge.

C. The Respective Functions of the Judge and the Jury

. . . .

29   As a corollary of the trial judge's duty to instruct the jury on the law, it is a well-established principle that a judge should withdraw a defence from the consideration of the jury when there is no evidence upon which a properly instructed jury acting reasonably could find in the accused's favour. In these circumstances, it only stands to reason that there is no need to direct the jury on an issue not raised in the case. It would only serve to confuse the jury and detract from their duty to return a true verdict. This threshold test, requiring that a defence be put to the jury only if there is an evidential foundation for it, is often referred to as the "air of reality" test.

30   It is important to note that the "air of reality" test has no application in respect of the question of whether the Crown has proved beyond a reasonable doubt each essential element of the offence. By his plea of not guilty, the accused in effect advances the "defence" that the Crown has not met its burden in respect of one or more of the necessary ingredients of the offence. In every trial where there is no plea of guilty or an admission by the accused as to one or more of the essential elements of the offence, the question of whether the Crown has met its burden is necessarily at play and must be put to the jury for its determination. This "defence" is squarely before the jury. There is no further threshold to meet. The imposition of any additional hurdle would run counter to both the presumption of innocence and the burden of proof on the Crown.

31   Hence, it is never the function of the judge in a jury trial to assess the evidence and make a determination that the Crown has proven one or more of the essential elements of the offence and to direct the jury accordingly. It does not matter how obvious the judge may believe the answer to be. Nor does it matter that the judge may be of the view that any other conclusion would be perverse. The trial judge may give an opinion on the matter when it is warranted, but never a direction.

32   The "air of reality" test applies, rather, in respect of affirmative defences that may or may not arise depending on the particular facts. For example, it is not in every case that defences such as the following will arise: intoxication, necessity, duress, provocation, alibi, automatism, self-defence, mistake of fact, honest but mistaken belief in consent or defence of property. It is not incumbent on the Crown in every trial to negative all conceivable defences no matter how fanciful or speculative they may be. A certain threshold must be met before the issue is "put in play": *R. v. Cinous*, [2002] 2 S.C.R. 3, 2002 SCC 29, at para. 52. A defence will be in play whenever a properly instructed jury could reasonably, on account of the evidence, conclude in favour of the accused: *R. v. Fontaine*, [2004] 1 S.C.R. 702, 2004 SCC 27, at para. 74.

33   The basic features of the "air of reality" test and the evidential standard that must be met were thoroughly canvassed by this court in *Cinous* and the analysis need not be repeated here. In the context of this case, it is important, however, to repeat what the threshold test is not aimed at. At para. 54, McLachlin C.J. and Bastarache J. stated:

> The threshold determination by the trial judge is not aimed at deciding the substantive merits of the defence. That question is reserved for the jury. See *Finta, supra*; *R. v. Ewanchuk*, [1999] 1 S.C.R. 330. The trial judge does not make determinations about the credibility of witnesses, weigh the evidence, make findings of fact, or draw determinate factual inferences. See *R. v. Bulmer*, [1987] 1 S.C.R. 782; *Park, supra*. Nor is the air of reality test intended to assess whether the defence is likely, unlikely, somewhat likely, or very likely to succeed at the end of the day. The question for the trial judge is whether the evidence discloses a real issue to be decided by the jury, and not how the jury should ultimately decide the issue.

D. Application to This Case

34   It is important to note at the outset that Mr. Gunning did not offer a plea of guilty to the lesser and included offence of manslaughter and made no admission in respect of the underlying offence of careless use of a firearm. The Crown argues and, to a certain extent the British Columbia Court of Appeal accepted, that the trial judge's instructions to the jury essentially accorded with the position adopted by counsel for Mr. Gunning at trial. References are made to counsel's closing address and to the exchange that followed in support of the position that counsel himself could not articulate a possible route to an acquittal. With respect, counsel's closing address and the exchange that followed must be viewed in context. By that time the trial judge had already ruled that he saw no air of reality to any defence to the underlying charge of careless use of a firearm, including defence of property. Indeed, in light of this ruling, there was no other possible route to an acquittal and counsel's position at that stage of the trial is hardly surprising. But it cannot be held against Mr. Gunning.

35   It follows from the foregoing analysis that the trial judge erred in instructing the jury that the fourth ingredient of the offence of murder, or alternatively of manslaughter, had been proven by the Crown. In making the finding of fact that Mr. Gunninguse of the firearm on the morning in question was careless within the meaning of s. 86 of the *Criminal Code*, and hence an unlawful act that caused the death of Mr. Charlie, the trial judge usurped the exclusive domain of the jury. Rather than deciding the issue himself, it was incumbent upon the trial judge to instruct the jury on the law in respect of the offence of careless use of a firearm, including any defences that arose on the evidence, and to leave for the jury the ultimate application of the law to the facts. That issue, together with the question of whether there was an intent to kill, were central in this trial. Mr. Gunning was entitled to have a jury of his peers, not the judge, determine whether his use of the shotgun was unlawful and

constituted a marked departure from the standard of care of a reasonably prudent person in his circumstances on the morning in question.

36   In my view, the trial judge's belated explanation to the jury was insufficient to cure the error. The Crown conceded as much before the British Columbia Court of Appeal, although not before this court. The trial judge's main instructions were forceful and definitive. They were given to the jury in writing. The instructions were repeated during the course of the later explanation. The purported correction described the jury's option of coming back with a not guilty verdict as a "possibility" that "technically", "hypothetically" could be reached. In addition, the unfortunate comment about the privilege on the part of a jury to reach a perverse verdict may have further detracted the jury from any serious consideration of Mr. Gunning's position in respect of the events that led to the tragic death of Mr. Charlie.

37   In my view, the trial judge also erred by failing to instruct the jury on the defence of property. As noted earlier, there are four elements to the defence. There was no question that Mr. Gunning was in peaceable possession of his dwelling-house and that Mr. Charlie, at least after he was told to leave, was a trespasser. The fourth element, the reasonableness of the force used, was more contentious. However, as stated in *Cinous*, at para. 54, "[t]he question for the trial judge is whether the evidence discloses a real issue to be decided by the jury, and not how the jury should ultimately decide the issue."

38   It is my view that the trial judge erred first, by taking too narrow a view of the scope of the defence advanced by Mr. Gunning and second, by deciding its merits. It is apparent from the above-noted excerpts of the pre-charge discussions that the trial judge initially misunderstood Mr. Gunning to be raising this defence in respect of the shooting. He then appeared to take the erroneous view that the defence could only be raised in respect of the "use" that actually caused the death (presumably the discharge of the weapon) and that it could not be raised in respect of Mr. Gunning's actions in taking and loading the gun for the purpose of intimidating Mr. Charlie into leaving the house. However, all of the events preceding the shooting had to be taken into account in determining whether Mr. Gunning had used reasonable force in his attempt to eject Mr. Charlie. In the end result, in determining whether there was any air of reality to this fourth element of the defence of property (i.e., the reasonableness of the force used to eject the trespasser), it becomes clear that the trial judge overstepped his role and decided the substantive merits of the defence. This is particularly apparent from his comment reproduced above that "a perfectly sober person having to load a gun because somebody is not only not leaving but being insulting may not be unlawful", but that the matter was otherwise in the case of this intoxicated accused. This weighing of the evidence and ultimate determination of the merits of the defence were matters for the jury to resolve.

. . . .

V. Disposition

43   For these reasons, I would allow the appeal, set aside the conviction and order a new trial.

5. NECESSITY

R. v. DUDLEY and STEPHENS

(1884), 14 Q.B.D. 273 (C.C.R.)

INDICTMENT for the murder of Richard Parker on the high seas within the jurisdiction of the Admiralty.

At the trial before Huddleston B., at the Devon and Cornwall Winter Assizes, November 7, 1884, the jury, at the suggestion of the learned judge, found the facts of the case in a special verdict which stated:

> that on July 5, 1884, the prisoners, Thomas Dudley and Edward Stephens, with one Brooks, all able-bodied English seamen, and the deceased also an English boy, between 17 and 18 years of age, the crew of an English yacht, a registered English vessel, were cast away in a storm on the high seas 1600 miles from the Cape of Good Hope, and were compelled to put into an open boat belonging to the said yacht. That in this boat they had no supply of water and no supply of food, except two 1 lb. tins of turnips, and for three days they had nothing else to subsist upon. That on the fourth day they caught a small turtle, upon which they subsisted for a few days, and this was the only food they had up to the 20th day when the act now in question was committed. That on the 12th day the remains of the turtle were entirely consumed, and for the next eight days they had nothing to eat. That they had no fresh water, except such rain as they from time to time caught in their oilskin capes. That the boat was drifting on the ocean, and was probably more than 1000 miles away from land. That on the 18th day, when they had been seven days without food and five without water, the prisoners spoke to Brooks as to what should be done if no succour came, and suggested that some one should be sacrificed to save the rest, but Brooks dissented, and the boy, to whom they were understood to refer, was not consulted. That on the 24th of July, the day before the act now in question, the prisoner Dudley proposed to Stephens and Brooks that lots should be cast who should be put to death to save the rest, but Brooks refused to consent, and it was not put to the boy, and in point of fact there was no drawing of lots. That on that day the prisoners spoke of their having families, and suggested it would be better to kill the boy that their lives should be saved, and Dudley proposed that if there was no vessel in sight by the morrow morning the boy should be killed. The next day, the 25th of July, no vessel appearing, Dudley told Brooks that he had better go and have a sleep, and made signs to Stephens and Brooks that the boy had better be killed. The prisoner Stephens agreed to the act, but Brooks dissented from it. That the boy was then lying at the bottom of the boat quite helpless, and extremely weakened by famine and by drinking sea water, and unable to make any resistance, nor did he ever assent to his being killed. The prisoner Dudley offered a prayer asking forgiveness for them all if either of them should be tempted to commit a rash act, and that their souls might be saved. That Dudley, with the assent of Stephens, went to the boy, and telling him

that his time was come, put a knife into his throat and killed him then and there; that the three men fed upon the body and blood of the boy for four days; that on the fourth day after the act had been committed the boat was picked up by a passing vessel, and the prisoners were rescued, still alive, but in the lowest state of prostration. That they were carried to the port of Falmouth, and committed for trial at Exeter. That if the men had not fed upon the body of the boy they would probably not have survived to be so picked up and rescued, but would within the four days have died of famine. That the boy, being in a much weaker condition, was likely to have died before them. That at the time of the act in question there was no sail in sight, nor any reasonable prospect of relief. That under these circumstances there appeared to the prisoners every probability that unless they then fed or very soon fed upon the boy or one of themselves they would die of starvation. That there was no appreciable chance of saving life except by killing some one for the others to eat. That assuming any necessity to kill anybody, there was no greater necessity for killing the boy than any of the other three men.

But whether upon the whole matter by the jurors found the killing of Richard Parker by Dudley and Stephens be felony and murder the jurors are ignorant, and pray the advice of the court thereupon, and if upon the whole matter the court shall be of opinion that the killing of Richard Parker be felony and murder, then the jurors say that Dudley and Stephens were each guilty of felony and murder as alleged in the indictment.

. . . .

Dec. 9. The judgment of the court was delivered by LORD COLERIDGE C.J.: —

. . . .

There remains to be considered the real question in the case — whether killing under the circumstances set forth in the verdict be or be not murder. The contention that it could be anything else was, to the minds of us all, both new and strange, and we stopped the Attorney-General in his negative argument in order that we might hear what could be said in support of a proposition which appeared to us to be at once dangerous, immoral, and opposed to all legal principle and analogy. All, no doubt, that can be said has been urged before us, and we are now to consider and determine what it amounts to. First it is said that it follows from various definitions of murder in books of authority, which definitions imply, if they do not state, the doctrine, that in order to save your own life you may lawfully take away the life of another, when that other is neither attempting nor threatening yours, nor is guilty of any illegal act whatever towards you or any one else. But if these definitions be looked at they will not be found to sustain this contention. . . .

Is there, then, any authority for the proposition which has been presented to us? Decided cases there are none. . . .

The American case cited by my Brother Stephen in his Digest, from Wharton on Homicide, in which it was decided, correctly indeed, that sailors had no right to throw passengers overboard to save themselves, but on the somewhat strange ground that the proper mode of determining who was to be sacrificed was to vote upon the subject by ballot, can hardly, as my Brother Stephen says, be an authority satisfactory to a court in this country.

. . . .

Now, except for the purpose of testing how far the conservation of a man's own life is in all cases and under all circumstances, an absolute, unqualified, and paramount duty, we exclude from our consideration all the incidents of war. We are dealing with a case of private homicide, not one imposed upon men in the service of their Sovereign and in the defence of their country. Now it is admitted that the deliberate killing of this unoffending and unresisting boy was clearly murder, unless the killing can be justified by some well-recognized excuse admitted by the law. It is further admitted that there was in this case no such excuse, unless the killing was justified by what has been called "necessity." But the temptation to the act which existed here was not what the law has ever called necessity. Nor is this to be regretted. Though law and morality are not the same, and many things may be immoral which are not necessarily illegal, yet the absolute divorce of law from morality would be of fatal consequence; and such divorce would follow if the temptation to murder in this case were to be held by law an absolute defence of it. It is not so. To preserve one's life is generally speaking a duty, but it may be the plainest and the highest duty to sacrifice it. War is full of instances in which it is a man's duty not to live, but to die. The duty in case of shipwreck, of a captain to his crew, of the crew to the passengers, of soldiers to women and children, as in the noble case of the *Birkenhead*; these duties impose on men the moral necessity, not of the preservation, but of the sacrifice of their lives for others, from which in no country, least of all, it is to be hoped, in England, will men ever shrink, as indeed, they have not shrunk. It is not correct, therefore, to say that there is any absolute or unqualified necessity to preserve one's life. "Necesse est ut eam, non ut vivam," is a saying of a Roman officer quoted by Lord Bacon himself with high eulogy in the very chapter on necessity to which so much reference has been made. It would be a very easy and cheap display of commonplace learning to quote from Greek and Latin authors, from Horace, from Juvenal, from Cicero, from Euripides, passage after passage, in which the duty of dying for others has been laid down in glowing and emphatic language as resulting from the principles of heathen ethics; it is enough in a Christian country to remind ourselves of the Great Example whom we profess to follow. It is not needful to point out the awful danger of admitting the principle which has been contended for. Who is to be the judge of this sort of necessity? By what measure is the comparative value of lives to be measured? Is it to be strength, or intellect, or what? It is plain that the principle leaves to him who is to profit by it to determine the necessity which will justify him in deliberately taking another's life to save his own. In this case the weakest, the youngest, the most unresisting, was chosen. Was it more necessary to kill him than one of the grown men? The answer must be "No" —

So spake the Fiend, and with necessity,
The tyrant's plea, excused his devilish deeds.

It is not suggested that in this particular case the deeds were "devilish," but it is quite plain that such a principle once admitted might be made the legal cloak for unbridled passion and atrocious crime. There is no safe path for Judges to tread but to ascertain the law to the best of their ability and to declare it according to their judgment; and if in any case the law appears to be too severe on individuals, to leave it to the Sovereign to exercise that prerogative of mercy which the Constitution has intrusted to the hands fittest to dispense it.

It must not be supposed that in refusing to admit temptation to be an excuse for crime it is forgotten how terrible the temptation was; how awful the suffering; how hard in such trials to keep the judgment straight and the conduct pure. We are often compelled to set up standards we cannot reach ourselves, and to lay down rules which we could not ourselves satisfy. But a man has no right to declare temptation to be an excuse, though he might himself have yielded to it, nor allow compulsion for the criminal to change or weaken in any manner the legal definition of the crime. It is therefore our duty to declare that the prisoners' act in this case was wilful murder, that the facts as stated in the verdict are no legal justification of the homicide; and to say that in our unanimous opinion the prisoners are upon this special verdict guilty of murder.[1]

The court then proceeded to pass sentence of death upon the prisoners.[2]

1. My brother Grove has furnished me with the following suggestion, too late to be embodied in the judgment but well worth preserving: "If the two accused men were justified in killing Parker, then if not rescued in time, two of the three survivors would be justified in killing the third, and of the two who remained the stronger would be justified in killing the weaker, so that three men might be justifiably killed to give the fourth a chance of surviving."— C.
2. This sentence was afterwards commuted by the Crown to six months' imprisoment.

PERKA v. R.

42 C.R. (3d) 113, [1984] 2 S.C.R. 233, 14 C.C.C. (3d) 385,
1984 CarswellBC 823

DICKSON J. (RITCHIE, CHOUINARD and LAMER JJ. concurring): — . . . .

I FACTS

The appellants are drug smugglers. At trial, they led evidence that in early 1979 three of the appellants were employed, with 16 crew members, to deliver, by ship (the Samarkanda), a load of cannabis (marijuana) worth $6,000,000 or $7,000,000 from a point in international waters off the coast of Colombia, South America, to a drop point in international waters 200 miles off the coast of Alaska. The ship left Tumaco, Colombia, empty with a port clearance document stating the destination to be Juneau, Alaska. For three weeks the ship remained in international waters off the coast of Colombia. While there, a DC-6 aircraft made four trips, dropping into the water shrimp nets with a total of 634 bales of cannabis which were retrieved by the ship's longboats.

A "communications" package was also dropped from a light aircraft, giving instructions for a rendezvous with another vessel, the Julia B., which was to pick up the cargo of cannabis from the Samarkanda in international waters off the coast of Alaska. En route, according to the defence evidence, the vessel began to encounter a series of problems; engine break-downs, overheating generators and malfunctioning navigation devices, aggravated by deteriorating weather. In the meantime the fourth appellant, Nelson, part-owner of the illicit cargo, and three other persons left Seattle in a small boat, the Whitecap, intending to rendezvous with the Samarkanda at the drop point in Alaska. The problems of the Samarkanda intensified as fuel was consumed. The vessel became lighter, the intakes in the hull for sea water, used as a coolant, lost suction and took in air instead, causing the generators to overheat. At this point the vessel was 180 miles from the Canadian coastline. The weather worsened. There were 8-to-10-foot swells and a rising wind. It was finally decided for the safety of ship and crew to seek refuge on the Canadian shoreline for the purpose of making temporary repairs. The Whitecap found a sheltered cove on the west coast of Vancouver Island, No Name Bay. The Samarkanda followed the Whitecap into the bay but later grounded amidships on a rock because the depth sounder was not working. The tide ran out. The vessel listed severely to starboard, to the extent that the Captain, fearing the vessel was going to capsize, ordered the men to offload the cargo. That is a brief summary of the defence evidence.

Early on the morning of 22nd May 1979 police officers entered No Name Bay in a marked police boat with siren sounding. The Samarkanda and the Whitecap were arrested, as were all the appellants except Perka and Nelson, the same morning. The vessels and 33.49 tons of cannabis marijuana were seized by the police officers.

Charged with importing cannabis into Canada and with possession for the purpose of trafficking, the appellants claimed that they did not plan to import into Canada or to leave their cargo of cannabis in Canada. They had planned to make repairs and leave. Expert witnesses on marine matters called by the defence testified that the decision to come ashore was, in the opinion of one witness, expedient and prudent and, in the opinion of another, essential. At trial, counsel for the Crown alleged that the evidence of the ship's distress was a recent fabrication. Crown counsel relied on the circumstances under which the appellants were arrested to belie the "necessity" defence; when the police arrived on the scene most of the marijuana was already onshore, along with plastic ground sheets, battery-operated lights, liquor, food, clothing, camp stoves, and sleeping bags. Nevertheless, the jury believed the appellants and acquitted them.

. . . .

II THE NECESSITY DEFENCE

(a) *History and Background*

From earliest times it has been maintained that in some situations the force of circumstances makes it unrealistic and unjust to attach criminal liability to actions which, on their face, violate the law. Aristotle, *Nicomachean Ethics*, translated by Sir David Ross, Book III, p. 49, 1110a, discusses the jettisoning of cargo from a ship in distress and remarks that "any sensible man does so" to secure the safety of himself and his crew. Pollard, arguing for the defendant in the case of *Renniger v. Fogossa* (1551), 1 Plowden 1 at 18, 75 E.R. 1, maintained:

> . . . in every law there are some things which when they happen a man may break the words of the law, and yet not break the law itself; and such things are exempted out of the penalty of the law, and the law privileges them although they are done against the letter of it, for breaking the words of the law is not breaking the law, so as the intent of the law is not broken. And therefore the words of the law of nature, of the law of this realm, and of other realms, and of the law of God also will yield and give way to some acts and things done against the words of the same laws, and that is, where the words of them are broken to avoid greater inconveniences, or through necessity, or by compulsion.

In *Leviathan*, Pelican ed. (1968), c. 27, at p. 157, Hobbes writes:

> If a man by the terrour of present death, be compelled to doe a fact against the law, he is totally excused; because no law can oblige a man to abandon his own preservation. And supposing such a law were obligatory: yet a man would reason thus, If I doe it not, I die presently; if I doe it I die afterwards; therefore by doing it there is time of life gained; Nature therefore compells him to the fact.

To much the same purpose Kant, in *Metaphysical Elements of Justice*, translated by Ladd (1965), discussing the actions of a person who, to save his own life, sacrifices that of another, says at p. 41:

> A penal law applying to such a situation could never have the effect intended, for the threat of an evil that is still uncertain (being condemned to death by a Judge) cannot outweigh the fear of an evil that is certain (being drowned). Hence, we must judge that, although an act of self-preservation through violence is not inculpable, it still is unpunishable.

In those jurisdictions in which such a general principle has been recognized or codified it is most often referred to by the term "necessity". Classic and harrowing instances which have been cited to illustrate the arguments both for and against this principle include the mother who steals food for her starving child, the shipwrecked mariners who resort to cannibalism (*R. v. Dudley*, (1884), 14 Q.B.D. 273 (C.C.R.)) or throw passengers overboard to lighten a sinking lifeboat (*U.S. v. Holmes*, 26 F. Cas. 360 (1842)), and the more mundane case of the motorist who exceeds the speed limit taking an injured person to the hospital.

. . . .

In Canada the existence and the extent of a general defence of necessity was discussed by this court in *Morgentaler v. R.*, [1976] 1 S.C.R. 616, 30 C.R.N.S. 209, 20 C.C.C. (2d) 449. As to whether or not the defence exists at all I had occasion to say at p. 678:

> On the authorities it is manifestly difficult to be categorical and state that there is a law of necessity, paramount over other laws, relieving obedience from the letter of the law. If [such a principle exists] it can go no further than to justify non-compliance in urgent situations of clear and imminent peril when compliance with the law is demonstrably impossible.

. . . .

In the present appeal the Crown does not challenge the appellants' claim that necessity is a common law defence preserved by the *Criminal Code*, R.S.C. 1970, c. C-34, s. 7(3). Rather, the Crown claims, the trial judge erred in: (1) instructing the jury on the defence in light of the facts; and (2) imposing the burden of disproof of the defence upon the Crown, rather than imposing the burden of proof on the appellants.

(b) *The Conceptual Foundation of the Defence*

In *Morgentaler v. R.*, *supra.* I characterized necessity as an "ill-defined and elusive concept". Despite the apparently growing consensus as to the existence of a defence of necessity, that statement is equally true today.

This is no doubt in part because, though apparently laying down a single rule as to criminal liability, the "defence" of necessity in fact is capable of embracing two different and distinct notions. As Macdonald J.A. observed succinctly but accurately in the *Salvador* case [*R. v. Salvador* (1981), 21 C.R. (3d) 1, 59 C.C.C. (2d) 521 (N.S.C.A.)], at p. 542:

> Generally speaking, the defence of necessity covers all cases where non-compliance with law is excused by an emergency or justified by the pursuit of some greater good.

Working Paper 29, Criminal Law — The General Part: Liability and Defences (1982), of the Law Reform Commission of Canada at p. 93 makes this same point in somewhat more detail:

> The rationale of necessity, however, is clear. Essentially it involves two factors. One is the avoidance of greater harm or the pursuit of some greater good, the other is the difficulty of compliance with law in emergencies. From these two factors emerge two different but related principles. The first is a utilitarian principle to the effect that, within certain limits, it is justifiable in an emergency to break the letter of the law if breaking the law will avoid a greater harm than obeying it. The second is a humanitarian principle to the effect that, again within limits, it is excusable in an emergency to break the law if compliance would impose an intolerable burden on the accused.

Despite any superficial similarities, these two principles are in fact quite distinct and many of the confusions and difficulties in the cases (and, with respect, in academic discussions) arise from a failure to distinguish between them.

Criminal theory recognizes a distinction between "justifications" and "excuses". A "justification" challenges the wrongfulness of an action which technically constitutes a crime. The police officer who shoots the hostage-taker, the innocent object of an assault who uses force to defend himself against his assailant, the Good Samaritan who commandeers a car and breaks the speed laws to rush an accident victim to the hospital, these are all actors whose actions we consider *rightful*, not wrongful. For such actions people are often praised, as motivated by some great or noble object. The concept of punishment often seems incompatible with the social approval bestowed on the doer.

In contrast, an "excuse" concedes the wrongfulness of the action but asserts that the circumstances under which it was done are such that it ought not to be attributed to the actor. The perpetrator who is incapable, owing to a disease of the mind, of appreciating the nature and consequences of his acts, the person who labours under a mistake of fact, the drunkard, the sleepwalker: these are all actors of whose "criminal" actions we disapprove intensely, but whom, in appropriate circumstances, our law will not punish.

Packer, *The Limits of the Criminal Sanction*, expresses the distinction thus at p. 113:

> Conduct that we choose not to treat as criminal is "justifiable" if our reason for treating it as noncriminal is predominantly that it is conduct that we applaud, or at least do not actively seek to discourage: conduct is "excusable" if we deplore it but for some extrinsic reason conclude that it is not politic to punish it.

It will be seen that the two different approaches to the "defence" of necessity from Blackstone forward correspond, the one to a justification, the other to an excuse. As the examples cited above illustrate, the criminal law recognizes and our *Criminal Code* codifies a number of specific categories of justification and of excuse. The remainder, those instances that conform to the general principle but do not fall within any specific category such as self-defence on the one hand or insanity on the other, purportedly fall within the "residual defence" of necessity.

As a "justification" this residual defence can be related to Blackstone's concept of a "choice of evils". It would exculpate actors whose conduct could reasonably have been viewed as "necessary" in order to prevent a greater evil than that resulting from the violation of the law. As articulated, especially in some of the American cases, it involves a utilitarian balancing of the benefits of obeying the law as opposed to disobeying it, and, when the balance is clearly in favour of disobeying, exculpates an actor who contravenes a criminal statute. This is the "greater good" formulation of the necessity defence: in some circumstances, it is alleged, the values of society, indeed of the criminal law itself, are better promoted by disobeying a given statute than by observing it.

With regard to this conceptualization of a residual defence of necessity, I retain the scepticism I expressed in *Morgentaler v. R.*, *supra*, at p. 678. It is still my opinion that "No system of positive law can recognize any principle which would entitle a person to violate the law because on his view the law conflicted with some higher social value." The *Criminal Code* has specified a number of identifiable situations in which an actor is justified in committing what would otherwise be a criminal offence. To go beyond that and hold that ostensibly illegal acts can be validated on the basis of their expediency would import an undue subjectivity into the criminal law. It would invite the courts to second-guess the Legislature and to assess the relative merits of social policies underlying criminal prohibitions. Neither is a role which fits well with the judicial function. Such a doctrine could well become the last resort of scoundrels and, in the words of Edmund Davies L.J. in *Southwark London Borough Council v. Williams*, [1971] Ch. 734 at 746 (C.A.), it could "very easily become simply a mask for anarchy".

Conceptualized as an "excuse", however, the residual defence of necessity is, in my view, much less open to criticism. It rests on a realistic assessment of human weakness, recognizing that a liberal and humane criminal law cannot hold people to the strict obedience of law in emergency situations where normal human instincts, whether of self-preservation or of altruism, overwhelmingly impel disobedience. The objectivity of the criminal law is preserved; such acts are still wrongful, but in the circumstances they are excusable. Praise is indeed not bestowed, but pardon is, when one does a wrongful act under pressure which, in the words of Aristotle in the *Nicomachean Ethics* p. 49, 1110a10, "overstrains human nature and which no one could withstand".

George Fletcher, *Rethinking Criminal Law* (1978), describes this view of necessity as "compulsion of circumstance", which description points to the conceptual link between necessity as an excuse and the familiar criminal law requirement that in order to engage criminal liability the actions constituting the *actus reus* of an offence must be voluntary. Literally this voluntariness requirement simply refers to the need that the prohibited physical acts must have been under the conscious control of the actor. Without such control, there is, for purposes of the criminal law, no act. The excuse of necessity does not go to voluntariness in this sense. The lost alpinist who on the point of freezing to death breaks open an isolated mountain cabin is not literally behaving in an involuntary fashion. He has control over his actions to the extent of being physically capable of abstaining from the act. Realistically, however, his act is not a "voluntary" one. His "choice" to break the law is no true choice at all; it is remorselessly compelled by normal human instincts. This sort of involuntariness is often described as "moral or normative involuntariness". Its place in criminal theory is described by Fletcher at pp. 804-805 as follows:

> The notion of voluntariness adds a valuable dimension to the theory of excuses. That conduct is involuntary — even in the normative sense — explains why it cannot fairly be punished. Indeed, H.L.A. Hart builds his theory of excuses on the principle that the distribution of punishment should be reserved for those who voluntarily break the law. Of the arguments he advances for this principle of justice, the most explicit is that it is preferable to live in a society where we have the maximum opportunity to choose whether we shall become the subject of criminal liability. In addition, Hart intimates that it is ideologically desirable for the government to treat its citizens as self-actuating, choosing agents. This principle of respect for individual autonomy is implicitly confirmed whenever those who lack an adequate choice are excused for their offences.

I agree with this formulation of the rationale for excuses in the criminal law. In my view this rationale extends beyond specific codified excuses and embraces the residual excuse known as the defence of necessity. At the heart of this defence is the perceived injustice of punishing violations of the law in circumstances in which the person had no other viable or reasonable choice available; the act was wrong but it is excused because it was realistically unavoidable.

Punishment of such acts, as Fletcher notes at p. 813, can be seen as purposeless as well as unjust:

> ... involuntary conduct cannot be deterred and therefore it is pointless and wasteful to punish involuntary actors. This theory ... of pointless punishment, carries considerable weight in current Anglo-American legal thought.

Relating necessity to the principle that the law ought not to punish involuntary acts leads to a conceptualization of the defence that integrates it into the normal rules for criminal liability rather than constituting it as a *sui generis* exception and threatening to engulf large portions of the criminal law. Such a conceptualization accords with our traditional legal, moral and philosophic views as to what sorts of acts and what sorts of actors ought to be punished. In this formulation it is a defence which I do not hesitate to acknowledge and would not hesitate to apply to relevant facts capable of satisfying its necessary prerequisites.

(c) *Limitations on the Defence*

If the defence of necessity is to form a valid and consistent part of our criminal law it must, as has been universally recognized, be strictly controlled and scrupulously limited to situations that correspond to its underlying rationale. That rationale, as I have indicated, is the recognition that it is inappropriate to punish actions which are normatively "involuntary". The appropriate controls and limitations on the defence of necessity are therefore addressed to ensuring that the acts for which the benefit of the excuse of necessity is sought are truly "involuntary" in the requisite sense.

In *Morgentaler v. R.*, *supra*, I was of the view that any defence of necessity was restricted to instances of non-compliance "in urgent situations of clear and imminent peril when compliance with the law is demonstrably impossible". In my opinion this restriction focuses directly on the "involuntariness" of the purportedly necessitous behaviour by providing a number of tests for determining whether the wrongful act was truly the only realistic reaction open to the actor or whether he was in fact making what in fairness could be called a choice. If he was making a choice, then the wrongful act cannot have been involuntary in the relevant sense.

The requirement that the situation be urgent and the peril be imminent tests whether it was indeed unavoidable for the actor to act at all. In Lafave and Scott, *Criminal Law*, at p. 388, one reads:

> It is sometimes said that the defence of necessity does not apply except in an emergency — when the threatened harm is immediate, the threatened disaster imminent. Perhaps this is but a way of saying that, until the time comes when the threatened harm is immediate, there are generally options open to the defendant to avoid the harm, other than the option of disobeying the literal terms of the law — the rescue ship may appear, the storm may pass; and so the defendant must wait until that hope of survival disappears.

At a minimum the situation must be so emergent and the peril must be so pressing that normal human instincts cry out for action and make a counsel of patience unreasonable.

The requirement that compliance with the law be "demonstrably impossible" takes this assessment one step further. Given that the accused had to act, could he nevertheless realistically have acted to avoid the peril or prevent the harm, without breaking the law? *Was there a legal way out?* I think this is what Bracton means when he lists "necessity" as a defence, providing the wrongful act was not "avoidable". The question to be asked is whether the agent had any real choice: could he have done otherwise? If there is a reasonable legal alternative to disobeying the law, then the decision to disobey becomes a voluntary one, impelled by some consideration beyond the dictates of "necessity" and human instincts.

The importance of this requirement that there be no reasonable legal alternative cannot be overstressed.

Even if the requirements for urgency and "no legal way out" are met, there is clearly a further consideration. There must be some way of assuring proportionality. No rational criminal justice system, no matter how humane or liberal, could excuse the infliction of a greater harm to allow the actor to avert a lesser evil. In such circumstances we expect the individual to bear the harm and refrain from acting illegally. If he cannot control himself we will not excuse him. According to Fletcher, this requirement is also related to the notion of voluntariness:

> . . . if the gap between the harm done and the benefit accrued becomes too great, the act is more likely to appear voluntary and therefore inexcusable. For example, if the actor has to blow up a whole city in order to avoid the breaking of his finger, we might appropriately expect him to endure the harm to himself. His surrendering to the threat in this case violates our expectations of appropriate and normal resistance and pressure. Yet as we lower the degree of harm to others and increase the threatened harm to the person under duress we will reach a threshold at which, in the language of the Model Penal Code, "a person of reasonable firmness" would be "unable to resist". Determining this threshold is patently a matter of moral judgment about what we expect people to be able to resist in trying situations. A valuable aid in making that judgment is comparing the competing interests at stake and assessing the degree to which the actor inflicts harm beyond the benefit that accrues from his action.

I would therefore add to the preceding requirements a stipulation of proportionality expressable, as it was in *Morgentaler v. R.*, *supra*, by the proviso that the harm inflicted must be less than the harm sought to be avoided.

(d) *Illegality or Contributory Fault*

The Crown submits that there is an additional limitation on the availability of the defence of necessity. Citing *R. v. Salvador*, *supra*, it argues that because the appellants were committing a crime when their necessitous circumstances arose they should be denied the defence of necessity as a matter of law.

. . . .

In any event, I have considerable doubt as to the cogency of such a limitation. If the conduct in which an accused was engaging at the time the peril arose was illegal, then it should clearly be punished, but I fail to see the relevance of its illegal character to the question of whether the accused's subsequent conduct in dealing with this emergent peril ought to be excused on the basis of necessity. At most the illegality — or, if one adopts Jones J.A.'s approach, the immorality — of the preceding conduct will colour the subsequent conduct in response to the emergency as also wrongful. But that wrongfulness is never in any doubt. Necessity goes to *excuse* conduct, not to *justify* it. Where it is found to apply it carries with it no implicit vindication of the deed to which it attaches. That cannot be over-emphasized. Were the defence of necessity to succeed in the present case, it would not in any way amount to a vindication of importing controlled substances or to a critique of the law prohibiting such importation. It would also have nothing to say about the comparative social utility of breaking the law against importing as compared to obeying the law. The question, as I have said, is never whether what the accused has done is wrongful. It is always and by definition wrongful. The question is whether what he has done is voluntary. Except in the limited sense I intend to discuss below, I do not see the relevance of the legality or even the morality of what the accused was doing at the time the emergency arose to this question of the voluntariness of the subsequent conduct.

. . . .

In my view the better approach to the relationship of fault to the availability of necessity as a defence is based once again on the question of whether the actions sought to be excused were truly "involuntary". If the necessitous situation was clearly foreseeable to a reasonable observer, if the actor contemplated or ought to have contemplated that his actions would likely give rise to an emergency requiring the breaking of the law, then I doubt whether what confronted the accused was in the relevant sense an emergency. His response was in that sense not "involuntary". "Contributory fault" of this nature, but only of this nature, is a relevant consideration to the availability of the defence.

. . . .

(e) *Onus of Proof*

Although necessity is spoken of as a defence, in the sense that it is raised by the accused, the Crown always bears the burden of proving a voluntary act. The prosecution must prove every element of the crime charged. One such element is the voluntariness of the act. Normally, voluntariness can be presumed, but if the accused places before the court, through his own witnesses or through cross-examination of Crown witnesses, evidence sufficient to raise an issue that the situation created by external forces was so emergent that failure to act could endanger life or health and upon any reasonable view of the facts, compliance with the law was impossible, then the Crown must be prepared to meet that issue. There is no onus of proof on the accused.

. . . .

(f) *Preliminary Conclusions as to the Defence of Necessity*

It is now possible to summarize a number of conclusions as to the defence of necessity in terms of its nature, basis and limitations: (1) the defence of necessity could be conceptualized as either a justification or an excuse; (2) it should be recognized in Canada as an excuse, operating by virtue of s. 7(3) of the *Criminal Code*; (3) necessity as an excuse implies no vindication of the deeds of the actor; (4) the criterion is the moral involuntariness of the wrongful action; (5) this involuntariness is measured on the basis of society's expectation of appropriate and normal resistance to pressure; (6) negligence or involvement in criminal or immoral activity does not disentitle the actor to the excuse of necessity; (7) actions or circumstances which indicate that the wrongful deed was not truly involuntary do disentitle, (8) the existence of a reasonable legal alternative similarly disentitles; to be involuntary the act must be inevitable, unavoidable and afford no reasonable opportunity for an alternative course of action that does not involve a breach of the law; (9) the defence applies only in circumstances of imminent risk where the action was taken to avoid a direct and immediate peril; and (10) where the accused places before the court sufficient evidence to raise the issue, the onus is on the Crown to meet it beyond a reasonable doubt.

(g) *The Judge's Charge*

The trial judge concluded that there was before him an adequate body of evidence to raise the issue of necessity and proceeded to direct the jury with respect to the defence. As I have earlier indicated, the Crown disputes whether the defence was open to the accused in the circumstances of the case and submits further that if it was in fact available the trial judge erred in his direction.

In my view the trial judge was correct in concluding that on the evidence before him he should instruct the jury with regard to necessity. There was evidence before him from which a jury might conclude that the accused's actions in coming ashore with their cargo of cannabis were aimed at self-preservation in response to an overwhelming emergency. I have already indicated that in my view they were not engaged in conduct that was illegal under Canadian criminal law at the time the emergency arose, and that, even if they were, that fact alone would not disentitle them to raise the defence. The question then becomes whether the trial judge erred in charging the jury in the terms that he did.

The summary of conclusions with regard to necessity in the forgoing section indicates that for the defence to succeed an accused's actions must be, in the relevant sense, an "involuntary" response to an imminent and overwhelming peril. The defence cannot succeed if the response was disproportionate to the peril or if it was not "involuntary" in the sense that the emergency was not "real" or not imminent or that there was a reasonable alternative response that was not illegal.

In the course of his charge on the issue of necessity the trial judge instructed the jury, using the specific words that appear in *Morgentaler*, to the effect that they must find facts which amount to "an urgent situation of clear and imminent peril when compliance with the law is demonstrably impossible" in order for the appellants' non-compliance with the law against importation and possession of cannabis to be excused. That is the correct test. It is, with respect, however, my view that in explaining the meaning and application of this test the trial Judge fell into error.

The trial Judge was obliged, in my opinion, to direct the jury's attention to a number of issues pertinent to the test for necessity. Was the emergency a real one? Did it constitute an immediate threat of the harm purportedly feared? Was the response proportionate? In comparing this response to the danger that motivated it, was the danger one that society would reasonably expect the average person to withstand? Was there any reasonable legal alternative to the illegal response open to the accused? Although the trial judge did not explicitly pose each and every one of these questions, in my view his charge was adequate to bring the considerations underlying them to the jury's attention on every issue except the last one, the question of a reasonable alternative.

This issue was the determining obstacle to the success of the defence of necessity in a number of the cases referred to earlier, including *Gilkes, Doud, Byng* and, for the present case most notably, because of the similarity of its factual basis, *Salvador*. Indeed, in most cases where the defence is raised, this consideration will almost certainly be the most important one.

In his charge, the trial judge did not advert to this requirement. He did tell the jury that they must find facts capable of showing that "compliance with the law was demonstrably impossible" but on his recharge he put before the jury a significantly different test. The test, he said, is:

> . . . can you find facts from this evidence, and that means all the evidence, of course, that the situation of the Samarkanda at sea was so appallingly dire and dangerous to life that a reasonable doubt arises as to whether or not their decision was justified?

And again, at the conclusion of the recharge:

> There is no need for the evidence to show you that a certainty of death would result unless the action complained of by the Crown was taken. It doesn't go so far as that. You have to look at it as reasonable people and decide on any reasonable view of the matter, would these people have been justified in doing what they did? That is all that necessity means.

Both of these passages imply that the crucial consideration was whether the accused acted reasonably in coming into shore with their load of cannabis rather than facing death at sea. That is not sufficient as a test. Even if it does deal with the reality of the peril, its imminence and the proportionality of putting into shore, it does not deal at all with the question of whether there existed any other reasonable responses to the peril that were not illegal. Indeed, aside from the initial repetition of the *Morgentaler* formula, the trial judge did not advert to this consideration at all, nor did he direct the jury's attention to the relevance of evidence indicating the possibility of such alternative courses of action. In these respects I believe he erred in law. He did not properly put the question of a "legal way out" before the jury.

In my view, this was a serious error and omission going to the heart of the defence of necessity. The error justifies a new trial.

. . . .

V CONCLUSION

On the basis of all the above, it is my conclusion that the Court of Appeal was correct in the result in ordering a new trial and was correct in sustaining the trial judge's decision to withhold the botanical defence from the jury.

I would dismiss the appeals.

Appeals dismissed.

[Wilson J. delivered a lengthy dissent. She accepted the distinction between justification and excuse but was of the view that necessity could sometimes be pleaded as a justification, not only as an excuse.]

Is it necessary to distinguish justification from excuse? What legal consequences flow from the distinction? How does one determine whether the situation should be labelled a justification or an excuse? Should consequences flow from labels?

R. v. LATIMER

[2001] 1 S.C.R. 3, 39 C.R. (5th) 1, 150 C.C.C. (3d) 129,
2001 CarswellSask 4, 2001 CarswellSask 5

The defence of necessity received another high profile test in this heartwrenching case. A father was on trial for the first degree murder of Tracy, his 12-year-old daughter, who had a severe form of cerebral palsy. Tracy was quadriplegic and her physical condition rendered her immobile. Her condition was permanent, caused by neurological damage at the time of her birth. She was said to have the mental capacity of a four-month-old baby, and could communicate only by means of facial expressions, laughter and crying. She was completely dependent on others for her care. She suffered five to six seizures daily. It was thought that she experienced a great deal of pain. This could not be reduced by medication since this would conflict with her anti-epileptic medication and her difficulty in swallowing. She had to be spoon-fed, and her lack of nutrients caused weight loss. There was evidence that Tracy could have been fed with a feeding tube into her stomach, an option that would have improved her nutrition and health, and that might also have allowed for more effective pain medication to be administered. The accused and his wife rejected this option as intrusive and the first step to artificially preserving her life. Tracy had a serious disability but was not terminally ill. She had undergone numerous surgeries including the implanting of metal rods to support her spine. The Latimers learned that the doctors wished to perform additional surgery on a dislocated hip which involved removing her upper thigh bone. According to the accused's wife they perceived this as mutilation.[1]

The accused decided to take his daughter's life. While his wife and Tracy's siblings were at church, he carried Tracy to his pickup truck, seated her in the cab, and inserted a hose from the truck's exhaust pipe into the cab. She died from the carbon monoxide. The accused at first maintained that she had simply passed away in her sleep, but later confessed to having taken her life. Charged with first degree murder, the jury found him guilty of second degree murder. The trial judge had withdrawn the defence of necessity from the jury by the following instruction:

> [W]hile the doctrine of necessity can sometimes operate to excuse criminal misconduct, I must tell you as a matter of law that the doctrine does not apply in this case. The defence of necessity exists only where the perpetrator's decision to break the law is inescapable and unavoidable and necessary to avert some imminent risk of peril. It arises only in cases where there is no option, no other choice. That was not the situation here. There was an option, albeit not a particularly happy one. The option was to persevere in the attempts to make Tracy comfortable in her life, however, disagreeable and heartwrenching those attempts may have been. (41 C.R. (4th) at 38)

---

1 The above facts are taken from the Supreme Court's review of the record. The tragic context has been further described by Professor Barney Sneiderman, "The Latimer Mercy-Killing Case: A Rumination on Crime and Punishment", (1997), 5 Health L.J. 1 at 1-2 as follows:

Gravely affected since birth by cerebral palsy, Tracy Latimer was a "totally body-involved spastic quadriplegic", whose constant muscle spasms and seizures had wrenched her body into a twisted frozen position. She had the mental age of a two- or three-month-old baby, weighed 38 pounds, wore diapers, often needed suppositories to unplug her bowels, had impaired vision, and could not sit up, talk, or feed herself. Her parents kept a bucket at hand when feeding her as she had difficulty in swallowing and would constantly vomit. She spent her days either in bed or propped in a wheelchair, tightly fitted to prevent her thrashing about during her daily seizure episodes.

Tracy had undergone a number of surgical procedures to relieve the painful muscular tension afflicting her grossly contorted body; muscles had been cut at the top of her legs, her toes, her heel cords, and knees. There was also surgery on her spine; stainless steel rods were inserted on each side to relieve the cramping of her stomach and lungs. Because Tracy was on anticonvulsant medication to control her seizures, her parents were fearful that using narcotics to control her pain could prove fatal by depressing her respiration (a concern shared by Tracy's orthopaedic surgeon). She was in constant pain from a dislocated hip, and Latimer was appalled at the prospect of impending surgery that would involve the removal of part of her hip and thigh bone. And there would be more surgery to come.

Sneiderman's sources are the reported decision in (1995), 41 C.R. (4th) 1 (Sask. C.A.), the trial transcript and newspaper accounts. The notion Tracy was in constant pain has been disputed: see Ruth Enns, A Voice Unheard. The Latimer Case and People with Disabilities (1999). An appendix at pp.166-170 shows that Tracy's mother's communication books had multiple entries as to her happiness and smiles.

The jury returned a verdict of second degree murder. The sentence was life imprisonment with no parole eligibility for ten years.

In dismissing Latimer's appeal the Saskatchewan Court of Appeal held that the trial judge had properly withdrawn the defence of necessity from the jury given the *Perka* criteria. A majority, over the dissent of Chief Justice Bayda, rejected the argument for a constitutional exemption from the mandatory sentence.

At the second trial, ordered by the Supreme Court for other reasons, the charge was second degree murder. The trial proceeded on the basis the accused had been motivated by concern for his daughter's present and future pain. For very similar reasons to those offered in the first trial, the trial judge, Noble J., withdrew the defence of necessity but only after the addresses by counsel. The jury again convicted but were visibly upset when asked to make a recommendation whether parole eligibility should be set at more than ten years. They recommended one year! This reality was a factor Noble J. took into account in opting for a constitutional exemption and imposing a sentence of one year followed by probation for one year less one day. During the second trial, defence counsel asked the trial judge for a ruling, in advance of his closing submissions, on whether the jury could consider the defence of necessity. The trial judge told counsel that he would rule on necessity after the closing submissions. Some of the defence counsel's address referred to the defence of necessity. The judge later ruled that the defence was not available.

The Saskatchewan Court of Appeal affirmed the conviction but reversed the sentence. It imposed the mandatory minimum sentence of life imprisonment without parole eligibility for ten years. The Supreme Court in a short unanimous judgment dismissed the accused's further appeals against conviction and sentence.

Per curiam: —

. . . .

(1) The Availability of the Defence of Necessity
(a) The Three Requirements for the Defence of Necessity

We propose to set out the requirements for the defence of necessity first, before applying them to the facts of this appeal. The leading case on the defence of necessity is *Perka v. The Queen* . . . .

. . . .

Dickson J. insisted that the defence of necessity be restricted to those rare cases in which true "involuntariness" is present. The defence, he held, must be "strictly controlled and scrupulously limited" (p. 250). It is well-established that the defence of necessity must be of limited application. Were the criteria for the defence loosened or approached purely subjectively, some fear, as did Edmund Davies L.J., that necessity would "very easily become simply a mask for anarchy": *Southwark London Borough Council v. Williams*, [1971] Ch. 734 (C.A.), at p. 746.

Perka outlined three elements that must be present for the defence of necessity. First, there is the requirement of imminent peril or danger. Second, the accused must have had no reasonable legal alternative to the course of action he or she undertook. Third, there must be proportionality between the harm inflicted and the harm avoided.

To begin, there must be an urgent situation of "clear and imminent peril": *Morgentaler v. The Queen*, [1976] 1 S.C.R. 616, at p. 678. In short, disaster must be imminent, or harm unavoidable and near. It is not enough that the peril is foreseeable or likely; it must be on the verge of transpiring and virtually certain to occur. In *Perka*, Dickson J. expressed the requirement of imminent peril at p. 251: "At a minimum the situation must be so emergent and the peril must be so pressing that normal human instincts cry out for action and make a counsel of patience unreasonable". The *Perka* case, at p. 251, also offers the rationale for this requirement of immediate peril: "The requirement . . . tests whether it was indeed unavoidable for the actor to act at all". Where the situation of peril clearly should have been foreseen and avoided, an accused person cannot reasonably claim any immediate peril.

The second requirement for necessity is that there must be no reasonable legal alternative to disobeying the law. *Perka* proposed these questions, at pp. 251-52: "Given that the accused had to act, could he nevertheless realistically have acted to avoid the peril or prevent the harm, without breaking the law? *Was there a legal way out?*" (emphasis in original). If there was a reasonable legal alternative to breaking the law, there is no necessity. It may be noted that the requirement involves a realistic appreciation of the alternatives open to a person; the accused need not be placed in the last resort imaginable, but he must have no reasonable legal alternative. If an alternative to breaking the law exists, the defence of necessity on this aspect fails.

The third requirement is that there be proportionality between the harm inflicted and the harm avoided. The harm inflicted must not be disproportionate to the harm the accused sought to avoid.

. . . .

Evaluating proportionality can be difficult. It may be easy to conclude that there is no proportionality in some cases, like the example given in *Perka* of the person who blows up a city to avoid breaking a finger. Where proportionality can quickly be dismissed, it makes sense for a trial judge to do so and rule out the defence of necessity before considering the other requirements for necessity. But most situations fall into a grey area that requires a difficult balancing of harms. In this regard, it should be noted that the requirement is not that one harm (the harm avoided) must always clearly outweigh the other (the harm inflicted). Rather, the two harms must, at a minimum, be of a comparable gravity. That is, the harm avoided must be either comparable to, or clearly greater than, the harm inflicted. As the Supreme Court of Victoria in Australia has put it, the harm inflicted "must not be out of proportion to the peril to be avoided": *R. v. Loughnan*, [1981] V.R. 443, at p. 448.

Before applying the three requirements of the necessity defence to the facts of this case, we need to determine what test governs necessity. Is the standard objective or subjective? A subjective test would be met if the person believed he or she was in imminent peril with no reasonable legal alternative to committing the offence. Conversely, an objective test would not assess what the accused believed; it would consider whether in fact the person *was* in peril with no reasonable legal alternative. A modified objective test falls somewhere between the two. It involves an objective evaluation, but one that takes into account the situation and characteristics of the particular accused person. We conclude that, for two of the three requirements for the necessity defence, the test should be the modified objective test.

The first and second requirements — imminent peril and no reasonable legal alternative — must be evaluated on the modified objective standard described above. As expressed in *Perka*, necessity is rooted in an objective standard: "involuntariness is measured on the basis of society's expectation of appropriate and normal resistance to pressure" (p. 259). We would add that it is appropriate, in evaluating the accused's conduct, to take into account personal characteristics that legitimately affect what may be expected of that person. The approach taken in *R. v. Hibbert*, [1995] 2 S.C.R. 973, is instructive. Speaking for the court, Lamer C.J. held, at para. 59, that:

> it is appropriate to employ an objective standard that takes into account the particular circumstances of the accused, including his or her ability to perceive the existence of alternative courses of action.

While an accused's perceptions of the surrounding facts may be highly relevant in determining whether his conduct should be excused, those perceptions remain relevant only so long as they are reasonable. The accused person must, at the time of the act, honestly believe, on reasonable grounds, that he faces a situation of imminent peril that leaves no reasonable legal alternative open. There must be a reasonable basis for the accused's beliefs and actions, but it would be proper to take into account circumstances that legitimately affect the accused person's ability to evaluate his situation. The test cannot be a subjective one, and the accused who argues that *he* perceived imminent peril without an alternative would only succeed with the defence of necessity if his belief was reasonable given his circumstances and attributes. We leave aside for a case in which it arises the possibility that an honestly held but mistaken belief could ground a "mistake of fact" argument on the separate inquiry into *mens rea*.

The third requirement for the defence of necessity, proportionality, must be measured on an objective standard, as it would violate fundamental principles of the criminal law to do otherwise. Evaluating the nature of an act is fundamentally a determination reflecting society's values as to what is appropriate and what represents a transgression. Some insight into this requirement is provided by George Fletcher, in a passage from *Rethinking Criminal Law* (1978), at p. 804. Fletcher spoke of the comparison between the harm inflicted and the harm avoided, and suggested that there was a threshold at which a person must be expected to suffer the harm rather than break the law. He continued:

> Determining this threshold is patently a matter of moral judgment about what we expect people to be able to resist in trying situations. A valuable aid in making that judgment is comparing the competing interests at stake and assessing the degree to which the actor inflicts harm beyond the benefit that accrues from his action.

The evaluation of the seriousness of the harms must be objective. A subjective evaluation of the competing harms would, by definition, look at the matter from the perspective of the accused person who seeks to avoid harm, usually to himself. The proper perspective, however, is an objective one, since evaluating the gravity of the act is a matter of community standards infused with constitutional considerations (such as, in this case, the s. 15(1) equality rights of the disabled). We conclude that the proportionality requirement must be determined on a purely objective standard.

(b)   The Application of the Requirements for Necessity in This Case

The inquiry here is not whether the defence of necessity should in fact *excuse* Mr. Latimer's actions, but whether the jury should have been left to consider this defence. The correct test on that point is whether there is an air of reality to the defence.

.   .   .   .

The question is whether there is sufficient evidence that, if believed, would allow a reasonable jury — properly charged and acting judicially — to conclude that the defence applied and acquit the accused.

For the necessity defence, the trial judge must be satisfied that there is evidence sufficient to give an air of reality to each of the three requirements. If the trial judge concludes that there is no air of reality to any one of the three requirements, the defence of necessity should not be left to the jury.

In this case, there was no air of reality to the three requirements of necessity.

The first requirement is imminent peril. It is not met in this case. The appellant does not suggest he himself faced any peril; instead he identifies a peril to his daughter, stemming from her upcoming surgery which he perceived as a form of mutilation. Acute suffering can constitute imminent peril, but in this case there was nothing to her medical condition that placed Tracy in a dangerous situation where death was an alternative. Tracy was thought to be in pain before the surgery, and that pain was expected to continue, or increase, following the surgery. But that ongoing pain did not constitute an emergency in this case. To borrow the language of Edmund Davies L.J. in *Southwark London Borough Council*, *supra*, at p. 746, we are dealing not with an emergency but with "an obstinate and long-standing state of affairs". Tracy's proposed surgery did not pose an imminent threat to her life, nor did her medical condition. In fact, Tracy's health might have improved had the Latimers not rejected the option of relying on a feeding tube. Tracy's situation was not an emergency. The appellant can be reasonably expected to have understood that reality. There was no evidence of a legitimate psychological condition that rendered him unable to perceive that there was no imminent peril. The appellant argued that, for him, further surgery *did* amount to imminent peril. It was not reasonable for the appellant to form this belief, particularly when better pain management was available.

The second requirement for the necessity defence is that the accused had no reasonable legal alternative to breaking the law. In this case, there is no air of reality to the proposition that the appellant had no reasonable legal alternative to killing his daughter. He had at least one reasonable legal alternative: he could have struggled on, with what was unquestionably a difficult situation, by helping Tracy to live and by minimizing her pain as much as possible. The appellant might have done so by using a feeding tube to improve her health and allow her to take more effective pain medication, or he might have relied on the group home that Tracy stayed at just before her death. The appellant may well have thought the prospect of struggling on unbearably sad and demanding. It was a human response that this alternative was unappealing. But it was a reasonable legal alternative that the law requires a person to pursue before he can claim the defence of necessity. The appellant was aware of this alternative but rejected it.

The third requirement for the necessity defence is proportionality; it requires the trial judge to consider, as a question of law rather than fact, whether the harm avoided was proportionate to the harm inflicted. It is difficult, at the conceptual level, to imagine a circumstance in which the proportionality requirement could be met for a homicide. We leave open, if and until it arises, the question of whether the proportionality requirement could be met in a homicide situation. In England, the defence of necessity is probably not available for homicide: *R. v. Howe*, [1987] 1 A.C. 417 (H.L.), at pp. 453 and 429; Smith and Hogan, *Criminal Law* (9th ed. 1999), at pp. 249-51. The famous case of *R. v. Dudley and Stephens* (1884), 14 Q.B.D. 273, involving cannibalism on the high seas, is often cited as establishing the unavailability of the defence of necessity for homicide, although the case is not conclusive: see Card, Cross and Jones, *Criminal Law* (12th ed. 1992), at p. 352; Smith and Hogan, *supra*, at pp. 249 and 251. The Law Reform Commission of Canada has suggested the defence should not be available for a person who intentionally kills or seriously harms another person: *Report on Recodifying Criminal Law* (1987), at p. 36. American jurisdictions are divided on this question, with a number of them denying the necessity defence for murder: P.H. Robinson, *Criminal Law Defenses* (1984), vol. 2, at pp. 63-65; see also *United States v. Holmes*, 26 F. Cas. 360 (C.C.E.D. Pa. 1842) (No. 15,383). The American *Model Penal Code* proposes that the defence of necessity *would* be available for homicide: American Law Institute, *Model Penal Code and Commentaries* (1985), at para. 3.02, pp. 14-15; see also W.R. LaFave and A.W. Scott, *Substantive Criminal Law* (1986), vol. 1, at p. 634.

Assuming for the sake of analysis only that necessity could provide a defence to homicide, there would have to be a harm that was seriously comparable in gravity to death (the harm inflicted). In this case, there was no risk of such harm. The "harm avoided" in the appellant's situation was, compared to death, completely disproportionate. The harm inflicted in this case was ending a life; that harm was immeasurably more serious than the pain resulting from Tracy's operation which Mr. Latimer sought to avoid. Killing a person — in order to relieve the suffering produced by a medically manageable physical or mental condition — is not a proportionate response to the harm represented by the non-life-threatening suffering resulting from that condition.

We conclude that there was no air of reality to *any* of the three requirements for necessity. As noted earlier, if the trial judge concludes that even one of the requirements had no air of reality, the defence should not be left to the jury. Here, the trial judge was correct to remove the defence from the jury. In considering the defence of necessity, we must remain aware of the need to respect the life, dignity and equality of all the individuals affected by the act in question. The fact that the victim in this case was disabled rather than able-bodied does not affect our conclusion that the three requirements for the defence of necessity had no air of reality here.

In *R. v. Morgentaler, Smoling and Scott* (1985), 48 C.R. (3d) 1 (S.C.C.) the court considered whether Dr. Henry Morgentaler could rely on the defence of necessity for having provided therapeutic abortions without complying with the law in force at the time concerning such abortions. The court held:

> . . . the defence of necessity is not premised on dissatisfaction with the law. The defence of necessity recognizes that the law must be followed, but there are certain factual situations which arise which may excuse a person for failure to comply with the law. It is not the law which can create an emergency giving rise to a defence of necessity, but it is the facts of a given situation which may do so.

> This was not a case where two or more doctors agreed to procure the miscarriage of a female person who was in immediate need of medical services in order to avoid danger to her life or health, and in which case the defence of necessity would be a live issue. The defence of necessity cannot be resorted to as an excuse for medical practitioners in Canada to agree in the circumstances of this case to procure abortions on their own opinion of the danger to life or health and at a place of their own choosing in complete disregard of the provisions of s. 251 of the *Criminal Code*.

The decision in *Latimer* that there was no evidentiary foundation for the defence of necessity to be put to the jury is in stark contrast to the three *Morgentaler* trials in Quebec where the necessity defence was weak but nevertheless left with the jury. **Should the defence of necessity have been put in *Latimer*?**

Latimer is clearly a hard case. It engages the emotions of disabled persons who understandably feel vulnerable if the accused was not to be punished for deliberately taking an innocent life without consent. There is also understandable fear that a lenient sentence would encourage other similar actions and moves to decriminalize assisted suicide and euthanasia. See further David Lepofsky, "The *Latimer* Case: Murder is Still Murder When the Victim is a Child With a Disability" (2001), Queen's L.J. 319.

In June 1995, the Special Senate Committee on Euthanasia and Assisted Suicide handed down its report, recommending that counselling suicide, assisting suicide, and non-voluntary euthanasia should all remain criminal offences. They also recommended, however, that "the *Criminal Code* be amended to provide for a less severe penalty in cases where there is the essential element of compassion or mercy". **Should the court have given Latimer a constitutional exemption from the minimum ten year sentence which his conviction carried?**

Chief Justice Bayda carefully considered public outrage expressed against the sentence and four other mercy killing cases, two involving consent, where the charges were reduced from murder and the sentences were probation. This is a powerful judgment: see, too, Tim Quigley, "*R. v. Latimer*: Hard Cases Make Interesting Law" (1995), 41 C.R. (4th) 89 at 96-98. At its heart the concern is for equal justice. Unfortunately, it was not even referred to by the Supreme Court. See, too, Barney Sneiderman, "The *Latimer* Mercy-Killing Case: A Rumination of Crime and Punishment" (1997), 5 Health L.J. 1 and "The Case of Robert Latimer. A Commentary on Crime and Punishment" (1999), 37 Alta. L. Rev. 1017. The latter article was relied on by defence counsel in the Supreme Court but is not even acknowledged by the court. For a wide range of views on the Supreme Court's decision see comments by Barney Sneiderman, Archibald Kaiser, Allan Manson and Stuart in the C.R.'s. In *R. v. Ferguson*, 54 C.R. (6th) 197, 228 C.C.C. (3d) 385, [2008] 1 S.C.R. 96 the Supreme Court firmly decided that constitutional exemptions were not available in the case of minimum sentences. See comments by Steve Coughlan and Paul Calarco.

In the United Kingdom the absolute authority of *Dudley and Stephens* that necessity can never be a defence to a deliberate killing may have been weakened by a ruling of the Court of Appeal: *Re. A (Children) (Conjoined Twins: Surgical Separation)*, [2000] 4 All E.R. 961 (C.A.). The court ruled that necessity would legalize an operation to separate conjoined twins against the wishes of their Catholic parents. The operation would result in the instant death of one of the twins but would likely save the other from death for a normal life. The defence of necessity is fully reviewed by Brooke L.J. and also relied on by Ward L.J. and Walker L.J. It somehow rests on the view that death was not intended. Brooke L.J. refers to a real life example:

> At the coroner's inquest conducted in October 1987 into the Zeebrugge [ferry] disaster, an
> army corporal gave evidence that he and dozens of other people were near the foot of a rope

ladder. They were all in the water and in danger of drowning. Their route to safety, however, was blocked for at least ten minutes by a young man who was petrified by cold or fear (or both) and was unable to move up or down. Eventually the corporal gave instructions that the man should be pushed off the ladder, and he was never seen again (at para. 311).

For a full review of *Latimer* and the *Conjoined Twins* case see Gary Trotter, "Necessity and Death: Lessons from *Latimer* and the Case of the Conjoined Twins" (2003), 40 Alberta L. Rev. 817. Professor Trotter argues that necessity should be rejected as a defence to intentional killings and that the *Conjoined Twins* case must be confined to its "idiosyncratic context".

For an argument that mandatory minimum sentences for murder are not appropriate in the context of euthanasia see Nadia E. Thomas, "Sentencing Murder: Did Robert Latimer Deserve the Mandatory Minimum?" (2002), 7 Can. Crim. L.R. 93.

---

1. The accused is charged with speeding and dangerous driving. He was clocked on radar at l20 k.p.h. in a 50 k.p.h. zone. He was operating his vehicle in a heavily built-up residential area and was observed maintaining this speed over a distance of several city blocks. During this time he was being closely followed by another automobile. The automobile alternately slowed and accelerated with the second vehicle always maintaining a distance of seven to eight feet from the lead vehicle. The accused testified that each time he speeded up he did so to ensure maintenance of interval between himself and the car behind him to avoid the hazard presented by the other driver's tailgating. The driver of the other vehicle admitted that he was crowding the accused intentionally as he was "out for thrills". The accused relies on necessity. What do you, as Crown counsel, argue?
Compare *R. v. Fry* (1977), 36 C.C.C. (2d) 396 (Sask. Prov. Ct.), *R. v. Kennedy* (1972), 18 C.R.N.S. 80, 7 C.C.C. (2d) 42 (N.S. Co. Ct.) and *R. v. Morris* (1994), 32 C.R. (4th) 191 (B.C. S.C.).

2. The accused is charged with fishing in a place where, at that time, fishing was prohibited by law. The waters had been closed to fishing from 1400 hours that day. The basis of his defence is that, owing to the very inclement weather the day before, his punts, used for collecting the herring from the gillnets, were beached. The accused was therefore unable to retrieve all his nets before 1400 hours although he worked all morning and did manage to retrieve some. Give judgment.
Compare *R. v. Pootlass* (1978), 1 C.R. (3d) 378 (B.C. Prov. Ct.).

3. The accused is a police constable and at the material time was driving a police cruiser. He received a radio call that a bank alarm had gone off at the Bank of Montreal a few blocks away. He was advised that the robbers were armed and still on the premises. He turned on the siren and roof lights and headed for the bank. As he approached the bank he was aware of a stop sign which required him to stop at the intersection. Because of the emergency and his concern for the safety of the people in the bank,

he decided not to stop. He slowed to 20 k.p.h., looked both ways, and entered the intersection without stopping. He collided with a car coming from his right. He was aware of his exemption under the circumstances from the speed provisions of the *Highway Traffic Act*, but realized there was no other exemption. The accused is charged with failing to stop and advances the defence of necessity. Result?

Compare *R. v. Walker* (1979), 48 C.C.C. (2d) 126 (Ont. Co. Ct.).

4. The accused is charged with having committed an assault on his wife. The assault allegedly occurred in the accused's truck as they were returning from an evening at the tavern. The accused was driving. He was sober but his wife was drunk. His wife became agitated about an occurrence earlier that evening and demanded that they return to town. The accused refused to turn around and his wife threatened to jump. She reached for the door handle and he grabbed her and pulled her back. She grabbed at the steering wheel and the truck nearly went into the ditch. The accused grabbed her around the neck and held her in that fashion all the way home. Grounds of necessity?

Compare *R. v. Morris* (1981), 23 C.R. (3d) 175, 61 C.C.C. (2d) 163 (Alta. Q.B.).

5. The accused was charged with trespassing contrary to a provincial statute. The trespass occurred on the grounds of Litton Industries. The accused testified that she believed Litton Industries to manufacture component systems for the Cruise missile and that the Cruise missile was aimed at targets in other countries which could trigger a nuclear conflict. She believed Litton Industries was committing a serious offence and she was prepared to commit the offence of trespass to avert this evil. She testified she was involved in the protest because "I have to!" The defence relied on necessity.

Compare *R. v. Young* (1984), 39 C.R. (3d) 290 (Ont. Prov. Ct.).

6. The accused, a 33-year old mother of five young children, was charged with defrauding the Ministry of Community and Social Services of more than $1,000. It was alleged that during a common law relationship over a ten year period she had misrepresented that her partner and the father of four of the children had not been living with her. It was further alleged that as a result she had obtained family benefits to which she was not entitled. Over the ten years until final separation she had received benefits of some $130,000. On the final separation the accused went to a women's shelter.

The trial judge found that the accused had failed to disclose that the parties were from time to time living together and that as a result she had received family benefits to which she was not entitled. However, there was evidence that he was abusive and spent any money he had on alcohol. She testified she was afraid to tell General Welfare that he was living with her in case the welfare cheque was made out to him. She feared he would drink away the money and they would be without food or shelter or both. Should the defence of necessity succeed?

Compare *R. v. LaLonde* (1995), 37 C.R. (4th) 97 (Ont. Gen. Div.) and see comment by Sheila Noonan, "*LaLonde:* Evaluating The Relevance of BWS Evidence" (1995), 37 C.R. (4th) 110.

7. The accused is charged with impaired driving and driving over the legal limit. He was found driving erratically on the streets of a small town at midday. He was trying to drive himself to hospital after an unsuccessful suicide attempt. He had been drinking heavily and he tried to poison himself with carbon monoxide from his truck inside his garage. He woke up, confused, to discover the truck had run out of gas. He decided to go for help in another vehicle. In his confused, highly emotional and drunk state it did not occur to him to go to a neighbour for help or to call 911. Should his defence of necessity succeed?

Compare *R. v. Desrosiers* (2007), 48 C.R. (6th) 85 (Ont. C.J.). See too *R. v. McCain* (2003), 15 C.R. (6th) 360 (Ont. C.J.).

8. The accused had a history of depression and moved into the forests and engaged in periods of fasting for spiritual cleansing. After a 60 day fast he walked for several hours in the cold to look for food. He believed he was in a desperate situation due to lack of food and hypothermia. He broke into a house where he ate some food and wrapped himself in blankets. The owner of the house found him unconscious. He is charged with breaking and entering a dwelling house and committing mischief. Should his defence of necessity result in acquittal?

Compare *R. v. John Doe* (2007), (sub nom. *R. v. Nelson*) 228 C.C.C. (3d) 302, 54 C.R. (6th) 393 (B.C. C.A.).

6. DURESS

(a) Section 17 and Common Law

See sections 17 and 18 of the *Criminal Code*.

R. v. CARKER (NO. 2)

[1967] S.C.R. 114, 2 C.R.N.S. 16, [1967] 2 C.C.C. 190, 1966 CarswellBC 169

RITCHIE J.: — This is an appeal by the Attorney-General of British Columbia from a judgment of the Court of Appeal of that Province, from which Mr. Justice MacLean dissented, and by which it was ordered that the respondent's conviction for unlawfully and wilfully damaging public property and thereby committing mischief, should be set aside and that a new trial should be had.

At the trial the respondent admitted having damaged the plumbing fixtures in the cell where he was incarcerated at Oakalla Prison Farm in British Columbia but, through his counsel, he sought to introduce evidence to show that he had committed this offence under the compulsion of threats and was therefore entitled to be excused for committing it by virtue of the provisions of s. 17 of the *Criminal Code* and that he was also entitled to avail himself of the common-law defence of "duress" having regard to the provision of s. 7 of the *Criminal Code*.

. . . .

I agree with the learned trial judge and with MacLean J.A. that in respect of proceedings for an offence under the *Criminal Code* the common-law rules and principles respecting "duress" as an excuse or defence have been codified and exhaustively defined in s. 17.

. . . .

At the outset of the proceedings at the trial in the present case and in the absence of the jury, Mr. Greenfield, who acted on behalf of the accused, informed the court that he intended to call evidence of compulsion and duress and he elected to outline the nature of this evidence which was that the offence had been committed during a disturbance, apparently organized by way of protest, to damage property at the Prison Farm in the course of which a substantial body of prisoners, shouting in unison from their separate cells, threatened the respondent, who was not joining in the disturbance, that if he did not break the plumbing fixtures in his cell he would be kicked in the head, his arm would be broken and he would get a knife in the back at the first opportunity.

. . . .

There can be little doubt that the evidence outlined by Mr. Greenfield, which was subsequently confirmed by the evidence given by the ringleaders of the disturbance in mitigation of sentence, disclosed that the respondent committed the offence under the compulsion of threats of death and grievous bodily harm, but although these threats were "immediate" in the sense that they were continuous until the time that the offence was committed, they were not threats of "immediate death" or "immediate grievous bodily harm" and none of the persons who delivered them was present in the cell with the respondent when the offence was committed. I am accordingly of opinion that the learned trial judge was right in deciding that the proposed evidence did not afford an excuse within the meaning of s. 17 of the *Criminal Code*.

. . . .

In support of the suggestion that the threat in the present case was "immediate and continuous" Mr. Justice Norris relied on the case of *Subramaniam v. Public Prosecutor*, in which the Privy Council decided that the trial Judge was wrong in excluding evidence of threats to which the appellant was subjected by Chinese terrorists in Malaya. In that case it was found that the threats were a continuous menace up to the moment when the appellant was captured because the terrorists might have come back at any time and carried them into effect. Section 94 of the Penal Code of the Federated Malay States, which the appellant sought to invoke in that case provided:

> 94. Except murder and offences included in Chapter VI punishable with death, nothing is an offence which is done by a person who is compelled to do it by threats, which, at the time of doing it, reasonably cause the apprehension that instant death to that person will otherwise be the consequence.

The distinctions between the *Subramaniam* case and the present one lie in the fact that Subramaniam might well have had reasonable cause for apprehension that instant death would result from his disobeying the terrorists who might have come back at any moment, whereas it is virtually inconceivable that "immediate death" or "grievous bodily harm" could have come to Carker from those who were uttering the threats against him as they were locked up in separate cells, and it is also to be noted that the provisions of s. 17 of the *Criminal Code* are by no means the same as those of s. 94 of the Penal Code of the Federated Malay States; amongst other distinctions the latter section contains no provision that the person who utters the threats must be present when the offence is committed in order to afford an excuse for committing it.

. . . .

The evidence outlined to the learned trial judge discloses that the criminal act was committed to preserve the respondent from future harm coming to him, but there is no suggestion in the evidence tendered for the defence that the accused did not know that what he was doing would "probably cause" damage. Accepting the outline made by defence counsel as being an accurate account of the evidence which was available, there was in my view nothing in it to support the defence that the act was not done "wilfully" within the meaning of s. 371(1) and 372(1) of the *Criminal Code* and there was accordingly no ground to justify the learned trial judge in permitting the proposed evidence to be called in support of such a defence.

In view of all the above, I would allow this appeal, set aside the judgment of the Court of Appeal and restore the conviction.

Appeal allowed and conviction restored.

R. v. PAQUETTE

[1977] 2 S.C.R. 189, 39 C.R.N.S. 257, 30 C.C.C. (2d) 417,
1976 CarswellOnt 415F, 1976 CarswellOnt 28

MARTLAND J.: — The facts which give rise to this appeal are as follows:

During the course of a robbery at the Pop Shoppe, in the City of Ottawa, on March 18, 1973, an innocent bystander was killed by a bullet from a rifle fired by one Simard. The robbery was committed by Simard and one Clermont, both of whom, together with the appellant, were jointly charged with non-capital murder. Simard and Clermont pleaded guilty to this charge.

The appellant was not present when the robbery was committed or when the shooting occurred. The charge against him was founded upon s. 21(2) of the *Criminal Code*. Section 21 provides as follows:

> 21(1) Every one is a party to an offence who
>   (a) actually commits it,
>   (b) does or omits to do anything for the purpose of aiding any person to commit it, or
>   (c) abets any person in commiting it.
>   (2) Where two or more persons form an intention in common to carry out an unlawful purpose and to assist each other therein and any one of them, in carrying out the common purpose, commits an offence, each of them who knew or ought to have known that the commission of the offence would be a probable consequence of carrying out the common purpose is a party to that offence.

The appellant made a statement to the police, which was admitted in evidence at the trial and which described his involvement in the matter as follows: On the day of the robbery Clermont telephoned the appellant for a ride as his own car was broken. Clermont asked the appellant where he used to work and was told at the Pop Shoppe. Clermont told him to drive to the Pop Shoppe because Clermont wanted to rob it, and, when the appellant refused, Clermont pulled his gun and threatened to kill him. Simard was picked up later and also a rifle. The appellant drove them to the Pop Shoppe. The appellant had been threatened with revenge if he did not wait for Clermont and Simard. The appellant, in his statement, stated he was afraid and drove around the block. After the robbery and homicide Clermont and Simard attempted twice, unsuccessfully, to get into the appellant's car. Three of the Crown's witnesses supported this latter statement.

The appellant did not testify at trial but relied on the above statement and two other statements also introduced at the trial by the Crown to support his argument that he had no intention in common with Simard and Clermont to carry out the robbery; *i.e.*:

    (1) an oral statement to a police officer on his arrest that he had been threatened with death "if he squealed";

(2) the written statement to the police outlined above in which he stated that he had only participated in the robbery by driving because he was threatened with death;

(3) a statement to his girlfriend the day after the robbery that he was forced to do it. The trial Judge charged the jury as follows:

> Now, the defence are asserting that Paquette participated in this robbery because he was compelled to do so, and in that connection I charge you that if Paquette joined in the common plot to rob the Pop Shoppe under threats of death or grievous bodily harm, that would negative his having a common intention with Simard to rob the Pop Shoppe, and you must find Paquette not guilty.

The appellant was acquitted. The Crown appealed to the Court of Appeal for Ontario [19 C.C.C. (2d) 154, 5 O.R. (2d) 1]. The reasons delivered by that court make it clear that the appeal would have been dismissed had it not been for the decision of this court in *Dunbar v. The King*, 67 C.C.C. 20, [1936] 4 D.L.R. 737.

The relevant portions of the majority judgment in that case are as follows [at pp. 27-8 C.C.C., pp. 743-4 D.L.R.]:

> On January 15, 1936, three men entered and robbed a branch of the Canadian Bank of Commerce in Vancouver and in the course of the robbery the teller was fatally shot. The appellant Dunbar was not among those who entered the bank but he had brought the robbers to the bank in an automobile and after the robery was over drove back for them and took them away to the house where they had all been living together. He subsequently shared with them in the proceeds of the robbery. He had a criminal record, had met one or other of the robbers in the penitentiary and had been living with them in the same house for some days prior to the robbery. He knew when driving the car to the bank that his associates were going there with the purpose of robbing the bank, that these men were armed and that in the course of such robbery it was not improbable that someone might be killed. His sole excuse for his conduct was that he had acted under compulsion as one of his associates had threatened his life unless he accompanied them and had further threatened that if he did anything to betray them that he would be killed. The point of alleged misdirection most stressed by counsel for the prisoner before us was a statement as follows:—
>
> "If you accept Dunbar's evidence that he was so bereft of reason that his reasoning faculties were suspended and that he was really in the position of having his hand held by somebody, that he had two men standing over him — you had this story of the thing put to you in the way that he would have you believe — well, then it seems to me there should be some evidence to show his mental condition."
>
> Section 20 of the *Criminal Code*, dealing with compulsion, excludes murder and robbery, and therefore is inapplicable to this case, but it was argued that if compulsion were shown it might be sufficient to negative any common intention under the provision of s. 69(2) of the *Code*. It seems to me that this argument fails to recognize the distinction between intention and the motive giving rise to intention.
>
> If Dunbar's story of the threat to him was true then he was faced with a choice between endangering his own life or assisting those about to commit a robbery which might, as he knew, be accompanied by murder of an innocent person. The motive giving rise to his choice between these two courses is irrelevant. This being so, in my opinion the issue was not unfairly put before the jury in the learned trial judge's charge. I would, therefore, dismiss the appeal.

Counsel for the Crown submits that the principles of law applicable to the excuse or defence of duress or compulsion are exhaustively codified in s . 17 [am. 1974-75-76, c. 105, s. 29] of the *Criminal Code*, and that the appellant is precluded from relying upon this provision because of the exception contained at the end of it. Section 17 provides:

> 17. A person who commits an offence under compulsion by threats of immediate death or grievous bodily harm from a person who is present when the offence is committed is excused for committing the offence if he believes that the threats will be carried out and if he is not a party to a conspiracy or association whereby he is subject to compulsion, but this section does not apply where the offence that is committed is treason, murder, piracy, attempted murder, assisting in rape, forcible abduction, robbery, causing bodily harm or arson.

In my opinion, the application of s. 17 is limited to cases in which the person seeking to rely upon it has himself committed an offence. If a person who actually commits the offence does so in the presence of another party who has compelled him to do the act by threats of immediate death or grievous bodily harm, then, if he believes the threats would be carried out, and is not a party to a conspiracy whereby he is subject to such compulsion, he is excused for committing the offence. The protection afforded by this section is not given in respect of the offences listed at the end of the section, which include murder and robbery.

The section uses the specific words "a person who commits an offence". It does not use the words "a person who is a party to an offence". This is significant in the light of the wording of s. 21(1) which, in para. (*a*), makes a person a party to an offence who "actually commits it". Paragraphs (*b*) and (*c*) deal with a person who aids or abets a person committing the offence. In my opinion, s. 17 codifies the law as to duress as an excuse for the actual commission of a crime, but it does not, by its terms, go beyond that. *R. v. Carker (No. 2)*, [1967] 2 C.C.C. 190, [1967] S.C.R. 114, 2 C.R.N.S. 16, in which reference was made to s. 17 having codified the defence or excuse of duress, dealt with a situation in which the accused had actually committed the offence.

The appellant, in the present case, did not himself commit the offence of robbery or of murder. He was not present when the murder occurred, as was the case in *R. v. Farduto* (1912), 21 C.C.C. 144, and *R. v. Warren* (1973), 14 C.C.C. (2d) 188, 24 C.R.N.S. 349, to which counsel for the Crown referred. In the former case the accused provided the razor with which the murderer cut the throat of the victim in his presence. The court was of the view that the trial judge could conclude that there was no case of such compulsion as would constitute an excuse. In the latter case the accused, the brother of the actual murderer was present with him over a period of time after the robbery occurred and before the deceased was killed in his presence. The report does not indicate the nature of the compulsion alleged. The emphasis appears to have been on the subnormal intelligence of the accused making him willing to go along with what was suggested to him.

The appellant could only be considered to be a party to the murder on the basis of the application of s. 21(2). Section 21(1) is not applicable because the offence to which he is alleged to be a party is murder, and it is clear that he did not commit murder, nor did he aid or abet in its commission.

Subsection (2) is only applicable if it is established that the appellant, in common with Simard and Clermont, formed an intention to commit robbery. The question in issue is as to whether the trial judge erred in law in telling the jury that if the appellant joined in the plot to rob under threats of death or of grievous bodily harm, this would negative such common intention.

I have already stated my reasons for considering s. 17 to be inapplicable. That being so, the appellant is entitled, by virtue of s. 7(3) of the *Code* to rely upon any excuse or defence available to him at common law. The defence of duress to a charge of murder against a person who did not commit the murder, but who was alleged to have aided and abetted, was recently considered by the House of Lords in *Director of Public Prosecutions for Northern Ireland v. Lynch*, [1975] A.C. 653, in which the decided cases were fully reviewed. The facts in that case were as follows [headnote]:

> The defendant drove a motor car containing a group of the I.R.A. in Northern Ireland on an expedition in which they shot and killed a police officer. On his trial for aiding and abetting the murder there was evidence that he was not a member of the I.R.A. and that he acted unwillingly under the orders of the leader of the group, being convinced that, if he disobeyed, he would himself be shot. The trial judge held that the defence of duress was not available to him and the jury found him guilty. The Court of Criminal Appeal in Northern Ireland upheld the conviction.

The House of Lords, by a three to two majority, held that on a charge of murder the defence of duress was open to a person accused as a principal in the second degree (aider and abettor) and ordered a new trial.

The conclusion of Lord Morris of Borth-y-Gest is stated at p. 677, as follows:

> Having regard to the authorities to which I have referred it seems to me to have been firmly held by our courts in this country that duress can afford a defence in criminal cases. A recent pronouncement was that in the Court of Appeal in 1971 in the case above referred to (*Reg. v. Hudson*, [1971] 2 Q.B. 202). The court stated that they had been referred to a large number of authorities and to the views of writers of textbooks. In the judgment of the court delivered by Lord Parker C.J. and prepared by Widgery L.J. the conclusion was expressed, at p. 206, that "it is clearly established that duress provides a defence in all offences including perjury (except possibly treason or murder as a principal)."

> We are only concerned in this case to say whether duress could be a possible defence open to Lynch who was charged with being an aider and abettor. Relying on the help given in the authorities we must decide this as a matter of principle. I consider that duress in such a case can be open as a possible defence. Both general reasoning and the requirements of justice lead me to this conclusion.

Lord Wilberforce, at pp. 682-3, cited with approval a passage from the dissenting reasons of Bray C.J., in *R. v. Brown and Morley*, [1968] S.A.S.R. 467 at 494:

> "The reasoning generally used to support the proposition that duress is no defence to a charge of murder is, to use the words of Blackstone cited above, that 'he ought rather to die himself, than escape by the murder of an innocent.' Generally speaking I am prepared to accept this proposition. Its force is obviously, considerably less where the act of the threatened man is not the direct act of killing but only the rendering of some minor form of assistance, particularly when it is by no means certain that if he refuses the death of the victim will be averted, or conversely when it is by no means certain that if he complies the death will be a necessary consequence. It would seem hard, for example, if an innocent passer-by seized in the street by a gang of criminals visibly engaged in robbery and murder in a shop and compelled at the point of a gun to issue misleading comments to the public, or *an innocent driver compelled at the point of a gun to convey the murderer to the victim*, were to have no defence. Are there any authorities which compel us to hold that he would not?"

I am in agreement with the conclusion reached by the majority that it was open to Lynch, in the circumstances of that case, to rely on the defence of duress, which had not been put to the jury. If the defence of duress can be available to a person who has aided and abetted in the commission of murder, then clearly it should be available to a person who is sought to be made a party to the offence by virtue of s. 21(2). A person whose actions have been dictated by fear of death or of grievous bodily injury cannot be said to have formed a genuine common intention to carry out an unlawful purpose with the person who has threatened him with those consequences if he fails to co-operate.

R. v. HIBBERT

[1995] 2 S.C.R. 973, 40 C.R. (4th) 141, 99 C.C.C. (3d) 193,
1995 CarswellOnt 117, 1995 CarswellOnt 530

The accused was charged with attempted murder, based on the allegation that he was a party to the shooting of C by B. The accused had gone with B to C's apartment and arranged for C to come to the lobby. When C entered the lobby, he was shot four times by B. The accused testified that B had threatened to shoot him if he did not cooperate and that he was terrified throughout the event. The accused believed that he had no opportunity to run away or warn C without being shot. The trial judge charged the jury that if the accused acted under fear of death or grievous bodily harm, he could not form a common intention with the person who had threatened him. The trial judge also said that if there was a safe avenue of escape, then the defence of duress was not available. The jury acquitted the accused of attempted murder but convicted him of the included offence of aggravated assault. His conviction appeal was dismissed and he appealed to the Supreme Court of Canada.

LAMER C.J. (LA FOREST, L'HEUREUX-DUBÉ, SOPINKA, GONTHIER, CORY, MCLACHLIN, IACOBUCCI and MAJOR JJ. concurring): —

. . . .

The "Safe Avenue of Escape" Requirement in the Common Law of Duress

The second and third issues raised by the appellant have to do with the so-called "safe avenue of escape" rule. The court must decide whether such a rule in fact exists, and, if it does, whether the availability of a "safe avenue" is to be determined on an objective or subjective basis. In my opinion, it is best to start the analysis by examining the juristic nature of the defence of duress and its relationship to other common law defences, since I am of the view that by so doing the answers to the questions posed in the present appeal will become clear.

(1) The Relation Between Duress and Other Excuses

As I have explained, the common law defence of duress, properly understood, is not based on the idea that coercion negates *mens rea*. Rather, it is one of a number of defences that operate by justifying or excusing what would otherwise be criminal conduct. Once duress is recognized as providing a defence of this type, it becomes apparent that much can be learned about its juristic nature by examining other existing legal excuses or justifications, such as the defences of necessity, self-defence and provocation, and by considering the extent to which analogies between these defences and the defence of duress can be drawn and sustained.

. . . .

The similarities between defences of duress and necessity have been noted on previous occasions by other commentators. . . . . In *Perka* the status of the defence of necessity in the common law of Canada was firmly established. In his majority reasons, Dickson J. summarized the considerable debate in the academic literature over the question of whether the defence of necessity should be conceptualized as a "justification" or an "excuse". Dickson J. described the justification-based approach to the defence of necessity . . . . He went on to reject this basis for the defence. Instead, he adopted an understanding of the defence of necessity based on the alternative concept of an "excuse" . . . . The common law defences of necessity and duress apply to essentially similar factual situations. Indeed, to repeat Lord Simon of Glaisdale's observation, "[d]uress is . . . merely a particular application of the doctrine of 'necessity'". In my view, the similarities between the two defences are so great that consistency and logic requires that they be understood as based on the same juristic principles. Indeed, to do otherwise would be to promote incoherence and anomaly in the criminal law. In the case of necessity, the court has already considered the various alternative theoretical positions available, in *Perka, supra*, and has expounded a conceptualization of the defence of necessity as an excuse, based on the idea of normative involuntariness. In my opinion, the need for consistency and coherence in the law dictates that the common law defence of duress also be based on this juridical foundation. If the defence is viewed in this light, the answers to the questions posed in the present appeal can be seen to follow readily from the reasons of Dickson J. in *Perka*.

(a) The Safe Avenue of Escape Requirement

The so-called "safe avenue of escape" requirement in the law of duress is, in my view, simply a specific example of a more general requirement, analogous to that in the defence of necessity identified by Dickson J. — the requirement that compliance with the law be "demonstrably impossible". As Dickson J. explained, this requirement can be derived directly from the underlying concept of normative involuntariness upon which the defence of necessity is based. As I am of the view that the defence of duress must be seen as being based upon this same theoretical foundation, it follows that the defence of duress includes a similar requirement — namely, a requirement that it can only be invoked if, to adopt Dickson J.'s phrase, there is "no legal way out" of the situation of duress the accused faces. The rule that the defence of duress is unavailable if a "safe avenue of escape" was open to the accused is simply a specific instance of this general requirement — if the accused could have escaped without undue danger, the decision to commit an offence becomes, as Dickson J. observed in the context of necessity, "a voluntary one, impelled by some consideration beyond the dictates of 'necessity' and human instincts".

(b) Is the Existence of a Safe Avenue of Escape to Be Determined Subjectively or Objectively?

How this question is answered depends, in my view, on how one conceives of the notion of "normative involuntariness" upon which the defence of duress is based. That is, is an action "normatively involuntary" when the actor believes that he has no real choice, or is this the case only when there is in fact no reasonable alternative course of action available?

Cogent arguments can be made in support of each of these positions. The issue can be framed in slightly different terms. The question of when a person "could not help doing what he did", and thus performs a normatively involuntary act can, however, be understood in two different ways. On the one hand, it can be argued that actors who perform acts that appear reasonable in relation to their knowledge of their surrounding circumstances "cannot help" what they did, even if their understanding of their situation is objectively unreasonable. Put another way, it can be argued that a person's acts are normatively involuntary if he or she honestly believes there are no reasonable alternatives, even if he or she has overlooked an alternative that a reasonable person would have been aware of. On the other hand, it can also be argued that an actor's failure to take steps to inform himself or herself of the true state of affairs is itself a choice, and that a decision based on the resulting erroneous view of the circumstances is thus not normatively involuntary, since it could have been avoided. In my opinion, the latter argument accords most closely with the view of normative involuntariness adopted by the court in *Perka*, which, as I have explained, should be seen as the theoretical foundation of both the defences of duress and necessity. As Dickson J.'s reasons in *Perka* suggest, a degree of objectivity is inherent to excuses that are based on the notion of normative involuntariness, to the extent that this concept turns on the objective availability, or lack of availability, of true choice. Indeed, Dickson J. clearly indicates that the operative standard for the defence of necessity is to be an objective one, based on whether "there is a reasonable legal alternative to disobeying the law".

However, simply adopting the second of the two arguments set out above does not fully resolve the issue of the standard to be applied in assessing whether a safe avenue of escape existed. Even if it is accepted that an actor's failure to take steps to acquire reasonable knowledge of his or her full range of options can, in itself, constitute a form of choice, it can still be argued that this only holds true when the actor is able to acquire and process additional information. That is, a person does not "choose" inaction when he or she is incapable in the first place of acting, or of knowing when to act. Thus, an argument can be made for framing the objective standard used in determining the availability of alternative options, such as "safe avenues of escape", in terms of the particular actor's capacities and abilities. This argument reflects a more general concern about the application of the negligence standard in criminal law, which Hart, *supra*, has summarized in the following terms:

> If our conditions of liability are invariant and not flexible, i.e. if they are not adjusted to the capacities of the accused, then some individuals will be held liable for negligence though they could not have helped their failure to comply with the standard.

This court has previously indicated that when assessing the reasonableness of an accused's conduct for the purposes of determining whether he or she should be excused from criminal responsibility, it is appropriate to employ an objective standard that takes into account the particular circumstances of the accused, including his or her ability to perceive the existence of alternative courses of action. For instance, in *R. v. Lavallee*, [1990] 1 S.C.R. 852, a self-defence case, Wilson J., writing for a majority of the court, declared (at p. 889):

> I think the question the jury must ask itself [in a case of self-defence] is whether, given the history, circumstances and perceptions of the appellant, her belief that she could not preserve

herself from being killed by [her "common-law" spouse] that night except by killing him first was reasonable.

The defences of self-defence, duress and necessity are essentially similar, so much so that consistency demands that each defence's "reasonableness" requirement be assessed on the same basis. Accordingly, I am of the view that while the question of whether a "safe avenue of escape" was open to an accused who pleads duress should be assessed on an objective basis, the appropriate objective standard to be employed is one that takes into account the particular circumstances and human frailties of the accused.

It should be noted that the question of what sort of objective standard is to be used when assessing the "reasonableness" of the conduct of persons raising an excuse-based defence is different in several key respects from the issue that was before the court in *R. v. Creighton*, [1993] 3 S.C.R. 3. In that case, in the course of considering the *mens rea* for "unlawful act manslaughter" under s. 222(5)(*a*) of the *Criminal Code*, a majority of the court was of the view that (at p. 61, per McLachlin J.):

> [C]onsiderations of principle and policy dictate the maintenance of a single, uniform legal standard of care for [offences with a mens rea of negligence], subject to one exception: incapacity to appreciate the nature of the risk which the activity in question entails.

Although I dissented on this point in *Creighton* (while concurring in the result), I now consider myself bound by the majority judgment. However, I do not believe that *Creighton* is applicable when what is at issue is the standard of reasonableness to be used in establishing the availability of an excuse-based defence, as opposed to the determination of liability under an offence that is defined in terms of a mental state of negligence. In my view, the relevant "considerations of policy and principle" in such cases are quite different from those identifiable in the context of negligence-based offences. Offences defined in terms of negligence typically impose criminal liability on an accused person for the consequences that flowed from his or her inherently hazardous activities — activities that he or she voluntarily and willingly chose to engage in. In *Creighton, supra*, the majority was of the view that people "may properly be held to [a strict objective standard] as a condition of choosing to engage in activities which may maim or kill other innocent people" (p. 66). Even if a person fails to foresee the probable consequences of their freely chosen actions, these actions remain the product of genuine choice. In contrast, excuse-based defences, such as duress, are predicated precisely on the view that the conduct of the accused is involuntary, in a normative sense — that is, that he or she had no realistic alternative course of action available. In my view, in determining whether an accused person was operating under such constrained options, his or her perceptions of the surrounding facts can be highly relevant to the determination of whether his or her conduct was reasonable under the circumstances, and thus whether his or her conduct is properly excusable.

. . . .

D. Assessing the Charge to the Jury

. . . .

It is quite possible that the jury determined that the appellant aided the assault "intentionally", in the sense that he performed acts that he knew would probably assist Bailey to commit the assault because he believed that if he did not Bailey would kill him. The jurors might have thus concluded that the appellant's *mens rea* was not "negated" by duress, under circumstances in which they might well have concluded that his conduct could be excused if they had been aware of the existence of the common law defence of duress, properly conceptualized.

Appeal allowed; new trial ordered.

(b)   *Charter* Standard of Moral Involuntariness

R. v. RUZIC

[2001] 1 S.C.R. 687, 41 C.R. (5th) 1, 153 C.C.C. (3d) 1,
2001 CarswellOnt 1239, 2001 CarswellOnt 1238 (S.C.C.)

The accused was charged with importing two kilograms of heroin into Canada. The accused admitted having imported the narcotics but claimed that she was then acting under duress. She conceded that her claim of duress did not meet the immediacy and presence requirements of s. 17 of the *Criminal Code* but challenged the constitutionality of s. 17 under s. 7 of the *Charter* and raised the common law defence of duress. She was acquitted at trial and the Crown's appeal was dismissed. The Crown appealed further. The Supreme Court was unanimous in dismissing the appeal and holding that s. 17 was in part unconstitutional.

LeBel J.: —

. . . .

An expert witness testified at trial that, in 1994, large paramilitary groups roamed Belgrade and engaged in criminal and mafia-like activities. The same expert maintained that people living in Belgrade during that period did not feel safe. They believed the police could not be trusted. There was a real sense that the rule of law had broken down. There was a series of encounters between Mirkovic and the respondent while she was walking her dog. Each time he approached her, he knew more about her, although she had shared no details of her life with him. He phoned her at home. He told her he knew her every move. Ms. Ruzic alleged that his behaviour became more and more intimidating, escalating to threats and acts of physical violence. On one occasion, he burned her arm with a lighter. On another, he stuck a syringe into her arm and injected her with a substance that smelled like heroin and made her nauseous. She indicated that these physical assaults were coupled with sexual harassment and finally threats against her mother.

On April 25, 1994, Mirkovic phoned the respondent and instructed her to pack a bag and meet him at a hotel in central Belgrade. Once there, he allegedly strapped three packages of heroin to her body and indicated that she was to take them to a restaurant in Toronto. He gave her a false passport, a bus ticket from Belgrade to Budapest and some money. He told her to fly from Budapest to Athens, and then from Athens to Toronto. When she protested, he warned her that, if she failed to comply, he would harm her mother.

. . . .

A. Are Statutory Defences Owed Special Deference by Reviewing Courts?

. . . .

The appellant now appeared to concede that the scope of s. 17 is susceptible to *Charter* review, but maintained that the courts should assume a posture of deference when undertaking such an assessment. The prosecution contends it belongs to Parliament to decide when otherwise criminal conduct should be excused, because determining who can rely on the statutory defence of duress and in what circumstances is an inherently policy-driven exercise. The appellant asserts that the legislature is best placed to determine what constitutes "morally involuntary" conduct for the purpose of invoking s. 17, given the difficult value judgments involved in defining duress. The appellant submits that the appropriate standard of review would restrict courts to consider simply whether the restrictions on the defence are irrational or arbitrary. As a corollary of its approach, the Crown did not seek to justify s. 17 under s. 1 of the *Charter*. Before the court, it argued rather that, if properly construed, s. 17 would not even infringe the *Charter*.

. . . .

Soon after the *Charter* came into force, Lamer J. pointed out in *Re B.C. Motor Vehicle Act*, that courts have not only the power but the duty to evaluate the substantive content of legislation for *Charter* compliance. In the realm of criminal law, the courts routinely review the definition of criminal offences to ensure conformity with *Charter* rights. This has included the *mens rea* element of an offence: *e.g.*, *R. v. Vaillancourt* and *R. v. Wholesale Travel Group*. These powers and responsibilities extend equally to statutory defences. courts would be abdicating their constitutional duty by abstaining from such a review. Defences and excuses belong to the legislative corpus that the *Charter* submits to constitutional review by the courts.

. . . .

[S]tatutory defences do not warrant more deference simply because they are the product of difficult moral judgments. The entire body of criminal law expresses a myriad of policy choices. Statutory offences are every bit as concerned with social values as statutory defences.

. . . .

B. Is it a Principle of Fundamental Justice That Only Morally Voluntary Conduct Can Attract Criminal Liability?

. . . .

The notion of moral voluntariness was first introduced in *Perka v. The Queen*, for the purpose of explaining the defence of necessity and classifying it as an excuse. It was borrowed from the American legal theorist George Fletcher's discussion of excuses in *Rethinking Criminal Law* (1978). A person acts in a morally involuntary fashion when, faced with perilous circumstances, she is deprived of a realistic choice whether to break the law. By way of illustration in *Perka*, Dickson J. evoked the situation of a lost alpinist who, on the point of freezing to death, breaks into a remote mountain cabin. The alpinist confronts a painful dilemma: freeze to death or commit a criminal offence. Yet as Dickson J. pointed out, the alpinist's choice to break the law "is no true choice at all; it is remorselessly compelled by normal human instincts", here of self-preservation. The court in *Perka* thus conceptualized the defence of necessity as an excuse. An excuse, Dickson J. maintained, concedes that the act was wrongful, but withholds criminal attribution to the actor because of the dire circumstances surrounding its commission.

Extending its reasoning in *Perka* to the defence of duress, the court found in *R. v. Hibbert* that it too rests on the notion of moral voluntariness. In the case of the defences of necessity and duress, the accused contends that he should avoid conviction because he acted in response to a threat of impending harm. The court also confirmed in *Hibbert* that duress does not ordinarily negate the *mens rea* element of an offence. Like the defence of necessity, the court classified the defence of duress as an excuse, like that of necessity. As such, duress operates to relieve a person of criminal liability only after he has been found to have committed the prohibited act with the relevant *mens rea*. Thus duress, like necessity, involves the concern that morally involuntary conduct not be subject to criminal liability. Can this notion of "moral voluntariness" be recognized as a principle of fundamental justice under s. 7 of the *Charter*? Let us examine possible avenues which have been put forward by the respondent towards such recognition.

1. Moral Voluntariness and Moral Blameworthiness

As we will see below, this court has recognized on a number of occasions that "moral blameworthiness" is an essential component of criminal liability which is protected under s. 7 as a "principle of fundamental justice". The respondent in the case at bar attempts to link the principles of "moral blameworthiness" and "moral voluntariness" as a means of securing the constitutional status of the defence of duress. Laskin J.A. in the court below has followed this line of reasoning. However, the appellant argues that "moral blamelessness" only arises in the absence of either the *actus reus* or the *mens rea* of an offence. One who acts under duress, he contends, remains a morally responsible agent whose behaviour is not blame-free. Further, the appellant submits that moral involuntariness is too vague and amorphous a concept to constitute a principle of fundamental justice. This controversy about the concepts of moral blamelessness and moral involuntariness brings us back to the foundations of criminal responsibility. In the analysis of duress and of its relationship with the tenets of the criminal justice system, is it appropriate to equate moral blamelessness with moral involuntariness?

. . . .

It should be emphasized that this court, in cases like *Sault Ste. Marie* and *Re B.C. Motor Vehicle Act*, has referred to moral innocence in the context of the discussion of the mental element of an offence. *Hibbert*, on the other hand, held that the defence of duress does not normally negate *mens rea*. Rather, it operates to excuse a wrongful act once the *actus reus* and *mens rea* components of the offence have been made out. Laskin J.A. conceded this point, but countered that moral blameworthiness is a broader concept, extending beyond the traditional elements of an offence. Both Laskin J.A. and the respondent rely heavily, in this respect, on Professor Martha Shaffer's article "Scrutinizing Duress: The Constitutional Validity of Section 17 of the *Criminal Code*" (1998), 40 C.L.Q. 444, in making this argument.

Professor Shaffer acknowledges in her article that moral blameworthiness is an ambiguous concept, the meaning of which this court has not had occasion to discuss in any significant way. I am reluctant to do so here, particularly since, in my opinion, conduct that is morally involuntary is not always intrinsically free of blame. Moral involuntariness is also related to the notion that the defence of duress is an excuse. Dickson J. maintained in *Perka* that an excuse acknowledges the wrongfulness of the accused's conduct. Nevertheless, the law refuses to attach penal consequences to it because an "excuse" has been made out. In using the expression "moral involuntariness", we mean that the accused had no "real" choice but to commit the offence. This recognizes that there was indeed an alternative to breaking the law, although in the case of duress that choice may be even more unpalatable — to be killed or physically harmed.

Let us consider again the situation of the lost alpinist: can we really say he is blameless for breaking into somebody else's cabin? The State refrains from punishing him not because his actions were innocent, but because the circumstances did not leave him with any other realistic choice than to commit the offence. As Fletcher puts it, excuses absolve the accused of personal accountability by focussing, not on the wrongful act, but on the circumstances of the act and the accused's personal capacity to avoid it. Necessity and duress are characterized as concessions to human frailty in this sense. The law is designed for the common man, not for a community of saints or heroes.

To equate moral involuntariness with moral innocence would amount to a significant departure from the reasoning in *Perka* and *Hibbert*. It would be contrary to the court's conceptualization of duress as an excuse. Morally involuntary conduct is not always inherently blameless. Once the elements of the offence have been established, the accused can no longer be considered blameless. This court has never taken the concept of blamelessness any further than this initial finding of guilt, nor should it in this case. The undefinable and potentially far-reaching nature of the concept of moral blamelessness prevents us from recognizing its relevance beyond an initial finding of guilt in the context of s. 7 of the *Charter*. Holding otherwise would inject an unacceptable degree of uncertainty into the law. It would not be consistent with our duty to consider as "principles of fundamental justice" only those concepts which are constrained and capable of being defined with reasonable precision. I would therefore reject this basis for finding that it is a principle of fundamental justice that morally involuntary acts should not be punished.

2. Moral Voluntariness and Voluntariness in the Physical Sense

The respondent's second approach, which relates moral voluntariness back to voluntariness in the physical sense, rests on firmer ground. It draws upon the fundamental principle of criminal law that, in order to attract criminal liability, an act must be voluntary. Voluntariness in this sense has ordinarily referred to the *actus reus* element of an offence. It queries whether the actor had control over the movement of her body or whether the wrongful act was the product of a conscious will. Although duress does not negate ordinarily *actus reus per se* (just as it does not ordinarily negate *mens rea* as we have just seen), the principle of voluntariness, unlike that of "moral blamelessness", can remain relevant in the context of s. 7 even after the basic elements of the offence have been established. Unlike the concept of "moral blamelessness", duress in its "voluntariness" perspective can more easily be constrained and can therefore more justifiably fall within the "principles of fundamental justice", even after the basic elements of the offence have been established.

Let us examine the notion of "voluntariness" and its interplay with duress more closely. As Dickson J. stated in *Rabey v. The Queen*, "it is a basic principle that absence of volition in respect of the act involved is always a defence to a crime. A defence that the act is involuntary entitles the accused to a complete and unqualified acquittal." Dickson J.'s pronouncement was endorsed by the court in *R. v. Parks*. The principle of voluntariness was given constitutional status in *Daviault*, where Cory J. held for the majority that it would infringe s. 7 of the *Charter* to convict an accused who was not acting voluntarily, as a fundamental aspect of the *actus reus* would be absent. More recently, in *R. v. Stone*, [1999] 2 S.C.R. 290, the crucial role of voluntariness as a condition of the attribution of criminal liability was again confirmed in an appeal concerning the defence of automatism.

In introducing the concept of moral voluntariness in *Perka*, the court specifically linked it to the more familiar notion of physical voluntariness discussed above. Dickson J. acknowledged that the two concepts are not identical. The lost alpinist, for instance, does not act in a literally involuntary fashion; he is physically capable of avoiding the criminal act. Fletcher puts forth another example, more pertinent to the defence of duress. Suppose someone puts a knife in the accused's hand and forces it into the victim's chest. The accused's body is literally overpowered, as is her will. Consider next the situation of someone who gives the accused a knife and orders her to stab the victim or else be killed herself. Unlike the first scenario, moral voluntariness is not a matter of physical dimension. The accused here retains conscious control over her bodily movements. Yet, like the first actor, her will is overborne, this time by the threats of another. Her conduct is not, in a realistic way, freely chosen.

What underpins both of these conceptions of voluntariness is the critical importance of autonomy in the attribution of criminal liability. The treatment of criminal offenders as rational, autonomous and choosing agents is a fundamental organizing principle of our criminal law. Its importance is reflected not only in the requirement that an act must be voluntary, but also in the condition that a wrongful act must be intentional to ground a conviction. *Sault Ste. Marie, Re B.C. Motor Vehicle Act*, and *Vaillancourt* all stand for the proposition that a guilty verdict requires intentional conduct or conduct equated to it like recklessness or gross negligence. Like voluntariness, the requirement of a guilty mind is rooted in respect for individual autonomy and free will and acknowledges the importance of those values to a free and democratic society: *Martineau*. Criminal liability also depends on the capacity to choose — the ability to reason right from wrong. As McLachlin J. observed in *Chaulk* in the context of the insanity provisions of the *Criminal Code*, this assumption of the rationality and autonomy of human beings forms part of the essential premises of Canadian criminal law.

Punishing a person whose actions are involuntary in the physical sense is unjust because it conflicts with the assumption in criminal law that individuals are autonomous and freely choosing agents: see Shaffer, *supra*, at pp. 449-50.

It is similarly unjust to penalize an individual who acted in a morally involuntary fashion. This is so because his acts cannot realistically be attributed to him, as his will was constrained by some external force. . . .

Although moral involuntariness does not negate the *actus reus* or *mens rea* of an offence, it is a principle which, similarly to physical involuntariness, deserves protection under s. 7 of the *Charter*. It is a principle of fundamental justice that only voluntary conduct — behaviour that is the product of a free will and controlled body, unhindered by external constraints — should attract the penalty and stigma of criminal liability. Depriving a person of liberty and branding her with the stigma of criminal liability would infringe the principles of fundamental justice if the accused did not have any realistic choice. The ensuing deprivation of liberty and stigma would have been imposed in violation of the tenets of fundamental justice and would thus infringe s. 7 of the *Charter*.

B. Do the Immediacy and Presence Requirements in Section 17 Infringe the Principle of Involuntariness in the Attribution of Criminal Responsibility?

. . . .

The appellant argues that the immediacy and presence requirements do not dictate that the threatener be physically present at the scene of the crime. Rather, they require a temporal connection between the commission of the offence and the threatener's presence, in the sense that the threatener must be able to execute the threat immediately should the accused fail to comply. The respondent replies that the appellant's proposed interpretation would stretch the language of s. 17 beyond recognition. As counsel for one of the interveners put it during the hearing of this appeal, it would amount to construing presence as absence and immediate as sometime later.

The plain meaning of s. 17 is quite restrictive in scope. Indeed, the section seems tailor-made for the situation in which a person is compelled to commit an offence at gun point. The phrase "present when the offence is committed", coupled with the immediacy criterion, indicates that the person issuing the threat must be either at the scene of the crime or at whatever other location is necessary to make good on the threat without delay should the accused resist. Practically speaking, a threat of harm will seldom qualify as immediate if the threatener is not physically present at the scene of the crime.

The court has in the past construed s. 17 in a narrow fashion. *R. v. Carker* and *Paquette v. The Queen*, are the two leading cases on the interpretation of s. 17. . . .

. . . .

I agree with the respondent that a threat will seldom meet the immediacy criterion if the threatener is not physically present at or near the scene of the offence. The immediacy and presence requirements, taken together, clearly preclude threats of future harm.

Neither the words of s. 17 nor the court's reasons in *Carker* and *Paquette* dictate that the target of the threatened harm must be the accused. They simply require that the threat must be made to the accused. Section 17 may thus include threats against third parties. However, the language of s. 17 does not appear capable of supporting a more flexible interpretation of the immediacy and presence requirements. Even if the threatened person, for example, is a family member, and not the accused person, the threatener or his accomplice must be at or near the scene of the crime in order to effect the harm immediately if the accused resists. Thus, while s. 17 may capture threats against third parties, the immediacy and presence criteria continue to impose considerable obstacles to relying on the defence in hostage or other third party situations.

Thus, by the strictness of its conditions, s. 17 breaches s. 7 of the *Charter* because it allows individuals who acted involuntarily to be declared criminally liable. Having said that, it will be interesting to see how the common law addresses the problem of duress, especially with respect to the immediacy component. In that regard, we will have the opportunity to see how the common law on duress in Canada, Great Britain, Australia, and even in some U.S. jurisdictions is often more liberal than what s. 17 provides and takes better account of the principle of voluntariness. This will confirm the view that s. 17 is overly restrictive and therefore breaches s. 7 of the *Charter*. We recall that the principles of fundamental justice may be distilled from the "legal principles which have historically been reflected in the law of this and other similar states" (*Seaboyer*). Examining the common law of other states like Great Britain and Australia to confirm our interpretation of s. 7 will therefore be relevant. The analysis of duress in common law will also be useful as it will shed some light on the appropriate rules which had to be applied to the defence of the accused in the case at bar and which will now be applied in all other cases, once s. 17 of the *Criminal Code* is partially struck down.

D. The Common Law of Duress

. . . .

[The court then examined the Canadian common law of duress as illustrated in *Paquette*, *Hibbert* and *Langlois*.[2] It then reviewed the English common law of

---

2 Editors' note: In *R. v. Langlois* (1993), 19 C.R. (4th) 87, 80 C.C.C. (3d) 28 (Que. C.A.) the trial judge, in opening the common law defence in this case, directed the jury that duress involved three essential requirements. First, there had to be either explicit or implicit threats of death or serious injury.
Second, the threats had to be "immediate": respondent had no right to yield to threats if he had an obvious safe avenue of escape. He had a duty to try by all possible means to avoid committing the crime, to escape.

. . . .

As to the third element, the judge directed the jury that a person subjected to threats was expected to show

duress which was seen as generally similar to its Canadian counterpart. The court found that in the Australian common law of duress there were some differences from state to state but that overall, the state courts appear to have followed quite closely the English courts' approach. Examining the American common law of duress, LeBel J. concluded that while in some states the defence is subject to quite strict constraints, several American cases have displayed a flexible view of the temporal criterion in the context of duress. While the common law was not unanimous in the United States, a substantial consensus had thus grown in Canada, England and Australia to the effect that the strict criterion of immediacy is no longer a generally accepted component of the defence.]

E. The Breach of Section 7 of the *Charter*: Conclusion in the Case at Bar

At the heart of Laskin J.A.'s decision is a concern that the immediacy and presence requirements are poor substitutes for the safe avenue of escape test at common law. In his view, their focus on an instantaneous connection between the threat and the commission of the offence misses the point in a number of special cases. He highlights two situations in particular. The first is the battered woman who is coerced by her abusive partner to break the law. Even though her partner is not present when she commits the offence and is therefore unable to execute it immediately, a battered woman may believe nonetheless that she has no safe avenue of escape. Her behaviour is morally involuntary, yet the immediacy and presence criteria, strictly construed, would preclude her from resorting to s. 17. There may also be other situations in which a person is so psychologically traumatized by the threatener that he complies with the threat, even though it was not immediate and to the objective observer, there was a legal way out. The second scenario described by Laskin J.A. is the case of a person like Ms. Ruzic, for whom effective police protection was unavailable. Do the immediacy and presence requirements demand that a person go to the authorities if he has the opportunity to do so, even when he believes it would be useless or even dangerous to do so? It should be noted that in this second scenario, a court might face a delicate task in assessing the validity of a claim that, in a foreign land, no police protection was available. It illustrates some of the difficulties in the practical implementation of a defence of duress which involves a risk of abuse through unverifiable assertions of danger and harm.

Nevertheless, s. 17's reliance on proximity as opposed to reasonable options as the measure of moral choice is problematic. It would be contrary to the principles of fundamental justice to punish an accused who is psychologically

---

reasonable courage:

> . . . la Loi ne protège pas une personne qui commet des infractions criminelles sous l'effet de menaces si cette personne n'est pas normalement et raisonnablement courageuse dans les circonstances particulières de sa situation.

The jury was then told that society expects a higher standard or additional degree of courage from someone who has chosen a calling that normally requires courage, such as a police officer. Penitentiary employees were also expected to show "the kind of courage one does not demand of an accountant or schoolteacher".

tortured to the point of seeing no reasonable alternative, or who cannot rely on the authorities for assistance. That individual is not behaving as an autonomous agent acting out of his own free will when he commits an offence under duress.

The appellant's attempts at reading down s. 17, in order to save it, would amount to amending it to bring it in line with the common law rules. This interpretation badly strains the text of the provision and may become one more argument against upholding its validity. The underinclusiveness of s. 17 infringes s. 7 of the *Charter*, because the immediacy and presence requirements exclude threats of future harm to the accused or to third parties. It risks jeopardizing the liberty and security interests protected by the *Charter*, in violation of the basic principles of fundamental justice. It has the potential of convicting persons who have not acted voluntarily.

F. Can the Infringement Be Justified Under Section 1?

Having found that the immediacy and presence requirements infringe s. 7 of the *Charter*, I turn now to consider whether the violation is a demonstrably justifiable limit under s. 1. The government, of course, bears the burden of justifying a *Charter* infringement. Consistent with its strategy in the courts below, the appellant made no attempt before this court to justify the immediacy and presence criteria according to the s. 1 analysis. I therefore conclude at the outset that the appellant has failed to satisfy its onus under s. 1.

Moreover, it is well established that violations of s. 7 are not easily saved by s. 1. Indeed, the court has indicated that exceptional circumstances, such as the outbreak of war or a national emergency, are necessary before such an infringement may be justified: *R. v. Heywood, Re B.C. Motor Vehicle Act*. No such extraordinary conditions exist in this case. Furthermore, I am inclined to agree with Laskin J.A. that the immediacy and presence criteria would not meet the proportionality branch of the s. 1 analysis. In particular, it seems to me these requirements do not minimally impair the respondent's s. 7 rights. Given the appellant's failure to make any submissions on the issue, the higher standard of justification for a violation of s. 7, and my doubts concerning proportionality, I conclude that the immediacy and presence conditions cannot be saved by s. 1.

. . . .

H. The Jury Charge

. . . .

Viewed in its entirety, the trial judge's charge explained adequately the elements of the defence of duress at common law to the members of the jury.

The charge contained all the elements required by the common law rules on duress. The criterion of the safe avenue of escape was well explained as was the objective component of this test. Notwithstanding the argument of the appellant, the law does not require an accused to seek the official protection of police in all cases. The requirement of objectivity must itself take into consideration the special circumstances where the accused found herself as well as her perception of them. Herold J. drew the attention of the jury both to that objective component and to the subjective elements of the defence. This argument must thus fail.

As to the immediacy of the threat, as Laskin J.A.'s reasons point out, Herold J. brought home to the jury the fact that the threat had to be a real threat affecting the accused at the time of the offence. This instruction at least implied that the jury had to consider the temporal connection between the threat and the harm threatened, although it would have been preferable to say so in so many express words.

There was no misdirection either on the burden of proof. The accused must certainly raise the defence and introduce some evidence about it. Once this is done, the burden of proof shifts to the Crown under the general rule of criminal evidence. It must be shown, beyond a reasonable doubt, that the accused did not act under duress. . . .

Disposition

The appellant's submissions cannot be accepted. The immediacy and presence requirements of s. 17 of the *Criminal Code* infringe s. 7 of the *Charter*. As the infringement has not been justified under s. 1, the requirements of immediacy and presence must be struck down as unconstitutional. The Court of Appeal and the trial judge were right in allowing the common law defence of duress go to the jury, and the trial judge adequately instructed the jury on the defence.

Is *Ruzic* consistent with *Stone*? Is *Ruzic* consistent with *Latimer*?

Does turning "moral involuntariness" into a principle of fundamental justice itself provide a broader defence than the court really intends? The defence of provocation, for example, (discussed below) requires that a reasonable person would have lost self-control in the circumstances. Would that amount to morally involuntary behaviour on the definition in *Ruzic*? If so, *Ruzic* seems to mean that provocation should be a complete defence, and applicable to any crime, rather than (as it is now) a partial defence applicable only to murder. See Steve Coughlan, "Duress, Necessity, Self-Defence and Provocation: Implications of Radical Change?" (2002) 7 Can. Crim. L.R. 147.

For critical comments on *Ruzic*, see Stanley Yeo, "Defining Duress" (2002) 45 Crim. L.Q. 293 and Ben Berger "Emotions and the Veil of Voluntarism: The Loss of Judgment in Canadian Criminal Defences" (2006) 51 McGill L.J. 99. In the years that have passed since *Ruzic* the new *Charter* standard of moral involuntariness has surprisingly yet to be applied in contexts other than duress. For an argument that *Ruzic* should inform the development of a substantive defence of entrapment see Paul M. Hughes, "Temptation and Culpability in the Law of Duress and Entrapment" (2006) 51 Crim. L.Q. 342.

In *Ruzic* the Supreme Court expressly left open the constitutionality of excluding the defence of duress in the case of the listed offences. **Do you think that a section 7 *Charter* challenge could succeed on the basis of the moral involuntariness standard or that of arbitrariness?**

In *R. v. Fraser* (2002), 3 C.R. (6th) 308 (N.S. Prov. Ct.), the court held that the exclusion of robbery from the s. 17 duress defence might result in the conviction of the morally involuntary. The exclusion of robbery was struck down. At trial both accused relied on the common law defence of duress. The court found the defence made out in the case of one of the accused who was therefore acquitted.

Justice Heeney in *R. v. Sandham* (2009), 70 C.R. (6th) 203 (Ont. S.C.J.) refused to strike down the exemption for murder on the basis that the argument was moot in that the common law did not allow the defence of duress for a murder perpetrator. Steve Coughlan, CR annotation, supports the exclusion of duress as a defence to murder and aiding murder. Professor Payan Akhavan "Should Duress Apply to All Crimes? A Comparative Appraisal of Moral Involuntariness and the Twenty Crimes Exception Under Section 17 of the Criminal Code" (2009) 13 *Can. Crim. L. Rev.* 271, however, argues that all of Canada's 20 crime exceptions are out of step with modern trends in other countries and should be struck down under *Ruzic* and the common law changed.

In *R. v. Li* (2002), 162 C.C.C. (3d) 360, 3 C.R. (6th) 173 (Ont. C.A.) the court held that the common law duress defence does not apply to individuals who voluntarily join a criminal organization.

Professor Martha Shaffer has persuasively argued that a revised law of duress must be broad to deal fairly with the experiences of battered women coerced into crime: see "Coerced into Crime: Battered Women and the Defence of Duress" (1999), 4 Can. Crim. L. Rev. 272 and "Scrutinizing Duress: The Constitutional Validity of Section 17 of the *Criminal Code*" (1998), 34 Crim. L.Q. 444.

The Law Reform Commission of Canada's Draft *Criminal Code* of 1986, s. 3(8) would codify the defence of duress as follows:

No one is liable for committing a crime in reasonable response to threats of immediate serious harm to himself or another person unless he himself purposely causes the death of, or seriously harms, another person.

Would this reform be wise? Consider whether the defence of duress would succeed under the present law and under that proposed by the Commission in the following situations:

1. The accused is charged with impaired driving. She admits that she was very drunk when she drove, but her defence is that she was compelled to do so to escape a sure beating at the hands of her enraged husband. She had been celebrating with fellow workers and her husband had discovered her with another male when he had gone to look for her four hours after he had expected her to return. In a state of rage he had smashed the window of the car in which she was seated and had also rammed the car when she drove off.

Compare *R. v. Smith* (1977), 40 C.R.N.S. 390 (B.C. Prov. Ct.).

2. The accused is charged with kidnapping contrary to s. 247(I)(*c*) of the *Criminal Code*. At the instigation of her husband she had lured a 20 year-old woman, whom she had previously known, into her husband's automobile on the pretext that she was going to a fashion show. The husband then grabbed the victim and tied her up while the accused drove her to a place where they were going to hold her. A ransom demand was made of the victim's father but the ransom was not paid and eventually the victim was released. Two weeks after the kidnapping and the failed extortion attempt, the accused confessed her participation to the police. Her defence was that she had acted entirely out of fear of her husband, who had previously assaulted her and had warned her that, if she did not do what he said, she would never see her daughter again, as the daughter would be kidnapped and taken to the United States.

Compare *R. v. Robins* (1982), 66 C.C.C. (2d) 550 (Que. C.A.).

3. The accused, Drazen Erdemovic, was indicted on May 29, 1996 before the Trial Chamber of the International Tribunal for the Prosecution of Persons Responsible for Serious Violations of International Humanitarian Law committed in the Territory of the former Yugoslavia since 1991. The case against Erdemovic was based on his own evidence. He had come forward to unburden himself and accept punishment. Erdemovic had been a member of a Sabotage Unit of the Serbian Army. On July 16, 1995, the Unit was ordered to a farm where they were told they would act as a firing squad to kill Muslims. Busloads of over 1000 Bosnian Muslim men and boys arrived and were executed that day. Erdemovic personally shot about 70 people. The accused pleaded guilty to a count of a crime against humanity but offered an explanation:

> Your Honour, I had to do this, they told me; "If you are sorry for them, stand up, line up with them and we will kill you too". I am not sorry for myself but for my family, my wife and son. . . and I could not refuse because they would have killed me. That is all I wish to add.

The Trial Chamber accepted his plea of guilt and sentenced him to 10 years: see *The Prosecutor v. Drazen Erdemovic*, Case No. IT-96-22-T, T.Ch.I, 29 Nov. 1996. Later the issue before the Appeals Chamber at The Hague, Netherlands (majority judgment issued on October 7, 1997) was whether duress was a defence to such a charge. If there is to be such a defence is it material that the Muslim civilians would in any case have been killed by other soldiers?

7. PARTIAL DEFENCES TO MURDER

(a) Provocation

Under s. 232 of the *Criminal Code*, provocation as there defined is a partial defence to a murder charge in that it reduces it to a conviction of manslaughter.

R. v. HILL

(1985), [1986] 1 S.C.R. 313, 51 C.R. (3d) 97, 25 C.C.C. (3d) 322,
1986 CarswellOnt 1005, 1985 CarswellOnt 132

DICKSON C.J.C. (BEETZ, ESTEY, CHOUINARD and LA FOREST JJ. concurring): —

Gordon James Elmer Hill was charged with committing first degree murder at the city of Belleville, county of Hastings, on the person of Verne Pegg, contrary to s. 218(1) [now s. 235] of the *Criminal Code*, R.S.C. 1970, c. C-34. He was found by the jury not guilty of first degree murder but guilty of second degree murder. He was sentenced to imprisonment for life without eligiblity for parole until ten years of his sentence had been served.

Hill appealed his conviction to the Court of Appeal of Ontario [32 C.R. (3d) 88, 2 C.C.C. (3d) 394]. He raised many grounds of appeal, but the Court of Appeal called upon the Crown with respect to one ground only, relating to the charge on the issue of provocation. The ground of appeal was that the trial judge failed to instruct the jury properly as to the "ordinary person" in s. 215(2) of the *Criminal Code*. Section 215 of the *Code* reads in part:

> 215.(1) Culpable homicide that otherwise would be murder may be reduced to manslaughter if the person who committed it did so in the heat of passion caused by sudden provoction.

> (2) A wrongful act or insult that is of such a nature as to be sufficient to deprive an ordinary person of the power of self-control is provocation for the purposes of this section if the accused acted upon it on the sudden and before there was time for his passion to cool.

These two subsections, given their plain meaning, produce three sequential questions for answer by the tribunal:

1. Would an ordinary person be deprived of self-control by the act or insult?

2. Did the accused in fact act in response to those "provocative" acts; in short, was he or she provoked by them whether or not an ordinary person would have been?

3. Was the accused's response sudden and before there was time for his or her passion to cool?

At this stage it is important to recall the presence of subs. (3) of s. 215, which provides:

(3) For the purposes of this section the questions

(*a*) whether a particular wrongful act or insult amounted to provocation, and

(*b*) whether the accused was deprived of the power of self-control by the provocation that he alleges he received.

are questions of fact . . . .

In the answering of these successive questions, the first, or "ordinary person", test is clearly determined by objective standards. The second, *de facto*, test, as to the loss of self-control by the accused, is determined, like any other question of fact as revealed by the evidence, from the surrounding facts. The third test, as to whether the response was sudden and before passions cooled, is again a question of fact.

At the time of the killing, Hill was a male 16 years of age. The narrow question in this appeal is whether the trial Judge erred in law in failing to instruct the jury that if they found a wrongful act or insult they should consider whether it was sufficient to deprive an ordinary person "of the age and sex of the appellant" of his power of self-control. Was it incumbent in law on the trial judge to add that gloss to the section? That is the issue.

I. THE FACTS

At trial both parties agreed that it was the acts of Hill which caused the death of Pegg, but disagreed otherwise. The position of the Crown at trial was that Hill and Pegg were homosexual lovers and that Hill had decided to murder Pegg after a falling out between them. The Crown argued that Hill deliberately struck Pegg in the head while Pegg lay in bed. This did not kill Pegg, who immediately ran from the bedroom into the bathroom to try and stop the flow of blood from his head. Realizing that he had been unsuccessful, Hill took two knives from the kitchen and stabbed Pegg to death.

Hill's version of the events was very different. He admitted to causing the death of Pegg, but put forward two defences: self-defence and provocation. Hill testified that he had known Pegg for about a year through the latter's involvement with the "Big Brother" organization. Hill stated that on the night in question he had been the subject of unexpected and unwelcome homosexual advances by Pegg while asleep on the couch in Pegg's apartment. Pegg pursued Hill to the bathroom and grabbed him, at which time Hill picked up a nearby hatchet and swung it at Pegg in an attempt to scare him. The hatchet struck Pegg in the head. Hill then ran from the apartment but returned shortly afterward. Upon re-entering the apartment, he was confronted by Pegg, who threatened to kill him. At this point. Hill obtained two knives from the kitchen and stabbed Pegg to death.

Hill was arrested, after a car chase with the police, at the wheel of a Pontiac automobile owned by Pegg. At the scene of arrest Hill denied knowing Pegg, but later he made a statement to the police which was substantially similar to his oral testimony at trial.

II. THE CHARGE

The trial judge instructed the jury on the defence of provocation in the following terms:

> The *Criminal Code* provides that culpable homicide that would otherwise be murder shall be reduced to manslaughter if the person who committed it did so in the heat of passion caused by sudden provocation.

> Under the *Code*, a wrongful act or insult that is of such a nature as to be sufficient to deprive an ordinary person of the power of self-control is provocation, if the accused acted upon it on the sudden and before there was time for his passion to cool.

The foregoing paragraphs are simply a recital of the *Code*. The judge continued [quoted at p. 90]:

> Provocation may come from actual words or a series of each or a combination of both, and it must be looked at in the light of all the surrounding circumstances.

> First, the actual words must be such as would deprive an ordinary person of self-control. In considering this part of the defence you are not to consider the particular mental make-up of the accused; rather the standard is that of the ordinary person. You will ask yourselves: Would the words or acts in this case have caused an ordinary person to lose his self-control?

After reviewing the evidence in support of the defence of provocation, the judge continued [quoted in part at p. 90]:

> You will consider that evidence and you will decide whether the words and acts were sufficient to cause an ordinary person to lose his self-control.

> The acts were rubbing the accused's legs and chest, grabbing him by the shoulder and spinning him around, and later Pegg grabbing his right wrist before the second stab. The words were: "I am going to kill you, you little bastard."

> If you find that they were, you will then secondly consider whether the accused acted on the provocation on the sudden before there was time for his passion to cool. In deciding this question you are not restricted to the standard of the ordinary person. You will take into account the mental, the emotional, the physical characteristics and the age of the accused.

> The incidents or the words upon which the provocation is based must be contemporaneous words or closely related to the tragedy. The killing must take place immediately after the acts or words constituting the provocation or so soon thereafter that the accused's passion had not time to cool.

> You will also ask yourselves: Was the provocation such that it would have led a person
> with the mental and physical condition and the age of the accused to respond in this way?

At trial, counsel for Hill objected to the instruction of the trial judge as to the objective requirement of the defence of provocation, submitting that the "ordinary person" referred to in s. 215(2) ought to have been defined as an ordinary person of the age and sex of the accused. Counsel submitted that the objective requirement would be satisfied if the judge were to recharge the jury by defining "ordinary person" as an "ordinary person in the circumstances of the accused". The judge refused to recharge the jury in those terms.

III. THE COURT OF APPEAL

The oral reasons Brooke J.A. (Martiqcand Morden JJ.A. concurring) noted that counsel for the defence, relying on *R. v. Camplin* (1978), 67 Cr. App. R. 14 (H.L.), submitted that the judge should have instructed the jury to consider whether the wrongful act or insult was sufficient to deprive an "ordinary person" of the age and sex of the accused of his power of self-control. The Court of Appeal held that because the trial judge declined to do so he erred. In reaching this conclusion, Brooke J.A. stated [at p. 90]:

> The age and sex of the appellant are not "peculiar characteristics" excluded from consideration
> of the "ordinary person" in the objective test in s. 215(2): see Fauteux J. (as he then was) in
> *Wright v. R.*, [1969] S.C.R. 335, [1969] 3 C.C.C. 258 at 264-65, discussing *Bedder v. D.P.P.*,
> [1954] 1 W.L.R. 1119 (H.L.).

He also added [at pp. 90-91]:

> In our respectful opinion, there is nothing in that judgment which precludes charging the jury
> as the defence requested. As the matter was left to the jury, the age of the appellant was a
> consideration only if and when the jury turned to the question of whether the wrongful act or
> insult deprived him of his power of self-control. The effect of the charge was that an ordinary
> person did not include a 16-year-old youth. If this is so, the jury may have rejected the defence
> judging the objective test on that basis.

In the result, the Court of Appeal held that the judge was in error and there may well have been misdirection which seriously prejudiced *Hill* and so the conviction could not stand. The appeal was allowed, the conviction set aside and a new trial on the charge of second degree murder ordered.

IV. THE ISSUE

The issue in this appeal is whether the Ontario Court of Appeal erred in law in holding that the trial judge erred in law with respect to the elements of the objective test relevant to the defence of provocation in failing to direct the jury that the "ordinary person" within the meaning of that term in s. 215(2) of the *Criminal Code* was an "ordinary person of the same age and sex as the accused".

V. The Defence of Provocation

The defence of provocation appears to have first developed in the early 1800s. Tindal C.J. in *R. v. Hayward* (1833), 6 C. & P. 157 at 159, told the jury that the defence of provocation was derived from the law's "compassion to human infirmity". It acknowledged that all human beings are subject to uncontrollable outbursts of passion and anger which may lead them to do violent acts. In such instances, the law would lessen the severity of criminal liability.

Nevertheless, not all acts done in the heat of passion were to be subject to the doctrine of provocation. By the middle of the 19th Century, it became clear that the provoking act had to be sufficient to excite an ordinary or reasonable person under the circumstances. As Keating J. stated in *R. v. Welsh* (1869), 11 Cox C.C. 336 at 338:

> The law is, that there must exist such an amount of provocation as would be excited by the circumstances in the mind of a reasonable man, and so as to lead the jury to ascribe the act to the influence of that passion.

The *Criminal Code* codified this approach to provocation by including under s. 215 three general requirements for the defence of provocation. First, the provoking wrongful act or insult must be of such a nature that it would deprive an ordinary person of the power of self-control. That is the initial threshold which must be surmounted. Secondly, the accused must actually have been provoked. As I have earlier indicated, these two elements are often referred to as the objective and subjective test of provocation respectively. Thirdly, the accused must have acted on the provocation on the sudden and before there was time for his or her passion to cool.

(a) *The Objective Test of Provocation and the Ordinary Person Standard*

In considering the precise meaning and application of the ordinary person standard or objective test, it is important to identify its underlying rationale. Lord Simon of Glaisdale has perhaps stated it most succinctly when he suggested in *Camplin, supra*, at p. 726, that:

> ... the reason for importing into this branch of the law the concept of the reasonable man [was] ... to avoid the injustice of a man being entitled to rely on his exceptional excitablity or pugnacity or ill-temper or on his drunkenness.

If there were no objective test to the defence of provocation, anomalous results could occur. A well-tempered, reasonable person would not be entitled to benefit from the provocation defence and would be guilty of culpable homicide amounting to murder, while an ill-tempered or exceptionally excitable person would find his or her culpability mitigated by provocation and would be guilty only of manslaughter. It is society's concern that reasonable and non-violent behaviour be encouraged that prompts the law to endorse the objective standard. The criminal law is concerned, among other things, with fixing standards for human behaviour. We seek to encourage conduct that complies with certain societal standards of reasonableness and responsibility. In doing this, the law quite logically employs the objective standard of the reasonable person.

With this general purpose in mind, we must ascertain the meaning of the ordinary person standard. What are the characteristics of the "ordinary person"? To what extent should the attributes and circumstances of the accused be ascribed to the ordinary person? To answer these question, it is helpful to review the English developments, I shall begin with the English cases.

(i) English Law of Provocation and the Ordinary Person Standard

In *R. v. Lesbini*, [1914] 3 K.B. 1116, the English Court of Criminal Appeal refused to take into account the mental deficiency of the accused in assessing the availability of the provocation defence. It confirmed the threshold objective test for provocation, whereby there must be sufficient provocation to excite a reasonable person. A reasonable or ordinary person was not one with mental deficiencies. In *Mancini v. Pub. Prosecutions Dir.*, [1942] A.C. 1, the House of Lords endorsed the *Lesbini* case and further elaborated the objective test of provocation. Viscount Simon L.C. stated, at p. 9:

> The test to be applied is that of the effect of the provocation on a reasonable man, as was laid down by the Court of Criminal Appeal in *Rex v. Lesbini*, so that an unusually excitable or pugnacious individual is not entitled to rely on provocation which would not have led an ordinary person to act as he did.

The ordinary or reasonable person, therefore, was one of normal temperament and average mental capacity.

In 1954, the House of Lords was faced with the question of whether, in applying the objective test of provocation, it should take into account certain physical characteristics of the accused. In *Bedder v. D.P.P.*, [1954] 1 W.L.R. 1119, a sexually impotent man killed a prostitute after she taunted him about his physical condition. The House of Lords had to determine whether, in applying the objective test of provocation, the sexual impotence of the accused should be taken into account. The test would then have been whether an ordinary person who was sexually impotent would have been provoked. The court rejected this approach and held that the peculiar physical characteristics of the accused were not to be ascribed to the ordinary person for the purposes of the objective test.

Despite the House of Lords' conclusion that the physical characteristics of the accused were irrelevant to the determination of whether a reasonable person would have been provoked, it appears that the court was primarily concerned with the difficulty of distinguishing "temperament" from "physical defects". As Lord Simonds L.C. stated, at p. 1121:

> It appears to that court, as it appears to me, that "no distinction is to be made in the case of a person who, though it may not be a matter of termperament, is physically impotent, is conscious of that impotence, and therefore mentally liable to be more excited unduly if he is 'twitted' or attacked on the subject of that particular infirmity". The court thereupon approved and reiterated the proposition that the question for the jury was whether on the facts . . . from the evidence the provocation was in fact enough to lead a reasonable person to do what the accused did.

The *Bedder* approach to the ordinary person standard is no longer the law in England. In *Camplin, supra,* the House of Lords expressly rejected the narrow objective test articulated in *Bedder*. The *Camplin* case involved a youth of 15 years of age who maintained that he had been provoked by a homosexual assault. The House of Lords unanimously concluded that the ordinary person, for the purposes of the objective test of provocation, was to be an ordinary person of the same age and sex as the accused. It should be noted that in *Camplin* the trial judge had specifically directed the jury to take age and sex into account and the appeal sought to establish that this was wrong. In the present case, there was no such instruction.

In justifying its shift away from the *Bedder* approach, the House of Lords relied in part on legislative changes in the law of provocation introduced after the *Bedder* opinion. Specifically, in 1957, s. 3 of the *Homicide Act, 1957* (5 & 6 Eliz. 2, c. 11), was passed; it provides:

> 3. Where on a charge of murder there is evidence on which the jury can find that the person charged was provoked (whether by things done or by things said or by both together) to lose his self-control, the question whether the provocation was enough to make a reasonable man do as he did shall be left to be determined by the jury: and in determining that question the jury shall take into account everything both done and said according to the effect which, in their opinion, it would have on a reasonable man.

The phrase "the jury shall take into account everything" was interpreted to allow a consideration of relevant characteristics in connection with the objective test.

Lord Diplock clarified the underlying rationale for expanding the notion of the ordinary person when he wrote, at p. 717:

> To taunt a person because of his race, his physical infirmities or some shameful incident in his past may well be considered by the jury to be more offensive to the person addressed, however equable his temperament, if the facts on which the taunt is founded are true than it would be if they were not.

On a similar note, Lord Morris of Borth-y-Gest held, at p. 721:

> If the accused is of particular colour or particular ethnic origin and things are said which to him are grossly insulting it would be utterly unreal if the jury had to consider whether the words would have provoked a man of a different colour or ethnic origin — or to consider how such a man would have acted or reacted.

Taking these considerations into account, Lord Simon of Glaisdale formulated the objective test as follows, at p. 727:

> I think that the standard of self-control which the law requires before provocation is held to reduce murder to manslaughter is still that of the reasonable person ... but that, in determining whether a person of reasonable self-control would lose it in the circumstances, the entire factual situation, which includes the characteristics of the accused, must be considered.

One conceptual difficulty was acknowledged by Lord Diplock. He recognized at p. 717 that:

> ... in strict logic there is a transition between treating age as a characteristic that may be taken into account in assessing the gravity of the provocation addressed to the accused and treating it as a characteristic to be taken into account in determining what is the degree of self-control to be expected of the ordinary person.

In most cases, it is appropriate to assume that the level of self-control or degree of reasonableness is the same regardless of certain physical differences. Age, however, in Lord Diplock's view posed a more difficult problem. He resolved this problem with respect to age by appealing to the acknowledged importance of the law's compassion to human infirmity. On a more general level, he rejected the solution of separating out the inquiry into two phases as overly complicated for the jury.

(ii) Canadian Case Law

The Supreme Court of Canada has also had occasion to provide guidance on the ordinary person standard for provocation. In *Taylor v. R.*, [1947] S.C.R. 462, 3 C.R. 475, 89 C.C.C. 209 [Ont.], a case in which the accused was drunk at the time of his alleged provocation, Kerwin J. at p. 471 made clear that for the purposes of the objective test of provocation the "criterion is the effect on the ordinary person ... the jury is not entitled to take into consideration any alleged drunkenness on the part of the accused".

This court again rejected a consideration of the drunkenness of the accused in connection with the objective test in *Salamon v. R.*, [1959] S.C.R. 404, 30 C.R. 1, 123 C.C.C. 1 [Ont.]. Fauteux endorsed the trial judge's instruction to the jury [quoted at p. 410] not to consider "the character, background, temperament, or condition of the accused" in relation to the objective test of provocation. Similarly, Cartwright J. (dissenting on another issue) wrote, at p. 415, that the trial judge correctly "made it plain that on this [objective] branch of the inquiry no account should be taken of the idiosyncrasies of the appellant and that the standard was that of an ordinary person".

Finally, in *Wright v. R.*, [1969] S.C.R. 335, [1969] 3 C.C.C. 258 [Sask.], a son was charged with the shooting death of his father. The evidence suggested that there had been some difficulties in their relationship. The father was said to have been a bad-tempered and violent man who had mistreated his son on a number of occasions. The accused had not seen his father for a period of about five years until a few days prior to the fatal incident. On the evening of the shooting, the accused had spent most of the day drinking with his friends. In considering the objective test of provocation, the court rejected the relevance of the quality of the accused's relationship with his father, the mentality of the accused or his possible drunkenness. Fauteux J. quoted, at p. 340, the words of Lord Simmonds L.C. in *Bedder, supra*, that the purpose of the objective test is:

> . . . to invite the jury to consider the act of the accused by reference to a certain standard or norm of conduct and with this object the "reasonable" or the "average" or the "normal" man is invoked.

The court went on to state, at p. 340:

> While the character, background, temperament, idiosyncrasies, or the drunkenness of the accused are matters to be considered in the second branch of the enquiry, they are excluded from consideration in the first branch. A contrary view would denude of any sense the objective test.

Appellate Courts at the provincial level have also considered the nature of the ordinary person standard of provocation. In *R. v. Clark* (1975), 22 C.C.C. (2d) 1 (Alta. C.A.), the "morbid jealousy" and "slight mental degeneration" [p. 15] suffered by the accused was held not to be relevant to the objective test. According to Clement J.A., at p. 16:

> In the first branch of the inquiry, the objective test, which in essence has to be determined as a standard of comparison is the reaction that might be expected from ordinary human nature to the wrongful act, or to the alleged insult in the present case.

In *R. v. Parnerkar* (1972), 16 C.R.N.S. 347, 5 C.C.C. (2d) 11, affirmed [1974] S.C.R. 449, 21 C.R.N.S. 129, 10 C.C.C. (2d) 253, the Saskatchewan Court of Appeal held that the cultural and religious background of the accused was not relevant to the determination of the objective test. The accused, born in India, was alleged to have been provoked by, *inter alia*, the deceased's statement: "I am not going to marry you because you are a black man." The court's ruling seems to narrow unduly the conception of the ordinary person and rigidly prohibit a consideration of the physical characteristics of the accused along the lines of the *Bedder* case. I should note that *Parnerkar* was affirmed by this court on appeal; however, this particular question was not addressed.

In more recent decisions, appellate courts at the provincial level appear to be moving towards the *Camplin*, *supra*, approach. The Ontario Court of Appeal's decision in the present appeal, and *Daniels v. R.* (1983), 7 C.C.C. (3d) 542 (C.A.), reflect this trend. In *Daniels* case, Laycraft J.A. held that in instructing the jury on the objective test of provocation the trial judge should tell the jury to take into account all of the external events putting pressure on the accused. He stated at p. 554:

> The purpose of the objective test prescribed by s. 215 is to consider the actions of the accused in a specific case against the standard of the ordinary person. Hypothetically, the ordinary person is subjected to the same external pressures of insult by acts or words as was the accused. Only if those pressures would cause an ordinary person to lose self-control does the next question arise whether the accused did, in fact, lose self-control. In my view, the objective test lacks validity if the reaction of the hypothetical ordinary person is not tested against all of the events which put pressure on the accused.

(iii) The Appropriate Content of the Ordinary Person Standard

What lessons are to be drawn from this review of the case law? I think it is clear that there is widespread agreement that the ordinary or reasonable person has a normal temperament and level of self-control. It follows that the ordinary person is not exceptionally excitable, pugnacious or in a state of drunkenness.

In terms of other characteristics of the ordinary person, it seems to me that the "collective good sense" of the jury will naturally lead it to ascribe to the ordinary person any general characteristics relevant to the provocation in question. For example, if the provocation is a racial slur, the jury will think of an ordinary person with the racial background that forms the substance of the insult. To this extent, particular characteristics will be ascribed to the ordinary person. Indeed, it would be impossible to conceptualize a sexless or ageless ordinary person. Features such as sex, age, or race do not detract for a person's characterization as ordinary. Thus particular characteristics that are not peculiar or idiosyncratic can be ascribed to an ordinary person without subverting the logic of the objective test of provocation. As Lord Diplock wrote in *Camplin*, *supra*, at pp. 716-17:

> . . . the "reasonable man" man has never been confined to the adult male. It means an ordinary person of either sex, not exceptionally excitable or pugnacious, but possessed of such powers of self-control as everyone is entitled to expect that his fellow citizens will exercise in society as it is today.

It is important to note that in some instances certain characteristics will be irrelevant. For example, the race of a person will be irrevelant if the provocation involves an insult regarding a physical disability. Similarly, the sex of an accused will be irrelevant if the provocation relates to a racial insult. Thus the central criterion is the relevance of the particular feature to the provocation in question. With this in mind, I think it is fair to conclude that age will be a relevant consideration when we are dealing with a young accused person. For a jury to assess what an ordinary person would have done if subjected to the same circumstances as the accused, the young age of an accused will be an important contextual consideration.

I should also add that my conclusion that certain attributes can be ascribed to the ordinary person is not meant to suggest that a trial judge must in each case tell the jury what specific attributes it is to ascribe to the ordinary person. The point I wish to emphasize is simply that, in applying their common sense to the factual determination of the objective test, jury members will quite naturally and properly ascribe certain characteristics to the "ordinary person".

(b) *The Subjective Test and Actual Provocation*

Once a jury has established that the provocation in question was sufficient to deprive an ordinary person of the power of self-control, it must still determine whether the accused was so deprived. It may well be that an ordinary person would have been provoked but in fact the accused was not. This second test of provocation is called "subjective" because it involves an assessment of what actually occurred in the mind of the accused. At this stage, the jury must also consider whether the accused reacted to the provocation on the sudden and before there was time for his passion to cool.

In instructing the jury with the respect to the subjective test of provocation, the trial judge must make clear to the jury that its task at this point is to ascertain whether the accused was *in fact* acting as a result of provocation. In this regard, a trial judge may wish to remind the jury members that, in determining whether an accused was actually provoked, they are entitled to take into account his or her mental state and psychological temperament.

VI. THE VALIDITY OF THE JUDGE'S CHARGE

To apply this statement of the law to the present appeal, we must return to the actual words of the trial judge. When instructing the jury on the objective test of provocation, he began by stating [quoted at p. 90]:

> First, the actual words must be such as would deprive an ordinary person of self-control. In considering this part of the defence you are not to consider the particular mental make-up of the accused: rather the standard is that of the ordinary person. You will ask yourselves: Would the words or acts in this case have caused an ordinary person to lose his self-control?

He later added:

> You will consider that evidence and you will decide whether the words and acts were sufficient to cause an ordinary person to lose his self-control.

In my view, this part of the charge was well-stated and correct in law. The trial judge did not err in failing to specify that the ordinary person, for the purpose of the objective test of provocation, is to be deemed to be of the same age and sex as the accused. Although this type of instruction may be helpful in clarifying the application of the ordinary person standard. I do not think it wise or necessary to make this a mandatory component of all jury charges or provocation. Whenever possible, we should retain simplicity in charges to the jury and have confidence that the words of the *Criminal Code* will provide sufficient guidance to the jury. Indeed, in this area of the law I take heed of the words of Lord Goddard C.J. in *R. v. McCarthy*, [1954] 2 Q.B. 105 at 112:

> No court has ever given, nor do we think ever can give, a definition of what constitutes a reasonable or average man. That must be left to the collective good sense of the jury . . . .

It has been suggested that the instruction of the trial judge on the subjective prong of the provocation defence had the effect of misleading the jury on the appropriate content of the ordinary person standard. The charge stated [quoted in part at p. 90]:

> . . . you will then secondly consider whether the accused acted on the provocation on the sudden before there was time for his passion to cool. In deciding this question you are not restricted to the standard of the ordinary person. You will take into account the mental, the emotional, the physical characteristics and the age of this accused . . . .

In my opinion, these words would not have misled the average juror with respect to the objective test, particularly when viewed in the context of the charge as a whole.

I have the greatest of confidence in the level of intelligence and plain common sense of the average Canadian jury sitting on a criminal case. Juries are perfectly capable of sizing the matter up. In my experience as a trial judge I cannot recall a single instance in which a jury returned to the courtroom to ask for further instructions on the provocation portion of a murder charge. A jury frequently seeks further guidance on the distinction between first degree murder, second degree murder and manslaughter, but rarely, if ever, on provocation. It sems to be common ground that the trial judge would not have been in error if he had simply read s. 215 of the *Code* and left it at that, without embellishment. I am loath to complicate the task of the trial judge, in cases such as the case at bar, by requiring him or her as a matter of law to point out to the members of the jury that in applying the objective test they must conceptualize an "ordinary person" who is male and young. The accused is before them. He is male and young. I cannot conceive of a Canadian jury conjuring up the concept of an "ordinary person" who would be either female or elderly, or banishing from their minds the possibility that an "ordinary person" might be both young and male. I do not think anything said by the judge in the case at bar would have lead the jury to such an absurdity.

VII. CONCLUSION

I find that the trial judge's charge to the jury on the ordinary person standard in the defence of provocation was consistent with the requirements of the *Criminal Code* and correct in law. It was not necessary to direct the jury that the ordinary person means an ordinary person of the same age and sex as the accused. I would therefore allow the appeal and restore the conviction.

McIntyre J. gave a concurring judgment. Three separate dissenting judgments were delivered by Lamer, Wilson and LeDain JJ. None of the dissenters unequivocally favoured a mandatory direction to the jury as had the House of Lords in *Camplin*. In general, the dissenting justices were of the view that this trial judge's direction had excluded age from consideration under the "ordinary person" test and that this had in the circumstances been unfairly prejudicial to the accused.

Should the Supreme Court have adopted the full *Camplin* approach?

In *R. v. Jackson* (1991), 68 C.C.C. (3d) 385 at 410, the Ontario Court of Appeal applied the "modified objective test" of *Hill* to consider "whether a reasonable young adult would have been deprived of self-control by an assault committed by a long-time friend, lover, provider and protector in the course of an argument which signalled the end of this long-standing relationship". This issue was not addressed when the Supreme Court dismissed the further appeal: [1993] 4 S.C.R. 573, 26 C.R. (4th) 178, 86 C.C.C. (3d) 385.

For a view that the present provocation defence contributes to homophobia and violence against gay men and lesbians see N. Kathleen (Sam) Banks, "The 'Homosexual Panic' Defence in Canadian Criminal Law" (1997), 1 C.R. (5th) 371.

R. v. TRAN

[2010] 3 S.C.R. 350, 2010 CarswellAlta 2281, 2010 CarswellAlta 2282, 261 C.C.C. (3d) 435, 80 C.R. (6th) 1

The accused suspected that his estranged wife was having a relationship with another man and had made attempts at surveillance. He entered his estranged wife's home unexpected and uninvited, using keys he had purported to return. He found his wife in bed with her boyfriend, and attacked the two of them. He then ran from the bedroom to the kitchen, returned with two butcher knives, and renewed his attack, stabbing the boyfriend several times. The accused then confronted his estranged wife and slashed her with the knife, during which time the boyfriend managed to crawl into the living room. The accused followed him to that room, renewing his attack. He eventually stabbed the boyfriend 17 times, killing him, and also injured his estranged wife.

At trial, the only defence raised was that murder should be reduced to manslaughter based on provocation. The trial judge held that the Crown had failed to disprove the elements of provocation, acquitted the accused of second degree murder, and convicted him of manslaughter. The Court of Appeal held that there was no air of reality to the defence of provocation and substituted a conviction for second degree murder.

CHARRON J. (for seven justices): —

[6] The preceding overview of the facts reflects the trial judge's findings and uncontested items of evidence. I agree with the Court of Appeal that, on those facts, there was no air of reality to the defence of provocation. In my respectful view, the trial judge proceeded on wrong legal principles concerning the requirements for the defence of provocation and, as a result, erred in law in finding that there was an evidential basis in this record for that defence.

[7] Specifically, there was no "insult" within the meaning of s. 232 of the *Criminal Code*, R.S.C. 1985, c. C-46. As rightly concluded by the Court of Appeal, the appellant's view of his estranged wife's sexual involvement with another man after the couple had separated — found at trial to be the "insult"— cannot in law be sufficient to excuse "a loss of control in the form of a homicidal rage" and constitute "an excuse for the ordinary person of whatever personal circumstances or background" (Watson J.A., at para. 64). In addition, the uncontradicted evidence about the appellant's knowledge that his wife was involved with another man and his own conduct in entering her home and bedroom, unexpected and uninvited, belied any notion that this supposed "insult" would have struck "upon a mind unprepared for it" as required by law (Hunt J.A., at para. 18). Finally, there was no air of reality to the appellant "acting on the sudden at the time of the killing" (Watson J.A., at para. 77).

[8] As a conviction for murder was inevitable, both on the law and on the trial judge's essential findings of fact, the Court of Appeal properly substituted a verdict of second degree murder and remitted the matter for sentencing. I would dismiss the appeal.

2. Analysis

[10] As the opening words of the provision make plain, the defence will only apply where the accused had the necessary intent for murder and acted upon this intent. Parliament thus carefully limited the application of the defence. The requirements of the defence contained in s. 232 have been described variously by the Court as comprising either two, three or four elements. For example, in *R. v. Hill*, [1986] 1 S.C.R. 313, Dickson C.J. identified three general requirements for the defence of provocation:

First, the provoking wrongful act or insult must be of such a nature that it would deprive an ordinary person of the power of self-control. That is the initial threshold which must be surmounted. Secondly, the accused must actually have been provoked. As I have earlier indicated, these two elements are often referred to as the objective and subjective tests of provocation respectively. Thirdly, the accused must have acted on the provocation on the sudden and before there was time for his or her passion to cool. [p. 324]

In *R. v. Thibert*, [1996] 1 S.C.R. 37, Cory J. for the majority of the Court collapsed these three requirements into two elements, one objective and the other subjective, describing them as follows:

First, there must be a wrongful act or insult of such a nature that it is sufficient to deprive an ordinary person of the power of self-control as the objective element. Second, the subjective element requires that the accused act upon that insult on the sudden and before there was time for his passion to cool. [Emphasis in original deleted; para. 4.]

Subsequently, in *R. v. Parent*, 2001 SCC 30, [2001] 1 S.C.R. 761, the Court reiterated the test in *Thibert* but framed it in terms of four required elements:

. . . (1) a wrongful act or insult that would have caused an ordinary person to be deprived of his or her self-control; (2) which is sudden and unexpected; (3) which in fact caused the accused to act in anger; (4) before having recovered his or her normal control . . . . [para. 10]

[11] These various formulations do not differ in substance. While it may be conceptually convenient in any given case to formulate the requirements of the defence in terms of distinct elements and to treat each of these elements separately, it is important to recognize that the various components of the defence may overlap and that s. 232 must be considered in its entirety.

[12] Before discussing the requirements contained in s. 232, it is useful to briefly review the historical development of the defence. As we shall see, prevailing social mores and judicial attitudes have played an important role in defining what amounts to provocation at law.

2.1 *Historical Development of the Defence*

[13] The defence of provocation, presently codified in s. 232 of the *Criminal Code*, has its origins in the English common law. More specifically, its precursor lies in the sixteenth century concept of "chance-medley" killings. As the English jurist Sir Edward Coke described it, "[h]omicide is called chancemedley . . . for that it is done by chance (without premeditation) upon a sudden brawle, shuffling, or contention" (*The Third Part of the Institutes of the Laws of England: Concerning High Treason, and Other Pleas of the Crown and Criminal Causes* (1817), at p. 56). During these killings, persons were considered to act "in the Time of their Rage, Drunkenness, hidden Displeasure, or other Passion of Mind" (*Statute of Stabbing (1604)*, 2 Jas I, c. 8). Such killings were considered less

morally reprehensible than deliberate "cold-blooded" killings and, informed by the value of honour that formed an important aspect of that period's social context, were viewed as partially excused.

[14] During the seventeenth century, another trend in the law of homicide emerged. It provided that anyone charged with murder was presumed to have acted with "malice aforethought", for which the punishment at the time was death. In response to the severity of the law, the courts resorted to the separate crime of manslaughter to take into account certain human frailties that would operate to rebut the presumption. One such concession to human frailty was that the accused had been provoked into committing the act (Department of Justice, *Reforming Criminal Code Defences: Provocation, Self-Defence and Defence of Property: A Consultation Paper* (1998), at p. 2). However, not any provocation would suffice; it had to be significant: see G. R. Sullivan, "Anger and Excuse: Reassessing Provocation" (1993), 13 *Oxford J. Leg. Stud.* 421, at p. 422.

[15] By the eighteenth century, the doctrine of provocation had become entrenched in the common law. Initially, the accused's state of mind, and in particular whether he was sufficiently deprived of self-control to have acted without malice in responding to the provocation, was the focus of the defence. Eventually, however, the courts set out to create greater certainty by establishing specific categories of "provocative events" that were considered "significant" enough to result in a loss of self-control. In the seminal case, *R. v. Mawgridge* (1707), Kel J. 119, 84 E.R. 1107, Lord Holt C.J. set out four categories of provocation. One category envisaged a husband catching a man in the act of adultery with his wife. The basis of the provocation, he wrote, was that "jealousy is the rage of a man, and adultery is the highest invasion of property" (p. 1115). Interestingly, while the killing of a sexual rival caught in the act of committing adultery with one's wife was seen as a proper basis for the defence, the killing of one's wife for infidelity was not: F. Stewart and A. Freiberg, *Provocation in Sentencing Research Report* (2nd ed. 2009), at para. 2.1.2. Another category included an "affron[t]" of "pulling . . . the nose, or filliping upon the forehead" (*Mawgridge*, at p. 1114). These categories carried the vestiges of a social view that privileged notions of preserving a man's honour. As Sullivan has described it:

> A violent response in such circumstances was not so much a matter to be condoned but to be required of a man of honour. The core perception of mitigating anger at this time was not of an emotion rendering the agent out of control but as a hot-blooded response informed and controlled by a rational understanding of the nature and degree of the provocation offered. It was a case of hot-blooded yet controlled vindication of one's honour rather than spontaneous, uncontrolled fury. [p. 422]

[16] By the middle of the nineteenth century, attempts to identify further categories were abandoned and the defence became more generalized. In *R. v. Hayward* (1833), 6 Car. & P. 157, 172 E.R. 1188, at p. 1189, Tindal C.J. told

the jury that the defence was derived from the law's "compassion to human infirmity". The Law Commissioners' Digest of 1839 provided that the provocative conduct must be "a wrongful act or insult", which required that the conduct be inherently offensive (Law Commission of Great Britain, *Partial Defences to Murder*, Consultation Paper No. 173 (2003), at para. 1.27, citing "Fourth Report of Her Majesty's Commissioners on Criminal Law", in *Reports from Commissioners* (1839), 235). These developments occurred at the same time as another critical one. While an objective standard was always implicit in the defence, a more formal standard of self-control expected to be exercised by the "reasonable man" in the circumstances was eventually proposed: *R. v. Welsh* (1869), 11 Cox C.C. 336. Ultimately, the objective element came to play a heightened role in the operation of the defence as the recognized grounds of provocation were abandoned (see T. Macklem, "Provocation and the Ordinary Person" (1987-1988), 11 *Dal. L.J.* 126, at p. 130).

[17] As this brief historical review demonstrates, the social context has always played an important role in defining what amounts to provocation at law. In 1949, Lord Goddard C.J. summarized the relationship between the defence and social context in the following manner:

> At a time when society was less secure and less settled in its habits, when the carrying of swords was as common as the use of a walking stick at the present day, and when duelling was regarded as involving no moral stigma if fairly conducted, it is not surprising that the courts took a view more lenient towards provocation than is taken to-day when life and property are guarded by an efficient police force and social habits have changed.

> (*R. v. Semini*, [1949] 1 K.B. 405, at p. 409)

[18] The common law defence of provocation was adopted and codified in the Canadian *Criminal Code* from its inception in 1892. The wording of s. 232 remains substantially unaltered. The same cannot be said of the social context in which it is embedded. The continued appropriateness of the defence has been a source of controversy, both in Canada and abroad. Some commentators and reviewing bodies have recommended that the defence be abandoned altogether, leaving provocation, when relevant, as a factor to be considered in sentencing. For a discussion of such reform proposals in Canada and elsewhere, see D. E. Ives, "Provocation, Excessive Force in Self-Defence and Diminished Responsibility", in Law Commission of Great Britain, *Partial Defences to Murder: Overseas Studies*, Consultation Paper 173 (App. B) (2003), 73, at pp. 78-81; Australia, Victorian Law Reform Commission, *Defences to Homicide: Final Report* (2004); New Zealand Law Commission, *The Partial Defence of Provocation*, Report 98 (2007).

[19] Parliament has not chosen this course and the defence continues to exist in Canada. This does not mean, however, that the defence in its present articulation should not continue to evolve to reflect contemporary social norms,

and in particular, *Charter* values. Just as at common law the notion of an "insult
. . . sufficient to deprive an ordinary person of the power of self-control", now
codified under s. 232, is not frozen in time. By incorporating this objective
element, the defence of provocation is necessarily informed by contemporary
social norms and values. These include society's changed views regarding the
nature of marital relationships and the present reality that a high percentage of
them end in separation.

[20] It is with these considerations in mind that I turn to an examination of the
defence as contained in s. 232 of the *Criminal Code.*

2.2 *Provocation Under Section 232 of the Criminal Code*

[21] Viewing the provision as a whole, I offer some preliminary comments
about the juridical nature of the defence. A criminal law defence is usually
characterized as providing either an excuse or a justification for the impugned
conduct. As Professor K. Roach rightly observes: "As a partial defence that
reduces murder to manslaughter, provocation does not fit easily into the excuse/
justification framework" (*Criminal Law* (4th ed. 2009), at p. 358). In *R. v.
Manchuk*, [1938] S.C.R. 18, at pp. 19-20, this Court explained that "provocation
. . . neither justifies nor excuses the act of homicide. But the law accounts the
act and the violent feelings which prompted it less blameable because of the
passion aroused by the provocation, . . . though still sufficiently blameable to
merit punishment — and it may be punishment of high severity — but not the
extreme punishment of death."

[22] Thus, the accused's conduct is partially *excused* out of a compassion to
human frailty. While the call for compassion was particularly compelling in
times when the alternative was the death penalty, the rationale subsists today,
given the serious consequences to the offender flowing from a conviction for
murder. It is not sufficient, however, that an accused's sudden reaction to a
wrongful act or insult may be explained from a purely subjective standpoint.
The provision incorporates an objective standard against which the accused's
reaction must be measured — that which may be expected of the "ordinary
person" in like circumstances. Not all instances of loss of self-control will be
excused. Rather, the requisite elements of the defence, taken together, make clear
that the accused must have a *justifiable* sense of being wronged. This does not
mean, and in no way should be taken as suggesting, that the victim is to be
blamed for the accused's act, nor that he or she deserved the consequences of
the provocation. Nor does it mean that the law sanctions the accused's conduct.
Instead, the law recognizes that, as a result of human frailties, the accused reacted
inappropriately and disproportionately, but understandably to a sufficiently
serious wrongful act or insult.

[23] In my view, the requirements of s. 232 are most usefully described as comprising two elements, one objective and the other subjective. As Cory J. for the majority of the Court put it in *Thibert*:

> First, there must be a wrongful act or insult of such a nature that it is sufficient to deprive an ordinary person of the power of self-control as the objective element. Second, the subjective element requires that the accused act upon that insult on the sudden and before there was time for his passion to cool. [Emphasis in original deleted; para. 4.]

[24] I will review each element in turn.

2.2.1 The Objective Element: A Wrongful Act or Insult Sufficient to Deprive an Ordinary Person of the Power of Self-Control

[25] For the purpose of discussion, the objective element may be viewed as two-fold: (1) there must be a wrongful act or insult; and (2) the wrongful act or insult must be sufficient to deprive an ordinary person of the power of self-control.

[26] While the concepts "wrongful act" and "insult" are not defined, the following limitation is set out in s. 232(3):

> **232.** . . .
>
> (3) For the purposes of this section, the questions
>
> > (*a*) whether a particular wrongful act or insult amounted to provocation, and
> >
> > (*b*) whether the accused was deprived of the power of self-control by the provocation that he alleges he received,
>
> are questions of fact, but no one shall be deemed to have given provocation to another by doing anything that he had a legal right to do, or by doing anything that the accused incited him to do in order to provide the accused with an excuse for causing death or bodily harm to any human being.

The second branch of s. 232(3) is not at issue in this case and I do not propose to discuss the limitation on the defence in circumstances where the accused himself incites the act of provocation with a view to providing himself with an excuse for committing the offence. The "legal right" limitation on the defence, however, merits further discussion in the context of this case.

[27] It is well established that the phrase "legal right" does not include all conduct not specifically prohibited by law. For example, the fact that a person may not be subject to legal liability for an insult directed at the accused does not mean that he or she has the "legal right" to make the insult within the meaning of s. 232(3) and that provocation is not open to the accused. To require

that an insult be specifically prohibited by law would effectively render the word "insult" under s. 232(2) redundant, as any such "insult" would necessarily be a "wrongful act". The phrase "legal right" has been defined, rather, as meaning a right which is sanctioned by law, such as a sheriff proceeding to execute a legal warrant, or a person acting in justified self-defence (*Thibert*, at para. 29, citing *R. v. Haight* (1976), 30 C.C.C. (2d) 168 (Ont. C.A.), at p. 175, and *R. v. Galgay*, [1972] 2 O.R. 630 (C.A.), at p. 649). Interpreted in this manner, the notion of legal right serves to carve out from the ambit of s. 232 legally sanctioned conduct which otherwise could amount, in fact, to an "insult".

[28] There has been academic criticism of this approach. Professor Roach argues, for example, that the concept of legal right could be rethought in the context of domestic violence. He writes: "It could be argued that people have a legal right to leave relationships and even to make disparaging comments about ex-partners. The Court's continued refusal to recognize this broader interpretation of a legal right could deny women the equal protection and benefit of the law" (p. 359).

[29] In my view, these concerns, while legitimate, are better addressed at the stage when the gravity of the "insult" is objectively measured as against the ordinary person standard. In other words, while one spouse undoubtedly has a legal right to leave his or her partner, in some circumstances the means by which that spouse communicates this decision may amount *in fact* to an "insult", within the ordinary meaning of the word. However, to be recognized *at law*, the insult must be of sufficient gravity to cause a loss of self-control, as objectively determined. The fact that the victim has the "legal right", in the broad sense of the term, to leave the relationship is an important consideration in the assessment of this objective standard.

[30] The "ordinary person", as a legal concept, has generally been assimilated in the case law to the well-known "reasonable person" and the two terms are often used interchangeably: e.g., *Hill*, at p. 331. While I believe that the two fictional entities share the same attributes, at first blush some may question this as a logical inconsistency, given that a "reasonable" person would not commit culpable homicide in the first place. Indeed, "reasonableness" often defines the standard of conduct which is expected at law, and conduct which meets this standard, as a general rule, does not attract legal liability. The inconsistency is resolved when it is recalled that the defence is only a partial one, and that the defendant, even if successful, will still be guilty of manslaughter. The use of the term "ordinary person" therefore reflects the normative dimensions of the defence; that is, behaviour which comports with contemporary society's norms and values will attract the law's compassion. Meeting the standard, however, will only provide a *partial* defence. In this context, it seems to me that the label "ordinary person" is more suitable and this may explain Parliament's choice of

words. Cory J. for the majority of the Court in *Thibert* explained how the ordinary person standard should be interpreted:

> Yet, I think the objective element should be taken as an attempt to weigh in the balance those very human frailties which sometimes lead people to act irrationally and impulsively against the need to protect society by discouraging acts of homicidal violence. [para. 4]

[31] Applying this objective standard has not been without difficulty. A central concern has been the extent to which the accused's personal characteristics and circumstances should be considered when applying the "ordinary person" test. Traditionally, Canadian courts, endorsing the approach of their English counterparts, adopted a restrictive approach, prohibiting any reference to the accused's characteristics or circumstances (*Bedder v. Director of Public Prosecutions*, [1954] 1 W.L.R. 1119 (H.L.); *Salamon v. The Queen*, [1959] S.C.R. 404; *Wright v. The Queen*, [1969] S.C.R. 335). However, this approach required the court to completely ignore relevant contextual circumstances in making its determinations.

[32] Recognizing this deficiency, a broader approach was eventually adopted in conceptualizing the "ordinary person" so as to account for some, but not all, of the individual characteristics of the accused. As Dickson C.J. explained in *Hill*, this more flexible approach is essentially a matter of common sense:

> ... the "collective good sense" of the jury will naturally lead it to ascribe to the ordinary person any general characteristics relevant to the provocation in question. For example, if the provocation is a racial slur, the jury will think of an ordinary person with the racial background that forms the substance of the insult. To this extent, particular characteristics will be ascribed to the ordinary person. Indeed, it would be impossible to conceptualize a sexless or ageless ordinary person. Features such as sex, age, or race, do not detract from a person's characterization as ordinary. Thus particular characteristics that are not peculiar or idiosyncratic can be ascribed to an ordinary person without subverting the logic of the objective test of provocation. [Emphasis added; p. 331.]

[33] I emphasize the words of caution that, in adopting this more flexible approach, care must be taken not to subvert the logic of the objective test. Indeed, if all of the accused's characteristics are taken into account, the ordinary person *becomes* the accused. As Dickson C.J. noted, this approach would lead to the anomalous result that "[a] well-tempered, reasonable person would not be entitled to benefit from the provocation defence ... while an ill-tempered or exceptionally excitable person would find his or her culpability mitigated by provocation and would be guilty only of manslaughter" (p. 324).

[34] Further, an individualized approach ignores the cardinal principle that criminal law is concerned with setting standards of human behaviour. As Dickson C.J. put it: "It is society's concern that reasonable and non-violent behaviour be encouraged that prompts the law to endorse the objective standard"

(p. 324). Similarly, McIntyre J. in concurring reasons expanded upon this purpose, stating:

> The law fixes a standard for all which must be met before reliance may be placed on the provocation defence. Everyone, whatever his or her idiosyncracies, is expected to observe that standard. It is not every insult or injury that will be sufficient to relieve a person from what would otherwise be murder. The "ordinary person" standard is adopted to fix the degree of self-control and restraint expected of all in society. [p. 336]
>
> It follows that the ordinary person standard must be informed by contemporary norms of behaviour, including fundamental values such as the commitment to equality provided for in the *Canadian Charter of Rights and Freedoms*. For example, it would be appropriate to ascribe to the ordinary person relevant racial characteristics if the accused were the recipient of a racial slur, but it would not be appropriate to ascribe to the ordinary person the characteristic of being homophobic if the accused were the recipient of a homosexual advance. Similarly, there can be no place in this objective standard for antiquated beliefs such as "adultery is the highest invasion of property" (*Mawgridge*, at p. 1115), nor indeed for any form of killing based on such inappropriate conceptualizations of "honour".

[35] Finally, the particular circumstances in which the accused finds himself will also be relevant in determining the appropriate standard against which to measure the accused's conduct. This is also a matter of common sense, as it would be impossible to conceptualize how the ordinary person might be expected to react without considering the relevant context. Again here, however, care must be taken not to "subver[t] the logic of the objective [inquiry]" and assimilate circumstances that are peculiar to the individual accused into the objective standard (*Hill*, at p. 331). For example, in determining the appropriate objective standard, it will be relevant for the trier of fact to know that the alleged provocation occurred in circumstances where the deceased was wrongfully firing the accused from his long-term employment. This context is necessary to set the appropriate standard. But the standard does not vary depending on the accused's peculiar relationship or particular feelings about his employer or his employment. Personal circumstances may be relevant to determining whether the accused was in fact provoked — the subjective element of the defence — but they do not shift the ordinary person standard to suit the individual accused. In other words, there is an important distinction between contextualizing the objective standard, which is necessary and proper, and individualizing it, which only serves to defeat its purpose.

2.2.2 The Subjective Element: The Provocation Must Have Caused the Accused to Lose Self-Control and Act While Out of Control

[36] Once it is established that the wrongful act or insult was sufficient to deprive an ordinary person of the power of self-control, the inquiry turns to a consideration of the subjective element of the defence. The subjective element can also be usefully described as two-fold: (1) the accused must have acted in

response to the provocation; and (2) on the sudden before there was time for his or her passion to cool.

[37] The inquiry into whether the accused was in fact acting in response to the provocation focuses on the accused's subjective perceptions of the circumstances, including what the accused believed, intended or knew. In other words, the accused must have killed because he was provoked and not because the provocation existed (*R. v. Faid*, [1983] 1 S.C.R. 265, at p. 277, citing Professor G. L. Williams in his *Textbook of Criminal Law* (1978), at p. 480).

[38] The requirement of suddenness was introduced into the defence as a way of distinguishing a response taken in vengeance from one that was provoked. Therefore, suddenness applies to both the act of provocation and the accused's reaction to it. The wrongful act or insult must itself be sudden, in the sense that it "must strike upon a mind unprepared for it, that it must make an unexpected impact that takes the understanding by surprise and sets the passions aflame" (*R. v. Tripodi*, [1955] S.C.R. 438, at p. 443). Further, the intentional killing must have been committed by the accused "before there was time for his passion to cool": s. 232(2) of the *Criminal Code*.

2.3 *The Role of the Judge and Jury*

[39] As noted earlier, s. 232(3) provides that determining whether a particular wrongful act or insult amounted to provocation and whether the accused was deprived of the power of self-control by the provocation are questions of fact. Consistent with the wording of this provision, it remains with the jury, and not the trial judge, to weigh the evidence in order to determine whether the Crown has discharged its burden of disproving that the killing was caused by provocation (*R. v. Fontaine*, 2004 SCC 27, [2004] 1 S.C.R. 702, at para. 56, citing *R. v. Schwartz*, [1988] 2 S.C.R. 443).

[40] However, the interpretation of a legal standard (the elements of the defence) and the determination of whether there is an air of reality to a defence constitute questions of law, reviewable on a standard of correctness. The term "air of reality" refers to the inquiry into whether there is an evidential foundation for a defence. Statements that there is or is not an air of reality express a legal conclusion about the presence or absence of an evidential foundation for a defence: *R. v. Cinous*, 2002 SCC 29, [2002] 2 S.C.R. 3, at paras. 50 and 55; *R. v. Osolin*, [1993] 4 S.C.R. 595, at p. 682; *Parnerkar v. The Queen*, [1974] S.C.R. 449, at p. 461. Thus, this inquiry is not a review of the trial judge's assessment of the evidence but of the judge's legal conclusions in relation to the defence of provocation: *R. v. Ewanchuk*, [1999] 1 S.C.R. 330, at para. 21.

[41] In a jury trial, the judge is the gatekeeper and judge of the law and must therefore put the defence to the jury only where there is evidence upon which a "reasonable jury acting judicially" could find that the defence succeeds (*Faid*, at p. 278). For the defence to succeed, the jury must have a reasonable doubt about whether each of the elements of provocation was present. This necessarily requires that there be a sufficient evidential basis in respect of each component of the defence before it is left to the jury: the evidence must be reasonably capable of supporting the inferences necessary to make out the defence before there is an air of reality to the defence (*Fontaine*, at para. 56; *R. v. Reddick*, [1991] 1 S.C.R. 1086, at p. 1088, citing *Pappajohn v. The Queen*, [1980] 2 S.C.R. 120, at p. 133). In a trial by judge alone, the trial judge must instruct himself or herself accordingly. Therefore, the trial judge errs in law if he or she gives effect to the defence of provocation in circumstances where the defence should not have been left to a jury, had the accused been tried by a jury.

3. Application to the Case

[42] As stated at the outset, I agree with the Court of Appeal that there was no air of reality to the defence of provocation in this case. The conduct in question does not amount to an "insult"; nor does it meet the requirement of suddenness.

[43] As for the objective element of the defence, the appellant does not suggest that he was provoked by a "wrongful act". Rather, his contention is that, in the context of his relationship with Ms. Duong, his discovery of her sexual involvement with Mr. An Tran amounted to an insult at law. The facts do not support this contention.

[44] First, it is difficult to see how the conduct of Ms. Duong and Mr. An Tran could constitute an insult on any ordinary meaning of the word. The general meaning of the noun "insult" as defined in the *Shorter Oxford English Dictionary on Historical Principles* (6th ed. 2007), vol. 1, at p. 1400, is "[a]n act or the action of attacking; (an) attack, (an) assault." Likewise, the action of insulting means to "[s]how arrogance or scorn; boast, exult, esp. insolently or contemptuously. . . . Treat with scornful abuse; subject to indignity; . . . offend the modesty or self-respect of." Here, Ms. Duong and Mr. An Tran were alone in the privacy of her bedroom, neither wanting nor expecting the appellant to show up. In these circumstances, I agree with Hunt J.A. that "[n]othing done by the complainant or the victim comes close to meeting the definition of insult. Their behaviour was not only lawful, it was discreet and private and entirely passive vis-à-vis the [appellant]. They took pains to keep their relationship hidden. . . . Their behaviour came to his attention only because he gained access to the building by falsely saying he was there to pick up his mail" (para. 17).

[45] Further, there was nothing sudden about the discovery. The appellant is the one whose appearance came as a total surprise to Ms. Duong and Mr. An Tran, not the other way around. On the factual findings made by the trial judge, the appellant had not only suspected his wife's relationship with another man, but he made deliberate attempts to surveillance her activity, including by eavesdropping on her conversations. The night before the tragic events, the appellant told his godmother that he now knew who the man was whom his wife was seeing (trial judge's reasons, at p. 26). Therefore, it cannot be said that his discovery, upon entering Ms. Duong's bedroom unannounced and uninvited, "str[uck] upon a mind unprepared for it".

[46] Finally, I also agree with Watson J.A. that on "the subjective side of the question", the trial judge's findings of "[o]utward excitement and anger" could not be decisive (para. 76). The appellant did not testify about his state of mind. The evidence shows, as Watson J.A. notes, that he

> was measuring his actions on what he was saying and doing. The trial judge should have addressed whether he could have regained his self control by the time he went into the living room and finished off the victim — not merely whether he was still angry and excited. The trial judge found his anger continued but she failed to direct herself to consider whether the continuation of his anger amounted to a continuing lack of the power of self control without an opportunity to recover it. [para. 76]

As Watson J.A. rightly concluded, "there was on the trial judge's fact findings no air of reality to his acting on the sudden at the time of the killing" (para. 77).

4. Disposition

[47] The Court of Appeal properly substituted a conviction for second degree murder and returned the matter to the trial court for sentencing. As Watson J.A. stated: "In light of the law, and of the trial judge's findings of fact, and of the overwhelming evidence, a conviction for murder was unavoidable" (para. 81). I would dismiss the appeal.

Appeal dismissed; conviction for second degree murder upheld.

The Court says in *Tran*:

it would be appropriate to ascribe to the ordinary person relevant racial characteristics if the accused were the recipient of a racial slur, but it would not be appropriate to ascribe to the ordinary person the characteristic of being homophobic if the accused were the recipient of a homosexual advance. **Does this mean that *Hill* is wrongly decided?**

This case is an important and helpful review of the long controversial partial defence to murder and is now the starting place for judicial analysis.

This defence has little to do with theories of justification or excuse but is all about a long-established doctrine to sometimes avoid the rigours of the fixed penalty for murder—in Canada, formerly death and now life imprisonment. Without the fixed penalty we would not need the partial defence of provocation. This legislative change seems unlikely so the courts must soldier on.

On the facts the Supreme Court unanimously finds that there was no air of reality to the provocation defence as there was no insult given that the new couple were discrete and that the accused did not act on the sudden because he had suspicions in advance of his discovery. It is arguable that the Court has become too restrictive. **What if a wife has suspicions that her husband is abusing a daughter? She investigates and opens a door to find him touching his daughter inappropriately. If she loses control and kills him can she not have the benefit of the partial defence to reduce her criminal culpability?** The child abuse will constitute a wrongful act for these purposes but, applying *Tran*, she did not act on the sudden. This result may seem severe. **Is *Tran* authority that the suddenness requirement can never be met if there is any prior suspicion?**

It will be important not to generalise *Tran* to other defences such as self-defence and duress where the individualised approach to tests of objective reasonableness is now well established and not subject to the special limits characterising the uneven law of provocation.

R. v. PARENT

[2001] 1 S.C.R. 761, 41 C.R. (5th) 199, 154 C.C.C. (3d) 1,
2001 CarswellQue 851, 2001 CarswellQue 852

The accused and his estranged wife were involved in divorce litigation over the division of their assets, some of which were held in a corporation. Their financial situation had deteriorated to the point the accused's shares were seized and put up for sale. The wife attended the sale, allegedly intending to buy the shares. The accused was also present. He carried a loaded gun with a locked security catch in his pocket. His wife suggested that they speak and they went into a nearby room. He testified that she said in effect "I told you that I would wipe you out completely". He then felt a hot flush rising and he shot. He said he did not know what he was doing any more and did not intend to kill her. She died from six wounds.

At trial on a charge of first degree murder he argued that the verdict should be reduced to manslaughter on the basis of lack of criminal intent or provocation. The jury found him guilty of manslaughter. The Court of Appeal upheld the verdict.

The Supreme Court allowed the appeal and ordered a new trial on second degree murder.

McLachlin C.J.C. for a unanimous court: —

The jury had three possible offences before it: first degree murder, second degree murder and manslaughter. All three offences require proof of an act of killing (*actus reus*) and the corresponding criminal intention (*mens rea*). In relation to murder, the defence of provocation does not eliminate the need for proof of intention to kill, but operates as an excuse that has the effect of reducing murder to manslaughter.

The Crown argues that the trial judge erred in suggesting that anger is capable of negating the intention to kill and that the jury could reduce the offence to manslaughter on this basis. More particularly, the Crown suggests that the judge's directions wrongly treated anger as a matter that could negate the criminal intent or *mens rea* of the offence; wrongly suggested that negation of intent can reduce the offence to manslaughter; and wrongly left open the suggestion that anger alone can establish provocation, when in fact other requirements must be met pursuant to s. 232 of the *Criminal Code*, R.S.C. 1985, c. C-46. The gravamen of the Crown's submission is that the trial judge's direction on intention was confusing and wrong and left it open to the jury to convict the accused of manslaughter, not on the basis of provocation (which the trial judge correctly defined), but on the erroneous basis that a high degree of anger short of provocation, as defined in law, could negate the criminal intent or *mens rea* of the offence.

The Crown objects to the portions of the jury charge in which the trial judge stated that the jury must take into account [TRANSLATION] "evidence surrounding the defence of provocation raised by the accused" in determining the accused's intent to kill. The Crown also objects to the trial judge's treatment of *mens rea* in the following passages:

> [TRANSLATION] For example, murder may be reduced to manslaughter where a person's state of mind is affected by alcohol consumption, drug consumption or where a person's state of mind is obscured or diminished by an outside force, by an incident like, for example, a fit of anger.

> . . . .

> You no doubt appreciate that we are not talking about an arbitrary reduction.

> . . . .

> In other words, it is not sufficient for a person to simply say "I was drinking" or "I took some drugs" or "I was really angry".

> . . . .

> That alone, that's not enough, and all that always depends on the circumstances. It always depends on the nature of the facts at issue, of external influences, or outside influences capable of affecting one's state of mind.

> . . . .

> It depends on the nature of the fact at issue, of its importance, its seriousness, its intensity

in relation to the action that was taken by the person who committed the crime, all the while taking into account the evidence as a whole and all the circumstances.

. . . .

So, you must look at the accused's state of mind when he killed Suzanne Bédard, you look at the entire evidence, including the elements surrounding the provocation defence with a view to determining whether he acted with the criminal intention that I defined earlier.

. . . .

Here, the accused, when he testified, described to you his state of mind when Suzanne Bédard said the words in question.

. . . .

You must then decide if this incident was sufficiently serious, important, intense so as to cause him to lose his faculties to the point of reducing the crime of murder to manslaughter.

. . . .

You will ask yourselves if his state of mind was affected, diminished, and if so, the intensity, the degree to which, taking into account all the circumstances at the time when he did what he did.

. . . .

To reduce murder to manslaughter, you must come to the conclusion that the influence of the events that occurred was *strong enough, important enough, intense enough* to cause the accused to *not know or not want what he was doing by reason of his state of mind, that his faculties were too diminished to fully assess the situation, or that raise a reasonable doubt in his favour, in this respect.* [Emphasis added.]

The Crown argues that this passage creates a halfway house defence of anger, between non-mental disorder automatism and provocation. I agree. This passage suggests that anger, if sufficiently serious or intense, but not amounting to the defence of provocation, may reduce murder to manslaughter. It also suggests that anger, if sufficiently intense, may negate the criminal intention for murder. These connected propositions are not legally correct. Intense anger alone is insufficient to reduce murder to manslaughter.

The passage cited overstates the effect of anger. Anger can play a role in reducing murder to manslaughter in connection with the defence of provocation. Anger is not a stand-alone defence. It may form part of the defence of provocation when all the requirements of that defence are met: (1) a wrongful act or insult that would have caused an ordinary person to be deprived of his or her self-control; (2) which is sudden and unexpected; (3) which in fact caused the accused to act in anger; (4) before having recovered his or her normal control: *R. v. Thibert*, [1996] 1 S.C.R. 37, 104 C.C.C. (3d) 1, 131 D.L.R. (4th) 675. Again, anger conceivably could, in extreme circumstances, cause someone to enter a state of automatism in which that person does not know what he or she is doing, thus negating the voluntary component of the *actus reus*: *R. v. Stone*, [1999] 2 S.C.R. 290, 134 C.C.C. (3d) 353, 173 D.L.R. (4th) 66. However, the accused did not assert this defence. In any event, the defence if successful would result in acquittal, not reduction to manslaughter.

So it seems clear that the trial judge misdirected the jury on the effect of anger in relation to manslaughter. His directions left it open to the jury to find the accused guilty of manslaughter, on the basis of the anger felt by the accused, even if they concluded that the conditions required for the defence of provocation were not met. The directions raise the possibility that the jury's verdict of manslaughter may have been based on erroneous legal principles, unless they were corrected in the recharge to the jury.

. . . .

The trial judge erred in his charge to the jury on the effect of anger on criminal intent or *mens rea* and its relationship to manslaughter. This error was not corrected on the recharge and we cannot infer from the way the trial proceeded that the jury's verdict of manslaughter was not based on the erroneous initial direction. It follows that the conviction for manslaughter must be set aside and a new trial directed.

As indicated earlier, the Crown in this appeal, relied solely on the trial judge's misdirections on anger and criminal intent. It is therefore unnecessary to comment further on the applicability of the defence of provocation as it may be tendered at the new trial. It will be for the judge on the new trial to determine whether, on the evidence there presented, the defence of provocation should be put to the jury.

I would allow the appeal and direct a new trial on second degree murder.

For a full analysis of *Parent* see Gary Trotter, "Anger, Provocation, and the Intent for Murder: A Comment on *R. v. Parent*" (2002), 47 McGill L.J. 669. See too, Wayne Gorman, "*R. v. Parent*" (2002), 45 Crim. L.Q. 412.

The partial defence of provocation is presently extremely controversial and has been under review by the Department of Justice for years: see, *Reforming Criminal Code Defences: Provocation, Self-defence and Defence of Property* (Department of Justice, 1998) pp.1-20. There is no legislative resolution in sight, no doubt because of a lack of consensus on reform options. A study by a Federal-Provincial-Territorial working group, reported in the Justice study at pp. 5-6, of 115 reported cases in which the defence of provocation was raised, warns against generalizations or special interest solutions. Sixty-two cases involved domestic homicides. In 55 cases men killed women and in 7 women killed men. The remaining 53 cases involving men killing men. Sixteen of these cases involved alleged homosexual advances. In all types of cases the study revealed that the defence of provocation was more often than not unsuccessful.

Some see the solution as being the abolition of the mandatory life sentence for murder. See Peter MacKinnon, "Two Views of Murder" (1985), 53 Can. Bar Rev. 130; "Annotation to Latimer" (1996), 41 C.R. (4th) 6; and Tim Quigley, "*R. v. Latimer* : Hard Cases Make Interesting Law" (1995), 41 C.R. (4th) 89 at 98). The law and order mood of the times makes this change unlikely.

The Supreme Court has recently spoken to the issue of sentencing in provoked murder cases. In *Stone* (1999), 24 C.R. (5th) 1 (S.C.C.), the accused stabbed his wife 47 times after she verbally insulted him and a "whoosh" came over him. The defence of provocation was left with the jury and they returned a verdict of manslaughter. The trial judge imposed a sentence of four years, taking into account 18 months pre-trial custody as equivalent to three years. On the sentence appeal, Justice Bastarache for a court unanimous on this point rejected the Crown's position that an accused should not gain a "double benefit" of considering provocation in reducing a verdict from murder to manslaughter under s. 232 of the *Code* and then again on sentencing. Rather, s. 232 provided an accused with a single benefit of a reduction of a verdict of murder to one of manslaughter to allow for consideration of the provoked nature of the killing in the determination of the appropriate penalty. A spousal connection between offender and victim was recognized as an aggravating factor in sentencing under s. 718.2(*a*)(ii) and previously under the common law, which applied to this case (the sentencing had been before the new section came into effect). However, the Crown had failed to establish that the sentencing judge did not properly consider the domestic nature of this offence in reaching his decision on sentence.

R. v. CAMERON

(1992), 12 C.R. (4th) 396, 71 C.C.C. (3d) 272,
1992 CarswellOnt 85 (Ont. C.A.)

The accused was convicted of second degree murder. He appealed, arguing that the statutory defence of provocation set out in s. 232 of the *Criminal Code* contravened ss. 7 and 11(*d*) of the *Charter* in that it is premised in part on an objective standard. The Ontario Court of Appeal dismissed the constitutional challenge.

DOHERTY J.A. (DUBIN C.J.O. and GRIFFITHS J. concurring): —

. . . .

The appellant contends that the "defence of provocation operates by negativing an essential element of the *mens rea* for murder". He goes on to argue that as provocation is premised in part on an objective standard, the statutory definition of provocation cannot stand in light of the authorities which hold that liability for murder cannot be determined by reference to an objective fault standard: see *R. v. Martineau*, [1990] 2 S.C.R. 633, 79 C.R. (3d) 129, 58 C.C.C. (3d) 353.

The argument misconceives the effect of s. 232. The section does not detract from or negative the fault requirement for murder, but serves as a partial excuse for those who commit what would be murder but for the existence of the partial defence created by s. 232. As the opening words of s. 232 plainly indicate, the defence only need be considered where the Crown has proved beyond a reasonable doubt that the accused committed murder: see *R. v. Campbell* (1977), 38 C.C.C. (2d) 6 (C.A.), at p. 15; *R. v. Oickle* (1984), 11 C.C.C. (3d) 180 (C.A.) at p. 190.

The statutory defence of provocation does not detract from the *mens rea* required to establish murder, but rather, where applicable, serves to reduce homicides committed with the *mens rea* necessary to establish murder to manslaughter.

The appellant also argues that, even if the statutory defence of provocation stands apart from the *mens rea* required for murder, ss. 7 and 11(*d*) of the *Charter* render the section inoperative insofar as it imposes an objective standard on the availability of the defence. He argues that for constitutional purposes there could be no distinction between a statutory provision which imposes liability for murder on an objective basis (*e.g.*, s. 230(*d*)) and a statutory provision like s. 232 which limits the availability of a defence to murder according to an objective criterion.

I disagree. The former imposes liability in the absence of a constitutionally mandated minimum level of fault. The latter provides a partial excuse despite the existence of the constitutionally required level of fault. Section 232 does not impose liability where subjective fault does not exist, but reduces the liability even when that fault exists.

The objective component of the statutory defence of provocation serves a valid societal purpose (see *R. v. Hill*, [1986] 1 S.C.R. 313, 51 C.R. (3d) 97, 25 C.C.C. (3d) 322, at pp. 330-331 [C.C.C., pp. 108-109 C.R.]) and cannot be said to be contrary to the principles of fundamental justice.

Resort to s. 11(*d*) of the *Charter* does not assist the appellant. Section 232 does not place any burden of proof on an accused to disprove anything essential to the establishing of his culpability. Indeed, the onus is on the Crown to negate provocation beyond a reasonable doubt: *Linney v. R.*, [1978] 1 S.C.R. 646, 32 C.C.C. (2d) 294. Nor, for the reasons set out above, does s. 232 modify the statutory definition of murder so as to eliminate an element of the offence required by s. 7 of the *Charter*.

The constitutional argument fails.

(b)   Voluntary Intoxication

At common law there are two partial defences to murder. We earlier saw that voluntary intoxication may reduce a murder charge to manslaughter since murder is considered to be a specific intent crime.

(c) Cumulative Effect on Intent

There is also the possibility, especially under Ontario case law, of what has become known as the "rolled up" charge which asks the jury to consider the cumulative effect of all the factors on whether the Crown has proved the intent required for murder.

R. v. NEALY

(1986), 54 C.R. (3d) 158, 30 C.C.C. (3d) 460,
1986 CarswellOnt 136 (Ont. C.A.)

CORY J.A.: —

. . . .

A brief history of the facts will suffice for the purposes of this appeal.

During the early morning hours of 20th August 1982 the appellant, Patrick Nealy, stabbed and killed Larry Casimiri. At the time, Nealy was 23 years old and Casimiri was 33 years old, married, with three children.

Earlier, during the afternoon of 19th August, Nealy injected into his arm a drug known as "stovetop". He thought that the plateau from that injection occurred late in the afternoon. In the evening, he and his girlfriend, Alison McKinley, drank together at the St. Charles Tavern. This is a bar which was frequented by members of the gay community and was well known to Nealy. While at this tavern, Nealy and his girlfriend met the deceased and two friends of the deceased. Some time around 11:00 p.m., Nealy and his girlfriend, together with the deceased and his two friends, proceeded to the Albany Tavern. This tavern as well was often frequented by members of the gay community.

Both the appellant and the deceased continued to drink at the Albany Tavern. The deceased danced with Nealy's girlfriend. According to Nealy, after dancing with her, Casimiri repeatedly said that Nealy's girlfriend "had nice tits and that he was going to fuck her". Nealy told Casimiri to keep quiet. Eventually, the two men began pushing and then punching each other. Nealy suggested to Casimiri that they continue their fight outside. Casimir left the Albany Tavern and Nealy followed him.

Before Nealy left the tavern, he removed a knife from his girlfriend's purse and placed it in his belt with the handle exposed. Once out on the street, the men continued to fight. To many of the witnesses, it appeared that Nealy was the aggressor and better-co-ordinated. Casimiri, although heavier-set, appeared drunk and unco-ordinated. It was Nealy's evidence that he was upset by what Casimiri had said about his girlfriend and that he was afraid of Casimiri, who came at him, as he said, "like a grizzly bear".

Nealy stated that he had the knife only to frighten Casimiri and he warned Casimiri to "back off". In any event, he stabbed Casimiri several times — on his evidence, three times. With the last stroke of the knife, Casimiri collapsed in front of a van parked on King Street and Nealy fled. Nealy testified that he had not intended to kill Casimiri and that he was angry with himself for what had happened and sorry for what he had done.

At the opening of the trial, Nealy entered a plea of not guilty to the charge of murder but guilty of manslaughter. This plea was not accepted by the Crown and the trial proceeded. Despite the plea, Nealy raised the issue of self-defence at trial.

At the conclusion of the evidence it was clear that the jury would have to consider: first, the issue of drunkenness and the effect upon the accused of the alcohol consumed; second, the question of self-defence; third, the question of provocation; and fourth, the effect that the alcohol he had consumed, coupled with the fear and anger experienced by the accused, would have upon the issue of whether he ever formed the requisite intent to murder Casimiri.

. . . .

The trial judge, early in his charge, read to the jury s. 212(a)(iii) and advised them of the intent that was required in order to find the accused guilty of murder.

Later he told the jury that he was going to deal specifically with self-defence, provocation and drunkenness. He dealt first, in an exemplary manner, with self-defence. He then said that the second defence was drunkenness, and gave instructions with regard to it, and lastly dealt with what he termed the "third defence" of provocation. Each of these aspects of the charge was, to a certain extent, "compartmentalized". It is conceded that he did not at any time instruct the jury as to the cumulative effect that the consumption of alcohol and the fear and anger that were experienced by Nealy as a result of his dispute with the deceased might have had upon Nealy's ability to form the requisite intent to commit murder.

It would, I think, have been better if the trial judge, at the conclusion of his reference to these three specific elements, had advised the jury as to the possible cumulative effect of the evidence.

In this case, it would have been preferable if the jury had been instructed along these lines: first, that, in considering whether the accused formed the requisite intent, they were to take into account the alcohol that had been consumed by Nealy; further, that they were to consider the evidence which Nealy had given as to his fear and anger as a result of the words uttered by Casimiri in the Albany Tavern and the punching and shoving which followed both inside the tavern and on the street. The jury should have been told that, even if the words spoken by Casimiri, coupled with his actions, did not raise in their minds a reasonable doubt as to whether or not Nealy had been "provoked" as that term is defined in s. 215 of the *Code*, or that Nealy was incapable of forming the required intent by reason of the consumption of alcohol, the jury was still to consider all these surrounding circumstances in coming to a conclusion as to whether Nealy possessed the requisite intent needed to commit murder pursuant to s. 212 (*a*) of the *Code*.

That, I believe, is the position that has been adopted by this court. In *R. v. Clow* (1985), 44 C.R. (3d) 228 at 231 (Ont. C.A.), there appears a statement of this court which is applicable to the facts of this case:

> It is respectfully submitted that the learned trial Judge erred in failing to instruct the jury as to the cumulative effects of consumption of alcohol or drugs, provocation and excessive force in self-defence as it might relate to the requisite specific intent 'to mean to cause death or to mean to cause bodily harm which she knew was likely to cause death and was reckless as to whether death ensued'.

We agree.

In *R. v. Trecroce* (1980), 55 C.C.C. (2d) 202 (Ont. C.A.), Martin J.A. stated at p. 211:

> That is not to say, of course, that a jury, if they consider that the accused was honestly defending himself, may not entertain a reasonable doubt whether acting instinctively in the excitement of the moment he really contemplated the consequences of his actions and actually had the requisite intent for murder even though that inference might normally be drawn from his acts apart from the circumstances that he was defending himself.

And in *R. v. Campbell* (1977), 17 O.R. (2d) 673, 1 C.R. (3d) 309, S-49, 38 C.C.C. (2d) 6 (C.A.), Martin J.A. again stated at p. 683:

> Provocation may, of course, inspire the intent required to constitute murder. There may, however, be cases where the conduct of the victim amounting to provocation produces in the accused a state of excitement, anger or disturbance, as a result of which he might not contemplate the consequences of his acts and might not, in fact, intend to bring about those consequences. The accused's intent must usually be inferred from his conduct and the surrounding circumstances, and in some cases the provocation afforded by the victim, when considered in relation to the totality of the evidence, might create a reasonable doubt in the mind of the jury whether the accused had the requisite intent. Thus, in some cases, the provocative conduct of the victim might be a relevant item of evidence of the issue of intent whether the charge be murder or attempted murder. This, I take it, was the view of Eveleigh, J., in *R. v. Bruzas, supra,* at p. 369. Provocation in that aspect, however, does not operate as a 'defence' but rather as a relevant item of evidence on the issue of intent.

The case referred to, *R. v. Campbell, supra,* was one of attempted murder. The argument there advanced on behalf of the accused was that provocation within the meaning of the *Code* would reduce the offence to attempted manslaughter. That argument was rejected because provocation is applicable only to reduce an act which would otherwise be murder to manslaughter. Nevertheless it was held in that case that acts of provocation, whether in murder or attempted murder, and by implication whether or not sufficient to satisfy the *Code* definition, might be relevant to the issue of intent.

R. v. Clow, supra, was relied upon and followed by this court in *R. v. Desveaux* (1986), 51 C.R. (3d) 173, 26 C.C.C. (3d) 88. In that case as well the statement of principle contained in *R. v. Clow* was a fundamental element in the decision of the court.

Although the question has not been specifically considered by the Supreme Court of Canada, there are some statements in various reasons of that court that lend support to the position set forth in *R. v. Clow* and *R. v. Desveaux*. In *R. v. Faid*, [1983] 1 S.C.R. 265, 33 C.R. (3d) 1, 2 C.C.C. (3d) 513 at 517-18, Dickson J. was considering the question as to whether or not excessive force in self-defence could result in a conviction of manslaughter. He stated:

> ... though the facts on which the defence of self-defence was unsuccessfully sought to be based may in some cases go to show that the defendant acted under provocation or that, although acting unlawfully, he lacked the intent to kill or cause grievous bodily harm. In such cases a verdict of manslaughter would be proper.

In *Brisson v. R.*, [1982] 2 S.C.R. 227, 29 C.R. (3d) 289, 69 C.C.C. (2d) 97 [Que.], the court was once again considering whether excessive force in self-defence could reduce a charge of murder to manslaughter. Dickson J., speaking on behalf of the court, stated at p. 258-59:

> To summarize, I would reject the notion that excessive force in self-defence, *unless related to intent under s. 212 of the Code* or to provocation, reduces what would otherwise be murder to manslaughter. [The italics are mine.]

In *R. v. Gee*, [1982] 2 S.C.R. 286, 29 C.R. (3d) 347, 68 C.C.C. (2d) 516, 43 N.R. 128 at 137, Dickson J., speaking for the majority, stated:

> In my view, it cannot be said that force can be partially justified. Success under s. 27 leads to acquittal. If the defence under s. 27 does not succeed, the jury should render the verdict which would have been rendered, absent s. 27. This may be a verdict of manslaughter, not because of partial justification under s. 27 but because the special mental element required for guilt of murder has not been proven. In other words, the half-way house is not to be found in s. 27 but, if at all, in s. 212.

These authorities emphasize the importance of the issue of intent. Further, they indicate that all the circumstances surrounding the act of killing must be taken into account in determining whether or not the accused had the intent required for the commission of murder. It may well be that the evidence does not give rise to a reasonable doubt as to whether there was provocation or whether the accused lacked the ability to form that intent as a result of consuming alcohol or drugs. Nevertheless, the evidence adduced on these issues, viewed cumulatively, may be of great importance in determining the crucial issue of intent.

Not every case where the consumption of alcohol and some form of provocation is involved will require a specific direction as to the cumulative effect of these factors. Still, it will be preferable in most cases and essential in some that such a direction be given. In the circumstances of this case, fairness required no less than the addition to the charge of two or three sentences which would be sufficient to bring to the jury's mind the necessity of considering all the pertinent facts in resolving the issue of intent.

The omission of the trial judge to give such a direction coupled with the improper aspects of the cross-examination of the accused, are sufficient to require a direction for a new trial. In the result, I would, with some regret, allow the appeal and direct a new trial.

In *R. v. Kent* (2005), 29 C.R. (6th) 33 (Alta. C.A.) Justice Low, writing for the B.C. Court of Appeal, could find no clear advice from the Supreme Court as to the use of a rolled up charge. The Court found that in the circumstances of this case a rolled up charge was unnecessary and might have confused the jury into thinking provocation was not available where there was a murderous intent. The accused's wife became angry when the accused returned home with drugs he had bought with money she had given him for groceries. According to the accused she said many mean things, including that her ex-husband would not have slept with his sister, as the accused had. This made him mad and he strangled her. The Court found that there was an air of reality for provocation and ordered a new trial.

In *R. v. Mohamed,* 2011 ONCA 260 (Ont. C.A.) the Ontario Court of Appeal noted that the concern that the jury will compartmentalise the evidence in a murder case is the greatest where a discrete defence has been left to the jury. The danger is that the jury, having rejected a defence such as provocation, will not consider the provocation evidence when dealing with intent. In *Mohamed* the trial judge had rightly found no air of reality to the defence of provocation and there was no concern that the jury would not consider all the circumstances in the face of explicit and repeated instructions to do so. See too *R. v. Flores* (2011), 83 C.R. (6th) 93 (Ont. C.A.).

8. GENERAL REVIEW QUESTIONS

1. **Jack and Jill have had a tempestuous love affair for over a year. Jack had always been highly strung. He had also endured periods of acute depression for which he had received several weeks of psychiatric counselling. He always seemed to fear the worst. Actually his often expressed suspicions that Jill was dating another man were well-grounded. Her other boyfriend, Bill, with whom she was much more emotionally involved, demanded that she "ditch"Jack. She decided on the strategy of first calming him with alcohol and then playing him a pre-recorded message on a cassette, during which she would leave his apartment. She carried her unloaded pistol in her purse for "protection". They had about five whiskys each at a local pub in less than two hours. As Jack was driving Jill to his apartment, Jill for some unknown reason — probably as a result of her intoxication — departed from her plan and started to play her cassette tape in the car. The message began brutally: "Jack, I've had enough. You are physically repulsive and a mental wreck. I love Bill and have done so**

passionately for two months . . .". It is not clear what happened next. All that is known is that Jack's car suddenly veered off the road, somersaulted and struck a fence. Miraculously Jack and Jill were unhurt. According to Jack, he was devastated by the message and he might well have lunged at Jill while he was still driving. In any event his mind was blank until he realized he had been in an accident, that Jill was pointing a gun at him and that he then stabbed her repeatedly with a screwdriver, which had been on the dashboard. A third party on the scene says Jack had a dull glazed look about him, was shouting "You bitch! You bitch!" hysterically and that it was extremely difficult to stop Jack's convulsive-like assault. Jill later died of the multiple wounds. Her pistol was found on the front seat of the car.

Jack stands charged with second degree murder. His defence counsel asks you for a brief as to his viable total or partial defences. Discuss relevant authorities and comment on the strength or weakness of each defence.

2. Jamie has had a tortured adolesence struggling with his sexual identity. At the age of 16 he recently came to terms with the fact that he was gay. Until his arrest he was living with his lover, Fred, a chartered accountant, aged 28. One of Jamie's former girlfriends, Bettie, realized Jamie's preference had changed. She became partly jealous and partly plain vicious. Whenever she saw Jamie she taunted him with anti-gay remarks. One night Jamie and Fred had been at a bar for several hours. Each had consumed about ten beers. Bettie came up to them. Just the sight of her made his blood boil. She again taunted him with several anti-gay remarks before moving off. Jamie told Fred he'd had enough. "The next time", said Jamie, "I'll thrash her to teach her a lesson she'll never forget." Fred said, "She deserves it." Jamie found a stick used to prop up a window and put it on the bar table. An hour and two beers later — during which time Jamie was morose — Bettie again arrived. She went up to Jamie and said all deserve AIDS. It's God's way of disapproving." Jamie would testify, "This was the last straw. I saw red again, picked up the stick and hit, hit, hit." In fact Bettie was knocked unconscious with about six very heavy blows. She died in hospital several days later. The fatal assault took less than a minute. Fred just watched, only intervening after the sixth blow, saying "That's enough".

You are an articled clerk to the prosecutor. She has charged both Jamie and Fred with first degree murder on the basis that they committed murder contrary to s. 229(a) that was planned and deliberate under s. 231(2). She is incensed by the wanton violence and will press hard for a conviction of first degree murder. She asks you for a legal memorandum assessing the strengths and weaknesses of all possible full and partial defences and the likely verdict. She notes there is no possibility of the defence of insanity.

9.   ENTRAPMENT

R. v. MACK

[1988] 2 S.C.R. 903, 67 C.R. (3d) 1, 44 C.C.C. (3d) 513,
1988 CarswellBC 701, 1988 CarswellBC 767

LAMER J.: —

INTRODUCTION

The central issue in this appeal concerns the doctrine of entrapment. The parties, in essence, ask this court to outline its position on the conceptual basis for the application of the doctrine and the manner in which an entrapment claim should be dealt with by the courts. Given the length of these reasons due to the complexity of the subject, I have summarized my findings on pages 964 to 966 of these reasons.

The Facts

The appellant was charged with unlawful possession of a narcotic for the purpose of trafficking. He testified at trial and, at the close of the case for the defence, brought an application for a stay of proceedings on the basis of entrapment. The application was refused and a conviction entered by Wetmore Co. Ct. J., sitting without a jury, in written reasons reported in (1983), 34 C.R. (3d) 228. A notice of appeal from that decision was filed with the British Columbia Court of Appeal but the appeal books were not filed within the time prescribed. Counsel for the appellant sought and obtained, with the consent of Crown Counsel, an order dispensing with the requirement that transcripts of evidence be filed and permitting counsel to base their arguments solely on the reasons for judgment of Wetmore Co. Ct. J. The Chief Justice of British Columbia directed that a panel of five judges hear the appeal. For the reasons given by Craig J.A., on behalf of the court, the appeal was dismissed. This decision is now reported at (1985), 49 C.R. (3d) 169. Leave to appeal was granted by this court.

It is necessary to describe in some detail the relevant facts. In view of the particular procedural history of this appeal, I think it is appropriate to reproduce in its entirety the summary of the evidence provided for in the reasons for judgment of Wetmore Co. Ct. J. (at pp. 234-37):

Through information obtained from an officer of the Ontario Provincial Police, one Momotiuk was brought to British Columbia. This man had apparently been dealing in narcotics in Kenora, Ontario. He was placed under police "handlers" in Vancouver, he visited the accused on a number of occasions, and eventually a transaction was set up whereby the accused would deliver cocaine to Momotiuk.

The accused testified. He first met Momotiuk in 1979 in Montreal where the accused was visiting one Franks. The accused understood Franks and Momotiuk to be associated in some clothing franchise.

The accused at this time was attempting to develop some property for sale near De Roche, British Columbia, and told Franks and Momotiuk of this and both expressed some interest in buying. Both arrived in British Columbia in October 1979. In the course of this visit the accused says that Momotiuk told him he was a drug trafficker in Kenora and wanted some "Thai pot". The accused says he had no interest.

Momotiuk, according to the accused, called later still wanting to make drug deals, and the accused told him he was interested only in real estate deals.

The accused again went to a yoga retreat near Montreal in December 1979. Franks and Momotiuk visited him there. Momotiuk produced some cocaine, which he and Franks used, and again asked the accused to become a supplier. A few days later they met again. At this time conversation was directed to show Momotiuk as an importer of drugs on a large scale, and again the accused was invited to join in and refused.

In January and February there were approximately seven telephone calls from Momotiuk to the accused soliciting his involvement. The accused says he refused.

In mid-February 1980 Momotiuk visited the accused again, asking him to supply drugs. The accused says he told Momotiuk he was not interested and asked to be left alone. Momotiuk continued to visit two or three times and also telephoned.

In March the accused says Momotiuk arrived again. They went for a walk in the woods. Momotiuk produced a pistol and was going to show the accused his marksmanship. He was dissuaded because of the probability of startling the horses nearby. The accused says that at this remote area Momotiuk said, "A person could get lost." This the accused says was a threat. He says the matter of drugs was again raised and the accused says he was adamant that he had no knowledge of drugs sources.

The accused was asked to phone him twice and did not. One Matheson attended at the accused's residence on 13th March with a message that Momotiuk was very excited and wanted to see him at the Biltmore Hotel. The accused says he wanted nothing to do with Momotiuk but was terrified of him and agreed to go into town to the Biltmore. He also says that Matheson told him Momotiuk had some friends with him. This the accused took to be other members of this illegal syndicate.

While en route to the city he twice noted a car which seemed to be following him. This was probably so, because undercover police officers were doing a surveillance at the time. On arrival at the hotel he met Momotiuk. Again he was informed of the syndicate. He was asked then if he wished to see the buying power. The accused agreed. He was directed to a car outside the hotel. In this car was an open briefcase with $50,000 exposed. The custodian, unknown to the accused, was an undercover policeman.

The accused returned to the hotel, Momotiuk asked him to get a sample and gave him $50 for this purpose.

The accused left and went to a supplier he had known of from years back. This supplier, one Goldsmith, now dead, heard the accused's story and agreed to supply "in order to get Doug (Momotiuk) off me". He obtained the sample and delivered it to Momotiuk, who tested it and said to get as much as he could. He returned to the supplier and offered $35,000 to $40,000 for a pound.

At the meeting the following day the accused had still not acquired the drugs and he says that at this point he was told to get his act together, in a threatening way.

I need not detail the accused's evidence of the following two days. He obtained 12 ounces of cocaine, and was to pay $27,000 for it. This credit, he says, was extended to him by

Goldsmith on the basis of payment when delivered to Momotiuk. It was in the course of this delivery that he was arrested.

It is on the basis of this testimony that the accused says he was entrapped. Momotiuk, Matheson and Franks did not testify. Neither did "Bonnie", the accused's former wife, who was apparently present at one of the Montreal meetings, where cocaine was produced and some discussion took place.

The accused has drug convictions in 1972 and 1976, two in 1978 and one in 1979. Those in 1976, one in 1978 and one in 1979 involved cocaine. He says his former use of drugs arose to relieve back pain, but in 1978 he discovered relief from yoga and gave up the use of narcotics. The offence in 1979 was a fall from grace when he met up with old friends.

Decisions of the Courts Below

Wetmore Co. Ct. J. held that the judgment of Estey J. in *Amato v. The Queen*, [1982] 2 S.C.R. 418, and of the British Columbia Court of Appeal in *R. v. Jewitt* (1983), 34 C.R. (3d) 193 (rev'd on other grounds, [1985] 2 S.C.R. 128), established that entrapment is recognized as part of the abuse of process doctrine and a stay of proceedings arising from a finding of entrapment is not a "defence" in the traditional sense of that word. This distinction between a "stay" and a "defence" was important in terms of the burden and standard of proof. Wetmore Co. Ct. J. decided the evidential burden rested on the party seeking the stay to satisfy a court on a balance of probabilities that there had been entrapment which would constitute an abuse of the courts' processes. He stated at p. 232:

> To ask the court to preclude either side — the state, represented by the prosecution, or the defence — from the adjudication of their differences must involve satisfying the court that its processes cannot result in the attainment of justice through the traditional avenue of a full and open trial. To make that finding, it seems fundamental to a system of justice in a free and democratic society that the court must be satisfied that its processes have been so abused that those very processes are precluded from attaining justice. Satisfaction in such a state of affairs existing must be more than a reasonable suspicion.

In Wetmore Co. Ct. J.'s view, the presumption of innocence until proven guilty beyond a reasonable doubt was not violated. He stated that this presumption applied at trial while a motion for a stay was to really determine whether the appellant would have a trial. It was not significant that in this case the motion came at the end of the proceeding: "What counsel is asking is that I stop the proceedings before a verdict. This amounts to aborting the trial" (p. 234). Wetmore Co. Ct. J.'s view of the nature of the entrapment claim may be discerned in the following passage, at p. 234:

> This evidentiary burden is of great importance in the matter of entrapment because fundamental to any such finding is the conclusion that the accused had no disposition to commit the crime but succumbed to improper enticement by authorities of the state. As in all matters of the mental element in criminal matters, the state of mind usually comes from inferences from established facts. I must test those facts to say then which is more probable as to the accused's predisposition, not merely if something is rationally possible.

After reviewing the evidence, Wetmore Co. Ct. J. noted, at p. 237, that the appellant's evidence found support in the testimony of the police officers to some extent: "They agree that Momotiuk was difficult to 'handle'". The stay was refused, however, because the appellant had not met the burden of proof. Wetmore Co. Ct. J. concluded, at p. 237:

> In fairness to the accused, I should say that, if I were to decide this issue on the basis of the Crown having to negate entrapment beyond a reasonable doubt, I would have such a doubt.
>
> I find, however, that it is far more probable that the accused became involved in this transaction for profit, rather than through persistent inducement and fear. Given his record and the alacrity with which he produced on seeing the $50,000 in March 1980, I find it much more probable that he then saw a situation of profit and acted upon it. There is no doubt in my mind that the opportunity was made available through the tactics of the police and their agent, but that falls short of entrapping a person into the commission of an act that he had no intention of doing.

The British Columbia Court of Appeal held that having regard to this court's decision in *Jewitt, supra*, and the opinion of several of the Justices in *Amato, supra*, entrapment is available in response to a criminal charge as an aspect of abuse of process but not as a substantive defence. It was further held that the determination of the existence of entrapment is a question of law to be decided by the trial judge. The appellant bore the onus of proof on a balance of probabilities, since an accused claiming entrapment is seeking to have the case disposed of on the basis of police misconduct as opposed to the merits.

Having decided the applicable legal issues, the Court of Appeal referred to the trial judge's conclusion that the appellant acted out of a desire for profit. Craig J.A. then stated at p. 183: "I think that the judge was right in concluding that there was no entrapment in this case." The appeal was therefore dismissed.

[Justice Lamer then thoroughly reviewed the American and Canadian jurisprudence and summarized his conclusions.]

. . . .

Summary

In conclusion, and to summarize, the proper approach to the doctrine of entrapment is that which was articulated by Estey J. in *Amato, supra*, and elaborated upon in these reasons. As mentioned and explained earlier there is entrapment when,

(a) the authorities provide a person with an opportunity to commit an offence without acting on a reasonable suspicion that this person is already engaged in criminal activity or pursuant to a *bona fide* inquiry;

(b) although having such a reasonable suspicion or acting in the course of a *bona fide* inquiry, they go beyond providing an opportunity and induce the commission of an offence.

It is neither useful nor wise to state in the abstract what elements are necessary to prove an entrapment allegation. It is, however, essential that the factors relied on by a court relate to the underlying reasons for the recognition of the doctrine in the first place.

Since I am of the view that the doctrine of entrapment is not dependent upon culpability, the focus should not be on the effect of the police conduct on the accused's state of mind. Instead, it is my opinion that as far as possible an objective assessment of the conduct of the police and their agents is required. The predisposition, or the past, present or suspected criminal activity of the accused, is relevant only as a part of the determination of whether the provision of an opportunity by the authorities to the accused to commit the offence was justifiable. Further, there must be sufficient connection between the past conduct of the accused and the provision of an opportunity, since otherwise the police suspicion will not be reasonable. While predisposition of the accused is, though not conclusive, of some relevance in assessing the initial approach by the police of a person with the offer of an opportunity to commit an offence it is never relevant as regards whether they went beyond an offer, since that is to be assessed with regard to what the average non-predisposed person would have done.

The absence of a reasonable suspicion or a *bona fide* inquiry is significant in assessing the police conduct because of the risk that the police will attract people who would not otherwise have any involvement in a crime and because it is not a proper use of the police power to simply go out and test the virtue of people on a random basis. The presence of reasonable suspicion or the mere existence of a *bona fide* inquiry will, however, never justify entrapment techniques: the police may not go beyond providing an opportunity regardless of their perception of the accused's character and regardless of the existence of an honest inquiry. To determine whether the police have employed means which go further than providing an opportunity, it is useful to consider any or all of the following factors:

— the type of crime being investigated and the availability of other techniques for the police detection of its commission;

— whether an average person, with both strengths and weaknesses, in the position of the accused would be induced into the commission of a crime;

— the persistence and number of attempts made by the police before the accused agreed to committing the offence;

— the type of inducement used by the police including: deceit, fraud, trickery or reward;

— the timing of the police conduct, in particular whether the police have instigated the offence or became involved in ongoing criminal activity;

— whether the police conduct involves an exploitation of human characteristics such as the emotions of compassion, sympathy and friendship;

- whether the police appear to have exploited a particular vulnerability of a person such as a mental handicap or a substance addiction;
- the proportionality between the police involvement, as compared to the accused, including an assessment of the degree of harm caused or risked by the police, as compared to the accused, and the commission of any illegal acts by the police themselves;
- the existence of any threats, implied or express, made to the accused by the police or their agents;
- whether the police conduct is directed at undermining other constitutional values.

This list is not exhaustive, but I hope it contributes to the elaboration of a structure for the application of the entrapment doctrine. Thus far, I have not referred to the requirement in *Amato, supra*, per Estey J., that the conduct must, in all the circumstances, be shocking or outrageous. I am of the view that this is a factor which is best considered under the procedural issues to which I will now turn.

Procedural Issues

The resolution of the issues surrounding the manner in which an entrapment claim should be considered at trial is, in my view, entirely dependant upon the conceptual basis for the defence, outlined earlier. If I were of the opinion that there was a substantive or culpability-based defence of entrapment, I would readily come to the conclusion that the defence raised a question of fact, which should be decided by a jury when there is a sufficient evidentiary basis on which to raise the defence, and I would hold that the onus would rest on the Crown to disprove the existence of entrapment beyond a reasonable doubt. Having come to the opposite viewpoint on the rationale for recognizing the doctrine of entrapment, I am not persuaded that the adoption of rules which historically, and by virtue of the *Charter*, conform to most substantive defences is either necessary or correct. It seems to me, however, that this court must be clear on how an entrapment claim is to be handled, as a brief review of some lower court decisions suggests that there is, at present, and understandably so, a great deal of confusion on the matter.

A. Who Decides: Judge or Jury?

Both the appellant and respondent agree that objective entrapment, involving police misconduct and not the accused's state of mind, is a question to be decided by the trial judge, and that the proper remedy is a stay of proceedings. I too am of this view. The question of unlawful involvement by the state in the instigation of criminal conduct is one of law, or mixed law and fact.

. . . .

Supporting the view that a judge should decide is the decision of the Court of Appeal in the present case, referred to earlier. Further, Tallis J.A. (Cameron J.A. concurring) in *R. v. Mistra* (1986), 32 C.C.C. (3d) 97 (Sask. C.A.), at p. 122, appears to have approved the decision of the British Columbia Court of Appeal in the present case and in *R. v Showman*, (unreported). In *Jewitt, supra*, at the level of the Court of Appeal, Anderson J.A. gave four reasons for his conclusion that the issue of entrapment is one to be decided by a trial judge (*supra*, at pp. 219-20). I am in complete agreement with the first and the fourth of these reasons. Anderson J.A. began by observing, at p. 219:

> . . . the courts have always been the masters of their own process and it is for the courts alone to determine whether there has been an abuse of process. All issues relating to abuse of process require a factual determination but it does not follow that such a determination should be made by a jury.

And he concluded at p. 220:

> . . . as a matter of policy, the issue of entrapment should be left to the courts so that standards and guidelines may be established by case law. Such a development will be impossible if issues of entrapment are left to juries.

Anderson J.A. made reference to potential prejudice arising should the issue go to the jury, for the jury may find the accused guilty because of the accused's criminal record or bad reputation (citing Frankfurter J. in *Sherman, supra*, at p. 382). I am not concerned by this for two reasons: firstly, as I noted earlier, in most cases the accused will have committed the offence and his or her guilt is not in issue; secondly, in my view the past criminal conduct of the accused is not relevant to the analysis, except where it relates to the reasonable suspicions of the police. The last point made by Anderson J.A. was that an accused could ask for evidence to be excluded by a trial judge under s. 24(2) of the *Charter* because of entrapment, and be denied that request and yet, in the same case, a jury may find that the police conduct brought the administration of justice into disrepute. He felt that such a result should be avoided. I prefer to express no opinion in this case on the propriety of a s. 24(2) application to exclude evidence because of entrapment. I am, however, of the view that the reasons which support a judicial determination of applications under s. 24(2) for the exclusion of evidence are equally relevant to the present discussion.

This court has held that the determination of whether the admission of evidence obtained in violation of a *Charter* right would bring the administration of justice into disrepute is one which should be made by a trial judge (*R. v. Therens*, [1985] 1 S.C.R. 613, per Le Dain J., at p. 653). In articulating how a trial judge should engage him or herself in that analysis, I stated in *Collins, supra*, that a judge should consider the question from the perspective of a reasonable person, "dispassionate and fully apprised of all the circumstances", and I commented that "The reasonable person is usually the average person in the community but only when that community's current mood is reasonable" (*supra*, at p. 282). The issue there, as here, is maintaining respect for the values which, over the long term, hold the community together. One of those very fundamental values is the preservation of the purity of the administration of justice. In my opinion a judge is particularly well suited to make this determination and this finding should be guided by the above quoted comments from *Collins, supra*. Further, as noted by Anderson J.A. in *Jewitt, supra*, and commented on by Vallerand J.A. in *Baxter, supra*, if one of the advantages of allowing claims of entrapment is the development of standards of conduct on the part of the state, it is essential that decisions on entrapment, and those allowing the claim especially, be carefully explained so as to provide future guidance; this is not something the jury process lends itself to. Accordingly, I am of the firm opinion that the issue of entrapment should be resolved by the trial judge for policy reasons.

Finally, I am of the view that before a judge considers whether a stay of proceedings lies because of entrapment, it must be absolutely clear that the Crown had discharged its burden of proving beyond a reasonable doubt that the accused had committed all the essential elements of the offence. If this is not clear and there is a jury, the guilt or innocence of the accused must be determined apart from evidence which is relevant only to the issue of entrapment. This protects the right of an accused to an acquittal where the circumstances so warrant. If the jury decides the accused has committed all of the elements of the crime, it is then open to the judge to stay the proceedings because of entrapment by refusing to register a conviction. It is not necessary nor advisable in this case to expand on the details of procedure. Because the guilt or innocence of the accused is not in issue at the time an entrapment claim is to be decided, the right of an accused to the benefit of a jury trial in s. 11(*f*) of the *Charter* is in no way infringed.

B. Who Bears the Burden of Proof and on What Standard?

. . . .

I have come to the conclusion that it is not inconsistent with the requirement that the Crown prove the guilt of the accused beyond a reasonable doubt to place the onus on the accused to prove on a balance of probabilities that the conduct of the state is an abuse of process because of entrapment. I repeat: the guilt or innocence of the accused is not in issue. The accused has done nothing that entitles him or her to an acquittal; the Crown has engaged in conduct, however, that disentitles it to a conviction. This point was made by Dickson C.J. in *Jewitt, supra*, in a passage cited earlier. This court in *Jewitt*, and more recently in *R. v. Keyowski*, [1988] 1 S.C.R. 657, affirmed that a court may only enter a stay for an abuse of process in the "clearest of cases" (*Jewitt, supra*, at p. 137; *Keyowski, supra*, at p. 659). It is obvious to me that requiring an accused to raise only a reasonable doubt is entirely inconsistent with a rule which permits a stay in only the "clearest of cases". More fundamentally, the claim of entrapment is a very serious allegation against the state. The state must be given substantial room to develop techniques which assist it in its fight against crime in society. It is only when the police and their agents engage in a conduct which offends basic values of the community that the doctrine of entrapment can apply. To place a lighter onus on the accused would have the result of unnecessarily hampering state action against crime. In my opinion the best way to achieve a balance between the interests of the court as guardian of the administration of justice, and the interests of society in the prevention and detection of crime, is to require an accused to demonstrate by a preponderance of evidence that the prosecution is an abuse of process because of entrapment. I would also note that this is consistent with the rules governing s. 24(2) applications (*Collins, supra*, at p. 277), where the general issue is similar to that raised in entrapment cases: would the administration of justice be brought into disrepute?

Before turning to the particular case at bar I would like to comment on the requirement in *Amato, supra*, that "In the result, the scheme so perpetrated must in all the circumstances be so shocking and outrageous *as to bring the administration of justice into disrepute*" (at p. 446, emphasis in original). I would, upon reconsideration, prefer to use the language adopted by Dickson C.J. in *Jewitt, supra*, and hold that the defence of entrapment be recognized in only the "clearest of cases". The approach set out in these reasons should provide a court with the necessary standard by which to judge the particular scheme. Once the accused has demonstrated that the strategy used by the police goes beyond the limits described earlier, a judicial condonation of the prosecution would by definition offend the community. It is not necessary to go further and ask whether the demonstrated entrapment would "shock" the community, since the accused has already shown that the administration of justice has been brought into disrepute.

In conclusion, the onus lies on the accused to demonstrate that the police conduct has gone beyond permissible limits to the extent that allowing the prosecution or the entry of a conviction would amount to an abuse of the judicial process by the state. The question is one of mixed law and fact and should be resolved by the trial judge. A stay should be entered in the "clearest of cases" only.

Disposition

In determining whether the doctrine of entrapmemt applies to the present appeal, this court is restricted to the summary of evidence provided by Wetmore Co. Ct. J. in his reasons. I am of the view that a stay of proceedings should be entered in this case. While the trial judge had the advantage of hearing the testimony of the appellant, and normally findings on entrapment cases should not be disturbed because of this, I am concerned that in this case too much emphasis was placed on the appellant's state of mind. Earlier in my summary of the decisions below I cited a passage from the trial judge's reasons wherein he stated that the fundamental issue was the appellant's state of mind and his predisposition to crime. This, perhaps, explains why in his conclusion the trial judge stated the appellant was not entrapped because he acted out of a desire to profit from the transaction. If the trial judge had been permitted only to evaluate the conduct of the police objectively, I think he might well have, and in any event, ought to have come to the conclusion the police conduct amounted to entrapment.

From the facts it appears that the police had reasonable suspicion that the appellant was involved in criminal conduct. The issue is whether the police went too far in their efforts to attract the appellant into the commission of the offence.

Returning to the list of factors I outlined earlier, this crime is obviously one for which the state must be given substantial leeway. The drug-trafficking business is not one which lends itself to the traditional devices of police investigation. It is absolutely essential, therefore, for police or their agents to get involved and gain the trust and confidence of the people who do the trafficking or who supply the drugs. It is also a crime of enormous social consequence which causes a great deal of harm in society generally. This factor alone is very critical and makes this case somewhat difficult.

The police do not appear, however, to have been interrupting an ongoing criminal enterprise, and the offence was clearly brought about by their conduct and would not have occurred absent their involvement. The police do not appear to have exploited a narcotics addiction of the appellant since he testified that he had already given up his use of narcotics. Therefore, he was not, at the time, trying to recover from an addiction. Nonetheless, he also testified that he was no longer involved in drugs and, if this is true, it suggests that the police were indeed trying to make the appellant take up his former lifestyle. The persistence of the police requests, as a result of the equally persistent refusals by the appellant, supports the appellant's version of events on this point. The length of time, approximately six months, and the repetition of requests it took before the appellant agreed to commit the offence also demonstrate that the police had to go further than merely providing the appellant with the opportunity once it became evident that he was unwilling to join the alleged drug syndicate.

Perhaps the most important and determinative factor in my opinion is the appellant's testimony that the informer acted in a threatening manner when they went for a walk in the woods, and the further testimony that he was told to get his act together after he did not provide the supply of drugs he was asked for. I believe this conduct was unacceptable. If the police must go this far, they have gone beyond providing the appellant with an opportunity. I do not, therefore, place much significance on the fact that the appellant eventually committed the offence when shown the money. Obviously the appellant knew much earlier that he could make a profit by getting involved in the drug enterprise and he still refused. I have come to the conclusion that the average person in the position of the appellant might also have committed the offence, if only to finally satisfy this threatening informer and end all further contact. As a result I would, on the evidence, have to find that the police conduct in this case was unacceptable. Thus, the doctrine of entrapment applies to preclude the prosecution of the appellant. In my opinion, the appellant has met the burden of proof and the trial judge should have entered a stay of proceedings for abuse of process.

I would accordingly allow the appeal, set aside the conviction of the appellant and enter a stay of proceedings.

Appeal allowed.

For a comment, see Stuart, "*Mack:* Resolving Many But Not All Questions of Entrapment" (1989), 67 C.R. (3d) 68.

The defence on entrapment has rarely succeeded. For an example of a stay for entrapment see *R. v. J.S.* (2001), 152 C.C.C. (3d) 317 (Ont. C.A.).

R. v. BARNES

[1991] 1 S.C.R. 449, 3 C.R. (4th) 1, 63 C.C.C. (3d) 1,
1991 CarswellBC 915, 1991 CarswellBC 11 (S.C.C.)

1   LAMER C.J. (WILSON, LA FOREST, SOPINKA, GONTHIER, CORY and STEVENSON JJ. concurring): — This case involves a consideration of the defence of entrapment as set out by this court in *R. v. Mack*, [1988] 2 S.C.R. 903. In particular, this court is asked whether the accused was subjected to random virtue-testing by an undercover police officer in the city of Vancouver. . . . .

Facts

2   On January 12, 1989, the appellant sold one gram of hashish to an undercover police officer near the Granville Mall area of Vancouver. The parties do not dispute the facts surrounding the sale, which are as follows.

3   The undercover officer was involved in a "buy-and-bust" operation conducted by the Vancouver Police Department. In a buy-and-bust operation, undercover police officers attempt to buy illicit drugs from individuals who appear, in the opinion of the officers, to be inclined to sell such drugs. If an officer is successful, the individual is immediately arrested for trafficking.

4   This particular operation was undertaken by the Department with respect to the Granville Mall area in the city of Vancouver, which covers a six-block

section of Granville Street. On the day of the arrest, the undercover officer approached the accused, Philip Barnes, and his friend, as they were walking towards Granville Street. The officer testified at trial that she approached the accused and his friend because she had "a hunch, a feeling that they'd—possibly might be in possession". She believed that he and his friend fit the description of persons who possibly had drugs in their possession and who would be willing to sell to her: "I had a feeling. They fit my general criteria. I look for males hanging around, dressed scruffy and in jeans, wearing a jean jacket or leather jacket, runners or black boots, that tend to look at people a lot." The officer indicated that there was nothing else that aroused her suspicions.

5   The officer approached the accused and asked him if he had any "weed". He said "no", but his friend repeated to him: "She wants some weed." The accused again responded negatively. The officer persisted and the accused then agreed to sell a small amount of cannabis resin to the officer for $15. Shortly afterwards, the accused was arrested by another officer and small amounts of cannabis resin and marijuana were seized from his person.

6   The accused was tried in the County Court of Vancouver before Leggatt Co. Ct. J., and was found guilty of trafficking in cannabis resin, of the included offence of possession of cannabis resin for the purpose of trafficking, and of possession of marijuana. The accused conceded that he sold illicit drugs to the officer, but argued that a judicial stay for entrapment should be directed. He claimed that he had no intention of selling drugs on the day in question, but felt sorry for the undercover officer; he agreed to sell only because he believed that his friend wanted to meet a woman and that this was a way of gaining an introduction. The trial judge held that the police officer had engaged in "random virtue testing", which was unacceptable according to the judgment of this court in *Mack*, *supra*, and therefore ordered a judicial stay of the proceedings.

7   The British Columbia Court of Appeal allowed the Crown's appeal and ordered a new trial.

. . . .

Analysis

Did the police officer engage in random virtue-testing?

14   To resolve this appeal, this court must consider whether the conduct of the undercover police officer was acceptable in light of the guidelines set out in *Mack*, *supra*. In *Mack*, I attempted to define the circumstances in which police conduct in the course of investigating and uncovering criminal activity ceases to be acceptable and, instead, amounts to the unacceptable entrapment of

individuals. The defence of entrapment is based on the notion that limits should be imposed on the ability of the police to participate in the commission of an offence. As a general rule, it is expected in our society that the police will direct their attention towards uncovering criminal activity that occurs without their involvement.

. . . .

16   It is apparent that the police officer involved in this case did not have a "reasonable suspicion" that the accused was already engaged in unlawful drug-related activity. The factors that drew the officer's attention to this particular accused—his manner of dress, the length of his hair—were not sufficient to give rise to a reasonable suspicion that criminal acts were being committed. Furthermore, the subjectiveness of the officer's decision to approach the accused, based on a "hunch" or "feeling" rather than extrinsic evidence, also indicates that the accused did not, as an individual, arouse a reasonable suspicion.

17   Consequently, the police conduct in this case will amount to entrapment unless the officer presented the accused with the opportunity to sell drugs in the course of a *bona fide* inquiry. In my opinion, the police officer involved in this case was engaged in such a *bona fide* investigation. First, there is no question that the officer's conduct was motivated by the genuine purpose of investigating and repressing criminal activity. The police department had reasonable grounds for believing that drug-related crimes were occurring throughout the Granville Mall area. The accused was not, therefore, approached for questionable motives unrelated to the investigation and repression of crime.

18   Secondly, the police department directed its investigation at a suitable area within the city of Vancouver. As I noted in *Mack, supra*, the police may present the opportunity to commit a particular crime to persons who are associated with a location where it is reasonably suspected that criminal activity is taking place. I stated, at p. 956:

> Of course, in certain situations the police may not know the identity of specific individuals, but they do know certain other facts, such as a particular location or area where it is reasonably suspected that certain criminal activity is occurring. In those cases it is clearly permissible to provide opportunities to people associated with the location under suspicion, even if these people are not themselves under suspicion.

The police department in this case focused its investigation on an area of Vancouver, a section of Granville Street covering approximately six city blocks, where it was reasonably suspected that drug-related crimes were occurring. In my opinion, they would not have been able to deal with the problem effectively had they restricted the investigation to a smaller area. Although there were particular areas within the Granville Mall where drug trafficking was especially serious, it is true that trafficking occurred at locations scattered generally throughout the Mall. It is also true that traffickers did not operate in a single place. It would be unrealistic for the police to focus their investigation on one specific part of the Mall given the tendency of traffickers to modify their techniques in response to police investigations. The trial judge admitted that the Mall was "known as an area of considerable drug activity". Similarly, the Court of Appeal found support in the evidence given at trial by Staff Sergeant Davies of the Vancouver City Police. In discussing the police department's activities in 1988, Staff Sergeant Davies indicated, at p. 370, that:

(a) Of the 2,294 persons charged with drug offences, approximately 22% were from incidents in the Granville Mall area;

(b) 506 arrests were made on the mall resulting in 659 charges—289 for trafficking, 199 for possession for the purpose of trafficking;

(c) 315 arrests were made in "buy and bust" operations resulting in 475 charges.

The Court of Appeal concluded, at p. 372:

The evidence at trial disclosed that sales of narcotics took place up and down the mall and it was for that reason that the undercover officer walked up and down the mall approaching persons and providing an opportunity to sell illicit drugs to her.

19   It is, therefore, my opinion that the police department was engaged, in these circumstances, in a *bona fide* inquiry.

20   I note that in many cases, the size of the area itself may indicate that the investigation is not *bona fide*. This will be so particularly when there are grounds for believing that the criminal activity being investigated is concentrated in part of a larger area targeted by the police. In this case, however, for the reasons discussed above, it was reasonable for the Vancouver Police Department to focus its investigation on the Granville Mall.

21   The accused argues that although the undercover officer was involved in a *bona fide* inquiry, she nevertheless engaged in random virtue-testing since she approached the accused without a reasonable suspicion that he was likely to commit a drug-related offence. She approached the accused simply because he was walking near Granville Street.

22   In my respectful opinion, this argument is based on a misinterpretation of *Mack*. I recognize that some of my language in *Mack* might be responsible for this misinterpretation. In particular, I stated, at p. 956:

In those cases [where there is a particular location where it is reasonably suspected that certain crimes are taking place] it is clearly permissible to provide opportunities to people associated with the location under suspicion, even if these people are not themselves under suspicion. This latter situation, however, is only justified if the police acted in the course of a bona fide investigation and are not engaged in random virtue-testing.

23   This statement should not be taken to mean that the police may not approach people on a random basis, in order to present the opportunity to commit an offence, in the course of a *bona fide* investigation. The basic rule articulated in *Mack* is that the police may only present the opportunity to commit a particular crime to an individual who arouses a suspicion that he or she is already engaged in the particular criminal activity. An exception to this rule arises when the police undertake a *bona fide* investigation directed at an area where it is reasonably suspected that criminal activity is occurring. When such a location is defined with sufficient precision, the police may present any person associated with the area with the opportunity to commit the particular offence. Such randomness is permissible within the scope of a *bona fide* inquiry.

24   Random virtue-testing, conversely, only arises when a police officer presents a person with the opportunity to commit an offence without a reasonable suspicion that:

(a) the person is already engaged in the particular criminal activity, or

(b) the physical location with which the person is associated is a place where the particular criminal activity is likely occurring.

25   In this case, the accused was approached by the officer when he was walking near the Granville Mall. The notion of being "associated" with a particular area for these purposes does not require more than being present in the area. As a result, the accused was associated with a location where it was reasonably believed that drug-related crimes were occurring. The officer's conduct was therefore justified under the first branch of the test for entrapment set out in *Mack*.

26   For these reasons, it is my opinion that the officer did not engage in random virtue-testing in this case. I would, therefore, dismiss the appeal and uphold the decision of the Court of Appeal ordering a new trial.

. . . .

65   MCLACHLIN J. (dissenting): — This appeal raises the question of when undercover police should be allowed to interfere with members of the public who are not under suspicion. This court laid out the basic principles governing undercover intrusion into private activity in *R. v. Mack*, [1988] 2 S.C.R. 903. The present case raises issues as to the ambit of the *Mack* test and its application. With the greatest respect, I cannot agree with the application of the *Mack* test adopted in this case by the Court of Appeal and endorsed by my colleague, Chief Justice Lamer. To accept this application would, in my considered opinion, represent endorsing a measure of state intrusion into the private affairs of citizens greater than any heretofore sanctioned by this court under the *Canadian Charter of Rights and Freedoms* and out of step with the philosophy and principles which

guided the decisions of this court in *R. v. Dyment*, [1988] 2 S.C.R. 417; *R. v. Duarte*, [1990] 1 S.C.R. 30; *R. v. Kokesch*, [1990] 3 S.C.R. 3; and *R. v. Wong*, [1990] 3 S.C.R. 36.

. . . . I . . . take the view that determining whether the police were acting pursuant to a *bona fide* inquiry requires consideration of more than the two factors referred to by Lamer C.J. More particularly, it involves consideration of whether the state's interest in repressing criminal activity in the particular case outweighs the interest which individuals have in being able to go about their daily lives without courting the risk that they will be subjected to the clandestine investigatory techniques of agents of the state. . . .

70   *Mack* therefore stands for the proposition that determination of entrapment must involve a balancing between the individual interest in being left alone and the state's interest in the repression of crime. Only where considerations such as fairness, justice and the need for protection from crime tip the balance in favour of the state will police conduct which offends the individual interests at stake be acceptable.

72   To paraphrase La Forest J. in *Wong, supra*, the notion is that individuals should be free to go about their daily business — to go shopping, to visit the theatre, to travel to and from work, to name but three examples — without courting the risk that they will be subjected to the clandestine investigatory techniques of agents of the state. A further risk inherent in overbroad undercover operations is that of discriminatory police work, where people are interfered with not because of reasonable suspicion but because of the colour of their skin or, as in this case, the quality of their clothing and their age.

73   It follows, from the fact that the concept of unlawful entrapment represents a balancing of conflicting interests, that the test for entrapment must likewise permit the measuring of relative harms. A test which does not permit weighing of the infringement on individual freedom and privacy in determining whether entrapment has occurred is to that extent deficient. As Lamer J. put it in the passage cited in *Mack*, what must be determined "in any given case" is where the proper balance lies.

74   While comments of Lamer J. in *Mack* on what constitutes a *bona fide* inquiry leave room for consideration of the individual interest in being left alone and not being induced into crime, the application of *Mack* proposed by him in this case permits little or no recognition of the interest of the individual in being left alone. All that is required is that the police act from a proper motive and that there be a suspicion of criminal activity within a general geographic area targeted by the police. That established, there is no room for consideration of factors vital to the balancing process, for example, the size of the area, the

number of innocent people going about legitimate activities who might be interfered with by the operation, and the seriousness of the crime in question.

75   In advocating a more refined test for *bona fide* inquiry than does Lamer C.J., I am motivated by concern for the implications of the test he proposes. That test would permit the police to extend their Granville Mall operation to all of Vancouver if statistics could be found to suggest that drug offences were occurring throughout Vancouver generally. The example is extreme. Yet it indicates the deficiency I see in the test proposed by Lamer C.J. In my view, a more sensitive test than that proposed by Lamer C.J. — one which permits appreciation of all relevant factors — is required.

76   I conclude that determination that the police were operating in the course of a bona fide inquiry within the meaning of *Mack* requires the court to consider not only the motive of the police and whether there is crime in the general area, but also other factors relevant to the balancing process, such as the likelihood of crime at the particular location targeted, the seriousness of the crime in question, the number of legitimate activities and persons who might be affected, and the availability of other less intrusive investigative techniques. In the final analysis, the question is whether the interception at the particular location where it took place was reasonable having regard to the conflicting interests of private citizens in being left alone from state interference and of the state in suppressing crime. If the answer to this question is yes, then the inquiry is *bona fide*.

77   In proposing a test that involves the balancing of conflicting interests, I am not insensitive to the criticism sometimes made that balancing formulas may lack certainty and predictability and accord too much discretion to reviewing judges. Notwithstanding such criticisms, a balancing approach remains the only rational way to address problems such as that presented in this case. Balancing formulas provide a way of channelling diverse information into an analytic framework, a framework which, while perhaps less than precise, is far superior to voting by "gut reaction". A balancing process, where conflicting interests are articulated and weighed against each other, forces us to face squarely the real policy issues involved in the case, to make explicit what otherwise, rightly or wrongly, may be assumed. Our constitutional law is embedded in the notion of defining and balancing strongly felt interests in society. The rules which elaborate that law must address the same concerns.

78   In point of fact, the test which I propose offers sufficient guidance to the police, in my view. It may reasonably be predicted, for example, that where there is no evidence of the likelihood of offences being committed at the place where the undercover operative is stationed, the interception is unlikely to be *bona fide* in the absence of a countervailing state interest of compelling proportions.

79   Having set out the considerations which should be addressed in determining whether an inquiry is *bona fide*, I turn to the facts of this case. In my view, the factors to which I have referred negate Lamer C.J.'s conclusion that the entire Granville Mall represents a suitable area within the city of Vancouver for the carrying out of a *bona fide* police inquiry. Granville Mall, located in downtown Vancouver, occupies a six-block stretch of Granville Street, a major north-south thoroughfare running through the entire city. The diversity of the Granville Mall area—which features theatres and restaurants, major department stores, large office towers, and within the radius of one block, the Vancouver Art Gallery, convention facilities and the Law Courts—means that on a daily basis literally thousands of individuals will frequent the Mall and thus fall subject to the clandestine investigatory techniques of the police on the policy proposed in this case.

80   Lamer C.J. bases his conclusion that targeting the entirety of Granville Mall as a site for undercover operations constituted a *bona fide* police inquiry, on the absence of improper motive and the fact that it was reasonably suspected that drug-related crimes were occurring on the mall. He refers to the trial judge's observation that Granville Mall is "known as an area of considerable drug activity". With the greatest respect, I cannot agree with Lamer C.J.'s conclusion at p. 461 that "[it] would be unrealistic for the police to focus their investigation on one specific part of the Mall". There is no evidence whatsoever that trafficking took place at the location of the undercover interception. Nor is there any evidence that traffickers systematically rotated locations to avoid detection. Indeed, the trial judge, in ordering a stay of proceedings, noted the legitimate character of much of the mall and held that the accused "was not at the immediate centre of drug trafficking". What evidence there is, established that the Granville Mall Skytrain station is known to the police as the "hub" of drug activity on the mall. That information suggests that it would be perfectly realistic for the police to focus their investigation on one specific part of the mall — namely, the very hub of drug activity, the Skytrain station.

81   As indicated above, I cannot agree that the fact that crime may be said to occur generally within a given area suffices to establish a *bona fide* inquiry, given proper police motives. Other factors must be considered. The first is the likelihood of crime in the particular area targeted. There was no evidence that trafficking was likely to occur in the intersection where the accused was intercepted—the intersection between a major hotel, an office tower and two department stores. On the contrary, as the finding of the trial judge reflects, drug trafficking was centred elsewhere on the mall. The fact that trafficking occurred at different locations in the six-block area of the mall does not establish that trafficking was likely to occur at the intersection where the accused was intercepted.

82   What evidence there is of drug activity on Granville Mall came from Staff Sergeant Kenneth Michael Davies, who, significantly, was called as "an expert in the areas of police enforcements [sic] practice and techniques regarding drug enforcement in the Granville Mall area and the downtown Vancouver area and, in particular, the operation of undercover operations". Staff Sergeant Davies noted that the hub of drug activity on Granville Mall had migrated northward from the McDonald's restaurant to the Skytrain station. He also stated that recently a greater proportion of the drug trafficking has been occurring indoors, in bars and restaurants along the mall. He offered no evidence whatsoever that the particular intersection in question here—Granville and Georgia—had ever been a known site of drug activity. Moreover, in cross-examination, he appeared to disapprove expressly of the conduct engaged in by the undercover policewoman:

> *Q* [The suspects] are noticed walking across the street in a crosswalk; that's it. They're not standing — not seen standing where a bunch of people were standing. They haven't come from a place where there is any suspicion of drug trafficking. They're just walking across the street?
>
> *A* If that's all there was, I personally wouldn't direct my operator to approach these people, given the very limited information you're giving me.

83   The statistics produced by Staff Sergeant Davies all relate to the entirety of the mall, with no attempt to discriminate between different locations where or times when the offences in question were committed. To rely on these numbers in support of the view that the police were justified in extending their operation to the entire six-block area of the mall is fraught with peril. Statistics are only as good as the questions upon which they are based. We have absolutely no idea what questions were asked in order to produce the numbers relied on by the Crown. It is entirely possible that the vast majority of the drug offences which occurred on Granville Mall took place close to the Skytrain station on Granville Street, the acknowledged hub of drug activity on Granville Mall. It is equally possible that none of the offences occurred at the intersection where the accused was intercepted. Again, it is possible that the vast majority of the drug offences which occurred on Granville Mall occurred on certain days or at specific times of day—weekends or late evenings, for example—and not at 6:00 p.m. on a weekday, which is when the transaction in question here occurred. I conclude that the statistics relied on in this case fall far short of justifying granting to the police unfettered licence to carry out their operation anywhere within a six-block stretch of downtown Vancouver without restriction as to the area and the times of day to be covered. In short, it is not established that the police could reasonably have suspected trafficking at the place and time where the accused was intercepted.

84   A second factor relevant to determining the appropriateness of the investigation is the impact that the investigation may have on law-abiding

citizens pursuing legitimate activities. Here the possibility of this undercover operation's interfering with legitimate activities was high. As already noted, the intersection in question is bounded by department stores, an office tower and a major hotel. Theatres, the Art Gallery and the Law Courts are nearby. This factor, while not in itself conclusive, weighs against the right of undercover police to intercede at will.

85 On the other side of the balance must be weighed the seriousness of the criminal activity which the police have targeted. It is apparent that the state interest in repressing crime may receive greater weight when the police target serious criminal offences. The offence here in question, while not to be condoned, cannot be considered as serious. In *Kokesch, supra,* Sopinka J. for the majority took judicial notice of the fact that narcotics offences involving marijuana are generally regarded as less serious than those involving "hard" drugs such as cocaine and heroin. The same might be said of offences involving hashish, the substance involved in this case. The amount, moreover, was small. In short, this was not the sort of serious drug offence which would more readily tip the balance in favour of the state.

86 I turn finally to the availability of alternative investigatory techniques for detecting the sort of criminal activity at issue. There were alternative ways of apprehending drug pedlars such as the appellant. Simple observation by undercover operatives (as opposed to interception) is one. I am left with some doubt as to whether the apprehension of drug pedlars on Granville Mall requires giving the police carte-blanche to intercept large numbers of law-abiding citizens as these citizens visit the theatre or leave major office towers or department stores.

87 I arrive then at the conclusion that in the case at bar the individual interest in being left alone and free to pursue one's daily business without being confronted by undercover police operatives vastly outweighs the state interest in the repression of crime. It follows that the police officer in this case cannot be said to have been acting pursuant to a *bona fide* inquiry. Any other conclusion would be, in my respectful opinion, unfitting in a society which heralds the constitutional protection of individual liberties and places a premium on "being left alone".

88 I would allow the appeal and restore the stay of proceedings.

———————————

L'Heureux-Dubé J. agreed with the majority on the merits but dissented on the issue of jurisdiction. She would have substituted convictions.

Chapter 8

PARTIES TO A CRIME

1. CO-PRINCIPALS

R. v. BALL

(2011) 82 C.R. (6th) 72, 267 C.C.C. (3d) 532 (B.C. C.A.)

The two accused were among a larger group of people who got into an altercation at a bar with two brothers; eventually the group of four or five pursued the brothers from the bar and assaulted them in an alleyway. One of the brothers died from the injuries suffered, but the evidence against the accused only established that they had struck the surviving brother. The accused were convicted of manslaughter, and one issue on appeal was whether they could be convicted of that offence not merely as aiders or abettors, but as principals.

RYAN J.A.: —

21   Section 21(1) of the *Criminal Code* provides:

> Every one is a party to an offence who
> (a) actually commits it;
>
> (b) does or omits to do anything for the purpose of aiding any person to commit it; or
>
> (c) abets any person in committing it.

22   Section 21(2) is not directly engaged by this appeal, but as there is some reference to it in the case law I reproduce it here for ease of reference:

> 21(2) Where two or more persons form an intention in common to carry out an unlawful purpose and to assist each other therein and any one of them, in carrying out the common purpose, commits an offence, each of them who knew or ought to have known that the commission of the offence would be a probable consequence of carrying out the common purpose is a party to that offence.

23   Two persons may both be actual committers for the purposes of s. 21(1)(a) (referred to in the case law variously as "co-principals", "joint-principals", "co-perpetrators" or "joint-perpetrators") even though each has not performed every

act which makes up the *actus reus* of the offence. As Martin J.A. explained in *R. v. Mena* (1987), 34 C.C.C. (3d) 304: 57 C.R. (3d) 172 (O.C.A.) at page 309:

> Unquestionably, more than one person may actually commit an offence. Perhaps the simplest example of joint perpetrators is where two accused attack the victim intending to kill him or her and the combined effect of the blows struck by the two accused is to kill the victim. In those circumstances, both the accused have murdered the deceased: see Smith and Hogan, *Criminal Law*, 5th ed. (1983), at p. 120.
>
>> At common law, a principal in the first degree is one who has committed the fact with his own hands, or through an innocent agent: see Russell on Crime, 12th ed. Vol. I (1964), at p. 131. It was well established that, if several persons combined to commit a crime and each person committed a different part of the crime, every such person was a principal in the first degree. In Russell on Crime, supra, the author states at p. 131:
>>
>>> All the facts of the case must be taken into account, so that where it appears that there is a joint enterprise afoot between two (or more) persons in which each has an active part to perform in order to effect the criminal purpose then each participant is equally a principal in the first degree. Thus in burglary if A hoists B through a half-open window and B then goes to the closed door of the house and opens it from the inside thus admitting A, both are principals in the first degree to burglary. So also there may be joint action in cases of stealing and other crimes. In certain circumstances each of the participants may do his part in the absence of the others and even may not know by whom the other parts were executed. [Footnotes omitted.] [Emphasis added.]

Glanville Williams in *Criminal Law: The General Part*, 2d ed. (1961) states at p. 349:

> Two persons may be guilty as joint perpetrators. Hence where a body of men beat a constable (some with sticks, some by throwing stones, some with their fists), and the constable died of the aggregate violence, the judge directed the jury that "If several persons act together in pursuance of a common intent, every act done in furtherance of such intent by each of them is, in law, done by all" (*R. v. Macklin* (1838), 2 Lewin 225).
>
> Part of a crime may be committed by one principal, another by another. Thus, in burglary, one may break and the other enter. Other illustrations are in forgery, where different persons execute different parts of the document (though in the absence of one another), and in libel, where D composes, E prints, and F publishes. In these cases, it is not necessary for the various perpetrators to be present at the same time. It is even possible for two persons to manipulate the controls of a car at the same time so that both are driving. [Footnotes omitted.]

In *Textbook of Criminal Law*, 2d ed. (1983), Glanville Williams says at p. 330:

> Two persons may be guilty as joint perpetrators; and part of a crime may be committed by one perpetrator, another by another. Thus, in robbery, which involves the two elements of theft and threat, one person may steal while his companion makes the threat of force, and the two are co-perpetrators.
>
> It is, I think, clear that in the above passage the author is referring to the case where two people have acted in concert to commit a robbery as a joint enterprise.

24   This conclusion is logical. Where two people rob a bank with a gun, only one person can carry and point the weapon, and it may be more convenient for a second, not occupied with a weapon, to scoop up the cash. The robbers have not, individually performed all elements of the offence, yet they both have committed the crime in the sense that they are co-perpetrators. There is no need in such a case to turn to accessorial principles to determine guilt. So also with an attack by two or more on two (or more) victims - an attacker may strike only one victim while others strike the second, or they may all strike both. The attackers are all actual committers. Again, there is no need to resort to accessorial principles to find a basis for conviction.

25   Where two persons commit a crime as co-perpetrators it may be the case that they have agreed to do so before embarking on the endeavour. For purposes of liability under s. 21(1)(a) of the *Code*, however, agreement to carry out a common purpose is not necessary. The question is whether there is an indication of common participation, not a common purpose.

. . .

28   It follows that where co-perpetrators engage in a deadly assault, the Crown need not prove which of the attackers struck the fatal blow or blows...

29   In the case at bar the trial judge found that the Clarke, Ball and Rosborough, members of the Woolnough party, jointly participated in an attack on the Johnston brothers as they left the Rec Room after they were advised by staff to leave. If this conclusion is not wrong, all of the attackers are responsible for the injuries received by both men.

30   In my view the trial judge was entitled to reach the conclusion that he did on the evidence. The Woolnough party was together in the Rec Room when Mark Woolnough and Ian Johnston almost came to blows. Bradley Johnston was nearby when this confrontation occurred and left with his brother when advised to do so. Both men were attacked at the same time by a group of individuals after they left the pub. The trial judge found that the group that attacked the Johnston brothers consisted of members of the Woolnough party. It matters little that each attacker did not lay a hand on each person assaulted. What matters is that all played a part in the attack, whether it was striking one brother or the both of them. In such a case the blow of one is the blow of them all.

31   I would not accede to this ground of appeal.

The Court of Appeal concluded that the accused could be found guilty as principals. They also found that the accused could be found guilty as either aiders or abettors under ss. 21(1)(b) and 21(1)(c).

In the mass first degree murder case of *R. v. Pickton* (2010), 77 C.R. (6th) 12 (S.C.C.) a 6-3 majority found that a direction to find guilt if "he was otherwise an active participant" in killings adequately conveyed the law on potential routes to criminal liability.

2.   AIDING AND ABETTING

See sections 21-23 of the *Criminal Code*.

DUNLOP and SYLVESTER v. R.

[1979] 2 S.C.R. 881, 8 C.R. (3d) 349, 47 C.C.C. (2d) 93,
1979 CarswellMan 91, 1979 CarswellMan 158

DICKSON J. (LASKIN C.J.C., ESTEY and SPENCE JJ. concurring): — The appellants were twice tried and convicted on a charge of rape. The indictment alleges that on June 26, 1975, they did unlawfully have sexual intercourse with B.R. without her consent. They were sentenced to serve six years in penitentiary. In an appeal taken following the second trial, the Manitoba Court of Appeal found error on the part of the trial judge, but by a three to two majority sustained the conviction by applying s. 613(1)(*b*)(iii) of the *Code* [37 C.C.C. (2d) 90]. It is from that judgment that the present appeal is taken.

[The complainant in the case had been raped by a group of about 18 members of a motorcycle gang. She identified Dunlop and Sylvester as two of the people who had raped her. They both denied the assault, and testified that although they had delivered beer to the location where the rapes occurred and had observed a woman having intercourse, they stayed for only three minutes, did not have intercourse with the complainant, and did not in any way assist anyone else to do so.

There was no dispute that if the Crown had proven beyond a reasonable doubt that the complainant's version of events was true, then the accused were guilty as principals to the offence. However, the trial judge also instructed the jury that an alternative way in which the accused could be found guilty was as parties to the offence under s. 21(1) or 21(2) of the *Criminal Code*. If that were correct, it could only be relevant if the jury did not accept the complainant's identification evidence, but nonetheless could find the accused guilty based on their testimony as to their behaviour.]

Section 21(2) of the Criminal Code

The first ground of appeal is that the trial judge erred in charging the jury on s. 21(2) of the *Code*, common intention, when there was no evidence that the appellants Dunlop and Sylvester had formed any common intention with those involved in the gang rape to commit rape upon B.R. It is common ground that the trial judge erred in this respect. Crown counsel concedes as much. There was no evidence that the appellants participated in a plan or scheme to lure the complainant to the dump as part of the initiation proceeding. In the Court of Appeal for Manitoba, Mr. Justice Matas, writing for the majority of the court, considered that there was "merit in the appellants' argument that the comments were inappropriate in the circumstances of the case". Mr. Justice Hall, writing the minority opinion, said [at p. 96]:

> In my respectful opinion, there was no evidence upon which a jury, properly instructed, could find or infer that the accused were parties to an offence under that subsection. In my view, it was a pure invitation to the jury to resort to surmise, speculation and conjecture, as opposed to proper legal inference, against which they were cautioned not to do in the general charge.

Section 21(1) of the *Criminal Code*

The second ground of appeal was set out in the formal judgment of the Court of Appeal in this manner:

> 2. That the Learned Trial Judge erred in charging the Jury with respect to Section 21(1) of the *Criminal Code*, as there was insufficient evidence in law to make the Appellant . . . a party to the offence.

In ascertaining the real ground upon which dissent is based, if the formal judgment fails to make that clear, this court may look to the written reasons of the dissenting judges: *Roy v. The King*, 69 C.C.C. 177 at pp. 188-9, [1938] S.C.R. 32 at p. 43, *per* Crocket J., and *Savard and Lizotte v. The King*, 85 C.C.C. 254 at pp. 255-6, [1946] S.C.R. 20 at p. 23, *per* Taschereau J.

Mr. Justice Hall in his dissenting judgment left no doubt that the "insufficient evidence in law", of which he spoke, was insufficient in the sense that the trial judge ought not to have charged the jury at all with respect to s. 21(1) [at p. 98]:

> The presence of the accused at the dump, and their passive observation of a girl having sexual intercourse is not sufficient in law to make them parties to an offence under s. 21(1) of the *Code*.
> The case for the Crown should have been allowed to stand or fall on the issue of whether the Crown had proved beyond a reasonable doubt that the accused were two of the Spartans who had sexual intercourse with B.R. against her will. She said they did, and identified them as two of the attackers. They denied any involvement and pointed to her uncorroborated testimony and to the unreliability of her identification of them. The trial judge fully and clearly exposed that issue. The charge should have stopped there.

As I read this passage, there is no suggestion that the evidence was insufficient to support a conviction, which is a question of fact or, at best, a question of mixed fact and law. That was the situation in *R. v. Warner*, 128 C.C.C. 366, [1961] S.C.R. 144, 34 C.R. 246. The error alleged in the dissent here is that there was insufficient evidence to go to the jury under s. 21(1), as opposed to insufficient evidence to support the jury's verdict. The question of whether there is sufficient evidence to go to the jury, *i.e.*, any evidence upon which a jury, properly instructed, could find the appellants guilty as parties to the offence under s. 21(1), is a question of law, which can found an appeal to this court under s. 618(1)(*a*) [am. 1974-75-76, c. 105, s. 18]: *R. v. Decary*, 77 C.C.C. 191 at pp. 194-5, [1942] S.C.R. 80 at p. 83, and *Calder v. The Queen*, 129 C.C.C. 202 at pp. 202-3, [1960] S.C.R. 892 at pp. 896-7, *per* Cartwright J.

On s. 21(1) of the *Code*, the jury was instructed as follows:

> Secondly, I should also instruct you on the law relating to parties to an offence. Section 21(1) of the *Criminal Code*, reads as follows:
> "Every one is a party to an offence who:
> (*a*) actually commits it,
> (*b*) does or omits to do anything for the purpose of aiding any person to commit it, or
> (*c*) abets any person in committing it."
> Abets, that word abets means encourages, supports, upholds. It is another way of expressing a person giving assistance to someone committing the offence. Everyone who aids and encourages the person in the commission of the offence is as guilty as the person who commits the actual criminal act.
> To find that the accused is guilty of aiding or abetting the commission of an offence by another person, it is only necessary to show that he understood what was being done and by some act on his part assisted or encouraged the attainment of that act.

Mere presence at the scene of a crime is not sufficient to ground culpability. Something more is needed: encouragement of the principal offender; an act which facilitates the commission of the offence, such as keeping watch or enticing the victim away, or an act which tends to prevent or hinder interference with accomplishment of the criminal act, such as preventing the intended victim from escaping or being ready to assist the prime culprit. Thus, in an early work, *Foster's Crown Law*, p. 350, we read:

> in order to render a person an accomplice and a principal in felony, he must be aiding and abetting at the fact, or ready to afford assistance if necessary, and therefore if A. happeneth to be present at a murder, for instance, and taketh no part in it, nor endeavoureth to prevent it, nor apprehendeth the murderer, nor levyeth hue and cry after him, this strange behaviour of his, though highly criminal, will not of itself render him either principal or accessory.

The leading case of *R. v. Coney* (1882), 8 Q.B.D. 534, decided that non-accidental presence at the scene of the crime was not conclusive of aiding and abetting. The accused were present at a prize fight, then illegal, though taking no part in the management of the fight. It did not appear that the accused said or did anything. The Chairman of the Quarter Sessions directed the jury that, prize fights being illegal, all persons who went to a fight to see the combatants strike each other, and being present when they did so, were guilty of assault unless they were casually passing by. If they stayed at the place, they encouraged it by their presence although they did not say or do anything. Eight of the 11 judges hearing the case reserved were of the opinion that the direction was not correct. Two passages from the judgment of Cave J. at p. 539 bear repeating:

> Now it is a general rule in the case of principals in the second degree that there must be participation in the act, and that, although a man is present whilst a felony is being committed, if he takes no part in it, and does not act in concert with those who commit it, he will not be a principal in the second degree merely because he does not endeavour to prevent the felony, or apprehend the felon.

and [at p. 540]:

> Where presence may be entirely accidental, it is not even evidence of aiding and abetting. Where presence is *prima facie* not accidental it is evidence, but no more than evidence, for the jury.

Hawkins J., in a well-known passage had this to say, pp. 557-8:

> In my opinion, to constitute an aider and abettor some active steps must be taken by word, or action, with the intent to instigate the principal, or principals. Encouragement does not of necessity amount to aiding and abetting, it may be intentional or unintentional, a man may unwittingly encourage another in fact by his presence, by misinterpreted words, or gestures, or by his silence, on non-interference, or he may, encourage intentionally by expressions, gestures, or actions intended to signify approval. In the latter case he aids and abets, in the former he does not. It is no criminal offence to stand by, a mere passive spectator of a crime, even of a murder. Non-interference to prevent a crime is not itself a crime. But the fact that a person was voluntarily and purposely present witnessing the commission of a crime, and offered no opposition to it, though he might reasonably be expected to prevent and had the power to do so, or at least to express his dissent, might under some circumstances, afford cogent evidence upon which a jury would be justified in finding that he wilfully encouraged and so aided and abetted. But it would be purely a question for the jury whether he did so or not. So if any number of persons arrange that a criminal offence shall take place, and it takes place accordingly, the mere presence of any of those who so arranged it would afford abundant evidence for the consideration of a jury of an aiding and abetting.

In this court the question of aiding and abetting was canvassed in *Preston v. The King*, 93 C.C.C. 81, [1949] S.C.R. 156, 7 C.R. 72. The appellant and another were accused of having set fire to a school. Mr. Justice Estey delivered the majority judgment in this court, in the course of which he stated (p. 159) that in order to find the appellant guilty of aiding, abetting, counselling or procuring, it was only necessary to show that he understood what was taking place and by some act on his part encouraged or assisted in the attainment thereof. Later he said (p. 160) that mere presence does not constitute aiding and abetting, but presence under certain circumstances may itself be evidence thereof. He proceeded to review the evidence and concluded, p. 85 C.C.C., p. 161 S.C.R.:

> If appellant's explanation was not believed by the jury there was *evidence in addition to his mere presence* upon which they might well conclude that he was guilty of aiding, abetting, counselling or procuring. (Emphasis added.)

Two Canadian cases make the distinction between presence with prior knowledge, and accidental presence. In *R. v. Dick* (1947), 87 C.C.C. 101, 2 C.R. 417 (Ont. C.A.), the accused was charged with the murder of her husband.

According to her own statement, she met her husband and Bohozuk, a friend, and they went with her in a borrowed car, her husband in the front seat and Bohozuk in the back. The two men began to quarrel, both were drinking; Bohozuk pulled a gun and shot Mr. Dick. It was not a happy marriage, nor were Mr. Dick and Bohozuk on best of terms. There was some surrounding evidence casting doubt upon the non-involvement of the accused. As Chief Justice Robertson noted, she did not admit that there was any design, nor that she knew Bohozuk intended to shoot Dick, nor even that she knew Bohozuk had a weapon with him. Yet the trial judge gave only general directions on aiding and abetting to the jury. Robertson C.J.O. concluded at p. 116 C.C.C., pp. 432-3 C.R.:

> Now, while it may be that a jury might infer from the evidence a good deal that is not expressly admitted, it is not at all certain that this jury did infer that the appellant knew more than she admits knowing of Bohozuk's then present purpose. This jury should have been instructed that if they found that the appellant was no more than passively acquiescent at the time of the shooting, and that she had no reason to expect that there would be any shooting until it actually occurred, then s. 69 did not apply:

In the result, a new trial was ordered.

In *R. v. Hoggan*, [1966] 3 C.C.C. 1, 47 C.R. 256 (Alta. C.A.), the charge was that the accused aided and abetted in wilfully attempting to defeat the course of justice by attempting to dissuade a witness from giving evidence. Johnson J.A. concluded at p. 5 C.C.C., p. 260 C.R.:

> There are two things that must be proved before an accused can be convicted of being a party by aiding and abetting. It must first be proved that he had knowledge that the principal intended to commit the offence and that the accused aided and abetted him. Where there is no knowledge that an offence is to be committed, the presence of an accused at the scene of the crime cannot be a circumstance which would be evidence of aiding and abetting.

The basis for Johnson J.A.'s approach to aiding and abetting is found in *Preston* and *Coney*, both of which he cites.

The case of *R. v. Salajko*, [1970] 1 C.C.C. 352, 9 C.R.N.S. 145 (Ont. C.A.), is like the instant case in many respects. A girl was raped by 15 young men in a lonely field. Three were charged. Two of these were identified as having had intercourse with the girl. She admitted, however, that the third accused, Salajko, though seen to be near the girl with his pants down while she was being raped by others, did not have intercourse with her. The Crown placed its case against him on s. 21 (1)(*b*) and (*c*) of the *Criminal Code*. One might be forgiven for thinking that it was open to the jury to infer encouragement by conduct, but the Ontario Court of Appeal thought otherwise. Chief Justice Gale, delivering the judgment of the court, stated that in the absence of evidence to suggest something in the way of aiding, or counselling, or encouraging on the part of the accused with respect to that which was being done by the others, there was simply no evidence upon which a jury could properly arrive at a verdict of guilty against the particular accused. The learned Chief Justice also found error in the trial judge's charge which seemed to indicate that a person could abet another in the commission of an offence if, knowingly, he stood by while the offence was being committed.

Finally, there are the cases of *R. v. Black*, [1970] 4 C.C.C. 251, 10 C.R.N.S. 17, and *R. v. Clarkson*, [1971] 3 All E.R. 344. The victim in *Black's* case was conveyed to a clubhouse where he was subjected to various sordid indignities. Many of the accused took an active part in torturing the victim while others stood around laughing and yelling. The British Columbia Court of Appeal confirmed the convictions, being of the view that the spectators furnished encouragement to the perpetrators of the outrages and their mere presence in the circumstances of the case ensured against the escape of the victim. There was thus something more than "mere presence", as in *R. v. Coney, supra*. Most important, the trial judge directed the jury in language drawn from the judgment of Hawkins J. in *Coney* and reviewed the evidence relating to the presence of the accused in clear terms.

In contrast to *R. v. Black* is the case of *R. v. Clarkson*, a decision of the Court Martial Appeal Court. A girl was raped in a room in a barracks in Germany by a number of soldiers. Another group of soldiers clustered outside the door and later "piled in" to the room. They remained there for a considerable time while the girl was raped. There was no evidence that the appellants had done any physical act, or uttered any word, which involved direct physical participation or verbal encouragement. There was no evidence that they touched the girl, or did anything to prevent others from assisting her or to prevent her from escaping. The Appeal Court held that it was not enough that the presence of the accused, in fact, gave encouragement, "It must be proved that the accused intended to give encouragement; that he *wilfully* encouraged" (p. 347). There must be, the court held, an intention to encourage and encouragement in fact. The convictions were quashed.

The case at bar

In the case at bar I have great difficulty in finding any evidence of anything more than mere presence and passive acquiescence. Presence at the commission of an offence can be evidence of aiding and abetting if accompanied by other factors, such as prior knowledge of the principal offender's intention to commit the offence or attendance for the purpose of encouragment. There was no evidence that while the crime was being committed either of the accused rendered aid, assistance or encouragement to the rape of B.R. There was no evidence of any positive act or omission to facilitate the unlawful purpose. One can infer that the two accused knew that a party was to be held, and that their presence at the dump was not accidental or in the nature of casual passers-by, but that is not sufficient. A person cannot properly be convicted of aiding or abetting in the commission of acts which he does not know may be or are intended: *per* Viscount Dilhorne in *Director of Public Prosecutions for Northern*

Ireland v. Maxwell, [1978] 3 All E.R. 1140 at p. 1144 (H.L.). One must be able to infer that the accused had prior knowledge that an offence of the type committed was planned, *i.e.*, that their presence was with knowledge of the intended rape. On this issue, the Crown elicited no evidence.

In concluding that there was evidence of a nature which would permit the jury to draw an inference that the accused were more than merely present at a crime and had done nothing to prevent it, Mr. Justice Matas referred to the earlier meeting of the Spartans at the dump (with Sylvester and Dunlop present) when Douglas was introduced as a prospect, the presence of members of the group at the Waldorf beverage room where the complainant and her friend were spending some time, the bringing of the complainant by Douglas to the dump, the reappearance of a group of Spartans at the same location (where the gang rape took place), the arrival of the accused with a substantial quantity of beer, and the observation by both accused of intercourse taking place by the complainant and one male, but with other men nearby.

The activities of Douglas are twice mentioned by Mr. Justice Matas, but it must be recalled that Douglas was not one of the accused. Dunlop and Sylvester bear no responsibility for what he may or may not have done. Apart from presence earlier in the evening at the dump and at the Waldorf beverage room, the evidence Mr. Justice Matas marshalls against Dunlop and Sylvester is (i) their arrival at the dump with a substantial quantity of beer, and (ii) their observation of intercourse. In my view, for the reasons I have earlier sought to express, neither of these facts is capable in law of affording evidence that the appellants aided and the commission of the crime of rape. They go only to mere presence and not to complicity.

With great respect, I am unable to find in the evidence to which Mr. Justice Matas alludes, or elsewhere, any facts as distinguished from surmise or suspicion, upon which any jury could conclude beyond reasonable doubt that the accused had assumed a role which would qualify them as aiders and abettors under s. 21(1) of the *Code*.

In these circumstances, in my view, the trial judge erred in charging the jury on the alternative bases of (i) principal offender, and (ii) aider and abettor.

Question by the jury

The error, unfortunately, was compounded when the jury, which had retired at 3:15 p.m., returned at 5:40 with the following question:

> If the accused were aware of a rape taking place in their presence and did nothing to prevent or persuade the discontinuance of the act, are they considered as an accomplice to the act under law?

That question should have been answered in one word — "No".

A person is not guilty merely because he is present at the scene of a crime and does nothing to prevent it: Smith & Hogan, *Criminal Law*, 4th ed. (1978),

p. 117. If there is no evidence of encouragement by him, a man's presence at the scene of the crime will not suffice to render him liable as aider and abettor. A person who, aware of a rape taking place in his presence, looks on and does nothing is not, as a matter of law, an accomplice. The classic case is the hardened urbanite who stands around in a subway station when an individual is murdered.

The judge here initially intended to respond to the jury's question with a "No" answer, but during argument, he was persuaded to the point of view, advanced for the first time on behalf of the Crown, that the accused might be guilty as parties to the offence under s. 21 of the *Code*. As a result, the judge recharged in these words:

> Now, I have decided that the best way to reply to your query is to refer again to a portion of the law that I gave you in respect to parties to an offence, and to make one or two further comments on it.
>
> Under section 21(1) of the *Criminal Code*, everyone is a party to an offence who; (a) actually commits it, (b) does or omits to do anything for the purpose of aiding any person to commit it — and I will come back to that, or (c) abets any person in committing it. And abets, I told you before means encourages, supports, upholds, is another form of giving assistance to a person committing the offence.
>
> Everyone who aids and encourages another person in the commission of a criminal offence is as guilty as the person who actually commits the criminal act. To find that an accused is guilty of aiding or abetting in the commission of an offence by another person, it is only necessary to show that he understood what was being done, and by some act on his part, assisted or encouraged in the attainment of what was being done.
>
> But when you are considering what I have said, going back to that middle section of the definition I read, everyone is a party to an offence who does or omits to do anything for the purpose of aiding another person to commit it, I should say the phrase omitting to do anything, that phrase, omitting to do anything means intentionally omitting to do something for the purpose of aiding another to commit an offence, that if it had been done, would have been prevented or hindered the person from committing an offence. Intentionally omitting to do something for the purpose of aiding another to commit an offence, that if it had been done, would have prevented or hindered the person front committing the offence.
>
> So that if you find an accused person knew that an offence was being committed and intentionally omitted to do something, for the purpose of aiding another to commit the offence, that if he had done it might have hindered or actually prevented the offence, then presumably you can find that the person was a party to the offence. But unless it reaches that level, then you cannot find him a party.

I think, with respect, that this recharge is in error in three respects: (i) it is not responsive to the question asked; (ii) on the facts of the case, it might leave the jury with the impression that the accused could be parties to the offence if they knew that an offence was being committed and failed to do anything to hinder or prevent it, and (iii) the jury received no help in applying the instruction given; no act or omission is identified as providing a possible factual underpinning to the operation of s. 21.

Conclusion

If the trial judge was in error in charging upon s. 21(2), which is admitted and, as I believe, in error in his recharge on s. 21(1), what disposition is to be made of the case? The majority view in the Manitoba Court of Appeal was that the trial judge had not erred in his answer to the jury's question. As to the admitted error in charging as to common intention under s. 21(2), Mr. Justice Matas said [at p. 101]:

> But it is apparent from the juror's question that the members were not troubled by the concept of common intention. In any event, in light of all the evidence and the whole charge, I am satisfied that no substantial wrong or miscarriage of justice occurred.

The difficulty one faces is that we do not know, and will never know, whether the jury found the appellants guilty because they had had intercourse with the complainant, or by reason of the operation of s-ss. (1) or (2) of s. 21 of the *Code*. We do know from the question of the jury, and its timing, that after two hours and 25 minutes of deliberation the jury had not accepted the evidence of the complainant as to direct participation by the appellants. Fifteen minutes after resuming deliberation, following the recharge, the guilty verdict was returned.

I do not think this is an appropriate case for the application of s. 613(1)(*b*)(iii). I am unable to say that the verdict would have been the same in the absence of error. For the following reasons given by Mr. Justice Hall, I would direct a verdict of acquittal, rather than have the applicants undergo a third trial [at p. 98]:

> The accused have been subjected to two trials and a like number of appeals. They have been in custody over a year. The doubt raised on their innocence or guilt should be resolved now. The substance of the case is their denial against the testimony of B.R., without much more. In the circumstances, the needs of justice would be met by directing a verdict of acquittal, rather than having the accused submit to a trial for the third time.

I would allow the appeals, set aside the judgment of the Manitoba Court of Appeal, and direct a verdict of acquittal in respect of each appellant.

MARTLAND J. (dissenting) (RITCHIE and PIGEON JJ. concurring): — The appellants were convicted by a jury on a charge of rape. The facts giving rise to this charge are stated in the reasons of my brother Dickson.

It is not disputed that mere presence at the scene of a crime is not, in itself, sufficient to establish aiding or abetting the commission of an offence, but the trial Judge did not instruct the jury that it was. He charged the jury that "it is only necessary to show that he understood what was being done and by some act on his part assisted or encouraged the attainment of that act".

. . . .

In my opinion, there was evidence on which the jury could conclude that the appellants had aided and abetted the commission of the offence. The jury had been properly instructed as to what was necessary in order to establish aiding and abetting. The sufficiency of that evidence was solely a matter for the determination of the jury and was not a matter to be decided by the Court of Appeal.

Martland J. regarded the response of the trial judge to the jury in question as not offensive when read in the context of the evidence of that evening's events. The minority accordingly would have dismissed the appeal. Pratte J. (Beetz J. concurring) agreed that the appeal should be disposed of in the manner proposed by Dickson J. but on the narrower ground relating to the response of the trial judge to the jury's question.

Appeals allowed; acquittals entered.

Kulbacki, a 20-year-old man, owned a motor vehicle and was sitting in the front passenger seat while a 16-year-old female drove the car at speeds over 90 m.p.h. on an unimproved municipal highway. He did and said nothing to stop, prevent, or attempt to stop or prevent the driver from driving in that manner. **Is he guilty of dangerous driving?** See *R. v. Kulbacki*, 47 C.R. 233, [1966] 1 C.C.C. 167, 1965 CarswellMan 41 (Man. C.A.).

R. v. LAURENCELLE

(1999), 28 C.R. (5th) 157, 1999 CarswellBC 2109 (B.C.C.A.)

1   ESSON J.A. (orally):— The appeal by Ms. Laurencelle is against her conviction by a Provincial Court judge on a charge of unlawful confinement.

2   The facts of the case are these. At about 10:30 on a Saturday evening in July, Robert McCarron was kidnapped by four men from the parking lot of a grocery store. They used knives to force him to go with them to a nearby house. Two of the men were never identified; one of them was identified as Bradley McCandless ("McCandless") and another as Jeromy Biron ("Biron"). McCandless subsequently pleaded guilty to charges of kidnapping and unlawful confinement and, I believe, two other charges that arose out of the overall incident.

3   The victim was kept in the house from Saturday evening until the following Tuesday when he escaped. He was the only witness at the trial of the appellant. He surmised from what he observed that the house was the home of the appellant and Biron and, as well, the appellant's daughter was there at times. In the course

of the original kidnapping, the complainant was threatened by two of the men and assaulted by McCandless. All of this took place without the appellant knowing anything about it at that stage. At about 11:00 p.m. McCandless forced the victim to turn over various items, including his bank card and keys, and also forced him to reveal his personal identification number so that his bank card could be used. With the bank card and that information, McCandless was able to liberate some $2,400 from the bank account apparently in several stages over the period of time the victim was held.

4   During the time of his confinement, the victim was kept bound by tape around his legs and his hands were also bound with tape. McCandless was the prime player in taking those steps. The victim was allowed to use the washroom on a number of occasions by McCandless, who would cut the tape from him and escort him to the washroom, then re-apply the tape after he came out of the washroom.

5   The appellant first had knowledge of anything to do with this at about 11:30 p.m. on the Saturday evening when she arrived home with her daughter. She was heard by the victim to say "What's going on?", and it appeared to him that they then went to another room and had a conversation of which he did not know the contents. The appellant's contact with the complainant consisted of her providing him with water on more than one occasion, and on one occasion removing the tape from his hands so that he could smoke a cigarette. She attempted to comfort him. The victim said that, after her first conversation with McCandless on the Saturday evening, she appeared to be afraid of McCandless, and she told the victim that she was afraid of McCandless and Biron. The evidence of that statement by her, I note, was led by the Crown in his direct evidence. She was asked by the victim when he would be let go, she assured him that he would be let go and that he would be okay.

6   From time to time between the Saturday evening and the Tuesday when the escape took place, McCandless left the residence to re-appear with new clothing and other personal items which the victim assumed were purchased with his bank card. There is no evidence that the appellant shared in any way from the fruits of these crimes. The victim could not say definitely whether he and the appellant were ever alone in the house, although as far as he knew, they were not. She took no part in tying him up, assaulting or threatening him, other than the one incident of untying him so that he could smoke a cigarette. The victim said he was not afraid of the appellant and that he did not believe that the appellant was involved in the kidnapping or the confinement. In his evidence, he said this:

> Q And, in fact, her involvement with you to the limited extent that it was, appeared to you to make—an attempt to make you more comfortable, is that right?

A That's right.

Q And she expressed concern to you for your wellbeing, your health, your safety, etcetera?

A Yeah, she did.

. . . .

Q And you didn't see Ms. Laurencelle with any new belongings?

A No I didn't.

. . . .

Q So if I understand you correctly, Ms. Laurencelle took no active part in anything relating to you, isn't that right?

A Yeah, I don't think so.

7   The appellant alleges these errors on the part of the trial judge:

> 1. The learned Trial Judge erred in finding that the Appellant's act of caring for the Complainant made her a party to the offence.

> 2. The learned Trial Judge erred in finding that the Appellant's omission of failing to leave the Residence made her a party to the offence.

> 3. The verdict was unreasonable and unsupported by the evidence.

8   It is common ground that the applicable law is as stated by the Supreme Court of Canada in *Dunlop and Sylvester v. The Queen* (1979), 47 C.C.C. (2d) 93 (S.C.C.). Dickson J. (later C.J.C.) said at p. 106:

> In order for an accused person to be convicted as a party to an offence, the Crown must prove that accused actually committed the offence, or that she aided or abetted another to commit it within the meaning of s. 21 of the *Criminal Code*. The Crown must therefore prove that an accused who was present during the commission of an offence was more than passively acquiescent to the commission of the offence.

The principal submission of the appellant is that there was nothing that went beyond passive acquiescence on her part.

9   The trial judge in convicting the appellant on this count said this:

> There was no indication that the accused was aware that the kidnapping and confinement was going to take place, but upon entering her own home some short time after the offence she saw the complainant or the victim bound. She knew what had occurred and unfortunately for her made a wrong decision.

> At that point in time she could have left and there would have been no burden on her to do anything else and she could not have become involved in this matter. She did not leave

immediately. In fact, she did not leave at all. She stayed. She stayed in the home. She allowed the victim and Bradley McCandless and Biron to remain, which is more than passive acquiescence. She helped in the care of the victim and as I said she allowed her home to be used as a place of confinement, thereby encouraging the other co-accused in their venture.

It was reported by the victim that she said she was afraid of Brad and Jeromy. It is left open to the court to wonder why she said that. Was she afraid or equally plausible, was this said to instill fear in the victim? She was free to come and go at any time. There was a safe avenue of escape available at all times. There was no evidence before me to indicate any reason why she could not walk out the door. She chose not to do that.

She may have been doing it in a kindly manner, but nonetheless, she was unlawfully confining the victim under all the circumstances that I heard this morning and I find her guilty of count two.

10   I should mention that the Crown laid the same charges against the appellant as they did against McCandless, which included kidnapping and robbery and I believe a fourth count, thus the reference to count two. The trial judge did dismiss the other counts so we are dealing only with unlawful confinement.

11   It is my view, with respect, that the passage which I have quoted from the judge's reasons indicates that she lost sight of the principle that the burden of proving participation was on the Crown. She appears to have imposed a duty on the appellant to leave the house, and perhaps more importantly, she found that the appellant "allowed" McCandless and Biron to remain. In my view, the evidence provides no reasonable basis for finding a duty to leave or for finding that the appellant allowed McCandless and Biron to remain and continue the confinement. The evidence, since it all comes from the victim, is very hazy as to what the appellant's relationship was to the house but, from what little evidence there is, it can be taken that she and Biron were both living there and both, to that extent, had some control over the premises. There is no basis for asserting that the appellant had sole control, and certainly no basis as a matter of common sense for suggesting that she had any effective way of requiring McCandless and Biron to leave. This case is quite different from the various cases which have found that control can lead to a person being found a party by allowing premises or automobiles to be used in an unlawful manner.

12   The judge's observation that she was left to wonder whether the appellant said to the victim that she was afraid in order to instill fear in him is mere speculation. It would almost seem to imply an assumption that the accused should have given evidence, since it was only the accused who could have "left it open to the court to wonder" why she said that. However that may be, it was not an appropriate basis upon which to reject the otherwise contradicted evidence that she had expressed fear. I will observe finally on that point that the suggestion that she was being devious in saying she was afraid is inconsistent with her other behaviour towards the victim.

13   The Crown submits that the acts of kindness amounted to aiding and abetting the offence of confinement. With respect, I can find no adequate basis for making that connection. For those reasons, I would allow the appeal, set aside the conviction, and direct that an acquittal be entered.

R. v. BRISCOE

[2010] 1 S.C.R 411, 2010 CarswellAlta 589, 2010 CarswellAlta 588, 73 C.R. (6th) 224, 253 C.C.C. (3d) 140

The accused was charged with kidnapping, aggravated assault and first degree murder. He had been one of a group of five people who had lured a 13-year-old girl to a secluded area. Two of the other male members of the group raped her and she was killed by the application of various types of force by several members of the group. Briscoe did not apply any force which contributed to her death, though he stood by and watched the rape and murder. The Crown's theory was that another member of the group, Laboucan, was the mastermind who had formulated the plan, selected the victim and communicated the plan to the others. Briscoe's actions constituted aiding the offences. He had driven the group to and from the crime scene, chosen a secluded location, provided and transported weapons (a wrench and a mallet), at an early point held the victim and told her to shut up, and had threatened a friend of the victim who was also present. The Crown also submitted that, even apart from Briscoe's acts of assistance, his presence coupled with his knowledge of the plan made him an abettor. His presence could lend courage to the attackers, discourage rescue, and give the victim further reason to feel helpless and lost and futile. The trial judge agreed that the external elements were proven but held that the Crown had not proven the *mens rea* for party liability beyond a reasonable doubt. The Supreme Court of Canada ordered a new trial.

CHARRON J. (for the Court): —

[13] Canadian criminal law does not distinguish between the principal offender and parties to an offence in determining criminal liability. Section 21(1) of the *Criminal Code* makes perpetrators, aiders, and abettors equally liable:

> 21. (1) Every one is a party to an offence who
>
> (a) actually commits it;
>
> (b) does or omits to do anything for the purpose of aiding any person to commit it; or
>
> (c) abets any person in committing it.

The person who provides the gun, therefore, may be found guilty of the same offence as the one who pulls the trigger. The *actus reus* and *mens rea* for aiding or abetting, however, are distinct from those of the principal offence.

[14] The *actus reus* of aiding or abetting is doing (or, in some circumstances, omitting to do) something that assists or encourages the perpetrator to commit the offence. While it is common to speak of aiding and abetting together, the two concepts are distinct, and liability can flow from either one. Broadly speaking, "[t]o aid under s. 21(1)(*b*) means to assist or help the actor. . . . To abet within the meaning of s. 21(1)(*c*) includes encouraging, instigating, promoting or procuring the crime to be committed": *R. v. Greyeyes*, [1997] 2 S.C.R. 825, at para. 26. The *actus reus* is not at issue in this appeal. As noted earlier, the Crown argued at trial that Mr. Briscoe was both an aider and an abettor. The trial judge's finding that Mr. Briscoe performed the four acts of assistance described above is not disputed.

[15] Of course, doing or omitting to do something that resulted in assisting another in committing a crime is not sufficient to attract criminal liability. As the Court of Appeal for Ontario wrote in *R. v. F. W. Woolworth Co.* (1974), 3 O.R. (2d) 629, "one does not render himself liable by renting or loaning a car for some legitimate business or recreational activity merely because the person to whom it is loaned or rented chooses in the course of his use to transport some stolen goods, or by renting a house for residential purposes to a tenant who surreptitiously uses it to store drugs" (p. 640). The aider or abettor must also have the requisite mental state or *mens rea*. Specifically, in the words of s. 21(1)(*b*), the person must have rendered the assistance *for the purpose* of aiding the principal offender to commit the crime.

[16] The *mens rea* requirement reflected in the word "purpose" under s. 21(1)(*b*) has two components: intent and knowledge. For the intent component, it was settled in *R. v. Hibbert*, [1995] 2 S.C.R. 973, that "purpose" in s. 21(1)(*b*) should be understood as essentially synonymous with "intention". The Crown must prove that the accused intended to assist the principal in the commission of the offence. The Court emphasized that "purpose" should not be interpreted as incorporating the notion of "desire" into the fault requirement for party liability. It is therefore not required that the accused desired that the offence be successfully committed (*Hibbert*, at para. 35). The Court held, at para. 32, that the perverse consequences that would flow from a "purpose equals desire" interpretation of s. 21(1)(*b*) were clearly illustrated by the following hypothetical situation described by Mewett and Manning:

> If a man is approached by a friend who tells him that he is going to rob a bank and would like to use his car as the getaway vehicle for which he will pay him $100, when that person is . . . charged under s. 21 for doing something for the purpose of aiding his friend to commit the offence, can he say "My purpose was not to aid the robbery but to make $100"? His argument would be that while he knew that he was helping the robbery, his desire was to obtain $100 and he did not care one way or the other whether the robbery was successful or not.

(A. W. Mewett and M. Manning, *Criminal Law* (2nd ed. 1985), at p. 112)

The same rationale applies regardless of the principal offence in question. Even in respect of murder, there is no "additional requirement that an aider or abettor subjectively approve of or desire the victim's death" (*Hibbert*, at para. 37 (emphasis deleted)).

[17] As for knowledge, in order to have the intention to assist in the commission of an offence, the aider must know that the perpetrator intends to commit the crime, although he or she need not know precisely how it will be committed. That sufficient knowledge is a prerequisite for intention is simply a matter of common sense. Doherty J.A. in *R. v. Maciel*, 2007 ONCA 196, 219 C.C.C. (3d) 516, provides the following useful explanation of the knowledge requirement which is entirely apposite to this case (at paras. 88-89):

> . . . a person who is alleged to have aided in a murder must be shown to have known that the perpetrator had the intent required for murder under s. 229(a): *R. v. Kirkness* (1990), 60 C.C.C. (3d) 97 (S.C.C.) at 127.

The same analysis applies where it is alleged that the accused aided a perpetrator in the commission of a first degree murder that was planned and deliberate. The accused is liable as an aider only if the accused did something to assist the perpetrator in the planned and deliberate murder and if, when the aider rendered the assistance, he did so for the purpose of aiding the perpetrator in the commission of a planned and deliberate murder. Before the aider could be said to have the requisite purpose, the Crown must prove that the aider knew the murder was planned and deliberate. Whether the aider acquired that knowledge through actual involvement in the planning and deliberation or through some other means, is irrelevant to his or her culpability under s. 21(1).

[18] It is important to note that Doherty J.A., in referring to this Court's decision in *R. v. Kirkness*, [1990] 3 S.C.R. 74, rightly states that the aider to a murder must "have known that the perpetrator had the intent required for murder". While some of the language in *Kirkness* may be read as requiring that the aider share the murderer's intention to kill the victim, the case must now be read in the light of the above-noted analysis in *Hibbert*. The perpetrator's intention to kill the victim must be known to the aider or abettor; it need not be shared. *Kirkness* should not be interpreted as requiring that the aider and abettor of a murder have the same *mens rea* as the actual killer. It is sufficient that he or she, armed with *knowledge* of the perpetrator's intention to commit the crime, acts with the intention of assisting the perpetrator in its commission. It is only in this sense that it can be said that the aider and abettor must intend that the principal offence be committed.

. . .

[25] In this case, I agree with Martin J.A. that the trial judge erred in law by failing to consider wilful blindness. As he noted, even Mr. Briscoe's own

statements to the police suggest that he had a "strong, well-founded suspicion that someone would be killed at the golf course" (para. 30) and that he may have been wilfully blind to the kidnapping and prospect of sexual assault. His statements also show that he deliberately chose not to inquire about what the members of the group intended to do because he did not want to know. As he put it, "whatever you guys wanna do just do it. Don't do it around me I don't want to see nothing I don't know what the fuck you're gonna do." The trial judge relied heavily upon the statements in his reasons but did not refer to the doctrine of wilful blindness. Of course, whether Mr. Briscoe had the requisite *mens rea* for the three offences was a question for the trier of fact, and Mr. Briscoe is entitled to the benefit of any reasonable doubt on this issue. However, from a legal standpoint, it is my respectful view that the evidence cried out for an analysis on wilful blindness. In these circumstances, the Court of Appeal rightly concluded that the trial judge's failure to consider Mr. Briscoe's knowledge from that perspective constitutes a legal error which necessitates a new trial on all charges.

In *R. v. Simpson* (1988), 62 C.R. (3d) 137 (S.C.C.), the Supreme Court unanimously held that the unlawful purpose in s. 21(2) must be different from the offence actually charged. The "unlawful purpose" and the "offence" committed in the course of the pursuit of the unlawful purpose were different. This settled a long-standing conflict of opinion in lower courts.

R. v. LOGAN

[1990] 2 S.C.R. 731, 79 C.R. (3d) 169, 58 C.C.C. (3d) 391,
1990 CarswellOnt 1002, 1990 CarswellOnt 110

The accused were convicted of attempted murder. During a robbery a person was shot and severely injured. Neither accused did the shooting. Johnson admitted to being one of the robbers but stated that he had no intention to shoot and that there had been no discussion concerning the use of guns. Logan had boasted of being involved in planning the robberies. The trial judge instructed the jury that there could be convictions, under s. 21(2), if the Crown established beyond a reasonable doubt that the accused knew or ought to have known that someone would probably shoot with the intention of killing. The Court of Appeal allowed appeals with respect to the convictions for attempted murder and substituted convictions for robbery. The Crown appealed.

LAMER C.J.C. (DICKSON C.J.C., WILSON, GONTHIER and CORY JJ. concurring): —

. . . .

The appellant is challenging the constitutionality of s. 21(2) in general and, in particular, of the objective component of the section ("ought to have known"). However, the Court of Appeal, quite correctly, did not declare the objective component of s. 21(2) inoperative for all offences. They dealt specifically with the operation of the provision in relation to the offence of attempted murder and the possibility that a party to an attempted murder could be convicted upon proof of objective intent, whereas a conviction of the principal would require proof of subjective intent. More generally, as a basis for their decision, the court determined that it is a principle of fundamental justice that a party to *any* offence cannot be found guilty of the offence based on a lower standard of requisite *mens rea* than that required for convicting the principal.

For this proposition, the court relied on our judgment in *Vaillancourt*. In that case, this court held that for a few offences the principles of fundamental justice require that a conviction cannot stand unless there is proof beyond a reasonable doubt of a minimum degree of *mens rea*, and that legislation providing for any lesser degree violates the *Charter* and is inoperative. Murder was one of those offences.

With respect, I cannot construe *Vaillancourt* as saying that, as a general proposition, Parliament cannot ever enact provisions requiring different levels of guilt for principal offenders and parties. Although I readily admit that, as a matter of policy, the proposition seems more equitable than not, I am not ready to characterize it as a principle of fundamental justice. It must be remembered that within many offences there are varying degrees of guilt, and it remains the function of the sentencing process to adjust the punishment for each individual offender accordingly. The argument that the principles of fundamental justice prohibit the conviction of a party to an offence on the basis of a lesser degree of *mens rea* than that required to convict the principal could be supported only, if at all, in a situation where the sentence for a particular offence is fixed. However, currently in Canada the sentencing scheme is flexible enough to accommodate the varying degrees of culpability resulting from the operation of ss. 21 and 22.

That said, however, there are a few offences with respect to which the operation of the objective component of s. 21(2) will restrict the rights of an accused under s. 7. If an offence is one of the few for which s. 7 requires a minimum degree of *mens rea*, *Vaillancourt* does preclude Parliament from providing for the conviction of a party to that offence on the basis of a degree of *mens rea* below the constitutionally-required minimum.

Requisite mens rea for conviction pursuant to s. 21(2)

Therefore, the question whether a party to an offence had the requisite *mens rea* to found a conviction pursuant to s. 21(2) must be answered in two steps. Firstly, is there a minimum degree of *mens rea* which is required as a principle of fundamental justice before one can be convicted as a principal for this particular offence? This is an important initial step because if there is no such constitutional requirement for the offence, the objective component of s. 21(2) can operate without restricting the constitutional rights of the party to the offence. Secondly, if the principles of fundamental justice do require a certain minimum degree of *mens rea* in order to convict for this offence, then that minimum degree of *mens rea* is constitutionally required to convict a party to that offence as well.

Step 1: Section 7 and Attempted Murder

With respect to the case at bar, then, the first question which must be answered is whether the principles of fundamental justice require a minimum degree of *mens rea* in order to convict an accused of attempted murder. *Ancio* established that a specific intent to kill is the *mens rea* required for a principal on the charge of attempted murder. However, as the constitutional question was not raised or argued in that case, it did not decide whether that requisite *mens rea* was a *constitutional* requirement. The case simply interpreted the offence as currently legislated.

In *R. v. Martineau*, a judgment handed down this day, this court has decided, as a constitutional requirement, that no one can be convicted of murder unless the Crown proves beyond a reasonable doubt that the person had *subjective* foresight of the fact that the death of the victim was likely to ensue. Because of both the stigma and the severe penal consequences which result from a conviction for murder, the Constitution requires at least that degree of intent.

As defined in *Ancio*, the elements of *mens rea* for attempted murder are identical to those for the most severe form of murder, murder under s. 212(*a*)(i) [now s. 229 (*a*)(i)]. For each, the accused must have had the specific intent to kill. All that differs is the "consequences" component of the *actus reus*. Quite simply, an attempted murderer is, if caught and convicted, a "lucky murderer". Therefore, it would seem logical that the requisite *mens rea* for a murder conviction, as described in *Martineau*, must be the same for a conviction of attempted murder. However, logic is not sufficient reason to label something a "constitutional requirement". As I have stated in *Vaillancourt*, the principles of fundamental justice require a minimum degree of *mens rea* for only a very few offences. The criteria by which these offences can be identified are, primarily, the stigma associated with a conviction and, as a secondary consideration, the penalties available.

The stigma associated with a conviction for attempted murder is the same as it is for murder. Such a conviction reveals that, although no death ensued from the actions of the accused, the intent to kill was still present in his or her mind. The attempted murderer is no less a killer than a murderer: he may be lucky — the ambulance arrived early, or some other fortuitous circumstance — but he still has the same killer instinct. Secondly, while a conviction for attempted murder does not automatically result in a life sentence, the offence is punishable by life and the usual penalty is very severe.

It should be noted that, as a basis for a constitutionally-required minimum degree of *mens rea*, the social stigma associated with a conviction is the most important consideration, not the sentence. Few offences have a high minimum sentence such as that for murder. For some offences there is a high maximum and a low minimum penalty available; for other offences the maximum penalty is much reduced and there is no minimum imposed whatsoever. In either situation, the fact that a lesser sentence is available or imposed, by statute or through the exercise of judicial discretion, in no way ends the inquiry. The sentencing range available to the Judge is not conclusive of the level of *mens rea* constitutionally required. Instead, the crucial consideration is whether there is a continuing serious social stigma which will be imposed on the accused upon conviction.

For example, the offence of theft in the most serious circumstances is punishable by a maximum of ten years or, in less serious circumstances, a maximum of two years if the Crown proceeds by indictment; if the Crown proceeds summarily, the maximum is six months. The constitutional *mens rea* requirement would not, under s. 7, be triggered by any punishment within these ranges which the sentencing Judge decided to impose. Whether the actual or available punishment is severe or not, the social stigma associated with being labelled dishonest will be automatically and unavoidably imposed upon conviction. It is because of this stigma that the principles of fundamental justice will require a minimum degree of *mens rea*, that is, as I said in *Vaillancourt*, at p. 653, "proof of some dishonesty".

For these reasons, the *mens rea* for attempted murder cannot, without restricting s. 7 of the *Charter*, require of the accused less of a mental element than that required of a murderer under s. 212(a)(i), that is, subjective foresight of the consequences. While Parliament, as I have already implied, could well extend our definition of attempted murder in *Ancio* to include the unsuccessful murderers of s. 212(a)(ii), it cannot go further and include objective foresight as being sufficient for a conviction without restricting s. 7 of the *Charter*.

Step 2: *Mens Rea* for Attempted Murder Pursuant to S. 21(2)

Having completed the initial step of the inquiry, one can proceed to the second step in determining the requisite *mens rea* for the conviction of a party pursuant to s. 21(2) on a charge of attempted murder. When the principles of fundamental justice require *subjective* foresight in order to convict a principal of attempted murder, that same minimum degree of *mens rea* is constitutionally required to convict a party to the offence of attempted murder. Any conviction for attempted murder, whether of the principal directly or of a party pursuant to s. 21(2), will carry enough stigma to trigger the constitutional requirement. To the extent that s. 21(2) would allow for the conviction of a party to the offence of attempted murder on the basis of objective foresight, its operation restricts s. 7 of the *Charter*.

Section 1 Analysis

Given the finding that s. 7 is restricted in the present case, can that restriction be found to be a reasonable limit demonstrably justified in a free and democratic society? The s. 1 analysis to be followed in answering this question has been set out in the decision of this court in *R. v. Oakes*, [1986] 1 S.C.R. 103, 50 C.R. (3d) 1, 24 C.C.C. (3d) 321.

. . . .

However, even though Parliament has sought to achieve an important legislative objective by enacting the restriction in issue in this appeal and even though such restriction is rationally connected to that objective, I am of the view that it does not satisfy the proportionality test because it unduly impairs an accused's rights under s. 7 of the *Charter*: see *Vaillancourt*, *supra*, at p. 651.

The objective component of s. 21(2) unduly impairs rights under s. 7 of the *Charter* when it operates with respect to an offence for which a conviction carries severe stigma and for which, therefore, there is a constitutionally-required minimum degree of *mens rea*. The words "ought to know" allow for the possibility that while a party may not have considered and accepted the risk that an accomplice may do something with the intent to kill in furtherance of the common purpose, the party, through this negligence, could still be found guilty of attempted murder. In other words, parties could be held to be criminally negligent with respect to the behaviour of someone else. For most offences under the *Criminal Code*, a person is convicted for criminal negligence only if consequences have ensued from their actions. While a person may be convicted, absent consequences, for criminal negligence (*e.g.*, dangerous operation of a motor vehicle), none of these forms of criminal negligence carry with them the stigma of being labelled a "killer". In a situation where s. 21(2) is operating in relation to the offence of attempted murder, no consequences have resulted from the actions of the party, and yet the party could be convicted of this offence and suffer severe accompanying stigma and penalty.

Because of the importance of the legislative purpose, the objective component of s. 21(2) can be justified with respect to most offences. However, with respect to the few offences for which the Constitution requires subjective intent, the stigma renders the infringement too serious and outweighs the legislative objective, which therefore cannot be justified under s. 1.

Conclusion

I would, therefore, as did the Court of Appeal, declare inoperative the words "or ought to have known" when considering under s. 21(2) whether a person is a party to any offence where it is a constitutional requirement for a conviction that foresight of the consequences be subjective, which is the case for attempted murder. Once these words are deleted, the remaining section requires, in the context of attempted murder, that the party to the common venture know that it is probable that his accomplice would do something with the intent to kill in carrying out the common purpose.

I would dismiss the appeal. I would restrict my answers to the constitutional questions as follows:

> 1. Does s. 21(2) of the *Criminal Code* contravene the rights and freedoms guaranteed by section 7 and/or section 11(*d*) of the *Canadian Charter of Rights and Freedoms*?

> Yes, on charges where subjective foresight is a constitutional requirement, to the extent that a party may be convicted if that person objectively "ought to have known" that the commission of the offence would be a probable consequence of carrying out the common purpose.

> 2. If the answer to question 1 is in the affirmative, is section 21(2) of the *Criminal Code* justified under section 1 of the *Canadian Charter of Rights and Freedoms*, and therefore not inconsistent with the *Constitution Act, 1982*?

> No.

L'Heureux-Dubé and Sopinka JJ. delivered separate concurring opinions.

R. v. PORTILLO

(2003), 17 C.R. (6th) 362, 176 C.C.C. (3d) 467,
2003 CarswellOnt 2972 (Ont. C.A.)

DOHERTY J.A.: —

. . . .

On this record, there was a basis upon which to leave liability under s. 21(1)(b), s. 21(1)(c) and s. 21(2).

As I understand the evidence, even if the jury was satisfied that the appellants were somehow involved in the death of the deceased, they may well have been unable to determine the exact nature of each appellant's participation in the homicide. Specifically, even if the jury were satisfied that both appellants were involved in the killing, they may have been unable to determine whether one, the other, or both actually participated in the strangling of the deceased.

In these circumstances, I suggest that potential liability under s. 21(1) might be explained along the following lines:

- The liability of each accused under s. 21(1) must be determined separately. Each accused may be found not guilty, guilty of murder, or not guilty of murder but guilty of manslaughter. The verdicts with respect to each accused do not have to be the same.

- To convict an accused of murder or manslaughter, the jury must be satisfied that the accused participated in the killing.

- Participation means doing something that caused the death of the deceased or doing something for the purpose of helping another person to do something that caused the death of the deceased.

- If the jury is satisfied that an accused participated in the killing as described above, it is unnecessary for the jury to determine the exact nature of that participation.

- If the jury is satisfied that an accused participated in the killing of the deceased, he is guilty of either murder or manslaughter. He is guilty of murder if he did so with the necessary blameworthy state of mind and manslaughter if the Crown has not proved the blameworthy state of mind.

- The blameworthy state of mind consists of intending that the deceased should be killed; or intending that he should suffer bodily harm of a kind likely to result in death and yet proceeding despite knowledge of that risk: *R. v. Kirkness* (1990), 60 C.C.C. (3d) 97 at 127 (S.C.C.).

The jury would also have to be instructed on potential liability for murder and manslaughter under s. 21(2). Liability for murder under s. 21(2) requires that the Crown prove beyond a reasonable doubt that:

- the accused was a party to a common design to steal from the deceased;
- another person who was a party to that same common design committed murder as defined in s. 229(a) in the course of carrying out the theft; and
- the accused knew that murder was a probable consequence of carrying out the common design to steal from the deceased.

If the Crown proves the first two of the three elements described above, but fails to prove that the accused knew that murder was a probable consequence of carrying out the common design, the accused is not guilty of murder but is guilty of manslaughter if a reasonable person would have foreseen the risk of harm to the deceased as a result of carrying out the common design to steal from him: *R. v. Jackson*, [1993] 4 S.C.R. 573.

---

3. COUNSELLING

Section 22 of the *Criminal Code* provides that:

(1) Where a person counsels another person to be a party to an offence and that other person is afterwards a party to that offence, the person who counselled is a party to that offence, notwithstanding that the offence was committed in a way different from that which was counselled.

(2) Every one who counsels another person to be a party to an offence is a party to every offence that the other commits in consequence of the counselling that the person who counselled knew or ought to have known was likely to be committed in consequence of the counselling.

(3) For the purposes of this Act, "counsel" includes procure, solicit or incite.

The court has noted that although "counsel" could have the ordinary meaning simply of advising, for criminal law purposes it must be limited to cases of actively inducing (*R. v. Sharpe*, 2001 SCC 2, [2001] 1 S.C.R. 45, 150 C.C.C. (3d) 321, 39 C.R. (5th) 72, para 56).

The court has also described, in *R. v. Hamilton*, 2005 SCC 47, 198 C.C.C. (3d) 1, 30 C.R. (6th) 243, [2005] 2 S.C.R. 432 the external and fault elements of the offence:

29 In short, the *actus reus* for counselling is the deliberate encouragement or active inducement of the commission of a criminal offence. And the *mens rea* consists in nothing less than an accompanying intent or conscious disregard of the substantial and unjustified risk inherent in the counselling: that is, it must be shown that the accused either intended that the offence counselled be committed, or knowingly counselled the commission of the offence while aware of the unjustified risk that the offence counselled was in fact likely to be committed as a result of the accused's conduct. (emphasis in original).

Hamilton is discussed at greater length in Chapter 9 under "Liability for Offence not Committed".

4. ACCESSORY AFTER FACT

R. v. DUONG

(1998), 15 C.R. (5th) 209, 124 C.C.C. (3d) 392,
1998 CarswellOnt 1784 (Ont. C.A.)

The accused was charged with being an accessory after the fact to a murder committed by one L. Two people were killed in December 1993. There were reports in the newspapers and on television connecting L to the homicides. The accused and L had been friends for five or six years. L called the accused and asked if he could stay at the accused's apartment. L indicated he was in trouble for murder and had no place to go. The accused had seen the media reports of the homicides and knew that L was in trouble. The accused allowed L to hide in his apartment for about two weeks. The police raided the apartment and found L hiding in the bedroom. The accused was specifically asked by the police what L told him about the homicides and he replied that he had told him he was in trouble but that the accused said he didn't want to know anything more because he knew he would be in trouble for helping him hide.

L was charged with two counts of first degree murder and three counts of attempted murder. After a lengthy trial he was convicted of two counts of second degree murder and two counts of attempted murder. The accused was convicted and appealed.

Section 23(1) of the *Criminal Code* provides:

An "accessory after the fact" to an offence is one who, knowing that a person has been a party to the offence, receives, comforts or assists that person for the purpose of enabling that person to escape.

DOHERTY J.A. (CATZMAN and AUSTIN JJ.A. concurring): —

There is little Canadian case law dealing with the knowledge requirement in s. 23(1), perhaps because the language of s. 23(1) is unambiguous. In *R. v. Vinette* (1974), [1975] 2 S.C.R. 222, 19 C.C.C. (2d) 1 (S.C.C.), the accused was charged with being an accessory after the fact to manslaughter. Both the majority (per Pigeon J. at p. 231 S.C.R., p. 7 C.C.C.) and the dissent (per Laskin C.J.C. at pp. 225-26 S.C.R., pp. 2-3 C.C.C.) accepted that the Crown had to prove that an accused charged with being an accessory after the fact to a homicide had knowledge of "the unlawful killing." Similarly, in *R. v. A. (M.)*, released March 22, 1996, this court proceeded on the basis that knowledge of the offence committed by the person aided was an essential element of the charge of being an accessory after the fact. See, also, D. Watt, "Accesssoryship After the Fact: Substantive Procedural and Evidentiary Considerations" (1981), 21 C.R. (3d) 307 at pp. 308, 318-19; V. Rose, *Parties to an Offence* (1982) at pp. 164-66, 194.

In other jurisdictions where provisions like s. 23(1) were in effect, or the common law prevailed, courts required that the Crown prove that the accessory after the fact knew of the specific offence committed by the person assisted: *R. v. Levy*, [1912] 1 K.B. 158 (Eng. Ct. of Crim. App.) at p. 160; *R. v. Tevendale*, [1955] V.L.R. 95 (Australia Vict. Sup. Ct.); *R. v. Carter* (1990), 47 A. Crim. R. 55 (Queensland C.A.) at p. 63; P. Gillies, *Criminal Law* (1990) at pp. 765-66. For example, in *R. v. Carter*, *supra*, Carter J. said at p. 63:

> It follows that in this case it was incumbent upon the Crown to establish the fact that the principal offender had done the acts said to constitute the offence of murder, that the accused knew that and, with that knowledge, received or assisted Carter in order to enable him to escape punishment.

The authorities referred to by Crown counsel rely on statutory language which is very different from that found in s. 23(1). These statutes create a more generic offence involving the hindering of an investigation, or interference with the apprehension or conviction of a person. For example, in *R. v. Morgan*, [1972] 1 Q.B. 436 (Eng. C.A.), the relevant statutory provision provided:

> Where a person has committed an arrestable offence, any other person who, *knowing or believing him to be guilty of the offence or of some other arrestable offence,* does without lawful authority or reasonable excuse any act with intent to impede his apprehension or prosecution shall be guilty of an offence. [Emphasis added.]

Parliament could have enacted similar legislation. It has not, however, done so and it is beyond the authority of the courts to enact such legislation by judicial fiat. I am not moved by the Crown's further contention that the requirement that the Crown prove that the accessory had knowledge of the offence committed by the person aided will allow individuals to escape justice when they aid someone believing that person has committed crime "x" when in fact the person has committed crime "y". If that is the effect of the present legislation, it is for Parliament to decide whether the statutory prohibition should be expanded. Moreover, it seems to me that the circumstances posited by the Crown would give rise to a charge of obstructing justice under s. 139(2) of the *Criminal Code*.

A charge laid under s. 23(1) must allege the commission of a specific offence (or offences) and the Crown must prove that the alleged accessory knew that the person assisted was a party to that offence. The Crown will meet its burden if it proves that the accused had actual knowledge of the offence committed. Whether wilful blindness will suffice is addressed below. The further question of whether recklessness as to the offence committed by the principal would be sufficient need not be decided in this case.

The appellant argues that wilful blindness can only be relied on by the Crown if the Crown proves that an accused whose suspicions were aroused had the means available to verify the accuracy of those suspicions. The appellant goes on to contend that he could have turned only to Lam to verify his suspicions and that the record does not suggest that Lam would have admitted his culpability in the murders. It follows, says the appellant, that he did not have the means available to him to verify his suspicions and should not, therefore, be held culpable on the basis of wilful blindness. The appellant cites no authority for this proposition.

Wilful blindness is explained in *Sansregret v. R.*, [1985] 1 S.C.R. 570 at p. 584, 18 C.C.C. (3d) 223 at p. 235:

> . . . wilful blindness arises where a person who has become aware of the need for some inquiry declines to make the inquiry because he does not wish to know the truth. He would prefer to remain ignorant. The culpability in recklessness is justified by consciousness of the risk and by proceeding in the face of it, *while in wilful blindness it is justified by the accused's fault in deliberately failing to inquire when he knows there is reason for inquiry.* [Emphasis added.]

More recently, in *R. v. Hawkins*, [1995] 4 S.C.R. 55 at pp. 110-11, (*sub. nom. R. v. Jorgensen*) 102 C.C.C. (3d) 97 at p. 135, Sopinka J. described wilful blindness in these terms in reference to a charge of selling obscene material:

> . . . *It is well established in criminal law that wilful blindness will also fulfil a mens rea requirement.* If the retailer becomes aware of the need to make further inquiries about the nature of the videos he was selling yet deliberately chooses to ignore these indications and does not make any further inquiries, then the retailer can be nonetheless charged under s. 163(2)(a) for "knowingly" selling obscene materials. *Deliberately choosing not to know something when given reason to believe further inquiry is necessary can satisfy the mental element of the offence.* . . .
>
> A finding of wilful blindness involves an affirmative answer to the question: Did the accused shut his eyes because he knew or strongly suspected that looking would fix him with knowledge? [Emphasis added.]

These authorities make it clear that where the Crown proves the existence of a fact in issue and knowledge of that fact is a component of the fault requirement of the crime charged, wilful blindness as to the existence of that fact is sufficient to establish a culpable state of mind. Liability based on wilful blindness is subjective. Wilful blindness refers to a state of mind which is aptly described as "deliberate ignorance" (Don Stuart, Canadian Criminal Law, 3rd ed. (1995), at p. 209). Actual suspicion, combined with a conscious decision not to make inquiries which could confirm that suspicion, is equated in the eyes of the criminal law with actual knowledge. Both are subjective and both are sufficiently blameworthy to justify the imposition of criminal liability.

The appellant's submission misunderstands the basis upon which liability is imposed where wilful blindness exists. Liability turns on the decision not to inquire once real suspicions arise and not on the hypothetical result of inquiries which were never made. Where an accused chooses to make no inquiries, preferring to remain "deliberately ignorant", speculation as to what the accused would have learned had he chosen to make the necessary inquiries is irrelevant to the determination of the blameworthiness of that accused's state of mind.

The appellant also submits that even if wilful blindness has application in the circumstances of this case, the trial judge erred in finding that the appellant was wilfully blind to the fact that Lam was a party to murder. This is in essence an argument that the trial judge's finding is unreasonable. It was urged that the appellant's statements to the police suggested only that he suspected that Lam had some connection, perhaps as a witness, to the homicides. The appellant submits that a finding of knowledge that Lam was a party to murder based on those statements was more speculation than reasonable inference.

It was certainly open to trial counsel to advance the argument now urged upon this court. I cannot say, however, that the trial judge's rejection of that argument and his conclusion that the appellant's suspicions extended to a suspicion that Lam had been a party to murder was unreasonable. It was open to him to infer that the appellant's statements revealed a state of mind which encompassed the suspicion that Lam was in trouble because he had been a party to murder. The fact that the appellant may have contemplated other possible connections between Lam and the murders afforded no bar to a finding that he was wilfully blind to the fact that Lam was a party to murder.

See also *R. v. Shalaan*, [1998] 1 S.C.R. 88, 121 C.C.C. (3d) 223, where the Supreme Court of Canada affirmed the decision of the Nova Scotia Court of Appeal in a murder case. The accused's husband had been killed in his home, while only the accused and a young person were present, and only one of those two people could have committed the killing. The trial judge ((1996), 153 N.S.R. (2d) 35, 108 C.C.C. (3d) 220 (N.S.S.C.)) had held that he was not persuaded beyond a reasonable doubt that the accused had performed the killing, and in fact was convinced that it was the young person who had committed the offence. He also held that the Crown had not proven that the accused had aided or abetted the crime, or had known in advance it would be committed. If she was guilty, then, it was only as an accessory after the fact, which he held required the Crown to prove:

     (i) The identity of Fayezah Jassim Shalaan as the offender;
     (ii) The time and place of the offence as set out in the Indictment;
     (iii) That T.A. committed murder;
     (iv) That Fayezah Jassim Shalaan knew that T.A. had committed murder;
     (v) That Fayezah Jassim Shalaan helped T.A. to escape from justice by receiving, comforting, or assisting him;
     (vi) That the purpose of Fayezah Jassim Shalaan in receiving, comforting, or assisting T.A. was to help him escape from justice. (para 18)

The trial judge held that the Crown had proven all the elements but (iii). With regard to that element, he noted that the young person had already been tried for the offence in a different court and had been found not guilty. In those circumstances, he held, a conviction of the accused as an accessory after the fact was not possible:

¶ 22...Section 23.1 refers to where the principal "cannot be convicted of the offence." Although the section does not describe or limit the basis upon which a conviction of a principal cannot be convicted, various legal texts and cases have referred to specifics such as the ability to locate or compel the attendance of such a person, an incapacity based on infancy under Section 13 of the *Code*, and even the death of a principal before indictment or trial...In my opinion Section 23.1 refers to these types of specifics and not a situation where the principal has been previously acquitted.

¶ 23 In my opinion we are all still left with the common law, and the obiter in *Vinette*, as interpreted by Moir J.A. in *Anderson*, and that is, if the principal was acquitted, the accessory must be acquitted.

¶ 24 Under these circumstances for me to find the accused guilty on this charge would, in my opinion, be perverse and result in inconsistent verdicts. It might well be inclined, I submit, to bring the administration of justice into disrepute.

The Nova Scotia Court of Appeal ((1997), 159 N.S.R. (2d) 285, 115 C.C.C. (3d) 450)) overturned this verdict. After an extensive review of the history of the provision and case law from Canada, the United States and Great Britain, the Court of Appeal concluded:

¶ 29...It is clear from [s. 23.1] and s. 592 of the *Code* it is not necessary to convict a principal in order to convict an accessory. While the language does not refer to the acquittal of the principal, in my view the words "whether or not the principal" is convicted, are broad enough to encompass the acquittal of the principal. Those provisions have changed the common law.

The Supreme Court of Canada affirmed this result.

5.   GENERAL REVIEW QUESTION

1. **A group of five youths, aged 17 to 19 and including A and B, are in a Kingston bar watching the televising of a National Hockey League play-off game between the Montreal Canadiens and Quebec Nordiques, won by Quebec 4-1. During this game each consumes only about three beers. During the second period a Quebec supporter, Pierre, is discovered in the bar. He is sitting alone. His actions are limited to smiling a lot and applauding Quebec goals. After the game the group of five corner Pierre outside the bar and begin deriding him and elbowing him. B shouts "Let's beat up the Frog". A leaves the group momentarily, goes to the back of the bar premises, picks up a four-foot-long loose fence picket, returns and proceeds to savagely beat Pierre, who has fallen to the ground. B removes his leather belt from his jeans and is about to join the attack when Pierre lapses into unconsciousness. The group runs off. C, a passing pedestrian who is a doctor, turns Pierre over, starts to examine him but then departs. Later C explains "Ontario doctors were on work-stoppage". An ambulance is summoned by another passer-by. It only arrives 35 minutes later as the ambulance service is involved in a rash of hospital transfers due to the doctors' work-stoppage. Pierre dies in transit. The autopsy assigns the death to a combination of the beating, the delay and Pierre's previously undiagnosed heart aneurism.**

The responsible Crown Attorney is appalled by the incident. He asks you for a memorandum of law and advice as to the maximum viable charges (discussing possible defences) against A (the attacker), B (the bystander) and C (the doctor).

Chapter 9

INCOMPLETE CRIMES

1. ATTEMPTS

See sections 24 and 463 of the *Criminal Code*.

R. v. ANCIO

[1984] 1 S.C.R. 225, 39 C.R. (3d) 1, 10 C.C.C. (3d) 385,
1984 CarswellOnt 41, 1984 CarswellOnt 799

McINTYRE J. (DICKSON, BEETZ, ESTEY, CHOUINARD, LAMER and WILSON JJ. concurring): — This appeal [from 63 C.C.C. (2d) 309] involves consideration of the mental element required for proof of the crime of attempted murder, the subject of this court's earlier judgment in *Lajoie v. R.*, [1974] S.C.R. 399, 20 C.R.N.S. 360, [1974] 10 C.C.C. (2d) 313, affirming 16 C.R.N.S. 180, 4 C.C.C. (2d) 402.

At the date of the events which give rise to this appeal the respondent had been married some 25 years. His wife had left the matrimonial home and was living with one Kurely. The respondent was depressed and had been drinking to excess on the date in question. He telephoned his wife at Kurely's residence and told her he was afraid that their 23-year-old son was about to commit suicide and asked her to meet him. She refused to co-operate. Later the same evening the respondent broke into a friend's home while its owners were absent and took away three shotguns. He sawed off the barrel of one, loaded it and, taking some extra ammunition with him, went to Kurely's apartment building and gained entry by breaking the glass in the front door. On hearing the noise caused by the breaking glass, Kurely came from his bedroom to investigate, carrying a chair with a jacket hanging on it. He saw the respondent, carrying the shotgun, ascending the stairs to the second floor. He threw the chair and jacket, hitting the respondent. The gun went off. The blast missed Kurely by some three feet but put a hole in the jacket, which had been on the chair. A struggle followed, in which Kurely appears to have wrestled the gun from the respondent. When the police arrived, having been called during the course of the fight between the two men, Kurely was on the floor with his head partly under a bed and with the respondent upon him striking him weakly.

Shortly after his arrest the respondent stated to the police:

> I just went over to see my wife. I had phoned her earlier. I broke the window and went in. Then I heard what sounded like a gun go off. You are lucky you got there when you did. I had him by the throat and I would have killed him.

According to the respondent's account of events, the gun was discharged accidentally, although under tests conducted by the police the weapon was not found to be prone to accidental discharge.

The respondent was charged with a number of offences arising out of this affair but only one, that of attempted murder, is involved in this appeal. It was contained in the first count of the information and was in these terms:

> . . . did attempt to murder Michael Kurely by discharging a sawed off shotgun at him contrary to s. 222 of the *Criminal Code* of Canada [R.S.C. 1970, c. C-34].

He elected trial by judge alone and was convicted. The conviction was quashed in the Court of Appeal and a new trial directed. This appeal is taken by leave of this court.

· · · ·

The Crown contended in this court that the Court of Appeal was in error in holding that the *mens rea* in attempted murder was limited to an intention to cause death (s. 212(*a*)(i)), or an intention to cause bodily harm knowing it to be likely to cause death and being reckless whether death ensues (s. 212(*a*)(ii)). The Crown's position was stated in its factum in these words:

> . . . the intention for attempted murder is not restricted to an actual intention to kill or an intention to cause grievous bodily harm that one knows is likely to cause death and is reckless whether death ensues or not, but *extends to an intention to do that which constitutes the commission of the offence of murder as defined in ss. 212 and 213 am. 1974-75-76, c. 93, s. 13; c. 105, s. 29; since am. 1980-81-82-83, c. 125 s. 15 of the Criminal Code. It is the Crown's position that s. 24 and s. 213(d) in combination can form the basis for a conviction of attempted murder.* (The italics are mine)

The respondent supported the judgment of the Court of Appeal, which followed the judgment of this court in *Lajoie v. R.*, *supra*. In that case it was held that a conviction for attempted murder could be sustained where the Crown had shown on the part of the accused either an intent to kill the potential victim or an intent to cause bodily harm which he knows is likely to cause death and is reckless whether death ensues or not. Although reference was made in *Lajoie* to the possibility of committing attempted murder as defined in s. 213 (see the concluding sentence on p. 408), the respondent and the Court of Appeal in the case at bar adopted the view that this was merely obiter. . . . .

. . . .

The respondent submitted that the Crown's position, that s. 213(*d*) coupled with s. 24(1) described a further intent sufficient to warrant a conviction for attempted murder, should not be accepted because there was no authority to extend the concept of a constructive intent further than *Lajoie* had taken it. While contending on the facts of this case that he was not obliged to go further, he argued that in reason and logic a specific intent to kill should be the only intent sufficient to ground a conviction for attempted murder. It was said that the effect of the Crown's argument in extending the concept of an attempt to s. 213(*d*) of the *Criminal Code* would be to justify a conviction for attempted murder in the absence of any mental element with respect to the causing of death which would be to ignore the words of s. 24(1) specifically requiring an intent to commit the offence in question.

Lying at the heart of the controversy which arises in this case is the judgment of this court in *Lajoie, supra*.

. . . .

A great deal of the confusion surrounding the nature of the intent required to found a conviction for attempted murder may well stem from an assumption that murder and attempted murder are related offences which must share the same mental elements. A brief review of the historical development of the law relating to the two offences demonstrates that the crime of attempt developed as a separate and distinct offence from the offence of murder.

In very early times murder was simply the killing of a human being. The law was concerned with the injury done to the family of the deceased and the compensation which should follow. The consequence of the killing was the important feature and the intent or *mens rea* was of little if any significance. Special mental elements were recognized in statutes as early as the 13th Century, and by the 14th Century the concept of malice aforethought had developed: see *Act of the King's Charters of Pardon, 1389* (13 Ric. 2, star. 2), c. 1. Thus two elements came to be recognized in murder: the killing, and the malice aforethought, which in modern times has come to mean the necessary intent or intents.

As the common law developed, the mental element required for the commission of murder expanded to include both constructive intent and knowledge of the likelihood of death as a result of a person's acts, with recklessness as to whether death ensued or not.

. . . .

The offence of attempts developed much later than the offence of murder. In early times an attempt to commit an offence was not itself a crime. It was considered that in the absence of a guilty act intention alone was not punishable.

The modern offence of attempting the commission of a crime is said to have its origins in the Court of Star Chamber. An early venture into this field is found in the *Case of Duels* (1615), 2 State Tr. 1033, which involved proceedings against one William Priest for sending a written challenge to duel and one Richard Wright for carrying it and a stick that was to be the measure of the length of the weapons to be employed. It was asserted by Sir Francis Bacon, then Attorney General, at p. 1041, that:

> For the Capacity of this court, I take this to be a ground infallible: that wheresoever an offence is capital, or matter of felony, though it be not acted, there the combination or practice tending to that offence is punishable in this court as a high misdemeanor. So practice to impoison, though it took no effect; waylaying to murder, though it took no effect; and the like; have been adjudged heinous misdemeanors punishable in this court. Nay, inceptions and preparations in inferior crimes, that are not capital, as suborning and preparing of witnesses that were never deposed, or deposed nothing material, have likewise been censured in this court, as appeareth by the decree in *Garnon's Case*.

The court in its decree gave effect to the Attorney General's submission saying, in part, at p. 1046:

> And the court with one consent did declare their opinions: That by the ancient law of the land, all inceptions, preparations, and combinations to execute unlawful acts, though they never be performed, as they be not to be punished capitally, except it be in case of treason, and some other particular cases of statute law, so yet they are punishable as misdemeanors and contempts: and that this court was proper for offences of such nature.

The practice of the Court of Star Chamber in this respect became firmly established in that court (see Hall, *General Principles of Criminal Law*, 2nd ed. (1960), p. 565 *et seq.*) and was in time adopted in the Court of King's Bench. It has been said that the origin of the doctrine of criminal attempt as it is known in the common-law was Lord Mansfield's judgment in *R. v. Scofield* (1784), Cald. Mag. Rep. 397. Scofield was charged in an indictment with "wickedly, unlawfully and maliciously intending devising and contriving to feloniously set fire to, burn and consume a certain house".

. . . .

Whether *Scofield* was the starting point for the common-law doctrine is doubted by Hall (pp. 569-70) but the question seems to have been settled in *R. v. Higgins* (1801), 102 E.R. 269 (K.B.), where it was said, at p. 274, by Grose J.:

> First, as to the offence itself, it must be admitted that an attempt to commit a felony is in many cases at least a misdemeanor . . .

Any doubt remaining regarding the existence of the offence of attempted murder in England was set to rest by the enactment of the *Offences Against the Person Act, 1861* (24 & 25 Vict.), c. 100, ss. 11 to 15. These sections made it a felony to attempt the commission of murder in the various ways described.

In Canada the common-law offence of attempt was codified in the *1892 Criminal Code* as s. 64.

. . . .

A minor change in the 1953-54 *Code* changed the section to its present form in s. 24.

. . . .

The section has therefore covered the law of attempt in general since the codification of the law in 1892. In addition, particular provision has been made in the *Criminal Code* for the offence of attempted murder . . . .

. . . .

It is clear from the foregoing that in common law and under the criminal law of Canada criminal attempt is itself an offence separate and distict from the crime alleged to be attempted. As with any other crime, the Crown must prove a *mens rea*, that is, the intent to commit the offence in question, and the *actus reus*, that is, some step towards the commission of the offence attempted going beyond mere acts of preparation. Of the two elements the more significant is the *mens rea*. In *R. v. Cline* [(1956), 115 C.C.C. 18], Laidlaw J.A., speaking for the Ontario Court of Appeal, said, at p. 27:

> Criminal intention alone is insufficient to establish a criminal attempt. There must be *mens rea* and also an *actus reus*. But it is to be observed that whereas in most crimes it is the *actus reus* which the law endeavours to prevent, and the *mens rea* is only a necessary element of the offence, in a criminal attempt the *mens rea* is of primary importance and the *actus reus* is the necessary element.

And in *Russell on Crime*, 12th ed. (1964), vol. 1, p. 175, it is said:

> Since the mischief contained in an attempt depends upon the nature of the crime intended, the criminality lies much more in the intention than in the acts done.

This proposition was accepted by Goddard L.C.J. in *Whybrow* [(1951), 35 Cr. App. R. 51], at p. 147, where he stated that "the intent becomes the principal ingredient of the crime".

The common-law recognition of the fundamental importance of intent in the crime of attempt is carried forward into the *Criminal Code*. A reading of s. 24 of the *Code* and all its predecessors since the enactment of the first *Code* in 1892 confirms that the intent to commit the desired offence is a basic element of the offence of attempt. Indeed, because the crime of attempt may be complete without the actual commission of any other offence and even without the performance of any act unlawful in itself, it is abundantly clear that the criminal element of the offence of attempt may lie solely in the intent. As noted by

Glanville Williams, *Criminal Law: The General Part*, 2nd ed. (1961), p. 642, para. 207, in discussing attempts:

> An *actus reus* . . . need not be a crime apart from the state of mind. It need not even be a tort or a moral wrong or a social mischief.

The question now arises: What is the intent required for an attempt to commit murder? As has been indicated earlier, the Crown's position is that the intent required for a conviction on a charge of attempt to murder is the intent to do that which will, if death is caused, constitute the commission of murder as defined in ss. 212 and 213 of the *Code*, so that a combination of ss. 24 and 213(*d*) can form the basis for a conviction of attempted murder. The respondent, on the other hand, argues that, although the authorities presently limit the intent to that which would constitute murder as defined in s. 212 of the *Code*, logic and principle dictate that the intent should be limited to the specific intent to kill described in s. 212(*a*)(i).

While it is clear from ss. 212 and 213 of the *Criminal Code* that an unintentional killing can be murder, it is equally clear that, whatever mental elements may be involved and whatever means may be employed, there cannot be a murder without a killing. Section 24 of the *Code* defines, in part, the offence of attempt as "having an intent to commit an offence". As Estey J. observed in *R. v. Quinton*, [1947] S.C.R. 234 at 235-36, 3 C.R. 6, 88 C.C.C. 231, in referring to the then s. 72 (now s. 24):

> This section requires that one to be guilty of an attempt must intend to commit the completed offence and to have done some act toward the accomplishment of that objective.

The completed offence of murder involves a killing. The intention to commit the complete offence of murder must therefore include an intention to kill. I find it impossible to conclude that a person may intend to commit the unintentional killings described in ss. 212 and 213 of the *Code*. I am then of the view that the *mens rea* for an attempted murder cannot be less than the specific intent to kill.

As I have said earlier, there is a division of opinion upon this point and strong arguments have been raised in favour of the Crown's position that a "lesser intent", such as that provided in s. 212(*a*)(ii), or even no intent at all relating to the causing of death, as provided in s. 213(*d*), may suffice to found a conviction for attempted murder. This view is supported in *Lajoie, supra*. In my view, with the utmost respect for those who differ, the sections of the *Criminal Code* relied on in that case do not support that position.

As noted above, Martland J.'s analysis of the intent required to found a conviction for attempted murder is based primarily on the change in wording of s. 222. In my opinion, emphasis on the amendment of this section is unwarranted, for two reasons. Firstly, s. 222 does not define or create the offence of attempted murder. The scheme of the *Criminal Code* in relation to attempts has been the same from its inception. One section defines the offence of attempts generally

(s. 72 of the 1927 *Code*, now s. 24). Another sets out the penalties of attempts (s. 57 of the 1927 Code, now s. 421), and a third creates a separate penalty for attempted murder (s. 264 of the 1927 *Code*, s. 210 in *Lajoie*, now s. 222). Rather than defining or creating an offence, s. 222 merely fixes a penalty for a specific attempt. Despite the categorization of the various means of committing murder set out in the old s. 264, there is no essential difference between the old and the new sections in this respect.

Secondly, the elimination of the words "with intent to commit murder" from s. 264 is not significant. Section 24 defines an attempt as "having an intent to commit an offence". Because s. 24 is a general section it is necessary to "read in" the offence in question. The offence of attempted murder then is defined as "having an intent to commit murder". This does not differ from the old s. 264 reference to "with intent to commit murder", which Martland J. acknowledged was interpreted, in *R. v. Flannery* [[1923] 3 W.W.R. 97], to require the specific intent to kill.

Martland J. placed further emphasis on s. 222 of the *Criminal Code* by relying on the words "attempts by any means" to support his conclusion that murder may be attempted in any of the "ways" set out in ss. 212 and 213. In my view, the reference to "any means" in s. 222 refers to ways in which a murder could be accomplished, such as by poisoning, shooting, or stabbing. The earlier version of s. 222 (s. 232 in 1892, s. 264 in 1906) listed the various methods by which a killing could be effected, but the illustrations were replaced in the 1953-54 revision with a general reference to murder "by any means". In any event, ss. 212 and 213 have nothing to do with the means of killing. They are concerned solely with describing the mental elements which will suffice to make a completed killing murder. The fact that certain mental elements, other than an intent to kill, may lead to a conviction for murder where there has been a killing does not mean that anything less than an intent to kill will suffice for an attempt at murder.

It was argued, and it has been suggested in some of the cases and academic writings on the question, that it is illogical to insist upon a higher degree of *mens rea* for attempted murder, while accepting a lower degree amounting to recklessness for murder. I see no merit in this argument. The intent to kill is the highest intent in murder and there is no reason in logic why an attempt to murder, aimed at the completion of the full crime of murder, should have any lesser intent. If there is any illogic in this matter, it is in the statutory characterization of unintentional killing as murder. The *mens rea* for attempted murder is, in my view, the specific intent to kill. A mental state falling short of that level may well lead to conviction for other offences, for example, one or other of the various aggravated assaults, but not to a conviction for an attempt at murder. For these reasons, it is my view that *Lajoie, supra*, should no longer be followed.

I would accordingly dismiss the Crown's appeal and confirm the Court of Appeal's order for a new trial.

RITCHIE J.: — I am unable to distinguish this case from that of *Lajoie v. R.*, [*supra*], which is a unanimous judgment of this court and by which I feel bound. I would therefore allow this appeal.

Appeal dismissed.

R. v. SORRELL and BONDETT

(1978), 41 C.C.C. (2d) 9, 1978 CarswellOnt 1205 (Ont. C.A.)

Ontario Court of Appeal, DUBIN, MARTIN and BLAIR JJ.A. April 27, 1978.

BY THE COURT: — The Attorney-General of Ontario appeals against the acquittal of the respondents on a charge of attempted robbery.

The respondents were tried at Kingston before His Honour Judge Campbell, sitting without a jury, on an indictment containing three counts.

Count 1 charged the respondents jointly with, on or about March 3, 1977, attempting to rob Peter Mason of Aunt Lucy's Fried Chicken store at 240 Montreal St. in Kingston. Count 2 charged the respondent Sorrell with carrying, at the time and place aforesaid, a concealed weapon, to wit: a Smith and Wesson revolver. Count 3 charged the respondent Sorrell with having in his possession, at the time and place aforesaid, a Smith and Wesson revolver, knowing the same was obtained by an offence committed in Canada punishable on indictment. The respondent Sorrell, on arraignment, pleaded guilty to the charge of carrying a concealed weapon contained in count 2; his plea of guilty was accepted by the trial judge after the evidence was completed, and he was sentenced to imprisonment for 18 months. The trial judge acquitted the respondent Sorrell on count 3, on the ground that the Crown had failed to prove the necessary element of guilty knowledge. The Crown does not appeal the acquittal of Sorrell on count 3, and we are not further concerned with it.

On the evening of Thursday, March 3, 1977, Miss Dawn Arbuckle was the cashier at Aunt Lucy's Fried Chicken store at 240 Montreal St. in Kingston. The store is located at the corner of Montreal and Markland Sts., the customer entrances being on Montreal St. Mr. Peter Mason was the manager of the store. The regular closing time for the store was 11:00 p.m., but, on the evening in question, since almost all the chicken had been sold, the manager decided to close the store earlier, and locked the customer entrances at approximately 10:45 p.m. Around 10 minutes to 11:00 Miss Arbuckle noticed two men, wearing balaclavas, on the Markland St. side of the store; they then came to one of the customer entrances in Montreal St. The area outside the store was illuminated, and the lights normally on in the store, when open, were still on.

One of the men was wearing a blue ski jacket and the other was wearing a brown coat. The balaclavas worn by the two men were pulled down completely over their heads, and one man was also wearing sunglasses. Miss Arbuckle said that the balaclava worn by one man was blue and white in colour, and that worn by the other man was brown and white.

One of the men rapped on the door and on the window. The manager, who had been mopping the floor, turned around and said, "Sorry we are closed", and returned to his mopping. The two men turned toward each other, and made a gesture of surprise. At this time Miss Arbuckle noticed that one of the men had a silver-coloured gun in his hand. The two men then walked away on Montreal Street in the direction of Princess St.; whereupon Mr. Mason, the manager, telephoned the police. Two officers in a cruiser responded to the call, drove to the area and saw two men, whose clothing corresponded to the description that the officers had been given, walking on Montreal St. The officers drove past the two men, then made a U-turn and drove back towards them.

As the officers passed the two men, before making the U-turn, they saw one of the men throw "an article of material" towards a snow bank on the side of the street. The two men, who proved to be the respondents, were then arrested. The respondent Sorrell had a loaded .357 Magnum revolver concealed in his waistband. The gun was loaded with six Dominion .38 shells, and another five Dominion .38 shells were removed from the respondent Sorrell's pants' pocket.

An officer conducted a search of the immediate area where the respondents had been arrested, and found a brown balaclava on a snowbank on the side of Montreal St. The point on Montreal St. where the respondents were arrested was some 411 yards from the Aunt Lucy's store, where the attempted robbery is alleged to have occurred. The officer proceeded along Montreal St. in the direction of the Aunt Lucy's store, and found a blue balaclava in the middle of the sidewalk on Montreal St. at the intersection of Raglan St.

Neither of the respondents testified in his defence.

The Crown appeals against the acquittal of the respondents on the charge of attempted robbery on the ground that the trial judge erred in law in holding that the acts of the respondents did not go beyond mere preparation, and hence did not constitute an attempt.

Section 24 of the *Code* defines an attempt as follows:

> 24(1) Every one who, having an intent to commit an offence, does or omits to do anything for the purpose of carrying out his intention is guilty of an attempt to commit the offence whether or not it was possible under the circumstances to commit the offence.
>
> (2) The question whether an act or omission by a person *who has an intent to commit an offence* is or is not mere preparation to commit the offence, and too remote to constitute an attempt to commit the offence, is a question of law. (Emphasis supplied.)

In order to establish the commission of the offence of attempted robbery charged, it was necessary for the Crown to prove that the respondents:

(i) intended to do that which would in law amount to the robbery specified in the indictment (*mens rea*), and

(ii) took steps in carrying out that intent which amounted to more than mere preparation (*actus reus*).

By virtue of s. 24(2) of the *Code*, the existence of element (i) is a question of fact, but whether the steps taken are sufficient to satisfy element (ii) is a question of law.

In *R. v. Cline*, 115 C.C.C. 18 at p. 29, Laidlaw J.A., in his much-quoted judgment, said:

> (1) There must be *mens rea* and also an *actus reus* to constitute a criminal attempt, but the criminality of misconduct lies mainly in the intention of the accused. ... (5) The *actus reus* must be more than mere preparation to commit a crime. But (6) when the preparation to commit a crime is in fact fully complete and ended, the next step done by the accused for the purpose and with the intention of committing a specific crime constitutes an *actus reus* sufficient in law to establish a criminal attempt to commit that crime.

Thus, proof of the respondents' intention to commit the robbery particularized in the indictment, which is a question of fact, was the central issue in the case. Mr. Doherty for the Crown contended before us that on the facts found by the trial judge, he erred in law in failing to draw the legal conclusion of guilt required by the facts accepted by him as proved, and, in particular, erred in law in holding that the acts of the respondents, found by him to have been proved, had not gone beyond mere preparation. Counsel for the respondents, on the other hand, contended that the trial judge's reasons for judgment, considered in their entirety, show that he acquitted the respondents because he entertained a reasonable doubt whether they had the intent to rob the Aunt Lucy's store, the existence of which intent was essential to constitute the attempt charged.

A detailed examination of the trial judge's reasons for judgment is necessary in order to endeavour to ascertain the basis upon which he acquitted the respondents. The trial judge said:

> Turning to count 1, that is the count that affects both Sorrel and Bondett, namely, this attempted robbery count. There are many conclusions that I have drawn from the credible evidence, beyond a reasonable doubt, and I say that those conclusions complete substantially the Crown's case subject only — and I say only — to the thorny question as to whether or not the events in question constitute an attempt within the meaning of the *Criminal Code*.

After referring to certain discrepancies in the evidence of the Crown witnesses, which he did not consider material, the trial judge continued:

> The Crown's case on count 1 has been proved beyond a reasonable doubt in my finding on the matters of identity of the accused, the date, the place and, subject only to what I am going to be saying on the matter of attempt, as to the allegation that the attempted robbery, if there was an attempted robbery, was committed in respect of Peter Mason of Aunt Lucy's Kentucky Fried Chicken.

He then held that Mr. Mason, as the manager of the store, had the custody of the money in the store, and said:

It brings me down then to the sole remaining question, did what took place at the time and at the place, as referred to by the witnesses Arbuckle and Mason, constitute an attempt at robbery? I may say that I found the evidence of both of those witnesses to be satisfactory, credible, and my findings are based on that evidence. I as well look to the evidence at the trial as to the manner of departure from the premises — from in front of the premises — by the two accused and the actions that they were performing when seen and practically immediately apprehended by the police. I am finding that between them they rid themselves of the balaclavas which could raise the inference of guilty mind; but that, of course, raises the question: a mind having a sense of guilt of what? They may have thought that what they did at the front of the store was criminal in some way and that they should take some steps to cover up — whether they were right in that belief or not. Was what they had actually done illegal as being an attempt to rob, whether they believed it or not, that still leaves to me the question: was what they did within the ambit of an attempt to rob? The inference is pretty plain, and I think I would be naive to conclude otherwise, that they were up to no good on that occasion, that they may well have had robbery of the store in mind. But, again, I am driven back to the provisions of the *Code* that differentiate between mere preparation and the actual commencement of steps to commit the robbery

I am obliged to counsel for their references to cases on the point, one of which endeavours to lay down tests for the assistance of the court, and subsequent cases, but all of which have their own set of facts and circumstances with which the court then in those cases had to deal. It is an extremely thin line, but whether thin or otherwise, if my finding is that that line had been crossed beyond mere preparation, the finding — if it were to be made — that the line had been crossed would be sufficient to bring me to a conclusion beyond a reasonable doubt. Nevertheless, the fineness of the line is a bother to me. I am conscious of the fact that the accused timed their arrival at the store such that they could expect a fund of money to be in the till, such they could expect there would likely be few if any persons there other than the store personnel, and that they had costumed themselves for the purpose of disguising their features to render subsequent identification difficult, but I am also of the view that it is important for me to consider the fact that apart from rattling the door and perhaps rattling on the window — that would be consistent with an innocent person's endeavour to get in the food store — there was no gesture of threat of violence or threat of force. The case before me is attempted robbery and not attempted break, enter and theft, or break and enter with intent, or conspiracy, or whatever. So that the endeavour to open the door would — were one of those other charges to have been before me, and I am not saying in any way that it should have been before me — what was done by way of attempt to open the door could relate more to a charge of attempted breaking rather than the charge of robbery. In brief, in my finding, the accused by virtue of I suppose good luck of not having been able to progress further in doing whatever they were going to do had not yet crossed the line between preparation and attempt. Accordingly, I am finding that count 1 as regards both accused has not been proved on that narrow ground, and I have endorsed the indictment on count 1: both accused not guilty.

It will be observed that while the trial judge made an express finding that he was satisfied beyond a reasonable doubt that the respondents were the two men who had approached the store, and that one of them had a gun, he made no similar finding with respect to the existence of the necessary intent to rob. Mr. O'Hara, on behalf of the respondent Sorrell particularly emphasized the following passages in the trial judge's reasons, relative to intent, which Mr. O'Hara characterized as "powerful expressions of doubt", namely: ". . . they may well have had robbery of the store in mind", and ". . . what was done by way of attempt to open the door could relate more to a charge of attempted breaking rather than the charge of robbery". In our view, the trial judge's reasons are more consistent with a finding that the necessary intent to commit robbery was not proved beyond a reasonable doubt, than with a finding that such intent was established by the evidence. In any event, the Crown has not satisfied us that the trial judge found the existence of an intent to rob.

The Crown's right of appeal under s. 605(1)(*a*) of the *Code* is confined to a ground of appeal that involves a question of law alone. The failure of the trial judge to draw the appropriate inference of intent from the facts found by him, is an error of fact, and does not raise a question of law.

. . . .

If the trial judge had found that the respondents intended to rob the store, the acts done by them clearly had advanced beyond mere preparation, and were sufficiently proximate to constitute an attempt: see *Henderson v. The King*, 91 C.C.C. 97, [1948] S.C.R. 226, *per* Kerwin J., at p. 98 C.C.C., p. 228 S.C.R., *per* Estey J., at pp. 114-16 C.C.C., pp. 243-6 S.C.R., *per* Locke J., at pp. 116-17 C.C.C., p. 246 S.C.R.; *R. v. Carey*, 118 C.C.C. 241, [1957] S.C.R. 266, 25 C.R. 177, *per* Kerwin C.J.C., at pp, 246-7, *per* Rand J., at p. 251. If the trial judge had found that the respondents had the necessary intent his finding that the acts done by the respondents did not go beyond mere preparation and did not constitute attempted robbery, would constitute an error of law that would not only warrant, but require our intervention.

Because of the doubt that he entertained that the respondents had the necessary intent to commit robbery, however, his error in law in holding that the respondents' acts did not go beyond mere preparation, could not have affected the verdict of acquittal, unless, of course, his self-misdirection with respect to what constituted mere preparation, led him into error in entertaining a reasonable doubt whether the requisite intent had been proved. This question is one of considerable difficulty. The following passage (included in those previously quoted), would tend to support the conclusion that the trial judge was led into error with respect to the existence of the necessary intent by self-misdirection that the respondents' acts had not gone beyond mere preparation:

> It is an extremely thin line, but whether thin or otherwise, if my finding is that that line had been crossed beyond mere preparation, the finding — if it were to be made — that the line had been crossed would be sufficient to bring me to a conclusion beyond a reasonable doubt. Nevertheless, the fineness of the line is a bother to me.

The trial judge then proceeded, however, to refer to the matters in the passages previously quoted, relating to the issue of intent, which gave him difficulty in finding that the required mental element was present. The issue of intent was basic and, the trial judge, in our view, could not logically or appropriately make a determination whether the acts of the respondents went beyond mere preparation until he had first found the intent with which those acts were done.

The issue whether the acts of the respondents went beyond mere preparation could not be decided in the abstract apart from the existence of the requisite intent.

In the present case, there was no evidence of the intent to rob other than that furnished by the acts relied on as constituting the *actus reus*. There was no extrinsic evidence in the form of statements of intention, or admissions by the respondents showing what their intention was.

The prosecution in this case was forced to rely exclusively upon the acts of the accused, not only to constitute the *actus reus*, but to supply the evidence of the necessary *mens rea*. This court in *R. v. Cline, supra*, rejected the so-called "unequivocal act" test for determining when the stage of attempt has been reached. That test excludes resort to evidence *aliunde*, such as admissions, and holds that the state of attempt has been reached only when the acts of the accused show unequivocally on their face the criminal intent with which the acts were performed. We are of the view that where the accused's intention is otherwise proved, acts which on their face are equivocal may, none the less, be sufficiently proximate to constitute an attempt. Where, however, there is no extrinsic evidence of the intent with which accused's acts were done, acts of the accused, which on their face are equivocal, may be insufficient to show that the acts were done with the intent to commit the crime that the accused is alleged to have attempted to commit, and hence insufficient to establish the offence of attempt.

Counsel for the respondents while conceding that the trial judge's reasons are not free of ambiguity, submitted that they are reasonably open to the interpretation that he was searching for evidence that satisfied him beyond a reasonable doubt that the accused intended to rob the store in question, and at the end of his quest was not satisfied beyond a reasonable doubt, that the acts done by the accused supplied the necessary proof of intent.

We think that this submission accurately states the basis upon which the trial judge acquitted the respondents, and the Crown has not satisfied us that, but for the self-misdirection with respect to which complaint is made, the verdict of the trial judge would not necessarily have been the same. It is not to the point that, on the evidence, we would have reached a different conclusion with respect to the respondent's intentions.

. . . .

Appeal dismissed.

R. v. DEUTSCH

[1986] 2 S.C.R. 2, 52 C.R. (3d) 305, 27 C.C.C. (3d) 385,
1986 CarswellOnt 120, 1986 CarswellOnt 1009

LE DAIN J.: — This appeal, which involves a charge of attempting to procure a person to have illicit sexual intercourse with another person contrary to s. 195(1)(a) of the *Criminal Code*, raises two issues: the distinction between attempt and mere preparation, and the meaning of "illicit sexual intercourse".

The appeal is from the judgment of the Ontario Court of Appeal on March 17, 1983 setting aside the acquittal of the appellant by Graburn Co. Ct. J. on August 13, 1982 of the charge of attempting to procure a person to have illicit sexual intercourse with another person and ordering a new trial of the appellant on that charge.

During the period covered by the indictment, which is the three months ending on or about September 3, 1981, the appellant was carrying on a business known as Global Franchises Marketing, which was engaged in selling franchises of various kinds. During this period the appellant placed an advertisement in newspapers in Ottawa, Hamilton and Toronto inviting applications for the position of secretary/sales assistant and conducted interviews with three women who responded to the advertisement and with a police officer who posed as an applicant for the position and recorded the interview on a tape recorder. The advertisement read as follows:

ENJOY TRAVEL

SECRETARY — Sales Assistant to Sales Executive. $600-$800 per month to start plus commission, bonuses, company benefits and expenses. Must be free to travel extensively. Call 746-2440 ask for Mel.

In the interviews the appellant indicated that a secretary/sales assistant would be expected to have sexual intercourse with clients or potential clients of the company where that appeared to be necessary to conclude a contract. The appellant also indicated that a successful secretary/sales assistant could earn as much as $100,000 per year through commission or bonus on the sale of franchises. The appellant did not make an offer of employment to the three applicants who testified at his trial. After hearing what the position required they said they were not interested and the interviews terminated. Nor did he make an offer of employment to the police officer who posed as an applicant, but when she told him she was interested in the position, despite its requirements, he told her to think it over and let him know.

The appellant was tried upon an indictment containing two counts: attempting to procure female persons to become common prostitutes, and attempting to procure female persons to have illicit intercourse with another person. Graburn Co. Ct. J. acquitted the appellant on both counts. He found that the appellant intended that a person hired for the position should have sexual relations with clients or potential clients, but he held, as a matter of law, that the acts or statements of the appellant did not, in the absence of an offer of employment, constitute the *actus reus* of an attempt to procure. In his opinion they were mere preparation. He accordingly did not find it necessary to decide whether the sexual intercourse contemplated by the appellant would be illicit sexual intercourse within s. 195(1)(*a*) or make those who engaged in it common prostitutes within s. 195(1)(*d*), as it then read.

The Ontario Court of Appeal (Martin, Houlden and Robins JJ.A.) (1983), 5 C.C.C. (3d) 41, dismissed the appeal from the acquittal on the charge of attempting to procure female persons to become common prostitutes, but allowed the appeal from the acquittal on the charge of attempting to procure female persons to have illicit sexual intercourse with another person and directed a new trial of the appellant on that count of the indictment. The court held that the trial judge erred in concluding that the acts or statements of the appellant could not, in the absence of an offer of employment, constitute an attempt to procure rather than mere preparation. It held that there was evidence from which the trial judge could have concluded that there was both the *mens rea* and the *actus reus* required for an attempt to procure. The court also held that the sexual intercourse contemplated by the appellant would be illicit sexual intercourse within s. 195(1)(*a*). The appellant appeals from the judgment of the Court of Appeal with respect to the second count of the indictment.

The appellant, who appeared in person on the appeal, expressed his grounds of appeal in several different ways, but in my opinion there are only two issues that require consideration by the court:

1. Whether the Court of Appeal erred in holding that the acts or statements of the appellant could, as a matter of law, constitute an attempt to procure rather than mere preparation; and
2. Whether the Court of Appeal erred in holding that the sexual intercourse contemplated by the appellant would be illicit sexual intercourse within s. 195(1)(*a*) of the *Code*.

. . . .

[The Court first considered the second issue and concluded that the Court of Appeal did not err in holding that the sexual intercourse contemplated by the appellant would be "illicit sexual intercourse" within s. 195(1)(a) of the *Code*.]

. . . .

I turn now to the question whether the acts or statements of the appellant could, as a matter of law, constitute the *actus reus* of an attempt to procure a person to have illicit sexual intercourse with another person, contrary to s. 195(1)(*a*) of the *Code*. The general provision of the *Code* defining the constituent elements of an attempt to commit an offence is s. 24, which provides:

> 24. (1) Every one who, having an intent to commit an offence, does or omits to do anything for the purpose of carrying out his intention is guilty of an attempt to commit the offence whether or not it was possible under the circumstances to commit the offence.
>
> (2) The question whether an act or omission by a person who has an intent to commit an offence is or is not mere preparation to commit the offence, and too remote to constitute an attempt to commit the offence, is a question of law.

The issue is whether, if there was the necessary intent, the acts of the appellant were mere preparation to commit the offence of procuring a person to have illicit sexual intercourse with another person or whether any of them was a step in the commission of the offence, and the extent to which that distinction is to turn on the relative remoteness of the act in question from what would have been the completion of the offence. This issue, as s. 24 indicates, is a question of law. The appellant contends that the Court of Appeal erred in holding that one of the acts of the appellant could, if there was the necessary intent, constitute the *actus reus* of an attempt to procure.

The trial judge found that the appellant "intended that the women in question should have sexual relations with prospective customers and clients", but that the acts of the appellant consisting of the advertisements, the interviews and what was said during the interviews concerning the requirements of the position and the money to be earned, were mere preparation and too remote from the complete offence of procuring to constitute the *actus reus* of an attempt to procure. He said:

. . . .

> I consider that the interview and its content was an act remotely leading to the commission of the offence, and was not an act immediately connected with it, nor sufficiently proximate to it so as to constitute an attempt; the latter language being used by the Ontario Court of Appeal in the case of *Sorrell and Bondett* which was decided in 1978 and is reported in 41 C.C.C. (2d) at p. 9.

. . . .

Several different tests for determining whether there is the *actus reus* of attempt, as distinct from mere preparation to commit an offence, have been identified as reflected at one time or another in judicial decisions and legislation. All of them have been pronounced by academic commentators to be unsatisfactory in some degree. For a thorough analysis of the various tests, with suggestions for an improved test, see Meehan, *The Law of Criminal Attempt — A Treatise*, 1984, chapter 5, and Stuart, *Canadian Criminal Law*, 1982, pp. 529ff. There is a succinct appraisal of the various tests in the English Law Commission's Report No. 102 of 1980 entitled, Criminal Law: Attempt, and Impossibility in Relation to Attempt, Conspiracy and Incitement. It has been frequently observed that no satisfactory general criterion has been, or can be, formulated for drawing the line between preparation and attempt, and that the application of this distinction to the facts of a particular case must be left to common sense judgment.

. . . .

In my opinion the distinction between preparation and attempt is essentially a qualitative one, involving the relationship between the nature and quality of the act in question and the nature of the complete offence, although consideration must necessarily be given, in making that qualitative distinction, to the relative proximity of the act in question to what would have been the completed offence, in terms of time, location and acts under the control of the accused remaining to be accomplished. I find that view to be compatible with what has been said about the *actus reus* of attempt in this court and in other Canadian decisions that should be treated as authoritative on this question.

The most recent expression of opinion in this court on what constitutes an attempt to commit an offence is the judgment in *R. v. Ancio*, [1984] 1 S.C.R. 225, where the issue was the intent required for attempted murder. McIntyre J., in the course of a review of the development of the law of attempt, said with reference to the *mens rea* and the *actus reus* of attempt at p. 247:

> As with any other crime, the Crown must prove a *mens rea*, that is, the intent to commit the offence in question and the *actus reus*, that is, some step towards the commission of the offence attempted going beyond mere acts of preparation. Of the two elements the more significant is the *mens rea*.

McIntyre J. referred with approval to the judgment of Laidlaw J.A. in *R. v. Cline*, *supra*, particularly for what it said concerning the relative importance of *mens rea* in attempt, but that judgment has also been treated as helpful for what it said concerning the application of the distinction between preparation and attempt. With reference to this question Laidlaw J.A. said at p. 28:

> The consummation of a crime usually comprises a series of acts which have their genesis in an idea to do a criminal act; the idea develops to a decision to do that act; a plan may be made for putting that decision into effect; the next step may be preparation only for carrying out the intention and plan; but when that preparation is in fact fully completed, the next step in the series of acts done by the accused for the purpose and with the intention of committing the crime as planned cannot, in my opinion, be regarded as remote in its connection with that crime. The connection is in fact proximate.

Laidlaw J.A. offered six propositions by way of guidance for determination of the requisite *mens rea* and *actus reus* of attempt, the last two of which, with reference to the *actus reus*, are as follows:

> (5) The *actus reus* must be more than mere preparation to commit a crime. But (6) when the preparation to commit a crime is in fact fully complete and ended, the next step done by the accused for the purpose and with the intention of committing a specific crime constitutes an *actus reus* sufficient in law to establish a criminal attempt to commit that crime.

The extent to which some version of the proximity test, which was formulated in *R. v. Eagleton* (1854), Dears. C.C. 376 (C.C.R.), and applied in the much-criticized case of *R. v. Robinson*, [1915] 2 K.B. 342 (C.C.A.), as a "last step" or "last stage" test (*cf.* English Law Commission, op cit., pp. 335-36), is to be applied in drawing the distinction between preparation and attempt has also been the subject of commentary in this court. In *Henderson v. The King*, [1948] S.C.R. 226, where one of the issues was whether there had been an attempt to rob a bank, Estey J., who was one of the majority holding that there had been an attempt, said at p. 244:

> Counsel for the accused referred to a number of cases in which the attempted crime was either against the person or that of obtaining by false pretences. He contended that any act not "immediately connected with" the completed crime would be too remote to constitute an attempt. Even under the cases which he cited the accused may still have one or more acts to do, and these may be separated by an intervening period of time, in order to complete the offence and yet may be guilty of an attempt.

Among the cases referred to by Estey J. in support of this statement were *R. v. Cheeseman* (1862), 169 E.R. 1337, where Blackburn J. said at p. 1339, "But, if the actual transaction has commenced which would have ended in the crime if not interrupted, there is clearly an attempt to commit the crime", and *R. v. White*, [1910] 2 K.B. 124, where Bray J. said at p. 130: " . . . the completion or attempted completion of one of a series of acts intended by a man to result in killing is an attempt to murder even although this completed act would not, unless followed by other acts, result in killing. It might be the beginning of the attempt, but would none the less be an attempt." Taschereau J., dissenting, in *Henderson*, although he differed in the result, would not appear to have applied a different concept of proximity. He said, after referring to the authorities, including *Eagleton* and *Robinson*, at pp. 234-35:

> Although it may be said that no one could doubt the express purpose of the bandits, I do not believe that it can be held that the mere fact of going to the place where the contemplated crime is to be committed, constitutes an attempt. There must be a closer relation between the victim and the author of the crime; there must be an act done which displays not only a preparation for an attempt, but a commencement of execution, a step in the commission of the actual crime itself.

In *Detering v. The Queen*, [1982] 2 S.C.R. 583, which involved a conviction for attempted fraud, Laskin C.J. raised a question, as I read his reasons, as to the weight to be given to the proximity test in the essential task under s. 24 of the *Code* of distinguishing between preparation and attempt. With reference to the contention of counsel that "proximity was an essential requirement in the sense, to put it generally, that the actions of the accused must go beyond mere preparation and close (a question of degree) to the realization of his purpose", Laskin C.J. said at p. 586:

This leaves for consideration the so-called proximity principle. It may well be that this is envisaged by the reference to remoteness in s. 24(2), but I do not see that it advances the essential issue in attempt which requires going beyond mere preparation. Nor do I find cogency in the appellant's submission that if there is impossibility this does not bring any act of the accused closer to realization so as to establish proximity. I read s. 24(1) as making a different distinction, one merely requiring proof of intent and of accused going beyond mere preparation by making, as in this case, a false representation even though not resulting in full realization of his objective.

In my opinion, relative proximity may give an act which might otherwise appear to be mere preparation the quality of attempt. That is reflected, I think, in the conclusion of the majority in *Henderson* and in the conclusion of the Ontario Court of Appeal with respect to *actus reus* in *R. v. Sorrell and Bondett* (1978), 41 C.C.C. (2d) 9. But an act which on its face is an act of commission does not lose its quality as the *actus reus* of attempt because further acts were required or because a significant period of time may have elapsed before the completion of the offence.

In the case at bar the Court of Appeal agreed with the trial judge on the applicable meaning of "procure". The meaning selected by the trial judge and approved by the Court of Appeal was "to cause, or to induce, or to have a persuasive effect upon the conduct that is alleged." Martin J.A. expressed his agreement at p. 49 with the following statement of the issue by the trial judge: "The question for decision is did Mr. Deutsch attempt to cause or attempt to induce or attempt to have a persuasive effect upon the woman in question to have illicit sexual intercourse with another person. . . ." I agree that the sources referred to by the trial judge and Martin J.A. support the meaning given by them to the word "procure".

The Court of Appeal differed with the trial judge as to what would have constituted the completed offence of procuring a person to have illicit sexual intercourse with another person. The trial judge held that the offence of procuring would have been completed, in the particular context of this case, by the acceptance of an offer of employment. The Court of Appeal held, citing *R. v. Johnson* (1963), 48 Cr. App. R. 25, and *R. v. Gruba*, [1969] 2 C.C.C. 365, that the offence of procuring a person to have illicit sexual intercourse with another person is not committed unless sexual intercourse actually takes place. In the appeal to this court the respondent accepted this statement of the law as to what is required for the complete offence of procuring a person to have illicit sexual intercourse with another person. It was not challenged, and I accept it for purposes of deciding whether the acts of the appellant could, as a matter of law, constitute the *actus reus* of an attempt to procure.

I agree with the Court of Appeal that if the appellant had the necessary intent to induce or persuade the women to seek employment that would require them to have sexual intercourse with prospective clients then the holding out of the large financial rewards in the course of the interviews, in which the necessity of having sexual intercourse with prospective clients was disclosed, could constitute the *actus reus* of an attempt to procure. It would clearly be a step, and an important step, in the commission of the offence. Before an offer of employment could be made in such circumstances an applicant would have to seek the position, despite its special requirement. Thus such inducement or persuasion would be the decisive act in the procuring. There would be little else that the appellant would be required to do towards the completion of the offence other than to make the formal offer of employment. I am further of the opinion that the holding out of the large financial rewards in the course of the interviews would not lose its quality as a step in the commission of the offence, and thus as an *actus reus* of attempt, because a considerable period of time might elapse before a person engaged for the position had sexual intercourse with prospective clients or because of the otherwise contingent nature of such sexual intercourse.

For these reasons I would dismiss the appeal. I agree with the Court of Appeal that because the trial judge did not make a finding as to whether or not there was the necessary intent to procure there must be a new trial.

A defence which can arise in relation to attempts (but is not limited to that context) is "abandonment". The Alberta Court of Appeal considered this defence in their judgment in *R. v. S.R.B.*, which concerns a different co-accused in the same incident as in *Briscoe*, above. A group of people took part in varying ways in the rape and murder of a 13-year-old girl. Bird had helped with the rape but left the scene before the murder took place, saying that she was taking the victim's friend to the car because the friend "did not need to see this". The trial judge found that there was an air of reality to abandonment and acquitted the accused of murder. The majority of the Alberta Court of Appeal upheld this result, but the dissenting judge held that there was no air of reality to abandonment on the facts. On a subsequent appeal (*R. v. Bird*, 2009 SCC 60) the Supreme Court of Canada briefly agreed with the dissenting judge.

In articulating the requirements of the defence of abandonment, the majority in the Alberta Court of Appeal held as follows:

R. v. S.R.B.

2009 ABCA 45, 243 C.C.C. (3d) 419, 2009 CarswellAlta 157

[7] In *R. v. Gordon and Carey*, (1957), 116 C.C.C. 252, the accused embarked on a robbery (or in the alternative, an expedition to "case" a location for a robbery); Gordon shot and killed a patrolling policeman and the two accused fled (one of whom had been masked). The following observations of Coady J.A. (concurred in by Sheppard J.A.) at para. 95 inform the "air of reality" issue:

> With due respect, it seems to me that there was some evidence for the jury to consider, assuming the intent and attempt to rob Watkins Winram Ltd. was established. The man who

had put the mask on his head had removed it and both accused had walked away from the premises of Watkins Winram Ltd., without apparently having been disturbed or alarmed. This was evidence which the jury could consider; it might not satisfy them, but it might raise a reasonable doubt as to whether the two accused were or were not still continuing their attempt. If they were not, then there was no common intention at the time Sinclair was shot and they were not then engaged in the carrying out of the unlawful purpose. In the circumstances to tell the jury there was no evidence, was it appears to me, with respect, a misdirection. [emphasis added]

[8] This accords with the view of the Criminal Division of the England and Wales Court of Appeal as set out in the following passages of the Court's judgment in *R. v. O'Flaherty, Ryan and Toussaint*, [2004] 2 Cr App R 20 at paras. 58, 60, 63 and 64:

... A person who unequivocally withdraws from the joint enterprise before the moment of the actual commission of the crime by the principal, here murder, should not be liable for that crime, although his acts before withdrawing may render him liable for other offences.

. . .

[F]or there to be withdrawal, mere repentance does not suffice. To disengage from an incident a person must do enough to demonstrate that he or she is withdrawing from the joint enterprise. This is ultimately a question of fact and degree for the jury. Account will be taken of *inter alia* of the nature of the assistance and encouragement already given and how imminent the infliction of the fatal injury or injuries is, as well as the nature of the action said to constitute withdrawal.

. . .

For these reasons a defendant who effectively disengages or withdraws before the fatal injury is [sustained] or injuries are inflicted is not guilty or murder because he was not party to and did not participate in any unlawful violence which caused the fatal injury or injuries. We consider that the question whether or not the violence formed one evolving incident or was two separate and discreet incidents is only relevant in helping to decide whether a particular defendant disengaged before the fatal injury or injuries were caused or joined in after they had been caused.

. . .

Accordingly, we consider ... that the jury should have been directed that they must be satisfied (a) that the fatal injuries were sustained when the joint enterprise was continuing and that the defendant was still acting within that joint enterprise, and (b) that the acts which caused the death were within the scope of the joint enterprise. [emphasis added]

[9] In my view, the "air of reality" test is well articulated in paras. 7 and 8 above. If the evidential test is satisfied, the trier of fact considers whether or not the defence is made out and adjudicates accordingly. If the trier of fact has a reasonable doubt, appellate interference is not warranted.

[10] Counsel are agreed that there are two elements to the defence of abandonment. The first is that there is a change of heart or an abandonment of

the common purpose. Secondly, the change of heart or abandonment of common intention, where it is reasonable and practical to do so, must be communicated in a timely manner. See *R. v. Whitehouse* (1940), 75 C.C.C. 65 (B.C.C.A.). The communication may be through words or actions or both and must be "unequivocal". See K.J.M. Smith, *Withdrawal in Complicity: A Restatement of Principles*, [2001] Crim. L.R. 769 at pp. 774-775...

One of the most heated debates in Anglo-American criminal law has been as to whether courts should acquit in some cases of attempting the impossible. The embers were fanned by a complex decision of the House of Lords in *Haughton v. Smith*, [1974] 3 W.L.R. 1 (H.L.), to the effect that there were distinctions to be made. It is generally accepted by writers that a court should be able to convict of an attempt to commit a crime which, in the circumstances, was physically impossible to commit. One example is a would-be assassin throwing a bomb that will never explode. The major difference of opinion is between those who favour criminal responsibility and those who do not for cases of attempts which would only be criminal if the facts were as the accused wrongly supposed them to be. The classic examples are stealing an umbrella that turns out to be your own or stabbing a corpse thinking it was a live person. Glanville Williams urged Canadian courts:

> to lend no ear to the arguments of those who would persuade them, notwithstanding the clear and wise words of the *Code*, to introduce questions of impossibility into the law of attempt and its associated crimes: "Attempting the Impossible — A Reply" (1979), 22 Crim. L.Q. 49 at 57.

The Supreme Court agreed with Glanville Williams' position with its decision in *Dynar*.

UNITED STATES v. DYNAR

[1997] 2 S.C.R. 462, 8 C.R. (5th) 79, 115 C.C.C. (3d) 481, 1997 CarswellOnt 1981, 1997 CarswellOnt 1982

The U.S. government requested the extradition of D, a Canadian citizen who had been the subject of a failed "sting" operation by the FBI. D had agreed to launder money which he had been told were the proceeds of crime. Since it was a sting, the money was not in fact the proceeds of crime: under Canadian (but not American) law at the time, this meant that had D actually received the funds and laundered them, he would not have committed any offence. In fact the money was never delivered to him. The issue for the Supreme Court was whether D's conduct would have amounted to a criminal attempt under Canadian law.

CORY and IACOBUCCI JJ. (LAMER C.J.C., LA FOREST, L'HEUREUX-DUBÉ, and GONTHIER JJ. concurring): —

. . . .

(2) The Law of Attempt

The *Criminal Code* creates the crime of attempt to commit an offence:

> 24. (1) Every one who, having an intent to commit an offence, does or omits to do anything for the purpose of carrying out the intention is guilty of an attempt to commit the offence *whether or not it was possible under the circumstances to commit the offence*. [Emphasis added.]

On its face, the statute is indifferent about whether or not the attempt might possibly have succeeded. Therefore it would seem, at first blush, not to matter that Mr. Dynar could not possibly have succeeded in laundering money known to be the proceeds of crime. So long as he attempted to do so, he is guilty of a crime.

In our view, s. 24(1) is clear: the crime of attempt consists of an intent to commit the completed offence together with some act more than merely preparatory taken in furtherance of the attempt. This proposition finds support in a long line of authority. [Citations omitted.] In this case, sufficient evidence was produced to show that Mr. Dynar intended to commit the money-laundering offences, and that he took steps more than merely preparatory in order to realize his intention. That is enough to establish that he attempted to launder money contrary to s. 24(1) of the *Criminal Code*.

However, the respondent argues that Parliament did not intend by s. 24(1) to criminalize all attempts to do the impossible, but only those attempts that the common law has classified as "factually impossible". An attempt to do the factually impossible, according to the respondent, is an attempt that runs up against some intervening obstacle and for that reason cannot be completed. The classic example involves a pickpocket who puts his hand into a man's pocket intending to remove the wallet, only to find that there is no wallet to remove.

Traditionally, this sort of impossibility has been contrasted with "legal impossibility". An attempt to do the legally impossible is, according to those who draw the distinction, an attempt that must fail because, even if it were completed, no crime would have been committed. See Eric Colvin, *Principles of Criminal Law* (2nd ed. 1991), at pp. 355-56.

According to the respondent, the *Criminal Code* criminalizes only attempts to do the factually impossible. An attempt to do the legally impossible, in the absence of an express legislative reference to that variety of impossibility, is not a crime.

As support for this interpretation, the respondent offers two arguments. The first is that Parliament based s. 24(1) on an English provision whose purpose was to overrule a decision of the House of Lords that had made factual impossibility a defence. See Barry Brown, "'Th'attempt, and not the deed, Confounds us': Section 24 and Impossible Attempts" (1981), 19 *U.W.O. L. Rev.* 225 at pp. 228-29. On the strength of this argument, the New Zealand Court of Appeal accepted that New Zealand's equivalent to s. 24(1) criminalizes attempts whose completion is factually impossible but not those whose completion is legally impossible. See *R. v. Donnelly*, [1970] N.Z.L.R. 980 (C.A.) at pp. 984 and 988.

The respondent's second argument is that Parliament, had it intended to criminalize attempts to do the legally impossible, would have used the words "whether or not it was factually or legally impossible" in s. 24(1). As examples of statutes that were intended to criminalize attempts to do the legally impossible, the respondent cites provisions of statutes from the United Kingdom and from the United States . . . .

. . . .

A third argument, which the respondent does not advance, is that the words "under the circumstances" restrict the scope of s. 24(1) to attempts to do the factually impossible. An attempt that is not possible "under the circumstances", according to this argument, is by implication possible under some other set of circumstances. Otherwise, there would be no need to mention circumstances — the mere mention of impossibility would suffice.

. . . .

In addition there is another way of turning the same language to the respondent's advantage. "Circumstances", in ordinary parlance, are facts. Laws, by contrast, are not circumstances. Accordingly, applying the rule that *expressio unius est exclusio alterius*, the mention in s. 24(1) of attempts that are circumstantially or factually impossible may be taken to exclude attempts that are legally impossible. The question, as one Canadian writer has framed it, is whether "'the circumstances' referred to in [s. 24(1)] include the legal status of the actor's conduct". Brown, *supra*, at p. 229.

Still another argument in favour of the respondent's position, though one that reflects judicial policy rather than the strict ascertainment of legislative intent, is that penal statutes, if ambiguous, should be construed narrowly, in favour of the rights of the accused. "[T]he overriding principle governing the interpretation of penal provisions is that ambiguity should be resolved in a manner most favourable to accused persons". *R. v. McIntosh*, [1995] 1 S.C.R. 686, at para. 38.

Although some of these arguments have a certain force, what force they have is greatly attenuated when it is realized that the conventional distinction between factual and legal impossibility is not tenable. The only relevant distinction for purposes of s. 24(1) of the *Criminal Code* is between imaginary crimes and attempts to do the factually impossible. The criminal law of Canada recognizes no middle category called "legal impossibility". Because Mr. Dynar attempted to do the impossible but did not attempt to commit an imaginary crime, he can only have attempted to do the "factually impossible". For this reason,

Mr. Dynar's proposal that s. 24(1) criminalizes only attempts to do the factually impossible does not help him.

As we have already indicated, an attempt to do the factually impossible is considered to be one whose completion is thwarted by mere happenstance. In theory at least, an accused who attempts to do the factually impossible could succeed but for the intervention of some fortuity. A legally impossible attempt, by contrast, is considered to be one which, even if it were completed, still would not be a crime. One scholar has described impossible attempts in these terms:

> Three main forms of impossibility have set the framework for contemporary debate. First, there is impossibility due to inadequate means (Type I). For example, A tries to kill B by shooting at him from too great a distance or by administering too small a dose of poison; C tries to break into a house without the equipment which would be necessary to force the windows or doors. . . .
>
> The second form of impossibility arises where an actor is prevented from completing the offence because some element of its *actus reus* cannot be brought within the criminal design (Type II). For example, A tries to kill B by shooting him when he is asleep in bed, but in fact B has already died of natural causes; C tries to steal money from a safe which is empty. . . .
>
> The third form of impossibility arises where the actor's design is completed but the offence is still not committed because some element of the *actus reus* is missing (Type III). For example, A may take possession of property believing it to have been stolen when it has not been; B may smuggle a substance for reward believing it to be a narcotic when it is sugar. (Colvin, *supra*, at pp. 355-56.)

According to Professor Colvin, factually impossible attempts are those that fall into either of the first two categories. Legally impossible attempts are those that fall into the third category.

Colvin's schema appears attractive. But in fact it draws distinctions that do not stand up on closer inspection. There is no legally relevant difference between the pickpocket who reaches into the empty pocket and the man who takes his own umbrella from a stand believing it to be some other person's umbrella. Both have the *mens rea* of a thief. The first intends to take a wallet that he believes is not his own. The second intends to take an umbrella that he believes is not his own. Each takes some steps in the direction of consummating his design. And each is thwarted by a defect in the attendant circumstances, by an objective reality over which he has no control: the first by the absence of a wallet, the second by the accident of owning the thing that he seeks to steal. It is true that the latter seems to consummate his design and still not to complete an offence; but the semblance is misleading. The truth is that the second man does not consummate his design, because his intention is not simply to take the particular umbrella that he takes, but to take an umbrella that is not his own. That this man's design is premised on a mistaken understanding of the facts does not make it any less his design. A mistaken belief cannot be eliminated from the description of a person's mental state simply because it is mistaken.

If it were otherwise, the effect would be to eliminate from our criminal law the defence of mistaken belief. If mistaken beliefs did not form part of an actor's intent — if an actor's intent were merely to do what he in fact does — then a man who honestly but mistakenly believed that a woman had consented to have sexual relations with him and who on that basis actually had sexual relations with that woman, would have no defence to the crime of sexual assault. His intention, on this limited understanding of intention, would have been to sleep with the particular woman with whom he slept; and that particular woman, by hypothesis, is one who did not consent to sleep with him. Substituting the one description ("a woman who did not consent to sleep with him") for the other ("the particular woman with whom he slept"), it would follow that his intention was to sleep with a woman who had not consented to sleep with him. But of course, and as we have already strenuously urged, intention is one thing and the truth is another. Intention has to do with how one sees the world and not necessarily with the reality of the world.

Accordingly, there is no difference between an act thwarted by a "physical impossibility" and one thwarted "following completion". Both are thwarted by an attendant circumstance, by a fact: for example, by the fact of there being no wallet to steal or by the fact of there being no umbrella to steal. The distinction between them is a distinction without a difference. Professor Colvin himself agrees that "[t]he better view is that impossibility of execution is never a defence to inchoate liability in Canada" (p. 358).

There is, however, a relevant difference between a failed attempt to do something that is a crime and an imaginary crime. [Citation omitted.] It is one thing to attempt to steal a wallet, believing such thievery to be a crime, and quite another thing to bring sugar into Canada, believing the importation of sugar to be a crime. In the former case, the would-be thief has the *mens rea* associated with thievery. In the latter case, the would-be smuggler has no *mens rea* known to law. Because s. 24(1) clearly provides that it is an element of the offence of attempt to have "an intent to commit an offence", the latter sort of attempt is not a crime.

Nor should it be. A major purpose of the law of attempt is to discourage the commission of subsequent offences. See Williams' *Textbook of Criminal Law, supra,* at pp. 404-5. [Citations omitted.] But one who attempts to do something that is not a crime or even one who actually does something that is not a crime, believing that what he has done or has attempted to do is a crime, has not displayed any propensity to commit crimes in the future, unless perhaps he has betrayed a vague willingness to break the law. Probably all he has shown is that he might be inclined to do the same sort of thing in the future; and from a societal point of view, that is not a very worrisome prospect, because by hypothesis what he attempted to do is perfectly legal.

Therefore, we conclude that s. 24(1) draws no distinction between attempts to do the possible but by inadequate means, attempts to do the physically impossible, and attempts to do something that turns out to be impossible "following completion". All are varieties of attempts to do the "factually impossible" and all are crimes. Only attempts to commit imaginary crimes fall outside the scope of the provision. Because what Mr. Dynar attempted to do falls squarely into the category of the factually impossible — he attempted to commit crimes known to law and was thwarted only by chance — it was a criminal attempt within the meaning of s. 24(1). The evidence suggests that Mr. Dynar is a criminal within the contemplation of the Canadian law and so the double criminality rule should be no bar to his extradition to the United States.

2. CONSPIRACY

See section 465 of the *Criminal Code*.

R. v. CELEBRITY ENTERPRISES LTD. (NO. 2)

(1977), 42 C.C.C. (2d) 478, 1977 CarswellBC 607 (B.C. C.A.)

APPEAL by the Crown from the accused's acquittal by Trainor Co. Ct. J., [1977] 4 W.W.R. 144, on a charge of conspiracy to produce a public mischief. The indictment contained two counts: count 1, conspiracy to live on the avails of prostitution; and count 2, conspiracy to produce a public mischief. The accused were convicted on count 1 and acquitted on count 2. The accused appealed from their conviction on count 1 and the Crown appealed the acquittal on count 2. The court dealt with the accused's appeal first, and the judgment in that appeal is reported at 41 C.C.C. (2d) 540. Following are the reasons for *judgment on the Crown* appeal.

ROBERTSON J.A. (orally): — The learned trial judge held that count 2 disclosed no offence known to the law and he accordingly entered an acquittal upon it. Against that acquittal the Crown has cross-appealed. Count 2 reads in part:

> they did conspire together and with Eleanor Harrigan and Tony Pizani and other persons unknown, to effect an unlawful purpose, to wit, produce a public mischief at or in the premises located at 1019 Seymour Street, and known as the New Penthouse Cabaret, with intent thereby to corrupt public morals, contrary to the form of the Statute.

I am unable to see how one can eliminate from the count the words "produce a public mischief". If then the offence charged is conspiracy to produce a public mischief at common law, it is bad in view of the holding by the House of Lords in *Director of Public Prosecutions v. Withers*, [1975] A.C. 842, that there is no such offence. If the offence charged is conspiracy to produce a public mischief under the *Criminal Code*, it is bad because, while the *Code* makes certain defined kinds of public mischief offences, it does not provide that public mischief with intent to corrupt public morals is an offence.

As an alternative argument Mr. Jaques submits that one may treat the count as a charge of conspiracy to corrupt public morals. Assuming — contrary to my view — that one can so read the charge, the question arises whether a conspiracy to corrupt public morals is a conspiracy to effect an unlawful purpose within the meaning of s. 423(2)(*a*) of the *Criminal Code*. An unlawful purpose must be a purpose which is unlawful by the law of Canada, and it is of no significance that counsel for the accused has conceded that a conspiracy to corrupt public morals is by the common law of England an indictable offence, because s. 8 of the *Criminal Code* provides that

> 8. Notwithstanding anything in this Act or any other Act no person shall be convicted (*a*) of an offence at common law . . .

If something that someone does is not something of which he can be convicted, that something cannot, in my opinion, be "unlawful" in the sense in which the word is used in s. 423(2)(*a*).

It is consistent with this that, since s. 8 came into force in 1955, there is no reported case in Canada where there has been conviction of conspiracy to effect an unlawful purpose where there has not been a breach of either a Dominion statute or a provincial statute.

I would, therefore, dismiss the cross-appeal.

McFarlane and Taggart JJ.A. concurred.

R. v. GRALEWICZ

[1980] 2 S.C.R. 493, 54 C.C.C. (2d) 289,
1980 CarswellOnt 661F, 1980 CarswellOnt 661

CHOUINARD J. (RITCHIE, DICKSON, BEETZ and ESTEY JJ. concurring): — Upon motion of the appellants the following information was quashed by order of Judge Brown of the Provincial Court (Criminal Division) of the District of York:

> That Roman Adolfe Gralewicz, John Royce, Roy Norris Willis, Roger Desjardins, Richard Thomasson, Edwin Aldon Williams, Hedley Harnum, Andre Bansept, William Lisenchuk, Walter Mercer, and George Baldo between the 1st day of January, 1971 and the 21st day of January, 1977, in the Province of Ontario and elsewhere in the Dominion of Canada, unlawfully did conspire and agree together, the one with the other and with John Robert Lazarus, John Pearson, Glen Patrick Milley, Ian Joseph Vickers, Lawrence Carey, George Keagan, Donald Roy Swait, Arthur Hunt, Michael Dabour, John Richard Wood, Kenneth Henry McGuire, and with another person or persons unknown to effect an unlawful purpose, to wit: to prevent members of the Seafarers' International Union of Canada from participating in the lawful activities of their Union, in accordance with Section 110(1) of the

Canada Labour Code, R.S.C. 1970, Chapter L-1 as amended, by committing the following acts, to wit:

(1) Threats and assaults upon members of the said Union;
(2) Possession and use of offensive weapons;
(3) Defrauding members of the said Union through falsifying expenses;
(4) Violations of the articles of the said Union's Constitution as they relate to elections, trials and individual rights,
(5) Unlawfully preventing the said Union members from obtaining employment,

Thereby committing an offence contrary to Section 423(2)(a) of the *Criminal Code,* R.S.C. 1970, Chapter C-34.

. . . .

In the appellants' submission an agreement to prevent anyone from exercising his freedom under s. 110 of the *Canada Labour Code,* R.S.C. 1970, c. L-1, to participate in the lawful activities of his union does not amount to a conspiracy to effect an unlawful purpose within the meaning of s. 423(2) of the *Criminal Code.*

Section 110(1) [rep. & sub. 1972, c. 18, s. 1] of the *Canada Labour Code* reads as follows:

110(1) Every employee is free to join the trade union of his choice and to participate in its lawful activities.

The first submission advanced on behalf of the appellants is that:

The *Canada Labour Code* is a complete and exhaustive code provided by the Parliament of Canada for the conduct of those industrial relations which come under federal jurisdiction. It was not the intention of Parliament that its provisions should be enforced by resort to the *Criminal Code* or to any other statute since it provides its own mechanisms for enforcement.

In the appellants' submission, s. 110 is merely declaratory and contains no requirement and no prohibition. It does not create an offence. Various offences are created by ss. 184 and 185 [rep. & sub. *idem*] relating to interference with the freedoms of employees and employers recognized by s. 110 but none in the nature of that alleged in the information. Section 186 [rep. & sub. *idem*] enacts a general prohibition to the effect that "no person shall seek by intimidation or coercion to compel a person to become or refrain from becoming or to cease to be a member of a trade union." This deals with membership, not with participation in the lawful activities of a union.

The only section of the Act under which a prosecution could be contemplated for preventing members of a union from participating in the lawful activities of their union would be s. 191(1) [rep. & sub. *idem*]:

191(1) Subject to section 190, every person other than an employer or a trade union who violates or fails to comply with any provision of this Part other than section 148, 184 or

185 is guilty of an offence and liable on summary conviction to a fine not exceeding one thousand dollars.

Counsel for the respondent conceded however, and rightly so in my opinion, that this section could not apply because the words "violates or fails to comply" imply a prohibition or a requirement and there are none in section 110.

I see little merit in the appellants' first submission and I can but conclude as suggested by the respondent that "the fact that within a code of labour relations there is no specific sanction to enforce the rights of employees to participate in the lawful activities of their union does not sanctify otherwise criminal conduct".

The appellants further submit that their conduct as charged in the information does not constitute an offence under the *Criminal Code*. In their submission:

> If a statute does not expressly provide a penalty then, the only possible offence one can commit with respect to it, is the one set out in s. 115(1) of the *Criminal Code*.
> 115(1) Every one who, without lawful excuse, contravenes an Act of the Parliament of Canada by wilfully doing anything that it forbids or by wilfully omitting to do anything that it requires to be done, is, unless some penalty or punishment is expressly provided by law, guilty of an indictable offence and is liable to imprisonment for two years.

Section 115(1) has no application here since s. 110(1) of the *Canada Labour Code* contains no prohibition and no requirement.

The only specific offences in the *Criminal Code* related to interference with union membership are those by employers under s. 382.

As regards interference with the right of a person to do something or to abstain from doing something s. 381 enacts:

> 381(1) Every one who, wrongfully and without lawful authority, for the purpose of compelling another person to abstain from doing anything that he has a lawful right to do, or to do anything that he has a lawful right to abstain from doing,
>
> (a) uses violence or threats of violence to that person or to his wife or children, or injures his property,
> (b) intimidates or attempts to intimidate that person or a relative of that person by threats that, in Canada or elsewhere, violence or other injury will be done to or punishment inflicted upon him or a relative of his, or that the property of any of them will be damaged,
> (c) persistently follows that person about from place to place,
> (d) hides any tools, clothes or other property owned or used by that person, or deprives him of them or hinders him in the use of them,
> (e) with one or more other persons follows that person, in a disorderly manner, on a highway,
> (f) besets or watches the dwelling-house or place where that person resides, works, carries on business or happens to be, or
> (g) blocks or obstructs a highway,
> is guillty of an offence punishable on summary conviction.

> (2) A person who attends at or near or approaches a dwelling-house or place, for the purpose only of obtaining or communicating information, does not watch or beset within the meaning of this section.

The appellants have not been charged under section 381. We were told by counsel that the respondent never relied on this section and that any similarity between allegations in the information and s. 381 is purely coincidental.

On the other hand, as recognized by counsel for the appellants, "it is evident that there may be interference with the rights of a person to do what he has the right to do other than by the means set out in section 381. However, those other means of interference do not attract criminal law sanctions unless, of course, they constitute crimes in themselves."

In this case what the appellants have been charged with is conspiracy "to effect an unlawful purpose, to wit: to prevent members of the Seafarers' International Union of Canada from participating in the lawful activities of their Union, in accordance with s. 110(1) of the *Canada Labour Code*".

It is, therefore, necessary to determine whether preventing members of a union from participating in the lawful activities of their union is an unlawful purpose within the meaning of s. 423(2) of the *Criminal Code*, or what is the meaning of unlawful purpose.

According to the appellants' counsel an unlawful purpose can only be one prohibited by statute either federal or provincial:

> In our respectful submission, the law does not create offences consisting of conspiracies to do acts not themselves prohibited by law under the guise of a conspiracy to effect an unlawful purpose. If the act which is the subject of the conspiracy is not prohibited by statute, it cannot form an unlawful act or purpose as the subject of a conspiracy.

They rely principally on *R. v. Celebrity Enterprises Ltd. et al., supra* [at p. 146], where Judge Trainor acquitted the accused of a count of conspiracy "to effect an unlawful purpose, to wit, produce a public mischief . . . with intent thereby to corrupt public morals, contrary to the form of the statute".

Analyzing the sections of the *Criminal Code* dealing with public mischief (s. 128 [rep. & sub. 1972, c. 13, s. 8]), mischief (s. 387) and offences tending to corrupt morals (ss. 159 and following) as well as other sections, Judge Trainor determined that none applied to the case and that consequently the unlawful purpose charged did not relate to an offence under the *Criminal Code*.

It would relate, however, to an offence at common law. While no such generalized offence as conspiracy to effect a public mischief was known to the law (*R. v. Withers*, [1975] A.C. 842), a conspiracy to corrupt morals was indictable (*Shaw v. Director of Public Prosecutions*, [1962] A.C. 220; *Knuller (Publishing, Printing and Promotions) v. Director of Public Prosecutions*, [1973] A.C. 435).

Judge Trainor was of the opinion that unlawful purpose does not extend to common law offences and he stated at p. 176:

I cannot accept the Crown's invitation to follow *Shaw* and *Knuller* and either extend the meaning of "unlawful purpose" to include a purpose not authorized by law or to hold that a common law offence can be an unlawful purpose. In my view our law has developed clearly and surely to the point that the "unlawful purpose" in s. 423(2) must be one contrary to law. Although the point is not before me I would think this reasoning applies equally to "unlawful means" in s. 423(2)(*b*).

By contrary to law I mean prohibited by federal or provincial legislation. Thus would be included all summary conviction offences under the *Criminal Code* and other federal legislation and offences created by provincial legislation.

That decision was upheld by the British Columbia Court of Appeal (1979), 42 C.C.C. (2d) 478, where speaking for the court Robertson J.A. states at p. 480:

If something that someone does is not something of which he can be convicted, that something cannot, in my opinion, be "unlawful" in the sense in which the word is used in s. 243(2)(*a*).

Leave to appeal to this court was refused, [1978] 1 S.C.R. xi.

All the Canadian cases in which conduct was held capable of being the subject of a criminal conspiracy to effect an unlawful purpose were based on conduct prohibited by legislation: see *Wright, McDermott and Feely v. The Queen*, [1964] 2 C.C.C. 201, [1964] S.C.R. 192, *R. v. Layton, Ex p. Thodas et al.*, [1970] 5 C.C.C. 260, 10 C.R.N.S. 290; *R. v. Chapman and Grange* (1973), 11 C.C.C. (2d) 84; *R. v. Jean Talon Fashion Centre Inc.* (1975), 22 C.C.C. (2d) 223. Counsel for the respondent recognized that there are no Canadian cases where a charge of conspiracy was upheld based on conduct not prohibited by legislation.

The respondent relies, however, on the following passage by Fauteux J., as he then was, in *Wright, McDermott & Feeley, supra*, at p. 202 C.C.C., pp. 193-4 S.C.R.:

While marginal notes in the body of an Act form no part of the Act, the marginal note appended to s. 408(2) accurately designates as "Common-law conspiracy" the offence described in this section which, as defined by Lord Denman C.J. in *R. v. Jones* (1832), 4 B. & Ad. 345 at p. 349, consists in a combination "to do an unlawful act, or a lawful act by unlawful means". Common-law conspiracy is one of the few common-law offences which, upon the 1954 revision of the *Cr. Code*, Parliament thought advisable to perpetuate by codification: *Martin's Criminal Code*, 1955, p. 35. Hence the law pertaining to this offence, its elements and the wide embracing import of the term "unlawful purpose", remains unchanged.

But all that was decided in that case was that unlawful purpose extends to a breach of a provincial statute, in that case the Ontario provincial *Police Act*. After the above passage, Fauteux J. continues:

While the term, as shown in *Harrisons Law of Conspiracy*, 1924, encompasses more than criminal offences, sufficient it is to say, for the purpose of this case, that the purpose alleged in the charge, to wit, the obtention from a constable of information which it is his duty not to divulge, is an unlawful purpose. In the language of Lord Mansfield, in *R. v. Bembridge* (1783), 3 Doug. 327 at p. 332, ". . . a man accepting an office of trust concerning the public, especially if attended with profit, is answerable criminally to the King for misbehaviour in his office." The fact that the purpose or the breach of trust contemplated by the conspirators, whether as their ultimate aim or only as a means to it, be, it carried into effect, punishable either under s. 103 of the *Cr. Code (vide, R. v. McMorran* (1948), 91 C.C.C. 19 at pp. 26 *et seq.*, 5 C.R. 338 at pp. 345 *et seq.*) or under s. 60 of the *Ontario Provincial Police Act*, adequately manifests the unlawfulness of the purpose within the meaning of the law attending common-law conspiracies.

When the *Criminal Code* was revised in 1954, s. 8 was introduced:

8. Notwithstanding anything in this Act or any other Act no person shall be convicted
    (*a*) of an offence at common law
    (*b*) of an offence under an Act of the Parliament of England, or of Great Britain, or of the United Kingdom of Great Britain and Ireland, or
    (*c*) of an offence under an Act or ordinance in force in any province, territory or place before that province, territory or place became a province of Canada,
but nothing in this section affects the power, jurisdiction or authority that a court, Judge, Justice or Magistrate had, immediately before the 1st day of April 1955, to impose punishment for contempt of court.

It follows that common-law conspiracy would have ceased to be part of Canadian criminal law had it not been retained as a statutory offence. But to make it a statutory offence does not necessarily mean that it was embodied with all its implications and uncertainties recognized by the decisions of the English Courts when no decisions in Canada had ever gone as far as those of the English Courts. And Fauteux J. in the above cited passage clearly does not say that.

The *Withers* case, *supra*, is authority to the effect "that it is not open to the courts nowadays either to create new offences or so to widen existing offences as to make punishable conduct of a type hitherto not subject to punishment". The more so in Canada and Cartwright J., as he then was, speaking for himself and five other members of this court, stated in *Frey v. Fedoruk et al.* 97 C.C.C. 1 at p. 14, [1950] S.C.R. 517 at p. 530:

To so hold would, it seems to me, be to assert the existence of what is referred to in Stephen's *History of the Criminal Law of England*, vol. 2, p. 190, as "*the power which has in some instances been claimed for the Judges of declaring anything to be an offence which is injurious to the public although it may not have been previously regarded as such*".

The writer continues: "*The power, if it exists at all, exists at common law.*"

In my opinion, this power has not been held and should not be held to exist in Canada. I think it safer to hold that no one shall be convicted of a crime unless the offence with which he is charged is recognized as such in the provisions of the *Criminal Code*, or can be established by the authority of some reported case as an offence known to the law. I think that if any course of conduct is now to be declared criminal, which has not up to the present time been so regarded, such declaration should be made by Parliament and not by the courts. [Emphasis added.]

It is difficult for me to see how the mere enactment of conspiracy as a statutory offence would have the effect of extending its scope beyond what it had been held to extend to at common law by the Canadian courts prior to its becoming a statutory offence while at the same time Parliament enacted s. 8 to exclude common-law offences from the ambit of the criminal law of Canada. I am, therefore, of the opinion, that in s. 423(2)(*a*) unlawful purpose means contrary to law, that is prohibited by federal or provincial legislation.

But even assuming that the meaning of unlawful purpose could be extended as far as it was at English common law prior to the 1977 amendments I do not believe that it would comprise a purpose to prevent members of a union from participating in the lawful activities of their union. (The law concerning conspiracy has been modified in England by the *Criminal Law Act*, 1977 (U.K.), c. 45, and in brief it now relates to the commission of an *offence*, meaning an offence triable in England and Wales.)

In Kenny's *Outlines of Criminal Law*, 19th ed. (1966), to which reference is made in the *Withers* case, *supra*, unlawful purpose as it then stood is described as follows at pp. 428-30:

451. The term "unlawful" is here used in a sense which, unhappily, has never yet been defined with precision. The purposes which it comprises appear to be of the following species.

(i) Agreements to commit a substantive crime; *e.g.* a conspiracy to steal, or even merely to incite someone else to steal. This extends to all cases where it would be criminal for any of the conspirators to commit the act agreed upon, even though there be in the gang other persons in whom it would be no offence to commit it; and to all "crimes", even non-indictable ones, *e.g.* non-payment of poor rates. A conspiracy to obstruct the *course of justice* can exist without there being any obstruction of the *police* (*e.g.* to fabricate evidence, or to keep witnesses away from the court). It therefore differs from a conspiracy to *obstruct the police* in the execution of their duty, for this may not be concerned in any way with the course of public justice, but have as its object, for example, to prevent the police from maintaining public order or keeping the highway clear.

(ii) Agreements to commit any tort that is malicious or fraudulent. Some say that agreements to commit any tort, of whatever kind, are indictable as conspiracies. But the weight of authority seems to be in favour of limiting the rule to torts of fraud or malice thus excluding, for instance, a trespass committed *bona fide* by persons eager to assert their supposed right of way.

(iii) Agreements to commit a breach of contract under circumstances that are peculiarly injurious to the public.

(iv) Agreements to do certain other acts, which (unlike all those hitherto mentioned) are not breaches of law at all, but which nevertheless are outrageously immoral or else are, in some way, extremely, injurious to the public. We may quote, as instances, agreements to facilitate the seduction of a woman; or to run slackly in a race so as to enable a confederate to win his bets: or to hiss a play unfairly; or to defraud a shipowner by secretly putting stowaways on board. Similar criminality would arise in agreements to raise by false reports the price of the Funds or of any other vendible commodity; or so to carry on trade as to diminish the revenue; or to persuade a prosecutor not to appear at the trial; or to give false information to the police; or to indemnify a prisoner's bail. On the other hand, it is doubtful whether an agreement to make loud noises for the purpose of disturbing an invalid neighbour would be indictable as a conspiracy. And a thrifty combination of poor-law authorities to marry a female pauper to a pauper of another parish, in order to relieve the ratepayers of the woman's parish, is not a conspiracy. Yet some combinations for procurement of marriage will amount to conspiracy; *e.g* taking a young woman of property from the custody of her relations in order to marry her to one of the conspirators. And although some combinations "in restraint of trade" may be so far illegal as to be unenforceable, it is now settled that they do not necessarily constitute a criminal offence. As to the question whether a conspiracy formed in England to effect some unlawful purpose abroad would be indictable here, the House of Lords has laid it down that a conspiracy to commit a crime abroad is not indictable in this country unless the contemplated crime is one for which an indictment would lie here, and that a conspiracy to attain a lawful object by unlawful means, rather than to commit a crime, is not triable here when the unlawful means and the ultimate object are both outside the jurisdiction. (I have omitted the footnotes and the references thereto.)

Reviewing this extensive list I do not see one head under which would come the conduct described in the information.

This is understandable because as it appears to me, to prevent members of a union from participating in the lawful activities of their union is not necessarily unlawful nor "outrageously immoral", nor "extremely injurious to the public". It is possible to conceive of many situations where to do that would not be so. This seems to be recognized by the Court of Appeal when speaking for the Court, Brooke J.A. says [at p. 191]:

The *Canada Labour Code* is silent as to acts by others outside of the employer-employee relationship which may interfere with the exercise by the employee of the right or freedom to participate in lawful activities of the union. This is no doubt in recognition of the right or freedom of others to perhaps peacefully persuade such employee as to his participation in the lawful activities of the trade union.

But then Brooke J.A. goes on to say:

But that is quite a different matter than acts or an agreement which has the purpose of preventing or depriving an employee from exercising his right or freedom to participate in the lawful activities of his union.

The distinction that is drawn here appears to me to relate to the means rather than to the purpose. The purpose in either case is the same, namely, that there be no participation by an employee in the lawful activities of his union. Only the means differ: persuasion in the first case, intimidation or other unlawful means in the other.

But we are not here concerned with the means. This information is not laid under s. 423(2)(*b*), nor under s. 381, nor under any other section charging a specific crime. It is laid under s. 423(2)(*a*) and, in my opinion, as laid it does not set out an offence known to the law of Canada.

I would allow the appeal, set aside the judgment of the Court of Appeal and that of the Supreme Court of Ontario, and restore the order of the Provincial Court quashing the information.

McINTYRE J. (dissenting) (MARTLAND J. concurring): —

. . . .

The principal question raised in this appeal is whether the information discloses an offence known to the law. The fact that Crown counsel considered that a particular section of the *Criminal Code* was not relied upon in drafting the information does not preclude this court from considering the effect of the section and finding that the unlawful purpose, alleged in the information, falls within the terms of s. 381 of the *Criminal Code*. While the information, to disclose an offence, must allege a conspiracy to effect an unlawful purpose, specific reference to a numbered section of the *Criminal Code* is not necessary.

Section 110 [rep. & sub. 1972, c. 18, s. 1] of the *Canadian Labour Code*, R.S.C. 1970, c. L-1, confers rights upon employees to join trade unions and participate in their lawful activities. While it may be doubtful if any effective sanction for the enforcement or protection of such rights appears in the *Canada Labour Code*, s. 381 of the *Criminal Code* makes it an offence and, therefore, an unlawful purpose to use the means therein described to compel a person to abstain from doing anything he has a lawful right to do. The information alleges a conspiracy to prevent members of the Seafarers' International Union of Canada from participating in the lawful activities of their union by committing the acts described in the infomation, thereby making the use of the described means a part of the unlawful purpose alleged. Such a conspiracy would, therefore, be a conspiracy to effect an unlawful purpose, and would be an offence within s. 423(2)(*a*) of the *Criminal Code*. I am, of course, far from saying that the Crown would be able to prove its case at trial, but I am of the view that an offence has been alleged in the information and the trial should proceed.

To the argument, which could be raised by counsel for the appellants, that reliance on s. 381 of the *Criminal Code* could take the appellants by surprise and prejudice them in their defence, there is a short answer. This argument might well have force where a previously unmentioned issue is raised after the completion of the evidence at a trial and before judgment, or even where it is produced during a trial when the defence has already adopted a position without consideration of the effect or influence such a change in the Crown position might have. However, that does not apply here where no trial has been commenced, and the appellants would have, from the outset, abundant notice of the problems they face.

. . . .

Appeal dismissed.

R. v. INNOCENTE

(2004), 187 C.C.C. (3d) 533, 2004 CarswellNS 260 (N.S.C.A.)

In May 1995 Innocente hired a person named Craig Henneberry to do work at his house. Eventually Innocente and Henneberry became involved in an enterprise transporting illegal narcotics from Montreal to Halifax. Henneberry flew with Innocente to Montreal and met Francois Germain: Henneberry subsequently made about a dozen trips in which he picked up drugs at Germain's apartment and drove them back to Innocente's home in Nova Scotia. In early July of 1995 Innocente and Henneberry had a falling out and Henneberry stopped his involvement in transporting the drugs. Innocente was charged with and convicted of having conspired with Craig Henneberry to traffic in cannabis resin between June 1, 1995 and July 30, 1995.

In this later case, Innocente was charged with having conspired with five people (including Francois Germain but not including Craig Henneberry) to traffic in cannabis resin and cocaine between March 25, 1996 and May 17, 1996. At this later trial, he sought to plead "autrefois convict": that is, that he had already been in jeopardy for this behaviour at the earlier trial and had been convicted of it, and so could not be placed on trial a second time for the offence. The decision is heavily fact-dependant, but the basic issue is straightforward. The Crown argued that there were two separate and independent conspiracies: the earlier one of which Innocente had already been convicted, and this second, later one. Innocente argued that there was only one conspiracy, which stretched through the entire period from June 1, 1995 to May 17, 1996, and included, at various times, all of the co-conspirators named in the two indictments, and different drugs at different times.

BY THE COURT: —

1   Daniel Joseph Innocente pleads the special plea of *autrefois convict* to a charge of conspiracy to traffic in a narcotic. He relies upon a previous conviction and sentence on a charge of conspiracy to traffic in a narcotic as the basis for the plea. Pursuant to S. 607(3) of the *Criminal Code*, I am deciding whether he has established the special plea, without a jury, before calling upon him to plead further.

. . . .

72   I am satisfied that the two conspiracies alleged - that for which the accused was convicted on the first count of the Henneberry indictment and the conspiracy alleged in the Poirier indictment - are, in fact, one and the same conspiracy. It seems clear, based on the information that was available to the Crown at the time of the Henneberry trial, that the indictment could have been amended at that time to reflect (at the very least) a time period extending into 1996 and the involvement of Mr. Germain as a co-conspirator with Mr. Innocente.

73   Another basis for the Crown's submissions that there were two conspiracies rather than one is that the indictments referred to different narcotics. The Henneberry indictment referred only to cannabis resin, while the Poirier indictment referred to cannabis resin and cocaine. The Crown submits, essentially, that the addition of cocaine to the later indictment creates a new conspiracy. However, the conspiracies alleged involved the supply of drugs to enable Mr. Innocente to traffic in drugs. There was no limit to the types of drugs that would be involved in these transactions. Mr. Henneberry did not specifically

recall all of the drugs that might have been involved, but he did testify that he had transported cannabis resin in the Thunderbird on the first trip.

74   I conclude that the likely introduction of cocaine in the period after March 26, 1996, did not trigger a new conspiracy or the end of the previous one. The enterprise commenced in May 1995 with the purchase of the Thunderbird and its registration in the name of Hélène Guitard, with Mr. Innocente retaining control and ownership of the vehicle, and with Mr. Innocente's discussions with Mr. Germain and Mr. Henneberry. Mr. Innocente engaged Mr. Henneberry to drive the vehicle, but only as driver. As Mr. Henneberry said, he was not a partner of Mr. Innocente, but was working for him. The conspiracy of which Mr. Henneberry was a part was one involving Mr. Innocente and Mr. Germain, for the sale and purchase of drugs, as opposed to the mere movement of drugs. Even if the introduction of cocaine represented the introduction of another object of the conspiracy, this does not necessarily end the existing conspiracy. A conspiracy can have more than one object.

75   The decision in *R. v. Saunders* (1990), 56 C.C.C. (3d) 220 (S.C.C.) (*sub nom. R. v. Rooke and De Vries*) does not assist the Crown. In that case the accused were charged with conspiracy to import heroin, but the evidence at trial was that one accused had been involved in the importation of cocaine rather than heroin. The trial judge instructed the jury that it could convict as long as the accused had conspired to traffic a narcotic, regardless of which narcotic. The Court of Appeal, [1987] B.C.J. No. 1351, ordered a new trial, and the Supreme Court of Canada dismissed the further appeal. McLachlin J. (as she then was) wrote (at p. 223):

> It is a fundamental principle of criminal law that the offence, as particularized in the charge, must be proved.... [O]nce the Crown has particularized the narcotic in a charge, the accused cannot be convicted if a narcotic other than the one specified is proved. The Crown chose to particularize the offence in this case as a conspiracy to import heroin. Having done so, it was obliged to prove the offence thus particularized. To permit the Crown to prove some other offence characterized by different particulars would be to undermine the purpose of providing particulars, which is to permit "the accused to be reasonably informed of the transaction alleged against him, thus giving him the possibility of a full defence and a fair trial": *R. v. Côté* (1977), 33 C.C.C. (2d) 353 at p. 357....

> Crown counsel suggests that the import of the decision of the Court of Appeal is that the Crown will necessarily fail in every case if it cannot prove that the conspiracy related to a particular narcotic, as opposed to and prohibited narcotic. I cannot accept that suggestion. I agree with Crown counsel that the gravamen of the offence is conspiracy to import a narcotic, rather than a particular kind of narcotic. The purpose of specifying the narcotic in a case such as this is to identify the transaction which is the basis of the alleged conspiracy. The fundamental requirement that the charge must provide sufficient particulars to reasonably permit the accused to identify the specific transaction may be met in a variety of ways. Where the Crown has evidence of the particular drug involved, this may properly be required to be provided as a particular identifying the transaction. But where the Crown is uncertain as to the particular drug which was the subject of the conspiracy, it may properly decline to give

particulars of the drug. The charge may nevertheless stand, provided that it sufficiently clearly identifies the alleged conspiracy in some other way. There must be a new trial in this case, not because a conviction for conspiracy to import a narcotic cannot be supported without proof of the type of narcotic involved, but rather because the Crown chose in this case to particularize the drug involved and failed to prove the conspiracy thus particularized.

76   Relying on *Saunders*, the Crown claims that because it did not specify cocaine in the Henneberry indictment, such an allegation would substantially alter the charges against Mr. Innocente and increase his jeopardy without any evidence to support a request for an amendment. However, it does not appear to me that the court said it was impossible to find a conspiracy as alleged on the indictment providing the indictment was properly amended during the trial. In *Saunders*, the court pointed out that no amendment had been sought at trial or at the Court of Appeal, and that it would be unfair and prejudicial to the accused to permit an amendment that fundamentally and retroactively changed the nature of what the Crown was required to prove (pp. 223-224).

77   *Saunders* stands for the proposition that if the Crown specifies a particular narcotic, it must prove that narcotic, and that the Crown can seek to amend the particulars in the indictment pursuant to section 601. The basis for the position the court took in *Saunders* was the necessity for the accused to be aware of the transaction upon which the Crown relies to found the charge. The Crown is bound by its own particularization of the offence. This does not mean that the Crown can rely on that particularization in order to defeat a plea of *autrefois convict*.

78   Once again, I find the reasoning in *A.A.B.* helpful on this point. As in that case, the transaction that forms the basis of the *autrefois* plea was a continuing transaction which could have captured both indictments had the necessary amendments been sought.

79   Another instructive case is the Ontario Court of Appeal's decision in *R. v. Paterson, Ackworth and Kovach* (1985), 18 C.C.C. (3d) 137 (affirmed at 39 C.C.C. (3d) 575 (S.C.C.)). In that case, the three accused were charged with conspiracy to traffic in cannabis resin. One accused was also charged with conspiracy to traffic in methamphetamine. The trial judge concluded that there had been a single conspiracy to traffic in both methamphetamine and cannabis resin, rather than the two conspiracies charged in the indictment. Martin J.A. quoted the following comment of the trial judge (at pp. 141-142):

... I am forced to reject the central arch-stone of the Crown's case, namely, that there were two conspiracies and not just one. To me, the Crown has totally failed to show that there were separate conspiracies in methamphetamine and cannabis resin. Indeed, it is my view ... that the Crown has proved one conspiracy to traffic, with two objects - the selling of a mix of so-called hard and soft drugs.

> The Crown, in attempting to breathe life into the two-conspiracy theory, has artfully attempted to segregate the evidence - especially the wire-tap evidence - into two separate segments or compartments, but, as I review that evidence, it simply cannot be jammed into the allegedly water-tight compartments raised in the Crown theory....
>
> The result I am driven to on this aspect of the case is that the Crown has totally failed to establish a "two conspiracy" case, as charged in the indictment. As it seems to me, the Crown has tried to package and compartmentalize the totality of the evidence to suit a preconceived theory, but the evidence does not, in my view of it, fit the artificial structure invented by the Crown. Rather, the Crown has proved a single conspiracy with two objects and multiple participants....

80   Martin J.A. went on to state the following propositions, among others (at p. 143):

> A single conspiracy may have more than one illegal object and it is proper to allege in one count a conspiracy to commit several crimes. If the prosecution proves a conspiracy to do any one of the prohibited acts alleged in the indictment as the objects of the conspiracy, that is sufficient to support a conviction....
>
> Where there is but one agreement, and not separate agreements as to the different unlawful objects, there can only be one conviction....

81   The Court of Appeal took no issue with the trial judge's finding that there was actually a single conspiracy where the Crown had charged two separate conspiracies (nor, indeed, did the Supreme Court of Canada). In this case, as in *Patterson*, I am forced to the conclusion that the Crown has forced an "artificial structure" of two conspiracies onto what is, in fact, an allegation of a single conspiracy to traffic in narcotics. The two indictments - the Henneberry and Poirier indictments - as formulated by the Crown in fact allege a single conspiracy. The details include the participation of Mr. Innocente and Mr. Germain in a scheme to transport narcotics from Montreal to Halifax by way of couriers (such as Mr. Henneberry) driving a Thunderbird automobile modified to conceal drugs in a secret compartment, and by other drivers and other means until the arrest of Mr. Germain and Mr. Poirier on May 15, 1996.

CONCLUSION

82   I conclude that Mr. Innocente's plea of *autrefois convict* in relation to the Poirier indictment must succeed. Accordingly, Mr. Innocente is discharged in respect of the charge before the court. The charge is dismissed.

3. LIABILITY FOR OFFENCE NOT COMMITTED

R. c. DÉRY

2006 SCC 53, 2006 CarswellQue 9479, 2006 CarswellQue 9480, 213 C.C.C.
(3d) 289, [2006] 2 S.C.R. 669, 43 C.R. (6th) 94

The judgment of the court was delivered by Fish J.: —

5   December brings with it, in Canada and elsewhere, a holiday season widely and joyously celebrated by "raising a glass". Liquor merchants must frequently replenish their shelves to keep the glasses filled. In the Quebec City region, the Société des alcools du Québec ("SAQ") is forced by the increased demand to stock more of its products than its secure warehouses can contain. The inevitable overflow is stored temporarily in trailers parked outdoors at an SAQ compound.

6   An unrelated investigation resulted in the interception of discussions between Mr. Déry, Daniel Savard and others, concerning the possibility of stealing this liquor stored outdoors. On the strength of the intercepted conversations, Messrs. Déry and Savard were both charged with conspiracy to commit theft and conspiracy to possess stolen goods.

7   There was no evidence that either accused had taken any steps to carry out the proposed theft, and the trial judge was not persuaded that they had at any point agreed to steal or possess the liquor that was the object of their covetous musings: (2002), 7 C.R. (6th) 325. In the absence of a proven agreement, the judge quite properly felt bound to acquit the accused of the conspiracies charged. On each count, however, he convicted both co-accused of attempting to conspire, which he believed to be an included offence.

8   A majority of the Court of Appeal of Quebec affirmed their convictions at trial: [2005] Q.J. No. 5350 (QL), 2005 QCCA 483; [2005] Q.J. No. 5351 (QL), 2005 QCCA 484. Forget J.A., dissenting, would have allowed their appeals on the ground that attempted conspiracy is an offence unknown to Canadian law.

9   This further appeal, by Mr. Déry alone, comes to this court as of right. The decisive issue is whether there is any legal basis for concluding that attempt to conspire to commit an indictable offence is a crime in Canada. In the absence of a statutory basis for concluding that the crime exists, there is of course no need to find authority that it does not: s. 9(a) of the *Criminal Code*, R.S.C. 1985, c. C-46, makes clear that no one in Canada may be convicted of "an offence at common law". To affirm Mr. Déry's convictions, we must therefore find that attempt to conspire has until now lain dormant within the statutory confines of the *Criminal Code*, ready to be roused by a proper sounding of its governing provisions.

10   Like Forget J.A., I would let sleeping laws lie.

. . . .

40   The argument in favour of attempted conspiracy is that the provisions governing inchoate liability can be stacked one upon the other, like building blocks. Pursuant to s. 463(d), attempting to commit any "offence for which the offender may be prosecuted by indictment" is an indictable offence punishable by half the maximum penalty for the attempted offence. Conspiracy to commit an indictable offence is itself an indictable offence, punishable by the maximum penalty provided for the underlying substantive offence: s. 465(1)(c). Likewise, it is argued, attempt to conspire is an offence punishable by half the penalty provided for the completed conspiracy.

41   I agree with Forget J.A. that this argument is seductive in appearance but unsound in principle (para. 79). It assumes, but does not establish, that attempt to conspire is an offence under the *Criminal Code*, and it leaves unresolved the question whether the definition of attempt in s. 24 captures, as a matter of law, an attempt to conspire.

42   In virtue of s. 24, a test of proximity separates "mere preparation" from attempt:

> 24. (1) Every one who, having an intent to commit an offence, does or omits to do anything for the purpose of carrying out the intention is guilty of an attempt to commit the offence whether or not it was possible under the circumstances to commit the offence.
>
> (2) *The question whether an act or omission by a person who has an intent to commit an offence is or is not mere preparation to commit the offence, and too remote to constitute an attempt to commit the offence*, is a question of law.

43   The intent of the legislator in s. 24(2) is to fix the threshold of criminal responsibility. Applying the test provided, courts must situate on a continuum from antisocial contemplation to prohibited conduct — or bad thought to substantive crime — the point where the criminal law intervenes. This continuum was aptly described a half-century ago by Laidlaw J.A. in *R. v. Cline* (1956), 115 C.C.C. 18 (Ont. C.A.):

> The consummation of a crime usually comprises a series of acts which have their genesis in an idea to do a criminal act; the idea develops to a decision to do that act; a plan may be made for putting that decision into effect; the next step may be preparation only for carrying out the intention and plan; but when that preparation is in fact fully completed, the next step in the series of acts done by the accused for the purpose and with the intention of committing the crime as planned cannot, in my opinion, be regarded as remote in its connection with that crime. The connection is in fact proximate. [p. 28]

44   In *Dynar*, Cory and Iacobucci JJ. observed that conspiracy is an act that precedes the next step after preparing to carrying out a plan:

Conspiracy is in fact a more "preliminary" crime than attempt, since the offence is considered to be complete before any acts are taken that go beyond mere preparation to put the common design into effect. The Crown is simply required to prove a meeting of the minds with regard to a common design to do something unlawful . . . [Emphasis added; para. 87.]

And they explained that "the reason for punishing conspiracy before any steps are taken towards attaining the object of the agreement is *to prevent the unlawful object from being attained, and therefore to prevent this serious harm from occurring*" (para. 90 (emphasis added)). The serious harm referred to is not the conspiracy but the substantive offence. By criminalizing conspiracy, the legislature has intervened earlier along the continuum because of the increased danger represented by a cohort of wrongdoers acting in concert. See G. Côté-Harper, P. Rainville and J. Turgeon, *Traité de droit penal canadien* (4th ed. 1998), at pp. 661-63.

45   The question this court must now answer is whether acts that precede a conspiracy are sufficiently proximate to a substantive offence to warrant criminal sanction. In *Dungey*, Dubin J.A. answered this question in the negative:

Notwithstanding that the charge was one of conspiracy, the conduct of the respondent should be viewed as a step preparatory to committing the substantive offence of fraud and, in that sense, what he did would be too remote to constitute an attempt. [p. 98]

In *R. v. Chan* (2003), 178 C.C.C. (3d) 269 (Ont. C.A.), Simmons J.A. was of a similar view:

Strictly inchoate crimes are a unique class of criminal offences in the sense that they criminalize acts that precede harmful conduct but do not necessarily inflict harmful consequences in and of themselves. It can thus be appreciated that it could extend the criminal law too far to reach behind those acts and criminalize behaviour that precedes those acts. [para. 69]

46   I agree with these observations. In *Dungey*, Dubin J.A. left the door open to a possible exception for substantive conspiracy precisely because, in that context, "the question of remoteness would not arise" (p. 99) since substantive conspiracies are themselves the legislative focus of the perceived harm, and not simply the risk of its possible commission.

47   Given that conspiracy is essentially a crime of intention, and "[c]riminal law should not patrol people's thoughts" (*Dynar*, at para. 169, per Major J.), it is difficult to reach further than the law of conspiracy already allows. Even if it were possible, it has never been the goal of the criminal law to catch all crime [Translation] "in the egg", as the Attorney General for Canada has put it in this case (factum, at para. 58). In this sense, conspiracies are criminalized when hatched. And they can only be hatched by agreement.

48   This basic element of conspiracy — agreement — exposes the otherwise hidden criminal intentions of the parties to it. This demonstrates their

commitment to a prohibited act. By contrast, the criminal law intervenes later in the progression from thought to deed where someone acts alone. Overt steps are then thought necessary to disclose and establish with sufficient certainty the criminal intention that is an essential element of the attempt to commit an offence.

49   By its very nature, moreover, an agreement to commit a crime in concert with others enhances the risk of its commission. Early intervention through the criminalization of conspiracy is therefore both principled and practical.

50   Likewise, the criminalization of attempt is warranted because its purpose is to prevent harm by punishing behaviour that demonstrates a substantial risk of harm. When applied to conspiracy, the justification for criminalizing attempt is lost, since an attempt to conspire amounts, at best, to a risk that a risk will materialize.

51   Finally, though Mr. Déry discussed a crime hoping eventually to commit it with others, neither he nor they committed, or even agreed to commit, the crimes they had discussed. The criminal law does not punish bad thoughts of this sort that were abandoned before an agreement was reached, or an attempt made, to act upon them.

52   For these reasons, I would allow the appeal, set aside Mr. Déry's convictions and order that acquittals be entered instead.

R. v. HAMILTON

[2005] 2 S.C.R. 432, 30 C.R. (6th) 243, 198 C.C.C. (3d) 1,
2005 CarswellAlta 1037, 2005 CarswellAlta 1038 (S.C.C.)

FISH J. (MCLACHLIN C.J., BASTARACHE, BINNIE, LEBEL and DESCHAMPS JJ. concurring): —

1   The respondent, René Luther Hamilton, offered for sale through the Internet access to a "credit card number generator" — in terms that extolled its use for fraudulent purposes. As part of the same package of "Top Secret Files", he also offered for sale bomb "recipes" and information on how to commit burglaries.

2   Mr. Hamilton was charged under s. 464(a) of the *Criminal Code*, R.S.C. 1985, c. C-46, in four separate counts, with counselling the commission of indictable offences that were not in fact committed.

3   The trial judge was not satisfied that Mr. Hamilton had acted with the requisite *mens rea*, or culpable intent, and she therefore acquitted him on all

four counts: (2002), 3 Alta. L.R. (4th) 147, 2002 ABQB 15. The Court of Appeal for Alberta dismissed the Crown's appeal: (2003), 25 Alta. L.R. (4th) 1, 2003 ABCA 255.

4   The Crown now appeals to this court on the ground that the trial judge erred as to the *mens rea* of counselling. In the Crown's view, it is unnecessary to prove that the person who counselled the offence intended that it be committed; recklessness is sufficient.

5   The Crown contends that even if recklessness is insufficient, the trial judge erred in confounding "motive" and "intent." With respect, I agree that the trial judge erred in this regard and that her verdict, but for this error, might very well have been different, at least on the count for counselling fraud. She acquitted Mr. Hamilton of that offence because, in her own words, "[h]is *motivation* was monetary" (para. 53; emphasis added).

6   I would therefore allow the Crown's appeal, order a new trial on the count for counselling fraud and dismiss the appeal with respect to the three remaining counts.

7   Mr. Hamilton was charged under s. 464 of the *Criminal Code* with counselling four indictable offences that were not committed: making explosive substances with intent; doing anything with intent to cause an explosion; break and enter with intent; and fraud.

8   The charges resulted from an advertisement, or "teaser", sent by Mr. Hamilton through the Internet to more than 300 people whose addresses he had acquired from published lists. His advertisement read, in part:

> HAVE YOU EVER HEARD OF A SOFTWARE PROGRAM THAT CAN PRODUCE AND DISPLAY VALID WORKING CREDIT CARD NUMBERS AT THE TOUCH OF A KEY!!!!
>
> WELL IT'S ARRIVED ..... THE TIME IS NOW!!
>
> THE AUTOMATIC CREDIT CARD NUMBER GENERATOR!!!!!!!!!
>
> ...
>
> *ALL VALID AND FULLY FUNCTIONAL!!*
>
> ...
>
> *YOU CAN ALSO Extrapolate NEW CREDIT CARD NUMBERS OFF OF YOUR EXISTING ALREADY VALID REAL CREDIT CARDS!!!! 100% valid numbers!
>
> *SIMPLE TO USE??? - ABSOLUTELY!!*
>
> ...

IMAGINE THE THINGS THAT YOU COULD DO WITH THIS PROGRAM, AND THE VALID CREDIT CARD NUMBERS IT GENERATES!!

THE POSSIBILITIES ARE ENDLESS!!!

...

ALSO AVAILABLE IS THE OVERSEA'S AT&T CALLING CARD NUMBER GENERATOR!!!!!

FREE LONG DISTANCE??? YUPPERS! YES INDEED, ABSOLUTELY!!!!!

*THIS SIMPLE EASY TO USE PROGRAM PRODUCES VALID OVERSEA'S AT&T CALLING CARD NUMBERS.. WITH ONE STROKE OF THE KEY!!! ....

...

*GET ANY CREDIT CARD YOU WANT

...

ALL OF THESE METHODS *HAVE BEEN PROVEN TO WORK OVER AND OVER, TIME AND TIME AGAIN!!* THESE ARE THE SECRETS THAT MILLIONAIRES AND GOVERNMENT INSIDERS ONLY TELL THEIR FRIENDS ABOUT!!

Don't delay ... This Extraordinary and Valuable Information including the Card Generator Programs can be yours Today for ONLY $50 (US FUNDS).

...

IF YOU DOWNLOAD THE PROGRAMS AND USE THEM ... WE ACCEPT NO LIABILITY FOR YOUR ACTIONS!

...

DON'T MISS OUT ON THIS CHANCE TO GET YOUR HANDS ON THESE TWO AMAZING PROGRAMS, THAT WILL FOREVER CHANGE YOUR LIFE .. ! IF YOU MISS THE CHANCE NOW, IT MIGHT NOT COME AROUND AGAIN ..... AS THESE SOFTWARE PROGRAMS ARE NOT SOLD IN RETAIL STORES, FOR OBVIOUS REASONS!!

...

Looking forward to seeing you well on your way to a wealthy lifestyle!! [Emphasis added.]

9   Mr. Hamilton also created a web site advertising the Top Secret files, and was shown to have made at least 20 sales.

10   The trial judge found that Mr. Hamilton had seen a computer-generated list of the contents of the Top Secret files. They contained document descriptions such as "bombs.txt", "bombs2.txt", "bombs3.txt", "How to Break into a House.txt", and "visa hacking.txt". Mr. Hamilton testified that he had not read these files, and the trial judge, without making an express finding, appears to have accepted his evidence in this regard. The Top Secret files were organized

into two zip files, which consisted of roughly 2000 pages of text. Only 13 pages related to the counselling charges that concern us here.

11   A document describing a credit card number generator that was not part of the Top Secret files was also discovered on Mr. Hamilton's computer. As well, a handwritten list of Visa numbers was seized in his possession. Of the listed numbers, all but one were found by the judge to be "valid" (para. 15), in the sense of "usable". But no complaints were received by the bank regarding their improper use. The trial judge accepted Mr. Hamilton's evidence that he did not use the credit card numbers he had generated.

12   The trial judge acquitted Mr. Hamilton on all counts and the Court of Appeal affirmed the acquittals.

III

13   The Crown contends that recklessness satisfies the fault requirement of counselling and that, even if intent (as opposed to recklessness) must be proved, the trial judge erred in grafting onto the required element of intention an additional requirement of motive.

14   At common law, counselling or procuring a felony was a substantive offence, whether or not the felony was subsequently committed: *R. v. Brousseau* (1917), 56 S.C.R. 22. The charges that concern us here are now codified in s. 464(a) of the *Criminal Code*, which provides:

> 464. . . .(a) every one who counsels another person to commit an indictable offence is, if the offence is not committed, guilty of an indictable offence and liable to the same punishment to which a person who attempts to commit that offence is liable;

15   The *actus reus* for counselling will be established where the materials or statements made or transmitted by the accused actively induce or advocate — and do not merely describe — the commission of an offence: *R. v. Sharpe*, [2001] 1 S.C.R. 45, 2001 SCC 2, McLachlin C.J., at para. 57.

16   The *mens rea*, or fault element, for counselling was recently considered in *R. v. Janeteas* (2003), 172 C.C.C. (3d) 97, which involved an appeal by the accused against his conviction on one count of counselling murder and two counts of counselling unlawful bodily harm. The trial judge had instructed the jury that they could convict the accused of these offences only if they were satisfied beyond a reasonable doubt that he had counselled their commission "with the intent that his advice or counselling ... *be accepted*" (para. 14; emphasis added).

17   The Ontario Court of Appeal found this instruction to be inadequate. In the court's view, it was not enough for the jury to conclude that the accused

intended that his counselling of the offences "be accepted" or "be taken seriously" (para. 43) by the persons counselled to commit then; the accused must have intended as well that the offence counselled be in fact committed (para. 46).

18   In the present case, the trial judge described counselling as a "dual *mens rea* offence" (para. 37) and the Court of Appeal in *Janeteas* cited this characterization of the requisite mental element in its reasons (at para. 19).

19   *Janeteas* was decided on an unusual set of facts and in light of concessions by Crown counsel as to the inadequacy of the trial judge's instructions to the jury. Moreover, authorities cited by the Court of Appeal – none of them binding on this court – do support the proposition that counselling is a "dual intent" offence. But the court in *Janeteas* did take care to say that it would have reached the same result even if it were found sufficient for conviction that the accused, in counselling the commission of the offences, was reckless as to the consequences.

20   In my respectful view, a judicial determination of the fault element for counselling should not be made to depend on whether the required *mens rea* is characterized as "dual". I find it preferable to begin instead by considering why the counselling of crime is prohibited and then to examine the ordinary meaning of the words used by Parliament to achieve its purpose.

21   Our concern here is with the imposition of criminal liability on those who counsel others to commit crimes. In this context, "counsel" includes "procure, solicit or incite": see s. 22(3) of the *Criminal Code*.

22   In their relevant senses, the *Canadian Oxford Dictionary* (2nd ed. 2004) defines "counsel" as "advise" or "recommend (a course of action)"; "procure", as "bring about"; "solicit", as "ask repeatedly or earnestly for or seek or invite", or "make a request or petition to (a person)"; and "incite", as "urge". "Procure" has been held judicially to include "instigate" and "persuade": *R. v. Gonzague* (1983), 4 C.C.C. (3d) 505 (Ont. C.A.).

23   Those who encourage the commission of crimes in any of these ways are criminally responsible for their conduct by way of "secondary liability".

24   The rationale underlying secondary liability was described by the Law Reform Commission of Canada as "straightforward, obvious and justifiable" – in principle, though not always in practice: Working Paper 45, *Secondary Liability: Participation in Crime and Inchoate Offences* (1985), at p. 5.

25   According to the Commission (at pp. 5-6):

. . . the rationale for secondary liability is the same as that for primary liability. Primary liability attaches to the commission of acts which are outlawed as being harmful, as infringing important human interests and as violating basic social values. Secondary liability attaches on the same ground to their attempted commission, to counselling their commission and to assisting their commission.

This is clear with participation. If the primary act (for example, killing) is harmful, then doing it becomes objectionable. But if doing it is objectionable, it is also objectionable to get another person to do it, or help him do it. For while killing is objectionable because it causes actual harm (namely, death), so too inducing and assisting killing are objectionable because of the potential harm: *they increase the likelihood of death occurring.*

The same arguments hold for inchoate crimes. Again, if the primary act (for example, killing), is harmful, society will want people not to do it. Equally, it will not want them even to try to do it, or to counsel or incite others to do it. *For while the act itself causes actual harm, attempting to do it, or counselling, inciting or procuring someone else to do it, are sources of potential harm – they increase the likelihood of that particular harm's occurrence.* Accordingly, society is justified in taking certain measures in respect of them: outlawing them with sanctions, and authorizing intervention to prevent the harm from materializing. [Emphasis added.]

26   These passages, in my view, aptly explain why Parliament has imposed criminal responsibility on those who counsel, procure, solicit or incite others to commit crimes, whether or not the crimes are in fact committed.

27   And it seems to me that the plain meaning of the terms used by Parliament to achieve this purpose point to a fault element that combines advertent conduct with a "conscious disregard of unjustified (and substantial) risk" that it entails: L. Alexander and K. D. Kessler, "*Mens rea* and Inchoate Crimes" (1997), 87 J. Crim. L. & Criminology 1138, at p. 1175 (emphasis in original).

28   The "substantial and unjustified risk" standard of recklessness has venerable roots in Canada and in other common law jurisdictions as well: see, for example, *Leary v. The Queen*, [1978] 1 S.C.R. 29 at p. 35 (Dickson J., as he then was, dissenting on other grounds); and, generally, M.L. Friedland and K. Roach, *Criminal Law and Procedure: Cases and Materials* (8th ed. 1997), at pp. 508 ff, where Herbert Wechsler explains, at p. 510-11, why the American Law Institute required in its Model Penal Code that the risk consciously disregarded be both "substantial" and "unjustifiable".

29   In short, the *actus reus* for counselling is the deliberate encouragement or active inducement of the commission of a criminal offence. And the *mens rea* consists in nothing less than an accompanying intent or conscious disregard of the substantial and unjustified risk inherent in the counselling: that is, it must be shown that the accused either intended that the offence counselled be committed, or knowingly counselled the commission of the offence while aware of the unjustified risk that the offence counselled was in fact likely to be committed as a result of the accused's conduct.

30   I would resist any temptation to depart in this case from that relatively demanding standard. The Internet provides fertile ground for sowing the seeds of unlawful conduct on a borderless scale. And, at the hearing of the appeal, Crown counsel expressed with eloquence and conviction the urgent need for an appropriate prophylactic response.

31   In my view, however, this task must be left to Parliament. Even if they were minded to do so, courts cannot contain the inherent dangers of cyberspace crime by expanding or transforming offences, such as counselling, that were conceived to meet a different and unrelated need. Any attempt to do so may well do more harm than good, inadvertently catching morally innocent conduct and unduly limiting harmless access to information.

. . . .

IV

34   In determining that the *actus reus* of counselling was made out, the trial judge stated:

> In my view the teaser, viewed objectively, actively promotes the use of the credit card generator. The legal disclaimers do not discourage use. Rather they serve as a message that the use of the numbers generated is illegal, and attempt to limit liability, which furthers rather than limits the message which is to use the numbers in a cautious fashion.
>
> The Top Secret files sent out by Mr. Hamilton which relate to the charges amount to "How To" guides. The bomb documents contain recipes for bombs together with instructions for assembly and then instructions on how to detonate the bomb. "How to Break into a House" gives instructions in a step by step fashion for a style of break in and theft. The [Visa] hacker, or credit card number generator, is similar. [paras. 20-21]

35   The trial judge appears to have accepted Mr. Hamilton's evidence that he did not read the files relating to bombs and to burglaries and found as a fact that he had no intention to induce the recipients of his "teaser" to either build bombs or commit burglaries. This finding of fact was not reviewable in the Court of Appeal and is not subject to review in this court, since the Crown's right of appeal is limited in both instances to questions of law alone.

36   Mr. Hamilton's acquittal on the count for counselling fraud does not stand on the same footing.

37   At least as regards the credit card number generator, the trial judge concluded that the documents offered for sale — and sold — by Mr. Hamilton "actively promote or encourage the actions described in them" (para. 22). Applying the test set out in *R. v. Dionne* (1987), 79 N.B.R. (2d) 297 (C.A.), she found that the documents "are likely to incite and are 'with a view to' inciting the offence" (para. 22).

38   Nothing in the evidence suggests that Mr. Hamilton intended these documents to be read in a different manner or that they be used for a different purpose. Moreover, the trial judge expressly found that Mr. Hamilton had "subjective knowledge that the use of false credit card numbers is illegal" (para. 53).

39   The trial judge nonetheless acquitted Mr. Hamilton on the charge of counselling fraud because she had "a doubt that Mr. Hamilton had subjective intent to counsel fraud" (para. 53). And she explained her conclusion this way:

> . . . His *motivation* was monetary, and he sought to pique the curiosity of readers who might acquire the information in the same way that he was initially attracted to the information. Further, he struck me as utterly unsophisticated and naïve to the point that he cannot be said to have been wilfully blind or reckless. [Emphasis added; para. 53.]

40   Essentially, on my reading of this passage, the trial judge acquitted Mr. Hamilton on this count because his motivation was mercenary as opposed to malevolent.

41   In my respectful view, this was an error of law requiring our intervention.

42   The distinction between motive and intent has been well understood by Canadian courts since at least 1979, when Dickson J. stated:

> In ordinary parlance, the words "intent" and "motive" are frequently used interchangeably, but in the criminal law they are distinct. In most criminal trials, the mental element, the *mens rea* with which the court is concerned, relates to "intent", i.e. the exercise of a free will to use particular means to produce a particular result, rather than with "motive", i.e. that which precedes and induces the exercise of the will. The mental element of a crime ordinarily involves no reference to motive: ...(*Lewis v. The Queen*, [1979] 2 S.C.R. 821, at p. 831)

43   Cory and Iacobucci JJ. also underlined this distinction in *Dynar v. United States*, [1997] 2 S.C.R. 462, emphasizing the importance, as a matter of legal policy, of maintaining it with vigilance: "It does not matter to society, in its efforts to secure social peace and order, what an accused's motive was, but only what the accused intended to do. It is no consolation to one whose car has been stolen that the thief stole the car intending to sell it to purchase food for a food bank" (para. 81). See also *R. v. Hibbert*, [1995] 2 S.C.R. 973.

44   In this case, of course, the motive attributed to the accused was far less laudable. He sought to make "a quick buck" by encouraging the intended recipients of his Internet solicitation to purchase a device that generated credit card numbers easily put to fraudulent use.

45   The trial judge's conclusion that Mr. Hamilton did not intend to induce the recipients to use those numbers is incompatible with the plain meaning of the "teaser" e-mail and with her other findings of fact, including her finding that

Mr. Hamilton well understood that use of the generated numbers was illegal. Her assertion that "[h]is motivation was monetary" immediately after her reference to these facts demonstrates an error of law as to the *mens rea* for counselling the commission of a crime, and warrants a new trial.

V

46   I would for these reasons allow the appeal on the count for counselling fraud and order a new trial on that count, but dismiss the appeal in relation to the three remaining counts.

CHARRON J. (MAJOR and ABELLA JJ. concurring) (dissenting):

[The dissenting judges disagreed that recklessness could be a sufficient basis for convicting an accused of counselling an offence, arguing that only actual intention should be sufficient.]

· · · ·

C. The *Actus reus* for Counselling an Offence not Committed

67   As stated earlier, only *mens rea* is at issue on this appeal. However, in order to properly determine the fault requirement for any offence, it is necessary to consider the *actus reus* of the offence so as to identify the circumstances and consequences to which the offence is directed. The *actus reus* under s. 464 consists of "counsel[ling] another person to commit an indictable offence" (or an offence punishable on summary conviction). Hence, there must be:

(a) an act of counselling;
(b) communicated to another person;
(c) in respect of the commission of an offence.

It is readily apparent from the language of the provision that the interpretation of the word "counsel", in large part, will determine the scope of criminal liability.

68   In its ordinary sense, counselling means simply to advise. If given that meaning, the scope of targeted activity would potentially be very wide. The simple communication of information on "how to" commit an offence would suffice to make out the *actus reus* of the offence. The criminalization of all such communications could easily be justified on the basis that society seeks to protect itself against the potential harm occasioned by acts of counselling — the increased likelihood that the counselled offence be committed. After all, it is at least arguable that the communication of this kind of information may plant a seed in the recipient's mind and increase the likelihood of the crime materializing. Should then all such communications be banned? More significantly, should they be subject to society's severest sanction, the criminal law?

69   We must ask ourselves if the resulting encroachment on freedom of speech would exact too high a cost. If "counsel" meant simply to advise, a lawyer's advice to a client on the law with respect to the various means of committing an offence could potentially be caught. Movies, video games, textbooks, and other literary works that describe or depict the commission of an offence may be subject to state scrutiny. I would think it obvious that such a prohibition on expression would be too wide. It is for this reason, as we shall see, that such an interpretation of the word "counsel" has been rejected in the criminal context.

70   The requisite *actus reus* of the offence of counselling was considered in *R. v. Dionne* (1987), 79 N.B.R. (2d) 297 (C.A.). Mr. Dionne was charged with counselling indictable offences that were not committed. He was alleged to have counselled an undercover officer to commit the offences of threatening and assault causing bodily harm. The trial judge instructed the jury on the requisite elements of the offences as follows, at para. 20:

> [Translation] Taking each count individually, the offence is complete if, first of all, the accused had the intention of having injury caused, or of having threats made by telephone, as the case may be, and secondly, if the accused conveyed his intention to someone else with a view to having that person cause the injuries, or make the threats by telephone.

71   On appeal, the New Brunswick Court of Appeal held that these instructions were erroneous. The *actus reus* of the offence of counselling could not be made out on the basis of a mere passive communication by an accused of his desire that an offence be committed — more was required. Ayles J.A. stated as follows, at para. 21:

> [Translation] In my opinion, those instructions are incorrect since the offence of incitement implies actions which are more serious than those of conveying one's intention to have injuries inflicted upon someone, with a view to having those injuries inflicted. *The actions or words must be capable of inducing a person to commit the intended offences, and passive communication of one's intention does not constitute an offence even if the object is to have injuries inflicted upon someone.* [Emphasis added.]

72   This court considered *Dionne* and expressly adopted this "stronger meaning of actively inducing" in *R. v. Sharpe*, [2001] 1 S.C.R. 45, 2001 SCC 2, at para. 56. In order for the *actus reus* to be proven, the words communicated by the accused, viewed objectively, must be seen as actively inducing, procuring or encouraging the commission of an offence. This restricted interpretation of the meaning of counselling is not only consonant with the definition of "counsel" under s. 22(3), it ensures that the scope of the offence remains within the justifiable limits of the criminal law. It is this concern of potential overbreadth that informed this court's adoption in *Sharpe* of a more restricted meaning of counselling.

73   The need to carefully circumscribe the scope of an offence prohibiting a form of communication was discussed at length in *R. v. Keegstra*, [1990] 3 S.C.R. 697. In that case, the constitutional validity of s. 319(2), which prohibits communications that wilfully promote hatred against an identifiable group, was challenged on the basis that it unduly restricted the freedom of expression under s. 2(b) of the *Canadian Charter of Rights and Freedoms*. This court, by majority decision, upheld the constitutional validity of the provision. It did so on the basis that s. 319(2) possessed sufficient definitional safeguards to ensure that it captured only the harm to which the prohibition is targeted and, as such, did not unduly restrict the s. 2(b) guarantee.

74   Hence, as held in *Sharpe*, nothing short of active inducement or encouragement will suffice to make out the *actus reus* of the offence of counselling. In other words, when viewed objectively, the communication must be one that actively seeks to persuade the person counselled to commit the crime. In this way, the scope of targeted activity is not extended to the mere possibility of planting a seed in the recipient's mind; it is limited to those communications that are likely to cause that seed to sprout, creating a resolve to commit the crime. It is only then that the potential risk justifies the criminal prohibition. However, it is well established that it is not necessary that the person counselled be in fact persuaded: *R. v. Walia* (1975), 9 C.R. (3d) 293 (B.C.C.A.), at pp. 293-95; *R. v. Glubisz* (1979), 47 C.C.C. (2d) 232 (B.C.C.A.), at pp. 235 and 241-42; *R. v. Gonzague* (1983), 4 C.C.C. (3d) 505 (Ont. C.A.), at pp. 508-9. The focus on a prosecution for counselling is on the counsellor's conduct and state of mind, not that of the person counselled.

D. The *Mens Rea* for Counselling an Offence Not Committed

75   No constitutional challenge is raised in this case. Nonetheless, the court must be mindful of the potential overbreadth of a criminal sanction whose sole target is speech. As reiterated in *Sharpe*, Parliament is presumed to have intended to enact legislation in conformity with the *Charter* (para. 33). This concern over the potential sweep of the provision does not end with the analysis of the requisite *actus reus* and the level of risk targeted by Parliament. The persons who could potentially fall within the reach of the criminal law must be considered. Because of the stigma attached to a criminal prosecution and to a conviction, it is important that the offence not catch the morally innocent.

76   The requisite *mens rea* is not expressly set out in s. 464. However, this is not unusual. The mental element of an offence is not always described in the enactment. Often it must be inferred from the nature of the prohibited activity and the harm it is meant to guard against. In this case, because of the nature of the offence, our earlier discussion on the requisite *actus reus* can largely inform the determination of the necessary *mens rea*. As we have seen, it is not sufficient that the communication simply raise the possibility of affecting its recipient; it

must actively seek to persuade that person to commit the crime. It follows that the counsellor must, at the very least, intend to persuade the person counselled to commit the offence. In this respect, it is my view that mere recklessness as to the counselled person's reaction to the communication is insufficient. In other words, it is not enough that the counsellor, knowing that the communication is objectively capable of persuading a person to commit an offence, goes ahead and does the act anyway. If mere recklessness as to the communication's potential power of persuasion were to suffice, some may argue that the publication of Shakespeare's *Henry VI*, with its famous phrase "let's kill all the lawyers", should be subject to state scrutiny!

[The dissenting judges also disagreed that the trial judge had erred by confusing "motive" and "intention".]

84   The trial judge concluded that Mr. Hamilton did not have the necessary *mens rea* on any standard. The Court of Appeal saw no reason to interfere with her conclusion. Nor do I. My colleague Fish J. is of the view that the trial judge erred by confounding "motive" and "intent". He rests this conclusion on the trial judge's finding that Mr. Hamilton's motivation was monetary. With respect, I disagree. The trial judge's consideration of Mr. Hamilton's motivation must be examined in the context of the evidence before her, and her reasons must be read as a whole.

85   Mr. Hamilton testified that he had not intended to induce the commission of any criminal offence. He had not written any of the files; he had himself purchased them off the Internet and did not even know what much of the information was about. The files consisted of roughly 2,000 pages of text, only 13 of which related to the charges before the court. In particular, he had not read any of the files about bombs or break and enters. The teaser made no reference to these files. As for the material on the credit card generator, he thought readers would simply be interested, as he had been, in discovering how easy it was to generate valid credit card numbers. He did not think anyone could use the credit card numbers without a valid name, expiry date or security number. Notably, at the relevant time Mr. Hamilton had never owned a credit card. The trial judge, as she was entitled to do, accepted Mr. Hamilton's testimony. She concluded as follows, at paras. 53-54:

> On all the evidence I find that Mr. Hamilton ought to have known he was counselling fraud. The teaser and his subjective knowledge that the use of false credit card numbers is illegal make this conclusion irresistible. However, I have a doubt that Mr. Hamilton had subjective intent to counsel fraud. His motivation was monetary, and he sought to pique the curiosity of readers who might acquire the information in the same way that he was initially attracted to the information. Further, he struck me as utterly unsophisticated and naïve to the point that he cannot be said to have been wilfully blind or reckless.
>
> I also find that Mr. Hamilton did not intend the fraud be carried out nor was he wilfully blind or reckless as to the risk of deprivation which would result (to use the *Theroux* test). In my

view the evidence points to a conclusion that Mr. Hamilton was inviting others to do as he had done: to satisfy their curiosity by seeing how easy it is to generate the numbers and to expect that they cannot use them without the expiry date. In other words, he did not specifically intend that the fraud would be carried out. Nor, in all of the circumstances, ought he to have known that the fraud would be carried out. It follows that there could not be a conclusion that he was wilfully blind or reckless as to the consequences of the fraud. Rather, Mr. Hamilton was trying to make money by selling information on the Internet. In my view, on all of the evidence, it cannot be found he counselled fraud.

86   The trial judge was entitled to consider motive. It is a piece of circumstantial evidence that may assist in determining an accused's state of mind. In reading her reasons as a whole, I see no reason to interfere with the conclusion reached by the Court of Appeal on this issue, at para. 44:

> The trial judge did not err as alleged by the Crown. As she was entitled to do, the trial judge considered motive as part of her fact findings. But her decision was based on other facts relating to the respondent's knowledge. She found, for example, that the respondent had not read most of the "Top Secret" files. She also found that he was not interested in their contents and that he was, overall, "naive, lazy or ignorant". Dealing with the credit card number generator, the trial judge accepted the respondent's testimony that he did not think any generated numbers could be used because they lacked an expiry date. On the basis of these facts, she found the respondent lacked sufficient knowledge of the consequences of his actions to satisfy the *mens rea* requirement. It is clear that she understood the nature of the test she was bound to apply and did not err in law.

IV. Disposition

87   For these reasons, I would dismiss the appeal.

Chapter 10

GROUP RESPONSIBILITY:
CORPORATIONS, CRIMINAL ORGANIZATIONS AND TERRORIST GROUPS

1. CORPORATIONS

(a) Common Law

CANADIAN DREDGE AND DOCK CO. v. R.

[1985] 1 S.C.R. 662, 45 C.R. (4th) 289, 19 C.C.C. (3d) 1, 59 N.R. 241,
1985 CarswellOnt 939, 1985 CarswellOnt 96

This is the leading decision on the difficult issue of the "identification doctrine" under which Canadian courts for many years imputed fault, including *mens rea*, to corporations. The case concerned appeals of several corporate accused against their *Criminal Code* convictions for conspiracy to defraud. The charges stemmed from bids for dredging contracts found to have been collusive. The Supreme Court rejected arguments that the companies were not guilty as the bids had been conducted by managers acting in fraud of the companies or contrary to corporate instructions.

The Supreme Court confirmed the convictions and took the opportunity to assert and justify the identification doctrine for holding corporations responsible for *mens rea* offences.

ESTEY J.: —

The position of the corporation in criminal law must first be examined. Inasmuch as all criminal and quasi-criminal offences are creatures of statute the amenability of the corporation to prosecution necessarily depends in part upon the terminology employed in the statute. In recent years there has developed a system of classification which segregates the offences according to the degree of intent, if any, required to create culpability.

(a) *Absolute Liability Offences*

Where the Legislature by the clearest intendment establishes an offence where liability arises instantly upon the breach of the statutory prohibition, no particular state of mind is a prerequisite to guilt. Corporations and individual persons stand on the same footing in the face of such a statutory offence. It is a case of automatic primary responsibility. Accordingly, there is no need to establish a rule for corporate liability nor a rationale therefore. The corporation is treated as a natural person.

(b) *Offences of Strict Liability*

Where the terminology employed by the Legislature is such as to reveal an intent that guilt shall not be predicated upon the automatic breach of the statute — but rather upon the establishment of the *actus reus*, subject to the defence of due diligence, an offence of strict liability arises. See *R. v. City of Sault Ste. Marie*, [1978] 2 S.C.R. 1299. As in the case of an absolute liability offence, it matters not whether the accused is corporate or unincorporate, because the liability is primary and arises in the accused according to the terms of the statute in the same way as in the case of absolute offences. It is not dependent upon the attribution to the accused of the misconduct of others. This is so when the statute, properly construed, shows a clear contemplation by the Legislature that a breach of the statute itself leads to guilt, subject to the limited defence above noted. In this category, the corporation and the natural defendant are in the same position. In both cases liability is not vicarious but primary.

(c) *Offences Requiring Mens Rea*

These are the traditional criminal offences for which an accused may be convicted only if the requisite *mens rea* is demonstrated by the prosecution. At common law a corporate entity could not generally be convicted of a criminal offence. Corporate criminal immunity stemmed from the abhorrence of the common law for vicarious liability in criminal law, and from the doctrine of *ultra vires*, which regarded criminal activities by corporate agents as beyond their authority and beyond corporate capacity. At the other extreme in the spectrum of criminal offences there are certain crimes which cannot in any real sense be committed by a corporation as a principal, such as perjury and bigamy, whatever the doctrine of corporate criminal liability may be. As a corporation may only act through agents, there are basically only three approaches whereby criminal intent could be said to reside or not reside in the corporate entity:

(i) a total vicarious liability for the conduct of any of its agents whatever their level of employment or responsibility so long as they are acting within the scope of their employment;

(ii) no criminal liability unless the criminal acts in question have been committed on the direction or at the request, express or clearly implied of the corporation as expressed through its board of directors;

(iii) a median rule whereby the criminal conduct, including the state of mind, of employees and agents of the corporation is attributed to the corporation so as to render the corporation criminally liable so long as the employee or agent in question is of such a position in the organization and activity of the corporation that he or she represents its *de facto* directing mind, will, centre, brain area or ego so that the corporation is identified with the act of that individual. There is said to be on this theory no responsibility through vicarious liability or any other form of agency, but rather a liability arising in criminal law by reason of the single identity wherein is combined the legal entity and the natural person; in short, a primary liability. This rule stands in the middle of the range or spectrum. It is but a legal fiction invented for pragmatic reasons.

. . . .

This [median] rule of law was seen as a result of the removal of the officer or managerial level employee from the general class of "inferior servants or agents" for whose acts the corporate employer continued (as in the case of the human employer) to be immune from vicarious liability in criminal law. This result is generally referred to as the "identification" theory. It produces the element of *mens rea* in the corporate entity, otherwise absent from the legal entity but present in the natural person, the directing mind. This establishes the "identity" between the directing mind and the corporation which results in the corporation being found guilty for the act of the natural person, the employee. . . . The essence of the test is that the identity of the directing mind and the company coincide so long as the actions of the former are performed by the manager within the sector of corporation operation assigned to him by the corporation. The sector may be functional, or geographic, or may embrace the entire undertaking of the corporation. The requirement is better stated when it is said that the act in question must be done by the directing force of the company when carrying out his assigned function in the corporation. It is no defence to the application of this doctrine that a criminal act by a corporate employee cannot be within the scope of his authority unless expressly ordered to do the act in question. Such a condition would reduce the rule to virtually nothing. Acts of the ego of a corporation taken within the assigned managerial area may give rise to corporate criminal responsibility, whether or not there be formal delegation; whether or not there be awareness of the activity in the board of directors or the officers of the company; and, as discussed below, whether or not there be express prohibition.

. . . .

Generally the directing mind is also guilty of the criminal offence in question. Glanville Williams, in *Textbook of Criminal Law* (1978), states, at p. 947:

> . . . the director or other controlling officer will almost always be a co-perpetrator of or accessory in the offence . . . .

. . . .

The corporation is but a creature of statute, general or special, and none of the provincial corporation statutes and business corporations statutes, or the federal equivalents, contain any discussion of criminal liability or liability in the common law generally by reason of the doctrine of identification. It is a court-adopted principle put in place for the purpose of including the corporation in the pattern of criminal law in a rational relationship to that of the natural person. The identity doctrine merges the board of directors, the managing director, the superintendent, the manager or anyone else delegated by the board of directors to whom is delegated the governing executive authority of the corporation, and the conduct of any of the merged entities is thereby attributed to the corporation. . . . A corporation may, by this means, have more than one directing mind. This must be particularly so in a country such as Canada where corporate operations are frequently geographically widespread. The transportation companies, for example, must of necessity operate by the delegation and subdelegation of authority from the corporate centre; by the division and subdivision of the corporate brain; and by decentralizing by delegation the guiding forces in the corporate undertaking.

The court in *Dredge and Dock* decided that there could be corporate responsibility on the identification doctrine whether or not there had been formal delegation, awareness of the activity in the board of directors or offices of the company, or express authorization or prohibition. However, the court also noted that the identification doctrine could not be used where the criminal act of the directing mind had been totally in fraud of the corporation or where the act was intended to, or did result in, benefit exclusively to the directing mind.

The Australian scholar, Professor Brent Fisse (see, for example, "Corporate Criminal Responsibility" (1991), 15 Crim. L.J. 166 and "Criminal Law: The Attribution of Criminal Liability to Corporations: A Statutory Model" (1991), 13 Sydney L. Rev. 277) and others have called for a new approach for holding corporations responsible for intentional crimes. The argument is that under the identification doctrine the imputing of intent of employees to the corporate entity misses the point. Corporate behaviour is not just the sum of individual employee behaviour but must be considered in the context of the organizational structure and culture.

Professor Pamela Bucy, "Corporate Ethos: A Standard for Imposing Corporate Criminal Liability" (1991), 75 Minnesota L. Rev. 1095, has recently proposed a standard of corporate criminal liability which turns on whether there was a corporate ethos which encouraged the commission of crime. The inquiry is not only into whether the actors were sufficiently high in the hierarchy but also looks at such aspects as company goals and practices, the reaction to past offences and the existence and sufficiency of compliance programs.

(b) New *Criminal Code* Provisions for Organizations (2003)

Twenty-six miners died in the Westray mine explosion in Nova Scotia. Manslaughter charges were laid against two mine managers based on breaches of health and safety regulations. After protracted proceedings they were dropped. In 2003 the federal government, with all party consent, responded by enacting[1] a new and severe regime to hold corporations and other organizations criminally responsible.

There are now two avenues to criminal responsibility:

Offences of negligence — organizations

22.1 In respect of an offence that requires the prosecution to prove negligence, an organization is a party to the offence if

(a) acting within the scope of their authority

(i) one of its representatives is a party to the offence, or

(ii) two or more of its representatives engage in conduct, whether by act or omission, such that, if it had been the conduct of only one representative, that representative would have been a party to the offence; and

(b) the senior officer who is responsible for the aspect of the organization's activities that is relevant to the offence departs — or the senior officers, collectively, depart — markedly from the standard of care that, in the circumstances, could reasonably be expected to prevent a representative of the organization from being a party to the offence.

Other offences — organizations

22.2 In respect of an offence that requires the prosecution to prove fault — other than negligence — an organization is a party to the offence if, with the intent at least in part to benefit the organization, one of its senior officers

(a) acting within the scope of their authority, is a party to the offence;

(b) having the mental state required to be a party to the offence and acting within the scope of their authority, directs the work of other representatives of the organization so that they do the act or make the omission specified in the offence; or

---

1 S.C. 2003, c. 21, s. 2.

(c) knowing that a representative of the organization is or is about to be a party to the offence, does not take all reasonable measures to stop them from being a party to the offence.

The massive width of these new provisions becomes clearer when one reads the definitions in section 2 of the *Criminal Code* of the terms "organization" and "senior officer":

"organization" means

(a) a public body, body corporate, society, company, firm, partnership, trade union or municipality, or

(b) an association of persons that

(i) is created for a common purpose,

(ii) has an operational structure, and

(iii) holds itself out to the public as an association of persons;

"senior officer" means a representative who plays an important role in the establishment of an organization's policies or is responsible for managing an important aspect of the organization's activities and, in the case of a body corporate, includes a director, its chief executive officer and its chief financial officer;

The responsibility of the organization is no longer dependant on establishing fault in the "directing mind" but extends to a much lower level.

For a full analysis of the new law, see Todd Archibald, Kenneth Jull and Kent Roach, "The Changed Face of Corporate Liability" (2004), 48 *Crim. L.Q.* 306 and Paul Dusome, "Criminal Liability under Bill C-45: Paradigms, Prosecutors, Predicaments" (2007) 53 *Crim. L.Q.* 98. The authors suggest that the expansion of corporate liability is overdue. However they criticise the new regime as being too broad, for a counter-intuitive extension of corporate liability for subjective intent offences to senior officers, and for blurring the distinction between regulatory and criminal liability. Surprisingly, there is as yet no judicial interpretation to consider.

2   CRIMINAL ORGANIZATIONS[2]

In 1997 the *Criminal Code* was amended[3] to include a wide variety of measures against "criminal organizations". Before considering the new substantive provisions we need first to assess their political origins in gang violence in Quebec.

---

2 Many of the notes in this section first appeared in Stuart, "Politically Expedient but Potentially Unjust Criminal Legislation against Gangs" (1998), 69 *Int. Rev. Penal Law* 245. This was a much expanded version of a paper of like name first published in (1997), 2 *Can. Crim. L.R.* 207. See too Michael Moon, "Outlawing the Outlaws: Importing R.I.C.O.'s Notion of Criminal Enterprise into Canada to Combat Organized Crime" (1999), 24 *Queen's L.J.* 451.

3 S.C. 1997, c.23.

(a) Biker Violence

The immediate context was the eve of a 1997 federal election and the perceived need to respond to a plea by the Quebec Attorney General and Quebec mayors for measures to address a violent and protracted fight between two biker gangs: the Hells Angels and the Rock Machine. That strife, focused in Quebec, had led to bombings and some thirty deaths. One bomb blast killed an innocent passer-by, a young boy. Members of the public were understandably outraged and frightened.

The federal Minister of Justice and the Solicitor General of Canada described[4] the new Bill C-95 as "tough new measures to target criminal gang activity" which had been developed through "extensive consultations with police across Canada" and a two-day national forum. That forum, held in Ottawa on September 27-28, 1996, had brought together "police, representatives from provincial and federal governments, the legal community, private industry and academics". The purpose of the forum had been to "examine the increasingly complex problem of organized crime in Canada, and to recommend integrated, effective measures to address it".

Consideration of whether any measures were necessary was thus a question not on the agenda.

The centrepiece, explained the Ministers, was a new offence of "participation in a criminal organization". This did not criminalise mere membership in a criminal organization and laid the groundwork for the targeted use of new investigative tools to be directed against criminal organizations. These included special peace bonds, new powers to seize proceeds of crime, including access to income tax information, a new possession of explosive offence, tougher and consecutive sentencing provisions, greater powers to resort to electronic surveillance and a new reverse onus bail provision for those charged with the new offences. Bill C-95 was extremely complex, consisting of over 50 pages of detailed *Criminal Code* amendments. It passed with all party consent through Parliament in a day with no meaningful committee review, for example, of the extensive police powers which read like a police wish list.

(b) Participation in Criminal Organization (Gangsterism) (1997)

The new crime in s. 467.1(1) of participation in a criminal organization, often dubbed gangsterism in the media, extended criminal responsibility beyond the already wide net for accessories or conspirators. Under s. 467.1(2) there must be a mandatory consecutive sentence and double criminality for a participant in a criminal organization who is a party to an offence committed in association with the organization.

The lynchpin is the definition of "criminal organization" inserted in 1997 into the *Criminal Code* definition section 2 as follows:

---

4 Department of Justice News Release, "Federal Government Introduces National Anti-gang Measures", April 17, 1997.

"Criminal organization" means any group, association or other body consisting of five or more persons, whether formally or informally organized,

(a) having as one of its primary activities the commission of an indictable offence under this or any other Act of Parliament for which the maximum punishment is imprisonment for five years or more, and

(b) any or all of the members of which engage in or have, within the preceding five years, engaged in the commission of a series of such offences.

This extended far beyond a cohesive gang committed to violence. This legislation does not just reach such broadly-structured gangs as the Mafia, the Hells Angels[5] or the Triads. It could certainly be applied to low level members of a highly organised gang, to those only very loosely associated in crime and to those who have never been violent. Only one of the group has to have committed a series of offences within five years. There is no requirement of gang continuity.

Consider the following hypothetical example of drugs distribution in a predominantly black area of Toronto. A buys a quantity of drugs from a high level drugs dealer. Rather than attempt to sell the drugs himself he approaches fellow black friends, B and C, and acquaintances, D and E, with an offer of easy money. A is the only one with a criminal record of three offences within the last three years — selling marihuana and two breaking and entry. A arranges for the five to meet in a park to split up the cache. The meeting takes place but B and D do not attend. A subsequently meets with them separately. Under Bill C-95 this is a criminal organization. It does not matter that there was no meeting of the minds required for the crime of conspiracy or that this was not an ongoing or structured group. The possible application of Bill C-95's array of strong new measures to such a group came at a time of a major Commission Report documenting systemic racism against black youths in Toronto,[6] particularly in the enforcement of drugs laws.

At its widest the complex new crime of participation in organized crime was committed by proof of

1. an association with an informal group of five or more;

2. knowledge that at least one of the group has been committing serious crimes within the last five years; and

3. being a party to an indictable offence in association with the group.

Section 467.1 has breathtaking scope and could surely be applied to most engaged in criminal conduct. It could certainly be applied to the above-described

---

5 In *Brown v. Durham Regional Police Department* (1996) 106 C.C.C. (3d) 302 (Ont. Gen. Div.), a civil action against the police, the court heard detailed evidence about motorcycle gangs in Canada. Ferguson J. noted that "the evidence showed that even organized clubs like the Hells Angels chapters appear to operate more as a brokerage of criminals than as a cohesive vertical hierarchy of criminal activity" (at 317).

6 *Report of the Commission on Systemic Racism in the Ontario Criminal Justice System* (1995).

temporary group of drugs traffickers.[7] It is expressly a form of guilt by association long shunned by common law jurisdictions which normally require proof by the state of an individual act with personal fault relating to that act or a shared purpose. The requirement of being a party to an offence does require proof of some individual act and personal fault. However this could merely be that required for liability as an accessory rather than perpetrator and could include anyone assisting another to commit a crime such as driving the getaway vehicle, or even merely providing it.

The new Canadian anti-gang provision is unlike the Italian *associazione di tipo Mafioso*,[8] which criminalizes membership in certain criminal associations. It is also distinguishable from the French *association de malfaiteurs*,[9] which penalises group preparation equally to the completed offence.

The Canadian scheme appears to be a much wider version of the United States RICO model. Passed in 1970 as a weapon against organized crime, the *Racketeer Influenced and Corrupt Organizations Act*[10] requires proof of an "enterprise"[11] and a connected "pattern of racketeering activity".[12] Although the RICO net is itself notoriously wide, there is, in contrast to the Canadian model, a requirement of an ongoing structure of persons associated in time and purpose and organized for consensual decision-making.[13]

It has been suggested[14] that a proper definition of organized crime should embrace the elements of corruption, violence, sophistication, continuity, structure, discipline, ideology, multiple enterprises, involvement in legitimate enterprises and a "bonding" ritual.

Professor Christopher Blakesley reviewed[15] several national studies presented at an international conference in Alexandria, Egypt from November 8-12, 1997, as to the dangers of adopting ill-considered criminal legislation on organized crime and concluded as follows:

---

7   Robert Gordon, "Criminal Business Organizations, Street Gangs and "Wanna-be Groups": A Vancouver Perspective", (2000) 42 Can. J. of Crim. 39 distinguishes the highly organised for-profit crime business, organised street gangs and the "wanna-be" unorganised groups which are typically young offenders.

8   In the 1987 show trial of alleged Sicilian Mafia members in Palermo, 344 were convicted and sentenced to a total of 2665 years in prison. By 1989 only 60 persons remained in prison: see Jean-Paul Brodeur, "Organized Crime: Trends in the Literature", a report to the Departments of Justice and the Solicitor General (May 1966), pp.28-29.

9   There are so few prosecutions that the crime is not listed in the French Department of Justice statistics: Brodeur, ibid., p.28.

10 18 U.S.C. ss.1961-1964.

11 Under s. 1961(4) an "enterprise" may be "any individual, partnership, corporation, association, or other legal entity, or any union or group of individuals associated in fact although not a legal entity".

12 A wide list of federal and state offences are enumerated as predicate offences ranging from murder to mail fraud: s.1961.

13 See Christopher Blakesley, "The Criminal Justice System Facing The Challenge of Organized Crime: Section II. The Special Part", at p.14 of an unpublished explanatory note written in preparation for the XVIth International Congress of Penal Law held in Budapest, Hungary, September 5-11, 1999.

14 Michael Maltz, "Defining Organized Crime", in Handbook of Organized Crime in the United States (1994) p.26

15 "General Report. The Criminal Justice System Facing the Challenge of Organised Crime", (1998) 69 Int. Rev. Penal Law 69.

It is easy to fall into the trap: politicians gain popularity and votes by looking "tough on crime", especially organised crime. They become even more popular when they are able to say bad things about courts that try to rectify the constitutional problems created by bad laws. Sadly, often the news media exacerbate the problem by pandering to public fear and appetite for salacious material. Outcries from interest groups are shrill, raising the cost to anyone who wishes to promote reasoned and constitutional laws. This all creates an atmosphere that tends to ignore the larger picture and which may actually hurt the battle against crime, while damaging human rights and democracy.[16]

(c) Fiasco of Manitoba Warriors Trial[17]

That the new anti-gang measures were not narrowly targeted became clear in the case of gangsterism charges laid in the trial of the Manitoba Warriors in Winnipeg.

In October 1998, police and prosecutors threw the new book at 35 accused. Most were charged with drugs and weapons charges and the new participation in a criminal organization offence involving the Manitoba Warriors. This was alleged to be a predominantly aboriginal street gang. The Crown proceeded by direct indictment. Of those charged, all but two were aboriginal. The hype and complexity escalated to such an extent that the Manitoba government constructed a custom-built high security court in an old mustard-seed cleaning plant. Many applied for bail. None succeeded. Review applications also failed. The new reverse onus bail provision for organised crime may have contributed to this extraordinary detention. The remand centre conditions were severe with contact visits severely limited. At appearances in the special courthouse accused were chained to the floor in special separate cubicles.

The public gallery was limited to 35 seats with an obstructed view which would not have permitted them to see the jury. After 20 months of pre-trial motions and guilty pleas only 15 accused remained. Finally outside counsel were employed to reach a plea bargain. As part of the deal the participation in a criminal organization charges were withdrawn. In all 32 guilty pleas were entered on drugs charges including trafficking of cocaine in Winnipeg hotels. Only two guilty pleas were entered at an early stage to the participation in a criminal organization charges and these only involved lesser participants. The cost of building the courthouse was $3.3 million and the total cost of this trial has been estimated at $7 million.

The final outcome of this show trial is a monument to State folly. Roland Penner, a former Attorney General for Manitoba, has described it as "politically motivated, expensive and constitutionally invalid".[18] Professor David Deutscher

---

16 At p. 4.

17 This account was first published in Stuart, "Time to Recodify Criminal Law and Rise Above Law and Order Expediency: Lessons from the Manitoba Warrior Prosecution", (2001) 28 Manitoba L.J. 89. The major sources for this account are the judgment of Krindle J. in *R. v. Pangman* (2000), 32 C.R. (5th) 272 (Man. Q.B.) dismissing the application for a change of venue, a CBC Magazine program "The Indian Courthouse" of November 15, 1999 and "Gang-related Charges Dropped Against Alleged Warriors", Globe and Mail, July 8, 2000.

18 *Globe and Mail, ibid.*

suggests it was "too complex, with too many accused and too many charges to have a chance of success".[19]

Only the most avid and self-congratulatory prosecutor could pronounce this trial as a success and a vindication of the anti-gang measures.[20] In terms of organised crime this street gang was, as even the Crown counsel put it, "in the junior leagues". Having endured this extraordinary use of state power, the Manitoba Warriors has been given notoriety and experienced an extraordinary use of state power which may lead, in a counterproductive way, to a more cohesive group in the future. As suggested by defence counsel Richard Peck:

> This has given them identity, empowerment and a sense of belonging which has been denied to them by society at large.[21]

Shouldn't this matter have been treated as a routine drugs conspiracy trial with discretion exercised to target only the major participants? At worst this was state action based on false stereotypes of aboriginal people.

(d) Widening Gangsterism Laws (2001)

The political cycle started again on the eve of another federal election in 2001. On September 12, 2000, a Montreal crime reporter was shot several times the day after he had published an expose of organised crime. By September 14, 2000, a Quebec Minister, Serge Menard, was calling for new and clearer organised laws to prohibit mere membership in criminal gangs like the Hells Angels and the Rock Machine and the use of the notwithstanding clause to trump any *Charter* claim of freedom of association. It is stunning that this initiative came from a province in which the invocation of the *War Measures Act* in 1970 and the banning of the F.L.Q. terrorist group led to the arrests of hundreds of innocent Quebecois. Canada does not need laws of guilt by association or any overriding of *Charter* rights.[22]

On the eve of the election a Parliamentary sub-committee on organised crime[23] held *in camera* hearings. Some MP's seemed troubled by the experience of the Manitoba Warriors trial. But no MP subsequently saw this test case as pointing to the dangers of Parliament's overbroad anti-gang quick fix. The Committee released a hastily drafted report with numerous recommendations to toughen the anti-gang laws. During the election campaign all politicians agreed that something more needed to be done about gangs. No politician dared to raise questions.

---

19 *Ibid.*

20 "Fontaine made fool of himself", *Winnipeg Free Press*, July 12, 2000. The remarks are attributed to Crown Attorney Bob Morrison at the final sentence hearing and were directed against remarks of Phil Fontaine, then National Chief of the Assembly of First Nations, who had been critical of the process.

21 *Winnipeg Free Press*, July 13, 2000.

22 See too Kent Roach, "Panicking over Criminal Organizations: We Don't Need Another Offence" (2000), 44 *Crim. L.Q.* 1.

23 Sub-committee on Organised Crime of the Standing Committee on Justice and Human Rights, *Combatting Organised Crime* (October, 2000).

After the election Bill C-24 proceeded rapidly through a committee hearing. It contained 70 printed pages of complicated amendments to the *Criminal Code* and other federal statutes. The *Proceeds of Crime (Money Laundering) Act* was substantially widened to embrace the seizure, freezing and confiscation of proceeds of most indictable offences rather than the 40 previously listed as "enterprise crimes". There are new offences to single out intimidation against people in the justice system including witnesses, jurors, prosecutors, guards, judges and politicians.

It also snuck in a Ministerial power to designate in ss. 25.1 and 25.2 police officers to break the law whether the target was organized crime or not. This power to designate can even be delegated to other police officers and is general rather than case specific. It is the antithesis of the rule of law. Despite the opposition of the CBA and others it also became law. Critics were fobbed off on a promise of Parliamentary review.

We concentrate here on the bill's widening of the criminal organization definition and the anti-gang offences. Since Bill C-24 the new definition of a criminal organization is found in s. 467.1 as follows:

> "criminal organization" means a group, however organized, that is composed of three or more persons and that has as one of its main purposes or main activities the facilitation or commission of one or more serious offences that, if committed, would likely result in the direct or indirect receipt of a material benefit, including a financial benefit, by the group or by any of the persons who constitute the group. It does not include a group of persons that forms randomly for the immediate commission of a single offence.

Under the same section

> "serious offence" means an indictable offence under this or any other Act of Parliament for which the maximum punishment is imprisonment for five years or more, or another offence that is prescribed by regulation.

The Department of Justice Backgrounder "Highlights of the Organized Crime Bill" released on its website on April 5, 2001 explains that a new definition of criminal organization was drafted to respond to concerns expressed by police and prosecutors that the current definition was "too complex and too narrow in scope". Ironically by this time convictions had been registered in Quebec under the new gangsterism laws against members of the Hells Angels and Rock Machine.[24] The Department of Justice nevertheless pressed on with the broadening of the existing definition in three ways by:

1. reducing the number of people required to constitute a criminal organization from five to three;

2. removing the requirement that at least one of the members be involved in committing crimes for the organization within the past 5 years; and

---

24 Two mega-trials of bikers in Quebec produced huge problems of cost, drain on legal aid, severance motions, disclosure, delay and complexity: see Anne-Marie Boisvert, "Mega Trials: The Disturbing Situation in Quebec" (2004), 15 C.R. (6th) 181.

3. extending the scope of offences which define criminal organizations, previously limited to indictable offences punishable by five years or more, to all serious crimes.

The bill removes the feeble limits on the definition of organized crime previously in place. To speak of a criminal organization of three seems laughable until we remember the huge scope of State power this definition will authorise. The Backgrounder explains that the inclusion of serious offences is to include "signature" crimes such as prostitution or gambling. This glosses over the reality that prostitution *per se* is not a crime. The power to add a list of crimes by regulation unreviewable by Parliament is the antithesis of democracy or the rule of law. The new definition does add one limit exclusion of a group formed "randomly for the immediate commission of a single offence". This is a welcome recognition of the need for continuity but it is very weak protection and is unlikely to exclude loose collectivities to distribute drugs to others and thereby involving multiple offences.

The Backgrounder also stresses that what is made criminal, subject to consecutive penalties as before, is *knowing participation* in activities that further the organizations objectives. Here the Backgrounder is shockingly misleading. When three new offence definitions the Bill creates are examined[25] it is clear that these elements of knowledge and participation are so comprised as to be a sham:

Participation in activities of criminal organization

467.11 (1) Every person who, for the purpose of enhancing the ability of a criminal organization to facilitate or commit an indictable offence under this or any other Act of Parliament, knowingly, by act or omission, participates in or contributes to any activity of the criminal organization is guilty of an indictable offence and liable to imprisonment for a term not exceeding five years.

Prosecution

(2) In a prosecution for an offence under subsection (1), it is not necessary for the prosecutor to prove that

(a) the criminal organization actually facilitated or committed an indictable offence;

(b) the participation or contribution of the accused actually enhanced the ability of the criminal organization to facilitate or commit an indictable offence;

(c) the accused knew the specific nature of any indictable offence that may have been facilitated or committed by the criminal organization; or

(d) the accused knew the identity of any of the persons who constitute the criminal organization.

Factors

(3) In determining whether an accused participates in or contributes to any activity of a criminal organization, the court may consider, among other factors, whether the accused

---

25 See too the further definition of criminal organization. Under ss. (2) facilitation of an offence does not require knowledge of a particular offence the commission of which is facilitated, or that an offence actually be committed. Under ss. (3) committing an offence means being a party to it or counselling any person to be a party to it.

(a) uses a name, word, symbol or other representation that identifies, or is associated with, the criminal organization;

(b) frequently associates with any of the persons who constitute the criminal organization;

(c) receives any benefit from the criminal organization; or

(d) repeatedly engages in activities at the instruction of any of the persons who constitute the criminal organization.

Commission of offence for criminal organization

467.12 (1) Every person who commits an indictable offence under this or any other Act of Parliament for the benefit of, at the direction of, or in association with, a criminal organization is guilty of an indictable offence and liable to imprisonment for a term not exceeding fourteen years.

Prosecution

(2) In a prosecution for an offence under subsection (1), it is not necessary for the prosecutor to prove that the accused knew the identity of any of the persons who constitute the criminal organization.

Instructing commission of offence for criminal organization

467.13 (1) Every person who is one of the persons who constitute a criminal organization and who knowingly instructs, directly or indirectly, any person to commit an offence under this or any other Act of Parliament for the benefit of, at the direction of, or in association with, the criminal organization is guilty of an indictable offence and liable to imprisonment for life.

Prosecution

(2) In a prosecution for an offence under subsection (1), it is not necessary for the prosecutor to prove that

(a) an offence other than the offence under subsection (1) was actually committed;

(b) the accused instructed a particular person to commit an offence; or

(c) the accused knew the identity of all of the persons who constitute the criminal organization.

It can be seen that knowledge is expressly not required to be proved of the crime to be facilitated or committed or of the identity of the members of the criminal organization. That is a knowledge requirement that has no real meaning and points to absolute responsibility which is unconstitutional where the liberty interest is at stake.[26] So too it is express that no crime need to have been facilitated or committed by the criminal organization or even made more likely. Even the Backgrounder acknowledges the "provisions could target anyone (not just members)". Contrast the focus in conspiracy jurisprudence on a meeting of the minds on a common purpose. As Justice Dickson put it in *Cotroni, Papalia* (1979):[27]

---

26 *Motor Vehicle Reference* (1985), 48 C.R. (3d) 289 (S.C.C.); *Pontes* (1995), 41 C.R. (4th) 201 (S.C.C.).

27 45 C.C.C. (2d) 1 (S.C.C.).

The word "conspire" derives from two Latin words, "con" and "spirare", meaning "to breathe together". To conspire is to agree....There must be evidence beyond a reasonable doubt that the alleged conspirators acted in concert in pursuit of a common goal".[28]

Charter challenges to the new scheme based on vagueness, overbreadth and lack of fault were rejected by Fuerst J. in *R. v. Lindsay* (2004), 20 C.R. (6th) 376 (Ont. S.C.). The court however read into the knowledge requirement a requirement of proof of knowledge of the composition of the criminal organization although not of the identity of those in the group. In contrast in *R. v. Accused No. 1*, 2005 CarswellBC 2982, 134 C.R.R. (2d) 274 (B.C. S.C.), Holmes J. struck down the new definition of criminal organization as too vague and too broad. However her decision was soon reversed by the B.C.C.A. in *R. v. Terezakis* (2007), 51 C.R. (6th) 165, 223 C.C.C. (3d) 344 (B.C. C.A.), leave to appeal refused (2008), 226 C.C.C. (3d) vi (note) (S.C.C.). In 2009 the Ontario Court of Appeal had little difficulty rejecting the appeal in *Lindsay* (2009), 245 C.C.C. (3d) 301 (Ont. C.A.).[29] Even if the new laws survive *Charter* challenge, the blunderbuss laws will do no credit to the Canadian justice system and may lead to injustice.

The new three category approach to participation in organized crime is anything but simple and will itself add to the complexity of trials. Quite apart from the Manitoba Warriors prosecution, gangsterism trials in Alberta and Quebec have followed the pattern of excessive length, complexity and cost. Even before this legislation it was never desirable to have mass trials.

3. TERRORIST GROUPS[30]

(a)   9/11 Attacks

Seeing those planes explode into the World Trade Center buildings, the towers falling and the horrifying destruction of life are memories we will always have. We all feel more vulnerable. Most expected our government to be proactive on our behalf. It is easy to support the allocation of significant sums of government money for preventive measures such as better airport security, medicine to counteract anthrax, more anti-terrorist police and CSIS personnel, and even for our military assistance to the United State's uncomfortable war in Afghanistan. Those planning or committing acts of violent terrorism should be arrested, prosecuted and severely punished.

However the complex new criminal laws which Bill C-36 added to our permanent laws led to opposition in some quarters at the time they were rushed

---

28 At 17-18.

29 See the comprehensive and highly critical review by Miles Hastie, "The Separate Offence of Committing a Crime 'In Association with' a Criminal Organization: Gangs Symbols and Signs of Constitutional Problems" (2009) 14 *Can. Crim. L. Rev.* 79.

30 Most of the notes in this section first appeared in Stuart, "The Anti-Terrorism Bill C-36: An Unnecessary Law and Order Quick Fix that Permanently Stains the Canadian Criminal Justice System" (2002), 14.1 *Nat. J. of Const. L.* 153. Compare however Stanley Cohen, "Safeguards and Justification for Canada's New Terrorism Act" (2002), 14.1 *Nat. J. of Const. L.* 99. See too 24 conference essays from a U. of T. conference in Daniels, Macklem and Roach (ed.), *The Security of Freedom. Essays on Canada's Anti-Terrorism Bill* (2001, U. of T. Press).

through Parliament, opposition which still continues. Some argue that when the State turns to its power to investigate, detain, punish and imprison, the standard of justification should be high, even in extraordinary times. Basic principles of a criminal justice system that deserves the name require the state to prove both that the individual acted and was at fault, that responsibility be fairly labelled and that any punishment be proportionate to the accused's actions.

(b)   Definition of Terrorism

To many critics the fatal flaw in Bill C-36 is its very wide definition of "terrorist activity" in s. 83.01. It decides who can be charged as a terrorist and against whom extensive new investigative powers can be exercised. In one respect the definition may be unduly narrow. There is no wisdom in requiring proof of a motive under s. 83.01(1)(b)(i)(A) of "a political, religious or ideological purpose, objective or cause". For years criminal law has sought to avoid proof of a bad motive as a requirement for criminal responsibility. It is too hard to prove and may, as here, lead to curious results. Why should a violent terrorist with unfathomable motives not be included? On this point the government was stubbornly adamant. Perhaps the political problem may be that if the government had conceded that point, its case for special new laws would have been even weaker. The unfortunate reality of retaining the motive clause is that there will be religious and political targeting.

A most contentious aspect of the new definition remains the wide extension in s. 83.01(1)(b)(ii)(E) to those who intend to cause "serious interference with or serious disruption of an essential service, facility or system, whether public or private, other than as a result of advocacy, protest, dissent or stoppage of work that is not intended to result in the conduct or harm referred to in any of clauses (A) to (C)" [which include intending to cause a serious risk to the safety of the public].

At first reading the bill purported to exempt "lawful protest". That exemption was not worth the paper it was written on as most protesters in Canada have, when charged, been convicted of at least obstruction offences. The government finally removed the word "lawful" from "protest". This may afford some protection to protesters. However it refused to remove clause (E) altogether as so many, including then Liberal backbencher Irwin Cotler,[31] had urged. The overbreadth dangers have been reduced but remain a serious concern.

Do you think that the following activities could still be investigated, charged and punished as terrorism?

1. Aboriginal groups' blockading of logger roads to assert aboriginal title.

2. Anti-globalisation protests, such as those which occurred in Quebec City.

3. Disruptive passive resistance inspired by Mahatma Gandhi.

---

31 See Cotler, "Thinking Outside the Box: Foundational Principles for a Counter-Terrorism Law and Policy", in *The Security of Freedom, ibid.,* pp. 111-129.

4. Labour union stoppages of many types.

5. Sending aid to an Afghanistan refugee group later determined to be involved in terrorist activity.

6. Community groups sponsoring Muslim immigration into Canada where an immigrant is allegedly involved in terrorist activities in the country of origin, even if this was some time in the past.

7. A person claiming refugee status in Canada has to establish fear of political persecution from his or her country of origin. It would not be difficult for opponents in that country to provide intelligence to Canada that the refugee had participated in terrorism.

8. Gangs of bikers or even a couple of youths out to disrupt the town.

Equally, if not even more contentious, is the alternative way the legislation permits persons to be branded as terrorists. The Governor-in-Council, on the recommendation of the Solicitor General, is now empowered to name by regulation a list of terrorist entities (s. 83.05). This designation is based on a determination by the Government, in private and without public debate and based merely on reasonable grounds rather than proof in a court of law. There is strong argument that this power violates the presumption of innocence in s. 11(d), which requires proof beyond reasonable doubt of essential elements before a fair and independent tribunal.[32] The Government amendments did include a provision (s. 83.05(5)) for after-the-event review by a judge but there is a power for a judge to prevent disclosure of information for reasons of national security. In this definition of terrorism, there is a great difference between what the Government told Canadians it intended and what the bill says. In its original Backgrounder entitled "Highlights of Anti-Terrorism Act" the claim was that:

> This definition and designation framework will provide clear guidance to police, prosecutors, the courts and the public on what constitutes a terrorist group or activity while protecting the lawful activities of legitimate political or lobby organizations.

> Recently UN Secretary General Kofi Annan has urged UN members to agree on a definition of terrorism as any action:

>> intended to cause death or serious bodily harm to civilians or non-combatants with the purpose of intimidating a population or compelling a government or an international organization to do or abstain from doing any act.[33]

Similarly in *Suresh v. Canada*,[34] in the context of a review of the controversial power to detain on security certificates without any charge, the Supreme Court adopted as a definition of terrorism for the *Immigration Act* that from the International Convention for the Suppression of Terrorism of any:

---

32 See further Kent Roach, "Listing and the Law" (2009) 55 *Crim. L.Q.* 1.
33 Report of March 21, 2005.
34 [2002] 1 S.C.R. 3

act intended to cause death or serious bodily injury to a civilian, or to any other person not taking part in the hostilities in a situation of armed conflict, when the purpose of such act, by its nature or context, is to intimidate a population, or to compel a government or an organization to do or abstain from doing any act.[35]

These definitions are considerably narrower than those to be found in the very complex definition in ATA.

(c)   Broad New Offences

Being branded as a terrorist in one of these ways is not an offence. The bill creates new offences of Participating, Facilitating, Instructing and Harbouring.[36] We will focus critical attention here on the new offence of knowingly participating or contributing to terrorist activities. Similar criticism could be advanced against the other three offences. So what on earth, some might say, is wrong with creating a crime of knowingly participating in terrorist activity? The Backgrounder gives as an example the act of knowingly recruiting into the group new individuals for the purpose of enhancing the ability of the terrorist group to aid, abet or commit indictable offences.

The problem is that Parliament, just as it did earlier in the case of the creation of a crime of knowingly participating in a criminal organization, has cynically legislated out of existence any meaningful test of knowledge or meaningful test of participating or contributing. Here again the devil is in the detail.

The definition section is s. 83.18(1):

Every one who knowingly participates in or contributes to, directly or indirectly, any activity of a terrorist group for the purpose of enhancing the ability of any terrorist group to facilitate or carry out a terrorist activity is guilty of an indictable offence and liable to imprisonment for a term not exceeding ten years.

So there is here a fault requirement of actual knowledge plus a purpose of enhancing the terrorist group's ability to facilitate or carry out a terrorist activity. Yet consider the next subsection, which had a strange and revealing heading "Prosecution" in the original bill:

(2) An offence may be committed under subsection (1) whether or not

(a) a terrorist group actually facilitates or carries out a terrorist activity;

(b) the participation or contribution of the accused actually enhances the ability of a terrorist group to facilitate or carry out a terrorist activity; or

(c) the accused knows the specific nature of any terrorist activity that may be facilitated or carried out by a terrorist group.

---

35 Para. 98.

36 For a full analysis see Kent Roach, "The New Terrorism Offences and the Criminal Law", *The Security of Freedom*, *supra* note 30, pp.151-172. See too Martha Shaffer, "Effectiveness of Anti-Terrorism Legislation. Does Bill C-36 Give Us What We Need?" *The Security of Freedom*, *supra* note 30, pp. 195-204. She also called for withdrawal of the bill.

Then we find a definition of participating or contributing which includes acts as vague as

> (b) providing or offering to provide a skill or an expertise for the benefit of, at the direction of or in association with a terrorist group

> (d)...remaining in any country for the benefit of, at the direction of or in association with a terrorist group.

Bar Association representatives pointed out to the Parliamentary committee that clause (b) is inconsistent with the proper legal representation of those affected by these new terrorist laws. The Government did not bother to respond. Clause (d) is particularly stunning. It establishes guilt by association wherever you are in the world and whatever you are doing! The maximum sentence on conviction for such knowing participation in terrorism is 10 years (s. 83.18). This must be served consecutive to a sentence for any other offence (s. 83.26).

When such criminalization is read in conjunction with the wide ways you can be branded as a terrorist, there would be good arguments that such provisions violate section 7 *Charter* protections requiring meaningful act and fault requirements. The Supreme Court has held that you cannot substitute elements to avoid fault standards[37] and that minimum fault standards established by the court cannot be watered down.[38] Excluding a mistaken belief defence respecting an essential element of a crime has been held to be unconstitutional.[39] The court has re-asserted as a fundamental principle that the State prove a voluntary physical act.[40] In Bill C-36 there is often no real act requirement and there is no clear requirement that the accused knew that the group is involved in the acts which constitute terrorism. Other *Charter* arguments would be vagueness and overbreadth and disproportionate punishment contrary to the cruel and unusual punishment protection of section 12.

Charter challenges were rejected by the Ontario Court of Appeal in the 2010 appeals of *Khawaja* and *U.S. v. Nadaraj*.[41] The Court seemed little interested in taking the *Charter* arguments seriously and much more concerned to impose long prison sentences. It contented itself with a detailed analysis of the complex ATA provisions and found that the *mens rea* provisions required a specific and high degree of moral culpability, and that the scheme was not too vague or overbroad. Section 7 *Charter* challenges based on vagueness or overbreadth long recognised by the Supreme Court are admittedly unruly. Lower courts have, as here, almost always dismissed them.

Even if these new provisions are *Charter*-proof the larger issue is whether the new offences risk injustice in the form of unfair labelling and huge and dangerous overreaching of State power.

---

37 *Vaillancourt,* [1987] 2 S.C.R. 636.
38 *Supra* note 34.
39 *Hess and Nguyen,* [1990] 2 S.C.R. 906.
40 *Ruzic* (2001), 41 C.R. (5th) 1 (S.C.C.). The court also speaks of no criminal responsibility where there is "moral involuntariness".
41 (2011), 81 C.R. (6th) 285 (Ont. C.A.) and (2011), 82 C.R. (6th) 122 (Ont. C.A.).

(d) Three-Year Review

In 2006, the three-year review proceeded through Parliament. Some argued that the government of the day should withdraw the whole ATA as thorough overkill and unnecessary given existing *Criminal Code* offences and state powers. This did not occur. Canadian governments of any stripe have clearly fallen for the worldwide lure of special anti-terrorist laws. It is interesting to note proposals made by then backbencher Irwin Cotler that were not accepted by the Liberal government at the time of passage:[42]

1. Removal of the motive requirement of a religious or an ideological purpose as this provides an unnecessary defence and could be relied on for discriminatory law enforcement;

2. Delete clause E, which ensnares those intending to disrupt essential services, as this could be stretched to characterise as terrorist acts of protestors never intended to be caught;

3. Prior notice before being listed as a terrorist group;

4. Crime of facilitation should require that the facilitator know the group is engaged in terrorism;

5. Meaningful oversight by a Parliamentary officer or the Security Intelligence Review Commission;

6. Judicial rather than ministerial authority to authorise foreign intercepts originating or ending in Canada;

7. No suppression of information depriving an accused of the right to know and contest State evidence; and

8. The inclusion of an anti-discrimination clause

The government did not respond to such conerns or to the amendments urged in such detail and with such persuasive force by Professor Kent Roach before the Senate ATA Review Committee.[43]

A major problem with a broad definition of terrorism and broad offences is that this can be used for racial profiling. Professor Ed Morgan[44] has suggested that the approach to this complex issue being developed by our courts should not be applied in other contexts such as immigration and border crossing, given

---

42 *Wholesale Travel Group Inc.*, [1991] 3 S.C.R. 154.

43 Kent Roach, "The Three Year Review of Canada's Anti-terrorism Act: The Need for Greater Restraint and Fairness, Non-Discrimination and Special Advocates" (2005). See too Kent Roach, "The Parliamentary Review of the Anti-Terrorist Act" (2007) 52 *Crim. L.Q.* 281. See also Kent Roach, "Ten Ways to Improve Canadian Anti-Terrorism Law", (2005) 51 *Crim. L.Q.* 102, Stuart, "Avoiding Myths and Challenging Minister of Justice Cotler to Undo the Injustices of Our Anti-Terrorism Act" (2005), 51 *Crim. L.Q.* 53 and Maureen Webb, "Essential Liberty or a Little Temporary Safety? The Review of the Canadian Anti-Terrorist Act" (2005), 51 *Crim. L.Q.* 53.

44 "Racial Profiling as an Investigative Tool", *Law Times*, October 15, 2002,

ubiquitous threat of mass violence since the 9/11 attacks. This view is surprisingly insensitive to the experience of Muslim and Arab Canadians who have presented significant anecdotal and survey evidence to Parliamentary committees that they have been, and continue to be, racially targeted under ATA and immigration powers. Principles being developed in the context of criminal trials seem equally applicable.[45]

---

45 See too Sujit Choudhry and Kent Roach, "Racial and Ethnic Profiling: Statutory Definition, Constitutional Remedies and Democratic Accountability" (2003), 41 *Osgoode Hall L.J.* 1 and Teem Bahdi, "No Exit : Racial Profiling and Canada's War Against Terrorism" (2003), 41 *Osgoode Hall L.J.* 293. See especially David Tanovich, *The Colour of Justice* (Irwin Law, 2006) pp. 105-118.

Chapter 11

SENTENCING

1. PRINCIPLES OF SENTENCING

See, generally, Allan Manson, *The Law of Sentencing* (Irwin Law, 2001), and Manson, Trotter, Healy, Roberts and Ives, eds., *Sentencing and Penal Policy in Canada* (2nd ed.) (Emond Montgomery, 2008).

R. v. SWEENEY

(1992), 11 C.R. (4th) 1, 71 C.C.C. (3d) 82,
1992 CarswellBC 460 (B.C. C.A.)

Sweeney was convicted of one count of criminal negligence causing death, one count of driving with a blood alcohol level in excess of .08 and one count of failing to remain at the scene of an accident. The incident took place on September 1, 1989, when Sweeney drove his motor vehicle into another while being chased by the police. The driver of the other vehicle was killed. Sweeney was 20 years old at the time of this offence. He was sentenced to four and one-half years' imprisonment on the first count, six months concurrent on the second and six months consecutive on the third. His right to drive was suspended for 15 years. The court allowed the appeal from sentence. The majority opinion was written by Hutcheon J.A., concurred in by McEachern C.J.B.C., Lambert, and Toy JJ.A. The court decided there was an error in principle when the trial judge used a sentencing starting point of five years' imprisonment for all drinking and driving offences causing either death or bodily harm. The court substituted a sentence of 18 months' imprisonment less one day for the sentence of four and one-half years imposed on the count of criminal negligence causing death, but did not interfere with the sentence of six months concurrent for impaired driving or the sentence of six months consecutive for failing to remain at the scene of the accident. The reason for deducting a single day from the 18 months was to indicate that, for this offender, provincial time would have been more appropriate than federal time. The driving prohibition of 15 years also remained. The majority judgment was relatively short. Separate and concurring reasons for judgment were delivered by Wood J.A.

Wood J.A. (McEachern C.J.B.C. concurring): —

These appeals presented the court with a rare opportunity to undertake a thorough re-examination of the principles governing the imposition of sanctions in our criminal justice system. We sat five judges so that we could embark upon that exercise free from the constraints imposed by previous decisions. I believe that it is important, not only for the guidance of trial judges, but also for the information of the public, that such an opportunity not be missed.

II

While the proper role of this court on a sentence appeal is to determine the fitness of the sentence imposed in the court below according to the application of recognized legal principles, we do not perform that function in a legal vacuum devoid of any understanding of the realities of life to which our decisions must be applied. In order to understand the approach which I have taken on these appeals, it is necessary to consider some of those realities which cannot be ignored while en route to a principled determination of the fitness of the sentences imposed below.

I start with the fact that the drinking driver is an enormous social problem. The numbers alone tell us that. Every year over 10,000 convictions are recorded in this province for drinking/driving offences. The experts agree that these numbers represent only a fraction of the number of such offences actually committed. While only a small number of those who are caught have caused death or bodily harm, it is beyond dispute that in most cases that is more the result of good luck than it is an accurate reflection of the risk or danger created by such an offender.

. . . .

Ordinary, reasonable and fair-minded people expect that any punishment meted out under our criminal law will bear some direct proportionality to the moral culpability of the offence for which it is imposed. For reasons which I will explain more fully later, the moral culpability of the offence of impaired driving *simpliciter* is the same as that of the same offence, committed by the same individual, which causes either death or bodily harm to an innocent victim, irrespective of whether the latter offence is characterized as impaired, dangerous or criminally negligent driving. That is because, apart from the personal circumstances relating to that offender, the moral culpability of both offences lies in the intention to drive a motor vehicle after having voluntarily consumed more alcohol than the law permits, together with a reckless disregard for the foreseeable consequences of such driving.

And yet the maximum penalties which Parliament has set for simple impaired driving and related offences are very much lower than those which it has mandated where an impaired driver causes either death or bodily harm. And while the tragic consequences of motor vehicle accidents caused by impaired drivers continue to shock and outrage our community, the daily parade of those convicted of simple impaired driving continues to pass with little comment. Furthermore, while the sentences imposed upon drinking/driving offenders who have caused either death or bodily harm have increased dramatically in the last decade, the average penalty imposed for the simple impaired driving or related offence, despite various Parliamentary initiatives, has not.

. . . .

Prior to 1985, at the discretion of Crown counsel, an impaired driver who caused death could face a charge of either criminal negligence causing death (s. 203), for which the maximum penalty was life imprisonment; manslaughter (s. 219), for which the maximum sentence was also life imprisonment; or criminal negligence in the operation of a motor vehicle (s. 233(1)), for which the maximum penalty was imprisonment for five years. By virtue of s. 589(5) of the *Criminal Code*, R.S.C. 1970, c. C-34, dangerous driving (which was also an offence under s. 233(4), and punishable as an indictable offence by imprisonment for up to two years) was an included offence of all three charges. For the impaired driver who caused bodily harm, the only available charge was criminal negligence causing bodily harm, for which the maximum punishment was imprisonment for 10 years.

The 1985 amendments, which did away with the offence of criminal negligence in the operation of a motor vehicle, increased the range of charges that can now be laid in a drinking/driving case resulting in either death or bodily harm:

s. 220	Criminal Negligence Causing Death	Life
s. 236	Manslaughter	Life
s. 221	Criminal Negligence Causing Bodily Harm	10 yrs.
s. 249(4)	Dangerous Driving Causing Death	14 yrs.
s. 249(3)	Dangerous Driving Causing Bodily Harm	10 yrs.
s. 255(3)	Impaired Driving Causing Death	14 yrs.
s. 255(2)	Impaired Driving Causing Bodily Harm	10 yrs.

The stated purpose of this Parliamentary initiative was to enhance the role of the criminal justice system in the war against the drinking driver. Thus it is important to note that the maximum sentences set for the offences created to address that specific problem, *i.e.*, impaired driving causing death and impaired driving causing bodily harm, were 14 years and 10 years respectively.

. . . .

In 1988, Parliament amended the *Criminal Code* by enacting subss. 735(1.1) to (1.4), which permit a judge to consider a written statement by the victim of an offence, or by the victim's close relatives, in which the harm done by the commission of the offence is described. By this amendment Parliament sought to ensure that the courts would not overlook the consequences to the victims of a crime when considering the seriousness of the offence committed.

Several things need to be said about these provisions. First of all, it is important to note that they are permissive, not mandatory. Thus, while they confirm the admissibility of victim impact statements in the sentencing process, they do not require that such statements be before the court. The result is that they will be present in some cases and not in others, a circumstance which necessarily minimizes the role which they can play in a principled approach to sentencing.

Secondly, they do not purport, and I do not believe that they were ever intended, to require the sentencing court to take a retributive approach when sentencing an offender. In *R. v. Hinch* (1967), 2 C.R.N.S. 350, [1968] 3 C.C.C. 39, Norris J.A., for a majority of this court concluded that there is no role for revenge in a principled system of sentencing. I endorse that view. Such a system requires a balanced, objective approach, separate and detached from the subjective consideration of retribution.

This does not mean, of course, that the tragic consequences to innocent victims are to be ignored when passing sentence on the convicted drinking driver. Indeed, as already noted, with the 1985 amendments Parliament specifically made those consequences part of the *actus reus* of the crime itself. And, notwithstanding the view of some, the courts have never been insensitive to the suffering which victims of crime must endure. The dilemma facing the sentencing court is to balance a proper consideration of the consequences of a criminal act against the reality that the criminal justice system was never designed or intended to heal the suffering of the victims of crime.

In few cases is that dilemma more acute than it is in connection with the offences under consideration in these appeals. The terrible consequences of drinking and driving shock the sensibilities of all of us, so much so that not only the surviving victims of such crimes, but also many impartial, reasonable and fair-minded people instinctively cry out for the harshest form of punishment for the offender.

But if the tragic consequences to innocent victims were to become the standard by which appropriate sentences for such offences are determined, the courts would soon be reduced to choosing between either imposing the maximum legal term of imprisonment in all cases or embarking upon a comparative analysis of the seriousness of the consequences in individual cases. The first alternative would be an abdication of our responsibility and the second is unthinkable.

(c) The Principles of Sentencing

Much has been written in recent years about the purpose of sentencing. In February of 1987 the Canadian Sentencing Commission, under the chair of Judge J.R. Omar Archambault, published its report entitled *Sentencing Reform: A Canadian Approach* (Ottawa: Supply and Services, 1987). That study was devoted to recommending legislative initiatives designed to correct perceived inadequacies in the existing sentencing process. While it would not be proper for the courts to implement specific legislative proposals, particularly when Parliament has chosen not to do so, the report nonetheless contains much information and learned discussion which is of assistance when searching for a principled judicial approach to sentencing within the existing legislative framework. Although I do not accept all of the commission's conclusions, much of what I have to say in this part of my reasons borrows heavily from the theoretical content and the informational material contained in its report.

At p. 153 of that report the Commission suggested the following "Fundamental Purpose of Sentencing":

> It is recognized and declared that in a free and democratic society peace and security can only be enjoyed through the due application of the principles of fundamental justice. In furtherance of the overall purpose of the criminal law of maintaining a just, peaceful and safe society, the fundamental purpose of sentencing is to preserve the authority of and promote respect for the law through the imposition of just sanctions.

This philosophical statement, which I adopt, finds a more practical equivalent in the simple proposition that the purpose of sentencing is to enhance the protection of society. That purpose is achieved if the imposition of legal sanctions discourages both convicted offenders from re-offending and those who have yet to offend from doing so at all. Overlying and influencing the ability of the legal sanction or sentencing process to achieve this purpose, however, is the extent to which that process enjoys the acceptance and respect of the community at large.

A number of factors govern the community's acceptance of the sentencing process. There is a prevailing belief that sentences should reflect, and be proportionate to, both "the gravity of the offence and the degree of responsibility of the offender". In my view the gravity of the offence and the degree of responsibility of the offender are determined by the moral culpability of the offender's conduct.

As a society, we long ago opted for a system of criminal justice in which the moral culpability of an offence is determined by the state of mind which accompanies the offender's unlawful act. Thus the consequences of an unlawful act when either intended, or foreseen and recklessly disregarded, aggravate its moral culpability. But consequences which are neither intended nor foreseen and recklessly ignored cannot aggravate the moral culpability of an unlawful act, except and to the extent that Parliament so decrees.

As I noted earlier, for the same offence committed by the same offender, the moral culpability of the offence of impaired driving *simpliciter* is the same as that of impaired driving causing either death or bodily harm. That is because in both cases the mental element of the crime consists of the intention to drive with a reckless disregard for foreseeable consequences. The fact that death or bodily harm does or does not result when any such offence is committed is more likely to be due to chance than to any circumstance of foreseeability, for such consequences are always foreseeable whenever a person impaired by alcohol gets behind the wheel of a car and drives.

The degree of moral culpability will, of course, vary from offender to offender according to a number of factors which will be discussed later in these reasons, all of which relate in some way to that person's state of mind. But, except to the extent that Parliament has made the consequences of impaired driving part of the *actus reus* of the offences under consideration, I do not accept that the moral culpability of an impaired driver who unintentionally, albeit recklessly, causes either death or bodily harm is greater than it would otherwise have been if he had been caught before such tragic consequences occurred.

And even though Parliament has made the consequences of impaired driving part of the *actus reus* of the offences under consideration, as a civilized society we recognize that the criminal justice system alone cannot be expected to eliminate criminal wrongdoing, a circumstance which necessarily means that we must show restraint when imposing punishment. Accountability of the offender, not punishment for the sake of punishment, must be the primary focus of the sentencing process. Thus any sentence imposed should be the least onerous sanction appropriate to the circumstances of both the offence and the offender.

Another factor which enhances community acceptance of the sentencing process is the extent to which it reflects consistency in the ultimate sanctions imposed upon like offenders for similar offences. However, while consistent treatment of like cases is an important goal in a principled approach to sentencing, the principle of accountability requires that the aggravating and mitigating circumstances peculiar to each offence and each offender be taken into account. Therefore, each sentence must, to some extent, be tailor-made for the circumstances peculiar to its own case. Any adherence to the principle of consistency which denies such legitimate variation would necessarily result in the imposition of arbitrary sanctions.

The respect which the community at large has for the sentencing process will also depend on the extent to which the specific goals of any sanction imposed can be seen to serve the ultimate purpose of sentencing. Those goals have traditionally been described as (i) general deterrence, (ii) specific deterrence, (iii) isolation, and (iv) rehabilitation. In recent years some cases and literature on the subject have suggested a fifth, which has come to be known as "denunciation". The Archambault Commission suggested a sixth called "just deserts". Each of these goals must be examined more closely, with particular reference to the offences under consideration in these appeals.

(i) General Deterrence

The theory behind the general deterrence goal of sentencing is that the legal sanction imposed on actual offenders will discourage potential offenders. While there is little empirical evidence to support such a theory, common sense tells us that to some extent, that must be so. Indeed, there can be little doubt but that the very existence of a criminal justice system acts as a deterrent which prevents many people from engaging in criminal conduct.

The problem with the theory lies in its extension to the conclusion, which I believe has been too easily accepted in the past, that the greater the sanction imposed in any given case, the greater will be its general deterrent effect. There is an increasingly persuasive body of evidence and learned opinion to the contrary.

In its report, at p. 136, the Archambault Commission noted:

> With regard to general deterrence, the overall assessment of the deterrent effects of criminal sanctions ranges from an attitude of great caution in expressing an opinion to outright scepticism.

. . . .

The Commission concluded that it is extremely doubtful that an exemplary sentence imposed in a particular case can have any perceptible effect in deterring potential offenders.

. . . .

(ii) Specific Deterrence

While it is easier, from a historical vantage, to determine whether any particular sanction has been successful in persuading an individual not to re-offend, there are also reasonable limits to the specific deterrent effect which can be expected from a sentence of imprisonment in connection with the offences under discussion. In many cases, of course, imprisonment will not be necessary to ensure that the individual does not re-offend. But in those cases where the court finds that such a sanction is necessary to meet the goal of specific deterrence, it would be unreasonable, in the absence of any cogent evidence to the contrary, to conclude that the specific deterrent value of a sentence of imprisonment will be any greater than its over-all general deterrent effect. Any person who would not likely be deterred by such a sentence falls into the category of offender for whom an isolative sentence must be considered.

(iii) *Isolation*

Isolation is achieved primarily by a sentence of imprisonment. It is justified as a "goal" of sentencing by the simple proposition that so long as an offender is separated from society, he or she cannot re-offend. In terms of the protection of society, it is the option of last resort. Even as such, it suffers from the ultimate weakness that if the fundamental requirement of proportionality is observed, the individual concerned must eventually be released from jail. Experience teaches us that most people emerge from prison a worse threat to society than when they entered. Thus care and restraint must be exercised when imposing a sentence of imprisonment even when the goal is to isolate the offender.

In relation to the offences under consideration, of course, the chronic alcohol abuser, whose inability to refrain from driving a motor vehicle while intoxicated is demonstrated by a number of previous convictions for drinking/driving-related offences, presents as a candidate for an isolative sentence unless the court is persuaded that rehabilitative treatment can and will be undertaken with a reasonable prospect of success. Even in such cases, however, the fundamental requirement of proportionality must be observed.

(iv) *Rehabilitation*

It has long been recognized that rehabilitation, as a goal of the sentencing process, cannot be achieved through the imposition of custodial sentences. That does not mean that rehabilitation should be regarded as a less important goal of sentencing. Indeed, in my view it is self-evident that rehabilitation remains the only certain way of permanently protecting society from a specific offender.

Thus if the rehabilitation of a specific offender remains a reasonable possibility, that is a circumstance which requires the sentencing court to consider seriously a non-custodial form of disposition. In some cases, even those involving serious criminal offences, where the chances of rehabilitation are significant, or its benefits to society substantial, the importance of imposing a rehabilitative non-custodial form of sentence may outweigh the perceived general deterrent advantages of a custodial sentence. If so, a court should not hesitate to impose the former, for in such circumstances the requirements of accountability and proportionality can be met with carefully crafted terms and conditions which both restrict the individual's freedom and enhance supervision of the rehabilitative process.

I have previously noted that while minimum penalties are provided in the *Criminal Code* for simple impaired driving and its related offences, Parliament has so far seen fit not to impose any such requirement on drinking and driving offences which result in death or bodily harm. Thus it clearly remains open to a court to impose a non-custodial sentence upon conviction for offences of this sort where the circumstances in favour of such a disposition are sufficiently compelling to overcome the need for a sentence of imprisonment, which would otherwise be required to meet the other goals of sentencing.

(v) *Denunciation*

This court first gave formal recognition to denunciation, as a goal of sentencing in *R. v. Oliver*, [1977] 5 W.W.R. 344, a case in which a lawyer was convicted of converting trust funds to his own benefit with the intent of defrauding his clients. Chief Justice Farris, speaking for the court, said at p. 346 of the report:

> Courts do not impose sentences in response to public clamour, nor in a spirit of revenge. On the other hand, justice is not administered in a vacuum. Sentences imposed by courts for criminal conduct by and large must have the support of concerned and thinking citizens. If they do not have such support, the system will fail. There are cases, as Lord Denning has said, where the punishment inflicted for grave crimes should reflect the revulsion felt by the majority of citizens for them. In his view, the objects of punishment are not simply deterrent or reformative. The ultimate justification of punishment is the emphatic denunciation by the community of a crime.

. . . .

As pointed out in the report of the Archambault Commission, the notion of denunciation as a goal of sentencing is one associated with the retributive theory of sentencing. I would affirm this court's rejection of that theory of sentencing as declared in *R. v. Hinch*. That means that denunciation as a goal of sentencing must be strictly limited to ensuring that sentences imposed for criminal convictions are proportionate to the moral culpability of the offender's unlawful act.

. . . .

(vi) *Just Deserts*

Notwithstanding the efforts of the authors of the Archambault Commission report to distinguish this "goal" of sentencing from that of retribution, I am of the view that, from a practical as opposed to a theoretical viewpoint, they are indistinguishable. Accordingly, I am of the view that it has no place in a principled approach to sentencing.

IV

I turn then to the fitness of the sentences under appeal.

. . . .

For those who would argue that these sentences do not adequately reflect the gravity of the offences committed, I point to the 10,000 or more convictions for impaired driving-related offences, which occur annually in the courts of this province, the majority of which result in a fine and a modest, albeit inconvenient, licence suspension. By contrast, the sentences I have set for these appellants are very much more severe, sufficiently so to reflect Parliament's mandate to treat such offences more seriously even though, in each case, the moral culpability of their crime is no greater than it would have been if they had been arrested before innocent victims had suffered.

For those to whom the call for more and longer sentences of imprisonment comes easily, I reiterate my determination not to sanction the imposition of retributive sentences. If retribution is to become a principle by which the severity of legal sanctions is to be determined in this country, then let Parliament say so in language which is clear and unequivocal and which can withstand close scrutiny under s. 12 of the *Charter of Rights and Freedoms*.

Most Canadians take pride in the belief that our criminal justice system responds in a balanced and reasonable way to the actions of the small minority of our population who offend against the law. But Canada has one of the highest per capita imprisonment rates of the so-called western industrialized world. In the last 35 years, nine separate national studies, royal commissions and parliamentary committees, which have considered in depth the question of a principled approach to sentencing, have all concluded that we jail too many people for too long. I believe that the fundamental purpose of sentencing can be achieved without contributing to that problem. Indeed, I am of the view that if the traditional principles of sentencing are applied with appropriate judicial restraint, we can reduce our resort to long terms of imprisonment in many cases without in any way reducing the protection which the public receives from the sentencing process.

For commentary, see Code, "Proportionate Blameworthiness and the Rule Against Constructive Sentencing" (1992), 11 C.R. (4th) 40.

R. v. C.A.M.

[1996] 1 S.C.R. 500, 46 C.R. (4th) 269, 105 C.C.C. (3d) 327,
1996 CarswellBC 1000, 1996 CarswellBC 1000F

The accused pleaded guilty to a number of counts of sexual assault, incest and assault with a weapon, arising from a largely uncontested pattern of sexual, physical and emotional abuse inflicted upon his children over a number of years. The trial judge, remarking that the offences were as egregious as any he had ever had occasion to deal with, sentenced the accused to a cumulative sentence of 25 years' imprisonment, with individual sentences running both consecutively and concurrently. The Court of Appeal reduced the sentence to 18 years and 8 months.

The appeal was allowed and a sentence of 25 years' imprisonment restored. In the course of his reasons Chief Justice Lamer wrote, for the court:

Did the Court of Appeal err in holding that retribution is not a legitimate principle of sentencing?

As a second and independent ground of appeal, the Crown argues that the Court of Appeal erred in law by relying on the proposition that "retribution is not a legitimate goal of sentencing" in reducing the sentence imposed by Filmer Prov. Ct. J. to 18 years and 8 months. In my reading of the judgment of the Court of Appeal below, I find little evidence that the passing remarks of Wood J.A. in relation to the legitimacy of retribution played a significant role in his conclusion that the respondent's sentence ought to be reduced to 18 years and 8 months' imprisonment. It should be noted that Rowles J.A., in her concurring reasons, did not even discuss retribution as a principle of sentencing. Similarly, there is no evidence that Filmer Prov. Ct. J. placed any explicit reliance on the objective of "retribution" in initially rendering his stern sentence. Accordingly, whether or not Wood J.A. erred as a strict matter of law in his discussion of the philosophical merits of retribution as a principle of sentencing, I conclude that Wood J.A.'s discussion of retribution was not a decisive element in the majority of the Court of Appeal's conclusion that the sentence of the respondent ought to be reduced to below 19 years. Therefore, I am persuaded that the remarks of Wood J.A. in relation to retribution did not constitute a reversible error.

However, given the continued judicial debate over this issue, particularly in recent judgments of the British Columbia Court of Appeal (see, e.g., *R. v. Hicks* (1995), 56 B.C.A.C. 259, at para. 14 (rejecting retribution), *R. v. Eneas*, [1994] B.C.J. No. 262, at paras. 45 and 46 (endorsing retribution); *R. v. M. (D.E.S.)* (1993), 80 C.C.C. (3d) 371, at p. 376 (rejecting retribution); *R. v. Hoyt*, [1992] B.C.J. No. 2315, at paras. 21 and 22 (rejecting retribution); *R. v. Pettigrew* (1990), 56 C.C.C. (3d) 390, at pp. 394-95 (endorsing retribution)), it would be prudent for this court to clarify briefly the existing state of Canadian law in this important area.

It has been recognized by this court that retribution is an accepted, and indeed important, principle of sentencing in our criminal law. As La Forest J. acknowledged in discussing the constitutionality of the dangerous offender provisions of the *Criminal Code* in *R. v. Lyons*, [1987] 2 S.C.R. 309, at p. 329:

In a rational system of sentencing, the respective importance of prevention, deterrence, retribution and rehabilitation will vary according to the nature of the crime and the circumstances of the offender. No one would suggest that any of these functional considerations should be excluded from the legitimate purview of legislative or judicial decisions regarding sentencing.

This court has since re-endorsed this passage on a number of occasions as a proper articulation of some of the guiding principles of sentencing in a number of subsequent cases. See *Luxton, supra,* at p. 721; *Goltz, supra,* at p. 503; and *Shropshire, supra,* at para. 23.

The Canadian Sentencing Commission in its 1987 Report on Sentencing Reform also endorsed retribution as a legitimate and relevant consideration in the sentencing process. While the Commission noted that strict retributivist theory on its own fails to provide a general justification for the imposition of criminal sanctions, the Commission argued that retribution, in conjunction with other utilitarian justifications of punishment (*i.e.,* deterrence and rehabilitation), contributes to a more coherent theory of punishment (*supra,* at pp. 141-42, 143-45). More specifically, the Commission argued that a theory of retribution centred on "just deserts" or "just sanctions" provides a helpful organizing principle for the imposition of criminal sanctions (at p. 143). Indeed, as the Commission noted, retribution frequently operates as a principle of restraint, as utilitarian principles alone may direct individualized punishments which unfairly exceed the culpability of the offender. As the Report stated at pp. 133-34:

> The ethical foundation of retributivism lies in the following principle: it is immoral to treat one person as a resource for others. From this principle it follows that the only legitimate ground for punishing a person is the blameworthiness of his or her conduct. It also follows that sanctions must be strictly proportionate to the culpability of a person and to the seriousness of the offence for which that person has been convicted.... According to these principles, all exemplary sentences (i.e. the imposition of a harsher sanction on an individual offender so that he or she may be made an example to the community) are unjustified, because they imply that an offender's plight may be used as a means or as a resource to deter potential offenders.

See, similarly, B. P. Archibald, *Crime and Punishment: The Constitutional Requirements for Sentencing Reform in Canada* (1988) 22 R.I.T. 307, at p. 18. With these considerations in mind, the Commission explicitly defined the fundamental purpose of sentencing with reference to the normative goal of imposing "just sanctions". As the Commission cast the guiding purpose of criminal sentencing, at p. 153:

> In furtherance of the overall purpose of the criminal law of maintaining a just, peaceful and safe society, the fundamental purpose of sentencing is to preserve the authority of and promote respect for the law through the imposition of just sanctions.

A majority of this court has since expressed approval of this passage as an accurate statement of the essential goals of sentencing. See *R. v. Jones,* [1994] 2 S.C.R. 229, at p. 291 (although I dissented on the merits of the case). Retribution, as an objective of sentencing, represents nothing less than the hallowed principle that criminal punishment, in addition to advancing utilitarian considerations related to deterrence and rehabilitation, should also be imposed to sanction the moral culpability of the offender. In my view, retribution is integrally woven into the existing principles of sentencing in Canadian law through the fundamental requirement that a sentence imposed be "just and appropriate" under the circumstances. Indeed, it is my profound belief that retribution represents an important unifying principle of our penal law by offering an essential conceptual link between the attribution of criminal liability and the imposition of criminal sanctions. With regard to the attribution of criminal liability, I have repeatedly held that it is a principle of "fundamental justice" under s. 7 of the *Charter* that criminal liability may only be imposed if an accused possesses a minimum "culpable mental state" in respect of the ingredients of the alleged offence. See *Martineau, supra,* at p. 645. See, similarly, *Re B.C. Motor Vehicle Act, supra; R. v. Vaillancourt,* [1987] 2 S.C.R. 636. It is this mental state which gives rise to the "moral blameworthiness" which justifies the state in imposing the stigma and punishment associated with a criminal sentence. See *Martineau,* at p. 646. I submit that it is this same element of "moral blameworthiness" which animates the determination of the appropriate quantum of punishment for a convicted offender as a "just sanction". As I noted in *Martineau* in discussing the sentencing scheme for manslaughter under the *Code,* it is a recognized principle of our justice system that "punishment be meted out with regard to the level of moral blameworthiness of the offender" (p. 647). See the similar observations of W.E.B. Code in "Proportionate Blameworthiness and the Rule Against Constructive Sentencing" (1992), 11 C.R. (4th) 40, at pp. 41-42.

However, the meaning of retribution is deserving of some clarification. The legitimacy of retribution as a principle of sentencing has often been questioned as a result of its unfortunate association with "vengeance" in common parlance. See, *e.g., R. v. Hinch and Salanski, supra,* at pp. 43-44; *R. v. Calder* (1956), 114 C.C.C. 155 (Man. C.A.), at p. 161. But it should be clear from my foregoing discussion that retribution bears little relation to vengeance, and I attribute much of the criticism of retribution as a principle to this confusion. As both academic and judicial commentators have noted, vengeance has no role to play in a civilized system of sentencing. See Ruby, *Sentencing, supra,* at p. 13. Vengeance, as I understand it, represents an uncalibrated act of harm upon another, frequently motivated by emotion and anger, as a reprisal for harm inflicted upon oneself by that person. Retribution in a criminal context, by contrast, represents an objective, reasoned and measured determination of an appropriate punishment which properly reflects the moral culpability of the offender, having regard to the intentional risk-taking of the offender, the consequential harm caused by the offender, and the normative character of the offender's conduct. Furthermore, unlike vengeance, retribution incorporates a principle of restraint; retribution requires the imposition of a just and appropriate punishment, and nothing more. As R. Cross has noted in *The English Sentencing System* (2nd ed. 1975), at p. 121: "The retributivist insists that the punishment must not be disproportionate to the offender's deserts."

Retribution, as well, should be conceptually distinguished from its legitimate sibling, denunciation. Retribution requires that a judicial sentence properly reflect the moral blameworthiness of that particular offender. The objective of denunciation mandates that a sentence should also communicate society's condemnation of that particular offender's conduct. In short, a sentence with a denunciatory element represents a symbolic, collective statement that the offender's conduct should be punished for encroaching on our society's basic code of values as enshrined within our substantive criminal law. As Lord Justice Lawton stated in *R. v. Sargeant* (1974), 60 Cr. App. R. 74, at p. 77:

> society, through the courts, must show its abhorrence of particular types of crime, and the only way in which the courts can show this is by the sentences they pass.

The relevance of both retribution and denunciation as goals of sentencing underscores that our criminal justice system is not simply a vast system of negative penalties designed to prevent objectively harmful conduct by increasing the cost the offender must bear in committing an enumerated offence. Our criminal law is also a system of values. A sentence which expresses denunciation is simply the means by which these values are communicated. In short, in addition to attaching negative consequences to undesirable behaviour, judicial sentences should also be imposed in a manner which positively instills the basic set of communal values shared by all Canadians as expressed by the *Criminal Code*.

As a closing note to this discussion, it is important to stress that neither retribution nor denunciation alone provides an exhaustive justification for the imposition of criminal sanctions. Rather, in our system of justice, normative and utilitarian considerations operate in conjunction with one another to provide a coherent justification for criminal punishment. As Gonthier J. emphasized in *Goltz*, *supra*, at p. 502, the goals of the penal sanction are both "broad and varied". Accordingly, the meaning of retribution must be considered in conjunction with the other legitimate objectives of sentencing, which include (but are not limited to) deterrence, denunciation, rehabilitation and the protection of society. Indeed, it is difficult to perfectly separate these interrelated principles. And as La Forest J. emphasized in *Lyons*, the relative weight and importance of these multiple factors will frequently vary depending on the nature of the crime and the circumstances of the offender. In the final analysis, the overarching duty of a sentencing judge is to draw upon all the legitimate principles of sentencing to determine a "just and appropriate" sentence which reflects the gravity of the offence committed and the moral blameworthiness of the offender.

2. SENTENCING REFORM: REDUCED USE OF INCARCERATION

Major amendments to the *Criminal Code* came into force on September 3, 1996 when Bill C-41 was proclaimed in force. Mr. Justice Vancise of the Saskatchewan Court of Appeal hails the amendments as providing a framework under which there should be less custodial sentencing: "To Change or Not to Change — That is the Issue" (1996), 1 Can. Crim. L.R. 263. In addition to a number of specific amendments to sentencing powers, Bill C-41 declared the Purpose and Principles of Sentencing in ss. 718, 718.1 and 718.2. These were first considered by the Ontario Court of Appeal in *Priest*.

R. v. PRIEST

(1996), 1 C.R. (5th) 275, 110 C.C.C. (3d) 289,
1996 CarswellOnt 3588 (Ont. C.A.)

The accused was a 19-year-old first offender. He had no prior record. He pleaded guilty to breaking and entering a convenience store and stealing computer games and accessories worth approximately $2,700. He confessed when confronted by the store owner. All of the stolen property was recovered and there were no aggravating features involved in the offence. There was no violence or vandalism. There was no breach of trust involved. All of the stolen property was recovered. At the sentencing hearing, which lasted for less than five minutes, the accused was unrepresented by counsel. There was no presentence report or other information about the accused's background, family, roots in the community, education or work history. Crown counsel suggested a sentence of 30 to 60 days. Taking judicial notice of the prevalence of the crime of breaking and entering in the community and stating that general deterrence was for that reason the primary sentencing consideration, the trial judge imposed a sentence of one year's imprisonment. The accused appealed. The sentencing of the appellant took place on July 15, 1996. On August 22, Carthy J.A. ordered the appellant released on bail pending appeal and ordered that the appeal be expedited. Thus, when the appeal came before the Court of Appeal on August 30, the accused had already served five weeks in jail. Crown counsel conceded that the sentence could not stand and suggested that it be reduced to time served and probation for one year, with conditions that the accused report to a probation officer and seek and maintain employment.

ROSENBERG J.A: —

It is obvious that the original sentence of one year imprisonment cannot stand. In imposing the sentence that he did, the trial judge ignored principles and procedural guidelines that have been laid down by this court on many occasions.

Prevalence of the Crime

In imposing the sentence, the trial judge found that general deterrence was the paramount consideration. In stressing general deterrence to the exclusion of all other objectives, he relied upon the apparent prevalence of the offence of break and enter in Hearst. It is not necessary to decide in this case whether the trial judge had sufficient information before him from which he could safely conclude that there was a serious problem of break and enter in Hearst. I note, however, that unlike some cases that have come before this court, there were no statistics placed before the trial judge and he based his opinion on the court dockets of persons accused of the crime of break and enter.

The principles to be applied where there appears to be an unusually high incidence of a particular crime in the community have been set down by this court. In 1978, Arnup J.A. in *R. v. Sears* (1978), 39 C.C.C. (2d) 199 at p. 200, (Ont. C.A.), pointed out that prevalence of a particular crime in the community can never be more than one factor to be taken into account .... This court has specifically spoken on this principle in relation to break and enter in *R. v. Rohr* (1978), 44 C.C.C. (2d) 353 (Ont. C.A.). In that case the youthful appellant had broken into an aquatic centre, done considerable damage, and stolen some $600 worth of goods from the snack bar. The 16-year-old appellant had no prior record but was sentenced to six months imprisonment pursuant to the trial judge's policy of imposing lengthy jail terms even on first offenders for break and enter because of the increase in the number of break-ins in the community. Martin J.A. made it clear that even where break and enter is prevalent in a particular community, it is a circumstance to be taken into consideration, but not the exclusive consideration.

The trial judge was entirely wrong to state that due to the apparent prevalence of the crime of break and enter in Hearst, general deterrence was the paramount objective in sentencing this accused. This was a serious error in principle and wholly distorted the decision as to the appropriate disposition.

This court has stressed that before imposing a sentence of imprisonment upon a first offender, the trial judge should have either a presentence report or some very clear statement with respect to the accused's background and circumstances. That principle has particular application in the case of a youthful offender like this appellant. This requirement of a presentence report or statement about the offender is not a mere formality. As discussed below, the trial judge has a duty to consider whether any disposition other than imprisonment would be appropriate. Without some understanding of the accused's background, the trial judge cannot possibly make that determination. Based on the scanty information before him, the trial judge would have no means of determining that imprisonment was the appropriate sanction for this appellant.

Youthful First Offender

The primary objectives in sentencing a first offender are individual deterrence and rehabilitation. Except for very serious offences and offences involving violence, this court has held that these objectives are not only paramount but best achieved by either a suspended sentence and probation or a very short term of imprisonment followed by a term of probation .... It has been an important principle of sentencing in this province that the sentence should constitute the minimum necessary intervention that is adequate in the particular circumstances. This principle implies that trial judges consider community-based dispositions first and impose more serious forms of punishment only when necessary. These principles have now been codified in the recently proclaimed ss. 718 and 718.2 of the *Criminal Code*, R.S.C. 1985, c. C-46. Section 718(*c*) instructs that separation of offenders from society is an appropriate objective of sentencing "where necessary". Section 718.2(*d*) directs that an offender should not be deprived of liberty "if less restrictive sanctions may be appropriate in the circumstances". The principle embodied in now s. 718.2(*e*) was of particular significance in this case. It provides that "all available sanctions other than imprisonment that are reasonable in the circumstances should be considered for all offenders, with particular attention to the circumstances of aboriginal offenders". Although these sections had not been proclaimed when the appellant appeared before Judge Cloutier, the provisions to a large extent codify existing practice and principles in this province, especially in relation to first offenders.

. . . .

Proportionality

In the recently proclaimed s. 718.1, Parliament sets out the fundamental principle of sentencing:

> 718.1 A sentence must be proportionate to the gravity of the offence and the degree of responsibility of the offender.

Although only now codified, this principle is well established in this country. Chief Justice Lamer in *R. v. M. (C.A.)*, [1996] 1 S.C.R. 500 at p. 530, 105 C.C.C. (3d) 327 at p. 349, noted that this principle now has a constitutional dimension:

> Within broader parameters, the principle of proportionality expresses itself as a constitutional obligation. As this court has recognized on numerous occasions, a legislative or judicial sentence that is grossly disproportionate, in the sense that it is so excessive as to outrage standards of decency, will violate the constitutional prohibition against cruel and unusual punishment under s. 12 of the *Charter*.

The principle of proportionality is rooted in notions of fairness and justice. For the sentencing court to do justice to the particular offender, the sentence imposed must reflect the seriousness of the offence, the degree of culpability of the offender, and the harm occasioned by the offence. The court must have regard to the aggravating and mitigating factors in the particular case. Careful adherence to the proportionality principle ensures that this offender is not unjustly dealt with for the sake of the common good.

The sentence imposed by the trial judge in this case was wholly disproportionate to what occurred. This was a break-in of non-residential premises. There were a number of mitigating factors that were completely ignored by the trial judge. The appellant had no prior record; he confessed to the offence; he returned all of the stolen goods; and he pled guilty at an early opportunity. The trial judge was required to give effect to these mitigating factors in imposing sentence on this appellant.

While I hesitate to label the sentence grossly disproportionate, it approaches that standard. It was well above the threshold of the "clearly unreasonable" or "demonstrably unfit" sentence requiring intervention by this court.

The Role of the Courts

In his reasons for sentence, the trial judge stated that the citizens of Hearst must know that the court is doing its job. He was rightly concerned with the need to protect society and that the courts be seen to be doing their part. The courts of this country must accept the fundamental purpose of sentencing that imposition of appropriate sanctions can contribute to the maintenance of a safe and peaceful society. As Parliament has stated in the recently proclaimed s. 718 of the *Criminal Code*, the purpose of sentencing is also to contribute to respect for the law and maintenance of a just society. Respect for the law is not enhanced when overly harsh sanctions are imposed and a trial court ignores well established sentencing principles. The trial court does not fulfil its duty to fashion a sanction that will contribute to the maintenance of a more just society when it imposes a sentence on the offender that is far beyond the usual penalty imposed for this offence in other parts of the province and the country. The offender and the offender's family would harbour a well-justified sense of grievance over the offender's treatment by the judicial system. Chief Justice Lamer made this crucial point in *R. v. M. (C.A.)*, *supra*, at pp. 558-59 S.C.R., p. 369 C.C.C. He was there discussing the rationale for the objectives of denunciation and retribution in a just system of punishment. His statements, however, have a broader application. He said:

> The relevance of both retribution and denunciation as goals of sentencing underscores that our criminal justice system is not simply a vast system of negative penalties designed to prevent objectively harmful conduct by increasing the cost the offender must bear in committing an enumerated offence. Our criminal law is also a system of values. A sentence which expresses denunciation is simply the means by which these values are communicated. In short, in addition to attaching negative consequences to undesirable behaviour, judicial

sentences should also be imposed in a manner which positively instills the basic set of communal values shared by all Canadians as expressed in the *Criminal Code*.

This positive aspect of sentencing, reinforcing the basic values of the society, can only be achieved if the court exercises its broad discretion in sentencing in a just manner having regard to established principles. Section 717(1) (now s. 718.3) of the *Criminal Code* emphasizes that the sentence to be imposed is in the discretion of the trial judge. That discretion is, however, not unfettered. The various principles and objectives of sentencing set out by this court and in the *Criminal Code* are designed to guide the exercise of the discretion. The substantial deference that appeal courts are required to pay to the exercise of the trial judge's discretion is not unlimited. In *R. v. M. (C.A.)*, *supra*, at p. 374, Chief Justice Lamer described the imposition of sentence by the trial judge as a "delicate art" where the judge attempts to balance carefully the societal goals of sentencing against the moral blameworthiness of the offender and the circumstances of the offence, "while at all times taking into account the needs and current conditions of and in the community". Regrettably, the sentencing judge failed to exercise his discretion in this careful and measured way.

For the foregoing reasons, we allowed the appeal and reduced the sentence to time served (approximately five weeks) and one year probation on the statutory terms and on the special terms that the appellant report forthwith to a probation officer and thereafter once per month if required and that he make reasonable efforts to seek and maintain employment or education.

The sentencing reforms in Bill C-41 contained s. 718.2(e), aimed at reducing the use of incarceration. That section provides:

718.2 A court that imposes a sentence shall also take into consideration the following principles:

...(e) all available sanctions other than imprisonment that are reasonable in the circumstances should be considered for all offenders, with particular attention to the circumstances of aboriginal offenders.

The correct approach to applying s. 718.2, and in particular the issue of sentencing aboriginal offenders, was discussed in the following case:

R. v. GLADUE

[1999] 1 S.C.R. 688, 133 C.C.C. (3d) 385, 23 C.R. (5th) 197,
1999 CarswellBC 778, 1999 CarswellBC 779 (S.C.C.)

The judgment of the court was delivered by CORY and IACOBUCCI JJ.:—

. . . .

52   Canada is a world leader in many fields, particularly in the areas of progressive social policy and human rights. Unfortunately, our country is also distinguished as being a world leader in putting people in prison. Although the United States has by far the highest rate of incarceration among industrialized democracies, at over 600 inmates per 100,000 population, Canada's rate of approximately 130 inmates per 100,000 population places it second or third highest: see Federal/Provincial/Territorial Ministers Responsible for Justice, *Corrections Population Growth: First Report on Progress* (1997), Annex B, at p. 1; Bulletin of U.S. Bureau of Justice Statistics, *Prison and Jail Inmates at Midyear 1998* (March 1999); The Sentencing Project, *Americans Behind Bars: U.S. and International Use of Incarceration, 1995* (June 1997), at p. 1. Moreover, the rate at which Canadian courts have been imprisoning offenders has risen sharply in recent years, although there has been a slight decline of late: see Statistics Canada, "Prison population and costs" in *Infomat: A Weekly Review* (February 27, 1998), at p. 5. This record of incarceration rates obviously cannot instil a sense of pride.

[In particular, the court held that the section's specific reference to the circumstances of aboriginal offenders was meant to respond to the overrepresentation of aboriginal persons in Canadian prisons.]

58   If overreliance upon incarceration is a problem with the general population, it is of much greater concern in the sentencing of aboriginal Canadians. In the mid-1980s, aboriginal people were about 2 percent of the population of Canada, yet they made up 10 percent of the penitentiary population. In Manitoba and Saskatchewan, aboriginal people constituted something between 6 and 7 percent of the population, yet in Manitoba they represented 46 percent of the provincial admissions and in Saskatchewan 60 percent: see M. Jackson, "Locking Up Natives in Canada" (1988-89), 23 *U.B.C. L. Rev.* 215 (article originally prepared as a report of the Canadian Bar Association Committee on Imprisonment and Release in June 1988), at pp. 215-16. The situation has not improved in recent years. By 1997, aboriginal peoples constituted closer to 3 percent of the population of Canada and amounted to 12 percent of all federal inmates: Solicitor General of Canada, Consolidated Report, *Towards a Just, Peaceful and Safe Society: The Corrections and Conditional Release Act—Five Years Later* (1998), at pp. 142-55. The situation continues to be particularly worrisome in Manitoba, where in 1995-96 they made up 55

percent of admissions to provincial correctional facilities, and in Saskatchewan, where they made up 72 percent of admissions. A similar, albeit less drastic situation prevails in Alberta and British Columbia: Canadian Centre for Justice Statistics, *Adult Correctional Services in Canada, 1995-96* (1997), at p. 30.

[The court also held that the traditional approach of many aboriginal peoples to societal problems corresponded well with the amendments to *Criminal Code* aimed at incorporating more restorative principles. Ultimately they laid down a series of guidelines to assist judges in applying s. 718.2(e).]

93   Let us see if a general summary can be made of what has been discussed in these reasons.

1 Part XXIII of the *Criminal Code* codifies the fundamental purpose and principles of sentencing and the factors that should be considered by a judge in striving to determine a sentence that is fit for the offender and the offence.

2 Section 718.2(*e*) mandatorily requires sentencing judges to consider all available sanctions other than imprisonment and to pay particular attention to the circumstances of aboriginal offenders.

3 Section 718.2(*e*) is not simply a codification of existing jurisprudence. It is remedial in nature. Its purpose is to ameliorate the serious problem of overrepresentation of aboriginal people in prisons, and to encourage sentencing judges to have recourse to a restorative approach to sentencing. There is a judicial duty to give the provision's remedial purpose real force.

4 Section 718.2(*e*) must be read and considered in the context of the rest of the factors referred to in that section and in light of all of Part XXIII. All principles and factors set out in Part XXIII must be taken into consideration in determining the fit sentence. Attention should be paid to the fact that Part XXIII, through ss. 718, 718.2(*e*), and 742.1, among other provisions, has placed a new emphasis upon decreasing the use of incarceration.

5 Sentencing is an individual process and in each case the consideration must continue to be what is a fit sentence for this accused for this offence in this community. However, the effect of s. 718.2(*e*) is to alter the method of analysis which sentencing judges must use in determining a fit sentence for aboriginal offenders.

6   Section 718.2(*e*) directs sentencing judges to undertake the sentencing of aboriginal offenders individually, but also differently, because the circumstances of aboriginal people are unique. In sentencing an aboriginal offender, the judge must consider:

(A) The unique systemic or background factors which may have played a part in bringing the particular aboriginal offender before the courts; and

(B) The types of sentencing procedures and sanctions which may be appropriate in the circumstances for the offender because of his or her particular aboriginal heritage or connection.

7   In order to undertake these considerations the trial judge will require information pertaining to the accused. Judges may take judicial notice of the broad systemic and background factors affecting aboriginal people, and of the priority given in aboriginal cultures to a restorative approach to sentencing. In the usual course of events, additional case-specific information will come from counsel and from a pre-sentence report which takes into account the factors set out in #6, which in turn may come from representations of the relevant aboriginal community which will usually be that of the offender. The offender may waive the gathering of that information.

8   If there is no alternative to incarceration the length of the term must be carefully considered.

9   Section 718.2(e) is not to be taken as a means of automatically reducing the prison sentence of aboriginal offenders; nor should it be assumed that an offender is receiving a more lenient sentence simply because incarceration is not imposed.

10   The absence of alternative sentencing programs specific to an aboriginal community does not eliminate the ability of a sentencing judge to impose a sanction that takes into account principles of restorative justice and the needs of the parties involved.

11   Section 718.2(e) applies to all aboriginal persons wherever they reside, whether on- or off-reserve, in a large city or a rural area. In defining the relevant aboriginal community for the purpose of achieving an effective sentence, the term "community" must be defined broadly so as to include any network of support and interaction that might be available, including in an urban centre. At the same time, the residence of the aboriginal offender in an urban centre that lacks any network of support does not relieve the sentencing judge of the obligation to try to find an alternative to imprisonment.

12   Based on the foregoing, the jail term for an aboriginal offender may in some circumstances be less than the term imposed on a non-aboriginal offender for the same offence.

13   It is unreasonable to assume that aboriginal peoples do not believe in the importance of traditional sentencing goals such as deterrence, denunciation, and separation, where warranted. In this context, generally, the more serious and

violent the crime, the more likely it will be as a practical matter that the terms of imprisonment will be the same for similar offences and offenders, whether the offender is aboriginal or non-aboriginal.

Times have changed. The current Conservative Government constantly repeats a mantra of "serious time for serious crime" and has introduced a number of new mandatory minima prison sentences for various offences, particularly for firearms and drug offences. Kent Roach, "Rates of Imprisonment and Criminal Justice Policy" (2008) 53 *Crim. L. Q.* 273, raises concerns that this will substantially increase Canada's imprisonment rates. He notes that Canada's current rate of imprisonment is 110 per 100,000 whereas that in the United States is a staggering 738 per 100,000.

In *R. v. Ferguson* (2008), 54 C.R. (6th)197 (S.C.C.) the Supreme Court added further rigidity in deciding that constitutional exemptions were not available in the case of minimum sentences. See C.R. comments by Steve Coughlan and Paul Calarco. Coughlan sees the decision as consistent with the rule of law. Calarco suggests that the rigidity may make claims of cruel and unusual punishment under s. 12 of the *Charter* more likely to succeed.

The message of the 3-2 majority Court of Appeal in *R. v. Arcand* (2010), 83 C.R. (6th) 199 (Alta. C.A.) delivered at the start of a lengthy analysis of Canadian sentencing policies and realities, is that courts of appeal need to be far more aggressive in intervening to control rampant sentencing disparity through a scheme of starting-point prison sentences for particular crimes:

FRASER C.J., COTE and WATSON J.J.A.—

We must face up to five sentencing truths. First, it is notorious amongst judges, of whom there are now approximately 2,100 in this country at three court levels, that one of the most controversial subjects, both in theory and practical application, is sentencing. That takes us to the second truth. The proposition that if judges knew the facts of a given case, they would all agree, or substantially agree on the result, is simply not so. The third truth. Judges are not the only ones who know truths one and two, and thus judge shopping is alive and well in Canada - and fighting hard to stay that way. All lead inescapably to the fourth truth. Without reasonable uniformity of approach to sentencing amongst trial and appellate judges in Canada, many of the sentencing objectives and principles prescribed in the Code are not attainable. This makes the search for just sanctions at best a lottery, and at worst a myth. Pretending otherwise obscures the need for Canadian courts to do what Parliament has asked: minimize unjustified disparity in sentencing while maintaining flexibility. The final truth. If the courts do not act to vindicate the promises of the law, and public confidence diminishes, then Parliament will. [para. 8]

This is a concern not evident in sentencing judgments of other courts of appeal. See, for example, *R. v. Tuglavina* (2011), 83 C.R. (6th) 356 (N.L. C.A.) and *R. v. Kummer* (2011), 83 C.R. (6th) 379 (Ont. C.A.), which assert an approach of setting flexible guidelines, and accept and justify the Supreme Court's approach that appeal courts should show deference to sentencing decisions of trial judges. The message of the majority of the Alberta Court of Appeal can be read as encouraging the current Parliamentary trend to fixed minimum sentences. Although this would make sentencing easier it is likely that many judges at all levels, and including Alberta judges, would not favour such rigidity or lack of trust in the judiciary. Not all crimes are the same and minimum sentences allow for no individual factors to be taken into account.

3. TOOLS OF SENTENCING

Discharges

See section 730 of the *Criminal Code.*

In *R. v. Derksen* (1972), 20 C.R.N.S. 129, 9 C.C.C. (2d) 97 (B.C. P.C.), on a charge of possession of cannabis resin, the prosecutor asked that the court grant an absolute or conditional discharge since it was a first offence. Ostler J. expressed concern that it could not be in the best interests of an accused and not contrary to the public interest to approach all unremarkable cases of this sort with a uniform policy of a discharge; to do so would be seen by many as condoning the offence and inviting a further breach. He concluded:

> In fine, it is my opinion that the discharge — the finding of guilt without the usual concomitant of conviction — should never be applied routinely to any criminal offence, in effect labelling the enactment violable. It should be used frugally, selectively and judiciously, as Parliament obviously intended. If it is considered that an absolute or conditional discharge is the appropriate penalty for a first offence under this section, then Parliament should so declare. The courts should not compromise or circumvent the law.

In *R. v. Fallofield* (1973), 22 C.R.N.S. 342, 13 C.C.C. (2d) 450 (B.C. C.A.), the defendant had been convicted of possession of stolen goods of a value of less than $200; while delivering refrigerators to a new apartment building, he took some left-over pieces of carpet of a value of $33.07. Evidence at the trial showed the defendant to be a corporal in the Armed Services, married, no previous record, and that a conviction could very possibly affect his future career in the Navy. The Court of Appeal reviewed the discharge cases to that date and, with the caveat that the discretion to grant a discharge should not be fettered, offered the following conclusions respecting what is now s. 730:

(1) The section may be used in respect of *any* offence other than an offence for which a minimum punishment is prescribed by law or the offence is punishable by imprisonment for 14 years or for life or by death.

(2) The section contemplates the commission of an offence. There is nothing in the language that limits it to a technical or trivial violation.

(3) Of the two conditions precedent to the exercise of the jurisdiction, the first is that the court must consider that it is in the best interests of the accused that he should be discharged either absolutely or upon condition. If it is not in the best interests of the accused, that, of course, is the end of the matter. If it is decided that it is in the best interests of the accused, then that brings the next consideration into operation.

(4) The second condition precedent is that the court must consider that a grant of discharge is not contrary to the public interest.

(5) Generally, the first condition would presuppose that the accused is a person of good character, without previous conviction, that it is not necessary to enter a conviction against him in order to deter him from future offences or to rehabilitate him, and that the entry of a conviction against him may have significant adverse repercussions.

(6) In the context of the second condition the public interest in the deterrence of others, while it must be given due weight, does not preclude the judicious use of the discharge provisions.

(7) The powers given by s. 662.1 [now s. 730] should not be exercised as an alternative to probation or suspended sentence.

(8) Section 662.1 should not be applied routinely to any particular offence. This may result in an apparent lack of uniformity in the application of the discharge provisions. This lack will be more apparent than real and will stem from the differences in the circumstances of cases.

The granting of a discharge does *not* mean that an accused has no criminal record. Under s. 730(3) of the *Criminal Code* a discharged accused "shall be deemed not to have been convicted of the offence". A 1972 amendment to the *Criminal Records Act* prescribed that one subject to a discharge could apply to the Parole Board, subject to a shorter waiting period, for a pardon. A pardon "vacates" a record. This amendment thwarted the aim of the discharge provisions and risked misinformation and confusion. It was only amended in 1992. Under s. 6.1, after one year following an absolute discharge and three years following a conditional discharge, no disclosure of such a record can be made without the approval of the Minister and all reference must be removed from the automated criminal conviction records retrieval system maintained by the R.C.M.P. This provides only partial relief to one discharged and there is no remedy for breach.

What, then, is the legal effect of a discharge? If the question is "Have you been convicted?" it would appear that the discharged accused can answer "No", relying on the *Criminal Code* deeming provision. If the question is "Do you have a criminal record?" it seems that the answer still has to be "Yes" unless the time period for non-disclosure has arrived. Presumably a discharged accused can still apply for a pardon. After such a pardon the answer could presumably be "No" to both questions, otherwise the application for pardon would be meaningless.

Fines

See s. 734 of the *Criminal Code*, and compare the counterpart provisions with respect to summary conviction offences in s. 787.

Probation

See section 731 of the *Criminal Code*.

In *R. v. Sangster* (1973), 21 C.R.N.S. 339 (Que. C.A.), the trial judge had given a suspended sentence of five years' imprisonment and placed the accused on probation for three years. Kaufman J.A. dismissed the Crown's appeal but noted:

> I do, however, wish to point out that the true intent of s. 663 (1)(*a*) of the *Code* is to suspend "the passing of sentence", and not the sentence itself. With respect, I therefore consider it unwise to indicate to an accused the precise sentence which might be imposed on him should he fail to observe the conditions set by the court. To do so may well put the judge in a predicament: keep his word and sentence an accused to a term of imprisonment which might be considerably longer than the circumstances would warrant or, in the alternative, give a proper sentence, but lose credibility. Neither situation is good — the first an injustice to the accused, the second an unnecessary embarrassment to the court.
>
> This should not be taken to mean that an accused cannot be told that failure to abide by the conditions might entail serious consequences, indeed even imprisonment for a lengthy period. But I do think that no court should bind itself in so absolute a fashion that all room for discretion will have vanished.

The court may suspend the passing of sentence and place the accused on probation when there is no minimum punishment provided (cf. *R. v. Bradshaw*,

[1976] 1 S.C.R. 162, 29 C.R.N.S. 221, 21 C.C.C. (2d) 69). The court may fine the accused and place him on probation or the court may imprison the accused and place him on probation. (The imprisonment in such a case cannot be for a period longer than two years: *R. v. Nutter, Collishaw and Dulong* (1972), 7 C.C.C. (2d) 224 (B.C. C.A.)). The court cannot fine the accused and place him on probation and imprison him: *R. v. Smith* (1972), 7 C.C.C. (2d) 468 (N.W.T.) and *R. v. Blacquiere* (1975), 24 C.C.C. (2d) 168 (Ont. C.A.).

Section 732.1 provides that the court may prescribe, besides the statutory conditions listed, "such other *reasonable* conditions as the court considers desirable for securing the good conduct of the accused and for preventing a repetition by him of the same offence or the commission of other offences". The condition imposed then cannot be as additional punishment. In *R. v. Ziatas* (1973), 13 C.C.C. (2d) 287 (Ont. C.A.), the trial judge, on an assault charge, fined the accused and placed him on probation for one year with the condition that he not operate a motor vehicle during that period. The condition was struck out on appeal because:

> we are all of the view that he proceeded upon a wrong principle, inasmuch as he imposed this term of the probation order as an additional punishment to be imposed upon the accused, whereas his only power, if he had any jurisdiction to impose the condition under s. 663(2) of the *Criminal Code*, was to impose such reasonable conditions as he considered desirable for securing the good conduct of the accused and for preventing the repetition by him of the same offence or the commission of other offences.

In *R. v. Gladstone* (1978), 2 C.R. (3d) S-9, 40 C.C.C. (2d) 42 (B.C. Co. Ct.), the accused was convicted of breach of a regulation made under the *Fisheries Act* and the court made it a condition of probation that he surrender his permit to fish for a period of one month. The appeal court allowed the accused's appeal and noted:

> A condition of probation based upon s. 663(2)(*h*) [now s. 732.1] should be reasonable and it should be designed to secure the good conduct of the accused and to prevent a repetition by the accused of the same offence or the commission of other offences. The primary purpose of a condition of probation attached under 663(2)(*a*) to (*h*) inclusive, should be for the rehabilitation of the accused, not the imposition of punishment. That is particularly relevant when a condition of probation has been prescribed following the suspension of sentence, as distinct from a condition of probation being imposed following the passing of sentence, be it the imposition of a term in jail, or of a fine.
>
> In this case the comments expressed by the learned Provincial Court Judge in sentencing the accused indicate that his primary purpose in directing the accused to surrender his permit to fish was to punish the accused, because he had violated his privilege to fish under the permit, and also to deter the accused and other native people from a repetition of the offence.
>
> In my respectful view, the condition attached by the learned Provincial Court Judge to the probation order was inappropriate for several reasons. First, having suspended sentence, he in effect punished the accused by depriving him of his permit to fish for a period of 30 days. Secondly, in view of the particular circumstances of the accused — that he was a native Indian, no longer employable, in receipt of Social Assistance, and who represented that he was catching fish to smoke for winter food for himself and his family — I am not persuaded that it was a "reasonable condition" within the general purview of s. 663(2)(*h*). Thirdly, the primary purpose of the condition was not directed to the rehabilitation of tlhe accused. Fourthly, the effect of the condition was to prohibit the accused from fishing under his permit for one month, as distinct from restricting the accused from fishing under the permit for specified periods of time within the period of one month.
>
> In view of the accused's alleged lack of understanding of the precise terms of his permit to fish, including the requirement that fish be "marked" (which may have been caused by his difficulty

in hearing), a condition of probation under s. 663(2)(*a*), that the accused be required to report to and be under the supervision of a fisheries officer for a fixed period of time would have been more appropriate. It would have had the primary purpose of encouraging the rehabilitation of the accused. It would have enabled a fisheries officer to ensure that the accused clearly understood the terms of his permit. Alternatively, a condition of probation under s. 663(2)(*h*) that the accused report for several weeks to a fisheries officer on the completion of each weekly period of fishing under the permit, to demonstrate to such fisheries officer that any fish caught had been "marked" properly, would have complied with the scope and purpose of s. 663(2)(*h*).

In *R. v. Pawlowski* (1971), 5 C.C.C. (2d) 87 (Man. C.A.), the accused's probation order which provided for restitution also contained a condition that he pay costs of $1000. The magistrate said he was assessing heavy costs to indicate to the accused disapproval of his actions and because of his lack of remorse. Dickson J.A., struck out the condition as illegal and said that s. 737(2)(*h*) did not authorize the imposition of punishment by means of a fine nor a requirement to pay costs.

In *R. v. DeKleric*, [1969] 2 C.C.C. 367 (B.C.C.A.), the magistrate suspended the passing of sentence and imposed a condition of probation that the accused pay the sum of $500 in favour of the Vancouver Superannuated Police Officer's Association. Davey C.J.B.C. noted:

> However, I cannot part with this case without some remarks about condition (3), which required the respondent to pay the sum of $500 to the Vancouver Superannuated Police Officers' Association at the rate of $100 per month. It seems to me, with the greatest respect to this experienced Magistrate, that that is quite wrong. If the circumstances required a fine, it should have been imposed as a fine. If the circumstances required as a condition of suspended sentence, restitution or reparation to the injured parties within the meaning of the provisions of the *Code* which allow such a condition to be imposed as a term of the suspended sentence, then it should have been done that way. This innovation is a most dangerous one. It can lead to the greatest abuses, and for myself I hope it is the last time we see such a condition imposed as a term of any suspended sentence.
>
> I have considered whether we should impose a fine or not. If we impose a fine, then this is no longer a suspended sentence. The only consequence of breach of the recognizance will be an action to recover the amount of the recognizance. Under a suspended sentence, if the respondent is in breach of the conditions of the recognizance, he may be brought before the court to have an appropriate sentence imposed in the light of the conditions which then exist. That is what I think should be done.

Restitution

Sections 738-741.2 authorize orders of restitution. In *R. v. Dashner* (1974), 25 C.R.N.S. 340, 15 C.C.C. (2d) 139 (B.C. C.A.), the accused, convicted on two counts of assault causing bodily harm, was fined and placed on probation. One condition of the probation order required the accused to pay each victim $500 within two months. This condition was struck out on appeal and McFarlane J.A. noted:

> I think, however, that great care should be taken to ensure that restitution or reparation will not be made a condition of a probation order unless the court is satisfied that the convicted person is able to pay and that the circumstances come clearly within the paragraph, particularly that the amount ordered represents "actual loss or damage sustained". My reason for this view is that breach of a probation order is itself an offence under the *Criminial Code* which may involve very serious consequences.

I think assistance in the task of interpretation and application of s. 737(2)(e) may be found in para. (h) which authorizes:

> (h) . . . such other reasonable conditions as the court considers desirable for securing the good conduct of the accused and for preventing a repetition by him of the same offence or the commission of other offences.

> It appears that the general purpose of probation orders is to secure the good conduct of the convicted person as opposed to compensating victims of crime. The remedies available to them by ordinary civil suit and under the *Criminal Injuries Compensation Act*, 1972 (B.C.), c. 17, should not be overlooked: nor the difference between compensation on the one hand and restitution or reparation on the other.

So, too, in *R. v. Groves* (1977), 39 C.R.N.S. 366, 37 C.C.C. (2d) 429 (Ont. H.C.), where McEwan P.C.J. had made it a condition that the accused pay to his victim, a police officer, $500 for his pain and suffering which resulted from the accused twisting and bending the officer's little finger. The officer had received workmen's compensation for his injury during his absence from duty. He was still experiencing discomfort at the date of the trial. On appeal, O'Driscoll J. noted the lack of discovery mechanisms in the criminal process for accurately determining extent of loss and concluded:

> In my view, had Parliament intended to confer upon the criminal courts a remedial power to order an offender to compensate a victim for pain and suffering, it would have set out its intent in clear language. Indeed, it seems to me, that the word "actual" as used in the section suggests that Parliament intended to restrict its scope to those damages that are relatively concrete and easily ascertainable and as such exclude such vague, amorphous and difficult matters as "pain and suffering". Consequently, I am of the opinion that an order under s. 663(2)(e) should be restricted to those damages in the nature of special damages.

The amount of restitution is to be fixed by the sentencing judge. In *R. v. Shorten* (1976), 29 C.C.C. (2d) 528 (B.C. C.A.), the accused were convicted of welfare fraud. The trial judge fined the accused and placed them on probation with a condition requiring restitiution in such amounts and at such times as the probation officer should order. In striking out this condition McIntyre J.A. stated:

> It seems to me that the condition in question can be attacked from either of two angles: (1) Because the judge has delegated to the probation officer the duty to form a judicial opinion of the convicted person's ability from time to time to pay. (2) Because the judge has delegated to the probation officer the power to make an order or orders. It is apparent that the trial judge, in what may well have been a commendable effort to make a realistic order which would offer some hope of compliance did attempt to delegate his functions in dealing with sentence. This part of his order cannot stand.
> In reaching this conclusion I am not overlooking the provisions of s. 738(3) of the *Criminal Code* which provide for the modification of a probation order after its making. The operation of this section, however, depends upon an application by prosecutor or accused. No such application has been made and the possible operation of that section in these circumstances is therefore not before us.

In addition to the restitution that can be made as part of a probation order, a number of recent changes to the *Code* provide for compensation: see ss. 725-727.

Community Service

See s. 732.1(3)(*f*): provides for conditions of community service not exceeding 240 hours over 18 months.

In *R. v. Stennes* (1975), 35 C.R.N.S. 123 (B.C. C.A.), the accused was sentenced to a six-month term to be followed by probation for two years with a number of conditions including the condition that he do 40 hours of community work per month. The Court of Appeal noted:

> Counsel for the appellant took the initial objection that the probation order was a nullity under the provisions of the *Criminal Code*, R.S.C. 1970, c. C-34, s. 663(l)(*b*) [am. 1972, c. 13, s. 58], for the reason that the condition which I have mentioned as being that numbered 7, that the appellant do 40 hours of community work per month, was the equivalent of a fine, and that a probation order could be given only in addition to fining or imposing a term of imprisonment, and that as imprisonment had already been imposed in this case no fine could be also imposed.
>
> I find no substance to that argument. In my view a condition in a probation order to do certain work, if appropriate, is not a fine, and I so hold. Accordingly, that submission must fall to the ground. I will have something to say later about the terms of the condition itself.

Later in the judgment, however, the condition was struck out as "inappropriate" with no discussion as to why.

By contrast, in *R. v. Shaw* (1977), 36 C.R.N.S. 358 (Ont. C.A.), the Ontario Court of Appeal approved of conditions of community service projects in respect of two youths convicted of trafficking in marihuana and L.S.D. The court added:

> Not only do I think that the provisions in the probation orders relating to this matter are valid, but in appropriate cases should be more extensively used.

Intermittent Sentence

See section 732, available for sentences not exceeding 90 days. Note that if an intermittent sentence is imposed, then the court must order probation. It might be advisable to consider as a term of the probation that the offender attend at the detention centre on time and in a sober condition.

Recognizance to Keep the Peace

See sections 810, 810.1 and 811 of the *Criminal Code*. Along with the authority specified in these sections the magistrate has a common-law jurisdiction to bind over a person to keep the peace: see *R. v. White; Ex parte Chonan* (1969), 5 C.R.N.S. 30, [1969] 1 C.C.C. 19 (B.C. S.C.).

Imprisonment

Maximum sentences for indictable offences range from life (*e.g.* manslaughter: s. 236), 14 years (*e.g.* incest: s. 155(2)), ten years (*e.g.* obstructing justice in a judicial proceeding: s. 139(2)), five years (*e.g.* for an offence for which no punishment is specially provided: s. 743), and two years (*e.g.* wilful obstruction of a peace officer: s. 129). The maximum is generally six months in the case of offences punishable by summary conviction (*e.g.* assault: s. 266(*b*) and s. 787). In 1994 Parliament increased the maximum penalty for several hybrid offences when proceeded against by way of summary conviction to 18 months: see, *e.g.* assault causing bodily harm (s. 267) and sexual assault (s. 271).

For a long time Canada had just a few minimum imprisonment sentences (eg. life for first or second degree murder and 14 days for a second conviction for impaired driving). In recent years Parliament has, however, added a number notably for firearms and drug offences.

Where the accused is convicted of more than one offence and receives more than one prison sentence the judge has a discretion to declare that the sentences be served concurrently or consecutively (s. 718.3(4)).

Conditional Sentences

See ss. 742-742.7. If a court has decided to impose a sentence of imprisonment of less than two years, these sections, which came into force in September, 1996, permit a court to order that the offender serve the sentence in the community where the court is satisfied that such an order would not endanger the safety of the community. The court is obliged to impose certain conditions and also may impose others. The pattern for granting conditional discharges is controversial and inconsistent: see, for example, Tim Quigley, "Uneven Deference on Conditional Sentencing", (2003) 12 C.R. (6th) 117.

R. v. PROULX

2000 SCC 5, [2000] 1 S.C.R. 61, 140 C.C.C. (3d) 449, 30 C.R. (5th) 1,
2000 CarswellMan 32, 2000 CarswellMan 33

The judgment of the court was delivered by LAMER C.J. — ...

127   At this point, a short summary of what has been said in these reasons might be useful:

1. Bill C-41 in general and the conditional sentence in particular were enacted both to reduce reliance on incarceration as a sanction and to increase the use of principles of restorative justice in sentencing.

2. A conditional sentence should be distinguished from probationary measures. Probation is primarily a rehabilitative sentencing tool. By contrast, Parliament intended conditional sentences to include both punitive and rehabilitative aspects. Therefore, conditional sentences should generally include punitive conditions that are restrictive of the offender's liberty. Conditions such as house arrest should be the norm, not the exception.

3. No offences are excluded from the conditional sentencing regime except those with a minimum term of imprisonment, nor should there be presumptions in favour of or against a conditional sentence for specific offences.

4. The requirement in s. 742.1(a) that the judge impose a sentence of imprisonment of less than two years does not require the judge to first impose a sentence of imprisonment of a fixed duration before considering whether that sentence can be served in the community. Although this approach is suggested by the text of s. 742.1(a), it is unrealistic and could lead to unfit sentences in some cases. Instead, a purposive interpretation of s. 742.1(a) should be adopted. In a preliminary determination, the sentencing judge should reject a penitentiary term and probationary measures as inappropriate. Having determined that the appropriate range of sentence is a term of imprisonment of less than two years, the judge should then consider whether it is appropriate for the offender to serve his or her sentence in the community.

5. As a corollary of the purposive interpretation of s. 742.1(a), a conditional sentence need not be of equivalent duration to the sentence of incarceration that would otherwise have been imposed. The sole requirement is that the duration and conditions of a conditional sentence make for a just and appropriate sentence.

6. The requirement in s. 742.1(b) that the judge be satisfied that the safety of the community would not be endangered by the offender serving his or her sentence in the community is a condition precedent to the imposition of a conditional sentence, and not the primary consideration in determining whether a conditional sentence is appropriate. In making this determination, the judge should consider the risk posed by the specific offender, not the broader risk of whether the imposition of a conditional sentence would endanger the safety of the community by providing insufficient general deterrence or undermining general respect for the law. Two factors should be taken into account: (1) the risk of the offender re-offending; and (2) the gravity of the damage that could ensue in the event of re-offence. A consideration of the risk posed by the offender should include the risk of any criminal activity, and not be limited solely to the risk of physical or psychological harm to individuals.

7. Once the prerequisites of s. 742.1 are satisfied, the judge should give serious consideration to the possibility of a conditional sentence in all cases by examining whether a conditional sentence is consistent with the fundamental purpose and principles of sentencing set out in ss. 718 to 718.2. This follows from Parliament's clear message to the judiciary to reduce the use of incarceration as a sanction.

8. A conditional sentence can provide significant denunciation and deterrence. As a general matter, the more serious the offence, the longer and more onerous the conditional sentence should be. There may be some circumstances, however, where the need for denunciation or deterrence is so pressing that incarceration will be the only suitable way in which to express society's condemnation of the offender's conduct or to deter similar conduct in the future.

9. Generally, a conditional sentence will be better than incarceration at achieving the restorative objectives of rehabilitation, reparations to the victim and the community, and promotion of a sense of responsibility in the offender and acknowledgment of the harm done to the victim and the community.

10. Where a combination of both punitive and restorative objectives may be achieved, a conditional sentence will likely be more appropriate than incarceration. Where objectives such as denunciation and deterrence are particularly pressing, incarceration will generally be the preferable sanction. This may be so notwithstanding the fact that restorative goals might be achieved. However, a conditional sentence may provide sufficient denunciation and deterrence, even in cases in which restorative objectives are of lesser importance, depending on the nature of the conditions imposed, the duration of the sentence, and the circumstances of both the offender and the community in which the conditional sentence is to be served.

11. A conditional sentence may be imposed even where there are aggravating circumstances, although the need for denunciation and deterrence will increase in these circumstances.

12. No party is under a burden of proof to establish that a conditional sentence is either appropriate or inappropriate in the circumstances. The judge should consider all relevant evidence, no matter by whom it is adduced. However, it would be in the offender's best interests to establish elements militating in favour of a conditional sentence.

13. Sentencing judges have a wide discretion in the choice of the appropriate sentence. They are entitled to considerable deference from appellate courts. As explained in *M. (C.A.)*, *supra*, at para. 90: "Put simply, absent an error in principle, failure to consider a relevant factor, or an overemphasis of the appropriate factors, a court of appeal should only intervene to vary a sentence imposed at trial if the sentence is demonstrably unfit".

The majority Conservative Government's *Safe Streets and Communities Act*, Bill C-10 of 2011, when it passes, will limit conditional sentences by enacting the following *Criminal Code* provision:

742.1 If a person is convicted of an offence and the court imposes a sentence of imprisonment of less than two years, the court may, for the purpose of supervising the offender's behaviour in the community, order that the offender serve the sentence in the community, subject to the conditions imposed under section 742.3, if

    (*a*) the court is satisfied that the service of the sentence in the community would not endanger the safety of the community and would be consistent with the fundamental purpose and principles of sentencing set out in sections 718 to 718.2;

    (*b*) the offence is not an offence punishable by a minimum term of imprisonment;

    (*c*) the offence is not an offence, prosecuted by way of indictment, for which the maximum term of imprisonment is 14 years or life;

    (*d*) the offence is not a terrorism offence, or a criminal organization offence, prosecuted by way of indictment, for which the maximum term of imprisonment is 10 years or more;

    (*e*) the offence is not an offence, prosecuted by way of indictment, for which the maximum term of imprisonment is 10 years, that

        (i)   resulted in bodily harm,

        (ii)   involved the import, export, trafficking or production of drugs, or

        (iii)   involved the use of a weapon; and

    (*f*) the offence is not an offence, prosecuted by way of indictment, under any of the following provisions:

        (i)   section 144 (prison breach),

        (ii)   section 264 (criminal harassment),

        (iii)   section 271 (sexual assault),

        (iv)   section 279 (kidnapping),

        (v)   section 279.02 (trafficking in persons — material benefit),

        (vi)   section 281 (abduction of person under fourteen),

        (vii)   section 333.1 (motor vehicle theft),

        (viii) paragraph 334(*a*) (theft over $5000),

        (ix)   paragraph 348(1)(*e*) (breaking and entering a place other than a dwelling-house),

        (x)   section 349 (being unlawfully in a dwelling-house), and

        (xi)   section 435 (arson for fraudulent purpose).

APPENDIX A

The Canadian Bar Association formed a Task Force in 1990 to comprehensively consider the reform of the General Part of the *Criminal Code*. In its 190-page report, it re-assessed the proposals of the Law Reform Commission Report: *Recodifying Criminal Law* (rev. ed., 1987).

C.B.A. TASK FORCE REPORT
PRINCIPLES OF CRIMINAL LIABILITY (1992)

PART VIII: SUMMARY OF RECOMMENDATIONS

The Canadian Bar Association's *Criminal Code* Recodification Task Force recommends that the General Part of the new *Criminal Code* contain provisions to the following effect:

DECLARATION OF PURPOSE AND PRINCIPLES

WHEREAS the purpose of the criminal law is to ensure the protection and security of all members of Canadian society;

AND WHEREAS that purpose is fulfilled by setting standards which represent the limits of acceptable conduct and by proscribing culpable conduct which falls outside those limits;

AND WHEREAS the criminal law should be used in a manner which least interferes with the rights and freedoms of individuals;

AND WHEREAS the purpose of the *Criminal Code of Canada* is to set out the principles of the criminal law in a single document;

It is declared that the following principles will guide the interpretation and application of the *Criminal Code of Canada*:

(a) no one shall be criminally sanctioned unless that person has the requisite wrongful state of mind;

(b) the criminal law should only be resorted to when other means of social control are inadequate or inappropriate;

(c) persons who commit crimes must bear the responsibility for their actions;

(d) the criminal law is to be administered in a fair and dispassionate manner while recognizing the principles of tolerance, compassion and mercy that are integral values of Canadian society.

Principle of legality

1. No one is criminally liable for conduct that, at the time of its occurrence, was not an offence under this *Code* or under any other Act of the Parliament of Canada.

Criminal liability

2. Except where otherwise specifically provided, no one is criminally liable for an offence unless that person engages in the prohibited conduct, with the required blameworthy state of mind, in the absence of a lawful justification, excuse or other defence.

Prohibited conduct

3. Prohibited conduct consists of an act, omission or state of affairs committed or occurring in specified circumstances or with specified consequences.

Omissions

4. No one is liable for an omission unless:

   (a) that persons fails to perform a duty imposed by this Act, or

   (b) the omission is itself defined as an offence by this Act.

Causation

5. (1) A person causes a result when that person's acts or omissions significantly contribute to the result.

   (2) A person may significantly contribute to a result even though that person's acts or omissions are not the sole cause or the main cause of the result.

   (3) No one causes a result if an independent, intervening cause so overwhelms that person's acts or omissions as to render those acts or omissions as merely part of the history or setting for another independent, intervening cause to take effect.

Conscious involuntary conduct

6. (1) No one is liable for prohibited conduct which, although conscious, is involuntary.

   (2) Prohibited conduct is involuntary if it was not within one's ability physically to control. Without limiting the generality of the foregoing, this includes:

(a) a spasm, twitch or reflex action,

(b) an act or movement physically caused by an external force, and

(c) an omission of failure to act as legally required due to physical impossibility.

(3) This section does not apply to conscious involuntary conduct due to provocation, rage, loss of temper, mental disorder, voluntary intoxication or automatism.

(4) If the involuntary prohibited conduct occurred because of a person's prior, voluntary blameworthy conduct, then that person may be held liable for that prior blameworthy conduct.

Automatism

7.   (1) No one shall be convicted of an offence where the prohibited conduct occurred while that person was in a state of automatism.

(2) For the purposes of this section, automatism means unconscious, involuntary behaviour whereby a person, though capable of action, is not conscious of what he or she is doing, and includes unconscious, involuntary behaviour of a transient nature caused by external factors such as:

(a) a physical blow,

(b) a psychological blow from an extraordinary external event which might reasonably be expected to cause a dissociative state in an average, normal person,

(c) inhalation of toxic fumes, accidental poisoning or involuntary intoxication,

(d) sleepwalking,

(e) a stroke,

(f) hypoglycaemia,

(g) a flu or virus, and

(h) other similar factors.

(3) Subsection (1) does not apply to automatism which is caused by:

(a) mental disorder,

(b) voluntary intoxication; or

(c) fault as defined in subsection (5).

(4) For the purpose of this section, automatism is caused by mental disorder when the unconscious, involuntary behaviour arises primarily from an internal, subjective condition or weakness in the accused's own psychological, emotional or organic make-up, including dissociative states caused by the ordinary stresses and disappointments of life.

(5) Notwithstanding subsection (1), automatism is not a defence:

(a) to an intentional offence if a person voluntarily induces automatism with the intention of causing the prohibited conduct of that offence,

(b) to a knowledge offence if a person voluntarily induces automatism knowing that it is virtually certain that he or she will commit the prohibited conduct of that offence while in that state of automatism, or

(c) to a reckless offence if a person voluntarily induces automatism, notwithstanding the fact that the person is aware of a risk that he or she will commit the prohibited conduct of that offence while in that state of automatism, and it is highly unreasonable to take that risk.

Mental elements of an offence

8. (1) For the purpose of criminal liability, the mental elements of an offence are:

(a) intent,

(b) knowledge, and

(c) recklessness.

Intent

(2) A person acts intentionally with respect to prohibited conduct when the person wants it to exist or occur.

Knowledge

(3) A person acts knowingly with respect to prohibited conduct when the person is virtually certain that it exists or will occur.

Recklessness

> (4) A person acts recklessly with respect to prohibited conduct when, in the circumstances actually known to the person:
>
> > (a) the person is aware of a risk that his or her act or omission will result in the prohibited conduct, and
> >
> > (b) it is highly unreasonable to take the risk.

Prescribed state of mind applies to all aspects of prohibited conduct

> (5) When the law defining an offence prescribes the state of mind required for the commission of an offence, without distinguishing among aspects of the prohibited conduct, that state of mind shall apply to all aspects of the prohibited conduct of the offence, unless a contrary intent plainly appears.

Residual rule

> (6) Where the definition of a crime does not explicitly specify the requisite state of mind, it shall be interpreted as requiring proof of intent.
>
> (7) Where the definition of a crime requires knowledge, a person may be liable if the person acts or omits to act intentionally or knowingly as to one or more aspects of the prohibited conduct in that definition.

Greater culpability requirement satisfies lesser

> (8) Where the definition of a crime requires recklessness, a person may be liable if the person acts, or omits to act, intentionally or knowingly as to one or more aspects of the prohibited conduct in that definition.

Mistaken belief in facts

9. No person is liable for an offence committed through lack of knowledge which is due to mistake or ignorance as to the relevant circumstances; but where on the facts as the person believed them he or she would have committed an included offence, the person shall be liable for committing that included offence.

Caution respecting belief

10. A court or jury, in determining whether a person had a particular belief in a set of facts, shall have regard to all the evidence including,

where appropriate, the presence or absence of reasonable grounds for having that belief.

11. No one is criminally liable for conduct if, through disease or mental disability, the person at the time:

    (a) was incapable of appreciatng the nature or consequences of such conduct, or

    (b) believed what he or she was doing was morally right, or

    (c) was incapable of conforming to the requirements of the law.

Defence of the person

12. (1) Every person is justified in using, in self-defence or in the defence of another, such force as, in the circumstances as that person believes them to be, it is reasonable to use.

Excessive force

    (2) A person who uses excessive force in self-defence or in the defence of another and thereby causes the death of another human being is not guilty of murder, but is guilty of manslaughter.

Defence of property

13. (1) A person is justified in using such force as, in the circumstances which exist or which the person believes to exist, is reasonable:

    (a) to protect property (whether belonging to that person or another) from unlawful appropriaton, destruction or damage, or

    (b) to prevent or terminate a trespass to that person's property.

    (2) In no circumstances is it reasonable, in defence of property, to intend to cause death.

Necessity

14. (1) No one is criminally responsible for acting to avoid harm to oneself or another person or to avoid immediate serious damage to property, if the danger which he or she knows or believes to exist is such that in all the circumstances (including any of his or her personal characteristics that affect its gravity) he or she cannot reasonably be expected to act otherwise.

    (2) Clause (1) does not apply to anyone who has knowingly and

without reasonable excuse exposed himself or herself to the danger.

Duress

15. No one is liable for committing a crime in response to a threat of harm to oneself or another person if the threat is one which in all the circumstances (including any of his or her personal characteristics that affect its gravity) he or she cannot reasonably be expected to resist.

Intoxication

16. (1) No person is liable for a crime for which, by reason of intoxicaton, the person fails to satisfy the culpability requirements specified by its definition.

    (2) Clause (1) does not apply where the voluntary consumption of an intoxicant is a material element of the offence charged.

    (3) Notwithstanding clause (1), a person charged with a Schedule 1 offence who would, but for voluntary intoxicaton, be found guilty of that offence shall instead be found guilty of the included offence of criminal intoxication.

    (4) A person found guilty under clause (3) is liable to the same punishment as if found guilty of an attempt to commit the offence charged.

Mistake of law

17. No one is liable for a crime committed by reason of mistake or ignorance of law:

    a. concerning private or other civil rights relevant to that crime, or

    b. resulting from:

        i. ignorance of the existence of the law, where the law has not been published or otherwise reasonably made known to the public or persons likely to be affected by it,

        ii. reasonable reliance on a judicial decision, or

        iii. reasonable reliance on a statement by a Judge, government official or person in authority.

Provocation

18. (1) An accused is provoked if, as a result of another's act or statement, the accused loses self-control where a person in the accused's situation, under the circumstances as the accused believes them to be, would lose self-control.

    (2) An accused who, while provoked:

    a. commits murder, shall be convicted of manslaughter, and

    b. commits any offence included in the Schedule, shall be convicted of committing that offence under provocation, and shall be liable to half the penalty of the offence charged.

Trivial violations

19. Where the Crown has proved all the essential elements of an offence the court may, before a finding of guilt is entered, stay the proceedings against the accused with respect to that offence, where the accused satisfies the court on the balance of probabilities that, having regard to the nature of the conduct and all the attendant circumstances, the violation was too trivial to warrant a finding of guilty, the entering of a conviction or the imposition of a criminal sanction.

Entrapment

20. (1) Where:

    a. the trier of fact is satisfied that the Crown has proved beyond a reasonable doubt all the essential elements of an offence, and

    b. the court is satisfied that the accused has established, on the balance of probabilities, that he or she was entrapped into committing that offence,

    the court shall stay the proceedings against the accused respecting that offence.

    (2) Without limiting the generality of subsection (1), entrapment includes committing an offence when the authorities:

    a. not having a reasonable suspicion that the accused is already engaged in that particular criminal activity, or not acting in the course of a bona fide investigation directed at persons present in an area where it is reasonably suspected that the particular criminal activity is occurring, provide the accused with the opportunity to commit that offence; or

b. having a reasonable suspicion that the accused is already engaged in that particular criminal activity, or acting in the course of a *bona fide* investigation directed at persons present in an area where it is reasonably suspected that the particular criminal activity is occurring, go beyond providing an opportunity and induce the accused to commit that offence.

Common-law defences

21. No defence, justification or excuse shall be unavailable unless expressly prohibited by this *Code*.

Attempts

22. (1) Every one who, having an intent to commit an offence, does or omits to do anything for the purpose of carrying out that intention is guilty of an attempt to commit the offence, even if it was factually or legally impossible under the circumstances to commit the offence.

    (2) The question whether an act or omission by a person who has an intent to commit an offence is or is not mere preparation to commit the offence, and too remote to constitute an attempt to commit the offence, is a question of law.

    (3) Except where otherwise expressly provided by law, every one who aids or encourages another person to commit an offence is, if that offence is not committed, guilty of an attempt to commit that offence.

Conspiracy

23. (1) Every one is liable for conspiracy who agrees with another person, whether or not they are married to each other, to commit a *Criminal Code* offence which is indictable or which may be proceeded with by indictment.

    (2) A person does not conspire unless he or she intends to commit an offence described in clause (1).

    (3) A person who abandons a conspiracy to commit an offence described in clause (1), before that offence is attempted or committed, is not liable for the conspiracy.

(4) In determining whether a person abandoned a conspiracy the court shall consider all relevant circumstances, including whether the person communicated his or her desistance to the other conspirators or to the authorities, or both.

(5) Every one who conspires to commit an offence described in clause (1) is liable, even if it was factually or legally impossible under the circumstances to commit the offence.

(6) Subject to diplomatic and other immunity under law, this *Code* applies to, and the courts have jurisdiction over:

    a. conduct engaged in outside Canada which constitutes a conspiracy to commit a crime in Canada, where the conduct took place on the high seas or in a state where the crime in question is also a crime in that state, and

    b. conduct engaged in inside Canada which constitutes a conspiracy to commit a crime outside Canada if the crime in question is a crime in Canada and in the place where the crime is to be committed.

Parties

24. Every one is a party to and guilty of an offence who:

    a. actually commits it,

    b. does or omits to do anything knowing that it will aid any person to commit it, or

    c. does or omits to do anything with the intent of encouraging any person to commit it.

Multiple convictions

25. No person shall be convicted twice for the same delict.

APPENDIX B

Text of a General Part Suggested by Don Stuart

The following is an amended version of a draft first presented to a conference of academics, judges and lawyers entitled "Making Criminal Law Clear and Just: A Criminal Reports Forum", held in Kingston, Ontario, on November 6-8, 1998. The papers and proceedings of that conference have been published: see Stuart, Delisle and Manson, eds., *Towards a Clear and Just Criminal Law* (Carswell, 1999).

Preamble

Whereas the Criminal Code of Canada has not, since it was first enacted in 1892, comprehensively declared basic principles under which persons can be justly held criminally responsible,

Whereas Criminal Law should be clear and accessible to all,

Whereas the declaration of such principles by the courts has become unduly complex and sometimes inconsistent, and

Whereas the Criminal Code should reflect minimum constitutional standards declared by the courts to be mandated by interpreting the Canadian Charter of Rights and Freedoms,

Parliament hereby enacts a new Part 1 of the Criminal Code entitled Principles of Criminal Responsibility.

Principle of Legality

1. No one can be found guilty of conduct that is not an offence under this Act or another Act of Parliament.

Principles of Interpretation

2. In the absence of clear legislative intent to the contrary, the principles in the General Part are to be applied in the interpretation of any offence in the Criminal Code or other Act of Parliament

3. Where a provision of the Criminal Code is reasonably capable of two interpretations, the interpretation which is more favourable to the accused must be adopted.

Criminal Responsibility

4. Except where otherwise specifically provided, no one is criminally

responsible for an offence unless that person engages in the prohibited conduct with the requisite fault and in the absence of a lawful justification, excuse or other defence.

Prohibited Conduct

5. Prohibited conduct consists of an act committed or omission occurring in specified circumstances and sometimes with specified consequences.

Omissions

6. No one is criminally responsible for an omission unless

    (1) there is a legal duty declared by the offence definition in the Criminal Code or other Act of the Parliament of Canada, or

    (2) that person created danger to life or safety of others and rectification was reasonably within that person's control.

Involuntary Conduct

7. (1) No one is criminally responsible for involuntary conduct.

    (2) Conduct is involuntary if it was beyond that person's ability to control.

    (3) This section does not apply to conduct resulting from rage, mental disorder, or where the accused getting into the involuntary state satisfied the fault requirement for the offence charged.

Causation

8. (1) A person causes a consequence when that person's acts or omissions significantly contribute to the result.

    (2) A person may significantly contribute to a consequence even though that person's acts or omissions are not the sole or main cause of the consequence.

    (3) No one causes a consequence if an independent, intervening cause so overwhelms that person's acts or omissions as to render those acts or omissions as merely part of the history or setting for another independent, intervening cause to take effect.

Minimum Fault for Criminal Code Offences

9. Unless the law creating the offence specifies to the contrary, criminal

responsibility under the Criminal Code requires proof of fault in the form of intent, recklessness or criminal negligence.

10. Unless the law creating the offence specifies to the contrary, recklessness is the fault element required in relation to each element of the offence.

Intention

11. A person acts "intentionally" with respect to

   (1) a circumstance where that person hopes or knows that it exists or will exist;

   (2) a consequence when that person's purpose is to cause it, or that person knows that it would occur in the ordinary course of events if he or she were to succeed in his or her purpose of causing some other consequence.

Recklessness

12. A person acts "recklessly" with respect to

   (1) a circumstance when that person is aware of a risk that it exists or will exist;

   (2) a consequence when that person is aware of a risk that it will occur; and it is, in the circumstances known to that person, unreasonable to take the risk.

Criminal Negligence

13. A person is "criminally negligent" where a reasonable person in the accused's situation would have been aware of the risk and the failure to avoid it constituted a marked and substantial departure from the standard of care a reasonable person would have exercised in the circumstances.

Reasonableness Standard

14. For the purposes of section 13 and the application of any reasonableness standard under this Criminal Code the trier of fact must take into account the person's awareness, if any, of the circumstances and also factors the person could not have controlled or managed such as race, gender, age and experience, where relevant, but not self-induced intoxication.

Mistake of Fact

15. (1) Where the fault requirement is intent or recklessness, to excuse a mistaken belief need not be reasonable although reasonableness is relevant to determining whether the belief existed.

(2) Where the fault requirement is criminal negligence, to excuse a mistaken belief must be reasonable.

(3) Where the accused has a mistaken belief within the meaning of subsections (1) or (2) he or she may nevertheless be convicted of an included or attempted offence where the belief constitutes the requisite fault for that offence.

Fault for Offences Under Other Acts of Parliament

16. (1) Unless Parliament expressly requires intent, recklessness or criminal negligence as a fault requirement or expressly imposes absolute liability, negligence is required for penal liability.

(2) A person acts "negligently" where he or she departs from the standard of care expected of a reasonable prudent person in the circumstances.

(3) Before imprisonment can be imposed, intent, recklessness or criminal negligence must be proved.

(4) Where the Crown has proved the conduct specified in the offence for which the fault requirement is negligence, the accused is presumed to have acted negligently in the absence of evidence to the contrary.

Common Law Defences

17. No defence, justification or excuse shall be unavailable unless contrary to an express provision of the Criminal Code.

Mistake or Ignorance of Law

18. Ignorance or mistake of law is not an excuse.

19. No one is criminally responsible for a mistake or ignorance of law resulting from.

(1) the law not being properly made known to those likely to be affected, or

(2) reliance on a judicial decision or official advice.

Age Incapacity

20. No person is criminally responsible for conduct while under the age of twelve years.

Mental Disorder Incapacity

21. (1) No person is criminally responsible for conduct while suffering from mental disorder that rendered the person incapable of appreciating the nature and quality of the conduct or of knowing that it was morally wrong.

    (2) For the purpose of subsection (1), every person is presumed not to suffer from a mental disorder, in the absence of evidence to the contrary.

Self-induced Intoxication

22. Self-induced intoxication is not a ground of incapacity nor may it be considered in any determination of reasonableness under this Act.

Defence of Person

23. A person is not criminally responsible for using force against another person if he or she

    (1) reasonably believes that force is necessary for self-protection or the protection of a third party from unlawful force or the threat thereof;

    (2) the degree of force used is reasonable, although no one is expected to weigh with nicety the degree of force needed.

Defence of Property

24. A person is not criminally responsible for using force against another person if he or she

    (1) reasonably believes that force is necessary to protect property, whether belonging to that person or another, from unlawful appropriation, destruction or damage, or to prevent or terminate a trespass to that person's property; and

    (2) the degree of force used is reasonable, although no one is expected to weigh with nicety the degree of force needed.

Duress

25. A person is not criminally responsible for conduct under threat where

(1) that person reasonably believes

    (a) that a threat has been made to cause death or serious personal harm to that person or another if the conduct is not performed;

    (b) that the threat will be carried out if that person does not act or before that person or that other can gain official protection; and

    (c) that there is no other way of preventing the threat being carried out;

(2) the threat is one which in all the circumstances that person cannot reasonably be expected to resist; and

(3) the person has not recklessly exposed himself or herself to the risk of threat.

Necessity

26. A person is not criminally responsible for conduct under necessity where

(1) that person reasonably believes that it is immediately necessary to avoid serious personal harm to that person or another or serious harm to property;

(2) in all the circumstances that person cannot reasonably be expected to do otherwise; and

(3) the person has not recklessly and without reasonable excuse exposed himself or herself to the danger.

Accessories

27. Every one is an accessory to an offence and liable to the same penalty as a perpetrator who

(1) does or omits to do anything with intent to procure, assist or encourage another to commit an offence;

(2) with the fault required for that offence; and

(3) that other person commits the offence, whether or not that person can be convicted of it.

Corporations

28. (1) Corporations may be held criminally responsible for any offence if, on consideration of that corporation's organizational structure

and culture, the corporation can be justly held to have acted with the fault specified for the particular offence, whether this be intention, recklessness or criminal negligence.

(2) For the purpose of the determination under subsection (1), consideration is to be given to acts of authorization or delegation, corporate goals and practices, past practices, any past offences and the existence and sufficiency of compliance programmes.